TURMOIL AND TRIUMPH

George P. Shultz

TURMOIL AND TRIUMPH

My Years as Secretary of State

A ROBERT STEWART BOOK

Charles Scribner's Sons
New York

Maxwell Macmillan Canada
Toronto

Maxwell Macmillan International
New York   Oxford   Singapore   Sydney

Charles Scribner's Sons　　　　　　Maxwell Macmillan Canada, Inc.
Macmillan Publishing Company　　　1200 Eglinton Avenue East, Suite 200
866 Third Avenue　　　　　　　　　Don Mills, Ontario M3C 3N1
New York, NY 10022

Macmillan Publishing Company is part of the Maxwell Communication Group of Companies.

Library of Congress Cataloging-in-Publication Data
Shultz, George Pratt, 1920–
　　Turmoil and triumph: my years as secretary of state / George P. Shultz.
　　　p.　cm.
　　"A Robert Stewart book."
　　Includes index.
　　ISBN 0-684-19325-6
　　　1. Shultz, George Pratt, 1920–　　　2. Statesmen—United States—Biography.
　　3. United States—Foreign relations—1981–1989.
　　I. Title.
　　E840.8.S535A3　1993
　　973.927′092—dc20
　　[B]　　　　　92-35247

The epigraph is a quotation from Isaiah Berlin and Ramin Jahanbegloo, *Conversations with Isaiah Berlin* (New York: Charles Scribner's Sons, 1991), p. 34.

Macmillan books are available at special discounts for bulk purchases for sales promotions, premiums, fund-raising, or educational use. For details, contact:

　　　　Special Sales Director
　　　　Macmillan Publishing Company
　　　　866 Third Avenue
　　　　New York, NY 10022

10　9　8　7　6　5　4　3　2

Printed in the United States of America

At crucial moments, at turning points,
when factors appear more or less equally
balanced, chance, individuals and their
decisions and acts, themselves not
necessarily predictable—indeed, seldom
so—can determine the course of history.

ISAIAH BERLIN

Contents

Foreword

On January 20, 1989, I left Washington on the five o'clock flight for San Francisco to take up private life once again, combining association with Stanford University's Hoover Institution and Graduate School of Business and several businesses where I knew and respected the management. I was tired after six and one-half tumultuous years, and I felt that memoirs could easily become self-serving. Turn over the documents to the historians, I thought, and let them write the record of foreign policy during the Reagan years.

Soon my energy returned and, as I looked into my records, I felt a renewed sense of excitement about what had happened on my watch, and a desire to set out the flow of events, the hows and the whys, as they appeared from my own angle of view. Much had been accomplished during those crucial years. The process was at times exhilarating, at times fractious, in an administration often at odds with itself. I wanted to present the reality as I experienced it, warts and all: a foray into how things happened in Washington during years that were on the hinge of history. When I started as secretary of state, the world was in turmoil, and when I left office, the cold war was over and, after a struggle lasting over four decades, the idea of free and open political and economic systems had triumphed.

And so I began what turned out to be three years of hard but fascinating work. My objective has been to produce a living history, re-creating the scene as I experienced it. I was exposed to a fire hose of information and a kaleidoscopic round of action, day after day, week after week—with an unrelenting pressure to perform and an opportunity to make a difference. My adrenaline started to rise again but, in the telling, I could also reflect more fully on these experiences.

As I prepared to write, I found at hand an unusually rich record about a period of extraordinary importance in our county's foreign affairs: not just official papers that flowed in and out of my office, but careful notes about my meetings with key leaders and a contemporaneous, on the spot record of what went on in my office wherever I was, my readouts of meetings

I attended elsewhere, and my own musings about what I thought there and then.

Presentation confronted me with the problem of capturing the flow and interplay of developments in different parts of the world at one moment in time and in one aspect of our foreign policy at different points in time. There are, unfortunately, no literary techniques to convey the simultaneity of events. Most chapters take up a subject over a defined period, simply for the sake of coherent presentation. Nevertheless, a sense of development was needed and all the connections had to be remembered. I tried to do that as I went along.

I have been blessed with an editor of extraordinary talent, Cynthia Fry Gunn. I first worked with Cynthia sixteen years ago when she edited my book *Economic Policy Beyond the Headlines*. She encouraged me to undertake this memoir in the first instance and has seen me through from early, tentative efforts to completion of the book. She provided challenge, debate, and sound advice on the entire manuscript in endless iterations, making extensive and essential editorial transformations, reorganizations, and critiques. I owe her an enormous debt of gratitude for contributing her keen intelligence and insight, her laser-beam focus and drive for excellence, and her boundless energy to this demanding project. With unswerving dedication she held me to the highest standards and aspirations, and has kept me at it these past three years.

This book bears the imprint of Robert Stewart, who has been a source of patient support and genuine encouragement, providing helpful suggestions and allowing me the time I needed to do this job right.

I also thank a tireless and talented group that has assisted me as well. Grace Hawes has been a resourceful archivist whose capacity for detective work and organization has made my vast records readily available. Romayne Ponleithner has been a wonder at managing and typing the massive flow of drafts, keeping the flood of changes and reorganizations straight, and meticulously indexing the book. Kiron Skinner has been an unflagging provider of the public record, critic, and manager of a rotating group that relentlessly checked the manuscript for factual accuracy. Maren Leed was especially helpful in this effort. The Hoover Institution has graciously put at my disposal the necessary facilities. Phyl Whiting, Juanita Nissley, and June DeVille have helped me organize my life so that I could save the blocks of time needed for this endeavor.

Four friends have provided penetrating and constructive criticism in their reading of the entire manuscript: Ken Dam, Andrew Knight, Don Oberdorfer, and, until his sudden death, George Stigler. John Whitehead provided helpful recollections of our efforts to stimulate change in the countries of Eastern Europe. Tony Motley provided me vital information and his account of the Grenada effort. Ray Seitz, my executive assistant, who broke me in during my first two years as a new secretary of state, provided especially helpful recollections.

Charlie Hill, a senior research fellow at Stanford's Hoover Institution, served as my executive assistant for two-thirds of my time as secretary of state and was a close associate during the two years before taking up that post. With the perspective gained from his experience as a senior foreign service officer and with great ability, he took extensive notes in my office and other places where I happened to be. These notes constitute a remorselessly precise record and a vivid picture of a "slice of history in the making." Charlie drew from his notes to provide invaluable and unique raw material for this book. I am deeply grateful to him, both for his critical role while I was secretary of state and for his essential work with me on this manuscript.

Many friends and associates have read parts of the draft manuscript dealing with subjects familiar to them and have given me the benefit of their reactions. I thank Mike Armacost, Harry Barnes, Jerry Bremer, Chet Crocker, the late Phil Habib, Jim Hodgson, Geoffrey Howe, Bob Kagan, Max Kampelman, Henry Kissinger, Clay McManaway, Dick Murphy, Paul Nitze, Nick Platt, Roz Ridgway, Harry Shlaudeman, Gaston Sigur, Abe Sofaer, Bill Stanton, and Jim Timbie.

In my stewardship at the State Department and in writing about those times in this book, I have been fortunate to have been surrounded by talented colleagues. I could not do without them. I thank them for being special friends and partners in what I regard as great endeavors.

GEORGE P. SHULTZ
Stanford, California
December 1992

Part I

GATHERING THE THREADS

CHAPTER 1

The World in Turmoil

Someone handed me a note: a George Clark from the White House was calling. I did not know any George Clark and pushed the slip of paper aside. It was Friday morning, June 25, 1982. As president of Bechtel, an engineering and construction company with global reach, I was in the midst of an important meeting in London. When my presentation was over, the call came through again. This time the note said Bill Clark was on the line. Judge William P. Clark, Jr., President Reagan's California friend and now his national security adviser. I had telephoned him a week earlier to express my concerns over the Israeli invasion of Lebanon and the destruction of Beirut, which was now in full fury. I left the room and took the phone. "The president wants to talk to you about something of great importance," he said. "Can you go to the American embassy, where you can talk on a secure phone?"

The rumor that Secretary of State Alexander Haig was about to resign was circulating again, but I had no idea what was behind this request. Soon after I arrived at our embassy on Grosvenor Square, President Reagan's call came through. "Al Haig has resigned," he told me, "and I want you to be my secretary of state."

"Haig has already resigned? That is a fact?" I asked. "It has already happened?" I did not want to get into the position of saying yes to the president's request and then having Al Haig told that he was out.

"He has resigned," the president responded. "It hasn't been announced, but it has happened. I have accepted his resignation, and I want you to replace him."

As we talked, it dawned on me that President Reagan wanted me to say yes then and there. "Mr. President, are you asking me to accept this job now, over the phone?"

"Well, yes, I am, George," he replied. "It would help a lot because it's not a good idea to leave a post like this vacant. When we announce that Secretary Haig has resigned, we'd like to announce that I have nominated you to be secretary of state." For a brief moment, flashes of California raced through my mind—my life at Bechtel and Stanford was wonderful. I had been out of office for about eight years. I loved what I was doing and the people I was working with. I knew from experience the tensions, the lack of privacy, and the demands on time, energy, intellect, emotion that come with a cabinet post. But I had come to regard public service as something special, more an opportunity and a privilege than an obligation. I supported the president and his ideas. I felt well prepared. "Mr. President, I'm on board." So back I would go to the pressures of Washington, this time to what I knew would be the toughest, most demanding, and yet potentially most exhilarating and gratifying of jobs.

Danger and Disarray

Early the next morning, my wife, O'Bie, and I were off on the Concorde headed for Washington. I used the four-hour flight to gather my thoughts and assess the world scene:

The year was 1982, but the 1970s were still with us. The mood at the end of that decade had been captured by Jimmy Carter, unfortunately for him, in an unforgettable way: America was suffering from a bad case of "malaise," he said. Americans could no longer be optimistic. At the end of the 1970s the predictions were for rising oil prices, more inflation, and stagnation: the United States would simply have to get used to a lower standard of living. An escalation of cold war tension was taken for granted. Moscow's military might grew yearly. The nuclear arms race proceeded unharnessed. The Soviet army's invading forces were grinding through Afghan villages. So much for détente.

Throughout the cold war era, America's responsibilities as a superpower had been fulfilled with impressive success. But fear of flagging will or failure had become pervasive. The American presidency had become a story of successive agonies: the assassination of John F. Kennedy; the anguished departure of Lyndon Johnson at the nadir of the Vietnam War; Richard Nixon's de facto impeachment; Gerald Ford's healing but brief stewardship; and Jimmy Carter's miseries, which, with a weak smile, he spread across the American and international scene. In June 1980, I had said in a speech to the Business Roundtable, "All around us, and plain for all the world to see, is confusion about our aims, deterioration in our world position, and deep concern, perhaps fear, that we are no longer able to establish a tough-minded sense of direction and stick to it."

Now, in mid-1982, we were still besieged by problems and buffeted by events. Ronald Reagan's program, off to a strong start at home, was struggling abroad. President Reagan had set out to restore America's strength, optimism, and "can do" spirit. He was strengthening our defense capabilities, invigorating the morale of our men and women in uniform, and carrying the message of political and economic freedom around the world. But the president's foreign policy refused to lift off and soar. I felt the United States held the winning hand, but it was proving a difficult hand to play.

Bitterness marked the discord between the United States and our European allies over the proposed construction of a gigantic 3,500-mile pipeline running from Siberia through rugged terrain to carry gas, Soviet gas, into Europe. The American and European economies were in a recession, and the pipeline contract meant good jobs during a time when they were hard to get.

But suddenly, in mid-December of 1981, the Polish government, with clear Soviet support, cracked down on the Polish labor union Solidarity and its courageous leaders. The Reagan administration was determined to register its views forcefully, to use the events in Poland as the basis for action against the Soviets. On December 29, the president ordered all U.S. firms to break any direct contract involving the Siberian pipeline and not to enter into any new ones. Six months later, on June 18, 1982, in the acrimonious aftermath of the Versailles economic summit, President Reagan carried his policy further: any European firm operating on a U.S. license or any American subsidiary operating in Europe must break all pipeline contracts. Our European allies harshly attacked the United States for this "retroactive action." We were, they cried, an "unreliable supplier," applying "extraterritorial" reach to American foreign policy that encroached upon their sovereignty.

The Europeans were enraged, as were important segments of the U.S. business community. Yet the upcoming year, 1983, would be critical for nuclear arms negotiations: close U.S.-European coordination would be essential. New Soviet missiles, SS-20s, had been deployed and, since the 1970s, explicitly and directly targeted on Europe. These intermediate-range missiles could not reach the United States. Their purpose was to intimidate West Europeans as part of an ongoing Soviet effort to drive a wedge between the United States and our NATO allies. U.S. missiles, as agreed by all NATO members, were scheduled to be deployed beginning in late 1983 on European soil as a counter to these Soviet deployments. Crucial negotiations would determine whether the arms race would be speeded up or scaled back. The pressing need for coherence and unity in the alliance would be practically impossible to manage, I knew, unless we could dissipate the acrimonious atmosphere with the Europeans created by the pipeline dispute.

U.S.-Soviet relations had gone into the deep freeze when the Soviets invaded Afghanistan just after Christmas of 1979. Now the Soviet-backed crackdown in Poland further deepened the cold. Relations between the two superpowers were not simply bad; they were virtually nonexistent. West German Chancellor Helmut Schmidt said to me in May 1982, "The superpowers are not in touch with each other's reality. The Soviets can't read you. More human contact is needed."

"The Soviet system is incompetent and cannot survive," I had said in a speech at Stanford in 1979. "In the struggle with communism freedom is the ideological victor in the world." Now, three years later, in 1982, I had not changed my mind. The Soviets had to be made to realize that they could not succeed with aggression, nor could they win an arms race. But we did not want to spark conflict through fear or miss opportunities to resolve outstanding problems. President Reagan recognized the Soviet Union for what it was: aggressive, repressive, and economically bankrupt, but militarily powerful, with an arsenal of strategic nuclear weapons able to devastate us in thirty minutes. We must recognize that reality, I knew, but we should also be ready to deal with the Soviets more constructively if the opportunity arose. We had to gather support for this approach: from Congress, the press, and the public. Global stability depended on how we dealt with the Soviets. This was an issue I was eager to talk over with the president.

As I looked to Asia, it struck me that the opening to China achieved by President Nixon and Henry Kissinger was closing. An array of minor differences had been blown up to become major items of tension. The immediate dilemma was how to fulfill our responsibility to help Taiwan with its defense while standing behind our agreements with Beijing when U.S.-China relations were reestablished. With our important economic and political interests in Asia, I saw an uneasy state in our relationship with Japan. Trade issues were endless and difficult, and we were pressing Japan, somewhat against their better judgment, to undertake greater defense efforts. As a marine, I had fought the Japanese in World War II, and I was uneasy with encouraging Japan's renewal as a military power. Elsewhere in the Asia-Pacific region, I knew concern about a rearmed Japan was widespread.

Turning to Africa, the scene all across the southern continent was grim. Apartheid in South Africa was abhorrent and oppressive. Could the United States fashion a policy to slow the expansion of communism beyond Angola and Mozambique, provide a chance for independence in Namibia, and somehow make white South Africans realize that change must come?

In the Muslim world, the rise of Ayatollah Khomeini's radical fundamentalism had the Arab nations in a panic, and with good reason. Even the Grand Mosque in Mecca had been attacked, in November 1979, by extremists. Iran's military drive into Iraq was raising the specter of a new and fearsome force across the world of Islam—from Marrakesh to Bangladesh.

In our own part of the world, I could see that President Reagan was giving sharper attention to the Caribbean and Central America as well as Canada and Mexico. U.S. foreign policy started in our own backyard:

anything rotten there could infect the United States. So we must pay attention. "Another Vietnam": that's what critics called U.S. support for El Salvador. Democracy in Central America was showing sparks of life, but setbacks there were too often magnified into an imperative for American disengagement. The Soviets observed our domestic discord with relish, expecting that an America divided in rancorous debate over emerging Marxist revolutionary movements to its south would be less inclined to act to contain Moscow's advances elsewhere in the world.

Then there was Lebanon: there was no point in philosophizing over whether this country was a vital U.S. interest. A war was raging there, and war in the Middle East meant trouble for everybody. Only a few weeks earlier, the Israelis had launched an invasion into southern Lebanon and by now had beaten the Syrians back and had pinned down the Palestine Liberation Organization (PLO) in the city of Beirut. The trauma in Lebanon reverberated throughout the Middle East. Any notion of a peace process going forward between Arabs and Israelis, with the Israeli army at that moment laying siege to an Arab capital, was impossible. Perhaps even worse, the relationship between Israel and Egypt, given life by the Camp David Accords of 1978, was swiftly deteriorating.

The Arab world had been infuriated by Egyptian president Anwar Sadat's courageous visit to Jerusalem in 1977. Egypt's subsequent peace treaty with Israel further heightened tensions. Arab League nations broke off relations with Egypt. Sadat was assassinated. Now, with an Arab-Israeli war raging, Egypt's leaders were under enormous pressure. Egypt's large Arab population was deeply aggrieved and was muttering about its own government in Cairo. The negotiations for autonomy called for in Camp David—as a step toward a solution to the Palestinian problem and to the status of the occupied territories on the West Bank and Gaza—were dead. The keystone of peace, the Egyptian–Israeli Peace Treaty, was under the gun. The United States had to act quickly, I knew.

The four-hour flight passed like a flash. Upon arrival, O'Bie and I were met at Dulles Airport by what would now be my security detail and by the president's top White House advisers: Chief of Staff Jim Baker, Counselor to the President Ed Meese, Assistant to the President Mike Deaver, and National Security adviser Bill Clark. It was noon on Saturday. The president and the first lady had gone to Camp David for the weekend. Someone pointed to a U.S. Marine helicopter, its rotors turning slowly. "The president wants you to chopper up to Camp David for a meeting. There's a car over there to take Mrs. Shultz into Washington, or wherever she wants to go. She can scare up a hotel room for the two of you."

"Thanks a lot," I replied, "but we come as a package deal. Either we both go to Camp David or we both go scare up a Washington hotel room—take your choice." So off we went together to Camp David.

Early Associations

On the brief helicopter ride, earlier associations with the president flashed through my mind. His telephone call to me in London was not the first time Ronald Reagan had asked me to help. I remembered an invitation from him, when he was governor of California, to come to Sacramento in August 1974, after I resigned as secretary of the treasury in the Nixon administration. He knew I had moved to California and invited me to lunch. We sat together with a few other people and talked for several hours. He grilled me about how the presidency worked. He was interested in nuts and bolts: the process of assembling the budget, dealing with the cabinet and individual cabinet members, ideas for reform of the executive branch, prospects for containing federal spending—on and on. I came away convinced that this man did not simply want to be president: he had an agenda, and he wanted to know how to carry it out.

I remembered having Ronald Reagan to dinner at my house on the Stanford campus in July 1978, when he was a presidential candidate. He was questioned, argued and agreed with, lectured and listened to, by among others Milton and Rose Friedman, Bill Simon, Martin and Annelise Anderson, Ezra Solomon, and Alan Greenspan. Years later he remarked, "I noticed you watching me closely that evening, and I wondered what you were thinking." I had been trying to decide whether he had real views or canned statements. I could see his views were real and ran deep.

I could talk to Ronald Reagan candidly, and he would listen. He had strong views, and I respected them. I felt we could work together. So during the presidential campaign I became chairman of his economic policy advisers and, after his inauguration, chairman of the President's Economic Policy Advisory Board. And in May 1982, just a month before the president telephoned me in London, I had traveled, at his and Secretary of State Haig's request, to meet each allied head of state in preparation for the Versailles economic summit. The president wanted me to give the allied leaders a reading of his personal views and to find out what was on their minds.

Camp David

When our chopper arrived at Camp David, the president and Nancy Reagan greeted us. The natural, relaxed attitude of the president at Camp David that Saturday contrasted with my encounter in late 1968 with President-elect Richard Nixon. Nixon had asked me on the telephone to become his secretary of labor. I said yes, but I also requested a meeting, which soon took place at the Century Plaza Hotel in Los Angeles. I wanted to be sure the president-elect knew my views on labor matters and saw what kind of labor secretary I would be. I would get along with the unions, try to make collective bargaining work, play down high-level and White House intervention in strikes, work on retraining programs for displaced or disadvantaged workers, advocate equal employment opportunity. If he was uncomfortable with these views, well, my appointment hadn't been announced, and he could go on to someone else. Of course, I wanted to know his ideas on these subjects and what he hoped to accomplish in the White House.

Instead, I was struck to hear an uneasy, defensive statement about why I, as a university man, would feel comfortable in his cabinet. Was he afraid of rejection from a person in the academic community? I had supported him during the campaign. I thought to myself, this man has just been elected president of the United States and yet he is selling himself to me. The complexity of Nixon and his insecurities, as well as his brilliance and his keen instinct for strategy, were in my mind as I talked with Reagan, who was invariably so comfortable with himself.

President Reagan and I had lunch under a canopy of trees outside Aspen Cottage at Camp David. Bill Clark, Jim Baker, and Ed Meese joined us. The shells were falling in Beirut, the press was howling, and pressure on the United States was mounting at the United Nations to take some kind of action against Israel. The president was calm and affable. But he and his aides, I could see, were also gripped with a sense of urgency, frustration, and crisis. The Fourth of July holiday coming up would be no holiday for me. The president wanted me involved right away, but I could not be in the action officially until I was confirmed by the Senate, at the soonest in two to three weeks' time. Until then I would study the issues and assemble my State Department team.

As President Reagan and I surveyed the world from this relaxed country setting, the challenges I faced were daunting. The president and his White House team talked less about those challenges than about organization and working relationships. I could detect ongoing institutional tensions between the White House and State Department. They assured me of their wholehearted support. I remembered the importance of the easy contact I had developed with President Nixon when I had been in his cabinet. "I consider myself to be part of the White House and of your team. I'm working for you, Mr. President. I'll make use of the talent at the State Department to get our job done. I've always been able to work with career people in government, and I know they'll work hard for us if we give them leadership and involvement." These were welcome sentiments. They all seemed to be looking for calmer seas after their tempestuous time with Al Haig.

Washington insiders were saying that the foreign affairs system in Washington wasn't working after a year and a half of the Reagan presidency and Haig's secretaryship. Former National Security adviser Zbigniew Brzezinski had just said in an interview that the United States had a choice in making foreign policy: the president does it all, and he and the NSC (National Security Council) adviser overshadow the secretary of state; or the secretary of state, in close communication with the president, is allowed to go to work. "What has surprised me about the last 18 months is that we have had neither the first nor the second system," Brzezinski said. "The president has not been actively involved, but the secretary of state has not been permitted to run foreign policy. I hope now, with Mr. Shultz coming on, that the president will decide to let the secretary of state run foreign policy and be recognized as the man in charge."[1]

I could not yet judge this organizational issue, but I had signed on with Ronald Reagan because I supported his principles and felt that we agreed on the direction our foreign policy should take. Despite the uneasy state of the U.S. economy and the world economy, I felt that the president was profoundly right to stress that economic progress and development would spring from free and open markets, free enterprise, and an open trading system. The president was also right to stress the importance of our ability to defend ourselves. Whatever the merits and demerits of the scale and composition of the defense buildup President Reagan had launched, our defensive capabilities were improving, and morale in the armed services was rising. From a military standpoint, the United States was back in business. From the standpoint of diplomacy, that renewed capability was important. Power and diplomacy work *together*. Political pressures in Washington tend to push toward one extreme or the other; operating both at the same time would require great care and skill.

Most important, I was convinced that the West was winning the ideological battle. Communism had failed: as an economic model, it simply didn't work, as demonstrated in the dramatic contrast between West Germany and East Germany, North Korea and South Korea, and through other comparisons between thriving market-based economies and foundering command-and-control economies. As a political model, communism had failed as well. And on a moral dimension, Communist countries exhibited such gross violations of human rights that any prospect of communism's further spread was chilling to contemplate. Yet in the military dimension, the Soviet Union had proved itself able to develop awesome power and use it ruthlessly and skillfully.

The crux of the issue, I had said in my speech at Stanford in 1979, was time and will: to hold off the Soviet military threat long enough for America to regain its resolve internationally, to demonstrate how to use freedom and open markets as the organizing principles for economic and political development, and to do so long enough to allow communism's failures to be fully recognized and to play themselves out. America had much more going for it than was commonly perceived. The question was whether our

1. As quoted in the *Atlanta Constitution*, June 27, 1982.

will and resolve, and that of our allies, were sufficiently strong to contain Soviet aggression and challenge its ideology.

Upon our return from Camp David, O'Bie and I didn't have to scare up a hotel room after all. We were offered the town house on Jackson Place set aside for former presidents when they visit Washington. On Sunday, we went to see Vice President George Bush, my second call after hitting the ground in Washington. He and Barbara were at home at their official residence on the grounds of the Naval Observatory in northwest Washington and had invited us to lunch. They were gracious in welcoming us to the administration. I stressed that I intended to work closely with the White House and for the president. My way would be supportive and collaborative.

Getting Started at State

I then went to work. Ready and waiting for me was what the security agents who now led me everywhere called "the secure package": a Cadillac limousine—heavy and creaky with armor plate—driven by a young agent, with another riding shotgun beside him, and a follow car, a high-chassised Chevy Blazer carrying four agents and a small arsenal. They kept a constant radio chatter going between the two vehicles and with our destination, the Department of State.

Larry Eagleburger, the under secretary of state for political affairs, was waiting for me in my office. A voluminous, white, long-sleeved turtleneck inadequately disguised his bulk but apparently kept him comfortable in the cold, air-conditioned drafts of the place. Eagleburger got on the phone and with exaggerated profanity, and in tones of mock irritation and impatience that were his trademark, summoned Charlie Hill, a foreign service officer who apparently was good at writing things down. The appearance of this hollow-eyed figure in a sawed-off sweatshirt, who had obviously been at it all night, and his sidebar briefing of Eagleburger on what was happening at this moment in Beirut underscored that I had walked into a hands-on operational outfit in the midst of a crisis. The contrast between the peaceful summer day, with tourists strolling outside the State Department, and the tense situation within could not have been more stark.

I could quickly see that the State Department's operations center was on full alert. Through cables, tickers, television, and telephones—secure and open—State Department officers were maintaining instantaneous contact with a dangerous situation in war-racked Beirut and, at the same time, were engaged in intensive diplomatic efforts to deal with it in Jerusalem, Riyadh, Tunis, Damascus, Paris, New York, and who knew where else. From our ambassador's residence in Yarzé on a hill overlooking Beirut, Phil Habib, presidential envoy to the Middle East, was conducting negotiations to try to evacuate leaders and fighters of the PLO from the city and, simultaneously, to hold back the Israelis from demolishing this capital of an Arab country with air and artillery bombardment. Such an act could incite political upheaval all across the Middle East and fuel terrorist retaliation that would threaten American lives and America's interests.

This was not yet my challenge, however, for I was not yet secretary of state. Until confirmed, I would study, learn, listen, and wait. Al Haig and I talked for two hours that Sunday afternoon. Haig had no gripe with me, nor I with him. Our styles and approaches were different, but our general outlook on many issues was similar. I was surprised, as I looked around during my conversation with Haig, at the unchanged appearance of the secretary of state's office. It looked just as it had almost six years earlier when I had met there with Henry Kissinger. Large but not impressive, the room was dark and gloomy with the draperies drawn, its colonial furniture somehow out of place in the impersonal "Eisenhower modern" style of the walnut-paneled room. At the end of this chamber was a small, ancient desk, which I was told had been fashioned from the timbers of Captain Oliver Hazard Perry's flagship at the Battle of Lake Erie in 1813. I could easily hear "We have met the enemy and they are ours!" coming from Al Haig, so commanding was his bearing. In fact, this instinct for command had apparently generated many of his problems. He reviewed for me the range of issues worldwide, emphasizing Lebanon, Central America, the Soviet Union, and China.

I had heard and read that Haig's resignation was the result of clashes with the White House staff over both style and substance. He wanted to run things himself, but others wanted in—including Ronald Reagan. Haig's bristling manner did not suit the Meese-Baker-Deaver circle, and bureaucratic turf battles were constantly being waged between the White House and the State Department.

This was a different Washington from the one I had experienced a decade earlier as secretary of the treasury. The number of aides that surrounded the president and each of the top appointed officials had ballooned. Staffs of organizations, supposedly following the same administration policy, waged perpetual battle on behalf of—and often without the knowledge of—their principals. And, as I had sensed in the days when Henry Kissinger was national security adviser, a cult of secrecy verging on deception had taken root in the White House and NSC staffs. Beyond that, the secret and spectacular Kissinger trip in July 1971 reopening relations with China cast the NSC adviser in an operational role. When he became secretary of state, he retained for some time the title and role of NSC adviser as well. Henry's brilliance and skill carried the day, but the potential for conflict between the secretary of state and the NSC adviser was evident.

I had learned a few things over the years about struggles between the

White House staff and cabinet officers.[2] I also knew from my days as Office of Management and Budget director and treasury secretary how easily a White House office can be translated into authority: President Nixon had installed me in a suite of offices on the floor above Henry Kissinger's to give me a White House perspective to bring to my tasks. Nixon didn't like budget work or economics much and wanted me to run the details, subject to his policy direction. I retained the confidence of my cabinet colleagues because I did not abuse this power, but I could see then how the White House staff can easily overreach unless cabinet officers and the president refuse to let that happen.

Throughout the next week I operated from my transition office, physically only about twenty yards away from the secretary of state's suite but operationally far removed from the action. I spent the week performing the Washington rites of passage. Appointed officials of the administration, high and low, came to call on me, to inform and get to know the secretary of state–designate, the third-ranking position in the executive branch. But I went up to Capitol Hill to call on the senators who would be giving their advice and consent on my appointment and with whom I would work in the development and support of our foreign policy.

Over the July Fourth weekend O'Bie and I went to the farm in western Massachusetts that my father had bought some forty years earlier. Deliberately not remodeled or modernized, this simple house has always been a place for me to unwind and get away from it all, to enjoy family and old golfing buddies. My rural neighbors and the Cummington volunteer fire company were amused by my new notoriety and by my retinue of security agents, who were rigging up the farm to an alarm that would go off in the local firehouse should "the perimeter" be breached. I was resigned to the intrusive nature of their job. From Massachusetts I flew to San Francisco to organize personal and financial matters for my new life in Washington. As I made these moves around the country, I was kept generally abreast of events in Lebanon.

Yasser Arafat, leader of the PLO, was reported to be jubilant about Haig's resignation, seeing it as giving new life to the PLO presence in Israeli-surrounded Beirut. In contrast to "pro-Israel" Haig, I was being stereotyped as an "Arabist," because Bechtel Corporation had big con-

---

2. When I took office as labor secretary, I was acutely conscious of the days when John Steelman, President Truman's aide, completely preempted the labor secretary by making clear that the way to the exercise of presidential clout ran through him. A Republican administration would have a different relationship with organized labor (as George Meany, president of the AFL-CIO, told me, "I got no chips on that table"); nevertheless, the labor movement, and George Meany as the personification of organized labor, had considerable political power and would therefore be sought after from time to time. I told George Meany that I would see that he had quiet access to the president. He told me that he would deal with the White House only through me. I knew my system was working when White House staffers came to me in frustration for help with organized labor. They said that Meany's office had sent them.

struction jobs under way in Saudi Arabia and around the Persian Gulf. The shift from Haig to Shultz, others speculated, might undermine the cease-fire by leading Israel to conclude that a negotiated departure of the PLO was now impossible and that an assault to capture the city was the only way to finish off the Palestinian leader.

At dawn on July 1 the White House had received an urgent, very restricted message from Phil Habib: the United States should insist on an unequivocal pledge from Israeli Prime Minister Menachem Begin not to invade Beirut and to allow efforts aimed at a political and diplomatic solution to proceed without any deadline whatsoever. If Begin refused, Habib recommended, the United States should stop all military supplies to Israel and support a UN resolution calling for Israel's total withdrawal from Lebanon and for international sanctions against Israel. Haig differed sharply: take the pressure off the PLO and you founder in your diplomatic effort to get the PLO to leave.

"To escape the postresignation curiosity of Washington," as he put it, Haig had taken up residence at the Greenbriar, a grand secluded resort in West Virginia, where he continued to monitor the cable traffic. Notwithstanding the gulf between Habib, Haig, and the White House over the war, Al Haig was still managing the U.S. role in dealing with the Beirut crisis. Haig had resigned, but he remained. Decisions were being taken in which I had no hand but with which I would be compelled to work as soon as I was confirmed. It made no sense for Al Haig to keep trying, between sets of tennis, to run a negotiation in war-stricken Beirut from a telephone in the West Virginia mountains.

As I talked with the president in person and later by phone during the first days of July, I could see that he was increasingly uneasy with Al Haig's continuing role. I didn't want to act as though I was already secretary of state, and Al didn't want to relinquish control. He had particularly strong views about the ongoing situation in Lebanon, and he wanted to give the directions. Not everybody agreed with those views. The president and his advisers wanted Haig to leave now that he had resigned, but somehow nobody was ready to tell him. I talked with President Reagan on July 5 while he was in California. He clearly wanted Al out of the loop. Finally, I volunteered. "Well, maybe you'd like me to call him and tell him." The president quickly took me up on the offer. So I called Al and told him that the president felt that it was time for him to turn over the reins.

"Well, George, do you think you're ready?" Haig asked.

"Al," I said, "I'm not going to become acting secretary of state. Walter Stoessel, your deputy, will be the acting secretary until I'm confirmed."

Haig said he wanted to hear the word directly from the president. The president made a further call.

"What George told you is true," he confirmed. So Haig did finally leave.

But I saw in this episode a little suggestion about how Ronald Reagan, who could be as tough as nails, didn't like picking up the phone and telling Al Haig, "It's time to go."

As I worked my way through the first two weeks of July, Beirut kept breaking in. I was now getting briefed on the situation two or three times a day. Phil Habib was raging over the secure telephone that negotiations had been halted because of Israeli shelling and harassment of the Lebanese go-betweens. The cease-fire kept breaking down. As of Tuesday, July 13, the day my Senate confirmation hearings began, all fronts looked bad. The PLO was stalling and complicating the negotiations because no Arab country wanted to take them. The Israelis, seeing Habib's effort as likely to fail, were threatening to capture Beirut and rout the Palestinians. Yet they were hesitant, realizing that house-to-house fighting in Beirut would cost the lives of many Israeli soldiers. They preferred a negotiated outcome. But the multinational force (MNF) needed as part of the deal to get the PLO out of Beirut was not coming together easily.

Beirut was capturing the headlines, but, far from being an isolated problem, it seemed almost a symbol of a world in disarray. Daniel Southerland wrote in the *Christian Science Monitor* on July 15: George Shultz "faces a world in turmoil, and the world will not wait. Rarely has a new secretary of state had to deal with so many upheavals occurring in so many places around the world." He was right. As I headed for my confirmation hearings, I knew I would face stiff and difficult questions, but they were the least of my problems. The world *was* in turmoil, and creative engagement from the United States of America was desperately needed.

CHAPTER 2

Confirmation:
Prepare and Defend

I remember thinking to myself after completing my final exam for a Ph.D. degree in economics at MIT that it would be my last. From now on, as a faculty member, I'd be giving the exams, not taking them. How wrong could I be? No exam I had taken before compared with the demands and the tension that surrounded my confirmation hearing for the post of secretary of state.

The personal side of my life would be open for inspection, including my finances, prior affiliations, and any potential conflict of interest. Not just individual acts would be in question; everything would be scrutinized— my whole life record: my reputation, my demeanor under pressure, as well as my thoughts, plans, and hopes for the future.

I had been through the confirmation process in the Nixon administration as nominee for secretary of labor in 1969 and again for secretary of the treasury in 1972. I remembered Senator Jacob Javits taking me aside just before my hearings for secretary of labor were to begin. "Remember, George, what you don't say can't be held against you," he said with a wry smile. I knew a great many of the senators personally, Democrats and Republicans, and they knew me. I figured I was clean as a hound's tooth, as President Eisenhower used to put it; nevertheless, I had given careful thought to the problems of confirmation. I was a university professor, but also a businessman who had served on the boards of multinational corporations. I was president of Bechtel, a vast enterprise engaged in huge engineering and construction projects all over the world. I knew that many supporters of Israel were concerned that Bechtel's projects and connections in the Arab world would bias me against Israel. I had no such bias, but I knew that I had to be ready to state my positions clearly and thoughtfully.

So despite what I regarded as a clean and open record, I took an unusual step: I decided to get legal counsel. I wanted to start right out in a way

16

that would build confidence in my unencumbered dedication to the job. I called Lloyd Cutler, one of Washington's wise men, who had the added advantage of being a Democrat and having served in the Carter White House. He agreed to help, and his counsel was invaluable. I made all the details of my activities and my finances known to him. I decided to make an absolutely clean break, resigning from all my business and organizational responsibilities, putting all my financial holdings in a blind trust, and, of course, disassociating myself completely from Bechtel. Everyone agreed that it was fine for me to be a professor on leave from Stanford University, and the trustees agreed to give me leave for as long as I was secretary of state. I doubt that they foresaw six and a half years.

I set up within the State Department what the lawyers call a recusal process, which would take effect automatically when the Senate voted to confirm my nomination. Under that process everyone would understand that if any matter involving Bechtel came into the department, I would not even know that the issue was under discussion.

When Lloyd Cutler laid out for the White House, State Department, and Senate ethics units all the steps I was taking, they were astonished. On the whole, with his good work and these decisions, potential accusations or concerns about conflicts of interest arising from my business background were defused or put to rest. The process helped build trust and confidence.

My preparation also involved reading mountains of briefing books and listening as waves of experts gave me their views on an incredible range of issues. I submitted to a State Department specialty—the murder board. I would pick a subject—Soviet relations, El Salvador, nuclear nonprolif-eration, refugee policy, pipeline sanctions—and do my homework. Senior officials would then fire questions, often hostile, at me as they thought senators might. We had a little rock and sock, just to give me a feel for what was to come. A little went a long way. My confirmation hearings, I concluded, would be not so much an exam as an opportunity to reestablish myself, my views, and my presence in high-pressure Washington. I knew I had to project confidence without arrogance, to be my own man while supporting the president, to speak candidly and substantively without pre-suming expertise where my background was scanty. I had no chip on my shoulder, but the senators must see that I would not be bullied. Once a person can be bullied and turned apologetic, there's no end of trouble.

Where I had clear views on hot topics, I wanted to set them out candidly and clearly. I wanted the senators to feel that "what you see is what you get." If they didn't like what they saw, they could argue, and if they didn't like it at all, they could vote against me. But if I was confirmed, there I would be, out in front, having put my views forward. I recognized that plenty of minefields lay ahead, so I should not make my passage through them more difficult by ill-considered or offhand commentary.

The confirmation process would let the American people see and hear and judge me as a person who would be conducting a substantial part of their business, and it would impose on me accountability. If confirmed, I would be on the firing line again and again in hearings and sessions on Capitol Hill, where I would give and get information, and explain and defend our policies on behalf of the president. This accountability, through continuing public interaction with the Congress and the public, critically distinguishes cabinet members from staff members in the White House, the National Security Council (NSC), or elsewhere in the executive branch who have no such requirement or tradition of public accountability.

The Hearings Begin

July 13, 1982: the hearing room was jammed, the atmosphere electric with anticipation of what might come—a circus, an assault, an explosive argument. I sat alone at the center table, arranged so that I looked up at the senators seated around a horseshoe table above me. My wife, two of my children, Margaret and Alex, and Lloyd Cutler sat behind me. Hot, bright lights illuminated the room, with the television cameras whirring away and reporters leaning forward to scrutinize my every facial expression for signs of inner feeling.

A number of senators made positive noises in their opening statements. I decided the natives were friendly. In the years ahead, my knowledge would increase tremendously as I was exposed to the fire hose of information that was pointed at me day after day. But, remarkably, the attitudes and ideas that I expressed at the hearings had a staying power throughout my time as secretary of state. I set out in my prepared statement what were to me bedrock principles. I stressed the importance of economic strength at home, the crucial need for a strong defense to back up a strong diplomacy, and the vital role our allies played as we pursued our objectives of peace, freedom, and stability.

I was impressed, and said so, with the complexity and global nature of economic and strategic developments and the impact of the revolution in communications and information technology on our world. "The international economy is no longer managed from a few world capitals but has developed into a global network of mutually dependent partners," I said. "Extensive trade in goods and services, the international flow of critical raw materials, the emergence of new technologies, and the revolution in communications have created a world in which no nation is immune from the influence of the international economy."

The problems of our tense relations with the Soviets would, I knew, come up again and again in the hearings, so I set out my views: "Diminished

American strength and resolve are an open invitation for Soviet expansion into areas of critical interest to the West and provide no incentive for moderation in the Soviet military buildup. Thus it is critical to the overall success of our foreign policy that we persevere in the restoration of our strength; but it is also true that the willingness to negotiate from that strength is a fundamental element of strength itself . . . and as we enter a potentially critical period of transition in Soviet leadership, we must also make it clear that we are prepared to establish mutually beneficial and safer relationships on the basis of reciprocity."

Finally, I discussed my views on the Middle East, especially Lebanon. I had known Beirut when it was a beautiful and thriving city. Now it was being consumed by a devastating conflict between Israel and the Palestinians. I knew from my own experience what a great problem this war posed in other Arab countries. I had visited Israel, first in 1969 and again in 1977. I had former students and many friends there, and I admired and liked the Israelis. I knew Palestinians, too, hardworking, able, and creative people, somehow lost in the tangle of Middle East developments. I ended my prepared statement with a pledge: "We must dare to hope that with effort and imagination, we can arrive at an agreement that will satisfy the vital security interests of Israel and the political aspirations of the Palestinians, meet the concerns of other parties directly involved, and win the endorsement of the international community."

Questions and Answers

For two days the senators probed and questioned in purposeful and thoughtful ways. I also took some jabs that caused the temperature to rise a bit. A hot issue was my Bechtel association and a presumed pro-Arab tilt. Very early in the hearings I had a testy exchange with Senator Alan Cranston from my home state of California. Cranston was very close to Jewish groups in the United States and to Israel, and he spoke for many of the reservations about me that were being expressed behind the scenes. Earlier I had called on Cranston to set out my views, and we had a friendly, forthright discussion. I was surprised, under those circumstances, that during the hearing, Senator Cranston took me on, attacked my association with Bechtel, and implied that Bechtel was in some way reprehensible and unprincipled.

The best approach, I decided, was to hit back directly. Hearings are used in part by politicians to score points with the voters back home. So I had to stand up for myself.

MR. SHULTZ. First of all, Senator, let me say that I resent what I regard as a kind of a smear against Bechtel. I think it is a marvelous company, an honorable company, a law-abiding company, a company that does credit to our country here and all over the world. Now, first of all, about your implication—

SENATOR CRANSTON. Well, let me—

MR. SHULTZ. Well, now, wait a minute. You had your say. Let me have my say.

SENATOR CRANSTON. All right. I said that I have great respect for the company. I have questions about one pursuit of policies by that company at one particular time.

MR. SHULTZ. You inferred that Bechtel continues—that Bechtel violates the law insofar as the Arab boycott is concerned. That is not correct. Bechtel abides by the law. . . . So in your question you said will I part company with Bechtel and not encourage violation of this law, I just reject that. Bechtel abides by that law.

Questions about Bechtel didn't end there. Cranston and a few others poked away at the Arab boycott of Israel, Bechtel's lobbying activities, and its work in the nuclear field. Bechtel was easy to defend; it had handled these issues honorably and well. In the end, Senator Paul Tsongas, Democrat from Massachusetts, concluded, "The Bechtel issue is basically a non-issue." That captured the prevailing view.

Senator Charles Mathias described a foreign policy sea that was not only "stormy" but "flecked with some very dangerous chunks of ice, ice floes that could founder us. . . . But the big iceberg, the real iceberg that threatens the navigation of the ship of State continues to be our relationship with the Soviet Union," he said. "Never before have two nations commanded such enormous destructive power. We are in a unique position for which there is no precedent in the whole history of mankind, and the management of that relationship will in a very large measure fall to you. . . . No. 1, do you think that is a danger? No. 2, how do we cope with it?"

Our relationship with the Soviet Union would go best, I said, if "everyone, ourselves, them, our friends around the world," sees that we proceed on the basis of "realism about what is going on around the world, and the implications of Soviet behavior" and second, "that we are clear in our minds and in our actions that we will provide ourselves with the strength that we need to defend our interests, not to be aggressive, but to be able to deter any [Soviet] aggression. . . . I think on the basis of realism and on the basis of strength, part of that strength itself is the self-confidence to undertake negotiations when they are called for." I felt confident that this was President Reagan's view, but few people at the time would have agreed; the president was under attack for taking unrealistic negotiating positions with the Soviets. Ours "is not a strategy of aggression," I said. "It is not a strategy of confrontation. It is a strategy of confidence and strength and realism about the nature of their system and what they are trying to do."[1]

A refrain heard throughout the hearing concerned the theme of negotiations. When to negotiate? With whom? How to go about it? The Soviets, the PLO, Central America, China, Japan—almost every topic featured this refrain. In a comment all too prophetic of the perpetual battles ahead, I said I was struck whenever I was involved in negotiations that the most important bargaining took place *within* one's own negotiating team and that those internal negotiations were the most difficult of all.

The questions put to me ranged the globe, but the most intense concerned the Middle East.

SENATOR BOSCHWITZ. The President has also said that the cornerstone of our effort and our interest in the Middle East is a secure Israel. Do you agree with that as well? . . .

MR. SHULTZ. Yes. But I think that we and everybody else involved weaken Israel when we do not insist and work and strive to bring about a peaceful situation there. We do not do anybody any favor by letting this thing drag on. So I believe that strength is not simply military strength, but what you do with it and what you do with the situation that may be created by it.

It is not military strength that we want; it is peace that we want.

Senator John Glenn of Ohio asked about sending marines to Lebanon as part of a multinational force. "I favor the use of U.S. forces if it can be done properly and safely," I responded, "in order to resolve the problem we see in Beirut. If we can remove the PLO fighters from Beirut peacefully, get them somewhere else, and avoid an explosion in Beirut, we will have accomplished something very important for the long-run cause of peace, and we will have avoided a tremendous amount of bloodshed. So if we can do that properly and in conjunction with the forces of another country which I think shows that it is not just us, I would favor doing that, yes, sir."

"You used the word 'safely,' " Glenn followed up. "I would submit that if it can be done safely, we do not need the Marines. And if it cannot be done safely, then we are going to be attending some funerals over in Arlington with Marines coming back in body bags one of these days. It is one or the other."

1. I was not a neophyte in dealing with the Soviets. In 1973, my talks with Premier Alexei Kosygin underlay the evolution of what became the Long-Term Grain Agreement, first negotiated in 1975: the Soviets committed publicly to buy a stated amount of grain during a crop year, a commitment that our farmers wanted; then, if the Soviets wished to buy above that amount, they could do so up to a certain specified point, but beyond that point they had to obtain permission and publicly announce their intended purchases. This arrangement gave the Soviets assurances of their access to our market but also gave information to the market that would prevent Soviet exploitation of the monopsony power that goes with a big buyer— a point I had gotten across to Kosygin two years earlier.

"Well, we certainly do not want that," I responded. "But I do not agree with you. I think that on our streets, if there are some police, it helps safety. It is not a question of saying if things are safe, we do not need the police, and if they are not safe, we cannot use them. I think the presence of people who are capable of maintaining peace contributes to it."[2]

I had said in my opening statement, "The crisis in Lebanon makes painfully and totally clear a central reality of the Middle East: the legitimate needs and problems of the Palestinian people must be addressed and resolved, urgently and in all their dimensions." At the same time, in a region where hostility was endemic and where so much of that hostility was addressed against Israel, its preoccupation with matters of security was essential. No one, I stressed, should question the depth and durability of America's commitment to the security of Israel or our readiness to assure that Israel had the necessary means to defend itself. "We owe it to Israel," I said, "in the context of our special relationship to work with her to bring about a comprehensive peace acceptable to all the parties involved, which is the only sure guarantee of true and durable security."

High-sounding talk, and I meant every word of it.

---

2. I have thought about this exchange many times, especially after the tragedy of the car bombing of our inadequately secured marine barracks in Beirut in October 1983 in which 241 marines were killed.

CHAPTER 3

How I Think
and How I Got That Way

No one can ever be fully prepared for the job of secretary of state. But as I reflect on my life and experiences, I can see that certain stages of my career have been particularly helpful. As a dean at a major university, I learned to exercise responsibility in a sea of uncertain authority. As an economist, I learned that important results emerge from an unfolding process and that good policy must therefore have a sense of strategy, pace, and timing. As the incumbent in three cabinet posts in the Nixon administration, I had been exposed to the special ways of Washington and to the role of Congress and the press. I had good experiences with able and supportive career public servants. As secretary of the treasury, I developed important friendships with people in many parts of the world and, in my work with them, got a feel for the world economy. As a leader in a large international business, I expanded my sense of variations and similarities in countries and people throughout the world. In short, I brought with me a diverse knowledge of my own country and how it works, as well as how it works with others, from my experiences as a university man, a cabinet official, and a business and financial man. I also had been a resident at times on both coasts and in the Midwest, an arbitrator and mediator in labor disputes, and a worker on the problems of civil rights. My early life, too, was important.

My Early Life

My parents loved me, and I knew it. They made me a part of their life, so I was surrounded by whatever the conversation was when we were all at home. I was born in New York City in midtown Manhattan. When I was two or three years old, we moved across the Hudson River to Englewood, New Jersey, to a house where we lived until I went to college.

I have vivid memories of my mother reading to me as a young child, especially *When We Were Very Young* by A. A. Milne. I can still quote verses here and there from that book. I am sure this experience has something to do with my love of and respect for books. My parents paid a lot of attention to me, and throughout my childhood I was in a very supportive environment.

I can remember clearly my grade-school teachers, particularly Mr. Metzger, who taught English and history, and Mr. Beaumont, who taught mathematics. They set high standards and had the attitude "Good is not good enough." They also made me pay attention. I remember looking out the window one day and having an eraser hit me behind the ear. Good marksmanship by Beaumont.

The academic program was strong, and the teachers were top-notch. I liked school, and I did well. When I was about twelve years old, I decided to start a newspaper with the imaginative title the *Weekly News*; it came out on Saturdays. I would get up my copy and use a gelatin-based reproduction process. I priced my paper at five cents. The main thing I remember about this endeavor, which didn't last long, was going around peddling my paper. One day when I arrived at my neighbor's front door with my latest edition, he walked over to a nearby table and picked up a copy of the *Saturday Evening Post*, which also cost five cents in those days. He placed the magazine in my hand and said to me, "I bought this for five cents. Do you think I should pay the same price for your paper?"

I was devastated. But I learned something about the marketplace.

My mother, Margaret, like me was raised as an only child. She was the daughter of a Presbyterian missionary, who with his wife had gone west to establish a church in Shoshone, Idaho, where my mother was born. When she was four years old, both of her parents died. She then moved to New York, where her aunt and uncle brought her up. Her uncle, George Pratt, was an Episcopalian minister. Uncle George and Aunt Margaret were like grandparents to me. We would often go to Uncle George's church on Sundays, and afterward we would have lunch in their New York apartment. As a small boy, I didn't particularly enjoy this, but I liked them.

My father, Birl, was one of seven children. He was raised as a Quaker on a farm in Indiana and managed somehow to get a scholarship and by working, waiting on tables and such, put himself through DePauw University. My father loved sports and passed his enthusiasm and competitive instincts on to me. At DePauw he played on the football team. The high point of his football career was the game with Notre Dame. Whenever we listened on the radio to a Notre Dame football game, my father would always remind me that he played against Notre Dame. He never told me the score. After DePauw, my father got another scholarship, to study for a Ph.D. in history at Columbia University. In connection with his dissertation, he wound up writing a book jointly with Charles A. Beard, the famous historian. I think my father always regretted he did not somehow stay in university teaching, because he enjoyed it and enjoyed history.

In the early 1920s my father took a job with the New York Stock Exchange, where he developed an educational program that taught the basic procedures, the nuts and bolts, of how the Stock Exchange worked as well as more advanced subjects relating to security analysis and investment management. In those days, people worked a five-and-a-half-day week, so often on Saturday mornings, particularly in the fall and spring, I would go into work with my father. He would give me things to do around the office, and then we would go out to lunch together. I remember the most wonderful triple-decker sandwiches I ever had in my life at a restaurant called BMT. I would look forward to them all week long.

I loved playing football, and in the summer before my senior year at Princeton, I was determined to make the first team, so I worked hard. When the early practice time came before school started, I was in great physical shape. I knew I impressed the coaches and had a crack at making the team. Then, in one of those early scrimmages, I got clipped: my left knee was very badly injured, and I was unable to play at all in my senior year. After my injury, I was asked to be coach of the freshman backfield. It was, in a sense, my first teaching job.

I suppose this experience in coaching had something to do with my own orientation to the university and to a teaching career. It also marked the beginning of my own style of management. I always have found that if I could create an environment around me in which everybody felt they were learning, I would have a hot group. I have always tried to include people in what I was doing, to encourage them to say what they think, to let them see the problems that were confronting us all, and to create an atmosphere in which everyone could feel at the end of the day, or the end of a week or a month, that he or she had learned something.

As a child of the 1930s and of the depression, somehow I was attracted to economics and to what I thought of as the real side of the economy. At Princeton I had an experience in doing my senior thesis that left a permanent mark on me. I decided to write it on the agricultural program of the Tennessee Valley Authority (TVA), which was then both an exciting and controversial initiative in public policy. My major was economics, but my minor was in public and international affairs. So studying the TVA was right up my alley. During the summer of my junior year, I got a fellowship that enabled me to go down to the Tennessee Valley, where I gathered information from the headquarters in Knoxville and then went to live with a so-called hillbilly family in the mountains of Tennessee. I wanted to learn about how the TVA's effort to improve farm practices actually worked.

The family took me in but initially was very slow to give me real answers to my questions. Gradually, I learned from them and others that they knew the government information gatherers wanted to hear certain kinds of things, and that was precisely what the farmers told them, whether the information was accurate or not. The farmers wanted to continue receiving the fertilizer and other benefits the government was supplying them. So I came to see the distinction between the material that I eventually was able to gather and the statistics that had been compiled by the government, based on flawed raw material. I learned that if you are going to get people to talk candidly, they have to trust you, and trust takes time to develop.

Midway through my senior year at Princeton, the Japanese attacked Pearl Harbor on December 7, 1941, and America entered World War II. Although much of the senior year still lay ahead, my classmates and I were eager to get into the war. The dramatic aerial combat of the Battle of Britain had impressed us deeply. I tried to enlist in the Royal Canadian Air Force as a way of getting over there and doing my part, but my eyes weren't good enough to pass their test. As I was about to graduate, I heard a lot about the bright young economists at MIT. Somehow it appealed to me that a place like MIT, with its orientation toward the practical, would also be a place where there would be first-class economics. I applied to MIT for admission to the Ph.D. program in industrial economics and was accepted. Then I went to war.

I joined the marines, then turning the tide against Japan at Guadalcanal. I left for boot camp in Quantico, Virginia, in August 1942 and from there went to New River, North Carolina, for artillery training, after which I was shipped directly overseas. By April 1943, I was in Samoa, then on to a couple of battles in the Pacific islands.

When I came back to the States in the fall of 1945, after the war ended, I was assigned to the Boston Navy Yard. The marines didn't want to discharge people like me, but there was nothing for us to do. So I went to my commanding officer. "You don't have anything for me to do, so to get off your hands, why don't I just go over and enroll at MIT?" I asked him. "I won't be here during the day, but if you have something for me to do, you can get ahold of me." That was fine with him.

So I went to MIT. "You admitted me before the war, and here I am," I said to Doug Brown, one of the professors. I asked about the GI Bill of Rights, and he sent me over to see the MIT treasurer, who reacted very negatively toward me: "You people who come back from fighting in the war think the country owes you everything. Here you come to MIT and the first thing you ask about is how you are going to get money out of the GI Bill. What kind of an attitude is that?" My adrenaline rose, and though I felt like socking him, I just turned around and walked out.

I enrolled and soon found out there was hardly anyone else in the program. I took a class taught by Paul Samuelson, later to become Nobel Laureate, in which I had only one classmate. And I was the only student in the class of a wonderful professor of statistics named Harold Freeman. He liked to walk, so we would stroll outside and discuss the material, and he would quiz me. Then he would say, "Now it's time for some work at the blackboard," so we would find an empty classroom, and I would go to work at the blackboard on various statistical problems. I had professors who were absolutely the finest, and I had them practically to myself. This sort of graduate education was virtually unique.

I had met Helena O'Brien, O'Bie, on Kauai, where she was an army nurse. I was there for rest and recreation and re-forming our battalion between operations. We were married between MIT semesters in February 1946, two months after she returned to the States and two years after we met. Nurses were scarce after the war, so we figured she would get a job as a nurse. She worked for one day in a hospital in Cambridge, where the conditions were not as sanitary as she felt necessary. She left in tears and came home. "I'm a veteran, and I have the GI Bill of Rights. I can go to school, too," she said. So she went to the Fannie Farmer Boston Cooking School on the GI Bill. When I came home at night, having had half a hamburger for lunch somewhere and somehow eking out a meager existence with a part-time job while I studied, she might say, having eaten a lot of what she cooked that day, "Well, I don't feel too hungry." So the GI Bill of Rights was a two-edged sword, I discovered.

When I finished my Ph.D. in 1949, MIT and several other universities offered me a job. It was considered a compliment if the university where you got your Ph.D. asked you to stay on and become a member of the faculty. I was flattered and stayed. In 1955, I left for a year to become a senior staff economist for the President's Council of Economic Advisers and had the great good fortune of serving under Chairman Arthur Burns. Arthur liked to talk and stayed around the office late. So whenever I prepared a memorandum for him, I would bring it up to his secretary around four o'clock in the afternoon, hoping that he would look at it about 4:30 or 5:00 and ask me to discuss it with him. He often did, providing me the opportunity to sit and talk, sometimes for lengthy periods of time. This was a great education.

In the Nation's Service, the Princeton motto, was a favorite of my father's. He was never more thrilled than when I was appointed to the President's Council of Economic Advisers. When my family and I drove down to Washington, where I would begin that service, my mother and father drove down, too, forming a little caravan of sorts. My father saw my office in the Executive Office Building, right next to the White House, and he beamed.

Later that year he died. "Whatever you do," he told me, "do what you think is right for you. Somehow, the material side of life will take care of itself." I have always followed that advice.

My Life in Teaching, Business, and Government

As a dean at a big, high-powered university, the University of Chicago, from 1962 to 1968, I had a role with many parallels to that of a cabinet officer. I had to create an environment conducive to learning but could not order students to learn. I worked with faculty members who could be prima donnas (which was all right if they could sing), and who could become difficult when brought together in a meeting, somewhat like a congressional committee. I had a central administration to persuade about my budget and appointments. I had alumni whose loyalty I needed and whose money I sought. Here I was as dean, with a variety of constituencies, none of which was under my control. I had the responsibility for the health of the organization, but my only real authority came from my persuasive powers. I learned early on that I must be able to persuade if I was going to be effective.

In the three cabinet posts that I held in the Nixon administration, I learned the complexities of the interplay between the White House and Congress, between politicians and bureaucrats, and between the press and the public. As a cabinet officer, I could not just tell people what to do. I was working for the president; he was the one who got elected. My policies were his policies. But even with the president behind me, I had to persuade people, including those who worked directly with and for me. Of course, as events are breaking, you make decisions and expect that they are going to be carried out—and they will be, especially if you have built an atmosphere of inclusion and a record of performance. Performance creates legitimacy for a leader.

I was fortunate to have started initially as secretary of labor. I had come to the office in 1969, and I knew the subject cold. The department itself was small enough to let me get my arms around it and understand it well. I was a labor economist. I had worked as an arbitrator and mediator of labor disputes. I had undertaken one of the most extensive private efforts ever at retraining displaced workers. I had struggled with the issues that were at the heart of the department.

I encountered plenty of controversy in my time as secretary of labor, not only with labor disputes but with such undertakings as the drastic reform of the Job Corps, and to my complete surprise, the assignment in March 1969 from President Nixon to chair a Cabinet Task Force on Oil Import Control, a challenge that combined economic policy with political dynamite—from Texas to Massachusetts. After this assignment was announced, I received a short note from Edward Levi, president of the University of Chicago, from which I was on leave. "Dear George," he wrote, "I see that you have reformed the Job Corps and are now tackling the oil import control system. What do you want to teach next fall?"

When an early reorganization of the executive office of the president created the Office of Management and Budget (OMB), building on the old Budget Bureau, President Nixon asked me to become its first director. I took office in July 1970. He decided he wanted the director close to him, and so I had my office suite in the White House. My deputy director, Caspar Weinberger, occupied the traditional suite of the director in the Old Executive Office Building. I was responsible for the budget but interacted continuously with the president's immediate advisers in domestic and national security areas. This juxtaposition gave me a sense of what life was like in the White House, particularly as distinct from a cabinet department. A cabinet department is organized around the secretary and the programs of the department. The secretary is the boss. The White House is organized around the president, and from what I have seen of the White House in different administrations, it is an egocentric kind of operation that varies tremendously from one president to another, as each puts on it his own personal stamp. Everyone in the White House is staff to the president.

From director of the OMB, I went on in June 1972 to become secretary of the treasury at a time when the international monetary system was in turmoil. The Bretton Woods system of fixed rates of exchange between currencies had broken down, and a flexible-rate system emerged in its place. In the process of helping achieve a major transformation in the international monetary system, I traveled abroad extensively and became well acquainted with important government leaders all around the world, forming friendships that were deepened by working together on difficult problems in an atmosphere of great tension. After all, the price of money is the most important price in an economy, so the system for establishing that price will command intense attention. When you work through such hard problems with others, you form bonds that hold. Among the close friends I made during this period were Helmut Schmidt, finance minister of West Germany, soon to become chancellor, Valéry Giscard d'Estaing, minister of finance for France, soon to become its president, and Takeo Fukuda, finance minister of Japan, later to become its prime minister.

After I left the Nixon administration and had joined Bechtel, I traveled the world, acquiring firsthand experience with the world of work in many countries and making friends with people in unions, business, and finance. For example, I first met Bob Hawke, who became prime minister of Australia in 1983, when he was head of the Australian labor movement and I was concerned with major construction jobs in that country. In these years I gained a practical and operational angle of vision on foreign countries different from that accessible to a government official.

A Sense of Strategy

My training in economics has had a major influence on the way I think about public policy tasks, even when they have no particular relationship to economics. Economics deals with markets and how they work and seeks out the wide ramifications of policies and events across industries and over time. Economic policies are partially anticipated and continue to affect the economy long after they have been put in place. Results occur, but with a lag. The key to a successful policy is often to get the right process going. While the economist is accustomed to the concept of lags, the politician likes instant results. The tension comes because, as I wrote, "The economist's lag is the politician's nightmare."[1]

A good illustration came at the start of my first job in the cabinet. When I came into office as labor secretary in 1969, a major strike of longshoremen all along the East and Gulf coasts had been the center of attention for months. President Johnson had intervened, invoking the Taft-Hartley law, which allowed him to seek and get an injunction to stop the strike for eighty days. He did this after finding and declaring the strike a "national emergency." The unions contested this finding, and the issue went on a fast track to the Supreme Court, which upheld the president. By the time I took office in January 1969, the Taft-Hartley time period had run out, and the strike had started again. All of the statutory measures available to deal with it had been used. So when I arrived, I had a stubborn strike on my hands that had been authoritatively declared a national emergency.

I went to President Nixon, then preoccupied with the Vietnam War. "I have a strategy for how to handle this strike," I told him. "Let the pressures produced by the strike cause the union and management to settle it themselves through the collective bargaining process. We should announce that we will *not* intervene." By saying that, I was also saying, in effect, that the former president of the United States and the Supreme Court were wrong in their finding that the strike was a national emergency. I argued to Nixon that the economy was resilient and that while disruptions could be expected, buyers and sellers had all sorts of ways of finding substitutes for scarce goods: "There will be no dire emergency, and in the end the pressures will work to bring about a private settlement."

If we avoided direct intervention here, we would deliver a forceful message signaling the administration's commitment to the free collective bargaining system. We would also teach labor and management an important lesson about allowing private economic processes to work. The president

---

1. I summarized this idea, and the difficulty of implementing it, in an earlier book, *Economic Policy Beyond the Headlines*, which I wrote with Kenneth Dam (Stanford, Calif.: Stanford Alumni Association, 1977; New York: W. W. Norton, 1978).

supported me in this strategy. He successfully withstood tremendous pressure on the White House to intervene.

Meanwhile, pressure continued to mount on labor and management. Finally, lo and behold, after about six weeks, labor and management got together and settled the strike. The longshoremen went back to work. The result was much as I had predicted: the collective bargaining process was reinvigorated. By allowing the pressures inherent in the market to have their effect, people were forced to find their own solution. This approach was a sharp contrast to that taken in the Kennedy-Johnson period, when high-level intervention and "jawboning" in major disputes were routine. The result then had been a predictable flow of cases right into the White House. As I said to Nixon: "If the president hangs out his shingle, he'll get all the business."

So an economist is by training a strategist who will try to understand the constellation of forces present in a situation and try to arrange them to point toward a desirable result. A sense of strategy is critical in any negotiation: when to make concessions, when to hold firm, when to let things cool off, when to be intransigent. Coming into office as secretary of state at a time when we confronted tremendous problems, the economist in me asked, "Where are we trying to go, and what kind of strategy should we employ to get there?" recognizing that results would often be a long time in coming.

I could easily foresee that the year 1983 was going to have as one of its dominant motifs the critical negotiation on intermediate-range nuclear forces (INF) missiles and that success would require a cohesive NATO alliance. But we would never achieve the needed cohesion in the atmosphere of acrimony with our allies that had been generated by the Siberian pipeline dispute and other disagreements. I was alarmed that this problem did not seem adequately recognized within the administration. I knew that the right kind of negotiating atmosphere for us demanded that we get the pipeline dispute behind us as a clear matter of priority. Yet we had to resolve the dispute in a way that strengthened, not weakened, our hand with the Soviets.

This instinct for thinking ahead and trying to develop a sense of strategy had an institutional counterpart in the Department of State, known as the policy planning staff. This organization had been put in place in General George Marshall's day and had been staffed by such luminaries as George Kennan, Paul Nitze, and later Winston Lord. Its purpose was to give the secretary of state and the administration an ability to look beyond the moment, to anticipate, and to design policies from a long-term perspective. Much of the thinking that resulted in the Marshall Plan and the policy of containment so central to post–World War II developments is associated with the policy planning staff. The people involved in this innovative work were among those "present at the creation," to use Dean Acheson's phrase about the seminal period in post–World War II diplomacy when he was secretary of state.

Actually my own instincts had led me to establish first in the Department of Labor and later at Bechtel a unit like the policy planning staff. I was persuaded to do so partly as a result of an incident in 1968 at a quiet, isolated haven on the Stanford campus called the Center for Advanced Study in the Behavioral Sciences, where each year some fifty scholars are invited to do whatever they want. Some called it the Center for the Leisure of the Theory Class. When I arrived, the director took me to my study. The room was small, about fifteen feet to a side, with one glass-paneled door that overlooked San Francisco Bay. A simple desk and chair, a side chair, and a little settee were the furnishings. That was it. I looked around and I said, "Where's the telephone?"

"There is no telephone," he said with a smile. "If you get a call, a buzzer will sound, and you go down the hallway to a little booth to take the call." I looked at the telephone booth. It was the only unpleasant, clammy place in the whole complex. "If you want to make an outgoing call," he told me, "you can use a pay phone, and you'll need to have the right amount of change."

"If you don't have the money to pay for telephones, I'd be glad to pay for the installation," I told him.

"No, we don't believe in telephones. Try it. You'll like it." He laughed.

After a couple of weeks, it dawned on me that for the first time in a long while I was working completely from the inside out. What I did was what *I* decided to do, not what somebody rang me up on the telephone and asked me to do. I carried this lesson over into my later work. In any day, or certainly in any week, I would block out periods of time when nothing was scheduled and I wasn't going to deal with the things in my "in" box. I was going to sit with a piece of paper and think ahead about key problems, ways of getting at them, what I wanted to work on, and what I wanted to cause others to work on. This was my own personal version of policy planning.

Getting the Right People

Lessons learned when I started out as secretary of labor served me well. It had been the easiest transition imaginable. My predecessor, Bill Wirtz, a good friend from Chicago, wanted me to jump right into substantive issues, particularly the crisis of the moment: the longshoremen's strike. I knew I would have to find a way to handle the strike, but my first priority was to put together a team of top people. The work of the department interacted with many groups, and I wanted as much access as possible to their grapevines. I needed diversity: someone from labor, from management, and from the mediation and arbitration, the legal, and the black communities. I quickly gathered first-class people to fill the political-level positions in the department. A critical ingredient was the diverse blend of experience that I was able to assemble. As for the professional civil servants at the department, I was warned that all were Democrats and that they would not cooperate with me in a Republican administration. That prediction turned out to be absolutely wrong. When career people, whatever their political bent, see serious, responsible effort at the top, they work their hearts out. That has always been my experience.

I sought the same kind of team at State. I was warned that the foreign service officer corps was incorrigibly biased toward the liberal side of politics and that I could expect either to be captured or sabotaged by them. I doubted the latter was true; I was certain the former would not happen.

Foreign service officers bring a fund of knowledge and institutional memory not available anywhere else. The selection process is about as rigorous as any in the nation, so the level of talent and energy is first-class. And they possess a skill, a mentality, and an instinct for the record that are exceptional. As Senator Daniel P. Moynihan put it, "The true diplomatist [is] aware of how much subsequently depends on what clearly can be established to have taken place. If it seems simple in the archives, try it in the maelstrom."[2]

At the same time, a secretary of state has to have people around him who are sensitive to the political currents in Washington, people who have a deep understanding of the crucial give-and-take of politics within the halls of Congress. In the end, it is the president's foreign policy, so key people who help him shape it and carry it out—including in the State Department—should be on his political wavelength. They should be expected to recognize the political moment and know how to seize it. As I reviewed the roster, though, I noticed that there were almost no political appointees around as holdovers from Alexander Haig's time. Too many positions were vacant, perhaps an indication that the president's political supporters were reluctant to join the Haig State Department as relations with the White House worsened.

The deputy secretary, my alter ego and acting secretary when I traveled, should be, in my view, a political appointee attuned to the White House. I called Ken Dam right off. He was then provost at the University of Chicago, where he had been a professor of law. Ken had a brilliant mind, honed to a keen edge in the seminar rooms of Chicago; he had as well the common sense associated with Kansas, his home state. He had worked with me when I was director of the OMB and later when I was treasury secretary. We were joint authors of *Economic Policy Behind the Headlines*,

2. Daniel Patrick Moynihan, *A Dangerous Place* (Boston: Little, Brown & Co., 1978).

drawing on my experiences with economic policy in the Nixon administration. For the vacant post of under secretary for economic affairs I recruited Allen Wallis, recently retired as chancellor of the University of Rochester. Decisions might not go his way for political reasons, but as a forceful advocate of the free market, he never failed to leave his mark.

Larry Eagleburger, as Haig's under secretary for political affairs, was responsible for tapping the department's institutional memory and talent and for knowing how to use those resources effectively. Eagleburger talked as though he simply assumed that I would want to replace him. With a cigarette in one hand and a medicinal inhalator in the other, his mouth opening fishlike to accept one or the other, he was convincing as he talked about the need to find less stressful employment and break out of the paltry foreign service officer's salary chart that was keeping his family strapped for funds. Yet I also knew that he had the affection and respect of the service—and the Congress—and that duty to country was his compelling priority. I asked him to stay, and he said yes. The other principals in the department were people I wanted to keep; they had strong reputations, and I did not believe in turning a place upside down when I walked into a new job.

The Problem of Management

I was determined from the moment the president nominated me to do more than direct the policies and their implementation at State. I wanted to make the nuts and bolts of the department work well, too. So management would get my close attention. I had learned more than a few things from my experience at Bechtel, a superbly managed outfit. I wanted to produce a well-run organization at State that would serve the nation's interests efficiently and effectively. I had no illusions that it would be easy. In government the emphasis is on policy. That's where the excitement and the attention are, and that's where the talent goes. But I was determined I would find a way and find the people to "mind the store."

Stanford students often asked me about the differences between managing in business, in government, and in the university. I had a somewhat flip answer. "In business," I said, "you have to be very careful when you tell someone working for you to do something, because chances are high that he or she will actually do it. In government, you don't have to worry about that. And in the university, you aren't supposed to tell anyone to do anything in the first place."

I asked Jerry van Gorkom, who had just sold his company to the Pritzker family of Chicago, whether he would like to bring his track record of effective management to Washington and give it a try. He was delighted and accepted. Soon, however, I sensed his frustration. "You've given me this job," he told me one day, and then let loose. "I look over a problem and decide what to do. No sooner have I sent out an instruction than it's overridden by the White House or leaked to the press, or a call comes in from some congressional staffer irately challenging what we're doing. In business, when we decided to do something, we did it. In government nothing ever gets settled. I can't stand this atmosphere." So I knew that Jerry would not be with us for long. His plight was a dramatic illustration of how different business and government are. In each, you have to decide what to do, but in government, if the decision is going to stick, the divergent and divisive constituencies with a stake in the decision have to be persuaded—or, if not fully persuaded, at least consulted—so they feel that their views were considered. Even then, they can give you plenty of grief.

Congress and the Press

Two positions of great significance in any government department are the director of congressional relations and the press spokesman. For the first position, I decided to keep on Powell Moore, a Haig selection and a southerner who had a deft congressional touch. For press spokesman I recruited John Hughes, who had been editor of the *Christian Science Monitor* and was now heading up the Voice of America. Both Moore and Hughes were top-notch. But I had my own models to draw upon when it came to the Congress and the press.

In my book, the best congressional strategist ever to hit Washington was Bryce Harlow. I recalled going to an instructional session that he chaired. Bryce was diminutive, and he had with him Rogers Morton, a huge man, who measured at least six feet six. "I want all you new people to realize how tough it is to deal with the Congress," Bryce said. "Rogers, will you please stand up?" Rogers Morton stood up, and Bryce from his five-feet-four height then said, "Twenty years ago, when I came to Washington, I was as tall as Rogers Morton."

Bryce had a number of simple rules: "Return your calls promptly; deal straight with members of Congress." He had a complex web of intense relations with people. Sometimes a person was on his side, sometimes not. He was constantly forming and re-forming coalitions to work on a particular subject. People had to know, he felt, that you were a tough adversary and would fight hard and skillfully for your point of view. "Never agree to do something unless you know that you can do it" was one of Bryce's maxims. "If you give your word, then you better deliver. That way you develop trust. Trust is the coin of the realm."

The press spokesman is important in any department, but particularly so in the Department of State. The press is briefed every day, usually at noon, and it's done on the record, on camera, in the State Department briefing room. Sometimes the briefings are very short; sometimes, when it's a big news day, the briefing can go on for hours. So the briefer is standing there with a book full of what is called guidance—written questions and answers—and is speaking for the government of the United States to a worldwide audience.

I brought to my thinking about press spokesmen the experience from my earlier times in the cabinet, most particularly from my first brush with the press as secretary of labor. Herb Klein, President Nixon's press adviser, wanted to send me somebody from Nixon's California entourage, but I decided to get my own man.

I chose Joe Loftus, the premier labor reporter in the United States, having worked for the *New York Times* for some twenty-five years. Joe had seen press spokesmen come and go. "The spokesman has credibility only when reporters know that he is on the inside," he told me. As spokesman, he would have to know what was going on, be able to attend any meeting, be well informed; he would have to be able to conduct himself in accordance with "Loftus's Laws":

- Don't lie. Don't mislead. Credibility is very precious; it can never be misused. Once destroyed, it cannot be recaptured.
- Respond to questions directly.
- Help reporters get their facts straight. The press is an important way you communicate with the public. Don't act as if they are your enemy, however tempting at times.
- Get on top of breaking stories. Be part of the original story. Nobody reads the reaction story. So be quick and don't hold back. In practice, this means a constant tug-of-war between the spokesman and substantive officials, who all too often are reluctant or slow to provide needed information.

Bryce Harlow and Joe Loftus were of another era. In their day, Congress was "the other branch," and the press was the "Fourth Estate." Since then, Vietnam and Watergate had soured the atmosphere, and each part of Washington saw enemies as it looked out at the others. Despite the intervening history, I still looked to Harlow's and Loftus's guiding principles. A free press is still vital to, and a guarantor of, good government, and trust is still the coin of the realm.

How the State Department Works

When I walked into the State Department, I didn't fully appreciate what an action-oriented operation it was. Events of moment were taking place all over the world all the time, and the United States, as a world power, was monitoring and influencing those events, or trying to. Some 5,000 cables came in each day, and about 1,200 went out. Almost 40 percent of them were "action" messages calling for virtually immediate response in Washington or in the field. The responses ran from visa applications to questions of high policy, matters often, but not always, routine: try acting on Yasser Arafat's application for a visa. Of course, only a tiny fraction of the cable traffic came my way. The sheer volume emphasized to me the importance of my close contact with the people who handled this massive flow of the nation's business.

A cadre of "desk officers" of the department tracked developments in other countries around the clock, and because much of the world was waking up when we went to sleep, the operations center was always on the job and ready to wake me or others up if need be. The flow of information, background knowledge, and options for action involved the assistant secretaries of state for each sector of the world (Africa, Latin America, Asia, Europe, and the Near East and South Asia). These operational units were joined by the so-called functional bureaus, whose expertise was not in geographic areas but in subjects like economics, law, intelligence, political-military affairs, international organizations, narcotics, science, or human rights. Working together, these bureaus, in constantly shifting groupings as the needs of the moment indicated, sorted out what was routine and what needed to be sent up the line to the secretary and other principals of the department.

All of this rested on the broad base of embassies and consulates spread all over the world, managed (under difficult circumstances, given budget restraints and congressional demands) by the geographic bureaus. From these posts came a torrent of information about the world as it relates to America, and to these posts went instructions for action from Washington.

As secretary, I could see I had at hand an extraordinary information machine: it could produce a flow of reports on what was happening in real time, background on what had been done before and how that had worked, analyses of alternative courses of action, and ideas on what might be done. The department is a great engine of diplomacy for the secretary to use in carrying out the president's foreign policy. But the heart and soul of the department comes from the enormous crush of work to be done and from everyone's commitment to do it well. The problems were difficult, with high stakes riding on success in handling them with a sense of strategic purpose and tactical skill. I could already see that the lights burned late in the State Department building and that people there loved being part of the action.

First Efforts

By the time the Senate had confirmed my nomination, my new people were coming on board, and the accelerating pace of work in the State Department was assaulting me with a fire hose of information on a daily basis. At the same time, I was struggling to develop a pattern of interaction between the day-to-day work of the world and longer-range efforts to think out strategically what should be our course farther ahead. On Wednesday, July 14, the Senate Foreign Relations Committee voted unanimously to confirm me, and the full Senate confirmed me unanimously the next day. The president swore me in on Friday, July 16. It was time to go to work.

In fact, I had gone to work even before I was sworn in: I had met privately with the president first thing that morning to talk about the Middle East. The problem of Lebanon was front and center; Beirut was being shelled as we spoke. We were seeking a cease-fire and agreement on the departure from Beirut of the leadership and fighters of the PLO, which would close its headquarters in Beirut and remove any reason for Israeli forces to enter this Arab capital. Lebanon would then have a chance to settle down, the security threat to Israel originating from there would diminish, and some beginnings of a relationship between Israel and Lebanon might follow.

But my primary focus with the president that morning was on the problems of the West Bank and Gaza, which lay at the center of the Arab-Israeli dispute. Some people argued that the problems of Lebanon had to be solved before the peace process could resume. This, I felt, would leave us in a quagmire and encourage opponents of the peace process to prolong Lebanon's agony. I had been working hard on these issues in my preconfirmation period and had already had many discussions with President Reagan about them: the president was receptive to my ideas.

After our private talk, President Reagan and I walked out to the Rose Garden, where I was sworn in, in the presence of my whole family, followed by pictures with the president in the Oval Office. My children were captivated by his easy manner and his sense of humor. Many friends attended, going back to my time in the Eisenhower and Nixon administrations. From there I went on to a meeting of the National Security Council principals[3] about East-West trade and the Siberian pipeline problem.

When I returned to the State Department, I started to assemble a diverse group to confer with me on Mideast issues, a task made easier by the help of the White House telephone operators, who can find anyone, anywhere, anytime. My first call was to Irving Shapiro, then president of Du Pont. I had toured the Middle East with him, going from Saudi Arabia to Jordan

---

3. In addition to myself, the principals were President Reagan, Vice President Bush, and Secretary of Defense Cap Weinberger. CIA director Bill Casey and Chairman of the Joint Chiefs of Staff Jack Vessey were present as advisers. NSC adviser Bill Clark acted as coordinator of the meeting.

to Israel, just a week after Anwar Sadat's historic visit to Jerusalem. Next I called Bob Ames, a Middle East expert at the CIA with extensive knowledge of Palestinian matters. Larry Silberman, who had been my general counsel in the Labor Department, was next on my list. Finally, I called Henry Kissinger, whom I had known since our days in the west wing of Nixon's White House and whose font of knowledge and depth of insight on this and other areas of foreign policy were unparalleled. Each of them agreed at once to join me the next day, Saturday, at the department.

Early that Saturday morning, Moshe Arens, the Israeli ambassador, came in at my invitation. He was the first ambassador to call on me, and the symbolism was not lost on him. We talked about the U.S.-Israeli relationship, now sorely strained by the crisis in Beirut. It was a tense conversation, candid, good-tempered, but with an edge.

I then met with my Middle East group.[4] We worked and took our meals in the diplomatic reception rooms on the eighth floor of the State Department. The rooms are named after early statesmen, Thomas Jefferson, John Adams, Benjamin Franklin, James Monroe, and James Madison, all of whom had served as president as well as secretary of state except Franklin, America's first diplomat. The setting is imbued with a sense of history, standards, and achievement. Here we were surrounded by the artifacts of the founding years, including the stand-up desk Thomas Jefferson had designed and at which he had written portions of the Declaration of Independence.

I had to step out first to see Ambassador Ashraf Ghorbal of Egypt and then Prince Bandar, Saudi Arabia's ambassador in Washington. They both banged away at me about Israel's bombing and shelling of Beirut. I banged back about Arab reluctance to take in the PLO leaders and fighters we were seeking to evacuate from Lebanon. When I rejoined my group, the discussion continued through the afternoon and dinner. No one hung back. How could we talk to the Palestinians? What was necessary for Israel's security? Were interim arrangements for governance on the West Bank possible? Could we get attention to these issues when Lebanon was under siege? It was almost 9:00 P.M. when, on my way home, I dropped off Henry Kissinger at National Airport so that he could catch the shuttle for New York.

This gathering inaugurated what became a trademark of my time as secretary of state: the Saturday seminar. In my six and a half years in office I convened on at least twenty occasions a diverse group of people, many

---

4. In addition to the outsiders, the administration people involved were Larry Eagleburger, Bud McFarlane, who came over from the NSC staff, Dick Fairbanks, who was working as a special ambassador on Middle East matters, Nick Veliotes, the assistant secretary for Near Eastern Affairs, Deputy Secretary Walt Stoessel, and Paul Wolfowitz, who was at the time the director of the policy planning staff.

from outside the government, to explore a particular topic in an informal and open way as a help to me in formulating policy and advancing our objectives. Following this first Saturday seminar, I assembled a small group in the State Department to work secretly to develop a comprehensive approach to the deep-seated issues dividing Israel, its Arab neighbors, and the Palestinians.

I was determined not to be pinned down by the Beirut crisis. There were other problems that couldn't be postponed. I had to negotiate with the People's Republic of China a communiqué on our arms sales to Taiwan. I had to take decisions on our policy designed to move countries of Eastern Europe away from the Soviet Union by adjusting our behavior toward those countries, depending on the degree to which they might take positions at variance with Moscow. When I arrived at work the next Monday, I had to prepare for the state visit of Prime Minister Indira Gandhi of India. As the week went on, I met with Chancellor Helmut Schmidt of West Germany on the pipeline dispute, with Prime Minister Lee Kuan Yew of Singapore on issues in the Asia-Pacific region, and with Italian Foreign Minister Emilio Colombo on missile deployments in Italy, as well as the MNF in Beirut and the Italians' distress over the pipeline. I was enmeshed in an immense flow of issues, events, and people that the secretary of state encounters on a typical day, in a typical week, whether just entering office or not. The sweep ranged from close to home to Europe, the Americas, the Middle East, Africa, and Asia and included security issues, economic issues, just about anything else imaginable. All of this was piled into my first week in office.

Meanwhile, all the problems of the world in turmoil that I inherited pressed in upon me: acrimony with the Europeans and at home over the Siberian pipeline and with China over arms sales to Taiwan; tension in Central America; friction with Japan and other countries in the Pacific; stalemate with the Soviets. Virtually every day found me in a kaleidoscopic round of activities involving two or three or four of these issues. The days were hectic, intense, and demanding on my stocks of energy and intellect. Almost immediately I found myself embroiled in the daily pulls and hauls among key players on the Reagan team. So this is life, I thought, in the cockpit of the free world.

Part II

THE MIDDLE EAST: PROGRESS AND DESPAIR

CHAPTER 4

The Siege of Beirut

In my confirmation hearings, I had told the Senate that the crisis in Lebanon made painfully clear the urgent need to resolve the problems of the Palestinian people. The peace process had collapsed, and a war process continued to gather momentum. Now the Israeli army was laying siege to the capital of an Arab land: they were poised on the southern edge of Beirut. Palestinian fighters ran raids against their front lines and lobbed mortars in their rear areas; the Israel Defense Forces (IDF) pounded back at the city with artillery, tank forays, and air strikes.

The United States was caught in the middle. The Arab world blamed us, as Israel's great ally and financial supporter, for all of Israel's deeds and looked to us to end the fighting in a responsible way. The Lebanese government particularly relied on us to save them from outside predators and to help them restore Lebanese central authority over their country. The Israelis took our material support for granted while defying any criticism of their chosen course of action; yet they also clearly wanted the United States to negotiate an end to the war that would keep the IDF out of inevitably bloody street-to-street fighting in Beirut.

The problems to be faced had been around for a long time. The Palestine Liberation Organization (PLO), expelled by Jordan after bloody battles back in late 1970, had established its headquarters in Beirut and based its fighters in Lebanon. Their cross-border attacks on northern Israel and Israeli retaliatory strikes led to a cease-fire negotiated on July 24, 1981, after long efforts by Phil Habib. The border had been generally quiet for eleven months, although the sense of mutual antagonism was intense. The PLO wanted to disrupt Israeli society, and the Israelis could not bear their enemy in a sanctuary so close to their border.

With the fighting across the Lebanese-Israeli border greatly reduced, PLO terrorism beyond the Middle East increased. The cease-fire applied only to the border area; the Israelis screamed "foul" as the PLO hit elsewhere. On June 3, the Israeli ambassador to Britain, Shlomo Argov, was shot and critically wounded in London. The Israelis bombed PLO targets in Lebanon in retaliation, killing 45 people and wounding more than 150, according to the Lebanese government. The PLO responded with artillery attacks on northern Israel. On June 5, the UN Security Council, meeting at Lebanon's request, issued a unanimous call for a cease-fire. On June 6, massed Israeli tanks and infantry crossed into Lebanon, supported by air strikes and sea landings. This was war, and not only between Israelis and Palestinians: the Israeli forces were taking on the army and air force of Soviet-backed Syria as well. Initially announced by Prime Minister Begin as an operation to clear out terrorists from a zone forty kilometers (twenty-five miles) deep into southern Lebanon, the invasion kept rolling northward until, by June 9, Israeli forces were within sight of Beirut. Israel's real objective was the destruction of the PLO and its leadership of the Palestinian movement.

The U.S. response and objectives evolved rapidly: attain a cease-fire between the Israeli and Syrian forces; use the Israeli presence and threat as a means to negotiate the evacuation of the PLO from Beirut, and in turn use that prospect to keep Israeli forces out of that Arab capital; lay the groundwork for putting in place an international peacekeeping force, as the Lebanese were requesting; work for a diplomatic arrangement that would get all foreign forces out of Lebanon; and use the opportunity to help Lebanon get back on its feet, assert its national identity, and, if possible, develop some sort of stable relationship with Israel.

In those first two weeks of July 1982, I could only watch the crisis as it careened back and forth between progress and chaos; I could not take decisions on it until I was confirmed by the Senate. As reports were passed to me, I became aware of an acute problem with the State Department's system of crisis management: the pace of events had outstripped the traditional methods of receiving cabled messages from overseas and responding with written instructions to our posts. There simply was not time to draft, type, code, transmit, decode, process, and read written telegraphic traffic. This was the first diplomatic crisis handled by instant voice communications via satellite. The central and novel piece of equipment was the tacsat, a regulation-issue army backpack field telephone whose radio signal was beamed up by a little open-umbrella-like device by a window in the State Department and then down to Habib at his army field radio, set up in our ambassador's residence in Yarzé on a hill overlooking Beirut. Diplomatic decision makers were in immediate contact with all points of a swiftly changing situation half the globe away. I could see that the technology of communication and massive, instantaneous information flows were transforming the way Washington handled a foreign policy challenge. We were operating in a world of real-time diplomacy with the telephone and tacsat overtaking cable traffic. Our ability to respond quickly increased, but so did the possibilities for error, confusion, and inadequate record keeping. We were in a new age, an information age, and we would have to learn how to make the most of it.

Al Haig was convinced, he had told me, that he had sound assurances from Israel that if the United States negotiated a PLO departure from Beirut, Israel would agree to a cease-fire and would not send its troops into the city. The Israelis were well aware, he said, that their entry into an Arab capital would be a cataclysmic event, with the potential of inflaming the entire Arab world. They would also pay a heavy price in the casualties of street-to-street fighting.

The president's special envoy to the Middle East happened to be on his way there when the war broke out. He was on the job instantly, arriving in Jerusalem for talks the day after Israeli forces crossed into Lebanon on June 6. It was, inevitably, Phil Habib, recently retired for health reasons, back on the job as America's top diplomatic pro. Over a long foreign service career he had turned himself into the State Department's preeminent negotiator, first in the Far East and then in the Middle East. His dynamism, political savvy, and judgment had taken him to the highest job traditionally available to a career diplomat: under secretary of state for political affairs.

This was an odd destiny for an Arab-American kid from a Lebanese Christian family who grew up in a Jewish neighborhood in Brooklyn and satisfied his curiosity about distant lands by attending the University of Idaho to study forestry. The joke was that Phil Habib had chosen his life's work by thinking he was signing up with the Forest Service. But now he was—retired or not—the "Godfather of the Foreign Service."

Habib's personal style was direct, forceful, no nonsense. Although he was working his way through a series of multiple bypass coronary operations, Habib never ceased to rave and rant and wave his arms in perpetual motion as he shouted imprecations at anyone in range. Habib's tantrums were at once theatrics and persuasively serious. Beneath the surface noise everyone discerned a just and good-natured gentleman. So I would silently chuckle and quietly, patiently smile as Habib stood before me roaring in outrage. He had, to say the least, an unusual diplomatic style, but it worked. Habib could convey unpleasant truths and stark realities in a manner that would often ultimately win agreement without resentment. He knew both the Lebanese and the Israelis well, and he enjoyed the bargaining process as much as they did. He also enjoyed—too much for his own good—the Lebanese food. I had known him for many years. I knew we could talk straight to each other and that he was absolutely trustworthy.

On Friday, July 2, Phil had met with Lebanese intermediaries, who had just seen PLO chairman Yasser Arafat. The PLO had taken "a decision in principle" to accept U.S. proposals for their evacuation, but they demanded that we produce a place for them to go. The government of Lebanon now formally requested an international presence; specifically, they wanted a multinational force (MNF), if possible, to oversee the departure of the PLO, not a UN peacekeeping operation. Menachem Begin, in any case, would have nothing to do with a UN role in any form for Beirut, a view traced back to 1967, when the United Nations pulled its peacekeeping troops out of the Sinai at Gamal Abdel Nasser's demand, a step toward the war that followed. Moreover, a multinational force separate from the United Nations could be formed more quickly and would be composed of forces from major countries whose involvement the ever-bargaining Lebanese regarded as advantageous.

When Larry Eagleburger telephoned Al Haig at the Greenbriar to relay Habib's report, Haig said that an American presence in the multinational force "would be no problem. Do it quietly." The Joint Chiefs of Staff and Secretary of Defense Cap Weinberger were very negative about a U.S. role, but on Saturday, July 3, State got word from the White House: "The president approves a U.S. contribution to the multinational force."

At that moment, everything seemed to be falling into place. The general assumption was that within a few days the PLO would leave Beirut, by ship or overland, to be received by and remain in Syria. After the PLO withdrew, a multinational peacekeeping force, including an American contingent, would enter Beirut for a strictly limited time, say, thirty days; Israeli troops would pull back five or so miles from the city. The government of Lebanon would regain control of its capital and, with international support, could start the long process of getting all foreign forces out and reestablishing its national integrity.

Then Habib called in on the tacsat, shouting, "There's a firefight going on. Flares are coming down. The Israelis are moving forward northeast of the airport, across the railroad track. They're putting the squeeze on the city. If they break the cease-fire, it could screw it all up! This deal could be set in the next twenty-four to seventy-two hours. Israeli pressure now won't help!"

Within minutes, Ambassador Sam Lewis in Jerusalem reported in by secure telephone. He had just met with Prime Minister Begin, Defense Minister Ariel Sharon, and Foreign Minister Yitzhak Shamir to discuss the favorable news of the PLO's decision to leave. The Israelis were delighted by the president's approval of U.S. participation in the multinational force. As to where the PLO would go, they didn't really care. "Just get them out of Lebanon and leave no seed," Begin said. The discussion had taken place, Lewis reported, in Begin's bedroom. The prime minister had pulled open a drawer, taken out a bottle of scotch, and poured everyone a drink: a toast "to General Alexander M. Haig, Jr." They had laughed to see that the brand of scotch was Haig and Haig.

Lewis had broken the happy mood by asking about the shelling that night. Begin was annoyed. "Habib is hysterical," he said. "It is all highly exaggerated; we are just returning fire." Lewis pointed out that the firing would disrupt critical meetings in Beirut to move forward a solution quickly.

"It will be quiet the rest of the night," Sharon told Lewis.

The *Washington Post* on July 4 ran the headline "Arafat Reportedly Signs Agreement to Withdraw." That same day, Lebanese President Elias Sarkis gave Habib a paper signed by Arafat and dated July 3.

> The leaders of the PLO do not wish to remain in Lebanon. However, it must be understood that in spite of the desire of the leaders to leave Lebanon, they cannot depart until after the period necessary for the application and execution of the arrangements agreed upon. This decision, which stems from our desire to prevent bloodshed of the innocent citizens in Beirut, comes with a reminder to your Excellency of our insistence in obtaining guarantees for the protection of our Palestinian refugees in their camps during and after the disengagement operation. In addition to what we received from your Excellency concerning guarantees, we request that an international-Arab or international force participate in these guarantees with the Lebanese Army.
>
> With warmest greetings and revolution until victory,
>
> Yasser Arafat, Chairman
> PLO Executive Committee

Despite what Begin had said to Lewis in his bedroom, the breakdown of the cease-fire paralyzed Habib's work. The Lebanese officials who were acting as go-betweens with the PLO could not travel back and forth because of the danger from falling shells or because they refused to cross checkpoints that Israeli troops set up between Christian East Beirut, where Habib was located, and Muslim West Beirut, where Arafat had his headquarters. Habib and Sharon were railing at each other.

Meanwhile, Haig was still at the Greenbriar and was still secretary of state. Eagleburger telephoned him on Monday morning, July 5—a government holiday in Washington. The Saudis had informed us that they had persuaded Syrian President Hafez al-Assad to accept the PLO in Syria. In time, this pressured promise did not hold, and in any event, the PLO now refused to go to Syria. So the cease-fire had fallen apart, and the negotiations had stalled. No Arab country wanted to accept the PLO. We now had to put together a multinational force with U.S. participation, which was bound to be opposed within the U.S. government and at the United Nations. And getting other nations to join us, as we must, would not be easy.

We had sent a message, I learned, to King Fahd of Saudi Arabia pointing out that while the Arabs had long criticized the United States for inattention to the Palestinian problem, it was now the Arab states that were unwilling to take the PLO in and that therefore "we are now at a point where the very survival of the PLO as a potentially constructive political force in the region is at stake." Our ambassador to Saudi Arabia, Dick Murphy, said that with this message we had "put in the maximum needle." On the Israeli side, Sam Lewis reported, the atmosphere suddenly had changed markedly. Menachem Begin was sinking into a mood of deep depression, "a recognition that he is in a real box."

Walking into a War

On July 14, the day the Senate Foreign Relations Committee recommended my confirmation as secretary of state, word came in of a massive Iranian military assault into Iraq, with Iranian troops advancing some twenty miles in six hours. The Arabs in the Persian Gulf area were more immediately concerned about the threat of Iranian Shiite fundamentalism than about the siege of Beirut, but to help advance a solution for Lebanon, King Fahd welcomed the willingness of the United States to commit troops to a multinational force. He agreed to send Prince Saud, his foreign minister, to Washington to join Syrian Foreign Minister Abdel Khaddam and to meet directly with the president and me.

PLO supporters in Washington were fervently lobbying congressmen and senators on Capitol Hill. Senator Chuck Percy, chairman of the Senate Foreign Relations Committee, telephoned urging me to seize "the great opportunity that now exists." Some kind of messenger from Arafat had told him that the PLO was ready to meet the U.S. conditions. (In 1975, Secretary of State Henry Kissinger had declared that the United States would not negotiate with the PLO until it recognized Israel's right to exist and accepted UN Security Council Resolution 242, the "territory-for-peace" resolution, as a basis for negotiating peace with Israel.)

Jeane Kirkpatrick, our ambassador to the United Nations, rushed to the State Department to argue vehemently against Percy's idea. "Covenants made under duress are not binding," she said. This was "the deathbed confession of the PLO." But, she added, "I would not dismiss the possibility of dealing with the PLO. Let the military drama play out. Break their military power, get them out of Beirut, and then—if they accept 242 and Israel's right to exist—we talk to them."

At this point I realized for the first time that the CIA's top specialist on Arab affairs, Bob Ames, had been carrying on a dialogue with the PLO leadership through envoys and intermediaries for at least a year. In the steady round of Mideast briefings I received, Ames had appeared several times. I was impressed by his understanding of the Arab political and cultural scene. The bottom line Ames described was that the PLO was now ready to meet our conditions if we would make some gesture indicating we would support Palestinian "self-determination," really a code word for support of an independent Palestinian state. That would be a gigantic step, not a gesture, and I was unwilling to consider it. Furthermore, as was so often the case, the PLO messages were vague, inconsistent, and delivered through a variety of channels. When specifics were requested, the PLO ducked; they would meet the American conditions, for example, not by making a direct statement but by attaching themselves to a resolution then being drafted at the United Nations. Such indirection was all too slippery and vague and therefore unsatisfactory to me. Bob Ames wanted to meet his PLO contact. I instructed that there must be no such meeting.

I decided to ask Israeli Ambassador Moshe Arens to come to see me. Knowing this, Sam Lewis called in from Israel. Prime Minister Begin, he said, was very unhappy about my confirmation testimony and was even more upset about Phil Habib's negotiation. "He is the worst negotiator I've ever seen," Begin told Lewis. In reality, Lewis said, "the Israelis now are frightened and nervous."

At 9:00 A.M. on Saturday, July 17, the day after I was sworn in as secretary of state, Arens came into my office. It was the Jewish Shabbat, and normally Arens might have come under attack in Jerusalem if it had been known he was at work, but this was a war. His hair was clipped short, and his speech was brisk. From my days on the faculty at MIT, I saw in him what he once had been: an aeronautical engineer with a Ph.D. from MIT. I could see him with his slide rule. Born in Lithuania, he had, in fact, been brought up in New York City. No foreign representative ever seemed more American than Moshe Arens. But he had long since given up his American citizenship. And I was soon to realize that no Israeli was more resolute in pursuit of Israel's objectives than Arens. I told him I knew his reputation and trusted his ability to hear my views and transmit them accurately to his government. Assure Jerusalem, I said, that if your government wants to get a message to me, you can do so at a moment's notice. "The excessive Israeli shelling is making it almost impossible to work out the agreement that everyone wants," I told him in the direct language he understood.

Arens went straight to his points. He characterized U.S.-Israeli relations as perplexing: we used to have the same views about how to achieve shared goals; now those views are different. "The U.S. claims that diplomacy can work in Beirut—that Israel's military pressure is interfering with diplomacy. So two weeks ago I recommended to Jerusalem that we comply with the president's request and ease the situation for diplomacy. But today I am pessimistic. Israel does not want one square inch of Lebanon, nor does it have any idea of installing a puppet government," Arens claimed.

After Arens left, I launched into my first Saturday seminar with Henry Kissinger, Irving Shapiro, and Larry Silberman, along with key people from State, the CIA, and the National Security Council (NSC) staff. The object was to explore ways to get the Mideast peace process back on track. Everyone agreed on the importance of getting a credible process going and not letting the problems of Lebanon overwhelm everything else. On the question of how to deal with the Palestinians, I was skeptical. So, I could sense, was Henry Kissinger. The consensus of what I had heard that day was that we should offer to have Habib meet Arafat to make final arrangements for the PLO's departure from Lebanon. In return, the PLO would publicly and authoritatively accept UN Security Council Resolution 242 and Israel's right to exist. We would tell Arafat that the United States would be ready to discuss broader Middle East issues with the PLO after they had reached their destination outside Lebanon—and we would set a twenty-four-hour deadline for Arafat's answer. With a positive answer from Arafat, we would be in a better position to get some Arab state to receive the Palestinian evacuees.

I thought over this strategy for dealing with the PLO on my way back to Jackson Place. I decided it was a bad idea. The Lebanon crisis was one problem; an Arab-Israeli solution for the West Bank and Gaza was another. I would not try to bargain one for the other. Remarkably, no one leaked the hot news that direct U.S.-PLO discussions had been under consideration. What *was* the subject of speculation in the press—as reporters had observed the participants coming and going around the State Department on Saturday—was the idea, totally unfounded, that I had asked Kissinger to go to Beirut to replace Habib.

On Tuesday afternoon, July 20, just before Prince Saud of Saudi Arabia and Foreign Minister Khaddam of Syria were about to come into my office, I learned that Bob Ames of the CIA had gone ahead, against my instructions but with CIA director Bill Casey's approval, and had met with a PLO representative the previous day. The CIA report—supposedly advance notice of what my visitors were about to tell me—turned out to be quite wrong. I saw then that Bill Casey and the CIA acted independently and provided information on which I could not necessarily rely.

Saud and Khaddam said they had come on a mission for the Arab League and that the entire Arab world had high hopes for the outcome of their meetings with me and with President Reagan. Prince Saud was a tall and dramatic figure in white burnoose and black flowing robes; his hawklike profile and aura of desert nobility and his erudite manner of the Princeton graduate left my outer office staff agog as he swept through the corridors. Khaddam was short, bullet-headed, and aggressive. As our meeting started, he pulled out a pad to make notes, and I handed him a pencil. "Ha!" he exploded. "To Israelis you give warplanes, and to Arabs you give pencils!"

After unloading on me about the Israeli shelling of Beirut, they told me that no Arab country was willing to take the PLO. Both Saudi Arabia and Syria genuinely feared that if they accepted the few thousand PLO fighters, they eventually would have to take all the 400,000-some Palestinians living in Lebanon; that if the PLO fighters evacuated Beirut, the families they left behind would be slaughtered; and that Israel would not withdraw an inch after the PLO left, thus humiliating the country that took them. They thought—and feared—that Israel intended to stay in Lebanon, creating a North Bank to add to the other occupied territories. Saud and Khaddam suggested that the PLO "relocate elsewhere in Lebanon," something neither the government of Lebanon nor Israel nor I would accept. I told them that idea was "a nonstarter."

In New York, UN Ambassador Jeane Kirkpatrick was irate about a joint French-Egyptian draft resolution to revise UN Resolution 242 to recognize "the legitimate rights of the Palestinian people," including their right to "self-determination." That would cut across Habib's work at a critical time, mix the outcome in Beirut with the Middle East peace process in general, turn the negotiations over to the United Nations, and be the vehicle for a PLO assertion that it had met U.S. conditions for direct discussions. "You can't imagine what the pressures are like here," she said. "The Soviets are demanding UN action." The Saudis were furious at this blatant French effort to take credit for getting the United States and the PLO together. And now word had come that David Dodge, acting president of the American University of Beirut, had been kidnapped on July 19. The university was a highly regarded institution serving not only Lebanon but also the entire eastern Arab world, and this act against a respected American friend of the community seemed ominous, especially since Dodge was reportedly in the hands of pro-Khomeini Iranian "revolutionary guards" now in Beirut.

Former Israeli Prime Minister Yitzhak Rabin came to Washington on July 27, and I stressed two imperatives to him: the Israeli military must stay out of Beirut, and a political approach to the Palestinian issue must be pursued in a different way, but consistent with the Camp David Accords. Israel, I told him, was in tough shape around the world; the war was increasingly undermining Israel's relationship with its friends and what had been a vital consensus in its favor. Rabin had spent time with me during my first trip to Israel in 1969, and I saw him in Washington when he was Israel's ambassador to the United States. Our talks always went to the core of current problems. Yet Rabin always conveyed a sense of being vastly preoccupied with something deeper than the topic of conversation. I soon concluded that his preoccupation was with the concept and future of Israel itself: its significance as a Jewish state and the dilemma of security and democracy in a country with a large and growing Arab population surrounded by a hostile Arab world. In office—any office, military, diplomatic, or government—his preoccupation charged him with physical and intellectual energy; out of office, as now, it gnawed at him from within. When on active service, his deep voice carried weight and authority; now it seemed tired and slow. Rabin was a force that needed to be utilized.

At this point I felt it was crucial for us to move along two tracks at once. First, we had to keep Phil Habib's negotiations going until the PLO was out of Beirut and in another Arab country. We could then turn to the problem of getting both the Israeli and Syrian armies out of Lebanon so that Lebanon could stand on its own again. Second, at the same time, we had to revive the Arab-Israeli peace process in a way that would satisfy Israel's needs for security and also give the Palestinians a sense of identity and a serious avenue toward gaining more control over their lives.

Israeli shelling of Beirut started again. Habib called in that the biggest barrage of the war so far was under way. "Their guns are firing only a few hundred yards from me. I could have walked down the hill myself from here and told them to stop!" Arafat, through channels in Cairo, passed a message that reached Bob Ames: Habib talks only about our going but never about how and where. Where are we to go? Syria will not take us. I am not interested in saving only my life.

On July 29, Arafat sent Habib a paper outlining steps for a PLO departure. This seemed to be a breakthrough—an unequivocal and firm decision by the PLO to leave Beirut. We now had indications that the PLO might be dispersed among several Arab countries, including Jordan, Egypt, Syria, and Sudan.

The bombardment by the Israelis stopped, but they kept the city's power and water turned off. Too much Israeli pressure now would bring everything to a halt. Lebanon's president, Elias Sarkis, warned that if the Israelis resumed bombing, the negotiations would stop. The Lebanese intermediaries were pleading with Habib to get the water and electricity back on.

At 3:00 on Sunday morning, August 1, all hell broke loose. Israeli tanks attacked in the southern suburbs of the city and spread across Beirut International Airport. A Middle East Airlines Boeing 707 on the tarmac was hit by a shell and destroyed. On the tacsat Habib was threatening to resign: "It is indecent for the U.S. to go along with this!" Smoke was hanging over the city. Israeli aircraft and artillery hits were observed in the vicinity of the refugee camps and the Shiite neighborhoods. I put our diplomatic capabilities into action again on all fronts—in Jerusalem, Washington, and New York—demanding that the Israelis call off their assault.

During this same period, Habib and Begin had exchanged correspondence about a matter deeply disturbing to Begin—the possibility that as the last arrangements were to be worked out for the PLO's departure, Habib might be close to making direct contact with PLO representatives. Habib had assured Begin that, in the interest of efficiency and speed, he would set up "proximity talks" so the Lebanese intermediaries could quickly move back and forth between Habib and the PLO to exchange proposals and replies on the final details of the departure. As Israeli forces rolled over the southern suburbs of the city, Habib received another message from Prime Minister Begin:

Thank you for your prompt reply. . . . In the second part of your most recent message to me you confirm completely the information given to me by Professor Arens, our Ambassador in Washington. You speak about an upper floor from which you will conduct negotiations whereas in the lower floor there will be located Lebanese and terrorist representatives. This "flooral" arrangement is totally unacceptable to us. I therefore repeat my most urgent request for reconsideration. At twelve noon I left our cabinet session and telephoned Professor Arens as follows:

a.) The Israeli Cabinet has decided to accept a ceasefire provided, as a *sine qua non*, that the ceasefire be mutual and absolute. b.) Our action in the early morning was a reaction to repeated violations of the ninth ceasefire, which came into effect 1030 Thursday night. There was no plan or intent today to conquer Beirut.

Regards.

M. Begin

My First Visit with Shamir

Later that Sunday, August 1, the day the media were calling "black Sunday," Israeli Foreign Minister Yitzhak Shamir arrived in Washington. "Are you losing patience with Israel?" a reporter asked President Reagan.

"I lost patience a long time ago," the president replied. "The bloodshed must stop."

Habib called in on the tacsat on Monday, August 2. "It's now clear that the IDF is moving forward from the cease-fire lines of last night. They are trying to get a line north of the airport. They did not get up into Burj al-Brajneh. They are moving slowly, not many of them. As they move up, PLO fighters fire a few rounds and withdraw toward the city. So there is not a cease-fire *in place*. Then artillery comes in to cover the Israelis. It has not escalated yet, but if the PLO fires their mortars, then off we go again. We can't take it again. When I was in Jerusalem and told Begin I could manage a cease-fire, he agreed to a cease-fire *in situ*. This is *not* a cease-fire *in situ*. The Israelis took over the airport."

Habib reported that the water and power, just restored, had now been cut off again by the Israelis and that the IDF was blocking UN efforts to look at the situation. In Jerusalem, Habib's deputy, Morrie Draper, met with Prime Minister Begin. Begin said that he had ordered the city's water turned back on. On the question of proximity talks with the PLO, Begin said that American and Palestinian negotiators would have to be at least 300 yards apart; Israel would not agree to delegations in side-by-side buildings or "floorally" in the same building. As for UN observers, Begin said Jeane Kirkpatrick had "betrayed" him and voted in favor of "them."

At this moment, if a cease-fire could hold, we could move forward in our negotiations. The Lebanese government agreed not to press for the deployment of observers (which in any event would be impossible to interpose between the IDF and the PLO fighters); two Lebanese army generals were to meet with the PLO to take up Habib's ideas for the conduct of an evacuation; and we had a UN Security Council resolution on observers that could provide endorsement for an international peacekeeping force.

Ambassador Sam Lewis reported that Menachem Begin was in a very good mood: "He keeps referring to 'the beautiful letter' that President Reagan sent him on his birthday." Begin sent a reply to President Reagan:

> I feel as a Prime Minister empowered to instruct a valiant army facing "Berlin," where among innocent civilians Hitler and his henchmen hide in a bunker beneath the surface . . . so that that which happened once on instructions from Berlin—the proclamation of intention to destroy the Jewish people—will never happen again.

But at that same moment, Habib was reporting artillery rounds of three to five per minute. The Israelis were again moving forward on the ground. Habib feared the Lebanese talks with the PLO on evacuation would collapse.

President Reagan's meeting with Yitzhak Shamir on August 2 was grim. I had discussed it carefully ahead of time with the president. We knew it would be a tough encounter. Reagan did not smile. Shamir held his ground. Shamir raised the question of proximity talks; President Reagan said to take it up with me. Shamir argued Israel's case justifying the collapse of the cease-fire. The president didn't buy it. The president talked with intensity about what was being shown on television—hospital scenes, babies with their arms blown off. "If you invade West Beirut, it would have the most grave, most grievous, consequences for our relationship," the president told Shamir and added, "Should these Israeli practices continue, it will become increasingly difficult to defend the proposition that Israeli use of U.S. arms is for defensive purposes." This statement, given the circumstances, was a signal that President Reagan might soon cease to oppose the use of statutory provisions that could suspend the supply of American military equipment to Israel—the ultimate sanction.

Shamir quickly retorted, "All arms are being used only for Israel's defense." He was calm and tried to be friendly. President Reagan kept after him, stressing the disproportionality of Israel's response to relatively minor PLO cease-fire violations.

"The Soviets are profiting from the nature of your retaliation," the president told Shamir. "Fifteen hours of shelling make people forget who fired the first shot. The Soviets may even be stimulating it, and you are playing into their hands."

The *New York Times* coverage of the Reagan-Shamir meeting was headlined "U.S. Displays a New Face to the Israelis." Beneath it, side by side, were the two smiling broadly at their 1981 meeting and then, above, stony-faced one year later.

It was then my turn to deal with Shamir. This would be our first meeting. I returned to the department, and we started at 11:30 A.M. on August 2. I wanted him to understand me, to recognize my way of working at problems, and to get a feeling for my attitude toward Israel. I invited him to sit with me alone in my back office for a private talk. "I am an admirer and supporter of Israel," I told him. "I will be a supporter in tough times as well as good times, not a fair-weather friend. When the going gets tough, some people you think are your friends won't be there: I'll be there. But I also believe in direct statements, so you will know my views of the issues we are dealing with. When I am critical, you will know it; I will also not hesitate to be openly supportive when I feel that is deserved. Our relationship will emerge out of the work we do together, but I want you to know at the outset how I view Israel myself."

Just before Shamir's arrival, I had received a report that Prime Minister Begin had sent a somewhat threatening message to King Hussein, saying that after the PLO had been removed from Beirut, Jordan should not aid the PLO in the West Bank or it would be held responsible for future Palestinian activity there.

Shamir was a paradoxical presence. A small but powerful man with a large and leonine head, he seemed both shy and sure. He had been a warrior of the Zionist underground, accustomed to the anonymity of revolution. Now in the halls of diplomacy, he was quiet in manner and direct in his approach. He told me that we were "at an important moment for the free world." If security arrangements for Israel's northern border could be agreed on between Lebanon and Israel, the prospects for peace could be widened and the peace process advanced. The departure of the PLO from Lebanon was a precondition, Shamir said, for a solution that would make Lebanon stable and allow a Lebanon-Israel agreement on security that would then enable Israeli forces to withdraw.

The PLO, supported by a statement from the Arab League, had let Habib know that they were prepared to depart. The problem was where they could go and how. "I have the impression, " I told Shamir, "that you doubt that the PLO has decided to leave. So the conflict goes on and is extraordinarily disruptive to the process of arranging for the PLO's departure."

"We have doubts that the PLO is ready to leave," Shamir confirmed. "Leaving will change their position entirely. Nowhere else can they so effectively threaten Israel as in Lebanon, not in Syria or in Egypt. They will try not to leave." But, he said, Israel did not oppose Habib's effort to make them leave. "We can test their readiness; make a timetable. But we don't see the connection between a cease-fire and negotiations for their departure."

That was the crux of the problem. Habib required a cease-fire for negotiations to take place. Without a cease-fire, it would be physically impossible for negotiators to move back and forth to pass the necessary messages. Yet the Israelis regarded continued military pressure on the PLO as essential to convince them to leave. "If the PLO knows that the U.S. links a cease-fire and negotiations, then the PLO will keep violating the cease-fire in order to block the negotiations," Shamir argued.

"But," I responded, "you retaliate to any pinprick with a massive response." I bore in on Shamir to get a commitment that Israel would stop its massive retaliation whenever there was a cease-fire violation by the PLO.

"There is a difference of opinion between us," Shamir said. "Those who oppose a military solution take away the pressure for a peaceful solution. The problem of places for the PLO to go is not settled. And the problem of their wanting 1,500 to stay and wanting a political office to remain in order to settle the problem of the camps—these are very important questions for Israel," Shamir continued. "It would put the PLO in charge of the refugee camps, which are the source of manpower for the PLO. We won't accept such a solution. It is hard for Habib, but if the PLO decides to leave, a solution will be found for all other problems. And if they don't decide to leave, we must make clear to them that they are exposed to physical danger. The U.S. encourages them to think otherwise."

"We should test the PLO's—and Arab League's—assertions that the PLO will leave," I told Shamir. "If Israeli actions force Habib to focus on water and power or on repeatedly renegotiating broken cease-fires, then he can't get to the real negotiations to get the PLO to leave. We face a cycle of self-denying factors."

"The main obstacle is the U.S.'s clear position that there is no alternative to a diplomatic solution," Shamir repeated. "If the PLO knows this, they will never leave." We both knew that there was an alternative and not a pleasant one.

"A military solution will cost many lives, Israeli as well as Palestinian," I said. "We can do better."

At the end Shamir gave a bit. "If we arrive at a conclusion—and there is no problem of a week or ten days, set a time limit—then it would be wise perhaps to try to negotiate them out. It will be hard because the PLO will try to sabotage the effort. But maybe it's reasonable to try."

I summed up for Shamir what I wanted from the Israelis: "We agree on the importance of maintaining the cease-fire and in using restraint in doing so; we agree on the need to create conditions such that Habib can work on the basic problem; we agree to take the limited time available to try to work out the places and procedure for the evacuation of the PLO."

Over lunch Shamir talked about Israel's desire that Bashir Gemayel be elected as Lebanon's next president. Shamir wanted the U.S. view. "Outsiders talking about who they want elected is a delicate matter and has a tendency to backfire," I said. "So the United States is constrained, while we have a similar view that Bashir would be a good choice. He must be able to win the support of Muslims," I said. "The more that he is seen as his own man, the better off he will be in the election."

Shamir was not being cautious. "But Lebanon is in an exceptional situation," he said. "The Lebanese need support. Israel does not want to dictate but to give help and advice. We want to leave Lebanon as soon as possible and to have an agreement with the government of Lebanon. It will be easier to make such an agreement with Bashir. For us, it is sufficient to know that the U.S. does not oppose such a development."

"Our advice," I responded, "is to let the Lebanese achieve a delicate balance. Bashir should be free of being seen as the candidate of Israel or of the U.S."

When Phil Habib got a readout of our meetings, he noted, "The IDF consolidated its lines at the airport today; they now control the entire airport and a large area beyond. They could take Burj al-Brajneh tomorrow. So I can see why they now could agree to restrain their forces—they are in a pretty position now." Habib was working with a Lebanese army officer, Abu Walid, who would then be in touch with the PLO's representative, Hani al-Hassan, to discuss arrangements for the PLO's departure.

Getting Somewhere?

Our reports from Beirut were that movement on key issues was beginning. The PLO had made a counterproposal on the details of their departure. They were clearly serious about leaving. The key for them was how and when the multinational force was to be put into Beirut. Habib and Draper were buoyed by their current meetings. Discussions were serious and operational. Habib was putting the burden of finding a place to go on the PLO itself, but at the same time we intensified our contacts with the Arabs to find a place willing to take Arafat and his organization. I telephoned Shamir to say that the signs were good and to urge that the cease-fire be maintained. Shamir said he still doubted that the PLO really intended to leave.

Habib sent a new proposal to the PLO outlining details of departure. The Palestinians were no longer calling for an Israeli troop pullback but were entirely focused on the multinational force as the crucial issue. The PLO insisted on the international force and wanted assurances on the details of its deployment. It was Tuesday, August 3. Habib hoped to get liaison officers from the troop-contributing countries into Beirut by Friday. The most likely country to accept the PLO now looked to be Egypt, but President Hosni Mubarak was insisting that the United States make policy concessions regarding the overall Arab-Israeli peace process that were out of the question.[1] Clearly, Arab governments did not trust the PLO and, for all their pro-Palestinian rhetoric, worried more about a potential PLO threat to them than about the fate of the besieged PLO. This presented us with a diplomatic problem: just as we were beginning to make progress in the negotiations to get the PLO to leave Beirut, the Arab nations were fervently backpedaling away from accepting them. Israel might well start calling this process a conspiracy to keep the PLO in Beirut despite the Israeli siege.

At 3:45 A.M., Washington time, on Wednesday, August 4, Habib was on the tacsat. Once again, massive shelling was taking place. Tank movements, too, were massive. Israeli troops were moving forward to Beirut, up the coast road north of the airport. An Israeli attempt to cut off the Palestinian refugee camps in the southern suburbs from the city of Beirut itself appeared to be in the making. President Sarkis was begging Habib to get the Israelis to stop. The Israelis were now inside West Beirut. All this was happening as the PLO was presenting a workable departure scenario: they would leave before the MNF was fully deployed and would turn all their heavy weapons in to the Lebanese army.

Beginning at about 10:00 in the evening of August 3, I had begun to receive reports of heavy shellings by the Israelis. I conferred with Nick Veliotes and Sam Lewis by phone and called Shamir, who was still in the United States. Shamir told me the reports were gross exaggerations. I told Shamir my reports were based on direct observation. We had a sharp exchange.

At 4:00 the next morning, Saudi Prince Bandar was on the telephone to me. King Fahd, he reported, said the Israeli attack "is the beginning of the disaster. The United States must do something. U.S. prestige is on the line, and so is Saudi Arabia's." King Fahd "asks the president to intervene immediately so that drastic steps are not necessary."

I came into the department at 5:00 A.M. Habib was screaming in rage on the tacsat. The shelling was the worst he had seen in eight weeks of war. We had to get the Israelis to stop. Charlie Hill was talking to Habib in Beirut on a telephone in one hand and to Deputy Chief of Mission Bill Brown in Jerusalem on a telephone in his other. Brown was also holding two receivers: talking to Hill on one and to Prime Minister Begin on the

---

1. Mubarak's conditions were not clear to us, but he seemed to want the United States to declare it favored self-determination for the Palestinians or to announce directly that there should be a Palestinian "homeland" on the West Bank and in Gaza.

other. Begin was calmly denying that any shelling was taking place; this had just been confirmed by Defense Minister Ariel Sharon. "There is no intent today to occupy West Beirut. If we had such an intent, I would write to Ronald Reagan," Begin said. The United States was being fed hysterical, inflated reporting, Begin said.

Hill relayed this to Habib. "Oh, yeah?" Habib said, and held his tacsat earpiece out the window so that we could hear the Israeli artillery firing. Hill counted eight shells within thirty seconds from IDF artillery batteries located just below Habib's position. When Bill Brown reported Begin's assurances, we told him to tell Begin that at the very moment he was reassuring us, we could hear the noise of the Israeli guns.

Begin telephoned Bill Brown again. It was now 5:10 A.M. in Washington. The Israeli chief of staff had reported that the PLO had been using "a great variety of weapons." The IDF had fired back, but only at the origin of the firing against them. The Israelis were not advancing at all, Begin said. "Do you think the chief of staff of the Israel Defense Forces is misleading me?" Begin asked.

Sam Lewis told us his opinion was that we were seeing "a spasm leap forward by Ariel Sharon," probably carried out under some blanket Israeli cabinet decision that he should keep the pressure on Beirut.

At 5:30 A.M., Habib relayed a message from President Sarkis of Lebanon: "President Sarkis requests your intervention in the present situation in Beirut in order to save innocent lives and the destruction of the capital. The president is asking himself to whom he can address himself other than to the president of the United States?"

Habib said that this Israeli advance undermined the present working plan for PLO departure. Prior to this advance, the PLO had dropped its demand for an IDF pullback; now a major Israeli withdrawal would have to be achieved before the PLO agreed to leave. "We cannot now honestly pursue the plan we have presented to the PLO," Habib said.

I did not know who was to blame on the Israeli side, but I was clear in my mind that Israel in its official voice was either uninformed or deliberately trying to mislead us. In either case, I was disappointed and angry.

I called NSC adviser Bill Clark in the White House to request a crisis meeting for 7:15 A.M. in the Situation Room. Habib urged that we impose sanctions on Israel unless they ceased firing, withdrew, and restored power and water. Ambassador Lewis offered a draft letter for President Reagan to send to Begin disassociating the United States from Israeli actions. Meanwhile, back in Israel, Ariel Sharon was on the phone to Bill Brown, heaping scorn on our reports: they are false, hysterical, unprofessional; the IDF has done nothing like what is being claimed, Sharon said. The IDF had observation posts on the heights of Beit Mary, where they could overlook Beirut. But Habib, at the U.S. ambassador's residence on the heights above Beirut, could also observe every move against the city below.

In reality, President Reagan was more hesitant than anyone else about cracking down on the Israelis. I wanted stronger pressure on Israel; so did George Bush, Jim Baker, and Ed Meese, but the president would not go along. Cap Weinberger was at the extreme; he seemed almost ready to sever relations. Three points had emerged from this episode. First, our intelligence about what was happening on the ground (apart from what Habib could see) was terrible; Bill Casey had nothing better than Reuters reports of what was going on. Second, Cap Weinberger was ready to cut off the pipeline of U.S. assistance to Israel. And third, Begin's—and Israel's—credibility had sunk abysmally low. High U.S. officials now began to *assume* that reports from Israel were simply not accurate, whether through confusion or purposely.

The White House meeting went on for hours, but the public statement that emerged from President Reagan was woefully inadequate in my view, mild and pedestrian. Much stronger in substance was Ronald Reagan's private message to Menachem Begin: a cease-fire in place must be established until the PLO leaves Beirut. "The relationship between our two nations is at stake," Reagan said starkly.

The situation as I saw it now was this: President Reagan had given his views to Shamir in strong language, and I had followed up with Shamir, telling him of the PLO's decision to depart and getting from him a commitment to give us time to arrange the details. The negotiations in Beirut with the PLO took a turn for the better, getting down to operational details. Then came the escalation of fighting the previous night. We communicated our information to Begin, who told us that not much was going on, but, again, Habib could see the fighting with his own eyes. We informed Begin again; he said we were imagining things. After a special White House Situation Room meeting early the next morning, President Reagan sent another message to Begin, stressing that Habib's negotiations must continue. I wanted it made clear to Begin that the cease-fire reference in the president's message meant a *rollback*. That is, a cease-fire *in place* must be established as of the lines of August 1, not the lines resulting from the escalated fighting on August 3.

I called in Ambassador Arens, handed over the president's letter to Prime Minister Begin, and went over all of these points with him. I told him we were both in an increasingly intolerable position. I said Israel simply had to realize that it was better to get the PLO out without devastating Beirut. It was one thing for the United States to be pilloried by our Arab friends, but this situation did not bode well for the United States' and Israel's ability to work out a more general peace in the region.

Arens argued the merits of continuing military pressure on the PLO. "Doesn't turning the screw help?" he asked.

"Now when it's turned," I said, "it mostly digs in to noncombatants and treats the world to a picture that is abhorrent. The symbol of this war has become the baby with its arms blown off. So stop turning the screw. And let the situation have a chance to work itself out. There is no doubt whatsoever in the PLO's mind about Israel's ability or will. Don't let another night like last night happen or it all will break down. Israel's original move into Lebanon and its subsequent advances have been against the advice of the United States," I told Arens. "We want the PLO out, and the negotiating track has a reasonable chance of achieving that objective." I stressed that the last sentence of the president's letter to Begin had been written by the president himself: "The relationship between our two nations is at stake." "Ronald Reagan is an agreeable man but decisive," I said. "Don't push him."

A bruised Habib set about trying to pick up the pieces of the negotiations. "I will soon learn," he said, "whether the Lebanese will continue to deal with me after this." The critical questions remained: Where would the Palestinians go? When would the multinational force arrive? The PLO wanted it to arrive early; the Pentagon wanted it to arrive late. The French appeared willing to enter Beirut before the PLO evacuation began. Where would the MNF be deployed? What would its function be? How would we assemble the PLO for departure? What about their heavy weapons? Would there be UN observers?

Late Thursday afternoon, on August 5, at Senator Chuck Percy's urgent request, I went to Capitol Hill to brief all the senators on the situation. The majority of them were deeply hostile to Israel's actions. The few who defended what the Israelis had done—Senators Kennedy, Metzenbaum, and Boschwitz—took the position that the PLO would never leave Beirut and that Israel had no choice but to go into the city to dig them out.

That same day, UN Security Council Resolution 517 censured Israel. The United States abstained because the text did not mention the necessity of a PLO departure from Beirut.

Habib, on the tacsat, expounded that we were not being tough enough on the Israelis. He called the latest Reagan-to-Begin message "a wet noodle." But he again proceeded to put together the negotiations for departure. "We are in the homestretch," Habib predicted.

I thought so, too. Habib was as aware as I was of the president's tough private message to Begin. Just as the Israelis were convinced that willingness of the PLO to leave Beirut was created by their incessant pounding on that city, I was convinced that a tough U.S. posture was necessary to keep that pounding under control. The right combination of strength and diplomacy was the essential ingredient for agreement, and it was up to me to see that Habib—in the field and on the verge of achieving the negotiation for departure—had as strong a hand as possible.

CHAPTER 5

The PLO Moves Out of Beirut

On August 5, 1982, we got a breakthrough of sorts from the Saudis. Prince Bandar reported that King Fahd had declared, "Wherever the PLO elects to go, we will work to assure it is accepted." At this point the situation in Beirut looked promising. The newspaper headlines gave the Arabs the sense that the United States was working hard, so the Arabs had better do their part to find a new home for the PLO. The Israeli cabinet had just rejected a call for UN observers and was feeling tough and satisfied. We could count on extremists at the United Nations to concoct outlandish language for all resolutions on this topic, so we could abstain or veto at little political cost. This gave Phil Habib some time to work.

Habib was making good use of his time. The PLO was now active in its own behalf to find a place to relocate. Arafat and his men were focusing on Egypt and had sent messages to President Mubarak asking him to drop his efforts to link acceptance of the PLO to political or policy changes by the United States on other Middle East peace issues. They agreed to turn over their heavy weapons and wanted international observers to be present, and the multinational force (MNF) to come into Beirut on the day of their departure. Their concern was what would happen to them once they turned their backs and started the process of evacuation. Also on their minds were those who would be left behind in the Palestinian refugee camps just south of Beirut.

Habib, in turn, sought assurances of safety from the Lebanese government and the likely new president of Lebanon, Bashir Gemayel, and from the Israelis at both the political and military level. He received them. On this explicit basis, he gave the PLO the assurances that it wanted. He continued to refine the details of departure, asking the PLO to give him their proposed schedule by unit, destination, and route chosen. Habib was starting detailed talks with the advance liaison officers from the French, Italian, and U.S. militaries that would make up the multinational force. He was also making strenuous efforts to restore water, power, and other services to West Beirut. The Israeli soldiers who now ringed the city with checkpoints were stopping all cars and were confiscating medicines that physicians sought to bring into the devastated area. Habib raged at this as inhumane and worked to get fuel and medicine to the hospital at the American University of Beirut via the Red Cross. I supported Habib from Washington, and gradually services were restored to Beirut.

The bad news was that the Israeli cabinet had decided to name Defense Minister Ariel Sharon as the sole decision maker for the Israelis with regard to Habib's Beirut negotiations. Habib met with Sharon on the evening of August 6 and briefed him on the state of discussions with the PLO about its evacuation. Each was on his best behavior. Habib reported that it was "Mr. Minister" and "Mr. Ambassador" and not acrimonious. Sharon zeroed in on the deployment of the MNF, insisting that it not come into Beirut until all the PLO had left. The Israelis still pictured the PLO standing behind a protective screen of international peacekeepers, thumbing its nose at the Israelis and altering the terms for departure. Habib said no dice, and as he explained the whole plan to Sharon, the Israeli concerns faded. The operational plan was a good one and addressed the needs of all sides.

At the end of the day on Saturday, August 7, Habib reported that he was feeling some satisfaction from his meeting with Sharon and from a communication he had from Bashir Gemayel confirming that his Lebanese Forces (LF) would not interfere with the departure of the PLO and would not harass or attack the Palestinians who would be left behind in the refugee camps. The Lebanese in West Beirut were eager to have the MNF come in, as was the PLO, who desperately wanted an international force in place before its leaders and fighters started leaving the city.

I knew that France wanted its troops in the MNF as a way to reassert its traditional influence in the Levant. The Israelis just as avidly wanted to keep the French out. The French had a favorable view of the PLO, and the Israelis distrusted them. To maneuver for diplomatic advantage, the French played hard to get, while the Israelis played hard to give. I stonewalled both, confident that in the end we would get both the French and the Israelis to come around. By August 6, Claude Cheysson, the French foreign minister, had confirmed French participation. And by August 8, American, French, and Italian military liaison officers were meeting with Lebanese representatives in Beirut.

Just how and when the MNF would enter was still not settled. We now had a carrier offshore, and our helicopters shuttled U.S. liaison personnel back and forth to meetings with Habib. On Sunday, August 8, two Israeli fighter aircraft circled around and "buzzed" the U.S. choppers as they returned our liaison officer to our carrier. Tempers on our side were getting dangerously short. The pilots shrugged it off, but the entire U.S. military chain of command, from the Mediterranean to Europe to Washington, D.C., was furious; so was I, and so was Cap Weinberger. We protested strongly, and Prime Minister Begin personally apologized for the incident.

Late in the day I received a cryptic message regarding the PLO from King Fahd: "There is no longer any problem about their destinations." Whether that meant Egypt had come around or that several Arab governments had agreed to take PLO contingents, I did not know. We gathered all available information and tried to list the approximate number of Palestinian fighters that would have to be moved out. The total came to about 10,700.

The PLO was desperate to get out of Beirut now, but the Israelis kept putting obstacles in the path of completing a negotiation. Officials on their way to liaison meetings were roadblocked and delayed. The use of the airport by the Italian contingent of the MNF was denied. No "approval" was forthcoming for French participation at all, and Israeli forces occupied the port of Juniyah, north of Beirut, where the French contingent had planned to land. Israeli paranoia was making everyone so jumpy that it was necessary to go over every step of the departure in detail with Israeli officials in order to reassure them that their security was not threatened and to get their approval, since they held the balance of military power on the ground. Of course, such veto power is just what Israel wanted.

Habib had his final plan drawn up in every detail by August 8. D-Day would be August 14. It looked as if we had assigned destinations for some 7,000 PLO in Jordan, Syria, Iraq, and Egypt. Habib met with Ariel Sharon for three and a half hours at Israeli army field headquarters just outside Beirut. The Israelis listened attentively as Habib, in his friendly but "don't dare challenge me" way, set forth the details of how the PLO was to retreat from its part of Beirut, the scene where it so long had held sway over politics, money, and the life of a once-thriving and glamorous capital.

Sharon, in a businesslike way, stated the Israeli position, which he described as a decision of the cabinet: no Israeli agreement to the entry of the MNF until all the PLO had left Beirut. Habib said that matters had gone too far for that. The government of Lebanon wanted the MNF, and continuing Israeli shelling had caused the PLO to insist that the MNF be on hand before their departure movement began. Why, Habib rhetorically asked Sharon, do the Israelis think the PLO would expose itself to an unsheltered withdrawal after the Israeli military attacks of the last few days? Habib pointed out that in terms of the MNF mandate, if the MNF deployed and the PLO then refused to move, the MNF role would terminate immediately, and it would depart. Habib said he was proceeding on the basis of Israel's word that Israel wanted a political-diplomatic solution.

"Yes," Sharon replied.

Habib told Sharon that Israel now had every possible detail of the plan and asked Sharon to take it to Prime Minister Begin. If Begin wanted,

Habib would fly down to Jerusalem to go over it with him. "It's only four hours door to door," Habib said.

The PLO, it now appeared, would leave by boat from the port of Beirut. Attention turned to the details of drafting the departure agreement. Every word was scrutinized. In paragraph sixteen the Israelis objected to the words "vacate the route," meaning that the IDF, which now controlled the port, would allow the PLO to get to the boats. The words were changed to "clear the route"; the PLO objected because this would allow the Israeli troops to be visible to the TV cameras as the PLO boarded. Debate continued over the issue of whether Israelis would be out of sight at the time of evacuation. Prime Minister Begin sent me a letter on August 9 concerning these details. "It's inaccurate in every paragraph," Habib said. "They are either massively misinformed or twisting the record. But at the end of the letter the prime minister says that Mrs. Begin sends her regards to Mrs. Shultz; that part is probably accurate," Habib said.

On the other hand, Begin was conveying a new message to the Israeli people. "There is a basis for the assumption that they [Arafat and the PLO] will leave soon and we will not have to go into West Beirut," he had told a military audience on August 8.

The Israelis were now running occasional air strikes on the Sabra and Shatila refugee camps, the airport circle, and other selected targets south of the city center. They informed Lebanese intelligence that this "softening up" would continue for a day or two. On the other side, Habib was reporting to me that "bad actors" within the PLO, under Syrian influence, had been violating the cease-fire. Habib was raising hell about it with Muslim leaders who supposedly had influence with these people. We urged the Israelis to hold back their retaliatory measures. We were suspicious that "softening up" shelling was a prelude to an IDF assault into the refugee camps. Sharon had mentioned to Habib on August 8 the "need to clean out" the camps. Habib protested violently and was deeply alarmed.

The Pentagon was now actively preparing for entry of the U.S. contingent. Rear Admiral Jon Howe, one of the Defense Department's most promising flag officers, now assigned to my staff to head State's Bureau of Political and Military Affairs, was working to get our military's views written into the MNF agreement. The main issue was over how long the MNF would assist the Lebanese armed forces and internal security force to maintain order after the PLO departed.

At midday August 9, a Monday, I was surprised by a telephone call from the Israeli embassy. Sharon was coming to Washington. He requested three meetings on Thursday: with me, with Cap Weinberger, and with President Reagan. Habib's first reaction to the news was calm: let Sharon come, let him raise any topic; but we will not delay the departure timetable because of his Washington trip. We will proceed as planned. To me Sharon's maneuver looked like a classic diplomatic end run. I didn't like it. On reflection, Habib didn't either. Sharon, I thought, was coming to try to convince us that Habib had been duped, that the PLO had no intention of leaving Beirut, and that Habib should be taken off the job. I decided to cable back through Israel's Deputy Chief of Mission Benjamin Netanyahu the following message:

> Minister Sharon would be welcome, as always, in Washington. We would not, however, be prepared to take up any matters pertaining to the current problem of West Beirut. To deal with that situation, the President's personal emissary, Ambassador Habib, has produced a negotiated package arrangement that is reasonable and capable of being put into effect as early as the end of this week. Time is of the essence if the momentum toward the outcome we seek is to be maintained and built upon. We do not want anything to delay us in these crucial final days. We hope that Israel will give its cooperation to this package arrangement as quickly as possible. Ambassador Habib and Ambassador Lewis are ready to answer whatever questions Israel may have and to transmit messages as may be desired.

Sharon decided not to come after all. I was glad to see his trip derailed. In Jerusalem, Sam Lewis was meeting Prime Minister Begin to discuss our plan, first in private and then in a larger group. Lewis reported to me that Begin took umbrage at the use in the departure agreement of the expression "D-Day." That signified the Allied invasion of Europe, Begin said; there should be no hint that this would be a victory day for the PLO. "Call it E-Day," Begin said. Begin also said that he was highly offended by the use of the phrase "Palestinian forces," as it suggested they were a legitimate armed force. "Use 'PLO members,'" he said. "Also, don't use the word 'died'; use 'killed.'"

In the larger official meeting that followed, Sharon, Shamir, and Arens were also present. Begin said he had read the plan and agreement carefully. He was "prepared to accept it in principle, subject to important changes." Begin made his points: Israel is "adamantly opposed" to the MNF going in on day one, the day of withdrawal. Let the Lebanese army go in. Begin called this "a great concession" by Israel. He then unleashed a long tirade against the French and said that Israel was "categorically opposed" to any UN observers. There must be a detailed schedule for the withdrawal of all Syrian forces from Lebanon. There must be a detailed accounting of the numbers of PLO members and of the countries to which they would go.

Begin and Sharon then got into a dispute about what to do about Syrian forces' heavy weapons. Begin did not insist on an impossible requirement as part of this arrangement. Throughout the meeting, Begin showed annoyance and animosity toward Sharon, Sam Lewis said. For his part, Sharon was visibly miffed that the story was out that he had tried to go to Washington to "end run" Habib and had been rebuffed by me. Begin asked

Lewis to convey the points to Habib. If Habib accepted them, all was agreed; if not, Habib should come to Jerusalem to talk to Begin directly. Begin was not looking well. He seemed anxious to approve a political solution in order to forestall pressure for an outright Israeli assault into Beirut. In Sam Lewis's view, Begin was pleading for help from us in getting a negotiated departure for the PLO.

When Habib and I heard Begin's points, we knew that the PLO would not accept them: Arafat and his men would never trust the ability of the Lebanese army to protect them from the Khataeb (the militia of the Maronite Christians) as they left. So I sent Habib by helicopter to Israel to see Begin and to urge him to drop his demand for these changes.

On Tuesday, August 10, the president and I had meetings with Shimon Peres, the head of Israel's Labor party. The Israel Air Force provided a context for the meetings: they were running air strike after air strike against PLO positions south of Beirut. According to press reports, the aircraft struck at 2:00 P.M., "the exact moment that residents of Beirut listened to Israeli radio announce from Jerusalem that a special meeting of the Israeli cabinet had given its conditional approval to the Habib plan."[1] The meetings with Peres had long been scheduled and were part of the regular round of calls paid on the president and the secretary of state by top Israeli leaders whenever they were in town. Peres was upbeat. I worried that his optimism might infect President Reagan and mislead him to think that work on the Arab-Israeli peace process would move ahead easily in Israel. "The U.S. has never had a better opportunity to bring peace than it has today," Peres said. The war had been awful, but it offered a chance for Lebanon to free itself from all foreign forces, including Israel's and Syria's, and to become a real nation again. At the same time, the peace process could be given a needed boost. He impressed the president with his thoughtful and reasonable manner and his support for UN Resolution 242 as the basis for a peaceful outcome in the Arab-Israeli dispute. The present plight of the PLO could help, he said. "The PLO's record is hopeless. It is a Mafia whose structure is riven by blackmail, jealousy, terrorism; it leads the Palestinian people only to a dead end."

I made myself clear to Peres: "The war is not a blessing. The Arabs feel helpless. They blame the U.S. The war has shown how quickly military action and death can come. It will be difficult to draw the Arabs into the peace process unless they can see an end to it that is constructive. The Arab world now has zero confidence that there is any give in Israel. They are sure that Israel will never leave Lebanon. Why are Israeli administrative and financial people entering Lebanon? Why is the IDF stocking winter clothing in Lebanon? There is a total lack of trust."

1. Loren Jenkins in the *Washington Post*, August 11, 1982.

Peres understood. "I am sure we will leave Lebanon," he told me.

That afternoon, I received two positive reports: Yasser Arafat had accepted the Habib package, and the PLO departure schedule had been set. And the Tunisian ambassador to Lebanon had informed Morrie Draper, Habib's deputy, that Tunisia was prepared to take all the PLO if the United States so desired. Tunisia was a "moderate" Arab state. This was good news; we did not want to see the PLO relocate to an extremist state.

Menachem Begin sent a private message to me, conveyed orally by the prime minister to Sam Lewis. Begin's emotional intensity had been extraordinary, Sam recounted. Begin was deeply concerned that the U.S.-Israel relationship was coming apart at the seams. "Please understand the nature of our people and of me. Sanctions will never change our decisions. Please prevail over those in the president's entourage who seek to impose military and economic sanctions on Israel."

Lewis said Begin was clearly frightened that the arrangements for evacuation of the PLO all could be falling apart. Begin was highly sensitive to the growing charges that Ariel Sharon was leading him around by the nose and ordering military operations on his own. "Approval of the Habib plan for PLO departure would help, would it not?" Begin asked Lewis.

"It would be a step on the right road," Lewis replied.

Suddenly, the sands of the Arab world shifted regarding the PLO. Syrian President Assad told Saudi King Fahd that Syria would take "the maximum possible number of PLO." Iraq then let it be known that it would "take them all." Everywhere in the region people and governments seemed to be adjusting their thinking to the plan and to the reality of the PLO's departure. Only the Egyptians were still seeking linkage to other issues in the peace process. Osama el-Baz, Mubarak's key aide, a foreign affairs operator and a Harvard man, said that Egypt would not take any PLO except in the context of "a clear and unequivocal commitment by the United States to reach a comprehensive settlement to the Palestinian question in all its aspects on the basis of recognizing the Palestinian people's right to self-determination." This we would not do; it would be tantamount to recognizing an independent Palestinian state.

Habib met in Jerusalem with Begin and the many Israeli officials who would be responsible for implementing their part of the departure plan. The meetings were flexible, friendly, and businesslike. Everyone seemed ready to address practical details seriously. Begin's concerns seemed to have narrowed down to his obsessive dislike of the French, their votes at the United Nations, and what he regarded as their record of anti-Semitism. Begin was determined that if the French were part of the MNF, at least they would not enter Beirut as the first contingent. The French told Habib that if Israel vetoed their arrival on the first day, then they wouldn't be part of the MNF at all. Our Defense Department, as shy as the French were bold, was making it clear that U.S. forces would not go in on the first day and was insisting that some other nation's military take the lead.

The PLO side was working seriously as well, but the effort was showing gaps in its organizational capability. Arafat had sent his nominal foreign minister, Faruq Khaddumi, to Tunis to lay the groundwork for the PLO move there. It appeared that Tunisia would be the PLO's new home and headquarters.

Revealingly, the Israelis had started to "background" the press on an upbeat note, a sign that they were ready to settle matters. The Israelis had been convinced that Phil Habib was wrong in his approach, but now they were reversing themselves. The Israeli planners were obviously shifting their thinking to Phase II. Israel's armed forces, we were told, would never move out of Lebanon until Syria's left as well. "There will have to be simultaneous withdrawal," Begin told Habib. As for Phase I, the planners were now poring over maps of the port area in north Beirut with the four piers from which the PLO would board ships bound for Tunis—the first real sign that the Israelis were taking the withdrawal seriously. As for the PLO, I knew that they were actually serious about departing when I heard their request that they be allowed to take their Mercedes-Benzes with them. They presumed, they said, that the boats used in the evacuation would be car ferries.

One Last Shot and a Tough Response

In the early morning hours of August 12, as we in Washington slept, intense shelling broke loose again in Beirut. At dawn, Washington time, Habib called in on the tacsat: "The city is being destroyed, and America is being blamed for it. It is all going up in smoke! Tell Begin to stop it or else! Israel is destroying the negotiation in its final moments!"

Israeli radio was reporting that the IDF was moving forward in a combined air, sea, and land offensive. Twenty-five Israeli soldiers were reported wounded so far. Sam Lewis called in to say that he had found Begin's young friend Dan Meridor in the Knesset, where the cabinet was meeting, and gave him a terrific blast. "Nobody can understand what Israel is up to," Lewis said. "Stop it now, this minute! Your friends can't understand what you are doing!"

I talked to Habib at 8:45 A.M., Washington time. "While I was negotiating today," Habib told me, "there were constant heavy air strikes and artillery. Eight hours of air strikes. The Lebanese president and prime minister have made an urgent appeal to us. They can't negotiate under these conditions. So I can't get to the PLO. I'm making my own plea." Habib said, "There has to be a three-day cease-fire for me to be able to negotiate seriously. Tell the Israelis to stop using air strikes; they are using heavy artillery and air strikes in the museum area and near the French embassy. The fire from the Palestinians is minute. Some radicals tried to start this and have succeeded. The Israeli response is unwarranted and not proportional. There have been fifty sorties today at a minimum. The city is progressively being destroyed, and the Lebanese are asking me what there is to negotiate about."

I was enraged. The reputation and word of the United States were being compromised. The Lebanese and PLO now believed that Habib's negotiations were a sham, an effort to hold the PLO's neck while Israel swung the ax. I went over to the White House and gave President Reagan my report. My agitation showed. He, too, was visibly angry. He said another Holocaust was taking place. I urged him to telephone Begin. The president did, but Begin was in the midst of a cabinet meeting and did not take the call.

Meanwhile, at 10:15 A.M. Washington time, we heard that the director general of the Israeli Foreign Ministry, David Kimche, had informed Ambassador Lewis that the cabinet "has ordered an immediate cease-fire and will hold it as long as there is no untoward military action by the other side." At 10:20, Habib called in to say that he had just met with Mother Teresa, who was in Beirut and who said she would pray to the Virgin Mary for him. "I then went outside," Habib said, "and watched the Israeli air force drop sticks of bombs on Beirut from 10,000 feet."

The Soviet Union called for an urgent meeting of the UN Security Council.

A few minutes later, at 11:05, President Reagan got through to Prime Minister Begin, who had just concluded a cabinet meeting. Reagan's tone was the harshest possible, and his words were followed by a written cable:

> At this most crucial moment in Ambassador Habib's mission, when he is only a few days away from working out the final detailed points of his package plan for the departure of the PLO from Beirut and Lebanon, Israeli air strikes and other military moves have stopped progress in the negotiations. I find this incomprehensible and unacceptable. It raises troubling questions about the reality of Israel's commitment to a negotiated solution to this crisis in Beirut. The assurances which we hear from Jerusalem are not borne out by the actions of the Israel Defense Forces, who erupt massively to any provocation. Israel must adhere to an immediate, strict cease-fire. Furthermore, what is the purpose of moves by Israel's forces toward Jubayl and the north of Lebanon? I cannot accept this new military offensive as compatible with the pledges of Israeli withdrawal from Lebanon and support for the emergence of a strong Lebanese government. I cannot stress enough to you how seriously I regard this situation. Ambassador Habib must be enabled to fulfill these last steps in his mission. The cease-fire must be kept. Our entire future relations are at stake if this continues. He has already achieved a fully

comprehensive and reasonable package agreement. Israeli military actions of the past several hours may have made further alteration of that package impossible. If so, or if for any other reason the package must stand as it is, we will look to Israel to accept it fully without further discussion, so that the agony of Beirut may be ended.

Begin called President Reagan back within several minutes. "I have just talked with the minister of defense and the chief of staff. Now there is no firing at all," he told the president. "I don't want to cause you any problem with public opinion. Let's hope Phil Habib can get the other side to hold the cease-fire; then we can have no firing at all until the terrorists leave in the next few days."

President Reagan's anger must have come through on the telephone. Such anger, particularly toward Israelis, was rare for Ronald Reagan. His message was clear as a bell. Finally, Begin and the Israelis must have realized that enough was enough. They were alienating their best friends and stood a chance of losing an agreement with Lebanon that they wanted and needed.

Final Steps

Sam Lewis reported that the Israeli cabinet voted 16 to 2 for the cease-fire. Defense Minister Ariel Sharon had one supporter in voting for continued military action. Begin spoke strongly to the cabinet, saying he knew nothing of these latest military moves until they were well under way. Begin was angry and talked of defense ministers who had been removed from office in the past. Some cabinet ministers charged that the IDF action had been contrary to the decisions of the government of Israel. Reports coming in were that in the course of eleven hours the Israeli air force had run 220 sorties, that 44,000 shells had been fired, that an estimated 200 were dead, 400 wounded.

Ambassador Dick Murphy in Saudi Arabia reported that Arafat had contacted King Fahd about Israel's objection to any foreign peacekeeping forces to protect the PLO on its departure. Arafat and Fahd share the view, Murphy said, that "Israel now intends to wipe out the PLO as they are leaving." They asked the Saudis to contact the United States about this. In Washington, some of our Middle East specialists were speculating that Sharon was starting to feel that Arafat's departure would in fact be seen as a brilliant escape and a political victory and that Sharon therefore wanted it known that *he* had always been in favor of wiping out the PLO. Sharon did not want the ultimate failure of Israel's "Peace for Galilee" invasion of Lebanon to be blamed on him.

On Friday, August 13, the Beirut scene was relatively quiet once more.

Habib left at 8:00 A.M. to talk to Begin. The issue was still the PLO's fearful need for foreign forces to cover them as they left and Israel's refusal to let the French do that job. The opinion coming from our embassy in Israel was that Begin had been deeply embarrassed by Sharon and the IDF attack on August 12. It was increasingly looking as if Begin had been something of a victim of Sharon's manipulation throughout the war. Sharon, our embassy said, was now isolated in the cabinet.

Habib met Begin to review all the plans and emerged, he said, in a mood of "dour optimism." There were many Israeli complaints, he said, but they were talking of the plan as a foregone conclusion. Israel wanted a negotiated removal of the PLO from Beirut. By this point, several hundred Israelis had been killed and many more wounded, and the Israelis knew that a battle for the city itself would be bloody. The departure of the PLO, they seemed to think, would be the political end of Arafat and his organization. At that moment, Begin, deeply embarrassed by Sharon's independent actions, appeared to have regained the upper hand. The recent air strikes on Beirut, we were told, had not been approved by the Israeli cabinet, and "air strike authority" had now been taken out of Sharon's hands. On that same day, the government of Lebanon accepted the plan and called for the arrival of the MNF. We all pointed to daybreak Saturday, August 14, as the moment when the French MNF contingent would come into a Beirut port.

A crucial issue centered around Syria's troops in Lebanon. They had entered Lebanon in force in the late 1970s to restore order among the warring factions, militias, and the Palestinians. The Syrian presence, designated the Arab Deterrent Force, had been legitimized years before by an Arab declaration in Cairo in 1979. The Israelis wanted the Syrians to withdraw entirely from Lebanon. The United States wanted this, too, as did the Lebanese. But Syrian withdrawal would not be possible without an IDF commitment to withdraw as well. I could see that a joint withdrawal of both these major regular armies was essential for the Lebanese central government to regain control of its country. This would require a tricky diplomatic effort. For the moment, however, we needed a Syrian commitment to pull its troops back from the Beirut area as the MNF arrived. Phil Habib was working with his Lebanese contacts to get Syrian President Assad's agreement to this. At the same time, the government of Lebanon was seeking to get Arab governments to state that the Cairo declaration of 1979 was no longer in effect—in order to deprive the Syrian army of any semblance of legitimacy for its now-permanent presence on Lebanese soil. I instructed Dick Murphy to ask the Saudis to help get Syrian cooperation in this.

At the end of the weekend, the Lebanese reported that Assad would not agree that the Arab Deterrent Force mandate was over, but Lebanese leader Saeb Salam told us the Syrians did agree to redeploy their forces within Lebanon and to accept the return to Syria of Palestinian troops under Syrian military command. Getting the Syrians out of Beirut and possibly out of Lebanon altogether as a result of a Lebanese government request was, we thought, potentially the most important and far-reaching aspect of this whole affair. The Lebanese had girded their loins for the first time in a long time in their attempt to regain control over their own country.

The chief remaining concern of Arafat and the PLO was for their safety as they departed, for the safety of Palestinian prisoners who were held by Israel, and for the safety of those left behind in the refugee camps. We told Habib to have the Lebanese tell the PLO that we would maintain an interest in seeing that Palestinian prisoners held by Israel would be treated in accordance with the Geneva Convention.

For the Israelis, the chief remaining concern was for the return of their downed pilot, said to be in Syrian hands. He had piloted a Skyhawk fighter which had dispensed chaff to blind Syrian surface-to-air missiles and permit the devastatingly successful Israeli air force victory over Syrian MIGs at the start of the war. The "backseater," the other Israeli airman on the plane, had, because of his crucial technical knowledge, committed suicide as his plane went down rather than allow himself to fall into Syrian hands, where torture surely awaited him. Ambassador Moshe Arens told me, in a nighttime meeting on August 16, that Israel would consider trading the 300-some Syrian prisoners of war held in Israel. To Begin, the release of Israeli prisoners was essential for them to agree with the entire arrangement.

The next morning, Phil Habib reported that Ariel Sharon, on Begin's instructions, had raised *eleven* new issues, which, according to Habib and Draper, only skimmed the surface of their demands: the Israelis had "twenty million" other proposals for the conduct of the departure. They demanded that we provide them with a letter of assurances covering many of these points. As Habib would make a little progress, Sharon would step up the military pressure by shelling, air strikes, and once again the shutting off of food and water. The PLO, who had their own wells and vast supplies, were not hurt much, but the Lebanese negotiators were paralyzed by such tactics. Instead of Israeli military pressure speeding Habib's work, Sharon's actions kept retarding progress at critical moments. Sharon's heavy-handedness extended to Habib himself. Habib reported that when he held meetings in a house near our ambassador's residence, the Israelis would lob shells directly overhead.

Israeli President Yitzhak Navon, who held the ceremonial position of head of state, had been scheduled to visit Washington to meet with President Reagan in mid-September. We got word at this time that Navon wanted to postpone his visit until November or December. He was "personally appalled" by Israel's actions in Lebanon and indicated to Sam Lewis that he did not want to be put in a position of having to defend Begin's policy while the Lebanon war was still in progress.

An additional matter was the election of the next president of Lebanon, tentatively set for Thursday, August 19. There would have to be a continuity of government in Lebanon in order for authority to exist to ask the MNF to enter Beirut on Saturday. The Israeli army had been surrounding the presidential palace in Baabda and the Palais Mansour, the parliament building. We pressed them to pull away. As soon as they did, however, the PLO, Palestinian troops fighting under Syrian command, and units of the Lebanese army took up positions in the same locations, which threatened the holding of the elections as scheduled. Habib went into high gear with the key Lebanese to urge them not to postpone the vote.

We proceeded to charter three of the big car ferryboats that would normally be plying the eastern Mediterranean loaded with tourists at this time of year—the *Sol Georgios*, the *Alkyon*, the *Aphrodite*—and arranged for them to be lying off Beirut port by first light Saturday.

The current plan for the PLO evacuation was for the boats to take the entire group from Lebanon to Yemen (North and South). On Wednesday, August 18, a "flash" telegram from Ambassador Dick Murphy came in. The Saudis, he said, had become desperately afraid of having the PLO relocate on the Arabian Peninsula, so close to their kingdom; the Saudis saw the Palestinians as a threat to Saudi security and were therefore blocking the entire departure plan by ruling out the only recipient places available. King Fahd told Murphy that if the PLO went to Yemen, it would not be for the cause of Palestine but to subvert the entire Gulf area. Fahd proposed that the PLO evacuation by sea go from Beirut to Latakia, on the coast of Syria, and that some PLO departees go to Cyprus en route to Iraq.

On Thursday, August 19, the Israeli cabinet approved our departure plan but would not implement it until their downed pilot and all Israeli prisoners and bodies in Palestinian and Syrian hands were returned to Israel's control. At this point there could scarcely have been any remaining concern of any party about the PLO evacuation that had not been discussed and dealt with at excruciating length. But despite the care in working out the details, many aspects of this undertaking were still uncertain and likely to become the issue on which the whole enterprise might collapse. So we approached the departure as a classic "Middle East solution," meaning: do not inquire too deeply or press too hard on the most sensitive and intractable of issues. The more we said about the plan, the more trouble we were inviting; many incompatible aspects would be "understood" and lived with if they were largely left alone—especially in public. If we were explicit, we would just force others to retort that that was *not* what they agreed to or understood. The Arabs were able to proceed this way; it did not come naturally to either Americans or Israelis, but it is a wise strategy in moments of possible progress in the Middle East.

Actually, in diplomacy, many problems are solved by not being too precise and public about the solutions. I have said, and others have told me, in a negotiation, "Don't try to pin me down on this. I'll work the problem out to your satisfaction, but I'll do so in my own way and in my own time."

In the midst of all this, Cap Weinberger informed me that he wanted to start serious discussions of tank sales with the Saudis. Would I clear a message he wanted to send them? He brought this up at our weekly breakfast meeting. I sat listening and eating my eggs for fifteen minutes while Cap argued for this move. I was incredulous at the disruptive timing of the idea. At the end of his presentation I looked up, "Cap, I find everything you said incomprehensible." Cap seemed unable to understand that such a move at this moment could be the joker in the deck that could destroy our Lebanon and Middle East negotiations at their most delicate moment.

Meanwhile, Israeli demands kept rolling in. The IDF wanted to set up a post on top of the grain silos at the port, an elevation from which they could command the entire evacuation scene. These grain elevators were the dominating feature of the port and were located right in the center of the pier area. You could spit on the evacuation ships from a post atop them, and such a position would be inside the perimeter of the multinational force. We said no, but the Israelis would not stop pressing.

The Lebanese also began to play the departure for their own purposes. Sunni Muslims let Habib know that they would not attend the election assembly because they would not accept Bashir Gemayel as president; the Sunnis proposed that President Sarkis continue in office for another year. Bashir countered by letting the Lebanese Muslims know that his militia, with Israeli support, would control the port of Beirut and would not allow the French to land unless the Sunnis agreed to make up the assembly quorum needed to hold the presidential election. No quorum, no MNF; no MNF, no PLO departure—and the Israeli siege of Beirut would continue. Habib went to see Bashir to insist he abandon this position; the PLO departure was bigger than Bashir's election at this point. The Saudis told Dick Murphy that they favored a postponed election. They were not opposed to Bashir Gemayel as Lebanon's president but felt that he should not be elected at this time in this way.

Late that night, Habib reported in. Bashir had had a confrontation with Israeli Lieutenant General Rafael (Raful) Eitan and had obtained IDF acquiescence for Bashir's troops to take up positions at the port. "If the Muslims want to save Beirut, then they have to produce a quorum by

Monday," Bashir said. "If the election is held Monday, then we will let the PLO departure take place," Bashir said. The Syrians were putting heavy pressure on the Lebanese Sunnis to prevent a quorum. Any potential interference at the port would mean that the MNF would refuse to enter and the PLO would stay: neither the PLO nor the Lebanese nor Israel nor the United States wanted this. Bashir was risking a loss of support all around, Habib stressed. I sent a message to Israel to urge them to help back Bashir off. Word came back from Jerusalem in the middle of the night that the PLO and the Red Cross had gathered the two Israeli prisoners and the remains of nine others in preparation for turning them over to Israel.

I looked at the *New York Times* with my first cup of coffee at home at 6:00 A.M.. Friday, August 20. Its banner headline read: "ISRAELIS ACCEPT PLAN TO END BEIRUT SIEGE; GOAL IS TO BEGIN P.L.O. PULLOUT TOMORROW."

By 7:30 A.M. I was in the department at breakfast with Senator Scoop Jackson when I got word that Morrie Draper was on the tacsat with a checklist rundown:

- Prisoners and remains are in Red Cross control, ready for turnover.
- Bashir may be neutralized now. We have backed him off.
- The election and PLO departure have been delinked. The Lebanese government is ready to announce that French, Italian, and U.S. forces are all ready to come in as the MNF.
- The *Sol Georgios* will be the first boat to arrive. To build confidence that all is in order, it is vital that the people of Beirut be able to see her lying off the port overnight in advance of an early-morning docking.
- Verification of the PLO personnel departing will be done by regular Lebanese immigration officials; not perfect but workable.

We seemed close at last. At 9:00 A.M. I headed over to the White House to inform President Reagan. After a brief discussion in the Oval Office, I went into the Cabinet Room with the president for a briefing of congressional leaders. The president then telephoned Phil Habib on an open international line and instructed Phil to go ahead and sign the departure agreement for the United States. At 9:30 A.M. President Reagan went to the White House pressroom to announce that the United States had accepted Lebanon's request and would provide troops for the MNF. The president then took questions, and one of his responses held the potential for real trouble. He said that U.S. forces would be withdrawn if they were fired upon. I hoped this would not become an invitation to anyone intent on disrupting the proceedings.

Reports of disputes and demands flooded into the State Department as all parties jockeyed for some new marginal advantage. The Soviet embassy in Washington came at us with a strong demarche, claiming that Israel intended to massacre the Palestinians as they boarded the boats, thus allowing the Soviets to take credit if violence did not occur, or blame the United States if it did. The Syrians said they would cooperate with Saudi Arabia to revitalize the 1947 General Assembly Resolution 181, which proposed a two-state—Arab and Jewish—solution on the West Bank.

Israeli troops took the grain silos at the port and set up a firing post there; we insisted that the Ministry of Defense order them off. The French insisted that their MNF troops occupy the Beirut power station; they wanted to show that after months of failure by others, the French would restore reliable electric power to the city. I cabled Sam Lewis to tell the Israelis to do it first and get the credit for it. The Israelis needed to clean up their image in Lebanon if they were to achieve any positive result from their invasion. "That's right: the hell with the French," Habib said sarcastically, feeling that the French deserved some credit. American forces, I could see, would stand to the side, at Cap's insistence; he wanted the marines encapsulated in the port area. I was upset but unable to change Cap's orders. So the French Foreign Legion and the Italian *Bersaglieri*, with feathered plumes on their helmets, would move out into Beirut to establish the international presence. I had argued in vain for a more active role for the marines, but the president put Cap in control of the disposition of troops, and Cap was determined. I felt that we were sending just the wrong message—a message of weakness—throughout the Middle East.

The IDF dismantled their grain-elevator post but inserted a company of mechanized infantry and some armor inside the main east entry gate of the port. This put them next to positions of the Lebanese army, who feared the press would photograph them in physical proximity to the Israelis, suggesting Israel-Lebanese complicity in the war. Israeli Foreign Ministry officials told us that Sharon had ordered this out of spite for having been overruled by the United States and the Israeli Defense Ministry on the grain-silo post. And the PLO insisted that their rifle-powered grenades (RPGs) were "individual" rather than "crew-served" weapons and therefore did not have to be turned in before departure. Habib ran a mini-negotiation; the Palestinians were allowed to take 12 RPGs per 100 men on board the ships.

I went down to the State Department auditorium to meet the press: "The President today announced that a plan to resolve the crisis in West Beirut has been agreed upon by all the parties, and that in connection with that plan the Government of Lebanon has asked the United States, and the President has agreed, to the deployment of U.S. forces as part of a multinational force to help the Government of Lebanon to implement the plan. He also expressed his admiration and thanks to Phil Habib, and I would like to take this occasion to add my thanks to Phil, a truly great

American." Phil's efforts had been magnificent. His patience and his perseverance, his knowledge and professional performance, had been a marvel.

Arrival and Departure

At dawn on Saturday, August 21, the French forces landed on the docks of Beirut port. PLO fighters were firing their "individual" weapons—AK-47s—into the air as they departed the port in trucks, shouting, "Revolution to victory!" The French ambassador was posturing to political effect and insisted on marching at the head of the column of PLO moving toward the port. The *Sol Georgios* was loading, with a sailing time of 2:00 P.M., Beirut time. These PLO fighters felt, and said so at every turn, that they were fighting the 1948 war against the Jews that their fathers had not fought, leaving the battle then to forces of Arab nations that had lost the war.

At the power plant, Morrie Draper and General Amir Druri, the IDF commander of the Northern Front, were struggling over who controlled the switch, Draper wanting to restore power to the city. Sharon was nearby and ordered the shutoff to continue. He seemed to have no sense of the need in the future for the Lebanese to regain a modicum of confidence in the Israelis. Israeli soldiers were also causing a multitude of minor but irritating problems, generally getting in the way and obstructing efforts to clear the port area and maintain order. Phil Habib insisted on being on the spot in the port; his presence was calming, preventing what could have been violent flare-ups in the tense atmosphere.

The Israelis were especially sensitive to the image projected by the PLO—that it was a regular army with top-class equipment and discipline. The Palestinians had loaded one car ferry with jeeps and Land Rover–type vehicles. The Israelis would not let it sail. Sam Lewis approached Begin about it, and the prime minister exploded: "They are not an army! They are rabble! Let Bourguiba [the president of Tunisia] take them in and buy them Cadillacs." Sharon had made the decision to keep the ship in port, and Begin would not overrule him. Sam Lewis then went to see Sharon, who was mild and polite but "terribly sorry" that he couldn't accommodate us. The departure of PLO vehicles had not been mentioned in the agreement, and that was that. The vehicles would have to be off-loaded, Sharon said. The Israelis were beginning to see that winning a war did not mean they had gained a victory.

We told the Israelis that the ship was going to leave. I talked to Cap Weinberger, and he agreed to bring U.S. Navy destroyers in close, put our helicopters overhead, and escort the car ferry out under our naval protection. It was a moment of potential American-Israeli confrontation. The French were the MNF's unit on the scene, and the Lebanese were in charge of clearing departees. In our view, Israel had no say in this matter. We told Sam Lewis to inform Sharon that we had a legitimate difference with Israel over the interpretation of the agreement on this point. Habib thought it covered vehicles; Sharon did not. We would tell the Beirut harbormaster to clear the ship to sail, and we would impound the vehicles either in Cyprus, Crete, or in Tunis, pending a later solution. We hoped that Israel would not try to block the departure of the vessel, which would be under U.S. Navy escort. The tension was extreme as we waited to see whether the IDF would challenge us on this. There was no way the United States could back down, having gone this far. The Joint Chiefs of Staff instructed our naval assets in the area to prepare to defend the car ferry, and themselves, against Israeli attack. Habib called in to tell me, "If we decide to do this, we must be prepared to go all the way to back up our decision." We were prepared.

At 11:00 A.M. on Sunday, a report came in that Sharon had ordered the vehicles seized and unloaded from the ship. Sam Lewis tried to defuse the situation through approaches in Jerusalem. "Tempers are running high in Washington," Lewis told the Israelis in the Foreign Ministry. "The U.S. is on the verge of decisions that will be very unfortunate for Israel." Lewis was advised by the Israeli Foreign Ministry to speak directly to the prime minister. The Israeli "inner cabinet," their counterpart to our National Security Council, was reviewing the situation.

As Lewis was seeking to get through to Begin, he got a telephone call: Sharon had decided that the U.S. proposal to have the ship sail and the vehicles impounded later was "unacceptable." Lewis went to Begin and argued that the ship must sail on schedule. It was not a matter of the PLO trying to cheat but a decision by Habib that the vehicle shipment was permissible under the agreement. We would ask that the vehicles be impounded in Cyprus, Crete, or Tunisia, pending their proper disposal. So, Lewis told Begin, we would give the order to sail, and we hoped that Israel would not try to block the ship's departure. We did not want Monday morning's headlines to shout about an American-Israeli conflict over this.

Begin agreed, and the ship sailed with Israeli cooperation. This had been a highly dangerous confrontation over a relatively small point, but trivial points at crucial moments become weighted with significance. Nearly a year later, when the dangerous U.S.-Israel confrontation had been long forgotten, we got a cable from Nicosia asking, "What are we supposed to do with that warehouse full of jeeps gathering dust"?

On Monday, August 23, the election for the new president of Lebanon was held at eleven in the morning. A quorum was present to vote, and Bashir Gemayel was elected president. The Israelis were ecstatic. We told them to tone it down and leave Bashir alone. "You could crush him with your embrace," I told Arens.

Habib now wanted the U.S. Marines to enter Beirut on Wednesday, August 25. The Palestinian forces under Syrian command wanted to turn over their positions to the Americans, not to the Lebanese army. They feared that the Lebanese army would not be strong enough to stand up to the Khataeb, the Christian militia; they were afraid that the Khataeb would take over the PLO positions and attack the Palestinian civilians left behind. For this reason, Habib argued for mixing elements of all three MNF forces—French, American, and Italian—with the Lebanese army and having them on post and patrolling throughout the city. The Defense Department wanted none of this: they did not want American forces exposed to danger in a situation of mixed command.

"The U.S. Marines can't just sit on their ass all the time," Habib howled. That afternoon, I put the case strongly to Weinberger that the marines should come in on Wednesday, deploy southwest along the Green Line that divided Christian East Beirut from Muslim West Beirut, and take up positions vacated by the Palestinians. Weinberger flatly refused. Wednesday was okay, but the marines should not even leave the port compound, he said. Such a nondeployment would be humiliating and would convey the dangerous impression that our marines were cowering in a corner and would not resist if attacked, I countered. I went to the president to argue the case, but he did not want to intervene with his secretary of defense on matters of tactical deployment of troops. Habib sent a blistering cable to Weinberger arguing for an active marine role along the Green Line. Cap would not hear of it. He would not listen to me or, I felt by this time, to anyone else. So Habib went to the French, and the Foreign Legion did the job.

Habib had sent Draper to Tel Aviv to talk to Sharon about ways to speed MNF deployment and alleviate the fears of the Palestinians about the safety of those they were leaving behind in Beirut. Draper found that Sharon was in full accord with Weinberger, but for totally different reasons. Sharon would not agree to the U.S. Marines entering early, nor would he agree to the marines or other MNF contingents taking up positions with the Lebanese army along the Green Line. He wanted the marines to stay in the port, the French at the museum crossing point, the Italians at the Galerie Simaan crossing point, and wanted them nowhere else.

Habib was steaming over the Weinberger-Sharon approach, which was slowing down the evacuation, alarming the Palestinians, denigrating the marines, and generally raising the possibility that something could go wrong dramatically. The French and Italian forces were ready and willing to take up positions all along the Green Line and to patrol actively; it was the Pentagon and Sharon who were holding the MNF in check. "The French won't take it," Habib said. "They will do the job alone—and the IDF can go to war with the French." I was desperately frustrated. So was Habib.

"This is the absolute low point in these ten weeks of hell," Habib told me. "The United States will be laughed at; it's an international disgrace."

"Weinberger and Sharon are co-vetoers," I responded. "We can't take a stand against Sharon's veto of our deployment because Weinberger has already vetoed our deployment." So we would have to look to the French and Italian forces to take the lead and hope for the best.

As this was all developing, Yasser Arafat sent word to Habib that he wanted to leave Beirut quickly. He would travel with an entourage of twenty bodyguards and aides. He wanted Habib to arrange a safe departure. Habib did not respond quickly, and word followed that Arafat had approached the Greek government to get him (plus fifty followers) to Greece as soon as possible. The Greek and French ambassadors in Beirut came to see Habib and said they had agreed to Arafat's request and proposed that a French naval or commercial ship transport the group to Piraeus, the port of Athens. Habib said it would take at least a week to arrange a safe departure; Israel would have to agree not to try to kill Arafat as he left the port. Meanwhile, the evacuation ships were arriving on schedule and departing with Palestinians bound for Latakia, Larnaca, Tartus, Port Said, and the ports of Yemen, Tunisia, and Sudan. It appeared that the entire evacuation could be completed by August 31. The U.S. Marines still had not landed, but Sharon informed Habib that Israel would not agree to the marines docking at the port of Beirut on Wednesday, August 25.

Habib reported that his French contacts were "livid" about the American and Israeli refusals to allow the MNF the scope they needed to do their job. At the same time, Habib's Lebanese contacts were "white with fear and anger." Didn't we realize, they asserted, that the curtailment of the MNF mission was a plot by which the Israelis either intended to invade the city themselves or send in the Khataeb to attack the remaining population? And the PLO now was becoming afraid to continue withdrawing in the absence of a protective presence by the MNF. "I have a furor on my hands," Habib told me.

In Beirut, Habib was flooded by messages from intermediaries stating that Arafat wanted to get out fast. Most of his Fatah followers had now left, and he was fearful; his messengers variously said he wanted to go to Saudi Arabia via Cyprus, or to Yemen on the next ship leaving port, or to leave on Friday the twenty-seventh in order to get to the Arab summit in Fez. Habib said it was all too confusing; the earliest we could arrange his departure would be 11:00 A.M. on Monday on a French or Greek ship to Piraeus, as discussed earlier. In the meantime, the French said they were prepared to offer him protective custody or asylum.

At 5:00 A.M. on Wednesday, August 25, the U.S. Marines landed in the port of Beirut. French troops handed over the port area to the marines and moved down into checkpoints between the port and the Hippodrome to the south of the city. The PLO was frantic to get out and now proposed a stepped-up schedule with nearly 4,000 to depart overland to Syria. Because of the need for safe procedures for overland travel, Habib had to tell the PLO that a swifter schedule could not be established right away.

Habib saw Sharon to discuss Arafat's departure, set now for Monday, August 30, by commercial vessel to Piraeus and then by air to Tunis. Sharon agreed. For safety reasons, Habib said, the U.S. Navy would escort the vessel carrying Arafat and provide air cover from the Sixth Fleet as well. The Israelis wanted Arafat out but did not like this approach. "Too much like a triumphal departure," they said.

On Friday, August 27, we organized the first overland convoy from Beirut to Syria. The Italian contingent of the MNF did a professional job of escorting the convoy all the way to the Syrian border. Israeli troops were unrestrained, hooting and making obscene gestures at the departing PLO columns as one IDF squad car dashed in and out, weaving through the line of 350 vehicles carrying 1,351 Palestinians out of Lebanon. As for the departure by sea, Cap Weinberger would helicopter in from a carrier to the port of Beirut to visit our marines there, and the marines would oversee the departure of the last PLO fighters from the piers as Weinberger looked on.

On Monday, August 30, Yasser Arafat finally left Beirut, escorted by five Greek officers and the secretary general of the Ministry of Merchant Marine of Greece. His ship was the *Atlantis*, a Greek merchant vessel escorted by the Greek warship *Croesus*. The Sixth Fleet provided general air cover. The final issue was whether Arafat would be allowed to take his communications jeep with him. He pressed repeatedly, saying, "I would leave my glasses behind but not my jeep." The French ambassador said the French would take responsibility for Arafat's "imponderables" (two jeeps, an armored Mercedes-Benz, and a crate) and ship them to him at some future time and place. When Arafat's departing column arrived at the Beirut docks, the French units of the MNF tried to enter the port area in order to be seen escorting him off, but the U.S. Marines blocked the French, and an ugly, nondescript mob that followed, from entering what was now the marines' area of operations. This tough stance raised the marines' morale; they had been feeling low because of snide criticism of the restricted role of "no responsibilities" imposed on them by the Pentagon.

On Wednesday, September 1, the *Mediterranean Sun* left the port of Beirut with the last group of PLO. The MNF, feeling its primary mission had been achieved with the evacuation of the PLO, began to prepare its own departure. Altogether, some 8,500 PLO personnel were evacuated, a number that exceeded earlier Israeli estimates of the number of PLO fighters in the city. Added to these was the departure of 2,500 of the

Palestine Liberation Army and 3,600 Syrians from the Arab Deterrent Force who went out overland.

The entire PLO evacuation bore out General Dwight D. Eisenhower's saying, "Plans are useless, but planning is essential." Every detail of the movement had been negotiated down to the nub before evacuation day, but what was planned was not what happened. As our embassy in Nicosia cabled to me, "Virtually nothing in the transit of PLO evacuees through Cyprus . . . went according to plan, but everything went well." Indeed, everything went beautifully. Some 15,000 armed Palestinians and Syrians moved out by sea and over the mountains to Syria without a hitch.

Phil Habib returned to Washington a hero. I went out to National Airport to greet him and proudly accompanied him to the White House on September 7, where the president awarded him our country's highest civilian honor, the Medal of Freedom. President Reagan, who returned early from his California vacation for the ceremony, hit a responsive chord in saying, "His successful negotiation of the cease-fire in Lebanon and the resolution of the West Beirut crisis stands out as one of the unique feats of diplomacy in modern times."

Phil expressed his thanks to his deputy, Morrie Draper, and to the president and me for our strong support of his mission. He went on to say that peace in the Middle East was tenuous and that much remained to be accomplished. But, he added, "I'm a chronic optimist, Mr. President, and I'm convinced that it's going to stay on track." I gave a dinner for Phil at my home in Bethesda; all the weary band of foreign service officers who had supported Phil's mission were there. We were riding high. For the first time in a long time, our diplomacy was the toast of the town.

The *Washington Post* editorial the next day, September 8, was headed "One of the Best":

> You can put aside the cracks about those effete cookie pushers, the ones in striped pants, over at the State Department. Yesterday President Reagan awarded the Medal of Freedom to one of their best, Philip Habib, for his "truly heroic work" in conducting the negotiations that halted a war in Lebanon and transformed the prospects for peace in the area as a whole. . . .
>
> This man who is pleased to be called a rug merchant had something better going for him than magic, which is not reliably on tap to ordinary mortals. He had the imagination, toughness and perseverance to see the game through.

"Mr. Habib had as well the confidence of the president. This is to the point," the editorial continued. "Many people see Ronald Reagan as a strong-armer. Much of what he has said over the years conveys that impression. From the start in Lebanon, however, and now more widely in the Middle East, Mr. Reagan has emerged as a leader trying to use American power in its various dimensions to shape a political accommodation. We find no irony in his celebrating an achievement of diplomacy. We see an apt symbol for the larger quest he is engaged in now."

This tough negotiating experience had been a searing one for me. I saw the excruciating complexity of the Middle East. I saw the interplay of power and persuasion. But the Israelis had overplayed their power, and Beirut, a city I had known in better days, lay shattered.

I hoped for far better prospects in the Middle East. An extended war between Israel and Syria had been avoided, the PLO leaders, fighters, and headquarters had been removed from Beirut, and a chance for a more stable Lebanon was on the horizon. I had learned a great deal. President Reagan, I saw, could be decisive, but was slow to boil. Cap Weinberger and the Pentagon were extremely wary and reluctant to use the formidable capabilities lodged in the Department of Defense. The CIA and Bill Casey were as independent as a hog on ice and could be as confident as they were wrong. I also learned, once again, that negotiations can succeed if you work hard and smart. Most of all, I could see how ready everyone was for diplomatic engagement by the United States and for a U.S. diplomatic success.

CHAPTER 6

A "Fresh Start" in the Middle East

The Arab-Israeli peace process, started in 1967 by UN Security Council Resolution 242, reborn in the Camp David Accords, and brought to initial reality in 1979 in the the Egyptian–Israeli Peace Treaty, was a casualty of the Israeli invasion of Lebanon. The wounds would be fatal, I knew, unless we planned for peace while the war still raged. This was the message of Egyptian demands linking their willingness to accept PLO evacuees from Beirut to U.S. progress on resolving Palestinian issues. They urged on us "self-determination" for the Palestinian people, a formulation that we could not accept. This amounted to endorsement of an independent Palestinian state, an outcome unacceptable to the United States, Israel, and, in truth, to most of the Arab world as well. But I well understood that Israel's invasion of Lebanon put a severe strain on Egypt and its relationship with Israel.

Simultaneously with our efforts to get the PLO out of Beirut, I started work on the thorny issues of governance over the West Bank and Gaza. President Reagan, in our early conversations, had encouraged me to develop my ideas as well as a strategy to reinvigorate Middle East diplomacy. My first Saturday seminar on July 17 got the ball rolling. I then collected a small core group to work with me on the details of a new strategy. I knew that total secrecy would be required. Any premature hint that the United States was reconsidering its position on the Palestinian issue would have disruptive effects not only on Phil Habib's work in getting the PLO out of Beirut but also on the ability of the United States to make something positive emerge from this terrible war. I called together a very few of our people, swore them to total secrecy, and told them we needed to hammer out a new approach within a few weeks. What I wanted was a fresh start to the Middle East peace process. I wanted to avoid giving any political bonus—acceptance of Palestinian self-determination or PLO recognition of some sort—to Yasser Arafat in return for his decision to leave Beirut.

But that was exactly what all other parties wished to deliver to him: the French wanted it in return for joining the multinational force, the Arab nations wanted it in return for accepting the PLO evacuees, and the PLO wanted it in return for leaving Beirut and was sending spurious messages everywhere to try to pull this off.

To work on our fresh start I gathered an informed, experienced, talented, and volatile lot with divergent views: Bud McFarlane, Larry Eagleburger, Nick Veliotes, Bob Ames, Paul Wolfowitz, Charlie Hill, Bill Kirby, and Alan Kreczko. We held our meetings in the conference room across the inner corridor from my office. Unchanged in its furnishings since Henry Kissinger's time, the room featured a twenty-foot-long abstract painting with a red line falling from one end to the other. Someone had mockingly titled it "Chart of State Department morale during the time of Henry Kissinger." I learned quickly that morale was always said to be falling in the State Department no matter which transient appointee reigned on the seventh floor. I had the painting removed. My group began meeting regularly there in late July and continued through the end of August 1982. There were no leaks.

"When the last ship sails out of the port of Beirut with the last PLO fighter on board," I said to the group, "we must be ready to move on the larger Palestinian issue, or we will have lost any chance of turning the course of this war into an avenue toward peace. We must avoid the trap of putting the peace process to one side until Lebanon's problems are solved. We need to get quickly to the substance of a new approach."

"Anything we come up with will be unacceptable to Israel," someone interjected.

"Nothing that is worthwhile is acceptable to anyone in the Middle East," I responded, "but everyone looks to us for ideas. It is up to us to set the agenda."

A Peace Initiative Takes Shape

While we were working in secret throughout July and August, arguing and debating among ourselves, a stream of callers came to us with a variety of messages. I heard and learned from them all, but without revealing that we were attempting to produce a new policy. The Saudi ambassador, Prince Bandar, brought me word from King Fahd: Arafat and his colleagues are "prepared to take the steps necessary to stimulate the peace process"; and Fahd's recent statement—citing "the right of all people in the area to live in peace"—was a deliberate effort, Bandar said, to make clear that Saudi Arabia is willing to live in peace with Israel.

The Egyptian foreign minister, Kamal Hassan Ali, and General Zeid Bin Shaker, commander in chief of the Jordanian armed forces, called on me. Both were in a state of great anxiety about Israel's intentions. Hassan Ali emphasized that our preoccupation with Lebanon should not deter us from dealing promptly with the fundamental problem of the Palestinians. He urged that we endorse the idea of Palestinian self-determination and a dialogue with the PLO. Bin Shaker desperately wanted reaffirmation of our military and political support for Jordan. King Hussein, he said, feared that Israel intended to carry out Defense Minister Sharon's threat to create a Palestinian state in Jordan by overthrowing the king. His fears had been heightened by the lengths to which Israel had gone in Lebanon. I told Bin Shaker that he could count on our support for Jordan's territorial integrity and independence.

By July 30, I was able to show President Reagan an initial draft of a new peace inititiative on the Middle East. I went over all aspects with him carefully. I wanted him to provide his own ideas and reactions directly to me, to make this initiative his own, and to be a part of, and completely comfortable with, what I was doing. I sensed that earlier in the administration, under Haig, President Reagan was kept out of direct involvement far too much. I wanted him in all the way. I emphasized to the president the importance of secrecy in our deliberations. In order to ensure security, knowing full well how pieces of paper moved around in the White House, I suggested to the president that I take my draft back from him after our meeting. He laughed, but he agreed with me and handed back the draft. The question that weighed most on his mind was Israeli security. How could it be guaranteed? At the same time, he was getting increasingly fed up with the Israeli shelling of Beirut. That afternoon, NSC adviser Bill Clark called: "The president's friendship for Israel is slipping. Enough is enough." I knew that President Reagan's friendship ran deep, as did mine. But we were both disturbed by the Israelis' disproportionate military actions, the destruction of Beirut, and the resulting casualties among the Lebanese.

On the first of August, when Israeli Foreign Minister Yitzhak Shamir came to Washington, he got a frosty reception from President Reagan and from everyone else. On August 2, I had a private talk with Shamir over lunch. The lesson of the Lebanon conflict was that the lack of a solution to the issue of Palestinian rights, or even a visible and credible search for one, was a formula for unrest and continued violence. "There has to be a process in which the Palestinians have real participation," I told him. "They can't be represented by someone they have no control over. Their representatives must be legitimate so that those represented can see some validity in the negotiations. We should work within the Camp David Accords for a definitive and creative solution for the West Bank and Gaza."

"Israel is ready to resume the autonomy negotiations at any time," Shamir responded, "and we hope to convince Jordan to join. Israel wants Palestinian Arab representatives among the negotiating parties as part of a Jordanian or Egyptian delegation." After I listened to Shamir describe all of the political advantages that the Palestinians would gain in his version of autonomy talks, I said to him sardonically that I was starting to think he might even go so far as to use the word "self-determination."

I assembled my core group on August 7, a Saturday, in the early evening. One way to keep things secret in Washington is to work on a weekend, and we did plenty of that. At this session we focused on the problem of "self-determination." The phrase expressed an American ideal, enunciated to the world to resounding applause by President Woodrow Wilson. How could the United States fail to support it for the Palestinians? We could and did, of course, point to the fact that the United States had fought a civil war against the aspiration of the Confederate States of America for self-determination. But when it came to the Palestinians, "self-determination" had acquired too many barnacles: it had become a "code" that no longer meant simply self-determination but signified agreement in advance that there would be a Palestinian state. Negotiations for Palestinian self-rule would never begin if the outcome had to be agreed upon in advance. Somehow we had to give hope to the Palestinians that a diplomatic process could produce as its outcome a just solution, but that conclusion would have to be negotiated over time, not dictated at the start. This was one of the thorny problems that we scratched away during our late Saturday session.

Again and again my group engaged in heated argument, under the pressure of the increasingly imminent deadline—the PLO departure date—established by me. A set of generally held views emerged.

First, each party, Arab or Israeli, should be able to enter the negotiations with any position it wanted to take. Israel, for example, could assert the view that the occupied territories should be part of Israel; the Palestinians could assert that their aim was to achieve an independent state. But neither could demand recognition of such aims as a precondition to begin negotiations.

Second, there must be a Jordanian role, and the PLO must give Jordan, with Palestinians in its delegation, a green light to negotiate on behalf of the Palestinians. This would require a reversal, or deft avoidance, of the 1974 Rabat Declaration by which the Arabs put such a role solely in the hands of Arafat's PLO. Israel would never negotiate with the PLO, so a way around this was needed.

And third, I could see that the achievements of Mideast diplomacy since 1967 had been swept from the board by the Israeli invasion of Lebanon. I had to find a way to put them back and add some new elements that would get the parties moving again. I felt that the moment had come for the United States to put forth our own view of what the outcome of the peace process should look like—even though we insisted that no party would be allowed to require its final position to be a prerequisite for sitting down at the negotiating table. An American position could pull the two sides in toward a sensible center position and away from extremes. This would be a big—indeed, explosive—step to take. Up to this point, the United States had carefully refrained from suggesting an outcome, fearing such an action would compromise our role as mediator. "If we are going to take a stand," I said to the group, "we have to be ready to take a lot of flak. I have to go to the president to make sure he stands there and that he will stay there. And to win the inevitable confrontation with the Begin government, we have to prove that we are consistent with the Camp David Accords."

Finally, in view of the location, small size, and barren character of the land involved, I felt that the West Bank and Gaza could not realistically compose an independent Palestinian nation-state. That territory could not perform as a workable economic entity, and its people would strain constantly against the tight confines of its borders. The Palestinian people would find it more promising to find their national rights within a broader and more workable setting through association with Jordan. Furthermore, for economic reasons, if no other, they would need a link with Israel as well. The key was Jordan's King Hussein, and the critical question was whether he would be bold enough to buy into this "Jordanian option" and stand up to it when the radical and terrorist elements in the PLO targeted him for doing so.

The President Engages

I met with President Reagan on Friday, August 13, at 10:00 A.M. I was concerned that he was almost too enthusiastic about the initiative, and I wanted to be sure he fully appreciated the difficulties involved. He had met with Shimon Peres, leader of Israel's Labor party, the previous day and heard him talk positively about possibilities on the West Bank and about the UN Resolution 242 formula of "territory for peace."[1] I did not want the president to be misled into thinking more optimistically than was warranted. Although Peres and many others in the Labor party were pre-

1. The key sections of Resolution 242, adopted on November 22, 1967, by the UN Security Council, are as follows:
   "(i) Withdrawal of Israeli armed forces from territories occupied in the recent conflict [**territory**];
   "(ii) Termination of all claims or states of belligerency and respect for and acknowledgment of the sovereignty, territorial integrity and political independence of every State in the area and their right to live in peace within secure and recognized boundaries free from threats or acts of force [for **peace**]."
The omission of the word "the" before territories has left ample room for argument about the extent of withdrawal envisaged in the resolution, but Peres's endorsement of the 242 formula was a declaration by him of the Labor party's willingness to accept a compromise that involved some territorial concessions.

pared to relinquish large parts of the West Bank in the course of a negotiation with neighboring Arab states, principally Jordan, Prime Minister Begin and the Likud party, now in power, took a much harder line. "We are on a head-on collision course with the Israeli leadership," I told the president, "so we must be absolutely sure about our position and we must demonstrate that we are not threatening Israel's security."

For the first time, in this meeting, I felt that the president was fully engaging himself in this major foreign policy question. To put this proposal across, President Reagan would have to achieve an easy mastery of the complicated details. Beyond this, the overall success of the administration, I thought, would be greatly enhanced if the president displayed to the world the broad vision, the close-in touch, and the flair for timing that was expected of American diplomatic leadership. To put it bluntly, if Ronald Reagan looked good here, it would bring international opinion, and cooperation, into play for us on our full agenda.

The president invited me to Camp David for lunch on Saturday, August 14, to continue our talk. He now seemed comfortable with what we were proposing and fully aware of likely problems with the Israelis. A new strategy paper was now in order, I could see. I should provide the president with a better understanding of the interrelated dynamics of Lebanon and the wider peace process. Whatever the outcome of these briefings, I was determined that we would not lift a finger until the president said go. Ed Meese kept emphasizing that it must be the president's program and that President Reagan had to be involved. "Why do you think I am pushing for all these meetings?" I replied.

When I left for Camp David, I took with me Nick Veliotes, Bob Ames, Paul Wolfowitz, and Dick Fairbanks. I asked Veliotes and Ames to "role play" the way we would present our plan to Prime Minister Begin, to King Hussein, to President Mubarak, and the way they might react. The actors were effective. The play was tense and presumed no sure outcome. The president engaged and became part of the process. When it was over, he gave me the go-ahead I needed. He agreed that when the time came to make a statement on Lebanon, he would use the occasion to underscore the importance of moving ahead on the broader issues of the Arab-Israeli conflict. Ed Meese and Mike Deaver, who watched all this unfold, said they had never seen anything like the effort I had mounted to get the president involved in the full depth of the issues. "The president was ready for this a year ago, but Al Haig kept the Middle East away from him," Meese told me.

On August 17, with the president's endorsement, I met in a closed session with the Senate Foreign Relations Committee to consult on every key question we were addressing in the upcoming initiative. "The senators," I reported to the president, "did virtually all of the talking." Their major themes were: the West Bank–Palestinian question should be addressed quickly, regardless of the state of play in Lebanon; Jordanian involvement was essential to effective negotiation; the Camp David process provided a means of continuity that had Israeli acceptance; Israeli settlement activity in the occupied territories had been the major cause of Arab cynicism, and a settlement freeze there would do the most to reinvigorate the peace process. All these points were consistent with my own thinking. On August 18, I went through the same process at a breakfast meeting with the House Foreign Affairs Committee, where similar points were made to me.

Preliminary Probes:
Arab and Israeli Reactions

I felt that at this moment we were now launched on our new initiative. The plan remained secret, but the press was now aware that meetings on the peace process had taken place, and nervous phone calls of inquiry started coming in. I had Ambassador Sam Lewis briefed on the initiative and told him that the president had approved it. Lewis called it "a sure disaster," made worse by our secrecy. "Israel will learn of it and screw it up," Lewis predicted. I told Nick Veliotes to brief Vice President Bush before I sent Nick flying off to talk secretly with King Hussein. Nearly everyone who was brought into the effort worried that we were moving too fast; they feared that the initiative would leak and the negative reaction to it—especially from the Israelis—would cut across the Beirut evacuation plan and stop it in its tracks. I did not agree at all. We could not make the peace initiative hostage to the crisis in Lebanon or put planning on hold until the PLO had departed. Both the peace initiative and the PLO departure plan, I felt, had to go forward simultaneously, and as quickly as possible.

Nick Veliotes left Thursday night, August 19, for London. There King Hussein's aircraft would pick him up and take him to Amman for two days of undisclosed talks. I told Nick to be clear, concise, and positive. I asked Larry Eagleburger to call Ambassador Arens to start sounding out Israel on the need to revitalize the peace process. Arens resisted; Lebanon should be stabilized first, he told Eagleburger, and turned into a pro-Western nation. There should be a peace treaty signed between Lebanon and Israel. Then the United States and Israel might cooperate on larger peace issues. If we were to go ahead now, Arens said—and he claimed that he saw signs that we were preparing to do so—our proposal "could crash on takeoff." "Look," said Arens, "we have wiped the PLO from the scene. Don't you Americans now pick the PLO up, dust it off, and give it artificial respiration."

The analysis I got from Bob Ames of the CIA was different: Arafat had solidified his leadership position as a result of the war with the Israelis.

He would now take "a grand tour" of Arab capitals; his removal from Beirut would give him new flexibility, as he would no longer be directly under Syria's thumb. Records and organizational structure were already in place in Tunis, Ames said, as the site of the new PLO headquarters. "The PLO has plenty of life in it." He did not agree with the Israeli view that they had been finished off: Palestinian "moderates" now had a chance to be heard. Contrary to the official Israeli line, Israeli intelligence analysts, Ames said, agreed with ours that Arafat had gained in strength and control. Whether the PLO was strong or not, I did not regard the PLO as reliable or as moderate—that was why our initiative sought to bring King Hussein and Jordan back into the center of the scene.

In the afternoon on August 24, I assembled in my conference room Irving Shapiro, Bud McFarlane, Dick Murphy (in from Saudi Arabia), Roy Atherton (in from Egypt), Charlie Hill, Dick Fairbanks, Larry Eagleburger, Paul Wolfowitz, and Bob Ames. I had gathered them to hear Nick Veliotes report to me on his secret mission to King Hussein.

Veliotes said he had met with King Hussein on the previous Saturday night. The king was interested. His main concern was "Did we mean it? Would we see it through?" On Sunday they met again for two hours. Again, the king talked with emotion about the importance of the staying power of President Reagan. He said he had seen too many similar initiatives "collapse for want of American political will." King Hussein wanted to be sure we would stick with the three key elements: that the United States would oppose a Palestinian state, oppose Israeli sovereignty over the territories of the West Bank and Gaza, and favor a link between the Palestinian authority in those territories and the kingdom of Jordan. "The king," Veliotes concluded, "is a potential player; we may be able to bring another Arab leader to the negotiating table." King Hussein said he would write a letter to President Reagan with questions about the major aspects of our proposal. Hussein assured Veliotes he would not reveal our initiative to any other Arabs until we agreed to make it public.

I would await King Hussein's formal response to the proposal. If the king's reply was positive, I would move quickly and on all fronts at once. Within twenty-four hours, a message from King Hussein arrived by close-hold cable. Despite the understanding of secrecy, the message clearly was drafted so that if it did leak, its contents would not risk harm to the king, politically or otherwise. The king called on the United States to be resolute; he said we had to get wide Arab support, go far toward meeting PLO needs, and make clear that this initiative was not linked to Camp David. Between the lines, King Hussein was telling me that the United States had to negotiate with the PLO, walk away from the Camp David Accords, and see to it that Israel withdrew from the West Bank and Gaza. "It's a very upbeat letter," Nick Veliotes said. "The king is very interested; it's just that he has to cover his ass."

"Hussein is always this way in first meetings," Bob Ames said. "He'll come around."

I said that the letter amounted to one word: "No." I was not impressed. The king was telling us to stay the course but was not going to get on course himself. His letter certainly was not supportive enough for me to take to the president and tell him that the king was ready to work with us. I also felt that I was seeing some of the professional optimism, even wishful thinking, for which the Arabists in the government were known.

At just that time, word came in that the Israeli newspaper *Ma'ariv* was carrying a story headlined "Shultz Advisor: 'Begin Intransigent and Uncompromising.' " It was referring to Irving Shapiro. Irving had given an interview to an American weekly, the *Jewish Exponent*, saying Prime Minister Begin "has a penchant for being on the extremes" and telling the Israelis they'd better declare themselves ready for serious dealing on the peace process. The Baltimore *Jewish Times* had repeated the story under the headline "No Alternative to Palestinian State." Irving had thereby dealt himself out of the pack as a possible envoy to Begin and the Israelis. Another setback followed. In one of those paradoxes so agonizingly familiar in the Middle East, Israeli Foreign Minister Yitzhak Shamir, in an article in the *Washington Post* on August 26, called for Jordan to join the peace process. This call from Israel would make our own effort to get King Hussein to step forward all the more difficult. I prepared a hard-line letter for President Reagan to send to King Hussein, the essence of which was, *we* have stood up to be counted; now so should *you*.

Israel was now getting wind of our peace plan. We owed it to the Israelis to give them the full thrust of our thinking. Prime Minister Begin had taken the first week of September to vacation in Nahariya, a coastal resort in northern Israel. I told Sam Lewis to prepare himself to see Begin privately there. I knew Lewis would meet with trouble. Ariel Sharon had sent a message to Bill Casey at the CIA. The gist was: if the United States has a peace plan that the Israelis don't like, Israel will annex the West Bank! Our ambassador to Jordan, Dick Viets, cabled that King Hussein had decided to give the full green light to our proposal. Hussein had told the Saudis, the Egyptians, and the PLO that the United States planned a major shift in policy and that he had to have their support in cooperating with us on it. Hussein also urged the Arab world to support our approach at the soon-to-be-convened Fez summit.

This seemed to be good news, but it also showed that Hussein was laying the groundwork to back out if he did not get an Arab consensus behind him. And consensus was clearly an impossible requirement. "This is another way for King Hussein to tell us, 'I am not ready to take these risks, but I am ready for you to take them,' " I said. I felt that my Arabist advisers did not appreciate my reaction and considered me lacking in the sophistication necessary to plumb the Arab mind. Foreign service officers, out of long years of trying to read King Hussein's tea leaves, felt that the king was being forthcoming. I was dubious.

Our timetable was being accelerated by the pace of events and the spread of knowledge about the forthcoming initiative. President Reagan, I felt, needed to give the speech announcing our initiative within the next few days. I called Phil Habib on the tacsat to inform him that our peace plan was about to be unveiled. It bore, I told him, the "footprints" of Habib himself, who had discussed many of the ideas with me at Stanford months ago, while I was still a private citizen. I asked him to inform Bashir Gemayel about it before Bashir left for the Fez Arab summit.

On Monday, August 30, we were ready to go. I told Dick Murphy to depart immediately with Prince Bandar to brief King Fahd in Jiddah. I called Bandar in to provide him with my own sense of the importance and urgency of our report. I told Roy Atherton to leave for Cairo that afternoon and to see President Mubarak as soon as possible.

I called President Reagan. "The shoes will start to drop on Tuesday," I told him. We agreed that he should make a television speech announcing the peace initiative soon, and I promised him a draft text by that evening. I assured the president that his plan would be acclaimed in most quarters, including parts of Israel, but I wanted to forewarn him that there would be a hot, harsh reaction from the Israeli government. The president told me that the tone of the speech should not anticipate Israeli combativeness.

The following day, the first shoe dropped: on August 31, Dick Murphy in Saudi Arabia reported in, giving us King Fahd's reactions. Fahd did not understand some of the subtleties of our position. He seemed disappointed that we didn't recognize the PLO. King Hussein was about to arrive in Saudi Arabia, and Murphy hoped that Hussein would bring Fahd around to at least lukewarm support before the Arab League summit in Fez the following weekend.

That same afternoon, Sam Lewis met Menachem Begin at his vacation spot in Nahariya. He reported in: Begin reacted to the initiative with shock and outrage, conveyed in a calm, steely manner. The war had worn him down. He had been looking forward to his holiday. Now, he said, we were confronting him with a significant departure from the Camp David Accords. He would have to call an emergency session of his cabinet, bringing them up from Jerusalem to Nahariya. He requested that the president not announce the initiative until after the Israeli cabinet had met and we received their response. Begin, Sam Lewis reported back, was feeling "very put upon" by both the substance and procedure of what we were doing. As Lewis made his departure, Begin called after him in an angry and determined voice, "Don't worry, we know how to take care of ourselves, and we will."

I knew that Prime Minister Begin would be disturbed about our prior consultations with King Hussein, as Lewis also predicted, but I felt that the Israelis would try to block the initiative regardless of when they had been informed. The key to progress now would be the emergence of a credible Arab negotiating partner. The stakes were too high to stall. We had to get a peace process under way again. The United States had to put forth a new agenda. "Let people argue," I said, "but they will be arguing over our agenda, and that will be constructive."

I recognized that former President Jimmy Carter's comments on President Reagan's initiative would be significant. Begin would claim that the plan transgressed the Camp David framework. I sent a man Carter knew and trusted, Deputy Secretary of State Walt Stoessel, to Plains, Georgia, to brief Carter. I then called all of the former secretaries of state to brief them and heard positive responses, especially on the importance of re-establishing a peace process. Ambassador Atherton later reported in that President Mubarak's reactions were "generally positive."

Prospects were clouded. The tortuous experience of the siege of Beirut over the past month showed how remote the Middle Eastern reality was from the ideal of a negotiated peace. The Beirut evacuation plan had been entirely an American idea, drafted and negotiated by us. Arafat had not initiated anything. King Hussein saw negotiations as a trap. To survive, he had to appear willing while simultaneously planning his escape. The Saudis would promise to use their influence, but never seemed able actually to do so. The Israelis had mastered every detail of war and diplomacy but in each case carried their tactics to a point where they damaged their own self-interest. The Egyptian approach seemed to offer promise, but the Israeli invasion of Lebanon had deeply embarrassed the Egyptians; to the Arab world it seemed that the Egyptian–Israeli Peace Treaty had given Israel security on its southern front, only to free it to go into battle in the north. Some people in the region wanted peace with their neighbors; some did not. But whether for or against, active or passive, all seemed endlessly inventive about blocking progress toward peace. So be it. But leadership from the United States might be able to break through the endless intransigence. And the absence of any credible peace process would mean regression from what had been achieved, most especially between Egypt and Israel.

Throughout the next day, my team and I worked with the president and his speechwriters to put the finishing touches on the Middle East address he would deliver that evening. The president continued to worry about Israeli security, and I sent him some language he could use to highlight his commitment. In Israel the propaganda counterattack of the Begin government was well under way. The media barrage had started only hours after Sam Lewis had seen Prime Minister Begin. The question of acceding to Begin's request that we delay until the Israeli cabinet had met had been rendered moot by these Israeli leaks to the press. Nonetheless, the Israeli embassy sent us an official warning: "If the U.S. goes public on peace process issues with which Israel disagrees, it throws into question the entire role of the U.S. as an honest broker."

Banner headlines in Jerusalem papers made clear that our peace initiative was being received very badly. It was a "complete deviation" from Camp David; it would drive Israel back to the 1967 borders; it was a U.S. attempt to impose a solution rather than promote negotiations, and so on. There was no positive commentary. An American Jewish leader told us that Begin had been telephoning his American supporters to provide his view of the situation. Begin said what was happening was like the ancient Jewish story of Haman, who sought to destroy the Jews in Persia. The United States was Haman, but Begin would be like Queen Esther, who tricked Haman into giving the Jews the victory. The story was celebrated every year at the holiday of Purim, when Haman's fate was symbolized by eating pastry called *hamantaschen*, or Haman's ears. So Begin was after my ears, it seemed. Begin wasn't my only problem. Over at the White House, Mike Deaver was arguing strenuously that our initiative was unacceptable. It was, Deaver worried, a "sellout" of Camp David.

Just prior to the president's speech, I held a large press briefing in the Loy Henderson Auditorium at the State Department. The atmosphere was tense with anticipation. This was my first major substantive experience with the press since confirmation. They had copies of the president's speech, embargoed until after delivery. My briefing was piped live to the press corps accompanying the president in California, all this in an effort to present a coherent and consistent picture of the president's peace plan.

The President Speaks

President Reagan's nationally televised address on the evening of September 1, 1982, was seen and heard all over the world. "Today has been a day that should make us proud," the president began. "It marked the end of the successful evacuation of PLO from Beirut, Lebanon." The marines had accomplished their mission and would be out in two weeks. He then went on to describe how the war in Lebanon had demolished not only much of the city but the peace process as well. It also had demonstrated that "the military losses of the PLO have not diminished the yearning of the Palestinian people for a just solution of their claims" and "while Israel's military successes in Lebanon have demonstrated that its armed forces are second to none in the region, they alone cannot bring just and lasting peace to Israel and her neighbors. The question now is how to reconcile Israel's legitimate security concerns with the legitimate rights of the Palestinians. And that answer can only come at the negotiating table."

The president called for a "fresh start." For the first time, an American president set forth U.S. positions on key issues, thereby going beyond procedures and mediation activity, as a way to generate support for, and attention to, the peace process in the Middle East.

First, as outlined in the Camp David Accords, he endorsed the idea of a five-year period during which the Palestinian inhabitants of the West Bank and Gaza would have "full autonomy over their own affairs." A self-governing Palestinian authority would be constituted through free elections. If successful, the result would be "to prove to the Palestinians that they can run their own affairs and that such Palestinian autonomy poses no threat to Israel's security."

Second, he called for "the immediate adoption of a settlement freeze by Israel" in the occupied territories during the transition period to "create the confidence needed for wider participation in these talks." He assured the Israelis and informed the Arabs, however, of the U.S. view that Jews must have the right to live on the West Bank, historically Judaea and Samaria.

Third, he was clear and explicit about two well-known proposals: "The United States will not support the establishment of an independent Palestinian state in the West Bank and Gaza, and we will not support annexation or permanent control by Israel. There is, however, another way to peace" he continued. "The final status of these lands must, of course, be reached through the give and take of negotiations. But it is the firm view of the United States that self-government by the Palestinians of the West Bank and Gaza in association with Jordan offers the best chance for a durable, just, and lasting peace." His approach was based, he said, on the idea of an exchange of territory for peace set forth in UN Resolution 242. And when the time came to apply this formula to the border between Israel and Jordan, "our view on the extent to which Israel should be asked to give up territory will be heavily affected by the extent of true peace and normalization and the security arrangements offered in return."

He reaffirmed the long-standing U.S. position that Jerusalem must remain undivided but that its final status should be decided through negotiation.

He said that in the negotiations to come, "The United States will . . . oppose any proposal from any party and at any point in the negotiating process that threatens the security of Israel. America's commitment to the security of Israel is ironclad, and, I might add, so is mine. . . . It has often been said—and, regrettably, too often been true—that the story of the search for peace and justice in the Middle East is a tragedy of opportunities missed. . . . This time we must not let it slip from our grasp."

His speech was a dramatic development, particularly since the timing coincided with the completion of the PLO departure from Beirut. Why did I encourage the president to take this major American step on the West Bank and Gaza problem when so many other problems remained unresolved in Lebanon? There was no other way, I felt: America was central to any hope of progress in either case. We could not step away or stand back from either without abandoning our leadership role and succumbing to those who always are saying, "This is not in *our* interest," or "This is not the time." If the peace process was made hostage to a restored stability in Lebanon, who could say when that day would come? And, with no identifiable peace process in sight, the great achievement of peace between Israel and Egypt would be increasingly jeopardized.

The World Reacts

The *Washington Post* on September 2 headlined "U.S. Urges Palestinian Self-Rule Tied to Jordan." The *New York Times* banner read "REAGAN URGES LINK TO JORDAN AND SELF-RULE BY PALESTINIANS; ISRAEL REACTS ANGRILY TO PLAN." Reactions to the peace plan were very supportive in Congress, in the press, among our allies, and in the Arab world, where the Saudis, Egyptians, Moroccans, and PLO all were reported to be positive and upbeat. An Arab reporter called in: "This is the hottest thing in seventeen years. The Arabs should grab it." At the White House, Bud McFarlane said that the mood had gone from "traumatized" to "euphoric" and everyone was taking credit for it, even Deaver. In only a matter of hours it was evident that there was a new stature to our foreign policy. The *London Times* on September 3 called the president's speech "the best and most hopeful foreign policy move to come out of his Administration." Jimmy Carter praised the initiative and said it was fully consistent with Camp David. Senators Boschwitz and Cranston, two of Israel's staunchest friends, made supportive comments.

But the Israeli government was going all out to strangle the infant initiative in its cradle. The cabinet communiqué indicated that, if the Arab side accepted our plan, Israel would not participate. And a blistering "Dear Ron" letter came in from Prime Minister Begin: "A friend does not weaken his friend; an ally does not put his ally in jeopardy. This would be the inevitable consequence were the 'positions' transmitted to me on August 31, 1982, to become reality. I believe they won't."

On September 2, I had met with a group of Arab-Americans. They were disappointed that we seemed to rule out an independent Palestinian state. I said that it wouldn't work, that there was no support for it in America and implacable hostility to it throughout Israel, and that there were few responsible Arab leaders, rhetoric notwithstanding, who truly wanted to see an independent state.

I then went to a meeting with leaders of the American Jewish community.

They were disappointed, they said, that they had not been more fully consulted in advance. But they were clearly embarrassed by the vehemence of Begin's rejection. They worried about a settlement freeze but could not really oppose the principles the president had outlined.

Afterward, Nick Veliotes came into my office with a telephone report from Beirut that Bashir Gemayel had just returned from an extraordinary session in Jerusalem. Gemayel reported that Begin had demanded that he come to Begin's office immediately. A helicopter had been sent for this purpose. Gemayel found Begin in a rage. In the presence of Ariel Sharon, Begin demanded that Gemayel sign a peace treaty with Israel immediately, "if not on the twenty-third [the scheduled date for Gemayel's inauguration as president of Lebanon], then the twenty-fourth." Begin berated Gemayel for his ingratitude and implied threats about continued Israeli support. Gemayel was stunned by this outburst and was hardly able to respond. I, too, was stunned to hear this story and the portrait of Begin on the rampage. What he wants, Gemayel said, "is a puppet state."

After Nick had left, I said to Ray Seitz, my executive assistant, "What we have announced as a Middle East initiative must be shattering for Begin and the group around him. In recent days they must have felt at the height of their power. They have proven again the invincibility of their military machine. They have secured their southern border in a peace treaty with Egypt. They believe they have just devastated their bitter enemy, the PLO, and most of southern Lebanon is their playground. They think they have the power and influence to establish whatever kind of government they want in Beirut. They are wrong about that, but they see the road open to a unilateral implementation of restricted autonomy in the West Bank. Jordan is cowering. All of this has brought Israel, in their eyes, to a supreme position. As they see it, we have suddenly pulled the rug out from under them."

On September 8, B'nai B'rith called the Reagan peace plan "worthy of consideration." I was encouraged. In New York on September 12, I spoke at a friendly but uneasy dinner held by the United Jewish Appeal (UJA). The next morning over breakfast I found former Secretary of State Cyrus Vance supportive. I went on to meet with the editorial board of the *New York Times*, where the questions were probing and not at all hostile.

On September 14, Al Haig criticized some elements of the president's initiative in a speech to the UJA, and called the proposal for a freeze on West Bank settlements "a serious mistake." He was lambasted in an editorial headed "Two Mideast Bombs and a Flare" in the *New York Times* on September 16: "Simultaneously on Tuesday, two ugly bombshells and a bright diplomatic flare lit the Middle East sky. The bomb throwers—an unknown terrorist in Beirut and a former Secretary of State in New York— certainly damaged the promise in King Hussein's message from Jordan [praise for the American proposals]. Sabotage is always easy in a powderkeg." The *Times* went on: "The true enemy remains despair. President Reagan's bold bid for a West Bank deal is having the desired effects. His formidable critics in many places can promise only more violence. The President's only option is to persist. . . . He [General Haig] is entitled to his view of events and to his own peace plan—if he has one. But as someone who used to lecture others on their obligations to the Commander in Chief, the general must know that his public carping risks undermining the President's most considered diplomatic venture at a tense and dangerous time."

Meanwhile, the Arab world was doing its own job of making the peace process more difficult. The Arab summit meeting at Fez endorsed an all-Arab proposal calling for a Palestinian state. A message came in from King Hussein in which he stressed to us his unhappiness with the outcome in Fez and suggested that he might make a move on his own, perhaps as Egypt's president Anwar Sadat had once done in going to Jerusalem. I was skeptical. Prince Bandar, on the other hand, pointed to a sentence in the Fez declaration dealing with the rights of states in the area to live in peace and said it amounted to recognition of Israel's right to exist, a gigantic step for the Arabs.

Whatever the reactions, President Reagan's new initiative now commanded the high ground and had once again turned attention to the larger underlying problems in the Middle East. Our work was cut out for us, but at least we could see a structure and a set of ideas with which to work. With the PLO now out of Beirut and the president's "fresh start" inititative on the table, we could turn from damage control to positive efforts, seeking to draw the players themselves in the region toward our views, seeking with King Hussein a mandate for negotiations and Palestinians for his delegation.

If we actually could produce a genuine Arab partner to negotiate directly with Israel, I was convinced the Israelis would be drawn into those negotiations by the sheer force of Israeli public opinion, whether they liked the U.S. positions or not. In the Middle East, the odds are always against you, the obstacles to progress always formidable. But by having an agenda out there, we at least had everyone's attention. Without a credible process under way, a vacuum exists that inevitably draws more violence and extremism. With our new agenda and a process, we had filled the void and provided a reason for hope that peace, while not probable, was at least possible.

"Everything is going according to plan: the Israelis are very negative, the Arabs are very fuzzy, and we have a good, strong defensible position," Ray Seitz remarked to me.

"Better than that," I said, "for the first time in this administration, we have a Middle East policy."

CHAPTER 7

Lebanon After the PLO Exit:
Chaos Takes Another Form

With the departure by September 1, 1982, of the last PLO fighters from Beirut, Prime Minister Menachem Begin stepped up the pressure for the political gains Israel sought in Lebanon. Israeli Ambassador Moshe Arens came to see me on September 14: a peace treaty between Israel and Lebanon, he said, is "now or never."

"The United States unequivocally favors an Israel-Lebanon peace treaty," I told him. "But a peace treaty has to be signed between sovereign governments, and Bashir Gemayel's presidency is not yet sufficiently established to stand the test of legitimacy such a treaty would require."

Even as I was talking to Arens, the first reports were coming into State's operations center that an enormous bomb had gone off in Gemayel's Beirut headquarters. Bashir Gemayel was dead. My first concern was that Lebanon, already ravaged by war, not slide into total chaos. The State Department issued a strong statement urging adherence to the constitutional process there, and we sent messages to Israel, Syria, Saudi Arabia, France, Italy, and the Vatican urging their support for a proper constitutional succession. I instructed Morrie Draper, who was filling in for Phil Habib while Phil was home in California, to sound out Elias Sarkis to see whether he would remain as president for the time being. We urged the Israelis once again not to send troops into Beirut to try to control this new situation. Prime Minister Begin told Draper that Israeli forces had been ordered to make some minor positional adjustments—"limited and precautionary"— and that this was in the interest of security in the city. Specifically, the Israelis said they wanted to prevent the Phalange militia from raiding the Palestinian refugee camps south of the city to avenge Bashir Gemayel's death. No one knew who had placed the bomb that killed him. Lebanese Christians blamed the Palestinians; Palestinians blamed Israel; others claimed it was an inside job.

At midday, Washington time, Ariel Sharon telephoned U.S. officials to say that the American embassy in Beirut was "under fire" from PLO terrorists who had surrounded our chancery building; the Israel Defense Forces (IDF) would rescue our people in Beirut if requested to do so. By direct contact we knew that our embassy was, in fact, not under fire and was ringed protectively by a local Lebanese militia. When we sent word back to Sharon saying, "No thanks," to his offer, he replied that Israeli forces had "occupied all key points in Beirut and by so doing have prevented civil war." We contacted the Israeli Foreign Ministry. People there seemed confused, agonizing over a situation that was both diplomatically and militarily explosive and which they seemed to have no means of controlling or even tracking effectively. The Israelis, contrary to their repeated assurances to us, had indeed sent their troops into the heart of Beirut, where they now occupied key places, Ras (Point) Beirut, the Corniche, and the hotel area. On the tacsat Morrie Draper gave us his view: "Begin has been manipulated again by Sharon."

From Saudi Arabia, Ambassador Dick Murphy reported that Lebanese Muslim leaders had contacted King Fahd to discuss what to do to restore order in the aftermath of Bashir's assassination. The Saudis put the question to Murphy: would the U.S. support Amin Gemayel, Bashir's brother, as president of Lebanon? Our answer, relayed by Murphy, was that it was not for us to choose a successor, but we thought Amin Gemayel would be a good choice.

I called Arens back in my office on the next afternoon. "When the prime minister of Israel tells us something, we take it as fact," I told Arens. "When others complain to us, we take the prime minister's word as gospel and pass it on. We rely on it and tell others that they may rely on it. That credibility has now been undermined, repeatedly. People are no longer accepting Israel's word, and that's bad." We wanted to see Israeli troops located where Prime Minister Begin said they would be located. Arens said that there was no intention to mislead us and that, in fact, Begin had not done so; these were only precautionary moves, wise steps to prevent chaos.

"Israel's military occupation of an Arab capital will have a lasting emotional and symbolic impact," I said. "Occupation also carries with it responsibility for whatever might take place. You are making a big mistake. We worked hard to arrange the evacuation of the PLO from Beirut, so Israel has no reason to enter the city. This is bad business. The longer Israel stays in the city, the more vocal we will be," I told him. The United Nations was seething with anti-Israeli sentiment. "From your own interests, look at what is happening to you. You're getting clobbered. Israeli forces should be pulled out of the city." I said I looked for a fast Israeli response to my "words of counsel."

Italian Foreign Minister Emilio Colombo called me on September 16 with the report on his meeting with Yasser Arafat. The PLO leader accused the United States, France, and Italy of withdrawing the multinational force (MNF) prematurely. Arafat was deeply concerned about the Palestinians left behind in the Beirut refugee camps, fearing they would be slaughtered. He stressed that Phil Habib had given assurances for the safety of the camps after the PLO fighters departed, and he urged the Italians to try to get French and American agreement to keep the MNF in the city. The Lebanese wanted the MNF to stay, too, Arafat stressed.

I knew, however, that the MNF would *not* stay beyond the period agreed upon at the outset: long enough to get the PLO out of Beirut and little more. I had real difficulty getting Cap Weinberger and the Defense Department to deploy the marines in the first place, and, once deployed, they had not been permitted to take any meaningful part in the action. I had misgivings about such a quick withdrawal, but under all the circumstances, I realized that the marines would in fact leave as soon as possible after the PLO departure. The American MNF contingent had begun its withdrawal on September 10, and despite the assassination of Bashir Gemayel, the entire force would be out by September 16. Indeed, the more trouble there was in Beirut, the greater the pressure would be from the Pentagon and from the public to get our forces out swiftly. To Arafat the MNF meant protection for civilians but, in fact, the MNF's stated mission—to achieve the safe departure of the PLO—had been completed.

The word I received from Italy was followed by fury from the French, who told us Israeli tanks and bulldozers were at the French ambassador's residence in Beirut, tearing it to the ground. (This report proved to be vastly exaggerated, but at this time, when many inconceivable events actually were taking place, every report, however flimsy and hysterical, was given some credence in the first instance.) I talked on the phone to Claude Cheysson, the French foreign minister. He had just been in Beirut and was infuriated by Israeli actions; he was strongly considering whether to recommend sending a reconstituted MNF back to Beirut.

A mist of bitterness now hung over every American-Israeli official encounter. Our people felt that everything we had worked for through the evacuation of the PLO, the deployment of the MNF, and the plans for putting the Lebanese nation together again was being dragged down by preemptive Israeli military behavior and political deception.

The Israelis were furious with us. They had launched a brutal war in Lebanon for purposes that kept escalating in ambition and exploding in their faces: first it was security of Israel's northern border, then expulsion of the PLO from Beirut, then a peace treaty with Lebanon. Begin and the foreign ministry were outraged at any suggestion that they had misled us but were stung by an awareness that they themselves had been misled by Ariel Sharon. "You people don't know what you are doing," Moshe Arens told me on September 16. "Without Israeli forces in Beirut now, all hell would break loose in the wake of Bashir's assassination. You want Israelis to clean up the mess while you Americans stay clean with the Arabs!"

"The occupying power of a city is responsible for everything that takes place there; Israel should not want such a responsibility, nor can it possibly fulfill it," I told Arens. It was a tough, heated conversation. Arens was undeterred.

The United States had "needlessly complicated" the situation with the president's September 1 initiative, he said. A message came in from King Fahd of Saudi Arabia, who pleaded that his honor, name, and credibility were at stake: the United States had to get the Israelis out of Beirut. Saudi Arabia could not give us any help on our peace initiative until the Israelis were out, Fahd said.

By Friday, September 17, the Israelis had consolidated their grip on Beirut and were ringed around the Palestinian refugee camps in the southern suburbs. Morrie Draper was in close contact with Defense Minister Sharon and Foreign Minister Shamir, who were now willing to start planning for Israeli forces to hand over their positions in Beirut to the Lebanese army. At the United Nations, the United States voted for a Security Council resolution that condemned Israel's incursions into Beirut and demanded an immediate return to positions they held before September 15.

Saturday, September 18, was Rosh Hashanah; falling on the Jewish Shabbat, it was a double holy day. I looked forward to a quiet weekend. At 5:45 A.M., Washington time, I was awakened at home by a telephone call from Larry Eagleburger, who told me that our embassy in Lebanon was at that moment talking to foreign service officer Ryan Crocker. With a hand-held transmitter, he was walking through the Shatila refugee camp and describing as he moved scenes of a massacre of shocking magnitude. Crocker had counted some fifty dead bodies, including women and children. I dressed hurriedly and headed for the State Department.

When Crocker returned to our embassy, he reported that the Red Cross had been in the Sabra and Shatila refugee camps and concluded that the massacres had been carried out by a special unit of the Phalangist Lebanese Forces. The French told us their officers had entered the Sabra and Shatila camps and reported "horrible destruction," with families lying dead in groups. The French said survivors claimed that Israeli bulldozers had come in to push rubble over the bodies, all of which had taken place while IDF forces were occupying positions surrounding the camps. Survivors in the camps told Crocker that gunmen had moved most women and children to a soccer field. The young men were then taken in small groups up narrow alleys and were executed at close range with automatic weapons and small-arms fire. In addition to those killed, hundreds had been taken away from the camps—it was not known where. Red Cross officials told our people that hundreds of refugees had fled to a hospital south of the Shatila camp.

Gunmen had pursued them there, shooting some and seizing others, including some medical personnel. The events they described were horrifying. I was shaken and appalled.

Our embassy in Tel Aviv's telegram 14040 arrived on my desk that Saturday morning. It reported Draper's conversations with Ariel Sharon on Friday—the day the majority of the killings took place, although they had begun even the night before, on Thursday. Sharon had told Draper that Israeli forces would remain in the areas where "the terrorists" were located until the Lebanese Armed Forces (LAF) cleaned them out. "Let the LAF go into the camps," Sharon said. "They can kill the terrorists. But if they don't, we will." I was stunned by this cable. We got Draper on the tacsat. He said that Major General Drori, the Israeli Northern Commander, had asked the Lebanese Armed Forces to enter the camps and clean them out, but the LAF commander had refused. Drori then said that the Lebanese Forces (LF) would do the job and pointed to sixty-some trucks lined up to transport such a force in and out.

The Israelis had said they had to enter Beirut after Bashir was assassinated in order to prevent a bloodbath: now it appeared they had facilitated—and perhaps even induced—just that. The entire Israeli justification for their actions was in shreds. Israel faced a tremendous moral charge. Our own position was serious; Phil Habib had assured the Palestinians that all precautions would be taken to protect those left in the camps after the PLO departed. Habib had relied on Israeli and Lebanese assurances. The MNF had not been designed to perform such a job, and our own marines had come and gone in short order.

"The brutal fact is, we are partially responsible," I told Eagleburger. "We took the Israelis and the Lebanese at their word." I told Draper to get to the Israelis and demand they pull back immediately and turn the camps over to the protection of the Lebanese army. I could not believe that the people of Israel would in any way support what their army had allowed to happen in Beirut.

I went to the White House on Saturday morning and told President Reagan what we were learning about the massacres. I would call in Ambassador Arens. The president was deeply shaken and asked whether we had been too cautious with the marines. Had we withdrawn them too quickly?

Late that afternoon I met in my office with Arens, who had come directly from Rosh Hashanah synagogue prayers when he got my message. "The president has instructed me to demand that Israeli forces get out of Beirut; we have asked the government of Lebanon to order its armed forces to take over Israeli-held positions in the city. One fact is undeniable," I said: "Israel, against all our advice, had taken control of the city, and now it is the scene of a massacre."

Arens told me he, too, was appalled by what had happened. For the first time in any of our meetings, he was subdued. After Arens left, I called together the people who had been gathering reports to construct a picture of what had happened. It was this: the Israel Defense Forces had let Phalange militiamen into the Sabra refugee camp Thursday evening and had fired illumination rounds through the night to enable the Phalangists to conduct what amounted to a massacre. The Israeli forces on the scene were well aware of what was taking place. At some point on Friday, a similar scourge of the Shatila refugee camp took place.

In an agitated state, I went back to the White House at 5:30 that Saturday evening. I found the president more than ready to send the marines back. I agreed with him, but I knew that Cap Weinberger and the Pentagon would be opposed. The president said we had inherited a responsibility and was worried by what he called "the Vietnam problem," the reluctance of the United States to use its troops again in tough spots and the perception that we would not. I said that the French and Italians felt we all had taken a black eye by having pulled out the MNF just before this massacre. The president was ready to reconstitute and reinsert the multinational force. "If we show ourselves unable to respond to this situation, what can the Middle East parties expect of us in the Arab-Israeli peace process?" he said to me.

Back in my office, I telephoned former President Carter to tell him what we knew. "You have to throw the book at Begin," he said. "Tough talk is the only talk Begin understands."

The following morning, Sunday, September 19, a political firestorm was breaking out in Israel as a result of the gruesome revelations of massacre in the refugee camps. Television pictures showed bodies piled in heaps. Ray Seitz, my executive assistant, told me he was revolted by the report that bulldozers had been used to push rubble over piles of bodies. As a boy, he said, he was seared by the image of bulldozers pushing piles of Jewish bodies into mass graves. Additional reports came in of Israeli lawlessness in West Beirut. The Israel Defense Forces were conducting house-to-house searches and arresting or detaining many people and breaking into apartments and offices, allegedly looking for material of intelligence value for use against the PLO. The IDF broke into Lebanese Prime Minister Shafik al-Wazzan's home. The Soviet embassy was violated. Israeli troops had entered banks in the financial district.

The French and Italians were similarly outraged. Italian Foreign Minister Colombo telephoned me and raised the idea that we reconstitute the MNF and send it back in. The Lebanese government was crying for any international support to help restore stability, but specifically hoped the MNF would come back. UN Ambassador Jeane Kirkpatrick called in to say the PLO at the United Nations favored reconstitution of the MNF. The UN Security Council had just that morning passed a resolution stating it was appalled by the massacre and calling on the secretary-general to consider the possible deployment to Lebanon of UN forces. I knew that a UN force was unlikely, so I felt that we should hold the idea of the return of the MNF in reserve. At the request of the secretary-general, I sent a message to Israeli foreign minister Shamir urging that Israel agree to deployment of UNIFIL (United Nations Interim Force in Lebanon), which had been stationed in southern Lebanon since 1948, to Beirut to serve as peacekeepers as the IDF left the city.

I telephoned Howard Baker, the Senate majority leader. I knew he would be appearing on "This Week with David Brinkley" at 11:30 A.M., so I went over to his home to brief him. His support would be key if we decided to go ahead with the MNF again.

At 11:00 A.M. on Sunday the president and his chief advisers met in the White House Situation Room. I briefed on the situation. It was de facto a NSC session. I had called NSC adviser Bill Clark earlier to be sure Cap Weinberger would be there. I wanted Cap to hear the president's views directly, not subsequently from me. Cap tried to set the tone with his total reluctance for the United States to do anything more in Lebanon. "Israel has gotten itself in a swamp, and we should leave it at that," he said.

President Reagan picked up on that and agreed that Israel must realize it had gotten itself into a terrible swamp and the sooner it got out of Lebanon, the better. World opinion was crushing. "Let's go for broke right now," the president said. He was ready to make a statement within the next twenty-four hours that would seek not only to have Israel withdraw from Beirut but to begin a process for full withdrawal of all foreign forces from Lebanon, and he was more than ready for U.S. participation in a reconstituted MNF. The president asked me to convene top officials from State, Defense, and the CIA to prepare for a second session with him in the evening. By this time, it was clear to all that President Reagan and I were on the same wavelength.

Before our evening meeting with the president, a large crowd convened for a preliminary 4:00 P.M. session in the State Department's operations center. I seated Cap Weinberger next to me. I acted as chairman, calling on various people for their views on what could and should be done. Everyone knew that President Reagan was ready to send the marines back to Beirut, so the Pentagon had at least to appear to be responsive. Cap accordingly shifted his approach.

What I then heard Cap advocate gave me my first experience with what I would come to recognize as a standard Pentagon tactic: when you don't want to do something, agree to do it—but with such an impossible set of conditions and on such a preposterously gigantic scale that the outcome will be to do nothing. So Cap set forth the Defense Department proposal: there should be no MNF redeployed anywhere in Lebanon until all foreign forces had agreed to depart and, in fact, had done so. All foreign forces—Syrian, Israeli, Iranian, and Palestinian—would leave Lebanon. (How they would be induced to leave was *my* problem.) Once all such troops were gone, U.S. armed forces would form a giant cordon around the entire perimeter of Lebanon's borders and coastline so that the Lebanese army would be undisturbed as it retook control of internal security.

The Defense Department, Cap said, could do nothing until the State Department produced the comprehensive international agreement that would rid Lebanon of its foreign presences. I was, under this "plan," supposed to conduct diplomacy without strength, with no military backup—and in pursuit of a ludicrously impossible ideal.

Bud McFarlane, representing the NSC staff, said that the MNF was a political signal to the government of Lebanon as well as to the Arabs in the context of the peace process. The deployment of the MNF was a political act, he said, not a military act, and if we didn't do it, we would lose credibility in the Middle East and any hope of success with the president's peace initiative.

After Weinberger, for the third or fourth time, made his point about the precondition of an agreement, I summed up: "If you can't deploy until a general withdrawal agreement, then you have to ask how quickly, if at all, such a diplomatic process can be completed. My guess is many months at best, if ever. Look how long it took Phil Habib to get the PLO out of Beirut."

Weinberger said once again that we needed all the agreements for withdrawal before a deployment. It was too uncertain, he said, to put the MNF in Beirut and then simply hope for the best. The mission needed to be defined. I said the mission was defined—help the Lebanese get control of and stabilize their situation—but it could be narrower, perhaps limited just to Beirut. Fred Ikle, under secretary of defense, made the same point. Admiral James Watkins, the acting chairman of the Joint Chiefs of Staff, said the U.S. component would need to be an "enriched force," perhaps 5,000 men. Weinberger insisted there was great danger from the Phalange. He thought we might need a division (some 16,000 to 20,000 men) in order to be prepared for major hostility.

The real possibilities seemed to come down to a Phase I, namely, an MNF presence in Beirut, and a Phase II, dealing with the larger issues of Lebanon. "We shouldn't be the Beirut police department," Cap insisted.

I called on the CIA's Bob Ames. He reiterated the need for action and stressed his concern that if we didn't move rapidly, we would lose the momentum in the Arab world in support of the president's peace initiative: "We need action quickly."

"That's for the president to say," Cap interjected.

"We need to have a record, a clear record, of what the Israelis and the

Syrians have already said about their respective commitments to withdraw," I said.

Cap continued to stress that "a limited Beirut mission is too risky." At the end of the meeting, Bud McFarlane and Fred Ikle both let me know they supported a Beirut-only operation for the MNF.

"The president wants teeth in whatever he does, and it is up to the Department of Defense to provide the teeth," I said.

After the meeting, I assembled my Middle East group in my office. We were not five minutes into our review when Phil Habib walked through the door, fresh from two weeks in California. I described the Weinberger concept to Habib, who proceeded to blow it out of the water as impractical and unnecessary. The Lebanese borders could not be guarded without tens of thousands of men, he said.

"The military wants to do what the diplomats don't think is necessary, and the diplomats want the military to do what the military is too nervous to do. Our military is nervous that Ronald Reagan isn't," I said, venting the frustration I felt during the wider meeting in the operations center.

Phil Habib stated the MNF mission: "Through its presence the MNF will assist the government of Lebanon to reassert its authority in Beirut. It will provide assurance during the period of disengagement of Israeli forces from Beirut. It does not have responsibility for internal security." Just before departing for the White House, I gathered my papers together. To me the decision for the president was straightforward and simple. Did the political and diplomatic benefits of an immediate reestablishment of a multinational force in Beirut outweigh the military risks? Certainly there were risks, and the president should know them. Lebanon was a tough place, often a quagmire.

That Sunday night we went back to the president. I again insisted that Cap be present so that he would hear the president's decision firsthand. The president was decisive: the United States would participate in the return of the multinational force to Beirut at the invitation of the government of Lebanon. The president felt that the United States must contribute to a visible, definite, constructive, international effort to help the central government of Lebanon begin to regain control over its own country. The United States sought a Lebanon free of foreign forces and with control over its own territory. Such a legitimate government, we hoped, could negotiate a meaningful agreement with Israel.

We had to move quickly to consult with the French and Italians, whose concurrence was required before the president could issue a statement. We also needed to talk to the secretary-general: the UNIFIL option had been overtaken. Cap heard the president. Ronald Reagan called for a firm, strong, and active U.S. Marine presence in Beirut. But at every turn the attitude of the Defense Department seemed to me to transmit the wrong message. It was almost as though they would have our forces shrink back, duck, and cover until it became clear to anyone with a gun in Beirut—and that was just about everybody—that you could take a poke at the Americans and not worry much about getting hit back.

After the meeting, I returned to the State Department. We estimated that it would take four days for the marines to reach Beirut from Naples. They would probably arrive on Thursday, September 23, the day Amin Gemayel, Bashir's younger brother, was to be inaugurated as president of Lebanon. I called in French Ambassador Vernier-Palliez. He supported the president's position but felt that the French government would want the UNIFIL alternative clearly eliminated before signing on to a new multinational force. He commented privately that the French felt particularly burned as a result of the massacre because French troops removed the mines around the refugee camps. "We do not trust the Israelis," he said sharply.

At 10:30 P.M., I met with Italian Ambassador Petrignani. His foreign minister, Emilio Colombo, had been the first to urge that the multinational force be reconstituted. When this meeting concluded and as the clock inched toward an 11:00 P.M. meeting with Arens, I reviewed the day's activities and observed to Ray Seitz, "Weinberger and Habib have the same strategy in talking about a point: they don't stop, they don't breathe, and you can't interrupt."

Before Arens arrived, in came Phil Habib again. I felt the Israelis should see the offer of a new multinational force as a way for them to get off a very sharp hook. Habib said that Sharon wanted his troops to go in and out of Beirut freely. "They won't leave without one hell of a fight." Habib then asked whether Sam Lewis would be giving the same message to the Israelis in Jerusalem. Eagleburger told him that Lewis was in Cyprus. Habib exclaimed, "The ambassador to Israel is in Cyprus? The ambassador to Lebanon is in Washington? What kind of Foreign Service are you running here?"

My session with Arens went well past midnight. He seemed jolted by my demand that Israel vacate all of Beirut and the airport. "The president isn't demanding anything; events are," I said. Arens asked that the president delay his statement so that a response could come from Israel. "Time's a-wasting," I said. Arens's primary concern was the swiftly spreading public belief that Israel was responsible for the Sabra-Shatila massacres.

"I want to emphasize," Arens told me, "that any insinuation that Israel bears part of the responsibility for the killings will be a shadow across the U.S.-Israel relationship."

"Face the facts," I said. "You bear responsibility." And we shared it, I thought, because we took them at their word to ensure safety in the camps.

That same Sunday night, the Israeli cabinet convened in an extraordinary session. The cabinet rejected the idea of using UNIFIL in Beirut that I had proposed to Shamir. Most important, the cabinet issued a communiqué that rang with Menachem Begin's voice:

> A blood libel was plotted against the Jewish state and its government as well as the IDF [Israel Defense Forces] on Rosh Hashanah. In a place distant from an IDF position, a Lebanese unit entered a refugee camp where terrorists took shelter in order to arrest them. That unit attacked the civilian population, resulting in many losses of lives. . . . All the accusations—direct or hinted—claiming that the IDF has any responsibility whatsoever for the tragedy in the Shatila camp are groundless. The Cabinet rejects them with loathing. . . . Despite the instigation emanating from within our midst, we are calling on the people to unite around its elected government, fighting to provide security and peace to Israel and all its citizens. No one will preach to us values of morality and respect for human life, upon which we have and will continue to bring up generations of Israeli fighters.

I was appalled. How could Begin and the cabinet issue such a statement? Were they all so dangerously ill informed? Was Sharon completely dominant? Did they think we, let alone Israeli citizens, would believe simply anything, however outrageous? The statement suggested that either they were unhinged from reality or totally carried away with their momentarily commanding position.

On Monday, President Reagan announced that the marines would return to Beirut with the multinational force. On Tuesday, September 21, Amin Gemayel was elected president of Lebanon, and the Israeli cabinet approved the withdrawal of Israeli forces from Beirut and the redeployment of the MNF. On Thursday, Amin Gemayel was inaugurated. On Friday, the French contingent came ashore at Beirut. On Saturday, Habib visited Ariel Sharon at his farm in the south of Israel and got agreement that the IDF would move out of Beirut sector by sector to enable a full-scale MNF deployment. Within a few days the marines were back in Beirut.

On September 24, 1982, Prime Minister Begin had asked that a judicial commission of inquiry be set up to investigate the Sabra and Shatila massacres. He had first opposed the idea but later reversed himself. The public outcry in Israel resulted in a demonstration in Tel Aviv numbering 400,000 people, 10 percent of Israel's population. Some of Begin's coalition partners had issued warnings that they might resign. The chairman of the commission was Chief Justice Yitzhak Kahan, and the other members were Supreme Court Justice Aharon Barak and Yona Efrat, a retired major general.

On September 30, I spoke at the opening of the UN General Assembly in New York. I had been in office little more than two months. In my address I summed up what little wisdom I picked up from the incredible events of August and September. We would start from realism. We would act from strength, both in power and purpose. We would stress the essential need to generate consent, build agreement, and negotiate on key issues. We would conduct ourselves in the belief that progress was possible, even though the road to its achievement was long and hard. I thought these points were straightforward and obvious, benchmarks for our foreign policy in the 1980s. They proved to be anything but easy to implement.

At the end of September, Habib was back at work, trying to get an agreement that would remove all foreign forces from Lebanon and put Lebanon back on its feet. In Jerusalem, talking to Begin, Habib was interrupted by Sharon, who informed Habib, "We already have an agreement with Lebanon." Taken aback, Habib broke off the talks and immediately returned to Beirut, where he confronted Amin Gemayel. It was true; Gemayel had signed a general agreement accepting a series of far-reaching Israeli demands that could not possibly stand the light of day. Sharon had gone too far in pressing, and Gemayel had given in too easily. He had accepted an agreement dictated by Israel. The result was worthless, and the process had wasted valuable time.

In early December, while the president and I were out of the country on a trip to South and Central America, I got word that a supplement was moving through the lame-duck session of Congress to provide a $250 million increase in the amount of U.S. military assistance granted to Israel: this in the face of Israel's invasion of Lebanon, its use of cluster bombs, and its complicity in the Sabra and Shatila massacres! We fought the supplement and fought it hard. President Reagan and I weighed in personally, making numerous calls to senators and congressmen. On December 9, I added a formal letter of opposition saying that the supplement appeared "to endorse and reward Israel's policies." Foreign Minister Shamir called President Reagan's opposition "an unfriendly act" and said that it "endangers, the peace process."

The supplement sailed right by us and was approved by the Congress as though President Reagan and I had not even been there. I was astonished and disheartened. This brought home to me vividly Israel's leverage in our Congress. I saw that I must work carefully with the Israelis if I was to have any handle on congressional action that might affect Israel and if I was to maintain congressional support for my efforts to make progress in the Middle East.

On February 8, 1983, the Kahan Commission issued its report on the Sabra and Shatila massacres, recommending the dismissal or censure of top Israeli officials, including Defense Minister Sharon. The *New York Times* on February 9, 1983, summarized: "The commission's conclusions fell into two broad categories: first, that Israeli officials, knowing the

Phalangists' violent history and the extreme tensions after the assassination of their leader, President-elect Bashir Gemayel, should have realized the probability of a massacre and should not have ordered the Phalangists into the Palestinian camps without effective supervision; and second, that officials should have acted decisively on reports of killings, and should have stopped the Phalangists immediately."

The Kahan Commission's own words were devastating: "It is evident that the forces who entered the area were steeped in hatred for the Palestinians, in the wake of the atrocities and severe injuries done to the Christians during the civil war in Lebanon by the Palestinians and those who fought alongside them; and these feelings of hatred were compounded by a longing for revenge in the wake of the assassination of the Phalangists' admired leader Bashir and the killing of several dozen Phalangists two days before their entry into the camps."

The Kahan Commission also reported, "In the course of the events and also thereafter, rumors spread that personnel of Major [Saad] Haddad were perpetrating a massacre or participating in a massacre. No basis was found for these rumors. The IDF liaison officer with Major Haddad's forces testified that no unit of that force had crossed the Awali River that week. We have no reason to doubt that testimony." Those who had done the job were Phalangist Lebanese Forces under Commander Elie Hobeika, the commission concluded.

Referring to the history of pogroms against the Jews, the commission observed: "the Jewish public's stand has always been that the responsibility for such deeds falls not only on those who rioted and committed the atrocities but also on those who were responsible for safety and public order, who could have prevented the disturbances and did not fulfill their obligations in this respect. . . . the decision on the entry of the Phalangists into the refugee camps was taken without consideration of the danger— which the makers and executors of the decision were obligated to foresee as probable—that the Phalangists would commit massacres and pogroms against the inhabitants of the camps and without an examination of the means for preventing this danger."

The Israeli cabinet voted 16 to 1 to accept the report of the Kahan Commission. Ariel Sharon resigned and was replaced as defense minister by Moshe Arens. Expressing its criticism of Sharon's role, the commission observed that after the assassination of Bashir Gemayel, "no prophetic powers were required to know that concrete danger of acts of slaughter existed when the Phalangists were moved into the camps without the I.D.F.'s being with them. The sense of such a danger should have been in the consciousness of every knowledgeable person who was close to this subject, and certainly in the consciousness of the Defense Minister, who took an active part in everything relating to the war."

Israel could not be exonerated from responsibility for what had occurred in Sabra and Shatila. But I believed that the people of Israel deserved credit for setting up the proper procedure under which the facts were brought to light and responsibility allocated for the Israeli role in these horrible occurrences. Unfortunately, the sad plight of Lebanon did not end with the massacres at Sabra and Shatila.

Part III

GARDENING

CHAPTER 8

The Soviet Union:
First Efforts

Remnants of détente were still apparent when Ronald Reagan took office. Secretary Haig ended the procedure begun by Henry Kissinger whereby Anatoly Dobrynin was the only ambassador in Washington who could come to the State Department unnoticed by using the underground entrance to the garage. After that, Dobrynin came the same way everybody else did—to the main entrance of the building. When I arrived on the scene, a special telephone, a hot line, in the secretary of state's office still connected directly to the Soviet embassy. I didn't see any use for it, and some of our security people thought it might even be a subtle kind of bug, so we took it out.

Despite an extended period of détente with the Soviet Union beginning in the Nixon administration, a sharp disenchantment had followed—brought about by the Soviet move into Angola in 1975, their deployment in the mid-1970s of a new generation of powerful nuclear missiles aimed at Europe, the Soviet invasion of Afghanistan in 1979, and their complicity in the crackdown on Solidarity in Poland in 1981. Such aggressive actions created great tension between the two superpowers. Still, the central preoccupation of American foreign policy had to be the Soviet Union. A return to predétente estrangement would be unwise and self-defeating. This was the country that could wipe us out in thirty minutes with strategic nuclear missiles.

Unique among the people at the top in the Reagan administration, I had negotiated with the Soviets before, and successfully, as secretary of the treasury, and I had come to know some Soviet leaders in an informal way.

I remembered my first trip to Moscow, in 1973. I had been warned repeatedly by the Secret Service and the CIA that everything would be bugged. The only place to have a private conversation was in a boxlike room in the middle of our embassy with electronic countermeasures surrounding it. It was claustrophobic, but it was the one place in the whole city of Moscow, I was told, that was "secure." O'Bie and I were taken to our hotel room by Secret Service personnel. They pointed with some pride to the bugs they had identified in the living room, the bedroom, and the bathroom. They were not going to bother taking them out, they told us, because they were sure there were plenty of others. They just wanted us to see for ourselves that they were not kidding.

I had come to Moscow in connection with trade negotiations; my counterpart then was the Soviet minister of foreign trade, a salty old Communist named Nikolai Patolichev. We had many meetings, both in Moscow and in Washington, and we reached some mutually satisfactory agreements. We got to know each other well enough for him to tell me some stories about his life. I remember one vignette vividly. In World War II, he was in charge of tank production. The Soviets were always working to make better tanks, he recounted, but whenever they changed the design, they slowed up the rate of production. On one occasion, Patolichev told me, he was called to Moscow to meet directly with Stalin, who gave him an explicit order: "Do not make any more changes. The tank we have is a good tank, and we must produce more volume, so my orders are, don't change again."

Patolichev no sooner had returned home than his people came in with designs for a sharply improved tank. What was he to do? He decided to have the new tank built surreptitiously, with a part taken from here and a part from there; few people would know what was going on. He and a small group constructed the tank to the new specifications, and when it was finished, they could see that it was significantly better. Inevitably, Stalin found out. Patolichev told me he was deathly afraid of what might descend on him. But the tank was so superior that military leaders said, "Well, all right, but this is the last time. No more changes." Stalin agreed.

"So," Patolichev said with a smile, "I got away with it." I had no idea whether this story was true, but I had no reason to doubt it. In any event, it gave me an insight: creative and independent people could make even a flawed Soviet system into a formidable foe and could have strength as individuals and a capacity to think for themselves. Earlier I had spent a weekend at Sochi, a Soviet resort on the Black Sea. We were taken to a very fine stone guest house that was relatively new, although on mature, well-landscaped grounds that clearly had surrounded a mansion in an earlier time. As we walked in, I remarked on what a handsome, well-built structure it was. My host from the Trade Ministry smiled and said, "Yes, we wanted to bring you here so that you could see that not everything good in the Soviet Union was built by the czars." He knew as well as I that most post-czarist construction in the Soviet Union was shoddy.

Patolichev insisted, on another occasion, that I accompany him to Leningrad. He made clear that the first official event would be a visit to the

Leningrad cemetery. I resisted at first, but once there, I appreciated why he was so insistent. We entered and looked down upon a long path between huge mounds where tens of thousands of Soviet citizens who died in the Battle of Leningrad were buried. He and I walked slowly down the path toward a memorial as funereal music played. I carried a wreath to lay there. As we were walking, Patolichev described the fighting to me and the numbers of people who were killed. "Every Russian family has some member who fought, died, or suffered as a result of the Battle of Leningrad," he told me. As he spoke, I noticed that the Soviet interpreter had dropped out and had been replaced; she had moved back with the rest of the party and was openly sobbing. This tough old guy, Patolichev, had tears streaming down his cheeks. When we were about to leave the cemetery, I said to him, "I, too, fought in World War II and had friends in arms killed beside me." Then I went to the middle of the terrace above the cemetery, raised my hand in a long salute, dropped it smartly, as an old marine, turned about-face, and left. The Soviets were moved by this salute far more than by the wreath.

So, from my time in the Nixon administration, I had learned something of the human dimension to the Soviet Union. I learned that World War II —the Great Patriotic War Against Fascism, the Soviets called it—was a matter of deep significance to them. I also learned that the Soviets were tough negotiators but that you could negotiate successfully with them. In my experience, they did their homework and had skill and patience and staying power. I respected them not only as able negotiators but as people who could make a deal and stick to it. They also, I realized, could turn negotiations into occasions for denunciation and deceit and shameless propagandizing. Their willingness to engage seriously would depend entirely on how they perceived their interests. Such occasions would come, I felt, when the Soviets concluded that we were not only strong and determined but also willing to make agreements that were mutually advantageous. I was determined to make American strength serve the cause of serious negotiation on behalf of American interests, and I was certain that Ronald Reagan shared this view.

Starting in with Gromyko

Prospective events have a way of stimulating and organizing activity. My upcoming meetings in New York with Soviet Foreign Minister Andrei Gromyko in late September 1982, at the start of the annual UN General Assembly, did just this. Preparations began even as I was being confirmed. I received endless briefings. Virtually everyone reminded me how many foreign ministers, presidents, secretaries of state, and other plenipotentiaries had met Gromyko and then departed the scene, while he remained. Finally, I threatened to throw the next person who spewed out this line right out of the room. "Let's just stick to content," I said.

Shortly after taking office, I blocked the resumption of negotiations with the Soviets on a long-term grain agreement, which had major congressional support. It was incredible to me that we would resume such negotiations, which we had suspended only eight months earlier as part of the sanctions imposed in response to Soviet-supported crackdown on the Polish trade union Solidarity. Such a move, I argued to senators from the farm states, would send entirely the wrong signal to the Soviets and would virtually destroy our efforts with our allies to defuse the raging dispute over the sanctions we had imposed on the building of the Soviet pipeline. "The West Europeans accuse the US of double-dealing by urging trade sanctions against Moscow while continuing to sell grain to the Soviet Union," Daniel Southerland reported in the *Christian Science Monitor* on July 15, 1982.

By midsummer, Paul Nitze's "walk in the woods" was well known to the president and all his top advisers. Paul, head of our intermediate-range nuclear forces (INF) negotiating team, had worked out on an informal basis—during a walk on July 16, 1982, in the woods outside Geneva— with Yuli Kvitsinsky, his Soviet opposite number, the structure of a deal to break the negotiating impasse. The result would have left both sides with some deployments, thus differing from our basic position of no INF nuclear missiles deployed by either of us, the so-called zero-zero option, and would have eliminated deployment in West Germany of Pershing II intermediate-range nuclear ballistic missiles.

Nitze's "walk" was studied throughout the rest of the summer; by early September, both the office of the secretary of defense and the Joint Chiefs of Staff had registered their negative opinions. The president, too, was opposed. The Pershing IIs, they felt, were the elements in our deployments most feared by the Soviets, and therefore we should not give them up prematurely through an agreement that allowed the Soviets to retain intermediate-range ballistic missiles while we had only our slower-moving cruise missiles. The absence of any word from Moscow regarding "the walk," moreover, suggested that the Soviets rejected the package. If we, on the other hand, reacted favorably, they would simply pocket our concessions.

Eugene Rostow, head of the Arms Control and Disarmament Agency, and Paul Nitze felt that an important opportunity was being missed. Rostow let his disappointment show and eventually was asked to resign. I argued to the president that private informal contacts were often useful in a negotiation like this. He agreed. The president's instructions to me for my meetings with Gromyko were the same as those given to Paul Nitze as he returned to Geneva: do not state our view of the package unless it is raised by the Soviets. If raised, say the proposed deal is not acceptable to us but that the channel is promising and should be kept open.

The president and all his advisers, including me, were concerned about a late-August report that the Soviets might position high-performance jet fighter aircraft in Nicaragua. At a meeting of the NSC principals in early September, we all agreed such a move would be unacceptable, and the president added that statement to my instructions for my meetings with Gromyko. I insisted firmly that I should not lay down such a marker unless the president made clear to the Defense Department and the Central Intelligence Agency that we would take action if the Soviets took this step. I wanted to know what that action would be. After a lengthy argument, Bill Casey put forward a credible way of destroying such aircraft immediately upon delivery, and the president affirmed that action would be taken if such planes were delivered. And so I proceeded. I remembered my instructions as a marine in boot camp when I was issued my rifle: "Never point this rifle at someone unless you are willing to pull the trigger."

I also wanted constructive proposals in my instructions. I had identified two areas—Southern Africa and nuclear nonproliferation—that bore at least some prospect of progress with the Soviets. The atmosphere was tense, but I was ready to be positive. An American businessman, Simon Chilewich, reported that the chairman of the Soviet State bank, Vladimir Alkhimov, a man I knew from my time as secretary of the treasury, had called me "a very reasonable man" and expressed the hope that the United States and the USSR, now that I was secretary of state, could "start talking business." Alkhimov, and perhaps some higher authority, doubtless expected this information to reach me. Was this an early signal that the Soviets were interested in talking business themselves? I didn't know, but I didn't rule it out.

As an important part of my preparation for the Gromyko meetings, I focused on human rights practices in the Soviet Union. I assembled lists of people who had been denied permission to emigrate, reviewed the special problems of Soviet Jewry, and expanded my knowledge of the full range of our human rights concerns. I met with Avital Shcharansky, the intense and compelling wife of the famous dissident. Afterward, I was wrung out. The woeful treatment of her husband, his courage, and my inability to provide any real assurance about his release made for immense frustration. Avital's pleas dramatized the human side of the tension in U.S.-Soviet relations. "The president and I will never give up on pressing the cause of human rights and the case for your husband's release," I told her.

I convened a Saturday seminar on the Soviet Union on August 21. Hal Sonnenfeldt, a canny specialist on the Soviet Union who had participated in meetings with me in Moscow during the Nixon years, organized and conducted the proceedings. Many of those people assembled had direct experience in dealing with the Soviets: Don Rumsfeld and Harold Brown, secretaries of defense in the Ford and Carter administrations, and Henry Rowen, Norman Podhoretz, Pete Peterson, Bill Hyland, and Brent Scowcroft joined a few key people from the administration, including Cap Weinberger and Bud McFarlane. Our talks continued through most of that day. The participants painted a picture of formidable Soviet military power, of an aggressive foreign policy, of intransigence on human rights, and of Gromyko as an unbending and often insufferable interlocutor.

As the date for my meeting with Gromyko approached, I thought about who should attend and what the arrangements should be. The earlier pattern had been for the American secretary of state and Gromyko to exclude others, except for interpreters and note takers. I wanted to increase the status of our ambassador and under secretary and let these key associates get a feel for what Gromyko was like in action. So we told the Soviets that Larry Eagleburger and Ambassador Art Hartman would join me. Gromyko said he would bring two people with him, although I felt that he did not like the idea of enlarging the group.

Art Hartman greeted Gromyko on September 28 as his car pulled up to the U.S. mission, just across from the UN building. I met him on the eleventh floor as he came out of the elevator. We went into Ambassador Jeane Kirkpatrick's office. I spoke with Gromyko for some three hours. I was struck by how somber and humorless he was throughout his presentation. Gromyko called our relations "politically tense." He asked me whether the United States wanted "peaceful coexistence or confrontation."

"The deterioration of our relations is the result of Soviet conduct," I replied, and went through their refusal to honor human rights agreements, their military buildup, their aggressive and repressive actions in Poland, Afghanistan, and elsewhere. I gave particular attention to the human rights area: problems of Jews, dissidents, and families divided by Soviet refusal to allow emigration, as well as the persecution of people monitoring Soviet compliance with their obligations under the Helsinki Final Act (the Helsinki Watch group). I noted Leonid Brezhnev's signature on the Helsinki Final Act, which the United States, Canada, and all the nations of Europe had signed in 1975 and which guaranteed a range of basic human rights. I regarded the Soviet signature as obligating them to live by its terms.

"Is it so important that Mr. or Mrs. or Miss so and so can or cannot leave such and such a country?" Gromyko responded. "I would call it a tenth-rate question." He expounded on the provision of the Helsinki Final Act "dealing with non-interference in the internal affairs of a sovereign country."

When his lecture finally ended, I said, "I am frankly disappointed that you call human rights a tenth-rate question. That is one of the difficulties facing our relationship. Human problems always enjoy the highest priority in the United States." I told him about my visit to the cemetery in Leningrad and the emotional response of Patolichev and the other Soviets present. "They must have felt," I said, that "the wellspring of human values should not be regarded as a tenth priority but rather should be emphasized." Gromyko did not respond.

I raised the issue of arms control negotiations involving intermediate-range (INF) and strategic (START) nuclear missiles as well as negotiations under way on conventional weapons, wanting him to see that we were serious in our approach. He agreed that the arms talks at Geneva were proceeding in a businesslike fashion, but he criticized our positions, particularly our position on INF—the zero option—calling for the elimination of this entire class of weapons. "This cannot be the basis for any U.S.-Soviet agreement," Gromyko said. The Soviets already had such missiles deployed, and the United States did not; so the zero option, he maintained, amounted to "unilateral disarmament" by the Soviets. He obviously did not want our meeting to provide a basis for any public impression that the negotiations were proceeding in a promising way.

As it turned out, I did not need to use my instruction about Paul Nitze's walk in the woods. Gromyko never raised the subject. I did tell him, however, that the private channel was useful. (The next day, in Geneva, Kvitsinksy told Nitze, "Neither the result nor the channel is acceptable to the Soviet Union.") Gromyko criticized our failure to ratify existing arms agreements, in particular the nuclear test ban treaties agreed to in the mid-1970s. At the end of the meeting I suggested to Gromyko that our staffs get together prior to our next meeting the following Monday to identify areas where we might be able to work together constructively. Gromyko agreed.

After Gromyko left, I reported back on the secure phone to President Reagan. Gromyko had talked for an hour and a half straight. He had tried to dominate the meeting through the technique of long, laborious monologues. "If they want a tense relationship, we can deal with that; if they want a constructive relationship, we are also ready for that," I said. Despite Soviet public claims that they had "written off" the Reagan administration, I told the president, "Gromyko clearly wants to keep talking to us."

On Monday I went to the Soviet mission in New York. One argument we did *not* have was over where to meet. We long ago had agreed to alternate when away from Washington or Moscow: one time on U.S. premises, the next time on Soviet premises, no matter what city we were in. The Soviet decor was heavy and somber. The chairs were too deep and soft to be comfortable. In a session lasting over four hours, we agreed that nuclear nonproliferation and Southern Africa were two areas where we might do some quiet, good work. Gromyko and I agreed to use the word "businesslike" to describe the tone of our sessions. "Stiff and formal" would have been more accurate. Gromyko was an actor. He knew the atmosphere he wanted to create, and he tried to impose it by talking severely and at great length. I tried to create a different atmosphere by shorter and more direct statements. The encounter had been a standoff, I felt.

Moscow and Andropov

On November 10 we got word of the death of Leonid Brezhnev and shortly thereafter of Yuri Andropov's accession to power as general secretary of the Communist party. Andropov had long been head of the KGB, also known as the Committee for State Security. This news reminded me of a report that I had received back in August about comments Andropov had made to a delegation of visiting Polish officials. "The Soviet economy is not in much better shape than that of Poland," he allegedly had said. "The Soviet Union faces a serious and increasing problem with [our] youth, who are becoming apolitical, pacifistic, and interested only in themselves." The Soviets had a "church problem," he said, "with more and more young people seeking out the church, perhaps as a means of dissent." Andropov's candid and pessimistic assessments reportedly had shocked the Poles.

The Western media quickly came up with a rich portrait of this man about whom very little was known: he liked jazz, scotch, and racy Hollywood novels, we were told. He was reportedly fond of the saying "A fish's head is the first part to rot." Was he asserting that the leaders were old and useless, while the young were disaffected and idle? Given his KGB background, I thought Andropov would try to reinvigorate the Communist system through stern discipline. I doubted such a tack could succeed.

I was scheduled to leave on Saturday afternoon, November 13, for Moscow, where I would join Vice President Bush, who was heading up the American delegation to Brezhnev's funeral. There we would meet with General Secretary Andropov. Early that same morning, I conducted another of my Saturday seminars, this time on Latin America, in preparation for a trip that the president and I were to take in two weeks' time. At lunch I choked on a fish bone, which I simply could not dislodge. As I continued to cough and cough, people in the room looked increasingly worried. I was worried, too. Finally, after about twenty minutes, Allen Wallis took me downstairs to my car and over to the emergency room of nearby George Washington University Hospital. There I was propped up on an operating table, given a muscle relaxant, and then some barium to swallow. My wife and my daughter Margaret had been summoned. "If there is an obstruction, minor surgery will be necessary," the doctor told me. If the tightness in my chest was *not* caused by an obstruction, that might indicate a more serious problem. When told that I was preparing to leave in a few hours for Moscow, the doctor declared in no uncertain terms that I was *in no condition* to travel.

Twenty minutes later, however, I sent word that I would be leaving for Moscow as planned. Somehow, in the process of swallowing the barium and being shaken around for X-rays, whatever had obstructed my breathing had been dislodged. I was actually feeling quite chipper. "This is all quite reminiscent of Lazarus," Ray Seitz reported back to the State Department.

As I left the hospital, I went over to some ten reporters who had gathered near the door. "Just a bone caught in my throat," I said vigorously but hoarsely. I headed straight to Andrews Air Force Base, where I walked across the tarmac on this windy, chilly day. I was relieved as I boarded the plane and was wheels up, after all.

In Moscow, I met up with Vice President Bush, who had arrived there after breaking off from his trip in Africa. The funeral was the occasion for a major gathering of leaders from throughout the world. The vice president and I called on President Mohammad Zia ul-Haq of Pakistan, and I received German Foreign Minister Hans-Dietrich Genscher, British Foreign Minister Francis Pym, and Chinese Foreign Minister Huang Hua. We all knew Russian ears were in the walls, which made for some odd conversations.

At Red Square on November 15, 1982, the delegations were grouped by political orientation, a kind of global caste system arranged by the Soviets. The democratic governments and those allied with them were placed together. For three hours, we watched the parade go by, militaristic in tone throughout. The speeches echoed that theme. The day was bitterly cold. I had on a pair of long underwear borrowed from Art Hartman. Still I was freezing. "Just be thankful it isn't February," remarked Francis Pym as we all shivered.

Once Brezhnev's coffin had been lowered into its grave, the tone of the ceremony changed drastically. The solemnity of Tchaikovsky was abruptly interrupted by upbeat martial music and a brisk march by of troops. Andropov's eulogy was vigorous, his voice strong and commanding, and he seemed very much in charge, acting as a master of ceremonies of sorts.

When the proceedings ended, everyone walked to St. George's Hall, a large and imposing structure on the Kremlin grounds containing the grand throne room of the czars. Here I handed over my overcoat, wondering whether, in this gigantic throng, I would ever see it again. Then I stood with our delegation in a line winding up a very wide staircase above which hung a huge portrait of Lenin in a dramatic revolutionary pose. We mingled and talked with people we knew or recognized but studiously avoided bumping into a Yasser Arafat, Fidel Castro, or Muammar Qaddafi. A photograph of such a sight could generate the erroneous conclusion that consultations were taking place.

A Soviet protocol officer proceeded down the line and approached Vice

President Bush, asking him and the rest of us in the U.S. delegation to follow. The vice president waved him off, reluctant to be singled out for special treatment and, as a politician, knowing the risks of butting into a line. This was pure George Bush: no special favors. The Soviet official insisted. The vice president, Art Hartman, and I were ushered along the line and placed directly in front of Prime Minister Pierre Trudeau of Canada. With some embarrassment I turned to Trudeau and suggested jokingly that we go together as a "North American delegation." Trudeau laughed, commenting dryly that he was accustomed to "following the Americans." We then shook hands with Andropov, who seemed to me genuinely pleased by the presence of the vice president and the secretary of state in the U.S. delegation.

We met with Andropov late in the afternoon. After assuring us that President Reagan's messages concerning the possibilities of a constructive relationship had been duly noted in the Kremlin, he followed with a litany blaming the United States for the sorry state of relations. Without ever using the words "human rights," Andropov made clear that no one should tell the Soviets how to run their internal affairs. He looked more like a cadaver than did the just-interred Brezhnev, but his mental powers filled the room. He reminded me of Sherlock Holmes's deadly enemy, Professor Moriarty, all brain in a disregarded body. The presence of Andrei Alexandrov-Agentov, who had been Brezhnev's foreign policy adviser, suggested to me continuity in Soviet foreign policy. I was struck by Andropov's comment: "Periodically, excesses of rhetoric will appear in our relationship, but it is important to pay attention to the real business at hand." Andropov had a concise script in front of him but seemed to speak in his own words. The substance was tough, but his manner was straightforward. He made no mention of a summit.

Andropov had covered in twenty minutes what Gromyko and I had spent seven and a half hours discussing in New York. He focused precisely. Gromyko did not speak, although he whispered to his new leader a few times. Andropov seemed to want to get something going. Whether he was constructing a mousetrap, I did not know. I had watched Andropov carefully. He projected immense intelligence and energy. This man was a powerhouse, I thought. I knew that Andropov, as head of the KGB for so long, must have a capacity for brutality as well as for skill in propaganda. I put him down as a formidable adversary.

In the informal banter at the end of the meeting, the vice president said to Andropov: "Well, you and I have something in common in our backgrounds."

"That's right," the general secretary said. "We're the men of peace. Have you ever read the transcripts of the discussions between Shultz and Gromyko—they're the men of war." Everybody laughed except me. At least they read the transcripts, I thought, so it matters to spell out our positions. While the vice president joked about the fact that each had headed his country's intelligence service, I didn't find it humorous. I was uneasy about this new Soviet leader.

In Washington on December 6, Soviet Ambassador Dobrynin asked to see me, if only for a few moments. He proposed that we start U.S.-Soviet discussions, potentially at all levels, beginning with systematic conversations between the two of us.

On December 21, General Secretary Andropov made his first major arms control speech. It contained several proposals but was mainly propaganda designed to affect European politics and to undermine our ability to proceed with deployments should INF negotiations fail in the latter part of 1983. We would, of course, address his ideas. But I told President Reagan, "1983 will be 'the year of the missile.' We will have to have all our wits about us if we are to succeed."

CHAPTER 9

Our Neighborhood

I deliberately planned my first trips out of the country as secretary of state to Canada, Mexico, and countries of Central and South America. I was making a point: we must recognize the importance of our own neighborhood. If relations with our neighbors are positive and the conditions around us are healthy, then the United States will be more secure and prosperous. So my approach was to pay attention. From all my prior experience, I appreciated how important it is to see people on their own turf, where they feel at home and where you meet the people with whom they work. I call this kind of work "gardening," and it is one of the most underrated aspects of diplomacy. The way to keep weeds from overwhelming you is to deal with them constantly and in their early stages. President Reagan was in full agreement with me. In fact, after the plans for my proposed journey south had been approved and were well under way, he called and said he would like to make it a presidential trip.

In the fall of 1982, Mexico was in the process of changing presidents. I had been distressed with the performance of outgoing President José López-Portillo. I had known him when I was secretary of the treasury in 1974. I was as surprised and disappointed as anyone when he suddenly nationalized the Mexican banks. He had seemed sensible. I heard that he walked off with a huge fortune. President Reagan and I hoped for something better from incoming President Miguel de la Madrid, and we wanted him to know that we were ready and anxious to work cooperatively with him. To make this point, we arranged for meetings with him on October 8, 1982, in San Diego and Tijuana, with the movement between an American and a Mexican city designed to show mutual interest and respect. There were plenty of issues to work on: trade, investment, immigration (legal and illegal), drug traffic, pollution along the border. We wanted to engage Mexico's new president. President Reagan and I were in fact both impressed with this modest, straightforward, yet strong and insistent man. I felt that we had made a good start.

My own first trip out of the country as secretary of state had been to La

Sapinière in Canada for a NATO foreign ministers' meeting held the previous week. Later in October, I went to Ottawa. I was acutely conscious of Canada—by far our largest trading partner, much larger than Japan—and I was frustrated that so few people in Washington appreciated Canada's significance to us. The new foreign minister, Allan MacEachen, was an acquaintance from my days as a young professor of economics at MIT, when he was a graduate student in my department there. I told President Reagan when I returned that we had our differences with Canada: over cross-border pollution, congressional initiatives that would threaten Canadian exports, and Canadian investment and energy policy. But, despite the problems, our shared objectives were of far greater importance than our differences. We were like-minded on the Middle East peace process, the importance of reaching an allied consensus on East-West economic policy, and on the need to combat protectionism. To give the U.S.-Canadian relationship the attention it deserved, I would meet informally with the Canadian foreign minister on a quarterly basis to address problems and opportunities.

The agreement to make a regular, scheduled effort to attend to "gardening" was the key outcome of my trip, but I found its importance hard to convey to the traveling press. On the airplane heading home, virtually all the questions were about the Middle East. "Why are you wasting time on Canada?" was the attitude. Still, in these quarterly meetings, which were especially productive after Brian Mulroney and Joe Clark came to office, I was determined to work through innumerable problems, large and small, dealing with them early on and transmitting the message to the Canadians that the United States recognized the importance of our relationship and would spend time and effort on it. The policy would pay dividends to both countries, but it wasn't easy to sell.

The hot spot of the hemisphere was El Salvador, where we supported a government struggling to be a democracy in the face of guerrillas on the left and generals on the right. Support from the Soviet Union via Cuba and Nicaragua provided the Communists in the countryside with ample military and logistic supplies. These guerrillas could be cruel terrorists. So could the military forces of El Salvador. A shocking number of killings by right-wing death squads spread havoc as well. Our aid was conditioned by Congress on progress in human rights practices in El Salvador and came in increments, calling for decisions on the next installment every six months. The State Department had to certify progress toward democracy and human rights as a condition for the release of funds. And I, as secretary of state, had to defend that certification against informed and critical questioning.

Frustrations, ambivalence, and political tension were evident both in El Salvador and in the United States as Salvadoran President Alvaro Magaña and Minister of Defense José Guillermo García were pitted against rightist members of the military linked to Constitutional Assembly President Roberto D'Aubuisson. We had to find the way to nourish democracy in El Salvador, improve the army's ability to deal effectively with the guerrillas, and, at the same time, persuade the army leaders and their right-wing supporters that violations of human rights by them would not be tolerated. This was no easy task.

We emphasized the importance of economic development in this impoverished part of the world. President Reagan had set out early in his administration a strategy emphasizing trade and investment in a market setting as the key to economic progress. He developed this theme in successive presidential speeches and comments at the Ottawa economic summit in July 1981, the International Meeting on Cooperation and Development in Cancún, Mexico, in October 1981, and, fully formed as a Caribbean Basin Initiative, before the Organization of American States (OAS) in February 1982. Legislation was proposed to Congress in March 1982.

The program as set out to the OAS would give exports from the countries of the Caribbean Basin, with the exception of textiles and apparel, duty-free treatment for twelve years and provide tax incentives to encourage investment in the region and a $350 million supplemental aid program to help with special projects. Technical assistance in private-sector business techniques and in methods to promote investment opportunities would be available. We wanted to work closely with Mexico, Venezuela, and Canada to coordinate our own development measures with the vital contributions of other countries in our hemisphere and to draw funds as well from the Europeans, the Japanese, and the multinational lending institutions.

The president also called the attention of the OAS to military-security problems: "Economic progress cannot be made while guerrillas systematically burn, bomb, and destroy bridges, farms, and power and transportation systems." He pointed to the Soviet-backed "totalitarian left" in Cuba, Grenada, and Nicaragua as the source of the security threat and called for security assistance to the free nations of the Caribbean.

My first appearance on Capitol Hill as secretary of state had come on August 2, 1982, before the Senate Finance Committee on behalf of the Caribbean Basin Initiative. "The program is not just good medicine; it is vital," I said. After a complex legislative battle, the sum of $350 million did become available to the Caribbean Basin countries on September 15. The trade and investment aspects of the program came harder: special interests are always wary and watchful of potentially competitive imports.[1]
By the fall of 1982, we had a positive program on the table, a part of it in

1. By August 5, 1983, these critical parts of the program had become law.

hand, and reasonable prospects for the balance of the program. It gave the president and me a strong basis for our talks with leaders in the region.

My First Major Trip with the President

On November 30, 1982, two weeks after returning from the Brezhnev funeral in Moscow, I set off with President Reagan on a four-country swing to South and Central America. The problems there were difficult and in some areas explosive. Ronald Reagan was a master of friendly diplomacy, imparting a strong, clear view on thorny problems with a light touch that could make friends, command respect, and cement relationships. He was easy to like.

I peered out the window of *Air Force One* as we flew in darkness over the unseen forests of Brazil. The moon was white and full, and the wing of the airplane gleamed like ice. Below I saw flashing rolls of heat lightning in the clouds high above the forest. The president came into our compartment with a letter in his hand, which he proceeded to read to us. It was from an American sailor in the Pacific who was describing his thoughts as he participated in the rescue of Vietnamese boat people discovered adrift on the ocean. The letter was sentimental and patriotic, and we were quiet as the president read aloud. He was genuinely moved. This impressed me. Afterward, the president chatted for a while. He said he had read the biography of Brazilian President João Baptista Figueiredo. "I like him already," he announced. "He was in the cavalry, too!"

Brasilia, our first stop, was spacious and spare. The architecture and city plan, once considered futuristic and fabulous, now reminded me of institutional project housing, cold and dehumanized. There were few traffic lights, but not much traffic either. I went to the Alvorada Palace on the first morning. The exterior columns of the palace were crescent-shaped— a graceful abstract of the sails of the early Portuguese explorers. The interior was a series of open reception rooms resembling attractive hotel lobbies. The French doors opening onto the terrace were twenty feet high. Breakfast was served in the presidential palace for all the key people, and I went with all my papers prepared for the day. After breakfast I had about half an hour of dead time before we were to leave for the first stop, the American embassy, where the president and I would greet the Americans stationed in Brazil. I sat myself down in a room that looked to be directly on the path between the presidential quarters and the entrance to the palace, thinking that I would know when it was time to leave by the commotion that would be stirred up by the president's movement. Everyone else disappeared, and I worked away, alone.

Suddenly I became aware that it was dead quiet. I looked out the window.

There I saw the last car of the presidential motorcade departing from the palace. The Secret Service, unknown and unannounced to me, had taken the president down a back elevator to the garage where his motorcade was located. No one had clued me in on this. I rushed out of the palace, spotted a lonely cab across the street, hailed it, and managed to get across the idea without knowing any Portuguese that I wanted him to "follow that motorcade!" And he did.

The presidential motorcade was so long—at least thirty-five vehicles—that it seemed the first car would arrive at its destination before the last one had left the point of departure. The motorcade moved slowly, so we were able to catch up. As the final car in the motorcade pulled up at the American embassy, my cab was on its tail. I jumped out, tossed the driver a twenty-dollar bill, and ran forward past scores and scores of cars to our embassy building, where I saw Ambassador Tony Motley at the podium, in the process of introducing me. Just as he finished, I stepped forward.

No one had even noticed that I had missed the motorcade. Then, and thereafter, I was fully aware that on a presidential trip the secretary of state is nobody. The Secret Service couldn't care less. Although I was surprised by this experience (after all, when I was secretary of the treasury, these guys reported to me!), I was glad I learned the lesson in Brasilia, where a cab driver came to my rescue.

In the course of our four days in Brazil, a genuinely warm relationship emerged between the two presidents. President Figueiredo had an agreeable, easygoing manner. He and Ronald Reagan hit it off immediately: pure chemistry. That sent an important signal down the line to bureaucracies that had previously produced a frosty relationship.

We moved during the visit from a relationship of chilly stalemate, held over from years of the Carter administration, to one of problem solving. And there were plenty of problems to work on with this country that accounted for roughly half of South America in terms of geography, population, and GNP.

Our visit in Brazil was punctuated with a fine state banquet at the Itamaraty Palace. President Reagan was tired. He concluded his toast by saying how pleased he was to be in "Bolivia," bringing forth an outcry in the press. The next day we traveled to São Paulo, a city of around 9 million people that accounted for almost half the domestic production of Brazil. We swooshed over field upon field of skyscrapers down onto a helicopter pad near the governor's palace for a speech and reception. The Brazilians have a sense of humor. When we landed, we were greeted by a huge banner that read "The people of Bolivia welcome the President of Canada." The Brazilian chief of protocol blanched. Ronald Reagan roared.

Soon we were off again on *Marine One, Nighthawk One,* and *Nighthawk Two*, beating through heavy fog. We could not see at all, and there was a vague sense of apprehension until we broke out of the clouds. We all said the president should not be flying in this kind of weather. I thought none of us should be flying in this kind of weather.

The next morning, I found a game of chicken under way between Assistant Secretary of State Tom Enders and NSC adviser Bill Clark. Clark didn't like the arrangements at our next stop: Bogotá, Colombia. We had seen a copy of the speech President Belisario Betancur intended to give when we were in Colombia. Clark didn't like one of the passages in it: condescending. Get it changed. Clark threatened to recommend that we overfly the country and go directly to Costa Rica. I didn't take him seriously. Our ambassador, Tom Boyatt, had already been in action. Some assurances about Betancur's speech were soon received from the Colombians.

Nevertheless, the scene when we arrived was chaotic. The presidential palace was surrounded by thousands of troops. Drug traffickers had blown up the Palace of Justice, home of the Colombian Supreme Court, in protest against extradition to the United States of one of their leaders. Jeeps with mounted machine guns were positioned at each street corner. Security was so tight that the inside of the palace was a chambered nautilus—once in a room, you could not get out. We were met with confusion, protesting Secret Service agents, bewildered guards. Finally, everything settled down, and the meeting began.

I had traveled to Colombia several times as a private citizen and businessman, but never in an atmosphere as tense as this. We talked about the importance of the fight against drugs and the drug traffickers as well as against the terrorists who did their dirty work. We talked about economic problems and about Central America. President Betancur seemed to want to be the mediator there, settle everything, win the Nobel Prize. His attitude *was* condescending. He was not really Ronald Reagan's kind of guy. The two men had a civil conversation, but the press came away with the impression that Betancur was strongly critical of Reagan's Latin America policy.

We arrived at night in Costa Rica, a model democracy, the wealthiest country per capita in Central America, a nation that had long ago eliminated its armed forces. Two rows of bleachers were filled with children waving Costa Rican and American flags. They were, I learned, from the George Washington School, the Thomas Jefferson School, and the Abraham Lincoln School. The Costa Ricans were very pro-American. Eyes moistened as "The Star-Spangled Banner" was delightfully tortured by their band of bright-eyed and enthusiastic musicians. The president instinctively went over to the children. It was a genuine gesture of warmth, not a "photo op."

In our chopper, *Marine One*, the next day, we passed over coffeed hills and banana groves under clear skies. Costa Rica has soft breezes and is lushly green. We experienced the red-and-gold splendor of the Teatro Nacional, an ornate nineteenth-century replica, I was told, of the Paris Opera House. I noticed a Secret Service agent who sat motionless in a tiny opera box, looking like a portrait. President Luis Monge delivered his welcoming speech.

President Reagan rose to give his return address. Suddenly, a man in the lower balcony leaped to his feet and began to read loudly his manifesto. He was a Communist member of the Costa Rican legislature. The rest of the crowd began to hiss and shout him down. They stamped their feet on the wood floor. They cried out, "*Cállate*," which means "shut up," and "*Huevón*," street language which means "big-balled bastard," an insult, I was told, because Costa Rican lore has it that large testicles indicate idiocy. The president was patient and unperturbed. The man finished. The president said that in a Communist country such freedom of speech would not be allowed. A tumultuous and spontaneous cheer filled the chamber.

We stopped in San Pedro Sula, Honduras, on the way back home, expressing by the president's presence and in his words our support for democracy, freedom, economic development, and the rule of law.

After we took off for Washington, I had a good stiff drink and dinner, then put my seat back, and went out like a light. The president came back to my cabin, took a look at me, and called the White House photographer. He struck a pose as though imploring me. The flashbulbs popped, but I never stirred. A couple of days later, the president surprised me with a print. There he was with his arms outstretched, and there I was dead to the world. He had inscribed on it, "But George, I have to talk to you— the Russians are calling!"

The president's idea from the beginning had been that he wanted to "drop in on friends." He wanted to listen to them, not lecture them. He was convinced, as was I, that foreign policy must pay special attention to our own neighborhood, our own hemisphere. We had—amid all the tumultuous issues so demanding of our time and energy in the second half of 1982—made a start. Canadians, Mexicans, and the people of Central and South American countries could see us reaching out to them and to their problems. We had demonstrated that we were ready to work with the Spanish-speaking countries of South America; we had made a positive start with Brazil; and we had carried, as dramatically as possible, the banner of democracy and the rule of law to show our beleaguered friends in Central America that we were on their side.

CHAPTER 10

Damage Control:
The Siberian Pipeline Dispute

I faced a poisonous problem as I took office as secretary of state: a dispute was raging between the United States and our European allies over the building of a 3,500-mile pipeline extending from western Siberia, north of the Arctic Circle, to seven countries of Western Europe—a huge commercial deal between European companies, with support from their governments, and the Soviet Union. Europe would receive gas and with it the vulnerability that stemmed from a degree of dependence on energy supplied from Siberian fields in the Soviet Union. By the end of the 1980s, Europe's dependence on Soviet natural gas supplies would rise on average from 15 to 20 percent. The Soviets would receive European and American help (credits, engineering, critical supplies) in constructing the pipeline. And as gas was delivered, they would receive hard currency, estimated to amount eventually to $10 billion to $12 billion a year, with which to buy Western goods, potentially including high-technology items. American companies were involved, along with their licensees and subsidiaries in Europe. Good jobs would be generated at a time when jobs were hard to get in the United States and in Europe. Unemployment in mid-1982 was high: 14 percent in Britain, 9 percent in France, almost 8 percent in West Germany, the highest level since 1954. And in the United States, unemployment rose to over 10 percent by the last half of 1982.

The Europeans decided in September 1981, after a long period of argument with us, to go ahead with their participation in the pipeline. Although the pipeline itself was a huge venture, it was only the tip of an iceberg. President Reagan was far more inclined than the Europeans to restrict trade with the Soviets, especially trade that carried with it access to Western technology. The president's prohibition on December 29, 1981, of direct involvement by American firms in the pipeline project affected some sixty U.S. companies. Caterpillar Tractor lost a $90 million order for pipe-laying equipment, and General Electric an order worth $175 million. But the real crisis arose in the acrimonious aftermath of the Versailles economic summit in June 1982, when Defense Secretary Cap Weinberger, CIA Director Bill Casey, and NSC adviser Bill Clark persuaded the president, on June 18, 1982, to extend the reach of the U.S. sanctions to the licensees and subsidiaries of American firms located in Europe. Bill Clark called the decision meeting when Secretary of State Haig, a strong opponent of this action, was in New York to see Foreign Minister Gromyko. Haig was informed only after the fact; he was livid.

The response from Europe was swift and sharp. British Prime Minister Margaret Thatcher, the president's strongest overseas supporter, said in the House of Commons, "The question is whether one very powerful nation can prevent existing contracts being fulfilled; I think it is wrong to do that." She and others focused on the problems of breaking existing contracts (retroactivity) and on the effort to force U.S. views on others by an order prohibiting the fulfillment of contracts by licensees and subsidiaries of U.S. companies operating abroad (extraterritoriality). "The outcries from the western European allies have been loud and angry, and the prestige of every major leader in the western alliance is now publicly impaled on this escalating dispute," wrote reporter Murrey Marder in the *Washington Post* on July 5. "Diplomats on both sides of the Atlantic are driven to find an elusive compromise, save an extraordinary amount of face and avoid shattering the western alliance. George P. Shultz, designated successor to Alexander M. Haig Jr., inherits a central American role in grappling with what a senior State Department official described last week as a 'monstrous problem.' "

The Soviets must have enjoyed the spectacle as the discord grew in America and Europe. Their encouragement and endorsement of the Polish government's crackdown on Solidarity had resulted in actions that were producing acrimony with our NATO allies at the very time when critical decisions were approaching. For 1983 would inevitably be the "year of the missile," the year when negotiations on intermediate-range nuclear missiles would come to a head: either in the form of a U.S.-Soviet arms control agreement or else in the actual deployment of these sensitive U.S. nuclear weapons on the soil of the five European basing countries (West Germany, Great Britain, Italy, Belgium, Netherlands), all of them involved in the pipeline controversy. There was also a Japanese dimension. Japan was in the process of negotiating with the Soviets to develop oil and gas prospects on nearby Sakhalin Island. The Japanese had been assured of, and were depending on, access to oil and gas equipment from the United States. Now they could see their project going down the drain too.

Confronting the Problem

This is where I had come in. How could we resolve this divisive issue in a constructive way, and quickly, before rancor so embittered the atmosphere that the cohesion needed to reach the hard decisions ahead was deeply impaired? I came to this subject with strongly held views of my own: as an economist I was skeptical of the effectiveness of sanctions, especially when applied unilaterally. The market is global and is simply too strong for sanctions applied by one country acting alone to have a decisive impact. The country applying sanctions can therefore wind up damaging its own trade more than that of the target country. My criticism of what I had called the Carter administration's "lightswitch diplomacy" had been quoted back to me in my confirmation hearings. In a speech to the Business Council in October 1978, I had said, "There is apparently a perception in our government that individual trades can be turned on and off like a lightswitch to induce changes in the domestic and foreign policies of a host government. As a result, the position of U.S. goods in world markets is eroding as our trading partners, increasingly, see evidence that we cannot be counted on as a reliable supplier. Increasingly, when the diplomat flicks the switch, the light will not go on. It will not go on because private firms cannot afford the cost, cannot make the investments to create the bargaining chips and then have the bargaining chips used. And self-respecting trading partners will not put up with it." I had not changed my view.

I knew President Reagan was uneasy about the combination of increased European dependence on Soviet energy, new credits to the Soviets, and prospective additions to their foreign exchange. Yet I also knew his respect for market forces. As secretary of the treasury in the Nixon administration, I had struggled with the issues of East-West trade, and a decade later, on the basis of discussions with heads of the Summit Seven countries on a presidential mission in May 1982, I had reported to Ronald Reagan, "Your views about credit to the Russians and their satellites have made a real impact and I sensed that sentiment on this issue is coming your way. No one will defend subsidizing the Soviet economy."

Soon after I became secretary of state, West German Chancellor Helmut Schmidt was my guest in the United States, first at my home and then at the Bohemian Grove, some sixty miles north of San Francisco. There, in a setting of magnificent redwoods and natural amphitheaters with great acoustics for musicals, we spent a long, relaxed weekend filled with candid and far-reaching discussion. Also present were Henry Kissinger and Prime Minister Lee Kuan Yew of Singapore. Schmidt was tremendously resentful about "extraterritoriality and retroactivity" and greatly concerned about the deployment of INF missiles. "Germany cannot be the only country to deploy," he said. "We must look beyond the pipeline dispute for positive things." Helmut and I managed to convey that more positive and constructive tone in an unusual joint press conference in San Francisco on July 22. The press expected an argument, but what they heard instead was a recognition of a problem and a desire to solve it. "Don't let us overdramatize the pipeline affair," Schmidt said. "We have some family problems, and we're going to overcome them."

I returned to Washington knowing full well that resolving the pipeline problem was a top priority for me. There was no reason to expect the Europeans to back down. At best, our sanctions might slow down the project while American parts and other American supplies were engineered out, itself an action setting a terrible precedent for our export capabilities. An unreliable supplier becomes a pariah in what is, increasingly, a truly global economy. At a Senior Interagency Group meeting on August 5, Cap Weinberger was militant. In response to comments about some of the legal issues involved, he said, "I don't want to hear about legalities." Cap was against the very idea of a negotiation to resolve this bitter dispute with our allies.

The next day, while I was having lunch with the president, I pointed out the long-term negative consequences to U.S. trade that would result from our current actions. I recounted my experience in the Nixon administration when export controls were imposed on soybeans. American farmers, I said, *never* recovered the markets lost because of that decision. Our soybean farmers no longer hold the dominant position in the Japanese market and other markets that they once did.

Truth and Consequences

Soon the momentum of events created new facts. Creusot-Loire, a French licensee of its U.S. partner, Dresser Industries, shipped sanctioned products, three sixty-ton compressors, on August 26. Dresser France had a gun to its head. France's minister of industry, Jean-Pierre Chevénement, threatened to "requisition" the company facilities if it refused to honor its contract. The British firm John Brown shipped gas turbines the next day. The Germans and the Italians were shipping, too. We would have to retaliate by issuing "denial orders" to the U.S. firms involved, prohibiting them from further pipeline-related dealings with their European subsidiaries and licensees.

With the fat now in the fire, even Cap Weinberger agreed that we should move quickly to engage the Europeans in working out the problem. We were willing to negotiate, but the aspects of our sanctions that were retroactive and extraterritorial were fighting issues to the Europeans and Japanese. We would seek to achieve a stronger agreement against subsidized credits and sales of strategic technology to the Soviets and their satellites, combined with greater sensitivity in Europe about not being overly dependent on energy supplies originating in the Soviet Union.

I recommended to President Reagan that we proceed with the denial orders against companies that violated our sanctions but also recommended that we proceed with immediate exploratory talks with our allies. The president agreed, with the caveat that we not seem "overly anxious" to talk. British Foreign Minister Francis Pym had called me from London suggesting that he might convene a meeting to discuss these issues. The president liked the idea that the Europeans would call the meeting rather than us. I agreed.

Our retaliatory actions brought home another reminder that government intervention in private market arrangements produces unanticipated consequences. Our initial action, in response to the first shipment in violation of the president's order, was against Creusot-Loire and its American partner, Dresser. I called French Foreign Minister Claude Cheysson in advance of the announcement to point out that our action was carefully limited to the specific cases and companies in question. He asked me whether our action against the British firm John Brown would be the same when they shipped. I assured him that it would.

On August 30, my colleagues and I confronted the likelihood that a straight denial order would probably put John Brown into bankruptcy. The company was totally dependent on its American relationships. I could see that we should "clarify" our denial orders against Dresser and Creusot-Loire—to narrow them to apply only to oil and gas technology. This would not really affect the impact of the sanctions in France but would make the parallel action against John Brown manageable.

I called Commerce Secretary Mac Baldrige, whose department actually issued the orders, explained the situation, and got his agreement to a joint memo of recommendation to the president. In the meantime, I explained to NSC adviser Bill Clark that this strategy was a "clarification, not a softening," of the president's position. He came on board.

Within an hour of sending this memo to the White House, a call came in to Baldrige from Clyde Farnsworth of the *New York Times* seeking confirmation of this whole agreement. The person who leaked the news no doubt wanted to stop my effort at damage control by implying that the president was being urged to "back down." It was the first time on my watch, but far from the last, that an effort was made to derail a policy through a leak. I had my suspicions of the source (somewhere in the Defense Department), but nothing definitive materialized.

Running Room and Forward Movement

The NATO foreign ministers had agreed to spend an early October weekend at La Sapinière in Canada. There would be no staff, no set agenda, no need for a communiqué. This, I knew, would be my moment of opportunity to resolve the pipeline impasse with the Europeans.

First I needed running room from the president. At a Senior Interagency Group meeting on September 16, I argued my points: "The sanctions are a wasting asset because substitutes for U.S. products will become available. The longer the sanctions last, the less they mean. They will unravel; that is predictable. American industry is against them, and so are most members of Congress on both sides of the aisle. We may be able to achieve what the president sought and failed to get before the extended sanctions were imposed. Remember the arguments at Versailles and other fruitless efforts to persuade the Europeans to join us in a stronger trade regime with the Soviets. Now we may be able to bring it off." Treasury Secretary Don Regan, in the chair, was helpful. Cap Weinberger finally came around, although on the basis of a written and detailed set of instructions. He wanted me on a short leash. This measure of agreement then went to President Reagan. He was increasingly on my side of the issue.

At La Sapinière, the combination of actions in defiance of U.S. sanctions by a few European firms and the strong retaliatory response by the president had a sobering impact. The NATO orientation at La Sapinière reminded us all that the issue should be defused before the critical year 1983, with its controversial missile deployments, arrived. The informal setting allowed me to talk to key people one at a time and then to put forward to the group the outline of a U.S. position. The problem had many dimensions: reliable trading relations, extraterritorial reach of U.S. foreign policy, the cohesion of the NATO alliance, the coming year of the missile. My aim was to get the solution to emerge from the mist.

I paid special attention to French Foreign Minister Claude Cheysson. He was informed, articulate, and combative, yet friendly. I knew from prior experience that the French always have a special point of view, often frustrating, but if I took the time to understand it, I could save myself a lot of grief. The French insisted that the stronger regime we sought governing trade and credits with the Soviets should be thought of as completely separate from the pipeline issue. Cheysson and the other Europeans regarded our sanctions as wrong to begin with, and the French would not go along with my idea of a solution: the United States would withdraw the sanctions, and the Europeans would adhere to a strengthened trade and credit regime. There should be, he argued, *no* linkage. I had no problem with separating the matters as long as the new, stronger trade and credit regimes were accepted by all the allies, including the French. I felt that we had reached a meeting of the minds, but as events unfolded, I learned to my distress that Cheysson could not deliver on our understandings because he did not necessarily speak for his president, François Mitterrand.

Out of the discussion among the NATO foreign ministers emerged a "nonpaper," setting out points of potential agreement. A nonpaper is a handy diplomatic device to facilitate precise discussion on an issue without the impediment of labeling the working paper as official and thereby making it more difficult to modify positions in the course of discussion.

I returned to Washington feeling good about my progress. I felt I was now in sight of achieving all of our objectives: a commitment to stronger controls over the sale of strategically important goods to the Soviet Union through a reinvigorated and more decisive COCOM (Coordinating Committee for Multilateral Export Controls),[1] with special attention to oil and gas technology; an agreement that other trade would not carry credits that subsidized the Soviets; a willingness to study alternative energy sources to avoid further European dependence on Soviet gas. The Europeans did not want a generalized trade war with the Soviets, and they let it be known that they expected the United States to abide by this "no subsidy" rule when it came to our own sales of U.S. agricultural commodities, as the United States was a huge supplier of grain to the Soviets.

I presented the results I had achieved to an October 15 National Security Council meeting called on the subject. "I don't know that this is enough to give up the pipeline sanctions," Cap Weinberger said, to my utter astonishment.

"You were here when we agreed on this approach, Cap," I said. This effort to block the whole process, to go back on a strategy that we had already agreed on was infuriating to me. "Look, I can get all this to fall apart if that's what you want," I responded.

My statement was greeted with a chorus of "No! No!" President Reagan gave me the green light to proceed.

After the meeting and back at State, I told Ray Seitz, "Cap loves those sanctions. He thinks the allies are like the air traffic controllers. But we can't fire the allies. We need them." I had known Cap well since the days when he was my deputy at the Office of Management and Budget and, later, when he was Bechtel's general counsel and I was its president. Cap before had always worked in a subordinate capacity to mine. Now we were on an equal footing organizationally. He was able, charming, and stubborn. His relationship with Ronald Reagan was close and considerably predated mine. He had been Governor Reagan's director of finance in California.

1. The Paris-based voluntary organization, founded in 1949, whose charter was to identify goods of potential critical military use by the Soviet Union and its satellites and other Communist countries and agree on restrictions of sales of such goods. Fourteen of the fifteen NATO countries were members. Iceland, because of its small size, was not. Japan joined in the early 1950s.

I respected and liked Cap, even though, as events unfolded, I argued with him increasingly across an ever-widening range of issues.

I moved forward during the next month through a negotiation based on the nonpaper and conducted through the European and the Japanese ambassadors in Washington. By Friday, November 12, we seemed to have an agreement. We cabled the European capitals and Tokyo saying that President Reagan would like to announce the agreement at noon on Saturday, November 13, in his regular radio talk and that he would also announce that we were lifting our sanctions. He would be careful *not* to link the two in any explicit way. We asked for replies by 8:30 the next morning. By that time we had heard affirmatively from all except the French. What's new? I thought. The president wanted to go ahead, anyway. At 10:45 A.M. I was called out of a Saturday seminar: Mitterrand's aide, Jacques Attali, said that the French wanted to "reopen the text" of the nonpaper.

I was amazed, as were the ambassadors of the other countries, when informed of this news. The French objected to having the lifting of the sanctions and the announcement of the trade agreement mentioned in the same speech, even though the wording would not link the two. I called Bill Clark at 11:00 A.M. and argued against making the announcement. If the president gave the speech before we had brought the French on board, we would lose all our leverage with them. "If we simply wait out the French, all the pressure from the other allies will fall on them. If we go ahead, the pressure is off, and we fail to accomplish what we intended." I knew an alternative speech on crime was already in the works at the White House. I could tell Clark's temperature was rising. So was mine. "Sit tight," I told Clark. "Let the president blow his top if he has to, but have him give the speech on crime." The president was set to go, however, and he did. He was tired of the sanctions issue and was convinced now that they were becoming counterproductive, as I had been arguing. The president had tried, unsuccessfully, to reach Mitterrand from Camp David before his speech at noon. At one o'clock I heard that Mitterrand still had not returned the president's call. Headlines in the *New York Times* on November 14, 1982, told the story: "REAGAN LIFTS THE SANCTIONS ON SALES FOR SOVIET PIPELINE; REPORTS ACCORD WITH ALLIES; FRENCH DENY ROLE; But President Says There Is Unity and Calls New Position Stronger."

The president's speech contained the essence of the agreement that I had painstakingly worked out: "First, each partner has affirmed that no new contracts for the purchase of Soviet natural gas will be signed or approved during the course of our study of alternative Western sources of energy. Second, we and our partners will strengthen existing controls on the transfer of strategic items to the Soviet Union. Third, we will establish without delay procedures for monitoring financial relations with the Soviet Union and will work to harmonize our export credit policies." He went on, "The understanding we and our partners have reached and the actions we are taking reflect our mutual determination to overcome differences and strengthen our cohesion. I believe this new agreement is a victory for all the allies. It puts in place a much needed policy in the economic area to complement our policies in the security area."

The president's announcement ended the controversial part of the pipeline sanctions, but the positive program we wanted and that the president announced had not yet been fully agreed upon. We had lost our leverage with the French: the sanctions were gone. I would have to take a different approach. With sanctions lifted, the French objection to linking the removal of the sanctions with the announcement of agreement on a program to regulate trade with the Soviets became a nonissue. I could now say to the French, "You have no excuses. Come on board."

In Moscow soon thereafter, on the occasion of Brezhnev's funeral, and unknown to me at the time, Danish Foreign Minister Uffe Ellemann-Jensen, then chairman of the European Community, took the unusual step of convening his French, German, Italian, and British colleagues in the secure room of the German embassy. He "considered it essential to back up the American Secretary of State," he told me later as he shared with me his notes of the session: "It became clear, however, during the discussion, that the majority felt that what ought to count was that sanctions had in fact now been lifted. A positive outcome had been obtained, and a trade war had been avoided. In the light of this, one ought not to think too much of the events preceding this result. In other words: Let bygones be bygones." In the end, said Ellemann-Jensen, all were "in full agreement on the substance," though "my French colleague had to contact his president before he could go this far."

Paris and the Pipeline

On Tuesday, December 14, after attending the annual meeting of NATO foreign ministers in Brussels, I left for Paris to complete the pipeline negotiations. I stayed in the U.S. ambassador's residence on the Rue du Faubourg St. Honoré, next to the British embassy and just down the street from the Elysée Palace, where I had a long, private meeting with President Mitterrand. Foreign Minister Cheysson was not present. I still could not quite get full agreement pinned down. So, knowing French sensitivities, I confined myself at an afternoon press conference to saying I was confident that the "right framework" would be found to coordinate U.S. and allied economic policies toward the Soviets.

The last event of the day was a large black-tie dinner in the magnificent rooms of the Quai d'Orsay, the French Foreign Ministry. Seeing it strictly as a social event, John Hughes, my press spokesman, had told our traveling press corps to take the night off and have a good time in Paris. No news.

The Quai d'Orsay was built for Louis Philippe and completed during the reign of Napoleon III. Its ornate ceiling is so heavily adorned with gold leaf, marble, cherubs, and crystal chandeliers that I wondered whether the ceiling might collapse from the sheer weight of it all. We dined at a table twenty yards long that glittered in silver, and we were treated to four fine wines and champagne toasts. My dinner conversation with Cheysson enabled me to work out the details with him of the framework I had referred to in my earlier press conference, elaborating upon and giving a further push to the program announced by President Reagan a month earlier. "Are you ready to state French agreements to these positions publicly?" I asked Cheysson. He said he was. That was precisely what I had sought. I wanted to close this issue out on the spot, so I persuaded Cheysson to join me in a joint press conference.

I called over John Hughes, who immediately sent out SOS messages to the press corps all over Paris. Soon most of the traveling press, along with some French reporters, assembled in another ornate room near the banquet hall. As Bernard Gwertzman described the proceedings in the *New York Times* on December 15: "The specific details were disclosed at an unusual news conference held close to midnight by Secretary of State George P. Shultz and Foreign Minister Claude Cheysson of France at the Quai d'Orsay, the French Foreign Ministry, after a black-tie dinner. The two men, apparently concerned that the degree of agreement reached by the two governments, which have been at odds in recent weeks, had not been made clear during an afternoon news conference by Mr. Shultz, decided to reveal more of the details. . . . Mr. Shultz, with Mr. Cheysson nodding in assent, outlined six points that are to form the basis for an overall alliance strategy on East-West relations. . . . The overall impact of the developments today suggested that the sharp dispute of recent weeks over East-West trade between France and the United States had been significantly eased."

The pipeline dispute, and the associated irritant with Japan, had finally come to an end. I was relieved that a serious problem had been defused. We could now look ahead to the critical year 1983 with a renewed cohesion in the alliance.

I had learned some important lessons about Ronald Reagan and his administration in my labors to resolve this rancorous dispute. Cap Weinberger exhibited a technique he used on many issues before and after: take a position and never change. He seemed to feel that the outcome, even if different from his position, would likely move further in his direction when he was difficult and intransigent. In many a battle, this technique served him well. But over time, as more and more people understood the technique, its effectiveness waned, and Cap's capacity to be part of final solutions declined. Another lesson concerned the pervasive presence of leaks. Leakers have many motives: general ill will, opposition to a policy or action, desire to curry favor with the press, self-importance. The problem of leaks had to be kept in mind, even though it was usually impossible to identify the culprits. Sometimes that was not even desired. As President Kennedy once remarked, "The ship of state is the only ship that leaks from the top."

My own views on the importance of the sanctity of contracts were also strongly reinforced as I saw how deep the resentment in Europe ran against being forced to break contractual agreements. We do American industry tremendous harm when we cause our companies to be viewed as unreliable suppliers. The issue of extraterritorial reach would not go away. I could see that as the global nature of trade and investment continued to increase, the problem would become ever greater. As foreign investment in the United States grew, we could very well find the shoe on the other foot.

Perhaps most important, Ronald Reagan, I had learned, could be perfectly comfortable in taking a highly controversial and even unpopular stand when he felt he was right. He was also willing to use a controversial position to bargain for other desired objectives. I saw President Reagan as a man ready to make trade-offs, a man who enjoyed and had a feel for the rhythm and timing of the bargaining process. This hard-line president combined a negotiator's instinct and common sense with tough views and staying power. But I also saw that once he got the bit in his teeth, he and his White House staff could act precipitously and thus complicate the achievement of our goals.

Allies and Friends in Europe

The United States, I knew, had no hope of dealing successfully with the Soviet Union and the turmoil around the world unless there was solidarity in the NATO alliance. I had forged some close relationships through the tough and traumatic process of defusing the Siberian pipeline dispute, and building on them would be crucial.

I planned a December 1982 visit to Europe, centered on the annual NATO foreign ministers' meeting in Brussels, to focus on the countries (Belgium, Great Britain, Netherlands, Italy, and West Germany) where our INF missiles would be deployed if our negotiations with the Soviets failed to produce an INF agreement by the end of 1983. In addition, I would go to France in the hope of finishing the final aspect of negotiation left over from the Siberian pipeline dispute and then to Spain, a fledgling democracy where a new government had just taken office.

Early Impressions from My Treasury Days

Germany was to be my first stop. My first experiences with Germany came from my time as treasury secretary, from June 1972 through May 1974, momentous years for international economic matters and particularly the international monetary system. Just as I was starting in at the Treasury, Helmut Schmidt shifted from his role as minister of defense in the West German government to become minister of finance. As it happened, Schmidt was scheduled to visit the United States, and he requested a meeting with me. When he arrived at my office, I saw immediately that we could communicate directly and easily. Our discussion was far ranging: the always controversial system of exchange rates, German-American relations, NATO, the Soviet Union, political conditions in our countries, as well as our personal outlooks. His penetrating intellect and great warmth and humor impressed me as those of a leader with an unusual breadth of vision. He was, I saw, both creative and energetic, deeply conscious of Germany's history and its place in history.

My tenure at the Treasury was a time when oil prices skyrocketed and immense financial flows to and from Saudi Arabia and other oil-producing nations rearranged financial markets on a global scale. The fixed-rate exchange system, as reestablished by the Smithsonian Agreement in late 1971, came apart: the monetary system of the world was in disarray. With such momentous events under way, the key finance ministers and central bankers met often, with high stakes riding on the policies they adopted and their ability to agree on what should be done.

When I came on board at the Treasury, I felt the United States was overdue to put forward a new plan for the international monetary system. Within a few months, the annual International Monetary Fund–World Bank meetings were to be held in Washington. So I developed a proposal. My co-workers were heavyweights: Federal Reserve Chairman Arthur Burns, Secretary of State Bill Rogers, Chairman of the President's Council of Economic Advisers Herb Stein, Special Assistant to the President Peter Flanigan, and Under Secretary of the Treasury for Monetary Affairs Paul Volcker. We worked under tight secrecy. The result was a novel proposal, having the appearance of a traditional par-value system, in which currency relationships were formally stated, but with automatic and symmetrical changes in par values triggered by changes in reserves. This automatic feature would make the system operate in the manner of a floating-rate system, even though it resembled the fixed-exchange-rate arrangement to which people had become accustomed.

Once the proposal was completed, I said to my colleagues and to President Nixon, who approved my suggestion, that I should show this paper in advance to the key finance ministers—of Germany, France, Britain, Japan, Canada, and Italy—to hear their reactions. So I engaged in a prior consultation that was unprecedented. The reaction was generally positive, but without commitment to the details. There was a collective sigh of relief that the United States once again was taking leadership and responsibility. And there was genuine appreciation for having been consulted and for knowing in advance what we were going to propose.

In the course of work on the monetary system, there was a tumultuous meeting in March 1973 in Paris at which French Finance Minister Valéry Giscard d'Estaing and I argued with each other vociferously but without rancor. At the height of one of these arguments, Helmut Schmidt intervened and verbally took us both by the scruff of the neck. "Settle down," he said. "We're going to have to work this out together. When we get through, we will have something that we have all agreed on and that we can present with a sense of shared commitment." In the end we did find our way to a new monetary system, with currency values reflecting market conditions and fluctuating far more than in earlier, more stable times.

From this meeting a feeling also emerged among us that the key finance ministers should meet privately before larger meetings took place. We could straighten out our thinking, understand each other better, and work through disagreements in a direct, informal, off-the-record setting.

Schmidt, Giscard, Chancellor of the Exchequer Tony Barber, and I agreed that on Sunday, March 25, 1973, before an important upcoming meeting in Washington, we would meet privately. I mentioned this to President Nixon, and he approved of the idea. "I'm going to be out of town on that weekend. Why don't you give your meeting a touch of class and hold it in the White House?" he offered. So we ended up in the library on the ground floor of the White House. A quiet fire was burning, and lunch was served in the best White House tradition and style, which provided a fine atmosphere for informal exchanges. We did not want any publicity about the meetings but needed a way to refer to them among ourselves. Taking our setting as the cue, we called ourselves "the Library Group." By the time a few more months had passed, I felt that this initial group of four should be at least five, and at the time of the mid-1973 World Bank–IMF meetings in Nairobi, Kenya, I proposed and got agreement to include the Japanese. This was the birth of what came to be called the Group of Five.[1] This close exposure to European leaders and their readiness to work informally and cooperatively impressed on me that I could deal directly with them, that small and frank discussions were desirable, and that people of vision and breadth could be found who could understand positions far wider than those of their own country.

Long before his election to the presidency, I had wanted to introduce Ronald Reagan to one of Europe's most forceful and influential leaders. In the summer of 1979, Chancellor Helmut Schmidt visited me in California. I had been working with Ronald Reagan and took the occasion to arrange a meeting of these two men, both of whom I admired. Somehow I could see that the relationship, even in the relaxed California atmosphere, was rather stiff. I sensed that these two friends of mine, the European man of intellect and the American man of instinct, would never really hit it off. Nevertheless, as leaders in office, they worked effectively together. Schmidt advised me in May 1982, when I was visiting him on behalf of President Reagan, "The superpowers are not in contact with each other's reality. They can't read you." Then he pledged, "The president must act as one among equals, but he is more than equal and must lead. I will support that leadership."

---

1. Canada and Italy were added in 1986 to become the Group of Seven, the Summit Seven of the annual economic summits.

Meeting with the Europeans

But now, as secretary of state, I would be meeting with the leaders of a new coalition government. Hans-Dietrich Genscher had taken his small but pivotal Free Democratic party out of the coalition with Chancellor Helmut Schmidt's Social Democratic party and formed a coalition with its opposition, the Christian Democratic Union, headed by Helmut Kohl. I had some forewarning of the problems in the German coalition, so I wasn't surprised when the Schmidt government fell on September 17, 1982. Helmut Kohl became the new chancellor. Yet I felt a certain sense of loss that Schmidt, a man I had regarded so highly for such a long time as both a close friend and a spirited leader, had been taken off the scene just as I reentered public life. I am sure that Kohl was aware of this. He went out of his way to show friendship to me and at first referred to himself to me as "the other Helmut." I could sense a certain unease in Kohl about my relationship with Schmidt. But I was glad to work with Kohl, and I respected his abilities.

Helmut Kohl had come to Washington for meetings on November 15 as the new chancellor. Kohl and President Reagan and I had similar impressions of Andropov, the new Soviet leader: formidable, experienced, tough; we agreed we needed to know him better. Kohl emphasized the importance of a firm and cohesive NATO alliance as the only hope for success in the crucial INF negotiations with Moscow. But it must be "a real negotiation, not just a show," he said.

My visit to Bonn was especially instructive: I was dealing with a new coalition government in which the new chancellor and his foreign minister were, as before, from different parties. When I arrived on December 7, 1982, unity was the word, but I would watch carefully for the reality. Genscher controlled the operational work of the Foreign Ministry, and Kohl controlled the chancellor's office.

My friend Arthur Burns had become ambassador only about nine months earlier. He had been my first boss in Washington during the Eisenhower administration, and we had also been close collaborators in the early 1970s when he was chairman of the Federal Reserve Board and I was secretary of the treasury. "I'm like a kid with a new toy. I'm learning a new language and a new country," he told me. I reflected that his zest for learning, still strong at the age of seventy-seven, was a key to the dynamism of his career and the extraordinary strength of his character.

The next morning, I got my first personal exposure to Hans-Dietrich Genscher. He let me know right off that he was born and grew up in Halle, East Germany, the German Democratic Republic. He visited there whenever he could. I realized the significance of his East German roots. Like Kohl and many other Germans, Genscher worried continuously about the Germans in the Soviet Union as well as in East Germany. If anyone would have suggested to Genscher that the division of Germany was a natural state of affairs, he would have thought they were crazy.[2]

In the capitals of the other basing countries, I listened to leaders and got a feel for their hopes and fears. At The Hague, banner-waving protesters demonstrated outside the Foreign Ministry, up in arms about U.S. efforts in El Salvador. Effigies hung from trees. As I left the meeting with Foreign Minister Hans van den Broek, the chant started: "Yankee, go home!" I went on to a meeting at the official residence of Prime Minister Ruud Lubbers. I felt a quiet strength in this man who would carry heavy responsibilities if the time came to deploy missiles in Holland.

From there, I went on to Italy, where our nuclear-tipped, ground-launched cruise missiles (GLCMs) were scheduled to be deployed in late 1983, depending on the status of our INF negotiations. The Italians were firmly committed to proceed if necessary but wanted an energetic and creative negotiation in Geneva. Toward the end of this visit, I had a private audience with Pope John Paul II. He seated me at the end of a table that seemed to serve as his desk. He pulled his chair up and leaned forward, engaging me intently with his eyes. We talked for about forty minutes. The Vatican took a great interest in Poland, the Soviet Union, our arms control negotiations, nuclear weapons, but most of all, the Middle East. Lebanon, a country where Christians and Muslims had once lived in peace, was now shattered. The Mideast peace process and the possibilities for peace in Lebanon were preoccupations of the Holy See.

I was then wheels up for France. A most extraordinary trio of motorcycle police escorted me into Paris, weaving in and out of traffic almost as if in a ballet. I called them the Three Musketeers. The French were always stylish. President Mitterrand exposed me to another European preoccupation: Africa. Mitterrand had an impressive grasp of the problems and possibilities, the personalities, the subtleties, of the region that had formerly been French West Africa in particular but Africa more broadly as well. He wanted me and the United States to devote more attention to Africa and, in doing so, to support French activities there.

In Spain, Prime Minister Felipe González had just entered office, along with a large Socialist majority in the Spanish Congress of Deputies. We

---

2. I had been impressed on an earlier occasion with the inhumanity of the division of Germany. I had taken Helmut Schmidt to a Bach concert in Carmel, California. A violinist from East Germany joined us after the concert. I witnessed a conversation that was deeply emotional and intense. After everyone left, I sat for a long while with Helmut, talking about his conversation with the East German musician. The violinist was encouraged to perform all over the world. He had a wife and two children, but they were never allowed to travel with him, in effect, held hostage at home so that he would always return. The pain engendered by the arbitrary division of Germans and the repressiveness of the East German system was striking. This experience made me feel that somehow, in the end, the yearning of the German people to come together would be fulfilled, that Germany would someday be reunified.

hit it off well, and our session was lively and animated. I remember vividly his description of how he would implement his policy. "I owe a great debt to President Mitterrand," he said.

"How is that?" I asked.

"President Mitterrand," González replied, "came in with a big majority on a Socialist ticket, just as I did. He put the Socialist program into place, and the result was a catastrophe for France. Therefore, I have learned something: don't implement the Socialist program. Use the marketplace. Encourage investors. That is what I am going to do." And that is what he did, with great success.[3]

Spain at this moment was energized by the spirit of freedom. I was struck by the respect and affection for King Juan Carlos I, who had played a strong and crucial role in bringing parliamentary democracy into being in 1978 and in aborting an attempted military coup in February 1981, thereby preserving the democratic opportunity. Memories in Spain were still vivid of the repressive dictatorial regime of Francisco Franco, spanning more than three decades. The struggle to retain control by elected civilian government had hung in the balance, and the king had swung that balance to democracy. The point was made to me again and again that Americans, who have so long enjoyed freedom, do not appreciate how much it means to the human spirit. The Spaniards knew all too well, because they had been deprived of it for so long. This made a special impression on me, reinforcing the importance of our efforts to make freedom a centerpiece in our diplomacy.

The Special Relationship

Every American secretary of state in recent history, at an early point, has had to think through the matter of the "special relationship" between Britain and the United States. That was dramatically the case with Al Haig, my immediate predecessor, who faced at the opening of his tenure Britain's war with Argentina over the Falkland Islands, a sudden and unexpected military conflict. Some in the Reagan administration had argued that U.S. interests lay on the side of maintaining good relations within the hemisphere and that Britain's decision to retake the islands in battle was a foolish attempt to prolong a colonial empire otherwise being voluntarily relinquished. Our ambassador to the United Nations, Jeane Kirkpatrick, argued the case and advocated American neutrality. To Ronald Reagan, however, Britain's response was a gallant resistance to an unjustified act of aggression. How could the United States do anything other than side with Britain,

---

3. The result was an explosion of economic growth in Spain, which became increasingly healthy as it joined the European Community and benefited from investment in Spain by companies looking to sell their products in the European Community.

our ally and sister democracy, against the Argentina of military dictators and human rights abusers? And the United States did lean heavily to the side of Great Britain.

When I took office, the Falklands fighting was over, but the war had made its mark on the Anglo-American alliance, now closer than at any time since World War II. Yet a great deal of resentment about the U.S. role in the war remained within some elements of the Reagan administration. Tom Enders, the assistant secretary of state for Latin America, in his early briefings to me, stressed the problems created for us in Latin America by our massive and visible support for the British. It would be hard to say, Enders argued, that the Falklands War had done serious damage to British interests, which were not large in Latin America; it was *American* interests that were damaged.

My reaction to Prime Minister Margaret Thatcher's decision and the British action in the Falklands was one of admiration, despite my misgivings about the apparent impact on our relationships throughout Latin America. The British decision to go to war for these desolate, wind-scoured, scarcely populated rocky islets 8,000 miles from London was the first marker laid down by a democratic power in the post-Vietnam era to state unambiguously that a free world nation was willing to fight for a principle. The world paid attention to this—and not just the Third World either; it was noted by the Soviets too. Attitudes everywhere were significantly affected. The Argentine military was discredited overnight, and the pressure for democracy in that country strengthened.

My first encounter with Prime Minister Thatcher's ambassador in Washington, Sir Oliver Wright, was stormy. I had persuaded President Reagan that we should vote in favor of a balanced UN resolution on the Falklands. Although our consultations had let her know what was coming and our negotiations produced a resolution she could live with, Margaret Thatcher was furious. We voted with Argentina and the rest of the Western Hemisphere for a resolution that she opposed. Her ambassador, on instructions, read me off like a sergeant would a recruit in a Marine Corps boot camp. I felt Mrs. Thatcher was wrong to oppose us for taking a reasonable position on a critical issue in our neighborhood. And Wright was wrong to lay it on so thick. I worried that President Reagan would be alarmed at Margaret Thatcher's reaction, but I found that he, too, was getting a little fed up with her imperious attitude on this matter.

I had met with Margaret Thatcher a few months earlier, in May 1982, on a Sunday at Chequers, the country house of the prime minister. I had come on a mission for President Reagan. She knew that our ambassador and others would try to sit in on our discussion. Preferring a private session, she extended an invitation to me to arrive an hour in advance of a larger scheduled luncheon. A car from our embassy came to pick me up; in it was the economic officer from the embassy. We rode together to Chequers.

When I got out of the car, the prime minister was standing in the doorway to greet me. I introduced her to the young man with me. "Oh, yes," she said, "he must be here to take notes, and, of course, I have people who can take notes, too." Then she turned directly to me and said, "Have you ever looked at the notes people take in meetings like this? They really don't bear much resemblance to what actually took place, at least to the subtleties of meaning." Then she turned to my man, "Have you ever had a good tour of Chequers?" He shook his head. She then turned to her assistant and said, "Well, why don't you show him around?"

With that, she locked her arm in mine and wheeled me off to a private room where we had an intense hour and a half together on the importance of free and open markets and of alliance strength and resolve to contain the Soviet threat. She was clear and forceful in expressing her ideas and strong in responding to questions that challenged her views. Freedom in political and economic life was her trademark. In that regard, she and Ronald Reagan were soul mates, and I was right with them. She left me with the feeling that right or wrong, there wasn't a shadow of doubt in her mind about where she was going and why.

On Thursday afternoon, December 16, 1982—some seven months after that visit—I landed in London, the last stop on my European swing. When I arrived at Number 10 Downing Street the next day for my first meeting as secretary of state with Margaret Thatcher, I was apprehensive that I would run into an argument about the Falklands.

Again, she met me at the door. We sat and talked in a living room where a fire burned brightly. The Falklands were on her mind, and she spoke of their strategic significance. What if the Panama Canal were to be closed, requiring shipping to go "around the Horn," as in clipper-ship days? The location of the Falklands in the shipping lanes of the South Atlantic would then be vital. I thought that was farfetched, but there was no point arguing about it. I agreed with our decision to support her, but I felt it was time to repair the damage done to our interests in South America. I stated my views firmly; she listened, but not sympathetically.

Mrs. Thatcher welcomed the end of the Siberian pipeline dispute and was vigorous in her support for the controls on trade with the Soviets that had by now been agreed on. Britain would be a genuine and strong ally on the INF negotiations. The British would deploy our nuclear weapons if need be, she said, despite the inevitable protests. She emphasized the importance of a clear and creative effort to negotiate an agreement on INF missiles, as had the other European leaders. But she was not optimistic about the possibility of a negotiated outcome and agreed wholeheartedly with the president on the necessity to demonstrate strength and unity in the Atlantic alliance.

That evening she gave a dinner in my honor at Number 10. The discussion soon turned to economics. As fellow devotees of free enterprise and free markets, Mrs. Thatcher and I got along well. In the course of the conversation, Foreign Secretary Francis Pym put forward an economic argument that made no sense to me. Before I could say a word, she verbally demolished what he had said. She was relentless and direct. She was right, too, but brutal. Pym was silenced and humiliated. He would not be a member much longer in her cabinet, I could sense. Some seven months later, he was sent to the back bench.

The special relationship between America and Britain was going to be stronger than ever, I felt, because it was flanked by the Reagan-Thatcher personal relationship, which was as close as any imaginable between two major leaders. As for me, I felt that the best way to get along with this indomitable leader was to know what I was talking about, to talk up, and to talk back. Thatcher's best points were often made in the course of vigorous debate. I enjoyed and admired her and looked forward to productive work together.

I left Europe for Washington eager to talk to President Reagan about my ideas for the year to come.

Reflections at Year-End: 1982

I met with the president on December 20. The world was still in turmoil, but some important problems had been put behind us, and a foundation had been established for work on others. I told him of how struck I was with the importance of the Middle East to the Europeans. President Reagan's September 1 peace initiative, the agreement to get the PLO out of Beirut, the work on the multinational force, the resolution of the Siberian pipeline dispute—all registered with Europe that the United States was engaged in a new diplomacy and leading the way. "They are willing— more than willing—to play a part, if asked. They are rooting for us to be successful," I said.

In Asia, there was at least a chance for a more positive relationship with Japan, and an early effort to develop that was under way. Japan's new prime minister, Yasuhiro Nakasone, seemed likely to be more dynamic than his predecessor. An agreement with the People's Republic of China on Taiwan arms sales, which we had reached on August 17, had calmed down a troubling issue. My discussions with the Chinese foreign minister in New York and Moscow had been testy but served to clarify positions. I would travel to China early in the coming year. A sensible strategy was emerging, the deterioration in our ability to work with the Chinese had stopped.

Then there was Central America. "Why are Europeans so skeptical of our efforts there?" I said in frustration to the president. "Aren't they for democracy, too? Don't they see why we can't stand for a Soviet beachhead in Nicaragua? Of course, there are problems in El Salvador. But we are working for democracy, the rule of law, and economic development. It almost seems as though they wish we would abandon our own neighborhood." The president shared my frustration. The Europeans would give us a hard time no matter what happened in Central America, I felt. We needed to persevere in what we regarded as the right course. But we also needed to persuade our friends in Central America that they, too, must help communicate to the Europeans how they were dealing with their problems. And the government in El Salvador needed to demonstrate its ability to get control of its military and to come down hard on human rights violations.

The U.S.-Soviet superpower contest was undeniably the central concern of our foreign policy. "The Soviet game is chess, and ours is poker. We will have to play a creative mixture of both games," I told the president. He liked the image but said he preferred poker. "We can win in 1983," I said, "although it is possible to lose. The year will be full of difficulties, and we can count on Andropov to create a few more. If we are successful in holding our allies together and sticking with the basic elements in our INF position, then the importance of that achievement cannot be overestimated."

"Deployment and negotiations," I said, "are intertwined: we won't get one without the other." We must have good-faith negotiations, from our side, on all fronts: the strategic nuclear arms and intermediate-range nuclear forces negotiations in Geneva (START and INF), the mutual balanced forces talks in Vienna (MBFR), and the human rights conference in Madrid (CSCE). "Let's stop talking about the zero option in INF," I said. "No one knows what that means. Let us say we are for the elimination of an entire weapons system. Let's make it our preferred outcome and ultimate goal, even when, as I feel is inevitable, we propose intermediate possible outcomes." The president was noncommittal on any change in our position.

"Here are the realities," I told the president. "Economic expansion is at last, even if barely, under way. Important for its own sake, it is critical in the East-West context, affecting everyone's attitude, and in particular, the European appraisal of the United States. They will complain about our interest rates and budget deficit, but they welcome economic expansion as vital to their own economies. And expansion is essential in the fight to keep the international trading system open. Protectionism is hard enough to contain in the best of times, let alone in bad times." The president agreed and asked me to give him my thoughts on economic policy as his administration proceeded.

"History is on our side," I said. "In terms of human values, there is no contest between our system and theirs. We must emphasize values. The weapons are a means to an end, not an end in themselves." In a refrain I used time and again, publicly and privately, I exhorted the president, "We have the winning hand, but we must play it for all it is worth."

The public and press reactions to my first months in office were generally favorable. Someone left on my desk a clipping from the *Christian Science Monitor*[4] calling me the "realist abroad" and editorializing:

> Little by little, Mr. Shultz appears to be pulling US foreign policy back toward the more moderate center and the bipartisan mainstream of past administrations. It is more focused on what is possible and practical. . . . These are but the beginnings of what the American public must hope will be continued efforts to give consistency and steadiness to the conduct of US policy. . . . There is no doubt American policy will continue to reflect Mr. Reagan's philosophical views. Mr. Shultz will not go against the President, even if and when he disagrees with him, and that is as it should be. But the secretary's professionalism and style should help ensure that US foreign policy is coherent, purposeful, and soundly grounded in international realities. His quiet influence on the President's thinking is already evident.

I went off for a Christmas holiday at Stanford to rest and prepare for what would be a demanding year ahead.

4. September 10, 1982.

Part IV

STRATEGIES
TAKE SHAPE

CHAPTER 12

A Move Beyond Rhetoric
with the Soviet Union

The beginning of a new year in Washington, let alone the start of a new Congress or a new administration, is always fresh. People are back from the holidays. Many have been home with their constituencies. The mood of the Congress often shifts, and the administration comes back with a sense of new possibilities and the president's State of the Union address in mind. Early 1983 was such a time. I wanted to develop a strategy for a new start with the Soviet Union. I felt we had to try to turn the relationship around: away from confrontation and toward real problem solving.

An opportunity had come to me in a message from Soviet Ambassador Anatoly Dobrynin in December 1982 proposing the start of U.S.-Soviet discussions at all levels. But I needed a much clearer sense of where Ronald Reagan stood if I was to be able to move us from rhetoric to real engagement with the Soviets. I knew the president's White House staff would oppose such engagement. There was lots of powerful opposition around town to any effort to bridge the chasm separating Moscow and Washington. It came from Bill Clark and the NSC staff, from Cap Weinberger and others at the Defense Department, and from Bill Casey and his soul mates at the CIA. Already there were voices in the administration warning the president that I, with my negotiating experience, and the State Department, with its bent to "better relations," posed a threat to the president's crusade against communism. I would have to be deft, but I was determined not to hang back from engaging the Soviets because of fears that "Soviets win negotiations."

Walter and Lee Annenberg had invited O'Bie and me to join their big New Year's Eve party for the president and Nancy Reagan at Sunnylands, the Annenbergs' Palm Desert home. When I arrived, Walter handed me an article from the December 12, 1982, London *Financial Times* naming me "Man of the Year." The article was flattering: "Mr. Shultz appears to have reversed the disintegration of the western alliance, helped to inject some realism into domestic economic policy and even restored some hopes that American leadership may yet galvanise the world into pulling itself out of the present economic crisis." Kind words. But I was well aware of how tenuous was even the slightest measure of success in these times. I was also alert to the tendency, over time, for the media to tear down whomever it has built up. The president and Nancy were relaxed and cordial, clearly enjoying themselves. The president and I sat together in Walter's study, surrounded by an assemblage of art, memorabilia, and photos. I had asked Bill Clark to be present, as I sought to avoid the NSC staff–State Department rivalry that had plagued so many of my predecessors.

Taking up the president's invitation to advise him on economic policy, I made a pitch for drastic tax reform, calling for massive elimination of deductions and sharp reductions in marginal rates of taxation. The president liked my ideas and told me to pass this proposal on to Don Regan. He wanted Treasury to work on it.

Moving on to arms control, I stressed that our negotiating posture in the coming year would be absolutely crucial. Our allies could not withstand the heat of political pressure against the installation of our INF missiles unless we, at the same time, were advancing reasonable and stabilizing arms control positions at the negotiating table. I felt that a dialogue with Soviet Ambassador Anatoly Dobrynin might be productive and would not have much, if any, downside. Given the frozen White House atmosphere, I took encouragement from President Reagan's willingness to hear me out, but he made no decision.

The Shift Begins

Two days later, back in Washington, I set to work. The president would give a radio address on U.S.-Soviet relations on January 8. At the State Department we helped produce for President Reagan what amounted to a message to Moscow:

> A new leader has come to power in Moscow. There's been much speculation about whether this change could mean a chance to reduce tensions and solve some of the problems between us. . . . If there are to be better mutual relations, they must result from moderation in Soviet conduct, not just our own good intentions. . . . We and our democratic partners eagerly await any serious actions and proposals the Soviets may offer and stand ready to discuss with them serious proposals which can genuinely advance the cause of peace. . . . We stand ready to work towards solutions to all outstanding problems.

I developed a few central propositions and sent them around to the Europeans and to colleagues at home. It was naive to think we could disarm the peace movement in Europe. The Soviets would not negotiate on INF until they were certain we would deploy. We were under attack from our own allies for not having achieved an arms agreement with the Soviets. We could expect the Soviets to play upon Western political fears in an attempt to block deployments and draw us into a bad agreement. But we would not allow substance to be driven by propaganda pressures. We would pursue a two-track approach: we would move with determination to get the missiles deployed—against vehement opposition from the left; we would move to create a serious American arms control negotiating position—against vehement opposition from the right. We must not give Andropov the impression that we or the alliance were in any way wobbly. By and large we had stymied the Communists, and the policy of firmness that brought that about should be continued. I realized, however, that I needed to have Ronald Reagan's full support for my plans to engage the Soviets and to turn our confrontational relationship into something more constructive.

Within days I became enmeshed in the problems surrounding the forced resignation of Eugene Rostow, the director of the Arms Control and Disarmament Agency. He had made known to his friends, including some Europeans, that he favored the "walk in the woods" formula worked out by Paul Nitze and felt that the United States should have followed up on this initiative more aggressively, despite Soviet rejection of the formula. In the process, he had alienated people in the White House and had lost the confidence of the president. Rostow had contributed a keen intellect, a broad base of knowledge, and a stature to our work. I was distressed to see him go, but there was no alternative. No one could be effective in such a job without the confidence of the president. I wound up being the one who had to give Rostow the word. I didn't relish the assignment. He appreciated the fact that I went to him directly, but it was a difficult meeting. I don't think he had ever been asked to leave a job before. He left with dignity and his head held high.

In the midst of the flurry over Rostow, I received a proposal from Secretary of Commerce Mac Baldrige about swapping nickel from the Soviet Union for butter from us. It was a clever business proposition, but it would not cost the Soviets any foreign exchange and would inevitably, given pressures from the farm bloc, carry an implicit subsidy, thus violating the agreement we had painstakingly worked out with the Europeans that we would not engage in subsidized trade with the Soviets. The Soviets would see that our agricultural sector was out of control politically and would play on that fact. They knew that our farmers were zealously eager to sell them food in every way conceivable, and this deal would set a precedent for others. I was opposed, and the proposal was soon shelved because of the subsidy issue.

On January 19, I sent a memorandum to the president outlining "U.S.-Soviet Relations in 1983." I proposed that we counter the "new Soviet activism by starting an intensified dialogue with Moscow." This would, I said, "keep the diplomatic initiative in our hands." Although we were adversaries, I said, "we must not rule out the possibility that firm U.S. policies could help induce the kind of changes in Soviet behavior that would make an improvement in relations possible." Let's put them to the test, I argued. I set out to him for the first time what was to become our four-part agenda: human rights, arms control, regional issues, and bilateral relations, including the problem of managing domestic (largely agricultural) pressures for increased trade. I set out four possible levels of contacts: specialists at "departments and desks"; ambassadors with Gromyko and me; foreign ministers directly; an eventual summit if substance warranted. "Should we later decide on a U.S.-Soviet summit," I cautioned, "you should probably meet with the Chinese first." Shortly after my paper reached the White House, Bud McFarlane let me know that the NSC staff over there was "fly specking" it. "There are so many ideologues around here that they are picking it to pieces," he said.

Dialogue with Dobrynin

Nevertheless, after considerable pulling and hauling with the naysaying NSC staff, the president authorized me to open a careful dialogue with Ambassador Dobrynin. We began on a pedestrian level, simply identifying agreements that we had on the books and going over what had happened to them. Some had expired; some were more or less in abeyance; some continued to be operational. We thought, let's try to work on these matters before taking on more weighty issues. "Walk before you try to run," I said. I noticed that Gromyko had been in Bonn in the middle of January and had threatened to deploy more Soviet missiles aimed at Europe if the U.S. deployments went forward in 1983. The Soviets were brandishing both the carrot and the stick at the Germans, and Hans-Dietrich Genscher was waffling, I was told, on the firmness of our deployment schedule.

Peter Dailey, our ambassador to Ireland and a man skilled in what we called public diplomacy, had been asked by the president to help out in the year of the missile, 1983. The Soviets were proceeding with a heavy hand, I told Dailey on January 18, but "they may have stepped in a hole by using threats," causing resentment by their overbearing approach. Dailey urged us to speak about the outcome we sought rather than the process. "The process, arms control, means weapons. What we want to talk about is peace," he said.

Three days later, the president met at the White House with our two chief negotiators, Ed Rowny and Paul Nitze, prior to their return to Geneva. President Reagan was determined to maintain our zero-zero position in INF but was willing to explore other options, should the Soviets show flexibility.

The president's State of the Union speech came on January 25. He suggested possible movement in INF negotiations. "At the heart of our strategy for peace is our relationship with the Soviet Union. The past year saw a change in Soviet leadership. We're prepared for a positive change in Soviet-American relations. But the Soviet Union must show by deeds as well as words a sincere commitment to respect the rights and sovereignty of the family of nations." The president then turned to reductions in arms, "For our part, we're vigorously pursuing arms reduction negotiations with the Soviet Union. Supported by our allies, we've put forward draft agreements proposing significant weapon reductions to equal and verifiable lower levels. We insist on an equal balance of forces. . . . In the case of intermediate-range nuclear forces, we have proposed the complete elimination of the entire class of land-based missiles. We're also prepared to carefully explore serious Soviet proposals."

This was new ground, giving me new flexibility. I could sense a growing sentiment among our European allies that we should adjust our position in the INF negotiations. They fully supported the basic principle of an equal outcome, but zero-zero was not the only place, they argued, where equality could be found.

Hans-Dietrich Genscher came to town. He met with the president and with me the day after the State of the Union message. The Soviet objective, he told me, was to get the deployment of Pershing II missiles in Germany postponed until 1985 in the expectation that such a delay would derail British and Italian deployments in 1983 and the whole deployment schedule would then unravel. Genscher wanted us to announce a counterproposal that would make a public splash. At the same time, he was steadfast about the deployment schedule of the Pershings. His words were strong and welcome. The report that he was "waffling" on deployments had proved wrong.

A President Ready to Engage

I returned to Washington on February 10, after a long trip to Japan, China, and South Korea. Snow was falling when my plane touched down at Andrews Air Force Base. The blizzard continued for days. By Saturday afternoon, February 12, Washington was covered by one of the heaviest snow-falls of the century. Traffic had virtually come to a halt. People were skiing in the streets. My telephone rang. It was Nancy Reagan inviting O'Bie and me to the White House for dinner. The snow had prevented the Reagans from going to Camp David. When we arrived that evening, the president and first lady were relaxed and talkative. The family dining room on the second floor of the White House imparts a sense of history, especially when the group is small and the atmosphere informal. The Reagans were gracious hosts. They like good conversation, a good story. If the president heard a story he liked, he never forgot it. And I would hear it again and again, further embellished and perfected with each telling.

President Reagan was fascinated by China and expressed openly his ideas about the Soviet Union. He recognized how difficult it was for him to move forward in dealing with either of these countries. He realized, I thought, that he was in a sense blocked by his own White House staff, by the Defense Department, by Bill Casey in the CIA, and by his own past rhetoric. Now that we were talking in this family setting, I could see that Ronald Reagan was much more willing to move forward in relations with these two Com-munist nations—even travel to them—than I had earlier believed. Reagan saw himself as an experienced negotiator going back to his days as president of the Screen Actors Guild. He was self-confident about his views and positions. He had never had a lengthy session with an important leader of a Communist country, and I could sense he would relish such an opportunity.

"I will be meeting with Dobrynin again late Tuesday afternoon," I told him. "What would you think about my bringing Dobrynin over to the White House for a private chat?"

"Great," he responded. "We have to keep this secret," he said. "I don't intend to engage in a detailed exchange with Dobrynin, but I do intend to tell him that if Andropov is willing to do business, so am I."

Monday morning at 7:40, a call came to me from Bill Clark. His nose was out of joint. He was very negative about a meeting between Reagan and Dobrynin. "I argued against the meeting to the president," he told me. President Reagan, however, had his own ideas and wanted to get more involved. The efforts of the staff at the NSC to keep him out, I thought, were beginning to break down. Mike Deaver made arrangements to send a White House car over to the State Department's basement garage to bring Dobrynin and me over to the relatively unwatched East Gate of the White House without the press's knowledge.

When Ambassador Dobrynin walked into my office at 5:00 P.M. on Tuesday, I greeted him with the question "Anatoly, how would you like to go see the president? Why don't we just go back down in my elevator, get in the car, and go over there?" Dobrynin immediately agreed, surprised but elated. Off we went.

Rather than the brief meeting I expected, the president talked with us for almost two hours. He clearly had thought about the meeting a great deal. Ronald Reagan is the master of the personal encounter, and he impressively engaged Dobrynin on all the issues and argued our positions effectively on START, on INF, and on Afghanistan and Poland. He spoke with genuine feeling and eloquence on the subject of human rights, divided families, Soviet Jewry, and refuseniks. He also talked with sincere intensity about the Pentecostals, a small group of Christians who had taken refuge in our embassy in Moscow almost five years earlier. The Pentecostals wanted to pursue their religion, and they wanted to emigrate from the Soviet Union. They had not been allowed to leave. "If you can do something about the Pentecostals or another human rights issue," Reagan told Dobrynin, "we will simply be delighted and will not embarrass you by undue publicity, by claims of credit for ourselves, or by 'crowing.' "

Afterward, Dobrynin and I went back to State and continued until almost 8:00 P.M. Before he left, Dobrynin said to me, "We should handle the 'special subject' [the Pentecostal families in our Moscow embassy] privately." I agreed.

After Dobrynin left, I thought over the day's events. It was apparent to me that Bill Clark and others at the White House were uneasy about how the president would perform. They didn't trust him to act on his own. I had no worries about that. Ronald Reagan knew what he wanted to say, was serious, had real substance to talk about, and wanted to make it clear to the Soviets, "If you are ready to move forward, so are we." I was impressed and reassured. The president was personally engaged. I felt this could be a turning point with the Soviets.

Larry Eagleburger came to my office on the next afternoon. He had just talked to Bill Clark and Bud McFarlane. They had reacted to the president's meeting with Dobrynin with a "substantial lack of enthusiasm." Bill Clark wanted to talk directly to me about the results of the meeting, Eagleburger said. He and others on the NSC staff were opposed to "détenteniks." My meeting with the president and Dobrynin had generated an internecine struggle in the White House between Clark, who saw it as bad policy, and Deaver, who saw it as good politics. I saw it as good policy and would leave the politics to the president.

"The president had the time of his life," I told Eagleburger, describing President Reagan in action with Dobrynin.

"That's why Bud and Bill are holding back," Eagleburger replied.

"The point is, Ronald Reagan wants to get involved. I'd love to see the cable Dobrynin sent to Moscow," I said. "I should talk with Weinberger, Casey, and Clark. The president is not a loner. He does not want to be the subject of an end run. In this instance, he end ran his own staff."

Problems with the NSC Staff

I thought over the difficulties I was having with the NSC staff. A president needs his staff. It is not simply another bureaucracy but the essential team that brings order to his time and priority items to his attention. I had been urged, right from the start, to work directly with the president. But whenever I did, I seemed to get in trouble with his staff. It is a fact of life that if the president's staff does not support a policy, the policy is not likely to succeed. The president by himself cannot make sure that a policy is being implemented, so the staff has to be brought along. "Bill Clark is feeling pressed now," I said to Ray Seitz. "He is devoted to the president, but his grasp of the substance is limited. Clark fears that Reagan, if given his head, will make mistakes, so Clark is reluctant to let the president move in new directions. Deaver concentrates on image: that's his job. But he is close to the president and Nancy and understands them as a couple. Deaver has no fear of Reagan's instincts and so is bolder in his recommendations." Clark and Deaver were destined to disagree. Their concerns often could not be reconciled.

The problem was crystallized now because the president wanted to be engaged but didn't quite know how to do it. President Reagan's staff in a way had cut him off. They had a lot of leverage because the president did not like to act in isolation. He liked his staff around him as he made decisions, and he liked general agreement. That was what had gotten Al Haig in trouble. Haig tried to get the president to make decisions on his own or let Haig make them. Ronald Reagan wanted to talk things through with others, and he disliked divisive meetings.

I had come to another realization. My current problem with the White House staff in a curious way was connected with my trip to the Far East. When I was away from Washington for a stretch of time, I started to lose the taste and feel of the White House, to get out of touch. If I had been in town over the preceding two weeks, I probably would have been more attuned to the growing friction between Clark and Deaver.

I had managed to develop a new Middle East policy and to achieve the lifting of the pipeline sanctions by putting in a great deal of time not only with the president but also with the White House staff and cabinet colleagues. I had done a lot of talking and a lot of listening. Out of this laborious process, I had developed a consensus. But U.S.-Soviet matters were too hot: a similar effort could not produce consensus. The views were too divergent and too fiercely held.

At the White House dinner with the president that snowy Saturday night, when I saw his interest emerge, I had seized an opportunity. Everything had been telescoped. It had been important to move, and the move had been productive. I recalled how Bill Clark had telephoned me the previous October in New York about the pipeline sanctions and wanted to reverse completely the mandate for discussions with the Europeans that had emerged, with the president's approval, after intense internal debate. I had to walk him back painstakingly. Process, I could see, was especially important in this administration because too many people at the White House didn't understand the complexities of the issues. Clark simply didn't comprehend the subtleties or the nuances.

I knew that I would have to insist on dealing directly with the president. I could not let the White House staff interpret me to him. That was especially true when it came to Clark, because his views and instincts were different from mine, and he could not translate me accurately. As for the immediate turn of events, even the blizzard that February evening had moved forward the affairs of state: if it hadn't snowed, the president would have gone to Camp David, and I would not have been invited to the White House to gain the insight and opportunity to help him engage directly with the Soviets.

An Overture: The Pentecostal Christians

On the afternoon of February 28, Ambassador Dobrynin called to say he was ill and wished to send his deputy, Oleg Sokolov, over immediately to deliver a message from the Soviet government. I agreed. Our European bureau objected strongly to my receiving Sokolov. They pointed out that Gromyko would never receive our deputy chief of mission and that it was hard enough for our ambassador to see him. For me to receive Sokolov would undercut the effectiveness of our people in Moscow, they argued. I was startled to see the impact of strained reciprocity. They agonized over this with me at length. I could see the logic of their argument, but my instincts told me to receive Sokolov. "It's not my way," I said, "to stand too much on ceremony."

Sokolov was in my office for only a few seconds. He handed over a message that he said had two parts. The second part was "constructive," he said. The full text dealt with the Pentecostals:

> We already explained to the American side our principled position on this subject. Keeping Soviet citizens in the U.S. Embassy for such a long time is clearly illegal and abnormal. Their further stay there only aggravates the situation, and the responsibility for that fully rests with the American side. The resolution of this issue depends precisely on the American side: the above-mentioned persons should leave the U.S. Embassy.
>
> In this connection we can say definitely that no one is going to persecute them, there are no such intentions. Accordingly, after those persons return to the place of their residence, the question of their leaving the USSR will be considered. It will be done with account taken of all the circumstances involved in this matter.

I sent this message over to the president at once, along with my initial reactions:

> Formally, this does not go beyond what the Soviets have said before. Nevertheless, the Soviets are obviously trying to be responsive to your deep interest in the Pentecostalists' plight. Thus, although the written message keeps their formal line intact, they may in fact be offering a kind of assurance that emigration will be permitted if the families return home first.
>
> There are two problems with this. First, the families have had several lifetimes of broken promises, and it may take a great deal more than this sort of vague and masked assurance (if that is what it is) to convince them to leave their refuge in the Embassy and apply for emigration from home. Second, given the vagueness of the message, we should be skeptical too.

What were we to make of this message from the Soviets? It did not provide anything approaching a real guarantee. On the other hand, it was a speedy response to the "special subject" the president raised with Dobrynin. It was unlikely the Soviets would dupe us to get the Pentecostals out of the embassy and then double-cross us. That would only enrage the president. Increasingly, I came to the view that this was a significant overture.

A breakthrough on the Pentecostal Christians could open other avenues for progress. I drew up a set of ideas for the president presenting a longer-term view of our relations with the Soviets. I urged that we work to set up a systematic dialogue, consider renewing some languishing agreements, point toward a possible Reagan-Gromyko meeting, reopen the idea of reciprocal consulates in Kiev and New York, and consider a new agreement on cultural exchange. Above all, we had to devise a clear strategy on human rights. We could not continue simply to vilify the Soviets publicly and expect them to respond by doing the things we wanted. It was time to start some quiet diplomacy. The critical element was to get the president heavily engaged. The more he was engaged, the better off we would be. "When he's engaged, he's good," I said.

If we urged the Pentecostals to leave the embassy, we would be taking their lives in our hands. We couldn't do it on the basis of vague assurances. In the early 1960s, Pentecostal Pyotr Vashchenko first appealed to the Soviet government for the right to leave the Soviet Union so that he could practice his religion freely. He had served prison sentences for his religious beliefs but had never given them up. In June 1978, Pyotr, his wife, Avgustina, and three of his daughters, Lidia, Lyubov, and Liliya, along with two other Pentecostals, Mariya Chmykhalov and her son Timofei, rushed past Soviet guards and entered the American embassy in Moscow. After they refused to leave, the "Siberian Seven," as they became known, were given refuge there. They were not Pentecostals in the American tradition;

they were Siberian Orthodox Old Believers, people unwilling to accept compromise or deal in any way with ungodly authorities. They wanted to leave the Soviet Union, and they knew that taking refuge in our embassy would dramatize the lack of religious freedom in their country.

Two and a half years later, in December 1981, still living in the American embassy basement, Avgustina and Lidia Vashchenko began a hunger strike. Lidia kept at it and became desperately ill in January 1982. She was taken to a Soviet hospital. When she was released, she returned to her home in Chernogorsk, Siberia.

Following Sokolov's visit to my office in late February 1983, we received in early March some indirect assurances. The Soviet vice consul in San Francisco had told a local lawyer that success on the issue of the Pentecostals depended on doing things quietly. This might be a test of us as well as the Soviets. President Reagan had said he would not "crow." Would he keep his word? This would tell the Soviets something about the president's intentions toward them.

By mid-March, President Reagan authorized me to go back to the Soviets. I called in Dobrynin on March 16. "The president is pleased with the prompt Soviet response," I said, "but wants more clarity about what would happen to the Pentecostals." I told Dobrynin that the Soviet message I was hearing was this: "If the Pentecostals in the embassy go home and apply for visas, their requests will be acted upon favorably. If I'm wrong, tell me." Persuading the Pentecostals to leave our embassy would not be easy, but if the Soviets let Lidia Vashchenko leave the country, this could offer persuasive evidence to the others to expect the same treatment when they left the protection of American officials in Moscow.

To my disappointment but not to my surprise, Dobrynin said simply that we should read the Soviet message carefully; the Soviet authorities would take into account all factors, including our appeal. He doubted that Moscow would give additional assurances. It was a matter of principle, he said, since they regarded their sovereignty to be involved, but he would report my message.

On March 23, Lidia was summoned by Soviet authorities in Chernogorsk and was told to submit a complete application and the sum required for an exit visa. "The quick response," I told the president, "suggests the importance with which Moscow views your personal interest in this case."

That same day, I told Dobrynin of President Reagan's appreciation for this. "Once Lidia actually leaves the Soviet Union," I said, "we will approach the other Pentecostals to leave the embassy and apply to leave the USSR."

"The less said publicly, the better," Dobrynin stressed.

"We will be as low-key as possible," I assured him.

By April 5, Lidia was in Moscow. She told our embassy that she would resettle in Israel and planned to fly to Vienna the following afternoon if she could complete the paperwork in time. The Israelis authorized the

Dutch embassy in Moscow to issue Lidia an Israeli visa, but they had not yet decided whether she would be permitted to settle there. By April 7, Lidia was in Vienna, but the Israelis had not yet granted her permission to enter. The Soviets had insisted that she apply for a visa to Israel, and the families in Moscow considered it essential that she go there. They insisted that Israel welcome her before they would leave the embassy.

Meanwhile, in Madrid, Max Kampelman had developed an interesting private dialogue with KGB General Sergei Kondrachev. Both of them were in Madrid for the Conference on Human Rights, sponsored by the Conference on Security and Cooperation in Europe (CSCE), set up by the 1975 Helsinki Final Act. Max was head of our delegation. Kondrachev was the nominal "number three" in theirs, but he was generally recognized as the man running their show. I thought that as a KGB man, he might have a special channel to Andropov, given his position at the helm of the KGB before becoming general secretary. After consultation with the president, I authorized Max to open a private dialogue on human rights. Kondrachev said he was authorized to talk but that Max must talk "only to him" about the issues in their private channel: in other words, the head of the Soviet delegation, Deputy Foreign Minister Anatoly Kovalev, was not to be in this loop.

Max took up the Pentecostal problem with Kondrachev and gave him a list of some sixty members of Pentecostal families. Kondrachev checked with Moscow and reported to Max that all who wished would be allowed to leave the Soviet Union. But Kondrachev gave Max an urgent message: "Lidia must go to Israel. Lidia is for it, and I have problems if she doesn't go to Israel." Our ambassador in Israel, Sam Lewis, went to work. With strenuous efforts in Jerusalem and Washington, we persuaded the Israelis. On the evening of April 7, the Israelis notified us that their ambassador in Vienna would give Lidia a visa early next morning. Max told this to Kondrachev, who said, "Thank you."

In the meantime, a man who would become a key player in this drama, Dr. Olin Robison, arrived at our embassy in Moscow. Robison, president of Middlebury College and a lay Baptist minister, had spent time in the embassy during the Carter administration and knew the Pentecostals well. He was the right person, we felt, to explain to the Pentecostals what had happened and to express our view that if they left the U.S. embassy, the Soviets would likely grant them permission to leave the Soviet Union.

Dr. Robison and others in our embassy had a strong set of arguments to work with and Lidia's departure was the clincher. On April 12, the Vashchenko and Chmykhalov families left the U.S. embassy, took flights to their village in Siberia, and applied for permission to leave. Lidia's invitation to her family to join her in Israel fulfilled the final condition imposed on the Vashchenkos for their departure from our embassy. Two consular officers accompanied the families to the airport and remained with them until they boarded their flights. I assured President Reagan that we would monitor developments in Siberia as closely as possible, but, of course, we had no American personnel there. We now had taken the fate of these human beings into our hands. And by this time we were dependent on the reliability of the inferences the Soviets had encouraged us to make from their statements.

During my periodic meetings with Dobrynin during May and June, I asked insistently about the Pentecostals. By the middle of June, we still had no certain information. But we had a strong stream of events going for us. The Williamsburg summit in late May had given the world an impressive display of Western unity and confidence. I had testified at length on our approach to U.S.-Soviet relations before the Senate Foreign Relations Committee on June 15. The president endorsed my statement and authorized me to say so to the committee, adding his authority to the views I expressed. By that time also, the CSCE conference in Madrid had reached a critical stage. While earlier discussions with the Soviets on human rights seemed to have progressed there, acccording to Kampelman, more recently the Soviets had become intransigent. I raised with Dobrynin the cases of Andrei Sakharov and Anatoly Shcharansky and the issue of Jewish emigration in general. Dobrynin responded, as before, that these were "internal matters."

The Soviet authorities announced on June 26 that the Vashchenko family would be allowed to leave the Soviet Union and that shortly thereafter the Chmykhalovs could leave. On July 18, the Chmykhalov family arrived in Vienna. The Siberian Seven were all out of the Soviet Union, along with many family members.

The president was as good as his word: he did not crow. Ronald Reagan's personal initiative had succeeded. Apparently, there were people in Moscow, perhaps General Secretary Andropov himself, who also wanted an improvement in superpower relations. In the span of a few months, Washington and Moscow had resolved a sensitive issue that had dragged on for almost five years! This "special issue" was the first successful negotiation with the Soviets in the Reagan administration. The president's own role in it had been crucial. I always felt it was significant that Ronald Reagan's first diplomatic achievement with the Soviets—largely unknown to the public all these years—was on an issue of human rights.

Was this episode also a test by the Soviet leaders of their ability to deal with Ronald Reagan? I thought so. It was, in a sense, a direct transaction. The terms were simple: the Soviets would release the Pentecostals on the condition that President Reagan didn't crow. He kept his word. If this was a test, he passed. This success, unnoticed because of its terms, encouraged President Reagan and me to continue to pursue our efforts to turn the superpower relationship into something far more positive.

CHAPTER 13

Japan: Strategic Partner and Economic Power

My relationship with Japan began with World War II. I fought the Japanese in the Pacific as a U.S. Marine. Like other Americans then, I saw Japan as the enemy. Nevertheless, as a fighting marine, I learned to view the Japanese fighting ability with great respect. We fought to win, and the Japanese did the same. We saw that they could be formidable. We also saw many instances of brutality and overbearing behavior when they were in control.

Two instances of combat stick in my memory. The first involved the island of Nanumea, where the United States wanted to establish an air base and a hospital before the imminent bloody assault on Tarawa. I was a second lieutenant and had just been moved up from Western Samoa to Funafuti with my antiaircraft artillery battery. With no advance notice, I was tapped on the shoulder and told that I would lead my group of about twenty marines to take Nanumea, which was thought to be lightly held. We would go up on a destroyer and land at daybreak, surprising the Japanese and taking the island. We boarded our destroyer, were carried to a point offshore Nanumea, and waded in just as day was breaking. I saw that the shore was lined with natives, and in the middle was a man in a white robe. I walked up to him. I remembered how to say hello in Samoan from my brief stay there, so I said to him, "*Talofa sole.*"

"Good morning, Lieutenant. We have been expecting you," he responded in clipped English. "The Japanese left two days ago."

They had left all right, but they were back by noontime. They dropped a bomb right in the middle of the only real structure on the island, a Roman Catholic church. No doubt they thought that was where we would go for shelter. We were impressed with their accuracy. As we were getting organized, and before we could set up good defenses and get our airfield built and hospital facilities established, there were many other bombing raids. We lost three people in my battery, one of them a close buddy. I

172

remember the shock when, in the midst of an attack, I ran over to a gun emplacement, looked around, and said, "Where's Patton?" The answer: "Patton's dead, sir."

In the battle for the Palau Islands a year later, there were heavy casualties, and I lost friends. It was a combined marine-army landing operation with support from a gigantic assembly of ships. I went in on one of the early waves and wound up for a while more or less directing traffic on the beach. Conditions were chaotic. Supplies were pouring in. The beach was crowded, so matériel had to be moved out to make room for more. As I worked to organize our beachhead, Japanese soldiers from the high ground fired down on us. That day I saw the savagery of war. When the Japanese snipers were finally talked into coming out with their hands up, they were hit by fire from all over the beach.

After we had taken the two lower islands of Palau, my antiaircraft artillery battery was set up to defend against Japanese air retaliation. When we got orders to come home, I went first to Guam and got on a troopship with about 1,200 marines. By that time I was a captain, so I was in charge of this large contingent headed for the States. We assumed that we would be recycled, put into new units, and sent on to what we all thought was the certain invasion of the main islands of Japan. It would be a bloody battle, we knew. While we were on our way to Pearl Harbor, we heard that something called an atomic bomb had been dropped on Japan. Before we docked at Pearl, the war was over. The marines on our ship had no idea what an atomic bomb was, but whatever it was, we felt that it probably saved many lives, including our own.

Having fought in the Pacific theater, I could not help but focus on Japan, although that is not the way Americans traditionally have looked at Asia. In many ways, American attitudes toward Asia and the Pacific were shaped by New Englanders who went to sea to trade or went to live abroad as missionaries. They centered their efforts in Asia on China, not Japan. In time, the strong feeling for China that had developed among the American people became a real fascination. In recent decades this fascination has tended to make U.S. foreign policy in Asia Sinocentric, especially after President Nixon's dramatic opening to China in February 1972. For me, the centerpiece has always been Japan. By far the largest economy in Asia, Japan is a key strategic partner and a dramatic example of successful democratic governance in an area where that is scarce.

The view of Japan that I brought to the job of secretary of state was this: if we underestimate the Japanese, we make a huge mistake, but we can compete successfully with them and try to come out ahead in a fair and peaceful competition that produces benefits all around. Japan at the end of World War II was beaten, its economy a shambles. The United States, in a great act of statesmanship, took special care not to repeat the

tragic error of the Versailles Treaty, which sought to perpetuate the punishment of the vanquished of World War I. We helped Japan transform
itself into a democratic society with an approach to economic development
based on free markets and enterprise.

This wholly novel approach to rebuilding relations between winners and
losers after a massive military encounter produced an outcome of immense
significance. Japan has achieved a new kind of status as a world power,
based on its strong economic accomplishments. Together, the United States
and Japan make up over one-third of the world GNP and are a prime source
of technology, finance, and managerial know-how for the world. So the
state of relations between the two is of global significance. The ups and
downs of this relationship must be dealt with carefully and the relationship
constantly attended to with good sense. America must ensure that Japan
is not tempted, because of Western neglect, shortsightedness, or hostility,
to build an economic and military zone of its own in Asia. A strong Japan
severed from America would be unnerving to Asia and the rest of the
world. The other side of the coin is that Japan, through its intense competitive challenge, can help keep the massive potential and achievements
of the American economy from declining through our own complacency.

Japan in the Nixon Years

When I became director of the Office of Management and Budget in the
Nixon administration, President Nixon seemed anxious that I be physically
part of the White House instead of across the street in the Old Executive
Office Building. He installed me in an office in the White House and
provided office space for my staff as well. I suspect that Nixon also wanted
John Ehrlichman, his domestic policy adviser, and me to get to know each
other and establish an ability to work together easily. So he sent us both
on a trip to the Far East in September 1970. "The Far East is the future,"
he told us, and we should get a sense of it in our roles in budget and
domestic policy.

This was my first trip on a big government airplane, and the plane had
no windows. As it turned out, Ehrlichman was a talented cartoonist, and
he made little sketches of each of our stops: Tokyo, Hong Kong, and Saigon.
He pasted them up in our cabin where the windows would have been. His
drawings gave us a lift during the long hours confined together in a small
space.

When we arrived in Tokyo, our ambassador, Armin Meyer, had a small
dinner for us, and he invited the minister of international trade and industry, Kiichi Miyazawa. It was one of the strangest evenings I have ever
spent in my life. In the first place, Ambassador Meyer divided the men

from the women during the cocktail period and the dinner. He clearly wanted to talk business. At that time, the big trade issue was textiles and the American desire to restrict the flow of Japanese-made textiles into the United States.

During the dinner Meyer proceeded to berate Miyazawa in a manner that astounded both Ehrlichman and me. We thought he was way out of line and started to distance ourselves from him. At one point, Miyazawa was so taken aback that he said, "Mr. Ambassador, if you persist in this line of discussion, I will have to leave." That brought the conversation back to a more sensible course. I was impressed by Miyazawa's strength and dignity. I couldn't really imagine what the ambassador was up to other than perhaps trying to impress his two visitors with how fierce he was in his attitude toward the Japanese. This was my first exposure to Japan bashing. I didn't like it.

The next day, I told him that a friend of mine, Hiro Uzawa, who had been on the University of Chicago faculty at one time and was now on the economics faculty at Tokyo University, had invited me to have lunch with a group of economists. I planned to go the following day. Could he provide transportation? The ambassador became very upset. He said that I could not go to the university because my presence would cause a riot—an anti-American riot. I told him I thought that was very doubtful, and I went, despite his misgivings. There was no riot. As it turned out, the university was not even in session. No students were around at all.

My experience with Ambassador Meyer left its mark on me. My way, I determined, would be different. Toughness and determination are one thing; bashing is something different. It is visceral and transmits a sense of disdain and dislike, if not hatred. It can lead to a reciprocal spiral of distrust and distance that is entirely counterproductive.

We, at that time, were on the verge of declaring economic war on Japan because of fear of being inundated by Japanese textiles. This pressure was generated largely by the U.S. textile lobby, which had great political clout. Not long after, however, the United States came to import almost no textiles from Japan, and Japan became a net importer of textiles. Japan transformed itself into a high-wage economy, and the textile industry chases low wages.

Japan's "Nixon Shocks"

No doubt the Japanese felt their interests were not sufficiently considered by the Nixon administration, which certainly took some actions that, though not motivated by animosity toward Japan, caused uncertainties and strains to develop in our relationship.

The first shock came with Nixon's decision to seek an opening to China,

which became public with the sudden announcement in July 1971 that
Henry Kissinger had secretly arrived in Beijing. For an event of this magnitude to occur, without warning, between the United States, Japan's democratic friend, and China, Japan's Communist neighbor, stunned them.

The second Nixon shock came with the announcement on August 15,
1971, of a major change in U.S. economic policy: the establishment of
wage and price controls, the imposition of a surtax on all imports, and the
end of our willingness to trade gold for dollars at a fixed price, as we
"closed the gold window." Eventually, this led to a new international monetary system of floating exchange rates. This change in policy came as such
a total surprise to Japan that it got its own name in Japanese—the *shokku*.
The surtax in particular seemed to them to be an attack on open trade and
their access to the vast U.S. market.

A third shock stemmed from our ill-fated effort with wage and price
controls. Wage and price controls have the characteristic that one move
leads to the next in an inexorable spiral of escalating disaster. In 1973, a
growing shortage of soybeans developed in the United States, and the price
of soybeans, of course, started to rise. In this atmosphere people assumed
that the president, who had imposed wage and price controls despite having
said he would "never" do so, would also be willing to impose controls over
exports. That, in turn, created speculation about whether or not export
controls would be imposed. Such speculation feeds on itself, as everyone
tries to tie up his supplies of the potentially controlled commodity before
such a move takes place. A speculative frenzy resulted.

There were far more contracts for future delivery of soybeans than there
were soybeans. The price skyrocketed. A decision then *was* made to impose
export controls on soybeans, as distinct from an alternative decision to
announce that controls would never be imposed, which would also have
pricked the speculative balloon. The Japanese, who had come to depend
on supplies of soybeans from the United States—anyone who has been to
Japan has seen the extraordinary number of ways in which they use soybeans as a staple of their diet—were hit with another Nixon shock, this
one affecting the breadbasket as well as the field of trade.

There came yet another shock—the fourth in the series—when in the
fall of 1973 oil prices skyrocketed as supply and demand for oil tightened
and an Arab oil embargo further disrupted oil markets. This was not the
doing of the United States, but we were regarded as the country that kept
the balance in the Middle East as well as the country whose responsibility
it was to see that international markets were orderly. So the Japanese tended
to hold the United States responsible.

All of these developments, I knew, would have an ongoing impact on
the Japanese psyche and their sense of confidence in the United States and
would be important for me, as secretary of state, to take into account in
my dealings with Japan.

Japan Joins the Club

After I became the treasury secretary in June 1972, I organized, along with my fellow finance ministers—Helmut Schmidt of West Germany, Valéry Giscard d'Estaing of France, and Tony Barber of the United Kingdom—an informal group to discuss in private the tumultuous developments on the international monetary scene. I urged my colleagues to agree to bring Japan into this group, given Japan's importance as an economic power. We did. Japan's finance minister, Kiichi Aichi, joined our meetings just before the International Monetary Fund and World Bank sessions in Nairobi, Kenya, in September 1973. Aichi was proud that this came about during his tenure as finance minister. Earlier he had won widespread confidence among his colleagues for his role at the opening of the Tokyo round of trade negotiations. A few months later, Aiichi suddenly and unexpectedly died.

I first met his successor, Takeo Fukuda, at a meeting of finance ministers in Rome in January 1974. He had been finance minister on an earlier occasion and later became prime minister. Fukuda, whose confident demeanor conveyed a sense of latent power, sought me out to talk privately. "I want you to know two things," Fukuda told me. "Keep them in mind. They will help you understand what you observe going on in Japan. First," he said, "I, Fukuda, am determined to wring inflation out of the Japanese economy." Inflation was then running at over 20 percent per year and was feared to be out of control. "Second," he said, "I took this finance portfolio with the clear understanding from the prime minister that *I would be completely in charge* of economic policy. I am the boss. And I want you to know that I am determined to get rid of inflation. You will probably hear from Japanese businessmen and politicians who will complain about the tough policies I will institute. But keep in mind my objective and its importance." He carried through on this, and he did Japan a tremendous service. Fukuda was the head of an important faction of the dominant Liberal Democratic party (LDP), so he had clout as well as brains. He exemplified Japanese determination and long-term purpose.

Two Contentious Issues: Trade and Defense

As I started in as secretary of state in July 1982, America's agenda with Japan had two contentious issues: trade and defense. Once noted for its cheap and shoddy exported goods and for riotous resistance to any security relationship with us, Japan now was a trading powerhouse and the object of Washington's campaign to see Japan expand its military might. I was not exactly on anyone else's wavelength when it came to either matter. Unlike many others, I was not in favor of protection against Japanese imports and was also not in favor of urging Japan to reestablish itself as a military power. I had met with Prime Minister Suzuki over dinner in Tokyo in May 1982 on my mission to help President Reagan prepare for the economic summit in Versailles. Suzuki, like other statesmen of the large industrial democracies, had adopted an almost automatic approach to such talks. Economic summit? Stress unity. Third World? Let us cooperate to respond to their needs. American economy? Express concern about a current problem, in this case, the U.S. deficit. U.S.-Japan relations? Together we account for over one-third of world GNP, and this "imposes on us great responsibilities." Japan's economy? Suzuki was passive and unresponsive when I raised the issue of their restrictions on imports.

It was the same old song. Suzuki personified the time-honored Japanese tactic of dealing with difficult problems by ignoring them, or studying them in the hope that they would go away, or by simply changing the subject. I reported to the president: "I don't think the Japanese government is prepared yet to face up fully to this issue." Under these circumstances, U.S.-Japanese relations would be enormously frustrating.

One feature of my weekly routine as secretary of state was a regular Wednesday breakfast with the secretary of defense, with the national security adviser usually present. Early on, Cap Weinberger made known his desire to pressure Japan to increase its spending on defense. The next thing I knew, I was cited in a memorandum from Cap to the president as agreeing to an insistent application of pressure on Japan to this end. I exploded. I had told Weinberger and Clark that I in no way agreed. I was willing to be convinced that Japan should do more in our joint defense effort, but just how was far from clear to me. "Let them contribute more to the maintenance of our bases in Japan, for example," I said. "But the last thing America should want is the re-creation of a massive Japanese military machine through a major increase in their defense spending." As time went on, pressure from senators and congressmen mounted on Cap's side of the argument, and I found myself leaning against the wind.

On October 12, 1982, I received the unexpected news that Prime Minister Suzuki would soon resign. I had no idea why. I knew he had almost been forced to resign a year earlier for allowing the word "alliance" to appear in a joint communiqué issued after discussions between the president and him in May 1981. But as far as I could tell, Suzuki's departure caught the Japanese political scene by surprise as well. Maneuvering among the elders of the Liberal Democratic party got under way promptly, but the outcome was murky.

It was not until November 26 that the Japanese Diet confirmed the new prime minister, Yasuhiro Nakasone, and a cabinet weighted heavily toward the faction of the LDP headed by Kakuei Tanaka, a man earlier discredited by his involvement in financial scandal but respected as a powerful and dynamic politician. Shintaro Abe, formerly minister for international trade and industry and known as a determined negotiator, was named foreign minister.

The new leadership was said to consider its ties with the United States to be of great importance. I told President Reagan that despite the constraints of the Japanese domestic political scene, he could expect Nakasone to be a far more vigorous leader than Suzuki. I had met Nakasone years earlier and retained a vivid impression of a forceful and dynamic man. Nakasone, I felt, was the kind of leader capable of making a real impact on the world scene as well as inside Japan. The president and I saw this as a moment of great potential importance. By mutual and quick agreement, a visit to Washington by the new prime minister was scheduled for January 1983. If we engaged with energy and imagination, I felt sure that we could move the relationship between our two countries out of its period of drift.

Ron and Yazu

On January 17, 1983, Yasuhiro Nakasone was due to arrive in Washington. We had prepared extensively. As a Californian, President Reagan saw the Asia-Pacific region as a key part of our future and Japan as of central importance in that region.

As part of my own preparation, I talked with our ambassador to Japan, Mike Mansfield. "Japan has successfully gone through the postwar period," I said to Mike, "but has somehow stood outside the political and economic system that has produced progress for everyone. In standing outside, Japan has avoided taking any real responsibility for the maintenance of the system, for defense or trade or general economic conditions. At meetings, the Japanese are generally silent. They have ideas, but they don't say much. We, on the other hand, are continually trying to cope with all the creaks and groans of the system, so one of our objectives must be to say to the Japanese, 'You can't stand outside any longer. You have such a size and scope that you must be one of the three or four nations responsible for the maintenance of the current order, not just for the benefit of Japan alone but for the benefit of the system itself.' Nakasone," I continued, "appears to be a decisive man, the kind of man who can take initiatives and induce in Japan a sense of responsibility that transcends their islands. We should encourage him. That should be our broad objective for his visit to Washington."

Mansfield agreed, but he pointed out that we were partly responsible for Japan's psychology. "Nakasone will be the best prime minister since Fukuda. He is a new type of leader," said Mansfield. Nakasone had already made a remarkable move. His trip to South Korea just six weeks after becoming prime minister was a bold step, given the deep animosity in

Korea toward Japan as a result of four decades of harsh Japanese occupation preceding World War II.

"The Japanese," I said, "are developing a troublesome reputation internationally. Whenever people go to Europe and talk to the Europeans, what they hear are increasingly anti-Japanese views. In the United States, protectionist sentiment is rising for the first time as a real force since the 1930s, when that helped lead the world toward war. We can no longer indulge in the parochial. We have to have a world view."

Mansfield tried to put this in perspective. He pointed out that the Japanese imported at that time about $6.7 billion worth of our agricultural products, and they accounted for 60 percent of our meat exports. "So," he said, "we want them to open their markets further, but we shouldn't forget that we do sell a vast quantity of agricultural and other goods to them."

I had attended a meeting at the Treasury of the key agencies involved and found that representatives from the Commerce Department and the U.S. special trade representative's office, charged with the frustrating job of conducting trade negotiations, were extremely hostile toward Japan. Our trade deficit with Japan then amounted to $20 billion a year. Our unemployment rate was near 10 percent. All signs indicated that our deep recession was coming to an end. Nevertheless, the climate was tense. The *Washington Post* editorialized on December 31, 1982, "The Japanese have been unusually shortsighted in failing to keep their trade with the United States more in balance. The same insensitivity is apparent in defense. Trade frictions and defense frictions are now growing and feeding each other. We think this is the situation Mr. Nakasone will find on his visit, and we hope it is the message he takes home."

Apparently, Nakasone had been well aware of the atmosphere that he would encounter. Three weeks before his arrival, it was announced that the Japanese defense budget would rise by 5.1 percent, the same percentage as many other components of the Japanese budget, which was itself in deficit. Four days later, on December 29, Nakasone overrode this figure and increased the defense budget by 6.5 percent. This would bring defense spending to .98 percent of Japan's gross national product, keeping it under but as close as possible to the magic 1 percent figure that long had been regarded as a barrier. While the real increase (taking inflation into account) of 4.3 percent was in excess of the NATO target of 3 percent, it nevertheless disappointed many people. Nakasone also decided that Japan should share its military technology with the United States. The export of military technology and arms had virtually been banned since 1967, reflecting Japan's aversion to participation, directly or indirectly, in military action other than the defense of their islands. The United States was interested in robots, lasers, large-scale integrated circuits and other components for weapons, fiber optics for communications, next-generation computers, and many high-quality but conventional products. The decision by Nakasone to export military technology was an important gesture, and it was not an easy one for him to make.

Four days before his arrival in Washington, Nakasone, at a meeting of key economic ministers, had set out a strategy for dismantling the labyrinthine customs, product standards, and testing procedures that U.S. businesses constantly complained about as blocking their ability to compete in the large Japanese market. A new round of trade measures was announced, reducing or eliminating entirely import duties on forty-seven farm commodities and twenty-eight industrial goods. At the same time, import quotas were expanded on a half-dozen agricultural items, including fruit puree, noncitrus fruit juice, tomato juice, and ketchup. "This is the reality of dealing with Japan," I said. "You go from grand strategy to fruit puree without catching your breath." Those of us working on the trade problem regarded all these steps by the Japanese as positive, but not nearly sufficient in view of the size of the problem.

Nakasone stepped out of his aircraft at Andrews Air Force Base on schedule, accompanied by his wife, his daughter, and Shintaro Abe, his foreign minister. Reagan and Nakasone, both high-spirited, self-confident individuals, hit it off immediately. It is Ronald Reagan's nature to try to get to know the other guy. The two leaders developed a special and personal rapport and mutual respect. Even across cultures, they somehow understood each other. Nakasone was pleased with the president's initiative to use first names in private, and he began to refer to "my friend, Ron."

The visit had lots of charm, much of it contributed by Nakasone's daughter, who had lived in the United States and spoke English well. She acted as his hostess and did much of the informal interpreting. She gave the whole visit a warm air of friendship. A year later, when I stopped briefly in Tokyo after a trip to China, who should greet me at the airport but Nakasone's daughter. It was Valentine's Day, and she gave me a big chocolate valentine.

I wanted to get to know Foreign Minister Abe, just as the president was getting to know Nakasone. I invited Abe to my home for an informal visit before one of the formal dinners. Such a personal gesture seemed to come as a surprise to the Japanese, who took it as a mark of respect, which it was. It was also the start of a friendship and of productive work with Abe that would extend over a period of almost five years. We met on well over thirty occasions.

During his visit, Nakasone addressed the defense issue squarely. Japanese territory taken by the Soviets after World War II was still in Soviet hands, and Japan felt threatened by strengthened Soviet forces. Nakasone realized Japan had several military missions: to devise an air defense against Soviet bombers; to gain the capacity to keep Soviet surface ships and submarines from traversing Japan's straits in an emergency; and to extend protection to Japan's sea lanes. These were important and entirely defensive undertakings, but the Soviets responded with brutal harshness to Nakasone's stated intent to carry them out. An official commentary in *Tass* warned Japan that "the authors of such plans make Japan a likely target for a retaliatory strike . . . this could spell a national disaster more serious than the one that befell it 37 years ago." The bullying tactics of the Soviets were not, we could see, limited to Europe. But Nakasone persevered, moving Japan one step further into the security network erected by the West and symbolized most dramatically by NATO.

All in all, in his meetings with the president, the Congress, and the press, Nakasone made a tremendous impression. The *Washington Post* wrote on January 23, 1983: "Yasuhiro Nakasone, visiting Washington last week for the first time as Japan's prime minister, turned out to be that unusual leader with a coherent vision and considerable political courage. Just as Japan's unchecked military expansion brought it isolation and ultimate disaster in World War II, he pointed out, so now the political leadership must ensure that Japan's economic expansion does not produce a contemporary isolation. He pledged to help Japan become 'a harmonious member of the international community.' "

Nakasone was as decisive a leader as any who had come to Washington in a long time. He was ready to take political risks and make clear statements of position. Unlike other Japanese leaders who waited for a consensus to form, he was ready to move out in front. One of his most striking characteristics was his impressive control of his brief. He studied and knew the issues in their full complexity and detail. And he was ready when discussions went beyond the agenda to issues that came up out of the blue.

What lay ahead, however, was an ongoing effort to pick away at and work out countless problems. One by one, issues would be resolved; then others would arise, in a virtually continuous process of negotiations, consisting of pressure, persuasion, and a good deal of frustration on both sides.

Meeting the Japanese on Their Turf

Only a week after Nakasone departed from Washington, I was bound for Tokyo for my first visit there as secretary of state. I had long scheduled a trip to China and wanted to dramatize my positive attitude toward Japan by going there first. We took off from Washington early in the morning and flew for hours over the northern wilderness of Canada, an endless expanse of undisturbed, harsh country, forbidding and featureless until we crossed the Yukon and met the mountains of the Alaska Range. Snow softened the sharp peaks and filled up the crevices and rocky bowls. The land around Anchorage was barren and frozen mud. It was three in the afternoon when we arrived there, and the sun looked as if it was about to set, but it didn't: it hung suspended just above the horizon, casting a diffuse white glow. We landed in Japan late Sunday afternoon, having crossed North America and the Pacific Ocean without once losing sight of the sun. Yet when we arrived in Tokyo, it was the day after we left. I will never get accustomed to the International Date Line.

I had seen Tokyo grow and change over a period of twenty years from a city of human scale into an architecturally nondescript hive of humanity. Many of the buildings had a bland modernity that reflected the fact that the Tokyo earthquake of 1923 and the firebombing some twenty years later created considerable latitude for urban renewal. Tokyo is not organized in a Western sense. Streets twist and curve and intersect at peculiar angles as they follow the pattern of old labyrinthine roadways that once surrounded the Imperial City and were designed less for the smooth flow of traffic than for the defensibility of the Imperial walls. Yet for all its impenetrability, the city is neat and clean. What it may lack in grandeur it makes up for in vitality. Tokyo reflects Japanese society—a Western veneer masking Oriental structure, intricacy, and purpose-directed energy.

We had lunch with Foreign Minister Abe at the Ikura House, an exaggerated example of shoji architecture—the fragile style of paper windowpanes set in wood-frame panels. I couldn't help but notice that the entire upper echelon of the Japanese Foreign Ministry wore glasses, somehow giving me the fleeting impression that there were more of them than us. Both Abe and I gave straightforward, if bland, toasts. All in the U. S. contingent were bone tired, and some could barely stay awake. I saw Paul Wolfowitz, the new assistant secretary for Far East Affairs, with his chin on his chest. He was passed a note during dinner that read: "Rule One for a new assistant secretary: *never* fall asleep during the secretary's toast." Paul later asked the note passer, an experienced foreign service officer, how he managed to stay awake.

"I have been sitting on my fork," he replied. Diplomacy is a cagey craft.

In Tokyo the next morning it was Sunday afternoon in Washington, and the Washington Redskins were playing in the Super Bowl. We all wanted to see the game, and the Japanese made special arrangements for it to be televised at a studio set up for us. At a crucial moment deep in the second half of the game, a messenger touched me on the shoulder. The time had come for me to depart for my audience with the emperor. I left the room of football fans just moments before John Riggins scored the game-winning touchdown for the Redskins.

I had visited the emperor on an earlier occasion, and I knew that this stylized visit was of great symbolic significance. He did not customarily see visiting foreign ministers. I had not seen the meticulously manicured grounds of the Imperial Palace since I had first visited as treasury secretary.

The palace itself is contemporary and elegant, though not palatial in a European sense. Emperor Hirohito, frail at his advanced age, conducted our meeting with pleasant dignity. I followed the script, but I could not suppress a flashback to my World War II experience, when Hirohito symbolized the enemy.

The following evening we were hosts to the Japanese at our ambassador's residence, a grand old structure used by General Douglas MacArthur when he arrived in Tokyo. A large, narrow hall looks onto the gardens. In this room General MacArthur, regal in bearing, received Emperor Hirohito, who in a symbolic, dramatic act, came to MacArthur rather than the other way around. That night, after having had my own meeting with Emperor Hirohito, I presented Foreign Minister Abe with a burgundy-and-gold Redskins pennant and we all sang "Hail to the Redskins." After the song, I pulled out a Redskins scarf and cap and put them on him. Flashbulbs popped. We all laughed. These two events—Hirohito and MacArthur, Abe and me—in the same hallway but a generation apart hardly carried equal historical weight, but they showed the dramatic change in attitudes of former enemies toward each other.

During my meetings, strong Japanese views emerged about the intermediate-range nuclear forces (INF) negotiations. When Nakasone was in Washington, we had sought to capture the interest and involvement of the Japanese. By this time, they realized not only that Soviet SS-20s were aimed at Japan but that if attention was given only to NATO's needs, Japan might wind up being uniquely targeted. Both Nakasone and Abe backed President Reagan's zero option in the Geneva talks, and Abe outlined specific negotiating requirements to advance Japan's interests. They wanted to be sure that we adhered to our stated position of global limits as a central concept in the negotiations. The Japanese were particularly concerned about the "walk in the woods" formula that would have reduced missiles in Europe but would have merely frozen existing levels of SS-20 nuclear missiles—estimated to be about ninety warheads—in Soviet Asia. That was more than enough to destroy all the key targets in Japan. Japan would not agree to any arms control arrangement under which the Soviets could move missiles from west to east or that required the destruction of Soviet missiles in Europe while leaving them in Asia at the current level. I assured Abe that the United States would never do something welcomed by Europe but destructive to the rest of the world.

Even a short visit to Japan imparts a sense of the Japanese aesthetic. The Japanese have a natural and graceful interest in doing things well. Beyond economy and efficiency, there is for the Japanese a precisely correct way of doing things, and practicing to achieve that perfection is an expectation and fulfillment. This aesthetic underlies the Japanese way of life in everything from shipbuilding to flower arranging. It gives structure and order to the manners of an individual or the militarism of a nation. It can be stylized, which explains a lot about Kabuki plays and sumo wrestling, but stylization in a sense is the object of the exercise. Originality is not necessarily valued. These are impressive people, reinforced by insularity and ethnic uniformity and centuries of repetition. Visiting Japan can sometimes make one feel clumsy.

That evening, after I went back to the Okura Hotel, I put on the blue-and-white yukata provided by the hotel management. It is a lightweight cotton robe and very comfortable. I couldn't help but notice, however, that there were no side loops to hold the belt when it is untied. Our own civilization, I mused, clumsy though it can be at times, has come up with an improvement in bathrobe design; we in the West are not without refinements of our own.

On the second of February, I flew to China and from there to Korea and to Hong Kong for a meeting with our ambassadors from throughout the region. I landed in Tokyo on my way home to report back to Foreign Minister Abe. Stopping first and last in Japan symbolized a special interest in our relations with Japan, and I made it my regular practice.

By this time, an additional and persistent practice was emerging. With the prime minister or foreign minister, and in innumerable other contacts, we always banged away on trade issues: identifying problems, setting deadlines, using an impending meeting to try to pry loose concessions of one kind or another. The process was frustrating, debilitating, and unending, but much was accomplished. Nevertheless, the trade imbalance kept growing, owing to macroeconomic factors, especially the imbalance of saving and investment rather than the rules of trade. We always talked about strategic matters, with the Japanese becoming increasingly aware of the importance of their role in the strategic equation with the Soviet Union. Then we would discuss our respective economic-assistance and security-assistance programs, sharing ideas about needs worldwide to see how we could make our efforts as complementary as possible. We sought continually to broaden Japan's sense of its global interests. China was always a subject of fascination to the Japanese, and we compared notes on developments in China each time we met.

The Relationship Strengthens

The year 1983 was one of close attention to Japan. The process of frequent contacts continued. Abe and I met again in Paris on May 11 at the annual ministerial meeting of the Organization for Economic Cooperation and Development (OECD). President Reagan was host for the economic summit in Williamsburg toward the end of May. This was a big event for the president. It was preceded by a special bilateral meeting with Prime Minister Nakasone. The two men once again shared an easy rapport. By way of assuring the president of his cooperation to make the summit meeting a success, Nakasone said, "Ron, you be the pitcher, and I'll be the catcher."

"You can be sure that I will throw them straight," Reagan responded.

The security communiqué from Williamsburg was notable in that it identified Japan with the security system of the West, not just through the bilateral strategic partnership with the United States. This was Nakasone's doing. It was a strong, bold, and important step for him to take.

The most dramatic expression, at least to me, of Nakasone's commitment to and involvement in the global agenda occurred two years later, at the May 1985 economic summit in Bonn. At one point, President François Mitterrand of France expressed his skepticism about the economic summits and said that he might not come anymore because they were worthless. No one took him all that seriously, feeling it was a bit of an act and a way of expressing his frustration. Nevertheless, Mitterrand spoke with apparent conviction. After a while, Prime Minister Nakasone asked for the floor.

Basically, what he said was, "Here you are, Mitterrand, living in a country that has been democratic for a long time, surrounded by other democracies. You meet with your peers all the time, so it's one thing for you to be cavalier about these meetings. Look at my situation. What other major country in Asia can you really call a democracy? Remember, Japan is struggling with this Western concept, and we're making it work, but there is no peer group around us. We have to go all the way to Australia and New Zealand to find a clear-cut democratic counterpart, so these annual economic summits of the major countries that are free and democratic are of tremendous symbolic significance in Japan. They mean a great deal to me and to us. And they should mean a great deal to you, because Japan is a country that is part of this democratic system."

This was a riveting moment for me. His statement had great significance, and I found his words very moving. The Europeans did not seem to get the point. No one said a word to Nakasone. So I went over and told him that I had listened carefully to what he said and that I had great respect for his message and its importance.

Throughout my time in office, we urged Japan to take its place on the world's stage. We said to the Japanese, you are a mighty economic power and have benefited greatly by the economic system put in place after World War II. Now it is time for Japan not simply to benefit from this system but to contribute to it: by opening your markets, by being generous with aid (and not merely aid tied to purchases from Japan), and by taking an interest in the world beyond the countries of your most immediate neighborhood. And you must be a contributing partner in the strategic alliance that contains Soviet aggression and maintains a world of economic openness and political freedom.

President Reagan in Japan

An important opportunity to move forward on these problems came with President Reagan's trip to Japan and Korea in November 1983. By the middle of 1983, the president and I had spent considerable time discussing his prospective travel. I felt strongly that a presidential visit to Japan should precede one to China. Japan should in no way be used as a kind of launching pad for a trip to China. The president agreed. I had gone over the president's agenda carefully with him well in advance of his departure for Japan. He was well prepared. So on November 8 we boarded *Air Force One* and left for Japan and South Korea. An injudicious member of the White House retinue handed me a few sheets of paper when we landed, giving his impressions of *Air Force One* and its occupants. Here is his fanciful account:

> I am flying with the Government of the United States. We cruise above the Canadian Rockies in the blue-grey flat light of arctic dusk. We are a caravan of five airplanes. Air Force One, which carries the President; AF-26000, which transports staff and is haunted by the memory of carrying John Kennedy's body from Dallas to Washington; AF-970, in which Lyndon Johnson installed what some regard as an airborne throne; a contracted Boeing 747 carrying some 200 press; and, hovering always somewhere above us, the NEACP (pronounced "kneecap"), which is the Command Post for the President in the event of war. It seems an elaborate assemblage for the stark wastes of the white Yukon.
>
> Still, we are the King and his Court traveling in procession to a distant land. The King himself works and naps in the forward compartment of the airplane. He is isolated and, although approachable, is not approached. As with all kings, he must struggle against his august isolation or it will eventually bring him down. In the second, open compartment sits the King's Council, those who know the ways of the land and the customs of the people but who are responsible only to the King.
>
> There, amidst cushions, is Prince George, who advises the King on how to treat with foreign monarchs. He is experienced, honest, and loyal, but he has never been a member of the inner circle of the Court and does not reside in the Palace. He has integrity and weight. The King's subjects sleep better in their villages at night because he reassures them. He is, however, the object of plots and intrigues which he can ignore so long as he retains the King's favor. But if the King frowns, he will be sent away to the western provinces, although he is the only true noble in the King's entourage.
>
> Across from Prince George, in a high-backed lounge chair, sits Duke Edwin of Meese. He is a clever, wily man, somewhat astonished that his seigneur is now the King. Duke Edwin, unfortunately, is incapable of organizing even the King's kitchen, though he still has the King's ear and he can contribute

common sense. Opposite him sits the Marquis of Baker, who is ambitious and cunning. He is skilled with daggers. He is shrewd in his political judgments and ruthless in his political decisions. He is effective and makes the White House run. He has, however, served rival kings before and is therefore always suspect. The Earl of Deaver is the Royal Chamberlain and guards the royal door. He has used the position of managing the household to accumulate great personal power and to assemble his own retinue. He is cunning. He bells cats. The Baron Bud, who comes from McFarlane, deals with the security of the realm. He is not comfortable in this forward compartment. His great strength is competence, which is irrelevant. He has no political base of his own in the Palace, and without a demonstration of the King's confidence, he is vulnerable to the vagaries of the Court. He is therefore unsure of himself, and rightly so because the King has had the heads of his two predecessors.

In the third and fourth compartments sit an assortment of knights, pages, and knaves, all of whom serve different members of the Council and, like mirrors, reflect the status and authority of their masters. In the fifth compartment is a detachment of the King's Guard, muscular, angular men with varieties of menacing metal protruding from their waists. From this particularly rocky soil, however, springs a delicate flower in a pale blue velveteen jumpsuit. He prances and swivels up and down the aisle; perhaps the jester, you say. But no, the Queen's hairdresser. And finally, in the rear sits a select group of scribes of the Court whose duty it is to record every word uttered by the King so that the people of the realm will know what he has spoken.

We had hardly landed in Tokyo before the official arrival ceremony took place at Akasaka Palace, where the president and Nancy would stay during their visit. The palace is gigantic and incongruous: pink-and-white rooms plucked lock, stock, and sconces from the eighteenth-century French countryside. The palace, whose design was based on the Palace of Versailles and the Louvre, benumbs the visitor's eye. President Reagan descended the grand red-carpeted staircase and was greeted outdoors by Emperor Hirohito, then eighty-two years old, slightly bent, his morning coat hanging loosely. He seemed to sway as he stood next to the president, as if a breeze could knock him over. As fragile as the emperor was, he represented an astonishing political and religious continuity in Japanese life. Legend has it that his family and its throne date back over 2,000 years of unbroken lineage. And in those millennia, Japan had never been conquered by outside invaders until 1945. Anthems played. The wind blew again over the gray stone courtyard, slapping flags, and the emperor swayed. Ronald Reagan graced these ceremonies with a style and a snap. He saluted, turned, and inspected the troops. He did it all smartly and made me feel proud.

At one point during the visit we were taken to join the crown prince and princess to view an ancient Japanese rite. At the Meiji Shrine archers on horseback plunged through the chill gray drizzle firing knot-tipped arrows at targets no bigger than dessert plates. They missed and missed again. The orange-tasseled horses charged as the rider set, in seconds, a third arrow in his long bow. Another rider charged, his black-and-yellow jacket billowing in the wind, the heavy thump of hoofs throwing clods of mud behind. The archer stood steady in the stirrups and took aim, firing at the instant of the pass-by and shattering the plate into a cloud of rainbow confetti. The drum beat in the forest as it did centuries ago when Japanese archers on horseback broke up the army of Genghis Khan.

Throughout the visit, the meetings between President Reagan and Prime Minister Nakasone, between Abe and me, and between others up and down the line and their Japanese counterparts carried forth the endless debate over our trade and security agenda. The mutual esteem between Ron and Yazu continued to grow. My own relationship with Abe helped settle a few problems. All in all, we had developed the best government-to-government relationship with Japan in many a year.

President Reagan, accorded the unusual opportunity of addressing the Japanese Diet, gave a stirring speech. He revealed a deeply rooted belief, one that was not remotely appreciated or given much attention at the time: "I say our dream is to see the day when nuclear weapons will be banished from the face of the Earth. . . . We want significant reductions and we're willing to compromise. . . . We must not and we will not accept any agreement that transfers the threat of longer range nuclear missiles from Europe to Asia." The Japanese loved it. The arms control community cringed, and they did not take seriously Reagan's views about banishing nuclear weapons. Nuclear weapons had kept the peace, and the genie could not be put back in the bottle, they felt. Nevertheless, President Reagan's instinctive rejection of Mutual Assured Destruction was powerful. "A nuclear war can never be won and must never be fought," he said.

Economic Issues and Their Strategic Significance

Issues surrounding the need for more open markets and the large imbalance of trade with Japan have been and remain great sources of tension between Japan and the United States and, for that matter, between Japan and countries throughout the world. As the buildup of foreign exchange in Japanese hands has emerged in the form of Japanese investments in the United States and elsewhere, Japanese ownership of important assets in the United States has also become an issue.

As an economist and a believer in the benefits of free trade, I worried less about such developments than did most people in Washington. If the Japanese, as a producer-dominated and protected society, want to pay astronomical prices for goods that are cheaper elsewhere, that is more their problem than ours. Our problem—and challenge—is to produce goods that are competitive in price and quality. If we are worried about foreign financing of investment in the United States, let us increase our own savings to finance our own investment. In other words, I felt, if we wanted to see our real problem, we should look in the mirror.

Nevertheless, my years in Washington had taught me that economics is one thing and politics is something else. So I worked hard to get the Japanese to open their markets and counseled quietly with the president and my colleagues on the importance of dealing with our own huge federal deficit, which amounts to a massive dissaving.

Our strategy with Japan was, in effect, to use a continuing series of action-forcing events to put the spotlight on Japanese restrictions on trade and to get those restrictions reduced. After the president's November 1983 trip to Japan, for example, we created a special task force to follow up on all the commitments made or implied during the visit and named Vice President Bush as its chairman. The Japanese have no counterpart to a vice president, so after struggling over who should be the Japanese opposite number, Prime Minister Nakasone took on the job himself. By doing so, Nakasone raised the political risks but also delivered a political message to the Japanese bureaucracy.

The process of negotiating reductions in Japan's restrictions on imports went on and on. After the Japanese and U.S. elections in late 1984, Prime Minister Nakasone met with President Reagan in Los Angeles on January 2, 1985. We identified a handful of key industries for attention, with the May economic summit in Bonn serving as a deadline for action. The effort marked a departure from earlier trade talks in which the issues simply emerged from the U.S. political process. This time we selected areas in which U.S. competitiveness was strong and real barriers were keeping us out of the Japanese market. These so-called MOSS (market-oriented, sector-selective) talks produced positive results in a painful, tooth-pulling effort that left everyone involved a little ragged and frustrated. Foreign Minister Abe and I were charged with the task of overseeing what became a year-long process.

Finally, on January 10, 1986, after some last-minute concessions by Japan on forest products, Abe and I issued a joint statement. The talks succeeded beyond our expectations in expanding U.S. access to Japan's telecommunications, medical equipment, and pharmaceutical markets and made substantial progress on forest products. Our joint statement not only set out the achievements in the negotiations but also outlined issues left on the table and steps still to be taken in Tokyo to implement what had been agreed upon.

As secretary of state, I made a point of trying to have my say on economic matters privately with the secretary of the treasury or the president. Having been treasury secretary and budget director, I felt frequent public statements by me would be a problem for those holding my former positions, so I didn't do much of that. At the same time, as 1985 moved along, no one seemed to be stating what the general economic problems were. I had been invited to speak at Princeton, my alma mater, to a convocation on April 11, 1985, at the Woodrow Wilson School of Public and International Affairs.

I addressed the problem of interrelated imbalances in the U.S. economy and in the world economy: our budget imbalance, our trade imbalance (especially with Japan), the United States's and Japan's imbalances of savings and domestic investment, and the related strong capital inflows to the United States and the excessively strong dollar. I was concerned about the tendency of people to think that the reason for our big trade deficit, including our big trade deficit with Japan, was the barriers to imports erected by Japan and other countries. I believed that Japan was, and is, far too restrictive against imports for its own good and far too attached to inefficient methods of distribution. Japanese consumers were paying the price. But it was not possible to explain the rise in our own trade deficit by changes in Japanese restrictions on trade. On the contrary, the period of our rising deficit with Japan coincided with the increased opening of Japan to international trade. Japan's economy was not as open as ours, but it was more open than it had been ten years before. Therefore, the increase in the U.S. trade deficit could *not* be blamed on a change in Japanese trade barriers.

I argued that Japan was a high-savings country, with savings far higher than domestic investment. Therefore, in order for Japan to maintain a high level of employment, it had to have a large surplus of exports over imports, thereby raising the level of final demand to the level of its production capability. It followed that if the trade surplus of Japan was to be brought down, this disparity between savings and investment needed to be corrected. How? Examine, for example, the rather substantial tax incentives in Japan for saving and examine the need for investment in infrastructure and housing to the benefit of the Japanese consumer.

At the same time, the United States's problem was the reverse. Our net savings, in considerable part owing to our large federal deficit, were small relative to our appetite for investment, so we had drawn capital in from abroad to finance that investment. That, in turn, made it possible for our total demand (consumption plus investment) to exceed our production, producing our large-scale trade deficit. The deficit would fall if our savings rose, so that we could finance our own investment. Our deficit would also fall if our economy slumped, lessening the demand for imports—though no one wants to cut the deficit that way.

My message was, if we are to cure the deficit-surplus problem, it will be necessary for both the United States and Japan to change the relative pattern of savings and investment. Without that, we would be in for continuing frustration.

My speech received considerable attention in Japan, particularly from Prime Minister Nakasone. We developed a little joke between us. Nakasone was one of the best-informed heads of government that I encountered. When he talked about a subject, he was worth listening to. So I called him my professor, and he enjoyed that. When he read my Princeton speech and thought it was good, he started calling me *his* professor. In October 1985, he appointed a commission headed by Haruo Maekawa. The commission's report, released on April 7, 1986, was far more detailed and sophisticated about Japan than I had been in my talk, but its basic line of analysis was consistent with mine. Subsequently, Prime Minister Nakasone pledged to President Reagan to make an "historic change" in Japan's economy, committing his government to transform its export-driven economy into one led by domestic investment and consumer demand. That proved easier said than done.

On March 6 and 7, 1987, I talked in Tokyo with Nakasone and Abe. From the standpoint of economic advice, I said, "Give the consumer a break. Produce a market where prices in Japan are as low as prices for the same goods elsewhere. And change the tax treatment of savings and the attitude toward infrastructure so the consumers get a fair shake." My advice to the United States was: let's raise our savings to finance our own investment; that means getting our federal budget deficit under control. At the same time, it was in our interest and Japan's for the Japanese to continue to open their markets. But we must not close our markets to the Japanese. Whenever I hear a U.S. politician talking about how we should close our borders to Japanese products, I say, "Watch your wallet, Mr. and Mrs. Consumer. When the politicians want to protect you from the goods you love to buy, they will rob you blind."

The opening of Japan's markets was and is important as a matter of fairness, not only for the United States but for the world. A great deal of headway had been made in opening those markets. At the same time, the continued large trade surpluses raised concern about what the Japanese were trying to achieve. Japan was developing huge surpluses of foreign exchange, which meant more resources and more power to exert around the world. Of course, because Japan had saved, it had the resources. But this saving had been achieved at the expense of Japanese consumers and Japan's own infrastructure. Perhaps that was beginning to change, but questions remained about Japan's objectives. Was Japan trying to achieve by sheer economic power what it wasn't able to achieve with military power? And if so, as it tried to exercise that power, would it do so with the same insensitivity—and sometimes, brutality—that characterized its military occupations and tactics?

So we saw a paradox: Japan was respected for its clear accomplishments, yet feared. The rise of Japan to a central place among the world's nations meant that just about everyone had to engage with the Japanese. The nature and quality of that engagement was a compelling concern. As I traveled around the Asia-Pacific region, I was impressed by the combination of respect for and fear of Japan. The Chinese, Koreans, Filipinos, Singaporeans, Malaysians, and Indonesians all had direct experience of an often brutal and overbearing Japanese occupation.

When it came to America, this paradox was presented most vividly when facing the question of Japan's military role in the security structure of the free world. The issue was particularly prominent in the Reagan years. The United States, with Secretary Weinberger pushing particularly hard, had sought to persuade Japan to increase its defense spending and to take on more of the burden of its self-defense, making more tangible the responsibility announced earlier for a 1,000-mile perimeter of defense out into the Pacific. When I visited in the Philippines, the Filipinos were anxious to know where that 1,000 miles began. If it started on the Japanese-owned island of Okinawa, then the arc would include the Philippines, but if it started in Tokyo, then it wouldn't include the Philippines. One thing was clear: the Filipinos didn't want to be included.

Everywhere I went in the Asia Pacific, the idea of a rearmed Japan was opposed, and the idea of a Japan with a strategic relationship with the United States, including the presence of American troops on Japanese soil, was welcomed. The close and daily contact of American with Japanese forces would provide a kind of window on what Japan was doing and a check to prevent any unmonitored buildup. It would give "transparency" to the sort of military measures that raise the greatest concern.

I have often wondered whether the Japanese trust themselves any more than other people trust them when they have large-scale power in their hands. There is a feeling that they don't have a rheostat, only a switch that can go on or off but is difficult to moderate.[1]

When I was visiting Pearl Harbor, Ron Hays, the commander in chief of the Pacific Command (CINCPAC), took me down to the dockside to see an impressive naval ship flying the Japanese flag from the fantail. As a former marine, whenever I see a warship with the Rising Sun on the white field of the flag of Japan, my emotions take me momentarily back to wartime; it is a wrenching feeling. But then I looked again and saw berthed alongside the Japanese warship destroyers of the Royal Australian Navy with their flag, and of the U.S. Navy with the Stars and Stripes flying.

These ships, berthed together, symbolized a different relationship and

1. I was struck, years later, by a statement Prime Minister Nakasone made in a speech at Stanford University on February 18, 1992: "The Japan-U.S. security arrangement serves as a stabilizer in the Asia-Pacific by providing a security guarantee and also preventing a resurgence of Japanese militarism."

a sense of partnership, a change welcomed throughout the Pacific and, I suspected, in Japan as well. Japan the enemy had become Japan the partner. One of our jobs was, and is, to provide the rheostat.

An Unnoticed Turning Point

Diplomacy shapes the future in two ways: by decisive action at critical historical moments when information is scanty but choices must be made; and by long, evolutionary work, often nearly unobserved by the public eye. The latter often produces more lasting and significant change.

The story of Japan and the United States in the 1980s holds little drama but great importance for the world's future. In those years, a turning point of world-historical force took shape. A third continent joined Europe and America in the vanguard of global progress. Nothing is more striking in recent international history than the phenomenal development of the Asia-Pacific region from the unstable, war-racked zone of the 1950s, 1960s, and 1970s to the impressive economies of today. The transformation occurred because of Asian talent, drive, and determination, but it would not have occurred had the United States not carried forward its objective of sharing, rather than seeking to monopolize, world power and leadership.

The United States created an environment for regional stability that fostered progress. Our effort in Vietnam bought time for other Asian nations to pursue open economic policies and it blunted Communist ambitions in the region. Our revival of U.S.-China relations in the Reagan era helped turn that nation toward a potentially constructive path. And the manner of our commitment to our friends and allies, from Jakarta to Manila and Seoul, fostered a sense of strong self-reliance.

Even more significantly, America provided the economic context in which Asian progress could take hold. Without the accessibility of American markets to Asian imports, this great transformation could not have taken place. Between 1981 and 1987, America's imports from Asian countries increased four times over. Without such U.S. willingness to buy from Asian countries, they would never have been able to expand their export trade, which was the engine of their economic growth. Despite strong congressional and public voices calling for import restrictions, the Reagan administration stuck to a nonprotectionist policy.

The story was not one of the rise of Asia and the decline of America but of the entry of a new community into world leadership. And it was undergirded by a vast cultural and demographic transformation: with the Americanization of Asia came the human movements that have created a certain Asianization of America. A global intertwining had begun. Viewed from a century ahead, it could well be one of the most remarkable changes of the twentieth century. And central to this turning point was the American approach to Japan that began anew in the early 1980s.

Can this relationship be maintained on a fundamentally constructive course? The answer is by no means clear. American public opinion toward Japan went from disinterest in the 1970s to admiration in the early 1980s to resentment and bashing by the end of the decade. The Omnibus Trade Bill passed in 1988 had Japan in its sights, as changes were made in the structure of our trade laws that amounted, I argued, to procedural protectionism. Japan's ability to generate a sense of common purpose internally was impressive. But a central question remained: could this formidable nation identify with international objectives that went beyond their islands but nevertheless affected them profoundly? Prime Minister Nakasone and his administration seemed to recognize the importance to Japan of goals for the global economy and body politic. Whether Japan could mount and sustain the necessary effort, whether Japan could avoid isolating itself, were open questions. The decades to come would be powerfully affected by the answers.

CHAPTER 14

An Agreement Between
Lebanon and Israel

On Sunday, April 24, 1983, I took off from Andrews Air Force Base, headed for the Middle East. My objective was clear and public—achieve an agreement between the Lebanese and the Israelis. The bottom line was an Israeli commitment to withdraw its forces from Lebanon. The timing came against a background of political bickering and backbiting in Washington. Critics in Congress and in the press—and, for that matter, within the administration—felt that we should have long since achieved an agreement on the withdrawal of all foreign troops from Lebanon and that real progress should be under way on President Reagan's September 1 Middle East peace initiative. I shared the frustration and feared that the passage of time had both diminished our opportunities and compounded our difficulties. The story of my trip would be written as one of success or failure. Whatever the outcome, I knew it would influence how effectively I would be able to operate in the months ahead. Failure would put me under a cloud; success would give me momentum. High stakes, the sense of pressure and deadline, the edginess of the gamble, reminded me of the sound of pads slapping in the locker room before a big game.

Obstacles Abound

Through the winter of 1982–83, Mideast leaders had embarked on a familiar, disheartening series of moves. In effect, every side wanted to squeeze the system for its own purposes, regardless of the cost to the Lebanese. Jordan wanted an Israeli settlements freeze; Israel wanted U.S. assistance stepped up. Lebanon grew fearful of renewed Syrian dominance as massive Soviet military resupply flowed to Syria, and warring militias battled each other beyond the control of the weak Lebanese central authority.

Of all the obstacles to our effort to help Lebanon become an independent country free of foreign forces, the greatest was Syria. Hafez al-Assad, Syria's president, had his own agenda and was relentless in pursuing it. He wanted a Lebanon under his thumb. If Syria was excluded from the diplomatic rounds, Assad did everything possible to undercut progress. But whenever Assad's regime was included, it regarded itself as having gained the upper hand and sidetracked the diplomatic effort with impossible conditions and endless new demands. No matter how we approached them, the Syrians played the spoiler. In late 1982 through early 1983, Syria led the Lebanese to feel that it supported their work with us. But by April 1983, the Syrians were pulling the rug out from under our effort. By then they had been heavily rearmed by the Soviets, and Assad could see that Israel was weakened by deep internal political division over the Lebanese war.

Phil Habib and I therefore took the only approach that we felt had a chance of getting us to an agreement. We decided to stay in touch with Syria but try to get its principal Arab backer, Saudi Arabia, to move it in the right direction when the time came. We wanted to convince Syria that Israeli troops would not withdraw from Lebanon unless Syria was also willing to withdraw, whether or not Syria accepted the agreement we sought. The Saudis were convinced that Israel would not pull out; they saw "Operation Peace for Galilee" as a war of conquest and feared that we could never get an agreement from Israel to withdraw. Israel was set, the Saudis said, on creating a North Bank. When Israel agreed to withdraw, we would expect the Arab nations to pressure Syria to withdraw as well. A key piece of information had emerged months before, in September, from the Arab summit at Fez: the Saudis had informed us then that Syria had agreed to leave Lebanon when Israeli forces left. So we kept Syria generally informed of the negotiations without inviting its participation in discussions over the precise form an agreement might take.

Although the Syrians did the most to obstruct progress, the Israelis were not far behind. In fact, a secret and abortive effort by Israeli Defense Minister Ariel Sharon in the weeks following the Palestine Liberation Organization (PLO) evacuation cost valuable time at an opportune moment. The Israelis, who were both gloating and troubled, wanted the maximum political benefit from their massive military operation: they wanted nothing short of a peace treaty and full diplomatic relations with Lebanon, as they had previously achieved with Egypt. Egypt had been able to make peace with Israel in exchange for the return of the Sinai and still remain at the heart of the Arab world, even if estranged. Egypt was large enough, strong enough, and independent enough to withstand this temporary estrangement. Lebanon was not and could not; this the Israelis simply would not understand.

*   *   *

Over seven months had elapsed—precious time—since the successful evacuation of the PLO from Beirut on September 1, 1982, and President Reagan's speech launching his Middle East peace initiative that same day. It had been a long time, too, since the assassination of Bashir Gemayel and the massacres at Sabra and Shatila. Meanwhile, the Soviets had not only reequipped the Syrians; they were themselves manning surface-to-air missiles in Syria and Lebanon. The Israelis had squandered much of the goodwill their expulsion of the PLO leadership had generated among some of the Lebanese, and they had emerged in the eyes of much of the world as heedless, dangerous, and arrogant. The European Community had condemned Israel's invasion of Lebanon and refused to complete an arrangement to provide Israel with some $50 million in aid. Phil Habib and his deputy, Morrie Draper, had been struggling to reach an agreement during all these months. A structure was in hand, but the essential political decisions, let alone the details of the agreement, were not in sight. The questions were tough. How much normalization, if any, between Lebanon and Israel could be expected? How should security for northern Israel be handled? Would this require an Israeli presence in southern Lebanon? Would the presence of Major Saad Haddad's Lebanese Christian militia, supported by Israel, be acceptable to the Lebanese and sufficient for the Israelis? Some such security arrangement would be essential to Israel. I knew both sides were formidable bargainers, and, in a sense, liked nothing better than to bargain—endlessly.

I also knew I would need to undertake a shuttle mission around Middle East capitals if we were to have any chance of reaching an agreement between Israel and Lebanon after all these months of delay, during which our opportunities to achieve a successful outcome had become ever more difficult. The Israelis would not be happy to see me: they feared they would be pressed to withdraw behind their borders without adequate provision for their security; they also feared that the conclusion of the Lebanon war would mark the beginning of a new campaign to push them to withdraw from the West Bank and Gaza. They knew that Syria and some other Arab nations would be hoping I would fail. Len Garment, a friend from my days in the Nixon cabinet and a strong supporter of Israel, telephoned me on the eve of my departure. He had just talked to Benjamin Netanyahu, deputy chief of mission in the Israeli embassy. "Tell Shultz not to come. He'll be destroyed," Netanyahu warned.

I was scheduled to represent the United States at the OECD (Organization for Economic Cooperation and Development) ministerial meeting in Paris that would open on May 9. This could be taken as a deadline. I decided to make that known in order to use the pressure of my inevitable departure to push the parties to the point of decision.

Just before I took off on this highly charged mission, President Reagan called to invite me to stop at the White House on my way to Andrews Air

Force Base. We talked about the trauma of the terrorist bombing of the U.S. embassy on April 18, which had killed sixty-three people, including seventeen Americans. The president and I had met with the bereaved families at Andrews the day before, when the bodies were returned from Lebanon. The experience was wrenching and emotional. He confided that the ceremony had choked him up.

The View from Cairo

Shortly after takeoff, I invited the traveling press to join me for a press briefing. I chose my words carefully. I noticed that the press attitude varied according to occupation. The network reporters sipped their drinks: no sixty-second spot tonight. The weekly news magazine reporters took only occasional notes: on a Sunday evening, this week's edition was already closed. But the daily newspaper reporters scribbled furiously trying to capture the half-life of the news coming their way, searching for the line that would give their story the lead for tonight's file. The traveling press plays an important role on such a trip, for what they write not only affects attitudes at home but is read closely abroad, providing clues on what to expect and how I myself assessed the situation.

My first stop would be Cairo—a departure from the usual practice of opening our official Middle East rounds in Israel. This was a signal to the Israelis of our displeasure over the war and a gesture of appreciation to the Egyptians for their courageous and constructive role in maintaining the peace treaty with Israel, despite the pressures on them generated by Israel's invasion of Lebanon.

Cairo was vibrant. The city swarmed with people transacting business, working deals, turning a coin in this elusively subterranean economy, filled with backdoor marketplaces for alleyway merchants whose profit was survival. This was the time of the *khamsin* in Cairo, when the wind whipped in from the western desert and blew a hazy cloud of fine yellow dust into the city. People covered their faces with scarves or the tail cloths of turbans. Automobiles were shrouded in large striped hoods and huddled by the pavement in these pajamas.

I had asked all of our ambassadors from the key Arab countries and from Israel to meet with me in Cairo. They had all convened and were ready to talk when I entered my hotel late Monday afternoon. A real sense of accomplishment and momentum had been created by our successful diplomacy to get the PLO out of Beirut and end the siege of that beleaguered city and from the president's Fresh Start initiative to breathe life back into the Arab-Israeli peace process. This was our chance to get all foreign troops out of Lebanon. Arab attitudes had shifted over the past several months: there now was a mainstream acknowledgment that Israel could not be displaced by force and that negotiation was needed. "You have a very determined Ronald Reagan on your hands," I told them. "I, too, am determined to get an agreement."

I was hit by a barrage of pessimism. One by one, our ambassadors to the Arab countries expressed the immense frustration with and hostility toward Israel, coupled with great fear of her, so evident in each of the Arab nations. All were doubtful that Israel would ever give up anything, despite its earlier return of the Sinai to Egypt. They also saw few prospects of hope from the Arab side. "Expect the Arabs to follow the most radical, rejectionist, and irrational positions," one ambassador warned me.

The only positive note came from our ambassador to Israel, Sam Lewis, who felt I had a good chance of breaking the impasse between Lebanon and Israel. "The Israelis want you to succeed, but they are skeptical." He speculated that it would take at least several rounds to do the job, "but there is a sense in Israel that you can crack the issues." He told me of the immense symbolism and significance to the Israelis of Major Haddad's friendly Lebanese force in southern Lebanon. As the Israelis saw it, Haddad's militia was a Christian Arab ally providing an essential security function for Israel in hostile territory just across the border. Why should Israel be asked to give this up as a consequence of its victory over the PLO in Lebanon? Lewis also told me that significant sentiment in the Israeli cabinet favored unilateral withdrawal from Lebanon, at least to the Awali River. "If King Hussein offers a real chance for peace, public opinion in Israel will respond dramatically," he said.

Again, there was much talk about the fear that a North Bank was being created in Lebanon, which concerned all Arabs and many others throughout the world. "The Israelis want better relations with us, and they know this cannot happen as long as Lebanon continues to divide the United States and Israel," Lewis said. "Begin will want to pour his heart out to you and will want to see whether you are indeed a friend of Israel," he told me. "Begin recognizes the tragedy of the Palestinians, but he feels no responsibility for it. The mood in Israel is turning sour about Lebanon." On the peace process, Lewis reported, "It doesn't seem to be going anywhere. The only way to get the Israelis to make concessions is to talk peace," he said. "The Arabs, however, don't talk peace. They talk territory."

So from the point men on the scene I received, with one exception, a heavy dose of gloom. When I convened with them later in the evening, they were in better spirits. Expressing their anxieties to me seemed to have relieved a lot of tension: I felt I had been a therapist of sorts. But I was particularly concerned by the view of our ambassador to Syria, Bob Paganelli, who said, bitterly, that the Arabs saw U.S. relations with Israel as overriding all other interests. "We don't discipline the Israelis," he said.

His presentation evolved into a virtual attack on everything that the United States did in the Middle East. If that was how the American case was being represented in Damascus, I worried that I was heading for real trouble.

The next morning, I talked for two hours with President Hosni Mubarak, who was still feeling his way in the aftermath of the assassination of his predecessor, Anwar Sadat. Mubarak had steadfastly adhered to the Egyptian–Israeli Peace Treaty while Israel's war in Lebanon raged. That took courage. Mubarak exuded immense energy, speaking directly and moving quickly from one subject to another. He was more than a bluff, straightforward military man: I found him to be politically sophisticated, with a clear sense of both the limits and possibilities of Egypt's special Middle East role. He emphasized the centrality of the U.S.-Egyptian relationship and said he was leery of the Soviets. "My experiences with the Soviets have been very unsatisfactory," he told me. He confirmed his continuing adherence to the Camp David Accords and his firm support for President Reagan's September 1 peace initiative.

Mubarak wanted to be sure we understood and appreciated the plight of the Palestinian people. "Talk about it, but don't overdo it," he counseled. He opposed strongly any PLO presence in Egypt. Again and again he underscored the importance of my achieving an agreement between Lebanon and Israel under which the Israelis would leave Lebanon. He would return the Egyptian ambassador to Tel Aviv, he said, when such an agreement was in hand. Mubarak expressed confidence in the possibilities for economic development in Egypt, a reflection of what a negotiated peace accord had achieved for his country. "These are the results of peace through negotiations," he said.

I picked this up. "That's our theme," I told Mubarak. "Peace can come through negotiations."

My Shuttle Starts

On Wednesday morning, April 27, I left for Israel. Foreign Minister Yitzhak Shamir greeted me at Ben-Gurion Airport, and we rode together to Jerusalem, through the orange groves and vineyards of the Israeli Mediterranean plain, where water means life. Israeli ingenuity had brought fertility to this crusty land. We drove up from the plain along the old Jerusalem road, riding through a limestone canyon where Israeli soldiers and the Arab Legion had bloodied each other in 1948. The wreckage of old trucks and armored cars, still strewn along the roadside, served as a reminder of the struggle for Jerusalem. At the top of the canyon was the Kastel, a strategic point occupied in turn by the Israelites, Romans, Crusaders, Turks, Arabs, and now the Israelis again, full circle after two millennia. Then, beyond the rocky hills, Jerusalem came into view, the gold dome in the center and minarets and steeples appearing like the masts of a great white ship.

Shamir assured me immediately that Israel wanted to withdraw from Lebanon. He said that his concern was that Amin Gemayel was making damaging public statements that gave the appearance of Lebanese backtracking, causing trouble in the Israeli cabinet. He also expressed his desire for a U.S.-Israeli side agreement. I listened carefully but did not comment on any of these points.

When I arrived at the Israeli Ministry of Foreign Affairs, I was struck by its appearance: a haphazard collection of low, prefabricated buildings, roofed with sheets of corrugated tin, it was more like a kibbutz than a ministry. It was the only ministry in the Israeli government, I learned, that was not located in new quarters, an orphan status of penury with which State Department officials could readily identify. The architectural humility of Israel's Foreign Ministry, I mused, was not reflected in Israel's foreign policy. We arranged ourselves on one side of the conference table, facing the Israelis in a closed and narrow room that hummed with window air conditioners.

Yitzhak Shamir, seated at the center of his side of the table, was our host. He sat hunched over the table, studying my delegation. His words were few, but he chose them carefully. On his right sat Yehuda Ben Meir, the deputy foreign minister, born in Brooklyn and holder of a doctorate in philosophy from Columbia. He was voluble; he could argue small change into a matter of principle. He was the only man in the room who wore a yarmulke. On Shamir's left sat David Kimche, director general of the ministry; his face was handsome, angular, hawklike. Kimche was urbane, almost prim. British born and educated, he was a grappler, using pure, cool reason. So there sat Shamir, the gut fighter, and on his right was an American philosopher and on his left a British pragmatist.

I knew some of the other people at the table and particularly focused on General Avraham (Abrasha) Tamir, a short, thick man in a rumpled olive uniform. He looked like a street fighter. When he spoke, he seemed explosive, the veins of his neck expanding over his collar. When he listened, he seemed on the brink of erupting, rolling his head and tapping his finger along his temples.

The key Israeli participants each gave set-piece presentations on the various outstanding issues. I responded briefly to each and took careful notes. I wanted to give a sense of objectivity, probing at problems, asking questions for clarification, and listening carefully. We had not yet completed our first review of the entire agenda when it was time to break to meet with Prime Minister Begin in the cabinet room adjacent to his office.

There I found myself in a crowd. Moshe Arens, now the defense minister, joined us, along with a number of military officials. This was my first encounter with Menachem Begin. His dress and deportment seemed almost like those of a European statesman of an earlier era. Yet I knew that he, like other founders of the modern state of Israel, had a past of revolutionary ardor and violence. At this moment, however, he seemed bored and distracted. The point was, Begin said, to achieve a free and independent Lebanon, free of all foreign forces. Such a Lebanon could live in peace with Israel, and Israel's security could thereby be advanced. Begin's colleagues then completed setting out the agenda as they saw it. Their key points were: (1) Major Haddad must have command responsibility in South Lebanon: only Haddad's forces were capable of keeping the area secure against Israel's enemies; (2) a working relationship between Israel and Lebanon must be achieved, and Lebanon would have to abrogate the Arab boycott on trade with Israel; (3) UNIFIL (UN Interim Force in Lebanon) must be kept out of the south: ever since the United Nations abandoned its peacekeeping role in the Sinai and the 1967 war followed, Israel had lost any confidence in the United Nations in the Middle East; (4) Lebanon must extend diplomatic recognition to Israel; (5) Israeli liaison offices must be established in Lebanon and Lebanese offices in Israel. All these, plus an assortment of other Israeli requests and requirements, seemed virtually impossible to resolve—let alone resolve in only a few days. The Israeli demands were too heavy; the Lebanese could not possibly accept them and retain support from their fellow Arabs. Israeli overreaching, I could see, would be one of my most intractable problems.

After completing the discussion of agenda items, in which Begin took no part, he introduced the chief of military intelligence, who briefed us on the Syrian military buildup and the increase in Soviet advisers in Lebanon. He concluded that the Soviet-manned surface-to-air missiles (SA-5s) now in Syria meant that the Soviets could be drawn into a conflict, even without their intent.

That evening, Shamir gave a large dinner for me at the King David Hotel. I knew that my toast would be carried live on Israeli television and would also be watched throughout the Arab world and in the United States. The occasion presented me with an important opportunity to set a tone for my negotiations. "The remaining issues," I said, "have been debated, analyzed, pored over, agonized over. Now is the time to resolve them. As the Bible tells us, to every thing there is a season. There is a time to debate and there is a time to decide. Now is the time to decide. As in every negotiation, there must be compromise. For every risk that is taken, there is gain. And the risks of failure are far greater than any of the risks of an agreement as it is now envisaged."

After dinner, I thought over my meeting with Prime Minister Begin. I had noticed a tattered map of the Middle East pinned on the wall of the cabinet room. For Israel, it was a map of the world. For Begin, it was his vision and his life. He seemed pale, his skin stretched tight over the bones of his sallow face, and he did not look well. He grieved for the loss of his wife, and his heart was said to be weak. Still, at the meeting, he sat erect, shoulders back, and his voice carried authority. His manner was distracted and disengaged as the discussion unfolded, although his chin periodically jutted forward in a defiance that reflected his spirit. His thick, round glasses and the swivel of his head conveyed an owlish air. He spoke deliberately, as if to make every word seem momentous, but he paid little attention.

The next morning, I met with Prime Minister Begin alone. He wanted to tell me why the relationship with the United States had soured. I decided to let him get all this off his chest. He spilled forth a long list of grievances: we had held up delivery of F-16 aircraft; we were reluctant about supporting the next generation of Israeli-made Lavi fighter aircraft; our marines were in tense confrontations with the IDF south of Beirut; the chairman of the Joint Chiefs of Staff had come to the Middle East but not to Israel—on and on. I did not want the existing tensions between us to undercut the negotiations I faced in the coming days. I told Begin that I had spent many hours with President Reagan, over many months, talking about Israel. I told him how strongly the president wished to get divisive issues behind us. I suggested that he and I have a series of conversations over the next few days, as I shuttled back and forth, not just on the Lebanese agreement but on the whole situation in the Middle East and on the U.S.-Israeli relationship. He welcomed the idea.

Beirut: A City of Tactics

By 11:00 A.M., on April 27, I was back at Ben-Gurion Airport and on my way to Beirut. At Beirut International Airport, the plane came to a jolting stop on the runway. "Evasive action," I was told, because of the danger of rocket fire from one of the contending militias in the area seeking to drive out the international peacekeeping effort. As I looked out the window, I was reassured to see marine positions behind sandbagged walls. Each position flew an American flag. I was greeted by Lebanese Foreign Minister Elie Salem, Ambassador Robert Dillon, and Colonel James Mead, the commander of the marines. We went over to a tent where I was greeted by the three ambassadors from the other MNF countries—France, Italy, and Britain. I expressed my deepest appreciation for their cooperation following the car bombing of the U.S. embassy two weeks earlier. The French MNF commander, in a gesture that was virtually unprecedented, had turned over command of his troops to Colonel Mead in the moments following the explosion at our embassy, and the British offered their embassy facilities so that we could have secure communications from Beirut to Washington.

We left the airport in Chinook helicopters, turning out to sea and out of range. I could see the Beirut shoreline passing tilted through the open ramp at the rear. The Chinooks circled over American warships on the blue water and then suddenly swooped down to the Corniche and landed. Each landing kicked up a tremendous dirt storm. My hair and clothes were covered with grit. A platoon of marines had cordoned off the area. Half-tracks, tanks, and armored personnel carriers stood by the seawall. Blue-bereted Lebanese commandos guarded the rooftops and balconies of surrounding buildings.

We walked one block to the American embassy site, which I remembered from some eight years earlier as a handsome structure with a circular garden in front. The devastation stunned me. The facing wall of the building had been sheared away in the blast, and the front rooms had collapsed in an avalanche of rubble. Oddly, only portions of the topmost floor of the eight-story building held in the explosion, sticking out like the ledge of a cliff over the slide of wreckage below. Morrie Draper pointed out Ambassador Dillon's office on that floor. Dillon had told me in Cairo that he had been standing near his desk, speaking on the telephone, when the concrete wall of his office suddenly caved in on the swivel chair where he customarily sat. He was shaken—no wonder. And he was lucky. I went to an open garage off a small courtyard nearby. Gathered there was our embassy staff, Americans and Lebanese. I talked quietly with each of them, one by one. I expressed my sympathy and tried to give a sense of reassurance.

Then I was taken back to the helicopter and to the billowing dirt as we lifted off. We swung out over the waters off Point Beirut and turned toward the hills to the east of the city. There, at the presidential palace at Baabda, I met Lebanon's young president, Amin Gemayel. The palace was modern, light, airy, and seemingly normal. President Gemayel's young son romped in its corridors. Gemayel, a Maronite Christian, was flanked on his right by Prime Minister Shafik al-Wazzan, a round, pleasant-looking man with a small gray mustache—a Sunni Muslim. On Gemayel's left was Foreign Minister Elie Salem, a Greek Orthodox, whose head almost tilted forward with the size and weight of his nose. Also present were Presidential Counselor Wadia Haddad, a Protestant, and General Hamdab, a Shiite Muslim. They reflected the politics of Lebanon. They made up a suave and polished group, elegant and cosmopolitan. Gemayel's greatest fear, I soon learned, was that he would wind up with an agreement that did not produce a withdrawal of Israeli troops. Lebanon in that case would have paid a great political price, yet would face continued Israeli occupation. "We can't sign a politically expensive contract with no reward," he told me.

Gemayel said he had received a letter just that morning from President Assad saying categorically that any advantage to Israel from an agreement was a threat to Syria. "We have reached our red line," Assad said in typical Middle East language. Gemayel had seen Soviet personnel about fifteen miles from Beirut, "one mile from my village." The Lebanese, he told me, had had enough of Syrian and Soviet presence and pressure.

This Soviet presence was backed by menacing public statements out of Moscow that had become so excessive that I instructed Larry Eagleburger in Washington to call in Ambassador Dobrynin to protest. I told President Gemayel that we must not give ground to the Soviets. "Wherever they are, there is no peace, no progress, no good night's sleep. You can ask a Pole or an Afghan. We cannot let them hinder our progress." I reaffirmed the statement that Begin had made to me: "Israel wants to withdraw."

"It is difficult to believe that Israel's security relies on one man, Haddad. We are mature," Gemayel said. "We will decide." Gemayel's government was fragile and could move only on the basis of consensus, if then. I could sense at the end of our session that Gemayel was deeply troubled. He faced not only internal disintegration but probable Arab rejection of any wide-ranging agreement. That afternoon, still in the palace, Salem and Wazzan took over the negotiations. Salem went over the outstanding issues. He postured, pointing out that one thing or another was unacceptable. I patiently took notes and asked questions for clarification. When we left the cabinet room and walked along a wide marble corridor, a caramel-colored cat scurried toward me, hovering next to the wall, then hurried past me to an unknown destination. "Beirut is a city of tactics," I observed.

Back in Jerusalem with a Working Draft

That evening I was back at Jerusalem's King David Hotel. There are few sights more lovely to behold than the setting of the sun in Jerusalem. The surrounding hills are embedded with golden rock and lined with stone terraces supporting groves of gnarled olive trees. The walls and buildings and towers of the old city are built with dusty, phosphorescent limestone that lies just below the surface. The stone of Jerusalem captures light almost magically, and when the sun sinks under the horizon, the city glows in warm shades of rose and gold.

I was tired, but by now I was working from a draft agreement, to which U.S. side letters of assurance would be added. Taken together, the documents were beginning to add up to a major agreement that could both give Lebanon a new start as an independent state and offer far greater security for Israel. The Syrians and the Soviets would resist both prospects, I knew.

At 9:00 A.M., I started in with Begin, Arens, Shamir, and their colleagues. I told them I had a deeper sense of the issues as a result of my meetings the day before. "The U.S. embassy tragedy had a tremendous impact on me when I saw the building for myself," I told them. It added to the importance of our present work. I had told the Lebanese, I reported, that the Israelis wanted an agreement and wanted to withdraw. "I can now say the same to you," I told the Israelis. "President Gemayel emphasized to me that the Lebanese will make their own decisions, and he firmly rejected Soviet influence or intimidation. Moreover, the Lebanese are committed to preventing the return of the PLO. In these respects, there is an identity of interests." I advised the Israelis, "It is important for Israel to nourish over the long run the generally positive attitude of many Lebanese toward Israel."

Prime Minister Begin, who was more active in this meeting than the day before, said, "Israel wants nothing more than a free and independent Lebanon. But," he added, "Israel's security must be assured." He welcomed Gemayel's sentiments but said there still remained many practical questions to be resolved. He stressed the need to expand the content of "Haddad's role," regardless of his title.

I explored the difficulties in nondiscriminatory trade between Lebanon and Israel. "We must look for practical ways to deal with the Arab boycott [an Arab League agreement to boycott anyone who traded with Israel] as far as Lebanon is concerned." Shamir immediately expressed Israel's distrust of oral commitments. We explored the notion of an observer role, as distinct from a policing role, for UNIFIL. The Israelis emphasized their objection to UNIFIL as a shield behind which the PLO might have sanctuary from which to infiltrate.

Prime Minister Begin excused himself, and we adjourned to the Foreign Ministry, where Arens launched a strong criticism of U.S. policies. He said the United States seemed to have been outflanked by the Soviets and the Syrians and that we were focusing on disagreements between the United States and Israel. All this gave the Lebanese the impression that the United States would solve their problem for them and they would not have to deal with Israel, he argued. If Lebanon insisted on its Arabism and on remaining in a state of war with Israel, then so be it. "We will draw our lines. What we want is real cooperation on real problems. If Amin thinks he has other alternatives, we won't get an agreement."

I responded carefully to Arens's heated attack on the United States and on what we were doing. "There are some areas where the Lebanese feel they can cooperate," I said. "There are some where the Lebanese feel they must work it out for themselves. The Lebanese capacity for cooperation, however defined, must be consistent with the Lebanese need for sovereignty and the Israeli need for assurance. Insofar as the Soviets and Syrians are concerned, I would extend the point further by saying that we will continue to lose ground if we don't reach an agreement promptly. We have spent many months since the PLO withdrew, and we don't have an agreement to a very considerable extent because you Israelis are overreaching yourselves."

The session was disturbingly acrimonious. I couldn't make out whether Arens wanted a watertight agreement or no agreement at all. We were all aware of the strong and rising public opinion in Israel for Israeli withdrawal from Beirut, if not all of Lebanon. Afterward, Sam Lewis speculated that Begin really wanted out of Lebanon and that only the status of Major Haddad was of importance to him because it represented to him Israel's security needs.

"If so," I said, "Begin should tell that to Shamir and Arens, who are after more than the traffic will bear."

The Shuttle Begins to Fly

On Saturday, April 30, I was back in Beirut, talking privately with Amin Gemayel in the garden behind the palace. He was vehement. "I have my red lines, and if anything, I have exceeded them. I cannot go further and expect to sell this agreement." I pointed out how important it was to Lebanon to get an agreement that called for Israeli withdrawal. It would be a major step for Lebanon. We moved to the cabinet room. Someone tried to break the ice with a light touch. The Lebanese interpreter produced a photograph of Phil Habib in a bathing suit in 1949. After numerous unflattering comments, I broke into song: "You can easily tell he's not my mother. My mother's too refined." This moment of broad relief was followed by a torturous review of the agreement, word by word.

The Lebanese were backing away from commitments already made or at least were reinterpreting the intent of those commitments. Prime Minister Wazzan had not been involved in all of the earlier discussions, and some of the commitments that Lebanon had made came as a surprise to him. Salem continued to posture. The Lebanese were toughening and backsliding, particularly on questions such as the duration of the agreement and the trade, post, and telecommunications provisions that stood at the heart of greater normalization. They wanted Israeli withdrawal at the minimum political price. I did not let them back away from their commitments.

At one point, the Lebanese protested to a sentence in one of the articles. Phil Habib pointed out that the sentence was a condensation of an article that the Lebanese themselves had introduced. Salem said it was introduced "ad referendum."

"When someone agrees to something introduced by the other side, it can be ad referendum, but if you introduce it yourself, it is not ad referendum," Phil, exasperated, said. There was a pause.

"We are very creative people," Salem replied. Everyone laughed. There was an astonishing difference in atmosphere between the two negotiations. In Israel, it was businesslike, precise, legalistic, and cool. In Lebanon, it was rambling, less structured, and sometimes lightened by humor.

                    *   *   *

By late afternoon I could see that the talks were not going well and that I would need to stay overnight and take another whack at the issues. The Lebanese negotiators were increasingly fearful that they might be assassinated if they made any agreement with Israel. "I understand the problems that Lebanon faces in the Arab world," I told them. "Any secret oral agreement is bound to be public. Good faith is necessary, and people must stand up to what they agree to. Peace and stability in the Middle East require peace and stability in Lebanon. It is to Lebanon's advantage to move in this direction. We are not insensitive to the effects of this agreement on you, but we have to stand up to the broader stakes in this process."

Wazzan replied that Lebanon could not accept that Israel, having agreed not to pursue a formal peace treaty, was now attempting to produce the same effect by its insistence on all these articles. "Peace for Galilee," he said, "a stated purpose of their invasion in June, does not depend on the movement of goods, or on the post, or telecommunications. We have never waged war against Israel. We are the only country that has been destroyed. Now we are asked to accept conditions. We cannot accept conditions which will prevent us from carrying out the agreement." He ended, "We are not before a broad door, but a narrow window." The Lebanese were trying to close that window to a crack even as the Israelis were trying to push all the attributes of a full-scale international relationship through it.

That evening, Gemayel, Habib, and I discussed the day's developments over dinner in the presidential palace. We realized that we must put negotiations back on a positive track. By the time I got back to the U.S. ambassador's residence at 11:30 P.M., I was discouraged.

I saw that we were well guarded by marines. Some were on duty; others were sleeping on bedrolls in a courtyard. I was bone tired and instantly fell fast asleep. I heard a little thumping during the night but didn't pay much attention.

In the morning, I awoke to the news that two Katyusha rockets just missed landing on the rooftop of the ambassador's residence, exploding in the garden. The marines outside had scrambled. Less than a mile away and farther up the hillside, Druse and Phalange militias had been firing at each other sporadically through the night. There was concern back in Washington as the story of the rocketing came in. We heard that Sam Donaldson in Washington had said on ABC that I had come under attack. The Dillons, who had only weeks before experienced the bombing of their embassy, were badly shaken.

At breakfast in the residence, with the marines patrolling the terrace, I reviewed the issues and instructed that we should draw up a clean document to reflect what we believed the Lebanese would agree to and then go through it article by article. "A neat copy makes a difference," I said.

Morrie Draper found a little cause for optimism. "The fact that Wazzan did not strangle himself yesterday is one of the great achievements of the negotiations," he said. Habib was despairing, feeling that the fulfillment of his months of work might be slipping out of reach. He had made an enormous contribution, but it was now my agreement to win or lose.

"I had to come to the Middle East," I told Habib. "If an agreement doesn't come off and I had not come here personally to try to get it, the president would get clobbered. Don't worry. I'm tired, but I haven't collapsed yet."

John Hughes, State's press spokesman, pulled me aside to get guidance for his talks to the press about the "harrowing events" of the previous night. "I think the story will run like this," he said: "The first wave of PLO infantry hit the fence of the residence at 11:30 P.M. The secretary and his staff engaged in hand-to-hand fighting until 1:30 A.M." Ray Seitz, my assistant, asked Hughes whether the press got the part about Ray carrying me on his back for two hundred yards "despite a gaping wound in his right leg."

After breakfast on May 1, our morning's meeting with the Lebanese began. Without even referring to their gloomy appraisals of the previous day, they began by commenting positively on the tremendous work that had been accomplished. The meeting actually made the situation seem brighter. So I headed back to Israel in a good posture.

In Israel I met in the late afternoon with Shamir and Arens to present a draft of what had evolved in Beirut. "This is what the Lebanese will agree to," I said. I stressed that Wazzan had sat through the entire proceedings and was on board, even if very reluctantly. Now, with the Israelis, my objective was to develop the same sort of draft: one that would reflect what Israel would agree to. I described for Shamir and Arens my version of such a document. I then went over to the prime ministry to see Begin, who was most interested in my report of Elie Salem's effort in Damascus to bring the Syrians along. Begin now wanted me to go to Damascus, "the sooner, the better."

As for the draft that Lebanon could agree to, I said, "There are no fundamental changes from what you have seen: it remains quite a document." The sticking point, again, was Begin's insistence that Major Haddad, Israel's surrogate, be authorized to control security in southern Lebanon.

"If we don't have Haddad, we don't have an agreement," Begin said.

"I can be more effective on the Haddad issue if the Lebanese know precisely where Israel stands on the other issues," I told Begin. I stressed that the Lebanese side was fragile and that everything could start unraveling. The security system for the northern border was a good one. "It has real bite," I said. Our talk was friendly, quiet, and intense. Begin sought to draw from me an affirmation that the United States recognized that Israel was negotiating in good faith.

That evening, talking with my negotiating team, I felt on the verge of a breakthrough. If so, there would be a huge emotional impact in Israel—and elsewhere—about the drama of a second Arab country willing to negotiate what amounted to a peace treaty with Israel. "We are at the hinge of the negotiation," I said. "Now we can either allow the parties to go down the road, haggling over each article, or we can declare that each side has gone about as far as possible and look for reconciliation of differences in a broader conceptual framework." This would be the way to get them to agree on the details as well as the framework. That, in effect, was my role.

I set out not to split the difference between the two sides but to develop a document of benefit to both, a document that looked especially to the security of Israel's northern border and that Lebanon could sell as being in its interest and consistent with its Arab character.

First thing the next morning, May 2, I spoke again with Prime Minister Begin: "I'm thinking about how to structure the day. I want to feel free to call you. I will start with Shamir and Arens and discuss the context with them rather than the details. Then in a larger group, we can go over the draft, paragraph by paragraph. I plan to emphasize two different questions: the agreement as a text and the surrounding circumstances. We can talk about when to go to Damascus. I understand very well that Haddad is a central issue. I want to go to Beirut tomorrow on that question. Therefore, I want to have these other issues worked through here before I leave. It is important to recognize that this text represents what the Lebanese can accept."

Begin said he understood; he was available any time that I wanted to talk with him. Begin's concerns were now nearly all focused on the military aspects of the agreement. If I had to push the Lebanese further, it would be in this area. The Israelis now accepted that their withdrawal from Lebanon would be verified by outside supervisory teams. The Lebanese accepted the concept of a limited number of Israeli patrols into Lebanon but worried about the number of soldiers crossing the border daily. The Israelis said they could not be confident that the government of Lebanon would hold together, in which case they wanted Haddad in place, with some forces under his control. I noticed that the Israelis were adjusting to the idea of Haddad's being in less than total command of the south and that they had awakened to the question of Syria's response to the agreement. Prime Minister Begin, in his most recent meeting with the press, talked about the negotiations as though success was imminent. The "atmosphere was wonderful," Begin said to reporters.[1] I began to feel that the Israelis were ready to wrap it up.

1. *New York Times*, May 3, 1983.

A Threat from Syria

Back in Beirut on May 3, our motorcade traversed the city at a violent speed, brakes screeching and wheels squealing. Range Rovers crammed with blue-bereted commandos darted in and out of the motorcade waving submachine guns out the window. Gunship helicopters flew low overhead. We followed the road of the old Green Line that had separated the PLO forces from the Phalange. The buildings on either side were gutted and pocked in the polka-dot pattern of heavy automatic fire.

At Baabda, Foreign Minister Elie Salem reported on his talks with President Hafez Assad the day before. Assad was attentive and polite but unmistakable in his threats. Syria's withdrawal, he made clear, would not be discussed in a context of Israeli withdrawal. Sadat, Assad said, had deviated from the Arab consensus, and the Egyptians had killed him. This Salem took as a threat to the Lebanese, should they deviate from the Arab "consensus." Assad said that Israel was arrogant and saw its frontiers as lying between Turkey and Pakistan. Assad claimed to want an independent, sovereign, and united Lebanon. But the draft agreement, he said, was a hundred times worse than the Camp David Accords. The military provisions provided for Israeli patrols into Lebanon on the ground and in the air. To sign such an agreement would be humiliating to Lebanon, Assad said. The Arabs would boycott Lebanon as they did Egypt. The termination of a state of war would be the same as peace with Israel. If Israel acquired political benefit, the Syrian army would not withdraw. If Lebanon signed an agreement, Assad said, it would cause him "great pain to see Lebanon suffer the consequences."

Salem said that Assad did not want to review the agreement; he wanted to send a message. The Syrians clearly had hardened in the last month, reflecting, Salem thought, Soviet influence. Assad told Salem that he "looked forward to seeing George Shultz." What Salem had heard in Damascus was a rehearsal for my forthcoming meeting.

"The Syrian position should not be a surprise," Wazzan said. He had been certain that the draft agreement would be received negatively.

Salem summed up the situation to me: "We have two lousy neighbors."

It was apparent that I once again must spend the night in Lebanon. I quickly discovered, however, that Ambassador Dillon's wife was concerned that my presence in the ambassador's residence would draw another Katyusha attack. She obviously did not wish me to stay overnight there again. I asked Elie Salem where I might spend the night, and he suggested that I stay at the palace as President Gemayel's guest. I was not sure I would be warmly welcomed there either. We had dragged on through a long, nervous, and exasperating session. At the end, the tone of the meeting had become gloomy. The Lebanese were feeling increasingly that they were about to "sign their own death warrants." Salem confided to me that

Wazzan feared for his life. "We are not talking about the fall of a government but the fall of a head," he said.

The Lebanese, as much as possible, wanted to avoid putting anything down in writing; the Israelis, by contrast, wanted to put everything in writing. "I feel like the broker between Talmudic lawyers and Levantine rug merchants," I remarked. We once again put together a clean draft and got prepared to cover the key issues that evening.

"There are a lot of loose ends," Ray Seitz remarked.

"And they're getting looser," I added, shaking my head. My prospective evening in the palace created considerable strain. They had arranged a special room in Gemayel's personal quarters. In the evening, a firefight raged in the hills above the palace. We could hear the intermittent cracking of weaponry up and down the valleys. Standing out on the terrace in the late evening, I watched the flashes of light. Incongruously, a Christmas tree, still adorned with colored lights, stood about halfway between the palace and the fighting.

The next morning brought disturbing reports. The Soviets had increased their presence in Syria and in Lebanon. Analysts warned that we should not underestimate the probability of war in Lebanon between Israel and Syria. Even more troubling was the report that Syria had been involved in the bombing of the American embassy in Beirut on April 18. I had requested a meeting with Assad some time ago, but the Syrians were dragging their feet. The current word was that Assad could not receive me until May 7. My deadline of May 8 to attend the OECD ministerial meeting was threatened.

"Should Deputy Secretary Dam take your place at the OECD meeting?" I was asked. Larry Eagleburger called to say that "the White House" was concerned over "the lack of precision" in my daily cable reports to the president on what I was doing out here. By now I had learned the lingo; this meant that the leakers on the White House staff were searching for ammunition to fire at me via the press.

The Lebanese were now backing off the agreement when out of earshot and getting back on board when Phil Habib and I spoke to them directly. "If the joint committee [on security matters] is governed by unanimity," Prime Minister Wazzan said, "then I agree, but the document prejudges the work of the committee. If I have to choose between starting a war by accepting this draft or simply seeing what happens, I prefer the latter, rather than being responsible for the former."

Breaking Through

After we adjourned, Habib and I met privately with Wazzan and Salem for a heart-to-heart talk. I pointed up quietly the risks of no agreement.

We agonized together over the potential problems. When the plenary session resumed, Wazzan said, "Great progress has been made on many points. We give our thanks to Mr. Shultz. We reaffirm our acceptance, although we are not happy. There will be real problems in convincing others. The new hardship period will begin for us. I apologize if we were sometimes harsh. It is possible that a man may insult his dentist when a tooth is being extracted. You also have a difficult period ahead of you. We hope you can achieve our sovereignty." He added, "We hope *we* can succeed also."

I thanked Wazzan. "Yes," I said, "we have a heavy load ahead of us in Israel, in Damascus, and elsewhere. The agreement is a strong affirmation of your desire for peace. We recognize the difficulties. If we can work these out, you will find the United States a strong partner. The phrase sticks in my mind, 'I would rather light a candle than curse the darkness.' Too many people curse the darkness; we try to light a candle. As you said, Mr. Prime Minister, this may be a preamble to real peace in Lebanon and throughout the Middle East. We will continue in that spirit."

Wazzan was pleased and positive. But, he added, "Peace in Lebanon will not last unless the greater problem of the Palestinians is resolved." That, I knew, was true.

Back in Israel, on May 5, I found great consternation. The Israelis could see they were up against the pin. Arens telephoned me. "What have we got from the invasion?" he asked. "At least before we had Haddad."

"What you have got is a Russian presence in Syria," I responded. I had pushed the Lebanese as hard as possible, I told Arens, particularly on the security arrangements. "I have almost no degree of freedom left." I emphasized that the right of the Israelis in the agreement is "the right of self-defense." I added, "It is not a license that says if you don't like something the Lebanese are doing, you can insist on changing it."

I felt it was time to call President Reagan. When he came on the line, I told him that I had pushed Begin to call a cabinet meeting for tomorrow but that I couldn't predict the outcome. I expressed my concern about the heavy emphasis in the agreement on Lebanon's responsibility for security. "We have to keep things proportional in terms of any Israeli response to a security violation," I told the president. "A single rocket does not justify the bombing of Beirut." I suggested that the president call Begin after the cabinet acted, and I gave him my view that Gemayel had been a real stand-up guy. "The Syrians are a tough crowd," I said, "and the Lebanese deserve lots of credit. Gemayel recalls every half hour his visit with you when he was in Washington last month."

With time running out before I would have to leave for Paris and with the Lebanese finally, if tenuously, on board, bitter wrangling now burst out within the Israeli government. Sam Lewis told me there must be forty requests for changes in the agreement. Shamir expected a strong attack from Ariel Sharon in the next day's cabinet meeting, and Phil Habib reported that influential cabinet member David Levy had recommended rejecting the agreement. Shamir wanted to see me after the reception that night. The handling of issues such as intelligence, security, and Haddad's role were politically unacceptable in high Israeli political circles, he told me.

Mike Deaver called from the White House. He and the president were excited by the idea of an Israel-Lebanon agreement. Deaver, in his never-ending quest for the ultimate photo opportunity, asked what I thought of a presidential visit to the area. "Maybe at some point, Mike," I said, "but not now."

All through the evening and into the night the last-minute bargaining continued. Finally, I said, "The cabinet should accept or reject the agreement *as it now stands*. The negotiations should not, and cannot, go on without end."

The next morning, May 6, the Israeli cabinet session began at 8:30 A.M. They met for seven hours. I sat and waited. I was coughing, having come down with a respiratory infection that I couldn't shake. At 3:25 P.M., Begin telephoned me at the King David Hotel and read me the decision: "The Israeli government accepts the agreement in principle." The vote had been by a majority of 17 to 2, but the minority was exceedingly vocal. I congratulated Begin, and we talked for a few moments. Afterward, I looked out the window and thought to myself, funny how the big moment, when it finally comes, is an anticlimax.

Habib was a little worried: "The Israeli response sounds too qualified."

"The Israelis have now agreed. They can't backtrack," Sam Lewis countered.

At 3:55, I put in my call to President Reagan. It seemed to take forever. I got through to the White House at about 4:15 P.M. and was put on hold. Finally, the president came on the line. "Prime Minister Begin just informed me that after seven hours, the Israeli government accepts the agreement, in principle," I said. Arens had come to my suite by this time, and I put him on the phone.

Arens confirmed Israel's agreement to the president. "In the land of miracles, Secretary Shultz has brought off a real miracle. Unfortunately, the Syrians and the Soviets remain," Arens said.

I left my room to talk to the press gathered downstairs. The King David is a large hotel with small elevators. It took a while to get one to my floor. When I finally reached the lobby, I said a few words to a swarm of reporters. "We're really pleased that the Prime Minister and the Cabinet of Israel have decided to accept this agreement. We recognize there's a tremendous amount of work to be done, but this is a milestone and we're determined to keep on and do these additional things that are necessary to see that it works." I felt a genuine sense of accomplishment. I knew that might not last long. There were some 30,000 to 40,000 Israeli forces in Lebanon, "We have to go on to the question of Syrian and PLO withdrawal," I told the reporters, adding, "For Israeli withdrawal to occur, there has to be evidence of what Syria will do."

So, minefields lay ahead. Still, I had gotten what I came for: a commitment that Israel would withdraw from Lebanon, a good arrangement for the security of Israel's northern border, and a possible start on a normalized relationship between Israel and Lebanon.

On to Jordan, Syria, and Saudi Arabia

Now that the Israelis, grudgingly, and the Lebanese, fearfully, had accepted the agreement, I set off for a round of discussions with key Arab leaders. I left in the late afternoon on May 6 for Jordan. In Amman, King Hussein was gracious but worried. After many questions and some agonizing, he agreed to support the Israel-Lebanon agreement. We then talked at length about the larger West Bank–Gaza peace process. Here he was discouraged. He felt that the United States had let him down because we had "no positive word" from Israel on a host of issues important to him. I emphasized and reemphasized to him how essential it was for a credible Arab partner to come forward ready to negotiate with Israel. Our hopes were still on him. We talked over his recent failed efforts to get PLO agreement for him to represent the Palestinians in negotiations with Israel. I reinforced President Reagan's support for his continuing efforts, recalling to him his phone conversation with the president a few weeks earlier when I had been at Camp David for the weekend.

The following morning, May 7, I arrived in Damascus. Airports are revealing. This was a Soviet bloc–style airport; there were few planes, and those were mostly antiquated; a few new jetliners were mysteriously unmarked; there were no signs of the big international commercial carriers. All in all, the scene was decayed, drab, and sterile. I expected a cool reception and got one. Foreign Minister Khaddam met me at the airport and escorted me to a microphone. As I began my arrival statement, he moved well out of the way, not wanting to be caught with me in the camera lens. As we pulled around the back of the air terminal, I noticed that an honor guard had been assembled, obviously withdrawn at the last moment.

I was taken first to a small room in the Foreign Ministry. There Khaddam grilled me like a prosecuting attorney, though he was polite. He pressed for specifics of the agreement, and I gave him detailed answers. As Khaddam lectured us on Syria's historical relationship with Lebanon, he gestured toward Phil Habib.

"So Habib's parents come from Syria," I said. "That explains a lot about his character." Everyone laughed except Habib, the Lebanese-American.

The Lebanese had negotiated the agreement under duress, Khaddam said. Lebanon suffered under two occupiers, the Israelis and the Christians, "Any agreement reached at gunpoint is not an agreement," he said. The Lebanese government did not represent the Lebanese people. Any such agreement affected Syria's security. "This agreement does great harm to Lebanon, Syria, and the Arab world, and therefore it cannot be accepted by us," Khaddam concluded.

"You are wrong. It is exactly the opposite," I countered, having sat through his long dissertation. "Withdrawal will permit stability. The agreement provides for Israeli withdrawal, depending on Syrian withdrawal."

As we adjourned for lunch, Khaddam told me he was "becoming a vegetarian because," he said, "it makes me peaceful."

"How is it working?" I asked. I had come to a reluctant regard for Khaddam's intellect, having met with him in Washington and in New York, where he explored carefully with me the president's September 1 initiative. He had studied it more carefully than any other Arab or Israeli that I had talked with on the subject.

President Assad received me in his audience room at the modest presidential palace. Green velvet chairs and sofas were lined up in the narrow room against opposite walls of a pale pistachio color. The Syrians sat in a row along one wall; the Americans, in a row along the other. The room was devoid of decoration other than a painting depicting the victory of Saladin over the Crusaders. The painting hung on the wall opposite the visitors: point taken. At the end of the room was a small table with two chairs for Assad and me. Assad is an Alawite, a mountain tribe of warriors, the largest minority group in Syria. He had managed to hold power in this violent region longer than any other leader. At fifty-five, Assad appeared delicate, his shoulders thin and slightly hunched. As he sat, his legs were immobile, almost as if paralyzed. He had the face of a bird and the mind of a cat. His jaw was narrow and the face expanded upward over long, sharp jaws and closely set eyes, mushrooming finally into a high, broad forehead. His skull was large and elongated. He spoke slowly and listened carefully, as if the words were a series of targets, and he struck at any vulnerable phrase.

I knew this meeting was important. I was ready to engage with Assad on his concerns as well as mine. He recounted the recent history of Lebanon. He understood that Israel had a security problem. But he felt the agreement went "too far" in its security concessions to Israel, and he opposed any "normalization" between Lebanon and Israel as an unacceptable "reward for aggression." His manner was pleasant and engaging, even though his message was negative. He did not say no, and he invited me to return for further discussion. The discussion had gone as well as I could have expected. The real tests lay ahead.

                    *   *   *

I had a little time after my session with Assad and before my departure.
I remembered Henry Kissinger telling me of his Middle East shuttles and
complaining that he never got to see anything outside of the suite and lobby
of his hotels. Larry Eagleburger recounted that when Henry Kissinger was
in Damascus, he was awakened in his hotel room by the sound of a muezzin's call to prayer coming from the mosque in the predawn hour. Henry
picked up the phone on his bedstand and buzzed Eagleburger, waking him
up. "Larry," Kissinger said, "will you please go over there and tell them
to stop that!" I decided to try to see something of cultural significance
wherever I went so that I could learn a bit about the host country. Damascus
is the oldest continuously inhabited city on earth. I asked Foreign Minister
Khaddam to take me to see Damascus's famous Umayyad Mosque, built
in the seventh century.

Inside the courtyard of the mosque is a well of marble decorated with
the imprints of fossils. The well, I was told, served as a baptismal font
1,500 years ago and for centuries was used by Muslims for ablutions before
prayer. The Christian basilica, in its turn, had stood atop the remains of
a colossal Roman temple to Jupiter. And that temple had been built on
the ritual site of animist pagans. People had worshiped there in one form
or another for over 3,000 years.

The courtyard of the mosque is an enormous square, broken only by
the small mosaic treasure house, where pilgrims on the Haj would deposit
their valuables before setting off by caravan on the treacherous journey to
Mecca. The mosque itself is vast, the second largest in Islam. The floor is
covered by hundreds of rich carpets. Thousands of people gather here on
a Friday. The arched windows are stained glass of red and blue, and under
the central scalloped dome is a shrine said to contain the head of John the
Baptist. The mosque gives a sense of immense openness, enhanced by the
simplicity of the decoration. Transported by this rich and complex history,
I was soon off again to the airport and my flight to Saudi Arabia.

Late in the evening I arrived at Jiddah and went directly to see King
Fahd. I had slept briefly on the plane, knowing that the king preferred
meeting late at night or in the early morning hours. I had first met King
Fahd when he was crown prince and had met with him several times since.
When I arrived, King Fahd, who was most friendly in his greeting, seemed
neutral about the agreement but wary. He understood Israel's concern
about the security of its northern border, but he did not like the idea of
normalized Israeli-Lebanese relations. He feared, as did other Arabs, that
Israel intended to create a North Bank.

"Now we have an agreement under which Israel guarantees it will leave,"
I told the king. Whether he liked the agreement or not, the departure of
Israel from Lebanon was something that King Fahd very much wanted. He
now had a way to achieve that objective, namely, persuade Syria to with-

draw its forces from Lebanon. "Syria does not have to accept the agreement or have anything to do with it. They just have to leave Lebanon," I said. My argument seemed to sink in. In the end, I felt that my only chance of gaining Syrian withdrawal was through pressure from the Saudis and other Arabs to take this opportunity to avoid the creation of an Israeli North Bank, which they so dreaded.

I wanted to press the Lebanese and Israelis to move promptly to ratify the agreement now: to lock it in. "The longer the agreement is dragged out, the more of a target it is for everybody," I told my negotiating team after the session with Fahd.

The next morning, after breakfast in Saudi Arabia, I flew to Israel. Shamir met me at the airport with a string of changes the Israelis wanted to make. I was immovable. "If there are points to be clarified, I will clarify them, but the agreement itself is closed." Period.

By early afternoon I was on the way to Beirut to touch base once more with President Gemayel at Baabda. Gemayel said he would go to the Parliament on Tuesday to seek what would amount to a preemptive ratification. Most of the firing around Beirut now was between Syrian and Israeli troops. Gemayel knew that he could not govern effectively under such circumstances. The continual shelling was unsettling him. He seemed lonely, frightened, and was hanging on desperately. The Arabs were holding him at arm's length. The Syrians were in Lebanon and intended to remain there as overlords unless, by some miracle, this agreement could stick and liberate Lebanon to run its own affairs. "The Syrians," Gemayel said to me, "won't do anything for nothing, and I cannot offer them anything."

"You and the Arabs, particularly Saudi Arabia, can offer them Israeli withdrawal," I responded. I could feel the poignancy of the moment and the depth of Gemayel's misgivings and his dilemma. He counted on the United States and on me to stay engaged in Lebanon. We would. But in the end, the Lebanese would have to solve their own internal problems. After a wild ride down the mountain, I got back on my plane and headed for the OECD session in Paris.

In Paris, my eyes soon adjusted to the lush green of spring. Chestnut trees were festooned with ivory cones of blossoms. Low and heavy foliage lined the edges of the boulevards. Lilacs bloomed. There were red flowers and empty benches in the parks. The streets were wet with May rain. Paris was another world. Once I had known Beirut when it was "the Paris of the East."

CHAPTER 15

Tension and Tragedy
in Lebanon

On May 17, 1983, Israel and Lebanon signed, at Qiryat Shemona in Israel and at Khaldah in Lebanon, "The Agreement on Withdrawal of Troops from Lebanon." Under the terms of the agreement, each country would respect the sovereignty and territorial rights of the other; the state of war between them was terminated. Israel would withdraw its armed forces from Lebanon in accordance with a procedure set out in the agreement (kept secret for security reasons). The two nations agreed to settle disputes by peaceful means; both would pursue specified security arrangements for south Lebanon; neither would allow itself to be used as a staging ground for hostile activity against the other or against a third state or permit movement through its territory by armed forces of states hostile to the other. Neither would intervene in the internal affairs of the other or propagandize against the other. The two countries would establish a joint liaison committee aimed at developing relations between them, and each would maintain a liaison officer in the other's territory to carry out the functions of the committee. The agreement would put the Lebanese army into southern Lebanon along with UN observers; I had insisted on this point for Lebanon's territorial integrity and achieved it despite Israeli complaints.

The May 17 Agreement had costs and benefits for both sides. It had the potential to be a foundation for Lebanon's return to stability and control over its territory and for widening the base of peace in the Middle East.

But no Middle East episode ends with complacency. There were soon indicators, which taken together were most serious, that the Soviets and Syrians were determined to see that the region remained a tense and dangerous place. The Soviets began to pull their dependents out of Jordan, Lebanon, and Syria; Soviet military personnel continued to be assigned to forward command sites in Syria and Lebanon. Syrian air defenses began to challenge Israeli reconnaissance flights, and a wartime command structure appeared to be taking shape in Syria.

And Hafez Assad did the expected. He again asserted that Syrian troops could not withdraw from Lebanon because they had been invited in to restore order in 1975. Amin Gemayel's government of Lebanon had asked him to withdraw, but he did not regard that request as legitimate. The Arab League had sanctioned Syria's presence in Lebanon, and only the Arab League could request its departure. Over eight months had passed since the Arab summit at Fez, at which Assad had told King Fahd that Syria would withdraw from Lebanon if Israel withdrew. Now, with Soviet help, Syria was much stronger. The length of time taken to negotiate the agreement came at a heavy price.

A key provision of the May 17 Agreement stated that Israel would not be obliged to withdraw its troops until Syria did. Although we would seek an arrangement by which the Israelis would, in fact, move first, they would do so only after the Arabs had prevailed upon Syria to agree to pull out as well. It was crucial now that Israeli troops remain in place in Lebanon until agreement for Syrian withdrawal was achieved. Only if the Arabs saw that Israel would not leave unless Syria agreed to go would the plan have a chance of succeeding.

Assad said no to withdrawal and made Phil Habib persona non grata in Damascus to underline his point.[1] He then stimulated the Druse militia, under Walid Jumblatt, to increase military pressure on the government of Lebanon's positions and on the U.S. Marines. The Shouf Mountains, strategic high ground overlooking the Beirut International Airport, were the stronghold of the Druse, and the Israelis now occupied the Shouf. Increasingly, the Israelis found that they could not control this territory without suffering casualties.

A Tragic End

The Israelis wanted to leave the Shouf and pull back south of the Awali River. This was ominous. A unilateral Israeli withdrawal would open up the threatening high ground above the marines' position at the Beirut airport. Because Syria was providing the Druse both weapons and support, an Israeli retreat would be interpreted as the first unequivocal success by Syria or Syrian-backed forces during the entire Lebanon debacle. And it would be a vindication of Assad's strategy in opposition to the May 17 Agreement.

1. This made it necessary to replace Habib. Bud McFarlane became special envoy in July 1983.

On August 25, 1983, a memorandum went to President Reagan for his decision on continued use of the multinational force (MNF). The secretary of defense and the Joint Chiefs of Staff were opposed. Cap Weinberger had privately turned sour on Bud McFarlane's work in the region. The memo included a sentence saying State and Defense were fully supportive of Bud's effort; Cap insisted that it be deleted. I favored continued use of the MNF in Lebanon. The president approved the further deployment of the MNF, but in a purely peacekeeping role, not a military one. McFarlane went back to the president, asking for approval for the MNF to carry out "civic action" as a substitute for an authorized military role. I thought this was a subterfuge. The president didn't buy it.

The focus of attention in Lebanon was now on the Shouf. The Israeli army held its key sectors. The task was to restore the Lebanese government to a position of authority there. To do this, an agreement had to be reached between the Druse and the central government under which the multi-confessional Lebanese Armed Forces would be permitted entry to the area. The Israelis were needed to stay in place until this was achieved. But the Syrians, through bribes and threats, were inducing the Druse to refuse to cooperate and to make life dangerous for the Israelis.

It was immediately apparent where the problem lay. Walid Jumblatt, the Druse leader, who had been primed toward moderation by the Saudis, told the Lebanese that he simply "could not withstand" the pressure he was under from President Assad, who sought to destroy the May 17 Agreement. I recommended to President Reagan that he ask Prime Minister Begin to delay the withdrawal of the IDF. He did so, in a letter flashed to Israel.

The next day, Sunday, August 28, before our message had even reached him, Menachem Begin announced that he was going to resign. Syria would see a shift in the balance of power in this development and would step up the pressure, political and military, even further. Reports were now coming in that the marines in the MNF were taking fire. President Reagan was awakened shortly after midnight and was told that the situation was unraveling.

By dawn on Monday, August 29, the marines had reported three killed in action, their first casualties in Lebanon. They still were not sure about the source of the firing, but the best indications were that hostile fire was coming from Druse militiamen. I heard that Jumblatt had met Foreign Minister Khaddam in Geneva, and I assumed the Druse action had Syrian support and stimulation. The Italians and French were also under fire. Our naval contingent offshore had been lofting illumination rounds throughout the night. Some in the administration felt that if the shooting continued, even at a low rate, the consensus of support for the MNF would fracture, and the force would have to be pulled out of Lebanon. I let everyone know that in my view the MNF should hang in there: we should coordinate with the Italians and French to reinforce our troops and give them the authority to fire back. We had to keep the pressure on the Lebanese government to achieve a foundation for national reconciliation. And we needed to hold to the May 17 Agreement as the best hope for restoring Lebanon's national integrity. But Israel's intention to withdraw was undermining the fulfillment of this hope from within as much as Syria was undermining it from without. It was important that we get the president's request *not* to pull out the IDF to Begin quickly—whether he was about to resign or not—and keep Israel from walking away from the Shouf, leaving chaos in its wake and Syria in the wings.

Congress now began to raise the issue of the War Powers Act, since our forces were taking hostile fire. The War Powers Act, approved by Congress in 1973 after U.S. involvement ended in Vietnam, calls on the president to notify Congress when U.S. troops are in combat situations and to withdraw them within sixty days of the notification unless both houses of Congress declare war or otherwise approve the use of troops.[2]

At midmorning, Cap Weinberger called me. He had "problems" with the president's letter to Begin asking that the IDF stay in the Shouf: this despite the fact that it had already been signed and sent and was now in Sam Lewis's hands awaiting delivery. Cap thought it would be best to let the IDF leave the Shouf. The Pentagon was "full of distrust" for the Israeli military, Cap said; he speculated that the Israelis were allowing the Druse in the Israeli-held areas to fire at our marines. I called the president on the secure phone. He said he didn't agree with Cap: give Begin the letter as is.

Bud McFarlane then called me from Beirut. Syria was behind this upsurge in violence, he said. We had to give Amin Gemayel support for a government of national reconciliation. We should move some of our offshore elements in to strengthen the MNF. We should "put the screws to Syria," Bud said. He felt that the time had come for a dramatic move on our part to show we meant business. Without it, he felt disintegration would come. The vitally important point was to hold the IDF in the Shouf. It was Monday, August 29, and the Israelis were indicating they would unilaterally start to pull out the next day. "Please call Sam Lewis and instruct him to give the president's letter to Begin," Bud said. I had already sent that instruction.

Within minutes after I hung up the phone, a cable came in from Bud saying that the government of national reconciliation that we were trying to form in Beirut would not necessarily honor the May 17 Agreement signed by the Gemayel government. The new government would review the agreement "in the light of other options for achieving the withdrawal of all foreign forces." This will "drive the Israelis bananas," Eagleburger said. It was infuriating.

2. The president may have up to ninety days if he states "unavoidable military necessity."

Nick Veliotes and Bob Paganelli, our ambassador to Syria, both said I had no choice but to accept the new government's review. If I did, the price of the reconciliation government we sought would be the shelving of the agreement we had achieved. I saw it as a capitulation to Syria without receiving anything in return. I was determined that the United States would *not* give up on the agreement, certainly not unless something genuinely satisfactory was put in its place. I knew, however, that if Israel weakened and pulled its troops back unilaterally, that would be close to a death blow for the May 17 Agreement. Formerly, our problem had been with an overly aggressive Israel; now it was with an all-too-passive Israel. Underlying this transformation was Israel's loss of confidence in its own cause in Lebanon and even greater loss of confidence that the Lebanese could take any decisions even to serve their own interests.

First thing Tuesday morning, August 30, press reports came in from Israel that the IDF would delay its pullout. Such reports often meant a deliberate Israeli government leak. Intelligence reports were saying that Syrian artillery was involved in shelling Beirut International Airport, where the MNF forces were located. Now, in addition, shells were falling around the French and Italian embassies in Beirut. Casualties were rising. Heavy fighting was now going on at three or four locations around the city. A dud round that hit the Italian compound appeared to be of Syrian origin. The Syrians were providing logistics, weapons, intelligence, and threats to the fighting factions. The Cadmos Hotel, where U.S. Green Beret trainers were lodged, was surrounded by a Shiite militia faction.

I went to the White House to brief the president. The situation was deteriorating rapidly. Under Syrian threat, the key Lebanese factions would not join a government of national reconciliation unless the May 17 Agreement was scrapped. Israel had agreed to delay its pullout from the Shouf, but only until Saturday. The Lebanese were killing each other at Syria's behest. The marines were hunkered down, taking hostile fire and doing little else. The Israelis were packing their bags. And all parties were heaping scorn on the one negotiated agreement that could help.

Fire against marine positions at the Beirut airport grew worse. On the ground, the multinational force, especially our marines, was by this time in an uncomfortable position. We had been drawn into Lebanon by Israeli military action and by the atrocities in Sabra and Shatila. We had brokered an agreement designed to get all foreign forces out of Lebanon and were trying to help the Lebanese government regain control of its country.

We had seen some real progress and were in no position simply to pull out, leaving the Lebanese to fend for themselves. From the time the MNF had returned after the Sabra and Shatila massacres until the late summer of 1983, Lebanon had, by Lebanese standards, been relatively quiet. The new government of Amin Gemayel had started to function. Gemayel had made a favorable impression, especially on President Reagan, during his visits to Washington. The Lebanese-American community in the United States had rallied round. Funds were becoming available for the massive rebuilding effort needed. Our military was working with the Lebanese army to develop its professional capability and to staff itself in a multi-confessional manner. Nevertheless, old hatreds die hard in Lebanon, and the Syrians, who had lived with the people of Lebanon over the centuries, had plenty to work with in their efforts to stir up trouble and arm private militias.

Our marines had been ordered not to be drawn into a combat role, but they did "return" fire from time to time. The situation improved when we got tough and deteriorated when we took punches without returning them. Bud McFarlane pushed for an increasing show of strength, particularly against the Syrians. His assessment, as far back as August 10, was that little positive was likely to happen "until the U.S. and the Arabs applied some sticks to Assad."

I called Senate Majority Leader Howard Baker about the escalating violence in Beirut. I told him that the Lebanese army was holding together well. "We have no need for reinforcements, but we have assets nearby that can be used if needed. The marines return fire only in self-defense. McFarlane is seeking to broaden the base of the government. Nevertheless, we have to be careful; there is a lot of whistling in the dark. The Shouf is about to blow. The impending Israeli redeployment has precipitated this crisis."

The administration was considering what our position should be under the War Powers Act. Meanwhile, Gemayel issued a statement calling for a government of national unity. I held a press conference on August 31 and answered questions, which were exclusively about Lebanon, the War Powers Act, and the three marine casualties that had occurred two days before.

When my phone rang at home at 6:30 A.M. on September 1, I assumed it was more bad news from Lebanon. Instead, I learned that the Soviets had shot down a commercial Korean airliner, Flight 007, an event that became a white-hot focus of attention. This was also the day the Druse first declared they would now regard our marines as "enemy forces." This pronouncement seemed to further undermine the confidence of the Israelis.

Three days later, on September 4, the Israelis moved out of the Shouf, leaving the marines vulnerable to fire and demonstrating to Syria and the rest of the Arab world that Israel was retreating without any corresponding concession from Syria. This was a critical moment: the Israeli pullout deeply undercut the May 17 Agreement. Nonetheless, I was determined to pursue the cause, with the aim of getting Syrian forces to withdraw once Israel's forces had departed from the Beirut area. The Israelis would not leave southern Lebanon, so Syria's success in Beirut would not translate into the south. Only the May 17 Agreement held out any prospect for an independent Lebanon in control of its own territory.[3]

I could see that without an agreement to broaden the government, violence would escalate and the Lebanese army could not control the situation. Furthermore, Syrian artillery was on hand and formidable. Israel had washed its hands of the Beirut area, but we had made a commitment to help Lebanon regain sovereign control over its own territory. The road ahead promised to be rough. I talked to Howard Baker again about the need for an expression of congressional support. At the end of our conversation, I asked, "Then you'll carry the banner for the president?"

"Absolutely," he replied.

The French, too, had been targeted in late August. Foreign Minister Cheysson called to tell me that their contingent had been fired at for about three hours, that he had called Syrian Foreign Minister Khaddam to say that French planes were available, had missiles, and would fire back. "The bombardment," he told me, "stopped eight minutes later." He raised the question of a new Security Council mandate for UNIFIL, as a possible substitute for the MNF. We both thought the Soviets would veto the idea but that it should be explored. After Cheysson's call, I was worried about the NSC staff. "Those people are losing their heads over there. Communications are lousy. The NSC staff has gotten so involved that they feel Bud's mission is their mission," I said.

We kept getting drawn into a more militant posture, but only in a hesitant way. We needed to stand firm, showing strength that was purposeful and steady. The NSC staff had become the most militaristic group in Washington, but it was pulling against a reluctant Pentagon. On September 17, U.S. warships fired on artillery positions in areas in Lebanon held by Syria. A few days later, the battleship *New Jersey* arrived off Lebanon's coast.

Howard Baker pressed for President Reagan to file a report with Congress under the War Powers Act. By September 21, I was testifying before both the House and Senate on the situation in Lebanon and on the War Powers issue. I stressed the adverse consequences of a failure to remain engaged in Lebanon and found support in Congress for that point of view. Chief of Staff Jim Baker reported a conversation with Congressman Lee Hamilton: I had been, if anything, "too gentle" on this point. Then Baker added, "But if things go badly and we do pull out, we've written the script for the Democrats."

In my private meeting with President Reagan that same day, I found him

---

3. On January 18, 1984, when I met with Soviet Foreign Minister Gromyko, he assured me that Syria "has repeatedly stated that if Israel and the other occupants withdraw, it will withdraw its forces as well. The Soviet Union has good relations with Syria," Gromyko said, and he was "in a position to reaffirm once again that the Syrians will pull out their forces if other foreign forces are withdrawn." This volunteered comment was interesting, though I could hardly take it at face value.

preoccupied with Lebanon: "Are we going to let the Syrians and the Soviets take over? Are we just going to let it happen?" he asked. I was, if anything, even more convinced than the president that we must stand firm in Lebanon, for worldwide as well as for Lebanese considerations.

The next day, after rockets were fired against French and Italian troops, French jet fighters ran air strikes against militia artillery emplacements inside Syrian lines in the mountains east of Beirut. A story President Reagan often told flashed to my mind. A frog and a scorpion are on the bank of the River Jordan, and the scorpion, who can't swim, wants to get across. He asks the frog, "Will you put me on your back and take me to the other side?" "But," the frog replies, "you might sting me and then I'd drown." "Why should I do that?" says the scorpion, "I'd drown too." So out they set. In the middle of the stream, the scorpion stings the frog. As they are both going down, the frog asks, "Why did you do that? Now we'll both drown." The scorpion replies, "This is the Middle East."

On September 28, 1983, the House voted 250 to 161 to authorize the deployment of marines in Lebanon for an additional eighteen months. The vote was of immense importance. It let everyone know that the United States had staying power. President Reagan expressed his appreciation, especially since the resolution had been supported by all of the House leadership, Democrat and Republican. On September 29, the Senate voted for a similar resolution 54 to 46, and the House, that same day, approved the Senate version, 253 to 156.

On October 13, the White House announced that Bill Clark would become secretary of the interior. A few days later, Bud McFarlane replaced Clark as national security adviser. Cap Weinberger, increasingly uneasy about the position of the marines in Lebanon, pressed to have them moved to ships, where they would lie offshore in case they were needed. President Reagan brushed the suggestion aside. I agreed with the president.

At 2:00 A.M. on Sunday morning, October 23, the president was sleeping soundly at the Augusta National Golf Club, where I had invited him for a weekend of relaxation. Bud McFarlane, who was also with us in Augusta, woke the president and me with devastating news: a truck carrying high explosives had rammed through the apparently light security perimeter of the marine compound in Beirut and had crashed into the large cement building where, all grouped together, our marines were sleeping. We knew immediately that the casualties were high. We lost 241 men in what would be the worst single disaster of the Reagan administration. That same day, the French unit of the MNF lost fifty-eight men to a suicide-squad attack.

Early that morning, the presidential party returned to Washington. We were shocked and grieved. But the president was determined not to be driven out of Lebanon by this terrorist attack. We replaced our marine contingent and continued our effort to help the Lebanese out of their civil war and into a process of national reconciliation among the traditional confessional groups. All the Lebanese factions met in Geneva in late November in an attempt that showed some promise but failed in the end to produce a stable agreement. Don Rumsfeld, former secretary of defense, replaced McFarlane as our special negotiator for the Middle East that same month. He struggled skillfully, working with the Lebanese on their problems and trying to structure our position to maximize our own leverage in the situation. Military action escalated as winter came on. On three occasions in mid-December the Syrians fired on U.S. reconnaissance planes, and U.S. naval gunfire was used in response, with the sixteen-inch guns of the battleship *New Jersey* employed for the first time since the Vietnam War.[4]

As the strife-filled days went by, we observed that when our forces were aggressive in reconnaissance and reacted sharply when fired on, the Syrians stepped back and sounded more accommodating. If our forces seemed to hesitate, Syria's statements and actions grew more hostile.

After our commanders on the scene told Rumsfeld that reconnaissance flights were essential, he talked tough to the Syrians, warning them against shooting at these unarmed aircraft. But without his knowledge, reconnaissance flights had been suspended, supposedly to encourage a "cease-fire" on the ground. Then, sometime at the start of December, again without the knowledge of Rumsfeld or me, the flights were resumed. On December 3, one such flight was fired on by the Syrians. The next day, fighter aircraft from the carriers *John F. Kennedy* and *Independence* flew retaliatory missions, and an A-7E Corsair and a two-seat A-6E Intruder were shot down by Syrian surface-to-air missiles.[5] The A-7 pilot ejected and was rescued. The A-6's two fliers also parachuted out. Lieutenant Mark Lange was killed. Lieutenant Robert Goodman was captured, and

---

4. Assertions that the *New Jersey* would eliminate risk to our pilots may have led the navy to order the battleship to open hostile fire. On December 14, the ship's 1,900-pound shells were directed at Syrian antiaircraft batteries. Press reports denounced the ineffectiveness of the *New Jersey*'s gunfire.

5. Some months later, during a visit I made on June 15, 1984, to the *JFK*, then off the Virginia coast, the captain described how he had been stunned to learn, long after the fact, that the carrier's orders as received did not resemble those originally issued. Flaws in the chain of command had led to confusion about reconnaissance flights as well as to our aircraft being launched with the wrong loads at the wrong time and with inadequate preparation. As a former marine officer in the military chain of command, I was troubled at this foul-up, and after these talks on the *JFK*, I discussed the chain-of-command issue with army officers at Fort Bragg, North Carolina, and air force officers at Nellis Air Force Base in Nevada. Something was seriously wrong. The orders issued by the president were not the orders received or implemented by commanders at the point of battle. At each layer, the orders could be made tighter, but not more flexible. At each layer, risk assessment created a bias against action and an increased rigidity in thought. Commanders always want to avoid mistakes, but this propensity in the system bred hesitation and confusion. From those days forward, I urged those in and around the Joint Chiefs of Staff (who were not in the chain of command) to look into this problem.

the Syrians said he would be held prisoner until all Americans were out of Lebanon. On the same day that Lieutenant Goodman was downed and captured, eight marines were killed by artillery fire from Syrian-held territory. By early January, with the high-profile entrance of the Reverend Jesse Jackson as a self-appointed Mideast negotiator, Lieutenant Goodman was back in Washington. The president welcomed Goodman and Jackson to the White House in what he called a "homecoming celebration," but the immense press and congressional uproar over the capture of Lieutenant Goodman and the highly publicized involvement of Jesse Jackson gave Syria a strong message: the United States could not stand the heat of even a small-scale confrontation with Syrian forces.

Rumsfeld, under the impression that reconnaissance flights had been continuing since Lieutenant Goodman's retaliatory sortie, was trying to win concessions from the Syrians for curtailment of such flights. He then discovered, in the second week of January, that no reconnaissance flights had been flown, by order of the Defense Department, since December 18, 1983. The Syrians dismissed Rumsfeld with contempt. The Pentagon had canceled reconnaissance flights when our policy was to stand firm in Lebanon, only to resume them in late January, when our policy was moving toward withdrawal.

I continued to argue, especially to the president, that the United States must persevere in Lebanon. Working feverishly, Rumsfeld telephoned on January 4 to say he was somewhat heartened that a security arrangement could be achieved. "Eighty percent done," he said. I noted that the Syrians welcomed Rumsfeld when the *New Jersey* was firing and scorned him when the firing stopped—and noted also that our forces in general were scaling down their action. On January 11, I had to report to the president that Rumsfeld's effort was unraveling: "Don believes the Syrians are ultimately responsible for [the militias'] last-minute demands. . . . Syrian views on Lebanon appear to have hardened in response to domestic criticism of the MNF here and in Europe."

Congressional support was eroding, and Democratic strategy, led by House Speaker Tip O'Neill, focused on actual withdrawal of U.S. forces rather than on reducing the duration of the mandate voted for in September. Public and congressional concern was mounting. I was convinced that Syria and the Lebanese opposition now believed that Congress would eventually force a U.S. pullout and that this had been a primary factor in Syrian intransigence during December.

On Monday, January 9, 1984, at a National Security Planning Group meeting, Vice President Bush was more than ready to get out of Lebanon. I could see the political handwriting on the wall. From this moment forward, my effort would be to maintain the strength and steadiness needed to enable U.S. forces to achieve an orderly departure and to give the government of

Lebanon and its army a fighting chance. But I could no longer hope to fulfill President Reagan's pledge of December 10, 1983, that only when "internal stability is established and withdrawal of all foreign forces is assured, the marines will leave." I told Admiral Jon Howe, director of State's political-military affairs bureau, to go to the Joint Chiefs of Staff right away: "We must have a plan to get the marines out but stay engaged. The vice president is panicked."

In Beirut, the situation deteriorated as an increasing flow of arms, terrorists, and PLO guerrillas poured through a gap left by the Israeli pullout in the protective ring around the city. Gemayel wanted to use the Lebanese army to close the gap but needed U.S. artillery and tactical air support. Rumsfeld returned from the region in mid-January convinced that we needed to take the initiative, to use our military to convince the Syrians that domestic pressures would not force us and our MNF partners to withdraw from Lebanon without achieving our goals.

I appeared before the Senate Foreign Relations Committee on January 25, 1984. I emphasized that state-sponsored terrorism was a new worldwide phenomenon. I said the United States should not let the terrorists force us to retreat from Lebanon. I stressed that we needed to concentrate on discreet diplomacy to create greater stability and expand the reach of the legitimate government of Lebanon. When Senator Chuck Percy raised the possibility of resolutions about withdrawal, I said they would undercut our ability to negotiate a reasonable settlement. Washington had "pullout fever." Foreign Minister Khaddam of Syria was scathing in his anti-American tirades, convinced that we would soon pack up and leave.

I reviewed our options. It would be devastating, I felt, for us to cut and run. The president agreed, and a plan emerged from interagency discussions to deploy an antiterrorist force that would have mobility and a more active mission than the marines. Most marines would go aboard ship, but some would remain to guard our embassy. The new deployment would maintain a U.S. presence, show U.S. staying power, and address the emerging issue of terrorism. Our fleet would lie offshore with a large contingent of marines on board. Expanded rules of engagement would allow naval and air firepower to strengthen the Lebanese armed forces.

"American power must have more to it than a massive deterrent against the Soviets or a relatively simple exercise like Grenada," I said. "The realities we face will have much more ambiguity. The nature of the challenge is different. We don't think in those terms. We're in a low-grade war with Iranian and Syrian terrorists."

The president left in early February for California. While I was on a long-scheduled trip to Central America, South America, and the Caribbean, the situation in Lebanon further deteriorated. Vice President Bush, with Cap Weinberger at his side, convened a series of crisis-management meetings out of which came decisions to move up and condense the schedule for departure of the marines with no compensating deployment. President Reagan was kept duly informed. I worked my telephones hard, but to no avail. I could see that the president was losing heart, and the telephone was no substitute for my presence.

By the time I got back to Washington on February 8, I found a virtual stampede just to "get out" of Lebanon. "The Defense Department," I said, "will try to get the marines out without putting new elements in. It's a rout. We haven't figured out how to cope with terrorism. The vice president said that there is nothing more important than getting those marines out. We need some thinking about our interests worldwide and what the stakes are, what it means to have staying power in difficult and ambiguous situations."

The reality of our departure turned out to be far different from my earlier redeployment plan, which the president had approved. Our troops left in a rush amid ridicule from the French and utter disappointment and despair from the Lebanese. The Italians left as they saw us departing. The French stayed until the end of March, saying that their peacekeeping mission was no longer possible in what was basically a civil war, supported, in effect, by Syria. They left with their flags flying and a band playing. I liked their style. And the dignity of their departure made an impact in the Middle East. Our own precipitous departure made an impact, too. I knew then that our staying power under pressure would come into question time and again—and not just in the Middle East. In all, the MNF had lost 343 men: the United States, 264; France, 77; and Italy, 2.

Assessment and Reflection

What went wrong? Should U.S. forces have gone into Lebanon in the first place? Should I have gone to the Middle East much earlier? Should I have discounted Israeli staying power? Was the May 17 Agreement a futile exercise? Should we have withdrawn when the Israelis left the Shouf? Should we have used much greater military capability?

The Defense Department appointed a commission, chaired by recently retired Admiral Robert Long, to investigate the tragedy of the bombing of our marine barracks. Its findings were severe: direct blame for inadequate security at the marine compound and for the concentration of troops in one building was assigned to the commanders of the two main marine units in Beirut, who shared "the responsibility for the catastrophic losses." The report deplored "a general attitude throughout the chain of command that security measures in effect ashore were essentially the sole province of the U.S. MNF commander and that it would somehow be improper to tell him how best to protect his force." The report contained a remark I regarded as a misjudgment of our extensive and sustained efforts: "A more vigorous and demanding approach to pursuing diplomatic alternatives" was needed. Its most urgent message was that the Pentagon was "inadequately prepared to deal with this threat," which amounted to "an act of war using the medium of terrorism." I agreed with that assessment.

My own feeling, in retrospect, was that we were right to have deployed the MNF and that we were right to have made the effort to help Lebanon. Success would have been of immense strategic value to us. A stable Lebanon could be a bridge country in the Middle East; a Lebanon dominated by Syria and the Soviet Union would contribute to tension and constitute a site for threats against Israel. Lebanon had taken the brunt of turmoil from Middle East problems. Peace in Lebanon could contribute to peace elsewhere.

Our most important missed opportunity came in September and early October 1982—a time when the situation was most fluid, when Syria was in a weakened position, and when the Lebanese could have best responded to a strong U.S. initiative. But at that moment, Defense Minister Sharon, flushed with the predominance of his military position, tried to negotiate a peace treaty with Lebanon on his own and without the knowledge of the United States. He was dealing in rough terms with Lebanon's designated but yet-to-be-inaugurated president, Amin Gemayel, younger brother of the just assassinated Bashir. At first Amin played along, but in the end he didn't—and couldn't—follow through on his ill-considered assent to an overbearing Sharon.

In the meantime, Phil Habib had returned to Washington in triumph but in need of a rest. I should have told Habib to play a round of golf, spend a few days in the California sun, and then get right back to shuttling around the Middle East. But Phil convinced me that his deputy, Morrie Draper, deserved a chance to operate on his own. I also knew that Phil's health was poor, and I was concerned that he might not be up to the stress involved. We both were also aware that President Assad was blaming Phil for a bad incident, which was not Phil's fault. The Israelis had told Habib back in June 1982, when the fighting was heavy, that they were agreeable to a cease-fire. Habib, taking them at their word, conveyed that to Assad, who acted on this information. The Israelis then advanced, saying they had not promised a cease-fire *in place*. Assad and Habib both felt deceived. As a result, Habib undeniably had been undermined, and it became increasingly evident that Assad would no longer deal with Habib. Morrie Draper had many good qualities, but his designation even as acting head man sent a signal to the region that Lebanon had been relegated to a lower level of priority. An aggressive player like Ariel Sharon took this to mean he had a free field in which to work.

Habib got back into the thick of the action in late September, but critical time had passed. He discovered the abortive effort that had been going on. He struggled to construct a negotiating process. Not until October 25,

1982, were we able to announce that the Lebanese and the Israelis had agreed on talks to be brokered by the United States. Even then, Habib and Draper had to contend with such extreme positions on both sides that negotiations dragged. As a result, we missed our moment, a moment when Syrian withdrawal might have been worked out in connection with an Israeli withdrawal *forced* by the United States against the background of the massacres at Sabra and Shatila.

I also misjudged Menachem Begin and other key Israeli players. When I came into office, Israeli forces were driving northward, flushed with victory. But bitter struggles and betrayals within the Israeli leadership over the aims of the conflict, coupled with the horrors of the massacres at the refugee camps of Sabra and Shatila, left Prime Minister Begin a drained man and the Israeli people with no stomach for sustained political engagement in or with Lebanon. The Israelis had negotiated like tigers for a conditioned withdrawal in the May 17 Agreement: the Syrians had to go, too, they said, or the Israelis would not withdraw. I took the Israelis seriously, only to find them desperate a few months later to move out unconditionally and unilaterally from the Beirut area to southern Lebanon, where they had established a permanent security zone.

At one time, Begin envisaged the transformation of Lebanon into the second Arab nation, following Egypt's example, to make peace with Israel. But by the time I was in the region in April and May 1983 to work out what would become the May 17 Agreement, many Israelis saw Lebanon as a swamp. In a private dining room of the Jerusalem Hilton in early May, Yitzhak Rabin held forth passionately and candidly with me on the fate that awaited anyone foolish enough to get involved in Lebanon in any way. "Lebanon is a quagmire," he told me. "Anyone there will get drawn deeper and deeper into the engulfing morass."

Critics asked why we did not give the pivotal, destructive figure of Syrian President Hafez Assad more attention in April 1983. By that time, his military losses at the hands of the Israel Defense Forces had been recouped by massive arms transfers from the Soviet Union. At the same time, Assad could correctly assess that while American policy had a diplomatic arm, our military arm was tied behind our back, by our own leaders. Beginning with the first deployment of the MNF—the Pentagon restricted our marines to a passive, tentative, and dangerously inward-looking role in Beirut. Assad and others in the region could see that. The secretary of defense was reluctant to contemplate or cooperate with even a limited application of military force to bolster our diplomacy. As a result, the crucial combination of strength and diplomacy required for success was not available.

I therefore tried to create leverage on Assad from a different angle, from pressure on him by other Arabs. The Saudis and others were concerned about prolonged Israeli occupation of Lebanon, and the Lebanese had formally requested that the Syrians withdraw. But Assad's waiting game, his use of force, and flagging Israeli will all worked together to remove this leverage. Had Israel been willing to reduce its forces in Lebanon in a measured way and had the United States been more confident and determined in our deployments, the outcome might have been different.

The May 17 Agreement did not achieve a Lebanon free of foreign forces. And, ultimately, as Israel withdrew unilaterally from central Lebanon to the south, the diplomatic concept underlying the agreement fell away.

Nevertheless, the May 17 Agreement did achieve several changes for the good. The clear commitment it contained for withdrawal of Israel from Lebanon was essential to Hosni Mubarak and the Egyptians in their determination to hold to their own peace treaty with Israel. The commitment was also important to other key Arab states, particularly Saudi Arabia and Jordan. The May 17 Agreement contributed to the stature of U.S. diplomacy, even though implementation on the ground proved beyond us. The agreement provided the basis on which members of the European Community resumed their dealings with Israel, which they had shunned to protest Israel's activities in Lebanon. The agreement also put to the side a set of problems that were debilitating to the U.S.-Israeli relationship.

My first year as secretary of state was dominated by the Middle East. Whenever I turned to one of the many other major world problems, the Middle East would reach out and pull me back in. I could not allow myself to be totally consumed by the Middle East. Too much elsewhere in the world needed urgent attention, particularly at this early stage of my time in office. Nevertheless, I certainly threw myself at this challenge. I made a major effort, and President Reagan and I had set out two frameworks—the September 1 Fresh Start peace initiative and the May 17 Agreement—which, if followed by the parties in the region, could have spared Lebanon a decade of anguish and could have put the Palestinians on the road to greater political rights.

But the book was not closed. Many people said that this searing experience would lead me to avoid the Middle East. On the contrary, I felt I had learned a great deal. And as far as I was concerned, the experience left me more determined, if more patient and careful, to work for peace and stability in this most volatile of regions.

CHAPTER 16

Iraq, Iran,
and Chemical Weapons

On March 29, 1984, Don Rumsfeld arrived back in my office from his latest round of discussions in the Middle East. Jaunty and aggressive as ever, he was nonetheless battered by his Beirut experience. "What has happened in Lebanon hurts," he said, "but there is a bigger disaster on the horizon." As envoy to the Middle East, Rumsfeld had gone often to the Persian Gulf, and what he saw there alarmed him. "The Gulf Arabs think the Carter Doctrine means we save their regimes and keep the oil flowing." In his State of the Union message to Congress on January 23, 1980, Jimmy Carter had said, "Let our position be absolutely clear: An attempt by any outside force to gain control of the Persian Gulf region will be regarded as an assault on the vital interests of the United States of America, and such an assault will be repelled by any means necessary, including military force."

Iran's forces now were pushing the Iraqi army back inside Iraq, and soon they could threaten Kuwait and Saudi Arabia. The U.S. military was not remotely geared up in attitude to take action if such a crisis erupted suddenly, Rumsfeld felt. He was disturbed by the timidity that had characterized Pentagon officials in Lebanon. "The president is out on a limb with this [Carter's] holdover commitment, but our defense orientation can't match it. The Gulf could cave in to Iran—a collapse. It would be Lebanon all over again, but on a huge scale. Lebanon is a sideshow," he said. "The Gulf is crucial, and we are neither organized nor ready to face a crisis there." If things got out of control there, Rumsfeld said, "it could make Lebanon look like a taffy pull."

Rumsfeld was not alone in this view. Iraq's retreat as the numerically far greater Iranian forces swept forward was all too apparent. If Iraq collapsed, that could not only intimidate but inundate our friends in the Gulf and be a strategic disaster for the United States. I was as concerned as Rumsfeld and also as uneasy about attitudes in the Pentagon toward the use of U.S. military capability.

The Reagan administration had adopted a neutral posture toward the Iran-Iraq War even before I arrived on the scene. Iraq had started the war in September 1980, apparently believing that Iran, embroiled in the Khomeini revolution, would be unable to prevent Iraq from seizing disputed territory on the Shatt-al-Arab River and nearby islands. (Iraq claimed the whole river; Iran insisted on a midchannel boundary line.) The conflict soon took on a far more fearsome aspect than a boundary waters dispute. By the time I took office, the Iranians had driven Iraqi forces back into their own territory, and the war had grown into a titanic struggle in which the Islamic but non-Arab Shiite fundamentalist regime of Ayatollah Khomeini was pounding hard on Iraq and thereby threatening the wealth, the religious legitimacy, and perhaps even the existence of Gulf Arab states.

Balance-of-Power Policy

During my early days in office in 1982, I had assessed the momentum of the fighting and the interests of the United States in the Iran-Iraq War. The temptation was to stand by and watch this dictatorial and threatening pair of countries pound each other to pulp. But such a posture by the United States would have been inhumane and unwise. We did have a major stake in the Gulf, and the horrors of the Iran-Iraq War fell on ordinary people, not on their leaders. U.S. policy, therefore, should be and was to try to stop the war. Forceful and unanimous action in the United Nations seemed unlikely in the light of East-West confrontation, and the United States did not have direct access to either country, as we had diplomatic relations with neither. Our only tactic, I felt, was to work to dry up the sources of weaponry that enabled both Iran and Iraq to render death and destruction in this seemingly endless war. From the start of my term, I recognized what an uphill struggle that would be. Wars mean big money for arms merchants the world over; a combatant never has to search very long for someone somewhere ready and eager to sell weapons.

Arms transfers can often be tracked through painstaking documentary investigation after the fact, but such transfers can be masked without much difficulty at the time they are taking place. Indications were that China and North Korea were selling arms to Iran in the early 1980s, while China, Britain, Italy, France, West Germany—and the Soviet Union—were big suppliers of Iraq. No nation seemed to care much about drying up this arms trade except the United States and the fearful Arabs in the Gulf States.[1] Although I was skeptical about our ability to choke off the flow of weaponry that fueled the war, it was the only avenue open to us, and we

1. The Arab League met in emergency session on March 14, 1984, to call for a halt to arms shipments to Iran.

could at least disrupt the arms trade, cause difficulty and delay in access to spare parts, and make the weaponry more expensive to the warring countries.

By the spring of 1983, I had President Reagan's support for an energetic effort to stop the arms trade through what was known as Operation Staunch. Late that year, Ambassador Dick Fairbanks became the coordinating official. With his leadership, this effort was moderately successful. While the United States basically adhered to the policy of not supplying arms to either side,[2] our support for Iraq increased in rough proportion to Iran's military successes: plain and simple, the United States was engaged in a limited form of balance-of-power policy. The United States simply could not stand idle and watch the Khomeini revolution sweep forward. Beginning in December 1982, prodded by U.S. agricultural interests, we provided Iraq with $210 million in credits to purchase American wheat, rice, and feed grains, as well as access to Export-Import Bank credits and continuing financing of agricultural sales by the Commodity Credit Corporation. Some intelligence was also provided to Iraq.

By early 1984, Iran was in a position to launch a huge series of attacks on Iraq along an almost 800-mile front. My concerns were heightened by the belief that the suicide bomb attack that destroyed the U.S. Marine barracks in Beirut was the work of Iran, acting through its surrogates, Shiite terrorist groups in Lebanon. Resentment of Iran still ran deep in the United States after the seizure of our embassy and people in November 1979 and the long agony of the hostage crisis that was so debilitating to the Carter administration. In this situation, a tilt toward Iraq was warranted to prevent Iranian dominance of the Persian Gulf and the countries around it. At the same time, I took the firm position that there should be no deviation from our policy of seeking to deny arms to both combatants and urging other nations to do so as well.

On January 5, 1984, Israeli Ambassador Meir Rosenne came to see me privately. Israel, he said—and he stressed to me that he was speaking for Prime Minister Shamir and that no one else in his embassy knew what he was about to propose—was willing to guarantee the flow of oil from Iraq to the Mediterranean through the pipeline that ran from Kirkuk and Haditha in Iraq through El Mafraq, Jordan, to Haifa, Israel. The pipeline, completed in 1934 when Haifa was part of British Palestine, had been closed early in the Arab-Israeli wars and had been inoperative for over three decades. "I will just leave the idea with you to take action or not," Rosenne said.

I favored the idea, primarily because the result would be a mutually beneficial link between Israel and one of Israel's most dedicated Arab foes.

---

2. The United States violated this policy in the arms-for-hostages effort that would become known as the Iran-Contra affair, discussed in Chapters 37–39 and 42.

Interweaving of economic interests would be a step toward peace in the Middle East. I sent Rumsfeld to Iraq with the message: "Israel might be persuaded to agree to make the pipeline available to them." The pipeline, a quick analysis showed, could be open, secure, and functioning within six months.

The answer came back from Iraq in early February. No. Distrust and enmity, apparently, were thicker than the flow of money that would come from oil.

At this same time, King Hussein of Jordan and the Iraqis were discussing construction of a new pipeline from Iraq to the Jordanian port of Aqaba on the Red Sea. The Iraqis approached our embassy in Baghdad with this idea, indicating that they would build the pipeline only if the United States could obtain a guarantee from Israel to refrain from any activities that would block construction or cut the pipeline.[3] Israel gave the assurances that it would not attack such a pipeline, but the idea faded away, apparently for lack of adequate financing.

Chemical Weapons in Iraq

But something sinister seemed to be going on in Iraq. In late 1983, reports drifted in that Iraq, desperate to stop the oncoming Iranian forces, had employed chemical weapons on the front lines. Their use was a violation of Iraq's commitment as a signatory to the Geneva Protocol of 1925 prohibiting the use of chemical agents in wartime. The agony of soldiers gassed in the trenches in France during World War I had led the world's nations to ban the use of such weapons, presumably forever. Now we were seeing that use revived in the Iraqis' struggle to counter assaults by human waves of young Iranians, sometimes mere children. The source of the chemical agents was not known with confidence. Some intelligence pointed to the Soviets as suppliers. Other sources said Iraq had developed its own production capacity, with crucial assistance from West German companies. This news prodded me to push forward quickly for a new international treaty banning not only the production and use of chemical weapons but monitoring with great care transfers of chemicals with legitimate uses that might be employed in the production of nerve gas and other deadly battlefield poisons.

I found a profound lack of enthusiasm for my views. The West German government seemed singularly indifferent and incurious about what their private companies were shipping to Iraq. Within the "national security community" in Washington, there was strong opposition to the prohibition

3. This report and all further reports of an Iraq-to-Aqaba pipeline were withheld from me at the time, as it appeared that the Bechtel Corporation might have a role in such a project and I had totally removed myself from knowledge of any matter that involved Bechtel.

of chemical weapons production. A principal and important argument was the formidable problem of verifying compliance with such a treaty. The United States would comply, the argument went, but others would cheat, thereby leaving us at a disadvantage. The only answer, and certainly not a perfect one, was a strong verification regime, including sudden on-site inspection on demand, without advance notice.

On March 5, 1984, the administration, through the State Department spokesman, formally accused Iraq of using "lethal chemical weapons" in its war against Iran. On March 7, I was stunned to read in an intelligence analysis being circulated within the administration that "we have demolished a budding relationship [with Iraq] by taking a tough position in opposition to chemical weapons." I thought this was a shocking comment; the United States had to speak the truth and speak out forcefully. A National Security Planning Group (NSPG) meeting was held on March 30 to address Iraq's use of chemical weapons and the need to move forward with a U.S. draft treaty on the prohibition of these weapons.[4] CIA director Bill Casey argued hard against me and the draft treaty. President Reagan sided with me. He, too, stressed the importance of verification.

That same day, the United States announced the imposition of stringent restrictions on the sale to Iraq of five chemical compounds that could be used in the production of chemical weapons. I pushed forward, cabling my counterparts in NATO and Japan, giving special attention to West Germany and Italy, and emphasizing President Reagan's agreement that the United States should take a strong position in favor of the prohibition of the production of chemical weapons. Vice President Bush brought energy and influence to the cause of a treaty by personally tabling a U.S. draft text at the forty-nation Geneva Disarmament Conference on April 18, 1984. The United States instituted export controls on "precursor" chemicals that could be transformed into chemical weapons. Although initially the United States was almost alone in taking up this cause, we had begun to move the Europeans in the direction of restraining such exports. Words were coming our way even though actions were yet to follow.

The United States continued the policy of trying to deny arms to the combatants. In June 1984 when, through Operation Staunch, military matériel was spotted in Italian ports destined for Iraq, we prevailed upon the Italians to stop the shipments. That same month, the National Security Council produced a policy statement tightening export controls on Iran. We had no desire to create a situation of permanent enmity with either country. In September 1984, when Iraqi officials at the United Nations

---

4. I had secured agreement in principle to such a treaty earlier in 1984. The president had authorized me to announce in Stockholm at the opening of negotiations on confidence-building measures in Europe (Conference on Disarmament in Europe) that the United States would soon table a draft treaty calling for the prohibition of the production of chemical weapons.

passed word to me that they would like to resume full diplomatic relations, I responded that we were willing to consider the idea.

I raised the issue of U.S.-Iraq diplomatic relations in early October with both Yitzhak Shamir and Shimon Peres, and they both agreed it could be a positive development insofar as Israel was concerned. They could see that a U.S. dialogue with Iraq constituted at least a means of communication with a state that rejected Israel. The idea was put forth publicly by Iraq on October 12, and with the president's approval, I responded positively to Iraq's overture for improved relations. On November 26, 1984, Iraq's foreign minister, Tariq Aziz, met with President Reagan and me at the White House. At that time, the Iraqis appeared to be taking steps that were welcome to us. Iraq had shut down the Baghdad headquarters of Abu Nidal and had been removed from the list of countries supporting terrorism; the Iraqis no longer appeared to regard themselves as a "rejectionist" adversary of Israel and had made generally positive statements about a diplomatically negotiated solution to the Arab-Israeli conflict.

Later that day, I told Tariq Aziz that the United States was unalterably opposed to the use of chemical weapons and that we would be watching Iraq carefully. I remained skeptical but was nevertheless willing to work to move Iraq toward a more responsible position. On arms, I would not bend from our policy of no shipments to either country. When the Republic of Korea sought a "license" for weapons manufactures for Iraq based on U.S. technology, I insisted that the United States say no and told our people to make sure that the Defense Department, with its close ties to the South Korean military, held to that position.

On that same day, the United States resumed diplomatic relations with Iraq after a seventeen-year hiatus dating back to the 1967 Arab-Israeli War. Don Oberdorfer reported in the *Washington Post* on November 27, 1984: "Describing the resumption of ties as 'a positive development,' a senior State Department official sought in a White House briefing to discourage expectations of large-scale changes in Washington's policies toward Baghdad. Specifically, he said there is no change in prospect in the U.S. refusal to supply weapons or other military gear to Iraq or to Iran, its foe in the four-year-old Persian Gulf war."

There were no stars in my eyes or in Ronald Reagan's. I simply thought we were better off with diplomatic relations with Iraq. I was deeply convinced by this time that the absence of diplomatic relations with another country works to America's disadvantage: the result is that we deny ourselves access to and information about the troublemakers of the world and the opportunity to engage them and seek to bring about change. After Israel's air attack in 1981 that disabled the Iraqi nuclear reactor under construction at Osirak, I felt sure that Iraq would not abandon its efforts to build a nuclear weapons capability. Iraq's ambitions and activities were not of a kind to breed confidence in Saddam Hussein. But the fact remained that a radical Iran now posed an immediate threat to the strategic Gulf area, and Iraq was the only military machine that could block the path of Khomeini's forces.

Reports of Iraqi use of chemical weapons persisted. I heard credible reports that Iraq was building a chemical weapons facility, and I authorized strong statements condemning this activity. On March 25, 1985, I told Tariq Aziz that clear evidence of Iraq's link to chemical weapons was emerging: "The U.S. deplores and deeply opposes the production, acquisition, and use of such weapons; Iraq must understand this and act accordingly." Intelligence analysts tried to reassure me, asserting that the safety standards the Iraqis were employing were so bad that they would gas themselves before they got to gas anybody else. That was little comfort to me.

Time passed. My concerns did not diminish. On March 20, 1986, the United States again denounced Iraq for its use of gas against Iran on the battlefield. The issue soon spread to the other side of the battlefield, and on June 5, 1986, the United States announced a ban on sales to Syria of chemicals that could be transshipped to Iran for use as nerve gas against Iraq. Our action was important, but we could not be effective acting only by ourselves. By 1987, the United States still was the only nation trying in a serious and systematic way to halt the traffic in precursors and components for chemical weapons.

The Iran-Iraq War was an increasingly gruesome slaughter as the scourge of chemical weapons had once again been unleashed, and with insidious effect, to turn back the Iranian onslaught.

Postscript on Chemical Weapons

In September 1988, press and private reports came to us that the Iraqis were using chemical weapons to smash the Kurdish insurgency in northern Iraq. On September 8, I instructed Chuck Redman, the State Department spokesman, to announce that the United States was convinced Iraq had used nerve agents against the Kurds and denounce Iraq's practice as "abhorrent and unjustifiable." The United States immediately sought permission from Turkey to send a team of foreign service officers to the Turkish-Iraqi border, across which Kurdish refugees had fled, to look for evidence of the use of chemical weapons. Ambassador April Glaspie delivered our formal protest to the Iraqi government in Baghdad, and I called in the Iraqi minister of state for foreign affairs, Sa'adoun Hammadi, and blasted him. I authorized Redman to say: "The Secretary stressed to Dr. Hammadi that we attach great importance to the further development of our relationship with Iraq but that we do not intend to pursue this course if illegal Iraqi use of chemical weapons and other human rights abuses continue."

The Turks reported that Kurdish refugees showed no signs of being gassed. Formal U.S. efforts to inspect the sites inside Iraq to gather evidence were not successful, but personnel from our embassy did manage to get to the area. They reported many Kurds with oozing sores at the mouth and nose, flaking skin, and difficulty in breathing: symptoms of exposure to mustard gas. Our public charges against Iraq were not strongly echoed in other capitals. I felt that the United States must rally other nations to take seriously the reports of the use of chemical weapons. On September 12, the United States, along with Britain, West Germany, and Japan, formally asked the secretary-general of the United Nations to dispatch a fact-finding team to Iraq, but I feared that by the time it got there— if it ever got there—the evidence would have been covered up by the Iraqis. Nevertheless, a resolution demanding access passed the Security Council, meaning that the Soviets and Chinese were at least willing to go along. Iraq rejected the UN request.

President Reagan took the highly unusual step, in an effort to build confidence abroad in the accuracy of our accusation, of authorizing the disclosure of U.S. intercepts of Iraqi military communications that revealed that Iraq's military had indeed used poison gas against the Kurds. I strongly supported him in taking this important step, even though we all knew our ability to collect additional information by this method would be compromised. We had to convince skeptics at home and abroad that we had hard evidence to back our claims. On Capitol Hill, a bill was moving forward to impose unilateral economic sanctions on Iraq. I preferred to try to broaden, to make collective and therefore more effective, any sanctions that might be imposed. I wanted to bring other countries to our view through work in the United Nations.

When President Reagan gave his final address to the UN General Assembly on September 26, 1988, he spoke out in the strongest terms: "It is incumbent upon all civilized nations to ban, once and for all, and on a verifiable and global basis, the use of chemical and gas warfare."

Iraq and Iran—and similar regimes—would never be induced to stop using chemical weapons unless a tough and comprehensive international effort was mounted. The work to be done by the United States and through the international community was urgent: nail down an end to the Iran-Iraq War by following up on the cease-fire finally agreed on in August 1988 under UN auspices; raise the profile of U.S. objections to the use of chemical weapons and press others to do the same; press forward to get a tough new treaty prohibiting the production of chemical weapons, signed by as many nations as possible (the United States had taken the lead by tabling a draft treaty back in April 1984 in Geneva and had continued to press the case); finally, be ready to confront other nations—often friends and allies—whose private commercial dealings were providing dangerous regimes with the chemical precursors that could be transformed into gases used as weapons.

With the end of the Iran-Iraq War, our interest in maintaining the balance of power in the Gulf to block Iran's threat was greatly diminished. There had been a period of twelve to eighteen months in the mid-1980s when I, and American foreign policy, gave the benefit of the doubt to the Iraqi regime of Saddam Hussein. Our Near East bureau compiled a list of indications that Iraq was, by fits and starts, moving away from its support of terrorism, toward the necessity for a negotiated Arab-Israeli outcome, and into the circle of responsible international citizens. Nizar Hamdoon, Iraq's ambassador in Washington, credibly portrayed his government as reforming and worthy of steps by us in recognition of that.

It was a notable example of the power of diplomacy and of the difference that a deft ambassador can make. But we no longer live in the age of Machiavelli, and even a skillful ruler and his envoy cannot deceive the world for long in the information age. When Abu Abbas was allowed to leave Italy in October 1985 following the hijacking of the *Achille Lauro*, he went to Yugoslavia and then made his way to Baghdad. This was followed by Iraq's use of chemical weapons and our increasing awareness that Saddam Hussein had not only not given up his pursuit of a "military option" against Israel but was seeking to construct a regionally dominant military machine that could not be explained by his fear of Iran alone. I came to regard Iraq, once again, as one of the enemy states of the responsible world community. By the end of the Reagan years, after our reflagging policy had turned the Gulf War toward its conclusion, it was clear to me that no further reason existed for the United States to give Iraq the benefit of the doubt for balance-of-power purposes against Iran. We were at sword's point with Iraq: over chemical weapons, the difficulty of obtaining compensation from Iraq for the victims of the attack on the U.S.S. *Stark*, and signs of Iraq's support for terrorists. This was the context in which we sought, in one of the transition books we prepared at the State Department for the incoming Bush administration, to point out that a new and tougher policy toward Saddam Hussein's Iraq was now appropriate.[5]

Looking the Other Way

One confrontation over chemical weapons produced the most disturbing encounter with the West Germans I ever experienced in my decades of dealing with their leaders, who were among our strongest and most reliable allies. When I first heard, in the mid-1980s, that Iraq was building chemical weapons facilities with the help of West German engineers and companies, I tried hard to get the Germans to stop. President Reagan was as concerned as I

5. Elaine Sciolino referred to our recommended new policy to contain Iraq in the *New York Times* on June 27, 1992, and identified as her source one of the transition books the State Department had prepared for the Bush administration.

was. What we ran into were excuses: "You haven't really shown clearly that your allegations are true" or "We really have no control over the exports of things that could be as much for benign use as for chemical weapons use."

Chancellor Helmut Kohl and Foreign Minister Hans-Dietrich Genscher publicly portrayed themselves as in the lead in their horror of chemical weapons and their desire to see a strong treaty prohibiting the existence and production of such weapons, let alone their use. Their reluctance to come to terms with the involvement of West German companies in the production of chemical weapons was deeply disturbing to me and to President Reagan.

In September 1988, clear evidence came to light regarding the development of a chemical weapons plant in Rabta, Libya. The Japanese were building a metal-working plant nearby that could readily be adapted to the production of canisters of one kind or another. We raised this issue with the Japanese, and they replied that their investigation showed that no Japanese laws had been broken. This, too, was disturbing and unsatisfactory. Even more serious was the involvement of West Germans in the construction of the Libyan chemical plant. President Reagan and I wanted to impress upon Chancellor Kohl and Foreign Minister Genscher the seriousness of this matter, so when Kohl visited the United States in mid-November 1988, the president asked him to spend an hour of his time with me on this issue.

At 3:15 in the afternoon on November 15, I went to the suite Kohl always used at the Watergate Hotel. NSC adviser Colin Powell, Assistant Secretary of State Roz Ridgway, Ambassador Rick Burt, and CIA director Bill Webster accompanied me. Genscher was present, too. I asked Webster to give the briefing. I knew Kohl well by this time. I had visited him twice at his home and had met with him on innumerable occasions. I wanted Webster's presentation to be more incisive than it was so I augmented it, interjecting here and there to make key points as sharp as possible and to emphasize the meaning of various bits of evidence Bill described.

Kohl listened, but he was very uncomfortable. I was, too. I felt he was hearing me out, simply because he had been asked to listen. My own feeling was that the head of a country that deplores chemical weapons and terrorism and hears a report that companies in his own country are helping the likes of Libya's Muammar Qaddafi to develop a chemical weapons capacity ought to be *avid* for that information and seek to deal with its implications. But that was not the spirit of the occasion.

Kohl did agree that the United States could send a technical team to West Germany and present our evidence, although he was apprehensive about even that step, fearing that the mere arrival of such a team might suggest West German involvement in poison gas production. In West Germany, the U.S. team learned that West German intelligence had been passing to the German leadership the same information that the United States possessed. The West Germans had resisted taking any action.

Later, when I was in Paris for the Chemical Weapons Conference on Disarmament during the final days of the Reagan administration, I met again with Genscher. By this time, reports of the involvement of West German firms in Libyan gas production were surfacing. Genscher was furious at the United States, accusing us falsely of leaking the information. I, too, was furious. "It's not up to the U.S. to prove West German involvement," I told Genscher. "It's up to Germany to look into it and do something about it."

Kohl and Genscher suggested that an international inspection team schedule a visit to the Libyan facility, an empty suggestion, since the essence of any chemical weapons treaty is on-site inspection without warning. With twenty-four hours' warning, such a plant can be altered very easily so that it appears to be making ordinary chemical products. I was deeply troubled by the willingness of these leaders to look the other way on a matter of such importance.

In Paris, after arguing with Genscher about the involvement of West German firms with Qaddafi, I addressed the Chemical Weapons Conference on January 7, 1989: "Must it take a fresh shock of human tragedy," I asked, "must more places like Flanders Fields earn their place in the history books through the particular ghastliness of their destruction— before governments work together to restore respect for the international norms against chemical weapons use?"

I concluded by quoting Carl Sandburg, whose poem "Grass," ends with these stark and bitter lines:

> Pile the bodies high . . . at Ypres and Verdun.
> Shovel them under and let me work.
> Two years, ten years, and passengers ask the conductor:
> What place is this?
> Where are we now?
> I am the grass.
> Let me work.

The world should be able to find a better answer. A treaty bearing signatures of all nations, an understood capacity for inspection at any time, and a willingness, on a global basis, to be vigilant in the event of violation are all necessary ingredients to jam this horrific genie back into the bottle and keep it there. I hoped that the momentum generated at the end of the Reagan presidency and the new possibilities for joint action with the Soviets might bring the problem of chemical weapons once again under control. When he was vice president, George Bush cared about and labored hard on this issue. I was encouraged by his emphasis on the issue during his campaign for the presidency, and therefore, as I left office, I felt confident of leadership from the White House on this issue of central humanitarian concern.

CHAPTER 17

The Strategic
Defense Initiative

My first intimation of what was to become the Strategic Defense Initiative (SDI), though I didn't realize it at the time, came on the snowbound Saturday evening of February 12, 1983, when the Reagans could not get to Camp David and asked O'Bie and me over for an informal dinner with them at the White House. Soviet and Chinese developments were not the only subjects of conversation. We were all relaxed, off-duty, so to speak.[1]

From my standpoint this spontaneous evening of far-reaching conversation—foreign policy, China, and the Soviet Union in particular, as well as possible travel by the president—provided me an important insight into Ronald Reagan's real feelings, his beliefs and desires: especially his desire to get involved personally in work on these key relationships. He talked about his abhorrence of Mutual Assured Destruction (MAD) as the centerpiece of the strategic doctrine of deterrence. The idea of relying on the ability to wipe each other out as the way to prevent war had no appeal to Ronald Reagan. How much better it would be, safer, more humane, the president felt, if we could defend ourselves against nuclear weapons. Maybe there was a way, and if so, we should try to find it. He hoped for the day when there would be no nuclear weapons. I later learned that he had received encouragement from the Joint Chiefs of Staff the previous day, February 11, that a defense against strategic nuclear missiles might prove feasible and that a major research effort was needed and justified.

I did not know much about the science involved in possible strategic defense, but from what little I knew, it seemed to present huge, perhaps insuperable, problems. As I listened to President Reagan that evening, I understood the importance of what he was saying, but I had absoutely no idea that the views he was expressing had any near-term, operational significance.

1. The dinner is discussed in more detail in Chapter 12.

What I did know was the immense importance of issues concerning nuclear weapons and of the strategic doctrine of deterrence surrounding them. The Soviet Union had been our enemy since the end of World War II. They and we, and by now Britain, France, and China—at the least—had nuclear weapons, the awesome destructiveness of which was combined with ballistic missiles having unprecedented range, speed, and accuracy. Bombers and cruise missiles, slower flying but also capable of great range and accuracy, added to the means of delivering nuclear warheads. Both were being designed with stealth technology to make them increasingly difficult to detect.

Peace had been kept in Europe and World War III averted by this system of nuclear deterrence. We and the Soviets each possessed the capacity to strike back in the event of a nuclear attack in a manner so devastating as to deter such an attack. The doctrine of Mutual Assured Destruction in its various iterations was the underlying idea, and its implementation through the deployment of nuclear weapons that could survive a first-strike nuclear attack and retaliate massively was the means of keeping the peace.

In Europe, where NATO conventional forces were vastly outnumbered by Soviet and Warsaw Pact tanks, artillery, and manpower, deterrence of the use of that conventional superiority was maintained by a doctrine of "flexible response," formally adopted by NATO in 1967. We and our allies would not agree to "no first use" of nuclear weapons, since the threat of first use of even battlefield nuclear weapons constituted an all-important equalizer against the Soviets' conventional advantage. We needed the capacity to respond with flexibility to any potential threat, and we wanted the Soviets to know that we had that flexibility.

The stakes in avoiding a nuclear exchange are of such overriding significance that all American presidents, Republicans and Democrats alike, have put one concern foremost: the prevention of nuclear war while preserving freedom. And this has meant, despite the most intense differences in systems and values, a continuing effort to negotiate about nuclear matters with the Soviet Union and to prevent the proliferation of nuclear weapons.

A milestone of central importance was reached in 1972 with U.S.-Soviet agreement on an Antiballistic Missile (ABM) Treaty in tandem with an interim agreement to limit strategic arms (SALT I). The MAD doctrine was enshrined in the ABM Treaty by agreement to forgo, with the exception, by 1974, of a limited system at one site in each country, deployment of defenses against ballistic missiles. The Soviets deployed and then modernized a limited defense around Moscow, but we decided, after deploying a limited U.S. system at Grand Forks, North Dakota, where many of our intercontinental ballistic missiles (ICBMs) are installed, that such defenses were not sufficiently effective to warrant their very considerable expense. As a result, we were defenseless, and so basically were they, against attack by ballistic missiles. We relied on our ability to wreak nuclear havoc on the Soviet Union as the deterrent against their attack on us or our allies.

SALT I assumed that further negotiations would reduce the levels of deployed strategic weapons. Not only did such reductions not materialize, but technological developments made the basic system of deterrence increasingly unstable. What SALT I limited (the unit of account) was launchers, but both sides got around that limit by placing more than one warhead on a launcher. These multiple independently targetable reentry vehicles (MIRVs), with ten or possibly more warheads on a single launcher, increasingly eroded the stability of the system of deterrence, in particular of the land-based ICBM forces. With one warhead on a launcher and, a common assumption, two warheads needed to destroy a launcher, equality in the number of launchers meant that a first strike would leave the other side with ample retaliatory capacity. Deterrence was made stable by that relationship. The proliferation of MIRVed ICBMs meant that we and the Soviets were increasingly able to threaten all of the other's land-based intercontinental launchers of ballistic missiles with only a fraction of our own. The destructiveness of such a strike makes a decision to strike first more profitable and a preemptive strike more tempting. Of course, what worried us was the temptation to the Soviets. They claimed the same concern about us.

Fortunately, we had ballistic missiles on submarines thought to be invulnerable. We also had a formidable nuclear capacity carried by bombers, kept constantly on alert by the Strategic Air Command. The Soviets, too, possessed a triad of delivery systems that added to the survivability of their deterrent forces, and they moved out in front of us in making their land-based systems more survivable by making some of them mobile instead of fixed in known locations. Our own efforts had not succeeded in finding a survivable way of basing the MX, our most advanced and accurate MIRVed system, able to reach the Soviet Union from bases on land in the United States. The problem was how to base the MX so that it could survive a nuclear attack. Without a survivable basing mode, the MX could add to instability rather than diminish it.

A series of proposals, for varying reasons, had been rejected. Just before the Joint Chiefs gave the president their view that defense against ballistic missiles merited a strong research effort, they had failed to support a proposal put forth by the president on the advice of Secretary of Defense Weinberger for a "dense pack" basing mode for the MX missile. The idea underlying dense pack was to deploy our missiles close together so that a Soviet warhead destroying one silo would interfere with warheads targeted on nearby silos, a "fratricide" effect, allowing a sufficient number of our missiles to survive and thereby allowing us to retaliate. Some of the chiefs doubted that dense pack would work and said so publicly. The unwillingness of the Joint Chiefs to support dense pack doomed the proposal.

This was a traumatic episode for President Reagan, Secretary Weinberger, and the Joint Chiefs. I was dumbfounded at this turn of events. I had no basis for an independent opinion on the workability of dense pack, but for the secretary of defense to make a recommendation to the president without knowing confidently in advance that the chiefs would give the proposal their support was astonishing. I wondered about the depth of Cap's relationship with his key military advisers.

Against this background, Ronald Reagan was determined to *reduce*, not merely limit, the nuclear stockpiles of both superpowers. Two negotiations had been under way in Geneva, one on intermediate-range nuclear forces (INF) and the other on strategic (intercontinental-range) arms reductions (START).[2] In INF, our position called for elimination of this entire class of weapons; and in START, for reductions of about 50 percent. Of central significance, the units of account in the president's proposals were no longer limited to launchers but emphasized warheads—what hits the target—and the lift capacity of a missile, "throw weight," a key determinant of how many warheads, and of what weight, can be put on a missile.

All this was in my mind when, in mid-March, I heard more about "strategic defense" from brief discussions with NSC adviser Bill Clark. I learned that physicist Edward Teller, father of the hydrogen bomb, and Jay Keyworth, the president's science adviser, had been talking to the president about defense against strategic weapons. I argued the issues of strategic doctrine briefly with Bill Clark on Friday, March 18, although I had no idea that anything regarding strategic defense was imminent on the president's agenda.

A New Departure

On Monday morning, March 21, Larry Eagleburger reported to me on a conversation he had just had with Bud McFarlane. "The president will give a speech on Wednesday, March 23," he told me. The Joint Chiefs had convinced the president, he said, that the MX would remain vulnerable but that there was an alternative. "The alternative is a high-tech strategic defense system that can protect us against ballistic missiles and thereby protect our offensive capabilities. The president is intrigued and wants to make strategic defense the subject of his speech."

"The chiefs," I countered, "are not equipped to make this kind of proposal. They are not scientists."

Eagleburger went on to say that the president had nevertheless decided that "by the close of the century we should turn to a strategic defense and

2. INF negotiations began November 30, 1981; START, on June 29, 1982.

by then banish all nuclear weapons." Bud McFarlane wanted to get up a message to our allies, said Eagleburger.

"We don't have the technology to say this," I interjected.

"The White House has a whole public campaign planned," Eagleburger responded. It sounded to me like Fortress America. "This changes the whole strategic view and doctrine of the United States," I said.

Rick Burt came into the meeting. When Eagleburger described to him the president's idea, Burt was flabbergasted. "Not only is a nuclear-free world a pipe dream, but a speech like this by the president will unilaterally destroy the foundation of the Western alliance," he said.

After this meeting, I confided to my executive assistant, Ray Seitz, that I had heard of the strategic defense idea before: first at my dinner with the president and subsequently when I had argued with Bill Clark about the strategic defense question the previous Friday. "There is an interplay between policy and technology," I said. "Technology can make policy obsolete. The president is saying that defensive measures have a lot of promise, and he's right. But they should redraft the speech to recognize the evolving technology without changing our strategic doctrine."

About eleven o'clock that morning, Bill Clark called on the secure line about the new defensive concept that was to be part of the president's speech on the defense budget.

"This is so sweeping," I told him, "that it must be carefully considered. It could hit the allies right between the eyes. This is the year when we especially need a cohesive alliance in our negotiations with the Soviets. Why place so much confidence in the Joint Chiefs of Staff? They are in no position to make what amounts to a scientific judgment."

Later in the afternoon I went to the White House for a meeting with the president. I found great resistance to any change in the words for the speech. "This paragraph is a revolution in our strategic doctrine," I told President Reagan. He had Keyworth called in. I asked him, "Can you be sure of an impenetrable shield? And what about cruise missiles? What about stealth bombers? Your language is sweeping. I'm not objecting to R and D, but this is a bombshell. What about the ABM Treaty? What about our allies and the strategic doctrine on which we and they depend? You don't say anything about those questions." His answers were not at all satisfactory to me.

After returning to my office, I learned that the president instructed Bud McFarlane, Clark's deputy, to cut back on the speech. This initiative will not be seen as a peaceful gesture, I thought; it will be seen as destabilizing. I respected the importance of the R and D effort called for in the speech, but I felt it was urgent that the speech say that our research would be consistent with the ABM Treaty and that we would continue to rely on existing strategic doctrine and the existing structure of our alliances.

The next day, March 22, we received a new draft of the strategic defense speech. The style and substance were toned down, but it still proclaimed, "Tonight we are launching a truly new beginning which holds the promise of changing the course of human history." The effect remained unsettling, and I continued to be disturbed. I favored the R and D effort but objected to the total lack of attention to our strategic doctrine and to our obligations under the ABM Treaty. Without dealing with these problems, we would set off alarm bells among our allies, let alone the Soviets, especially since the Soviet Union was called the "evil empire" in this draft of the president's speech.[3] I also wondered just how solid was the scientific and technological basis for these sweeping statements. I pointed out that we needed some very precise Qs and As to handle the difficult and tricky questioning that would inevitably follow. Without this, people would say that we didn't know what we were talking about.

I called Bill Clark. "The latest draft is an improvement, but we still have to be very careful," I said. "This is a big step." I pointed out to Clark that the message contained the seeds of a total reversal of our strategic doctrine. I would be interested in how Keyworth handled the scientific briefings, I told him. When Keyworth came over to the State Department to give us the word, I had not been impressed with reports of his answers to penetrating questions.

At 5:45 P.M. I received the packet of Q and A material to support the president's speech. Larry Eagleburger, Jerry Bremer, and Jon Howe joined me. I told them that we must consider the problems that we would confront as a result of the president's speech. "What are the positive things that can be emphasized? In a technical sense we have an R and D proposal which, if successful, might result in something in a decade or so. This envisages, if we ever get to the stage of deployment, the eventual abrogation of the ABM Treaty. Everyone will assume that the president would not make this statement unless we had solid evidence of a real breakthrough on defensive systems. People will want to know if there is a breakthrough. If the answer is no, then the president's statement could backfire. There may be new technical substance to it; there has been speculation about the uses of laser beams in space. The Soviets will assume that we are on the verge of some special technical innovation. Maybe that is the greatest benefit," I said.

Eagleburger was troubled by what this might mean for stealth technology, the promising but expensive effort to design planes and cruise missiles so that they would present the most minute image possible to radar detection. If a new defensive system could not be penetrated by such offensive weap-

3. The president had called the Soviet Union an "evil empire" in a speech on March 8 to the annual convention of the National Association of Evangelicals. His phrase caught wide attention in the United States and in Europe and stood in people's minds for a certain implacability in Ronald Reagan's approach to the Soviet Union (see Chapter 18).

ons, then the stealth technology was already obsolete. If a new defensive system could be penetrated by stealth, then the statements the president proposed to make were far too extravagant.

"If the defensive umbrella extends only to intercontinental ballistic missiles," I said, "then the whole concept has a big hole in it. New technology already means that intercontinental ballistic missiles are only *one* high-powered means of delivering nuclear warheads. Air- or sea-launched cruise missiles and bombers, particularly the prospective stealth bombers, can do the job, too."

I had raised the question of the coverage of the proposed defense shield with the president on Monday but received no clear answer. "Whenever I ask for a meeting with the president, a crowd collects, and the number of people makes an incisive and candid discussion difficult," I complained upon my return. I had told the president, "From what I know of history, competition in weaponry is a long story of measure and countermeasure. It is imprudent to put all your eggs in one basket." I feared the president might be relying too heavily on Keyworth, who seemed to have limited understanding of strategic doctrine and gave very superficial answers to extremely important questions, such as stealth.

"The president seems to be proposing an updated version of the Maginot Line," Eagleburger said. Jon Howe expressed his view that history also indicates that offense always overtakes defense.

"There are numerous questions about technology that must be addressed," I remarked. "We have to look at survivability and reliability and cost. There are also questions about deterrence: if we put a defensive system in place and continue to maintain our offensive weapons, the result is destabilizing. The Soviets will assume that we are on to something more than the president reveals in his address. Ironically, the address may make more dangerous our 'window of vulnerability' because the Soviets will see this as an effort to render their offensive capability obsolete by the end of the century. Once the system is in place, okay," I said, "at least for a while, but the run-up period to deployment will be highly dangerous." I wondered whether it would work politically. I would have a hard time supporting the initiative publicly, I confessed, because I didn't know enough about the technology. "I don't think the [Joint] Chiefs know about it either," I said. "The White House will expect me to defend it, and I will, but I'll have difficulty." I laughed and commented, "There isn't anyone else defending our position on El Salvador or working on the [nuclear] freeze movement or standing up for Ken Adelman."[4]

*   *   *

4. Kenneth Adelman was the president's nominee to head the Arms Control and Disarmament Agency. His confirmation prospects were in trouble, and the White House personnel and political offices, having picked him, were not giving him much support.

At 6:30 in the evening, the president called me. "I think the wording of the speech is better in this current draft, and some of the Qs and As are helpful," I told him, "but I still have great reservations, not about the R and D effort, but about advancing this as something of such tremendous importance and scope. It implies we are changing our strategic doctrine. There are a host of unanswered technical questions. There is tremendous strength in both offensive and defensive measures, but the former historically has the upper hand. I can't see being certain of one system defending against cruise missiles on submarines and stealth bombers, let alone ballistic missiles. I can see the moral ground you want to stake out, but I don't want to see you put something forward so powerfully, only to find technical flaws or major doctrinal weaknesses." I went on, "I have been sitting here trying to think it through. It raises questions about the B-1 bomber and stealth and INF deployments. I have to say honestly that I am deeply troubled. Of course, I will support you. I'm sure you know that."

President Reagan responded, stressing the overwhelming attractions to him of a defensive system.

"I agree that if we get there, we'll be in the catbird seat," I said. "So we must push our R and D if for no other reason than because the Soviets are. But it can be destabilizing as to what the Soviets do and how they respond. They will assume that we have a major scientific breakthrough. I don't know the implications of that."

The president interrupted to say that this was the part that would make a news item and attract the networks.

"It's more than a news item. It's a sweeping proposal," I said.

I looked over the draft text again and said, "A lot of weight is put on Keyworth. It suggests that we really have the technology. I don't have the information. Is stealth irrelevant? Perhaps I could redraft a few alternative paragraphs that support R and D, state that the research is consistent with the ABM Treaty and that we continue to rely on our strategic doctrine of deterrence. We don't want to make the prospect sound as if this is an overall and imminent solution to our problems. Should I give it a whirl?"

The president told me to go ahead.

Half apologetically I said, "I feel I would be derelict if I didn't tell you what I think." That was the end of the conversation.

I was impressed with the president's call. Again, I could see the depth of his feelings about this issue, his abhorrence of reliance on the ability to "wipe each other out" as the means of deterring war, and, of course, I could agree that if we could learn how to defend ourselves, that would be wonderful.

Eagleburger came back into my office to report that Bud McFarlane had just informed him that the strategic defense umbrella applies only to ballistic missiles.

What a disaster, I thought. "The idea and the rhetoric don't fit together. What about the other delivery systems?" I asked. "The rhetoric must be consistent with what is and is not being covered." I briefly described my conversation with the president and told Eagleburger to draft alternative language that would damp down what I regarded as the overblown aspects of the speech and would make the necessary strategic points.

Shortly afterward, I received an invitation from the president for dinner at the White House the next evening, when the speech would be given. Other guests would include the Joint Chiefs of Staff, a covey of scientists, and former national security advisers. At 7:10 that evening, I called Bud McFarlane. "If the defensive system that the president has in mind is only to counter ballistic missiles, then the concept is not as sweeping as has been described," I said. "I'm in the dark, but I'm leery about such promises in the face of such uncertainty. Anyway, I've been reworking the text as the president agreed and wanted you and Bill [Clark] to know that. I feel you guys are leading the president out on a limb and people will saw it off. The chiefs should have their necks wrung." Explaining my last statement, I told him that I was incredulous when I learned that the Joint Chiefs had called the White House only a few hours before to say that the idea would apply only to ballistic missiles and not to *all* offensive nuclear weapons. Apparently they, too, were suddenly aware of and disturbed by the overstated language in the speech.

At the end of the day, I felt that I had made some progress in toning down the draft and clarifying some of the underlying strategic concepts. I stood at my desk and looked at my call list. It was almost 7:30 P.M. My day wasn't over, but I had no stomach for what was left.

On Wednesday, March 23, first thing in the morning, I remarked that Bud McFarlane seemed increasingly annoyed with what he regarded as my "obstruction" of the speech. This attitude confirmed to me that Bud apparently had been deeply involved in pushing this idea. From what I learned, Fred Ikle and Richard Perle over in Defense also had only recently learned of the speech and were opposed. They had been calling around town since last night. Ikle had called me and commented that the proposal was mainly a White House contraption. Clark had told me the previous night he really didn't know much about the details behind the proposal. I had been tempted to say, "Buddy boy, you've got to get into substance."

Jerry Bremer said our alternative draft had gone over to the White House last night and cables to allies and instructions to Cap Weinberger in Portugal had been held up. He also said the origins of the idea remained obscure. It allegedly had been discussed with the President's Foreign Intelligence Advisory Board (PFIAB) and with the Joint Chiefs.

I was pleased to see how quickly and well our group at the State Department had come to grips with this proposal. I pointed out that apparently there was an astonishing disconnect between the office of the secretary of defense and the Joint Chiefs of Staff, although Weinberger's role was unclear to me. "The pattern of our thinking about strategic issues reflects the technology of twenty years ago," I remarked. "That technology has changed, and therefore we need new patterns of thought." When I raised some of these conceptual problems created by cruise missiles and stealth technology with the president and his advisers, they were not responsive. Actually, I had to admit to myself that the president was advancing a new pattern of thought in the light of potential new technology.

Larry Eagleburger walked into my office to tell me he had just spoken with McFarlane. "They have our draft, but Bud apparently has drafted something softer. McFarlane said that our draft and the new softer NSC draft would be put before the president this morning. Clark is talking to Weinberger now. The atmosphere in the front office at the NSC is sour," Eagleburger said.

"Bud and Bill Clark have clearly been the moving forces behind this," I said.

"Last night Bud said that Perle and Ikle had been 'duplicitous,' " Eagleburger reported. "Bud said they had tried to confuse the issue by claiming that the Joint Chiefs didn't support the president's initiative."

Bill Clark called at 8:00 A.M. I discussed the alternative draft State had sent over the previous night: "It's a draft paper based on the assumption you want to make a big point of research on an antiballistic missile defensive system, but it doesn't fall into the trap of saying something more comprehensive that can't be supported. This can be consistent with our current doctrinal posture. The president is right to press R and D, if only because the Soviets are. There's nothing wrong with the R and D effort, but we shouldn't say it will enable us right now to rearrange the way we think. That is shaky ground. Technology is already moving past the antiballistic missile system. Look at cruise and stealth. If you have a softer draft than ours, so much the better. I think we have done the president a great favor by cautioning him not to go too far out on a limb."

The conversation then turned to Ikle and Perle. I knew that Clark was angry that Perle and Ikle had been phoning a variety of people claiming that the Joint Chiefs did not support the SDI idea in the president's speech.

"They're liars," Clark told me. That ended the conversation.

"They'll probably be fired," I said when I hung up the phone.

After lunch, we heard from Larry Eagleburger, who had been summoned to the White House at 11:00 A.M. and given the latest draft. He was told that the president had decided on this text. When I looked at the draft, I saw it was better than, but still close to, the previous day's version. "The president has decided this. That's where we stand," Eagleburger told me.

"The president may have decided it," I said, "but it's not clear to me that the president even saw our proposal from last night or the McFarlane softer version." I had felt the strength of the president's views on the importance of strategic defense, however, so I had no doubt that the decision was the president's. Anyway, the decision had been made, and there was, I thought, consolation in the fact that the speech was much improved over what we had been looking at on Monday.

Later that afternoon I went over to the White House. Bill Clark told me that Larry Eagleburger had "looked at the final version and said it seemed fine to him." That, I knew, was simply not true.

I had been authorized to let Dobrynin see the speech in advance, and I wanted to see Dobrynin, anyway, to hear his response to the president's ideas for the negotiations on reductions of conventional forces (MBFR). We set the meeting for 4:30 P.M. I gave Dobrynin a copy of the speech and drew his attention to the section on defense against ballistic missiles, which was to form the basis of the president's Strategic Defense Initiative (SDI). I knew this issue was explosive, but I presented it in a straightforward manner. I stressed that this was a research and development effort consistent with the ABM Treaty, that we knew that the Soviets were pursuing such efforts as well, and that our proposed program for strategic defense would be designed to enhance stability. Dobrynin was disturbed. "You will be opening a new phase in the arms race," he said. I reiterated our objective—to enhance stability.

Ronald Reagan Speaks

Then came the speech itself, "Defense and National Security," delivered in a televised address to the nation on Wednesday, March 23, 1983. Ronald Reagan, one of the premier speechmakers in our nation's history, added a new dimension to the course of global strategic thought and practice. This was a speech about the defense budget, but the defense budget, the president said, was not about "spending arithmetic." America maintains a powerful military, he said, but America does not start fights: deterrence means making sure any adversary concludes that the risk of attacking us outweighs any political gain.

The president then reviewed the sustained Soviet accumulation of enormous military might. He talked about the spread of Soviet military influence and focused on Soviet intelligence and military activity in Central America and the Caribbean Basin. He put the spotlight on emerging problems in Grenada. Then came examples of Soviet encroachment in Angola, Afghanistan, Ethiopia, South Yemen, and Vietnam. In Poland they were denying the will of the people, and in the Pacific they were becoming a naval force to be reckoned with for the first time in their history. "The final fact," President Reagan said, "is that the Soviet Union is acquiring what can only be considered an offensive military force. They have continued to build far more intercontinental ballistic missiles than they could

possibly need simply to deter an attack. Their conventional forces are
trained and equipped not so much to defend against an attack as they are
to permit sudden, surprise offenses of their own." The president then talked
about our need to modernize our forces yet at the same time work seriously
on arms control.

Then he came to his dramatic point: "In recent months, however, my
advisers, including in particular the Joint Chiefs of Staff, have underscored
the necessity to break out of a future that relies solely on offensive retaliation for our security. Over the course of these discussions, I've become
more and more deeply convinced that the human spirit must be capable
of rising above dealing with other nations and human beings by threatening
their existence."

The president concluded, in words I quote here in their entirety, given
their importance and the hyperbole with which they were met from all
sides:

> Wouldn't it be better to save lives than to avenge them? Are we not capable
> of demonstrating our peaceful intentions by applying all our abilities and our
> ingenuity to achieving a truly lasting stability? I think we are. Indeed, we
> must.
>
> After careful consultation with my advisers, including the Joint Chiefs of
> Staff, I believe there is a way. Let me share with you a vision of the future
> which offers hope. It is that we embark on a program to counter the awesome
> Soviet missile threat with measures that are defensive. Let us turn to the
> very strengths in technology that spawned our great industrial base and that
> have given us the quality of life we enjoy today.
>
> What if free people could live secure in the knowledge that their security
> did not rest upon the threat of instant U.S. retaliation to deter a Soviet
> attack, that we could intercept and destroy strategic ballistic missiles before
> they reached our own soil or that of our allies?
>
> I know this is a formidable, technical task, one that may not be accom-
> plished before the end of this century. Yet, current technology has attained
> a level of sophistication where it's reasonable for us to begin this effort. It
> will take years, probably decades of effort on many fronts. There will be
> failures and setbacks, just as there will be successes and breakthroughs. And
> as we proceed, we must remain constant in preserving the nuclear deterrent
> and maintaining a solid capability for flexible response. But isn't it worth
> every investment necessary to free the world from the threat of nuclear war?
> We know it is.
>
> In the meantime, we will continue to pursue real reductions in nuclear
> arms, negotiating from a position of strength that can be ensured only by
> modernizing our strategic forces. At the same time, we must take steps to
> reduce the risk of a conventional military conflict escalating to nuclear war
> by improving our nonnuclear capabilities.

America does possess—now—the technologies to attain very significant improvements in the effectiveness of our conventional, nonnuclear forces. Proceeding boldly with these new technologies, we can significantly reduce any incentive that the Soviet Union may have to threaten attack against the United States or its allies.

As we pursue our goal of defensive technologies, we recognize that our allies rely upon our strategic offensive power to deter attacks against them. Their vital interests and ours are inextricably linked. Their safety and ours are one. And no change in technology can or will alter that reality. We must and shall continue to honor our commitments.

I clearly recognize that defensive systems have limitations and raise certain problems and ambiguities. If paired with offensive systems, they can be viewed as fostering an aggressive policy, and no one wants that. But with these considerations firmly in mind, I call upon the scientific community in our country, those who gave us nuclear weapons, to turn their great talents now to the cause of mankind and world peace, to give us the means of rendering these nuclear weapons impotent and obsolete.

Tonight, consistent with our obligations of the ABM [Antiballistic Missile] Treaty and recognizing the need for closer consultation with our allies, I'm taking an important first step. I am directing a comprehensive and intensive effort to define a long-term research and development program to begin to achieve our ultimate goal of eliminating the threat posed by strategic nuclear missiles. This could pave the way for arms control measures to eliminate the weapons themselves. We seek neither military superiority nor political advantage. Our only purpose—one all people share—is to search for ways to reduce the danger of nuclear war.

The Reaction

It was a stunning and dramatic speech. It expressed a deep vision: we had painted ourselves into a corner with the concept of Mutual Assured Destruction, and the president proposed a way out. Its bottom line was honest: a research program aimed at finding out how to defend against the threat of strategic ballistic missiles. And it was responsible: we would pursue it "consistent with our obligations of the ABM Treaty and recognizing the need for closer consultation with our allies." The BBC called the speech "skillful," calculated to demonstrate a commitment to seek a "way out" of the arms race.

The next day, we were assessing the immediate reaction. The Soviets were swift and negative. Perhaps they were apprehensive that the president was really on to something. Congressional opinion was mixed. The atmosphere at the White House the previous night had been thoughtful.

Zbigniew Brzezinski said he wished he had heard the speech before he had read it, "The president is so much more convincing orally."

By late afternoon, I compared notes with Clark. "A lot of people," I told him, "are saying that technology should be changing our thought patterns. The president said the same thing last night. The instinct is right. We at State should have been cut in earlier." I told him, "If we hadn't reacted vigorously, the president would be out on an impossible limb. I know the interagency process is full of leaks, but we have to manage broader consultation on a secure basis." Clark didn't say much, but he seemed to agree.

Over at the White House, I found that the president was pleased with the response to his speech. I had to agree that the concept put forth was that technology had overtaken the validity of our current strategic thinking. "Let's hope the president's instincts are right," I said when I returned.

People chose sides fast. Despite a mainstream of thoughtful discussion, people all along the political spectrum seemed determined to exaggerate the actual words of the speech for the purpose of either supporting or vilifying it.

Advocates of the Strategic Defense Initiative surrounded it with exaggeration, expounding "an impenetrable shield." Opponents of the concept mounted a massive publicity campaign to argue, in effect, that any thought of trying to deviate from Mutual Assured Destruction (MAD) as *the* sanctified nuclear strategy was itself mad. The critics and the Soviets both denounced the president. Skeptics said it was not a strategic defense initiative but "a pipe dream, a projection of fantasy into policy," as the *New York Times* editorialized on March 27. "Star Wars," the press dubbed it.

The battle lines for a long and bitter debate between the administration and Congress were drawn. President Reagan issued an executive order on March 25, 1983, in which he instructed Bill Clark to supervise an "intensive effort" to define a long-term research and development program for the system. Critics of the president pointed to Article V, Section I, of the ABM Treaty, in which "Each Party undertakes not to develop, test, or deploy ABM systems." The president's proposal would violate the treaty, they claimed, because the line between research and development (the term found in the treaty) was not clear. On that same day, I instructed the State Department's legal adviser, Davis Robinson, to take a serious look at the ABM Treaty and the Outer Space Treaty and to produce a solid paper on the treaty implications of the president's Strategic Defense Initiative.

The president's speech was an undeniable success with the public at large. It provided a potent argument against the increasingly forceful nuclear freeze movement—and against those who argued that the Reagan administration was heedlessly taking the nation down the path to nuclear disaster. Many Americans found the idea of a strategic defense shield a more appealing means of reducing the threat of a nuclear war than the idea of a mere nuclear freeze. And SDI spoke to traditional pride in American technological prowess while holding out the possibility at least of a country protected by a strategic defense rendering us less vulnerable to foreign powers in the twentieth-century world of space, just as two oceans had shielded us in the nineteenth-century world of sea power.

But President Reagan's speech was less successful when it came to persuading foreign leaders. The kind of consultation needed to explain, reassure, and seek support from them had not been possible, given such short notice. The White House, I was told, had briefed a few foreign leaders on the basis of the early, extravagant drafts. The very aspect of the speech that made it appealing to the broad spectrum of the American audience—the call for a shield—made it frightening to our allies, who feared that an America protected by a nuclear shield might be unwilling to fight the Soviets to protect Europe. The image of "Fortress America" leaped to their minds immediately, as it had initially to mine.

Most bitterly, the speech did not persuade the experts in nuclear strategy. Proponents of deterrence responded negatively to the president's vision of a world free of nuclear weapons; in their calculus, any ability to defend our population at large would raise the specter of an American first strike at the Soviet Union and a subsequent Soviet inability to retaliate effectively. The nuclear balance would be broken.

The new Soviet leader, Yuri Andropov, said that Reagan's "new conception" would heighten the arms race and that the United States had embarked upon "an extremely dangerous path." *Tass* called the speech an attempt to violate the ABM Treaty and achieve strategic superiority for the United States. In an interview with reporters on March 29, President Reagan said that if the United States developed a comprehensive defensive system, a future president could offer to share that defensive technology with the Soviet Union. He said, "In my opinion, if a defensive weapon could be found and developed that would reduce the utility of these [ballistic missiles] or maybe even make them obsolete, then whenever that time came, a President of the United States . . . could offer to give that same defensive weapon to them to prove to them that there was no longer any need for keeping these missiles. Or with that defense, he could then say to them, 'I am willing to do away with all my missiles. You do away with all of yours.' "5

The speech lit up the boards. The cover of *Time* magazine on April 4, 1983, depicted a determined president against a Buck Rogers backdrop of death rays in space. *Newsweek*'s cover read "Star Wars" and followed with "Will Space Be the Next Battleground?" For all the uproar, one point

5. As quoted in the *New York Times*, March 30, 1983, p. A14.

began to sink in: prior to the president's speech, even the possibility that the United States might seriously seek to defend itself from nuclear attack seemed outlandish. After President Reagan's speech, what had seemed "outlandish" became the agenda for debate.

Whose Vision Was SDI?

Whose vision was the Strategic Defense Initiative? I had been surprised by the idea. Bill Clark, Bud McFarlane, Cap Weinberger, and the Joint Chiefs of Staff had been given an earlier preview than had I of what was on the president's mind. But their performance at the moment of decision and during the debate over the president's dramatic speech led me to conclude that none of them had investigated or really thought through the president's proposal. The Joint Chiefs had supported the idea back in February but were taken by surprise with the timing of the announcement and some of the sweeping language in initial drafts.

The truth of SDI's origin was simple: the vision came from Ronald Reagan. For years he had felt that there must be something better than our long-standing nuclear policy of Mutual Assured Destruction. A few scientists and close associates had discussed the concept with him over the years, and he had made the idea his own. Physicist Edward Teller later told me that in 1967, when Ronald Reagan had just been elected governor of California, Reagan came to the Lawrence Livermore National Laboratory for a briefing on a topic of Teller's research: how to defend against nuclear attack by using nuclear explosives. Reagan listened intently, asked many questions, but made no comments pro or con. This may have become the first gleam in Ronald Reagan's eye of what later became the Strategic Defense Initiative.

I later learned, too, of another pivotal event that had shaped the president's thinking. In July 1979, Reagan visited the North American Aerospace Defense Command (NORAD) at Cheyenne Mountain, Colorado. He was accompanied by Martin Anderson, an economist and adviser to Reagan and later his counselor on domestic affairs, and a screenwriter-friend, Douglas Morrow. As Anderson later recounted the story to me, they walked through massive steel doors several feet thick into what amounted to an underground city carved out of Cheyenne Mountain. After a series of briefings in various rooms making up this maze, they were ushered into the command center, "a huge and cavernous room with a large display at one end showing the United States and the airspace around our country and an array of consoles attended by the men and women on duty." Here, they were told, ballistic missiles and other intruders into our airspace would be tracked. "You could not help but be impressed—it was awesome—with this massive center for command and control of our forces in the event of nuclear attack," Anderson told me. At the end of the tour, he asked Commanding General James Hill what would happen if a Soviet SS-18 hit within a few hundred yards of the steel front doors. Without a moment's hesitation, the general answered, "It would blow us away." Reagan was incredulous. "What can we do about it?" he asked. The answer was that we could track it, but we couldn't do anything to stop it. Reagan shook his head, deeply disturbed that America had no means of defense against nuclear attack. He was clearly stunned. "There must be something better than this," he said. The impression this experience made on him was indelible.

A few days after the visit, Anderson, a jack-of-all-trades in the early stages of the presidential campaign, was asked by John Sears, then Reagan's campaign manager, to draft some thoughts on foreign policy and national security. In his "Policy Memorandum No. 3, Reagan for President," Anderson wrote:

> *Develop a Protective Missile System*. During the early 1970s there was a great debate about whether or not this country should build an anti-ballistic missile system. The ABM lost, and is now prohibited by SALT agreements. But perhaps it is now time to seriously reconsider the concept. To begin with such a system concentrates on defense, on making sure that enemy missiles never strike U.S. soil. And that idea is probably fundamentally far more appealing to the American people than the questionable satisfaction of knowing that those who initiated an attack against us were also blown away. Moreover, the installation of an effective protective missile system would also prevent even an accidental missile from landing.

"If it could be done," he concluded, "it would be a major step toward redressing the military balance of power, and it would be a purely defensive step."

This idea was never used during the campaign. Mike Deaver and John Sears regarded the word "nuclear" to be as alarming to voters as the words "social security." Nevertheless, in July 1980, the Republican national convention, controlled by Ronald Reagan, pledged in its platform to proceed with "vigorous research and development of an effective anti-ballistic missile system, such as is already at hand in the Soviet Union, as well as more modern ABM technologies." Even more to the point, Reagan entered the White House with an idea in his mind that he had first encountered in 1967 and that had been jolted back into his consciousness in 1979. He was loath to accept the answer given him at NORAD that America's only options in the face of nuclear attack were to do nothing or retaliate massively. He felt some sort of defense against nuclear weapons must be better. In fact, by 1983, research in the fields of computer science and infrared sensors and some other advances in technology had laid the groundwork for a fundamental shift in thinking.

After Reagan became president, I later learned, a small group had been set to work secretly in the White House in September 1981. Ed Meese acted as its convener.[6] Anderson's notes of a meeting on September 9, 1981, summarize succinctly: "Shift from offense to defense; move to space, get copy of treaty, go with ABM defense." The project percolated along over the next year. Teller, among others, kept pushing.

In December 1982, at one of the president's periodic meetings with the Joint Chiefs, he had asked them whether they thought a system of strategic defense was feasible. After a few days' consideration, their answer was that with today's technology, there was genuine promise.

On a snowy February 11, the day before my first intimation from the president of what was in his mind, the Joint Chiefs, with Cap Weinberger, Bill Clark, and Bud McFarlane in attendance, gave the president further encouragement and a supportive report. McFarlane later told me that Jim Watkins, chief of naval operations, had taken the lead in advocating an investment in research about strategic defense.

But all along, the creation of what became the Strategic Defense Initiative was the vision of Ronald Reagan. The visit to Cheyenne Mountain had made a deep impact. Once he was sold on this idea, he stuck with it and looked for ways to persuade others that his idea was right. It was a Reagan characteristic that I would observe again and again on important occasions.

Ronald Reagan had visionary ideas. In pursuing them, he displayed some of his strongest qualities: an ability to break through the entrenched thinking of the moment to support his vision of a better future, a spontaneous, natural ability to articulate the nation's most deeply rooted values and aspirations, and a readiness to stand by his vision regardless of pressure, scorn, or setback. At the same time, he could fall prey to a serious weakness: a tendency to rely on his staff and friends to the point of accepting uncritically—even wishfully—advice that was sometimes amateurish and even irresponsible. There was potential greatness in the idea of strategic defense. There were also flaws in the way it was initially proposed. Despite the controversy at the time, the extravagant launching of the Strategic Defense Initiative gave the proposal a special visibility that dramatically caught the attention of the Soviets.

SDI was to become a dominant issue throughout the 1980s. First was the question of its credibility as a strategic factor. Would it really work and how? When Ronald Reagan first heard of the SDI idea, it was linked to the use of nuclear explosions: the best countermeasure against nuclear warhead missiles seemed at the time to be the X-ray laser, itself driven by

6. Included at one time or another were Martin Anderson, businessman Karl Bendetsen, retired General Daniel Graham (who formed a group called High Frontier to lobby for strategic defense), Edward Teller, Jay Keyworth, businessmen Jacquelin Hume and Bill Wilson, as well as Jim Jenkins and Edwin Thomas, assistants to Meese and Bill Clark.

a nuclear explosion. But the president did not want to accept that; at the core of his vision was his deep unease about nuclear weapons. (Later, in fact, nonnuclear approaches were developed that suited him far better.)

Second, SDI would become the focus of an increasingly bitter domestic debate over strategic doctrine, as opponents of SDI in Congress sought further to enshrine Mutual Assured Destruction and a reading of the ABM Treaty that would render any effort to build strategic defenses against nuclear attack impossible.

And third would be the role of SDI in arms control negotiations. Bud McFarlane later told me that he was deeply concerned about strategic instability and distressed that the failure of "dense pack" left us without a basing mode for our only modern land-based strategic missile. We therefore were more vulnerable and less able to deter; we were also without an important bargaining chip in the START talks. McFarlane supported the project, he said, not so much on the real prospect of success in strategic defense but as a way of giving the scientific community money and inspiration to get going, thereby getting the Soviets' attention to arms control. In this sense, he saw SDI as a "bargaining chip" in the broadest sense. Others were deeply committed to strategic defense and believed that the program would succeed. To some, this meant that SDI should never be mentioned in negotiations; to others, negotiations seemed a way of preserving the concept from being erased by its critics.

Ronald Reagan said that the Strategic Defense Initiative would never be a bargaining chip. In our subsequent negotiations with the Soviets, the integrity of the basic research and development program was never compromised. But SDI proved to be of deep concern to the Soviets. General Secretary Andropov's reaction had been immediate. The Soviets were genuinely alarmed by the prospect of American science "turned on" and venturing into the realm of space defenses. The Strategic Defense Initiative in fact proved to be the ultimate bargaining chip. And we played it for all it was worth.

CHAPTER 18

A Strategy
for Soviet Relations

By early March 1983, a halting dialogue was under way with Ambassador Anatoly Dobrynin, and the impact of President Reagan's meeting with him the previous month was evident, on the president as well as on the Soviets. The next step for me would be to design a broader and longer-term approach to U.S.-Soviet relations to put before the president. I knew I had to get him heavily engaged. As I had with the Middle East, I needed to be sure he saw the inherent difficulties. At the same time, I worried that if we warmed up the U.S.-Soviet relationship, our European allies might jump out in front of us and try to move much faster than would be warranted or wise. We would have to move together so that the Soviets would not get an opportunity to split our alliance.

The First Round

I produced a detailed memorandum in early March for the president: "U.S.-Soviet Relations: Where Do We Want to Be and How Do We Get There?" I reported, "I have now had a number of the sessions with Dobrynin that you authorized me to undertake. . . . There have emerged a few tentative signs of Soviet willingness to move forward on specific issues—the Pentecostalists and technical-level exchanges and consular matters." I expressed our minimum objective: "to make clear that we are determined to resist Soviet efforts to use their growing military power in ways which threaten our security. . . . There must be no doubt in Moscow or elsewhere that we will not permit a resumption of the Soviet geopolitical expansion of the 1970s in the Third World." I also argued that there was "a chance to go beyond this minimum objective and make some progress toward a more stable and constructive U.S.-Soviet relationship over the next two years or so."

I pointed to the necessity of sustaining the efforts we had under way—rebuilding American economic and military strength, maintaining the vitality of our alliances, stabilizing our relations with China, continuing regional peacekeeping efforts and the vigorous competition in ideas—and to the opportunity before us: "While the Soviet response to a successful demonstration of our resolve is not entirely predictable," I said, "I believe that the Soviet leadership might conclude that it had no alternative but to come to terms with us. In that event, opportunities for a lasting and significant improvement in U.S.-Soviet relations would be better than they have been for decades. If the Soviets remained intransigent, we would have nonetheless taken the essential steps needed to ensure our security."

I set out our four-part agenda, with some additional thoughts.[1] I argued that engaging with Moscow on key regional issues, particularly Afghanistan and Southern Africa, put us in a position to sustain diplomatic pressure and exploit whatever opportunities might emerge. We should push toward constructive involvement with the Soviets in negotiations that might lead to acceptable settlements on either of those issues. "A litmus test of Soviet seriousness in response to our concerns would be whether they are moving seriously toward a real pullback from one of the positions gained in the 1970s." Here I was thinking of Afghanistan, Angola, or Cambodia.

On human rights I argued, "Where it would enhance the chances of success, our focus should be on private diplomacy leading to results, not counterproductive public embarrassment of Moscow." And I added, "We also want to increase our ideological impact inside the Soviet Union through expanded exchange programs and access of Americans to Soviet society."

The Evil Empire

On March 8, President Reagan spoke in Orlando, Florida, to the annual convention of the National Association of Evangelicals. Unknown to me or others in the State Department, the end of the speech contained several passages on the Soviet Union and our relationship with it: "This doesn't mean we should isolate ourselves and refuse to seek an understanding with them. I intend to do everything I can to persuade them of our peaceful intent, to remind them that it was the West that refused to use its nuclear monopoly in the forties and fifties for territorial gain and which now proposes a 50-percent cut in strategic ballistic missiles and the elimination of an entire class of land-based, intermediate-range nuclear missiles."

The president argued forcefully against the nuclear-freeze movement and harked to a struggle between good and evil, invoking a phrase that

---

1. We were determined not to allow the Soviets to focus our negotiations simply on matters of arms control. So we continuously adhered to a broad agenda: human rights, regional issues, arms control, and bilateral issues.

instantly became a center of controversy: "I urge you to beware the temptation of pride—the temptation of blithely declaring yourselves above it all and label both sides equally at fault, to ignore the facts of history and the aggressive impulses of an evil empire, to simply call the arms race a giant misunderstanding and thereby remove yourself from the struggle between right and wrong and good and evil."

The "evil empire" phrase would take on a life of its own. Calling the Soviet Union an "evil empire" transformed this into a major speech, even though it had not been planned or developed through any careful or systematic process. No doubt Soviet leaders were offended, and many of our friends were alarmed. How conscious of the implications of their words the president and his speechwriters were, I do not know. Whether or not he was wise to use this phrase to describe the Soviet Union, it was in fact an empire and evil abounded.

I worked hard to develop talking points for a meeting with the president on March 10. I was determined to describe my ideas for a new approach to the Soviets and to set out a proposed agenda for achieving our objectives. I wanted to come out of my meeting with some running room from the president.

When I walked into the Oval Office, President Reagan took me aside. "I don't want these people to know about Dobrynin," the president said to me, referring to his private meeting with Ambassador Dobrynin and our subsequent effort to allow the Pentecostals, who had taken refuge in our Moscow embassy, to gain the freedom to emigrate. His remark reinforced my growing sense that the president was a prisoner of his own staff. The Oval Office was filled with people—Jim Baker, Ed Meese, Bill Clark, Bud McFarlane, as well as faces I didn't recognize. I started off by saying that I wanted to speak candidly, "But I don't even know who all these people are." I looked at one man I did not know.

Bill Clark jumped in, "This is Richard Pipes. He's an NSC member. He's on the payroll."

I could see the president didn't like the large cast of characters. The mood was intense and acrimonious. I could also see that he wanted to do what I wanted to do, but Bill Clark was standing in the way. I addressed my remarks to President Reagan, saying that he had already established the basics. The United States had improved its military strength, and our economy was moving forward. Our alliances were in good shape. Our work in China had caught the Soviets' attention, and democracy was gaining in Central America. "It is time to probe and test," I said.

We should push for Afghanistan and Southern Africa as regional problems where progress might emerge. "On bilateral issues, we can discuss the umbrella cultural-exchanges agreement, proposed consulates in Kiev and New York City, and an appraisal of the eight existing agreements with the Soviets and where they stand. If this goes well, we can start looking at a Shultz-Gromyko meeting in Moscow, and then Gromyko would come here to meet you at the time of the UN meetings in October," I said.

When I had finished talking to the president, Bill Clark called on Richard Pipes. I knew his name and recognized his scholarly distinction—and his hard-line reputation regarding the Soviets. Clark then called on Leslie Lenkowski, as another "Soviet expert." After they had their say, I remarked, "Perhaps we should also ask our ambassador in Moscow for his opinion." The attitude of Clark's cadre was that *after* the Soviets have changed, *then* maybe we can do something with them. I was irritated. Toward the end of the meeting, I said that I understood the view of all these staff people was that I should "stop seeing Dobrynin and leave things as they are." Everyone in the room protested that this was not the correct interpretation. The meeting broke up. I was annoyed by the fiasco, and it showed.

Back in the State Department, Larry Eagleburger told me that Bud McFarlane had been outraged by the meeting. Bud had not known that Clark had loaded the dice with his naysayers. "Bud gave me a memo before the meeting to read and destroy that was right down our alley," I said. "It was his idea of how the president should respond, positively, to my suggestions. Clark wouldn't send it forward. The president was posturing in front of those guys. That's why he told me he didn't want to talk about Dobrynin." That was part of the problem: the president could not simply talk to me alone in the Oval Office. Key people in his administration *would have to know* that the president wanted a change; he would have to say it openly and publicly. "If the president doesn't express himself, the bureaucracy won't react. All I can do now is just pick up the ball and say go or no go."

At 7:25 that evening, Bill Clark telephoned. He talked as if nothing unusual had happened that afternoon. He told me that the president would "let me know tomorrow," whatever that meant. After the conversation, I said to Ray Seitz, "How can the president understand what I was trying to present this afternoon? Yet there's going to be some kind of communication from the president tomorrow about all this. Clark wants to keep State on a tight rein. It's like a sergeant I had in the Marine Corps who said, 'Don't fall out till I say fall out! Fall out!' "

The next day, March 11, I told President Reagan privately that I needed to have direction from him on Soviet relations. I went through with him again what I was trying to achieve.

"Go ahead," he told me. Despite this I could see that the president was concerned, and Clark even more so, that if he gave a green light to the State Department, I would run off and initiate actions that would change the atmosphere with the Soviets when they perceived no change was warranted. So I would need to be careful. There was no road map. I would need to make my own. I would have to keep going over my proposed route with the president privately, receiving his agreement and then seeking ways to have him make his own administration *follow through* on his decisions. From what I had seen so far, I faced a steep, uphill battle.

Problems with the NSC Staff

The next day, at about one o'clock in the afternoon, Mike Deaver called. The president had told him before the big meeting that there were too many people and that he, Deaver, should call me. Deaver said that anytime that I wanted to see the president alone, "just contact me."

"I need to see the boss. It's hard to operate with the NSC staff and the White House," I told him. Deaver's offer, in effect, invited me to go around Clark. I was frustrated in my dealings with Clark. But I realized the offer presented a dilemma for me, and an end run around Clark could cause real problems. I had to have access to the president on a regular basis, but I needed to have a working relationship with the NSC adviser, too. That was proving difficult to achieve: I could never get Clark to set regular meetings for me with the president; Clark always blamed this on "the schedulers." Whether Deaver was trying to be helpful or to undermine Clark, I didn't know. I knew I needed to try to improve the NSC process, not undermine it. I felt I must keep Clark informed about everything. But if Deaver was the only way I could get to see the president, then that was the way I would go.

I had an interview that day with Don Oberdorfer and John Goshko of the *Washington Post*. "Are you happy in your job?" Oberdorfer asked.

"I didn't come here to be happy," I replied with a laugh. Oberdorfer, an astute, tenacious reporter, was alert to the chatter around town that my testiness reflected the tension and frustration I felt working in this administration. Given the split in the White House—with Deaver and Baker contending with Clark and Meese—I did feel that whatever I did scored a point for one side or the other.

On March 16, I sent the president an important memorandum entitled "Next Steps in U.S.-Soviet Relations." I outlined my proposed program and our four-part agenda. Instead of asking for the president's formal approval—and thereby allowing my memo to be funneled through the NSC staffing process—I gave the president my reading of our own private discussions, and I said, "Here is how I propose to proceed in our bilateral relations with the Soviets in the coming months. I will continue to report to you and seek your further guidance at each stage of the process."

On Thursday, March 24, Bill Clark called. He told me he had arranged a meeting the next afternoon with the president to discuss relations with the Soviets. It would be a small meeting. "You should be there," I said.

Clark said he would try to arrange to have that sort of meeting a couple of times a week. He told me he had a heart-to-heart talk with the president, urging him to spend more time talking about foreign policy issues. According to Clark, the president had told Deaver to put this on the schedule. He also passed on an invitation to come to the White House in the morning to listen to a report by Dick Wirthlin on opinion poll findings about foreign policy. I was also invited to have lunch with the president, along with Arthur Sulzberger. When I hung up the phone, I laughed—apparently my office was bugged by the NSC.

In my private meeting with President Reagan on the afternoon of March 25, a Friday, I recalled to him our earlier conversation on the snowy evening in February when we had dinner together at the White House. "If Andropov is willing to do business, so am I," he had told me then. He was ready to work with the Soviets. But one camp of his staff did not want him to try. The president told me he was "open to a summit meeting," but only if there was some substantive movement. I reminded him of my initial meetings with Dobrynin and the Soviets' prompt response on the Pentecostals. "We have to take that as a direct signal," I said. "If we are going to pursue this, we have to outline a series of steps that build on each other." We needed to "create the right background music on human rights and bilateral issues as precursors to the agendas on arms control and regional issues," I said.

We both knew that pressure from U.S. agricultural interests was building to renegotiate a long-term grain agreement with the Soviets. "We ought to be able to manage this if we don't have it forced on us by the farmers," I said. "Maybe we can start negotiations in April."

On INF and other arms control issues, the president told me to make sure Dobrynin realized that we were serious, and he agreed that I should talk to Dobrynin about arms control between the sessions of our negotiations in Geneva.

Bill Clark now urged that I put these things directly to the president without the intervention of the NSC staff. "Otherwise," he said, "we'll lose control." Clark's comment was revealing, particularly as it was made in the presence of the president. He was admitting that he knew his own staff was part of the problem. I had no illusions—Clark was *not* on board with the president's and my Soviet agenda—but I seized on this to say to President Reagan that we had to have a fast-track way to get decisions. "The Soviets will outmaneuver us at every turn if we have to refight the fundamental direction of policy with each and every action memorandum." We also needed, I said, a way to slip the existence of our dialogue with the Soviets into the public domain rather than have it emerge as a sudden and sensational discovery. My testimony on U.S.-Soviet relations before the Senate Foreign Relations Committee, then scheduled for mid-April, would be the way. The president said he agreed. "Let's proceed."

This meeting with President Reagan had been critical; without it, I could not have begun to go to work with the Soviets. I had received a green light to implement my policy—now the president's policy—step by step, with the potential for a real reversal of U.S.-Soviet relations. The process would be slow and laborious, I knew. But at least I was now in a position to start serious work on this relationship of vital importance and the full agenda of issues before us.

"Chilly" Progress

The following Monday, March 28, Dobrynin came in. The INF negotiations were the central topic. After careful consultations with our allies, we were laying down a new variation of equal limits on both sides, our guiding principle. The president proposed an interim solution: if the Soviets would reduce their deployments of intermediate-range missiles to, say, 300 warheads, we would limit our deployment of comparable weapons to that number.

"We will *never* agree to U.S. deployments in Europe, whatever the number," Dobrynin told me. His statement confirmed my judgment that the Soviets would not bargain seriously in Geneva until they were convinced we *would* deploy and that probably the only way of convincing them would be by *actually deploying* the weapons. The tone of our meeting was pleasant enough, but the content was hard. The United States was determined to deploy unless an outcome could be negotiated that eliminated intermediate-range missiles on both sides. The Soviets were determined to block those deployments but were unwilling to consider a zero outcome or any deployment of U.S. intermediate-range nuclear missiles in Europe.

On March 30, the president announced his proposal for an "interim solution." At an April 2 Moscow press conference, Gromyko took an uncompromising position on the key issues in the INF negotiations: British and French nuclear systems had to be included, as did aircraft; there would be no limits on deployments in global terms. He deepened the chill level in our relations by asserting that there were now no systematic contacts between the United States and the Soviet Union—a public statement designed to heighten allied pressure on the United States.

I got some help from the Department of Defense. They proposed on April 11 talks to upgrade the hot line linking our respective heads of government, military-to-military contacts, and discussions of nuclear terrorism. The Soviets gave a fast response. By mid-April, they had agreed to talks to upgrade the hot line and on nuclear terrorism.

On April 22 President Reagan agreed to resume negotiations on a long-term grain agreement, thereby lifting his suspension imposed in December 1981 in response to the Soviet support of the crackdown on Solidarity in

Poland. This was an important step for the president. He had held off for a long time in the face of intense pressure from the farm bloc. The Soviets were well aware that our farmers had pushed hard for this decision, so its usefulness as a signal and a step toward improved relations was muted. Nevertheless, "evil empire" or not, the Soviets could see that Ronald Reagan was ready to do business. Almost a month passed before Dobrynin informed me on May 16 that the Soviets were prepared to proceed.

My time during this period became increasingly consumed by the Middle East, most particularly with negotiations over Lebanon and with the struggle to keep the president's Middle East peace initiative alive. No one should think that a secretary of state can concentrate on just one or two issues.[2] The fire hose of information that hit me daily was relentless, and it required a broad engagement in issues on a world scale. On Thursday, April 21, I announced my first trip to the Middle East as secretary of state, with the objective of completing an Israel-Lebanon agreement, including provision for Israeli withdrawal from Lebanon. The trip would last for over two weeks.

My task in the Middle East was to seek a diplomatic step forward. But the backdrop was shaped by the presence of Soviet arms. I could not escape Moscow, even in the Middle East. The Soviet Union had gained great leverage there through its rearming of Syria. But the war in Lebanon had cast doubt on the quality of Soviet weaponry. Now the Syrians had new weaponry, and Soviet personnel were manning those weapons. From our standpoint, I told Dobrynin, Soviet-manned SA-5s in Syria raised the risks of conflict and escalation in the area to the point of superpower confrontation. "You are there," I told Dobrynin. "You support Syrian radical policies and their links to organized PLO fighters and to Iranian and other terrorist groups that are not easy to control. That raises the risks. These circumstances mean real difficulty in easing tensions with the United States."

2. A host of other matters took up my time: preparations for the economic summit meetings to be hosted by the president in Williamsburg at the end of May and early June; the granting of political asylum to Chinese tennis star Hu Na, with consequent loss of "face" by Deng Xiaoping at the "unfriendly act"; a weekend at Camp David with the president and Nancy Reagan, punctuated by calls to the Middle East and a telephone conversation of the president with King Hussein of Jordan concerning the failure of the king's negotiations with Arafat for Palestinian associates to join him in the peace process; a visit to the president by the sultan of Oman on April 13; work on the confirmation problems of Ken Adelman; visits from key Canadians, Israelis, and Egyptians; development of what would become an address by the president to a joint session of Congress setting out our policies on Central America; coping with disturbing developments in Suriname; a speech of my own on Central America in Dallas; testimony before the Senate Armed Services Committee and the House Select Committee on Intelligence (about Nicaragua); another Dobrynin meeting, with Paul Nitze, our INF negotiator, in attendance; and another with our START negotiator, Ed Rowny; a trip to Mexico, April 17–19, with meetings with Mexican President de la Madrid, Foreign Secretary Sepulveda, and Finance Minister Silva-Herzog, in which I was accompanied by cabinet colleagues dealing with economic and environmental issues.

Another Look, Another Channel

Our efforts with the Soviets were difficult to get off the ground. Direct relations were still cool, and I had trouble prying loose decisions in Washington that would allow us to move forward. But, in Madrid, Max Kampelman, our negotiator at the Conference on Security and Cooperation in Europe (CSCE), was getting messages through his KGB contact, Sergei Kondrachev, that did not come through Foreign Minister Gromyko and that suggested some positive movement. The Soviets were not living up to the words on human rights that they had agreed to in the Helsinki Final Act. We insisted on deeds, actions. At the least, a few controversial dissidents should be allowed to emigrate as a beginning. Max seemed to be getting somewhere. Through Max's discussions with Kondrachev in the spring of 1983, the Soviets agreed that they would release Anatoly Shcharansky unconditionally if he would write a letter to Soviet authorities requesting his release. Kampelman pointed out that any requirement of a confession of guilt or any use of a word such as "pardon" would be unacceptable to Shcharansky. Kondrachev asked Max to write down what he thought Shcharansky would be willing to sign. Max wrote, "I hereby request that I be released from prison on the grounds of poor health." That was all. Kondrachev understood that this meant release from the Soviet Union as well as from prison. He checked with what he described as "the highest authority," and, after checking, he agreed.

"Shcharansky will not believe he has a deal unless he hears from somebody who is credible," Max told Kondrachev. "He should hear it from his mother, Ida Milgrom." We soon got word from Warren Zimmerman, the deputy chief of mission in our Moscow embassy, that Ida had been called to KGB headquarters, was treated with dignity and respect, and was told that they would try to make arrangements for her to see her son.

This was, she said, in stark contrast to the way she was usually treated by the KGB. Another date was set for her to go to the prison, and Zimmerman gave her the text of a proposed letter. She had earlier discussed this with Andrei Sakharov, who authorized her to say to her son that "Sakharov recommends that you send the letter." That was Ida's view as well.

Back in Madrid, Max met with Shcharansky's wife, Avital, whose first reaction was positive. But she soon returned with friends from an orthodox Jewish group with which she was affiliated. She and they now opposed his sending any letter. Regardless of the wording, they felt a letter somehow was an admission of guilt. Max was "incredulous" and said that "Shcharansky should be allowed to make this decision for himself. It is presumptuous for those who are free, not in prison and not in danger, to make such a decision for someone who is suffering in jail."

When Ida Milgrom visited her son, she urged him to write the letter.

Shcharansky asked his mother how his wife, Avital, felt about this and Ida reported, accurately, that Avital was opposed. He then rejected the arrangement.

Max heard quickly of Shcharansky's decision from Kondrachev, who said, "Everything is off now." Max didn't accept that: he argued in vain that Shcharansky should be released, letter or no letter.

One morning, Kondrachev came to Max. "I'm in trouble," he said. "You Americans are talking too much." Max remembered that when he had been in Washington a few weeks earlier, Dobrynin had invited him to lunch and was fishing for information. Max sensed that Dobrynin was not aware of the Madrid discussions, and he did not disclose anything. When Max went back to Madrid, he reported this to Kondrachev, who laughed. "Dobrynin is always sticking his nose where it doesn't belong."

Not long after, Kondrachev came back to Max again. "We're in trouble here, but I think Moscow has worked it out. Deputy Foreign Minister Kovalev [the nominal head of the Soviet delegation in Madrid] wants to see you right away." When they met, Kovalev read out a statement, the gist of which was: the United States has no right to interfere in our internal affairs; the Helsinki Final Act guarantees no interference; we are a sovereign country; we can't be forced or blackmailed into changing our internal behavior. Then he added, "Of course, if the Soviet Union makes a decision that is consistent with what the United States would like, you should know that that is strictly coincidental." So Moscow had in fact "worked it out." I felt that a new departure in our dealings with the Soviets had just occurred.

But the new departure I sought at my end in Washington was not yet taking hold. For some time I had been seeking approval from President Reagan to propose to the Soviets that we open discussions on expanded cultural exchanges and on opening two consulates, one in Kiev by us and another in New York by them. Before my long trip to the Middle East, I had tried to set this up with the president. "If you decide yes on the objective, then there is an implied chain of actions that need to be taken in order to reach the objective." The president agreed. But on my return from the Middle East, I encountered yet another series of big interagency meetings, ostensibly on the consulates issue, but really on the same old fundamental question: should the United States have *any* contacts with the Soviet Union? The NSC staff answer was, as ever, a resounding no.

I was beginning to realize that nothing I could do or say, and nothing the president would decide, would ever change their minds. The task before me was to make them irrelevant: I would contend with them and grapple to prevail. "There is a management crisis in foreign affairs here," I said to my staff. Clark's behavior was invariably frustrating. He would not move fast. He wandered. He made deals behind my back. I knew that somehow I had to get back to regular and small meetings with the president. "Without decisions from the president," I said, "everything just sloshes around. People can set up hurdles at will." But even with small, private meetings, the problem would be difficult to resolve unless President Reagan paid continuing attention once he had made a decision. "I need regular meetings with the president so I can keep his eye on the ball. The NSC staff process is the worst I've ever seen. It's worse than a university," I said with a rueful laugh.

On May 19, I heard that Bill Clark had decided to bring Jack Matlock onto the NSC staff and put him in charge of NSC staff work with the Soviets. I regarded this to be a big step forward. Matlock, a tough-minded foreign service officer, had served two tours of duty in Moscow. He was experienced and practical and knew the reality well. But Clark had his own views about our policy toward the Soviets and showed no variation in them at all. Clark had made clear to Art Hartman that he opposed my effort to move in small steps to test the Soviets so long as they were in Afghanistan; Clark therefore would not agree to actions even to implement the cultural and consulates agreements. As for a summit, the president had just made a public statement that he was willing to meet General Secretary Andropov if the Soviet leader attended the UN General Assembly. I was pleased that the president was pointing in the direction he wanted to go. But between Clark, who categorically opposed U.S.-Soviet contacts, and Deaver, who would see political value in a summit even if it had been robbed of substance by naysayers on the NSC staff, I felt that I faced a potential disaster. "A summit should take place only when some real substance is worked out," I said.

On May 21, I reviewed for the president where we stood on each of the items in our four-part agenda and gave him another carefully drawn memorandum: "We are now in a position where we need to take further steps if we want to see whether a visit [by me] this summer to Moscow for meetings with Andropov and Gromyko, an invitation [from you] to Gromyko to Washington for a meeting with you at the time of the UNGA [UN General Assembly] this fall, and ultimately a meeting between you and Andropov would be in our interest. I believe the next step on our part should be to propose the negotiation of a new U.S.-Soviet cultural agreement and the opening of U.S. and Soviet consulates in Kiev and New York, as I suggested some months ago. Both of these proposals will sound good to the Soviets, but are unambiguously in our interest when examined from a hardheaded American viewpoint." By this time, Vice President Bush had let me know that my papers to Reagan on Soviet policy were being countered by "absolutely vicious" memos to the president from the NSC staff.

I reminded the president that in his formal directive on Soviet relations, National Security Decision Directive 75, issued on January 17, 1983, he had endorsed the exchanges idea, arguing that an adequate formal framework for exchanges was the only way to ensure reciprocity in cultural, academic, and media contacts with the Soviets and to penetrate the Soviet Union with our own ideology. I also pointed out that "opening of U.S. and Soviet consulates in Kiev and New York would have the advantage of getting us onto new Soviet terrain while increasing the Soviet presence here only marginally. The Soviets already have a big UN Mission in New York, while our new consulate would be the first Western mission in the capital of the Ukraine. There is growing interest in a Kiev consulate in Congress and among American Jewish and Ukrainian groups. A U.S. presence there would also help us broaden our access to and ideological penetration of Soviet society." My recommendation ran into intense opposition from the NSC staff.

I Testify on U.S.-Soviet Relations

My formal testimony before the Senate Foreign Relations Committee on U.S.-Soviet relations, postponed by my Mideast shuttle, came on June 15, 1983. I had worked on this testimony with great care. Jack Matlock had taken an important part in the effort. Several days before testifying, I took a copy over to the White House, gave it to the president, and went over it with him line by line. I got the committee's attention by telling them of President Reagan's personal involvement. "The President has taken the time not only to talk with me about this, but he has read through this testimony and made a few suggestions," I said, adding with a smile, "which I found it possible to accept." Everyone laughed. I continued, he "has signed off on the testimony, so I feel very confident in saying that I am speaking not only for myself but for the President in this statement."

No subject in American foreign policy generated such tension as the superpower relationship. The aggressive behavior of the Soviets and the threat of potential confrontation were both clear. One camp emphasized the need for negotiation; the other, the danger of any negotiation. All of the tension manifest in the relationship itself was represented in my Senate hearing. Not only had I been preparing for months, but so had the committee. They had assigned the topic to a group from their staff that had just produced a report calling the present state of relations between our two countries "worse than ever."

"Certainly the issues dividing our two countries are serious," I said. "But let us not be misled by 'atmospherics,' whether sunny or, as they now seem to be, stormy. In the mid-1950s, for example, despite the rhetoric and tension of the cold war—and in the midst of a leadership transition—the Soviet Union chose to conclude the Austrian State Treaty. It was an important agreement, which contributed to the security of Central Europe, and it carries an important lesson for us today. The Soviet leadership did not negotiate seriously merely because Western rhetoric was firm and principled, nor should we expect rhetoric to suffice now or in the future." I emphasized, "But adverse 'atmospherics' did not prevent agreement; Soviet policy was instead affected by the pattern of Western actions, by our resolve and clarity of purpose. And the result was progress."

My testimony was interpreted very differently by the *Washington Post* and the *New York Times* and their reporters, Don Oberdorfer and Philip Taubman. Oberdorfer thought my statement was confrontational, and Taubman thought it positive. I instructed State's briefers to go with the *Times* version. The keynote, as I saw it, was captured in my statement: "Strength and realism can deter war, but only direct dialogue and negotiation can open the path toward lasting peace."

I began with human rights: "We have made clear that human rights cannot be relegated to the margins of international politics," I said. "Our Soviet interlocutors have a different view; they seek to dismiss human rights." I recalled that Foreign Minister Gromyko had responded to my remarks on this subject by saying it was a " 'tenth-rate question,' not worthy of high-level attention." Referring to unfulfilled Soviet promises, such as freedom of emigration under the Helsinki Final Act of 1975, I said, "We believe that international obligations must be taken seriously by the governments that assume them."

I pointed up the sharply divergent goals and philosophies of political and moral order that divided us from the Soviets and said these differences would not soon go away. It was now time, I stressed, to move beyond containment and détente: "Where it was once our goal to contain the Soviet presence within the limits of its immediate postwar reach, now our goal must be to advance our own objectives, where possible foreclosing and when necessary actively countering Soviet challenges wherever they threaten our interests. The policy of détente, of course, represented an effort to induce Soviet restraint. While in some versions it recognized the need to resist Soviet geopolitical encroachments, it also hoped that the anticipation of benefits from expanding economic relations and arms control agreements would restrain Soviet behavior. Unfortunately, experience has proved otherwise."

I went on to say, "In response to the lessons of this global superpower's conduct in recent years, our policy, unlike some versions of détente, assumes that the Soviet Union is more likely to be deterred by our actions that make clear the risks their aggression entails than by a delicate web of interdependence.

"Our policy is not based on trust or on a Soviet change of heart," I said. "It is based on the expectation that, faced with demonstration of the West's renewed determination to strengthen its defenses, enhance its political and economic cohesion, and oppose adventurism, the Soviet Union will see restraint as its most attractive, or only, option."

These thoughts reflected my conviction that we needed to get away from the old concept of "linkage," of thinking that by exerting pressure or offering rewards in one area, particularly trade, we could induce a change in Soviet behavior in a regional conflict or in some other area, such as human rights. By contrast, we were taking the position that regional conflicts had to be confronted on their merits, place by place, with strength, realism, and determination, just as arms control agreements needed to be worked out on their merits. It was unrealistic to expect that the Soviets would back off, simply for the sake of their relationship with us, from a position in some part of the world from which they were gaining an advantage. Linkage, I felt, was inhibiting our disposition to move forcefully and, ironically, often seemed to be turned on its head by the Soviets, as they tried to use linkage to their advantage—to threaten that the relationship would suffer if we undertook some action that they opposed.

We had, I said, clear ideas on how to approach the so-called Third World problems. "First, in the many areas where Soviet activities have added to instability, we are pursuing peaceful diplomatic solutions to regional problems, to raise the political costs of Soviet-backed military presence and to encourage the departure of Soviet-backed forces. . . . Second, we are building up the security capabilities of vulnerable governments in strategically important areas." I reminded the committee that this had a budgetary implication, since we were pushing for funds to provide security assistance to key countries. "Third," I continued, "our program recognizes that economic crisis and political instability create fertile ground for Soviet-sponsored adventurism." Therefore, I said, we need to help people with their own development, and finally "there is the Democracy Initiative, an effort to assist our friends in the Third World to build a foundation for democracy."

I noted that in a speech just the day before, Konstantin Chernenko, secretary of the Communist Party Central Committee, had emphasized the importance to the Soviets of destroying President Reagan's ideological initiatives. "It seems we have their attention. But I think if we can put competition on the basis of ideological competition, of competition of economic systems, we'll walk away with it," I said.

Questions from the Senators

Senator Percy led off the questioning by asking about the prospect of a summit between President Reagan and General Secretary Andropov and urged that there be one:

SENATOR PERCY: I would like to see us issue an invitation in the reasonable near future. . . . When can we look forward to a summit meeting with a properly prepared agenda but no high expectations and the world put on notice, that its purpose is just to gauge each other to be sure there is no miscalculation or misunderstanding, and to try to better understand each others policies?

SECRETARY SHULTZ: The President's view is that a summit meeting could be a good thing. He is ready to have one if the meeting is well prepared and if there is a high probability of some significant outcome from it, so that it is substantive in nature. He fears that a meeting for the sake of a meeting would raise expectations very high, and if all that happened was that there was a meeting, it would do more harm than good.

So there is in principle a readiness to have that meeting, but an operational requirement, that it have a substantive content that is prepared and on which we can move forward.

Negotiations were on everyone's mind. "What is certain is that we will not find ourselves in the position in which we found ourselves in the aftermath of détente. We have not staked so much on the prospect of a successful negotiating outcome that we have neglected to secure ourselves against the possibility of failure," I said. "Our parallel pursuit of strength and negotiation prepares us both to resist continued Soviet aggrandizement and to recognize and respond to positive Soviet moves." I said further: "The direction in which that relationship evolves will ultimately be determined by the decisions of the Soviet leadership. President Brezhnev's successors will have to weigh the increased costs and risks of relentless competition against the benefits of a less tense international environment in which they could more adequately address the rising expectations of their own citizens. While we can define their alternatives, we cannot decipher their intentions. To a degree unequaled anywhere else, [the Soviet Union] in this respect remains a secret." I went on, "Its history, of which this secrecy is such an integral part, provides no basis for expecting a dramatic change. And yet it also teaches that gradual change is possible. For our part, we seek to encourage change by a firm but flexible U.S. strategy, resting on a broad consensus, that we can sustain over the long term whether the Soviet Union changes or not."

Are we eager to reach a negotiated agreement? Senator Pell asked. "We need to be very careful," I replied, "that we do not somehow get ourselves in the position of feeling that it is very important to get an agreement for its own sake . . . the minute you see the other guy really wants an agreement, you have got him."

The senators asked about the value of face-to-face negotiation.

SENATOR TSONGAS: Everybody else thought there was some value to face-to-face negotiation. You are going to end up as the only administration that did not see them.

SECRETARY SHULTZ: So be it. I do not think we want to get ourselves in a position where because we do not want to be the only administration that did not make an arms control agreement, therefore let us make one. That is no way to approach it. We should only be ready to make one if it is substantively sensible from our standpoint. If we are not able to make one, well, then, that is the way the chips fall.

Are we negotiating in good faith? was the incessant question. "We say we are," I responded. "We do not think that the test of good faith can be allowed to become whether we get an agreement, because then you undermine your capacity to negotiate. The test of good faith is the reasonableness of the positions, the posture of give-and-take."

As in my confirmation hearings, Senator Cranston was an antagonist.

SENATOR CRANSTON: . . . Can you tell us what the United States, for its part, has done to contribute to the tension that exists between the United States and the Soviet Union?

SECRETARY SHULTZ: Nothing.

SENATOR CRANSTON: You really believe we have done nothing that contributes to the tensions between us?

SECRETARY SHULTZ: The Soviets say, for example, that we are contributing to the tension by the program of deployment of Pershings and GLCMs [ground-launched cruise missiles] in Europe. I reject that argument totally. Those deployments are a response to the massive SS-20 deployments. They are not provocative on our part; they are responsive on our part. . . .

Our actions around the world have been the actions of a helping hand, not aggrandizing our own power. It is simply not the case that when we build our strength, given the background, that this contributes to tension, unless you say that the way to relieve tension is just to do whatever the Soviets want. Then, of course, they would not be so tense, but a lot of us would not like it very well to live under their system.

This testimony was heavily covered in the United States, but perhaps of even more significance, it was closely studied abroad. Foreign ministers in NATO and Japan and in other parts of the world remarked to me on it immediately afterward and many times in the years to follow.

I had laid out a blueprint in this testimony, and they observed in the years to come that we stuck to it.

A Cold War Minithaw

Finally, after my testimony and after a long battle inside the White House and NSC staff, President Reagan gave me the authority I was looking for: I could tell Ambassador Dobrynin that we were ready to start negotiations on a new cultural-exchanges agreement and on the opening of consulates in Kiev and New York. By July 15, about one month later, Dobrynin informed me that the Soviets accepted our initiative to start these talks. Shortly thereafter, the last of the Pentecostal families was released. And on July 28 we finally concluded a long-term grain agreement, formally signed in Moscow on August 25, under which the Soviets agreed to purchase, on market terms, 9 to 12 billion metric tons of grain in each of the next five years. Talks were also going forward on the hot line, on keeping nuclear capabilities out of terrorist hands, and on nuclear nonproliferation.

Meanwhile, in Madrid the Conference on Security and Cooperation in Europe was ending in an unusual way. As the conference had progressed, the language proposed by the nonaligned nations got better and better from our standpoint. By spring 1983, the language that Max Kampelman had arrived with in Madrid in 1980 as the U.S. position had been beefed up in reaction to the Polish crackdown on Solidarity. A call for free trade unions was added. By midsummer, a document emerged that was completely satisfactory to us except for its failure to address the problems of families divided by the unwillingness of the Soviets to permit a Soviet spouse to emigrate. The congressional members of our CSCE delegation proposed that two meetings of experts be authorized in the final document. One would take up family reunification; the other, human rights more generally.

The Soviets opposed both meetings. The nonaligned nations then proposed a text that included a human rights session but still omitted family reunification. Max and I were not satisfied. Max persuaded his NATO colleagues to support us. At that point, General Secretary Andropov, undoubtedly on the recommendation of Kondrachev, wrote a letter to all the other heads of state of the CSCE governments saying that the Soviet Union, in the interests of concluding the Madrid conference, would accept the nonaligned document as is, without changing a comma. Max was not satisfied, and he worked out a plan under which Felipe González, prime minister of Spain, invited the heads of all delegations to a meeting in his quarters. It is time to bring this to an end, González said; here is a concluding document that I believe all of us must accept. The document that he tabled was exactly the document Andropov had agreed to but with the addition of the meeting on family reunification. It was accepted by everyone. I was impressed with Max's negotiating skills and put this into my memory bank for future reference.

So by August it seemed that despite all the tension, despite the inability to negotiate an arms control agreement, we were witnessing a "minithaw" in the cold war. We were actually agreeing with the Soviets on certain issues and engaging in some practical negotiations. Perhaps we were getting somewhere.

The Berezhkov Case:
A Cold War Incident Defused

Then a sudden and tense confrontation with the Soviets erupted: Andrei Berezhkov, the sixteen-year-old son of the first secretary of the Soviet embassy in Washington, took his parents' car on August 10 and disappeared from their Friendship Heights apartment. His parents were worried, especially because they believed that Andrei did not know how to drive. The Montgomery County police in Maryland treated this as a teenage runaway case and posted a lookout for the boy throughout the East Coast. The situation took a new turn when the White House and the *New York Times* received letters apparently written by young Berezhkov. The *Times* published the letter on August 12, 1983. In it, the young man wrote, in English, "I'm a Russian kid. . . . I hate my country and its rules and I love your country. I want to stay here. I wrote to Mr. President and I hope he will help me. I'm afraid that if my parents find out they'll put me in Siberia." It was signed Andy Berezhkov.

We received a report that Soviet security agents somehow had apprehended Andrei and that he was back inside his parents' apartment. The Soviet embassy on August 11 had notified the State Department that Andrei was safe at home and that all was well. From experience, however, we had to assume that publicity given to this as a "defector case" meant the Soviets now would try to spirit the young man out of the United States before we could look into the case to ensure his rights and fulfill our responsibilities for his safety. We called the Soviets to insist that Andrei not be moved until we were permitted to interview him. As we then moved to seal off possible exit routes, we ran into the usual frustrations. We asked the FBI to set up agents around the Berezhkov home; they moved slowly. We asked the Immigration and Naturalization Service (INS) to prevent his involuntary departure through Dulles or other airports; the INS told us that they were authorized only to block arrivals, not departures.

We met with the Justice Department and ran into a set of complex issues: as a minor, was he able legally to decide for himself? Under what legal provision could we stop and search cars leaving the Soviet residence to see whether he was tied up in the trunk? Could we detain and question someone with diplomatic immunity? If we did gain the chance to interview him, who would do it? Would it have to be a nongovernmental person in order to ensure a fair assessment and have it stand up legally? Soviet embassy officials were stalling in order to buy time to get the boy out of his parents' home and, if not on his way to Moscow, at least secure him inside the

Soviet embassy compound. They claimed that we had forged the letters from "Andy," in effect accusing us of kidnapping him. I had a round-the-clock working group set up in State's operations center. It was soon evident that the young man had been taken to the Soviet embassy compound.

By this time, the FBI was overreacting: they had stationed agents around the Berezhkov home and the Soviet embassy compound and were peering into every car, fearing the boy might slip through their net. We still faced legal questions: Andrei was a minor, and he had diplomatic immunity. I did not want the incident to get out of control. We had to protect Andrei's rights, but we did not want to stop and search Soviet embassy cars for the next month. I wanted the Soviets to know my view that it was in our mutual interest to deal with the situation calmly. I asked the Department of Justice to ease the pressure at the scene, moving the police and FBI ring back across the street so that some of the tension of a close confrontation between security officials could be reduced. We did not have to search every vehicle leaving the Soviet premises; suspicious cars or vans could be followed. Our aim was that the boy not leave the United States until we could determine his true wishes.

On the morning of Wednesday, August 17, Deputy Chief of Mission Oleg Sokolov told Rick Burt that Moscow had agreed to make certain concessions: a small press interview with Andrei Berezhkov could take place in the Soviet embassy compound. Ken Dam could be present. The reporters invited would be Leslie Gelb, Roger Mudd, and John Wallach. Then, Sokolov said, Berezhkov would be taken to Dulles Airport to return to Moscow.

This was unacceptable to us, since the Soviet officials would control the entire event and the location on Soviet property meant that the young man could not have the sense of security that would enable him to speak freely. The Soviets apparently were prepared to go ahead with this scenario with or without our agreement and then proceed to take the young man to the airport. If so, we would block his departure at Dulles. At this point, Soviet behavior was beginning to solve our legal problems. The Berezhkov case was no longer so much a question of asylum and our legal right to grant it to a minor with diplomatic immunity, but a question of a possible immediate threat to his personal safety: a potential kidnapping. The FBI had all the authority needed to deal with that.

Sokolov told us that he had tried to get Moscow to back off from their "contrived event" but that they had refused: a press conference would be held inside the Soviet compound, after which the Soviets would take the young man to Dulles en route to Moscow. If we sought to interview Andrei at Dulles, the Soviets would bring him back to their compound and then take action in a "decisive way," we were told. I took this to mean Soviet retaliation against our embassy in Moscow. In Moscow, Deputy Foreign Minister Georgi Kornienko told our embassy that if we tried to remove young Berezhkov from Soviet control, there would be "very serious consequences."

*   *   *

What was new and surprising in this was not Moscow's attempt to stage a heavy-handed show to enable them to whisk Andrei Berezhkov away; that was standard. What was new was a Soviet embassy official *confiding to us* that he had tried to convince Moscow to take an easier stance on the matter in the confidence that we would not exploit it for cold war purposes. Sokolov realized that we felt a responsibility for the rights of the young man.

We made a proposal to the Soviets: they could hold their press conference for Berezhkov inside the Soviet embassy compound. If Andrei indicated that he voluntarily wished to return to the Soviet Union, he then would be driven by the Soviets to Dulles. There within view of reporters and removed from Soviet sanctuary, he would talk with Assistant Secretary for European Affairs Rick Burt. If he was satisfied that Andrei in fact wanted to go home, the matter would be resolved. If Andrei, on the contrary, indicated that he wanted U.S. protection or political asylum, the INS would take custody of him at the airport. The Soviets accepted our approach and explicitly recognized that we would not allow Andrei to leave the United States if he indicated he feared for his safety or if he did not wish to return to the Soviet Union. We had a safe house arranged where Andrei could go.

There was a mob of reporters at Dulles Airport, and Andrei was met by applause and cheers. Rick Burt met with the young man privately for about half an hour. Andrei said he felt he had acted in haste and unwisely and now just wanted to go home. Andrei talked to Burt about his interest in rock music and mentioned how much he liked the Rolling Stones. Rick told Andrei he liked rock music, too, and that he knew Mick Jagger, the Rolling Stones' lead singer, personally. When Andrei got to the top of the ramp and was about to step aboard the aircraft, he turned back and shouted to Rick, "Say hi to Mick Jagger for me!" Reporters wondered whether this was some kind of code signal.

We had been able to work out a potentially explosive issue in a way that let both Soviets and Americans see that not every problem was going to be exploited to its fullest detrimental extent against our cold war adversary. As the *Washington Post* noted on August 19, 1983, "From its inception, the affair swiftly spiraled into an international incident engaging the personal attention of Secretary of State George P. Shultz and President Reagan." But this time there was a new sense that it was possible to *solve* problems rather than *create* them. We had stood firm on our principles without being provocative. The Soviets recognized that we would not deviate and took their chances on knowing how Andrei would respond at the airport, preferring to see a potentially explosive issue defused before it escalated into unmanageable proportions. Straightforward and candid handling had helped avoid unnecessary problems. The cold war minithaw continued as I left for a week of vacation in California.

CHAPTER 19

The Intensity
of Central America

On December 21, 1982, just back from a trip to solidify relations with our European allies and with a new U.S. peace initiative under way in the Middle East, I was feeling reasonably good about our progress in dealing with thorny foreign policy problems. I was startled to be assaulted by CIA director Bill Casey just after finishing a meeting in the Roosevelt Room of the White House. Bill cornered me as I was leaving and unloaded: "The American people are not behind our policy in Central America," he growled. "Our support in Congress is fading. We're in danger of losing on what is by far the most important foreign policy problem confronting the nation. You shouldn't be traveling around Europe. You should be going around the United States sounding the alarm and generating support for tough policies on the most important problem on our agenda. Force is the only language the Communists understand." I was taken aback by his vehemence and by the emotion in his attack on me. Casey seemed suddenly obsessed with the issue.

The situation in Central America was a problem of immense importance to the United States, and I knew we had to confront it. This was our neighborhood. Growing Cuban and Soviet influence was alarming, especially in the context of the world situation. The Soviets were increasingly active in almost every quarter of the globe: Afghanistan, Cambodia, Angola, Syria, Ethiopia, as well as in the Caribbean and Central America. If the Soviets consolidated a Communist regime on the mainland of the Americas, they could tie us down and preoccupy us right on our southern border in the hope that we would not attend adequately to Soviet challenges in the farther reaches of the world. If the Soviets could establish a base on Nicaragua's or El Salvador's Pacific coast, they could affect the strategic situation by surveillance of our Pacific shores, comparable to what they could do in the Atlantic from bases in Cuba. At the same time, the Soviets knew full well that Central America and the Caribbean was the region

285

where the American press and American public opinion were the most sensitive to the possibility of "another Vietnam." Trying to forge policy was like walking through a swamp.

Here, in broad terms, is how the situation had unfolded. In the 1970s, Central America had only one democracy: Costa Rica. The other states were oligarchies ruled by a combination of landowners, who were the real powers, and the military, who had the muscle. Latin America is heir to a great revolutionary tradition in which liberty opposed despotism and founded a community of republics in the decades just after 1776. But an older pattern of dictatorship, economic oligarchy, political despotism, and military repression reasserted itself for most of Central and South America in the late nineteenth and the twentieth centuries. The countries, though poor and with very low incomes per capita, did have productive and large-scale agriculture in certain crops, and the big landowners were wealthy people.

On July 17, 1979, Nicaraguan dictator Anastasio Somoza was overthrown by a broad opposition coalition composed of many elements: business, the Catholic church, *La Prensa*, parties seeking democracy, and the Sandinista Liberation Front (FSLN). The Sandinista revolution was an event that excited people throughout the world. Before the revolutionary coalition came to power, it promised in a statement to the Organization of American States (OAS) on July 12, 1979, "the first free elections known by our country in this century." It promised political pluralism and nonalignment as well. President Carter requested $75 million in aid for the new revolutionary government, and an additional $105 million was loaned or donated over its first year and a half as a result of emergency appropriations signed by him. This was the highest per capita rate of U.S. assistance going to any country at that time. It became apparent even before the end of the Carter administration, however, that the revolution had been taken over by hard-line Communists among the Sandinistas who were intent on creating a Cuban-Soviet–style state. Two of the original revolutionary leaders—Alfonso Robelo and Violeta Barrios de Chamorro—resisted the Marxist-Leninist takeover within the Sandinista ranks. They were harassed and left the new government in protest against its totalitarian approach and actions. Every one of the original promises was betrayed. First the Sandinistas moved to squeeze the democrats out of the governing junta, then to squelch all political opposition, press freedom, and the independence of the church. The Communists took over. Their attempt to support a "final offensive" to overthrow El Salvador's government led President Carter, in the last days of his administration, to suspend American aid to the Sandinistas. When President Reagan took office, he reviewed this decision and, on April 1, 1981, confirmed it.

Disenchantment with Nicaragua's new government grew swiftly. The Contras, a resistance movement initially formed by former members of

Somoza's defeated national guard, soon became a magnet attracting the democratic forces that hoped to reclaim the anti-Somoza revolution from the Sandinistas. On April 15, 1982, Eden Pastora, the Sandinista hero of the revolution that overthrew Somoza and a figure known to the region and the world as "Comandante Zero," held a press conference to denounce the new regime in Managua as having betrayed the true Sandinista movement; Pastora called for the expulsion of Soviet and Cuban advisers from Nicaragua. A few weeks later, on May 10, 1982, Nicaragua announced that a five-year $166.8 million agreement for Soviet aid had been signed. The Sandinistas were now officially and publicly aligned with the Soviet Union and Cuba, and their aggressive posture toward their neighbors was apparent—most prominently in their determination to turn El Salvador into a Marxist-Leninist regime like their own. The Sandinistas openly boasted of building, with Soviet and Cuban backing, the largest armed force in Central America's history.

"The process of revolution in Central America is one. The triumphs of one are the triumphs of the other. . . . Guatemala will have its hour. Honduras its own. Costa Rica will live in a brilliant moment. The first note was heard in Nicaragua." That confident prediction came from Cayetano Carpio, a principal leader of the Salvadoran guerrillas, in the August 25, 1980, edition of the Mexican magazine *Proceso*. The old forces of dictatorship had taken a new form: that of a command economy, a self-appointed elitist vanguard, and guerrilla warfare. Nicaragua had become its base, all of Central America its target. El Salvador was first on the list. In 1980, at Cuban direction, several Salvadoran extremist groups were unified in Havana and established their operational headquarters in Managua. Cuba and its Soviet-bloc allies provided training and supplies, which began to flow clandestinely through Nicaragua to El Salvador to fuel an armed assault.

The picture in Central America when I became secretary of state in mid-1982 was deteriorating. Although Honduras was an emerging democracy and Costa Rica was healthy and free, we were losing ground in El Salvador, getting nowhere in Guatemala, and had absolutely no ability to affect events in Nicaragua. The danger to El Salvador was ominous because fledgling efforts to construct a democracy there were beginning to take root. An internationally supervised election for a Constituent Assembly was held in March 1982. An estimated 80 percent of the electorate came to the polls in the face of armed, violent efforts to prevent them from exercising the right to cast their vote. A new constitution was drafted, a government of national unity established, and a program of major land reform initiated.

The United States was active on the diplomatic front, though there was unease and opposition to diplomatic efforts within the administration. On October 4, 1982, a U.S.-organized forum, held in the capital of Costa Rica and attended by officials from most Central American nations, put forward the San José Principles. Assistant Secretary of State Tom Enders played a leading role. The document called for each country of the region, in words clearly understood to be aimed at Nicaragua, Cuba, and the Soviet Union, to "create and maintain truly democratic government institutions based on the people's will as expressed in free and regular elections," to "respect human rights," to "prevent the use of their territory for the purpose of supporting, supplying, training terrorist or subversive elements in other states; to put an end to traffic of weapons . . . or activity aimed at the violent overthrow of the government of another state; to limit armaments and the size of the military and security forces to the levels that are strictly necessary for the maintenance of public order and national defense," to "withdraw from the Central American area all foreign military and security advisers and troops and prohibit the import of heavy weapons of evident offensive capacity through procedures that will guarantee verification." These ideas, controversial with the Sandinistas and their supporters, as well as with Casey and hard-liners on the NSC staff, were nevertheless a solid potential basis for diplomatic efforts by the United States and by our friends in the region. The key was the call for "democratic government."

With the rapid transformation of the Contras into a resistance force against the Sandinista regime and with the growing threat posed by the Sandinistas to their neighbors, President Reagan in December 1981 decided to provide American support for the Contras. Aid began to reach the Contras by spring 1982.

On November 8, 1982, *Newsweek* had asserted that our ambassador in Honduras, John Negroponte, was involved in covert arming and training of Nicaraguan exiles there. In reply, we had acknowledged that the United States was indeed supporting small-scale military operations intended to put pressure on, but not overthrow, the Sandinista government led by Daniel Ortega. This revelation set off loud alarm bells in Congress. On December 8, 1982, the Boland Amendment, named for its sponsor, Congressman Edward Boland, was passed by the House of Representatives 411 to 0. It prohibited the Department of Defense and Central Intelligence Agency from providing military equipment, training, or advice for the purpose of overthrowing the Nicaraguan regime.

The administration view was straightforward. The legitimate government of El Salvador, acting in accordance with the UN Charter, had asked the United States for help in defending itself against guerrillas supported by and through Nicaragua with support from Cuba and the Soviet Union. Economic assistance and security assistance were helpful, but we also needed something to preoccupy and counter the Nicaraguan regime. Under the authority of a presidential finding,[1] which was shared and discussed

---

1. The president is required to "find" compelling national security reasons as a basis for a covert action undertaken by the CIA.

with the intelligence committees of Congress in accordance with all requirements, the administration put in place a modest program of covert assistance to the Contras, who did not want the Sandinistas to create another Cuba. They were ready to put military pressure on the regime in Managua and hoped to force it at least to hold honest elections. The Contras thought they would win such an election. By supporting the Contras, we were not seeking the overthrow of the junta but to create sufficient pressure on the Nicaraguan regime to distract it from adventures in El Salvador and to induce it to accept regionwide provisions for peace and stability.

Secrecy is an illusive concept; very few acts or plans today are truly kept secret, while a large body of open secrets are the focus of public controversy. The U.S. effort to support the Contras was discussed, analyzed, and criticized openly and in detail in the media and yet was branded a "secret war." These discussions, dissections, and debates reported in the press were not leaks but by then a standard way of conducting the business of Washington. A *covert* operation was being converted to *overt* by talk on Capitol Hill and in the daily press and television news coverage. But because the program was nominally secret, I and others in the administration could not openly defend it. The CIA officials managing the program were uncomfortable, too, but for different reasons: they saw political pressure building and did not want the CIA to be the main target once again of congressional wrath. As press attention mounted in mid-1983, the CIA favored going public with the program and transferring it to the Department of Defense. Defense resisted: the program was controversial in Congress, and Defense already had all too much controversy on its hands. All this being so, why did we *not* make our program public, where we could debate and defend our actions openly?

An open effort would have caused an entirely new set of problems: while we felt the effort was compatible with all our international responsibilities, "deniability" was important for countries in the region through which the Contra aid flowed. They simply could not stand up to a publicly disclosed involvement in a program designed to disrupt a neighboring government; other covert efforts around the world might also be forced into the open (and many people opposed to covert action in Nicaragua were in favor of it in Afghanistan). So the U.S. effort to help El Salvador defend itself—and stop Nicaragua's effort to march Central America into the Communist bloc—stayed covert, and political figures in Central and South America and in the U.S. Congress retained their options: they could privately acquiesce in one or another form of U.S. help for the region while publicly attacking our policy.

As 1982 came to an end against this background of actions and controversy, I consulted frequently with my Central America team to try to take the measure of this deepening morass. My chief action officer for the region was Assistant Secretary of State for American Republics Affairs[2] Thomas Overton Enders, who had played a leading role in producing the San José Principles. Enders was a foreign service officer, a prodigy of the diplomatic corps, Yale educated, who would have felt at home in the old Eastern establishment that once conducted the nation's foreign affairs. He was imperious, intellectual, and ironic. His analyses conveyed an aura of brilliance even when he stated the obvious. People were impressed by his talents, but his sometimes smug smile and style could irritate even those who admired him most.

When Enders, six feet six inches tall, entered my office in the company of Larry Eagleburger, it was like a tenpin and a bowling ball both bearing down on me. Eagleburger called Enders "Too Tall." Eagleburger had warned me that Enders was an independent operator. Most assistant secretaries eagerly sought to involve the secretary of state in even the smallest details of their region's problems: Enders did not. He went off doing deals on his own, and his trail was hard to follow. I would soon find that Enders was not unique in this way of doing business in Central America.

A major problem in our assistance to El Salvador was "certification," which could stop us dead in our tracks at any time. "Certification" was Congress's way of saying it would curtail the funds needed in Central America unless we could demonstrate that notorious problems in the countries we supported were being solved—particularly the implementation of land reform in El Salvador, the elimination of "death squads," and progress in bringing to justice those in El Salvador who had murdered American nuns and representatives of the AFL-CIO. What this amounted to was congressional micromanagement of the U.S. economic and security assistance program. Funds were appropriated which would be released for a period of six months. Before the next six-month increment could be released, the secretary of state had to certify that progress was being made on the human rights and rule-of-law aspects of life in El Salvador. We were constantly struggling with an excruciating dilemma: on the one hand, we could point to progress; on the other hand, there were still great and disturbing problems. So we would certify the progress, but we realized that many thorny and deeply troublesome difficulties remained.

At the same time, from the standpoint of the Salvadoran military, certification created a problem. The military had funds and resources available to them for six months; they did not know whether these resources would be renewed for another six months. Because of this uncertainty, quite

2. The bureau in the State Department that deals with the countries to our south does not have a geographic designation, as do the bureaus of Asian, European, Near Eastern, and African affairs, but is uniquely designated American Republics Affairs, or ARA. The difference is important; it is intended to suggest a sense of community in our hemisphere and of attraction of the nations in this sector of the world to the idea of government of, by, and for the people.

predictably they husbanded their resources and therefore did not use them as effectively as possible to contend with the guerrillas. And as a result, Congress said that the security assistance was wasted because it was not being effectively used. It was a vicious circle. We argued for a longer time horizon so that the Salvadoran military could plan ahead and make better use of their resources. But Congress was reluctant.

The governments of El Salvador, Honduras, and Guatemala contained and tolerated many unsavory characters. Still, serious people in those governments were engaged in a stalwart effort to move toward democracy and the rule of law. The American left would have us leave those governments to struggle on their own and not worry whether communism came to prevail. The American right would have us support the anti-Communists no matter how outrageous their behavior.

To me, the task was to encourage democracy, deny the Communists their goals, and gain greater American public understanding and support for the economic and security assistance that was needed. We faced two related challenges: first, to help alleviate long-standing political, economic, and social problems; second, to help counter a Communist strategy that sought to aggravate and exploit those problems and then seize power by force of arms.

Nicaragua was at the heart of the challenge. Cuban military and security advisers in Nicaragua numbered about 2,000. We needed to create an atmosphere of uncertainty about our response should Cuba and the Soviets escalate their already extensive intervention. We had to take some measures to thwart Nicaragua's military support for the pro-Cuban revolutionaries in El Salvador. We had to deal with Nicaragua's diplomatic tactics, which were designed to exploit political turmoil in the United States over our Central America policy and split the United States from the other governments of Central America. I was confident that if there ever could be an honest election in Nicaragua, Ortega's government would lose. But also from our perspective, trouble at home for Ortega would decrease his ability to disrupt El Salvador and increase his willingness to negotiate a reasonable regional peace plan. The media was giving considerable attention to Eden Pastora, who proclaimed that the Sandinistas had sold out the revolution. The trouble was that Pastora's fame was greater than his reliability; he was mercurial and mysterious—not the kind of leader that we would be able to work with in a long and difficult effort or one who would prove capable of crystallizing the opposition.

"So far," Tom Enders said to me as we continued our review of the area, "we don't see the endgame. Cuban-type communism is being consolidated in Nicaragua. Nicaragua is promoting a revolution against El Salvador, and Cuba is preparing to step up support for a similar insurgency in Guatemala." Without a doubt, Enders said, a long struggle lay ahead.

My primary political-military adviser, Rear Admiral Jon Howe, was more pessimistic than Enders. He reported that a great deal of concern was being expressed by the Joint Chiefs of Staff about El Salvador. "We are losing. It could be finished by the end of the year." Enders countered that while El Salvador's armed forces had suffered a 13 percent casualty rate in the last two years, recruiting was up, and the army had grown from 7,000 to 30,000. At the same time, the guerrillas were using better tactics and getting better supplies. "The worst is that the Salvadorans are uncertain about our intentions," Enders said. "The certification process constantly hangs over their heads, with its threat to cut off funds. There is a sense of stalemate, and morale is bad. Some new action by the U.S. is needed," Enders said. "We simply need more resources and more management from the embassy."

The Pentagon wanted more U.S. advisers on the spot—160 or so. This was to augment the fifty-five already there. Bill Casey supported this. "Congress won't take the risk of losing Central America for the sake of twenty or twenty-five advisers," Casey told me. "I'm in favor of doing what we can and not being afraid of Congress."

My view was different: we had to get a workable policy in place, and workable meant a policy with congressional support. We had about fifteen months to go. Otherwise, by the time the 1984 presidential election campaign was in full force, we would confront an avalanche of political opposition at home.

"If the Democrats deny us support," Casey had said, it would be good politics to say to the country: "the Democrats gave away the Panama Canal, and now they have lost all Central America."

I doubted that would work, but the point, I felt, was not to lose Central America in the first place. I felt that we needed three basic components to support our policy: first, some form of military pressure, direct or threatened, to make the Communists feel the heat; second, a vigorous negotiating track to reach an agreement if we could and, at the least, to demonstrate that we were working to achieve a peaceful solution (which would help us to get the resources we needed from Congress); and third, support from those who counted in the region—not only the democratic forces in Central America but the three major regional nations: Mexico, Colombia, and Venezuela.

Crisis in Suriname

As I agonized over what to do about Nicaragua and El Salvador, an unexpected crisis appeared on the south shore of the Caribbean: Suriname. On December 8, 1982, Desi Bouterse, a creole army sergeant major who had led a group of army sergeants to overthrow Suriname's elected gov-

ernment in 1980, rounded up twenty to thirty prominent citizens and murdered at least fifteen of them in Fort Zeelandia, the stronghold of
Suriname's capital city, Paramaribo. Bouterse's reported aim was to eliminate his most vocal and influential opponents and intimidate the civilian
population, which earlier in the year had sought unsuccessfully to overthrow
his regime and restore democratic institutions. Bouterse's December 8
killings came at the end of a rising tide of tension that began when Suriname's trade unionists vehemently protested the visit to Paramaribo of
Maurice Bishop, Grenada's Marxist strongman.

Suriname was a self-governing territory of the Netherlands and, through
its ties with the Dutch, an associate member of the European Community.
The Dutch government in The Hague was alarmed but unwilling to act
alone in response to these atrocities. They asked to consult with the United
States. It appeared that Bouterse was taking Suriname on a forced march
toward Cuba-style communism and that Suriname stood at the edge of
becoming the first Communist state on the mainland of South America.
Bouterse had formed an alliance with the left-wing government of Grenada
and was rumored to have reached an agreement guaranteeing him support
from Fidel Castro. As an immediate reaction to the killings, we and the
Dutch suspended our aid programs and announced that our relationships
with Suriname were under review. Bouterse immediately began to talk of
going to the Soviet Union for $70–$80 million in funds.

On December 23, at the start of the day's business, Eagleburger came
into my office. The Suriname situation was getting out of hand, he said.
The people of Paramaribo were living in daily fear of Bouterse's reign of
terror. The Dutch wanted our help; they were open to any effort to save
the situation, but only if it was "short of intervention."

Bouterse's regime was not strong in military terms. The light weapons
present in the hands of the relatively few people involved in his regime in
Paramaribo meant that the city could be captured and controlled fairly
easily by a small professional military unit. Nonetheless, all options seemed
to close one by one. A covert operation by the CIA or the insertion of a
commando U.S. Delta Force would have been politically explosive at home.
Later that day Enders proposed, on behalf of the State Department at a
Crisis Pre-Planning Group (CPPG) meeting, that despite the evident Dutch
misgivings, we approach them with a suggestion: if they would send a
military force into Suriname, the U.S. Navy would interpose itself between
Suriname and Cuba to prevent the Cubans from coming to Bouterse's
assistance. This idea was rejected by Cap Weinberger and the Joint Chiefs,
who, it was becoming increasingly clear to me, were still seared by their
Vietnam-era experience: they instinctively opposed the small-scale use of
American forces, fearing it might undercut their effort to equip themselves
as a counterpoint to the Soviets.

Meanwhile, another challenge was occurring far away. Muammar Qaddafi, employing Soviet weapons acquired with Libya's enormous oil wealth, had begun an invasion of Chad, Libya's neighbor to the south. Reports were also coming in that Qaddafi was seeking to foment a coup to overthrow the government of Sudan. To support President Hissen Habré of Chad, we worked with the French, who, as the former colonial power there, *were* willing to intervene directly. And with cooperation from Egypt, which had a strategic interest in Sudan as the land of the Upper Nile, the United States staged a show of force that scared the Libyans off. The lesson: if the challenge was far away and our involvement nearly invisible or deniable and if another nation of power would act with us, then success was possible. Closer to home, where the stakes were higher, we seemed to be stymied. Paradoxically, there were signs that Qaddafi was moving to support the new pro-Communist strongmen in Grenada and Suriname.

The Suriname challenge, insignificant in its own right and nearly ignored by the media, put us face-to-face with a continuing problem. The Vietnam War had left one indisputable legacy: massive press, public, and congressional anxiety that the United States—at all costs—avoid getting mired in "another Vietnam." News items datelined from Central America or the Caribbean raised the alarm that this or that country of the region was about to become our next quagmire. We knew that any covert action by the CIA would be severely scrutinized, probably disallowed by the Congress, and that any direct military action would require that the president enter the as-yet-uncharted thicket of the War Powers Act, passed in 1973 over the veto of a weakened President Nixon in the aftermath of the Watergate scandal that ultimately forced his resignation.[3] So the American agonies subsumed under the terms Vietnam and Watergate had us tied in knots.

On Tuesday, December 28, 1982, President Reagan approved, Cap Weinberger and the Joint Chiefs notwithstanding, sending an emissary to the Dutch: if the Netherlands would send in a force to take charge of Paramaribo, we would provide a blocking naval force to ensure that Cuba did not move to intervene directly to support Bouterse's forces. The next night, Steve Bosworth of State's Latin America bureau left for The Hague with a letter from President Reagan to Prime Minister Lubbers of Holland.

A fairly steady round of meetings at lower levels was now going on: the Crisis Pre-Planning Group (CPPG) would go first, followed, a step higher, by the National Security Planning Group (NSPG). So far, there had been

---

3. Many in the legal community regarded the War Powers Act as unconstitutional. It had never been tested. With its requirement that Congress be notified when U.S. forces are committed to hostilities and that the forces be automatically withdrawn if Congress did not vote affirmatively for their deployment within sixty days (an additional thirty days were allowed if the president declared "unavoidable military necessity"), it was bound to add an element of uncertainty to the use of force by the United States. The uncertainty of affirmative and prompt action by both houses of Congress would encourage adversaries simply to wait out the sixty-day period.

no meeting of the National Security Council itself on the question. I had already observed that the statutorily designated National Security Council—the president, the vice president, secretaries of state and defense, with adjunct participation by the director of the CIA and the chairman of the Joint Chiefs of Staff—seemed never to meet without a crowd. They, plus a slew of other officials—their deputies and an ever-changing round of agency heads, staffers, and assorted hangers-on—would gather in the tiny White House Situation Room. In those days, the room was always filled to capacity. The sessions would produce plenty of heated argument but no decisions.

The decisions would come later, after President Reagan had participated in informal discussions following the formal NSC sessions. It was the president who would ultimately decide. But I became increasingly worried that in the absence of a presidential decision, the participants at these lower levels would begin making decisions on their own, and putting measures into effect, without my knowledge and without the knowledge of others at the top. I began to realize that I would have to be constantly on the alert to prevent zealots from becoming free agents instigating actions on their own that should be reserved for the president or his topmost cabinet-level appointees.

On January 3, the Crisis Pre-Planning Group met again, and I made sure I reviewed its conclusions. We sent cables to Venezuela and Brazil asking to consult with them before any action was taken toward Suriname. We cabled our ambassador, William Dyess, in the Netherlands to say we were ready for contingency planning with the Dutch on the questions of threats to their and our citizens in Suriname. We instructed our ambassador to Suriname, Robert Duemling, to protest the recent expulsion of his deputy and his public affairs officer and to warn Desi Bouterse about his new turn toward Grenada, Cuba, and the Soviet Union.

On the next day, January 4, 1983, I reviewed the situation with Tom Enders. The Dutch, we had found, were unwilling to intervene themselves. Prime Minister Lubbers was under intense pressure from the Dutch left; even the suggestion that the Netherlands would work with the United States on an "anti-Cuba" policy could mean the collapse of his government. Such a collapse would have far broader ramifications: the Netherlands was a basing country for projected deployment of U.S. intermediate-range missiles if the INF negotiations that would come to a head in late 1983 did not succeed. If the Dutch government came under leftist control, the critical NATO effort to counter Soviet missile deployments could start to collapse.

But if the United States went into Suriname alone, Enders felt, the political price in the United States would be excessively high. Even if we did take action that brought Bouterse down, we could not easily help a successor government take over without support from The Hague. The Dutch said they would support anything short of intervention, and the

Brazilians and Venezuelans seemed eager that something be done. They felt, as we did, that the emergence of another pro-Soviet, virulently anti-American regime in the hemisphere would be a blow to stability throughout the region. It looked to me as though the best we could put together would be a combination of external economic pressure with, perhaps, some kind of covert support for Bouterse's remaining opponents in Suriname—if there were any.

At the National Security Planning Group meeting later that morning, President Reagan was willing to consider use of American troops to get Bouterse out of power even without Dutch support. I was sympathetic, but I could not conceive of this proving successful: opposing political pressures would be too strong without some triggering event of undeniable and immediate effect on American interests to spur the call for U.S. action.

Throughout January and February 1983 the agonized debate went on, but it was increasingly clear that the Dutch would not take direct military action and neither would we. The final blow came in early March when Tom Enders went up to the Hill to explore with the intelligence committees the possibility of a covert operation against Bouterse. He ran into a buzz saw.

Every conceivable counterargument was raised: we were accused of planning an assassination attempt; we were encouraged to compete with the Cubans and Soviets by offering more aid to Bouterse (which Congress certainly would not have approved); we were told that any step we took would violate the nonintervention provisions of the 1947 Rio treaty and our obligations to the Organization of American States; we were asked why we wanted to intervene in Suriname when we were not seeking to intervene in Liberia, where Master Sergeant Samuel Doe was brutally consolidating his power. And as a final threat, one committee member began to press Enders for the names of those in the administration who were proposing such action against Bouterse, building a record for a subsequent witch hunt. From then on, the effort degenerated into farce.

At the end of March, the CIA sent briefers to me to outline a plan under which a force of 50 to 175 Korean commandos would stage out of Venezuela and run an assault into Paramaribo to overthrow Bouterse. It was a harebrained idea, ill thought out, without any convincing likelihood of success and with no analysis of the political consequences at home or internationally. I discussed the proposal the next day with Eagleburger and Enders. "Here is a place," I said, "that is virtually defenseless, yet we can't generate local people to do anything. These kinds of plans have a way of taking on a life of their own. I'm not persuaded. We have to think about the Bay of Pigs and assassination plots." There would be fallout in Congress on Central America. The whole thing depended on impossibly intricate timing and a presumption that the Koreans would be taken as members of the local population. That was crazy. I was shaken to find such a wild plan put forward seriously by the CIA.

Bouterse continued to consolidate his brutal regime with Cuban support and Soviet backing. The problem festered, and the president and I stewed in frustration at our inability to produce effective counteraction.

Tension Rises Over Central America Policy

In early February 1983, I had gone to China to try to turn around a deteriorating relationship and reestablish it on a solid footing. Upon my return to Washington, I found that the fervor of the intellectual debate over Central America had ratcheted up once again and that control of our work on Central America had shifted from State to the NSC staff: we were heading for trouble. Such mischief making and grappling for control of policy occurred time and again whenever my schedule took me out of Washington. The political atmosphere was bitter. Tom Enders' enemies were telling the press that he was going "soft" on the Salvadoran guerrillas. A White House versus State Department battle was brewing. Bill Clark and his NSC staffers were talking tough. They felt El Salvador was about to fall and that it was time for the wholesale "Americanization" of the effort. I felt that the NSC's ineptitude, if unchecked, would set the administration up for a massive defeat in Congress. I was concerned about the situation in El Salvador, but I wanted to keep the focus of U.S. support on help to that country's own armed forces, which did well when adequately trained and equipped.

On the last day of February, I had testified before the Senate Appropriations Subcommittee on Foreign Assistance and, in tough exchanges, pointed out that El Salvador is critically located; it is "connected right up through to Mexico with whom we have a long border. So the emergence of another country added to Cuba, Grenada, and Nicaragua, another country and then perhaps others to Soviet-Cuban influence, is bad news for this country." Responding to a question from the chairman, Senator Daniel Inouye, I said, "It is clear that the military forces of El Salvador depend upon supplies coming from the United States. The military forces of the insurgency depend upon supplies coming from the Soviet Union. If we stop our supplies and the Soviets continue, I think that is not likely to yield a result which we want. I don't believe in dire predictions, but I think the conclusions from that scenario are fairly obvious."

In the meantime, Jeane Kirkpatrick, our UN ambassador, had been in Central America and had returned with word of a proposed regionwide meeting about Central American problems. Venezuela, Mexico, Colombia, and Panama were taking the lead and apparently looking toward multilateral negotiations that would involve them with the five Central American states, including Nicaragua. The United States and Cuba would be excluded. Kirkpatrick's judgment was that we should not oppose such a meeting. I agreed that a regionwide solution was desirable, but I worried that the initiative would undercut the San José Principles and seem to set Cuba up as an equivalent to us.

Within a few months, this effort would evolve into the Contadora process, named for the tiny island off the Pacific coast of Panama where the meetings first took place in January 1983. The participants aspired to shape a regional approach to a negotiated solution. The United States supported the process. At the same time, we were supporting on a small scale, with arms and training, the Contras. Our objectives were to disrupt the ability of Daniel Ortega's regime to cause trouble in El Salvador and to push the Sandinista's into a regional peace process.

Former Democratic Senator Richard Stone of Florida, who had been defeated in the 1980 election, came on the scene. He had been asked by the White House in early 1983 to look into the Central American situation and give his advice. Stone asked to see me so that I could hear his ideas. "You've been on the defensive, and you need something positive. Give me a few days to work on it—you'll love it," he told me.

"I can hardly wait," I said skeptically.

Stone's idea, I soon discovered, was to persuade the government of El Salvador to advance the date of the presidential election: a democratic election monitored by observers would put a leader in place who would have legitimacy. We could probably get congressional funding to support such an election. This was a good idea, and I sent Stone to Central America to explore the possibility. On the airplane from San Salvador to Miami, Stone was chatting about his idea with an aide and was overheard by a reporter sitting in the seat in front of him. The leak was embarrassing, since the idea would be more appealing if it were not seen as an initiative from the United States. On his return, Stone came to my office and was deeply apologetic.

"As we used to say in World War II," I told him, " 'Loose lips sink ships.' "

Dick Stone was an amazing sight to behold. I had never met a more nervous man. In meetings he would sometimes vibrate with tension. But he also possessed an immense energy, and the constant stream of ideas he emitted in bursts every once in a while yielded a really good one. Like Enders, Stone was a problem but also an asset. By March 3, Stone reported agreement in El Salvador to advance the date of the presidential election. The pope, who was about to visit Central America, would support this idea in his public remarks.

As a concrete marker of the self-confidence and growing strength of El Salvador's new democratic leaders, on March 6 President Alvaro Magaña announced, in the presence of Pope John Paul II, that national elections would be held in El Salvador that year and that they would be open to all political parties and groups. On March 17 El Salvador's peace commission, composed of a Catholic bishop and two civilians, proposed legislation for a general amnesty, and the president of the Constituent Assembly explicitly called for the main political unit of the guerrillas, the Revolutionary Democratic Front (FDR), to take part in the elections.

Meanwhile, I prepared myself for additional congressional testimony. I was worried about proposals from the Defense Department, the CIA, and the NSC staff for an increase in the number of U.S. military trainers in El Salvador. I told the president on March 4 that the proposal for additional trainers was a self-inflicted wound that would soon amount to suicidal behavior on our part. It played straight into the argument that El Salvador was the next Vietnam.

The president saw my point. In a speech on March 10, President Reagan had urged an additional $110 million in military aid to El Salvador, $60 million of which was to be reprogrammed from funds already formally appropriated. I had testified on his behalf before the Senate on February 28, saying the additional aid was crucial because the guerrillas were "dedicated to tearing the country up." I rejected the notion of negotiations for power sharing between the guerrillas and the Salvadoran government. "Having observed these people try by violence to prevent an election from happening, why should they by violence, and with our agreement shoot their way into the government? No dice," I said. "We will not support that kind of activity." Let them lay down their arms and enter into elections in a democratic process. I also tried to assure Congress that we were not going to "Americanize" the war by increasing the number of American trainers there.

My testimony seemed to have a positive impact. That was promptly undercut by a blundering Bill Clark. In a session with reporters aboard *Air Force One*, as he flew with the president to California, he said that more trainers, beyond the current limit of fifty-five, were under consideration.

"How stupid can you get?" I said. Clark's comment fanned congressional anxiety and stirred their opposition to our requests for funds. The amount of funds reprogrammed was cut from $60 million to $30 million, and the House initially declined to appropriate any more money.

So we were deeply divided within the administration and in Congress in identifying and pursuing our objectives in Central America. And we had trouble with our friends as well. In 1981, François Mitterrand had been elected president of France. As part of his new Socialist program, Mitterrand radically changed French foreign policy toward Central America, the Caribbean, and Latin America. Paris moved to a clear and close relationship with Sandinista Nicaragua and with the leftist guerrillas the Sandinistas and the Cubans supported in El Salvador. Mitterrand appointed as his personal adviser on these issues Régis Debray, a leftist intellectual and onetime companion of Ernesto "Ché" Guevara, the Cuban revolutionary and agitator for Communist movements in every part of the hemisphere. Debray's *Revolution in the Revolution? Armed Struggle and Political Struggle in Latin America* became a handbook for Latin American guerrillas and made Debray an influential celebrity in Marxist-Leninist intellectual circles worldwide. For Debray, Castro's victory in Cuba demonstrated that armed struggle was everything: "The socialist revolution is the result of an armed struggle against the armed power of the bourgeois state"; armed struggle was an "old historic law" and, in his view, the only way forward for Latin America.[4]

On March 31, 1983, at President Mitterrand's request, I agreed to see Debray. He brought me a "message" from the Communist guerrillas in the jungles of El Salvador. If I wanted a dialogue with them, Debray said, they were ready; he could assure me that the message came from the faction that should be dealt with. Our talks could be kept secret. The guerrillas in El Salvador, Debray said, were concerned by what was happening to "the revolution" in Nicaragua. It was becoming "Cubanized." I heard him out, made no response, and he departed. My advisers buzzed in like hornets. "Debray can't be trusted," Enders said. "Any contact with the Salvador guerrillas will destabilize the democratically elected government there."

"Debray is a liar," Eagleburger added. "Central America is an ideological freebie for the French. They can be as leftist as they want there. Whatever happens can do them no harm, but trouble there can weaken the United States in Europe."

After they had all left, I thought over our problems in Central America. Every political movement in Central America, whether in or out of power, wanted to deal with us separately, "one on one." But Central America presented regionwide problems that needed regionwide solutions. As we dealt with individual issues and nations, I felt we should do so within a framework of general concepts, such as those set out in the San José Principles. We needed strength *and* diplomacy in our policy: strength to show the Communists that we would not tolerate their advance into our hemisphere and diplomacy to pry the way open for solutions short of war. Debray's visit sharpened my awareness that France's interests in Central America's were not ours. I did not appreciate Mitterrand's authorization of this meddling.

On April 12, 1983, Enders described a modest covert program for Contra

4. *Revolution in the Revolution? Armed Struggle and Political Struggle in Latin America* (New York: Grove Press, 1967), p. 19.

aid to the Senate Foreign Relations Committee and the Senate Intelligence Committee in a closed hearing on the subject. In an earlier open session on Central America, the atmosphere was highly charged. In the closed session, Enders said, the mood was "clubby." Senators Pat Moynihan and David Durenburger spoke against our policy, but the committee was united in the view that the administration was not seeking the overthrow of the Sandinista government and therefore was not in violation of the Boland Amendment. The committee chairman, Senator Barry Goldwater, issued a public statement to that effect.

Despite this, the congressional consensus on Contra aid was collapsing under intense political pressure from the left. Representative Boland himself declared that the administration was violating his amendment—which was not so. By July 1983, the House had defeated Contra aid, a big step on the way to the total cutoff that would come in 1984.

A First Effort with Mexico

In Mexico City on April 18, 1983, I met with Foreign Minister Bernardo Sepulveda, a mercurial, irascible, but clever political operator who was no particular fan of the United States. He talked to me privately about his recent session in Managua with the Nicaraguan *comandantes*, describing to me what he had discussed with them. As we talked, a set of principles emerged that tracked well with what had been worked out previously in San José. If the United States and Mexico could cooperatively support these principles, a potentially new and positive force for change might be launched, I thought. I took careful notes as we formulated principles that we could both support and which could guide our effort to bring about peace and stability in our neighborhood. Each of four points dealing with military matters, we agreed, must take place on a mutual and verifiable basis:

- Avoid escalation of present warfare in Central America and stop what is now going on. [My mind was on El Salvador, his on Nicaragua.]
- Stop the buildup of armaments in Central America: the level is already too high. [I focused on the heavy influx of Soviet bloc arms; he worried about the relatively tiny flow of supplies coming from the United States.]
- End the movement of armaments and military capabilities from one Central American country to another. [I felt this, if it came about, would be of immense benefit to El Salvador.]
- Remove foreign military advisers from the host country without delay. [If the Soviets and Cubans left Nicaragua, we could do without our military advisers in El Salvador.]

We went on to argue that peace and stability could not be obtained simply by the removal of aggressive armed forces. They would emerge from more positive developments:

- the establishment of a continuing and constructive dialogue among countries of the region;
- the emergence of societies that are pluralist and open, with strengthened political institutions and conscientious efforts toward internal reconciliation;
- the prospect of a free expression of the political will of the population as the basis for government office; and
- economic development based on secure conditions in the region, efforts in each country to open opportunities for trade and investment, and a willingness in the broader international community to promote financial flows of investment capital and markets that are genuinely open to the products of these countries.

When I returned to Washington that night, I got the statement of principles over to Bill Clark and asked him to put them before President Reagan. Clark instantly objected. "We do not want the Mexicans to deal bilaterally with Central America," he said, entirely missing the point that a strong statement of principles with American, Mexican, and regional support might move us forward.

The next morning, Clark telephoned to say "no go" on the principles. Without saying so directly, he implied that he had put the issue to the president and received a negative response. I suspected that the statement of principles had never left his office, but I had no time to fight this issue; Lebanon demanded my urgent attention as I prepared to leave for the Middle East the next day to try to negotiate an agreement that could lead to a new beginning for Lebanon free of all foreign troops.

More Problems and a Presidential Initiative

Once again, my departure from the Washington scene proved to be an occasion for others to try to take control of Central America policy. I learned that Deputy Secretary of State Ken Dam had signed off on a letter from Bill Clark to Clarence "Doc" Long, chairman of the House Subcommittee on Foreign Operations, saying that the administration would name a "regional" negotiator on Central America. As Ken knew, I thought the idea was reasonable, but I was surprised at Clark's favorable attitude. He had been opposed to any negotiations at all over Central America. Apparently recognizing that a diplomatic track was inevitable, Clark was attempting to formalize the role of Dick Stone and bring Stone under his direct control.

Although Stone technically would be an ambassador-at-large, he and Clark were headed toward a "special negotiator" status that would in effect take Central America out of State's Latin America bureau and put it under Clark's NSC staff. Stone was not playing this squarely, nor was Clark: Stone would, in effect, become Clark's under secretary for Latin America. I could write off control over Central America policy. And I did not know the extent to which President Reagan was involved in these decisions or was aware of their implications for the management of the tough Central America issues.

So from the Middle East I sent a message to the president. "I am disturbed to learn that the proposed mandate for this special envoy would have the effect of superseding the relevant authority within the Department of State and removing the direction of the policy from my supervision. I do not see how such an arrangement would serve your interests in an integrated foreign policy nor how a secretary of state could continue to serve under such circumstances." I was putting everyone on notice, especially Clark, that I intended to discuss all of this carefully with the president when I returned.

Meanwhile, a major move was under way to have the president address a joint session of Congress on the subject of Central America. This would be a big event and would certainly call attention to the issues at stake. I made my comments on the proposed text before I left. Some of the ideas I had worked on with Sepulveda were in the speech. I had not been an enthusiast for the idea of the president's addressing a joint session of Congress on the subject of Central America, but when I saw the final draft of the speech, I had to admit that it was excellent. President Reagan delivered it on April 27. He set out a line of thinking and a comprehensive program that could stand us in good stead in the troubled times ahead. First he laid the groundwork: "We're all well aware of the Libyan cargo planes refueling in Brazil a few days ago on their way to deliver 'medical supplies' to Nicaragua. Brazilian authorities discovered the so-called medical supplies were actually munitions and prevented their delivery. You may remember that last month, speaking on national television [his March 23 speech in which he announced his SDI program], I showed an aerial photo of an airfield being built on the island of Grenada. Well, if that airfield had been completed, those planes could have refueled there and completed their journey."

President Reagan described the efforts "toward an orderly and democratic society" in El Salvador and the actions by guerrillas to block an election, "The guerrillas threatened death to anyone who voted. They destroyed hundreds of buses and trucks to keep the people from getting to the polling places. Their slogan was brutal: 'Vote today, die tonight.' But on election day, an unprecedented 80 percent of the electorate braved ambush and gunfire and trudged for miles, many of them, to vote for freedom."

The president referred to a speech I had made on April 15 about the same subject: "I think Secretary of State Shultz put it very well the other day: 'Unable to win the free loyalty of El Salvador's people, the guerrillas,' he said, 'are deliberately and systematically depriving them of food, water, transportation, light, sanitation, and jobs. And these are the people who claim they want to help the common people.' "

He referred to the record of first the Carter administration's and then the Reagan administration's efforts with Nicaragua and summarized: "The Sandinista revolution in Nicaragua turned out to be just an exchange of one set of autocratic rulers for another."

After reviewing the importance of support from the United States, he set out a program: "We will support dialog and negotiations both among the countries of the region and within each country. . . . The United States will work toward a political solution in Central America which will serve the interests of the democratic process."

Then he offered assurances that resembled the San José Principles and the ideas Sepulveda and I worked out: "The United States will support any agreement among Central American countries for the withdrawal, under fully verifiable and reciprocal conditions, of all foreign military and security advisers and troops. We want to help opposition groups join the political process in all countries and compete by ballots instead of bullets. We will support any verifiable, reciprocal agreement among Central American countries on the renunciation of support for insurgencies on neighbors' territory. And, finally, we desire to help Central America end its costly arms race and will support any verifiable, reciprocal agreements on the nonimportation of offensive weapons."

The president announced his intention to name an ambassador-at-large as his special envoy to Central America. "He or she will report to me through the Secretary of State." I knew I would have to work to make this chain of command take effect, but I was glad to see these words in the president's speech.

When my aircraft landed at Andrews Air Force Base on May 11, upon my return from my Middle East shuttle, Bill Clark was there on the tarmac to meet me. The moment I stepped into the limousine, he hammered right in on Central America. He did not say one word about the Middle East. Clark, I could see, was as obsessed as ever with Central America. And he and his staff were now micromanaging our policy. Enders had lost control, and Clark was operating virtually independently.

Clark, I was later informed, had persuaded President Reagan to send John Gavin, the former actor, a fellow Californian and now our ambassador to Mexico, on a trip to Central America. Clark also wanted to fire Enders, saying that the president had lost confidence in him. In reality, Casey, Clark, and hard-line staffers at the NSC wanted no part of a diplomatic effort to accompany the military effort to defeat the Communists in the region. To them, diplomacy was an avenue to "accommodation."

"George, don't be a pilgrim," Casey once told me.

"What's that?" I asked.

"An early settler," he said.

I was now associated with this dual-track approach, strength *and* diplomacy. So was Enders. It was the right approach. The NSC staff effort was to move Enders out of the picture—and move diplomacy out of the picture—by moving Central America policy out of the State Department.

Bill Clark was difficult for me to deal with. Ronald Reagan never struck me as seeming like a former movie actor: he was natural, himself. But Clark always struck me as artificial, as if he were acting: he seemed to relish the role of the frontier lawman—a taciturn Gary Cooper. He wore hand-tooled cowboy boots and a Stetson and had a U.S. marshal's badge and a Colt .45 on display in his office. He was laconic to the point of noncommunication. He did not appear on television and rarely gave an interview to the press. He wanted to be called "Judge." Over time, I came to the conclusion that he was deeply uncomfortable and insecure in his role in foreign affairs and national security. He had no background whatsoever in these areas. The complexity of reality was a threat to him. To avoid looking ill at ease and uninformed, Clark took refuge in two simple principles: all of his decisions or recommendations would be hard-line, and he would try to control real access to the president. But when I talked directly and privately with President Reagan, I often found that his views were sharply different from, and much more savvy and nuanced than, Clark's.

New Management for Central America Policy?

Back in my office on May 12, in the late afternoon, I was in a quandary about Central America. Ken Dam reported that Bill Clark believed "we are at war and losing."

"If we are at war and losing, we are losing because of them," I replied. An NSC staff takeover would be a disaster, I knew. They had no standing on the Hill. "They will foul things up and then State will have to pull their chestnuts out of the fire."

Somehow I had to regain control of our Central America policy. It was too important to relinquish, and I would be blamed in the end anyway. But I could not imagine getting hold without replacing Enders, despite all his talents. Enders had hurt himself by being such an independent operator and was reaping the whirlwind of having excluded so many people, including me, for so long. The most promising person to replace him, I thought, would be Tony Motley, our ambassador to Brazil. Tony had grown up in Brazil. He understood Latin Americans instinctively. He was fluent in Portuguese and Spanish. He had been involved in U.S. politics. I could see he was a shrewd operator and a good street fighter. I also liked him. And I knew that the president, Clark, and others in the White House liked him, too.

On May 25, I spent most of the day at the White House. I started off privately with the president. "Mr. President, you have a fed-up, frustrated secretary of state on your hands," I opened. I told him he could have the best policy in the world, but it would not succeed with the present organization.

The president was startled and said he was "absolutely unaware" of the problems I raised. I felt that he was rocked back on his heels and that he had not realized how much confusion there was and how unhappy I was. He approved all of my suggested rearrangements, which came down to my leading Central America policy with Enders' successor and to having Stone report directly to me.

At 4:15 in the afternoon, after I returned to my office, the president called me regarding personnel changes. We discussed the idea of Tom Enders as ambassador to Spain and Tony Motley as his replacement in the American Republics Affairs (ARA) Bureau. We were going to reorganize, and we were going to do it with new personnel.

As soon as President Reagan hung up, Mike Deaver called to confirm the president's agreement with my proposals. Soon after, Chief of Staff Jim Baker called. He said that he would not renew Dick Stone's White House pass. I laughed. Those guys over there got the message fast. A bit later, Clark called. He hemmed and hawed about the question of ambassadors. I insisted that we had to move ahead quickly and coordinate an announcement. We called Enders in New York and Motley in Brasília to let them know what was coming.

A Grab for Power

If I thought that these changes would turn the policy situation around, I was dead wrong. When the next surprise on Central America hit me, I was not on another continent but only seventy miles south of Washington, in Williamsburg. Just before the economic summit was to get under way, I received a cable on Saturday morning, May 28, saying that a Crisis Pre-Planning Group (CPPG) meeting "reached the following decisions." Never mind that CPPGs do not have the authority to make decisions. They had "decided," I was informed, that the CIA would conduct an operation to place limpet mines on vessels in Nicaraguan ports and to mine the river

On the practice
field, Princeton
University, 1940.

I accompanied my father on a business trip at the age of seven; we found time to take a look at Kezar Stadium in San Francisco, 1928.

Batting cleanup, I swing for the fences, 1935.

As a marine lieutenant—a photo for the folks back home, 1943.

Birl and Margaret Shultz, my parents, 1941.

O'Bie and I, World War II days, Kauai, Hawaii, 1944.

As the new secretary of the treasury, I shake hands with the first treasury secretary, Alexander Hamilton, 1972.

My first—and only—camel ride, Petra, Jordan, 1982.

President Reagan welcomes me to
Camp David, June 26, 1982.
Ronald Reagan Presidential Library

Lunch at Camp David: Jim Baker,
President Reagan, Bill Clark, Ed
Meese, and I (second from left)
confer on "the world in turmoil"
outside Aspen Cottage on June 26,
1982, soon after the president
asked me to become secretary
of state.

I am sworn in as secretary of state by Attorney General Bill Smith in the White House Rose Garden, July 16, 1982. Ronald Reagan Presidential Library

In my office at the State Department, August 1982.

Bud McFarlane, Ed Meese, Jim Baker, and I listen as President Reagan calls
Prime Minister Begin: "The air strikes on Beirut must stop," August 1982.
Ronald Reagan Presidential Library

Doodles by President Reagan, July 29, 1982.

My first major address at the UN General
Assembly, September 30, 1982.

President Reagan, flanked by Phil Habib and me, November 1, 1982. We had Lebanon on our hands. Ronald Reagan Presidential Library

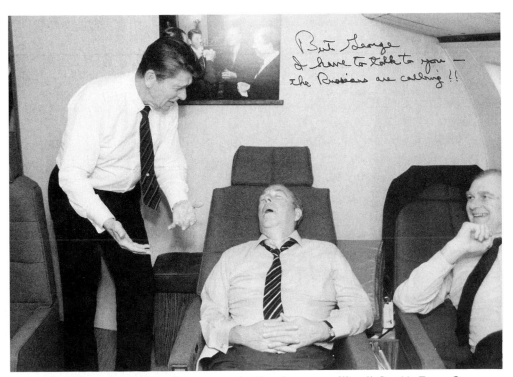

"But George, I have to talk to you—the Russians are calling." On *Air Force One*, somewhere over Central America, December 4, 1982. Tom Enders is at right. Ronald Reagan Presidential Library

My first trip to Japan
as secretary of state.
With Prime Minister
Yasuhiro Nakasone,
January 31, 1983.

After watching Super
Bowl XVII, I make
Foreign Minister Shintaro
Abe an honorary Redskins
fan. At the American
ambassador's residence,
Tokyo, February 1, 1983.

I inspect our troops
at Camp Liberty
Bell in the Demili-
tarized Zone, Korea,
February 1983.

Talking with Ray Seitz en route to China in February 1983.

The president and I toast Queen Elizabeth in San Francisco, California, March 3, 1983.
Ronald Reagan Presidential Library

Talking on the tacsat at Camp David, April 1983. Ronald Reagan Presidential Library

Looking over the American embassy in Beirut, bombed by terrorists, April 28, 1983. I am flanked by U.S. Ambassador Robert Dillon and State Department security detail head Bob O'Brien.

A critical moment at the Williamsburg economic summit, May 29, 1983. Ronald Reagan Presidential Library

After the May 17, 1983, Israel-Lebanon Agreement. Ray Osrin in *The Plain Dealer* (Cleveland)

Celebrating my first year as secretary of state. On the left is Clem Conger, the State Department's curator. On the right are O'Bie and Deputy Secretary Ken Dam. State Department, July 16, 1983.

With Ginger Rogers at the White House, October 4, 1983. "For a moment I thought I was dancing with Fred," she inscribed on the photo. Ronald Reagan Presidential Library

At Augusta, Georgia, as the Grenada crisis comes to a head, October 22, 1983. Bill FitzPatrick, White House

Awakened in the predawn hours, Bud McFarlane and I discuss the ominous situation in Grenada with the president, who gives his go-ahead for the Grenada operation. Augusta, Georgia, October 22, 1983. Ronald Reagan Presidential Library

I react to remarks by Marine Commandant General P. X. Kelley, testifying at hearings on the bombing of the U.S. Marine barracks in Beirut, October 24, 1983.

The ceremony for the marines killed in the bombing of the U.S. Marine barracks in Beirut. Camp Lejeune, North Carolina, November 6, 1983. Ronald Reagan Presidential Library

President Amin Gemayel of Lebanon arrives at the White House, December 1, 1983.
Ronald Reagan Presidential Library

Reporting to the president in Ireland, June 1984. Ronald Reagan Presidential Library

above El Bluff, a port on Nicaragua's Atlantic coast. High-speed patrol boats would be used to hit port facilities. This was outrageous. Clearly, the Washington bureaucracy was out of control. I telephoned Ken Dam at State: "The CPPG has *no authority* to reach such decisions. Call Bud McFarlane and tell him to put the decision on hold."

Ken later reported back that Bud would do so but was "unhappy."

The action by the Crisis Pre-Planning Group was more than astonishing; it was dumbfounding. Power was simply being usurped by the NSC adviser's staff. At the very moment President Reagan was putting Central America policy under my control, this covert action was proceeding as if nothing had changed. I had the directive ferreted out that states that the CPPG *has no decision-making role and no such mandate.* Saturday at noon, Clark, Baker, and Meese, all casually dressed, walked into my suite in Williamsburg. Clark handed me a revised Central America organization chart. The upshot of it was to negate my idea of line management, with which the president had agreed. I refused to accept it.

"I report to the president, not to the NSC staff," I told him. Clark and I then argued about who would be our next ambassador to El Salvador. I had thought this over at length and wanted Tom Pickering, one of our top foreign service officers. Clark would not give a straight reply but went on and on about various possible nominees for various jobs. Again, Clark had stubbornly strong opinions but lacked the depth of experience and judgment to back them up.

Our meeting ended with nothing resolved. A few hours later, I saw a report on the evening television news that a Mr. Thomas, who was unknown to me, would be appointed ambassador to El Salvador. We'll see, I thought. That evening, the Williamsburg summit was getting into full swing. There was no time to continue this battle, but the atmosphere between Clark and me was tense.

On Sunday morning, May 29, in the midst of managing the summit for the president, I thought over Clark's attempt to pick the new ambassador to El Salvador. Pickering would be the first test case: would I be able to pick our ambassador to El Salvador or not? The answer would indicate whether or not the president's assurances to me would stick. I also thought about the overreaching attempts of lower-level bureaucrats to decide on a step like mining the harbors of another country. Such a decision should not be made even with the secretary of state in the chair: only the president, or vice president in his absence, should decide such a matter. To have this approved by a meeting of people who had not even been confirmed by the Senate, let alone elected by the people, was dangerous. It was beyond my comprehension that staff people would take it upon themselves to assume such a responsibility.

By the time we returned from Williamsburg, I had won the battle to send Tom Pickering as ambassador to El Salvador, but even this victory soon became a problem. Pickering had been recommended to me as the quintessential foreign service professional, but when reached in London, where he was on leave from his post as ambassador to Nigeria, he was extremely reluctant to accept the job. Eventually, he did, but not until it had been reported to me that he had decided to say no and that he had misgivings about our whole Central America policy. So I got my man. And any doubts I had over his hesitation were later removed by his brilliant performance.

On May 31 the president chaired a National Security Planning Group (NSPG) meeting to review the CIA proposal to mine Nicaraguan waters. Again, I opposed this strongly. The CIA did not prepare its case well, and the president's innate common sense emerged. He did not approve the mining idea. President Reagan, I saw, was a cautious though decisive man, sensitive about being viewed as too pugnacious.

On Sunday, June 5, the president and Nancy Reagan had dinner with O'Bie and me at our home in Bethesda. The Williamsburg meeting had just ended, and we were feeling a glow about its success. The evening started with a general flurry of excitement in our neighborhood. The Secret Service had been insistent that, for security reasons, no prior notice be given that the president was coming our way. But they had gone through the neighborhood all day long, seeing to it that cars were not parked on the street, which alerted everybody that something special would be taking place. By the time Ronald and Nancy Reagan drove up with the large motorcade that always accompanies the president, the neighbors knew perfectly well what was up, and people turned out all along the street, waving and cheering. The president and the first lady waved back and enjoyed the outpouring of warmth.

The conversation that evening gave me an insight into the president's thinking about some key personnel decisions, just as my earlier dinner at the White House with the Reagans in February had given me insights into the president's thinking about China and the Soviet Union, and, as I later realized, SDI. I learned something else of interest that evening: the president was uneasy with Bill Clark, and Nancy had no time for him at all. This was in my mind as I found myself in the following week once again trying to establish a clear organization of Central America policy. I wanted to use the same system that worked in other areas. Interagency groups and senior interagency groups would discuss and pass options and judgments up the line. The Crisis Pre-Planning Group would be used only when there was a genuine crisis and in an advisory role only. Principal decisions would be made by the president after all relevant agencies had an opportunity for input. The NSC staff would coordinate this effort. Decisions would be implemented by the departments.

By the end of June, the idea of a bipartisan commission on Central

America had gathered a lot of momentum. We needed a way to gain bipartisan support for a sensibly tough and ambitious policy toward Central America. Senator Scoop Jackson had proposed the idea, saying that communism in Central America was a problem not only for El Salvador but for the whole region. "The real problem, the strategic problem, is Mexico. The real danger is the destabilization of Mexico," said Scoop in a telephone interview quoted in the *New York Times* on March 1. He continued: "My concern from the beginning has been that Mexico is the ultimate objective of those forces seeking to destabilize countries in Central America. Mexico's the ultimate target."

On July 11, the president called me to get my view about a potential chairman. "What about Henry Kissinger?" he asked, commenting that Henry's past gave him a considerable amount of political baggage. I felt that no one we could bring in would be better at coming to grips with a foreign policy issue in all of its dimensions. I liked the idea. "We should shape up the appointment so that we take the baggage off Henry's back," I said.

I had been told that Kissinger was worried about my reaction to his chairing of the bipartisan commission, so I invited him to lunch to express my wholehearted support. Henry wanted to be located in and administered by the State Department. He also wanted to include Mexico within the commission's mandate. Including Mexico made sense conceptually but would take the focus off our primary objective, Central America. Henry accepted the argument. His most important appointment would be that of the executive director, who would run the staff of the commission. He and I both knew and admired Harry Shlaudeman, the foreign service's most experienced Latin America diplomat and a man of great distinction. Harry accepted this tough assignment.

Counterproductive Proposals

Bill Clark meanwhile continued to press one idea after another on me, most of them ill formed or unwise. I found myself trying to stop or shape up the flow of suggestions. I had to keep him from simply having the president name the members of the commission without congressional consultation. Then he came up with an elaborate public affairs strategy requiring appearances by twenty-four assistant secretary–level officials in twelve media centers each month. I thought the idea was absolutely wild. "This cannot possibly be sustained. I don't like decisions that can't be implemented. I take these things seriously. I don't want someone six months from now telling me that Central America went down the drain because I did not carry out directives that were impossible," I told Clark.

Clark backed off, then returned to the sensitive question of U.S. military trainers in El Salvador. He raised the idea of a potential directive that would, he said, simply order a review and an increase in the number of trainers "if necessary." "We have established centers in Honduras to train men in the El Salvador armed forces," I replied. All this amounted to drastic action. I could see from my discussion that the implications had not been thought through at all. Under questioning, Clark seemed to back away from this attempt to increase the American advisory effort in El Salvador. During this conversation, I suddenly realized that Clark was holding a draft National Security Decision Directive (NSDD), which he had already gotten the president to sign. I read a sentence suggesting that Congress was not providing adequate security assistance and that, therefore, the executive branch had to make up for this inadequacy. I pointed out to Clark that this had major constitutional implications. "You cannot spend money that is not appropriated," I told him. Moreover, the draft NSDD stipulated that we study interdiction and quarantine.

The fact was that the crisis in El Salvador was beginning to be overshadowed by the crisis in Nicaragua. Some 2,000 Cuban military and security advisers were reported to have arrived following a visit to Managua by General Arnaldo Ochoa Sánchez, who had headed the Cuban expeditionary force to Angola. In the first six months of 1983, Nicaragua had received eleven shiploads of arms from Soviet-bloc countries, almost the same amount they had shipped in the entire previous year. In the Nicaraguan countryside, young men were rallying to an anti-Marxist Contra movement, but they would need training and support. And with the increasing opposition in the House of Representatives, our ability to provide that support was uncertain.

The situation called for very careful handling. The Pentagon wanted to conduct exercises in and around Central America, and Clark, too, seemed on the side of flexing American muscle. I was in favor of strength to support our diplomacy, but deployed in a way that would at least minimize congressional objections. Otherwise, the show of strength would turn into a display of weakness. In February, the United States and Honduras conducted a massive military exercise called "Big Pine." No combat troops were involved, but the movement caused irritation on the Hill, not least because of a lack of effective prior notice. In March the United States and selected allies conducted a joint maneuver off Puerto Rico that involved two aircraft carriers and scores of other naval craft.

The biggest shock for me came with the revelation, in late July, that the United States was planning "Big Pine II," a six-month-long exercise off both the Atlantic and Pacific coasts of Nicaragua during which American and Honduran troops would conduct war games on Honduran territory. Three thousand or more U.S. combat troops would be involved. The Pentagon had wanted to do it, and Bill Clark had approved it. I was totally blindsided, and I did not know the extent to which President Reagan had been involved. I knew that I had no chance to give him my views. The news cut right across Dick Stone's mission in the area, catching him completely by surprise, and it came just before an important congressional vote on Contra aid.

The situation was bizarre. Here we had a Pentagon that seemed to take any means to avoid the *actual use* of American military power but every opportunity to *display* it. We had an administration engaged in continuous, divisive debate about the use of strength versus diplomacy at a time when we needed *both* and had *neither* in Central America. We had a Congress whose most active members saw the specter of another Vietnam and seemed determined to prevent such an outcome by denying the United States the ability to use any aspect of national power to deal with Communist advances in Central America. Playing right into this were Bill Clark and Pentagon planners, who now sprung massive U.S. military movements on the world, heightening the worst fears in ways that would only further deprive the United States of the necessary range of options.

The news of Big Pine II caused the worst legislative defeat of the Reagan administration to that date. On July 28, 1983, the House voted 228 to 195 to shut off covert assistance to the Contras *just* as they were winning new adherents to their rebellion against the Sandinistas-turned-Marxists. To me this was a disaster. Congressman Trent Lott, the Republican whip, said that the decision to send troops to Central America for extended maneuvers had greatly upset members of Congress and damaged the administration's cause. "The timing of events this week certainly didn't help," he said.

The president was frustrated; he was determined to see communism blocked and democracy built in Central America, but his administration's *actions* in Central America were destroying his administration's *policy* with Congress.[5]

My Fight with Clark and the NSC Staff

I was even more troubled than President Reagan. At a NSC meeting on July 8, the chief of naval operations, Admiral James Watkins, had referred to "integral Cuban units" arriving in Nicaragua. If the admiral was right, I responded, then we needed to point to the marker I laid down with Gromyko in 1982[6] and tell the Cubans and the Soviets what we had seen.

---

5. We fought back in the Senate, and covert Contra aid later was continued by virtue of a compromise reached with the House in the House-Senate conference at the end of the year.

6. I told Gromyko in our meeting in New York during the UN General Assembly that the introduction of advanced aircraft into Nicaragua would be "unacceptable" to us and would be regarded as an "unfriendly act." Gromyko and I both knew these were strong words in diplomacy.

My advice was ignored. I later found that by general agreement in the intelligence community, there was no factual basis for Watkins's report. Whether Watkins's inaccurate statements had subsequently been clarified to the president, I did not know. Cap Weinberger at the same meeting had spoken of Soviet troopships, but these later turned out to be ships loaded with students.

I was concerned that President Reagan had made decisions about maneuvers and potential military actions on the basis of faulty intelligence. Tony Motley told me that there clearly had been a separate channel from the Defense Department to the NSC staff and then to the president. The president had been given a Defense Department paper of recommendations without any of the accompanying interagency papers. The press, Motley said, was reporting, on the basis of NSC staff and Defense Department backgrounders, that the purpose of the maneuvers was intimidation and interdiction. I was totally out of the decision loop.

Deeply disturbed by the series of decisions on Central America about which I was unaware, I was further rocked back by the news, on July 23, 1983, that Bud McFarlane had been sent on a secret mission to the Middle East the previous week: he had conferred with Syria's President Assad, the Lebanese, and Saudi King Fahd. Two days later, I was told that a decision "might have been made" to blockade Nicaragua and that Jeane Kirkpatrick had said as much publicly. On the telephone with Bill Clark on Monday, July 25, I asked point-blank, "Has there been a decision to form a blockade of Nicaragua?"

"No," he said.

I now realized that I could not trust the answers I got from the White House staff. The functions of the secretary of state were being usurped by the NSC staff. I was at the end of my rope.

I wondered whether Clark and his NSC staff at the White House could see what they were doing. I doubted it. They couldn't perceive how self-defeating their actions were. That was the irony. "They keep shooting themselves in the foot," Ray Seitz commented.

"In both feet," I corrected.

That afternoon, July 25, I went over to the White House for my 1:30 appointment with the president. I asked in advance that Vice President Bush, Bill Clark, Jim Baker, and Ed Meese be present, too. I told the president, "The process of managing foreign policy has gone completely off the track." I related the decisions about major military maneuvers in Central America as an example. Something of great importance was being done without my knowledge and behind my back and, quite possibly, was authorized by the president on the basis of faulty intelligence.

I brought up Bud McFarlane's trip to the Middle East. "When you do this, you undercut me. You undercut your Middle East negotiator, Phil

Habib. You send a message to Middle East leaders that if they don't like what they hear from the secretary of state, they can use another channel, a back channel to the White House. You make it very difficult to conduct foreign policy when you permit this," I told President Reagan. "There is no way I can do my job as secretary of state when secret missions like this take place without my knowledge. It completely undermines the confidence of foreign governments in dealing with me."

I told the president that he could have either of two kinds of secretary of state. One could be called upon to do whatever the NSC staff said the president wanted, to manage the humdrum work of foreign policy but to leave everything of consequence to the White House. "You can conduct foreign policy out of the White House if you want to, but you don't need me under those circumstances," I said. If he wanted an errand boy, he should get somebody else. The other way, I said, was to place confidence in the secretary of state as the central figure in the management of foreign policy for the president. Let the NSC staff be essentially staff to the president and, for that matter, to the secretary of state. "No foreign policy moves should go forward that the secretary of state does not know about and weigh in on. I do not expect to get my way all the time," I said. "That is not the point. The point is to know what is going on so that I can, at a minimum, give you the benefit of my advice."

I gave President Reagan some names he might wish to consider as my successor. "Bill Clark seems to want the job," I said, "because he is trying to run everything. There is also Jeane Kirkpatrick. Or Henry Kissinger. You can get lots of good people," I said. "But what is fundamental is that the process be open and legitimate and provide the secretary of state with a central part."

The president was visibly shaken. I was his choice to be secretary of state, he said. He wanted me to do the job; he had no idea how these things had happened; he could understand how they affected me. I had made myself clear in front of everyone, but even so, I left the Oval Office without a feeling that a definitive change would be made. In the Reagan administration I could not expect to be given a mandate and expect others to respect it; I would have to struggle incessantly to do my job.

That evening at about 6:00, Bill Clark called me on the telephone. He insisted that Tony Motley had been involved in drafting the July 18 memoranda that authorized the Big Pine II exercises and maneuvers. State's Latin America bureau, Clark said, was putting out the story that the maneuvers were going on without the president's knowledge.

I knew that Motley had *not* been involved, and I exploded. "No one in their right mind could put out such a 'story.' The military never does anything like that without orders," I said. "There has been a terrible erosion in the process, much more than people in the meeting this afternoon seemed to realize."

About 7:00 P.M., I received an invitation to an informal dinner with the president at the White House the following week. My visible unhappiness, I felt, had registered on him, and he was seeking to soothe me.

Larry Eagleburger came in to tell me that he had heard Bill Clark was about to ask him if he would replace Bud McFarlane as deputy over at the NSC. I told Larry I doubted Clark had "any intention" of asking him to take on the job. "It is simply a maneuver," I said. It reminded me of President Nixon, who tried to get Senator Byrd to do his bidding by putting the word out that Nixon was considering Byrd for the Supreme Court, which he wasn't.

Late that evening of July 25, I tried to reconstruct what had happened. Just after the president's April speech to a joint session of Congress, people at Defense and the CIA and Jeane Kirkpatrick all surged into a heightened state of alarm over Central America. At the controversial NSC meeting on July 8, Chief of Naval Operations Watkins, against a background of faulty intelligence, had laid out graduated military options. The president had asked, provocatively, "How do we stop Castro with exercises?" The July 12 memo issued as a result of the earlier NSC meeting said that Defense would develop a program of military actions, consulting with State. Defense proceeded to develop a draft, and Motley informally exchanged drafts with Fred Ikle, the under secretary of defense. Motley subsequently found out that Admiral Watkins was wrong about the nature of the Cuban presence in Nicaragua: there was no evidence to substantiate Watkins' claims. Nevertheless, the program went forward.

On July 16, at a Senior Interagency Group (SIG) meeting, Defense withdrew its draft paper and backed off. State should have smelled a rat, Motley realized later. The fact of the matter was that Defense people had already gone to the president. A July 18 memo from Clark to the president (essentially the draft prepared at Defense) triggered the decision to launch the Big Pine II maneuver in Central America. State did not see that memo until July 25. In other words, Clark used the Defense draft to send a decision memo to the president. "We did not see the memo going in, and we did not see the decision coming out," Motley told me. Shortly after July 18, Defense got orders to proceed. It was being said now that "these are normal exercises," but the events themselves suggested that this was not the original intent, and Defense Department spokesmen, on background, had been characterizing the exercises as much more militant.

I was the one who would have to answer questions from Congress as to "What the hell is going on down in Central America?" Defense did not really consider the exercises to be normal, so I could not assert to Congress that this was a "normal activity." We would be using combat troops in Honduras. Some of our ship movements would be new. It was also new that these would be coordinated exercises with an Atlantic and Pacific reach. They were combined sea-air-land exercises considerably beyond anything we had undertaken before in Central America. The White House staff and Defense had come on strong and then, with stories all over the press about escalation in Central America, they ran into a buzz saw in Congress. Now they were going soft.

Early in the morning of July 27, I met with Admiral Thomas Bigley, who briefed me on force dispositions for the Big Pine II exercises. He said they were "special deployments, but the exercises themselves are normal."

"If the president wanted you to interdict, put on a blockade, could you do it?" I asked.

"Yes," Bigley responded.

"So *training* for a blockade is ridiculous. You already have the know-how." The admiral agreed that this was not a training exercise. I told him that if we emphasized the Cuban presence in the region, "then the current exercises imply more in the offing. That's what's tricky. As a military man, I'm sure you don't believe in empty threats."

Shortly afterward, I left my office for the House and later the Senate, where some sixty senators in the Senate secure room awaited me for what turned out to be a highly charged session. Clark joined me, but all questions were directed at me during the session. I emphasized that the purpose of the exercises was deterrence, a warning to the Soviets, Cubans, and Nicaraguans that we could muster great power quickly. I described my earlier exchanges with Foreign Minister Gromyko and my marker, authorized by the president, that MIGs in Nicaragua were "unacceptable" and an "unfriendly act." The Senate audience was on the edge of their seats. I could have heard a pin drop. Oddly enough, at no time did anyone ask whether I knew of the president's decision in advance of the announcement of the actual exercises. That surprised me.

When I got back to my office later that day, Powell Moore, assistant secretary for congressional relations, telephoned to report on what happened after I had left the Senate: "Senators Byrd and Baker jumped all over Clark about the failure of the administration to consult with Congress. Clark responded that he was primed to get more and more active in dealing with Congress and left the impression that any lack of consultation had been the fault of the Department of State."

I was shocked at this bad faith, but I also knew I had a problem on my hands that far transcended an NSC staff–State Department turf fight. Clark was calling the shots in Central America and making dangerous errors. This was more than simple bureaucratic incompetence. The fact that I was not informed could not be dismissed as an oversight. Clark was attempting to run everything and was creating havoc in his wake. Cap Weinberger at Defense, by going along with this process, was also part of the problem.

At my Thursday, July 28, breakfast with Weinberger and others at Defense, I found Cap uninterested in the furor on the Hill and his deputy defense secretary, Paul Thayer, openly contemptuous of Congress. In an overbearing way, Thayer conveyed a sense that we could safely and properly simply "ignore Congress." I was amazed to find myself trying to make elementary points about civics to them. "Congress is provided for in the Constitution," I said. I realized that sometimes they were just blowing off steam in their frustration with Congress, but their rhetorical gunslinging had an underlying tone of conviction to it.

Jon Howe reported from his grapevine that Weinberger thought I had been informed. "Unhappily, he was wrong," I said. Despite our ongoing battles, if Cap said he thought I was informed, I believed him. But he himself had been misled or misinformed.

The perception of Clark's expanding influence over foreign policy was next enhanced by the need to replace Phil Habib as special negotiator for the Middle East. Phil had lost his ability to operate since President Assad of Syria had declared him persona non grata for spurious reasons. Bill Clark wanted Bud McFarlane to get the job, and Bud told me that he was tired of "paper pushing" and wanted to get "back in action." He told me he wanted to retain the title of deputy national security adviser to "increase his stature as negotiator."

State Department spokesman John Hughes told me pointedly, "It is getting into the mind of the press around here that the secretary of state is slowly being nibbled to death."

"No one," Ken Dam told me, "will believe that McFarlane reports to you if he is still deputy national security adviser."

Hughes predicted that the story would be "a shift of power from State to the White House."

"That's always the case," I replied. "That's where the president is. And now the president is much more interested than he was last year."

"But," Eagleburger warned, "perceptions have a great deal to do with your success in this town," and I knew he was right. I did not insist on a change in Bud's title. That would prove to be a mistake. But I had some suspicion that Bud had become too strong for Bill Clark and felt that he deserved a chance for a more operational role.

"I've always tried to avoid reacting to the press," I said to Ray Seitz after the group left. "The point is just to do the job."

"Don't allow yourself," he responded, "to get goaded by pygmies with spears. But there is some substance to what the press says, and some truth. State is not in control of Central America policy." The president was on the hard-line track, and we were trying to use that hard-line track as a basis for diplomacy. I called Bud, congratulated him, and noted that from a mechanical point of view, he would be on the State Department payroll. He would have the rank of ambassador and later ambassador-at-large. His office would be in the State Department.

The storm kept building. Clark was on the cover of *Time* magazine, with the story depicting him as the central figure of the administration in foreign affairs. "Clark takes charge in the White House" was the lead, and as for Central America, the cover featured Clark's "BIG STICK APPROACH," followed by the quote: "We don't want war, but. . . ." As for me, a separate article noted my "disappearing act" as "State Department influence continues to wane."

Later that day, July 29, Nancy Reagan called me. She was furious. She thought Clark ought to be fired. I could tell she was very upset. She knew about the meeting that I had had four days earlier with the president and his advisers. Clark did not have the president's best interests at heart, she said. I told her that I felt Clark was just "in over his head."

I was increasingly convinced that Clark was miserable in his role, but he considered Central America somehow to be familiar territory. Catching the sense from so many White House advisers that Nicaragua and El Salvador were of the utmost national security importance, he focused his efforts there. Every step he took was a misstep, however, and every misstep led him to blame someone else, which in turn led him to try to gather more power in his own hands—with the result that his errors were increasingly, undeniably, his own, and his machinations made the president look like a warmonger. "Deaver and Baker do not like Clark at all," I remarked to Ray Seitz. "In fact, Deaver, Baker, and Nancy want the president to be seen as a man of peace. They are pragmatic. Clark and Weinberger and Ikle want to throw down the gauntlet, but they chicken out when the other guy picks it up. They are confrontational, but when the clutch comes, they won't follow through."

I felt that Clark's departure was only a matter of time. I thought there would be four or five days of press stories about "Clark victorious." My strength is patience. I would let it emerge and choose my time.

Ronald Reagan, with his soft heart, would never fire Clark, but at some point, Nancy would prevail upon him to act in his own interest. I, too, would try again to get the president to come to grips with the problem. In a meeting with the president on Friday, August 5, I expressed again my discomfort and emphasized that it was essential for the two of us to have regularly scheduled discussions. That Sunday night, the president telephoned. He suggested that we get together privately on a regular basis, just the two of us, to talk over foreign policy. I agreed, but said that I thought it might be wise for the national security adviser to be present, as a listener.

"Let's try it with just the two of us first," President Reagan responded.

On Monday, August 8, Mike Deaver called to set up regular meetings for every Wednesday and Friday at 1:30 P.M. Vice President Bush had phoned me a few days before to assure me that I had all his support. "I'm on your side," he had told me.

I soon got word that Clark was asking questions about my private meeting with the president. What was it about? Clark seemed slightly panicky, I was told.

Even as the press was reporting that authority in foreign policy was flowing to Judge Clark, the reality was just the opposite. Within the administration, the inner circle recognized that Clark had botched the job. Authority had already begun to flow out of his hands. The *Time* magazine story on Clark had concluded: "With Shultz receding in influence, Clark will probably be forced into a more public role . . . and a few of Clark's rivals within the Administration relish the prospect, believing that such appearances will lay bare his shaky grasp of foreign policy. Says one detractor: 'I think he'll eventually hang himself.' " I thought it was a sound prediction. Clark was getting heavy publicity, but I knew his days were numbered.

That afternoon, to my relief, I got back to the real issues involving Central America. At the first meeting of the State group working on Central America, attended by our new ambassador to El Salvador, Tom Pickering, we were discussing the elections to come in early 1984. Some voices of concern were raised that elections would polarize the country. "Democracy starts with elections," I said. "We can't afford to delay, even though I understand there is no center, only extremes. My instinct is to push for a presidential election in El Salvador soon. Don't feel blue about the democratic process."

A Staff Reshuffle

And so we moved into the period of the August recess and vacation time. I needed some rest. I returned from my farm in Massachusetts toward the end of August, a few days before the president. All hell was breaking loose in Lebanon. The first three marine casualties occurred. And on September 1, the Soviets shot down Korean Air Lines Flight 007. The atmosphere was instantly supercharged with tension.

McFarlane by this time was well into his new job as Middle East envoy, and as predicted, he was in closer contact with Clark than with me. I did not like the way he was handling his mission. Trying to work out an agreed statement on security between Lebanon and Israel, Bud had lost his composure at a meeting with the Israelis outside Beirut. According to Sam Lewis's account, McFarlane had referred to the presence of Israeli Defense Minister Moshe Arens near Beirut as "an affront." Begin and Shamir were extraordinarily upset and communicated their feeling to Lewis that McFarlane's behavior was totally out of line. Bud was yelling, the Israelis told Lewis: "It was a barracks-room diatribe. He slammed the door, almost broke it. We are not children to be ordered around. There is no precedent for this in the history of U.S.-Israeli relations. After he [McFarlane] left,

Israel and Lebanon had a good bilateral meeting." When Phil Habib was our Middle East negotiator, he used theatrics to good effect; people got his point but didn't take it personally and were amused at his flair for the dramatic. Bud did not possess that gift. He was tied up, ill at ease, and often frustrated.

When McFarlane was back in town, I scheduled a lunch for October 13 with Bill Clark and Bud to make clear my concerns. Bud came into the session knowing that I was displeased with his performance and the way he had managed his role—including his direct calls to Clark rather than reporting back through me.

"I am a marine," Bud responded, upset. "And I report through the chain of command."

That was neither my perception nor the fact, I responded. I made it clear to Bud that I had dealt in Lebanon only through him. I did not undercut him by going around him and dealing with leaders directly. "Now the Saudis, the Syrians, and the Lebanese think the State Department is not in control. They believe the action is at the NSC." Bud, I knew, had met with Bill Clark when they were both in Rome. Bud had told Larry Eagleburger that he didn't go to Israel on that trip because he didn't want to upset the Arabs. "That's a terrible reason," I said. "We can't give so much to Syria that our own envoy won't go to Israel."

Despite the tension between me and McFarlane at lunch that day, Clark had been uncommonly pleasant. It struck me as unusual. That afternoon, Mike Deaver telephoned me, "Clark is being moved to become secretary of the interior." I thought about my conversation with the president and Nancy at my house in early June. The president was uneasy with Clark, and Nancy, I increasingly realized, viewed Clark as a liability and wouldn't even talk to him. At 5:00 P.M., the president publicly announced Clark's departure from the White House.

It was a day of lashing rain and high wind, the kind of day that seems to induce massive telephone use in Washington; the phone line rumor spreading around town was that I had given the president an ultimatum: me or Clark. It was not true.

Not long after the announcement, Mike Deaver telephoned again to ask me to support Jim Baker as Clark's replacement as NSC adviser; Deaver would then take over as White House chief of staff. At this point, everybody was calling me because they knew I had a private lunch scheduled with the president the next day. The evening news focused mainly on Clark's lack of experience for the Interior job. I thought, well, he loves the outdoors, he's a rancher, likes to be on a horse, and he's probably relieved to be out of the national security business.

The choice for national security adviser, I thought, came down to two people—Jim Baker or Bud McFarlane. The vice president, Mike Deaver, and probably Nancy wanted Baker, I figured, and the people in the NSC system wanted Bud. Deaver asked me to stop by his office before lunch the next day. There was a move afoot to postpone the decision, which I thought was a bad idea. The battle lines were drawn. The president had a huge stake in getting a top person who could work well with him and the rest of us. But he should decide as promptly as possible.

I felt Jim Baker performed an essential role in the White House. He was doing a tough job with brilliance. He had a deft touch. He might have some problems with the right wing, but Baker was by miles the most competent person over there and would be good to work with. Bud, I realized, got very uptight under pressure, but he was an experienced hand in national security affairs, had worked on the Hill, and knew Soviet and arms control issues well. Brent Scowcroft's name came up, but he had been critical of SDI, and he was not really on the president's wavelength on other issues. At lunch with the president, I told him that as far as I was concerned, Jim Baker would be an excellent selection for national security adviser. Afterward, we had a National Security Planning Group meeting on Lebanon, but the president was preoccupied with the question of Clark's replacement.

After the meeting, Bill Clark invited Cap Weinberger and Bill Casey into his office and rather obviously excluded me. At 3:10, Mike Deaver called and told me that opposition to Jim Baker had developed: Weinberger said appointing Baker would be politically unwise, and Casey said it would stir up "Debategate": the FBI was then investigating the 1980 Reagan campaign's acquisition of briefing books belonging to the Carter campaign. Baker and Casey were in bitter disagreement about what had happened and how. At 3:30, the president called to say he would be holding off on his decision for Clark's replacement for a short time. Ten minutes later, Nancy called. She was obviously troubled. The president, I felt, had in fact decided on Jim Baker when I had left the White House, but when he ran into opposition from Weinberger and Casey, he hesitated. I told Nancy that I could work with Baker. "Baker sparkles," I said. Bud, I thought, would be okay at the job.

The president called a few minutes later and asked me to talk to Cap Weinberger and Bill Casey. I set 5:00 P.M. for the meeting. Just before that time, both the president and the vice president telephoned, each obviously wanting to put Baker's candidacy across. I tried. But I did not succeed. Weinberger and Casey seemed to checkmate all candidates, although Jeane Kirkpatrick stood well with both of them. I respected her intelligence, but she was not well suited to the job. Her strength was in her capacity for passionate advocacy. She was not at all the dispassionate broker and faithful representative of divergent positions that the national security adviser needs to be. After meeting with Cap and Casey, I went over to Vice President Bush's office to have a drink with him before going home. He wanted Baker for the job. That was my preference, too. However, I was sure by now that would not happen: Casey knew that Baker would be impervious to his pressure and would downgrade his influence.

The next day, I heard that the opposition from Weinberger and Casey had eliminated Baker from the job, that Jeane Kirkpatrick was in the process of resigning as our ambassador to the United Nations, and that, over at the White House, there was talk about sending Jim Baker to the United Nations. I opposed that idea. If Baker wanted to get out of the chief of staff job, I hoped he would remain in the White House or at least in Washington. If he went to New York, he would be out on the margins. He was needed at the center. President Reagan called. He was now moving toward Bud for the job. I told the president that I could work with Bud; I wanted the president to make his own decision. I knew we would then have to select a new special negotiator for the Middle East to replace Bud, and I felt that would be for the best. On October 17, 1983, the president announced the appointment of Bud McFarlane as his national security adviser.

Usurpation of Power

With a new NSC adviser, I hoped the problems I encountered with the NSC staff under Clark would be dealt with. People on the NSC staff were so obsessed with the issues of Central America that their judgment had become flawed and their actions counterproductive. My struggle with the NSC staff centered on the problem of headstrong people who were over-zealous and all too eager to get involved in *operations*. Whenever they did so, they got the president—and our foreign policy—in deep trouble. I told Bud how important it was to keep the NSC staff *out of operations*. The job of coordination should give them plenty to do.

Time and again, I had seen White House and NSC staff members all too ready to take matters into their own hands, usurping power and authority that was not theirs and going off on their own. As one who had blown the whistle more than once, I became in their eyes an obstacle—someone to be eliminated or circumvented. Their answer seemed to be to proceed without my knowledge. So I knew I must be watchful. I suspected that they regarded the president in the same way, acting sometimes without his knowledge or at least without his full appreciation of what the foreign policy implications were or of congressional perceptions and reactions.

Central America policy was far more polarized politically than any other area of foreign policy. And my *procedural* struggles and frustrations were, in fact, struggles over *substance*. My private meetings with the president were crucial, I knew. But I also knew that there was no effective presidential policy without a supportive staff. I had to help the president make the NSC process work. Making the process work was the only way to explore the issues fully and to examine the alternatives carefully.

The NSC system seemed to work reasonably on many issues. Why not on Central America? The effort to answer that question and to come up with a solution was, and would continue to be, a central source of tension and frustration for me. More important were the real costs of a flawed NSC system: damage to the president and damage to policy. The stakes were high, and not just in Central America. The president and his policies were worth every ounce of effort and all the support I could muster. But Central America policy was a swamp.

CHAPTER 20

Grenada: A Shot Heard
Round the World

At 2:45 on Saturday morning, October 22, 1983, I was enjoying a good night's sleep in the Eisenhower cottage at the Augusta National Golf Club when I was awakened by a telephone call from Bud McFarlane with information about critical developments in Grenada. Bud then called and awakened President Reagan and we gathered in the solarium, where there was a secure phone. The situation was breaking fast, as we had known before leaving Washington. That was one reason why Bud, just a week into his new post as national security adviser, had come along on this golfing weekend. The president had considered briefly on Friday whether to go to Augusta at all, but he and the rest of us felt that the sudden cancellation of a long-planned trip would bring on intense and undesirable speculation.

Foreign service officer Frank McNeil, Bud told us, had just reported on his discussions in Barbados with the leaders of the island nations in the Eastern Caribbean. Formally constituting the Organization of Eastern Caribbean States (OECS),[1] they requested urgently that the United States help them bring order to Grenada and restore democratic government there. They were genuinely frightened that the emergence of a Soviet-Cuban–dominated state, through literally murderous events, would threaten their own democratic governments. Mrs. Eugenia Charles, prime minister of Dominica and chairman of the OECS, remembered well an abortive coup attempt launched against her from Grenada a year earlier.

---

1. The member states of the OECS were: Antigua and Barbuda, Dominica, Grenada, Montserrat, St. Lucia, St. Kitts-Nevis, St. Vincent, and the Grenadines.

Chaos Mounts in Grenada

The scene these leaders witnessed on October 22 was chaotic and ominous. We had seen the same picture and were also gravely concerned for the safety of a large contingent of American students—around 1,000—attending a medical school in Grenada, a nation of scarcely 100,000 people.

The Grenada problem had been of concern for some time and was now developing swiftly. Back on March 23, in a speech most notable for the announcement of his Strategic Defense Initiative, President Reagan had highlighted some alarming developments in Grenada and had shown an aerial photo of an airfield being built there by Cubans. Its potential military use was clear, and it was designed to accommodate large airplanes.

Grenada, a former British colony that attained internal self-government in 1967 and independence in 1974, had been dominated since the 1950s by the flamboyant populism and strong-arm tactics of its prime minister, Sir Eric Gairy. A major opposition party was formed in 1973, the New Jewel Movement, led by Maurice Bishop. It protested against economic and social conditions in Grenada and abuses of power by the Gairy regime. Its program stressed socialist and nationalist ideals. On March 13, 1979, in a nearly bloodless coup, Gairy was thrown out, and Bishop became prime minister. The new government was initially welcomed by Grenadians, as it promised to hold early elections and respect basic human rights.

These promises were never honored. The Bishop regime suspended the country's constitution, refused to call early elections, ridiculed English-style democracy as "Westminster hypocrisy," and turned instead to the Cuban model of "revolutionary democracy," which it tried to implement with Cuban aid. Human rights were violated regularly. Habeas corpus was abolished for political detainees, of whom there were almost a hundred by 1982. Freedom of the press and other political freedoms were abolished as well. Bishop established close ties with the Soviet Union and Cuba. In January 1980, for example, Grenada was the only Latin American country other than Cuba to vote against the UN resolution condemning the Soviet invasion of Afghanistan.

As far back as 1980, there were as many as a hundred Cuban military advisers in Grenada. There were also several hundred "construction workers" ostensibly engaged in helping to build the new airport in the southwestern corner of the island. Much of the construction was military in nature, and many of the construction workers were military personnel.

In May 1983, Prime Minister Bishop was invited to Washington in an effort on our part to size him up and see how committed he was to his present course. He met with Bill Clark and Ken Dam. They talked to him about improving relations between Grenada and the United States. These discussions apparently made the harder-line Communists in Grenada uneasy about Bishop. Cuba increased the number of its military advisers, with the notion that they would be able to take command of the hundreds of Cuban soldiers who were working on construction jobs, mostly at the airport. Meanwhile, Bishop attempted to burnish his Communist credentials. He made a trip to Eastern European capitals seeking support for his regime, which was foundering. Bishop then went to Cuba to meet with Fidel Castro in early October.

On October 12, a long-standing conflict between Prime Minister Bishop and Deputy Prime Minister Bernard Coard, who headed a more radical faction of the government, erupted in a fight in the Grenadian cabinet. Ostensibly, as the result of a rumor that he sought Bishop's assassination, Coard resigned. But on the night of October 13, Bishop was placed under house arrest. On October 15, Radio Free Grenada, which was run by Coard's wife, Phyllis, announced the arrest of three cabinet ministers and the replacement of Bishop as prime minister by Bernard Coard. An angry crowd of 300 gathered outside the government-controlled newspaper to protest. By October 18, five cabinet members had resigned, and one of them, Unison Whiteman, the foreign minister, said that "Comrade Coard, who is now running Grenada, has refused to engage in serious talks to resolve the crisis." On October 19, the airport at Grenada was closed, and flights from Barbados were turned back. Radio Free Grenada, the only source of news, went off the air. School children demonstrated for Bishop's return to office.

A crowd of thousands, apparently led by Whiteman, on October 19 marched to Bishop's residence, freed him, and proceeded to the downtown area toward Fort Rupert, also the police headquarters and the point guarding the entry to St. George's quiet, horseshoe-shaped harbor. There troops loyal to Coard, some in armored personnel carriers, surrounded Bishop and others, separated them from the crowd amid gunfire, killing bystanders and supporters of Bishop. Bishop and his circle were marched to Fort Rupert with their hands over their heads. There they were all executed by a firing squad. Radio Free Grenada came back on the air and announced the deaths and the formation of a Revolutionary Military Council headed by the army's chief general, Hudson Austin. An around-the-clock shoot-on-sight curfew was also announced. Journalists from the international press who arrived at the airport were immediately deported. Bernard Coard himself was placed under "protective custody."[2] Apparently, General Austin and his Cuban-trained comrades were in charge.

We were genuinely concerned that a large number of the some 1,000 American students attending medical school in Grenada could be taken hostage either as a group or one by one. The other Caribbean nations

---

2. Coard was tried and convicted in 1986, along with thirteen other codefendants, of killing Bishop and ten others.

worried that the Cubans would take over Grenada and threaten their own democracy and independence. We made an effort to evacuate the students through a Pan Am charter, but the plane was refused the right to land. We made another effort by chartering a cruise ship; it was denied permission to dock.

On October 20, the prime minister of Barbados, Tom Adams, declared, "I am absolutely horrified at these brutal and vicious murders." Describing the new regime, he said, "I do not think it will be possible to accommodate so wide a range of governments within the Caribbean. It goes far beyond ideological pluralism. This is the difference between barbarians and human beings." Other leaders in the Caribbean spoke in similar terms, and Prime Minister Charles, condemning the killings in Grenada, said her government would have no dealings with those who now "unlawfully" constituted the government of Grenada.

Meanwhile, we, too, had been busy. Back in the middle of the week of October 10, Assistant Secretary Tony Motley and his colleagues in our Latin America bureau had convened an interagency group meeting to evaluate developments. Then, on October 13, and again on the next day, the State Department drew up evacuation plans for the American students and reviewed them with the Joint Chiefs of Staff, as the evacuation would have to be carried out by the U.S. military. We could see by Saturday, October 15, that the situation was deteriorating. On October 18, after a discussion with Tony Motley, I authorized the establishment of a special task force on Grenada in the State Department. This put into place a round-the-clock watch and, with Tony as our leader, got us all mentally and administratively ready as the problem became more grave. An oral request had come in from Mrs. Charles on October 17 for help from the United States, and by the following day, on behalf of President Reagan, I asked her for a formal evaluation by the OECS. This served two purposes: first, it attended to her request and showed her that we were responsive and alert, and, second, it set the stage for the United States to act in a manner consistent with our national interests and with international law. With the situation becoming increasingly ominous in Grenada, Mrs. Charles went to the French and the British on October 19, but they declined to help her.

Tony Motley, who had spent ten years in the air force, including service during the Vietnam War, had several long sessions during this period with Jack Vessey, chairman of the Joint Chiefs of Staff, and his aide, Admiral Art Moreau, who attended the interagency group meetings. Tony had attended a Crisis Pre-Planning Group (CPPG) meeting chaired by Bud McFarlane on Thursday, October 20. The possibility of having to use force in Grenada had been discussed. Lieutenant Colonel Oliver North, a member of the group, mentioned that the marine replacement force for Lebanon, a sizable force, fully equipped, had left Norfolk, Virginia, that morning, steaming south before turning east. Motley suggested that as a matter of prudence the force continue steaming south for a day or so. Moreau, representing the Joint Chiefs, said absolutely not.

In the subsequent discussion, Tony informed me, the question was raised again with Moreau: wasn't the decision on the marine contingent a prudent, low-profile, low-risk move? Wasn't the only downside perhaps one or possibly two days' delay in the rotation of marines in Beirut while gaining us valuable reaction time if we needed it? Moreau continued to say no. He finally said the chairman of the Joint Chiefs would not consider changing the route of the marines without a written order from the president. The meeting broke up on that note. Immediately afterward, Bud McFarlane drafted an order from the president to the chairman, directing him to keep that convoy going south. The president quickly signed it, and the Joint Chiefs complied.

We had no embassy on Grenada but charged our ambassador on Barbados, Milan Bish, to keep track of events there through occasional visits and other means. We found that Bish had recently prohibited embassy political and U.S. Information Agency officers from even visiting Grenada to do the normal contact and reporting work. His rationale, as we learned it, seemed to be: these are Communists; therefore, they are evil and not trustworthy; therefore, we shouldn't talk to them. This was hardly what we needed. The upshot was that we had neither current information nor good contacts with whom to talk. Accordingly, we came to depend on the British on Barbados, who did keep in contact with Grenada, for information about what was happening there. Unfortunately, our ambassador to Barbados was inexperienced in government and diplomacy, and the British high commissioner there had an American wife who was said not to be shy about expressing her views in opposition to Ronald Reagan. So the relationship between the American and British contingents in Barbados was chilly rather than cooperative. Tony Motley suspected at the time, and later confirmed, that the British high commissioner's reporting to London was consistently that the Americans were typically making much ado about nothing.

The intelligence picture was different, however. The British and American working relationship meant that analysis was shared, as was the conclusion that developments on the scene in Grenada were alarming. Tony Motley and Larry Eagleburger met with the British ambassador to Washington, Sir Oliver Wright, who provided detailed information in writing on the Grenada constitution and on the precise line of authority from the queen to the Commonwealth, the governor-general, and the Grenada government. This information would be invaluable to us in defining the options for helping Grenadians establish a government on their island in the event of U.S. intervention.

A Decision for the President

Before leaving for Augusta on Friday, October 21, I met with Tony Motley. He brought me up-to-date on the rioting and gunfire in Grenada and the mood of the leaders of the Caribbean countries. The Caribbean leaders were out in front, he said, and we wanted to keep them that way. His view was that Venezuela was not likely to get involved, so it would be a Caribbean effort if anything went forward.

As we talked, I found that Tony and I were both increasingly convinced we had run out of ways to accomplish a peaceful evacuation of the American students and that the situation on the ground was deteriorating into total anarchy. Conditions were ripe, as both Tony and I saw it, for hostage taking. We both had the searing memory of Tehran and the sixty-six Americans seized from our embassy on November 4, 1979, and held hostage for well over a year. We both knew what Ronald Reagan's reaction would be to such a development in Grenada. He would not stand still while American hostages were held for 444 days. In fact, he probably wouldn't stand still for a week. With as many as 1,000 students scattered between two campuses, the town, and the countryside, much blood would be shed if our forces had to go in to rescue students or other American citizens taken hostage or held in some sort of forcible detention. We had to avoid such a situation.

"I want to make sure you are on board," Tony said.

"If we can bring this student rescue off, it would be a damn good thing," I replied. "We should think about Suriname, too." I had in mind the murderous regime of Desi Bouterse in Suriname, his Cuban orientation, and our frustration over our inability to deal decisively with that development. I commented that Bud McFarlane would be in Augusta, so I would be able to go over our plans further with him there.

Motley told me that the OECS meeting would take place in Barbados while we were in Augusta and that we would be sending foreign service officer Frank McNeil to be on hand. McNeil was to get a clear idea of what the OECS nations wanted and what they were prepared to say publicly.

As Motley put it, "Our mission just has to be either to get the students out, peacefully if possible, or to get 100 percent assurance that they are safe." One hundred percent is a hard number to approach, particularly under the chaotic conditions that prevailed in Grenada.

On October 21, Mrs. Charles convened the emergency meeting of the Organization of Eastern Caribbean States, plus Jamaica and Barbados, in Barbados. At this meeting, the assembled nations unanimously resolved to intervene by force in Grenada if the United States would assist them. The intervention would conform to the OECS charter provision that the heads of government could collectively agree to take whatever measures were necessary to defend the region and preserve the peace. Grenada, a member of this organization, did not attend the meeting. That same day, Grenada's ambassador to the Organization of American States resigned, and Cuba issued a statement asserting its noninvolvement but reaffirming its support for the "revolutionary process" in Grenada.

The urgent request for help from the small democratic nations of the Caribbean was presented to the president and me when we were awakened in Augusta at 2:45 A.M. on Saturday, October 22. We came up to speed quickly. Bud McFarlane and I discussed emerging developments briefly, then gave the president a summary of the events that had transpired, leading up to this request. Frank McNeil had reported that the OECS states, and particularly Barbados, were prepared to call publicly for U.S. intervention in Grenada in order to restore democratic institutions and bring order to the island. We were confronted with life-threatening danger to some 1,000 American students. We were also presented with an urgent and forthright request and with a stated willingness on the part of those states to make their request publicly.

President Reagan's reaction was decisive. What kind of a country would we be, he asked, if we refused to help small but steadfast democratic countries in our neighborhood to defend themselves against the threat of this kind of tyranny and lawlessness? Furthermore, Americans were in serious danger of being killed or taken hostage. We had to respond positively. By 3:35 A.M., Vice President Bush had put together a secure conference call with General Jack Vessey, chairman of the Joint Chiefs of Staff, Cap Weinberger, Tony Motley, Jim Baker, Ed Meese, John Poindexter, and John McMahon. I urged that we take action. Weinberger said that we didn't know enough to act. Vice President Bush was worried that an all-English-speaking rescue would look bad; he wanted us to try to enlist Venezuelan help. President Reagan gave his views, which were clear and unambiguous. A request to Venezuela would delay our action and might well leak, thereby forgoing the advantage of surprise. Ronald Reagan was ready to go.

After the conference call had been completed, I suggested to the president that he call Jack Vessey back and ask him what the numbers of troops were that would be required for this operation. "After he has told you, Mr. President, I suggest that you tell him to double it." He did call, and that helped reinforce the message to our military leaders that the president meant business. He also ordered the State Department and the Defense Department to move beyond a "warning order" status and prepare for a noncombatant evacuation order, including an invasion plan. This, too, served to keep the Defense Department moving.

So, in the early morning of Saturday, October 22, President Reagan, with McFarlane and me at his side supporting him fully, made the decision to go ahead with a rescue operation, to be launched on Monday night or Tuesday. The president, Bud, and I discussed whether, in the light of this impending major action, we should return to Washington. We decided it would be inadvisable, as it would only stir up intense speculation about what was in the offing. We knew that if this military operation was to be successful and if it was to take place before the Cubans on Grenada got around to thinking about hostages, it would have to be carried out quickly and secretly.

I talked to Tony Motley in Washington at 4:30 A.M. and gave my guidance to him and his deputies. We had to move quickly, before this window of opportunity closed. We couldn't let the Pentagon drag out our preparations until it was too late, which I feared they might do. Then, with Bud McFarlane constantly in touch by secure phone and calling us periodically, President Reagan and I, along with Senator Nick Brady and Treasury Secretary Don Regan, set out on our planned schedule, to tackle the Augusta golf course. To cancel would have started rumors. We played nine holes in the morning, checked our phones again over lunch, and started out again in the early afternoon. As we arrived at the sixteenth hole, the Secret Service suddenly descended on us. As if by magic, an armored car appeared into which they stuffed the president, then me, then Don Regan. "What about Brady?" I asked. They then brought him in, too. Within ten minutes a helicopter was hovering overhead, and I was told that *Air Force One* was on the tarmac, ready to go.

An intruder, we were told, had broken into the Augusta National Golf Club and was at that very moment in the pro shop, holding three people at gunpoint, having fired one round through the door just to show he meant business. He was demanding to see President Reagan. The Secret Service didn't know at this point whether this was just an isolated individual or whether there was a group behind him, so they were taking no chances. He was finally disarmed and placed under arrest. It turned out that he was alone. That was the end of our golf game. We went back to the cottage, where we had dinner.

At 2:30 the next morning, Sunday, October 23, Bud McFarlane again awakened President Reagan and me, this time with the devastating news that our marine barracks in Lebanon had been demolished by a car bomb. Casualties were heavy. We packed up and headed back for Washington. No one suspected there was any reason for our early departure other than the disaster in Lebanon. We were wheels down at Andrews at 8:20 A.M. as word came in that the high-rise building housing the French contingent in the multinational force (MNF) also had been hit by a terrorist suicide bomber. I went right to the Situation Room in the White House, where we dealt with both crises—in Beirut and in Grenada—at once. President Reagan dispatched a message to President Mitterrand about Beirut and one to Prime Minister Thatcher about Grenada; we decided to send Marine Commandant General P. X. Kelley to Beirut and Frank McNeil to the

Eastern Caribbean. The Defense Department people, who were unhappy about being ordered into Grenada, saw the Beirut barracks bombing as an opportunity to get us out of Lebanon, something they had long wanted. In the White House meeting, the president confirmed that we should not change our policy toward Lebanon because of this terrorist attack, but I knew that Cap Weinberger did not agree and would not give up.

One result of the Beirut bombing was that it provided a plausible reason for me to cancel my scheduled trip to El Salvador and Brazil, which had to be put aside because of our Grenada plans. At 2:45 P.M., before I went back over to the White House, Jon Howe, director of State's political and military affairs bureau, came into my office to review the situation in Grenada from a military standpoint. He emphasized what I had been saying to the president: if we are to make a move, we need to do it soon. The question was whether to use SEALs (navy commandos) and airborne rangers at night, followed by marines landing on the beach. Jon Howe recalled President Carter's failed effort to rescue American hostages in Iran, blamed in part on a breakdown of interservice coordination. "Timing is important," Howe said, "and we are losing time. Some reconnaissance flights have been sent out. There are some advance CIA elements under way. But the Pentagon officers are still saying that if we invade, we have to do it right. They are reflecting Cap Weinberger's mood."

Cap was continuing to say that there had to be far greater preparation and a much larger force before an operation could begin. I knew this was the counsel of no action at all. A little before four o'clock, I left for a National Security Planning Group (NSPG) meeting with President Reagan on the crises in Beirut and Grenada. Cap resisted on both fronts. He had not yet approved the dispatch of replacements or reinforcements to Beirut, which shocked even General Vessey. On Grenada, Cap again made clear his preference for a delay and reconsideration of the president's decision to proceed with a rescue operation. The debate was intense. President Reagan held firm.

The prospect of slippage surfaced again early on Monday morning, October 24. Cap was still arguing: now for an ultimatum rather than intervention. Ambassador Oliver Wright informed us that Britain was opposed to any military action. Margaret Thatcher, he said, preferred economic and political pressure. At the same time, however, we received reports that Britain had activated a Special Air Services Commando team and had ordered ships of the Royal Navy to stand offshore Grenada during the coming night. And the governor-general of Grenada, Sir Paul Scoon, was said to be ready to issue an official call for external military assistance.

I spent all afternoon on Monday, October 24, on Capitol Hill, talking about the marine barracks tragedy with senators and congressmen assembled in large rooms. It was a tough day. I was glad that the congressional vote had already been taken to retain our forces in Lebanon. Under the circumstances, I felt that members of Congress were reasonable and sympathetic. We discussed how the United States would proceed now. On the basis of the meeting with the president on the previous evening, I said that we would reinforce our marine presence in the multinational force, that I would be meeting on Thursday in Paris with the foreign ministers of the countries composing the MNF, and that we would be pushing hard for the warring factions in Lebanon to come together in a process of national reconciliation. "The president is not about to be driven out of Lebanon by this kind of terrorist attack," I told them.

A Plan of Action

Shortly afterward that same Monday evening, October 24, I proceeded to the Situation Room at the White House for another National Security Planning Group meeting with the president. Tony Motley accompanied me. Because of the work of Tony and his colleagues, I was able to set out a detailed series of steps that would become the basis for our activities in the hectic time to come. We had a ten-point checklist of plans and actions ready to go:

1. We had compiled a detailed and documented accounting of measures we had taken, short of the use of force, to assure the safety of the American students. These steps had included preleasing a Pan Am jet and chartering a cruise ship in the Caribbean (which, respectively, had been denied landing and berthing rights) and, on several occasions, unsuccessful efforts to get assurances of the safety of U.S. citizens from responsible governmental representatives in Grenada.

2. We had in our possession a signed, formal request from the Organization of Eastern Caribbean States asking for U.S. assistance in assuring their collective security and in restoring democracy to Grenada.

3. We had prepared a fully researched and coordinated legal opinion on our rights and obligations under the UN and OAS charters, including those that flow from legitimate requests for assistance from friends and allies, such as those in the OECS. We also had a succinct paper on our obligations under the War Powers Act, talking points for the president to use in initial briefings of congressional leaders, and a press briefing paper on all of these matters.

4. We had a complete file of coordinated, prioritized cables to be sent to all our diplomatic posts once U.S. forces had landed in Grenada. Craig Johnstone, Motley's deputy, wrote all the cables,

and I had Larry Eagleburger clear them on behalf of all the different bureaus that would normally be involved. We thereby finessed a great deal of bureaucratic haggling.

5. We had prepared a complete set of press statements and Qs and As with assigned roles for Defense, State, and the White House: the top press people in all three agencies were briefed in Tony Motley's office after the evening news broadcasts on Monday and were given assignments.

6. After a lot of hassling, State had obtained a firm understanding with the Joint Chiefs of Staff and our commander in chief of Atlantic Forces (CINCLANT) that the Caribbean Defense Force (CDF), composed of people, primarily policemen, from the East Caribbean countries, would "land" at a respectable time, not after everything was over, and that they would be properly utilized. (They were, in fact, quickly put to work guarding some 600 Cuban and 2,000 Grenadian prisoners, freeing up U.S. forces to do mopping-up work. Being mainly policemen, they were ideal for this role, and when the time came, they performed it well. This early, visible presence showed that it was not just a "Stars and Stripes" operation and gave the CDF the status and prestige necessary to take over security and law enforcement activities when the U.S. forces withdrew.)

7. We had developed a complete plan for an immediate transition to civilian power in accordance with the Grenadian constitution (which had been discarded by Bishop in 1979) and with the British Commonwealth system. The plan had two options: one assuming the British governor-general was alive and able to carry out his constitutional duties and another assuming the contrary. In the latter case, we had lined up what we called a shadow government. We had identified a number of respectable Grenadians living in the United States and, with their agreement, positioned them nearby in case they were needed. Either way, we were determined from the outset to put civilians and Grenadians forward quickly and simultaneously.

8. We also had developed a clearly defined understanding between State and the Joint Chiefs of Staff on an early and staged withdrawal of U.S. forces. That had been essential to gaining the Joint Chiefs' reluctant agreement to the operation in the first place.

9. The president had authorized the establishment of an embassy on Grenada and named Tony Gillespie, an experienced foreign service officer, ambassador. We wanted to get Gillespie there and in control quickly.

10. We had placed foreign service officers in key places: Gillespie went to Barbados to ride herd on Ambassador Bish in the em-

bassy there and was poised to go on to Grenada. Frank McNeil was in a shuttle between Barbados, Dominica, Jamaica, St. Lucia, and Washington, ensuring close communication with the OECS governments. Craig Johnstone was sent to the commander in chief of the Atlantic Forces (CINCLANT), to convince him and his staff of the seriousness of the problem. When Johnstone arrived at the headquarters in Norfolk, Virginia, at noon the previous Saturday, he was told that they needed more time. Johnstone and a brave navy commodore, Jack Darby, turned them around. Rich Brown went to New York to identify the shadow government and also to handle Charles Modica, the chancellor of the medical school, who seemed mainly concerned about tuition dollars having to be refunded. Larry Rossen was poised to go in with the navy commandos, the SEALs, to rescue the governor-general. Rossen was a young officer in our Latin America bureau who had spent considerable time on Grenada while stationed in Barbados. He was well known to the governor-general. We wanted to make sure that when the SEALs, in black uniforms and blackened faces, woke the governor-general up in the middle of the night and said, "Hi there, we've come to help you," he would see a friendly face. It was important to bring the governor-general, whom we assumed had been incommunicado, up to speed on the combined Eastern Caribbean–U.S. operation and assist him while he took over. His first public statements would be critical.

We had assigned Ashley Wills to Vice Admiral James Metcalfe's staff on the USS *Guam*. Admiral Metcalfe, with only four days' notice, would command the whole operation. Wills, a USIA officer stationed on Barbados, knew Grenada. Wills and Rossen pointed out the need for a plan to rescue the second campus and the critical need to rescue the governor-general. Metcalfe was glad to have their help. Tony Motley positioned himself in a back room in our State Department operations center and was in touch with everyone by tacsat.

At about six o'clock that Monday evening, October 24, President Reagan gave the final order to proceed, although the initial decision had been made early the previous Saturday at the Eisenhower cottage in Augusta. With the National Security Planning Group meeting and the decision behind him, the president then asked the congressional leadership to come to the White House. They arrived at about eight o'clock. I was there, along with Cap Weinberger, Jack Vessey, and Bill Casey. In turn, we briefed them on various aspects of the situation on Grenada. Then the president told them of his plan: (1) secure Point Salines and Pearls airports; (2) secure other key installations; (3) protect and rescue American citizens; (4) deter Cuban intervention. The Grenada operation would begin during the course of this night.

As he was speaking, the president was interrupted by a phone call. It was Margaret Thatcher: her message was negative and uncompromising. Our decision to save American lives, she said, would endanger the lives of British subjects and the life of the governor-general. She said she knew of no request from the Organization of Eastern Caribbean States for help. No such request had been made to her, she said. I could only conclude that she had not been kept well informed by people in her own government. Others lower down in the British government knew perfectly well that such a request had been made. I told Motley to produce a detailed message with all the facts that we could flash to her over the cabinet line.

The Republicans present supported the president, but Howard Baker seemed worried. The Democrats, particularly Tip O'Neill, were cool. Tip said that he had met a Grenadian who told him that the harbor and airfield there were for the use of Cuba and the Soviet Union, but this wasn't enough for Tip.

"Mr. President, I have been informed but not consulted," O'Neill said. With that, he stomped out of the family quarters of the White House. A couple of minutes later, as we were standing around talking, Tip came back. "Mr. President," he said, "I just wanted to say that I've been coming to these family quarters for a great many years, and I've never seen them in such wonderful shape. You and Nancy have made them look and feel like a real home." Then he turned and left.

The Rescue Begins

On Tuesday morning, October 25, I was in my office before dawn to study the situation emerging in Grenada. The intervention had begun the previous night, but the story hadn't broken. By 6:00 A.M., I heard from Eagleburger, Howe, and Motley that the landing had been effective and on time. The marines had used helicopters at the small Pearls airport in the middle of the island. The SEALs did not get into Point Salines, they said, but the rangers had landed and taken the large Point Salines airport. I told State's press spokesman, John Hughes, that we were not trying to establish a U.S. base on Grenada or to maintain any permanent presence. In our public comments, we should stress the restoration of law and order and the safety of our students. Although the Caribbean nations genuinely feared aggression from the Grenadian regime backed by the Cubans and Soviets, this was "not an East-West confrontation," I said. And we must keep our statements in line with our legal position: our action was undertaken at the request of the Organization of Eastern Caribbean States and its central purpose was to rescue the American students.

At 6:40 A.M., October 25, Frank McNeil came in to report. He had flown to Barbados the day before to meet with Eugenia Charles and other Eastern Caribbean leaders. McNeil had told them the United States took their request seriously and would act. He found them concerned about peace and security in their region and ready to act if they could get assistance. McNeil had arrived back in Washington at 2:00 A.M., accompanying Mrs. Charles, who would meet with President Reagan at 7:30 A.M. She was impressive and articulate, he reported. By 7:00 A.M., CBS had the first shred of a story: then the news began to break.

The British were in a terrific uproar. Margaret Thatcher was furious. Foreign Secretary Geoffrey Howe had embarrassed himself in the House of Commons by assuring the members that nothing would be happening in Grenada; he felt that we had misled him. Ambassador Oliver Wright came in to State at dawn under instructions "urgently to reinforce" Mrs. Thatcher's message. I was annoyed. We had turned ourselves into pretzels for Mrs. Thatcher over the Falklands crisis. "If we said no to those [Eastern Caribbean] people, we wouldn't be worth a plugged nickel," I said.

At 7:20 I met with Mrs. Charles, and at 9:00 she appeared with President Reagan on television. She was outstanding and vigorous. I came back to my office afterward and called Geoffrey Howe. He was my friend, and I felt terrible about his embarrassment in the House of Commons. "There was no intent to mislead you. I'm sorry if it appeared that way. It was only early on Saturday morning that we got the plea from the OECS to intervene."

I went off to the Hill for briefings of the full Senate and then the full House. This was the second day in a row that I had been there. I emphasized the atmosphere of violent uncertainty and the danger to American citizens on Grenada. "The president," I said, "had to ask himself whether to act before there was harm or hostage taking of U.S. citizens, and the president decided not to wait." This was also a response to Article 8 of the OECS charter. Scarcely a good word was said to me by the members of Congress. I returned to my office at 7:00 P.M. Jon Howe was waiting for me to report. "It's been tough going. No one says, 'Great!' You just get reamed," I remarked.

"We may have stumbled on to a much greater Cuban-organized resistance than we had foreseen. This is turning into a major operation," Howe told me. The CIA was estimating there might be as many as two Cuban battalions on Grenada; 2,000 to 2,500 Cubans were thought to be engaging our forces near the prison. Moreover, there were numerous Soviets and East Germans. The 82nd Airborne was arriving, a major reinforcement for our forces. I told Eagleburger to get a message through to John Ferch, the foreign service officer at the U.S. Interests section in Havana, to tell the Cubans that they would be better off to stop fighting. The Cubans were going to be overwhelmed; we didn't want to see a slaughter. We would evacuate those who surrendered and return them to Cuba. The road to safety lay in surrender.

By Wednesday morning, I learned that the governor-general was safe, and I called Geoffrey Howe to inform him and found that he already knew. He told me that he had taken a severe ridiculing in Parliament for being uninformed about our action. He did not like the way the intervention had been handled, but now that it had happened, he said, the British wanted it to succeed. President Reagan telephoned Prime Minister Thatcher to give her a firsthand report.

By 9:00 A.M., I was getting indications from Havana that the Cubans were looking for a way out. They had told Ferch that they wanted "a dignified solution" and asked for a cease-fire. We got in telephone contact with Cuban officials in Havana and began to put together a surrender-and-departure process for both Cubans and Soviets who were now in our hands. We informed Cuba by cable that "if [the senior Cuban on Grenada] will identify himself to us, we are prepared to arrange an immediate cessation of hostilities followed by repatriation of Cuban forces under arms in Grenada." This was nearly fouled up by CIA director Bill Casey, who had telephoned Ken Dam to say that he had encouraged General Manuel Noriega, Panama's strongman, to go to Cuba to act as our representative. Noriega had in fact done so, I was told.

I passed word to Casey to "forget it." I told our press office that "we should reaffirm that our aim is the safety of all foreigners." There would be a desire to get out a lot of information about the Cuban presence, and we should. "But we have to continue to make clear that our objective is to secure the island for the safety of Americans as well as to get the Cubans out of there," I said.

Jon Howe reported that most of the students were out of the second campus and that Fort Frederick and the prison had still not been taken but should be under control by the end of the day. I could see that we were already at a mopping-up stage. "As we wind up the operation," I said, "we should disarm everyone: deep-six the weapons." I wanted Mrs. Charles to supervise this. "Boy, is she tough," I said. "Too tough for the Black Caucus." She had met with the congressional Black Caucus on Tuesday afternoon, and they couldn't lay a glove on her.

I authorized Eagleburger to inform the Soviets of what we were doing. We had assured them as the operation began, that it was not aimed at Cuba. "Tell the Soviets we will get their diplomats out and to Barbados promptly. There should be no message suggesting that we are prepared to negotiate with the Soviets about the Cubans who are still fighting," I said.

The logistics were negotiated with Moscow and Havana: we would fly the Soviet and Cuban diplomats and a group of Cuban soldiers who had sought refuge in the Soviet embassy to Mexico City, where an Aeroflot plane would pick them up, stop in Havana to drop off the Cubans, and proceed on to Moscow. The Cubans had rejected our offer of flying them straight to Havana International Airport, care of the U.S. Air Force.

Tony Gillespie was at the Grenada airport with the U.S. Army commanding general, the airlift task force commander, the diplomats and their baggage, and the Cuban soldiers. Tony Motley was in a side room at State's operations center in Washington, linked to Gillespie by a tacsat. The Soviet "baggage" was more voluminous than what was normal for personal possessions and diplomatic papers and was packed in a variety of bags, trunks, and boxes. Although the Soviet ambassador made representations that there were no weapons, the airlift task-force commander felt it prudent to check, because the aircraft being utilized would have passengers and cargo all in one area. After some discussion, Motley and Gillespie concluded that given these circumstances, we should override the ambassador's objections regarding diplomatic immunity and search the luggage.

On top of one of the first trunks opened was an AK-47 fully loaded with a round in the chamber. Other bags then were opened, and in several there were AK-47s and some handguns similarly configured. The Soviet ambassador acted dismayed and said they must belong to his Cuban guests. We then opened all the bags and proceeded with a body search of all passengers, which turned up a variety of knives and knucklebusters and one hand grenade.

By this time, about an hour and a half had passed, and word of what we were finding was spreading around Washington. Some NSC hard-liners wanted to detain the diplomats and interrogate them for a while—never mind their somewhat dubious claim to diplomatic protection. The Joint Chiefs had a different view; they wanted to get them out of there. They had enough problems with 2,600 Cuban and Grenadian prisoners that needed care and feeding and with the sporadic fighting that was still going on. Tony Motley was thinking about holding on to them and mentioned this to Gillespie over the private secure phone. Gillespie expressed a residue of doubt over the wisdom of that decision.

Just at that moment, a young foreign service officer present in the room spoke up. Motley unkeyed the mike and listened to him. He had been in charge of coordinating the negotiations and arrangements for the exchange of diplomats and asylum seekers. In a very quiet but firm manner, he took Tony through the negotiations with the Soviets. He pointed out the precedents we were setting the next time a U.S. diplomat or dependents were snapped up by somebody, either behind the Iron Curtain or elsewhere. He pointed out the risk we would run that the Soviets might escalate the situation and grab one of our people under some pretext—at the very least the Soviets would protest violently and immediately. The secretary of state and the president would then be responding tomorrow or the next day without the benefit of the involvement of the past two hours and, in the cold light of day, would have to defend this seeming breach of normal and proper diplomatic conduct. Tony, having heard this young man out, told Gillespie to let the airlift go as planned and told the hard-liners to forget it. As Tony put it, "We've already won. Let's show a little style."

By 6:00 P.M. Wednesday night, as I was about to fly to Paris to meet for a few hours with the foreign ministers of the nations in the multinational force, we got news that Fort Frederick had been captured and the American students rescued, We had taken about 600 Cubans prisoner at that point and were arranging to ship them back to Cuba on a vessel ironically named *Vietnam Heroica*.

In Paris, the French told me Syria feared a U.S. attack—more so now that they had witnessed our action in Grenada. The French pressed me for reassurance that we would not strike a Syrian target. "Let Damascus worry," I said. It was fascinating to see this sudden effect of our Grenada operation halfway round the world. I assured my colleagues privately that we had no plan to retaliate against Syria, but "I would not want to reassure the Syrians."

While in Paris, I received reports on American media coverage and on congressional attitudes toward our Grenada operation: in general, it was snide, scathing, and condemnatory. The Grenada decision had been made on October 22, the day before the bombing of our marine barracks in Lebanon. But by the time the operation got under way, we were embattled: everyone was devastated by the bombing; 241 marines were dead, and this seemed to deepen the hostile congressional reaction to the Grenada rescue.

On Thursday afternoon, October 27, the nation watched the televised landing of the first aircraft at Charleston Air Force Base bringing back the American students from Grenada. We were all aware that how those students behaved and what they said to the media would greatly affect how the intervention in Grenada would be perceived in the United States. We watched the large transport plane wheel up to the front of the Charleston terminal, where a crowd was gathered. The stairs were rolled over to the door, but there was a delay before anyone emerged. Finally, one student came out and went down the front stairs.

At the bottom of the stairway, he fell to his knees and kissed the tarmac: all this live, in color, on all three major networks. We flipped around the channels. The TV anchormen kept trying to push the students to say that they were never in danger; it didn't work. Suddenly I could sense the country's emotions turn around. Our effort in Grenada wasn't an immoral imperialist intervention: it was an essential rescue and a job well done.

At that moment, I knew that we had won a clean sweep: on the ground in Grenada and in the hearts of America. People, still reeling from Lebanon, watched that spontaneous, grateful, emotional act that said "Thank you, President Reagan." And it did not matter what carping or spin Sam Donaldson and Tip O'Neill wanted to put on it. Americans had seen it for what it was.

Early the next morning, Friday, Senate Majority Leader Howard Baker telephoned me. "Things are looking a lot better on the Hill," he told me.

"Well, Howard, was I so persuasive last Tuesday?" I asked him.

"No, George, they've heard from the folks back home," he replied with a laugh.

Assessment: A New Departure

The facts soon emerged that Grenada, like the Falklands, was a shot heard round the world by usurpers and despots of every ideology. The report was sharp and clear: some Western democracies were again ready to use the military strength they had harbored and built up over the years in defense of their principles and interests.

The British

The British position remained a puzzle. Whatever the reasons for Prime Minister Thatcher's opposition, she did not exhibit any particular concern for "the special relationship" between Britain and America. President Reagan and I felt that she was just plain wrong. He had supported her in the Falklands. He felt he was absolutely right about Grenada. She didn't share his judgment at all. He was deeply disappointed.

Why did Mrs. Thatcher react so negatively to the American effort? I could only speculate. She had been needled hard two days earlier, in the rough-and-tumble of question time in the House of Commons, about being "Ronald Reagan's poodle." She may also have had a special sensitivity about a former British colony "going bad" and the Yanks having to go in there and clean up the mess. And her government was embarrassed, having declared too confidently that no Grenada operation was imminent.

At any rate, Margaret Thatcher and her government opposed the American rescue operation and did so vehemently: "We in the Western countries, the Western democracies, use our force to defend our way of life. We do not use it to walk into independent sovereign territories. . . . If you're going to pronounce a new law that wherever communism reigns against the will of the people, even though it's happened internally, there the USA shall enter, then we are going to have really terrible wars in the world."[3] She came very close to saying in her radio broadcast about Grenada that there were no circumstances in which intervention of one country in the affairs of another was justified, even to rescue its own citizens whose lives were threatened. The reality was that in the fog of chaos, Americans were clearly in danger. I was also dismayed to hear her taking a position similar to Cap Weinberger's. A Shultz-Weinberger "debate" on the question of whether and when force was required and justified was now well known. The debate, I knew, would continue long after our Grenada intervention.

Intelligence

A torrrent of information rushed in as the operation came to a close, and it tended to support our earlier intelligence. We found that there had been at least 600 Cubans with military training building the new airport runway, which obviously was for military use, not for "tourism," as had been stated. We knew the length of the runway. We knew about revetments along the taxi way, fueling points that were scattered around the terminal, and warehouse layouts. The runway would have served a very useful and immediate purpose. The Cubans were heavily engaged in Angola and Ethiopia. Their airplanes could not fly to Angola nonstop from Cuba. The Cubans had to refuel in places where they were not permitted to transport military aircraft and people. This meant elaborate subterfuge: putting the soldiers in mufti and putting weapons, uniforms, and other military gear in the baggage holds of civilian aircraft. A military field in Grenada, which was within nonstop distance of Angola, would solve this fairly major problem.

We had timely and accurate reports from our intelligence on the Bishop-Coard fight and Bishop's arrest. We knew that the Coard faction and General Hudson Austin were very much in the Cuban camp. There were two pieces of information that we didn't know in advance: the degree of military training and battle experience of the Cubans (who acquitted themselves well once the shooting started); and the existence of a huge cache of arms, more than one hand grenade for every man, woman, and child on the island, plus tons of small arms, ammunition, uniforms, and even artillery. The following April, a million rounds of ammunition were found under a false floor in the vacated Cuban embassy. Moreover, a great many papers were subsequently discovered showing the extensive contacts between Soviet, Cuban, and Grenadian officials. A vivid one reported a meeting of Chief of Staff Marshal Nikolai Ogarkov of the Soviet Union

3. Statements made by Prime Minister Thatcher in a highly publicized phone-in program on BBC World Service on Sunday, October 30.

and his Grenadian counterpart, Major Einstein Louison. Ogarkov said, "Over two decades ago, there was only Cuba in Latin America, today there are Nicaragua, Grenada, and a serious battle is going on in El Salvador."[4]

After the operation, when the question of this amount of matériel was raised with the Grenadians, they told us that under the cover of frequent and expected power shortages, every time a Cuban or Soviet merchant ship would pull up at the dock at night, the lights would go out, and a stream of trucks would run from the docks to hidden caches. The Cubans and their Grenadian partners thereby avoided detection by any overflights and reduced exposure of what was going on to any human observation.

Overall, the CIA did a creditable job. When it came to reports on hardware, I had far more confidence than when the CIA gave me political assessments and projections. Given President Reagan's statements about Grenada earlier in the year, the CIA should have had a better estimate of Cuban strength and more accurate and detailed maps of the island. It would have been helpful to know more about Cuban capabilities and intentions. But the CIA scrambled pretty successfully during the short period before the operation. If our ambassador in Barbados had been more aggressive and alert, he could have provided far more useful information.

The Military

The military performed with great skill, given such little time to prepare. Admiral Metcalfe and his forces were very flexible in reacting to new information and a changing situation. They were exceptionally good at following rules of engagement that required special care against incurring civilian casualties, often using light infantry rather than calling in the formidable aerial and naval gunnery that we had available.

The military was harshly criticized for the one bomb that landed on an asylum for the mentally ill, killing several people. The asylum was on a hill overlooking the governor-general's residence. Helicopter-borne SEALs were trying to rescue the governor-general in his residence. Communist forces were using the parapet wall that was the outer structure of the asylum to protect machine guns that were firing at the helicopters and pinning down the handful of SEALs who had managed to get to the governor-general. The Grenadians were flying their flag above the machine-gun emplacements. Calling in a fighter strike was absolutely correct. The bomb landed twenty-five yards from the target. It is too much to ask that those who directed the fire should have known that the Grenadians were using an asylum as a firing position.

4. *The Grenada Papers*, edited by Paul Seabury and Walter A. McDougall (San Francisco: ICS Press, 1984), p. 189.

We lost eighteen men. No one wants casualties; it was a mark of good battlefield management, however, that the casualties were kept low.

The Joint Chiefs of Staff were reluctant, because of their Vietnam War experience, to attempt the Grenada operation. They and other officers of that generation had been colonels, commanding brigades and wings and serving in planning and operations in Vietnam and Washington. They had seen, from one perspective or another, the dark side of the Vietnam War: sound tactical and strategic decisions overturned for "political reasons"; restrictions on winning; the military, individually and collectively, trashed on the campuses, in the news, and in Congress. All this left a bitter taste for many years, and especially among the military professionals, who spent years rebuilding the pride, prestige, and capabilities of their institutions. The result was that the Joint Chiefs of Staff did not just resist mounting an operation; they could take forever to put one together. I had argued effectively, I felt, for the necessity of going in.

Tony Motley did a terrific job in bringing the Joint Chiefs along. He convinced them that the problem was severe. And he showed them the way to get out quickly once the job had been done. He convinced them that all alternative means had been exhausted and that if we didn't go in quickly, we would have to do so eventually under much worse conditions.

The State Department

The entire Grenada operation was driven by the State Department. Tony Motley and his colleagues operated under my direction and with my encouragement. I trusted Tony and his people. I gave them a long leash, confident that they would make good tactical judgments and come back to me on any issue of policy. Most of them were foreign service officers, and their performance was magnificent. They demonstrated an ability to think and act under pressure during two very long weeks. They were able to act independently and carry out instructions. Equally important, they did not hesitate to question Tony or me or anybody else if they thought something was being done wrong. Sometimes political appointees and even senior civil servants get irritated by such questioning. Tony and I both welcomed it, because time and again it saved us from mistakes. Frank McNeil, Tony Gillespie, and Craig Johnstone on different occasions displayed professional courage; Larry Rossen, personal courage. When the helicopter flying Rossen in was initially turned away by enemy gunfire that wounded the copilot and others, Rossen got in on another pass, quickly linked up with the governor-general, and in essence became his principal adviser. He was the first foreign service officer, Motley told me, to be on the scene in advance of an invading force since Ambassador Robert Murphy had welcomed General Mark Clark to North Africa in 1942.

There were many signals sent by the Grenada operation. In many different parts of the world, people began to get the message: Ronald Reagan is capable of action beyond rhetoric. Latin Americans in particular saw that if a country went nose to nose with Uncle Sam, Fidel Castro could not, or would not, come to its rescue.

A few days after the Grenada operation, Desi Bouterse in Suriname abruptly changed course. He threw out the large Cuban contingent and all but broke diplomatic relations with Cuba. Within a week of the Grenada operation, Tomás Borge, a Nicaraguan *comandante*, called on our ambassador, Anthony Quainton, to inform him that if the United States ever wanted to evacuate Americans from Nicaragua, please call Borge and he would facilitate their departure. I saw some of the same reactions in my meeting in Paris when I heard reports of Syrian concerns that they might be next. Grenada had a strong rippling effect in faraway places.

The President

I was in close consultation with President Reagan throughout and insisted that every key decision be made by him. His role was pivotal in every respect. He had appreciated the problem early on. He had agonized about intervention in Suriname, and that frustrating experience probably prepared him to move definitively in Grenada. He was decisive, despite the distraction of our tragedy in Lebanon. He held firm against the Pentagon's desire for more time to prepare. His firmness probably was bolstered by the fact that, by chance, he had been in Augusta with McFarlane and me, two strong supporters of the action, and therefore was insulated somewhat from the Pentagon's reluctance. The president placed full confidence in his key people: in me, Tony Motley, and our colleagues on the diplomatic side and in Cap Weinberger and the military for the operation itself. He was instinctively proud of our men in uniform, and they reciprocated: they did a great job for him and for the country.

The Use of Force

Reflecting on this operation and the speed with which it was planned and carried out leads to another observation. No doubt, if the military had more time to plan the operation, they might have performed even better than they did. Problems of field communication and battlefield management, perhaps stemming from interservice rivalry, received much attention after the operation. No doubt such problems needed to be addressed. At the same time, delay would undoubtedly have meant leaks and much more opposition. Quite possibly, time and leaks could have meant that U.S. hostages would have been taken.

Often one hears the argument "Force should be used only as the last resort." This makes people feel good, and it sounds statesmanlike. In fact, I feel strongly that it is poor public policy and an unsound application of the law. The use of force, and the credible threat of the use of force, are legitimate instruments of national policy and should be viewed as such. Waiting to use force as a last resort would have meant possibly enduring hostage taking and having to use force then. The use of force obviously should not be taken lightly, but better to use force when you *should* rather than when you *must*; *last* means *no other*, and by that time the level of force and the risk involved may have multiplied many times over.

I recalled my early argument back in 1982 in the Situation Room of the White House involving a marker with the Soviets and Nicaraguans about MIGs coming to Nicaragua. When I told Gromyko that such a development was unacceptable to us, the threat was credible: the president had agreed on a plan to take them out. The Soviets, the Cubans, and the Nicaraguans sensed that we meant it. Therefore, the marker worked.

The United States took a lot of heat over the Grenada operation. We were opposed by the British and the French and many others throughout Europe and by Congress, particularly before they heard from the folks back home. On the other hand, we received some interesting support. Journalist Carl Rowan wrote a thoughtful column ending, "Given the context of crisis in the East Caribbean, the United States could not honorably refuse to respond. A remarkable number of liberals and blacks understand this." He for one.

George Will, in his column in *Newsweek* on November 7, 1983, headed "The Price of Power," opened, "Grenada, although small, is 15 times the size of Iwo Jima and of large symbolic value. U.S. soldiers' boot prints on Grenada's soil have done more than the MX will do to make U.S. power credible and peace secure. President Reagan's defense budgets are not, by themselves, a fully effective signal to the Soviet Union of U.S. seriousness. The boot prints prove that the United States will not only procure sophisticated weapons systems but also has recovered the will to use the weapon on which its security rests: the man with a rifle."

CHAPTER 21

The Missile
and the Alliance

The Soviet Union, beginning in 1977, started to deploy a new and impressive weapon, the SS-20 ballistic missile, aimed at Europe. It was "intermediate" in range, meaning that it could not reach the United States and therefore could not be classed as a "strategic weapon." But it could reach anywhere in Europe from secure bases in the Soviet Union, and when deployed in the early 1980s in the vast Asian reaches of the Soviet Union, it could devastate targets in Japan, South Korea, and China. It was accurate. It was mobile and therefore far more survivable against attack than ballistic missiles in fixed silos. It had three independently targetable nuclear warheads. By the U.S. count, 140 SS-20s with 420 warheads had been deployed by the end of 1979, and deployments were continuing.

For forty years, nuclear war had been prevented by "deterrence." To deter the Soviets required that our alliance match, in general terms, Soviet nuclear missile strength on two geographic levels. Since the Soviets' intercontinental ballistic missiles (ICBMs) could reach North America from the USSR, we had to have strategic missiles that could reach the Soviet Union either from our territory or from our submarines at sea. Since the Soviets' intermediate-range forces could strike our allies in Western Europe, NATO had to have somewhat equivalent forces in place in Western Europe to deter such a threat. The deployment of SS-20s upset the West European–Soviet balance because it represented a major qualitative advance in favor of the Soviets. The SS-20 deployments, as they proceeded, were one part of the continuing Soviet effort to intimidate our friends and allies, thereby causing them to move away from us and toward a political accommodation with Moscow.

The aim was to undermine Western Europe's confidence in us. By putting the SS-20s in place, the Soviets seemed to be saying: we now have created an imbalance; we can hit the capitals of Europe from our soil, and we dare the United States to say that it would respond with a strategic nuclear strike, a nuclear exchange risking demolition of the United States itself. That would seem highly implausible to many of our European friends. If they could not look to America to ensure their security, perhaps they should accommodate the Soviet Union's wishes.[1]

Helmut Schmidt had taken the lead even before the first SS-20 was in place. He convinced President Carter and other NATO leaders that action was needed, that we must insist on regaining the balance either by persuading the Soviets to dismantle their SS-20s or through deployments by NATO countries of weapons of comparable range and destructive power. If such a strong step was not taken, he argued, Europe would be subject to Soviet blackmail, and their efforts to split the Europeans from the United States would be relentless.

The responses came after intense discussion among alliance leaders throughout the year of 1979. NATO foreign and defense ministers, on behalf of their governments, formally adopted what came to be known as the "dual-track" decision. On one track, the United States would begin to deploy in late 1983—first in West Germany, Britain, and Italy, subsequently in Belgium and the Netherlands—single-warhead intermediate-range (INF) missiles. These five "basing countries" would host a total of 464 U.S. ground-launched cruise missiles, slow flying but hard to detect and capable of penetrating deep into the Soviet Union. West Germany would also provide bases for 108 U.S. Pershing II ballistic missiles whose warheads could reach well into Soviet territory (the Soviets claimed the warheads could target Moscow) in less than twenty minutes, replacing a like number of older, shorter-range Pershing Ia missiles. The ministers adopted a set schedule for these deployments. At the same time, on a second track, the United States would attempt to negotiate limits on the U.S. and Soviet INF missiles to an equal level, the lowest possible.

The American Peace Strategy: The Zero Option

On November 18, 1981, in a speech at the National Press Club in Washington, President Reagan proposed what would become known as the "zero option" for the negotiations: we would refrain from deploying our INF missiles if the Soviets agreed to dismantle all their INF missiles currently deployed. Explicit criteria were established to guide the negotiations to what would be an acceptable agreement: equality of deployment rights between the United States and the Soviet Union; coverage of the negotiations limited to U.S. and Soviet missile systems (meaning that the nuclear weapons systems possessed by Britain and France were not on the table);

1. With Soviet SS-20s being deployed in the Asian regions of the USSR as well, similar fears and uncertainties were being raised in the minds of our partners in Japan and South Korea.

a global scope to any agreed limits (so that the Soviets could not transfer the nuclear threat from Europe to Asia, or vice versa); no adverse effect on NATO's current conventional defense and deterrent capability; effective verifiability of the terms of any agreement. From the outset, the U.S. position also called for constraints on Soviet missiles with shorter range than the SS-20 but with range long enough to reach European and Japanese targets from Soviet-controlled bases.

President Reagan's proposal was endorsed by both Houses of Congress, in the Senate by a unanimous vote, and by our NATO allies. Helmut Schmidt characterized it as "the American peace strategy," and Margaret Thatcher called it "supremely important," the most significant message of the Reagan presidency. Editorial opinion in the United States and Europe was supportive and thoughtful. The *Washington Post* reported on November 19: "The President gave an awfully good speech yesterday. He was well prepared, forceful and he made a lot of sense. . . . How will it come out? That will depend in the first instance on the temper of the Europeans. Each great power is playing to them. The Soviets, as they observe the European 'peace movement,' may be sorely tempted to play to it in the hopes that eventually NATO will have to reduce or call off the new deployments without Moscow's having to make any concessions in return. No one can say confidently that this will not happen. The Europeans, however, have to ponder what then might result."

But the "arms control community" reacted with skepticism bordering on derision, arguing that the proposal was so unlikely to gain acceptance that it showed that President Reagan was not really serious about arms control negotiations. Former Secretary of State Al Haig was one of the doubters. Walter Slocombe, deputy under secretary of defense for policy planning and an arms control specialist in the Carter administration, said, "There's a school in this Administration that hopes the proposal is so brilliant that the Soviets will never accept it and that rather than advancing the negotiations, it will stop them." And William Hyland, who had served on President Nixon's NSC staff, warned, "Reagan's proposal is a clever tactic that buys about six months, but it puts the U.S. on a negotiating slope that will end in disaster. . . . Thanks to the zero option, the preparation of even one site for one missile will make a mockery of zero, and the Soviets and the disarmament demonstrators will have a field day."[2] General Secretary Leonid Brezhnev sneered that "those in the United States who advance this kind of 'proposal' apparently do not for a minute expect that the Soviet Union might agree to them," and *Tass* called the proposals "a mere propaganda ploy." Against this background, the first round of negotiations started in Geneva on November 30, 1981, with vet-

2. Slocombe and Hyland are quoted in *Deadly Gambits* by Strobe Talbott (New York: Alfred A. Knopf, 1984), pp. 80–81.

eran negotiator Paul Nitze heading the U.S. delegation and Yuli Kvitsinsky in the chair for the USSR.

Meanwhile, President Reagan and his advisers were working out a position for negotiations with the Soviets over nuclear forces with strategic range, with the capability of reaching from the United States to the Soviet Union or vice versa. On May 9, 1982, in a speech at Eureka College in Illinois, President Reagan set out the U.S. position on strategic arms. As he had repeatedly advocated, his concern was to achieve reductions, not limitations, and by at least one-third (to 5,000 land- and sea-based ballistic missile warheads on each side). He emphasized warheads—that's what hits you—and throw weight, or lift capacity, of the launcher as well as the launcher itself as the units of account. As with his INF position, the proposal met with skepticism from experts that such a sharp departure from past practice was in any way negotiable and with rejection by those who depicted America as the source of all global tensions. President Reagan was proposing a revolution in ways of thinking about arms control, but in many eyes his proposals were a smokescreen. Behind his proposals for large reductions, his critics felt, lay a reluctance to engage genuinely in arms control negotiations stemming from the president's skepticism of negotiated outcomes in the past.

On May 18, Leonid Brezhnev affirmed Soviet readiness to negotiate on strategic arms while calling President Reagan's proposal one-sided. Strategic arms reductions (START) negotiations got under way in Geneva on June 29, 1982, with negotiator Ed Rowny leading the U.S. delegation and Victor Karpov the Soviet delegation.

By mid-January of 1983, Foreign Minister Gromyko was in Bonn warning the West Germans not to accept the new U.S. missiles and calling on the United States to go beyond its "zero option" opening proposal. At the same time, *Tass* called unacceptable a rumored "interim solution" calling for each side to maintain a small number of missiles if total elimination could not be achieved. "The placement of the first Pershing II on West German territory and the first cruise missile in Sicily creates a new situation," *Tass* said, depriving the INF arms talks of "the realistic basis upon which they are now being conducted." In other words, the Soviets would never agree to any U.S. deployments of INF missiles, and the implementation of such deployments according to the schedule adopted by NATO would probably end the arms control negotiations so greatly valued in German public opinion.

Also in January, two months before major West German elections, Hans-Jochen Vogel, who would succeed Helmut Schmidt as head of West Germany's Social Democratic party, visited Moscow and seemed impressed by the prospects set forth by the Soviets of benefits Germans would enjoy if they rejected the deployment of U.S. Pershing II missiles. Vogel's trip was part of his election campaign and the Soviet responses part of their continuing effort to stir up the German people and cause the government of West Germany to cancel or postpone deployments. "It looks to me," I remarked, "as though Vogel bought a used car from Andropov."

On January 20, 1983, President François Mitterrand made a dramatic speech to the German Bundestag, commemorating the twentieth anniversary of the French-German friendship treaty that capped the two countries' postwar reconciliation. He made powerful points: he warned about the dangers of any division in the alliance and said that any diminution of defense ties between the United States and Europe would jeopardize the security of Europe. "The joint determination of the alliance and its solidarity must be confirmed so that the negotiations can succeed," he said; and he endorsed the president's "zero option" and defended NATO's decision to deploy missiles in Europe at the end of the year if no agreement was reached. He stressed that French nuclear systems "could not be taken into account," since the Geneva talks between the United States and the Soviet Union were about the "excessive armament of the superpowers, which had to be radically reduced." At the end of his speech, this man who had escaped from a Nazi prison camp and fought in the underground resistance, in a dramatic moment, as recounted in the *Washington Post* the next day, "leaned forward from the podium and, in a voice hushed with emotion, described the Germans as 'a great, noble and courageous people' whom he had come to know and love."

Vice President Bush arrived in Bonn on January 30 on the first stop in a swing that included the Netherlands, Belgium, Switzerland (where the START and INF arms talks were taking place), Italy, France, and Great Britain. He visited all the basing countries, assured them of U.S. resolve, invited their suggestions, and received confirmation of their support for the deployment schedule. In a dinner speech in West Berlin on the first night of his trip, he read a letter from President Reagan that Bush would deliver to the Soviet delegation in Geneva. The president offered to meet the Soviets' new general secretary, Yuri Andropov, "wherever and whenever he wants" to "sign an agreement banning U.S. and Soviet intermediate-range land-based nuclear missile weapons from the face of the earth." Vice President Bush picked up the phrase "banning . . . nuclear missile weapons from the face of the earth" and used it to great effect on this and a subsequent swing around Europe.

On March 6, 1983, Helmut Kohl's Christian Democratic Union (CDU) won a resounding victory in the national elections despite Soviet threats during the campaign of "social unrest" should the CDU win. This effort to interfere in West Germany's political process backfired. Kohl had firmly supported President Reagan's positions, the dual-track decision, and the importance of deployment on schedule if negotiations did not succeed. The opposition Social Democratic party (SPD) under Vogel, having abandoned the position of Schmidt, opposed Kohl's firm stance and was badly defeated.

By mid-March, President Reagan had about decided that it was time to suggest an "interim agreement," according to which we would accept deployment at equal levels without giving up "zero" as our ultimate goal. The president proposed to reduce our planned deployments if the Soviets cut back to an equal number of warheads on a worldwide basis. With strong support from our NATO allies and Japan, the president announced this proposal on March 30.

On May 3, General Secretary Andropov stated that the Soviets would consider reducing their numbers of missiles in Europe on the understanding that there would be no U.S. deployments. He also, significantly, offered to consider warheads as a unit of account. We welcomed Andropov's statement proposing reductions but continued to insist on equal numbers of U.S. and Soviet warheads. Then, on May 27, the Soviets made a threat, clearly intended to affect the summit meeting of leaders of the seven large industrial democracies, due to convene in Williamsburg, Virginia, on May 28. Just as the seven heads of government were gathering for their annual review of economic and security issues, the Soviets put out what I called "a very threatening shot across the bow of this meeting." *Pravda* had stated,

> The decision of the United States and NATO to start the deployment of new American missiles in Europe, if it will be carried out, will force the Soviet Union to reconsider the decision it adopted last year concerning the unilateral moratorium on the further deployment of medium-range systems in the European zone. The need would also arise to implement, on arrangement with other Warsaw Treaty member countries, other measures as well. . . . It would also be necessary, as it has been repeatedly warned by the Soviet side, to take other necessary reply measures with a view to the territory of the United States itself."

At least this threat covered all of us, rather than just the Europeans. But if the West did not deploy Pershing II and cruise missiles, there would be no incentive for the Soviets to negotiate seriously for nuclear weapons reductions.

So the challenge to the Williamsburg summit would necessarily transcend economic issues and go directly to security, the Soviets, the inviolability of the dual-track decision, and support for U.S. positions in Geneva, especially on INF issues.

The Williamsburg Summit

President Reagan had, by the time I joined him as secretary of state, gone through two economic summit meetings, first in Ottawa and then in Versailles. He found both unsatisfactory. He was frustrated by the excessive time spent arguing about the prearranged communiqués that had emerged from negotiations among the sherpas, the officials charged with preparing the way to the summit. President Reagan was frustrated, too, by the small amount of time spent by the heads of government alone with each other. With the next summit set to be held in the United States, we could, as the hosts, give the president a fresh and more productive approach.

I had never attended an economic summit, but I did have a hand in the inception of these events. Eight years earlier, President Gerald Ford and Secretary of State Henry Kissinger had received a proposal from Chancellor Helmut Schmidt of West Germany, President Valéry Giscard d'Estaing of France, and Prime Minister Harold Wilson of Great Britain to convene an informal meeting of heads of government of leading Western democracies. Their idea was to explore informally the problems of the day, particularly economic issues. Ford and Kissinger were uncertain about how to appraise this suggestion and, knowing that I was on friendly terms with Schmidt and Giscard, dating back to my Treasury days, asked me to make a trip to Bonn, London, and Paris to see what the Europeans had in mind and report back my advice. So, in September 1975, I went first to Helmut Schmidt, who remembered from our earlier days "the Library Group," which became the Group of Five, and now favored something similar involving heads of government.

From Bonn I went to London, where Prime Minister Wilson invited me to Chequers for a long discussion. He, too, was looking for a way to sort out problems in a new forum. When I arrived in Paris, Giscard d'Estaing was also positive and interested. Schmidt, knowing that I was going directly from Bonn to see Wilson at Chequers and then on to France, suggested that he come to Paris after my meeting with Giscard for a dinner discussion among the three of us. By telephone from Europe I gave my evaluation to Secretary of State Kissinger and through him to President Ford. My instructions had been to be "neutral" on this new summit idea, but my message to President Ford was that we should take a positive attitude. The president agreed, and my dinner with Schmidt and Giscard advanced the momentum.

The dinner was held at Marly, a small, charming house near Versailles, now reserved for the president of France. Marly dated back some hundred years or so. Schmidt walked in, looked over the cozy living room where a large fire was blazing, and immediately asked Giscard, "Who built this for his mistress?" We spent the bulk of our time on prospects for international monetary reform. We identified the key elements in what eventually became a formal agreement on this subject. Not a word about the meeting ever leaked to the press. I was frankly amazed that two heads of government could meet with a friend from the United States for a four-hour discussion over dinner without any of it being reported or even being known by the world press. At this gathering, the "Summit Seven" concept was born.

From this background I remembered that the original idea of the economic summit had been to promote private, informal discussions among heads of government so that they could actually get to know each other and reach an understanding of each other's thinking about economic issues and other matters of mutual concern, particularly those involving security. I told all this to President Reagan. Out of our discussion came the president's two rules that would guide our preparation for and conduct of the Williamsburg summit.

First, there would be no prenegotiated communiqué. Whatever was announced at the end of the summit meeting would emerge from the meeting itself. Second, the maximum amount of time possible would be given over to the heads of government for meetings among themselves. We would set the agenda from the top down rather than from the bureaucracy up. Foreign ministers and finance ministers would hold their separate meetings concurrently. The arrangements at Williamsburg included a room with a table equipped with a microphone for each head of government. The microphones were connected to an adjoining and completely separate room where interpreters, as well as aides, were present. With the benefit of earphones, the heads of government were able to be in a room with nobody else present and converse with each other directly, since the translations would all be simultaneous. It made for a genuine conversational atmosphere. Nothing like this had been done before.

Margaret Thatcher, I had been told, felt that President Reagan had been poorly prepared at the Versailles summit, and she was sharply critical of his staff. So we decided to get the president's attention and involvement by putting on a little show. With Mike Deaver as the impresario, we selected people to play the parts of Mitterrand, Thatcher, Trudeau, Kohl, Nakasone, Fanfani, and Thorn (president of the European Economic Commission) and let the president interact with them. We'd have a little drama and fun. Deaver and I remembered how effective this technique had been at Camp David when we were working on the president's Mideast initiative. In this session, as before, we caught the president's interest, and he became increasingly involved. By the time we got to Williamsburg, he was in top form, limber and well prepared in his mind for the interplay of issues and personalities.

The leaders at Williamsburg faced two major issues. In this "year of the missile" it was already late May. Negotiations with the Soviets in Geneva on INF and START were not producing anything promising. We had made significant modifications in our INF position in an effort to reach an agreement, but Soviet responses left no one optimistic. At the same time, many economic issues confronted us. The U.S. economy was experiencing a vigorous expansion after a rather severe recession. With large flows of money coming into the United States, the dollar was very strong, the Europeans complained, excessively so, forcing them to pay very high prices for dollar-denominated commodities, particularly oil. They did not like the volatility of exchange rates that resulted from the regime of managed floating rates that had emerged a few years earlier.

We flew down to Williamsburg on *Air Force One* on Friday afternoon, May 27. I spent Saturday afternoon greeting incoming delegations and meeting individually with each of the foreign ministers in a special room in the Williamsburg Inn. The meetings themselves would start officially with dinner on that evening.

Colonial Williamsburg, a historically based reconstruction that portrays the living conditions of our colonial era, proved to be an ideal meeting place and provided a special flair to the summit. The central part of Colonial Williamsburg was allocated completely to the summit, so only the participants were present. Each head of government stayed in one of the colonial houses. Between meetings the leaders could walk around casually and talk informally, which created an atmosphere conducive to the kind of easy discussion that the president desired.

Mrs. Thatcher had called a British election to be held on June 9, which was now just two weeks away. She was in the midst of her campaign. When I met with her foreign secretary, Francis Pym, I was aware that he would in all likelihood be dropped as soon as the election was over. He and I discussed the desirability of an INF statement. He thought it would be more appropriate for a NATO meeting. I then learned that the British had a draft of what might be said. Apparently Margaret Thatcher agreed with us on the importance of a strong security statement at this time. I took a look at the British draft and thought it was quite good. Pym and I agreed to see what transpired among the heads of government at their dinner meeting and keep the draft in reserve.

We all gathered briefly at Carter's Grove, a graceful colonial mansion, where there was an informal reception for everyone. The three groups—heads of government, foreign secretaries, and finance ministers—then separated for their respective dinners. The foreign ministers met in an upstairs dining room, and the heads used the main dining room downstairs.

When I heard the heads-of-government meeting breaking up below, I tried to bring our foreign ministers' meeting to a close as well. The next thing I knew, the president came bounding up the stairs and into our room. He said that he wanted to report that every one of the heads had agreed that there should be a security statement. After the others had left, President Reagan talked from some notes he had made about their discussion. He turned the notes over to me for our use. He said that the content and tone of the dinner meeting were good and the give-and-take vigorous. He recounted to me what the leaders had said. On INF, there was a general emphasis on global limits and verifiability. He had led off the discussion, and Margaret Thatcher then talked at length, apparently along the lines of the British paper. She did not show it to the other guests.

Helmut Kohl had stressed the importance of unity and decisiveness and the need to confirm both tracks of the two-track decision. He could feel the decision to deploy coming at him and wanted to emphasize the importance of that fact but also of the reality as well as appearance of a serious negotiation. Nakasone stressed the importance of being willing to negotiate without changing the deployment timetable and, especially, the need for zero missile levels as a global goal, not just a regional one. Others were generally supportive, the president reported. He wanted something drafted on arms control that could be examined by the foreign ministers in the morning.

President Reagan was elated. I could see he knew his extensive preparatory effort was paying off, that he was really getting somewhere and convincing people of the importance of what we were doing. I could also see that he was asserting himself front and center. Tonight he had become, I thought, "the head of the free world" in his own right, not simply by virtue of being president of its strongest power.

After the president left, I called in Rick Burt, assistant secretary of state for European and Canadian Affairs, and Allen Wallis, our sherpa. I turned over the president's notes and said they should use the notes and the British draft as the basis for a security statement to be ready the first thing in the morning.

Early the next morning I went over the draft. Bill Clark stopped by my suite at 7:45 A.M., picked up the draft, and carried it off to the White House staff meeting with President Reagan. He came back at 8:30: the president had read the statement and thought it was good. I had my authorization to work on it with the foreign ministers in my morning session.

When I got to our meeting room at the Williamsburg Inn, I started to hand out our statement. Everyone was prepared to discuss it except Cheysson. He repeated the French view that security matters were not appropriate at an economic summit and that France was not connected with the INF negotiations. Cheysson obviously was under instructions not to assent to any agreement. As a result, the draft I presented to the heads of government at our noon meeting was not agreed upon by all the foreign ministers.

When we circulated the draft to the heads, it was clear that Mitterrand and Trudeau were dragging their feet. President Reagan was upset. He felt that they had agreed to go ahead the previous evening and were now going back on their word. At one point, he threw his pencil down on the table in exasperation. When the heads departed for lunch, the foreign ministers remained and once again worked on redrafting several paragraphs. I then met privately with the president so that I would be fully conversant with his views.

In the afternoon plenary session, the heads continued their morning discussion of economic matters but then turned back to the security communiqué. I drafted some additional language in an effort to satisfy the French and the Canadians. We took a break, and the heads and the ministers milled around together. I showed Cheysson some new language, and he said, "No." Mitterrand was sitting across the room, seeming sour and imperial. I had listened for a while to the Europeans beating up on us about our budget deficits. I finally fired back and hoped that the president agreed with what I said.

The president and I were standing together when Genscher and Kohl came over, carrying a draft with language they said the French had approved. Genscher said the Germans agreed, as did Pym. At that moment, Mrs. Thatcher joined us and overruled Pym, much to his embarrassment. Pym said weakly that he only meant to agree "subject to agreement by the prime minister." Mrs. Thatcher accused Kohl of accepting language that was too weak. They argued for a bit. Then she exclaimed, "I'm in the middle of an election. I bent over backwards for your election. Now it's your turn. I have taken a strong position, and I want a strong statement here." The Germans and British finally did agree, but then the French fell off. President Reagan felt double-crossed.

Before long, I found myself over in a corner with Margaret Thatcher and François Mitterrand. We puzzled together over the language, and suddenly Mitterrand produced something that, from my perspective, strengthened the language while, by referring to "the countries concerned," also made clear that France was not undertaking a commitment to deploy missiles on behalf of another country. I looked at Margaret Thatcher, saw that she was on board, and said, "I think the president will buy this." I hustled over and found him completely satisfied with the solution.

Meanwhile, John Hughes, my press spokesman, and David Gergen, White House director of communications, were straining to get a statement out, as the press was growing negative, ready to write stories about a "summit in disarray." I went over to the U.S. press center, delivered our statement, and responded to questions. The security communiqué had emerged from the meeting itself and was very much a product of the heads of government themselves. It was the solid allied statement that our INF negotiations required. For the first time it brought the

Japanese formally into the Western security system. The language was strong and unambiguous:

> Effective arms control agreements must be based on the principle of equality and must be verifiable. . . . Our nations express the strong wish that a balanced I.N.F. agreement be reached shortly. Should this occur, the negotiations will determine the level of deployment. It is well known that should this not occur, the countries concerned will proceed with the planned deployment of the U.S. systems in Europe at the end of 1983. . . . The security of our countries is indivisible and must be approached on a global basis. Attempts to avoid serious negotiation by seeking to influence public opinion in our countries will fail.

David Gergen sought me out and said that he hoped that Don Regan and I could give a little "color" on how effective the president had been. That was easy to do. President Reagan had come into his own as a forceful and effective leader at this summit. He had really put himself into it. The *Washington Post* editorialized on June 1: "With both Japan and France on board, the seven endorsed a statement giving Mr. Reagan the boost for new missile deployment in Europe that he was eager to receive, and a pledge of fidelity to arms control that he was eager to give. The Kremlin sought to deter such a statement by a missile-rattling threat of its own on the eve of the summit, but the seven heads of government held firm. From all accounts, Mr. Reagan personally acted very much the leader of the alliance. He was 'up' for the summit, he set its tone of constructive engagement with common concerns, and he mastered all the theatrical possibilities available in the splendid Williamsburg setting. The president will take political credit for his performance, and he has every right to."

I recalled my meeting with Helmut Schmidt before the Versailles summit the year before. "The alliance needs a leader, and President Reagan must lead," he had told me. I had reported this to the president on my return and said to him, "A leader is needed, and you're elected." Now I felt, after the Williamsburg summit, that he not only had been elected, but he had performed brilliantly in the job. "Mr. President," I told him, "you've earned your spurs."

Strategic Ebb and Flow

After Williamsburg, a progression of point and counterpoint followed. We and our allies worked toward the set date—November 1983—to start deploying our missiles in Europe, and we worked to keep negotiations with the Soviets going forward. If one track fell out of line with the other, the effort risked failure. At the same time, the meetings with the Soviets contained their own movement of proposal and response but with no emergent harmony.

America's strategic deterrent had for years been at some disadvantage because of domestic opposition to locating intercontinental ballistic missiles (ICBMs) on American soil. Our heavy ballistic missile, the MX, was not deployable without a survivable basing mode. "Domestic opposition" was a political problem the Soviet Union never had to consider.

President Reagan had earlier appointed a commission chaired by Brent Scowcroft, former national security adviser to President Nixon, to review our problems with finding a suitable basing mode for the MX and with the concept underlying this weapon. On April 11, the commission recommended basing 100 MX missiles in existing silos, a further emphasis on reducing the total number of nuclear warheads, and development of a new strategic missile, the Midgetman, carrying only one warhead. The report was well received among the experts, who hoped to break the logjam on defense modernization and on appropriations for the production of the MX. We made adjustments in our START position in May and early June, but no further progress was made in the INF talks, and the spring round adjourned on July 14, scheduled to resume on September 6.

Meanwhile, Genscher gave me a report on a visit to Moscow he made in early July. He questioned whether we could really talk to Moscow through Gromyko. "There are others," he said, counseling me that I should travel to Moscow, since that was the only way to see Andropov and his associates.

Known to only a handful of people, President Reagan had received a private letter from General Secretary Andropov saying that the Soviet people were interested in reducing the nuclear threat. While at Camp David, Ronald Reagan wrote out by hand his reply, dated July 11, saying that the American people shared the same desire and suggesting that we do something about it, perhaps in a more personal channel. The president told me of his letter a little sheepishly. I was glad he had gone ahead on his own. "If you had staffed that through the NSC process, it would never have happened," I told him. Here is the text of the president's letter:

THE WHITE HOUSE

WASHINGTON

July 11, 1983

Dear Gen. Secretary Andropov

I appreciate very much your letter pledging an, "unbending commitment of the Soviet leadership and the people of the Soviet Union to the course of peace, the elimination of the nuclear threat and the development of relations based on mutual benefit and equality with all nations."

July 11, 1983

Dear Gen. Secretary Andropov

I appreciate very much your letter pledging an, "unbending commitment of the Soviet leadership and the people of the Soviet Union to the course of peace, the elimination of the nuclear threat and the development of relations based on mutual benefit and equality with all nations."

Let me assure you the government & the people of the United States are dedicated to, "the course of peace" and "the elimination of the nuclear threat." It goes without saying that we also seek relations with all nations based on "mutual benefit and equality." Our record since we were allied in W.W.II confirms that.

Mr. General Secretary could we not begin to approach these goals in the meetings now going on in Geneva? You and I share an enormous responsibility for the preservation of stability in the world. I believe we can fulfill that mandate but to do so will require a more active level of exchange than we have heretofore been able to establish. We have much to talk about with regard to the situation in Eastern Europe, South Asia, and particularly this hemisphere as well as in such areas as arms control, trade between our two countries and other ways in which we can expand east-west contacts.

Historically our predecessors have made better progress when communicating has been private and candid. If you wish to engage in such communication you will find me ready. I await your reply.

Sincerely
Ronald Reagan

Let me assure you the government & the people of the United States are dedicated to, "the course of peace" and "the elimination of the nuclear threat." It goes without saying that we also seek relations with all nations based on "mutual benefit and equality." Our record since we were allied in W.W. II confirms that.

Mr. General Secretary could we not begin to approach these goals in the meetings now going on in Geneva? You and I share an enormous responsibility for the preservation of stability in the world. I believe we can fulfill that mandate but to do so will require a more active level of exchange than we have heretofore been able to establish. We have much to talk about with regard to the situation in Eastern Europe, South Asia, and particularly this hemisphere as well as in such areas as arms control, trade between our two countries and other ways in which we can expand east-west contacts.

Historically our predecessors have made better progress when communicating has been private and candid. If you wish to engage in such communication you will find me ready. I await your reply.

Sincerely
Ronald Reagan

I later discovered that the president had shown his first draft to Bill Clark and, on the advice of Clark, he had taken out the sentences "If we can agree on mutual, verifiable reductions in the number of nuclear weapons we both hold, could this not be a first step toward elimination of all such weapons? What a blessing this would be for the people we both represent." President Reagan was consistently committed to his personal vision of a world without nuclear weapons; his advisers were determined to turn him away from that course.

On August 26, anticipating the resumption of negotiations, Yuri Andropov offered to bring down the number of Soviet medium-range missiles in its European territory to the combined British and French level and to destroy those missiles rather than redeploy them in Asia. He made no commitments regarding other current or prospective deployments in Asia. On August 29, President Reagan was in California on vacation, and I had just returned to Washington. We talked at length on the secure phone about Andropov's proposal and his most recent letter to the president. I thought Andropov's letter was cold, I told him. The president was pushing for a response. He wondered whether we were on the losing side of the argument on British and French systems.

"We have to keep this negotiation limited to the Big Two," I said. We should welcome the offer in Andropov's letter to reduce their numbers of missiles and destroy those removed from deployment rather than redeploy them in Asia. But we must maintain our basic criteria of global limits and of unwillingness to include British and French strategic systems in the INF negotiations. Most important, we should continue to make clear that we will deploy our INF missiles on schedule if no agreement is reached.

Korean Air Lines Flight 007

For the Labor Day weekend and the days preceeding, I had invited close friends from California to stay at my home in Bethesda. "Nothing is going on. Congress is in recess. It will be quiet. We can relax and talk," I told them when they arrived Wednesday evening. When my phone rang the next morning at 6:30 A.M., September 1, my initial reaction was that the call must have something to do with Lebanon. Instead, I was told that a Korean airliner had "disappeared" over Soviet territory: it had probably been shot down by the Soviets.

By 7:45, I was at the State Department and getting more details. Two hundred and sixty-nine people had been aboard the plane, including Congressman Larry McDonald of Georgia and sixty other Americans. The first intelligence reports—American and Japanese—indicated that the Soviets had shot the airliner down somewhere near or over Sakhalin, the huge Soviet island in northeast Asia. The plane had been off course, was well into Soviet territory, but was about to leave Soviet airspace when the Soviet interceptors, who had followed it for two and a half hours, shot it down.

At 8:20 A.M., I called Bill Clark, who was with the president in California. President Reagan already had been notified. We exchanged information, as yet somewhat sketchy. I told Larry Eagleburger to call in Oleg Sokolov, the Soviet chargé. Within an hour, much more information was coming in: the CIA had a transcript, I was told, of the Soviet pilot's conversation with his ground control, who ordered him to shoot the aircraft down, the pilot's acknowledgment, and then his confirmation that he had been successful.

A heated internal debate bubbled up over whether we could use such intelligence without dangerously compromising the means by which we got it. I told Eagleburger to work on the CIA, and he convinced them that the stakes were so high that they must agree I could use it, both with the Soviets and in public.

The debate now shifted, with even greater intensity, to what our public statement should be and who should make it. The president agreed that I should hold a press conference and get the facts out quickly. How should we characterize them? A decision had to be made now about how the United States would treat this disaster. What was said in the next hour or so would shape our reaction in a fundamental way. People began to give me drafts of what I should say. I found them all dangerously overdrawn, couched in an ominous tone that might suggest some form of U.S. military reaction or retaliation. I rejected the confrontational rhetoric.

*   *   *

I held a press conference at 10:45 A.M. to address what had transpired. Among my objectives was to let the Soviets know that we knew the essential facts about what had happened so that they would not try to deny them. I wanted to be totally factual but at the same time to let there be no doubt in anyone's mind that the Soviets had committed a terrible, unwarranted act.

In my opening statement, I said:

> At 1400 hours Greenwich mean time yesterday, a Korean Air Lines Boeing 747 en route from New York to Seoul, Korea, departed Anchorage, Alaska. Two hundred sixty-nine passengers and crew were on board, including Congressman Lawrence P. McDonald.
>
> At approximately 1600 hours Greenwich mean time, the aircraft came to the attention of Soviet radar. It was tracked constantly by the Soviets from that time.
>
> The aircraft strayed into Soviet airspace over the Kamchatka Peninsula and over the Sea of Okhotsk and over the Sakhalin Islands. The Soviets tracked the commercial airliner for some two and a half hours.
>
> A Soviet pilot reported visual contact with the aircraft at 1812 hours. The Soviet plane was, we know, in constant contact with its ground control.
>
> At 1821 hours the Korean aircraft was reported by the Soviet pilot at 10,000 meters. At 1826 hours the Soviet pilot reported that he fired a missile and the target was destroyed. At 1830 hours the Korean aircraft was reported by radar at 5,000 meters. At 1838 hours the Korean plane disappeared from the radar screen. . . .
>
> The United States reacts with revulsion to this attack. Loss of life appears to be heavy. We can see no excuse whatsoever for this appalling act.

Roger Mudd called my presentation "controlled fury."

Shortly after the press conference, I called the president, at about 8:30 his time in California. He had seen my press conference and felt it was strong. He, too, felt it was important to keep getting the facts out quickly, as the story was breaking fast. "We should keep on top of the story," he said.

"If they thought this was a commercial airliner, there is no excuse," I said, "but if they thought it was a U.S. intelligence plane and tracked it and didn't contact us, that's also an extremely serious matter. This has great implications. We must think through carefully and quickly what our follow-on activities should be. We've called in Sokolov, the chargé now at their embassy in Washington. He didn't have any information or any instructions. We don't know what they'll come back with. If they stiff-arm us, we should be prepared to act, including at the United Nations. There are many actions that we can take. It's an urgent matter."

The president asked about the impact of this event on the progress we had been making with the Soviets in other areas. "This will no doubt lead to all sorts of questions and will set back our positive efforts toward the Soviet Union," I said. "So much depends, of course, on how they react to our statement. We can expect political pressure here at home for us to break off our effort for better relations. I think I should go ahead with my scheduled meeting with Gromyko in Madrid in a few days," I told the president. I had already said as much in my press conference in response to a question.

"I will let the press know that we've talked. I'll tell them that if they think my reaction was strong, they should hear what you said on the phone. I don't want to overplay this, but it's important for us to put this whole thing on a world—not just a U.S.—basis and to bring Congress into the boat with us," I closed off.

As soon as I hung up the phone, Ed Meese called. Larry Speakes got on the line. I told them that with the president's approval we were now trying to examine all the implications of this event. "The Soviets owe the world an explanation," I said. I started calling congressional leaders. I caught up first with Senate Minority Leader Robert Byrd and told him that there would be tremendous reaction against the Soviets over this.

By 12:30 P.M., we got the first response from the Soviets when Oleg Sokolov came into the State Department. Gromyko, he told us, said KAL 007 was warned off but kept on. Sokolov speculated that the plane probably crashed, adding, "This is what they told me to tell you," a highly unusual comment coming from a Soviet official. I told Sokolov to relay back that this reply was completely unsatisfactory.

By midafternoon, I had learned that the president was returning to Washington immediately. By late that evening, with support from the South Koreans, we had agreed that we would go to the UN Security Council with our views on this matter. My houseguests from California took me to the Four Seasons for dinner that evening. As we walked through the door, someone called out, "Mr. Secretary, give 'em hell."

Friday, September 2, brought sad news. Senator Henry (Scoop) Jackson had died suddenly late the previous night. Scoop had persistently and intelligently called the Soviet Union to account for its actions over the years. His death was a real loss to the country, all the greater coming at such a critical moment. I had known him for many years.

CIA and NSA (National Security Agency) briefers then came in to give me their latest information. They now said that they felt that the Soviets might have mistaken the identity of the aircraft. I said that if the Soviets shot down a 747 thinking that it was our intelligence plane, "that is still terribly disturbing." But it was obvious that our intelligence aircraft, the RC-135, bore no resemblance to the distinctive profile of KAL's Boeing 747. We also knew the Soviets had tracked and observed the 747 over a period of hours, so that a case of "mistaken identity" was not remotely plausible. That the CIA was advancing such a theory made no sense and raised my suspicions. The intelligence community was being very elusive again. I had the feeling there was something they were not telling me. "They have no compunctions about fooling you," I told my group of Soviet specialists—Art Hartman, Rick Burt, Larry Eagleburger, and Mark Palmer.

Already a rush to the barricades had started. I was being urged to avoid my meeting with Gromyko in Madrid, cancel the negotiations over a long-term grain agreement with the Soviets, walk out of the arms talks. I was determined *not* to be stampeded into such actions. Dean Rusk called to invite me to a meeting of former secretaries of state. I laughed. I told him I thought it was a little premature. "I will go ahead and meet Gromyko," I told my colleagues at State. "I'll concentrate on the Korean airliner, demand an accounting, and focus also on human rights."

"We've known the Soviets have a stinking system," our ambassador to Moscow, Art Hartman, chipped in, "but we have to deal with it. We should not be surprised at what they are capable of. That is the difference between our societies."

Early Friday afternoon we met with the U.S. and international airline pilots' associations. A *Tass* statement came in: the Soviets still did not admit that they shot the plane down but, incredibly, said that the plane was on a deliberate intelligence mission. It was ludicrous.

I was not surprised at this Soviet behavior, as Jimmy Carter had been by the Soviet invasion of Afghanistan.[3] On the other hand, I was not pleased by those in the administration who were pushing for drastic responses. The president in his statement before leaving California had referred to "the barbarous act committed yesterday." I thought of my experience the night before at the Four Seasons and the "Mr. Secretary, give 'em hell" remark. I called *Air Force One* and commented on the absurd *Tass* statement and said that we should get our response out quickly so that it would be on the evening news. By 5:30 P.M., I made a statement in our pressroom rebutting the *Tass* statement.

By late afternoon President Reagan was back in Washington, and I had met with him in the White House. "There is a great contrast between your administration's view of the Soviets and the Carter administration's before Afghanistan," I told him. "We are not surprised; we are incensed. At the same time, we need to keep our heads. The whole world is shocked, not

3. When the Soviets invaded Afghanistan, President Carter declared his surprise and said it had taught him more about the Soviets in two and one-half days than he had known before and that it had changed his opinion of them. He responded by canceling everything then in the works with the Soviets: he withdrew from the Olympics, imposed an embargo on grain sales to the Soviets, and pulled the SALT II agreement back from consideration for ratification by the Senate.

just the United States. We should not let this become a U.S. versus the Soviets issue."

The president was very strong on organizing people to take specific steps: the attorney general suggested taking the matter to the International Court of Claims. Don Regan argued for economic sanctions. The president listened but was negative on sanctions. "I've been there," he said, referring to the Siberian pipeline sanctions. The president agreed that we should drag our feet on such things as consular and cultural agreements. It would not be business as usual, but we would not be thrown off course, either.

When the discussion moved on to my imminent meeting in Madrid with Gromyko,[4] Cap Weinberger objected violently: "George should not go." The president did not agree. I suggested that I drop my planned lunch with Gromyko and limit the agenda for Madrid to KAL 007 and human rights. The president agreed. Weinberger next advocated sending Paul Nitze to Madrid with me to say to Gromyko that there would be no more arms control negotiations until we had a satisfactory explanation of the downing of the KAL. The president brushed this aside. I could see that he wanted to take a hard position with the Soviets but that he was not about to break off from important dealings with them. No decision was reached as to when to use the actual recording the CIA had obtained of the Soviet pilot talking with his ground control. I was authorized to internationalize our efforts to bring about a search-and-rescue effort in the area.

When I returned to the State Department that night, a report had come in that longshoremen in Long Beach were prepared to attack any Soviet seamen whose ships docked in that port and that the Coast Guard had turned two Soviet merchant ships away. I gave instructions that we tell Sokolov that the United States could not guarantee them protection at this time: we did not deny Soviet ships the right to sail into our harbors, but we warned them that they were better off not to do so at this tense time.

Early the next morning I talked to David Gergen about the president's radio address, scheduled to take place that Saturday. I told him that we had the same view of the Soviets now as we had a week ago. This incident highlighted the nature of the Soviet system. The president must come across as a man of peace and dignity.

Later, I had a long talk with Senator Howard Baker. He was struck by reactions throughout the country. He recounted a conversation he had with a lawyer friend in Tennessee who was an avid Democrat. His friend was furious because Ronald Reagan had been right about the Russians. "They're a bunch of bastards," Howard quoted him as saying. "The KAL incident is having a tremendous impact throughout the country. We

4. I would join the foreign ministers of all European countries and Canada in marking the conclusion of a three-year conference on human rights (CSCE).

shouldn't overplay it," Baker said. "This will become, on its own momentum, our best support for the administration's hard line." Baker recounted suggesting to the president that all Soviet airplanes be suspended from landing anywhere until they made reparations; the president had responded wryly, "Remember, Howard, I'm president, and you're not."

Our approach was still evolving, but already decisions had been taken on what *not* to do. We were not going to cancel my meeting with Gromyko. We were not going to pull out of the INF and START talks. This was not going to be easy to manage. The knee-jerk reaction of Cap and other hardliners was to stop all contacts. Others pointed to the Nixon-Kissinger "linkage" approach to U.S.-Soviet relations to argue that we must not move forward in any area when an outrageous act is committed in another area. I regarded President Reagan's support for Paul Nitze and Ed Rowny's return to the arms control talks as courageous in this charged atmosphere.

I told my staff I wanted four papers, one on financial claims against the Soviets, another on how to approach the United Nations, a third on civil aviation matters, and a fourth on the nature of potential boycotts. "We must bring other countries along with us," I instructed.

As we sought to prove what had happened, evidence mounted against the Soviets. Public emotions escalated correspondingly. By noon on Sunday, we received from the Japanese the actual tape recording of the Soviet fighter pilot talking with his ground controller: the pilot had followed the airliner, assessed and reported on its position, and under orders from his ground control, shot it down. The pilot's words, "The target is destroyed," would chill the world when it was played at the United Nations and subsequently on the news, worldwide.

At a meeting Sunday morning with the Republican leadership in the White House, Senator Strom Thurmond had suggested the expulsion of "269 KGB agents in the U.S." to calls of "terrific" from the assembled crowd. We speculated whether Gromyko would cancel our meeting in Madrid under these circumstances. Cap argued once again that we should be the ones to cancel.

Afterward, President Reagan telephoned to ask me about the idea of the KGB expulsions. He didn't think much of the idea; neither did I. The Soviets would retaliate with their own expulsions, I said, and that would hurt us, as an open society, more than it would hurt them. "We do not want to turn this whole thing into a U.S.-Soviet issue," I stressed once again. I made a note to check carefully the president's upcoming speech, which would be televised nationwide Monday evening, to be sure that someone didn't slip the KGB expulsion idea in at the last minute. Only I and a very few others knew how intent the president was on developing his relationship with the Soviets and that he had sent a personal letter to Andropov in early July.

*   *   *

Monday, September 5, was Labor Day. I learned that Bill Casey had made a reference, on background, to a U.S. Air Force RC-135 being in the area when KAL 007 was shot down, and the press was questioning American honesty about what had happened. I asked for a full intelligence briefing. At 8:00 A.M., I was informed that the RC-135 had flown a mission to monitor a Soviet missile test in the Soviet Far East. It was a means of verification to which the Soviets had agreed. The RC-135 had crossed KAL 007's flight path at one point only. The Soviet ground station had assigned each aircraft a different tracking number, and the two aircraft were some 1,700 kilometers apart when the Soviets shot down the Korean airliner.

The last time that the Soviets monitored the RC-135 had been at 1640 Greenwich mean time. They shot down KAL 007 at 1826, or about two hours later—at a time when the RC-135 was back on the ground in Alaska. The RC-135 had never approached Soviet territory closer than thirty-eight nautical miles. So the RC-135 story was a red herring. I decided that we should urgently get the facts out about the RC-135. "The key in all of our representations in this matter is the emphasis on *the facts*, combined with our genuine concern," I stressed.

The president spoke on national television on Monday evening, September 5. His speech contained stirring rhetoric and yet was also appropriately controlled about what actions we would take. We were on our way, I thought, to mobilizing a strong worldwide reaction, one coordinated as a world concern, not just a U.S.-Soviet matter. We had witnessed the beginnings of a cold war minithaw prior to the shooting down of KAL 007. The superpower relationship had been warming up. The KAL attack brought back the cold. But we had to continue to engage the Soviets. "We have to realize that the Soviets are producing and deploying missiles like they are stamping out cookies with cookie cutters," I told my staff, "and they're aimed at us." That is why, I said, "our interests are served by continuing the INF and START talks. If the INF talks do not succeed by November, this step will help us manage our deployments."

On Tuesday, September 6, at a morning meeting at the White House, the president authorized me to meet with Gromyko in Madrid. He agreed that we should keep the focus on human rights and KAL 007. "We will continue with the arms control talks, but we can't do anything more than that," he said. We discussed whether KAL 007 was shot down with full knowledge by the top Soviet political leadership. We didn't know for sure about that, but certainly the top political leadership orchestrated the Soviet response. "Their reaction to the event demonstrates the mentality that allowed it to happen in the first place," I said. "They still continue to blunder."

So I went to Madrid for the CSCE meeting, which before the KAL tragedy had all the potential of being a celebration of progress on human rights, including progress with the Soviet Union. On the plane I reviewed all the elements of our meetings in Madrid with Max Kampelman, our negotiator, Art Hartman, Rick Burt, John Hughes, and Jack Matlock, the new coordinator of Soviet affairs on the NSC staff. After some argument among them, I concluded that I had to be ready to play the tape, provided by the Japanese, of the actual conversation between the pilot and his ground control. I had planned early meetings, starting with breakfast, for representatives of NATO and of the neutral and nonaligned countries. I decided that the way to handle the meeting was to make the tape available after the breakfast and suggest that anyone who wished to hear it could do so.

I arrived in Madrid in the early hours of September 7. At the breakfast that morning with the NATO foreign ministers, I found the discussion discouraging. There was no sign of a vigorous response by European governments. They talked about the legalities of overflight rights in the Soviet Union. "Public opinion in the U.S. is running high," I pointed out. "We have been restrained, but action is called for. You can see the beginnings," I told them, of a "public demand that any country that allows its planes to fly to the Soviet Union or Soviet planes to use its airfields will not be allowed to fly planes to the United States." That would be devastating and was just the kind of unilateral action I wanted to avoid. As it turned out, everyone wanted to listen to the tape of the Soviet pilot and his ground control: its impact was undeniable.

We had another session over lunch at which I tried my best to organize a strong multinational protest accompanied by strong actions. Support was developing for a two-way moratorium on air traffic that would run for one or two weeks. "You are all way behind your publics," I told them. Geoffrey Howe had become aware of this. The unions in Great Britain were outraged. Rick Burt suggested that we try to nail down the moratorium concept but not the length of time it would last.

At 4:00 P.M. I reported back to the president. "There is a lot of indignation," I said. "The nonaligned nations are a little more moderate than the NATO ministers. Insofar as the refusal of landing rights to the Soviets is concerned, the duration is the key issue. The basic idea under discussion is a good one—a moratorium on two-way traffic: nobody goes to the Soviet Union and no Soviet planes are allowed to come to non-Soviet countries." I urged that the president write strong letters to allied leaders and send them off right away. I did not want reservations about action to mount. Some of the allies were concerned about losing their own overflight rights across the Soviet Union. Cheysson was negative about doing anything that would interfere with civil aviation. Once again he was under tight instructions, so there was no point arguing with him. I felt it was important to take some significant action, if for no other reason than to prevent a variety of ineffective responses and therefore a division among our allies.

We got a break. Margaret Thatcher had sent instructions that she wanted to achieve something big and broadly based. Later that day, Gromyko spoke to the General Assembly of the CSCE. His statement was astonishingly brutal: "Since the plane-trespasser did not obey the order to proceed to a Soviet airfield and attempted to evade, an air defense interceptor carried out the order of the command post to stop the flight. Such actions are in full conformity with the law on the U.S.S.R. state border." He continued, "We state: Soviet territory, the borders of the Soviet Union are sacred." Under similar circumstances, in other words, they would do it again. His words were chilling to his listeners and created an intense furor throughout the free world toward the Soviets and the brutality of their system.

At least by this time, the Soviets had acknowledged that they did shoot the plane down. I could soon see the impact of Mrs. Thatcher's new instructions to the British delegation. Others were now coming around to do something unified, quick, and important. In spite of all the arguments about precisely what we should do, the statements being made by foreign ministers, one after the other, were excellent. The harshness of Gromyko's speech had stunned people.

The airline pilots were getting into the act as well. It looked as if U.S. pilots would vote for a sixty-day moratorium and that they would try to extend that internationally among all pilots. "Maybe the pilots will take you off the hook," I said to my fellow foreign ministers in NATO, particularly directing my eye to the French, "But you shouldn't let private groups make your foreign policy for you. You should get out in front and recognize that something strong and definite needs to be done, right here and now." There was no respect for human life, I stressed, in what Gromyko had said. I also pointed out to our allies that the president had sent Paul Nitze back to the INF talks despite great pressure not to do so. We wanted to keep that element of our relationship going, but in order to do so, I argued, we and our allies had to take unified action in this crisis.

Nitze reported he had word that the Soviets intended to break off the INF talks by October 12. So be it, I thought: that would be the Soviets breaking off; the effect on world opinion would be entirely different if the United States was the side that walked out. I got strong support from Giulio Andreotti, the Italian foreign minister, that the missile deployment schedule would go forward if the INF negotiations did not succeed. The ministers from the other basing countries agreed as well.

My meeting with Gromyko was to take place on the afternoon of September 8. I went over to our ambassador's residence after lunch to prepare for Gromyko's arrival. I planned to take him into a small room with only our interpreters and try to talk to him directly, first about human rights and then about the KAL downing. When he arrived, we went into the study for half an hour. The atmosphere was tense. He was totally unresponsive. I told him that we felt they had made a commitment during the

Madrid negotiations and through Max Kampelman to release Anatoly Shcharansky. Gromyko denied that any such commitment had been made. He declared once more that human rights was an internal concern, inappropriate for discussion between our two countries. I pointed to the CSCE document, in which each signatory nation agreed to honor specific human rights, and said that their signature on it made such discussion proper. I then turned to the Soviets' attack on KAL 007. Once again, Gromyko was totally intransigent. I regarded this meeting as a last effort to come to grips with this crisis with him on a human level, but it was fruitless.

In the larger plenary session that followed, Gromyko was determined to discuss matters other than human rights and KAL 007. He, as the guest, spoke first and went into the arms control negotiations. In our private session, he had at least admitted that the Soviets were responsible for the shooting down of KAL 007 and that this act had been authorized at senior levels. But the plenary session developed into a brutally confrontational meeting. At one point, Gromyko stood up and picked up his papers as though to leave. I think he half-expected me to urge him to sit down. On the contrary, I got up to escort him out of the room. He then sat down, and I sat down. After the meeting ended, my interpreter, Bill Krimer, told me that he had been interpreting in high-level meetings with the Soviets for seventeen years and had never seen anything remotely like it.

I called President Reagan and told him that Gromyko couldn't bring himself to answer any of my questions. The meeting became so outrageous and pointless that we just ended it. But I told the president that the French and the other allies were hearing from their pilots' unions and I believed that by the time the night was over, most of our allies would agree on significant actions: amendments on air traffic control through the International Civil Aviation Organization (ICAO); prohibition of normal liaison operations with the Soviets by NATO military attachés; a call for better military and civilian coordination of flights; a move to take these matters to the UN Security Council; explicit support for the five South Korean demands of the Soviets; and support for a two-week moratorium in air traffic to and from the Soviet Union, starting on September 15. I added that I believed the Irish would go along. "That's a big thing for them," I said, "because they get so much revenue from the Soviet use of their airfield at Shannon."

By 10:45 that evening, the NATO ministers met once again. Finally, we got somewhere. My charged session with Gromyko and his outrageous remarks had made it easier to put together a strong allied response. I had to give a great deal of credit to Hans-Dietrich Genscher. He had quickly appreciated the importance and the political difficulty of the president's decision to send Nitze and Rowny back to the arms control talks, demonstrating the seriousness of purpose so necessary in West Germany to sustain a tough decision to deploy missiles. Genscher could see that our action needed a counterpoint in clear moves in other areas, particularly in the field of civil aviation. He worked hard and effectively to achieve practical and operational agreements.

Endgame

In the midst of this atmosphere of recrimination and developing actions, the drama moved to other fronts. With Gromyko due to arrive in New York toward the end of September for the start of the annual UN General Assembly, and with popular antagonism toward the Soviets at fever pitch in the United States, the governors of New York and New Jersey took it upon themselves, on September 15, to deny landing rights to Gromyko's aircraft. The governors thumped their chests and took political bows. Their actions were, however, counterproductive. Not only did they present us a problem stemming from our obligation to permit the representatives of UN member-states to come to New York; it also took Gromyko off the hook. We immediately offered landing rights at a convenient military airfield, but Gromyko spurned the offer, claiming we were violating our obligations to the United Nations. On September 17, he canceled his appearance in New York. He had been isolated at Madrid, where his words and behavior turned everyone against him. All the governors had done was to give him the reason he needed to duck out of an embarrassing UN appearance.

Genscher called me on Tuesday, September 20, urging that an announcement be made of new INF moves by Thursday or at least before Sunday's elections in West Germany. I knew that the Germans were uneasy and were looking for every scrap of evidence that they could find that we were serious about pursuing a negotiating track with the Soviets.

On September 26, President Reagan, speaking at the start of the UN General Assembly, called for global limits on intermediate-range nuclear forces (INF) and, without giving up on our ultimate goal of the complete elimination of these weapons, asserted that the United States was open to negotiation over the number of Pershings and GLCMs to be deployed in Europe. He also proposed discussions on verifiable limits on some Soviet and American land-based aircraft. The next day, Foreign Minister Gromyko called the president's new proposal "patently unacceptable." A day later General Secretary Andropov followed suit, sharply dismissing President Reagan's proposal as "militarist," arguing that the United States planned to deploy new missiles in Europe, and complaining that we still excluded the British and French nuclear systems from the discussion.

The president did all he could to be constructive and avoid a confrontation. On television on October 4, he addressed the strategic arms issue, setting forth a "mutual, guaranteed build-down" of nuclear weapons levels. The Soviets rejected it within twenty-four hours. The tension was palpable and virtually global.

At a long session with the president in mid-October I told him that the absence of dialogue, even though the reasons were well understood, was causing worry both here and among the allies. I proposed, and he approved, my inviting Ambassador Dobrynin over for lunch. I also called attention to the start of meetings on confidence-building measures in Europe (CDE), to be convened in Stockholm beginning in mid-January 1984. "I should go and probably meet with Gromyko if he shows up," I said. He agreed.

"If things get hotter and hotter and arms control remains an issue," the president said, "maybe I should go see Andropov and propose eliminating all nuclear weapons."

"Without an arsenal of nuclear weapons, the Soviets are not a super-power," I replied.

When I met with Ambassador Dobrynin on October 28, he told me it looked to Moscow as if the United States sought confrontation, not problem solving. He said he thought the Korean Air Lines incident had been handled provocatively by us.

"On the contrary, we were restrained," I said, "but you reacted in an irrational manner. It was not only the United States that was repelled by what you did and said but everybody around the world." I asked again about Shcharansky, and he hinted to me that the approach to Kampelman had not been fully authorized. We had been well aware that Kampelman's channel had been through the Soviet KGB agent assigned to the Soviet delegation in Madrid and had assumed that Gromyko and his Foreign Ministry didn't like it. From our standpoint, we thought a Soviet commitment had been made on behalf of the "highest authority."

"We do not have a policy of confrontation," I told Dobrynin. "We can have discussions on important problems, but they cannot simply be about arms control. We need a constructive atmosphere." To this end, I mentioned that we had learned that the Soviets had some cosmonauts in trouble in space and that it was at least conceivable that a U.S. shuttle mission might rescue them. "We are headed into a dangerous period, and we are not well equipped to manage it. There are lots of points of tension," I said. "Some are predictable and some are unpredictable. We know some of the events that will take place, such as deployments. The outcome of many of these things is not sure. Unforeseen events occur. There is tension ahead of us, and our communication process is poor."

Dobrynin recalled the president's letter to Andropov and its reference to communication through private channels. He said they didn't understand what that meant.

"It means official yet informal exchanges that are restricted and private," I told him.

As our late November deployment time approached, there was a flurry of negotiating. The Soviets offered, on condition that we not deploy, to reduce their SS-20 launchers in Europe from 243 to 140 and, as they had promised before, to liquidate the balance rather than redeploy those weapons eastward to Asia. This amounted to 420 warheads that would remain, exactly the number the Soviets estimated were on British and French systems. They had accepted our principle of counting warheads rather than just launchers, but the inequality of their proposal made it unacceptable to us. After considerable argument back and forth, we countered with a global ceiling of 420 warheads for both the United States and the Soviet Union. This had a cosmetic resemblance to the Soviet proposal but, of course, was vastly different in that we would deploy 420 missiles, whereas in their proposal the United States would have none deployed. They rejected our counteroffer.

Countdown to Deployment

If the Reagan administration had a "D-Day," it was November 23, 1983: the day the first American Pershing II missiles would be deployed in West Germany, where protests and opposition to deployments were at a fever pitch. The logic was simple: we had to deploy our missiles in allied European territory to pressure the Soviets to remove their own missiles already targeted on Europe. But to the propagandists in Moscow and the peace activists of the West, D-Day was an opening to denounce the United States politically as the cause of world tension and to undermine the U.S. militarily by causing disunity in our alliance. There was a real chance that demonstrations could break the will of allied governments and prevent deployment—or at least pressure NATO so severely as to undermine our resolve to stand up to the Soviets in the future.

Newspapers, television commentators, public events, were filled with the rhetoric of fear: fear of nuclear war. Activists opposed to American policy seized the opportunity. As the key month of November started, a conference of scientists in Washington focused on a newly emerging assertion: that "nuclear winter," meaning the end of life on earth, could result from even a small-scale nuclear attack. In Europe, more than 2 million people had demonstrated in protests on October 22 and 23. An around-the-clock political campaign by women protesters at the Greenham Common deployment site in England was given wide news coverage.

ABC television's "The Day After," a docudrama depicting the result of a Soviet nuclear attack, was scheduled to be shown nationwide on November 20, virtually on the eve of critical deployments. Extensive media advertising had begun weeks before. Contraband copies of the two-hour drama had been circulating as early as September. According to a description in the *New York Times* on September 3, "the film is relentlessly depressing, with scenes of enormous destruction by firestorm, people being vaporized, mass graves, the irretrievable loss of food and water supplies, vandalism and murder, the breakdown of medical care and disfigurement and death from radiation sickness."

Was the drama a political statement designed to create fear and timed to stir up popular protest to block deployment of U.S. missiles on European soil? Many people in the State Department were highly apprehensive of the potential impact on the American public and the effect abroad when the show was aired in other countries. I was concerned.

Our public affairs bureau had been given an advance videotape of the show, so I had a monitor set up in my conference room and invited people working on our floor in the State Department to come and look at it. In general, they found the program heavy-handed and simple-minded in its depiction of the nuclear problem and of official American behavior as well as in its characterization of how a nuclear holocaust would start. Still, more than a few were apprehensive that the American public would be launched into a state of trauma by this program.

I agreed to appear on the ABC news program "Viewpoint" after the drama, which was watched by an audience of some 100 million people. The real issue, I wanted to make clear, was to handle crisis situations to avoid nuclear confrontation in the first place. Our point was to develop a diplomacy and an arms control policy to make deep cuts in nuclear weaponry and reduce the possibility of nuclear conflict. As Ronald Reagan himself said starkly, "A nuclear war can never be won and must never be fought."

On November 21, the day after "The Day After," the *Washington Post* reported, "Although the producers claimed that the film was not meant to make a political statement, it did. . . . The film suggested that deployment of U.S. cruise and Pershing II missiles in Europe to counter Soviet missiles stationed in the eastern U.S.S.R. was viewed as a provocation by Moscow and some U.S. allies. It suggested that the Soviets started a conventional war and that the United States escalated it to atomic war." As it turned out, the episode showed the importance, among other things, of not underestimating the intelligence of the American public. Outside the Beltway and outside the media circuit, the reaction by and large was that the fictional drama itself, although frightening, had been hyped massively and its importance exaggerated.

On November 14, the first Tomahawk cruise missiles had arrived in Britain; shortly thereafter another shipment was delivered in Italy. On

November 15, in plenary session at Geneva, the United States elaborated our INF proposal; the Soviets rejected it. On November 16, the Italian parliament voted in favor of our NATO deployments, 351 to 219. Six days later, the Norwegians endorsed the step, 78 to 77, with no margin to spare. The same day, November 22, the German Bundestag, after a tumultuous two-day debate, approved the deployments, 286 to 226. Before the vote, Paul Nitze's opposite number, Yuli Kvitsinsky, had proposed a renewal of the "walk in the woods," this time as "a walk in the park," in a deliberate and deceptive attempt to convince the Germans that the Soviets had made concessions in the talks, which the United States had spurned because of our resolve to deploy. Their deception did not work. Our allies were with us and recognized deception as well as we did.

The Soviets Walk Out

Our deployments took place on schedule. Allied unity and resolve were demonstrated. A true turning point had come, and it favored our cause. Strength was recognized as crucial to diplomacy.

The Soviets kept at it. They had played hardball from the beginning, and their actions grew tougher and more menacing after deployments began. On November 23, the day Pershing II missiles arrived in West Germany, the Soviets dramatically walked out of the INF negotiations in protest over the NATO deployments, saying they would never return while our deployments were in place. On December 8, they declined to set a time to resume the suspended START talks, thus bringing that negotiation to a halt. And on December 15, they declined to set a date for resumption of the talks in Vienna on conventional arms (MBFR).

At a private meeting with Chancellor Kohl in Bonn, I assured him that Ronald Reagan would spare no effort to develop a constructive dialogue with the Soviets but that Moscow would have to come forward with some reasonable positions. I emphasized patience and determination on INF, and he agreed.

"We should continually emphasize the theme that the greatest idea we have is *freedom*," Kohl told me. "We must keep in mind that the international communications systems increasingly reach into the USSR and Eastern Europe, and people there see the stark contrast between themselves and people who are free."

At the annual NATO foreign ministers' meeting on December 9, we and our allies produced the Brussels Declaration, concluding: "We shall continue to do our utmost to sustain a safe and peaceful future. We extend to the Soviet Union and the other Warsaw Pact countries the offer to work together with us to bring about a long-term constructive and realistic relationship based on equilibrium, moderation and reciprocity." Our cohesion, our readiness to engage, and our self-confidence were all quietly evident.

On the way home, flying from Lisbon to Washington on my birthday, December 13, I was mulling over the coming presidential election year of 1984. It was likely to be a time of hot domestic politics with little activity in foreign policy. If there was any way to avoid a dangerous new period of superpower tension, it would have to be worked out at the upcoming session of the Conference on Disarmament in Europe (CDE) in Stockholm. "Globally, things are not going well for the Soviets," I told my team. "They are in trouble in Angola, Afghanistan, and Cambodia. We may see some movement in our direction in Mozambique. In Poland, the economy is in desperate shape. Poland is an exhibition of the bankruptcy of the Soviet system. They've had a setback in Europe, and there is a succession problem internally."

When we landed at Shannon to refuel on our way to Washington, everyone was primed for a birthday surprise: at a recent White House dinner, I had danced with Ginger Rogers; pictures had been taken. One had been sent to Ginger, and it was now presented to me. "Dear George, For a moment I thought I was dancing with Fred. Love, Ginger," she had inscribed. Then we all celebrated with smoked salmon and Irish coffee. As we taxied down the runway preparing for takeoff, Paul Nitze looked out at the green Irish countryside, sparkling with bright spots of water. "In the days when Shannon first opened," he said, "we had to spend quite a few hours here; there was time to get out and wet a line, kill a salmon or two." It was the voice of an earlier era of diplomacy.

On returning to Washington, I found President Reagan thinking again about his desire to eliminate nuclear weapons. No one in the arms control community shared Reagan's view. I told Rick Burt and Jon Howe, "This is his instinct and his belief. The president has noticed that no one pays any attention to him in spite of the fact that he speaks about this idea publicly and privately. I told the president yesterday that I would study the proposition. We owe him an answer. The president believes that this is the way to go. If we disagree, we have to demonstrate why."

When I met with the president on Saturday, December 17, he said he wanted to make a major Soviet speech and include in it his readiness to get rid of nuclear weapons. He told me he had noticed that Soviet Defense Minister Ustinov in a speech two days previously, had proposed a ban on all nuclear weapons. By Monday, December 19, we had a good draft speech in the president's hands. He decided to give it in early January as the first part of a one-two message, with the second part being my speech at the CDE conference in Stockholm.

Throughout this struggle involving INF negotiations and our deployments, the Reagan administration took a beating in the press for its deep internal divisions and disagreement. We did have fierce arguments about arms control. It was well known that Cap Weinberger and I debated about when and whether to change our position in the INF and START talks. Much of this debate leaked to the press, which described us as an administration in disarray. Strobe Talbott, among others, had put it in terms of a battle between the two Richards: Richard Perle in Defense and Richard Burt in State. Some aspects of these arguments and leaks were counterproductive and debilitating, but we had an identified process through which people expressed honest and divergent views. The process had resulted in a gradual change of our INF positions, with the timing and content of our moves being just about right. As long as the arguments were honest and substantive rather than personal, they didn't worry me. I would worry far more about an administration whose members agreed on every subject. These were tough issues, with important points to be made for and against any given position. Good arguments are healthy as long as decisions result that are timely and intelligent.

President Reagan had kept a cool hand and a cool head. Our moves in arms control negotiations had been well timed. Our INF deployments had begun. Our allies were with us. The Soviets had suffered a severe propaganda defeat throughout Europe. Now it was time for us to try to resume a dialogue with the Soviets if we could, but on the basis that Ronald Reagan advocated. With deployments under way, our position was one of strength. We had started the year 1983 with Soviet threats and efforts to decouple the United States from our European allies. We ended the year with our alliance stronger than ever, forged by a common effort that proceeded under conditions of enormous tension. But we and our allies would need to hold our posture of firm resolve. The Soviets had walked out of the INF negotiations, saying that they would not return until we removed the missiles we were then deploying. I didn't believe that for a minute.

Part V

ON THE MOVE

CHAPTER 22

China:
Dealing Across Ideologies

"I am not here to play cards," I would tell the Chinese leadership in the Great Hall of the People in February 1983. "I am here to build our bilateral relationship and to discuss issues of mutual concern around the world."

In the summer and fall of 1982 when I came into office, I started lining up my ideas and developing strategic priorities. Visits are an important expression of presidential priorities. I saw a need for a sequence: first our neighbors to the north and south, then our European allies and Japan, then China, then the Soviet Union. Our democratic friends should come first; without them we could do little. President Reagan had been to Europe and met frequently with European leaders. I wanted him to go to Japan next, because Japan was our democratic and strategic partner and an emerging economic giant. Then should come a Reagan trip to China, to repair relations and put them on a sustainable footing so that we could focus most effectively on the country that presented the most critical issues of strategic significance: the Soviet Union. Ronald Reagan's first trip to a Communist country would require him to "deal across ideologies." It would not be easy for someone with his political principles, but it was a skill he would have to develop if we were to succeed in our foreign policy.

A Different China Policy

President Reagan's instincts and my own views on the People's Republic of China (PRC) were similar. We well understood and appreciated the geostrategic importance of China: an ancient culture with large ethnic Chinese communities extending into many other countries of the region, a nuclear power with ballistic missile capability, an antagonist to the Soviets and a partner in efforts to counter them in Afghanistan and Cambodia, and a country with a permanent seat and veto power in the UN Security

Council and with an enormous population of tremendous talent and capable of becoming a large trading and investment partner. Recognizing this, we nevertheless sought to alter the thinking underlying our policy. My own attitude was a marked departure from the so-called China-card policy: the idea that the United States could maneuver back and forth, playing one big Communist power off against another.

When the geostrategic importance of China became the conceptual prism through which Sino-American relations were viewed, it was almost inevitable that American policymakers became overly solicitous of Chinese interests, concerns, and sensitivities. Indeed, while President Nixon's historic opening to China in 1972 gave both countries some leverage with the Soviets, it is also true that the opening gave the Chinese leverage against us. As a result, much of the history of Sino-American relations since normalization of relations in 1978 could be described as a series of Chinese-defined "obstacles"—such as Taiwan, technology transfers, and trade—that the United States had been tasked to overcome in order to preserve the overall relationship.

On the basis of my own experience, I knew it would be a mistake to place too much emphasis on a relationship for its own sake. A good relationship should emerge from the ability to solve substantive problems of interest to both countries. As an old labor hand, I had observed over the years that good relations deteriorate when the two sides start valuing the relationship itself too highly. That would lead the union leader to say, "Let's not push that grievance. It will upset management." Or it would lead management to say to a foreman, "Don't get so excited about that problem; you'll only stir up the union stewards." When problems are not addressed, the relationship unfailingly deteriorates. I am convinced that in international relations, as in labor relations, the road to a bad relationship is to place too much emphasis on the relationship for its own sake.

Furthermore, the moment the Chinese saw that we so highly valued our relations with them, they would use that assessment to gain concessions. It was therefore in the interest of the Chinese to have us believe in the geostrategic triangle and in our responsibility for sustaining it. Once those premises had been granted, we could then be expected to concede on other issues, which by comparison paled in importance. For example, a tacit understanding arose that the United States should excuse, or at least overlook, almost continuous, virulent public Chinese criticism of U.S. policies on almost all international and regional issues, with the partial exceptions of Cambodia and Afghanistan. It had become standard practice for Americans visiting China to be treated to fire-breathing speeches denouncing the United States, followed by toasts and a sumptuous and amiable banquet.

So it was not surprising when I arrived at the State Department in mid-

1982 that our relationship was in trouble. The Chinese seemed to complain about every detail of the relationship, but the immediate issue was Taiwan and, in particular, the question of U.S. arms sales to Taiwan.

U.S. Arms Sales to Taiwan

The issue had been there, of course, from the beginning. On February 28, 1972, in Shanghai, at the conclusion of his visit to China, President Nixon and Premier Zhou Enlai issued a joint communiqué outlining the intentions of both countries to normalize relations. The United States deftly deferred the recognition issue by acknowledging that "all Chinese on either side of the Taiwan Strait maintain there is but one China and that Taiwan is a part of China." The Shanghai communiqué also highlighted, however, a key disagreement over the U.S. security relationship with Taiwan stemming from the 1954 Mutual Defense Treaty. While the Chinese called for the withdrawal of all U.S. military forces and installations from Taiwan, the United States pledged only a progressive reduction in forces and facilities as "the tension in the area diminishes."

A further compromise on Taiwan was spelled out in the agreement on normalizing relations between the United States and the People's Republic of China, which President Carter announced on December 15, 1978. On January 1, 1979, diplomatic relations with Taiwan terminated as diplomatic recognition was shifted to Beijing. The U.S. defense treaty with Taiwan was ended, but the Chinese failed to win a U.S. commitment to end arms sales to Taiwan. While recognizing the government of the People's Republic of China as "the sole legal government of China," the agreement also stated that the American and Taiwanese people would "maintain commercial, cultural, and other relations without official government representation and without diplomatic relations."

The euphoria following senior leader Deng Xiaoping's subsequent January visit to the United States was short-lived. In the spring of 1979, a coalition of conservatives and liberals in Congress passed the Taiwan Relations Act to "preserve and promote" by law future unofficial relations between the American and Taiwanese people. It was signed by the president on April 10. What particularly angered the People's Republic of China was the act's assertion that the United States would maintain its capacity to "resist any resort to force . . . that would jeopardize the security . . . of the people on Taiwan" and "provide Taiwan with arms of a defensive character." Taiwan was at least as angry over its loss of recognition and was worried about the longer-term implications for its security.

The continuing dissatisfaction of the People's Republic over the unresolved issue of arms sales to Taiwan led to the Reagan administration's first Sino-American diplomatic crisis when the PRC threatened to downgrade relations with the United States unless the arms sales were stopped. A negotiation dragged along, with the U.S. proposing a gradual reduction of arms sales with no upgrading of the quality of arms involved and the PRC insisting that all sales be stopped. To underline their point, the Chinese had reverted to their earlier and objectionable practice of equating the United States and the Soviet Union as equally reprehensible "hegemonic" powers. This is where I came in. The atmosphere I inherited was described by Christopher Wren on July 14, 1982 in the *New York Times:*

> China is displaying fresh irritation with the United States over what Peking feels is Washington's failure to bring about a quicker resolution of their longstanding differences on Taiwan. Peking appears concerned that the abrupt resignation of Secretary of State Alexander M. Haig, Jr. and Washington's preoccupation with the Lebanon crisis may be undercutting its efforts to get the Reagan Administration to end the delivery of aircraft and other weapons to Taiwan. . . . The Chinese leadership also seems worried that conservatives in the United States are exploiting the vacuum created by Mr. Haig's departure to revive support for the Nationalist regime on Taiwan.

Al Haig had been a key player, as a member of Henry Kissinger's NSC staff, in the 1972 opening to China. He was an "old friend" to the Chinese, and they did not know me personally. I thought the demand that arms sales be stopped was unacceptable, and so did President Reagan. In a spirited exchange with Senator Jesse Helms at my confirmation hearings, I had asserted the importance of our relations with China but staunchly defended our arms sales to Taiwan. Just five days after this exchange, China responded with what appeared to be a breakthrough in this year-long negotiation. The Chinese for the first time agreed to drop their insistence that the United States cease all arms sales to Taiwan and agreed to proceed instead on the basis of the concept of gradual reductions in arms sales.

The breakthrough in the Chinese position in our arms sales negotiations was to me a powerful signal, after a year of futile talks, that China was ready to deal with a policy of firmness from Washington. I felt that we should move quickly to capitalize on this development. Thus began a period of intense negotiations. Our point men were two talented and experienced foreign service officers: U.S. Ambassador Art Hummel in Beijing, using detailed instructions and talking points in his meetings with the Chinese authorities (including Deng Xiaoping), and John Holdridge, assistant secretary for East Asian Affairs, on the other end working with me, and through me to President Reagan.

While in the midst of discussions with the leaders of China, we also kept the president of Taiwan, Chiang Ching-kuo, well informed, assuring the Taiwanese of continued sales of arms, as demonstrated by our readiness to go forward with the sale to Taiwan of an important fighter aircraft, the

F-5E. The Taiwanese, though preferring no restrictions on arms sales, realized their important stake in the U.S. relationship with China. Normal contact and a dialogue on trade, investment, and security issues were to their advantage, although they could not openly say so. But they also needed to have the ability to defend themselves to ensure that the Chinese would live up to their expressed peaceful intentions.

Consultations with members of Congress took the form of closed sessions with the Senate Foreign Relations Committee and parallel sessions with members of the House Foreign Affairs Committee. At a critical session with senators on July 27, Holdridge discussed both the arms sales negotiations and our plans for congressional notification of the availability of F-5E fighter planes for Taiwan. He assured senators, including skeptics Barry Goldwater and Jesse Helms, that any agreement we made with China would link the peaceful resolution of the Taiwan issue to our policy on arms sales. Our approach was accepted.

I authorized Ambassador Hummel to negotiate with the Chinese deputy foreign minister, Han Xu, as a way of breaking through the remaining issues. Han Xu was well known to the United States; he had been involved in the original opening to China made by President Nixon and Henry Kissinger. The Chinese willingness to put him to work in this manner was a good sign. A rapid-fire process began, with cables flowing daily between Beijing and Washington and meetings between Ambassador Hummel and Han Xu proceeding at the same pace.

On August 17, 1982, we issued a joint communiqué that settled down the issue of arms sales to Taiwan while allowing us to remain true to our friends there. In a compromise formula stemming from the U.S. position taken at the start of the negotiations, the United States stated that it did not intend "to carry out a long-term policy of arms sales to Taiwan," that future sales would not exceed past quantitative or qualitative levels, and that the United States intended to reduce gradually its arms sales to Taiwan. The Chinese stated their peaceful intent toward Taiwan, acknowledging that should their peaceful intent change, U.S. policy would also change.

The *New York Times* expressed it well in an editorial on August 19, 1982: "What only President Nixon could begin, only President Reagan can continue," and went on to point out that "Washington's words on arms for Taiwan were formally linked to China's declared policy of 'striving for a peaceful resolution of the Taiwan question.' Such linkage has been a goal of American negotiators for months."

My First Trip to China

As I prepared myself to go to China in early 1983, I worked with President Reagan to develop further our approach to the Chinese. Our aims with

China needed more definition: to resolve the most troublesome problems, stabilize relations, and make use of our common interests against Soviet actions in Cambodia and Afghanistan and against deployment of Soviet missiles aimed at Asian countries. We would do what we could to edge the Chinese regime toward a more open and just society. We would also work to develop an important intelligence exchange with the Chinese.

I felt strongly that we should avoid the extreme shifts in American attitudes toward China that had characterized much of our past relationship. We had a tendency to become euphoric at times and then, when events did not go as well as we expected, to become depressed and overreact. The swings in the pendulum were too exaggerated. And concern in the United States about a downward swing gave too much leverage to the Chinese. We needed to achieve and maintain a more stable attitude toward our relationship with China and realize that we had to build it block by block.

My first meeting, as secretary of state, with a high Chinese official had been on October 1, 1982, with Foreign Minister Huang Hua. He was crusty, prickly, and experienced. He kept coming back to the issue of Taiwan. I told him that we would live by our communiqué and expected the Chinese to do the same. Toward the end of our meeting, he raised what he called the "more serious obstacle" of the Taiwan Relations Act and said that even if it could not be revised or abolished, at least the president should show flexibility in its implementation.

I responded categorically. I told him that President Reagan and I supported the Taiwan Relations Act and it had widespread support in the Congress. I said there was no prospect of repealing it or changing it and that our communiqué undertakings were fully consistent with the Taiwan Relations Act. It was a testy exchange. Huang Hua retorted that we wouldn't like it if China were to support one state against our central government, sell arms to that state, or encourage it to become a separate political entity. I replied with a touch of mock indignation, "Just keep your hands off California."

It took a while, but Huang Hua eventually laughed. He then made a concluding statement: "From the long-term point of view, regardless of some present factors, the development of U.S.-China relations is in the front of the interests of our two countries. Let us view the relationship from the long-term point of view." I took it as a sign that however strained our earlier conversation had been, the United States had taken a stand on Taiwan, and the Communist Chinese had accepted it, even if they found it hard to swallow.

The outgoing Chinese ambassador, Chai Zemin, had assured me in December 1982 that my approaching visit to China would be a "success." But I wondered. In my two meetings in 1982 with Huang Hua, he had complained at great length about Taiwan. I was fed up with that, and Beijing encounters might get testy, I knew. The Chinese also alleged that various American commitments made in the past—on technology transfers and textiles—had not been fulfilled. I was determined to be careful and precise in my own statements and not allow any polite generalities to lead to misunderstandings. "Here's what we'll do; here's what we will not do; here are the problems" would be my approach, and that would, I hoped, help to deflate false and ultimately frustrating expectations.

The immediate omens, however, were not good. Only about two weeks before I was to leave, the Chinese announced their intention to cut imports of selected American products, principally cotton and soybeans, in apparent retaliation for the continuing deadlock in our talks about the level of permitted imports of Chinese textiles into the United States. I remarked to Art Hummel, "The Chinese like to think they are part of the Third World, but they are really the Third World's chief competitor. Wait and see what happens when they begin to receive aid from the World Bank." The bank's aid resources were limited, and such a large new claimant as China would strain the system.

Another looming problem was technology transfer. I recognized the importance of access to sophisticated technology for economic modernization in China, but I knew that China's problems were more fundamental and systemic and that their economy was being suffocated by their bureaucracy. Just before leaving on my trip, I got word that the president had approved the sale of a Hyshare 700 computer to the Chinese. This was a positive signal, but I intentionally instructed that the Chinese be notified in routine fashion. "They'll get the message," I said. I didn't want to come with a present: it would be a bad precedent.

I arrived in China early in the afternoon of February 2, 1983, for a four-day stay. Newly appointed Foreign Minister Wu Xueqian met me at the airport—a favorable sign—and escorted me to the Great Hall of the People in the center of Beijing. On the way I passed a poster that, translated, recommended "Panda Temple Heaven Low Suds Detergent." The Cultural Revolution had "succumbed to Madison Avenue," I remarked. Pack up the MX missiles, I mused, we can turn back the "Communist hordes" with low suds detergent.

As our motorcade passed before the Gate of Heavenly Peace in Tiananmen Square and approached the western entrance to the Great Hall of the People, I became tense. I half-expected the Chinese to begin by lecturing me about Taiwan, technology transfer, textiles, and unfulfilled commitments. My party and I were greeted in the foyer of the Great Hall by Foreign Minister Wu and our other Chinese counterparts, all in gray tunics. We walked down the line shaking hands the way football players do at the beginning of a game. Cameras whirred and clicked.

In the huge "Szechuan" meeting room, we were ranged along a baize-covered table with note takers arrayed behind us. The doily-draped arm-chairs on which we sat were uncomfortable, slung back and too low for the table. At every chair was a thumb-thick red pencil, which produced crayonlike marks on the notepad provided. On one wall hung a colossal black-and-white print of a Chinese landscape—craggy mountains, winding stream, willow tree. I also noted in each corner of the room an intensely green, stunted Chinese fir tree and at various convenient locations around the room large white spittoons, which the Chinese targeted with athletic gusto.

While press photographers clicked their cameras, Foreign Minister Wu observed that the weather in Beijing had been mild and that snow would help the wheat crop. The press was then summarily herded out and the tall paneled doors were closed. We were presented hot towels to wash our hands and faces. Tea and beer were served. Cool towels then followed. Finally, Wu suggested we begin our meeting with a review of regional issues—the Middle East, Namibia, Afghanistan, and Cambodia—and pro-posed that if time ran out, we should schedule another meeting. Given this "constructive agenda," I immediately knew the Chinese wanted the visit to go well. The tension in the cavernous room lifted into the high ceiling.

The Chinese were so well prepared that their briefing papers were printed in booklets, each page a neat block of compact ideographs. Foreign Minister Wu's hair was brushed straight back, and his long teeth flashed like a fan when he smiled. Two symmetrical pink birthmarks fell like flaps from both sides of his forehead to his temples. Appearing to be a serious, thoughtful, and even studious man, Wu hovered over his briefing papers and fidgeted with a sheaf of pencils before him. He listened intently and spoke so softly that it seemed as though he was running out of breath. Nearby sat Mr. Zhang, who must have had to develop a very flexible ideology in the thirty years he had spent in the American department of the Chinese Foreign Ministry. Rather incongruously, given the grandeur of our surroundings and the gravity of our talks, he used a small red plastic pencil sharpener to sharpen his pencil.

My wife and I were housed in one of the villas in the extensive Diaoyutai State Guest House compound on the western side of the capital. The room overlooked a frozen pond, fringed by bare willow branches, in the middle of which sat a gazebo in the shape of a small temple. Beyond it a large Chinese flag waved, and the next morning, the rising sun hung there like a red ball. Although I was comfortable in the guest house, I felt vaguely like a prisoner: high walls enclosed the compound and cut it off from the city, and soldiers patrolled the grounds. The villa was completely bugged. I had three "hush phones," which required putting one's face into a funnel-shaped mask and speaking through a tube connected to the mask of the other speaker. We looked like Siamese-twin elephants joined at the trunk.

They were of no use, for I wanted to have a discussion among a number of my group, and I felt ludicrous using them. I constantly reminded myself to turn my sensitive papers face down because of possible cameras in the ceiling. I was told that even the garden was wired and therefore provided no refuge.

There are over 1 billion people in China. One billion is a lot of anything, but of people it is almost incomprehensible. As Deng Xiaoping would say to me when I raised the issue of human rights, "You support the right to emigrate? We'll give you 10 million people today! Would you like 20 million?" In Beijing I was not immediately conscious of the huge Chinese population. Tiananmen Square can hold a million people but is so vast that I had a sense of emptiness, not congestion. Tiananmen Avenue runs across the top of the square in front of the Gate of Heavenly Peace (where hung, I was told, the last remaining portrait of Mao) and is a wide boulevard. There was not much vehicular traffic in Beijing. Half of the avenue was reserved for bicycles, and here I began to get a feel of numbers. A steady stream of bikes passed by, as placid and uninterrupted as a meadow brook.

Foreign Minister Wu hosted a welcoming banquet for me my first night in Beijing. The Chinese are among the world's most expert hosts. They specialize in putting guests at ease even though there may be sharp differences, and they have a special gift for handling such major protocol events. The toasts come first. They are passed out in both languages for all to read. Everyone involved in my visit was invited, no matter what their position, on the theory that if they were there, they had a role and if they had a role, they should be recognized by inclusion. My Chinese hosts constantly plucked delicacies from the ever-changing "lazy Susan" and put them on our plates, gestures both polite and yet intimate. If the long initial meeting with Wu set the positive tone for my visit, the toasts at the banquet that evening set forth in public our respective positions, as they would at my return banquet following the conclusion of our meetings in Beijing.

While the outlook each of us presented was positive, we both referred to continuing problems. Wu reminded everyone of "obstacles." I pointed up economic possibilities and the importance of regional issues but also cautioned the Chinese about nuclear proliferation. I also referred to the "thousands of students" from China in American universities and noted that "in this modern world even the strongest and most independent nations cannot live in isolation." To support this point, I cited a statement by General Secretary Hu Yaobang in his report to the recent Twelfth Party Congress that "China's future is closely bound up with that of the world as a whole."

The next day, before and after lunch, Foreign Minister Wu and I continued talking for six more hours, covering every topic on our agenda.

During my analysis of Soviet developments, comments about the Reagan approach of strength and realism as the basis for dialogue, and my appraisal of Yuri Andropov, the Chinese were totally silent and attentive.

So far, the atmosphere with the Chinese had been businesslike and amiable. My first confrontation came, surprisingly, when I met at noon with American businessmen sent by their companies to live in Beijing and be part of the new trade and investment relationship. After my initial remarks, which were cautiously positive in tone, the businessmen proceeded to put forward the standard Chinese line on Taiwan, technology transfer, and trade. I snapped back at them. "Some businessmen sign deals even though they know the technology cannot be exported and then say to the U.S. government, 'We made this financial commitment: now you've got to approve it.' Buddy, that's your problem when you do that. Don't complain to the government."

When I was asked about the U.S. refusal to license Westinghouse to sell nuclear power plants to China, a deal potentially worth billions of dollars, because China would not sign the Nuclear Nonproliferation Treaty, I said, "The question carries the implication, as most of your questions do, that there is something wrong with the United States. Our regulations are based on a deep concern about the problems of proliferation of nuclear weapons technology. That is a legitimate problem. The question suggests in a rather cavalier fashion that you brush it off. I don't brush it off." We knew that the meeting room was bugged, and I could see that some of the businessmen were trying to make points that would ingratiate themselves with the Chinese authorities. If so, the Chinese got a feel for my bottom line, too. The encounter left me with a sour taste.

"Visit diplomacy" in dealings between nations is both a necessity and a potential trap. The visits provide occasions when leaders are compelled to clear the decks of other matters and focus intensively on every aspect, positive and negative, of affairs between the two governments. Such visits are all part of what I think of as gardening. Weeds are easier to deal with before they grow than after they have firmly implanted themselves. The potential trap is that visits can produce through all the hospitality and personal contact, a false sense of well-being and progress. In the case of China, I was not so much tending a garden as replanting one, and I needed others in the U.S. government to get involved. So, during and in consequence of my visit to Beijing, I helped set up other such trips: by Commerce Secretary Mac Baldrige, Defense Secretary Cap Weinberger, and Treasury Secretary Don Regan. The next day, February 4, I handed Premier Zhao Ziyang President Reagan's letter inviting him to the United States. He accepted and extended an invitation for a return visit by the president.

The main event of my schedule in Beijing was to be a two-hour meeting with China's senior leader, Deng Xiaoping. In visit diplomacy a conscious game is played. The traveling press knows the time allotted to the meeting. If the meeting runs to time, the press takes it as a sign of a cool, stiff relationship. This gives the hosts, in this case the Chinese, the upper hand: they can signal "progress" simply by keeping the discussion going beyond its scheduled end. The guest, of course, does not have this option—a game, but one that conveys a reality as well. Deng kept me there talking for almost three hours.

As I entered the Great Hall of the People, the guard at the door screamed out a command of welcome. It was more a siren than a voice and seemed like some vestige from the days when emperors held audiences in the Forbidden City. Ever since he first came to prominence in the pages of the Western press as a reviled target of Mao's violent Cultural Revolution, Deng had been described as diminutive, bullet-headed, and blunt. He was all of these. Probably because he was denounced by Mao for his pragmatism (e.g., as embodied in Deng's famous quote "I don't care what color a cat is as long as it catches mice," referring to whether someone was as "red" as a Communist should be), Deng gained the reputation as someone who could lead China down a path away from Marxism-Leninism. His early reforms of the agricultural sector seemed to bear this out. He mentioned Taiwan but did not make an issue of it. We talked about the Soviet Union and he told me that the "three obstacles"[1] meant better relations between China and the Soviets would be a long time coming. With me, Deng stressed that China must modernize and that to do so successfully, China had a policy of two openings: to the outside because there was so much to learn and acquire, and on the inside so that the people could energize themselves and interact successfully with the outside world.

Deng seemed to see that Marxist ideology would not bring China the wealth and power it sought. But he was nonetheless a Leninist and as such did not expect to give up political power. Deng had poor hearing in his right ear, and his chair was placed to provide him with the maximum benefit of my voice. One of the "China watchers" on my delegation said that in the days before relations were opened, we would have analyzed the photograph of the seating arrangement and concluded that it must have some political significance.

For two hours Deng spoke with me in moderate, pleasant, jocular tones, punctuated by an occasional gobbet of spit arched toward the pot at his feet. He impressed me, as he did almost everyone who met him, with the strength of his intellect, his humor, his candor, and his ability to cut through to the essence of issues and talk bluntly about them. One could easily see in him the Red Army veteran of the Long March of decades before.

---

1. The three obstacles to better China-Soviet relations were the massive Soviet military presence on the Chinese border, the Soviet presence in Afghanistan, and the Soviet presence, through Vietnam, in Cambodia.

*   *   *

Then, as though a switch had been turned on in his head, Deng's voice grew loud and strident and imperious as with a contemptuous look on his face he launched a seemingly endless, scathing diatribe about those unnamed enemies who derided the power of "the Chinese people" and sought to deny them their due. "The Chinese people defy all laws!" he rasped almost triumphantly.[2] Over and over he spat out references with a mystic awe to "the Chinese people" until everyone in the room could visualize this vast array of humanity. It was a disturbing, unforgettable performance. Nothing in it was directed at the United States specifically, but at those who would underestimate China. It was a rhetorical spasm, undoubtedly polished by repeated performances, but nonetheless deeply and truly felt.

When it was over, the Chinese officials seemed to regard my meetings as having cleared the way for a new stage, for what I described in my final press conference as an attempt to build together an atmosphere of mutual trust and confidence by addressing real problems and resolving them. "I appreciate the warmth and the seriousness with which my hosts have received me here," I said. "I would like to say that a number of times, when very direct and candid statements were made to me, my hosts said that I should remember that candor was something that could take place among friends. And I would have to say that I received a great deal of friendship during my visit here." Everyone laughed.

The *Washington Post* headlined on Monday, February 7: "China Assails U.S. On Taiwan Policy, Rejects Better Ties." The Chinese had not, in fact, pressed hard on the Taiwan issue while I was in Beijing. Deng had mentioned Taiwan but had not made an issue of it. The *Post* based its story on a statement from the official New China News Agency saying that my visit had helped U.S.-China relations "to some extent," but unless the Taiwan issue was resolved, mutual trust between China and the United States was "out of the question." This was another feature of "visit diplomacy": the after-visit punch in the nose.

I understood and was ready for this tactic; my interpretation: the Chinese understood I had not given ground on Taiwan. That was good, because Ronald Reagan certainly wasn't going to give ground either. At the same time, the New China News Agency report went on to spell out more issues on which we were "close" than I had in my own final statement.

One of my China hands told me that the visit would prove to be a turning point. Maybe so, I thought, but it will take considerable time and effort to find out. One recognition came to me with clarity: the Chinese simply did not comprehend the pluralism of America. Our concepts of "checks

2. This was his response to my urging that the Chinese government take its case regarding imperial Chinese railway bonds to the American court system; I assured him China would get a just hearing. In fact, China did go into our courts, and justice was done.

and balances" and "separation of powers" were utterly alien to them and to their experience with government. Skepticism about Western concepts came easily from a people who assumed the superiority of their ancient culture. Many of the welter of problems between our two countries stemmed from this gap in perceptions. I had, however, achieved my objective of reviving the flagging fortunes of Sino-American relations and had moved to restore a climate of cooperation and problem solving.

Problem Solving

Since the early years of the century, Asia had been a source of destabilization affecting the whole world—from the Boxer Rebellion, the Chinese Revolution, Japan's drive for empire, the Korean and Vietnam wars to China's Cultural Revolution. Now a new moment had arrived. Would Asia become a model of stability and prosperity? This was already under way, but it could not go forward confidently unless China was to emerge as a society far different from what it had been for generations. In a speech on Sino-American relations in San Francisco on March 5, 1983, I said that nothing underscored the direct interest of the United States in this region more than two simple facts: "We trade more today with the nations of the Asia Pacific than with any other region on earth, and we have fought three wars in the Pacific in the last forty years. We do not want to fight another, and this is a reason why the United States will continue to maintain a presence there."

I had decided during my visit in Beijing to enlist the new Chinese ambassador, Zhang Wenjin, to help resolve problems. He arrived in Washington in early March and even before he presented his credentials to President Reagan, I started working with him. Late on a Friday afternoon, March 18, I invited him to my office at the State Department. I also asked Cap Weinberger, Mac Baldrige, Jay Keyworth, Bill Clark, and a few people at State to join me. My idea was to have an informal and personal discussion, a session over drinks to get acquainted. I encouraged my colleagues to receive the new ambassador, listen to him, and see what we could properly do to solve problems.

Our policy on technology transfers to China was the key starting point. China, like the Soviet Union and its satellites, was restricted through agreements with our allies in the COCOM organization from access to a wide range of modern technology. (The technology transfer control process was exceedingly complex. Basically, there were two types of controls: national security controls over which the Defense Department had a virtual monopoly and which they administered with great strictness; and foreign policy controls, which were much more flexibly administered by the Commerce Department. The State Department played a role in both. The Soviet

Union and its satellites, which were classified as potential military adversaries, were subject to the strictest controls. China, as a country not in the Soviet bloc or in a position to take us on militarily, nevertheless was a power that could have an independent influence in the world, so it fell somewhere in between.) Although we called China a "friendly and non-allied country," the complicated classification system had the effect of putting them in virtually the same category as the Soviets.

In early May, Ambassador Zhang made a courtesy call on Vice President Bush. A professional like Zhang would have prepared his remarks to the vice president very carefully, so we took what he said seriously. He commented that "the Taiwan issue will be there for some time to come." Not months, but much longer. He described it as "an issue left over from history" and said that "a transition period" was needed before it could finally be resolved. Zhang explained that his government had to voice dissatisfaction with the present situation; otherwise, the "Chinese people" would not accept their government's position. So, he continued, even though the Taiwan issue would exist for a long time, the United States and China still needed to build up "trust and confidence" and the best place to do that was in the area of technology. Zhang noted that China was not asking for the most sophisticated technology, "which we wouldn't be able to use, anyway."

Zhang said that while his government realized there had been progress in bilateral relations, the United States had to decide whether China was a friendly, nonallied country or a potentially hostile one. He pointed out that any concern about transfer of technology to the Soviet Unon from China was farfetched. In effect, Zhang was telling us, almost directly, that China accepted that the United States would not give any more ground on Taiwan. He was also indicating that the Chinese did not expect export restrictions to be dropped entirely.

Considerable debate raged within the administration as to whether China should be reclassified to make it possible for us to license a far greater range of exports to the PRC. Finally, the president decided on May 21, 1983, to approve the reclassification so that we could follow through on our pledge to support China's modernization program. In passing this information to Ambassador Zhang in Washington, and through Secretary Baldrige, who happened to be visiting Beijing, we sought to give the Chinese the good news in a way that guarded against excessive expectations.

By June 10, Paul Wolfowitz, assistant secretary for East Asian Affairs, reported to me that relations with China were, in fact, improving in several areas. The president's science adviser, Jay Keyworth, had completed a visit to China during which he signed four new science and technology protocols. Secretary Baldrige's visit had been a great success, especially since he was able to inform the Chinese of the president's decision to liberalize technology transfers. Art Hummel in Beijing described the atmosphere for Baldrige's visit as "the best in my nearly two years as ambassador here." Working-level contacts for the embassy also improved considerably.

In addition, the Chinese agreed to send a nuclear delegation to the United States in mid-July. This decision and reports of China's intention to join the International Atomic Energy Administration (IAEA) suggested that our concerns about nuclear nonproliferation and China's nuclear export policies were being taken seriously and might lead to a change of policies and eventually to an agreement on nuclear cooperation.

There were still problems, to be sure. With the Chinese, every day could bring a new source of tension: Pan Am flights newly scheduled to Taiwan; the attendance of Washington officials at Taiwanese events; the membership of Beijing or Taipei in the Asia Development Bank. But we had undeniably entered a new era. In the early days of the Reagan administration, the Chinese had wanted to show that they could make trouble for President Reagan. They had seen, however, that my own approach to China paralleled that of the president. "When they saw we would not be rattled," China watcher Art Hummel observed, "they turned to a more constructive approach. Even so, there are time bombs all over the place."

High-Level Visits

On January 10, 1984, Premier Zhao Ziyang arrived for a three-day visit in Washington. Zhao's trip would be the first time that the formal head of the People's Republic of China had come to the United States. The visit would give President Reagan a chance to register in a personal way his commitment to the consolidation of a strong U.S.-China relationship and his readiness to support China's ambitious efforts at modernization. We also had a number of specific goals in mind: to enhance U.S.-China coordination where our interests were parallel, as in Cambodia and Afghanistan, and, to a degree, in South Korea; to continue to press for Chinese assurances on nuclear cooperation; to ask for Zhao's attention on the POW-MIA issue in Vietnam; and to strike a positive note on Taiwan, reiterating our position while expecting the Chinese to tone down their rhetoric.

The first visit between President Reagan and Premier Zhao was striking: Reagan, the dedicated anti-Communist, and Zhao Ziyang, the prime minister of the world's most populous Communist country. Zhao was an engaging personality; unlike many East Asian officials, he proved capable of a genuinely relaxed attitude and showed flashes of humor. But, speaking first as a guest, he went right at the president on the issue of arms sales to Taiwan. The president heard him out and then said, in a quiet and direct way, that we would continue to work with our friends on Taiwan, we would live up to our agreements on arms sales, and there would be no changes in the Taiwan Relations Act. I sensed that Zhao could feel the steel in the president's backbone. That was the last we heard of the subject during Zhao's visit. Moving on to other topics, the president found himself warming up to Zhao as a person. The rapport developed easily.

By now we were in a position to move forward in constructing a relationship with China on a new basis. There were many positive developments on which we could build. Trade and investment were expanding. Travel between our countries, by both Chinese and Americans, particularly students, was increasingly commonplace. Military-to-military discussions had started, and a process of technology transfer was under way on a controlled basis. Our cooperative efforts to counter the Soviets and Vietnamese in Cambodia and the Soviet invasion of Afghanistan were valued by both our countries. The Chinese understood and appreciated the importance to them of the president's insistence on a global approach to the INF negotiations, and they were always anxious to exchange views of the Moscow scene and appraisals of the leading personalities there. Most of all, they respected Ronald Reagan's tough-minded approach to the Soviets.

At the same time, the president and I had no illusions about China. We knew that China wanted it both ways: to gain the benefits of a booming economy while maintaining state control over key aspects of economic and political behavior. They would have to face the reality that a society cannot be Communist and capitalist at the same time—and this they were not ready to do.

Before long, we were heavily engaged in preparations for the president's trip to China, scheduled to start in late April 1984. This would be Ronald and Nancy Reagan's first visit to a Communist country, and I wondered how they and the Chinese would react to one another. In addition to the endless stream of briefing books and memos that I and others produced, we gathered some outsiders to brief the president. One such occasion really registered. Winston Lord and his wife, Bette Bao Lord, and four China scholars were present. After the scholars had said their piece, we turned to Bette for some personal observations about the Chinese people. A high-spirited woman and best-selling author, Bette, who was born in Shanghai, vividly described how the Chinese deal with others and how she thought it best to respond. Putting herself in the shoes of the first lady and then the president, she role-played how conversations might proceed.

At the first meeting the Chinese would be politely warm; at the second meeting, you already would be an "old friend"; then the Chinese would start to "reel you in," because in China an old friend could be expected to "make concessions." Bette commented on Chinese attention to detail, their sense of decorum combined with their readiness to be blunt. When it came time to change ambassadors in Beijing, it was no surprise that the president turned to Winston Lord and his talented partner.

The trip to China was leisurely: the president was determined to be at his best, and so we went across the Pacific slowly, letting our circadian rhythms adjust. After stopping in California, we spent a few days in Hawaii, a night in Guam, and from there flew to Beijing. A continuing round of events gave the president a feel for different personalities, some images of China's history, and opportunities to reach China's people directly. The official arrival ceremony at the Great Hall of the People was on Thursday, April 26, 1984, followed by two days of meetings, lunches, and dinners with President Li Xiannian, Premier Zhao, and the general secretary of the Chinese Communist party, Hu Yaobang, and an address to Chinese leaders in the Great Hall of the People. On Saturday, April 28, the president was interviewed for Chinese television. Then, in the main event, he had a lengthy meeting and working luncheon with Deng Xiaoping. That afternoon, the president and Nancy walked on the Great Wall and on Sunday visited the site of the excavated terra-cotta warriors in Xi'an: extraordinary life-sized figures, each different, an archeological treasure in the city considered the cradle of Chinese civilization. On Monday, we were off for Shanghai, where we toured the Foxboro Company installation and attended a reception at Fudan University, where the president held a question-and-answer session with students. He also addressed students and faculty at the university and attended a banquet hosted by Mayor Wang Daohan at the Shanghai Exhibition Hall. The following day, after touring a child-care center and visiting a family farm, the president and Mrs. Reagan left China for home.

The visit was sensational. There was, of course, great imagery to be found in China, and Mike Deaver took advantage of it all—the Great Wall, the terra-cotta warriors, scenes with the various Chinese leaders, and the human-interest shots with Chinese children. The president was in top form throughout the visit. He charmed the students in his question-and-answer session. His speeches, which were major events, clearly impressed the Chinese.

President Reagan did not hide his own beliefs or tailor his comments to please his hosts. He spoke about America again and again, saying, "We have drawn tremendous power from two great sources—faith and freedom. . . . Our passion for freedom led to the American Revolution, the first great uprising for human rights and independence against colonial rule."

He quoted Abraham Lincoln saying, "No man is good enough to govern another man without that other's consent." He counseled that the key American concept of government was "Trust the people." He said that "these three words are not only the heart and soul of American history, but the most powerful force for human progress in the world today." He also indirectly suggested the future path the Chinese might best choose by quoting Premier Zhao, who had said that progress "lies in our efforts to

emancipate our thinking in a bold way—to carry out reform with determination, to make new inventions with courage, and to break with the
economic molds and conventions of all descriptions which fetter the development of the productive force."

At Fudan University he spoke about how much the United States had
gained from China, pointing out that An Wang, who founded Wang Computers, was a product of Shanghai University, that I. M. Pei first became
interested in architecture as a student in Shanghai, and that much of what
we know about the fundamental nature of matter had been the result of
work by the Nobel Prize–winning scientist Dr. Lee Tsung-Dao, who was
born in Shanghai. Drawing out the implications of these individual achievements, the president said; "We believe in the dignity of each man, woman,
and child. Our entire system is founded on an appreciation of the special
genius of each individual and the special right to make his own decisions
and lead his own life. . . . We say of our country, 'Here the people rule,'
and it is so."

The Chinese leadership did not like everything that the president said,
and they censored some of the passages in their broadcasts to the Chinese
people. The effect of this censorship, however, was to highlight those very
passages which, as a result, received even greater attention. Wherever the
president traveled, he wore American values on his sleeve and spoke of
them with pride. It was vintage Ronald Reagan.

In my final press conference summing up the trip, I highlighted the theme
of Ronald Reagan "dealing across ideologies." It had been his first visit
to a Communist country, and it had come off as a resounding success.
Even the New China News Agency described it as "a significant step forward," while the Soviet news agency described it as "the Peking Primary."
U.S. News & World Report on May 7, 1984, wrote in its lead article, "After
a decade of playing cat and mouse, the U.S. and China got down to serious
business during Ronald Reagan's historic five-day mission to the Communist nation and put their relationship on a new course."

All this took place well before Foreign Minister Gromyko's first visit to
Washington in the Reagan administration in late September 1984. In a
sense, China provided a training ground and confidence builder for President Reagan's subsequent dealings with the Soviets across ideologies.

Problems with China, of course, would continue to arise through the
end of the president's second term. Neverthelesss, we never altered the
fundamental course that we had set early on. We viewed China as a giant
crippled by its own ideology. So long as China pursued that ideology, there
would necessarily be restraints on the kind of relationship it could have
with the United States. There would always be a gap between what we
expected from one another and what we were willing to deliver. We would
continue to do what we could to maintain and, whenever possible, improve

relations, but we would not abandon our fundamental values or principles in dealing with the Chinese. This was a lesson the president would carry over into his dealings with the Soviet Union.

I returned to China on two occasions during the next four years, but one incident from President Reagan's visit stands out with particular clarity. By the time we got to the final farewell banquet in Shanghai, I was tired from my own talks with the Chinese leadership, briefing the press, and generally keeping track of everything. When we arrived for the grand banquet in the Shanghai Exhibition Hall, we entered by two huge staircases that embraced a large area filled with flowers and plants. I noticed many of the dwarf evergreens that you see arranged so artfully in Japan. As I sat down at the banquet table, I made a remark to my Chinese host that, once begun, I could not stop, even though I could see I was headed in the wrong direction. I commented on the striking entry display, noting that it had reminded me of scenes I had frequently seen in Japan. Without batting an eye, he replied, "Yes, I suppose so. We taught them that two thousand years ago."

My host was right, of course, to be proud of China's ancient civilization and historic cultural achievements, which give the Chinese a strong and abiding sense of their place in the world. Yet I could not help but think that it was the special and tragic misfortune of this great people who, unlike the Japanese, too often found solace and satisfaction in the past. The Chinese people are tremendously gifted. Even under communism there have been great achievements. As the Chinese are increasingly set free, their accomplishments could be spectacular.

CHAPTER 23

The Strength and the Struggle
to Negotiate in Central America

When my plane landed in El Salvador on May 31, 1984, bringing an impressive U.S. delegation to the inauguration of José Napoleón Duarte as the newly elected president of that country, I took the pilot aside and gave him a "heads up" and an instruction. "After the inaugural ceremony, we'll fly to Managua for a few hours of meetings before returning to Washington. This must be kept secret until we arrive there, but make your plans accordingly. Get enough fuel on board so that we don't need any servicing there. No one is to touch this airplane while we're on the ground in Managua."

I did not want news of our stopover in Nicaragua, as Tony Motley put it, to "rain on Duarte's parade." We asked the Mexicans to inform the Nicaraguans that there could be no preannouncement of the secret meeting; otherwise, it would not take place. For the same reason, knowledge within the State Department of the upcoming meeting was strictly limited to those who absolutely needed to know. If there was a leak about my imminent visit to Nicaragua, that would dominate all the news. We wanted the spotlight to be on Duarte and the democratic process in El Salvador.

My secret trip had been in the works for about two weeks. Harry Shlaudeman, now our special negotiator for Central America, had strongly advocated a new effort to break the negotiating logjam: a Shultz-Ortega meeting and then ongoing, direct U.S.-Nicaragua negotiations. During Mexican President Miguel de la Madrid's visit in Washington that began on May 15, President Reagan had agreed that I should explore de la Madrid's thinking about this possibility, without any commitments on our part and with the understanding that the Mexicans would not be involved if talks did take place.

The debt problems of Mexico were of great concern, and through Treasury Secretary Don Regan, we were hard at work to help the Mexicans and to contain potential damage to our banking system. In this atmosphere of

400

strain on many fronts, the state visit had started on a somewhat edgy basis between the two heads of government. President Reagan's welcoming statement was interpreted by some as critical of Mexico's tolerance of Nicaragua's behavior. De la Madrid's address to a joint session of Congress was viewed as critical of Ronald Reagan, as de la Madrid warned against "the illusion of the effectiveness of force" and called for a negotiated solution to the problems of Central America. Both men made their statements in good temper, and in private de la Madrid impressed President Reagan, as he had me on earlier occasions, with his realism about the repressive nature of the regime in Nicaragua and his underlying friendly attitude toward the United States.

By his last evening in Washington, the atmosphere was relaxed, and I had a chance for a lengthy discussion with de la Madrid. He was eager to talk with me about Nicaragua, its internal problems, and its desire, he felt sure, to talk on a reasonable basis with the United States. He volunteered to help arrange something. Typically, Latin American leaders would criticize us in public, sympathize with our policy in private, and do little to help solve the problem. I hoped Mexico would lend a hand, and de la Madrid appeared ready to do so. I told him I would get back to him.

President Reagan by this time had agreed that I would head the U.S. delegation to the inauguration of José Napoleón Duarte on June 1. I suggested that I could go to Nicaragua in the late afternoon, after the inaugural ceremony, before returning to Washington. We had a week of gestation: I found Bill Casey, Bud McFarlane, and Cap Weinberger willing to agree that I go, though unenthusiastic over the prospect. They could see how such an effort would help us argue to Congress that we were trying to find a negotiated outcome. That would strengthen our case for Contra aid as supplying the pressure needed to help negotiations succeed. But I wanted the reality of a negotiation, not just the appearance, and that made them uneasy. Gradually, the president leaned more and more toward making the effort. I assured him that we would keep our friends fully informed and that our talks would support the regional approaches that the Core Four countries—El Salvador, Honduras, Costa Rica, Guatemala—with U.S. support, sought in the Contadora process.

The Contadora Process

The Contadora process seeking a regional solution to the problems of Central America had started almost a year and a half earlier. Mexico was its prime mover, joined by Colombia, Venezuela, Panama, and five Central American countries. The United States and Cuba did not take part directly, but the support of the United States for any regional solution would be essential, everyone knew, so we were involved indirectly, as was Cuba through Nicaragua. It had become almost a worldwide litany for nations to assert: "We support the Contadora process." Still, most observers, let alone participants, were skeptics. I certainly was, especially at first. But the Contadora process kept alive the possibility of a negotiated outcome; it identified key problems; it worked out possible solutions; and it put Nicaragua, the United States, and the Core Four at one time or another on the spot by making us decide whether or not we would support important provisions in draft treaties that emerged from the negotiations.

The Contadora process reached a high point in September 1983 with its Document of Objectives, including what became known as the "twenty-one points." We supported them, most especially their call for "democratic, representative and pluralistic systems that will guarantee . . . fair and regular elections based on the full observation of citizens' rights; . . . negotiations for the control and reduction of current stocks of weapons and on the number of armed troops; . . . internal control machinery to prevent the traffic in arms from the territory of any country in the region to the territory of another."

The Document of Objectives also included, "To prevent the use of their own territory by persons, organizations or groups seeking to destabilize the Governments of Central American countries and to refuse to provide them with or permit them to receive military or logistical support." We supported this objective with ambivalence. For as long as the Sandinistas continued to pursue their aggressive ways, we wanted to support the Contras as the way to distract Nicaragua from its support of insurgents in El Salvador and as pressure to move Nicaragua toward democracy.

Since January 1984, Tony Motley and his deputy in State's Latin America bureau, Craig Johnstone, had been working on diplomatic steps to help implement the Document of Objectives. We had distilled Contadora's twenty-one points into four objectives to be pursued simultaneously: Cuban and Soviet advisers would leave Nicaragua; Nicaragua would end support for the guerrillas in El Salvador; a regional agreement would be reached on military balances whereby Nicaragua would shrink its huge army; free and fair democratic elections would be held in Nicaragua. In return, but only after the four steps were agreed upon and irretrievably in the process of being implemented, the United States would end its support of the Contras, who by this time would have become part of the electoral process. We would also reduce our armed presence in the region, cut back on our arms transfers to other Central American nations, and extend economic support to Nicaragua. The plan had to be carried out swiftly; it had to be verifiable; and it required that all four steps occur simultaneously. We were not going to give Nicaragua what it wanted until we knew that we would get what *we* wanted. The negotiation of this four-step process would proceed swiftly, on a ninety-day timetable.

While I was doubtful that such a plan would work, I was willing to give it a serious try. The Soviet Union was experiencing increasing economic trouble at home, and I felt their internal difficulties might make the Soviets more hesitant in their adventures abroad. This might be a moment when the Sandinistas could be induced to pull in their horns. Even if we failed, and I hoped we would succeed, the demonstration that I was seriously pursuing a diplomatic track was essential if we were to have any hope at all for support from Congress for our Central America policy. I would throw myself into the effort to obtain congressional funds for the Contras, but I did not want to see a series of big administration defeats over Contra aid on the Hill. As a movement popularly rooted, the Contras would survive and fight, I felt, with or without congressional aid, so that they could still generate significant pressure on the Sandinista regime.

Meanwhile, the negotiations in Contadora to convert the twenty-one objectives into treaty form proved far more difficult than defining those objectives had been. Nevertheless, this effort held the center of the negotiating stage, and both the United States and Nicaragua paid attention. The Nicaraguans did so in large part because they were under pressure from the Contras, who were growing in numbers even though funding from the United States amounted to only about $2 million per month in this late-1983-to-late-1984 period.

U.S. efforts included support for the Contadora process as part of our negotiating strategy, but even more important, we had to work effectively with the Core Four countries individually and as a group to strengthen democracy and the rule of law, to promote economic development, and to help them provide for their own security. We worked endlessly with Congress to get the funds necessary to implement a strategy of diplomacy backed by strength and based on the three Ds: democracy, development, and defense.

The Kissinger Commission, appointed in July 1983, reported to the president on January 11, 1984. Henry Kissinger, in an impressive tour de force, guided a genuinely bipartisan group to conclusions that were virtually unanimous—and basically in accord with our analysis of the problems in Central America and the prescriptions needed to deal with them. U.S. interests, the commission said, were served when we worked to improve the living conditions of the people of Central America and to advance the cause of democracy, when we helped resist the violation of democracy by force and terrorism, and when we helped prevent hostile forces from seizing and expanding control in this strategic area. The commission recognized it was vital to prevent "the Soviet Union from consolidating either directly or through Cuba a hostile foothold on the American continents."

Its recommendations were ambitious. When I got my first glimpse of them, I remarked, "Henry is proposing that we *solve* the problems by *buying* Central America. Eight billion dollars!" But, on reflection, I agreed with the commission's conclusion that bold action was necessary—and not just limited to money. By February 3, President Reagan converted its recommendations to proposals to Congress, including the expenditure of $8 billion in Central America over five years, a goal we never approached in actual appropriations. The proposed level of economic and security assistance was roughly double the annual rate of support to our friends in Central America in 1983 and was double the amount Congress had already approved for 1984. Aid to El Salvador, the commission concluded, should be made conditional on an end to activities of the death squads. Kissinger's report had been dedicated to the late Senator Scoop Jackson, and the president called his proposal the Jackson Plan.

The death squads and other violations of human rights were intolerable, and with pressure from the United States and from the president himself, progress was being made in correcting these problems. In December 1983, Vice President Bush came down hard on human rights abuses during a visit to El Salvador: U.S. support absolutely would not continue unless El Salvador dealt decisively with this problem. I pounded on this same necessity in visits to El Salvador and in sessions with its leaders visiting Washington. On January 31, 1984, in El Salvador I said to all the candidates in the impending presidential election, "Death squads and terror have no place in a democracy, and I mince no words in saying it here or anywhere else. The armed forces must act with discipline in defense of the Constitution. And the judicial system must prove its capacity to cope with the terrorist acts of extremists of the right or left." I went further, saying that improvement in human rights "is good for the people of El Salvador. Who wants to live in a country where murder takes place on such a scale and isn't punished?"

The CIA Mines Nicaraguan Harbors

With the tailwind of bipartisan support from the Kissinger Commission, with the Contras increasingly effective in disrupting military and government efforts in Nicaragua, and with the twenty-one points of Contadora working in our favor, we seemed to be on a roll. Then, in early April 1984, a storm erupted: a story broke that Americans working for the CIA aboard a ship off Nicaragua had been supervising the mining of Nicaraguan waters in recent months. I was astonished. Apparently this was not something the Contras were doing; the U.S. government was actively and directly involved. I found that this covert operation had been approved by the president at a time when I was in Europe attending the annual meeting of NATO foreign ministers.

Members of Congress expressed outrage at the act and at not having been informed of this secret operation. The Senate on April 10 voted resoundingly 84 to 12 for a nonbinding resolution opposing the use of federal funds to mine Nicaraguan harbors. The House Foreign Affairs Committee followed suit the next day in a vote of 32 to 3, with 2 abstentions. Republicans deserted the president in droves. Senator Barry Goldwater, the president's conservative stalwart, wrote to Bill Casey, "Dear Bill: All this past weekend, I've been trying to figure out how I can most easily tell you my feelings about the discovery of the President having approved mining some of the harbors of Central America. It gets down to one, little, simple phrase. . . ." After expressing his anger and his sense of having been personally betrayed by the CIA, he went on, "The President has asked us to back his foreign policy. Bill, how can we back his foreign policy when we don't know what the hell he is doing. Lebanon, yes, we all know that he sent troops over there. But mine the harbors in Nicaragua? This is an act violating international law. It is an act of war. For the life of me, I don't see how we are going to explain it."

By April 13, however, it appeared that briefings had, in fact, taken place, perhaps too casually, in the intelligence committees of both houses of Congress. Goldwater later came to say that Casey may have informed him in such an offhand way that he had not paid much attention. I know that I myself got to the point that I hated to get intelligence information directly from Bill Casey, because when he spoke he so muffled and garbled his words that I was never quite sure what he was saying. I sometimes thought his technique was intentional. I heard that at the CIA the running joke was that Casey didn't need a secure phone; his voice was already scrambled.

Probably Goldwater and others thought, as I did, that the Contras, not the CIA, were responsible for mining the harbors and for the reported damage to ships in Nicaraguan waters. Edward Boland, chairman of the House Select Committee on Intelligence, in a speech on the House floor, was highly critical of the mining but said that his committee had first been informed on January 31, 1984, that the waters off Puerto Sandeno had been mined. The remainder of the mining took place in February, Boland said. Philip Taubman wrote in the *New York Times* on April 14:

His [Boland's] comments added to growing evidence that Congress was informed about the mining by the Reagan Administration well before a flurry of reports last week about the C.I.A.'s role in the operation. Although most members of Congress were presumably aware that Nicaraguan harbors were being mined—Mr. Boland said the mining was first revealed by the Managua radio on Jan. 3—the current furor in Congress developed after the extent of direct American involvement was disclosed in news reports last week. . . .

Intelligence officials reiterated today that the Senate intelligence committee was notified about the mining in briefings on March 8 and March 13, although they said the subject was not discussed at length. On April 2, they said, committee staff members were given a detailed account of the mining.

Staff members have confirmed that a written report on the mining was prepared after the April 2 briefing, but they do not know how many members read it, if any.

I had called in Tony Motley on April 13 and asked whether he had informed me that the CIA was conducting this operation. He said he had told me in one of our morning meetings. Somehow this had not registered at all on me. It must have sounded to me like a Contra action, not a CIA-run operation. I had moved hard to block a similar proposal in June 1983.

The mines had been custom made, Motley subsequently told me, designed to create a large bang and to do more damage to the courage of the Lloyds of London underwriters than to the hulls of the ships they struck. The object, Motley said, was not to sink ships but rather to cause shipping to Nicaragua, especially of petroleum, to carry such high insurance rates that the harbors of Nicaragua would be avoided by the commerce of the world. Motley said that the evidence suggested that the mining was succeeding in limiting shipping to and from Nicaragua. Certainly, mining can successfully limit shipping, I well knew. But that was not the point. We were engaged in an effort that we should have left alone entirely or left to the Contras. The mining episode was a political disaster for the administration.

Even though I had not been present when the president approved the operation and had in fact blocked an earlier attempt to mine Nicaraguan harbors, I kicked myself. I felt I should have been more alert to what was going on. The whole episode gave the Sandinistas a major propaganda victory, and the United States took a beating in Congress and from our allies around the world. Our support for the Contras was not immediately cut off despite the sharp congressional reaction. We would pay the price, however, when the fiscal-year authorization came to an end in October 1984.

Support for Duarte in El Salvador

I prepared myself for major informal meetings with the full House of Representatives and then the Senate to put forward urgently the administration case for support for El Salvador. My big talking point was Duarte's victory in the run-off election. A graduate of Notre Dame, he was a popular figure in the United States as well as in El Salvador and seemed almost saintly in his concern for the impoverished people of his country. He talked about justice in a compelling way. He came to Washington and on May 22 spent the day on the Hill, where he was effective and persuasive. As for my own efforts, I arranged for informal sessions to supplement formal appearances in public hearings so I could argue our case to members of

Congress directly and emphasize the strength of the president's feelings on the issues involved and the high priority he accorded to support for democracy in Central America.

I had asked Tip O'Neill to let me make an informal appearance in the House chamber before any House members who wished to come. He said this was unprecedented, but he would think it over. A few days later, Jim Wright, the majority leader, telephoned me, saying he was uncomfortable about using the House chamber for an informal session but proposed an acceptable alternative: use the large Cannon Caucus Room for a meeting that would be sponsored by Dante Fascell and Bill Broomfield, the chairman and ranking minority member of the House Foreign Affairs Committee.

On the morning of May 23, 1984, I did my best to put across the idea that we could succeed: El Salvador could work as a country, I said. It was possible to win over some of the guerrillas; the guerrillas were supplied daily by Nicaragua through an intricate logistical system that was highly vulnerable; the existence of this supply line demonstrated that Nicaragua was the supporter of El Salvador's guerrilla problem; and the opposition in Nicaragua, the Contras, deserved our support. I found that the mood of the House had shifted toward support for Duarte but that strong opposition to the Contras remained. President Reagan weighed in heavily and repeatedly. Members of the Kissinger Commission, Henry and others as well in both political parties, were helpful. Our efforts to gain increased assistance for El Salvador were ultimately successful. In the course of the summer, an "urgent" appropriation was approved for $61.75 million, and another $70 million was added subsequently.

Preparations for Managua

On the afternoon of May 23, preparing for a meeting of NATO foreign ministers to be held at the Wye Plantation near Washington, I raised once again with the president the question of a meeting with Sandinista leader Daniel Ortega. He didn't say very much. I knew he was still mulling it over. At the Wye Plantation on May 29, I learned that the White House was pushing to have Jesse Helms included in my delegation to Duarte's inauguration. Jesse Helms? How ironic, since Helms had backed Roberto D'Aubuisson, the leader of the right-wing Arena party and a man who had been linked to death squads. But perhaps I could use Helms's inclusion to show broad support for the election process and to help bring D'Aubuisson into line. Senators Paul Tsongas of Massachusetts and Strom Thurmond of South Carolina were already part of the delegation.

I soon heard from Chief of Staff Jim Baker that the president was warming up to the idea of my stopping briefly in Managua as long as the governments of the Core Four did not object. I called Tony Motley and had him make a secret check. I heard back the next day that while there was some unease that we might make a separate deal with the Sandinistas, the responses were generally favorable, except for President Roberto Suazo of Honduras, who reacted rather negatively. The Hondurans were especially concerned, as they felt particularly vulnerable to Nicaragua's large military buildup. I told Motley to report that to Bud McFarlane but to tell him that I was still inclined to go ahead. We would keep the Core Four Central American nations fully informed and would adhere to the regional approach that they, and we, sought through the Contadora process.

Later that day, the president approved the possibility of my stop in Managua. I had Harry Shlaudeman, who was in Mexico, explore with Foreign Minister Bernardo Sepulveda possible flexibility in the Nicaraguan positions. At the end of their conversation, Shlaudeman told Sepulveda, "We're prepared to go ahead." At my request, Sepulveda called Managua to get Daniel Ortega's agreement to confidentiality and to the proposed date of the meeting.

"This is going to be terrific. Jesse Helms will love it," I remarked sardonically. Before long, Shlaudeman reported back that he had gotten a "go" from the Mexicans on the Managua stop.

I had spent two days in our NATO meeting at the Wye Plantation, and it rained cats and dogs throughout. We were cooped up, running from place to place under umbrellas. No one got to enjoy the lovely vistas and relaxed surroundings of the vast grounds. I met with the marines who had provided security. They were all in their dress blues and lined up two deep. I walked back and forth, inspecting the ranks as I had done in my days in the Marine Corps. At the end, I stood in front of the marines and called out, "Which one of you is responsible for this weather?"

There was a long pause before one young marine sergeant took a step forward and barked, "I am, sir."

Preparations for my meeting in Nicaragua had been going forward on a contingency basis. The goal was to develop ideas and points of agreement that would reinvigorate the Contadora process. If the meeting went well, I would suggest follow-on discussions with Harry Shlaudeman in the chair on our side. I went over all this with the president, and he approved my approach. I was now set to proceed.

An Inauguration in El Salvador

We were wheels up from Andrews Air Force Base on the afternoon of May 31. At 8:30 A.M. sharp the next morning, the inauguration of José Napoleón Duarte was scheduled to begin. The official delegations were all gathered in a large holding room, where we were to wait about three-quarters of an hour before marching together into the Assembly Hall. Just then, an announcement was made, no surprise to old Latin hands, that the inaugural ceremony would be an hour late. I looked around this room of people from all over the world and said to members of our delegation, "Each of the other delegations is standing around talking among themselves. We have a point of view about Central America that is fundamentally bipartisan, so why not use this time to talk to the other delegations. Let's let them know how pleased we are about what is going on in El Salvador and how important it is that democracy prevail in Central America. Let's do a little selling."

And so we did. I was particularly impressed with Senator Strom Thurmond. Watching him in action was a revelation. Here was a politician who had survived through being a Democrat, a Dixiecrat, and a Republican and won always by overwhelming margins in his home state. He worked the crowd tirelessly, introducing himself, making lively conversation, and forcefully presenting our views on El Salvador and the rest of Central America. I took with me the department's top Spanish interpreter, Stephanie von Reigersberg. We started with delegations that spoke Spanish. Then she interpreted in Portuguese. Then we went to French speakers, then to Italians. She handled all these with great skill and fluency. Then I said to her, "Well, let's go talk to the Koreans and the Japanese." At that point, she threw up her hands.

The inaugural proceedings in El Salvador were genuinely stunning. High excitement filled the air. I had a feeling that the country was turning a corner. Duarte was magnificent. He exuded a sense of decency and human concern that was apparent to everyone. Forty-three countries were represented. Even Bernardo Sepulveda, who had been a skeptic about El Salvador, showed up. I called on the outgoing president of El Salvador, Alvaro Magaña. He had taken some tough actions, especially in forcing the military to come to grips with human rights abuses within the military, including bringing charges against officers involved in earlier murders. I had a brief session with the Core Four foreign ministers, and once again I assured them that we would keep them fully posted on what transpired in Nicaragua and that our approach would support the positions they had taken in Contadora.

By this time, we had an extra airplane on the ground in El Salvador. I had told the three senators privately that we would stop in Managua to meet with Daniel Ortega. "If you don't want to come, you don't have to. It's your choice," I said. Anyone in our delegation who wanted to go back to Washington immediately after the ceremony was over could do so. Jesse Helms opted to return. The air of excitement at the inauguration was so great that no one suspected that there was some other move afoot. I made a courtesy call on Duarte after the inauguration and headed straight for the airport. State Department spokesman John Hughes had a bit of a problem rounding up the traveling press and letting them know they would be "well advised" to be aboard. Miraculously, considering all the consultation that we had had, the secrecy held. When our plane took off, no one outside our loop knew where we were going. The Nicaraguans also kept their word and issued no statement. That registered with me, and I told them so upon my arrival.

My Meeting with Ortega

In Managua, I was greeted courteously and taken to a special room the Nicaraguans had set up at the airport. I had not met Daniel Ortega before. We shook hands. He had set up a long table with low lounge chairs arranged on each side. At the head of the table was one straight-backed chair, which was perceptibly higher than anybody else's. There he seated himself and arranged the American delegation on one side of the table and the Nicaraguan delegation on the other. He clearly had positioned himself so that he could look down on the rest of us. It reminded me of the way Ferdinand Marcos arranged meetings in Manila. I thought immediately, here is a man who, in some deep way, is insecure.

Ortega was in his military uniform. The rest of us were in civilian clothes. The meeting itself went on for about two hours. We each made direct and candid statements. The Sandinistas were on their best behavior. The Contras were very much on their minds. Ortega reviewed the history of Nicaragua and its relationship with the United States. He criticized us in a quiet voice. I described the problems of Central America as I saw them, emphasized the potential importance of the Contadora process, and presented our four-point program distilled from the twenty-one points of Contadora.

This was our basic position, I said. I stressed that the plan proposed by the president on the basis of the Kissinger Commission recommendations was something like a Marshall Plan for Central America. If Nicaragua persisted in standing outside the free economic system of the hemisphere, it would become an economic failure while the region as a whole moved ahead. The movement toward democracy and away from repression would provide pressure on his regime, and no pressure could be greater.

By the time the meeting drew to an end, Ortega and I had agreed that the United States and Nicaragua would engage in a series of further discussions. I told Ortega that Ambassador Shlaudeman would represent us, and he designated Vice Foreign Minister Victor Hugo Tinoco. Both men were present. I emphasized to Ortega that the subsequent meetings should proceed with as little publicity as possible and that their content should be confidential, with each side able to give private information to key friends, in our case, the Core Four countries. The United States's four-point approach, I said, was based on the Contadora twenty-one points, which the Ortega regime had accepted in principle but showed no indication of putting into effect. We both agreed that the talks between our countries would be in support of, not in competition with, the Contadora process. At the end of the meeting I felt that I had accomplished what I had set out to do. This would be a serious negotiating effort on our part.

Reactions to My Effort

My meeting in Nicaragua delayed my arrival back in Washington, so I was too late to be aboard *Air Force One* as the president took off for the London economic summit, with a two-day stopover ahead of time in Ireland. When I got to Andrews, I walked across the tarmac to shift planes and went on to catch up with him. Upon arrival, I gave the president my full report. He was pleased and encouraged. The reaction to my meeting in Nicaragua was strongly favorable, in the Congress and around the world.

When I later called on Irish Foreign Minister Peter Barry, he asked, "Why is the United States getting such a bum rap on Central America? I'm surprised at the amount of anti-American sentiment. I can't see why you haven't been able to get more balanced reactions. There's a bishop not twenty miles from here who is on television every night spewing half-truths."

"We are dealing with the reluctance of people to recognize that counterforce is sometimes necessary," I responded. "There are also many problems in El Salvador: the death squads, the judicial process. But we can't just walk away. Our test is whether there is progress, not a millennium. There have been three years of improvement."

"Sometimes I despair," Barry concluded.

In London, British Foreign Secretary Geoffrey Howe told me that although Central America was a concern to a relatively small number of the British people, it registered high in the priorities of the politically articulate. "Central America gets a great deal of publicity and the U.S. is a direct player. The [Nicaraguan] harbor mining incident has had a disproportionate effect. It's hard to see how you will work this out without leaving the sense that you might move in and take over."

"Certainly, if the U.S. backed off from the situation and Nicaragua became the dominant country in the region, the U.S. would eventually not be able to tolerate it," I told him. "To back off would eventually mean a war. Now we have friends in the area who are ready to resist."

"We recognize your strong interest," Howe said. "The question is whether Nicaragua is over the brink and irretrievably in the Soviet camp."

"The way to find out," I said, "is to see what reactions we get in negotiations while we maintain the pressure. The Contra pressure is important. I could see that from the expression on Ortega's face, but the pressure is not free of charge. The Hondurans are nervous because the Contras use bases in their country and Nicaragua's armed forces are far larger than those of Honduras."

When I got back to Washington from the summit, Cap Weinberger and Bill Casey were all over me with criticism of my meeting in Managua. "Come on, you both supported it," I told them. "Furthermore, we managed to get exactly what we went after." I was also hearing sharp criticism from the Hondurans, who felt I was falling into a Sandinista trap that would break apart common regional resistance to Nicaragua. They feared my meeting with Daniel Ortega might lead the Core Four to try to reach an accommodation with Nicaragua. The Hondurans would need continuing reassurance, and we would need to proceed carefully.

After some jockeying around, the resort city of Manzanillo, on Mexico's Pacific Coast, was selected as the site for the follow-on talks, which were delayed a bit at the request of the Ortega regime—for "internal deliberations." I suspected the delay really was to give Ortega time to consult with Nicaragua's Soviet patrons. And, sure enough, he soon left for Moscow. Our own deliberations were conducted in the interagency process, which worked overtime to do what it did best: block diplomatic activity. "It's like those old Christmas tree lights; one bulb goes and they all go. Anyone can veto anything," I said to Tony Motley.

On June 18, Motley emerged from a bruising White House session that was supposed to approve the "terms of reference" for Shlaudeman's talks. NSC staff members Oliver North, Constantine Menges, and John Poindexter wanted to reverse the process I had started in Managua. They sought to write terms of reference for Shlaudeman that would cause a breakdown at the very outset at Manzanillo. If that happened and if we did nothing, I feared that the Contadora process would collapse, Contra funding would be cut off by Congress, and we would be left with no Central America policy whatsoever. I told Shlaudeman to proceed without regard to their bureaucratic obstructionism.

I felt that even if the covert aid program for the Contras was not renewed by Congress in October, I had some points of strength with which to support serious diplomacy: the Contras were still being funded now and so were still a significant problem for the Sandinistas; the existence of the Contras held out a hope for those opposing Ortega; the flicker of a free press fanned this hope, and the Catholic church was still functioning despite harassment. Through our diplomacy at Manzanillo, I hoped we could use the leverage provided by the Contras to create change: the Contras were the most important pressure point. I would work hard with the president to maintain at least minimal congressional funding for them.

Before his first meeting with Nicaraguan Deputy Foreign Minister Tinoco, Harry Shlaudeman held a round of discussions with the heads and foreign ministers of the Contadora governments. They recognized that the Contadora process had run into deep trouble. Only the Panamanians maintained an outward show of optimism. The Venezuelans told us that Contadora was going nowhere and they gave every sign of wanting to wash their hands of it. Most pessimistic of all was Colombian President Betancur. De la Madrid and Sepulveda stressed Mexico's view that Contadora could not be "strung out" or sustained much longer. The Mexicans were positioning themselves, it seemed, to throw the blame on the United States for Contadora's collapse. Shlaudeman also spent time with the Core Four countries and emphasized a point that seemed to be especially important to each of them: "We insist that all four aspects of our program must proceed simultaneously, and we are not prepared to drop democratization." The Costa Ricans told us, "Only the United States can obtain from the Nicaraguans the concessions the process requires."

On June 20, Cap Weinberger, Jeane Kirkpatrick, Bill Casey, John Poindexter, and Bud McFarlane met with me in my conference room to discuss funding for the Contras. Mike Armacost and Bill Schneider were there, too, along with Fred Ikle and Dewey Claridge. Weinberger and Kirkpatrick believed that Congress, including influential Democrats, could still be convinced to vote support for the Contras. "It's vital for the administration to stand tough," Kirkpatrick said; "Twenty-one million dollars is minimal." Bud McFarlane agreed with Jeane and suggested that we get President Duarte and Honduran President Suazo "to come to the well of the House and say 'this is the moment of truth.' " The consensus of the group was to go back up to the Hill and fight for Contra aid with confidence that we would win. If we did not win, Bill Casey said, as he had before, at least we could blame Congress for "losing Central America."

"I'm for trying," I said, "but let's face up to the possibility that Congress may not agree. I'm not attracted to saying, 'We lost [Central America] and it's the Democrats' fault.' We have to know what we will do if we lose in the Congress. And put aside the idea of other sources for the money. What then?"

Casey felt that some Contras would fight on anyway. Weinberger said that we must not let the Contras collapse. Kirkpatrick argued that the damage would not be controllable if Contra funding stopped. Nicaragua would consolidate itself as a new Cuba, and the others in the region would "Finlandize," accommodate to this new Communist power. Panama would go with Cuba, and "we will confront MIGs before November," she said. If so, I thought, we would get that congressional funding. Tony Motley started talking about soliciting third countries. I was strongly opposed, and McFarlane waved him into silence.

"Okay," I said, "let's tell the president we will keep going at the Congress with a hard-hitting campaign." I added, "I have an empty feeling in my stomach, like when the Israelis pulled out of the Shouf. The guts of our effort are slipping out." The Nicaragua mining fiasco, I realized, had given the opposition a telling argument to use on the swing voters in Congress on the issue of Contra aid.

Harry Shlaudeman was already on the road, consulting with the Core Four about his upcoming negotiations with the Nicaraguans in Manzanillo when Weinberger on June 21 told Tony Motley that we would have to "reverse the decision" to hold such talks. NSC staffer Constantine Menges had come to see him, Weinberger said, to urge again that the Shlaudeman effort be aborted. Cap was easy to persuade and now said he "would like to recall George's mission." Weinberger's chief assistant, General Colin Powell, told Motley that Menges's end run was an outrage: "a serious breach of discipline."

Colin Powell was right, but the problem was even worse. Mike Deaver telephoned me to say that Bud McFarlane had gone to President Reagan to argue strongly against my sending Shlaudeman to negotiate in Manzanillo. "The president didn't buy it," Deaver said.

"Nobody likes this negotiation," Bill Casey told Motley. I knew that almost everybody in the administration was opposed to any discussion or negotiation with Nicaragua. Our effort to obtain an extension of Contra aid from Congress was going nowhere. I worried about a negotiation without the strength supplied by pressure on Ortega's regime from the Contras. The prospects for democracy and economic growth in neighboring countries were, I felt increasingly, the ultimate source of pressure on Nicaragua, where repression was a way of life and economic conditions were deteriorating. Even so, my confidence would have been greater if political and economic conditions in the Core Four countries had been better.

Talk at the second level of the administration continued to focus on soliciting third countries to provide Contra aid. I spoke sharply to Tony Motley on June 21: "Don't get into *any* discussion or acts about alternative funding," I told him. "Jim Baker thinks such solicitation is an impeachable offense. So don't you or anybody else in ARA [State's Latin America bureau] or in the administration do it! Make it clear. Craig Johnstone, too. No games." Our strength, I said, could be shown in naval exercises, in intelligence overflights, in the assistance Congress votes for El Salvador, in our determination to stand by our friends. "If Congress withdraws support from the Contras, that will hurt our effort, but all is not lost without a Contra program," I told Motley. "We still have leverage. The Sandinistas are apprehensive. They know that *they* ran a revolution without congressional support, and so can the Contras. The amount the Contras need is pitifully small." I was convinced that the Contras could get along at some minimal level without our support. "We should keep working for the Contra program but not be sanguine about getting it. Things won't fall apart. It's not a catastrophe."

Negotiations Under Way

On Sunday, June 24, Shlaudeman was in Manzanillo. All Washington seemed to be watching him, ready to pounce on any misstep. I was watching intently, too. But Shlaudeman was a sure-footed pro. I went from my office to State's operations center four times that Sunday to take Harry's phone calls from Manzanillo. On Monday, Mexican Foreign Minister Sepulveda introduced Shlaudeman to Tinoco and then left the room. A frenzy gripped the Reagan administration over this event.

Even as Shlaudeman and Tinoco talked, the National Security Planning Group (NSPG) was convened in the Situation Room, with President Reagan in the chair, to consider whether to go forward at Manzanillo and whether to seek third-country aid for the Contras. I felt isolated in my opposition to solicitation of third-country aid. "Going to third countries is very likely illegal," I said. Nobody liked my views at all. The president said nothing on the subject. My desire to go forward at Manzanillo was even more strenuously opposed by Cap and Bill Casey. The debate proceeded: should Shlaudeman be allowed to discuss procedure only, could he paraphrase his instructed points but not read them in full, or could he table our position paper? Weinberger was opposed to any negotiation. He wanted it stopped now. McFarlane spoke as if trying to be helpful, but his vacillation on the subject from day to day made him ineffectual. He did not have a clear, settled view. At the end of the meeting, the president said, "George has merit in continuing the negotiation."

The outcome was very much to my liking. President Reagan came down on my side. He endorsed the continuation of the Manzanillo meetings and called for us to reaffirm the four goals I had summarized to Ortega: genuine implementation of democracy; a verified end to the export of subversion, verified removal of Soviet bloc and Cuban personnel from Nicaragua, and verified reduction of Nicaraguan military forces to regional parity. We continued also to recognize that economic development would be of critical importance and that we would support a regional settlement in accord with the twenty-one Contadora objectives. Defense Secretary Cap Weinberger and Chairman of the Joint Chiefs Jack Vessey were assigned the task of providing plans for U.S. military activities and exercises in Central America to demonstrate U.S. resolve and to enhance the confidence of our friends in the region.

"I give the chances of a positive negotiated outcome with Nicaragua as two in ten," I said at the meeting, "but if our effort doesn't succeed, it

needs to be clear where the responsibility lies and that we have tried to
help our Contadora friends obtain a positive outcome."

Afterward, in what was becoming a pattern in the administration, the
NSC staff produced a National Security Decision Directive (NSDD), signed
by the president, that appeared to prevent us from pursuing diplomatic
steps and ran directly counter to what the president had said in the meeting.
Bud followed up by telephone, trying to argue that the NSPG had concluded that Shlaudeman could put forward *no* substantive position to the
Nicaraguans until the Core Four had cleared the position. I disagreed
vehemently with what I regarded as a deliberate recasting of the president's
decision at the meeting. This was just one more attempt to abort a negotiation approved by the president.

Shlaudeman called in. The daytime session had been procedural; he and
Tinoco were to resume at 6:00 P.M. Washington time. What was he to do?
I telephoned McFarlane and reminded him that he himself had been a
negotiator, in Lebanon. "This is madness," I told him. "I will tell Shlaudeman to put our points out there to the other side." He did not disagree.
"We can't be in a position where our negotiator has to have all Washington
sign off on every sentence he utters." I told Tony Motley to instruct Shlaudeman to read out carefully—in Spanish—to Tinoco on Tuesday, June 26,
every word from the paper that summarized our key points.

Shlaudeman began by saying, "The United States believes that the period
of the next several months offers a unique opportunity for a peaceful
resolution of the conflicts in Central America, a resolution in keeping with
the Document of General Objectives agreed to by the nine nations participating in the Contadora process." We fully supported the Contadora
process, Shlaudeman told Tinoco. He called our four points "interrelated
and indivisible" and said that in our view "The most appropriate approach
to resolving these problems is through a careful definition of the outcome
desired by all parties and the development of a balanced step-by-step
calendar of reciprocal and verifiable actions to achieve a successful outcome
to the Contadora process."

The Nicaraguans, Shlaudeman reported, were clearly operating under a
tight rein, without authorization to discuss substance. At first they were
undecided whether further meetings should take place, but they showed
interest in the "step-by-step calendar of reciprocal and verifiable actions,"
a phrase that suggested how operational our thinking had become. He
guessed that their consultations with Managua and their decision to go
ahead with additional meetings reflected their reaction to our step-by-step
approach. He could see, even in this initial meeting, that disagreements
would emerge regarding the relationship of the U.S.-Nicaragua discussions
to the larger Contadora process.

I reported to President Reagan on June 27, right after Harry's talks, that the Nicaraguans were nervous and on the defensive, unable to respond to the substantive and procedural suggestions that we made. The talks proceeded about as expected, and we stayed on the offensive. I thought these results showed the wisdom of the course we were on. "Your instincts were right on approving my trip to Managua," I said to the president, "and you were right in agreeing that we could not abort after starting this process. We are doing the right thing." I was deeply disappointed in the quality of the NSC discussion. Since I came on board, I told the president, there had been nothing but running battles between me and the rest of the administration on virtually every foreign policy matter. Still, I felt I was giving him good advice. "This Nicaragua event is a ten-strike," I told him.

When I got back to the State Department, Shlaudeman was there, just back from Manzanillo. "It is a terrible, stinking hot, fly-blown place," he said. "Even the Nicaraguans were unhappy with the site." I visualized slowly rotating ceiling fans and scrawny chickens pecking on the cantina floorboards. The Nicaraguans had wanted the Mexicans to participate to prevent "distortion of the record." Shlaudeman proposed having a Spanish-speaking stenotypist present. Tinoco wasn't interested, so the issue of Mexican attendance at the sessions dropped out. The Nicaraguans had no authority from Ortega to negotiate, so, apparently following Cuban advice, they used the session for propaganda, trying also to impose procedural rules to their advantage. "A very bush league outfit," Shlaudeman reported.

The Nicaraguans scorned the Contadora process, while Shlaudeman referred to it as central on every possible occasion. "The transcripts will make the sessions sound harsh and tense," Harry said, "but actually they weren't. They said nasty things in a nice way. They had a KGB-type guy there. The others are decent fellows. They are all terribly young."

I told Shlaudeman that he had done a great job. "The president is pleased. He's on our side even if no one else is." At the end of the week, at a National Security Planning Group meeting with Cap and all my other adversaries present, the president announced that he was pleased and enthusiastic about the Shlaudeman negotiations. The president's support was essential, but I knew that opposition would continue. Nothing ever seemed to get settled.

Although McFarlane, Weinberger, and Casey all had been consulted carefully before we launched this negotiating effort and they all signed on, they had tried strenuously to stop it in mid-flight. Then they sent along an NSC staffer to watch Shlaudeman like a political commissar and report immediately, session by session, back to McFarlane. (As the process unfolded, the staffer, Ray Burghardt, a foreign service officer, turned out to be supportive of Shlaudeman.) The very idea of a negotiation with Nicaragua unnerved them. They feared I would give away the store. They did not understand the politics of the issue or the fact that our best diplomatic defense was a strong offense. "The step-by-step approach on which we embarked is achieving our objectives," I said. If the Nicaraguans accept, then we have changed the situation in a positive direction. "If they don't, which is probable, well, European and domestic opinion has been strongly supportive of our effort, and Nicaragua has been increasingly isolated and divided and put on the defensive at Manzanillo and by Manzanillo." The next Shlaudeman-Tinoco meeting was set for mid-July.

Through most of the first half of July, I was in Asia for meetings with the countries of ASEAN (Association of Southeast Asian Nations) and with leaders from Australia, New Zealand, Japan, and China. While traveling, I received regular reports that the Pentagon-CIA-NSC staff effort to stop Shlaudeman's negotiations was very active. In Canberra, I got a "privacy channel" message from Bud McFarlane that attitudes around the world and within the United States had sharply changed—adversely toward the Nicaraguans—since I had left on my trip. If there had been a change, Manzanillo, I felt sure, had contributed to it. The pope had criticized the Sandinistas; press and religious freedom there had been further suppressed; it would soon be revealed that Nicaragua was trafficking in narcotics. "So I'd like your thoughts on why we should go ahead [with the next scheduled meeting]," Bud asked.

I was incredulous. He suggested two options: cancel Shlaudeman's meeting on July 16 or allow him to say only that we would not negotiate anymore until Nicaraguan behavior changed. As I flew to New Zealand, I sent Bud my answer: "We should continue the dialogue and use the ill repute of Nicaragua to build support for our efforts in El Salvador and with the Congress—and at the same time we should be up front in denouncing the practices you outline in your cable."

Shlaudeman's second meeting took place as scheduled on July 16 at an airport hotel in Atlanta: it was entirely devoted to procedural issues raised by the Nicaraguans, especially their desire to have the Mexicans present during the negotiating sessions. The following day, Interior Minister Tomás Borge announced Daniel Ortega as the Sandinista candidate for president in elections to be held on November 4. Ortega's government also announced the easing of emergency powers in order to permit an "open" campaign. On July 25, various Nicaraguan opposition groups came together and named former Central Bank head Arturo José Cruz as their presidential candidate. One of the original members of the revolutionary junta, Cruz was a man of stature, intelligence, and compassion who had left the Ortega government in disillusion with the Sandinista Front. He was the candidate of a coalition that included several political parties, two labor federations, and six business groups.

Cruz said that the coalition would participate in the election only if the government met its demands regarding the conditions necessary to ensure an open election. He refused to register his name as a candidate until the election laws were changed. He toured Ecuador, Venezuela, Colombia, El Salvador, and Costa Rica and won support for this position. He insisted that the government allow freedom of the press, guarantee that pro-Sandinista demonstrators would not disrupt opposition rallies, take local election machinery out of the hands of Sandinista bloc committees, and place voting booths far from military installations.

When Cruz made his announcement speech in Managua on July 25, his audience was smaller than expected: several buses carrying his followers had been detained by the police. It soon became clear that the Sandinistas would not permit a fair election: participation was curtailed, the opposition frozen out, the registration period cut short, the press censored, and campaigning controlled.

On July 27, President Reagan chaired another NSC meeting on Nicaragua. Jeane Kirkpatrick took the lead for those arguing against continuation of the Shlaudeman-Tinoco talks: Communists win negotiations; they don't honor agreements; we are undermining our friends. I replied with some vehemence, since I felt we went back to ground zero at every meeting. It was maddening. At least she was in command of the facts, and she argued fairly. Cap, by contrast, used arguments that often were not relevant and sometimes produced facts that were concoctions or exaggerations. The meeting was heated and acrimonious, and the outcome was vague. I checked privately with the president and kept going. Without a negotiating track, we would be absolutely sunk with Congress; the Core Four would feel pressured to sign a soft, quick treaty with Ortega; and the Sandinistas would feel no pressure to moderate their behavior. I also felt that the Manzanillo talks could before too long be melded into the Contadora process.

What did President Reagan really want? Many conservatives professed to be puzzled by him, believing that he must seek the overthrow of the Communist regime and therefore should not go along with me or my negotiating track. "Communists win negotiations," they argued again and again. "If agreements are reached, the Communists will not observe their side of the bargain, and the process of negotiations will have led us into unwise concessions; better not to negotiate at all." I was not puzzled by Ronald Reagan. Unlike many in his administration and in Congress, he understood that you have to keep the heat on: you can be tough in a negotiation, but you should keep open a way for the other guy to change his position.

On vacation, at home on the Stanford campus in early August 1984, around my dining-room table with Bud McFarlane, Mike Armacost, Peter

Rodman (head of the policy planning staff), and Charlie Hill, I reviewed the coming season: the diplomatic year that kicks off in September with the opening of the UN General Assembly.

"We must focus on Contra funding drying up by the end of the year," Bud said.

"Where have alternative sources come from for the Contras? Are they fighting for less money, or have they faded away?" Armacost asked.

"They are getting a million a month. I'm not sure where it all comes from," Bud answered. (I much later learned that he did know the money was coming from Saudi Arabia.) "I'm confident they can get it for the next six months. But they can't carry on next year without a new source of funds," Bud continued. He estimated Contra needs at $15 million a year.

A week later, Bill Casey told me we now had no hope of getting support for the Contras out of Congress. As summer drew to an end, we were told by the CIA that Czech-built aircraft of a more advanced type than previously seen in Central America, the L-39, would be shipped from Bulgaria to Nicaragua. We had reports of Nicaraguan pilots being trained on MIG-21s in Bulgaria. To Nicaragua, such aircraft would be a symbol of a Soviet decision to treat Nicaragua in the same league as Cuba, implying a commitment from Moscow of similar political magnitude. For the Soviets, however, such a decision would mean a major confrontation with the United States—one that they did not need and one that almost surely would arouse a majority in our Congress.

The L-39 was not the high-performance aircraft that would alter the region's military balance, but the introduction of such an airplane would represent a significant military escalation by the Soviets. I was also concerned that this would lead Washington's Central America watchers to "hyperventilate." Shipment of the L-39 was a Soviet decision that, if unchallenged, might well be followed by the transfer of high-performance MIGs to the Sandinistas. The United States simply could not allow such an escalation. Some in the administration worried; others welcomed a possible chance to press for an American military move against Nicaragua. I was ready to support an immediate strike by the United States against the MIGs should they appear. I knew the Pentagon would hesitate, and that is why I had insisted on a presidential decision in 1982 before I had laid down my marker to Gromyko. If the shipment materialized, I was ready with tough recommendations.

On October 10, 1984, came the passage of the third Boland Amendment: "During fiscal year 1985, no funds available to the Central Intelligence Agency, the Department of Defense, or any other agency or entity of the United States involved in intelligence activities may be obligated or expended for the purpose or which would have the effect of supporting, directly or indirectly, military or paramilitary operations in Nicaragua by any nation, group, organization, movement, or individual." Congress thereby had done more than shut off appropriated funds. This vote was an attempt to immobilize any administration effort to find support from other countries for the Contras.

The impact of the new Boland Amendment was obvious in Manzanillo, and it was negative. The anticipation of this congressional action had been a factor in the withdrawal of Arturo Cruz from political activity in Nicaragua. Cruz had tried to get an agreement for conditions of electoral fairness and seemed close to doing so, but at the last moment, with the new Boland Amendment favoring their cause, the Sandinistas rejected the agreement: they now did not need to subject themselves to even the most elementary ingredients of a fair election. Faced with this, Cruz withdrew his candidacy, as did Independent Liberal party candidate Virgilio Godoy, who explained that there "were no conditions" for a free election. The election of Daniel Ortega was inevitable, but also illegitimate. Even so, Ortega received only 63 percent of the vote, further reinforcing my view that if a fair election was held, the Sandinistas would lose. Democracy did not come to Nicaragua, but the process of holding a rigged election undermined the credibility of the Sandinistas.

So in the fall of 1984, with the diplomatic season beginning anew, we had a negotiating track under way with Nicaragua and were working to embed the content of those negotiations into the Contadora process and thereby gain regional acceptance of our four-step summary of the twenty-one points. Even without American funding, I felt low-level Contra pressure and the Ortega regime's fear that the United States might try a Grenada-style operation in Managua gave our diplomacy at least some foundation in strength. On the other hand, the highly visible votes of defeat in Congress were giving the Sandinistas the heart to spurn our approaches at Manzanillo and to become increasingly blatant in their manipulation of public, regional, and international calls for elections, negotiations, and other processes of peaceful resolution. "Thinking of the congressional defeats," I said, "there are times when it is better to have fought and lost, but not all the time." Clear congressional opposition to the strength needed to support our diplomatic effort was undermining the very effort that, ironically, our opposition in Congress claimed to support.

Manzanillo and Contadora

Meanwhile, Harry Shlaudeman kept plugging away at Manzanillo. By Labor Day of 1984, the talks were already in their fifth round. Harry would make the circuit of the Core Four and Contadora governments again to make sure that our effort at Manzanillo was fully coordinated with them. Honduras was still uneasy about direct negotiations between the United

States and the Sandinistas. They wanted a regional solution. So did we, and we were trying to pull the Nicaraguans into such a regional settlement from the bottom up. And in every meeting Shlaudeman hammered at two basic points: national reconciliation based on democratic principles was the essential foundation for any real solution, and the only way to achieve reconciliation was through talks with the armed opposition, the Contras.

On September 7, the Contadora group tried to create a settlement from the top down. They met and put forward a draft treaty, an *Acta*, an effort to put the twenty-one Contadora points into treaty language. The document was most unsatisfactory. At first the Nicaraguans objected vehemently because the draft would require a halt to all arms deliveries to the region while an agreement was being negotiated on a regional military balance. Then they realized that the United States and its friends would seek revisions. This draft, if accepted, could spell an end to U.S. military assistance to El Salvador, Honduras, and the Contras, while the verification and monitoring weaknesses of the text would allow Nicaragua to avoid compliance. This was just the sort of trap we had sought to avoid by bringing stronger language into Contadora through our negotiating effort at Manzanillo. We would have to work with our friends in the Core Four to see that the trap, if ever sprung, would catch Nicaragua.

On September 21, the Ortega regime suddenly reversed itself and offered to sign the proposed *Acta* on condition that no changes be made in the text and challenged the United States to do the same. The treaty text in my view required critical, but easily identifiable, changes. The key issues were verification and timing: we must insist on irreversible steps on Nicaragua's part as we took actions ourselves. "Simultaneity" was the word for this objective. We were not alone in this view. Our friends, the Core Four, also saw that the treaty had to be sharpened and strengthened. The consensus was that Nicaragua's acceptance of the *Acta* was a political ploy and that if the text was corrected, it was unlikely that Nicaragua would sign on. I felt that the United States should support the work under way to strengthen the treaty and make it a sound document.

At his sixth meeting with Tinoco, on September 25, Shlaudeman proposed that the September 7 draft treaty be the basis for the negotiations. The Nicaraguans declared that the draft was not negotiable. They were reading the U.S. congressional votes. The seriousness of the Manzanillo negotiations consequently was ebbing.

As I was on my way to Central America and to the inauguration of Nicolas Barletta as Panama's president on October 10, 1984, I received an urgent message from Bud McFarlane: there was "great consternation" in Washington that I was about to sign a nonaggression pact with Ortega and "give it all away." Kirkpatrick, Weinberger, and Casey were in a lather, and many powerful senators were stirred up, Bud said. This tactic was familiar: having concocted what they most did not want me to do, they would then spread the story that I was about to do precisely that—and in the dumbest, most dangerous way possible. I considered this groundless charge to be yet another warning shot across my bow.

The analysts in State's Latin America bureau thought that the Contras would be able to maintain a minimal level of activity for at least another three months. I wanted to use those months to develop a negotiated settlement in Contadora if at all possible. My Washington opponents knew that well. Bud McFarlane was now supporting me in this effort, especially in working good textual changes to the proposed *Acta* through the administration bureaucracy. At a White House meeting on October 15, McFarlane ripped into Constantine Menges, attributing the unwarranted scare stories to him and giving him a stunning public dressing down. Don Gregg, Vice President Bush's adviser on national security, said, "I never saw anything like it. Menges was humiliated." Menges—Motley called him "constant menace"—seemed almost possessed. He suddenly appeared in the State Department operations center one October evening, I was told, asking in great agitation for documents that he "knew" existed and that would reveal the extent to which we were trading away essential positions in negotiations for a Central America solution.

White House Chief of Staff Jim Baker and I discussed this distressing state of affairs. "You're winning, so what's your complaint?" Baker told me. "Nothing will change. You just have to keep battling. I'm on your side and so is Deaver and so is the first lady and so, pretty much, is McFarlane." Baker probably felt he needed to lift my spirits. A short while later a message came over from Vice President Bush saying he was "wholly supportive" of me. I was determined to follow the president's approach: I was ready to defend our interests but also ready to make peace. Bill Casey was wildly upset, and many on the NSC staff were dead set against what we were doing, as was Cap Weinberger.

On October 19, El Salvador, Honduras, and Costa Rica drafted a substitute for the September 7 *Acta*, calling their effort the Act of Tegucigalpa, named for the capital of Honduras, where they released the text. With this in hand, and through further extensive consultations, the Contadora group worked to develop a strengthened *Acta*. Their work proceeded slowly because of obstruction from Nicaragua and because of concern among the other countries that they might be labeled interventionists. Shlaudeman kept plugging away for the same objectives at Manzanillo. He asked questions but got no answers. The Nicaraguans were stalling after their propaganda barrage for the flawed September 7 draft had not brought results and as they saw congressional support for the Contras on the wane. At an NSC meeting on October 30, Bill Casey, Jeane Kirkpatrick, and Cap Weinberger all said the United States should take no part in a negotiated solution.

"You are out of your minds," I countered. "We are there. Our voice matters. People in our own country, in Europe, and in Central America like it. Without negotiations we would face a catastrophe." At this point I felt that we had regained the diplomatic initiative and had wide support for the kind of settlement that met our objectives.

We were reaching out. So was El Salvador's new president, Duarte, who, in a dramatic peace initiative at the United Nations, offered to meet and negotiate with the guerrilla leaders in El Salvador. His initiative was welcomed throughout the world, and on October 15 in La Palma in northern El Salvador, Duarte and the guerrillas sat down together in a session mediated by the Catholic church. They produced an agreement to establish a commission that would include all sectors of that society in the search for peace. In both El Salvador and in the Contadora process, I felt, our message was getting across: work to achieve national reconciliation within the framework of democracy. The popularity of this message put the Ortega regime and the guerrillas Ortega backed in El Salvador under pressure to appear democratic, moderate, and accommodating. This they were trying to do, but whenever a moment of truth came in negotiations, they would not turn away from the path they had set for themselves, nor would they turn away from Cuban-Soviet patronage, as the strengthened *Acta* would have required.

MIGs to Nicaragua?

On election day in the United States, November 6, 1984, a report came in that a freighter bearing twelve crates thought to contain MIG-21s was off the northwest coast of South America headed for Nicaragua. If they were MIG-21s, we would take them out. The Soviets knew I had laid that marker down. The next morning, the ship was said to be 225 miles out of port and to have slowed to eight knots. By midday, the ship was off the Pacific Coast port of Corinto. Our ambassador in Nicaragua, Harry Bergold, dispatched some embassy people to snoop around the port town. They reported no unusual activity. "Look," I told Motley, "I'm making you responsible for determining whether those crates contain lawnmowers or MIGs." We made our concerns known to the Soviets: they said our worries were groundless. Ortega declared, "It is not the policy of the revolutionary government to announce the type of weapons we receive." He continued, "All of the weapons that we receive are for the defense of the revolution."

The Crisis Pre-Planning Group met on November 7 to consider military options. The Pentagon tried to block any order to act by saying the mission would require some impossibly vast campaign—"the bomb Moscow option" I characterized such presentations. In the far more militant NSC staff, the crates seemed to offer a hope for bringing on the military action against Nicaragua that the junior staffers desired. The "intelligence community" displayed a now familiar pattern: an alarming early report became increasingly vague and ordinary the more we pressed the CIA for details. Jeane Kirkpatrick telephoned from New York on November 9 to say the Nicaraguans had asked the Security Council to take up the matter of U.S. preparations for aggression against them. When the ship docked and the crates were opened, they contained high-performance helicopters, not MIGs. "Voilà," said Motley.

"Voilà?" I asked. "Motley, you've been in the State Department too long." I told deputy CIA director Bob Gates that the whole episode, from the standpoint of the intelligence community, had not only been a failure but had been very costly: it revealed to the Soviets how much we *don't* know and how much we *do* know.

The Soviets and Nicaraguans had outmaneuvered us: they had lured us into visible protests in opposition to MIG-21s and then supplied the kind of aircraft that, ironically, would do far greater damage to the Contras in the field than would jet fighters. Then, in the United Nations, they had pointed to our statement that we would not tolerate MIGs as evidence of aggressive intent. The trouble with drawing red lines, as with the MIG-21, is that everything not over the line is taken to be okay.

A letter from General Secretary Chernenko to President Reagan arrived on November 16, 1984. The language was civil, inquiring why we were so upset about Nicaragua and assuring us of Moscow's goodwill and their desire to straighten out relations between us. But between the lines, the Soviets were mocking us.

On November 26, 1984, we were set back by the World Court opinion that took jurisdiction over Nicaragua's charges against the United States for mining their harbors. State and Justice Department lawyers thought we had an open-and-shut case against the assumption by the court of jurisdiction over a political-military dispute between states. But the court came to a different conclusion, and one that we felt was politically motivated. The United States announced its refusal to participate in the subsequent proceedings on the merits of the case or to accept whatever verdict the court might ultimately render. Nevertheless, the fact was that we lost.[1]

1. The U.S. position on the case of *Nicaragua* v. *The United States*, which the Sandinistas brought to the International Court of Justice (ICJ), led many to denounce the United States for weakening the fabric of international law. I believe that the extension, on solid ground, of international law is one of the great endeavors of the modern era and one in which the American role, throughout this century, has been indispensable and leading. But I also believe that our decision to oppose the jurisdiction of the World Court in the Nicaraguan harbor mining case was the right decision—and what the ICJ did was detrimental to the progress and developing legitimacy of international law. Nicaragua invoked the ICJ's compulsory jurisdiction regarding the United States, without having accepted compulsory jurisdiction itself—and the ICJ agreed with Nicaragua. Nicaragua, in effect, argued that it could support guerrilla warfare against El Salvador but that El Salvador could not, in its own self-defense, accept help from the United States. The ICJ acquiesced in that narrowing of a nation's right

The decision to use CIA personnel to mine Nicaragua's harbors continued to be a costly one.

As the year drew to an end, there was no denying that domestic opposition to our Central America policy was taking a heavy toll. The cutoff of congressional funds to the Contras strengthened the Sandinistas' hands. By the end of the year, about half of the Contra forces inside Nicaragua had gone to bases in Honduras. Secret arms shipments from the Soviet bloc to Nicaragua were unprecedentedly high, and the helicopter deliveries made a noticeable shift in the balance of forces. Daniel Ortega was able openly to consort with his Communist backers and openly scuttle any hope of real elections; yet he paid no price for this when it came to attitudes in the Congress of the United States. I could see that under these circumstances the continuation of talks at Manzanillo was no longer productive from our point of view and would likely work to his advantage.

On December 18, Shlaudeman and I discussed our situation. Any attempt to get money from Congress for the Contras in the near future would be fruitless, I realized. As a result, there was no chance that the Sandinistas would negotiate seriously; they didn't need to in the absence of Contra funding. On January 4, I expressed my view at a Family Group lunch in the White House. On this occasion, I had no problem getting administration unity: Weinberger, Casey, McFarlane, and I all agreed that Shlaudeman should inform Tinoco that we saw no point in talking further; we weren't ending the talks, but we were suspending them under present circumstances.

On January 7, 1985, Shlaudeman embarked on three days of consultations with the Core Four countries in preparation for terminating the negotiations with Tinoco. No one was surprised to hear what Shlaudeman had to say. They, too, had been disturbed by the increasing tendency of the Nicaraguans to describe their bilateral discussions with the United States as making the Contadora process irrelevant and unnecessary.

As soon as the Nicaraguans got wind of the content of Shlaudeman's discussions, they started putting out the word that the Manzanillo talks were promising: they wanted the United States to be blamed for stopping a serious negotiation.

---

to defend its security. And just as American courts do not resolve "political questions," the World Court had not adjudicated issues regarding the lawfulness of a nation's resort to force, for such issues involve world politics and world security, matters that the UN Charter places in the UN Security Council, not in the World Court. The ICJ departed from this important practice. *Nicaragua* v. *The United States* was a case in which a Marxist-Leninist regime, which by definition despises law as "bourgeois," sought to use America's commitment to the principle of law to tie our hands and prevent assistance to El Salvador in its need to defend against a Marxist-Leninist takeover. The United States was correct in refusing to accept the ICJ's decisions in this case, and the ICJ, not the United States, dealt a blow to the cause of international law.

On January 18, 1985, we announced that the Manzanillo talks, insofar as the United States was concerned, were suspended. The termination of the talks provided a semicolon, but not a period, to the continuing efforts to implement a policy of strength and negotiation in Central America. Shlaudeman had met Tinoco in Manzanillo eight times and in Atlanta once between April and December 1984; he held 120 meetings with Contadora country foreign ministers and logged over 250,000 miles. He had engaged in intensive and genuine diplomatic efforts. But as the U.S. ability to array strength against Nicaragua diminished, the prospects for our diplomatic success did so as well. Manzanillo had worked in our favor for a time, but that time had now passed.

I was disappointed. We had taken some losses. Still, I told President Reagan that we had also made progress in Central America over the past three to four years. Our friends in Central America were stronger, and Nicaragua, despite its propaganda achievements, was weaker economically and more isolated politically. Costa Rica, El Salvador, Honduras, and Guatemala—the Core Four—were effectively defending their interests in the regional diplomatic negotiations. But Nicaragua still represented a threat to political stability in the region.

Where could we go from here? The forward movement in Central America toward more democratic government and brighter economic prospects was fragile, more so in some countries than others. Congress did provide support for administration efforts to help the Core Four countries, each with its special problems. Honduras and El Salvador deserved special attention. Honduras had seen its new pattern of democratic governance mature to the point that power passed peacefully from one political party to another. The Honduran economy was poor, but entrepreneurial spirit was easy to find. A large proportion of the Contras had moved to Honduras and operated from there, to the consternation of the Honduran government, which observed with trepidation the large Nicaraguan army so amply supplied by the Soviets as well as the unwillingness of Congress to support the Contras.

El Salvador, through an open political process, had a government that had earned political legitimacy at home and increasing respect abroad. And it had become increasingly capable, with our continued help, of preventing a guerrilla victory. President Duarte provided a political cohesiveness and a sense of moral uplift and of hope to his country, but he had no feel whatsoever for economics and business and for the importance of the role of free markets, private enterprise, and the incentives needed to encourage entrepreneurial development and a healthy economy.

In Guatemala and Costa Rica, the work ahead seemed doable and the resources available. Costa Rica was the jewel of the region, with a long-standing democratic tradition and, at least relatively speaking, a prosperous economy. Nicaragua, with all its armed capability, was the odd man out in terms of political and economic philosophy and practice. If economic progress was inadequate in the Core Four countries, economic decline was the contrasting pattern in Nicaragua. Our task was to sharpen the contrasts and make them increasingly apparent throughout Latin America and Europe, not to mention the United States. I did not favor continued futile efforts to obtain congressional funding for the Contras. That only underlined and contributed to our problem.

We should continue to make the case for the Contras, I felt, but wait for our moment with the Congress. When events caused opinion to shift, we should be ready to move quickly for Contra aid if and when that moment of opportunity came. Tony Motley felt that the Contras could scrape up enough money themselves to hold together. I heard about efforts within the NSC staff to drum up private donations to support the Contras, but I felt that the only significant source of support in the end would be Congress. We should conduct ourselves carefully so that we did not alienate that potent potential source. Sooner or later I felt that Congress would provide us the leverage we needed for a successful diplomatic effort to further stability, democracy, and economic development in Central America.

CHAPTER 24

The Continuing Search
for Peace in the Middle East

With the departure of the PLO from Beirut in September 1982 and President Reagan's speech setting out his September 1 Fresh Start initiative for peace in the Middle East, an opportunity arose to revive Lebanon's nationhood and revitalize the Camp David peace process, which had been badly crippled, if not destroyed, by Israel's invasion of Lebanon a few months earlier. This is the story of what happened to the September 1 peace initiative and to the peace process between the time of Reagan's speech and the early part of 1986.

The story is one of some significant achievements, of dashed hopes and frustration punctuated by violence, of a continuing effort to keep credible ideas in play, and to keep alive at least a flickering hope of the possibility, if not the probability, of a more stable, more predictable, more peaceful future in the Middle East. Throughout this period, President Reagan's touchstones were an unshakable support for the security of the state of Israel, a readiness to understand Arab views and engage personally with Arab leaders, and a willingness to support sensible negotiating efforts even when the probability of success was clearly not high. The president gave me a lot of tactical running room, which I always exercised in keeping with his strategic views and in full consultation with him. I pulled the laboring oar and usually called the beat as well. So this is my story of how events unfolded, but Ronald Reagan's views were deeply held and fiercely felt, and his presence was always there, even when unspoken. He yearned to be a peacemaker in the Holy Land.

He and I had important achievements and ideas with which to work. The Camp David Accords, reached in September 1978 with the work and imagination of President Jimmy Carter, President Anwar Sadat, and Prime Minister Menachem Begin, brought peace between Israel and Egypt, the return of the Sinai to Egypt, and an approach to realizing "the legitimate rights" of the Palestinian residents of the West Bank and Gaza.

*   *   *

Two ideas in that approach had staying power. A first substantive step in negotiations over the West Bank and Gaza territories occupied by Israel at the end of the 1967 war would address immediate changes that could be made to give Palestinians who lived there greater control over their daily lives. These negotiations were first known as "autonomy talks." In the Middle Eastern land of paradox, these talks have been suspect in the eyes of many Arabs and Palestinians who have regarded more "self-rule," which they want, as an Israeli "sop" to satisfy the Palestinians permanently by allowing them the privilege of "collecting each other's garbage" and to deflect their attention from their ultimate objective: achieving an independent Palestinian state. I and many others, including Israelis and Arabs, saw these negotiations for increased Palestinian self-rule differently. I called them "transition talks" in order to emphasize that further changes and negotiations were to come.

Second, and equally important, Palestinian self-rule providing control over many aspects of their daily lives—accompanied by stable relationships with the Israeli population—could build mutual confidence in the workability of a more far-reaching agreement on the "final status" of the territories under negotiation. So two important substantive ideas of continuing relevance were "transition arrangements" and their relationship to "final status."

Then there was the question of identifying the Palestinians who would represent Palestinian interests in any negotiations. They must have representation because they are the human beings directly affected, certainly more so than any other Arabs. The terrorist tactics of the PLO and its objective of eliminating Israel, set forth in its charter, meant that Israel would not deal with the PLO. Could Jordan represent the Palestinians? Could Palestinians be found who were acceptable to Israel and legitimate in the eyes of their constituents and who could therefore serve in a Jordanian delegation? The issue of Palestinian representation presented an intractable problem that would not go away.

The peace process had faced a fundamental quandary ever since 1974, when the Arab League at Rabat, Morocco, took the diplomacy of the Palestinian issue out of the hands of Jordan, with Jordan's reluctant assent, and gave it to the Palestine Liberation Organization as the "sole legitimate representative of the Palestinian people on any Palestinian land that is liberated." The PLO is a collection of disparate Palestinian factions, all part of the Palestine National Council (PNC), the governing body of the Palestinian movement, which advocates armed struggle as the means to retake the Palestinian homeland from Israel. The PLO refused to recognize Israel's right to exist, was responsible for terrorist acts against Israelis, and would not accept the indispensable foundation stone of the peace process:

UN Security Council Resolution 242. The PLO, by its own nature and policies, had not passed the entrance exam for admission to the diplomatic process. Israel would not try to work out an agreement with an organization openly dedicated to its destruction.

American efforts to draw King Hussein into the peace process repeatedly encountered his resistance or reluctance: the Arab world might turn against him—perhaps fatally—should he move to deal with Israel on the issue of the occupied territories. For this reason, the chief task of diplomacy since the Arabs' unfortunate decision at Rabat had been to try to find a way for an Arab state or states, together with Palestinian representatives, to engage Israel. When Egypt did so in the negotiations over the Sinai—largely un-populated desert Egyptian territory occupied by Israel after the 1967 war—Palestinians were not directly involved. Egypt under the Camp David agreement sought for a time to play the necessary role of nation-state counterpart for Israel in talks about the territories of the West Bank and Gaza, but this was not a natural role for Egypt to play. As home to a million or more Palestinians and as former ruler of the West Bank, Jordan was much better suited. Jordan was not a signatory to the Camp David Accords, however, and when negotiations for a considerable degree of Palestinian self-rule—autonomy talks—fell apart in 1982 after Israel's invasion of Lebanon, there was little reason for hope that these talks could be revived under Egyptian sponsorship.

The Arab League Comes to Washington

The president's September 1 initiative did stir the Arabs into motion. An Arab summit was convened on September 6, 1982, in Fez, Morocco, in large part in response to the president's dramatic speech. One of the outcomes of the Fez summit was the formation of delegations that would visit the capital of each permanent member of the UN Security Council. King Hassan of Morocco brought a delegation from the Arab League to Washington for meetings with the president and me on October 22, designed to ask about the president's initiative and to give their interpretation of developments at the Fez summit. "You have a great opportunity, and you must not let Begin's intransigence cause you to fail to produce a credible negotiating partner with Israel," I told King Hassan. The Arabs repeatedly urged us to deal with the PLO.

The following Tuesday, October 26, I was talking with members of my Middle East core group about our several meetings with King Hassan's Arab League delegation. Hassan had accepted Resolutions 242 and 338 as the basis for negotiations. His delegation was agreeable to negotiations with Israel. We had extensive discussion about the role of the PLO and the importance of King Hussein's receiving a mandate for negotiation from the PLO. In a side conversation with King Hassan, he told me, "You have to open this PLO file."

"The trouble is," I replied, "when you open that file, you find terrorism." He understood my response, but he didn't like my restatement of the U.S. position. The United States would talk with the PLO only after the PLO had met our well-known conditions: accept Israel's right to exist, accept UN Security Council Resolution 242 as the basis for negotiation with Israel, and renounce terrorism.

CIA analyst Bob Ames had emphasized in our core-group discussion the importance of the PNC conference that was due to take place soon in Tunis. PLO leader Yasser Arafat would have to grapple with two issues, he said. First, he would ask the PNC whether he had the authority to deal in the peace process on the basis of UN Resolutions 242 and 338 and the right of Israel to exist. Their answer would be yes, Ames predicted. Second, Arafat would ask the PNC whether he had the authority to mandate the Jordanians to negotiate on behalf of the PLO. Again, Ames predicted, the answer would be yes. What Arafat didn't know, Ames went on, was whether he could count on the determination of the United States to insist that Israel negotiate in good faith. Arafat was especially distrustful of us, and even more distrustful of the Israelis, after the devastating massacres in the Palestinian refugee camps of Sabra and Shatila that had occurred a month earlier, in September. The developments predicted by Ames did not come to pass. But I would hear again and again from credible people that the PLO and Arafat were "about to change." Again and again, the predicted developments proved elusive.

I told my core group my own views on where we stood. "The Arabs are aware of, and accept the difference between, a transition regime and final status arrangements. They seem to think that Begin and Sharon are impossible, but not Israel generally. There is a realistic acceptance of negotiations with Israel. The Israelis, on the other hand, have pushed hard with their military strength, and they have used it harshly. They have killed the PLO's military operation in Lebanon, but they have paid a gigantic price. They are isolated." I referred to my recent conversation with the Australian foreign minister, who said to me, "Unusual things are happening within the Australian Jewish community." Edgar Bronfman, a major supporter of Israel in Canada and the United States, echoed this: "People are worried [about Israel]," he had told me. "So Israel is dominant," I said, "but in its moment of dominance, by Sabra and Shatila especially, it has cut the moral ground out from beneath itself."

The Start of Work with King Hussein

All our efforts were focused on getting King Hussein to enter direct talks with Israel despite the threats of Arab radicals. Sometimes the king talked boldly of doing so; at other times, he sank into despair. But he took our initiative seriously and seemed to be actively seeking to bring Palestinians into the process. On September 20, in an address to his nation, King Hussein had called publicly for the PLO and Jordan to develop the outlines of confederation. He had accepted UN Resolution 242 since he, as king of Jordan, had helped negotiate it in 1967, he said. He was, thereby, at least implicitly recognizing Israel. His speech was read as a challenge to the PLO's ability or willingness to speak for the Palestinians. Most importantly, the king began in late 1982 to indicate to us that should his efforts to get the PLO to sign on with him fail, he would move without them, with his own Palestinians, to engage the Israelis directly: a bold step of the magnitude of Anwar Sadat's decision to go to Jerusalem.

In late December 1982, King Hussein came to Washington and in one brief visit displayed every dimension of the endlessly frustrating Middle East morass. At the king's suggestion, he reversed protocol and came to my office. "What is the United States prepared to do?" he asked. "Camp David is dead," he told me. "September 1 is dead, too."

Our ambassador to Jordan, Dick Viets, who had accompanied Hussein to Washington, took the king's part. "It is up to us to do more," he said, and in a phrase I would hear again and again over the years, "or risk losing the king." The meeting went nowhere. The king returned to the Four Seasons Hotel, where he was quartered for the visit, and after a bit, I went over to try to salvage the situation.

King Hussein is the most engaging of monarchs. Short, fit, muscular, and soft-spoken, with a deep baritone voice, he calls everyone "sir"—a trait ingrained by his days at Sandhurst, Britain's West Point. In his bearing he seems sometimes imbued with an expanse of sadness; at other times, petulance. He combines the dignity and gravity of an hereditary monarch with the charm of a father interested in his children. He has a deep sense of history and mission, but he rules an impoverished country and has a weak hand to play in regional politics.

When our talk at the Four Seasons was over, the king said he would continue his efforts to get the PLO to agree that Jordan engage in direct talks with Israel. The first step in those talks, he reluctantly accepted, was to try to establish a period of transitional self-government for residents of the West Bank and Gaza. He wanted a time limit on the duration of these transition negotiations, since he suspected Israel would attempt to drag them out. He also insisted on a freeze of Israeli settlements on the West Bank before he came to the negotiating table. If, under these circumstances, the PLO blocked his effort toward direct talks, he said that he would "go to the people." He seemed to agree that President Reagan's, September 1 initiative offered the most workable way forward, but I knew that he was deeply troubled and would be hard to keep in harness for this effort. A few weeks afterward, word came to us that King Hussein had been taken to the hospital with heart fibrillations. I didn't wonder: he was under near-constant emotional stress and political pressure. And the picture in his mind of his grandfather's assassination on the steps of the Al-Aqsu mosque on Jerusalem's Temple Mount seemed always with him.

I wondered whether King Hussein could move forward without the PLO, even if he wanted to. He would face internal opposition. Palestinians in his delegation would face possible assassination at the hands of the PLO. Syria was a threatening presence on his border. If he was to take such a step, he would need full-scale support, in security and economic terms, from the United States. And he could get it. If he entered direct talks with Israel, King Hussein would receive enthusiastic support from Congress as well as from President Reagan.

Throughout the winter of 1983, the scene in the Middle East was disheartening. The Saudis canceled a visit by British Foreign Secretary Francis Pym as retaliation against a British decision not to receive an Arab League delegation because it included PLO members. The Israelis, on January 17, notified four foreign lecturers at Hebron University in the West Bank that they must cease teaching immediately unless they signed a new work-permit application that included an anti-PLO declaration. I reacted sharply, and Israel backed off. Former Presidents Ford and Carter, supporting our concerns about settlements, called Israeli settlements on the West Bank a "major obstacle" to peace. The Israelis countered by announcing more settlements. We protested.

Nevertheless, King Hussein, in close communication with Phil Habib, our special envoy to the Middle East, kept working for an agreement with Yasser Arafat that would allow the king to lead a Jordanian-Palestinian delegation into negotiations with Israel. On February 6, 1983, the king informed us of encouraging news: Arafat had agreed to four essential points. He would support Hussein's move to negotiations on the basis of President Reagan's September 1 initiative, accept a negotiating team of Jordanians with non-PLO Palestinians, forswear any statement that would tar the Palestinians as representatives of the PLO, and work jointly with the king to gain Arab support for this course of action. An announcement, however, could come only after the next Palestine National Council meeting, expected shortly. In early April, Arafat was again in Amman, talking to the king. What would be the outcome of these talks? Would we be able to get the peace process going forward, or would Arafat's word prove illusory again? We eagerly awaited the king's report.

On Sunday, April 10, I was at Camp David for a weekend with the president. Word came through that King Hussein was calling. His negotiations with Arafat had failed, he told President Reagan. He could not move forward. The president expressed his regret and urged the king not to give up. When King Hussein publicly announced his disappointing news, he said he would not enter peace negotiations either with the Palestinians or alone and on their behalf.

The PLO had apparently backed off at the last minute from a plan on which King Hussein and Arafat had agreed. The king, however, was publicly critical of the United States for not being willing to deal with the PLO; in addition, he expressed skepticism that the United States, which had been unable to persuade Israel to stop new settlements, could persuade Israel to make even more difficult decisions. The president and I both firmly stated our determination to persevere.

Hussein and Mubarak

Bud McFarlane, who had followed Phil Habib in July 1983 as our special envoy to the Middle East, was named as the president's national security adviser on October 17, 1983. To replace him, I suggested that the president ask Don Rumsfeld, the former congressman, White House chief of staff, and secretary of defense, to become our special envoy to the Middle East. He agreed. Rumsfeld was plugged into Washington as a heavy hitter. The intelligence community provided him, as a former secretary of defense and a member of their club, with far more information than ever came my way. Rumsfeld was a brainy grappler. He still had the tough body of the collegiate wrestling champion he had been at Princeton, but this was mud wrestling and Rumsfeld was a realist. He pored over volumes of documents and talked to the experts endlessly to learn the complexities of the Middle East problem. He went to the region to learn more.

We stayed close to King Hussein. During the fall of 1983 we worked quietly and closely with Jordan on a logistics program that would position military equipment there in case security should break down in the Persian Gulf. Pressures from the Gulf Arab states were enormous for the United States to tilt toward Iraq because Iran had turned the tables and now threatened to break through and sweep into those states. The logistics plan with Jordan was prudent in these circumstances, and cooperation with the Jordanians was good. They appreciated the assurances about their security.

King Hussein, with continuing encouragement from us, had not given up. In October 1983, the king told us he might reconvene the long-dormant Jordanian Parliament. This would be a step of some consequence, in our view, because the Parliament had been comprised of West Bank Palestinians as well as representatives from Jordan proper. The Parliament was therefore a symbol and an institutional embodiment of Jordan's claim of legitimate political responsibility for the West Bank and for the Palestinians who lived there. The king had dismantled the Parliament in 1974, after the Arab summit decision at Rabat. To reopen the Parliament now could be a message that Jordan was reasserting itself, and, at the least, implied a rejection of the Rabat decision that made the PLO the "sole" representative of the Palestinians.

A factor in the king's—and our—thinking was the fate of Yasser Arafat. The Israelis had pulled out of the Shouf Mountains on September 3 and 4, 1983, thereby undercutting our effort to use their presence as leverage in the longer-term effort to achieve the withdrawal of both Syrian and Israeli forces from Lebanon. On September 16, Arafat arrived back in Lebanon for the first time since we had engineered the PLO evacuation a year earlier. He soon became enmeshed in trouble there again, not from the Israelis but from the Syrians. Syrian-backed Palestinian forces attacked Arafat's PLO faction around Tripoli in the north of Lebanon. Syria backed its own PLO factions and had fallen out with Arafat. Soon another siege was under way. It was Beirut all over again on a smaller scale, but this time the Saudis were the mediators. They arranged a cease-fire on November 23 that allowed Arafat and his PLO supporters to evacuate Tripoli, an evacuation that could not take place until almost a month later and only after the United States reluctantly prevailed on Israel to allow passage of Arafat and his supporters on Greek ships under French escort. This was the second time the United States had saved Arafat's skin. Three strikes and you're out, I felt. Where Arafat would come to rest this time and what his political fortunes would be, we could not imagine.

Meanwhile, we worked on the Israelis, for they would have to permit West Bank residents who became members of the Jordanian Parliament to travel to and from meetings if the king reconvened that body. Timing would be important. I went over the possibility with Foreign Minister Yitzhak Shamir in November when he was in Washington, and at about the same time with Israeli President Chaim Herzog, who came to Washington to get an honorary degree from Georgetown. The response was cautious but interested. In the end, the Israelis let us know they would not interfere with the travel of members of the Jordanian Parliament.

Yasser Arafat reached Cairo on December 22, where he met with President Mubarak, a meeting welcomed by us as further lessening Egyptian isolation and possibly moderating Arafat's views but understandably denounced by Israel. And by January 4, 1984, Osama el-Baz, director of political affairs for President Mubarak, announced that Egypt was ready to join Jordan and the PLO to develop a joint approach to negotiations with Israel.

King Hussein, half-antagonistic, half-collaborative in his behavior toward the United States, announced that for the first time in eight years, he would convene the Jordanian Parliament, on January 9, 1984, to consider constitutional provisions dealing with the West Bank. On January 16, the king addressed the Parliament, urging new Jordan-PLO cooperation on the peace process and indicating the return of Jordan to a central diplomatic role. Israel deplored the attention in the speech to the PLO and rejected any thought of Israel's dealing with the PLO. Nevertheless, the king's action was a bold and constructive step.

A few days later, on January 19, the Organization of the Islamic Conference[1] voted to reinstate Egypt, which it had suspended from membership following the Egyptian–Israeli Treaty of Peace. This was an important development, a big moment, showing that an Arab nation could make peace with Israel and retain its role in the Islamic, including the Arab, world. Egypt's diplomatic isolation was ending. The step also could facilitate the restoration of Jordanian-Egyptian relations, just the kind of normalization that we wanted to see.

On February 9, 1984, we heard that Yuri Andropov had died and that his funeral would take place five days later. The president had no intention of attending the funeral. I stayed in Washington as well. King Hussein and President Mubarak were due in town for carefully worked out overlapping visits that presented another opportunity for a step toward negotiations. The fact that the president and I had remained in Washington and that King Hussein and President Mubarak maintained their visit schedules gave extra importance to our meetings. I always looked forward to seeing Hosni Mubarak. A big, bluff man with an open face that usually bore a look of faint surprise, Mubarak had an earthy shrewdness and a sharp sense of what the Egyptian people would not accept and must be called upon to endure.

Mubarak was elated over Egypt's reacceptance by the Arab world; King Hussein was troubled by his inability to get PLO support for moves toward negotiations on the West Bank. Their moods were played out against the background of the imminent and abrupt U.S. withdrawal from Lebanon, interpreted in the Arab world as showing that the United States was "short of breath" when difficult Middle East issues were involved.

Again King Hussein told us that if Arafat would not cooperate with him on dealing with Israel about the territories, he would move without the PLO to build a pro-Jordanian constituency among West Bank Palestinians and try to form a delegation from among them. In other words, the king

---

1. This organization was founded in May 1971 following a summit meeting of Muslim heads of state in Rabat, Morocco. According to its charter, its purposes included the promotion of "Islamic solidarity among member States" and the coordination of efforts to "safeguard the Holy Places and support of the struggle of the people of Palestine, and help them to regain their rights and liberate their land." The organization maintained its headquarters in Jiddah, Saudi Arabia.

was seeking a way to cast off Arafat. Mubarak, by contrast, wanted to "adopt" Arafat and use the Egypt-PLO connection to move Egypt deeper into the Arab fold. The king talked as though he simply wanted to go through the motions with Arafat and then strike out on his own without the PLO. But he also called for a UN resolution to prevent Israel from establishing settlements in the occupied territories. U.S. support for the resolution was the latest "litmus test" we were asked to pass. We were against new settlements and said so, but we were not prepared to vote for UN sanctions on Israel.

Nevertheless, the king continued to profess his determination to win Arafat to his cause or, at the appropriate moment, to go ahead without him. The problem turned out to be Mubarak. At the end of this joint visit, President Reagan, President Mubarak, and King Hussein proceeded to the East Room of the White House to make public statements. Seeking further to enhance Egypt's acceptability in the Arab world in general, Mubarak asserted—in that most publicized setting and in the presence of the president of the United States and the king of Jordan—that no Arab nation could negotiate over the territories on behalf of the Palestinians without the participation or assent of the PLO; the PLO truly was the sole representative of the Palestinian people.

So despite our efforts, King Hussein had now created a new obstruction with his settlements resolution, and Mubarak had put the king in an impossible position by declaring in advance that any effort to pressure Arafat into agreeing that the king "go forward or else" was doomed. When I met with Mubarak before his departure, I lambasted him for what I regarded as an ill-considered statement. I felt he was obstructing the peace process for the sake of trying to hasten Egypt's return to the Arab world, an objective I supported as a help, not a hindrance, to the peace process. By riding the Arafat horse roughshod over the hopes of the peace process, he also infuriated the Israelis and undermined the tone of the crucial Israel-Egypt relationship. Mubarak lit into me in return. We parted in near anger.

The turn of events led once again to a now-familiar reaction from King Hussein. "This is the end of our dialogue," Ambassador Dick Viets reported from Jordan. "I've never seen the king so dismayed, frustrated, and bitter." I understood the corner that Jordan was in, a corner made tighter by Syria's big military buildup and threatening behavior toward Jordan. Congress, I knew, would authorize little or no aid to Jordan as long as the king took no step toward Israel. But neither the Arab states nor the PLO would give him a mandate to negotiate with Israel. And King Hussein was not bold enough or strong enough to do so on his own initiative, even with our support. On March 14, the king, in an interview, went to ground in a way we had seen before: he denounced the United States for being too close to Israel, and he himself rejected peace negotiations with Israel. This led Congress to make clear that our military relationships with Jordan—and Saudi Arabia—would have to reflect this downturn. Seeing the inevitable and not wishing to fight only to suffer a defeat on the Hill, the president on March 21, 1984, withdrew from congressional consideration the sale of antiaircraft missiles to Jordan. Just as inevitably, the Jordanians turned to the Soviet Union for weapons. This time, the king's position had a new underpinning. Reacting to the humiliating manner of our departure from Lebanon, he said that the United States had no staying power, no ability to stand firm on its principles, no consistency.

Other developments were also working to impede progress. Rapidly rising inflation in Israel and a sense of Israeli failure in Lebanon put the domestic Israeli political scene in disarray. Elections loomed. The tandem of elections in Israel in the summer and in the United States in November made serious work on the peace process difficult under the best of circumstances. On May 18, 1984, Don Rumsfeld, no fool, bowed out as special envoy to the Middle East. We did not replace him. The message to the region was clear. The Arabs and Israelis were going to have to stir themselves, show more effort and flexibility.

"We can't want peace more than you do," I said to King Hussein, to Mubarak, and to the leaders of Israel. "We're not going to chase you until you catch us." I wanted that to penetrate. Our strategy to pull them forward was realistic, if risky. I knew a vacuum in peace efforts itself could produce problems—and violence.

A New Turn of the Wheel

Late in the fall of 1984, with the outcome of our election obvious and the strain of our strategy apparent, King Hussein once again began to talk to us in ways that pointed toward possibilities for progress. I had put Dick Murphy, now assistant secretary for the Middle East, to work. Murphy knew the Arab world intimately, having been U.S. ambassador to Syria and, most recently, Saudi Arabia. He had a sharp mind, a keen sense of irony, and a wry wit. With support from the president and me, he won the confidence of the Israelis. Murphy could sit with unblinking attention while Arab representatives elaborately used hours to get to the point. And he had steely nerves that steadied him as Israeli representatives got instantly to the point and tried to stab him with it. The combination of his knowledge and his indefatigable and unflappable effort made for one of the best diplomatic "touches" I had encountered.

Murphy traveled around the Middle East throughout the fall, endlessly it seemed, returning to Washington after six weeks straight in the field.

His presence, his message, his persistence and patience made an impact. King Hussein, he said, was "excited." The PLO was not the legitimate or proper representative of the Palestinians, the king in his own cryptic way told Murphy. He wanted to go back to the pre-Rabat situation so that Jordan once again could play the central Arab role in negotiations with Israel over the West Bank and Gaza. The outcome, as the king and his advisers described it to Murphy, should be right down the line of our September 1 proposal: land for peace, but recognizing that there would be no return to the pre-1967 borders; no Palestinian state; realization of Palestinian self-determination through a Jordanian-Palestinian federation. If the PLO did not agree to work with the king along such lines, Murphy was yet again assured, the king would go forward without them. He would count on U.S. economic and security support.

At the end of the process, there would be an international conference to ratify the outcome. If the PLO was not a player, as such, at the beginning, their acquiescence in Jordan's leading role would be gained by holding out to the PLO the prospect of their presence at the end of the process, if, by that time, the PLO had met the U.S. conditions. The concluding international conference idea thus would be a lure to get the PLO to hang back while Jordan worked on the problem.

Although this sounded far too optimistic to be true, the king seemed to be determined this time. The most striking indication of his seriousness was an evident shift in his intellectual approach: King Hussein was thinking in terms of process rather than insisting on a guaranteed outcome of the process before entering it. If there was one shorthand way to sum up the stalemate in the Middle East, it was that the Arab side invariably insisted on a comprehensive solution to all aspects of the conflict, guaranteed up front. The Israelis wanted face-to-face negotiations, a form of recognition, and they wanted to work on the problem step by step, without even an implicit indication about the eventual result.

Neither side gave credit to the other's outlook: the Israelis saw the Arab view as a way to avoid negotiations and to impose a solution upon Israel by outside powers—namely, the United States. The Arabs saw Israel's view as a snare designed with American collusion to delay progress endlessly while "facts on the ground," particularly new Israeli settlements in the West Bank, pushed Arab interests increasingly beyond reach. Both sides had a point. But here was King Hussein apparently recognizing that the Arab approach of a "comprehensive" settlement and the Israeli "step-by-step" approach could be compatible and usefully pursued in tandem. I was encouraged and was ready to help the king move toward the necessary next decisions. Since those decisions involved the PLO, however, the king would necessarily have to be the prime mover. He agreed and indicated to Murphy that the United States should just give him some time to work. That made sense to me.

Shoring up the Foundations

But other aspects of the Middle East question also called for urgent attention. Israel was in trouble in its relations with Egypt and was caught in a morass in Lebanon. Its economy was performing badly, and its politics reflected a sense of stalemate. I feared that Israel, divided between the Labor and Likud parties, would not be in a strong position to respond if the opportunity to move toward agreement with the Arab world arose.

The July 1984 Israeli elections had ended in a split decision, with neither major party able to form a government. After much negotiating, a coalition government of national unity emerged in September 1984, with the leader of the Labor party, Shimon Peres, becoming prime minister and the leader of the Likud party, Yitzhak Shamir, foreign minister for two years; in October 1986 they would exchange positions for the following two years.

They agreed that Israel must extricate itself from the quagmire in Lebanon. In my view, Israel had made mistake after mistake in Lebanon: by starting the war in the first place, by misleading the world about its objectives in the war, by impeding Phil Habib's efforts to bring the Beirut siege to a swift and sensible conclusion, by demanding too much of the government of Lebanon and taking too long in postwar negotiations, and by pulling its troops unilaterally out of the Shouf, undercutting our ability to generate Arab pressure on Syria to withdraw its forces in tandem with those of Israel. So be it: the point now was to lift the albatross of Lebanon from Israel's neck. By mid-February 1985, the Israel Defense Forces had completed the first stage of its withdrawal, and Israel's acute problems in Lebanon were defused.

The most important issue was maintaining good relations between Israel and Egypt. The Israelis were persistently sour about the Egyptian–Israeli Peace Treaty, feeling that they had given up strategic territory by returning the Sinai but had not received in return the benefits in trade, tourism, friendly media treatment, and international acceptance that they felt should result from such a peace agreement. On the other hand, the Israelis had seriously strained their relationship with Egypt by their invasion of Lebanon, by building new settlements in the West Bank and Gaza, and by retaining the beach resort of Taba near the head of the Gulf of Aqaba. Even Israeli officials sometimes admitted that Israel had held on to this tiny piece of Sinai not because of any legitimate dispute over the boundary line but to avoid returning all the Sinai so that no "total withdrawal" precedent could be cited to them in future negotiations over the West Bank. Fostering good relations between Egypt and Israel had to be at the top of my list of Middle East concerns.

Israel's economy by early 1985 was in sorry shape. I had repeatedly called Israel's internal economic problems to the attention of its leaders, but they were too preoccupied by issues involving security to pay much attention. Shaped in large part by people whose views were formed in the Central European socialist tradition, the Israeli economy was heavily owned by the state and operated by a large and stifling central bureaucracy. Early on, Israel had prospered as a small economy driven by the inspiration and energy that sprang from the creation of a long-awaited Jewish homeland. By now, however, change was drastically needed to privatize and deregulate business life and to free up the creative capacities of Israel's talented and resourceful people. Events forced Israel's leaders to address economic issues: the rate of inflation greeted Shimon Peres, the new prime minister, by soaring to an annual rate of 1260 percent in October 1984 and threatened to spiral totally out of control; Israel's foreign exchange position deteriorated; and a general loss of confidence bordering on panic ensued.

The need for budget and monetary reform was urgent. With considerable help from the United States—including good advice from U.S. economists Allen Wallis, Herb Stein, and Stan Fischer, and heavy pressure from me—significant budget and monetary reforms were undertaken. The economy recovered at least to an even keel. By the last half of 1986, the rate of inflation was down to an annual rate of 15 percent, and the foreign exchange crisis had passed. I was able to bring needed pressure to bear because Israel's friends in the United States, including those in our Congress, well knew that drastic and difficult change was critically important and Israel's leaders themselves realized that as well. In those circumstances, I could play the "heavy" and be supported, even thanked, for forcing necessary if difficult decisions.

I wanted to go further. I started to push for a U.S.-Israel free trade agreement, which would give Israel access to U.S. markets while forcing Israeli companies to meet real competition and, I hoped, opening up the Israeli economy to American investment. If we wanted to enhance private enterprise in Israel, then private enterprise in the United States should take the lead, I thought. I asked Detroit industrialist Max Fisher to lead the way. Max had quietly advised presidents and secretaries of state for decades. In his seventies and immensely energetic, Max still had the hulking presence of the Ohio State football player he once had been. Max was a man to whom few people could say no. If anyone could persuade Israel to break free from the entrenched, constricting, socialistic nature of the economy, he could.

Max formed "Project Independence" and enlisted more than a hundred experienced and successful U.S. business and financial leaders, all strong supporters of Israel. Max told me that he said to the prime minister and other Israeli leaders, "When you ask a guy like me to make a contribution to Israel, that's one thing. I give. But when you ask Max Fisher, the businessman, to make an investment, that's a completely different matter: I want to see my way to a reasonable return, and I want to operate my business in a way that has been successful for me in the past." After considerable effort and with help from the many experienced and successful American entrepreneurs he had recruited, Max, however, had to acknowledge that the Israeli bureaucracy had defeated him. Tragically for Israel, the bureaucracy had defeated an important opportunity to open up the economy and unshackle and energize the creative capacities of its talented population.

Also, as part of this overall economic effort, I favored U.S. approval of the licenses required to enable Israel to design and build the next generation of Israel Aircraft Industries' fighter, the Lavi (lion), which would replace the Kfir (lion cub), an aircraft built on the model of a 1960s-era French Mirage. This project, of special interest to Defense Minister Arens and others in the Likud leadership, helped keep some high-tech jobs in Israel at a critical time. But in the long run it proved too expensive for the Israelis. My advocacy was a costly mistake in terms of wasted U.S. security assistance funds. I was wrong, and Cap Weinberger, who had opposed the project from the beginning, was right.

I had started in mid-1983 the fourth part of my effort to create a better environment for the peace process: an improvement in the conditions and quality of daily life for the Palestinians of the West Bank and Gaza. This meant working with—and on—Israel's military government for the territories, and Israel's political leadership, to ease up on the controls that restricted economic activities of the Palestinian inhabitants of the West Bank and Gaza. I asked the Israelis, through our embassy in Israel and through State's policy planning director, Peter Rodman, and Mideast hand Bill Kirby, to take a more liberal view toward some of the development projects proposed by private voluntary organizations (mostly American and church related) in the territories. Some of these were as small and simple as approval for the importation of machinery for a small factory to produce olive oil. I asked the Israelis to allow funds from Arab countries to come across the Jordan River to support municipal operations and development. I asked them to allow small Palestinian-owned enterprises to start up and grow without suffocating them with paperwork. And I worked on the establishment of indigenous financial institutions—an Arab bank— to provide a source of funds for business projects.

All this was a long, frustrating, uphill battle. The Israelis feared that every step in this direction would reduce their control over, and therefore their security in, the territories. They also feared that outside money and help coming in might provide funds for terrorists and entangle the territories with the larger Arab world, thereby skewing any negotiations down the line. The Palestinians—especially the radicals among them—were obstructionist, too: radicals denounced efforts to better their conditions as ploys to make them content under "occupation" and therefore willing to perpetuate Israel's control. "Less is better" seemed to be their creed. In an odd reversal of perceptions, Israel was reluctant because "quality of life" was seen as an effective step-by-step process that would give Palestinians more control over their lives and livelihood. Radical Palestinians carried forward the old Arab approach of "all or nothing at all," which was unrealistic. I feared that violence and bloodshed would break out if there was no visible improvement in the conditions of daily life for the Palestinians in the occupied territories.

A New Effort by King Hussein

On February 11, 1985, King Hussein and Yasser Arafat agreed on a common approach to entering a peace process involving Israel. The king apparently received what he had been seeking from the PLO: Palestinian self-determination exercised through a Jordanian-Palestinian confederation, a Jordanian-Palestinian delegation to negotiate with Israel, and an "out at the beginning, in at the end" formula for PLO participation that we had discussed earlier. But the central feature of the February 11 agreement, as reported to me, was the statement that "any process aimed at establishing a just and comprehensive peace in the Middle East should take place through an international peace conference in which the Palestinian people, represented by the PLO, should participate as a principal party along with the UN Security Council's permanent member-states and the states that are concerned with the cause of peace in the Middle East." Explanatory messages came in saying that such a conference would come only at the end of the negotiations, to ratify and guarantee whatever outcome would be reached by means of direct Arab-Israeli negotiations, and so we shouldn't worry about the conference. I was not reassured.

The Hussein-Arafat agreement seemed like a big step forward but could easily become a big step backward, I worried. King Hussein had felt that he could not go forward without Arafat on board, so he had gotten Arafat into the backseat while he occupied the driver's seat. But Arafat was a backseat driver who intended soon to take the wheel. He and the king had created the "international conference" idea. If some form of international event as an "opener" could lead right away to direct Arab-Israeli negotiations, that just might be all right. The danger was that this could soon become a vehicle packed with the "international community," assembled to pressure Israel into concessions. King Hussein had not yet found a way to go forward while Arafat hung back; he had allowed himself to get entangled with Arafat as a partner, and perhaps a leading partner. The Israelis were not going to deal with Arafat's PLO, and they would not join a "substantive" international conference where they felt the dice would be loaded against them. From the U.S. standpoint, such a substantive conference, with authority to weigh in on an outcome (as opposed to a purely ceremonial event), would only put us in the position of being Israel's only advocate against increasingly hostile Arabs: a losing proposition for the United States and a winner for the Soviets.

I wanted to see direct Jordanian-Israeli negotiations within a year, with Palestinians represented and given a voice at the outset through the Jordanian delegation. Preparations would have to be deft. King Hussein was a tightrope walker. His decision to walk was itself courageous, but he took each step with the utmost caution—and at times, when the wire swayed, he would dart back to the platform for safety and survival.

I felt in my bones that Hussein's international conference idea would become just one more obstacle for parties to use at crucial moments to obstruct the peace process. Once the idea was invented, we would not be able to uninvent it. From now on, I would have to try to work around the notion of an international conference or attempt to shape it in a way that would not obstruct progress. On February 24, in an interview, Hosni Mubarak proposed what in effect would be a "regional" international conference, to involve Egypt, Israel, a Jordanian-Palestinian delegation, and the United States. Israel welcomed the idea; the PLO denounced it. Maybe we were getting somewhere, I thought. And maybe I had registered with Mubarak in our tense conversation in Washington a year earlier when I objected vehemently to his excessive support of the PLO.

King Hussein was scheduled to come to Washington in late May 1985. My effort in the late winter and spring would be to urge the king to form a delegation of Jordanian officials and acceptable Palestinians seen as legitimately representative of their people but free of any terrorist connections and not so clearly linked to the PLO as to be anathema to Israel. I wanted Dick Murphy to go to the Middle East and spend the time needed to foster the creation of such a group. If such a delegation could be put together, Murphy would first meet with the group, thereby giving it a U.S. stamp of approval, and the group would then engage in direct negotiation with an Israeli delegation.

To set the stage for this and lock it in, we would try to get King Hussein while he was in Washington to state publicly his acceptance of direct negotiations with Israel. Such a statement would give Congress something to point to in approving U.S. arms sales to Jordan, which the king anxiously sought—not because of fear of Israel but because of Syria's threatening behavior toward Jordan. Jordan's Soviet option had not produced much. If we could get a "Murphy meeting" and a Jordanian commitment to direct negotiations, I then would seek to shorten the timetable set forth in the Camp David Accords so that Israeli-Jordanian discussions on the final status of the occupied territories would begin early in the transitional period. I sent Murphy off to the region knowing that I was very likely to be there myself before King Hussein came to Washington.

This is, in fact, what happened. The uproar over the president's trip to Bitburg had led me to want to pay tribute in a special way to the victims of the Holocaust. Prime Minister Peres asked me to speak at Yad Vashem, the Holocaust memorial, on May 10, at the inauguration of a new outdoor monument, marked by a dramatic sculpture of the Star of David emerging from the prison walls of the Nazi camps. The occasion was stirring in itself but also gave me a way to be in the Middle East without raising expectations.

At the end of my brief stay in Israel and after I had discussed with Prime Minister Peres and Foreign Minister Shamir and other Israeli leaders their ideas of how to move the peace process forward, I reviewed the situation with Ambassador Sam Lewis and others on my Mideast team. We sat on patio furniture on the lush lawn that ran to the edge of the cliff behind the ambassador's residence overlooking the Mediterranean. Dick Murphy reported that King Hussein's position had shifted markedly: he was now proposing that Murphy meet first with a Jordanian-Palestinian delegation in which the Palestinians would be members of the Palestinian National Council but not officially members of the PLO. Then the PLO, the king claimed, would meet "the U.S. conditions: accept UN Security Council Resolution 242 and Israel's right to exist, and renounce terrorism." A Jordanian-PLO delegation would then meet with a U.S. delegation. An international conference would follow, after which direct contacts with Israel could go forward.

This process wouldn't work. A substantive international conference would block any chance of progress. The whole point of a Murphy meeting with a Jordanian-Palestinian group was to produce direct Arab-Israel contacts immediately afterward. The king had decided to get into "process," perhaps, but this kind of process could easily become just another way to pressure Israel even before direct talks started, if indeed they did start.

Breakthrough at Aqaba?

On Sunday morning my aircraft took off from Ben-Gurion Airport and turned west to head out over the Mediterranean and then south to Cairo. My destination was the Jordanian port of Aqaba, right next to the Israeli port of Eilat on the Red Sea. It would have been a short, easy flight had we been able to go directly. But Israel and Jordan were belligerents, while Israel and Egypt had relations under a treaty of peace. So I had to fly to Cairo, refuel, and then continue on to Aqaba. In Cairo, I went briefly to Qubah Palace to see President Mubarak. Our irritation with each other now forgotten, we discussed the "international conference," and I gave all the arguments against it. Mubarak seemed to agree. "Maybe hold it at the end of direct negotiations," he said.

King Hussein's palace on the Gulf of Aqaba is a collection of beautifully appointed low-lying structures linked by flower-lined walks, lawns, and gardens. Every detail is exquisite. King Hussein and Queen Noor took O'Bie and me on a short evening cruise on the king's yacht. The air was clear, the sun was setting, and the horizon was vivid in hues of red. As we moved away from the dock, the king pointed to the port side. There was Saudi Arabia, a stone's throw away. He pointed to starboard. There was Israel, then Egypt. He pointed to Taba, a beautiful beach where Egypt's Sinai meets Israel. I needed field glasses to pick out this tiny but contentious piece of land.[2] Four countries, he pointed out, all in easy sight of each other at or near the head of the Gulf.

On board and afterward, alone with me, the king told me that he needed an international conference to provide cover for his dealings with the Israelis; other Arab leaders had to join him in this effort; it was far too dangerous for him to move alone. For the same reason, he needed to have the PLO with him in some fashion. I responded bluntly, presenting the reasons why an approach calling for a "substantive" rather than "procedural" international conference would not get us anywhere. All the while I was talking to the king, Murphy and others of my party were having dinner with the king's team. The Americans were struck by the scornful laughter and contempt of the Jordanians for Arafat, who was the butt of their jokes.

By midnight, as I compared notes with my colleagues, there seemed only one avenue that offered any hope: if a Jordanian-Palestinian delegation could be put together without a clear PLO presence but with PLO acquiescence, then a meeting between them and Dick Murphy conceivably could lead swiftly to that same Jordanian-Palestinian group meeting with an Israeli delegation. Just getting the Arabs and Israelis in direct face-to-face talks would be an immense breakthrough.

That night in Aqaba we picked up an Israeli radio report of the communiqué of Sunday's Israeli cabinet meeting in Jerusalem. Prime Minister Peres, knowing full well what I was trying to do, came through with a remarkable statement, one that launched us in Aqaba into high gear. According

---

2. The Israelis had not withdrawn from Taba when they left the Sinai in accordance with the treaty of peace. Israel claimed that the international boundary, marked by stones in Ottoman times, put the line west of the beach; Egypt pointed to modern maps showing Taba in Sinai. I suspected that Israel stayed in Taba simply to make the point that UN Security Council Resolution 242 did not require giving up all territory in return for peace. But the retention of Taba presented us with a complicated and time-consuming legal and diplomatic problem that State's legal adviser, Abe Sofaer, eventually solved: Egypt got sovereignty; Israel got users' rights.

to the Israeli report, the cabinet announcement had stated, "There is a readiness for direct negotiations between Israel and a Jordanian-Palestinian delegation that does not include persons belonging to an organization committed to the Palestinian charter." This offered us something important to work with. The charter was filled with anti-Israeli material; there undoubtedly were credible and influential Palestinians who, on an individual basis, would not subscribe to it. The Israeli cabinet formulation seemed to offer real hope that direct contacts could be arranged.

The first thing Monday morning, I showed the Israeli sentence to King Hussein, who regarded it as a "very positive signal." The king's advisers felt it was "a sophisticated formula." Whether it was or not, I took it as an opening, and my discussions with the king privately at breakfast that Monday could not have been better. I was due in Vienna that night for the celebration of the thirtieth anniversary of the Austrian State Treaty and a potentially important meeting with Gromyko. But by the time I left the palace for my airplane, the king and I had agreed on a package that held great promise.

King Hussein would produce names for a joint Jordanian-Palestinian delegation. The Palestinians on the list would not be people unacceptable to Israel. Murphy would get together with this group, followed almost immediately by a "working group" session: a Jordanian–Palestinian delegation and an Israeli delegation meeting face-to-face, not to negotiate but to make arrangements for direct negotiations to follow between the two sides. I felt that this would be acceptable in Israel. I had achieved, for the first time, a commitment from King Hussein to direct negotiations. I had done so using the tacit understanding of the Israelis that even if the PLO approved or acquiesced in the Palestinians who would participate, this would not wreck the process so long as those named were not clearly associated with the PLO or with terrorism.

The king told me privately that he wanted to be engaged in direct negotiations with Israel by the end of 1985. He said the initial meeting with Dick Murphy should take place right after the king's Washington trip in May. The PLO, he said, would be "out at the beginning and in at the end." International support would come at the end of the negotiating process, and the PLO would not be involved until that point and then only if they had accepted the American conditions. In the king's talk with me, "international conference" had become "international support" and had gone to the bottom of the list of priorities. Many in the PLO would oppose what he was doing, and so would Syria; he was prepared for this, the king said, and would see the process through. Certainly, if King Hussein followed through on all this, he would need American arms to deter Syria. If we could bring it all off, the drama would be comparable to Sadat's bold initiative seven years earlier.

As a final positive step, King Hussein told me as I departed that he would say publicly in Washington that Jordan was no longer in a state of belligerency with Israel. Shimon Peres had told me that could be a major step forward, and I had urged the king to make this move. Congress would also see this step as a basis on which to vote for the arms package that the king both wanted and needed. After our final session, I pulled all the points of agreement together and placed them before the king. "Is this a fair summary of our discussion?" I asked.

"It is, sir," the king replied. The situation looked promising as I flew off from Aqaba for Vienna, leaving Murphy to work out the problems and nail down the results of my meetings with King Hussein and Peres. I sent a message to Peres saying that the cabinet communiqué had been a gift from heaven. I sent a message to King Hussein saying that the communiqué had been a gift from the Israelis.

Upon my arrival in Vienna, I received bad news. The Israeli cabinet had reconvened on Monday, May 13, to revise the communiqué. In place of the wording that King Hussein had taken as "a very positive signal," the cabinet had now issued a new formulation that narrowed chances considerably: "Regarding Jordan: readiness for direct negotiations between Israel and a Jordanian-Palestinian delegation which will not include persons belonging to an organization which is committed to the Palestinian Covenant, and opposition to discussions within the framework of an international conference."

A cable soon came in from our embassy in Israel: the original Israeli cabinet communiqué was not as carefully contrived as we had thought. Nimrod Novik, an aide to Peres, told us that the discussion within the cabinet meeting was in fact along the lines of the revised communiqué. Somehow the cabinet spokesman got the outcome somewhat muddled, showed it to Peres as guidance for the spokesman to use, and received Peres's casual approval. That informal guidance apparently was in turn folded into the regular communiqué. When David Landau of the *Jerusalem Post* began to press for the meaning of the language, the spokesman rushed back to Peres, who agreed that the communiqué should be revised to bring it back in line with the thrust of the cabinet's actual discussion. The Israelis quickly divined that the mistake had in fact had some important impact.

Nothing is more important to diplomacy than care in choosing and reporting words. Whether the formulations are vague or precise, other nations must assume that they were selected deliberately and with thought. That is why such care must be given to statements made during official visits and in official speeches. In foreign ministries all around the world, what you say gets quoted back to you, and you are expected to stand behind your words. The Israelis were usually among the most professional and precise. So I was surprised at their blunder. The Sunday formulation had not been an impossible one for them, and the king and I were justified in taking it seriously. Even the revised communiqué held some promise, but the process of revision took the edge off our ability to use those words to move the peace process forward.

Soon I learned that the king, too, had started backtracking, even before he heard of the revised communiqué. Murphy reported that the king's follow-up recommendations had been distressingly empty. The king when alone would speak openly and flexibly of his desire for peace and his willingness to take some chances to advance toward it. His advisers, however, were a negative and fear-inducing force: they worked to pull him back whenever he seemed poised to go forward.

King Hussein arrived in the United States on May 20, 1985. He would stay, on an unofficial basis, in Washington for a few days, proceed to Providence, Rhode Island, for his son's graduation from Brown University, and then return to Washington for his official visit. Dick Murphy's job was to travel with the king and to work for the Aqaba package just as the king and I had reviewed it in our final meeting. "Ignore any backsliding that has taken place since," I told Murphy. I wanted to get the entire Aqaba package out in public, with Jordanian agreement and participation, during the king's official stay.

Murphy came in to see me after his first informal sessions with the Jordanians at the Four Seasons Hotel in Georgetown. I called our Middle East group together to hear Murphy's report. In his soft-spoken, deadpan way, he told me, "No problem whatsoever with the language we suggested except for the words 'Israel,' 'direct,' 'negotiations,' " and then went down the list of every crucial term in the lexicon of Middle East diplomacy. "So the worms are fresh and moving around," Murphy concluded. I told him to keep working.

To the extent that the Jordanians and Israelis weren't upsetting the apple cart, Cap Weinberger was. Cap wanted to send an arms-for-Jordan package up to Capitol Hill regardless of Jordan's position toward Israel. Without a real change by the king, this was sure to be rejected by Congress, become a big defeat for the president, and sour the atmosphere for the king and his advisers. A poorly received aid request would induce King Hussein to head in exactly the wrong direction and blame the United States for his problems.

In an attempt to pull the pieces back together, I invited King Hussein to join me on Tuesday night, May 28, the evening before the king's first official day at the White House, on board the admiral's barge, a moderate-sized yacht owned by the U.S. Navy and assigned to the chief of naval operations, Admiral Jim Watkins, who graciously let me use the boat for such occasions.[3] The king agreed, and I planned an evening cruise that would take us down the Potomac to Mount Vernon and back while it was light enough for us to see the monuments of the capital, old town Alexandria, and the green riverbanks on the way.

I wanted to try to get as much of the Aqaba package as I could. At the least, I wanted the king to make clear that Jordan was no longer in a state of belligerency with Israel. Shimon Peres put a very high value on this, and a statement of nonbelligerency would gain support for the transfer of arms to Jordan that the king saw as symbolically and substantively important. I was ready to guarantee the king that Murphy would meet with a Jordanian-Palestinian delegation if a realistic set of names could be found. I recognized that the king would have to get the PLO to accept some people more moderate than they would want, and I would have to get Israel to accept those closer to the PLO than they would think ideal. I thought I made real headway.

But Wednesday produced another disappointment. The king did not even make a helpful statement on nonbelligerency. The best he could do, in a question and answer session, was to express "a genuine desire for negotiations, proceeding in a nonbelligerent manner." This was not enough for Congress, not enough for Peres, not enough for me. In only a matter of a few months, the king had gone from a stated readiness to move boldly— as Sadat had—without the PLO, to a situation in which the PLO now seemed to call all the shots. The major press interpretation of the king's talks in Washington was that some new event had emerged: an international conference, an idea that would endlessly complicate efforts toward peace.

As for a Jordan arms package, President Reagan telephoned King Hussein on June 12 to say that Congress was deeply negative but that should an emergency arise, meaning a danger to Jordan from Syria, the president could assure the king that he would use his authority to transfer needed arms and equipment to Jordan. The king in reply was glum but courteous: "You're the best judge, Mr. President." The arms issue then took a predictably unproductive course. On September 27—at Cap's insistence and against my advice—the president notified Congress of the administration's intention to sell Jordan $1.5 to $1.9 billion in arms. Congress barred any arms transfers until March 1, 1986, unless Jordan and Israel began "direct and meaningful peace negotiations." That was that.

---

3. The admiral's barge, which I was told was listed in Pentagon inventory as a "Class C Buoy Tender" to protect it from the green eyeshade boys, soon was gone, like the presidential yacht *Sequoia* and so many other assets that added grace and grandeur to America's diplomacy and international stature.

A Surprising Development

On the evening of Monday, August 5, an emissary from Shimon Peres came to see me at my home. Simcha Dinitz, a former Israeli ambassador to Washington, brought startling news: Shimon Peres and "an envoy" from King Hussein had secretly met in London on July 19. Dinitz reported to me on the outcome. The sensitive nature of the discussion told me immediately that Peres had met King Hussein himself. Peres had probably promised the king not to reveal this fact, and so throughout his report to me Dinitz referred to "the envoy." In my mind I substituted "King Hussein" each time he did.

Peres had been told by "the envoy" that the PLO had given King Hussein a list of twenty-two names and the king had rejected almost all of them. The seven who remained were not prominent in the PLO, the king felt, or were not PLO members at all. The United States should now choose four of the seven. King Hussein's vision was of an eventual Palestinian-Jordanian confederation with one chief of government, one army, one diplomatic service. The West Bank and Gaza would be demilitarized and would not be an independent state; rather, those areas would be part of the confederated state based in Jordan. According to the king's scenario, Dick Murphy would meet the Jordanian-Palestinian delegation. Then the PLO would meet the American conditions for a dialogue. The king had to have an international conference as a cover; the conference need convene only once and in order to authorize direct Arab-Israeli negotiations. All of this could take place in accordance with the September 1, 1982, Reagan Fresh Start initiative. The Reagan plan "harbors a basis for an agreement," said the envoy.

Peres firmly rejected any kind of prenegotiation session, if that was what the "Murphy meeting" with a Jordanian-Palestinian team would amount to. And Peres again made clear that Israel would never sit down with the PLO under any circumstances. The envoy once again indicated that if Arafat would not give his go-ahead to the king's efforts at direct negotiations with Israel, then the king would go forward anyway.

Hussein had said this before and never was, in the end, ready to go forward, even with the prospect of massive support from the United States. Perhaps, I wondered, the king's direct contact and demonstrated ability to talk constructively with Prime Minister Peres would make the difference. The report from Dinitz suggested that a new and hopeful level of personal contact had been reached through this secret London meeting, and I was gratified to hear sounds of support for our September 1 initiative. But the same fundamental problem remained: who would represent the Palestinians. And the international conference, even structured with the aim of keeping such a forum under control, still sounded like trouble.

However, while Peres had told King Hussein that Israel could not explicitly agree to a meeting by Dick Murphy with a Jordanian-Palestinian group as a precursor of direct Arab-Israeli negotiations, at my home Dinitz informed me of something Peres had apparently not told the king. In Peres's view, if the Murphy meeting took place, Israel would have to live with it, although stating objections publicly.

I assured Peres, through Dinitz, that the United States was not going to deal with the PLO until it met the U.S. conditions for entry into the diplomatic process—and there was no sign that it was about to do this. "When it does, we'll talk to the PLO; if it doesn't, we won't," I said. There was only one immediate objective: to get the parties into direct negotiations. What was changing for the better, I noted, was King Hussein. He had dropped his preoccupation with a guaranteed outcome of negotiations and seemed finally to understand and accept that this was a process. "You can't get there all at once; you have to put one foot ahead of the other, one step at a time," I said.

I told Dinitz that I would instruct Murphy to get to work once again. I also told him if there was to be an international conference, I would advocate that participation be limited to "those governments which have given diplomatic recognition to both Jordan and Israel." Dinitz found this "fiendishly clever." That would, of course, exclude the Soviets. Dinitz noted as he left that neither the Israeli embassy in Washington nor the Israeli inner cabinet was aware that Peres had sent him to see me. After he had gone, I thought to myself that Prime Minister Peres was operating up to—and perhaps beyond—the limits of his political capability in his coalition government.

During this period, our continuing effort to get a U.S.-Jordanian-Palestinian meeting was consuming a good chunk of my time almost daily. It had taken us months to get a list of Palestinian names out of the Jordanians—and nearly all of those listed had PLO ties. "We can accept two people from this list and meet tomorrow," I said to Murphy, "but if the king wants four Palestinians, we should insist that the meeting be followed immediately by direct talks with Israel." In other words, the follow-on to the Murphy meeting had to be dramatic enough to squelch criticism of our association with people identified with the PLO in any way. Maybe the king couldn't handle the direct talks, but my proposition was a credible one.

On August 9, I put this possible approach to President Reagan. He did not want us to meet with anyone even *remotely* associated with the PLO. Murphy could agree to meet with one or two Palestinians from the West Bank or Gaza, and the session should be followed by a "working group" that would bring Arabs and Israelis into direct contact. That was all the running room I could get.

A few days later, Washington attorney Len Garment came to see me with "a message from Shamir." Garment said that Foreign Minister Shamir did *not* want Murphy to meet with *any* Palestinians. He questioned our judgment in even considering such a meeting, which he felt would: break the letter and spirit of the U.S. 1975 commitment not to meet with PLO members until the PLO met our conditions, lead to "tremendous tumult" in Israel, break apart the Israeli government, and jeopardize U.S.-Israeli relations. Despite this message, I kept Murphy at work to see whether *some* form of his meeting with *some* Palestinians could lead to direct negotiations.

I went back to the president again. I argued that we should let Murphy meet with Palestinians who were not tainted with terrorism or extremism, even if they had a slight association with the PLO, on two conditions: that King Hussein and selected Palestinians would then proceed with direct talks with Israel and that if the PLO refused any Palestinian participation, the king would proceed with Israel on his own, as Sadat had. The king was about to visit Washington again, and I wanted to use his visit to move forward. The president understood the issue well, both the problems and the opportunities, and he was genuinely torn. The president finally concluded that Murphy could continue to try to set up a meeting for himself with acceptable Palestinians if, and only if, it would lead immediately to direct Arab-Israeli negotiations.

On August 18, after extensive shuttling between meetings with Israelis, Jordanians, Saudis, and Palestinians, Murphy gave up on the effort to achieve a meeting with a joint delegation; even if the right Palestinians could be found, it had become clear that no follow-on or direct contact with Israel was in the Arabs' plan—and that, to us, was the whole point.

For all my frustration with King Hussein, I knew that the problem of Palestinian representation was a legitimate one for him, and a big one. He had not been able to solve the problem himself, and we had not been able to solve it for him. Somehow I had to keep a peace process visibly in play. I saw the president again on September 5, just to make sure our views were in alignment. He was unswerving: there should be no ambiguity about our refusal to deal with anyone genuinely associated with the PLO. Murphy could meet, but only with Palestinians from the occupied territories. And we should press the king toward direct negotiations with Israel. Ronald Reagan was taking a personal stand on this, and he was steadfast. The president, King Hussein, the Israelis, all had good reasons for their fervently held principles, but together they had squeezed out the possibility of progress at this point.

Within weeks, Margaret Thatcher, angry at the United States for failing to produce a "Murphy meeting," decided to meet with the PLO herself. Jordan was off the hook. But I decided to make still another attempt to find a formula that both the king and the Israelis might accept. The king was due in New York on September 23, 1985. I decided to put a test to him. If he wanted an international conference, I would offer him American support for one that would meet his needs *and* kick off direct contacts between Arabs and Israelis.

The King and the Cheeseburger

The king was to be my guest for dinner on September 24. I would set forth to him privately on that occasion, after dinner, a carefully crafted plan to meet his needs for an international conference as a means of getting to direct negotiations. The president agreed to the plan, especially since it involved no change in the conditions under which we would talk to the PLO. According to the plan, on October 1, Jordan and Israel would simultaneously but separately request the secretary-general of the United Nations to invite to a conference those permanent members of the UN Security Council that have relations with Israel and Jordan. Also invited would be Israel, Jordan, Egypt, Syria, and Lebanon. The conference would take place on October 31, 1985. Any permanent UN Security Council member-nation that did not at present have diplomatic relations with both Israel and Jordan but that entered or offered to enter relations with both by October 31 also would be invited. The United States would obtain guarantees from Jordan and Israel that they would enter direct negotiations under UN Security Council Resolutions 242 and 338 on November 1, 1985, on the basis of expressions of support by one-half or more of those nations attending the international conference.

The United States would also support direct Syrian-Israeli negotiations. Between October 1 and 31, Jordan would endeavor to persuade the PLO to accept—fully, clearly, and without comment, amendment, elaboration, or qualification—UNSC Resolutions 242 and 338 and recognize Israel's right to exist. Should the PLO do this, the United States would meet with PLO representatives immediately. If, in addition to this, the PLO publicly and unambiguously declared a moratorium on armed and violent means of opposition to Israel and declared its acceptance of negotiations as the sole avenue toward a solution to the Arab-Israeli conflict, then the PLO would be welcome to attend the international conference as part of the Jordanian national delegation. Should the PLO moratorium on armed and violent struggle be demonstrated to be in full and continuing effect at the end of ninety days following the start of direct Jordan-Israel negotiations, the United States would support PLO participation in those direct negotiations for as long as the moratorium continued. If, by October 7, the UN secretary-general was unable to assure the requesting parties that the international conference would convene on October 31 in Geneva under the terms of the request, the parties would agree to issue parallel invitations to Geneva, simultaneously but separately, on their own behalf. Should this effort prove not feasible, for whatever reason, the United States would offer to host such an international conference in Washington under similar terms. Jordan and Israel would agree in advance to all these contingencies.

In my thinking, if the PLO made no move to meet the conditions, the Palestinians could be represented by residents of the West Bank and Gaza or any diaspora Palestinians who would personally affirm acceptance of UN Resolutions 242 and 338, and of Israel's right to exist, and disavow terrorism.

The dinner was held in a room with a spectacular view in the UN Plaza Hotel. The king was emerging from a recent bout with the flu, and Queen Noor was protective of him. Upon learning that lobster was being served, the king said that he did not care for lobster and asked instead for the chef to prepare a cheeseburger for him. The staff at the Plaza seemed never to have heard of an item called a cheeseburger. It took forever for them to produce one as we all sat formally around the table, chatting awkwardly and with increasing frustration. The king would talk only about American arms sales to Jordan and why he could do nothing to help us politically in getting them through Congress. The king grew bored, tired, and unhappy, and the queen kept trying to get him to leave and go to bed. And I, along with the other guests, increasingly despaired.

I told the king that I wanted to propose to him a way to deal with his expressed need for an international conference. He was not interested. He was in no mood to work with us in a constructive fashion about anything. He would not make any move that would help the president help him with the Congress. We never got a chance to talk alone. The king simply was not prepared to engage that night. He clearly had no idea how difficult it was for the president to push for arms for Jordan—which Jordan could not pay for—and he was not prepared to take political risks for peace. The dinner was a fiasco.[4]

I had become used to the fact that the first meeting of any visit by or to King Hussein would have a certain predictable rhythm: the king would at first be aggrieved and negative; later, he would be more forthcoming. The trouble at this point was that we had no time to pay court to him and wait for his mood to pass. Foreign Minister Eduard Shevardnadze was in town, and I was booked to start in early the next morning to work with him to prepare for the upcoming Reagan-Gorbachev summit in November. I instructed Dick Murphy and Paul Boeker, our ambassador to Jordan, to present our ideas carefully to the king, but I knew that the moment for me to open up this complex plan with him personally had passed. Now,

4. Although he did not mention it at the time, the king, I later was told, was allergic to lobster. "If we had only thought to send someone over to the New York Bar and Grill across the street, we could have produced a cheeseburger for the king within minutes and the course of our diplomacy might have been different," I said with a laugh.

when we were poised to meet his newly created need for an international conference, we could not penetrate the royal personality.

The king had confided to Ambassador Boeker that he—not an envoy— had met Peres in London in July, confirming what I had already surmised from my meeting with Dinitz at my home. President Reagan was willing to devote time to the Middle East and had become increasingly ready to make tough decisions; he clearly hoped to advance the peace process before he left office. Dick Murphy and his team kept at the Jordanians, with familiar roller-coaster results.

At 8:00 A.M. on September 30, I had breakfast with King Hussein and then escorted him to a meeting with President Reagan. The session was bizarre. The king again urged that the process go forward and said that if the PLO would not meet the U.S. conditions and thus could not participate, he would go forward without the PLO. Instantly, Jordanian Prime Minister Zaid Rifai raised a host of objections. I could see that there was no coherent Jordanian position and that there would not be one. We got nowhere.

After King Hussein had left the White House, I apologized to the president for the lack of success. I said that I would continue to respond to the king's concerns but that no achievement ever held up for more than a few hours. "Sometimes," I told the president, "the king acts like a spoiled child."

"George, he's a king." The president sighed.

I sensed that the king was getting ready to leave the peace process altogether. It was "You can't fire me; I quit," and he and his followers were setting the stage for a self-righteous exit. I felt deeply frustrated. But I was determined to keep trying.

Israel Punctuates the Process

On Tuesday morning, October 1, I had breakfast with Simcha Dinitz, who again had come as Shimon Peres's private envoy. I hoped to talk to him about the process of getting to Arab-Israeli negotiations. Instead, Dinitz handed me a message from Peres stating that the Israel Air Force had just conducted an air strike on a suburb of Tunis. The target was Hamam el-Shaat, a PLO military compound. Dinitz said that the escalation of terror in the region attributed to Palestinians had created an impossible situation for Israel. Palestinian terrorists had murdered Israelis in the port of Larnaca, Cyprus. Those responsible were part of Force 17, a PLO group based in Amman. Ariel Sharon had demanded that Israel undertake an operation inside Jordan. I had urged Israel not to strike at Jordan. In fact, the Israelis themselves felt their hands were tied as far as Jordan was concerned. The Tunis operation had been substituted for that, Dinitz said.

Reports on the attack on Tunis showed it to be an Israeli attempt to knock out part of the PLO's command structure that had been directing terrorist operations. The air strike had hit a PLO command building cleanly and was clearly not aimed at civilians. I agonized that Tunisia—a moderate Arab state and a friend of the United States—had been the site of the attack. The Tunisians had accepted the PLO when Phil Habib negotiated their exit from Beirut, and we had appreciated that at a time when no other Arab state wanted Arafat and his followers. The PLO had then drawn Tunisia into the arena of violence, and Israel had, predictably, struck back at the source of the terrorist commands. I wanted in some way to reach out to Tunisian President Habib Bourguiba and his government. When the inevitable resolution came up in the Security Council denouncing Israel, though having no practical effect, I was among those who recommended to the president that the United States abstain rather than veto the resolution. A surge of criticism came at me from Israel and its friends when the United States did not exercise its veto.

The president readily agreed to a decision that alienated the Arab side, too: the United States would boycott the commemoration ceremonies for the fortieth anniversary of the United Nations if Yasser Arafat attended. As a result, the resolution inviting him was withdrawn on October 14, 1985.

The *New York Times* on November 11 revealed that Prime Minister Peres and King Hussein had secretly agreed to an international conference; this revelation caused severe political strains within Israel.

On November 21, U.S. authorities arrested Jonathan Jay Pollard, an American citizen working for the U.S. Office of Naval Intelligence, on charges of spying for Israel. For Israel to have done such a thing was shocking and chilling, even to Israel's staunchest American supporters. Prime Minister Peres called me seeking advice on how to handle this genuine crisis in U.S.-Israeli relations. "Apologize," I told Peres, "and pledge to cooperate fully in the U.S. investigation of the case." He took my advice, but this was only the beginning of a long effort to come to grips with the reality and implications of Israeli attempts to steal secrets from its one true friend in the world. American Jews, sometimes accused of being more pro-Israeli than pro-American, were particularly anguished and upset.

Syria and Jordan on December 11 produced a joint communiqué calling for an international conference that would have substantive powers, a proposal that Israel would never accept. At the end of the year, King Hussein and President Assad met for the first time in six years, in Damascus, which undercut entirely the argument in Congress in favor of American arms transfers to Jordan. King Hussein had gone to Damascus to secure his flank with Syria. Syria's price was a veto over the peace process. At year end, all efforts at diplomacy had been thwarted, the military confrontation had escalated, and the peace process was on the ropes again. U.S.-Israeli relations were severely strained by the devastating revelation of Israeli spying on the United States.

A Thorny Idea

In early 1986, King Hussein continued to push for his international conference. His requirement, which neither we nor the Israelis could accept, was that such a conference would continue in being, or reconvene, to consider cases of stalemate by the parties holding direct talks; in other words, a higher court of appeal to which a party could resort to get a matter adjudicated.

I was totally opposed to this. A simple fact of negotiating life is that *no* party will continue to negotiate in one forum if a higher forum is available for appeal. The king did not really want direct negotiations but rather a dressed-up version of the old vision of a grand, comprehensive settlement imposed on the situation from on high.

On Saturday afternoon, January 18, Murphy telephoned from London, where he had just seen King Hussein. The king was gloomy and sour. Murphy told him that I was ready to travel to the region, shape the kind of international conference event that Israel could accept, and then to try to get the Soviets to cosponsor it. The king was totally focused on the conference: he wanted the PLO to be in it after meeting the U.S. conditions. He wanted the Soviets there whether they recognized Israel or not. He wanted Syria there, but Syria insisted that the Arab side be able "to go back to the podium" of the conference should talks with Israel bog down. Neither the United States nor Israel could accept that. But when it came to a "working group" that could put Jordanians and Palestinians in touch with Israeli officials—and thereby give Congress a reason to vote for arms for Jordan—the king was unresponsive.

After meeting with King Hussein in London, Dick Murphy went to see Shimon Peres, who was also there. Out of Murphy's talks a more central focus emerged on what we called "the hang-back option," a more precise version whereby the PLO would be "out at the beginning, in at the end." The chief problem with the international conference—would it reconvene in case of stalemate?—was being sidestepped by Peres. Murphy saw that the possibility of reconvening was important to King Hussein, and he developed a formulation that he felt protected Israel but gave the king what he seemed to need. Peres said that no one could stop the king from going back to the conference or stop the conference from reconvening, but Israel would not go back. The conference would therefore have no authority, and the only avenue open would be direct negotiations. Murphy, shuttling back and forth, was impressed with the seriousness of both men.

Late on January 27, Prime Minister Rifai went to the American embassy in Amman, where we gave him access to a secure telephone, and talked to Murphy. The king had gotten a slippery proposition from Arafat: the PLO accepted President Reagan's September 1 Mideast peace initiative on condition that we accept the February 11 PLO-Jordanian accord of 1985. The two proposals were contradictory. Someone described Arafat as a "mud puppy," a bottom fish in southern state canals that flaps about to muddy the waters whenever anything approaches. He had done it again. Murphy thought that Rifai was asking us for a negative reply. I instructed Ambassador Paul Boeker to go to see the king and try to get a clearer picture.

Word of what was going on was circulating in Washington. One of Israel's most powerful and most articulate friends in Congress telephoned me. His words revealed the agonies that this moment brought forward. "It's a critical moment," he said. "The door will slam soon, and when it does, Israel is doomed. There are two years of the Likud ahead, and there's no turning back. Israel either stops being a Jewish state or stops being a democracy—and either is a catastrophe." The congressman said he hated the PLO but that we should tell King Hussein that if the PLO accepted the conditions, we would be ready to see them at the international conference. "The king can't move without them," he said. He urged that I give the PLO something on the self-determination issue by agreeing to the words within the framework of the PLO-Jordanian February 11, 1985, accord. "If I said this publicly, I'd have to resign," he said. I was impressed that this stalwart supporter of Israel was ready to take such a step, but I was not.

By this time, we had received a report of talks between King Hussein and Prime Minister Thatcher in London. She and the king envisioned a substantive conference, which would amount to the amassing of international pressure against Israel. This was no way to get direct talks under way. On this matter, Margaret Thatcher's thinking was quite different from Ronald Reagan's and mine.

At the very end of January 1986, Shimon Peres told the new U.S. ambassador to Israel, Tom Pickering, that King Hussein had sent him a note saying that the Americans had been pushing him to make "a dramatic act," but that the time was not ripe for such a step. Nevertheless, the king expressed his strong desire to continue his effort with Peres to reach a peace negotiation. The king was ready to meet the Israeli prime minister "at your place," that is, in Israel, secretly.

Arafat's meeting with King Hussein in Amman on Wednesday, February 5, 1986, was watched minute by minute; the betting was that this was "it"— the king would not let Arafat get away without a clear yes or no to the question of meeting the U.S. conditions. If, by some miracle, Arafat did issue a clear statement about Resolution 242, Israel's right to exist, and abjuring terrorism, we knew that Israel would still not sit down with the PLO. But such a PLO action would mean that Jordan would be able to engage with Israel and that an international conference with Palestinian participation was possible.

At the end of the day, we heard the results from Prime Minister Rifai. Arafat had produced three texts, all hinged on the PLO's accepting UN Resolution 242 in return for the U.S. accepting Palestinian "self-determination"—which we regarded as meaning an independent Palestinian state. The king had declared these texts unacceptable. The Jordanians had suggested that we try drafting a text that Arafat might adopt as the PLO text and which might break the logjam. We did so.

As the king described his session with Arafat to Ambassador Boeker and Wat Cluverius[5] the next day over lunch, Arafat had brought three texts of what he could agree to: bad, worse, and worst. Arafat had not made a serious effort, the king felt. The king then handed Arafat the text I had sent. "Abu Ammar, this will show how far off you are," the king said. Arafat rejected our text.

So the king's mood was downcast again, and this time for good reason. After two years of work on his part, there was no movement in the peace process, no U.S. military assistance was forthcoming, and his relations with the United States had in fact deteriorated. He contemplated "going public" to blame Arafat but held off. The king said he placed "about 15 percent" of the blame for all this on the United States. To Boeker, the king sounded as if he was seeing not the end of a phase but "the end of an era"—the end of Jordan's effort to play an important role in the search for a solution for the West Bank and Gaza. I sent King Hussein a message praising his steadfast and hard work for peace. I told him that in my contacts with Congress there was an appreciation of the difficulty of his position even among those who opposed arms sales to Jordan. They felt that he had made strenuous efforts at considerable personal risk to find a way to negotiate with Israel.

Arafat's refusal to go forward with King Hussein brought an end to another chapter in the search for a solution to issues of control over the West Bank and Gaza. The rotation of the Israeli government from Peres to Shamir was about to take place. We would need to work up a new model. I had, against my own instincts, worked hard on the format of an international conference as desired by King Hussein and accepted by Prime Minister Peres. With the end of this round, I would have to take this off

5. Deputy assistant secretary of state, a man to whom King Hussein talked easily and whom we therefore sent to Jordan at critical times.

the table. Arafat had stopped the process once again; he should not be able to pocket the inducements we had put out there and claim them at some later date.

Ambassador Sam Lewis had a private dinner with Peres on February 6 at which Peres said he was pondering whether to ask me to throw myself into the situation by a shuttle effort in the few weeks remaining before the Likud would come into power. Lewis urged Peres to ask me to come. Peres replied that he felt he could not, because to do so would signal that he, Peres, could be pressured to make concessions on behalf of Israel, and Peres did not feel able to do that. Peres said that he and King Hussein had "a close understanding" of how the peace process should go and even how it should come out. "But Hussein can't get the support of his crowd, and I can't get the support of mine," Peres told Lewis.

On February 19, 1986, King Hussein, in an eighty-eight-page speech, announced that he was ending his effort to construct a joint peace strategy with Arafat and the PLO. He characterized Arafat as untrustworthy and said that the problem lay in Arafat's unwillingness to accept unconditionally Resolutions 242 and 338: "I and the Government of the Kingdom of Jordan announce that we are unable to continue to coordinate politically with the PLO leadership until such time as their word becomes their bond, characterized by commitment, credibility and constancy."

King Hussein described in detail his dealings with the United States over the past year—to contrast American flexibility with PLO intransigence. As our embassy in Amman reported, "Hussein's speech bringing down the curtain on this act of the peace process clearly blames Arafat and the PLO for this premature ending." American flexibility was characterized as creating a major opportunity that the PLO muffed.

Here we were, seemingly back where we had started. I felt a sense of deep frustration. And yet, despite the frustrations, there had been important accomplishments. Our efforts had helped Egypt sustain its peace with Israel, however cool relations between them were. Progress had been made in our quality-of-life effort for the Palestinians on the West Bank and Gaza. Lebanon, though still explosive, had been defused as a time bomb threatening the entire region. The Israeli economy was recovering its balance. And the standing of the United States in the region, despite the debacle of our withdrawal from Lebanon, was strong.

I knew that without a peace process, a dangerous vacuum existed that would likely be filled by violence. Even against seemingly overwhelming odds, the peace process therefore must be pursued. With the coming of Yitzhak Shamir as prime minister would also come, I knew, a different and more difficult set of attitudes. We would need a new model. We would not give up.

CHAPTER 25

Realistic Reengagement
with the Soviets

Our deployments of nuclear missiles in Germany, Britain, and Italy in 1983 had been crucial, gut-wrenching moments. We and our allies were steadfast. There was a new confidence within the alliance and a sense of satisfaction and strength. Free and democratic nations had held together well in the face of threatening tactics from the Soviets. At the same time, we had begun to convince our critics in the West that the United States was ready for, and working toward, negotiated nuclear arms reductions. President Reagan had sent our negotiators back to Geneva despite the Soviet downing of Korean Air Lines Flight 007, a decision that brought an end to the era of "linkage," during which such an outrageous act would have put all aspects of our relationship on ice. And we had consulted closely with our allies to put forward reasonable positions in both the INF and START negotiations. The Soviets had threatened and cajoled and used our missile deployments as cause to walk out of, and suspend their participation in, all arms control talks. They would not return, they said, until we removed our INF missiles from European soil.

The atmosphere was tough by the end of 1983. In describing the end of the various negotiations, *Time* magazine said, "The suspensions left the superpowers for the first time in 14 years with no arms-control talks of any kind in progress and with even regular diplomatic contacts frosty."[1] The Reagan revolution in arms control—the effort to achieve deep cuts in nuclear warheads—was over: that was the "expert" view. *Time*, in naming Ronald Reagan and Yuri Andropov their "Men of the Year," pictured them as stern faced, backs to each other. In describing its choice, *Time* said, "In shaping plans for the future, every statesman in the world and very nearly every private citizen has to calculate what may come of the

---

1. This quotation and others in this paragraph appeared in *Time*'s "Men of the Year" issue on January 2, 1984.

face-off between the countries whose leaders—one operating in full public view, the other as a mysterious presence hidden by illness—share the power to decide whether there will be any future at all." In a press conference, Marshal Nikolai Ogarkov, chief of staff of the Soviet armed forces, charged that the United States "would still like to launch a decapitating nuclear first strike." Such a perception was incredible, at least to us.

Andropov had not been seen in public since August 18, 1983, when he had met with a delegation of U.S. senators. On December 26, he failed to appear at a meeting of the Communist Party Central Committee and sent a message attributing his absence to "temporary causes." Two days later, he was absent from the opening of the Supreme Soviet. It looked as though we once again would have to deal with a new leader in the Kremlin.

Despite the "war danger" talk coming out of Moscow, I did not believe the Soviets really anticipated a military confrontation with us. But such propaganda was increasingly effective in rousing public alarm, both in Western Europe and America. We were feeling political pressure against our continuing INF deployments and for concessions to the Soviets to lure them back to the table. President Reagan and I were not going to yield on either of these fronts, but we could not leave matters as they stood; an important reason for our success in maintaining a cohesive alliance and bringing about the deployment of INF missiles was a positive and engaged diplomacy. So we had to continue a policy of strength combined with a readiness to negotiate. Realistic reengagement, I called our objective.

I had spent the Christmas holiday in California, ending with what had become an annual golf game with President Reagan at the home of Walter and Lee Annenberg, followed by their New Year's Eve party. The occasion provided the opportunity for extended and relaxed talk with the president. He was still convinced of the desirability of a world without nuclear weapons. We also discussed Soviet violations of existing arms control agreements. Some violations were minor exploitations of ambiguous language; others were of potentially strategic signficance. The clearest and most important violation, in this case of the ABM Treaty, was the Krasnoyarsk phased-array radar station, located deep inside the Soviet Union, where it could serve a "battle management" function in a potential antiballistic missile system. The Joint Chiefs of Staff had told us that the fundamental balance of forces was not affected by these Soviet transgressions. In military terms, that might be true, but the political consequences were vast.

If the Soviets were violating the terms of agreements negotiated years ago, how could we proceed to negotiate new agreements with them with any serious expectation that they would be honored? We would never get an arms control treaty through the Senate unless the Soviets carried out their existing commitments. We were in a double bind: if we overplayed Soviet transgressions, they and our critics would accuse us of seeking to avoid negotiations; if we ignored their violations, the Soviets would have set a precedent of treaty interpretation that we would not be able to live with—and critics of any U.S. reengagement with the Soviets would have increased political leverage to try to derail our constructive efforts. So the question was how high a decibel level to put on these violations at this stage of the game. My preferred course of action, I told the president, was to keep the public decibel level down but to tell the Soviets flatly that their violations of solemn agreements would have to be rectified before any new understandings could be reached.

On the afternoon of January 3, 1984, just back from California, I met with Anatoly Dobrynin to see whether the Soviet leadership was in any shape to reengage with us. When Ambassador Dobrynin had returned to Moscow a few weeks earlier, I equipped him with a question: "Are you ready for a serious and private dialogue with us?" Yes, he now said. He was authorized to carry out such a dialogue in Washington with me, and he assumed we would authorize Ambassador Hartman to do the same in Moscow with Foreign Minister Gromyko.

Dobrynin went into great detail trying to convince me that General Secretary Andropov, while working from his house, was fully operative and setting the political agenda. I asked him whether working from his home was not itself a sign of illness. He had seen Andropov when he was in Moscow recently, Dobrynin said, and was not aware of any illness. But "such things are not discussed as openly in Moscow as they are in Washington," he added. I knew he was not being candid with me. I told Dobrynin the president's position on Soviet violations: we would get nowhere, I made clear, unless the Soviets rectified violations of previous arms control agreements.

For his part, Dobrynin probed. Was the American leadership in a position to reengage seriously? Would we be able to conduct a normal foreign policy in a presidential election year? I told him that President Reagan would do so and would call his shots as he saw them "on the merits." Despite continuing carping from hard-liners in the White House that the downing of the Korean airliner in September 1983 rendered any high-level U.S.-Soviet contact improper, I was scheduled to meet with Gromyko in Stockholm on January 18. The opening of the Conference on Disarmament in Europe (CDE) would take place there, and foreign ministers from every country in Europe, east and west, as well as Canada and the United States, would be present.

President Reagan and I had agreed that he would give a speech in early January on U.S.-Soviet relations before I went to Stockholm. My speech in Stockholm would be coordinated with his, building upon the president's themes and addressing the substance of the prospective negotiations. Our speeches would lay the groundwork for my meeting with Gromyko. I hoped that the president's speech would be given early enough to allow the Soviets some time to reflect upon it before Gromyko and I met. As always, however, the speechwriting process was an agony of pulling and hauling, and the days went by without agreement on a final draft. The president wanted to speak again about his hope for a nonnuclear world; the bureaucracy would not hear of it. "Every meeting I go to," I told Rick Burt and Jon Howe, "the president talks about abolishing nuclear weapons. I cannot get it through your heads that the man is serious. We either have to convince him he is barking up the wrong tree or reply to his interests with some specific suggestions."

Actually, I took on the "you're barking up the wrong tree" job myself. I told the president that I shared his dissatisfaction with our dependence on the threat of nuclear annihilation as the means of keeping the peace. "But nuclear weapons cannot be uninvented," I said. "The present structure of deterrence and of our alliances depends on nuclear weapons, and the best approach is to work for large reductions in nuclear arsenals." I made no real impact on the president with this argument. I gave him a paper with my line of reasoning, but he stuck with his own deeply held view of where we should be heading.

I had one of my regular meetings with the president on Friday the thirteenth, which I have never considered unlucky since I had been born on a Friday the thirteenth. I went over the outline of my talking points for my upcoming meeting with Gromyko in Stockholm. The president approved them, including greater flexibility in our approach to the START talks based on a recognition of the different structures of our respective strategic systems. "These are *not* points approved by the interagency group," I told the president candidly. He cocked his head in a so-what attitude—the changes didn't bother him at all. I told him I would go over our meeting with NSC adviser Bud McFarlane, who could inform the interagency group on arms control, which had proved to be a debilitating bottleneck. I recognized that this was risky footwork. I went over the START talking points with Bud, and he set out to get them approved in the interagency process. By the time we got through, I was clearly authorized by the interagency group, as well as the president, to start with a rather general statement of our START position, but if Gromyko seemed interested and wanted to talk about START, I could move on to develop the more expansive points I had gone over with the president. It was bizarre, I thought, that not only the president but the entire interagency group had to be brought on board before I could proceed.

The president gave his speech on January 16 in the East Room of the White House. It was comprehensive and operational. "Cooperation and understanding are built on deeds, not words. Complying with agreements helps; violating them hurts. Respecting the rights of individual citizens bolsters the relationship; denying these rights harms it. . . . Strength and dialogue go hand in hand. We are determined to deal with our differences peacefully, through negotiations," he said. "I support a zero option for all nuclear arms. As I have said before, my dream is to see the day when nuclear weapons will be banished from the face of the earth. . . . Our negotiators are ready to return to the negotiating table to work toward agreements in INF, START, and MBFR. . . . We seek to reduce nuclear arsenals."

A Turn in Stockholm

On that same day, January 16, I arrived in Stockholm. In response to a press question linking the president's speech to election-year politics, I said that the president "didn't need the Russian embrace to get reelected." I wanted things to settle down: there was, I thought, too much talk about a thaw with—and a softened tone toward—the Soviets. Such talk raised expectations that would lead to disappointment if nothing happened.

European reaction to the president's speech was genuinely positive. The *Daily Telegraph* on January 17, 1984, was typical: "His major address has effectively relaxed three years of the so-called confrontational, or more simply, hardnosed, approach to the Soviet Union. . . . Mr. Reagan is now calling for the resumption of dialogue allied to realism about East-West relations and Western nuclear strength."

Our strategy was easy to state but difficult to implement: we needed to maintain the strength of our position and the cohesiveness of our alliance, and we also needed to show that we were ready for any reasonable dialogue with the Soviets. The Soviets, by contrast, wanted to create an atmosphere of danger and confrontation, with the blame falling on us. Their objective was to scare the Europeans out of continuing to deploy INF missiles according to the NATO schedule. But the Soviets also had a tricky problem: too much bluster and intimidation would backfire. Aside from atmospherics, however, there were genuine problems; progress on at least some of them could be to the Soviets' advantage as well as to ours. Their hard line would therefore be under some strain.

My own speech at the CDE opening session on January 17 began with a tribute to Raoul Wallenberg, the Swedish diplomat who had saved the lives of thousands of Hungarian Jews during World War II. January 17 was the thirty-ninth anniversary of his arrest by the Soviets in 1945. The Soviets claimed he had died shortly after the war, but we did not believe that. At the top of our agenda for this conference, I said, was the topic of human rights, which were "central to any discussion of European security. . . . an artificial barrier has cruelly divided this continent—and indeed heartlessly divided one of its great nations. . . . This division is the essence of Europe's security and human rights problem, and we all know it." I then announced the controversial proposal that I had managed to get approved before leaving: "The United States negotiators will be presenting a draft treaty [in Geneva] for the complete and verifiable elimination of chemical weapons, on a global basis." This initiative was, I said, "part of a broader American effort to build a more stable, consistent, and constructive East-West relationship—a relationship not marked by the abrupt shifts, exaggerated expectations, and dashed hopes of the last decade. . . . Let us so conduct ourselves in our deliberations that historians of the future will mark this gathering as a turning point in East-West relations."

The next day, I listened to Gromyko deliver what was a truly brutal speech:

> The incumbent U.S. Administration is an administration thinking in categories of war and acting accordingly. Naturally, those who have assumed a course of war have no interest in reaching arms limitation agreements. . . .
> The American military machine is sowing death and destruction in Lebanon. . . .
> And can any upright person be indifferent to what has happened to Grenada? The piratic, terrorist action of the great neighbor against the Grenadian people is a challenge to the world at large. . . .
> It is an open secret who is sending bands of mercenaries, terrorists against Nicaragua, who is turning Honduras into its military base, who is keeping an antipeople regime of butchers in power in El Salvador. All that is absent in that country now are the bonfires of the Inquisition.

In a section of his speech dealing with confidence-building measures, Gromyko took a swipe at our proposals for on-site inspections by saying it was "unacceptable . . . [to] look for a crack in the fence to peep at one's neighbors." Gromyko's rhetoric was outrageous, but I was determined to go forward and pursue the positive talking points I had sought and the president had approved.

I went to the Soviet mission for my meeting with Gromyko. Scheduled to last for three hours, it wound up going for five. We sparred awhile about our respective speeches. He was clearly sensitive to my message regarding the "artificial division of Europe." He regarded both my speech and the president's as "hostile" to the Soviet Union.

I had been very disappointed in his speech, I told him. Some of his statements, I said, "were beyond the pale" and just plain unacceptable.

Gromyko was glad, he said, to hear that I found his speech unacceptable; he regarded that as praise for his speech. "I would have been put on my guard," Gromyko told me, "if you had said the Soviets were right about anything."

"I'm glad to hear that you're not on your guard," I interjected. He laughed, sneered, and scoffed all at the same time. It was an ugly dialogue, but as we argued back and forth about the differences between our systems, I began to feel for the first time that somehow, in this process of sparring and interrupting, we had managed to start a real conversation.

I outlined our reasoning in wanting to see private exchanges take place and said I had been glad to hear from Dobrynin that the Soviets, too, were interested. Gromyko replied it was "high time" for such private discussions to take place between responsible officials and without publicity. I outlined in broad terms our positions on strategic arms, intermediate-range arms, and conventional arms, and I explained our view that a global approach to chemical weapons agreements was needed. He did not press for more information about our ideas on strategic arms, so I kept our new ideas in my pocket. I could polish that option up and use it to good effect at a later time.

We set a date of March 16 as a time to resume the talks on conventional arms reductions (MBFR) but agreed not to announce this now. I had started my presentation, as I always did in my meetings with the Soviets, with human rights issues. Gromyko refused to respond and accused me of trying to interfere in Soviet "internal affairs." But for the first time Gromyko actually *listened* to what I said, and I was fascinated that later in the conversation he returned—on his own—to the subject of human rights. He was defensive, protesting too much about Soviet rectitude and American perversity. I was "blowing it all out of proportion," he said. My position was "entirely pervaded by falsehood," and the United States was "exploiting this matter for propaganda purposes." He added, "Nowhere else are human rights violated so much as in some of the places in the Western Hemisphere that are so dear to U.S. hearts, not to mention in the United States itself." Referring to my comments about emigration, travel, and family reunification, Gromyko claimed that he "did not know of a single instance where these matters caused wars to break out." Now that Gromyko, obviously provoked by my earlier presentation, had himself come back to the subject of human rights, I took the opportunity to amplify our positions, going through our concern about the right to emigrate and the large number of Soviet Jews denied that right, including Anatoly Shcharansky, Ida Nudel, and Josif Begun. Andrei Sakharov, I said, should at least be released from internal exile in Gorky and allowed to live in Moscow, where he could interact with his colleagues and with visitors from other countries. I expressed my admiration for the Soviets' decision to allow the Pentecostal families who had taken refuge in our embassy to emigrate. He did not respond.

Instead, Gromyko returned to arms control issues, saying that the Soviet Union would have to think long and carefully about how negotiations could resume. He cautioned me that our own discussion of this matter "in no way constituted continuation of the Geneva negotiations." He continued,

"In order for negotiations to resume, the United States would have to change its positions and express willingness to return to the situation existing before deployment of the new U.S. missiles in Western Europe." The Soviets, he said, considered our Pershing II missiles in Europe to be strategic in nature because they could reach the Soviet Union.

I sensed he was searching for a different "structure" in these talks that would allow the Soviets to return without losing face. In renewed negotiations, I replied, Soviet medium-range missiles must be included along with U.S. medium-range missiles. Soviet SS-20s could hit our allies. The Soviet Union, I said, should recognize the nature of a free alliance: "When you hit one country, you hit us all, because we are bound together as allies." So any negotiations would have to include the SS-20s if the Pershing IIs and ground-launched cruise missiles were included.

Gromyko and I noted some positive developments: hot-line negotiations, discussions on nonproliferation of nuclear weapons, work on agreement on navigation aids in the Pacific, continuing discussions about Southern Africa. Gromyko seemed preoccupied by the presence of our forces in Lebanon and said, "If you were to ask about Syria, it has repeatedly stated that if Israel and other occupants withdraw, it will withdraw its forces as well." The Soviet Union had good relations with Syria, and he "could reaffirm once again" that the Syrians would pull their forces out if other foreign forces withdrew. I seized on this statement as strengthening the significance of the May 17 Agreement I had negotiated between Lebanon and Israel in 1983 and which was now being undermined by Syria.

As our meeting drew to a close, Gromyko said that if he understood me correctly, I had spoken "in favor of more frequent exchanges of views between the two of us." He told me that he "shared this wish." He took up the question of consulates and cultural exchanges and said that he believed "some progress could be made" and would like to hear specific suggestions from me. We discussed briefly how we might agree to characterize our meeting. Gromyko suggested what I considered an interesting word, "necessary." Beyond that, he cautioned, if I were to suggest that we had in any way resumed negotiations about strategic or intermediate-range arms, he would have to deny it, although he looked forward to a continuation of our discussions. Gromyko wanted to have the fact of the discussion without the appearance of fruitful exchange. I decided not to say much publicly: the reality would emerge in a credible and convincing way soon enough. The exchange had provided a way to reengage the Soviets on what amounted to our four-part agenda and provide a quiet forward thrust to U.S.-Soviet relations.

This had been my best meeting with Gromyko by miles. In spite of the posturing, we had some real exchanges. He could sense that too, I was sure. About halfway through the meeting, I felt that I was in charge: the talk was about our agenda and our initiatives. "The Soviets feel the heat," I told my team on the aircraft going home. "No one is in their corner. But it would be a mistake to push too hard right now. They're too tentative. We need a strong position on conventional arms ready when the conventional arms talks begin. We need to get Jim Goodby [our negotiator in Stockholm] and his Soviet counterpart at the CDE talks to develop a private pattern of interaction.

"On nuclear issues, take the START positions that I didn't use and fill them out," I instructed. On INF, I noted that Gromyko hadn't argued with me about the necessity to include their SS-20s if our intermediate-range missiles were included. "Maybe there is a way," I reflected, "to put INF and START talks under some sort of common umbrella while keeping them in separate negotiating groups." I was beginning to feel a momentum building.

"Be careful," Ray Seitz, my executive assistant, said, looking toward the press in the back of the plane. "They may see a canary feather in the corner of your mouth."

The more time I spent with Gromyko, the more I came to see him as a symbol of communism's tragic flaw. He was a man of dignity and intelligence. I could imagine him, with his quizzical gaze, pursed lips, slight stoop, and sharp tongue, as a prelate in Rome or perhaps as the head of a Norwegian shipping dynasty. But as Moscow's most experienced diplomat, he lived a life of irreconcilable objectives. He believed the Marxist dogma he preached. To him, the laws, institutions, and values of the West were bourgeois deceptions. But he must have been able to see how at odds with the facts were his preconceived notions. He believed in the cause of peace, but a peace that could come only when all the world turned Communist. That was clearly not happening. He was comfortable with the cold war. His mind was lodged somewhere around 1948, but these were the 1980s. I could sense his growing inner conflict.

In truth, the meeting with Gromyko confirmed my sense that we were moving to a new stage. If so, I thought, that was a direct reflection of emerging U.S. strength and the cohesion in our alliance demonstrated by the first deployments of our intermediate-range missiles in Great Britain, Italy, and West Germany.

Andropov Dies, Chernenko Emerges

On February 9, 1984, normal programming on Soviet radio was replaced by funereal music, signaling that Yuri Andropov had died, passing from the scene after a brief sixteen months as general secretary of the Communist party of the Soviet Union. His replacement by another elder, Konstantin Chernenko, was taken to mean that, in all probability, the Soviets were unlikely to make much change in their policies.

Should President Reagan attend the funeral and thereby find the occasion for his first meeting while in office with the top man in the Soviet Union? There was a brief flurry of debate over the question. It was an election year. The politicians were in favor of the president's leading our delegation. I was opposed. We should not be running after the Soviets, I argued. King Hussein and President Mubarak were due in Washington. If the president went to Moscow, we would have to cancel their visits. The president could stay in Washington on their account, raising the stature of these visits as part of our continuing effort to bring sense and stability to the Middle East. The president was on his way back from California, and I learned upon his return that the debate was academic. His view was the same as mine. Beyond that, he felt instinctively, in a typically Reaganesque way, that to go to the funeral of a man he didn't know and who had been an implacable adversary would be insincere and inappropriate.

Vice President Bush led our delegation to Moscow. Senate Majority Leader Howard Baker accompanied him. I stayed home for the Hussein and Mubarak visits. There was intense speculation about Chernenko's health among the traveling party. The vice president cabled his opinion: Chernenko "looks almost as young as Reagan, ruddy, almost tanned in appearance, scar across forehead just below hairline, good pallor, hands puffy, but face not puffy. Features sharp, spoke quickly, long sentences without coughing or other problems. Not polemical, more relaxing to be with than Andropov. Twinkle in his eye, speech quick and precise. Fellow you feel you could talk to, no impression that he is slow of mind." Reporters on the trip, however, portrayed Chernenko as sickly, gasping from emphysema, and too weak to keep saluting as Soviet troops marched by Lenin's tomb.

Chernenko did almost all of the talking on the Soviet side, the vice president said, and what he had to say was encouraging: "We are not inherently enemies." Bush told Chernenko that President Reagan was ready for a real dialogue. "He's no pushover, but he does seem open and treated us graciously." The vice president concluded that after a period of uncertainty and immobility, there was now somebody at home in the Kremlin with whom we could have a real exchange. On February 23, a letter came to the president from General Secretary Chernenko. It was relatively warm in tone when compared to Andropov's letters but it contained no new substance. Chernenko highlighted to President Reagan, as Gromyko had to me in Stockholm, the Soviet interest in proposals for arms control in outer space.

And so, against this somewhat optimistic background, we in the State Department and others in the national security community put together a framework for U.S.-Soviet relations for the president, including a checklist of some thirty-nine items for U.S.-Soviet discussion, with the status and prospects noted for each. We developed a potential timetable of meetings between Dobrynin and me and between Gromyko and Hartman. We proposed to ask Brent Scowcroft, who was one of a group of private citizens—the "Dartmouth Group"—who held periodic meetings with Soviets, to serve as a private channel of communication during the week of March 8. If all went well, we foresaw a later meeting between Gromyko and me and then, conceivably, an invitation to Gromyko to come to Washington when he visited the UN General Assembly in September. This would be a major move, since Gromyko's invitations to Washington had been suspended since the Soviet invasion of Afghanistan in 1979.

I urged the president to address strategic arms reductions in his reply to Chernenko. In his letter dated March 6, President Reagan wrote:

> The strategic arms talks have always had as an important stumbling block the fact that our forces are not constructed—for understandable reasons of history and geography—along the same lines. We are concerned about the current imbalance in large, MIRVed, land-based systems in favor of the USSR, which we consider to be the most destabilizing category of nuclear systems. You have criticized our proposals as one-sided and an attempt to restructure your forces without any attendant change in our forces. This is not our intent. Our purpose is to achieve significant reductions in the strategic systems of both sides. Such reductions need not result in identical force structures. The balance we seek must obviously take account of the interests of both sides. That is why in my earlier communications I suggested that we explore what types of reciprocal concessions might bring our interests into better balance. . . . The trade-offs we are prepared to discuss would, I believe, bridge the proposals of both sides and provide, as I have said, a more stable balance at lower levels.

On March 7, in an hour-and-a-half meeting with Ambassador Dobrynin, I presented the president's letter to him, explained it carefully, and suggested follow-up steps. Dobrynin called our exchange "a good effort" and "the most detailed discussion of three or four years." We had gone through our entire four-part agenda.

But the tone soon shifted, and the Soviet preoccupation with the president's Strategic Defense Initiative, announced dramatically in March 1983, became more and more evident. A meeting between Hartman and Gromyko had been "very tough," and by March 20 Dobrynin delivered another letter from Chernenko: our deployment of missiles in Western Europe created "an additional strategic threat to the Soviet Union." The letter continued, "Attempts to somehow sidestep the deadlock will not be productive," and went on to point out that "the development of large-scale ABM systems [meaning SDI] would be in direct contradiction with the objectives of strengthening stability—and you in your letter speak in favor of strengthening stability. . . . the inescapable consequence of the implementation of such plans can be only one thing—an arms race in all directions whose magnitude it is difficult even to imagine today. What is needed is not the negotiations on what such systems might be, but a resolute and unequivocal renunciation of the very idea of creating such systems." Dobrynin then added some official "oral" remarks, which only underlined Soviet stiffening. The Soviet Union "will not permit the military balance to be upset," Dobrynin said, and pointed to our actions to protect shipping in the Persian Gulf. "No one has the right to arrogate to himself the role of some sort of traffic policeman over international lines of navigation," he told me.

By this time, the Soviets had given Scowcroft the cold shoulder. Brent had gone to Moscow and let it be known he was ready to meet privately; the Soviets offered only a deputy foreign minister—a level with no authority in their system. Ambassador Hartman, back in Washington in late March for consultations, took the occasion to see Dobrynin. "The Scowcroft mission was a U.S. trick: Gromyko viewed it as an effort to go around him," Dobrynin said. Hartman responded that he had personally gone over the mission in detail with Gromyko. Art asked Dobrynin why, all of a sudden, people who came to Moscow were being told that American efforts to stimulate a dialogue were merely election-year politics. Dobrynin made no real response. In his view, the "space issue" could become "the most dangerously destabilizing factor in our relationship." This Soviet concern about SDI as well as our INF deployments was accompanied by their deliberate effort once again to put a further public chill on an already cold relationship.

An Atmosphere of Strain

The Olympic Games were set for July 1984 in Los Angeles. We knew the Soviets, with their sense of reciprocity, would have the U.S. boycott of the 1980 Olympics in Moscow on their minds. Nevertheless, we proceeded on the assumption that the Soviets would attend. After an April 24 meeting of the Olympic Committee in Lausanne, the head of the Soviet National Olympic Committee announced, "There will be no boycott. That is our principal position. The Soviet Union never intended nor intends at the present to take a political decision of a boycott." But on May 8, the Soviets reversed themselves, issuing a statement in *Tass* saying that the United States was conniving with "extremist organizations" that aimed to create "unbearable conditions" for their delegation and athletes, an apparent reference to their fear that anti-Soviet demonstrations by human rights activists would embarrass them in Los Angeles. We had, in fact, bent over backward to meet all Soviet concerns and had developed a plan for 17,000 people to be involved in Olympic security. We were prepared to spend up to $50 million to assure security, $1 million of which was for the Soviet delegation, including $500,000 to be certain that the Soviet ship that was to house their officials and supporters would have the utmost security. The Soviets knew all this. Nevertheless, claiming inadequate security for their athletes, they announced that they would not attend the Olympics. We denounced their action as unjustified and a "blatant political action." We knew that security was not the problem: the Soviet action was their way of retaliating against Jimmy Carter's decision to boycott the 1980 Olympics in Moscow as a protest against the Soviet invasion of Afghanistan. The Soviet statement implied that Moscow hoped to heighten tensions and hurt President Reagan's chances for reelection. That didn't pan out for Moscow.

I told Dobrynin on May 10 that if the Soviets changed their minds, their athletes would be welcome at the games.[2] At this same May 10 meeting, Dobrynin raised again what the Soviets called the "militarization" of outer space: the president's Strategic Defense Initiative obsessed them. He proposed that official discussions on this subject be undertaken and announced publicly. I said we were willing to talk but that outer space was militarized by the fact that ballistic missiles go through it, and so if the subject was to be discussed, it should be within the context of strategic arms talks. "Defense and offense are related and need to be discussed together," I said.

The harsh Soviet line and the absence of renewed negotiations were beginning to fray nerves in Europe. On May 4, a worried Italian Prime Minister, Bettino Craxi, had suggested that NATO halt its INF deployments if the Soviets resumed negotiations. President Reagan wrote to Craxi, and I wrote to Foreign Minister Giulio Andreotti, opposing this significant break—without any consultation—with our NATO position. The general reaction to the Italian proposal among our other allies was negative, but the atmosphere of strain the Soviets were promoting was having an effect.

The Dutch coalition government, facing a crucial vote on the question of INF missile deployments on their soil, could not count on a majority in their Parliament in favor. By May 22, I began to fear that the Dutch government faced a real crisis on this issue. Hans van den Broek, the Dutch foreign minister and a man I admired, was making a valiant effort. But, he told me, "we simply cannot get a yes from the Dutch Parliament.

2. They did not change their minds, and all the Warsaw Pact countries except for Romania followed their lead and boycotted the Olympics. It must have been very painful for the talented and highly trained Soviet and East German athletes, as well as those from the other boycotting nations. The president attended the opening ceremony of the Olympics and invited me to go with him. It was a dramatic event. The cheers for the Romanian team were deafening.

Therefore the strategy is to avoid a no and also to avoid losing both the cabinet and the missiles. The only solution is time." They could go ahead, he said, with construction of the facilities and leave open the question of deployment. After some agonizing, I agreed that this was the best approach, with a final yes or no to come in 1988, when the deployments were actually scheduled to take place. "Everyone knows that the Dutch have blinked," I said afterward. The episode would no doubt encourage the Soviets in their hard line.

By this time, President Reagan had sent General Secretary Chernenko five letters laying out our view of the U.S.-Soviet relationship and identifying concrete steps forward that we could take. He had received as many replies. My meetings with Ambassador Dobrynin in Washington and Hartman's meetings with Foreign Minister Gromyko in Moscow had gone over all of the items on our agenda in some detail. Our effort was to show a reasonable face; theirs was to alarm our friends in Europe. Overall, the best that we could say was that the Soviets had for a time shown a wary willingness to work on some issues, followed by a stiffening. They seemed to be combining delaying tactics in private with propaganda in public. We had made an impressive record of U.S. efforts to negotiate with the Soviets, through proposals on a wide array of issues. Nevertheless, the shrillness of Soviet rhetoric was rising rapidly and reached its high point when, on May 10, *Tass* compared the president to Hitler and characterized a Reagan speech as "a shameless lie from beginning to end."

A June 6 letter from Chernenko to President Reagan, responding to the president's most recent communication about Andrei Sakharov and other human rights cases, concluded, "I must point out that introduction into relations between states of questions concerning solely domestic affairs of our country or yours does not serve the task of improving these relations—if this is our goal. I wish questions of such a nature did not burden our correspondence, which both of us, as I understand it, value."

Toward the end of June, the CIA produced a shotgun listing of reports citing increased Soviet aggressiveness in the political, propaganda, commercial, internal security, and military arenas. The CIA suggested a Soviet decision to move from civilian- to wartime-type activity, which could easily be read as a prediction of war. I told CIA director Bill Casey that I had problems with the report. It was a sloppy piece of work and more alarmist than the facts warranted. It appeared to be straining toward a conclusion of heightened Soviet aggressiveness. I pointed out to Casey that the Soviets had been trying to encourage divisions in the West, in part by seeking to scare people about the state of East-West relations. "We do not want to play *their* game," I told Casey. "Should this piece reach the press, it would do more harm to our policies in Western Europe than several months of Soviet propaganda."

SDI Rivets Their Attention

The Soviets' preoccupation with the president's Strategic Defense Initiative was intensifying. Dobrynin raised "the cosmos" at every meeting. In a letter to the president in early June, Chernenko wrote, "Let me remind you that these [earlier suggestions] included renouncing the construction of large-scale anti-ballistic missile defense systems, entering into negotiations on preventing the militarization of outer space." And on June 29, we received a private message from the Soviets that they quickly made public, proposing the start of talks on the militarization of outer space in Vienna on September 18, 1984. We turned around an answer within twenty-four hours, agreeing to undertake such talks but noting again that we would expect to discuss both offense and defense as they pertained to outer space.

At a breakfast meeting on July 3, Dobrynin told me that the Soviets had raised one issue, the demilitarization of space, and the United States had raised another, resuming negotiations on offensive nuclear systems, which the Soviets regarded as unacceptable. He requested clarification.

I pointed out to him that the Soviet Union had made a proposal and publicized it. We consequently publicized our response after notifying the Soviet embassy. Now, I told him, "President Reagan is writing confidentially to Chernenko to confirm that we accept the Soviet proposal without preconditions." But I wanted him to know what we expected to discuss. When our delegation showed up in Vienna in September, I said, "they will be led by broad-gauged negotiators who can take up all the relevant topics." Dobrynin was noncommittal, but he thought we could expect an official response quickly from the Soviet Union and that he "could not say that the Soviets accept your acceptance."

I told the president afterward, "Eventually I suspect they may be forced to take yes for an answer." But Chernenko wrote on July 26, "No doubt whatsoever now remains that the American side is not prepared to conduct negotiations with the aim of preventing the militarization of outer space. . . . I repeat, we regret that the current American position makes it impossible to conduct the negotiations."

Chernenko had proved me wrong: "The Soviets cannot take yes for an answer," I said publicly. But we continued to emphasize our readiness to meet in Vienna on September 18.

Taking Stock

As the summer proceeded and our elections approached, I began to think ahead to what we might accomplish in a second Reagan term. I discussed some key points with the president. He listened patiently. How much he absorbed, I couldn't tell at the time, but I considered these private discussions essential to conditioning him, and myself, for the work to come. I frequently heard him repeat back to me or someone else ideas or bits of information from these sessions.

The Soviet Union, I told him, was mired in a protracted and so far inconclusive process of succession in leadership and in the difficulties of a stagnant and foundering economy. Nevertheless, they could maintain their present rate of increase in military spending and their steady modernization in both nuclear and nonnuclear forces. Among the Soviets' biggest potential challenges, I told him, were the separatist tendencies among their nationalities, problems in the assimilation of their burgeoning Muslim population, and the rising anti-Moscow sentiment in the Baltics and the Ukraine.

Sooner or later the Soviets would have to face the hurdle of a generational turnover when the senior members of the Politburo retired or died and would be replaced by younger men who might have a significantly different outlook, I told the president. "Unlike the older men," I said, "those in the new generation will not have spent their early careers surviving or carrying out Stalin's purges. They will be post–World War II people. I suspect that ideology will be less of a living force for them, that they will believe more in technology and will look for policies that are genuinely effective. As new people on the scene," I speculated, "they will be even more sensitive than their elders to slights and to real or imagined challenges to Soviet 'equality' with the U.S. It will pay dividends to treat them with civility, whatever our differences might be and to recognize the importance of their country."

I speculated that the two most likely candidates to succeed Chernenko were Mikhail Gorbachev, a member of the Politburo and a protégé of Andropov, and ex-Leningrad party boss, Grigory Romanov. The conventional wisdom, I told him, was that Gorbachev was a more moderate candidate from the U.S. point of view and less insular in outlook than most of his Politburo colleagues. We had to recognize the prevailing Soviet view of the United States: extreme distrust verging, in some instances, on paranoia. The role of the Soviet military in high-level policy-making, I said, was likely to remain prominent. Transitional periods in Soviet history had always witnessed an increase in the military's influence. They would know that they confronted an administration that had built up its defense capability, deployed INF missiles, and developed an ideological offensive in favor of freedom and human rights. They would be wary of our intentions and wary of a president who had great political strength and demonstrated dexterity at seizing the diplomatic initiative from Moscow. The Strategic Defense Initiative, I told the president, and the possibility of successful space-based defense technologies "are of intense concern to them."

The Soviets could not feel too comfortable about the prospects on their perimeter, I noted. Political instability still roiled beneath the surface in

Poland, and economic stagnation continued to plague the countries of the Warsaw Pact. I pointed out, however, that Soviet success in Western Europe would grow if the left-wing parties that had broken with the NATO defense consensus supporting INF deployments came to power in the United Kingdom, Norway, Denmark, the Netherlands, or even the Federal Republic of Germany. The Soviets had not been able to develop their relations with China or with Japan, I told the president. They remained bogged down in Afghanistan. "The authority of the Kabul regime," I said, "extends no further than the range of Soviet artillery." Pakistan had remained stalwart in resisting Soviet pressures to curtail support for the mujaheddin resistance fighters in Afghanistan and to negotiate directly with the Soviet-supported government in Kabul.

I counseled the president that our objectives should remain to counter Soviet expansionism, to do whatever we could to encourage greater liberalization and pluralism within the Soviet Union, and to reach mutually beneficial agreements with the Soviets where we were able to do so. "We should continue to pursue a policy that is consistent and predictable, avoiding the wide pendulum swings of the past decade and a half," I said. We were still keeping alive the possibility of what we now called the "September talks," originally proposed by the Soviets, then backed away from by them after we accepted. If we were successful in engaging the Soviets in negotiations, I said, we would have both the forum and the signal we needed to begin discussing the complex trade-offs required to achieve an agreement on deep cuts in strategic arms. I felt that the Soviets would remain interested because of their great fear of potential U.S. technological breakthroughs in space weaponry.

I suggested to President Reagan that we prepare for a new level of U.S. activism toward areas on the Soviet borders, particularly Eastern Europe. We needed to stick with our policy of "differentiation," which sought to induce the Warsaw Pact countries to pursue policies that diverged increasingly from the Soviet line in both the domestic and foreign affairs areas.

The president needed no urging from me, though I encouraged him anyway, to continue his emphasis on human rights matters. I said that a summit meeting conferred the highest form of legitimacy on a Soviet leader, and a proposal for a serious summit after the elections would probably be well received in Moscow and could influence favorably the Soviet reaction to any accompanying U.S. proposals on arms control. A summit would be hailed by our allies, who would become increasingly nervous the longer the apparent stalemate in high-level U.S.-Soviet contacts persisted. I said that the prerequisites for an effective approach to Soviet affairs over the next four years would be the same as the prerequisites for the restoration of our position over the last four: steadiness and patience, continued economic recovery, steady growth and modernization of our military forces and the will to use them when warranted, and solid alliance relationships and international friendships. We had hard work ahead of us.

Feelers from Gromyko

During the first part of August, while I was in California, hints came in that Gromyko might be looking for a chance to meet the president. A Soviet diplomat—we thought it was probably Deputy Chief of Mission Oleg Sokolov—had told Washington correspondent John Scali that he thought Gromyko would like to be invited to meet with the president "this fall." Another Soviet diplomat in Berlin told Nelson Ledsky, one of State's German specialists, that a traditional Gromyko trip to Washington during the UN General Assembly depended on whether he would be treated in the same way as he had been "before Afghanistan." Shortly thereafter, Sokolov passed on to me Gromyko's "heartfelt gratitude" for my letter marking his seventy-fifth birthday. Sokolov also pointed to my reference to our prospective meeting at the United Nations in New York as an important gesture.

On August 13, I was in Los Angeles for a session between President Reagan and Italian Foreign Minister Giulio Andreotti. I sought a little extra private time with the president and told him of these feelers from Gromyko. I reminded the president that Gromyko had not been invited to the White House since the Soviet invasion of Afghanistan in December 1979 and that "we would be reinstating something without a change in Afghanistan." But "if we could get something going that would be a little more constructive, that would be helpful." There was no need for him to decide this right away, I said. "But perhaps you'd like to consider whether to invite Gromyko this fall."

The president said he didn't need to think about it. "It's the right thing to do. Try to work it out," he said. A diplomatic minuet proceeded: we didn't want to invite Gromyko unless we knew he would accept, and he didn't want to let us know he would accept unless he knew we would invite him.

Countdown

With almost predictable frequency, whenever a big meeting with the Soviets was about to take place, puzzling or potentially derailing developments would occur. On September 6, 1984, in a tersely worded announcement, the Soviet press said Chief of the General Staff and First Deputy Minister of Defense Nikolai Ogarkov had been replaced by Marshal Sergei Akhromeyev. Ogarkov had been known in military circles for his "independent of the party" tendencies. At sixty-one, Akhromeyev was the youngest marshal in the Soviet army. He reputedly had extensive arms control experience and major responsibilities for operations in Afghanistan. Art Hartman had met Akhromeyev and described him as candid, affable, and less prone to polemics than other Soviets, with an unusually sophisticated grasp of strategic and arms control issues. On September 11, we announced that Gromyko would be meeting with the president in Washington on Friday, September 28. This would be Ronald Reagan's first meeting with a member of the Soviet Politburo since he had become president almost four years earlier.

As the Gromyko meeting approached, the Soviets on September 12 seized an American barge, the *Frieda K.,* and its crew—which had strayed into Soviet waters. They detained the five crewmen, holding them in a hotel in the town of Urelik. The U.S. embassy in Moscow managed to get a phone call through to the captain of the barge, Tabb Thoms, and heard that all were safe and well. Then the phone "inexplicably" went dead when Thoms was asked whether he had been allowed to contact the embassy. Soviet authorities were handling the matter in a tough and uncooperative manner.

I told Dobrynin on September 17 that it was "ridiculous for an incident of this type to become an issue right now," that we should "get rid of it— solve it—right away." By September 20, I was able to report to the president that the five crewmen of the *Frieda K.* had been safely escorted by the Coast Guard cutter *Sherman* en route home. The five had been pressured to sign a statement admitting they had intentionally violated Soviet borders. They refused to do so. They were not physically mistreated. The seismographic tapes being carried as cargo by the barge were returned. The Soviet embassy in Washington had probably weighed in to solve the problem quickly.

On September 16, an American of Ukrainian descent, Victor Kovalenko, lobbed a jar of red paint against the wall of the Soviet embassy, creating a basketball-sized blotch. He was charged with "destruction of property," a felony. I told Dobrynin on September 17, "We take very seriously all threats against the security of the Soviet embassy, including vandalism," and that the person who threw the paint had been detained and charged.

Despite these distracting events, Dobrynin and I spent most of our time together discussing the impending Gromyko meetings. He told me Gromyko was eager to talk and that he accepted our agenda. "But is it really necessary to raise human rights?" he asked.

"Yes," I told him. "President Reagan will talk about human rights, as will I, and will explain to Gromyko why this subject is so important to us."

Ronald Reagan regarded his upcoming meeting with Andrei Gromyko as one of critical importance. He prepared intensely for it, listening to me and others in his administration, consulting with former President Nixon, former Secretary of State Kissinger, and others. I took him a set of talking points I had worked over personally and carefully. He thanked me and took them to Camp David.

On Monday morning he telephoned me and asked me to come over to the White House. "George, I've looked over your talking points, and they are very good. But I've been thinking about this all weekend up at Camp David, and I've written my own talking points, and I'm very satisfied with them. You can look them over if you want." In short, he was open to comments, but his mind was firm on how he would handle Gromyko.

Actually, the president had accepted the substance of the talking points I had given him; his personal effort was in setting the tone and atmosphere of his discussion. He was determined to make clear to Gromyko that the United States wanted peace and to explain why we and our allies were so apprehensive about the Soviet Union. This was vintage Ronald Reagan: it came from the inside out. Gromyko, as an astute observer of presidents over many years, would be able to see that President Reagan was speaking about deep-seated beliefs and meant every word that he said.

The president's speech to the UN General Assembly on Monday, September 24, was universally regarded as constructive, even conciliatory. There was not a word of criticism of the Soviet Union from the cold warrior. This was a far cry from the "evil empire" speech. And it was no election-year ploy: Ronald Reagan's reelection was virtually certain, and polls were already predicting a landslide. Walter Mondale called the president's speech "deathbed conversions," but the fact of the matter was that President Reagan had started on this process with Ambassador Dobrynin in the family quarters of the White House back in February 1983. I had been the only other person present.

The president returned to Washington on Tuesday; I stayed on in New York to work with Gromyko on the full range of our agenda. He gave no ground. When he left our building on First Avenue, he said through an interpreter that he would not answer questions because "the discussions are not concluded." A *Tass* dispatch, as always, put forward a negative assessment of the meetings.

On Thursday came Gromyko's address to the United Nations. It was uncompromising, filled with bombast and misrepresentations. He accused us of deceit, provocation, warmongering, and wrongdoing of every kind. He even accused us of interfering in the affairs of an Afghanistan struggling against "gangs of anti-Government bandits and saboteurs." He had the gall to say this when Soviet troops were ravaging the country.

I sat through this speech with a stony face and afterward commented to the press, "It is sad and disappointing that Mr. Gromyko should give us yet another misrepresentation of history and a distortion of the peaceful and constructive role of the United States in world affairs. We can only say, as the president did on Monday, that we will try, and try again, to bring forth a more constructive relationship with the Soviet Union."

That afternoon, Gromyko met with Walter Mondale, the Democratic candidate for the presidency. According to the *New York Times* account on September 28, 1984, Mondale reported that he had told Gromyko that if elected, he would order a freeze on all new weapons developments for six months to give an incentive for the Soviet Union to agree to a summit; Mondale also had "called for a negotiated, verified freeze at current levels of nuclear arms, to be followed by reductions." He had criticized President Reagan for not having had a summit meeting with a Soviet leader or having concluded an arms control agreement.

Tass issued a statement after the Mondale meeting: "It followed from what W. Mondale said that he, for his part, regarded a turn for the better in relations between the United States and the Soviet Union as important, and, in principle, possible. Some ideas suggested by him in this context, should they materialize in Washington's policy, would open up certain possibilities for bringing the positions of the two powers closer and for subsequent agreements on arms limitations and disarmament." Mondale had at once undercut Reagan's efforts with the Soviets and his own campaign. But Mondale's embrace by *Tass* was unlikely to do him much good with the American public.

Gromyko Returns to Washington

Friday morning, September 28, arrived, and along with it, Andrei Gromyko and an immense throng of photographers and reporters from all over the world. Nancy Reagan had called me earlier and asked what I thought about her being part of the luncheon group. I said that we were coming to her home for lunch, and I thought it would be most appropriate if she greeted Gromyko on his arrival and stayed until the reception was over, at which point she would leave the working lunch group. I could not help but note to myself that the treatment being accorded to Gromyko was of a magnitude greater than anything given to any other foreign minister and was on a scale with a visit of a head of government.

It took about twenty minutes for the meeting to get going because the press came through the Oval Office in waves, five in all, taking pictures and shouting questions. The president and Gromyko sat with their delegations ranged alongside them and smiled throughout this process. The president started the meeting in the Oval Office just as he had planned, and Gromyko listened to President Reagan elaborate on America's hope for peace and explain why we saw the Soviet Union as a threat to those hopes. He added that he had long believed that "difficulties arise when countries talk *about* each other rather than *to* each other." Gromyko replied with the Soviet view of world events. The president raised the idea of an umbrella arrangement for reestablishing discussions of arms control issues and said he thought a formula could be found covering all of the issues and making it possible to discuss both defenses in space and nuclear weapons. Gromyko was concerned that such a formula would relegate space weapons to a sideline. The president responded that there could be separate concurrent negotiations on these issues.

As we were about to leave for lunch, the president took Gromyko aside and had him stay back in the Oval Office, where the two of them conversed in English without interpreters. The president later told me that in their private conversation he had been struck by Gromyko's description of the two superpowers sitting on top of ever-rising stockpiles of nuclear weapons and by Gromyko's statement that the Soviet Union wished to reduce the size of those piles. "My dream," Reagan had told him, "is for a world where there are no nuclear weapons."

The two men walked together through the long colonnade separating the West Wing from the main mansion of the White House and came into the reception, where they were greeted by Nancy Reagan. Gromyko was not aware that she was going to be present, and he devoted all of his attention to her. As the short reception was coming to a close and we began to move into the dining room, Gromyko took Nancy to one side and whispered to her, "Does your husband believe in peace?"

Nancy replied, "Yes, of course."

"Then whisper 'peace' in your husband's ear every night," Gromyko said.

"I will, and I'll also whisper it in your ear," she said. And with that she leaned over with a smile and whispered softly, "Peace."

A national evening news broadcast in Moscow showed a two-minute videotape of President Reagan and Gromyko talking in front of a White House fireplace. This was the first the Soviet public had learned of the meeting. Gromyko issued a statement through *Tass*, saying that the Soviet Union was still unconvinced "about practical positive changes in the foreign policy course of the U.S. Administration." He continued, "The Soviet Union will continue to judge real intentions of the U.S. side by its practical deeds. The future will show whether Washington intends to adjust its political course."

At 10:00 A.M., Saturday, September 29, 1984, Gromyko arrived at the State Department for the first time since the Soviet invasion of Afghanistan five years earlier. I could see that my comments in Stockholm about an artificially divided Germany still rankled. "Why would you make such a statement?" he asked. "It is shocking. The results of the war have been written into history. They are firm and permanent. What does it mean to speak of 'division'? Prewar Germany is no more. Now there are two German states. There are fixed postwar borders between the two countries, as in the rest of Europe." He said that "the USSR would like the United States to know that no one—no one—can change the reality of the situation in Europe" and that statements like mine "poison the atmosphere" and "cast a dark shadow over the relations between the two major powers."

I responded that my comment was "a simple observation of a situation that, as we see it, is undesirable. The Berlin Wall is a symbol of the division. There should be an easy flow of people throughout Europe," I said, "as there is now in Western Europe."

Gromyko turned to the subject of Japan and said that he did not understand why Japan had to remilitarize and why the United States was attempting to foster hostile attitudes in Japan against the Soviet Union. I told him that Japan was seeking to build a defensive force. What affected Japan's thinking, I said, was the large number of Soviet ships and aircraft passing by Japan and the SS-20s within range of Japan—all of which Japan found disturbing. Then I reminded him about the islands just north of Japan, taken by the Soviets at the end of World War II and never returned. The islands historically had been Japanese, I said. I went on to say that Asia was a place of great dynamism. "The people there are smart; they have drive; they are very industrious and have strong goals. Japan is a key country in Asia," I said. (Why should I protest if the Soviets want to alienate the Japanese by their antagonistic actions toward Japan, I thought but did not say.)

Gromyko turned to the "question of questions," nuclear weapons. "This is the issue on which we should work night and day." At the end, in what I regarded as an important remark, he asked me to convey to President Reagan his thanks for the president's courtesy in receiving him and concluded, "If it appears appropriate for the two of us to meet again soon, I am ready to work that out." I told him the combination of meetings we had just had were by far our most productive to date and that we might just be seeing the emergence of genuine dialogue.

All in all, President Reagan and I felt that a great deal of progress had been made. We had engaged in a rigorous give-and-take on nearly every global and bilateral issue. The discussions had been direct and nonconfrontational. As the visit proceeded, the Soviets' public statements even started to change. In contrast to Gromyko's skeptical statement after his Friday meeting with the president, a *Tass* report on Saturday described future sessions between ministers as established and the discussion I had had with Gromyko as "a normal conversation" rather than as an argument about conflicting positions, as *Tass* had described our first meeting. I speculated, as did others, that Gromyko's mission had been to sound out the possibilities for the future without seeming to surrender any of the Kremlin's positions. Interpreted in this light, Gromyko's harsh speech to the United Nations had served the function of a fanfare to preclude any interpretation that his trip to the White House was a sign of weakness.

On November 6, Ronald Reagan was reelected by a landslide victory over Walter Mondale, who was defeated by a record electoral margin: Mondale carried only his own home state of Minnesota and the District of Columbia. The election was a stunning triumph for Ronald Reagan and for the clear agenda he advocated. Walter Mondale had challenged that agenda directly, and the people had spoken. The president now had a strong mandate to pursue his agenda his way in a second term. That mandate also made a deep impression abroad, including in the Soviet Union: Ronald Reagan was a man to be reckoned with and also a man who would be able to carry an agreement he negotiated with the Soviets through the Senate ratification process.

President Reagan, in his first comments after his victory, said that he planned to give the highest priority to seeking arms reductions with the Soviet Union. My job was to help the president in setting a course. I knew that the waters ahead would be turbulent and that the hazards we encountered from the Soviets would not be the only ones. There were rocky shoals and uncharted depths.

A fierce struggle within the administration and with many members of Congress lay ahead as well. Nevertheless, with the president strong and committed, the opportunity was there to achieve substantial change, a great turning in superpower relations was under way. If the first Reagan term could be characterized by a buildup of strength, in the second term we could use that strength for determined and patient diplomatic efforts to produce greater peace and stability in the world.

CHAPTER 26

Breakthrough
with Gromyko

The meetings that President Reagan and I had in New York and Washington with Andrei Gromyko marked a new turn in the superpower relationship. He had been invited to the White House for the first time since the Soviet invasion of Afghanistan. He came, and in the process, broke open the Soviet effort to heighten superpower tensions in response to our deployments of INF missiles in Europe. We agreed on a renewed process of diplomatic exchange. Gromyko sized up the president on a personal level, and President Reagan took the measure of Gromyko.

After my session with Gromyko on Saturday, September 29, 1984, I took stock. Before the dialogue we now had under way, we had endured a year of Soviet propaganda: the Soviet Union could never deal with Ronald Reagan; they were prepared to wait until he had departed from the presidency. Now they wanted to talk to us, perhaps seriously. I had suggested to Gromyko that each side assess the situation facing us and then exchange evaluations. I did this, setting out a detailed agenda for us to work on— and also responding to the immense array of misstatements of fact that I had heard from him.

I decided to make my views known in as open and public a way as possible. The Soviets had put out their line in an interview with General Secretary Konstantin Chernenko that appeared in the *Washington Post* on October 17, 1984. It was not encouraging; Chernenko seemed primarily interested in promoting the nuclear freeze movement.

Beyond Linkage and Détente

I was invited to address the opening of the new RAND/UCLA Center for the Study of Soviet International Behavior on October 18. I used my speech to develop the larger conceptual issues that faced us in managing U.S.-

Soviet relations over the long term and to make an important conceptual point: I put aside the Nixon-era concepts of "linkage" and "détente," and set out a new approach that I hoped would prove more effective and that reflected the reality of what we were in fact doing.

I had a hard time with the State Department's Soviet specialists, who did not share my views. They kept changing my words to the point that I stopped sending them drafts for comment. I sent Peter Rodman, director of State's policy planning staff and a man Richard Nixon knew well and respected, to see Nixon in New York to show him the draft. Nixon made good suggestions, liked the language, but was uncomfortable about my new approach to "linkage." He and most Soviet experts liked to link all aspects of our Soviet relationship together and try to use the presumed Soviet desire for progress in one area, such as trade, as leverage to achieve progress in another, such as arms control, regional issues, or human rights. I felt that we must be prepared to fight out each issue on its own terms, and that we would be better off if we thought of the relationship that way.

My observation was that linkage had too often become a trap. The Soviets used it against us. In the case of Soviet Jews, the Soviets were using human beings as pawns, encouraging us to believe that concessions to Soviet demands on issues of important substance, such as most-favored-nation treatment for their prospective exports to the United States, would lead to better treatment of Jews in the Soviet Union or to more permits for Jewish emigration. We would, I argued, avoid that trap by addressing every issue on its merits: we would press on what was right for Soviet Jews whether things were going well or poorly on other issues of concern. We would step up to each issue and assert our interests strongly.

The U.S.-Soviet relationship is a global one, I said. "We impinge on each other's interests in many regions of the world and in many fields of endeavor. A sustained and sound relationship, therefore, will confront the fact that the Soviets can be expected periodically to do something abhorrent to us or threaten our interests.

"This raises the question of linkage," I went on. "Should we refuse to conclude agreements with the Soviets in one area when they do something outrageous in some other area? Would such an approach give us greater leverage over Moscow's conduct? Or would it place us on the defensive? Would it confirm our dedication to fundamental principles of international relations? Or would it make our diplomacy seem inconsistent? Clearly, linkage is not merely "a fact of life" but a complex question of policy. There will be times when we must make progress in one dimension of the relationship contingent on progress in others. We can never let ourselves become so wedded to improving our relations with the Soviets that we turn a blind eye to actions that undermine the very foundation of stable relations. At the same time," I said, "linkage as an instrument of policy has limitations; if applied rigidly, it could yield the initiative to the Soviets, letting them set the pace and the character of the relationship.

"We do not seek negotiations for their own sake," I reminded my audience. "We negotiate when it is in our interest to do so. Therefore, when the Soviet Union acts in a way we find objectionable, it may not always make sense for us to break off negotiations or suspend agreements. If those negotiations or agreements were undertaken with a realistic view of their benefits for us, then they should be worth maintaining under all but exceptional circumstances. We should not sacrifice long-term interests in order to express immediate outrage. We must not ignore Soviet actions that trouble us. On the contrary, we need to respond forcefully. But in doing so, we are more likely to be successful by direct measures that counter the specific challenge."

I contrasted President Carter's reaction to the Soviet invasion of Afghanistan with President Reagan's after the shooting down of the Korean airliner. Carter froze the relationship and canceled everything from grain sales and participation in the Olympics to his annual meetings with Foreign Minister Gromyko. "But," I asked, "did his actions serve our economic interests? Did they further progress toward a better arms agreement? Did they get Soviet troops out of Afghanistan?" President Reagan never had illusions about the Soviet Union. "He made sure the world knew the truth about the incident. But he also sent our arms control negotiators back to Geneva, because he believed that reducing nuclear weapons was a critical priority."

"In the final analysis," I said, " linkage is a tactical question; the strategic reality of leverage comes from creating facts in support of our overall design. Over the longer term, we must structure the bargaining environment to our advantage by modernizing our defenses, assisting our friends, and showing we are willing to defend our interests. In this way we give the Soviets more of a stake, in their own interest, in better relations with us across the board."

I addressed the need for a long-term strategy: "Sudden shifts in policy, stemming from emotional and perfectly understandable reactions to Soviet behavior, are not the way to pursue our interests. It seems to me that the West, if it is to compete effectively and advance its goals, must develop the capacity for consistency and discipline and must fashion—and stick to—a long-term strategy."

I pointed to the difficulties of maintaining consistency and the implications of a failure to do so: "Historically, American policy has swung from one extreme to the other. We have gone through periods of implacable opposition—forgoing negotiations, building up our defenses, and confronting Soviet aggression. Then, concerned about confrontation, we have entered periods of seeming détente, during which some were tempted to neglect our defenses and ignore Soviet threats to our interests around the world—only once again to be disillusioned by some Soviet action that sent us swinging back to a more implacable posture."

"Therefore," I said, "we must come to grips with the more complex reality of our situation. A sustainable strategy must include all the elements essential to a more advantageous U.S.-Soviet relationship. We need to be strong, we must be ready to confront Soviet challenges, *and* we should negotiate when there are realistic prospects for success."

Divergent Views

As the November 1984 presidential election drew near, divisions of view within the administration made it difficult to make decisions quickly: a serious problem if we were to enter a period of real give-and-take with the Soviets. I felt that I had achieved a certain pacing in our diplomacy and had put some fundamentals in place. But I was not kidding myself. Cap Weinberger and Bill Casey wanted no dealings with the Soviets and were reluctant to make any changes in our negotiating positions once they had been laid down. Bud McFarlane, influenced by his experiences as an assistant to Henry Kissinger at the Vietnam negotiations, often voiced the view that in the last analysis there was no point in negotiating with Communists. Bill Casey's ideological bent on foreign policy issues was so strong that I worried about the objectivity of his and his agency's intelligence assessments. All three seemed to feel that any negotiated outcome would undermine the strength necessary not only to produce a useful result but also to ensure that the outcome would be fully observed.

The president was aware of these divergent views. When he decided in August 1984 that he wanted to meet Gromyko, he did not want to tell his White House staff right away about his decision because he did not want to gear them up to try to turn him around. But the wolves were out. A member of Vice President Bush's staff called over to say that the press had asked Bush whether I was out of line in my RAND/UCLA speech, and the vice president had assured them that my views were in accord with administration policy.

I knew that my own sense of procedure created a problem for me. I insisted on day-to-day dealing with the White House through the NSC adviser. I had told Bud McFarlane, now the third person to hold that position in the Reagan Administration, that he was my guy in the White House and that I would make no end runs. As a result, I did not create the leverage or fear over there that I would have if I had used my access to the president more aggressively.

But the real problem ran deeper than clashing personalities. An intellectual debate was raging. I needed to sharpen my argument so that the president would see clearly that an arms reduction agreement and a better U.S.-Soviet relationship were necessary objectives. I would have to state my views to the president directly and tell him he would have to make some big decisions and make those decisions clear to all his key people.

On Thursday, October 25, I had lunch with Bud McFarlane. My musings about trouble ahead suddenly seemed less abstract. Bud told me that in a long talk with the president "they" had come up with the idea of putting arms control into the hands of someone in the White House; it would be managed there by an arms control "czar"—an unfortunate term, I told Bud. McFarlane said the Soviets wanted to deal with us on arms control issues only: they didn't want to deal with any other aspects of a relationship.

"That is why," I countered, "we have to insist on our four-part agenda, to force them to deal with human rights and the explosive regional issues, as well as bilateral issues. If you pull arms control into the White House, you are giving the Soviets exactly what they want. All aspects of the U.S.-Soviet relationship should be managed together, and the center of gravity in working with the president should be the secretary of state."

"Well, I sort of agree," Bud said, and went on to describe a complicated policy-making structure.

"Procedure is not the main problem," I said. "There is a deep difference of opinion in the administration about whether arms control and a better Soviet relationship are in our interest. The president will have to decide. If his answer is yes, he will have to make compromises, to recognize that verification will not be perfect but that we can serve our interests with the right agreements."

Bud and I did agree on the text of a brief but important National Security Decision Directive approved and issued by the president the next day. It authorized explorations with the Soviets of ways to approach negotiations on the limitation of the antisatellite capabilities of both sides, on the more general topic of the militarization of space, and on the reduction of offensive nuclear arsenals. This meant we were prepared to discuss the U.S. Strategic Defense Initiative and Soviet ballistic missile defense programs in the context of the relationship between offensive and defensive capabilities. I, as secretary of state, was charged to solicit a Soviet position on the U.S. proposal to open "umbrella talks" about all these issues.

The very next day, I had a briefing from Lieutenant General James Abrahamson, the head of the SDI program. SDI was now central to our dealings with the Soviets, and I had to know where we stood. Only Paul Nitze, Lieutenant General Jack Chain, assistant secretary for political-military affairs, and I were there—we were the only State Department people cleared for the material. After a short while, I stopped him. "You are giving me the briefing that you give the *New York Times*." I asked him some pointed questions that had arisen in an earlier conversation I had with Paul Nitze. Abrahamson looked at his assistant and asked, "Is the secretary cleared for that material?" I was dumbfounded by his remark and his reluctance to answer even mildly penetrating questions. I asked him to leave and come back only when he felt comfortable to answer any question I might ask. I was a convinced supporter of SDI, but I was also concerned about inflated claims and overselling. Out of my long experience with high-powered scientists and engineers, I had also learned not to take claims at face value and to be uneasy when straightforward answers to straightforward questions were not forthcoming.

Insights from India

On October 31, 1984, Prime Minister Indira Gandhi was assassinated by two of her Sikh bodyguards. Her son Rajiv was sworn in to replace her. On November 1, I boarded an air force jet as head of the U.S. delegation to the cremation ceremony in New Delhi. Among those in my delegation were Senate Majority Leader Howard Baker and all living former ambassadors to India: Senator Pat Moynihan, Harvard Professor John Kenneth Galbraith, former Princeton President Robert Goheen, and former Senator John Sherman Cooper. India under Indira Gandhi had been basically pro-Soviet; relations with the United States had been generally sour and unproductive. Howard Baker said that he once spent "the worst three minutes of my life" with her. I recalled meeting with her myself. At first, she sat in silence; I waited for her to fill the vacuum. Eventually, she spoke up, and we wound up having a good talk.

India had made a major arms purchase from the Soviets just a month before Mrs. Gandhi's assassination. Our relations, nevertheless, had been improving since her State visit to Washington in July 1982 and my visit to India the following year, a development strengthened somewhat through our counterterrorism policy. In early July 1984, eight Sikh separatists had hijacked an Indian Airlines flight and demanded $25 million in reparations for the storming of the Golden Temple in Amritsar the previous month. When the hijackers surrendered in Pakistan, we helped persuade the Pakistanis to return them to India. Now I saw the occasion of this meeting with Rajiv Gandhi as an opportunity to build further and make a fresh start with this new leader.

On the aircraft I briefed Howard Baker and Pat Moynihan on my ideas about how we should proceed with the Soviets. Art Hartman had seen Gromyko in Moscow the day before. The Soviets were starting to bite on the idea of returning to arms control negotiations and were moving toward the way we wanted to structure them. But U.S.-Soviet relations overall remained chilly despite the promise shown by the Gromyko visit. When my delegation was briefed on arrival in Delhi by Ambassador Harry

Barnes, he told us of a Soviet propaganda campaign attempting to link the United States to Mrs. Gandhi's assassination, an outrageous notion.

The ritual cremation was a tough ceremony. Rajiv Gandhi poured ghee, clarified butter, over the corpse and then set the sandalwood pyre alight. He brushed his torch lightly over his mother's body. Loudspeakers blared, the crowd heaved and moaned. After the Vedic rite, in which the soul is said to be released to heaven as the skull cracks in the heat, the masses of people attending drifted away. The son stayed behind to gather the ashes and cast them into the sacred Jumna River, which flows into the Ganges, even more sacred.

After the ceremony, I went to the Soviet embassy in New Delhi to meet Soviet Premier Nikolai Tikhonov. My CIA briefing paper on him described an old, doddering man holding a ceremonial post and out of the action. In came a bouncy, lively individual, fully prepared to debate me energetically. I was amazed and startled; so much for our "intelligence." I told Tikhonov that President Reagan wanted the Soviets to know that if re-elected, he "will do everything he can to help bring about a relationship with the Soviet Union that will be a problem-solving relationship."

Tikhonov demurred. "If the president remains on the same course, it won't be good," he said, "but if he was to change course, that would be good. Now we have a different viewpoint on practically all issues between us: the arms race, the economic field, everywhere. So is this talk not a preelection tactic?"

I told Tikhonov that he missed my point: "I am giving you a private statement of intent by the president." Howard Baker and Pat Moynihan supported my statements, adding a senatorial perspective.

At the end, Tikhonov said, "I don't know one person in his right mind in the Soviet Union who would not want better relations with the United States. If President Reagan wants improved relations, we are ready."

"Let's shake on that," I replied. I told him to stop the propaganda broadcasts charging American involvement in the death of Indira Gandhi.

Tikhonov's reply was rambling. In effect what he said was "Soviet media have never suggested that the United States was behind Gandhi's murder, but we are going to stop."

My next call was to President Zia ul-Haq of Pakistan. It was getting on into the evening, and he and his entourage of note takers and experts were arranged in a semicircle all attired in tight black tunics over white leggings. Their appearance was elegant, their manner grand and gracious. I felt as if I had stumbled into the throne room of the emperor of all pandas.

Again the talk was of the Soviets—the Soviet occupation of Afghanistan and the continuing war in that beleaguered country. This was a military threat to Pakistan and a social burden, as 3 million Afghans had fled eastward across the border. American-Pakistani cooperation was crucial to support of the Afghan freedom fighters, who were giving the Soviets fits. The Soviets had enlarged their forces, Zia said, and were gaining more control over the country; in some areas they had been able to seal off the border against outside support for the resistance fighters. "But the Soviets cannot control Afghanistan unless Pakistan behaves," Zia said. So the Soviets, through their military and economic leverage with India, were using India to pressure Pakistan, to force the Pakistanis to worry about India as much as about Afghanistan. The Soviets thus sought to worsen relations between India and Pakistan.

This was a classic balance-of-power play and revealed how much a change in India's attitude under Rajiv Gandhi could mean for security in the region. Like me, Zia wanted to use the coming to office of Rajiv to make such a change. Zia's foreign minister, the suave and worldly Yaqub Khan, remarked about the current Soviet effort to portray the United States— and Pakistan—as implicated in the assassination of Mrs. Gandhi. "Their object is to sow discord and suspicion and negate your effort to better U.S. relations with India, which Pakistan favors."

I spoke to Zia about our worry based on evidence that Pakistan's nuclear program was developing a weapons capability. Senator Baker underlined our concern. "We are alive, sir, to the problem," said Zia. "We support your [nonproliferation] policy, and we implement it. But the difference for Pakistan is what is happening around here." He was referring to India's nuclear program and the established fact that India had set off one test explosion. When Pat Moynihan pressed about Pakistan's ability to make a nuclear weapon, Zia said, "We are nowhere near it. We have no intention of making such a weapon. We renounce our right to make such a weapon. But please do not discriminate against Pakistan. Look at what is happening in the region!"

Late that night, the three of us—Baker, Moynihan, and I—had almost completed the rounds. We had called on Rajiv Gandhi and had held bilateral meetings into double digits. We were exhausted. But our evening was not at an end. Our last stop was at the residence of the British high commissioner, where Prime Minister Thatcher was waiting to greet us. She briskly ushered us into the study. It was an English country house in India. Fine books and prints of rural churches lined the walls. A carved wooden hobbyhorse rocked at a touch in the corner. The fireplace was lit. Mrs. Thatcher clapped her hands, and servants in scarlet fan-topped turbans appeared: a bearer of scotch; a bearer of soda water; a bearer of brandy and cognac. A gold and glass clock struck midnight. Senator Moynihan spoke: "Prime Minister, you have not disappointed us. You are the first person we have seen today who has offered us a real drink!"

Mrs. Thatcher picked up a whiskey-soda. "One can take only so much orange juice," she said.

She looked around the room to make sure the servants had departed. She then engaged us in an energetic conversation, which she dominated, on the world's political scene. This was a great opportunity to reverse the trend of the last twenty years during which "India has been closer to the Soviet Union than to the Americans and you Americans have been closer to Pakistan," she said. "Now we have a chance to be close to *both* India and Pakistan and *they* closer to each other." Mrs. Gandhi hated communism, said Thatcher. "She only used it for India's international purposes while never adopting it for India's politics or society." She and Indira Gandhi had been at Somerville College, Oxford, at the same time, she noted. Then came a long Thatcher exposition on arms control. "I know you have thought all about this and already know what I'm about to say but . . ." She wore us down. As we left, Princess Anne emerged to chat. I began to wonder whether the English ever slept.

The Battle in Washington

Back in Washington on the day before our presidential election, I asked Bud McFarlane to come over late in the afternoon. I told him that I was not going to "give away" U.S.-Soviet diplomacy to the NSC staff. There would be no "czar." I said that we had to have one person to be the umbrella man over all the arms control issues. It should be Paul Nitze; he should be ambassador-at-large; and he should report to the president through me. Bud said he agreed it should be Nitze but thought that he "should be housed in the Old Executive Office Building." That way it would be easier to educate the president on the issues; it would show the press and Congress that Ronald Reagan was seriously involved; it also would make it easier for Bud "to coerce the system into more timely products."

"I'm not persuaded," I replied.

On Tuesday, November 6, Ronald Reagan was reelected in a landslide victory. I telephoned my congratulations to him the next day at the California White House: "Good morning, Mr. President for four more years!" I opened. "This is a terrific personal victory for you and also a mandate for your agenda, but how come you blew Minnesota?"

The president took the occasion of his electoral victory to send General Secretary Chernenko a forward-looking letter. Oleg Sokolov, the Soviet embassy's chargé, when delivering Chernenko's reply, stressed the extraordinary quickness of the general secretary's response. The letter itself was positive and upbeat. And wire services were reporting from Moscow that Soviet officials were expecting me to meet Gromyko in Moscow in January.

So the Soviets appeared to be getting more active as they faced four more years of Ronald Reagan.

We, at that very moment, seemed to be going the other way. Ken Adelman, director of the Arms Control and Disarmament Agency, went public in an interview in the *Wall Street Journal* on November 12, 1984, with his notion of "arms control without agreements": that a series of unilateral but reciprocated steps be encouraged, thus avoiding the complexities, the ambiguities, and the potential restrictions of formal agreements. Earlier he had shown me an article he had written and proposed to submit to *Foreign Affairs,* and I had told him that would be "very unwise." This was a topic for internal discussion. He went ahead and published it anyway.[1] It was outrageous that one of the president's appointees should argue in public for a major policy shift without putting it first to the president. This was a presidential-level decision, and the article sent an erroneous signal that the president was not interested in arms control negotiations. I knew the president's reluctance to fire anyone, so I took Adelman to the woodshed myself for his lack of judgment in taking his personal viewpoint public. I also gave him my own view that I thought his idea was dumb. He went away upset and an hour or so later sent back a note: "I appreciate your frankness. I am sensitive to the concern that some might misinterpret my article as saying the days of traditional, formal arms control agreements are over."

Jim Baker spoke to me about the article. A mess has been created, he said, but once again he said "you are winning, so what's your complaint?" Jimmy Carter appeared on a morning television show the next day, November 14, pointing to the notorious split in the administration and saying that the president must decide whether the United States will negotiate seriously on arms control or not. Within an hour or so, word came over that the White House wanted to hype my regularly scheduled meeting with the president—to show that the president "has decided on the direction we will go."

I asked Bud McFarlane to attend that key meeting, at 1:30 in the afternoon on Wednesday, November 14, at which I would give my detailed views to the president. We talked for a full hour, after which I spent another half hour with Bud. I told the president that his administration was deeply divided and that I wanted to set my views out for him. "Standing still with the Soviets is not an option. The choice is to negotiate new agreements or enter a world with no arms limitations. Opponents of negotiations are not troubled by the disappearance of arms control. They argue that nothing useful has resulted, that agreements will undermine public support for

---

1. Adelman's article appeared in the Winter 1984–85 issue of *Foreign Affairs.*

defense, and that arms control should be an exercise in public relations."
In fact, I said, "negotiations have produced security-enhancing agreements." I called attention to the Austrian State Treaty, the Berlin Accords,
the Atmospheric Test Ban, the Nonproliferation Treaty, and the Outer
Space Treaty as examples. I pointed out that the SALT I Treaty put a cap
on further growth in the number of Soviet launchers at a time when we
had no program to increase ours and that the ABM Treaty prevented costly
deployment of systems that would not have yielded reliable defense, given
the technology at the time.

I had asked the CIA to tell me what a world without current nuclear
arms limits and with no arms control agreements in force would look like
down the line. I got back the view that in such a scenario Soviet missile
warheads would likely double over the next ten years. I noted to the president that this doubling did not assume any vast new commitment of Soviet
resources but that the effort to keep pace with them on ballistic missiles
was very costly for us, politically as well as financially. An "unconstrained
environment," I argued, "is detrimental to the security interests of the
United States.

"We need to do better than existing agreements," I said, "and seek
reductions in the numbers of warheads, as you have proposed." I also
argued that the opponents of arms control misread the key relationship
between arms control efforts and public support for defense spending.
"Congress," I argued, "will not support key weapons systems without
meaningful negotiations. Similarly, allied support will be problematic if
arms control efforts unravel. Extreme positions and inflexibility will not
enhance our position but undermine it. Thanks to your policies, the United
States is confident and strong and the question now is whether we use
strength to achieve significant new accords with the Soviets or see an unlimited increase in nuclear weapons, along with greater tension. Most people in your administration are quite comfortable with the present situation,"
I said, "and are doing all they can to block any effort to engage with the
Soviets and to achieve arms control agreements."

The president interjected frequently as I talked, and it was clear he had
thought all this through. His point of view mirrored my own. It troubled
him that people within his administration opposed the kind of arms control
agreements he had advocated and even opposed an attempt to build a
constructive relationship with the Soviets.

At the end of our discussion, I told the president, "To succeed, we have
to have a team: right now there isn't one. Cap Weinberger, Bill Casey,
Jeane Kirkpatrick, and I just don't see things the same way." Leaks, end
runs, cutting people out, refusing to follow through on decisions—all these
tactics were constantly in use. "I have always been able to develop a team
wherever I have worked," I said. "Here I have been unable to do it. I can't

produce a team for you. I'm frustrated and I'm ready to step aside so you can put somebody else in at State who can get along with them. You will see no results without a team."

The president told me he wouldn't stand for any thought that I would leave. "I'm not ducking out," I said. "There's nothing I'd rather do than stay here with you and work out these problems. I have no hidden agenda." I left it at that.

I talked to Jim Baker the next day. "I'm concerned that though I've had this discussion with the president, the process will just drift along as before and nothing will happen," I said. Baker urged that when reporters at the State Department noon briefing asked the question "Will Shultz stay or go?" State's spokesman should answer clearly that I would stay. When John Hughes had been asked that question on the previous day, he had, on my instructions, resisted giving a clear answer. "The president will deal with the problem," Baker assured me. Baker said he thought that two new ambassadorial appointments would be made: Jeane Kirkpatrick to Paris and Cap Weinberger to London. I was sure that that would never happen. Actually, it could have been a great idea: Jeane loved France, and Cap loved England. Bud McFarlane telephoned to say that the president intended to speak personally to the others involved to get them to pull together and that Meese, Baker, and Deaver had asked Vice President Bush to weigh in after that. I had stirred things up, and that was to the good, but I had no illusions that the battle would end.

In the president's postelection letter to Chernenko, he suggested that we each appoint a high-level official, in whom we had special confidence, to deal with arms control. I was determined that Paul Nitze should be our man and that the chain of command should run from Nitze to me to President Reagan. Interagency committees would meet, and NSC members would fight for their views, but ultimately the decisions would be made through the Nitze-Shultz-Reagan lineup. This idea, I knew, would evoke more protest: Nitze had been considered "soft" and "uncontrollable" by many hard-liners in the administration ever since his walk in the woods.[2]

Larry Silberman, a colleague from my Labor Department days, came by to see me. His views were harsh but candid: the Shultz-Weinberger poison was draining the administration; the main battleground was Soviet relations and arms control; if control was put in White House hands, it would be disastrous; a "miasma of distrust" hung over Washington created by events such as Ken Adelman's *Foreign Affairs* article and Rick Burt's

---

2. See Chapter 11 for a brief account of Nitze's attempt to work out in 1982 the outline of an INF settlement during a walk in the woods with his Soviet counterpart. Nitze's effort was imaginative, but the results were not accepted in Moscow or in Washington.

leaks on the internal debate to Strobe Talbott. "Burt is the author of Talbott's book," Silberman observed.[3]

I told John Hughes, when he got the inevitable question at his noon briefing, to confirm that I would be staying on as secretary of state. I also told Bud McFarlane to make sure that no one at the White House took the announcement as a sign that I felt the problems had been resolved. At the end of the day, the president called to say that he had talked personally and separately to Cap Weinberger and Bill Casey and that now things "would work out okay."

Bill Casey was also in touch. "We've had a few disagreements, but I'm a great supporter of yours," he said. By this time, and of special significance to me, I had the president's go-ahead to pick Paul Nitze and to move toward a meeting with Gromyko.

On Saturday morning, November 17, in the White House staff dining room, I talked to Paul over breakfast. "I think this process is about to break open," I told him. He was raring to go.

An Exchange of Letters

By November 15, I had in President Reagan's hands a draft of a longer and more substantive message to General Secretary Chernenko than the one the president had sent right after the election. This became the formal vehicle for a tough-talking debate over the next few weeks. By November 16, the president had signed the letter, which went directly to Ambassador Hartman for delivery in Moscow. In it was a long and constructive review of the recent history of the U.S.-Soviet relationship with suggestions about all points on our four-part agenda. In the key paragraph, President Reagan wrote:

> In our correspondence and in your public statements, you have placed great stress on the question of negotiations on "preventing the militarization of outer space." In his discussions here Mr. Gromyko reaffirmed the importance the Soviet Union attaches to this issue. As I said in our meeting, the United States is ready to meet with you to discuss space weapons, and we have no preconditions as to the form or scope of the discussions. At the same time, we believe that the most pressing issue is how to begin the process of reducing offensive nuclear arms. I think your own experts would agree that these two areas are inherently related, even though we may ultimately choose, as was the case in the past, to discuss them in separate negotiating fora. The broader umbrella consultations I have suggested could give us a vehicle for agreeing on approaches to the interrelated issues.

3. Silberman believed that Rick Burt had provided much raw material for Strobe Talbott's *Deadly Gambits: The Reagan Administration and the Stalemate in Nuclear Arms Control* (New York: Alfred A. Knopf, 1984).

The Soviets did not give Art Hartman an immediate appointment. The next day we discovered why. A letter from Chernenko dated November 17 came in to the president:

> We propose that the Soviet Union and the United States of America enter into new negotiations with the objective of reaching mutually acceptable agreements on the whole range of questions concerning nuclear and space weapons. . . . There is an organic, and I would say, objective relationship between these issues and it is precisely in this way that they should be treated at the negotiations we are proposing. In other words, such negotiations must encompass both the issue of nonmilitarization of space and the questions of strategic nuclear arms and medium-range nuclear systems. In all these directions we are prepared to seek most radical solutions which would allow movement toward a complete ban and eventually liquidation of nuclear arms.

Chernenko then went on to say, "In order to settle these matters, we propose that A. A. Gromyko and George Shultz meet, let's say in the first half of January 1985. We would be prepared for this purpose to receive the Secretary of State in Moscow, or such a meeting could be arranged in a third country as may be agreed by the sides."

This letter was delivered to Rick Burt by the minister counselor at the Soviet embassy in Washington, Viktor Isakov, who explicitly noted how pleased he was to be delivering this message, since "for the first time in four years we can say we may be in business." I sent Chernenko's letter to President Reagan immediately with a covering memo, saying that Chernenko "accepts your approach of negotiations on both space weapons and offensive weapons, including both strategic weapons and what they call medium-range weapons, in other words INF." I also pointed out to the president that Chernenko's reply in fact specifically acknowledged an "organic" and "objective relationship" between defenses in space and offensive systems.

On Thanksgiving Day, November 22, we announced in both Washington and Moscow that Andrei Gromyko and I would meet in Geneva on January 7 and 8, 1985, "to enter into new negotiations with the objective of reaching mutually acceptable agreements on the whole range of questions concerning nuclear and outer space arms." I felt a sense of excitement that finally we were to embark on an effort of immense significance. The basic policy of strength, realism, and readiness to negotiate had paid off. Now the work would begin.

Prepare and Battle

From the moment of the official announcement, my life was dominated by preparations for the meeting to come. I faced a battle, I knew, with Cap

Weinberger and Bill Casey over the content of our positions at that meeting and over the attitude and spirit of our approach. I had a great advantage: I knew that I was on the president's wavelength, so my task was to get his views firmly embedded in my instructions.

I also knew that I would have to struggle to control the management of the U.S.-Soviet relationship in general and the conduct of the upcoming Gromyko meeting in particular. To be successful, I would have to deepen my knowledge of the intricacies of arms control. I installed Paul Nitze in an office as close to mine as possible, and the president nominated him to carry the rank and title of ambassador-at-large. I counted on Paul for ideas, advice, and representation to the Congress, the allies, and key people in other departments. I also counted on him to help me prepare personally for the Gromyko meeting and for the inevitable administration struggle as the date approached.

Nitze had been "present at the creation," when the post–World War II era was taking shape. He was one of the now almost legendary statesmen who had seen the promise of a peaceful, prosperous future turn suddenly cold. The Soviet Union emerged as a powerful totalitarian force determined to plow under the values and institutions of democracy. Throughout the difficult and testing time of the cold war, tough policies and strong allies had kept the West stable, growing, and able to deter a "hot" war. Of the key players involved in the development of the grand postwar strategy, the only one still in service was Nitze. From a half century of involvement, he was a walking history of the cold war as well as one of the creators of the doctrines by which the alliance of democracies had proved able to contain Soviet power. He had been involved in nearly every major decision of the U.S.-Soviet military confrontation. He was just the man to help me master the incredibly complex issues of arms control.

At age seventy-seven, Paul Nitze's face was tanned from winters on the ski slopes of Aspen, summers on his boat in Maine, and springs and autumns riding horses at his farm near Washington. His manner sparkled with a youthfulness that made colleagues forty years his junior seem tired and spent. He walked with an angular bend to his slender frame that did not impart an impression of age but rather the crafty wisdom of a character out of Shakespeare, whose plays Nitze carried with him on his almost constant travels. Some called him "the most underrated man in Washington," but everyone I knew who dealt with him rated him as formidable indeed.

We were smack in the middle of what was ever more clearly shaping up to be the endgame of the cold war. To me, the essence of it all was whether America and its allies would have both the will and resolve to conduct a policy toward the Soviet Union in which strength and diplomacy worked in tandem. In 1967, Pierre Harmel, then the foreign minister of Belgium, made a report to NATO that bore his name. The Harmel Report stated that NATO's fundamental task was to "maintain adequate military strength and political solidarity to deter aggression and other forms of pressure and to defend the territory of member countries if aggression should occur." It described the need for a suitable military capability to ensure the balance of forces in Europe and to create a climate of stability and confidence. Harmel's approach then outlined the second task for NATO: "to pursue the search for progress towards a more stable relationship in which the underlying political issues can be solved." That approach, strength *and* diplomacy, was key. In Paul Nitze I found a diplomatic soul mate who shared my view that strength and diplomacy had to be used together.

On Monday, November 19, I met Nitze for our first long, substantive discussion. Paul was eager to get to work but warned that he could not be out of the United States for long periods because of his wife's ill health. And at his age, he said, he could not fulfill the classic negotiator's "iron pants" role. I said I didn't want him for that: I wanted him for ideas and for close-in help to me, starting with an intense tutorial on all the ins and outs of the arms control process. As for the present "interagency process," Paul said, it was producing only "grief"; nothing could come out of it. I would use that process properly, I said, but decisions would be made by the president, not just emerge as the lowest common denominator of differing interagency views. So Paul and I had a deal, and our partnership was sealed.

President Reagan that day gave his full approval to a Shultz-Gromyko meeting in January. In diplomacy, location counts for something. We would propose Geneva, but the president was willing to accept Moscow if the Soviets resisted. I wanted to insist on Geneva to start and then move to a home-and-home (Moscow, Washington, Moscow) format. To get the Soviets to come back to Geneva after their highly propagandized walkout at the INF and START talks there in 1983 would be a significant symbolic step—and one that would not be easy for them. Even Richard Perle favored Geneva, although in earlier years he had argued against negotiations there, saying that Soviet spies were everywhere.

Later that day, I saw Foreign Minister Claude Cheysson, who told me privately that the French had invited General Secretary Chernenko to visit Paris in the spring. The Soviets had replied affirmatively, "depending on Chernenko's health." That was an astonishing revelation for the Soviets to make. If the Soviet general secretary was in poor health, I realized, decisions would be hard to get; if he died, another transition would delay progress and interrupt the momentum that I could feel building.

The interagency process that Nitze had derided was now taken over by Bud McFarlane. What had been called the Sack-pig (SACPG, or Strategic Arms Control Policy Group) was now reformed as Sack-gee (SACG or Senior Arms Control Group). I was determined not to let the interagency process divert us. It was a formula for stalemate. We were once again head-to-head with "the two Richards," Perle and Burt.

On November 25, Rick Burt was on one of the Sunday talk shows and said that we and the Soviets were starting "a negotiating process." Instantly, screams of alarm and anger came from the hard-liners. McFarlane called me to complain about Burt. "Whatever it is we are doing, I get told it's just too sensitive a matter even to *think* of it as a negotiation!" I exploded. It was absurd. Within a day or so, almost predictably, the issue of "slave labor" in the Soviet Union surfaced within the administration. This was a favorite of the hard-liners. By seeking to prove that forced labor existed in the Soviet Union—and, of course, it did—the opponents of a better relationship would periodically try to halt diplomatic progress in its tracks. The problem was that there was no way to connect forced labor to any of the trickle of imports to the United States from the Soviet Union. (The law required U.S. customs to bar products made with forced labor from entering the United States.) The resurfacing of this alarm indicated that the opponents of arms control negotiations were convinced that progress was on the horizon. They feared agreements. They thought the Soviets would outnegotiate us and then cheat. I disagreed. We could outnegotiate them and catch them if they cheated. But it meant we would have to compromise and have to realize that nothing is perfect or airtight.

On Wednesday, November 28, I went over to the Pentagon for a private breakfast with Cap Weinberger. I told him that I wanted to work with him, and that I knew he stuck to a position once he took it. Therefore, I said, "I would like to talk issues out with you as they come up—and before you make up your mind." I proposed that he, Casey, McFarlane, and I meet once a week for lunch in the White House so that we could talk over the big issues, particularly Soviet issues, but others as well. Cap agreed, in a reserved way. Later in the day, I went to see the president and put the idea to him. I suggested that he attend from time to time. He liked the idea and said we could use the Old Family Dining Room in the White House residence. That would give a special weight and feel to our gatherings. So that was the start of what became "the Family Group." Some family.

The next day, Jeane Kirkpatrick saw the president to hand in her resignation. Jim Baker had alerted me to this beforehand, and I had agreed with the idea, being boosted by Vice President Bush, that Vernon (Dick) Walters replace her as UN ambassador. I saw this as a chance to get the UN ambassador position out of the cabinet; it had become a job of greater stature than its substance warranted, and the tensions between our mission to the United Nations and the UN bureau at State made coordination of our policy and voting in New York a nightmare. Jeane Kirkpatrick was a powerful presence in the cabinet room. She would slowly take off her glasses, pause dramatically, toss them down on the table, compelling everyone's attention, and say, "Mister President," elongating the two words so that they filled a paragraph's length of time and seemed freighted with critical meaning. So one of my critics on Central America policy and on negotiations with the Soviets had decided to give up the contest.

Bud McFarlane, who had alerted me to his own impending resignation—this time on Friday, November 30—telephoned me to say, "Nothing dramatic will happen tomorrow." So he had decided to stay on for the time being.

Our first Family Group lunch in the White House residence took place on Saturday, December 1. Cap was impossible; he was not even willing to have us reiterate to the Soviets our own START and INF positions. He took up most of the time, elaborating endlessly on his positions, setting up straw men and knocking them down. When I spoke, he half-closed his eyes. Nothing was accomplished. As the lunch came to an end, Bud McFarlane was visibly shaking with frustration. Immediately he spoke to me again about resigning. He would stay to help get the arms control talks going and that would be it, he told me privately. "You should be able to see," he said, "no series of lunches is going to help us out of this mess."

It had now become known, at least internally, that Paul Nitze would be the top adviser on arms control. Ed Rowny asked to see me and accused Nitze of being soft on the Soviets and of exceeding instructions. Nitze would sell out, implied Rowny. "If you take Nitze, take me, too," he said; "otherwise you are asking for trouble." He was off-base on Nitze and making a deliberate threat. If I did not include him, Rowny was in effect warning me, he would mobilize the hard-liners against me. I did include him to the degree that he would not be embarrassed, but Nitze was the man of breadth, intellect, and experience on whom I relied.

If the hard-liners didn't like Nitze, their opponents didn't either. Rick Burt privately complained: "What's behind the Nitze thing? He's seventy-seven. He doesn't take orders. He's too iconoclastic." Burt sent me a memo with his suggestions for who should be in the meetings in Geneva: Shultz, Burt, Jack Matlock, and Art Hartman. He relegated Nitze to a marginal role. In accordance with the general unreality of this nondelegation to a nonnegotiation, we also had a non-Nitze. There was no announcement about his new role: at first because the Soviets did not respond well to the idea of each side having a trusted individual to serve as the umbrella holder over the entire range of issues, and later because the more publicity there was, the more political trouble would be stirred up. The domestic politics of arms control would be tougher to manage than the Soviets themselves. As I had learned long ago in the world of labor-management talks, the toughest negotiations take place within your own team, on your own side of the table. Finally, to reinforce Nitze's position, the president put his public imprimatur on Paul's role: he announced on December 5, "At the recommendation of the Secretary of State, I have today asked Ambassador

Paul Nitze to serve as the adviser to the Secretary for the Geneva talks. Ambassador Nitze has a long history of distinguished service to his country, and I am very pleased that he has accepted."

I then had to decide who would be in my delegation. Instantly, Bud let me know that I couldn't call it a "delegation" because that would imply a "negotiation" and politically the president couldn't take that. Whatever my group would be called, I decided I would include everyone in the administration with any serious claim to a piece of the arms control action. I had received lots of advice to the contrary, along lines that a large delegation would imply to the Soviets that we had not come to grips successfully with the known divisions in the administration. I thought the expertise just might be useful to have on hand and on the spot. I also thought it would present an opportunity to pull people together. If we reached an agreement, everyone would have been involved and therefore would be more likely to be supportive.

In the preparatory process, the senior interagency discussion would be run by Bud McFarlane. Periodically, results and issues would be brought to President Reagan and his top advisers. Parallel to that, I would meet alone with Nitze every day. Out of this process would come written instructions from the president. Once we had left for Geneva, I would expect my "delegation" to support the course decided on by the president. No more bickering. Once at work in Geneva, I would bring the delegation into every aspect of what was going on. I decided to rehabilitate Ken Adelman. He had made a mistake, but like other arms control specialists who seemed to oppose everything when on the outside, he turned helpful when included.

Meetings of the National Security Council were held in December to work over the core arms control issues and to get the president's attention and his guidance. Ronald Reagan's views were definite: all nuclear weapons should be eliminated, and strategic defense should take over the role of deterrence. He was annoyed with me for expressing reservations. I pointed out that offensive weapons were needed and that even the most far-reaching version of his dream of strategic defense was incomplete. What about defense against bombers, stealth aircraft, sea-launched cruise missiles? SDI wouldn't cover them. The Soviets didn't need to be convinced about the importance of strategic defense; they had always valued it. It was the United States that had deprived itself intellectually and actually of such defenses. SDI was essential, I agreed, but it was not everything. The president listened, but he didn't give any ground.

The Soviets now had been told about the unusually large number of people I was going to bring with me to Geneva and said they were confused. What did it mean? I told Rick Burt to tell them that it meant we would have all our expertise assembled and ready to work, but that only four people would join me at the table.

ON THE MOVE

Consultations with our allies were also part of my preparations for Geneva. On the way to the annual meeting of NATO foreign ministers in Brussels, I stopped on December 11 at Chevening, the British Foreign Office's country estate in Surrey. Originally given to the first earl of Stanhope by George I for his services in the War of the Spanish Succession, it was deeded to the nation when the Stanhope line ran out with the seventh earl. The American embassy in London was in the bequest: if the British didn't want it, the Americans could have it. We arrived in the evening as fog enveloped the mansion. Geoffrey Howe welcomed me and soon squired me into the library, showing me an autographed first edition of Adam Smith's *Wealth of Nations* and a note from Benjamin Franklin describing his stay at Chevening. My staff went to the nearby village for a pint at the local Frog and Bucket while Geoffrey and I reviewed Soviet affairs. The magnificent old house creaked like a pirate ship. I got little sleep. In the middle of the night a clock in the grand entry hall struck fourteen.

In Brussels the next day, I found the Europeans relieved that a U.S.-Soviet relationship was in the offing, but they revealed little confidence that we could make progress on any arms control initiative. SDI baffled them. I disagreed politely with my colleagues. I could sense that a new era in East-West relations was possible—not only because of changes that we were inducing in the Soviet Union, and which their own foundering political and economic system was imposing on them, but because of the realities of "the information age."

I outlined the U.S. approach to the Gromyko meeting, promised full consultation as we proceeded, and welcomed their advice. The communiqué stressed the allies' "determination to continue [INF] deployments" in the absence of a "concrete negotiated result" and welcomed the Gromyko meeting as part of an effort "to bring about an improved East-West relationship."

I also took the occasion to work on the Belgians and the Dutch about going forward with deployments in accordance with the NATO schedule. I said in a press conference, "It is harmful if undertakings are not adhered to. And it is certainly the case that if the Soviets could have their way without giving up anything or engaging in negotiations, it would be discouraging to negotiations." All in all, the NATO meetings were unusually free of contention. The cohesion of our alliance, so critical to security and progress, was holding fast.

I had left Paul Nitze in Washington to continue preparations for Geneva. When I returned, I found massive disagreement among the participants in the interagency process. "We must have something to say," I told the National Security Planning Group on December 17. "If my meeting with Gromyko breaks up in a huff, we must then go public with a credible position that *the Soviets* walked away from." But I did not like an approach of "preparing to fail." Tension was building from the clash of all the big and incompatible egos among the arms control mandarins. Jack Chain said of Ed Rowny, "He's been running around with his hair on fire" about what role he would get in the Geneva drama.

"That's a sure way to lose his part," I replied.

I met at length with Nitze, and we probed some of the scientific details of the SDI program. Paul had visited the laboratories, and his long experience enabled him to grasp the meaning of the technical complexities to which he was exposed. From his briefing to me it appeared that our scientists were working on a form of strategic defense that would not involve the use of nuclear explosions. If we were to ban all nuclear weapons in space—which seemed to be Gromyko's particular fixation—we could still proceed to develop a workable SDI. I felt we should pursue this differentiation between nuclear and nonnuclear. It might actually work in space negotiations.

Evidence was accumulating that Mikhail Gorbachev was "the man to watch" in the Soviet Union. The idea arose of inviting him to come to the United States so we could size him up as a person and expose him a little to America. The invitation would be extended through Don Kendall, the president of Pepsico, who did extensive business in the Soviet Union. He asked whether Gorbachev could be assured of being able to meet in Washington with the president and me. We were delayed in responding to Kendall by Bill Casey's objection that this would be "playing up" to Gorbachev and would anger Chernenko. I talked the matter over with President Reagan and McFarlane, and we decided to give the assurance and to tell Kendall to go ahead with the invitation. Our knowledge of the Kremlin was thin, and the CIA, I found, was usually wrong about it. In any case, we wanted to meet Gorbachev, and American foreign policy should not be the prisoner of an exercise in Kremlinology.

Our appetite was whetted by Gorbachev's performance on a visit to London. In an address at a luncheon hosted by Geoffrey Howe on December 17, he reiterated the readiness of the Soviet Union for significant reductions in nuclear arms but insisted on the related importance of halting development of defensive weapons in space. "Gorbachov [sic] links arms curb to star wars ban," headlined the London *Times* on December 18. In a sentence that caught President Reagan's attention, Gorbachev said, "The Soviet Union is prepared . . . to advance towards the complete prohibition and eventual elimination of nuclear weapons."

He also caught the imagination of the British public and their leadership. "I like Mr. Gorbachev. We can do business together," Margaret Thatcher declared.

On Friday evening, December 21, a letter from Chernenko to Reagan arrived. It called for the elimination of all nuclear weapons and of "strike weapons" in space. Was it the Soviet view, we wondered, that SDI aspired to place weapons in space designed to hit targets on earth? Dobrynin delivered the letter to me and pointed up the issue of "how the three aspects [outer space, INF, START] are going to be related and whether the U.S. is willing to negotiate on outer space or will continue to pursue its cosmos fantasy." He also said that Chernenko was disturbed by our refusal to call the Geneva meeting a negotiation.

The Soviets Move Toward Our Agenda

Nevertheless, I realized, the Soviets now were leaning toward us, moving toward *our* agenda. And the hard-liners in the administration were serving a purpose by worrying the Soviets that we might scrap the talks and just go on building up our military strength in ways that they could not match, either in money or in technology. SDI was our flagship in that regard.

That Friday, December 21, I convened what was to be my first productive Family Group lunch. Bill Casey admitted that our rhetoric on verification had carried us too far. Perfect verification simply could not be delivered, he argued, so we needed to be more careful and measured in our statements on the subject. I took this as a good sign that he was thinking in positive terms about the possibilities of negotiated outcomes.

I had also succeeded fairly well by now in my postelection attempt to get control of the personnel appointment process, to dump the deadwood and bring in quality people. In doing so, some protégés of right-wingers in the Senate and in the kitchen cabinet were on the outs. Evans and Novak's column had charged me with a purge.

Ed Feulner, head of the Heritage Foundation, said, "It's not unfair to say that there are very serious differences in this administration between what I call the true believers and the pragmatists. . . . Pragmatists want to resolve problems, and the true believers want to change institutions and leave a lasting legacy for this administration.[4] The term "pragmatist" had become a dirty word in some Washington circles. Art Buchwald called me a "closet pragmatist," but I was in no closet. I was proud to be a pragmatist. Principled pragmatism is America's philosophy. Evans and Novak began to talk of pragmatism as if it were some revolutionary doctrine of guerrilla fighters. It amused me to think of my State Department arms control colleagues as a bunch of "fire-in-the-belly pragmatists." I was reminded of a slogan attributed to the Argentine government, "Moderation or Death!"

Margaret Thatcher arrived for a whirlwind visit on December 22, a Saturday. President Reagan and Nancy were at Camp David, so, with Bud

4. Quoted in a *Washington Post* editorial by Philip Geyelin on December 27, 1985.

McFarlane, Ambassador Charlie Price, and Rick Burt, I went up by helicopter in the early morning to brief the president before she arrived. At 10:30 sharp, President Reagan drove his golf cart to the Camp David helicopter pad to greet her and take her to Aspen Lodge for a private talk. We convened an expanded meeting and working lunch beginning at 11:15. By 1:30, I was escorting her by helicopter back to Andrews Air Force Base, where her plane waited to take her back to London. She exuded intellectual energy throughout her time with us. The president had immense confidence in her, and her views carried great weight.

She was enthusiastic about Gorbachev, as had been clear from her public statements. But her real purpose was to register her views on my coming meeting with Gromyko. She was a firm supporter of research on strategic defense and wanted to make that clear to the Soviets: "Wedge driving is just not on." But she worried about the possibility that the United States might go it alone in eventual deployment, thereby "decoupling" itself from Western Europe.

The president said of Mutual Assured Destruction, "I don't think there's any morality in that at all." President Reagan wanted to transcend it with SDI; Margaret Thatcher considered it essential.

"Next year we will have had peace in Europe for forty years," she remarked. "That is a very long period of peace. We are going to have to live with that same doctrine for a considerable period of time." After intense discussion, President Reagan and Prime Minister Thatcher agreed on a four-point statement, and she announced it with enthusiasm: "First, the United States and Western aim is not to achieve superiority but to maintain balance, taking account of Soviet developments. Second, SDI-related deployments will, in view of treaty obligations, have to be a matter of negotiations. Third, the overall aim is to enhance and not to undermine deterrence. And fourth, East-West negotiation should aim to achieve security, with reduced levels of offensive systems on both sides."

It was an excellent statement: it differentiated between research and deployment of space-based defense and gave me some running room in Geneva. Since the president had signed on, my instructions would reflect what had been agreed upon. The argument coming from Cap and others at the Defense Department that we should not be willing to discuss SDI in any way was bypassed. I observed that Bud McFarlane had played a useful role in the meetings. I decided to ask him to be part of my Geneva delegation. I wanted him on board and to be a part of the outcome.

In late December there was a stirring in Congress about members being named to the delegation to Geneva and sitting in on the meetings. I said no—it verged on the unconstitutional in my view. Nonetheless, Senator Bob Dole kept pressing for a joint resolution that would recommend to the president that a congressional group accompany me as "official observers." Once again, as Jimmy Durante said, "Everybody wants to get into da act!"

Negotiations are not a spectator sport. If Congress didn't trust me to speak for the United States, they should ask the president to pick another secretary of state. On Friday, January 4, Senator Dole called me to say that a Senate observer group had been named (Stevens, Wallop, Lugar, Goldwater, Nunn, Moynihan, Pell, Kennedy, Gore), but they did not want to come with me to Geneva. He was frank enough to give me the reason: my session with Gromyko might fail.

As the year came to an end and the upcoming meeting in Geneva grew closer, I saw a parade of visitors who wanted to give me their thoughts. Many who followed Soviet affairs closely felt that a turning point had been reached, but no one really could say why. Hal Sonnenfeldt attributed it to Chernenko but thought that our chances to make arms control progress were slim. Others felt that the Soviets' hard line had produced the successful deployment of INF missiles by the allies in Europe and so Moscow was now turning to "a peace offensive" to try to divide the West.

I myself believed that the turning point had come in 1983, when we successfully deployed intermediate-range missiles in Europe despite Soviet maneuvering and a massive peace offensive. The Soviets, I thought, were realizing that the United States was pulling away in the competition: our military was better, our economy was better, our political will had been demonstrated in "the year of the missile," and on top of it came Ronald Reagan with his Strategic Defense Initiative and his massive electoral victory. The information age was well under way, and the Soviets were going to be left at the station as the train pulled out.

I got a readout from Jack Chain about the Dartmouth Group's encounter with Soviet officials. Former Chairman of the Joint Chiefs of Staff USAF General David Jones reported that the Soviet attitude had changed 100 percent. They now wanted a political atmosphere under which arms control negotiations could make progress. They seriously feared that the U.S. modernization program, along with SDI, meant that we were building a first-strike capability. Gromyko was a powerful figure on the current Kremlin scene, the "Dartmouth" people felt.

On to Geneva

The struggle now centered over my instructions for the upcoming Gromyko session in Geneva. While the focus would be on the scope and structure of renewed arms control talks, the underpinning, I persuaded the president, should be the substantive positions we had developed in 1983 on INF and the flexibility worked through on START over the past year but never presented to the Soviets. Beyond that, we had a philosophy to present about the emerging strategic reality and the need for a shift of emphasis toward defense. The final product—sixteen tightly packed pages—was discussed carefully with the president on December 31. Cap Weinberger, Bud McFarlane, and I were present. Cap argued. Bud and I met his points. The president approved the document, which carried the recommendation of all three of us. I finally had all the negotiating room I needed.

We held this document very closely, forever worrying about leaks that might give a leg up to Gromyko in Geneva. A paragraph was made available for public use that captured our fundamental concept:

> During the next 10 years, the U.S. objective is a radical reduction in the power of existing and planned offensive nuclear arms, as well as the stabilization of the relationship between offensive and defensive nuclear arms, whether on earth or in space. We are even now looking forward to a period of transition to a more stable world, with greatly reduced levels of nuclear arms and an enhanced ability to deter war based upon the increasing contribution of non-nuclear defenses against offensive nuclear arms. This period of transition could lead to the eventual elimination of all nuclear arms, both offensive and defensive. A world free of nuclear arms is an ultimate objective to which we, the Soviet Union, and all other nations can agree.

The instructions were then carefully translated into "talking points," arranged by topics and according to the time in the meetings when we judged they might come up. The talking points took up thirty-five single-spaced pages. I worked both documents over and over. I had never studied so hard in my life. I discovered a Nitze associate, Jim Timbie, a physicist and product of Stanford's Center for International Security and Arms Control. He had a wonderful talent for explaining complicated propositions in a simple and straightforward way. He, Nitze, Jack Chain, and Rick Burt were my tutors. The documents I had in hand were first-class. By the time I left for Geneva, I was master of my brief.

With the large delegation accompanying me to Geneva, pressure mounted over the question of who would actually sit in on the meeting for our side. Rowny wanted in and muttered threats. Adelman was in an uproar because he wanted a seat. Cap wanted Richard Perle. If Perle was in, Burt had to be in. I talked it over with the president. I told him that if we had ten or so people at the table, the message to the Soviets would be that we did not have our act together and that the extras were there as "political commissars." The president and I decided that I would be joined at the table by Bud McFarlane, Paul Nitze, and Art Hartman and that Jack Matlock, fluent in Russian, would be there to take notes. All the others would be nearby to be consulted if needed. I gave this news to the entire delegation and their principals[5] at breakfast in the State Department on Saturday, January 5. I said I was glad to have them all come with me. It was a mark of our seriousness of purpose. But there was no room for disagreements. We knew what the president wanted. "The guy who gets elected gets to make the decisions," I said. "So think more about the theme of elimination of nuclear weapons. Everyone thinks it is rhetoric, but rhetoric said often enough by important people tends to wind up with an operational character to it."

Rick Burt laughed. "Zero option. Let's start with eliminating just one missile," he said.

We would have only one spokesman, Bernie Kalb. "*No one else* is to talk to the press unless it is by my explicit decision," I said.

Cap interjected: "It's a novel idea, to control press contact."

I continued, "When it comes to criticism from within the group, I have a hide like a walrus, but I take a dim view of criticism that comes to me through the newspapers. You can tell me directly; you don't need the press as your intermediary."

Rowny came to see me yet again. He had to have a seat at the table, he pleaded. "It will ruin me not to be there," he said.

"No," I said. At one point he began to describe how he had written a book on *The Ten Commandments of How Not to Negotiate with the Soviets*.

"It must be autobiographical," Tom Simons interjected.

Later that day, January 5, we were on board USAF 972 on the way to Geneva. The press dubbed us "the ship of feuds." Just before takeoff, Cap had given me a memo from the Joint Chiefs saying I should not draw upon any material from our agreed START or INF negotiating positions with Gromyko. That was absolutely contrary to my instructions from the president, to which Cap had agreed. Cap was trying to use the chiefs as a way to narrow my authorized running room. It was too late. Rick Burt asked whether we could give Soviet embassy official Oleg Sokolov a ride to Geneva in our aircraft. It was a wild idea, as I am sure Burt well knew. If I had agreed, the KGB would have taken Sokolov into custody on arrival and debriefed him for forty years. On board the aircraft I gave copies of my talking points to everyone on the delegation. Richard Perle made some good suggestions but complained to McFarlane about the National Security Decision Directive, which was the official U.S. position. Over the Atlantic, Richard Perle spent a long, long time visibly talking with *Washington Post* correspondent Don Oberdorfer in the back of the plane. This created a

5. At breakfast were General Jack Vessey, General Jack Chain, Ron Lehman, Tom Simons, Bernie Kalb, Rick Burt, Ken Adelman, Richard Perle, Bud McFarlane, Cap Weinberger, Bill Casey, Jack Matlock, Doug George, Ed Rowny, Karna Small, Admiral Art Moreau, and Mark Palmer. (Nitze was absent.)

palpable tension all around, as everyone knew my instructions were that no one was to talk to the press except Bernie Kalb.

After we arrived in Geneva, I called Perle to my room and told him he had violated my instructions and that if he didn't like them, he could get on a plane and go home. He said he had not talked to Oberdorfer about arms control. I told him the rule is "no contact" about anything. He said okay. That cleared the air. He turned out to be one of the most helpful members of the delegation.

I then assembled the delegation—twenty-one in all—in the "security bubble" at the U.S. mission: a Plexiglas room with transparent floor, walls, and ceiling and with rushing air surrounding it to render it secure from listening devices. It was designed to hold about eight people and soon began to feel like the Black Hole of Calcutta. I opened by telling the team what the president of the Swiss Confederation had said to me in a brief arrival meeting: "The Swiss fully realize the good life of security, freedom, and prosperity they live is possible because America defends the free world." He had said this from the heart—it was something that few people seemed to realize and fewer still would openly admit. His remark provided a tailwind for our meetings.

I then told the group that there had been one misunderstanding about the press rules and that I had straightened it out with the individual involved. "The stricture is," I said again, "nobody talks to the press." We then embarked on yet another round on the endless complexities of arms control. I listened as Nitze described these horrible, cataclysmic weapons of mass destruction in his genteel, bland manner, as if he were talking about baby farm animals. My delegation was pessimistic and petulant.

The night before I was to meet Gromyko, the delegates roamed the hotel lobby and rode the elevators in rumpled suits and jogging togs. With no press contacts permitted, they seemed to have no purpose in life but to tell each other that the meeting was going to be a disaster and that *they* had told me so. "If only EUR's[6] interim measures approach had been adopted instead of Nitze's offense-defense idea, then we would have had a chance. Or if only . . ." On and on. They clearly were not pleased with Nitze's role. They liked the old approach of phases, or step-by-step movement toward an interim agreement. Paul wanted to bundle offense and defense together and talk about it all at once. If failure came, it would be because Shultz chose Nitze, they implied.

It was almost as if we had come to a wake: have a few drinks, see some old friends, sing some sad songs. All of the anecdotes were about Gromyko. Kvitsinsky had told Nitze, "Gromyko is a very stupid man. He remembers everything he has said and he has had said to him for forty years; he can't see the forest for the trees." I recalled Turkish Foreign Minister Vahit

6. State's Bureau of European and Canadian Affairs.

Halefoglu telling me that after each of three postings as ambassador to Moscow, Gromyko gave him the exact same farewell speech. "Every single time Gromyko sees me, he says, 'You've gotten taller,' " Art Hartman chimed in.

The Negotiation Begins

At 9:30 A.M. on Monday, we drove through the gates of the Soviet embassy in Geneva, which formerly had been the Latvian mission. A light snow covered the rolling grounds. Gromyko met me at the door, and we posed for a picture beneath a grim portrait of Chernenko. The Soviets were all, I was told, "American specialists" fluent in English: Obukhov, Karpov, Gromyko, Dobrynin, and the translator, Sukhodrev, who was still acting offended about our meeting in New Delhi, when Senator Moynihan had referred to him as "Sokolov."

If the U.S. delegation wasn't keen on Nitze, the Soviet delegation was. "He is a man of culture and learning," Lieutenant Colonel Ditinov said. "He grabs you by the throat intellectually." And in the first session the Soviets seemed of a similar mind on the format of our approach; they, too, were driving toward one forum under which all aspects of the nuclear arms control negotiations could be addressed.

Gromyko opened the session with an hour-long presentation. I raised the subject of human rights, and Gromyko declined to discuss it. There was no need to have a "human rights diversion," he said. I persisted enough to remind him of the importance I attached to this issue.

I made my presentation, noting that the president had been intensely involved in preparation for these meetings, and I wanted to read out many portions of my talking points so that he could get the full flavor of the president's views. The Soviets showed not a ripple of interest in our new ideas on strategic arms. Gromyko responded by taking the time for a full translation into Russian, even though everyone at the table understood English. I interpreted this as a sign of seriousness.

The germ of an agreement on the structure of renewed negotiations was apparent in each presentation, but there were also important differences. We each talked about three interdependent areas: space, strategic nuclear arms, and intermediate-range nuclear arms. The most fundamental difference involved what would be discussed under the heading "Space." Gromyko wanted the subject to be a "ban on the development, testing, and deployment of space strike weapons." I made it clear that "whenever research validates that a defensive technology would make a contribution to strengthening deterrence, the United States would expect to discuss with the Soviet Union the basis on which it would be integrated into force structures." And I insisted that our research effort would proceed. In any case, he eventually acknowledged that any agreement to ban research would be completely unverifiable. The one promising point was the forum. We could possibly get agreement to a "complex" approach in which START, INF, and space could be considered together even though worked on separately.

In the afternoon session I talked further about the essence of our idea. Each of the three areas was related. We would weave all of them into a concept of strengthened deterrence and equal security. We would restore the original basis for deterrence and reduce offensive systems—and ensure ABM Treaty compliance. I hit hard on what we regarded as clear treaty violations on their part, particularly their phased-array radar under construction at Krasnoyarsk. We would pursue a research program on strategic defense that might make deterrence more stable, I said.

Gromyko replied that he disagreed that an antimissile system was defensive. "SDI is not defensive," he said. "If you develop a shield against ICBMs, you could launch a first strike. We Soviets can do the same. But why do it at all? Why not just eliminate nuclear missiles themselves?" If the United States proceeded with SDI, the Soviets "would have to take countermeasures," he said. The Soviet Union would not participate with the United States to develop such a shield. "You just want superiority in order to blackmail us. If you don't stop your research, we will expose you for all the world to see. Reappraise your view. I asked your president, 'Why are we preparing for war in space?' Your president did not answer. Neither blackmailed nor a blackmailer be," Gromyko said. "Let's go up into a tower and think about the fate of the world."

"Let's go up and pretend we are aliens," I said. "What do we see? You have an impressive offensive and defensive capability. On our side, we have offensive but relatively little defensive capability. We see you getting worried about our defenses. Going to defense creates a less dangerous situation. Can we continue to rely on offensive deterrence given the nature of systems in the next years? We are concerned about the stability of deterrence. All three issues are interrelated," I said, "so we need three independent, interrelated groups: space, strategic arms, medium-range weapons. All will come together from time to time." Gromyko seemed to agree to the three forums but wanted to outlaw the subject of the first negotiation before it started.

At the reception that evening, Gromyko stood in the center of the room and allowed the American delegates to cluster around him. It was amusing to see hard-line cavemen with their muscle-bound approach to the Kremlin sporting big but uncertain smiles on their faces, elbowing each other to get close enough to be photographed with Gromyko. He was pleased, snide, and pompous as he told them how he stayed so fit: daily workouts with hand weights. As I assessed the day, I had not been impressed by Gromyko's performance. Everything he said was predictable, and he showed little disposition to engage in conversation that was genuinely creative. Whenever I asked for more details about one of his blustering assertions, he seemed to draw a total blank. Sometimes he would pontificate; at other times, he would simply look away and say, "I am silent, like fish."

Nevertheless, we were on track toward the result we came to achieve: get the arms talks started again within an acceptable structure and without the issues being prejudged.

Under all this there *was*, in fact, a dramatic change. These Soviet representatives were not those of a year or so ago. The "scientific progression of history" was obviously not on the Soviets' side: they had lost the fire of ideological, societal, and economic competition with us; they seemed to be looking for respect and treatment as equals. I knew that they would fight tooth and nail to keep those areas of strategic advantage over us that they now possessed and would keep trying to divide and demoralize the West. But we had come to a turning point.

Practically, this meant that the Soviets would accept our concept of dealing with all the arms control issues under one umbrella. Offense and defense would be considered together: allowing us to use the leverage of SDI to press them to reduce sharply their offensive weapons. This would be a long and bitter negotiation, but, to a degree, structure *was* substance. All this fully justified staying on for a second day of talks with Gromyko in order to design that structure of the negotiations about to begin. And it would be best to consider these as new negotiations; although the Soviets would actually be coming back to negotiations without any change or concession on our part, it would be wise for us not to "crow about it."

Gromyko asked me whether I had any problem with the idea of naming special representatives for each of the three main areas of the negotiations. "No," I said, "but to make progress, it cannot be left to negotiators; the high political level must stay involved."

"Yes," said Gromyko. "You have Paul Nitze. He is a wise man. But you need not designate him as a wise man. That is not wise."

At the first day's session at the Soviet embassy, nice, motherly Russian ladies pushed vodka on our security people and pushed it hard. The Americans all declined, but the Russians partook enthusiastically. In the afternoon session at the American mission, bottles of Jack Daniel's and Johnnie Walker Black Label had been set on a table outside the meeting room; the Soviet security guards drained them all. Back at the Soviet mission at the start of the second day, January 8, along came the Russian ladies again with the vodka. I took Gromyko aside and went over our human rights views with him at length. He raised both hands as if to shield himself from me and flapped his palms to make me go away. But I kept him in a corner, and he had to listen even though he pretended not to.

Gromyko's Bait and Switch

I had my team draft an agreed statement that we and the Soviets might release at the end of these meetings. When we reconvened in plenary session at 9:30 A.M., I just passed it around without saying anything so that nothing would appear in the transcript, as it would be read by others back in Moscow, to indicate that the Americans had proposed the language and the Soviets had agreed to it. Staying silent on the transcript can sometimes be crucial. We and the Soviets went back and forth that morning on our respective ideas for an agreement to begin arms reductions talks. At the end of the morning session, we exchanged draft texts and then adjourned for lunch. Their draft proposals were not bad, despite the convoluted language. I gave my delegation a complete readout after each meeting, and we talked over lunch about our response. We decided to proceed on the basis of the Soviet draft, with our bottom line being three interrelated but independent negotiating groups.

We reconvened in the U.S. mission at 2:35 for what we all knew would be the final session. As Gromyko was the guest, I gave him the floor. He criticized our draft and wound up saying that "the sides must look in a different direction to find acceptable wording." I responded to his critique point by point, especially his comments about defense. But I then said that their draft provided a basis from which to work and that we had worked out a revised version of it. Basically, we put our key points into the structure of their draft. I handed over our revised text, and after a brief discussion, Gromyko, at 3:05, asked for a break so that both sides could look over the various texts.

I had assembled our full delegation in a conference room adjacent to our meeting room so that everyone could be on hand for the time of critical decisions. The tension was high. When I opened the conference room door, I feared that my team was going to suffer from a mass of whiplash injuries, so swiftly did their faces snap toward me for the latest news. But, by this time, the psychology of our group had changed dramatically from pessimism to optimism that we would be successful. And everyone wanted to be identified with success.

At 3:25, Gromyko let us know he was ready to resume. He handed us an alternative statement saying that he and I had agreed to resume our discussion in "early March." I saw this as a prearranged ploy—bait and switch—designed to take the wind out of our sails and lead us to alter our position in order to get his agreement. I said I would be glad to meet him again in March if we could find a mutually agreeable date. I then asked him why he had in effect withdrawn the proposal that he had tabled in the morning. He responded but did not answer. At 3:40, I suggested another break.

My delegation was upset and alarmed. Their high hopes seemed to be getting dashed. "I hope you guys know I'm ready to walk out," I said. They all counseled another try. That, of course, was what I intended to do, and what I wanted to elicit from them. "I'm the only hard-liner here," I said with a grin.

I returned at 4:30 and was greeted by Gromyko's jest that he didn't expect to see me "until the second crow of the rooster." I said that if it had been Sunday, we would have been watching a football game. I then returned to my question about why he had pulled back from his earlier position. He became indignant. I got the feeling some members of his own delegation were dubious about his tactics. We went back and forth. He said that time was running out and that both sides should be brief. I felt that Gromyko had confused himself by his own maneuvering. "If the Soviet side is waiting for us to agree to stop our SDI research program, they will have a long wait," I told him.

Gromyko replied that this was not a precondition but that all aspects of space could be discussed in the appropriate negotiating group. "Okay, I said, "that's where we started." Then I asked him if he wanted to continue.

There is "plenty of time left before tomorrow morning," he said, and continued: "There is no one but Gromyko and the secretary to discuss these issues, and their leaders have charged them to do it. " At that point, I felt we were over the hump. At 5:50, Gromyko asked for another break to study the text further.

With my delegation fully engaged, we rearranged wording again, careful to maintain the identity of three negotiating groups underneath whatever umbrella emerged. I had a little time, so I asked Joyce Nesmith from my staff to slide out the identifying sign on the door of the room where we were negotiating and letter in on its reverse side, "Gromyko Room." When the Soviets let us know, at 6:35, that they were ready to resume, I held the door open and motioned for Gromyko to come over. "What's this?" I asked. "You have taken over this room, and pretty soon you'll want to take over our whole building!" He laughed lightly, but the distraction did seem to loosen things up a bit.[7] Two more breaks and several revisions later, we finally agreed on a text. By this time, it was approaching eight o'clock. I suggested we release the text at 10:00; he wanted midnight. Inevitably, we agreed on 11:00 P.M., which was five in the afternoon in Washington. Then we adjourned. Gromyko expressed his satisfaction with the "frank and businesslike" atmosphere we had maintained, and I reciprocated.

---

7. I took the "Gromyko Room" sign back to Washington, had it encased in plastic, and sent it to him with a note saying, "Any time you present this at the U.S. embassy in Geneva, you are entitled to the exclusive use of the room." I never got a reply.

*   *   *

The press blackout was over, and Bernie Kalb could not have been happier. "I've only been in this job three weeks, and you officials are the only friends I've got!" At least the reporters had been able to live it up in Geneva without fear of being scooped.

I called the president: "I can report to you that we have reached agreement with the Soviet Union to begin new negotiations on the questions we came here to discuss: nuclear and space arms. We will announce this at 11:00 P.M. here, which is 5:00 P.M. your time. We agreed to a set of points that are consistent with and supportive of your instructions. I think this is an opportunity for a good beginning. There is a wide difference of opinion on important topics, and the negotiations will be long and tumultuous. It will require patience, but we have an agreement."

The key paragraphs of the agreement, with all its convoluted language, were:

> The sides agree that the subject of the negotiations will be a complex of questions concerning space and nuclear arms, both strategic and intermediate range, with all the questions considered and resolved in their interrelationship. The objective of the negotiations will be to work out effective agreements aimed at preventing an arms race in space and terminating it on earth, at limiting and reducing nuclear arms, and at strengthening strategic stability.
>
> The negotiations will be conducted by a delegation from each side, divided into three groups. The sides believe that ultimately the forthcoming negotiations, just as efforts in general to limit and reduce arms should lead to the complete elimination of nuclear arms everywhere.

I now had a team. With the blackout over, I told them to talk to the press as much as they wished. And the next day I had them fan out all over the world—NATO headquarters in Brussels, Bonn, London, Paris, Tokyo, Beijing, Canberra—to tell allies and others about the new start to arms negotiations.

At the end of our session, I told Gromyko that we would welcome meeting Mr. Gorbachev when he came to the United States. The vice president would issue the invitation, and the president and I would be sure to meet with him. Gromyko replied, "Nonsense! This is total invention, total invention!" I didn't know what Gromyko was driving at, but he clearly was not in favor of a Gorbachev visit to Washington. I dropped the subject.

As I headed back to Washington the next day, I mulled over the enormous effort it took to bring about this agreement. But we had turned the corner. The president was fully engaged and fully behind what I was doing. With hard work, vision, and strategic thought, and with his continued involvement and support, we could capitalize on this turning point.

CHAPTER 27

New Man: New Ideas?

The agreement with Gromyko in Geneva to resume arms control negotiations was big news. I was taken completely by surprise by another piece of big news—a sudden development that was worked out while I was away and announced as I returned. Jim Baker and Don Regan would switch jobs, President Reagan announced on January 8, 1985. The political pro would become secretary of the treasury, and the man who made his fortune on Wall Street would become chief of staff in the White House.

As a believer in the importance of "repotting," of changing good people around so they don't go stale doing the same job forever, I could understand why both men might want the change, and I hoped for the best. I was glad to see that both men seemed enthusiastic about their new posts. But I had moved in the Nixon years from a cabinet secretary's office to the White House, and I expected Don Regan would have a tougher time with the transition than Jim Baker. Don was accustomed to running a tight ship his way and would inject his managerial style into the day-to-day work of the White House staff. But the White House is dominated by the man in the Oval Office and by politics. Sensitivity to the political implications and subtleties of developments large and small is essential. The chief of staff needs a nose and a feel for political nuance and personality, which was Baker's stock in trade. How would Don fit in this environment? Would he be good at it? Would a brusque managerial style fill the bill? I worried about these questions. But the two Irishmen, Reagan and Regan, seemed delighted with their working relationship.

At this point, the hard-liners were really laying into me. I had done the unthinkable—get the United States and Soviet Union on the road to a working relationship. They could not bring themselves to admit that I was carrying out Ronald Reagan's policy and that the president and I were in close accord. They could not attack the president, for he represented everything they believed in, so they attacked me and my "pragmatism." But when the far right wing attacked me, it actually was helpful. Public criticism of the administration was easing considerably—as it always did whenever something, anything, was moving positively with regard to the Soviets and arms control negotiations.

Strong Men for Tough Negotiations

We now had to pick a negotiator who would head the entire unified delegation and the three subheads. Nitze's wife was ill, and he was not able to move once again to Geneva, and anyway, I wanted to keep him close to me in Washington as my principal idea man. I favored Max Kampelman and told Cap so. Cap said he would prefer Edward Teller: no one else could be trusted to be totally committed to SDI. It was not a real struggle because Max Kampelman was so deeply respected. Within a few days, Bud, Cap, Casey, and even Richard Perle all accepted Max. We also decided that in addition to being overall head, Max would lead the space and defense talks. We wanted foreign service officer Mike Glitman to head INF negotiations and former Senator John Tower to head START. The president was enthusiastic about this slate, and in a meeting with Cap Weinberger, John Poindexter (sitting in for Bud McFarlane), and me on January 17, he assigned me the job of contacting each one and signing them up. I reached Kampelman and Glitman by telephone, and they both said yes.

Tower had just retired in some frustration from the Senate and his post as chairman of the Senate Armed Services Committee. He had already started a new life, looking, among other things, at the opportunity to enhance his income after a career on a government salary. He was just getting going. I asked him to come see me, and I put the proposition to him. The offer hit him like a ton of bricks. He would have to put aside his plans and aspirations for a private life once more. Yet he appreciated the importance of the job being offered to him. He asked whether he was the president's choice. I assured him that he was. His eyes welled up. He said yes.

Rowny, when I contacted him, could not bear the idea that the START talks, which he had headed for the United States and which had ended with a Soviet walkout in 1983, were now to be reorganized in a new form under Tower. Rowny resented that I was the one to bring him this news: "You are not high ranking enough to tell me this," he said. "I want to speak to the president alone." He had the right, I felt, to make his case, so I took him over for his moment with the president. The president and I had agreed that Rowny—and Nitze—would have the title of special adviser to the president and secretary of state on arms reduction negotiations. Rowny was hurt, but his bridges were behind him and in flames. He did try to make the best of his advisory role and became a contributing, if difficult, member of the team.

On January 18, on behalf of the president, I made the announcement of the three appointments in the White House pressroom. All three were respected, and the choices were well received on the Hill. When I was asked why Kampelman, who had no arms control experience, was selected, I responded, "He's smart. And he's a good negotiator. And he's experienced. He did an outstanding job in his [CSCE] work in Madrid. So he is really first class, as are the other two."

Meanwhile, on January 14, the prime minister of Belgium, Wilfried Martens, had made a critical official visit to President Reagan as part of our effort to help him, and his coalition government, win the support of the Belgian Parliament for the scheduled deployment of INF missiles on Belgian soil. With the new arms reductions negotiations just getting under way, the president was able to make a strong argument that this was not the time to give the Soviets what they wanted in exchange for nothing. Martens went home, used the president's argument, and prevailed. (On March 14, the Belgian coalition cabinet would vote to authorize immediate deployment of cruise missiles in accordance with its commitment under NATO's 1979 dual-track decision. The missiles arrived on site the following day. It was an important event. Our deployments would continue according to the established NATO schedule.)

We assembled the new team of arms control negotiators for a meeting with President Reagan on January 22, 1985. The president, in a written statement issued after the meeting, said, "I view the negotiating commitments we undertook two weeks ago with the Soviets in Geneva with the utmost seriousness. I have no more important goal than reducing and, ultimately, eliminating nuclear weapons." The president was happy with the new team, and I was exultant. They were all top people; they were my choices and the president's, and they knew it. We were in a negotiating stance with tough and sound positions and would be represented by a knowledgeable professional, a Democrat with hard-line foreign policy views and demonstrated negotiating skill, and a former Republican senator with strong conservative credentials.

On February 1, 1985, the Reagan administration filed a report to Congress charging the Soviets with a clear violation of the 1972 ABM Treaty and a number of other violations. (On January 23 of the previous year we had filed a report to Congress charging the Soviets with possible noncompliance with several treaties, and we had warned the Soviets that we would do so again if the violations continued.) I supported the idea of making these reports, though I regarded some of the charges as technical in nature and not of great significance. The most serious charge involved the phased-array radar[1] well into construction in Krasnoyarsk, a city deep in the interior

---

1. Instead of the traditional "dish" that rotates to view the horizon lighthouse-style, the phased-array radar watches everything all the time and never is "looking the other way."

of the Soviet Union. The ABM Treaty prohibited construction of these long-lead-time radars except on the periphery of the United States or the Soviet Union and oriented outward. The location and orientation of this large radar made it a clear violation of the ABM Treaty, and its potential role in an antiballistic missile defense made the violation important. Our objections were rendered all the more compelling by the increasing shrillness of the Soviet objections to our Strategic Defense Initiative, which was being conducted in strict conformity to the ABM Treaty.

By this time, Cap Weinberger seemed to be fixed on a new theme: the United States should exercise its option to withdraw from the ABM Treaty by giving the Soviets the six months' notice required by the terms of the treaty. Cap argued that compliance was inhibiting our research on SDI. We were, in fact, nowhere *near* the point in our research where such a step was needed for the sake of the program. Furthermore, our security interests would be jeopardized more seriously than those of the Soviets because the deployability of their far-less-sophisticated strategic defense system was further along than ours. The issue was explosive. If we tried to pull out of the ABM Treaty, our allies and Congress would be enraged, and our negotiations with the Soviets would blow up in our faces.

The State Department's seventh floor, including my offices, had just been completely rebuilt in a grand colonial style. It was a project planned long before I came to office but was carried out only when a secretary of state emerged who was ready to move into smaller quarters near the construction site so that the work could be done. I kept the contractors somewhere near their schedule by "walking the job" periodically. And so, in late January 1985, I moved in. I especially liked the fireplace in my large outer office, and I held many meetings and ceremonies in front of its blazing flames. I used it so much that John Crawley, who took care of my office, began telling people that he wanted a chain saw for his birthday. With the new bookshelves standing empty, I decided to inaugurate a secretary of state's library and solicited opinions on what books to put there. Columnist Joseph Alsop sent in a list of titles designed to educate secretaries of state about the cynical, hypocritical twists and turns of life in high politics, such as the memoirs of the Duc de Saint Simon at the court of Louis XIV. Joe Alsop's letter was delightfully snide and cutting. Nick Platt, whom I had just taken on as the State Department's chief of staff, remarked that "Uncle Joe is one of Washington's last civilized men; of course, it's turned him into a complete savage." I decided to put together a collection of works about American diplomacy.

The Soviets agreed to begin negotiations in Geneva on March 12. I brought the whole group of our arms control negotiators and advisers together before my new fireplace on Friday, February 1. I told them that INF was the area where we should push for progress. The Soviets, if they allowed progress to take place, would do so in order to reach a point when they could say, "No deal until you drop SDI." That would be the moment of truth. Since we would not drop SDI, it would be up to us to make it their moment of truth.

As for START, John Tower was pessimistic, primarily because of our continuing inability to deploy our big land-based missile, the MX. The problem of coming up with a suitable method of basing this missile so that it could survive a Soviet attack was still unsolved. Without the MX, we had no leverage with the Soviets. "I have never negotiated with our Slavic brethren," Tower intoned with his slow Texas drawl, "but I would not care to be sitting across the table from them when MX is defeated." Tower followed this with a scathing summary of his opinion of the "bastards" in the Senate. Someone noted that he had made a swift transition from the legislative to the executive branch. "The transition was completed some time ago," he said. "That is why I took my departure from the Senate."

As we went forward, I told our negotiators that we would do so with the awareness of Soviet violations of arms control treaty provisions. The domestic opponents of dealing with the Soviet Union were not going to let us forget Soviet noncompliance, and we would keep that issue squarely before the Soviets. These new negotiations "do not condone or ignore the past," I said. "By and large, the previous arms control agreements have been valuable, if flawed. The need is for tighter agreements that are verifiable. There is no responsible alternative. Treaties are not built upon trust, but treaties can be reached that themselves can be trusted."

The group was working fairly well, considering I had collected a lot of big egos with differing views. But Bud McFarlane was talking resignation again. Mike Deaver told me Bud had sent a note to Don Regan saying that the president had decided how he wanted foreign policy run, and he figured it was time to leave. Max Kampelman expressed a commonly held feeling: "I don't understand Bud's problem, but I have come to respect the fact that he has one." Bud seemed to want the NSC staff to run foreign policy, with the secretaries of state, defense, and treasury—and the director of central intelligence—as bit players. Bud was always tempted to go off on "secret" missions and to negotiate back-room deals. He seemed to want to pull off something akin to a Henry Kissinger-to-China deal, such as a secret mission to Cuba to work out a solution with Castro to the problems of Central America. Bud had said that he would stay until arms control negotiations were launched, and now they had been. Don Oberdorfer, in the *Washington Post* on February 8, 1985, had a story headlined: "Shultz Firmly in Command." The story quoted an "experienced observer" saying that I tended "to simplify, sometimes oversimplify, important issues." Maybe that was a good thing: I understood the complexities, but I wasn't going to drown in them.

A Different Kind of Gauntlet

I continued to work on the conceptual side of our approach to the Soviet Union and on February 22, 1985, at the Commonwealth Club in San Francisco, spoke on "America and the Struggle for Freedom," a statement that enunciated what came to be known as the Reagan Doctrine. I had gone over my speech carefully with the president, who approved wholeheartedly, and had shown it to Bill Casey, Cap Weinberger, and Bud McFarlane at one of our Family Group lunches. Casey said, "Don't put this into the interagency clearance process; don't let anyone change a word." I considered the speech an important complement to my June 1983 Senate testimony, which initially set out our four-part agenda, and my October 1984 RAND/UCLA speech calling for us to move beyond the concept of linkage in our policy toward the Soviet Union: "A revolution is sweeping the world today—a democratic revolution. This should not be a surprise. Yet it is noteworthy because many people in the West lost faith, for a time, in the relevance of the idea of democracy. . . . In the Western Hemisphere, over 90% of the population of Latin America and the Caribbean today live under governments that are either democratic or clearly on the road to democracy—in contrast to only one-third in 1979. . . . Democracy is an old idea, but today we witness a new phenomenon."

I made a point that the Soviets well understood: "For many years we saw our adversaries act without restraint to back insurgencies around the world to spread communist dictatorships. . . . any victory of communism was held to be irreversible. This was the infamous Brezhnev doctrine, first proclaimed at the time of the invasion of Czechoslovakia in 1968. Its meaning is simple and chilling: once you're in the so-called 'socialist camp,' you're not allowed to leave. Thus the Soviets say to the rest of the world: 'What's mine is mine. What's yours is up for grabs.' In recent years, Soviet activities and pretensions have run head-on into the democratic revolution. People are insisting on their right to independence, on their right to choose their government free of outside control."

I spoke about Solidarity in Poland, resistance forces in Afghanistan, Cambodia, Nicaragua, Ethiopia, and Angola, dissidents in the Soviet Union and Eastern Europe, and advocates of peaceful change in South Africa, South Korea, the Philippines, and Chile. All these people, I said, seek independence, freedom, and human rights.

"This new phenomenon we are witnessing around the world—popular insurgencies *against* communist domination—is not an American creation," I said. "The nature and extent of our support—whether moral support or something more—necessarily varies from case to case. But there should be no doubt about where our sympathies lie. It is more than mere coincidence that the last four years have been a time of both renewed

American strength and leadership and a resurgence of democracy and freedom. . . . If we shrink from leadership, we create a vacuum into which our adversaries can move. Our national security suffers, our global interests suffer, and, yes, the worldwide struggle for democracy suffers. . . . Today, however, the Soviet empire is weakening under the strain of its own internal problems and external entanglements. And the United States has shown the will and the strength to defend its interests, to resist the spread of Soviet influence, and to protect freedom. . . .

"How can we as a country say to a young Afghan, Nicaraguan, or Cambodian: 'Learn to live with oppression; only those of us who already have freedom deserve to pass it on to our children.' How can we say to those Salvadorans who stood so bravely in line to vote: 'We may give you some economic and military aid for self-defense, but we will also give a free hand to the Sandinistas who seek to undermine your new democratic institutions.'. . . What we should do in each situation must, of necessity, vary," I argued. "But it must always be clear whose side we are on—the side of those who want to see a world based on respect for national independence, for freedom and the rule of law, and for human rights. Wherever possible, the path to that world should be through peaceful and political means; but where dictatorships use brute power to oppress their own people and threaten their neighbors, the forces of freedom cannot place their trust in declarations alone. . . . We must, in short, stand firmly in the defense of our interests and principles and the rights of peoples to live in freedom. The forces of democracy around the world merit our standing with them; to abandon them would be a shameful betrayal—a betrayal not only of brave men and women but of our highest ideals."

I returned from California via Nellis Air Force Base in Nevada, where Lieutenant General Jack Chain had arranged what was to be an eye-opener for me. Having donned the special air force suit that inflates and deflates automatically when the speed of the jet changes rapidly, thereby preventing a blackout, I climbed into the rear cockpit of the F-15 Eagle, and we took off—straight up and right through the sound barrier. Lieutenant Colonel Bill Lamb, in the front seat, let me take over once we were well aloft, and I flew the plane for over half the time we were in the air, which made me the "official" pilot on the mission. I was amazed at the responsiveness of this great airplane and was exhilarated by the flight, even though the experience of breaking through the sound barrier was jolting. I could see Jack Chain's plane just off to my left, matching my every turn and roll. After we landed, I asked, "Who else ever had a general for his wingman?"

At a secret site I got a preview of the stealth fighter, the F-117 with its eerie angles and dull-windowed gaze, looking like a prehistoric flying reptile in the blasted desert setting surrounding its hangar. I also saw the "Red" air force—the Soviet MIGs that, one way or another, the U.S. Air Force had acquired and was training against. Although our stealth aircraft looked prehistoric, it worked futuristically. The Soviet planes looked modern, but when I sat in the cockpit of the Soviet MIG, its controls and capabilities were primitive by comparison. I realized why, pilot training aside, the Israelis had so devastated the Syrian air force in the skies over Lebanon in 1982. I came away from the desert with a new appreciation of the superiority of our equipment over that of the Soviets. The problem was that the Soviets were able to turn out big and accurate intercontinental ballistic missiles with nuclear warheads, and they were well ahead of us in making them mobile and therefore able to survive an attack from us. Given the political climate in the United States, we could not keep pace in modernization, production, and deployment of these deadly weapons.

A New Face: Mikhail Sergeyevich Gorbachev

At Bethesda Naval Hospital on Friday, March 8, 1985, doctors found a polyp in President Reagan's intestine. The procedure for a full examination and removal was delayed because the vice president was in Geneva lending support to our arms control negotiators. That weekend General Secretary Chernenko died, and on Monday, March 11, Mikhail Sergeyevich Gorbachev was named to succeed him. The funeral was set for Red Square on Wednesday, March 13, at 1:00 P.M. We asked Vice President Bush to remain in Geneva. A few weeks earlier, aware of Chernenko's poor health, the president had decided that the funeral delegation should be George Bush, myself, and Art Hartman.

Vice President Bush had been scheduled to attend the inauguration of an elected Brazilian president, Tancredo Neves, who was replacing a general and marking the return to civilian rule twenty-one years after a junta had brought the military to power. Neves was to be sworn in on Friday, March 15. Tony Motley said, "A Russian dictator dies every year, but Brazil has redemocratized only once in twenty-one years—keep that in mind. Three months from now, no one will remember who went to Moscow. Three years from now, the Brazilians will remember who went to their inauguration." But Neves abruptly became ill and died suddenly before he was even sworn in. He was an impressive and savvy politician, and Brazil would have been better off had he taken office.

I went to the White House to see President Reagan to go over ideas for the meeting our delegation would have with Gorbachev. There wasn't a thought in his mind of going to Moscow. I recommended that Vice President Bush deliver a letter to Gorbachev inviting him to the United States. The president agreed.

I arrived in Moscow on Tuesday evening, March 12, and joined George Bush at Spaso House, the residence of the U.S. ambassador, where Art

Hartman's birthday was being celebrated. In the entryway of Spaso House was a nineteenth-century carved and painted American eagle with the motto Live and Let Live on a ribbon dangling from its beak. Later in the evening, a staff aide completed this exhibit by showing me a passage from a book on communism from the shelves of the Spaso House library: " 'A general agreement to live and let live' . . . is inconceivable. The [Communist] Party is obliged to strive for the annihilation of its enemies. . . . Were it prepared to be delinquent in this, it would merely lay itself open to annihilation by its enemies: they would not imitate the Party's delinquency, but rather 'utilize' it to deprive of existence a Party which had ceased to strive for victory."[2] So much for peaceful coexistence. This was indeed the Communist creed and those in the Reagan administration who opposed negotiation with the Soviets based their position in recognition of it. I recognized it, too, but I knew that change was possible and that we could not simply acquiesce to some fated future decreed by Marx and Lenin.

Moscow was a round of meetings among attendees at the funeral, capped by the event itself, an initial handshake with Gorbachev, and then our extended meeting with him. The vice president and I visited President Zia of Pakistan, Chancellor Helmut Kohl, Prime Minister Margaret Thatcher, and Prime Minister Yasuhiro Nakasone. With India's new prime minister, Rajiv Gandhi, we talked of the importance to his subcontinent of getting the Soviets out of Afghanistan and improving relations between India and Pakistan. All conversation was awkward, since everyone knew the meeting sites were bugged and the Soviets were listening.

Vice President Bush, Ambassador Hartman, and I stood for two hours in our assigned area in Red Square for the funeral proceedings. We noticed that there were no military men on the reviewing platform at the top of Lenin's tomb. The military brass were in a separate area overlooking the space allotted to leaders of the Western world and our allies. I stood beside Zia and Yaqub Khan of Pakistan to show our unity in opposition to Soviet occupation of Afghanistan. Mikhail Sergeyevich Gorbachev, the new general secretary of the Communist party of the Union of Soviet Socialist Republics, spoke forcefully. We walked to the Great Kremlin Palace along with all other delegations to give our condolences to Gorbachev and his colleagues.

Our First Direct Encounter with Gorbachev

We waited at Spaso House for our turn to talk more extensively with Gorbachev. At 8:30 P.M., we got the call. Halfway to the Kremlin, the

2. Nathan Leites, *A Study of Bolshevism* (Glencoe, Ill.: Free Press, 1953), p. 29.

KGB lead car delayed and eventually returned us to Spaso House at 9:10. Gorbachev was running late. At 9:40 we departed again.

Gorbachev was accompanied by three familiar faces: Gromyko, Andrei Alexandrov-Agentov, a foreign policy adviser I remembered from meetings with Brezhnev during the Nixon administration, and Viktor Sukhodrev, the ubiquitous superinterpreter. Gorbachev started with a grace note, thanking us for "paying our respects to General Secretary Chernenko," and then launched into the most far-ranging statement on foreign policy that I had heard from a Soviet leader.

"It is natural," he began, "to wonder what might change with the departure of one general secretary and the appointment of a new one. The United States should proceed from the premise that there will be continuity in both the domestic and foreign policy of the USSR." Then he noted the chimes of an antique clock in the room and said, with a smile, that the clock was old and was not intended to serve as any kind of signal.

Gorbachev had an extensive set of typed notes that he shuffled around and at first looked at from time to time. He soon put them aside completely. He was articulate and spontaneous. He seemed to be thinking out loud. Maybe he was. With Vice President Bush carrying the ball for our side, I could listen intently and watch Gorbachev, trying to size up what kind of a person he was. Gorbachev later told me he had noticed me watching him in this first meeting and wondered what I was thinking.

Gorbachev talked in global terms, saying that our task was "to assist all countries in improving the international situation," which "had changed radically compared to the 1950s," with literally dozens of new countries, each with its own interests and aspirations. "No one, not even the USSR and the United States, could fail to take this into account. We have to learn to base our relations on these realities," and our interpretation of them must affect "the formulation and implementation of foreign policy." He referred to statements made "by very highly placed U.S. officials which attempted to explain events" throughout the world as "simply the result of Moscow's mischief making. Moscow would seem to be almighty. It seemed to have its hand everywhere. . . ."

"The USSR has no expansionist ambitions," he asserted. "It has all the resources it will need for centuries, be it in terms of manpower, natural resources, or territory." He embellished, smiling, as he said, "We have no territorial claims against the United States, not even with respect to Alaska or Russian Hill in San Francisco." He spoke of periods of past cooperation, particularly during World War II, as "a bright page in the history of Soviet-U.S. relations. It is especially appropriate to recall that cooperation now when we are approaching the fortieth anniversary of the victory." He went on to talk about the late 1960s and 1970s "when the two states had found it possible to cooperate to the benefit of international relations in general, and relations in Europe in particular." He singled out the 1972 nuclear arms control agreements as well as the 1975 Helsinki Final Act as examples of the benefits of cooperation. "That was a time when our economic, technical, and cultural relations began to develop extensively. Now we have to begin everything anew."

Gorbachev looked straight at Vice President Bush. "The USSR has never intended to fight the United States and does not have such intentions now. There have never been such madmen within the Soviet leadership, and there are none now," he said. "The Soviets respect your right to run your country the way you see fit. In the same way, it is up to the Soviet people to make such decisions on behalf of the USSR, and the USSR will never permit anyone to teach it how to govern itself." He added, "As to the question of which is the better system, this is something for history to judge."

He conducted a monologue on ending the arms race, "a problem that is particularly important and timely and has a direct bearing on the future relationship between the USSR and the United States." The Soviets, he said, were approaching the negotiations in Geneva "very seriously" and hoped that the negotiations would produce genuine results. "The two countries have now reached a point in their arms buildup when any new breakthroughs resulting from the scientific and technological revolution—not to mention shifting the arms race to space—could set in motion irreversible and uncontrollable processes." He probed: "Why are people in the U.S., including some participants in the present meeting, taking such a somber view of these negotiations? These negotiations are being depicted as requiring years and years. Is the U.S. side," he asked, "really interested in these negotiations? Is it interested in achieving results? Or does the United States find these negotiations necessary in order to pursue its programs for continuing the arms race, for developing ever new types of arms?" It would be "nothing but a pipedream, nothing but adventurism, for the United States to follow the advice of experts about wearing down and weakening the USSR economically, reducing its role in the world." Ironically, he accused the United States of "lowering an iron curtain to seal itself off from the USSR. . . . Contacts between the two countries have been curtailed," he asserted. "Technology can be transferred only with the express approval of the president. Trade is not permitted." He concluded, "What sort of relations will the two countries pursue in the future? Are we going to resort to the press in order to exchange views and assessments, or are we going to do this at the political level, giving an impetus to better relations between our two countries?"

Gorbachev's free-flowing monologue showed a mind working at high intensity, even at the end of a long, hard day. He displayed a breadth of view and vigor, I thought, but his basic positions were ones we had heard before.

*   *   *

Then came Vice President Bush's turn. "We have no aspirations of dictating how to administer the Soviet Union. This is the farthest thing from our thoughts." He handed the president's letter to Gorbachev and said President Reagan was ready for real give-and-take and for a meeting at the earliest convenient opportunity. Some progress had been made during the meeting between the president and Gromyko, he said. We hoped for further progress and positive results.

Bush hit hard on the importance of regional issues, specifically developments in Nicaragua and Afghanistan, and the potentially constructive role of the Soviet Union to further relief efforts in Ethiopia, where the Soviet-supported government was blocking humanitarian efforts to get food to starving people. He addressed possible cooperation on bilateral problems, noted progress under way in the housing, environment, and trade areas, and called attention to the importance of an agreement on Pacific air safety. On the question of human rights, he told Gorbachev that he must "understand that this issue is extremely important to the president and the American people." The denial of Jewish emigration, the persecution in the Soviet Union of Hebrew teachers, the treatment of dissidents, of Shcharansky, Sakharov, Begun, and Orlov, all presented central issues that we wanted to approach and discuss, consistent with the spirit and letter of the Helsinki Accords.

Gorbachev flushed slightly and interjected in an agitated way that he would "agree to think about appointing rapporteurs on human rights in order to discuss" this issue. "The United States violates human rights not only on its own territory but also beyond its borders," he asserted. "It disregards the human rights not only of individuals but of entire nations and countries. It brutally represses human rights. Just a few minutes ago we were talking about not teaching each other how to manage one's own affairs. . . . If necessary, we could establish a forum and have rapporteurs to demonstrate to the U.S. administration and the U.S. population how things stand with human rights in the United States and how the U.S. administration deals with that problem abroad." He no sooner made this proposal than he backed off and said he "did not think this was an appropriate subject for discussion between our two states" and complained that "every time there is a meeting involving our two countries, the United States proceeds to raise these questions. Thank God there is socialism, because with socialism the people of [former] capitalist countries have gained more rights."

Vice President Bush picked up the Gorbachev "rapporteur" suggestion. "We would be glad to present our problems and to hear out the Soviet side."

Bush then called on me. "President Reagan told me to look you squarely in the eyes and tell you: 'Ronald Reagan believes that this is a very special moment in the history of mankind,' " I said. "You are starting your term as general secretary. Ronald Reagan is starting his second term as president. Negotiations are beginning in Geneva. Over the past year we have found solutions to some problems, though not to the great problems, and if it is at all possible, we must establish a more constructive relationship between the United States and the USSR. President Reagan knows that he personally must work on this hard, and he is ready to do so. He expects the negotiators in Geneva to discuss the details, and there are many of them, but only people like those present in this room and the president can resolve the main issues. President Reagan is ready to work with you and in his letter is inviting you to visit the United States at the earliest convenient time. A letter from someone is one thing, but a personality with whom you can deal is something entirely different. If important agreements can be found, the sooner, the better."

Gorbachev said that it was important that our conversation "has been held not in the language of diplomacy but in the language of politics. Leaving aside the question of human rights, one could say that this exchange of views has been important and has included serious considerations which require thought." He concluded: this is "a unique moment; I am ready to return Soviet-U.S. relations to a normal channel. It is necessary to know each other, to find time for meetings to discuss outstanding problems, and to seek ways to bring the two countries closer together." The Soviet Union, he said, "advocates an honest dialogue which properly takes into account the 'ranking' of our two countries and of the officials leading these two countries."

"In Gorbachev we have an entirely different kind of leader in the Soviet Union than we have experienced before," I told Vice President Bush and others in our party. He was quicker, fresher, more engaging, and more wide ranging in his interests and knowledge. The content of our meeting was tough and his manner was aggressive, but the spirit was different. He was comfortable with himself and with others, joking with Gromyko in a way that emerged from a genuine confidence in his base of knowledge and in his political abilities. I pointed out that he used the big stack of notes in front of him only for a few minutes and then discarded them. "He performs like a man who has been in charge for a while, not like a man who is just taking charge." I came away genuinely impressed with the quality of thought, the intensity, and the intellectual energy of this new man on the scene.

Gorbachev impressed everyone, and the result was a certain Gorbachev euphoria in the air. People cited Margaret Thatcher's statement: "I like this man. We can do business together." I recalled Gromyko's remark, "Gorbachev has a nice smile, but he has iron teeth."

"Gorbachev is totally different from any Soviet leader I've met," I said to the press on Friday, March 15. "But the U.S.-Soviet relationship is not just about personalities," I cautioned.

I could sense instinctively in our hour-and-a-half meeting that he was out of a completely different mold. He managed the funeral so that it had a different feel from that of Brezhnev's, which was very military. (This time, their civilian leaders stood on the top of Lenin's tomb, and their military were placed in an area below them.) Would his ideas be out of a different mold as well? The answer to that question remained to be seen but might very well be influenced by our response to him.

Our Obstacle Course

Back in Washington, we faced a critical vote on appropriations and authorization for the MX missiles. We needed the vote badly for the sake of our security interests and for our negotiations. I had testified on the subject jointly with Cap Weinberger in an unusual three-hour session of the Senate Armed Services Committee on February 26. If we counted those "leaning our way," it looked like 52 to 48 in the Senate and even closer in the House. John Tower was pessimistic: "There are too many of faint heart. We need a 'Come to Jesus' meeting."

Max Kampelman, having just established himself in Geneva, made a quick trip back to Washington and spoke eloquently to a large group from Congress assembled in the East Room of the White House. The president, Cap, and I all pushed hard and talked to members of Congress individually and in groups and spoke publicly. In two votes on March 19 and 20, we won the Senate's approval, 55 to 45, and the House followed suit, by 219 to 213. Senator Lawton Chiles, one of our critics, said we had played "the Geneva card." Chiles said only about thirty senators thought we ought to build the MX, but "a lot of them say if anything [bad] happens at Geneva, we'd be blamed [in the Senate]." This vote was much like the deployments of INF missiles in Europe. Again we prevailed.

Just as real progress seemed to be possible, a brutal event occurred on March 24. An American army officer, Major Arthur D. Nicholson, Jr., assigned to the U.S. military liaison mission in Potsdam, was shot by a Soviet sentry in East Germany. The mission operated under the terms of a 1947 agreement between the United States and the Soviets, creating a "no man's land" where opposing cold war forces interacted to an understood set of rules. The event turned barbaric. The Soviets prevented first aid: by the time the medics arrived, the major had bled to death. As in the shooting down of the Korean airliner, the Soviets did something egregious and then blamed us for it. After expressing their "regret" over Major Nicholson's death, they accused him of "espionage activities" and failure to heed a warning from the sentry. We pushed strenuously to get the facts and see justice done. It was cold-blooded murder, and I said so. We protested vigorously and immediately. But I would not let "linkage" come into play; our movement toward a better overall U.S.-Soviet relationship would not be derailed. Cap took the opposite approach.

On that same day, a letter to President Reagan from General Secretary Gorbachev arrived. It was nonpolemical in tone and responsive to the letter from the president delivered by Vice President Bush during our meeting. Gorbachev said that the first priority should be to conduct business in such a way as to make clear that "both countries are not aiming at deepening their differences and whipping up animosity, but, rather, are making their policy looking to the prospect of revitalizing the situation and of peaceful, calm development." Such an approach "would help create an atmosphere of greater trust between our countries. It is not an easy task, and I would say, a delicate one. For trust is an especially sensitive thing, keenly receptive to both deeds and words. It will not be enhanced if, for example, one were to talk as if in two languages: one—for private contacts, and the other, as they say—for the audience."

Gorbachev asked President Reagan to "appreciate the seriousness of our approach to the negotiations, our firm desire to work towards positive results there," and concluded by saying that he attached great importance to contacts at the highest level. "For this reason I have a positive attitude to the idea you expressed about holding a personal meeting between us. And it would seem that such a meeting should not necessarily be concluded by signing some major documents. . . . The main thing is that it should be a meeting to search for mutual understanding on the basis of equality and taking account of the legitimate interests of each other." He thanked the president for his invitation to visit Washington and suggested that they "return again to the question of the place and time for the meeting."

The letter sounded like the Gorbachev I had listened to only a week and a half earlier. He had laid heavy emphasis in our meeting and his letter on the Geneva negotiations. Interest in these negotiations was strong in Congress and in the American public generally, but misperceptions of our approach were widespread. I had a speech to deliver on March 28 at the University of Texas at Austin: I used the occasion to make a comprehensive statement on our approach to the arms control issues being addressed in Geneva. My speech, I knew, would be read carefully by the Soviets.

Before the Austin Council on Foreign Relations, I set out our objectives: *stability* to "decrease and minimize the incentives one side might have to preempt or strike first in a crisis"; *reductions* rather than the previous concept of limitations; *equality* between ourselves and the Soviets, recognizing that our force structures are different and therefore a way of equating different weapons systems would be needed; and *verifiability*, so that we could be sure that agreements are being kept.

The president's Strategic Defense Initiative, I argued, "would take away incentives for an aggressor to attack first in a crisis" and would help in a world with fewer missiles, since "a strategic balance at sharply lower levels is more vulnerable to the risk of cheating. . . . But with feasible defenses in place, so many illegal missiles would be required to upset the balance that significant cheating could not be concealed." I addressed the criticism that SDI envisaged an impenetrable shield that could not be attained: "Even an imperfect but cost-effective defense system would vastly complicate any aggressor's first-strike planning." Patience would be required, I said. "We . . . are ready to move ahead as fast as possible. We will not be the obstacle." But there were obstacles, many of them within our own camp.

Back in Washington on Saturday, March 30, I called in Dobrynin about the fatal shooting of Major Nicholson. I told him of my revulsion at the unwillingness to allow the first aid that might well have saved his life, let alone at the shooting itself. We demanded an apology, restitution for the family, and steps to prevent another such incident from taking place. Dobrynin agreed to a military-to-military meeting between U.S. and Soviet commanders to arrange procedures that would bar the use of deadly force in such circumstances and so prevent further acts like this. Cap was angry and called this a "love and kisses" session with the murderers of a U.S. officer. Cap wanted a Soviet apology *before* any meetings of the kind I worked out with Dobrynin. I could understand that desire, but I knew that the absence of an apology would be used by Cap as a reason to refuse all dealings with the Soviets. It was better, I felt, to try to prevent a repetition of such awful occurrences. But Cap refused to allow our commanders to meet their Soviet counterparts. The Soviets would have to apologize first, he said, but he wouldn't allow a meeting to take place at which we could demand an apology.

When I next saw President Reagan, he was telling me how *he* was getting clobbered by Cap and the hard-liners for wanting to meet with Gorbachev. "We just have to go forward; we have made an impact on some Soviet minds, even though many minds in our own country will not change," I told the president. It was not a bad thing to have skeptics as long as they were not allowed to block efforts to improve the situation.

Two years ago, in 1983, our approach had been fragmented and the Soviets unrelentingly hostile. In the intervening period we had made the successful deployment of INF missiles in Europe *our* success. This year, I had gone to Geneva to meet Gromyko and had set a new arms control process in motion. Our allies were solidly with us. The concept of SDI—and its importance in negotiations to achieve arms reductions—was becoming better understood. A brand-new thought pattern had taken hold.

We had demanded that the Soviets return to Geneva without any concession from us. And now we had just gotten word that Gromyko was ready to meet me again, in Vienna on May 14, at the time when we would both be present to celebrate the thirtieth anniversary of the Austrian State Treaty. The president agreed with my analysis, but he also had his concerns. So did I. SDI gave the United States and our diplomacy an aura of potency; it was leading the Soviets toward the view that they could never match American strength and leading them as a consequence to the unavoidability of negotiations. But many in Congress and the press seemed intent on cutting SDI back or eliminating it altogether.

On Monday, April 15, Bud McFarlane told me again that he was about to resign. He would do so at the end of the week, and it would be effective June 1. He said he simply could not work with Chief of Staff Don Regan and Pat Buchanan, White House communications director. The tension of an administration in which so many key players were perpetually at odds with one another was too much for him. That evening, I went to see Bud. He was morose, as he had been for weeks. I told Bud that he was at the peak of his professional career. He was situated at the center of everything. This was not the time to trouble the president, I said, in the midst of a fight for a crucial vote on Contra aid and just before the president's state visit to Germany and the economic summit coming up in Bonn in early May. I left not knowing for sure what Bud would do, but my instincts told me he would stay.

Art Hartman was back from Moscow. He said that the new mood under Gorbachev was of Soviet preoccupation with their domestic problems. They were concerned as well with Eastern Europe and the Warsaw Pact. As for the United States, Gorbachev was taking his cue directly from the domestic political debate: Gorbachev had given visiting Speaker Tip O'Neill a two-hour monologue mainly aimed at stopping SDI. It would cost the Soviets twenty times less to inundate the United States with offensive weapons, Gorbachev said, than it would cost us to build SDI.

Art Hartman and I had a disagreement about security at our embassy in Moscow. I had become convinced, after discussions with Anne Armstrong and Marty Anderson, who had looked into staffing as part of their work on the President's Foreign Intelligence Advisory Board, that we should get the Soviet workers out of sensitive posts, such as switchboard operator and motor-pool driver, and replace them with U.S. citizens. Art said that doing so would be crazy: the more Americans in Moscow, the more targets for subversion the Soviets will have. "I have to pull U.S. Marines out of beds all over Moscow," Art said. He didn't want more Americans there to watch over and worry about. His argument didn't win me over.

The mood in the United States worsened at the end of April over a planned trade mission by Commerce Secretary Mac Baldrige to Moscow. The dispute over the death of Major Nicholson was souring the entire relationship. At breakfast at the White House on Saturday, April 27, a row erupted. Mac and I said that the trip should go forward; Cap, Bill Casey, and Don Regan said cancel. McFarlane and Richard Darman (sitting in for Jim Baker) were leaning toward canceling. The scene was bizarre. Here was the president ready to lead the charge to engage with the Soviets. At the same time, his secretary of defense and director of central intelligence were leading their own charge in exactly the opposite direction.

Reflecting these tensions within the administration and with the Soviets, President Reagan sent a lengthy letter to Gorbachev. "Mr. General Secretary," he wrote, "Certain recent events have begun to cast doubt on the desire of your government to improve relations." He reviewed at length and in severe tones the killing of Major Nicholson and the subsequent handling of the matter by the Soviets and concluded, "The American people see this tragedy through the eyes of the widow and an eight-year-old child. Consequently it will remain a penetrating and enduring problem until it is properly resolved." He went on to contrast Gorbachev's statement that "all people have the right to go their chosen way without imposition from the outside" with "Soviet military actions in Afghanistan." Referring to the call in Gorbachev's March 24 letter not to speak in two languages, President Reagan noted, "Soviet words and actions do not always seem to us to be speaking the same language."

He turned to our Geneva negotiations and to the Soviets' continuing criticism of SDI: "Defensive systems" can "provide the means of moving to the total abolition of nuclear weapons," he said. He referred to a statement from a 1962 Gromyko speech at the United Nations: "Anti-missile defenses could be the key to a successful agreement reducing offensive missiles," since they could "guard against the eventuality . . . of someone deciding to violate the treaty and conceal missiles or combat aircraft." The president argued, reflecting his discussion at Camp David with Margaret Thatcher: "If some options should at some time in the future be identified, development of them by the United States could occur only following negotiations with other countries, including your own, and following thorough and open policy debates in the United States itself. And if the decision to deploy should be positive, then further years would pass until the systems could actually be deployed. So there is no possibility of a sudden, secretive, destabilizing move by the United States."

President Reagan reviewed the full range of issues, including the importance of curbing the spread of chemical weapons, made more pressing by the "use of chemical weaponry in the Iran-Iraq War." He called for a procedure to review human rights problems, saying, "I am also prepared to appoint rapporteurs as you suggested to the Vice President."

On the question of the summit, he said,"Major formal agreements are not necessary to justify one. . . . I assume that you will get back in touch with me when you are ready to discuss time and place." He concluded with the hope that Gromyko and I could move "toward solutions of the problems" at our scheduled meeting in Vienna.

Against all this background, I prepared for my meeting in Vienna with Gromyko. The occasion was a celebration of a constructive and lasting agreement giving Austria its freedom and independence. What could be derived from the atmospherics of the occasion remained to be seen. A piece of good news came in: the Soviets ordered their forces no longer to employ live fire against our officers in East Germany, so perhaps another killing like that of Major Nicholson could be avoided in the future. I discussed strategy with the president. Ronald Reagan was steady on course despite all the turbulence. He was ready for a summit with Gorbachev but acutely conscious of all the problems that beset our relationship. My task was to play it straight, to use our ideas and positions to create flexibility on their part. But, as far as the summit was concerned, Gorbachev had the president's invitation. It was for him to respond.

As Washingtonians scrapped with each other over how to approach the Soviet Union, a storm was brewing over a matter of history and its power in the present that would soon embroil the president in a fever-pitch controversy in both Germany and the United States.

CHAPTER 28

Bitburg

No other event during my time as secretary of state caused such deep reflection about the emotionally charged complexities of Germany, past and present, and Germany's relations with the rest of the world as did the controversy over President Reagan's visit to Bitburg in 1985.

It all started with Chancellor Kohl's visit to Washington in late November 1984, but events earlier in the year made 1984 appear to be something of a turning point in the traditional search for German identity and in the relations between the two Germanies.

A tense human drama at the West German mission in East Berlin ended successfully in July 1984 on terms surprising to both West and East. Over a period of months, more than fifty East Germans had sought refuge in the mission, demanding the right to emigrate to the West. In earlier years, an event of this sort would have resulted in major strains to inner-German ties and months of frozen relations between the two German states. Instead, the two Germanies treated the issue as a joint problem that should be solved harmoniously. After much hectic negotiation, the asylum seekers did leave the mission with the promise that they would be allowed to leave East Germany in the coming months.

Might we be witnessing a new turn of the wheel in postwar German development and in Germany's ongoing search for identity? After consolidation of the two German states with their respective alliance systems, NATO and the Warsaw Pact, a careful process of renewed examination of their joint common interests was beginning. If well handled, I and many others thought, this national phase of German postwar development need not develop into a nationalist Germany-against-the-world trend.

I had intimations of such thinking from a talk with Chancellor Willy Brandt back in 1973 and from my extended visits with Helmut Schmidt, a friend for almost two decades and Brandt's successor as chancellor. And I could see that now Schmidt's successor Helmut Kohl believed that the Federal Republic's ties with the West would not remain healthy without a corresponding effort to expand ties between the two Germanies. The be-

ginning always involved improved possibilities for human and personal contacts: friends and relatives across the border and on the other side of the
wall. Kohl feared that stagnation of the inner-German relationship could
lead to the very anti-Western tendencies in the Federal Republic that he
was determined to avoid.

By the end of 1984, anxiety was growing about the upcoming fortieth
anniversary of the Allied victory in Europe and about how V-E Day would
be commemorated. The German government was particularly concerned
that Allied, or even U.S.-Soviet, ceremonies would project the image of
wartime victors in sharp relief against the vanquished Germanies. These
fears made the Germans seem uncharacteristically wary of U.S.-Soviet
commemorative steps, even though they might contribute to positive movement in East-West relations, a goal they otherwise strongly supported. Any
step, I could see, that would be interpreted as once again consigning West
Germany to outcast status was undesirable.

In 1984 the Soviet propaganda machine was attacking West German
revanchism at a high decibel level. The Soviets conveyed warnings about
the emergence, let alone the increased pace, of expanding contacts between
the two German states. By so doing, they again highlighted their own
refusal to consider change in the status of relations between the Germanies
and handed Helmut Kohl and Foreign Minister Hans-Dietrich Genscher a
means of rallying the country around a clear national issue. In contrast,
our desire was to demonstrate that we were working *with* the Germans to
deal with their deep preoccupation with the meaning of Germany and the
gnawing reality of its division.

Kohl to Reagan: Reconciliation

Chancellor Kohl came to Washington, at President Reagan's invitation, for
an official working visit November 29–30, 1984. We knew that Kohl would
want to address the handling of the V-E Day anniversaries. Despite pro-
testations to the contrary, many Germans had been deeply disturbed that
Kohl had not been invited to the June 1984 D-Day ceremonies in Normandy. Kohl had scheduled the 1985 economic summit (it was Germany's
turn) for May 2–4 in Bonn so that it would nearly coincide with V-E Day,
May 8—just leaving time for a state visit by President Reagan to West
Germany to take place between those dates. We knew that the Soviets
would mount a major campaign to support their thesis, as presented to me
by Andrei Gromyko, that "the results of World War II are a historical
reality that must never be changed."

I knew that President Reagan had been troubled as well as exultant at
the celebration the previous June marking the fortieth anniversary of the
Normandy landings. Germany could not be there, but Germany was now

part of what "the guys who hit the beach" were fighting for. Ronald Reagan, with his orientation to the future, wanted to look ahead *with* Germany rather than back *at* Germany. I, too, felt that these delicate anniversaries called for the closest possible consultation and sense of cohesion between Germany and America. Knowing the president's feelings and my own, I advised him to accept if Kohl invited him to make a state visit.

During his visit, Kohl did invite the president, and Reagan accepted. Kohl also handed over a list of sites that the president might visit. Somewhat surprisingly, it included Dachau, the infamous Nazi concentration camp near Munich. Kohl also suggested that he and the president visit a military cemetery where a "handclasp over the graves of the fallen" could be a symbol of reconciliation between onetime adversaries who had long since become allies. After Kohl's exclusion from the ceremony at Omaha Beach in Normandy, he and President Mitterrand of France had arranged in the autumn such a symbolic (and massively photographed) handshake over the graves at Verdun, the World War I battlefield. As Kohl recounted this ceremony to me and to the president, we could feel the intense emotional content in his voice and bearing. The chancellor's ideas were passed on to the White House and State Department staffs without presidential comment.

What happened then is what always happens when a summit or state visit is on the drawing board: the State Department is given the task of preparing the briefing material for the substance of the meetings, while the White House advance and security teams go to work on the scenarios, photo opportunities, and social occasions to be held. Within just a few days, the Kohl and Reagan staffs were reshaping the chancellor's proposals. Word came from Kohl's office that, on reflection, Dachau, or any other concentration camp, would not be a good idea. But the State Department did not accept the notion that such a visit should be dropped. Nazi horrors were a reality and a part of the past that must be remembered. At the same time, our research quickly revealed that there were no military cemeteries in Germany that held both German and American dead.

In January and February 1985 the issue was Dachau. In the German press, *Der Spiegel* reported German officials as saying that although a Dachau ceremony would be against Kohl's wishes, Reagan was pushing hard for it. In response, the White House spokesman's office said no, President Reagan did not want to include a concentration camp on the schedule. I knew that to be the case. Ronald Reagan wanted his state visit to be positive and forward looking.

At the end of January the Germans sounded out the State Department's European bureau to see whether we were continuing to plan for Dachau. I thought that it would be important to visit Dachau or another camp and that Kohl himself might favor it despite his staff, because I had heard him propose the idea back in November. I raised the matter with the president but got no definitive answer. At about this time I began a plan to continue on to the Middle East after the president's European trip in May. The Israelis had suggested, and I agreed, on a centerpiece event: a speech at Yad Vashem, the Holocaust memorial in Jerusalem, to inaugurate a compelling, new outdoor sculpture-monument.

Late in February Deputy Chief of Staff Mike Deaver led a White House advance team to survey the sites the president would visit. At State we were focusing on the policy papers for the economic summit and heard little about this trip other than that Deaver had gone to Dachau and that the chancellor's staff was furious that we were still considering a concentration-camp stop for the president. A story broke in the Washington press corps that, while in Germany, Deaver and others on the advance team had used diplomatic passports to get a 15 percent discount on the purchase of nine BMWs.

In mid-March a second White House advance team went to Germany to survey the scheduled sites again. Shortly after their return, the president, in a news conference, said that he would not be going to a concentration-camp site, as he felt very strongly about not reawakening the memories and passions of the time. He elaborated his rationale for the state visit in response to a question during a subsequent news conference on April 1: "Mr. President, you said in your last news conference that you didn't want to visit Dachau during your upcoming European trip because of an unnecessary guilt feeling that you said has been imposed on the present-day German people. How do you respond to those American Jews who have interpreted this remark as minimizing the Holocaust and as passing up an opportunity to dramatize this idea of 'never again' "?

President Reagan replied:

> I have made it very plain and spoken publicly on a number of occasions, and will continue to say, we should never forget the Holocaust. We should never forget it in the sense that this must never happen again, to any people, for whatever reason in the world.
>
> What I meant—and this time, to be a guest in that country at this particular time, when it is the coincident date with the end of the war, and recognizing that most of the population there—I grant you, there are some people there my age who remember the war and were participants in it on that side—but the bulk of the population, you might say everybody below 50 or 55, were either small children or were not born yet.
>
> And there's no question about their great feeling of guilt—even though they were not there to participate in it—of what their nation did. And then to take advantage of that visit, on that occasion, to go there—I just think is contrary to what I believe. We should all start recognizing the day of the end of the war, and make it more of a celebration of the fact that on that day, 40-odd years ago, began the friendship that we now know—40 years of peace

between us. And at the same time, you can say: And let us keep it this way and never go back to that other way.

And it just seemed to me that it would be just out of line to emphasize that when I was there, as a visitor in their country. I am supportive of the Holocaust Museum [in Washington, D.C.]; I've done everything I can to be supportive of that. And I will say anytime that anyone wants me to say it, as publicly as I can, that, no, we must never forget that chapter in the history of humankind and our determination that it must never happen again.

A Storm of Controversy

On April 11 the White House staff in Santa Barbara, California, announced that the president and the chancellor would lay a wreath at the German military cemetery at Bitburg. This was the first I had even heard of Bitburg. The cemetery had been chosen and proposed to Kohl, we were told, because it was located in Kohl's home state, the Rhineland-Palatinate, and close to the most populous state in Germany, North Rhine-Westphalia, where an important election was to be held the following month. There was also a U.S. Air Force base in Bitburg. The reaction to this announcement was immediate, and it was one of anger. Nathan Perlmutter, national director of the Anti-Defamation League of B'nai B'rith, was quoted in the *Washington Post* the following day: "I think his visit to the cemetery of German soldiers is an act of grace because it is good to express friendship to a former enemy. But the asymmetry of doing that while choosing not to visit the graves of that enemy's victims is insensitive, and it is not a healing act."

On April 12, as negative reactions to Bitburg were growing, I got word that the president and vice president would not be able to attend a ceremony in the rotunda of the Capitol on April 18 commemorating the fortieth anniversary of the liberation of the Nazi death camps by U.S. forces. The president had been invited to speak, but the White House now told me that his schedule would not permit his attendance. I got Mike Deaver on the telephone. "Look, Mr. Image Maker, you'd better get your president down to the rotunda Holocaust ceremony. This cold shoulder to the Holocaust makes no sense and is becoming a big story." Deaver was unable to shift the schedules, he said, and asked me to stand in for the president.

The Furor Builds

Two days later came the revelation that the cemetery contained graves of members of the Waffen SS, the military arm of the SS, which had been commanded by Heinrich Himmler. Some SS units had served as Hitler's bodyguard, and others had been involved in atrocities against civilians. The Waffen SS were among the German units that had launched the Battle of the Bulge and had infiltrated American lines disguised in American uniforms.

The furor over Bitburg grew to fever pitch. Peter Somer, an NSC staff specialist on Western Europe, had been on the advance team at the cemetery and had specifically asked whether SS were buried there and had been told they were not. "There are no painful surprises here," the Germans had assured them. There was a light covering of snow on the ground when they were there, he said, and no one had brushed it aside to read gravestone inscriptions.

Monday, April 15, Mike Deaver phoned to say that neither Reagan nor Kohl would budge from the idea of going to Bitburg. Helmut Schmidt was visiting in Washington at the time and told me he had just learned that one of his grandfathers was Jewish. He also told me that he thought Kohl had been "crazy" to schedule the Bonn summit in May, given the deep emotional content of V-E Day for the German people. But reacting to the information from Deaver, he said the president's instinct was right, though incomplete: a Holocaust site should be included.

If the president had told Helmut Kohl that he would go to Bitburg, I knew that he would go unless Kohl himself yielded in his insistence on this increasingly problematic visit. Ronald Reagan would not pull the plug unilaterally. I also knew that the earlier controversy over Dachau probably meant that there would be no visit there. But I felt the president *must* pay tribute to a Holocaust site. Shortly after Deaver's call, I went over to see the president to urge him to do so. Somewhat to my surprise I found that he had already changed his mind: he *would* go to a Holocaust site, and he was sending Deaver back to Bonn immediately to work it out with Kohl's staff.

Earlier that day President Reagan had received a long special-channel message from Chancellor Helmut Kohl. The message was extraordinary and put tremendous pressure on the president to follow through on the visit to Bitburg.

(To fully appreciate the pressure brought to bear on Ronald Reagan by Helmut Kohl, it is necessary to read Chancellor Kohl's letter in its entirety. I have not been allowed to reprint this letter here. The U.S. State Department refused to allow me to do so[1] despite my argument that West German "government spokesman Peter Boenisch had made known the contents of the letter from Kohl to Reagan" in Bonn on April 16, 1985.[2]

1. As required by law, as a senior public official with access to classified material, I had to submit my manuscript for clearance by the Department of State.

2. As reported by the Foreign Broadcast Information Service (a U.S. government publication) on April 17, 1985.

And the *New York Times* had reported on April 17, 1985, "The unusual step of publicizing Mr. Kohl's letter appeared to reflect the Bonn Government's irritation with Reagan aides' handling of the preparations for the visit to West Germany." I had explained to the State Department that I hoped the department would agree that we were breaching no confidence in printing a letter whose contents had in part already been made available by Mr. Kohl's own government.

The State Department, on its own initiative, referred the matter to the German government to see whether they would object to the publication of this letter. The German government decided that they did object to my reprinting of the text of the letter.)

Dated April 15, the "Dear Ron" letter stated flatly that if the Bitburg visit was canceled, such a decision would be fateful: it would have a serious psychological effect on the friendly sentiments of the German people for the United States of America and for the Reagan administration.

Chancellor Kohl said that the Bitburg cemetery, like all comparable German military cemeteries, contained the graves of mostly very young servicemen, many of them only eighteen, nineteen, or twenty years old, who lost their lives in the final days of the war. They included members of the Waffen SS who, Kohl said, were doing their duty as soldiers, and who died very young in the Bitburg area. At the age of eighteen or nineteen, Kohl said, they had no choice as to where the draft would send them. Were the few graves of those young men of that time, the chancellor asked the president, to serve as a pretext forty years after the war for us not to honor together all the dead of World War II? And, he argued, what are the Germans to think of a friendship that does not permit the American president and the German chancellor to lay a wreath together at a German military cemetery forty years after the war?

He said that he could understand the reaction of the Jewish organizations that still had very vivid memories of National Socialist terror. That was the reason, he said, why he had initially suggested that the president might visit Dachau, "although over 60 percent of the Germans living today were born after World War II." He renewed the proposal that the president visit Dachau or another site commemorating the "victims of fascist terror." He went on, "Even then you will not be able to satisfy all those now making public protests, but I am certain that you will meet with the understanding and support of all those who are serious about peace and friendship between our two nations."[3]

But he said that he felt strengthened in his attitude that the Bitburg visit should not be changed because of Soviet propaganda against President

3. I quote these passages directly because they are from a section of the letter released publicly by the German government at the time.

Reagan's visit. The Soviet leadership was, Kohl said, well aware that such a symbolic act over the graves of the war dead would foster friendship and understanding between our two peoples.

The impact of Kohl's letter was profound, and I regret that because of the decision of the United States and German governments, I have not been permitted to reprint its full and lengthy text here.

President Reagan was deeply affected by the strength and vehemence of Kohl's views. Kohl was adamant. In remarks to the press at the conclusion of a conference on April 16, the president again explained publicly his rationale for the upcoming state visit, which was provoking an ever-increasing storm of controversy. "My purpose was and remains not to reemphasize the crimes of the Third Reich in 12 years of power, but to celebrate the tremendous accomplishments of the German people in 40 years of liberty, freedom, democracy and peace," he said. "It was to remind the world that since the close of that terrible war, the United States and the Federal Republic have established an historic relationship, not of superpower to satellite, but of sister republics bonded together by common ideals and alliance and partnership."

The next day, the American embassy in Bonn reported that they had checked the Bitburg graves registry against SS records in the Berlin Documentation Center. Of forty-eight identified as Waffen SS, fifteen were listed in SS records; of these fifteen there were only two whose records contained more than rudimentary information: Ernst Schuler: an SS member since 1933, and at one time a member of the SS security service; Otto Beugel: awarded the Cross of Gold for, among other things, having killed ten Americans in combat. Overall, our embassy reported, a significant number of the 2,000 soldiers buried at Bitburg had been born before 1920 and therefore were not green recruits brought into battle in the final days of the war.

On Thursday, April 18, President Reagan, in a question-and-answer session with broadcasters and editors, made a statement that was immediately flashed out by the media: "I think that there's nothing wrong with visiting that cemetery, where those young men are victims of nazism also, even though they were fighting in the German uniform, drafted into service to carry out the hateful wishes of the Nazis. They were victims, just as surely as the victims in the concentration camps." The president's words drew immediate and heavy criticism for equating victims with perpetrators.

By high noon, I was at the Capitol rotunda. The atmosphere was as highly charged as at any event in which I had ever taken part. The crowd was large, the emotion tangible, and the hostility palpable. The virtual disbelief that the president would ever go to Bitburg was evident on all sides. Holocaust survivor and Nobel Peace Prize laureate Elie Wiesel spoke. I was seated only a few feet away. He turned to me from the podium and said, "I plead to you, please be our emissary. Tell those who need to know our pain is genuine, our outrage is deep, and our perplexity is infinite."

I could see that reading out my prepared statement would not in any way fit the occasion or serve the president well. When my turn came to speak, I put aside my prepared speech and searched for words. I said that Nazism "dealt an almost devastating blow to all our most fundamental hopes for the modern world. Those who prior to the war had maintained their faith in the possibility of human progress, in the idea that with high culture and high civilization would come the end of man's inhumanity to man . . . were stunned by the Holocaust. . . . I share with you also the deep conviction that there is no place within the deep spirit we feel of reconciliation . . . for understanding for those who took part in the perpetration of the Nazi horror." The visit to Bitburg was not going to be undertaken, I said, to try to "understand" what the SS did. The audience responded with a standing ovation. I was deeply moved.

The next day, April 19, the president was scheduled to award the Congressional Gold Medal of Achievement to Elie Wiesel at the White House. Tensions were building as to whether Wiesel would accept the medal or not. Don Regan, who was only a few months into his new position as White House chief of staff, was in a lather about it, feeling that the president was walking into political disaster. "Bitburg is killing us," he said. He instructed the White House advance team in Germany to ask the Germans to come up with a substitute event for Bitburg. I again emphasized to Don that the president simply had to go to a Holocaust site: if he was not going to visit a concentration camp, then he should take my place at the Yad Vashem Holocaust memorial ceremony in Israel. After intense consideration, the White House crew agreed that the president would go to Bergen-Belsen; Dachau was a problem because the president would have to spend time with Bavarian leader Franz Josef Strauss, whose frequently cited views on removing Germany from Hitler's shadow would diminish the occasion.

Reflecting on the day's events later in my office, I expressed my concern about the approaching ceremony honoring Elie Wiesel. "The president must take this as an opportunity. He must surround it with the right kind of words. He must be understanding and gentle. What he says will be tremendously important. There is unbelievable hostility; you can just feel it. He must be totally nonconfrontational." I feared that the White House speechwriters would *not* produce the right words. The attitude of White House Director of Communications Pat Buchanan was confrontational, as was his style—exactly what was *not* needed in this increasingly bitter atmosphere. I had asked Peter Rodman and Elliott Abrams to produce a draft for the president's use and I asked Bud McFarlane to get the White House speechwriters to consider it seriously. Bud said that he welcomed a draft text from us.

*   *   *

Reporters were calling the Bitburg controversy the worst blunder of the Reagan administration. On ABC's "World News Tonight," Sam Donaldson reported, "Not since White House visitors denounced the Vietnam War to Lyndon Johnson's face has a President publicly listened to such criticism of one of his decisions. Though Mr. Reagan listened attentively, he didn't change his mind. He talked on the phone with West German Chancellor Helmut Kohl for 20 minutes this morning. Kohl, knowing Mr. Reagan would have liked for him to have offered to cancel the cemetery visit, instead pleaded with the President to keep to his schedule. Mr. Reagan assured him he would, explaining to Elie Wiesel in a private meeting why he believed he had no choice."

I had told the president privately, "Bitburg is a disaster." The president was, in my view, hitting the most sensitive people at the most sensitive time, in the nation about which they were most sensitive. That night, Bud McFarlane used his newly established special communications channel to Chancellor Kohl's security adviser, Horst Teltschik. It was a long and unusual message, representative of Bud's thought process and style.

April 18, 1985

Subject: Message to Horst Teltschik

Dear Horst:

. . . . A number of unique and almost surreal factors have emerged which have so fundamentally altered the American people's perceptions of this visit as to risk real damage to the relationship unless we come to grips with it promptly. I refer to the truly overwhelming tide of criticism which has emerged in the American Jewish community over the president's acceptance of the chancellor's invitation to visit the cemetery at Bitburg.

Horst, I don't intend to argue the merits of the issue. Were it possible for the American people to understand the depth of the chancellor's sincerity in extending the invitation and the profundity of his commitment to reconciliation, there would be no issue. As matters stand, however, this appreciation does not exist. Nor can it be established in the extremely charged climate of outrage and bitterness that has been evoked in our country. It is truly sad that such a compassionate conviction has been so distorted. Yet distorted it is, and it is for this reason that I am sending this message. Horst, I am truly convinced that if the visit to Bitburg cemetery goes forward as now planned, it will lead to a groundswell of criticism that will not only seriously mar the quality of the visit but will also etch a scar of some depth on the basic character of US-German relations. (Looking back on this characterization, it reads as very extreme, but I must say, is justified.)

I want to ask your help, Horst, in seeking to find a way to remove what I

believe will be an unavoidable loss from the schedule. I believe we must find
a way to substitute another event for the visit to the Bitburg cemetery. . . . I
honestly believe that unless we do so, no amount of public explanations will
overcome the chorus of criticism which has reached a truly fever pitch here
in the States.

Horst . . . We are on the threshold of encountering real damage to the
relationship. President Reagan is deeply grieved over this. But he, too,
shares my sense of impending damage, albeit completely innocent and unintended. . . .

Unfortunately, the drumbeat of criticism gathers momentum with every
hour here. Indeed, on Friday morning the president will be called upon to
award a medal to one of the leading survivors of the Holocaust here at the
White House and it would be extremely timely were it possible to announce
an alternative site. As difficult as this may be to consider in such a short
time, could I ask you to give it your attention and let me know by return
cable. . . .

Bud McFarlane had not consulted the president before sending this message, although he had checked with Don Regan. The president was quite
irritated when he learned that Bud had asked the Germans to change plans
without consulting him directly. Nonetheless, the White House and State
Department staffs, by now working fairly closely together, rushed forward
for consideration a list of alternatives to Bitburg: the German War Memorial at Koblenz; the memorial to war dead at Bonn's North Cemetery;
the Adenauer memorial at Rondorf; the bridge at Remagen.

At 6:20 A.M. Friday, Ambassador Arthur Burns telephoned me from Bonn.
Teltschik had given McFarlane's message to Kohl, and Kohl had replied to
Burns. Kohl said that if the Bitburg visit was canceled, it would be unlikely
that he could remain as chancellor, and it would be terrible for U.S.-
German relations. Arthur Burns said he had already telephoned Elie Wiesel to tell him what Kohl had said and that he, Arthur, felt that the schedule
should not be changed. If Kohl was hurt politically, if his government fell,
Burns said, it would hurt the Federal Republic of Germany, and this ultimately would hurt the Jews, as they would be blamed for undermining a
fundamentally friendly government.

Arthur Burns's advice was very difficult for both of us. I knew that he
had come to this conclusion with the greatest reluctance, because he could
feel, as a Jew himself and as a refugee from that part of the world (he had
been born in Austria), the trauma of all those who saw the deep moral
meaning of Bitburg. But again this was characteristic of Arthur, who looked
at the situation with care, came to his own judgment of what was best for
the United States and for the president at that point, and gave his advice.
I told him, "Well, that is your view, Arthur. You should express it to the

president. You are his ambassador. You are the closest person we have to the situation in Germany and it's an important contribution to the president's thinking."

"Hitler is laughing in hell right now," I said. After arriving at my office early that morning, I had brought together a meeting of State's people most closely involved in the Bitburg trip. "The idea of the visit, reconciliation, has been destroyed. Kohl has butchered it. He told us there were no SS buried at Bitburg. Teltschik said there were none."

With the ceremony to honor Elie Wiesel due to take place in just a few hours, Elliott Abrams said White House speechwriter Tony Dolan had called to say that he found State's intervention in their speechwriting process offensive. "He said our [State's] draft was 'garbage, trash; butt out,' " Abrams recounted.

Arthur Burns called from Bonn again. Chancellor Kohl had just telephoned President Reagan directly to say that if the president did not go to Bitburg, it would be a political catastrophe for Kohl. He had a choice, Kohl said: President Reagan could go to Bitburg, or he could cancel and see the Kohl government fall.

True or not, I thought, that was an extraordinary—even unique—message for the head of one powerful nation to make to another. I regarded it as an expression of weakness, with or without Bitburg. "How strong is a government," I said, "that could be toppled by visiting a different cemetery?" But I also knew that the president could not ignore such an emotionally charged plea from Chancellor Kohl.

I headed right over to the White House to talk to the president. I could see that he had already made up his mind. I found him determined not to be pushed around further by anybody's pressure. His decision was firm: he would go to Bergen-Belsen, and he would go to Bitburg.

I came back to my office and again called a meeting of the people working on the visit: "The president is firm. So now let's make it work. No carping. No second-guessing." I knew very well that the president personally felt deeply about the Holocaust. Long before anyone in Washington ever heard of Bitburg, Ronald Reagan told me of how he first learned of the Holocaust. During the latter part of World War II, Reagan's job involved viewing film shot by military cameramen and war correspondent photographers. He assembled the selected shots into briefing films for senior officers. When he saw the first footage of the horror inside the concentration camps, filmed at the time the death camps were liberated, he was immensely shocked. Against regulations, he kept copies of the films because, he said, the scenes were so appalling that some people would later deny that it could have been so bad—or that it had taken place at all. Four years after the war, Reagan recounted, a guest at his house for dinner said he found the stories impossible to believe—it couldn't have happened that way. So Ronald Reagan got out the can of film and ran it for his skeptical guest.

When Prime Minister Yitzhak Shamir made his first visit to Washington during the Reagan administration, the president told this story to Shamir, who was deeply moved by it. Upon his return to Israel, Shamir told the story to Israeli journalists, who reported it in the Hebrew language press. English translations were picked up by American reporters. As the story emerged in American newspapers, it had become garbled, maintaining Ronald Reagan had said that he was present at the liberation of the camps as part of a U.S. army film crew. The president had said no such thing. But the critics then cited it as an example of Reagan's inability to distinguish fact from fantasy or real life from an actor's role that he had played or wished he had played. But I had heard the true version. I knew that the president back then had, in his own way, created his own Holocaust memorial.

At the scheduled time that Friday, April 19, the president presented the Congressional Gold Medal of Achievement to Elie Wiesel at the White House. The ceremony was carried live on television. The president did, after all, use much of the material we had sent him in his statement. He was compelling in his manner and delivery. Elie Wiesel then rose to speak. Showing a largeness of spirit, he expressed his awareness of the president's "commitment to humanity." Then he uttered what were to become the most famous words of the Bitburg controversy: "That place, Mr. President, is not your place. Your place is with the victims of the SS."

At that moment there was silence, but soon there was a deafening cacophony of the most varied assertions, reports, and declarations:

- The Senate voted 82 to 0 against the president's going to Bitburg. House Republican Whip Trent Lott informed us that the House was about to pass a near-unanimous resolution that the president cancel the Bitburg visit. At the same time, Bundestag deputies were writing to American members of Congress urging them to support the president's decision to go. The parliamentary majority leader of the Christian Democrats, Alfred Dregger, wrote to the fifty-three U.S. senators who had signed a letter calling on the president to cancel Bitburg. He described their request as an insult to his brother, who had died on the Eastern front fighting against communism.
- The Soviet press called the visit a "sacrilege," maintaining that the United States was allying itself with "past and present Nazis" to achieve world domination. "This is something to have been expected from the head of the Administration which proclaimed state terrorism its official policy," *Izvestia* reported on April 25.

- Religious leaders weighed in. The president received a telegram from Archbishop John J. O'Connor of New York urging him to cancel the Bitburg visit. We should be prepared to forgive, but never honor or forget, those who perpetrated the horrors of World War II, the archbishop said. President Reagan said that he was "not going to honor anybody," but to bring a visible awareness to a great reconciliation. Evangelist Jerry Falwell also opposed the visit and said that the president should admit that he was wrong.
- The American Jewish community was in an uproar. Benjamin Netanyahu, deputy chief of mission at the Israeli embassy in Washington, telephoned me to urge us to find an alternative quickly. "The groundswell is unbelievable," he said, "and building."
- Henry Kissinger telephoned President Reagan to support his decision to go ahead. Shortly thereafter, Kissinger said publicly that if the Bitburg visit was scrapped, "it would do enormous damage to our foreign policy" and "it would prove no particular point." "I believe," Kissinger said, "that the debate on this issue should stop."[4] And the top military man on my staff, General Jack Chain, told me that he had served at the U.S. Air Force base near Bitburg and that for years, every Memorial Day, American, German, and French commanders together had laid a wreath at Bitburg. So why the uproar now?

Our Own Past: Vietnam

Oddly, at the time of the public debate over how the United States should address this central question of Germany's past, a second debate was raging within the administration, unnoticed by the media, over how the United States should approach a central issue of America's past. April 29, 1985, was the tenth anniversary of the fall of Saigon. Should the administration say anything at all on the occasion, and if so, what? The overwhelming weight of opinion, expressed with increasing vehemence, was "don't open old wounds." I decided that a speech should be given, and I began to work on a draft, with the help of a few close associates, in a process that often became intense. The night before the event, I sent the draft around the administration for comment. Phone calls poured in: "Don't, for God's sake, give that speech." The NSC's staff specialist on Vietnam, Dick Childress, called in a rage, demanding to speak to me. The speech must not be given, he said. It would infuriate Hanoi and disrupt our efforts to make progress on the POW/MIA issue. I disagreed. I took my speech over to

4. As quoted in the *New York Times* on May 1, 1985, p. A18.

the president to read. He liked it and gave it his vote of approval: thumbs up.

In the vast diplomatic lobby of the State Department, I delivered the speech to a throng of several thousand people who packed the ground floor and the inside walkway above. "The tenth anniversary of the fall of Indochina," I said, "is an occasion for all of us, as a nation, to reflect on the meaning of that experience. As the fierce emotions of that time subside, perhaps our country has a better chance now of assessing the war and its impact. This is not merely a historical exercise. Our understanding of the past affects our conduct in the present, and thus, in part, determines our future."

In the course of America's involvement in Vietnam, there had been wrongdoing, and there had been error—political, military, and moral— but the true horror had come with the Communist takeover, as the 24 million people of South Vietnam became victims of a totalitarian state before which they stood naked, stripped of the most elemental human rights. And in Cambodia had come the worst horror of all: the genocide of at least 1 million Cambodians by the Khmer Rouge. "Events since 1975 shed light on the past: this horror was precisely what we were trying to prevent. . . . Whatever mistakes in how the war was fought, whatever one's view of the strategic rationale for our intervention, the *morality* of our effort must now be clear. Those Americans who served, or who grieve for their loved ones lost or missing, can hold their heads high: our sacrifice was in the service of noble ideals—to save innocent people from brutal tyranny."

I quoted from the grand old American diplomat Ellsworth Bunker: "No one who dies for freedom ever dies in vain." Emotions ran high. There were both cheers and tears. When it was over, I was wrung out. Reporters asked Ronald Reagan whether I was speaking for the administration in my comments on Vietnam. "Damn right he was," the president responded.

Arrival in Germany: Tension Mounts

The president and I arrived at Cologne-Bonn Airport on May 1 in a soft, cold drizzle. The president went off to Schloss Gymnich, the official West German guest residence, and my staff and I went to the Hotel Am Tulpenfeld, near the Bundestag. In my suite I found that someone had arrayed bottles of the well-known beer made in Bitburg and steins bearing its advertising slogan, *"Bitte ein Bit!"* The first people to come around to talk to me were our security agents. There was a special feeling of concern about this economic summit and state visit, a concern that extremist plots might be under way. Explosives in bars, clubs, and restaurants were especially feared. I asked all of our people to stick close by and take their meals in the hotel.

I followed my own advice and invited seven or eight of the State Department people on the trip to have dinner with me. Most of them had to keep working on papers or had other dinner commitments or press interviews scheduled, so it turned out that I was joined only by Paul Wolfowitz and State's spokesman Bernie Kalb. Paul and I listened to Bernie tell tales of the Jewish experience in America. I said to them that maybe we had gained some insight. "This uproar after forty years shows that the wounds are not healed; it shows instead how deep they run. To mark the war and the Holocaust we must say that we will never forget. But we must also remember that war and hatred can take anyone in their grip."

On May 3, General Matthew Ridgway telephoned Mike Deaver. Ridgway, then ninety years old, said, "I commanded the 18th Airborne Corps at the Battle of the Bulge. I am a soldier, and the president is in trouble. I am ready to come and lay that wreath myself." The White House took him up on his offer to help and arranged for General Ridgway to come to Bitburg for a solemn shake of hands with Johannes Steinhoff, a former *Luftwaffe* pilot who turned against Hitler and later, as a general in the West German Air Force, rose to become chief of staff of NATO air forces in Central Europe.

Media reports were coming in incessantly, and all were bad. Most of those buried in the forty-some graves marked Waffen SS had belonged to the Second SS Panzer Division, which went under the name *"Das Reich."* Some of those soldiers had participated in one of the worst regular army massacres of the war: at Oradour-sur-Glane in France in June 1944. All 642 residents of the village had been killed, including 207 children.

Chancellor Kohl's official spokesman said that President Reagan, in a meeting with Kohl, expressed regret that some Americans believed in collective German guilt. Larry Speakes, White House spokesman, denied that the president had said this, but many in the press interpreted it as an apology by the president to the chancellor for the position of American Jews. Teltschik told Rick Burt of his worries that all this furor would lead to more anti-Semitism in Germany. "Young Germans," he said "are saying that watching the power of the American Jews to pressure the president, they now understand the problem Germany faced prior to World War II." Such ugly sentiments emerging in Germany only reinforced to me the undesirability of a Bitburg visit in the first place.

The *New York Times* on May 3 reported, "SS Veterans Feel 'Rehabilitated' by Reagan Visit." There was at that time a reunion of the Waffen SS "Death's Head" Division going on in Nesselwang, in Swabia. The paper reported that this reunion would be followed by a reunion of the First Waffen SS Panzer Corps, part of which had formed Adolf Hitler's bodyguard. At the Death's Head Division reunion, *Times* reporter John Tag-liabue interviewed one veteran, who said, "The Zionists stop at nothing. But the President is an honest man. He made his decision, and he sticks to it." Another veteran said, "It took a long time, but this shows we were soldiers, just like the others. I never committed a war crime, and I don't know anyone who did. We didn't have time for that sort of thing. Our guys were disciplined, and we were too busy fighting."

The first event of the trip was the economic summit meeting, which was, after all, the primary reason we were in Bonn. On Sunday, May 5, before we all set off to go to Bergen-Belsen and Bitburg, I remarked to my staff about the battle we had had over our communiqué. The drafters had, as always, gone through the night wrangling over changes in wording. This year's fight was over how to refer to the Strategic Defense Initiative—would it be mentioned at all, and if so, with what language. My proposal was for the communiqué to state that we, the Summit Seven, "agree that SDI research is a prudent, justifiable, and useful step." The French refused. It was maddening. Finally, we got acceptable language.

All through the summit sessions it was evident that European leaders were following the Bitburg controversy closely. Prime Minister Craxi said there was "resonance" in Italy for what we were doing; Italians understood. Prime Minister Thatcher was appalled. She said that she for the first time felt a certain sympathy with Labour members of Parliament—those who had expressed shock over the Reagan decision to go to Bitburg. They wanted to see how the United States would handle the matter of "Germany-once-the-enemy and Germany-now-the-ally." As other leaders watched the process, they saw that President Reagan was willing to take tremendous political heat at home in order to help a friend abroad, and he was willing to follow through with his decision against great pressure. Even skeptics were impressed by his loyalty and staying power. It was an unusual per-formance, but characteristic of Ronald Reagan.

The President Speaks at Bergen-Belsen

Just before leaving for Bergen-Belsen, I pulled out of my pocket a small lapel pin with a German emblem on it. It symbolized a decoration, the Grand Cross of the Order of Merit, that I had received in 1974 from the German government. The event had been relatively unpublicized. Helmut Schmidt had pinned it on me. John McCloy, the great postwar statesman and once our high commissioner to Germany, had been there, along with a few other people interested in German-American relations. So this morn-ing, just before leaving, I asked Rick Burt, Bernie Kalb, and Charlie Hill whether I should wear this little button on my lapel. Immediately a fierce debate erupted. "Wear it; it symbolizes the alliance." "You don't need another controversy." "Don't be intimidated by the press. It's a gesture of reconciliation." "Good grief, it has the Iron Cross on it. Ask Arthur Burns what he thinks." I sighed and put the little pin away.

The weather at Bergen-Belsen was gray and unpleasant. It was drizzling lightly and muddy underfoot. After it was liberated by British troops on April 15, 1945, the camp was burned in order to stop a raging typhus epidemic from spreading among its 40,000 emaciated survivors. So no buildings stood at Bergen-Belsen. Instead, the president and Nancy Reagan walked among huge mounds of earth thrown up over mass graves, each marked with a small sign: "Here lie buried 8,000 bodies"; "Here lie buried 1,200 bodies," on and on. In one of them Anne Frank was buried. The scene was stark and somber.

Ronald Reagan spoke with power and emotion: "Here, death ruled, but we've learned something as well. Because of what happened, we found that death cannot rule forever, and that's why we're here today. We're here because humanity refuses to accept that freedom of the spirit of man can ever be extinguished. We're here to commemorate that life triumphed over the tragedy and the death of the Holocaust—overcame the suffering, the sickness, the testing and, yes, the gassings. . . . Out of the ashes—hope, and from all the pain—promise."

After quoting Anne Frank's eternally affecting words "In spite of everything I still believe that people are good at heart," the president concluded: "Such memories take us where God intended His children to go—toward learning, toward healing, and, above all, toward redemption. . . . We're all witnesses; we share the glistening hope that rests in every human soul. Hope leads us, if we're prepared to trust it—toward what President Lincoln called the better angels of our nature. And then, rising above all this cruelty, out of this tragic and nightmarish time, beyond the anguish, the pain and the suffering for all time, we can and must pledge: Never again."

When I returned to the aircraft, everyone who had not been there seemed to be speaking at once. "What happened?" "What was it like?" I could only shake my head. The experience was wrenching, the contrasts stark. I thought to myself, it was both unreal and yet all too real. You had to be there but couldn't wait to leave. It is too easy to forget. It is essential to remember.

We flew to the U.S. Air Force base at Bitburg. Members of my staff had been at the cemetery, where they recounted small skirmishes were being waged between the press and the government public relations officers. TV cameramen had bought cut flowers and had laid them on SS graves to be photographed, but the PR people would grab them away. The White House advance team had barred all television camera platforms or tripods so that cameramen could not pan from the president's wreath laying to a grave with an SS inscription. A White House official said to a network newsman,

"I don't care what you say as long as I control what you show." West German army reservists passed out leaflets: "*Say Yes to German-American Friendship*. Mr. President, we appreciate very much your courage to also visit the graves of German soldiers. We young Germans are very much aware of the brutal crimes committed in our recent history. They are a heavy burden on our conscience and we ask the victims to forgive."

Our motorcade came through the little town of Bitburg. It was by now a bright, warm, pleasant day. People lined the main street, most holding little American and German flags. At the crossroads, police in plastic riot shield helmets held back marching groups of people, each one wearing a yellow Star of David with the word *Jude* on it.

At 2:45 P.M. the president got out of his limousine at the gate of Kolmeshöhe, the name of the cemetery at Bitburg. The main impression was how tiny it was, about the size of a basketball court. The president walked down the gravel path flanking the graves and swung around in front of a squat stone, not a grave marker, and with the help of four German soldiers laid a tall wreath. Its message said: from "The President of the United States of America." (The message on the wreath he had laid at Bergen-Belsen had said: from "The people of the United States of America.") General Matthew Ridgway and Lieutenant General Johannes Steinhoff shook hands. A bugler sounded "*Ich Hatt' ein Kameraden*" ("Once I Had a Comrade"), the German "Taps." President Reagan and Chancellor Kohl did not shake hands. So there was no "photo op," as Kohl had wanted— no handclasp over the graves of the fallen—as he had with Mitterrand at Verdun. ("He who lives by the photo op dies by the photo op," quipped a journalist later on my plane.) Reagan never faced the Waffen SS graves. There were no speeches. Kohl brushed tears from his cheeks. Total elapsed time in the cemetery was eight minutes, but the brief moment left vast impressions:

- The mayor of Bitburg mentioned that there was another German military cemetery seven kilometers away with no SS graves. "Here," he said, "German history is clear. There's nothing hidden. There are no secrets."
- Banners in English by the road said. "Thank you. God bless you." A supporter of the visit, Hans-Peter Müller, grabbed a reporter, unfurled one of the banners, and said, "There is no half-reconciliation. We cannot be half-friend, half-enemy. I was never a Nazi."[5]
- At a simultaneous ceremony in New York, Elie Wiesel said, "Why not admit it, today we are wounded. . . . What was attempted at Bitburg [was] a denial of the past, a disregard of Jewish agony."
- Rabbi Henry Siegman of the American Jewish Congress said, "The

5. As reported by James Markham in the *New York Times* on May 6, 1985.

ugliest thing about the Bitburg lie is that the Germans and Americans are called on to falsify history in order to find a common base."

- In Israel, Menachem Begin said that the president's act had brought "one of the saddest days in the history of the Jewish people." Yitzhak Rabin said that President Reagan "will not be forgiven either by enlightened humanity or by the Jewish people."

- Richard Wirthlin, the polling expert, took a quick survey of American Jews and concluded, he told me later in one of our periodic meetings, that "the impact politically is immeasurable. Something broke, ripped, and is gone as a result."

- The *New York Times* lead editorial on May 6 said, "What now needs remembering is how quickly even a ceremonial error can develop a political, indeed geopolitical life of its own, persuading the most powerful leaders that they are helpless hostages of history. For all his pain at having to offend so many Americans, Mr. Reagan put it starkly: to abandon his promise to walk with Chancellor Kohl through the Bitburg cemetery would have looked as if he had 'caved in' under pressure. And as Richard Nixon and Henry Kissinger were summoned to testify, breaking even a small promise to an ally in the nuclear age would be a grievous sin. . . . This alliance will survive the folly of Bitburg, just as it would have survived the cancellation of Bitburg, because it is now deeply rooted in the democratic politics and prosperity of all its peoples."

President Reagan next returned to the U.S. Air Force base at Bitburg for one more emotional moment. He delivered a powerful, moving speech that summarized his view of this tumultuous day and lifted our sights toward his original objective:

I have just come from the cemetery where German war dead lay at rest. No one could visit there without deep and conflicting emotions. I felt great sadness that history could be filled with such waste, destruction, and evil, but my heart was also lifted by the knowledge that from the ashes has come hope and that from the terrors of the past we have built 40 years of peace, freedom, and reconciliation among our nations. . . . Some old wounds have been reopened, and this I regret very much because this should be a time of healing. . . .

To the survivors of the Holocaust: Your terrible suffering has made you ever vigilant against evil. Many of you are worried that reconciliation means forgetting. I promise you, we will never forget. I have just come this morning from Bergen-Belsen, where the horror of that terrible crime, the Holocaust, was forever burned upon my memory. No, we will never forget, and we say with the victims of the Holocaust, "Never again." . . . The evil world of Nazism turned all values upside down. Nevertheless, we can mourn the German war dead today as human beings, crushed by a vicious ideology. . . .

Too often in the past each war only planted the seeds of the next. We celebrate today the reconciliation between our two nations that has liberated us from that cycle of destruction. . . .

On this 40th anniversary of World War II, we mark the day when the hate, the evil, and the obscenities ended, and we commemorate the rekindling of the democratic spirit in Germany.

Five days after Bitburg and Bergen-Belsen, I was in Israel and about to speak at a special ceremony at Yad Vashem, the Holocaust memorial. On the drive through the hills toward Jerusalem, Ambassador Sam Lewis told me that the reaction of the Israeli public to Bitburg had in fact been low-key. "They see the president as a friend," he said.

At Yad Vashem, on a promontory of rock overlooking the wooded hills of Jerusalem, before a flame set in front of a massive sculpture that revealed, out of images of captivity and suffering, an emerging Star of David, I said: "The images of Jewish suffering still burn in our minds and our hearts. We must make sure those images never fade. For only by seeing and knowing that the capacity for evil exists in mankind can we do what we must to see to it that our humanity prevails. We do not avert our eyes. We do not forget. But neither do we despair. Let us be guided by both memory and hope. . . . Let us seek and never turn from the truth."

Retrospective: Understanding Bitburg

In many respects the centerpiece of the Bitburg drama was Ronald Reagan. Here he demonstrated his great capacity to stand against the political winds of the moment in favor of what he regarded—whether people agreed with him or not—as a primary obligation to Helmut Kohl, our close ally, a leader who had told the president starkly that his government would fall if the president changed his stand. This stubborn determination and willingness to do what he considered to be right, regardless of the apparent political fallout, was a distinguishing characteristic of Ronald Reagan and his presidency. I saw it time and again. I regarded this trait as one of his greatest strengths and an important reason why he had such tremendous popular support.

People felt that here was a man, whether you agreed with him or not, who had the ability to stand up for what he thought, even though there were many around counseling a different action on political grounds. Of course, the opposition to Bitburg was not primarily political but moral, and President Reagan *shared* the moral stance of those who opposed the visit. I am sure that this was an agonizing situation for him. Nevertheless, he was clear in his mind that he needed to proceed and that he would proceed.

*   *   *

I can only speculate about Helmut Kohl's motives in this. Perhaps he stated them fully enough in his cable to the president on April 15. He obviously wished to have some symbol of a new look at Germany and recognition of the democratic spirit in Germany that had emerged since World War II. He also had in his mind the positive response in Germany to his dramatic meeting with Mitterrand at Verdun. The visit to Bitburg, at least as it started out, was a way of putting the past to rest and moving on to a free and democratic future. As the whole episode devolved, I felt that Kohl overreacted to the threat to his government, although it is very difficult for an outsider to appreciate fully all the factors at play. The politician who runs for office has to make his own calls. But Kohl's unbending iron will did seem to demonstrate a massive insensitivity, on the one hand, to the troubles he was causing Ronald Reagan and, on the other, to the trauma this episode caused in the Jewish community around the world and, beyond the Jewish community, to all who remembered the Holocaust and its horrors.

The Bitburg episode made me and countless others ponder again the profound and agonizing issues involved: "the German question" and "the Jewish question"; the power of history in present events; the necessity to think through the meaning of forgetting, forgiving, reconciling, understanding—and their relationship to each other as concepts that humans must face. When the enormity of the event suddenly became inescapable, everyone involved seemed suddenly to grasp for words, for thoughts, for emotions, that could plumb these depths. So I had said that within a spirit of reconciliation there was no place for seeking to forgive the perpetrators of horror. Ronald Reagan himself felt that all mankind was victimized by these crimes; Elie Wiesel reiterated the undeniable uniqueness of the victims; Helmut Kohl proved both insensitive and yet more agonizingly troubled by Bitburg than anyone.

The lesson of Bitburg to me was that we must never forget, because so many do not want to remember. Ironically, the events that climaxed with the Sunday visit to Bitburg renewed more ardently than anything in decades the memory of the Holocaust. The Reagan state visit was undertaken to point up the achievements of West German democracy and its remarkable place in the Western alliance and the world economy as well as to celebrate forty years of freedom and friendship. Perhaps it achieved these goals in some measure. If it was a political plus for Helmut Kohl, it was a political disaster for Ronald Reagan. But also, as it gave rise to a fresh consideration of the Holocaust, the furor it caused showed that just such a fresh consideration was needed. Germany, its complexity, its agony, its achievements, its promise, its wrenching questions about itself, were all on vivid display.

CHAPTER 29

Rocks on the Summit Road

Bitburg was behind us. President Reagan flew to Strasbourg, where he addressed the European Parliament on May 8, 1985. With the decline of the left in Western Europe and with most national governments in the hands of the parties of the political center, the losing politicians had made their way to Strasbourg, where they pursued their ideological causes through rhetoric in what was in truth a politically powerless forum. The president's speech was thoughtful. He explained in detail our approach to the Soviets. Signs of protest were held high for the cameras by representatives in T-shirts. Hecklers yelling "U.S. out of Nicaragua" sporadically interrupted as the president spoke. At intervals, protesters walked out. The disruption continued throughout the president's talk.

Something went wrong with the teleprompter halfway through the speech. But the president found his place in his text with no problem and kept his cool throughout this bizarre scene. At the end, he addressed the protesters extemporaneously: "I admire this parliament and the chance for free speech here. And yet I can't help but remind all of us that some who take advantage of that right of democracy seem unaware that if the government they would advocate became a reality, no one would have that freedom to speak up again." Someone on my staff remarked, "Isolationism in America will take a big step forward today as TV viewers at home watch the European Parliamentarians flail about over Reagan's speech."

Aboard the aircraft bound for Lisbon I talked with President Reagan about my approaching meeting with Gromyko in Vienna. I wanted Bud McFarlane to sit in. He had been helpful in Geneva, and he liked the involvement. McFarlane agreed, but wanted to come so that the two of us could "talk to Gromyko privately." If Gromyko had something to say privately, I told him, that would come on his initiative, not ours. Again Bud yearned to undertake something secret. He wanted to go to Morocco to meet with King Hassan—a bad idea. Such a trip would imply approval of Morocco's new friendliness toward Libya and Qaddafi. He wanted to meet secretly in Rome with Jonas Savimbi, the leader of the Angolan

561

freedom fighters, to tell him that Chester Crocker really did represent the president's policy, but Savimbi ducked the meeting. Bud was not content with the tough and essential job the president had chosen him to do: coordinate the national security policy of the administration. He seemed unable to stay away from the press. He had "backgrounded" the president's Strasbourg speech in a way that clearly scooped the president. So it was Bud making news and not his boss; the White House crew was unhappy with him. Bud seemed to be drifting.

A Summit Comes into Focus

I had never been to Vienna before and wanted to go to the opera there. Upon my arrival, I dedicated four hours to *Der Rosenkavalier* with Leonie Rysanek. My hostess at the opera was Helene von Damm, now von Damm-Guertler after her recent marriage to the scion of the family that owned the Sacher Hotel, home of the Sacher torte. He was her fourth husband. Helene had started out with Ronald Reagan as his secretary in the governor's office in Sacramento and ran the personnel office in the White House in the early Reagan years. She had been born in Austria and now was back as our diplomatic envoy. She had many avid supporters, including at our embassy, and I felt that she was doing a fine job, as she had in White House personnel. But it was a disastrous step for our ambassador to marry a national of the host country.

Our press spokesman, Bernie Kalb, went to pay homage to Sigmund Freud at the consulting rooms at Berggasse 19, now kept as a museum. At our embassy, an elegant stone mansion from the imperial era, I was briefed by the deputy chief of mission (DCM) about the security bureaucracy's efforts to move our mission elsewhere so that the chancery could have a setback of fifty yards or so from any street; the Austrian government seemed inclined to deal with terrorists on the basis of "we will let you operate out of Vienna as long as you don't target Austrians." The DCM himself struck me as an odd duck: bright, precise, self-contained, but somehow mysterious. He, too, was Austrian-born. I inquired about him and was told that he was determined to keep his Vienna posting and was resisting the normal foreign service rotation to jobs elsewhere. His name was Felix Bloch. I encouraged the foreign service personnel system to move him on, but that did not happen.

Helene von Damm asked to see me alone. She was worried about "White House" unhappiness over her surprise divorce and marriage to Peter Guertler. "They were surprised because I did it quietly and privately to be discreet," she said. I told her that was not the problem. "You are a good ambassador. The problem is the nationality of your husband. People assume 'pillow talk.' Vienna is an international city. A lot goes on here;

people from all over the world are here to collect information and make deals." She said she understood this and had taken steps to "insulate" herself; for example, she never took classified documents home. I said that she should write out a statement about how she was handling this problem, but I was doubtful, I told her, of any way out. She could talk the situation over with me, I said, the next time she was in Washington. Helene did not know, nor did I at that moment, that the Austrian prime minister had sent a representative to the White House to tell Don Regan that the United States had to get her out of Vienna, as she was no longer a credible representative of America. I had earlier approached the president on this problem, but he waved me off.

The tone of U.S.-Soviet contacts had grown increasingly tense during the previous two months, and the killing of Major Nicholson in East Germany itself could not account for it. Gorbachev spoke in more moderate—and certainly more intriguing—language, but the underlying content of his statements was as tough as Brezhnev's. On the other hand, even as the Soviets talked and acted tough, they had been moving toward our agenda for almost a year now. This meeting in Vienna would be watched closely: could I use it to reverse a worsening situation? Would it moderate the atmosphere or contribute to the chill?

This would be the sixth time I had met Gromyko. The media was pressing to see whether our meeting would be a prelude to what they regarded as the *only* criterion of progress: a Reagan-Gorbachev summit. As far as I was concerned, the president had issued an invitation, and it was up to the Soviets to respond. I instructed my staff that absolutely *no one* was to raise the question of a summit with any Soviet counterpart, and I decided that I would not raise it with Gromyko. If I did, I knew, he would try to extract some concession from me as the price for a summit. That was a game I would not play.

Three hours had been scheduled for our meeting. I opened with highlights of my agenda, including human rights issues. Gromyko marched painstakingly and step-by-step through his list. Four hours passed. Then five. I was determined to go through every scrap of paper I had with me and to sit there until he broke. And he did. Finally, after six long hours, he said it was time to adjourn so we could be on time for the celebratory dinner to come. I agreed, gathered my papers, thanked him for his hospitality, and headed for the door.

Just then I felt a tap on my shoulder. "Gromyko would like a private word with you." I went over to the corner of the room where he was standing. "Is there anything else you want to talk about?" Gromyko asked me.

"No," I answered, "I've gone through everything."

"What about the summit?" he asked.

"What about it?" I replied.

"Gorbachev will not go to the United Nations [for the September opening of the General Assembly]," he said. "November would be better. President Reagan would be welcome in Moscow."

"It is your turn to come to Washington," I replied, as the most recent summits had been held in Moscow, Vladivostok, Helsinki, and Vienna.

"Out of the question!" Gromyko exploded. "It should be in Europe, in a third country."

"I will communicate that to Washington. Are you suggesting Geneva?" I asked.

"If you say Geneva, I'll have to say Helsinki," Gromyko growled.

So we were launched on our way to a summit. We agreed not to speak of this in public, and I held the information close: I did not even mention it in my cabled report to the president. I would ensure against a leak by reporting to President Reagan in person. Gromyko, I could see, had been instructed by Gorbachev to get the process started, to set the time and place. But Gromyko did not seem to have authority to engage on anything else. He was merely putting points down for the record. In six hours he turned not one new phrase, but simply waited for me to ask about a summit. The meeting had been sterile and peculiar—but at the final moment, productive.

My impression was that the Soviets were preoccupied with their domestic problems and this was forcing them to alter—for the better—the way they dealt with us. Yet the general assumption of the moment—quite to the contrary—was that the Soviets would agree to a summit only if they could extract a price from *us*: on arms control or Nicaragua, for example. If we didn't pay a price, they would shelve the whole matter for a couple of years. That notion was absolutely off the mark. Gorbachev, I felt, realized that the Soviet tactic of increasing superpower tension had not worked on Ronald Reagan. Gorbachev had far more to gain by seeking some form of accommodation.

That evening, I was seated next to Gromyko at dinner. He talked to me about the problem of alcoholism in the Soviet Union and the importance of Gorbachev's campaign against vodka. I told him we, too, were trying to curb excessive drinking, especially by drivers, but I reminded him of our disastrous experience with Prohibition. I told him rather spontaneously a joke going around. Two guys were standing in a long line to buy vodka. An hour went by, then two. One said to the other, "I'm fed up. I'm going over to the Kremlin to shoot Gorbachev." He left, and when he came back, his buddy asked him, "Well, did you shoot him?" "Hell, no," he responded. "The line there was even longer than this one!" Gromyko's face was motionless.

On May 15, we celebrated the thirtieth anniversary of the Austrian State

Treaty, which made Austria independent, neutral, and free from the circle of Soviet satellites. Over the past thirty years, Austria had prospered. Gromyko and I, along with Geoffrey Howe and French Foreign Minister Roland Dumas, represented the four powers that were signatories to the treaty. The ceremony was grand, making full use of the regal trappings of this once-imperial city.

Afterward, Gromyko asked to see me in private, with no interpreters. We went off into a side corridor. His mood was absolutely different from the day before—very upbeat. He told me that he wanted to tell me, "as another human being," that we must try hard between now and any summit to create a period of stability and an atmosphere with no major problems. We should also try to get a few agreements in hand to provide as much substance as possible for the summit.

I took his remarks as an important and positive sign. I told him I agreed. We should avoid any provocative incidents and try to keep any that did arise under control. I observed that the problems arose primarily from Soviet actions. "You owe us an apology about Major Nicholson and compensation for his family," I said. "You are threatening to restrict our access to Berlin. Don't let the Berlin air corridor become a problem. I will do my best to work with you to create a stable period." On the positive side, I said, "There are a number of areas where action is possible." As I hoped, Gromyko took this as a reference to human rights.

"Yes," he said, "but anything we do has to be in conformity with our laws."

"Fine," I said, "but then figure out how to *do it* in conformity with your laws." I urged him not to put Washington out of mind as the venue for the summit. It would be good for Gorbachev to see the United States.

"Not possible," he said. "We can find a European city."

I felt instinctively that Gromyko's world had changed dramatically since Geneva in January, when he so visibly displayed the arrogance of power. Now in Vienna, he had been reduced to going through pile after pile of talking points to mask the fact that he had no authority at all to say anything serious about the U.S.-Soviet substantive agendas. He had been sent to tell me that the Soviets wanted a summit and to make it appear, if possible, that the United States was the petitioner. Gorbachev had reduced him to an errand boy.

I was out ahead of the White House on the matter of a summit. "The president might not travel outside the U.S. for a summit," Bud McFarlane said to me.

"That would be insane," I responded. I would talk to the president myself. The struggle over setting the president's course was never-ending. I knew that Ronald Reagan's instinct was to work with the Soviets, but I also knew I had my work cut out for me.

*   *   *

Back in Washington on Friday, May 17, I went to the Oval Office to report. I found the president leaning backward. He wasn't sure about a summit in November. Maybe later. We should "think about it some more, play hard to get." I disagreed. There were big possibilities ahead, I told him, including in arms control.

"Many key people in your administration do not want a summit," I said. "You have to make up your mind. You have to step up to the plate. And when it comes to the divisions in your administration over this issue, you can't split the difference. Think about it," I said. "I will come back to you in a couple of days." I returned to my office and told Rick Burt to work up a full and detailed scenario: calendar, content, atmospherics, for a summit in November in Geneva. I would take it to the president in a few days and then, if he approved, present it to Gromyko in Helsinki in August.

Avital Shcharansky came in on May 22 on behalf of her husband; she had rebuffed an earlier attempt to gain his freedom. The Soviets were sending us signals that they had decided to move toward the United States and would use human rights decisions as a way to do it. Soviet representatives in the United States were paying attention to Jewish protests, asking prominent Jews in New York what their reaction would be if Shcharansky was released. The Soviets were toying with this man to serve their interests—keeping him incommunicado and then allowing him to contact his family—apparently to affect U.S. attitudes and decisions, in effect, once again trying to use "linkage" against us. Unknown to Avital, we were at that moment hard at work with a third country trying to arrange a complicated pattern of releases of people held in various countries by which her husband would himself be freed.

I went to President Reagan later that day with my full proposal for a November summit. He had thought it over further himself, I could see. He agreed with the plan—and also to inviting Gromyko to come to Washington at the time of the opening of the UN General Assembly, which Gromyko would attend in September. I now had the running room I needed to nail down time and place.

In early June, I lost one outstanding deputy and gained another. Ken Dam, the number two man in the State Department, decided to depart for a big job at IBM, and I persuaded John Whitehead, recently retired as chairman of Goldman Sachs, to take Ken's place. John was highly regarded as one of the top investment bankers on Wall Street. "He walks in the snow and leaves no tracks," Walt Wriston once said of John. I never knew quite what to make of that. Some smooth operator he was: he had great finesse and judgment.

Up in the eighth-floor dining room, a large group gathered to say farewell to Ken, who was widely and highly respected in Washington. Lloyd Cutler, in his tribute, said, "From the Democrat end of the table I can say that

I'm really not aware of which party Ken belongs to." When I saw the look on Jack Kemp's face, I could almost hear Jack saying, "I knew it!" That, in a way, was our built-in problem: we were conducting a U.S. foreign policy that was the president's, but to be effective, bipartisan support was essential. And my effort to forge a bipartisan foreign policy meant continual trouble within our own administration and with the right wing of the Republican party.

Managing Contention

The flow of events now precipitated renewed argument over the issue known as "interim restraint." The SALT II agreement negotiated by the Carter administration was unratified and therefore nonbinding, but the United States and the Soviet Union had adhered voluntarily to the limitations set forth in the agreement. Scheduled U.S. submarine deployments would put us beyond the number of launchers allowed by SALT II unless we disassembled one of our oldest nuclear submarines. There was evidence of Soviet violations.[1] And the end of the term of the treaty, had it been ratified, was approaching: December 31, 1985. Should we continue our "interim restraint," pending negotiation of a new treaty on strategic arms? That was the matter of debate. I favored continuation. Those who wanted to drop such restraint asked, "Does it make sense for the United States to adhere to a flawed treaty after the Soviets have violated it and after it has expired according to its own terms?" Others argued, "Ronald Reagan is the first president in years not to have concluded an arms control agreement with the Soviets. Does he want it on his record that he ended one of the major agreements that still exists? Do we gain from freeing the Soviets completely from the limitations of the treaty?"

I felt that if we scrapped SALT II, we should do so for military or security reasons: we should press the Soviets on their violations and adhere to both SALT I and II as long as we did not pay a military or security price for doing so. Most members of Congress and our allies agreed. The argument within the administration was fierce.

*   *   *

1. The principal violation was the Soviet development, prohibited by the treaty, we argued, of a "new type" of missile. The Soviets disagreed, arguing that this was a permitted modernization of an older existing missile type and did not fit the treaty definition of a new missile. They were certainly wrong in spirit, and probably technically as well. This was the sort of tactic that made many people wary of negotiations with the Soviets, and it was the type of misunderstanding that I was determined to avoid in any formal agreement I worked out with them. Compromises should be clear, and we should avoid the temptation to use words in a treaty that simply papered over differences and therefore led to disagreement down the line over interpretation.

At the NATO foreign ministers' meeting in Lisbon on June 7, I nevertheless set forth the arguments for ending our voluntary adherence to SALT II so that they would be prepared if the president followed that course. I, along with our whole delegation, also worked intensely to try to get the president's Strategic Defense Initiative endorsed in our communiqué. Bernie Kalb said of Rick Burt's efforts, "Rick has been trying to construct a skyscraper, and he may only get a hut. Did you get a skyscraper or a hut, Rick?"

When I saw the proposed communiqué, I said, "He got a latrine." Rick had fought a good fight, but the Europeans were being chickenhearted.

By Saturday, June 8, I was at Winfield House, our ambassador's residence in London. All our ambassadors from posts in Europe were there. I called Art Hartman, Jack Matlock, and Rick Burt together for breakfast upstairs, along with our host, Ambassador Charlie Price, to talk about further steps with the Soviets. I had another task as well. I was to tell Helene von Damm-Guertler that the White House had decided to take her out of Vienna. Because of the sensitivities involved, a careful ballet had been choreographed so that my Soviet team, arriving for breakfast, would not see Helene depart from an earlier meeting with me. The men were to be shunted into the Gold Room until Helene was gone. It was a long struggle; she did not want to accept the verdict. When she left, I watched as she walked past the security agents standing guard outside my sitting-room door. Down the parquet floors of the many-doored corridor, past bowls of dried flower petals on stands, the click of her departing heels mingled with the scratching of the claws of the King Charles spaniel that roamed the house.

The main topic at breakfast was a major speech given by Gorbachev a few weeks before at Leningrad's Smolny Institute, the academy commandeered by the Bolsheviks in 1917 at which Lenin had announced that the Communist party would "proceed to construct the socialist order." Under a large portrait of Lenin, in a hall designed like a church with pews and a pulpit, Gorbachev spoke "like a Baptist preacher," Art Hartman recounted. "Gorbachev would read a few sentences and then lean forward to explain what he meant. He was very effective. He must alarm the party bureaucracy who fear change. Gorbachev was clearly most concerned about the domestic crisis in the Soviet Union," Hartman said. He talked about "spiritual values" and the creation yet again of "a new Soviet man." He told his audience what they instinctively knew: their system was not working. The reason he gave was poor management and poor work habits; these he sought to change. With these reforms, he said, it would be possible to make the Soviet system work.

This brought to mind a remark Margaret Thatcher once made to me. "Gorbachev thinks there are problems with the way the system works; he thinks he can make changes to make it work better. He doesn't understand that *the system is the problem*." I fully agreed. I had made the same point myself.

*   *   *

Back in Washington the president announced on June 10 his decision on the issue of "interim restraint." The United States would continue to abide by the unratified SALT II Treaty. When I stopped by Don Regan's office in the White House, he was highly disturbed, saying he had to talk to me about "a personnel problem." Spread all over his desk were newspaper clippings about SALT and the interim restraint decision. Secrets had been revealed to the press, Don said, and they came from Bud McFarlane. He was appalled by Bud's incessant briefings to the press. "I gave him a piece of my mind," he said.

The president had been at a dinner party, Don told me, given by George Will for Richard Perle on his birthday. Perle and Will and others of like mind had "worked the president over," pressing him to abandon interim restraint.

On *Air Force One*, Don continued, the president had written out by hand his decision on interim restraint and told Regan that his decision would "shut up the right-wing critics." Bud had altered the president's wording and then had briefed the press to make himself look like a hero to those—certainly the majority in the media—who wanted to preserve interim restraint. I agreed with the decision to continue to abide by the SALT II limits, but I found Don's account deeply disturbing. Decisions of such magnitude *must* be made by the president. The people who serve the president should state their views, but they cannot arrogate presidential powers to themselves.

If I had been in the president's shoes, I would have fired Bud on the spot. Bud had the bit in his teeth. I concluded from this willful act that he really *was* ready to leave office. I looked further into the president's decision and came to the conclusion that the underlying reason why we stuck with interim restraint was the decision of the Joint Chiefs that the submarine to be dismantled was in fact obsolete: it had passed its useful lifetime and would be costly to maintain. By the time I caught up to all this, the public verdict was in. It was a split decision: Senator Dale Bumpers (Democrat from Arkansas) called Reagan's decision "the most statesmanlike act of his presidency." Senator Steve Symms (Republican from Idaho) called it "unilateral disarmament and appeasement."[2] The Soviets, in a statement issued by the Foreign Ministry, spoke as though the decision had gone *against* SALT II: "On the whole, the decision concerning the Poseidon submarine does not change the overall picture of the United States' undermining the positive [impact] that was created in the strategic arms limitation field through the efforts of the two sides."

The Soviets were undoubtedly reacting to the language supporting the

2. As reported in the *Washington Post*, June 11, 1985, p. 1, by George C. Wilson and Margaret Shapiro.

decision rather than the decision itself. I recalled the charge once leveled at me as a labor arbitrator: "You gave the language to the loser and the decision to the winner." Yet the Soviet reaction no doubt helped the president. He seemed content with the outcome.

Just then, a chance of movement emerged on an issue of genuine importance: Afghanistan. Rajiv Gandhi visited Washington from June 11 to 15. We were struggling to open a new chapter in American-Indian ties. Afghanistan was a major topic. If the Soviets pulled out their troops, not only would Afghanistan be freed of foreign occupation, but also an issue that was exacerbating Indo-Pakistani tensions would be resolved. The Indians thought Moscow might be ready to act quickly to get out of their Afghan quagmire. Our policy of aid to the Afghan mujaheddin, who were fighting fiercely against the Soviet occupiers and their Afghan collaborators, was paying off. The costs to the Soviets of their presence in Afghanistan were high. If Gorbachev was preoccupied with domestic Soviet problems, a top foreign policy priority might well be to get the Afghan war burden off his back. The Indians were ready to undertake a new diplomatic initiative with the Soviets, arguing for a change in Moscow's policy and removal of their troops from Afghanistan.

The Soviet Union's military standing was also suffering a setback in the Iran-Iraq War. At my Thursday morning staff meeting, the intelligence briefer reported that in Iran's most recent military offensive against Iraq, the Iraqis—Soviet armed and trained—had lost 300 tanks and 18,000 men killed in action in three days.

On Monday evening, June 17, I met with Dobrynin to discuss a date and a site for the summit and to plant the idea—an idea I had discussed fully with the president—that if offensive strategic weapons were drastically reduced, the needs for defenses against them would be far less. I was, in other words, linking the deployment side of SDI to deep cuts and indicating that the United States was not necessarily committed to a full-scale, deployed SDI no matter what: the Soviets could have an impact on the future if they would act reasonably about the present.

Dobrynin did not seem to get the point. "Dobrynin *does* know what we are talking about; the Soviets just don't want to acknowledge SDI in any form," Paul Nitze observed. I had presented this line of thought to Dobrynin on the basis of discussion, first with Nitze and McFarlane and then with President Reagan, in effect bypassing the contentious interagency discussion process. After each session with the Soviets, I went over everything carefully with the president. He knew and approved of what I was doing, and I knew it was essential to keep him fully engaged.

Changing of the Guard:
Shevardnadze Comes on the Scene

On Monday, July 1, Dobrynin came to see me: "The Soviet Union agrees to a Gorbachev-Reagan summit in Geneva on November 19 and 20, 1985." Dobrynin and I agreed to make the announcement. As for the concept of reducing offensive weapons and thereby reducing the need for defense (SDI), Dobrynin's reply from Moscow was negative: the Soviets wanted to stop SDI in its tracks, not just moderate it.

On July 3, as planned, we announced that President Reagan and General Secretary Gorbachev had agreed to meet in Geneva. The Soviets made the announcement as well, but with an added surprise: Gromyko had been elevated to the ceremonial post of the president of the USSR, and Eduard Shevardnadze, first secretary of the Communist party in the Republic of Georgia and a man with no prior experience in foreign policy, had been appointed to replace veteran diplomat Gromyko as foreign minister.

Gromyko, I felt, had by 1984 reached the pinnacle of his power in the making of Soviet foreign policy, especially so during my meetings with him in September 1984 and January 1985. (Our Soviet specialists regarded the rehabilitation of Vyacheslav Molotov, Gromyko's early mentor and patron, in 1984—when Molotov was readmitted to party membership—to be a consequence of Gromyko's heightened influence.) In Vienna, in May 1985, however, I had encountered a far different Gromyko, a man whose power had been cut back sharply. Referring to Gorbachev, Gromyko had said, "He has a nice smile but iron teeth." Now the bite of those iron teeth, I perceived, had been felt by Gromyko himself. To me, this change was all to the good. The people rising to the top in Moscow were coming from outside Moscow, from the republics, where they had to face, and deal with, the problems created by their system. Such people, I thought, would incline more to pragmatism than to ideology. "I bet Gromyko hasn't got a clue what's going on in the Soviet Union," I said. "He hasn't had to pay attention to it for decades."

I telephoned Dobrynin and asked him to call on me: "You have a new boss," I remarked. "I'm writing a message to him. We'll have our ups and downs, but let's try to get started on the right foot, maintain a high and professional quality of work between us, and guide this relationship in a more constructive direction. I look forward to getting to know him. I'll be in Helsinki in July. I hope he comes to New York for the UN General Assembly and, when he does, that he will come to Washington. I understand that he is interested in domestic economic problems, so we have a common bond."

Dobrynin, obviously miffed that someone with no foreign policy background had been picked, replied that he had already received a cable signed by Shevardnadze. "Our foreign policy is going down the drain. They have named an agricultural type," Dobrynin said. I was surprised by his candor, though not his disappointment.

"Fine," I said, "you just pay attention to what's going on in your country and let us worry about the rest of the world."

Once again, Bud McFarlane wanted to resign. This had long since become routine. He had come to my house on Monday evening, July 1, to tell me that he would submit his resignation on Friday, to become effective September 1, 1985. He seemed very tired. After I told him that Gorbachev had accepted a November summit date, he decided not to resign after all. He then adopted the attitude that we should "play it down": we should call it a "meeting," not a "summit," he said. He was reflecting his fear of the hard-line opposition to any kind of working relationship with the Soviets.

Just at this time, another new face with strength and intellect came on the scene. Rick Burt moved from his post as assistant secretary of state for European and Canadian Affairs to be our ambassador to West Germany. Rick had done a fine job, and I knew how important the post was. I worked hard to get the right replacement. Rozanne Ridgway, our ambassador to East Germany and an experienced foreign service officer, had been called to my attention by Larry Eagleburger. I had made a point of meeting with her early on and had put her to work on the contentious and delicate issue of Jewish claims against the East Germans. I found her to be creative, tough-minded, and perceptive. I chose Roz for this critical assignment. The president supported my choice, but we ran into trouble in the Senate with some of the Republican right, particularly Jesse Helms. Roz had been a presidential appointee in the Carter administration. Would she support Ronald Reagan's policies? Could a woman handle this tough and demanding job? some senators asked. Nonsense, I said. I was advised by the political side of the White House that I should consider withdrawing the nomination. I would not, I made clear. Finally, the opposition faded away because they saw that they could not weaken my resolve. I was dug in on this appointment, and the president stuck with me. Roz was confirmed by the Senate on July 16 by a vote of 88 to 9.[3]

On July 30 through August 1, the foreign ministers of the United States, Canada, and all the countries of Europe would gather to celebrate the tenth anniversary of the signing of the Helsinki Final Act. Shevardnadze

3. In Roz I found a kindred spirit in her skepticism about the concept of linkage in dealing with the Soviets. She told me about one of her earlier experiences in which she had not been permitted to enforce a fishery agreement she had negotiated with the Soviets because her superiors feared that such an action would upset what they regarded as a more important negotiation with the Soviets.

would be there. Information about him was scarce. He was from Georgia, and Georgians had the reputation of being gregarious, energetic, full of economic hustle, with more subterranean private enterprise than commonly found in the USSR. He was known as a strong leader who had dealt harshly with corruption. I heard he would bring his wife. O'Bie and I decided to make every effort to get to know these two people and establish a friendly personal relationship, however strained the relations between our two countries.

We assembled in Finlandia Hall, and while people were visiting before the formal opening, I asked a member of my staff where in the hall the Soviet delegation was seated and whether Shevardnadze was there. He was. I set out down one aisle, across the front of the hall, and up the aisle leading to the Soviet delegation. As I proceeded, more and more delegates saw what was happening. The room quieted. When I reached his seat, we shook hands. He broke into a broad smile. There was a sense of relief and shared drama. We chatted in a friendly, open manner. "I expect our meeting tomorrow to be constructive." He reciprocated in a natural, easy way. No reservations. No guarded wariness. Dobrynin hovered over him like a keeper, which Shevardnadze didn't appear to appreciate.

Early in the opening session I delivered a hard-hitting speech on Soviet violations of the human rights provisions of the Helsinki Final Act: denial of emigration and travel, suppression of religion, repression of individuals who constituted a Helsinki watch group (including Andrei Sakharov and Yuri Orlov), and jamming of radio and TV transmissions. I named names. The president had approved of this departure from our usual approach of private diplomacy. On the anniversary of this agreement to respect human rights, the United States had to speak out publicly about Soviet violations. I saw Shevardnadze again during a break in the session. "Did you have to deliver such a tough speech?" he asked me.

"I just stated facts, and I look forward to discussing this subject privately with you," I replied. Then I changed the subject. "I have a suggestion for you that will improve the quality of our meetings and allow us to use the limited time more effectively. We're set up so that we can make simultaneous translations of what we say. How about trying it? Any time you or I want to go over some point again or more carefully, we can just hold up a hand and go immediately to the traditional consecutive method." He agreed without hesitation. This meant an opportunity for a real conversation, for a chance to connect the words with the eyes, the hands, and the body language of the speaker, for the possibility of interruptions and the kind of exchange that is possible when both people speak the same language.

Our meeting, a preparatory effort for the coming Reagan-Gorbachev summit in Geneva, was a straightforward restatement of substantive positions. Since the session took place in our ambassador's residence, Shevardnadze, the guest, spoke first. He had a huge pile of notes and went through them. Dobrynin sat beside him. I interjected a question or two, responding to some of his points, and I described the scope of our four-part agenda. Afterward, I asked him how he liked the simultaneous translation. "We got eight hours' work done in four," he remarked happily.

We then met alone. I brought up the subject of human rights again. "Beyond the merits of individual cases," I said, "positive Soviet action in this field affects the atmosphere around all our relations. Until the Soviet Union adopts a different policy on humanitarian issues, no aspect of our dealings will be truly satisfactory, nor will your society be able to progress as it can and should."

Instead of reacting with indignation or rage, Shevardnadze asked with a smile, "When I come to the United States, should I talk about unemployment and blacks?"

"Help yourself," I replied.

Overall, the substance of the Soviet position was unchanged. But I was struck by Shevardnadze's tone: it was far less polemical. This might just be a different style, but it might also indicate that the Soviets were taking a new look at themselves. The next day, I heard of an interesting sidelight on the meeting. A member of the Soviet staff told one of our senior foreign service officers that Shevardnadze had wanted to "toss out" all of his prepared papers and just talk to me informally, to "wing it," as he put it. Dobrynin had nearly gone crazy trying to hold Shevardnadze to his script. I smiled. That was a good sign.[4]

The summer passed. With the arrival of fine fall days in Washington, the mood in the White House was still ambivalent. It would be a "meeting," not a "summit"; it should be played down. Retired Navy Chief Warrant Officer John Walker had been arrested in the spring by the FBI in the opening salvo of what would be a damaging spy case; we had not been given satisfaction on the death of Major Nicholson; there was evidence (subsequently discredited) that the Soviets were putting carcinogenic dust on U.S. diplomats as a means of tracking them; Gorbachev told interviewers from *Time* that the United States was waging a "campaign of hatred" against the Soviet Union. The downward drift about which Gromyko had expressed concern in Vienna seemed all too evident. I was determined to turn the mood around, and the place to start, I knew, was with the president himself.

4. In a visit with me at Stanford's Hoover Institution in May 1991, when we were both out of office, Shevardnadze reminisced about our first meeting: "I knew I was supposed to be tough, but I softened a few passages in my talking points because it was not in my nature to speak that way." At the end of the meeting, he had said, "You have experience on your side, but I have truth on my side." I remembered laughing when he said that, and he had smiled. The remarks showed up in the transcript and became a focus of attention for members of the Politburo, he recounted. "They complimented me. The remark established me in their eyes as someone who could 'talk tough' and who had a flair for a phrase," he said laughing.

I talked about this sour and uncertain mood with Paul Nitze and Roz Ridgway. Our view of the summit was positive. I also talked to Bud McFarlane: his downbeat attitude was infecting the White House. I reviewed a little history with him. "When I arrived," I told Bud, "people said I made a big difference for one main reason: I expressed *confidence* in the president—in contrast to Al Haig, who was always telling the president not to say anything, because Haig was always worried that the president would blow it and say the wrong thing. But now you people on the White House and NSC staff are surrounding the president with uncertainty: that's not Ronald Reagan," I said. "He's best when he's confident and comfortable; you people are making him uncomfortable. You are trying to convince the president that this Geneva summit is a big worry. It isn't. It's a good thing. Ronald Reagan's policy is clear and straightforward, and yet his staff makes it complicated and unclear."

On September 16, 1985, I told the president, "I believe we should take a much more positive and commanding attitude toward Geneva than is at present apparent to the public. We sought the meeting, and we got it. We have important objectives. We have a strong position from which to work and we are ready to engage with the Soviets and confident that we can represent ourselves and the free world strongly."

"I have always thought that letting Reagan be Reagan means a self-confident and positive approach," I concluded. "With the strong position we are in and the important objectives to be served, we should stop poormouthing this gigantic event and take it on as the important challenge and opportunity it really is. This is not the opening game of the little-league season. This is the Super Bowl. We can and must win, whether it turns out to be a propaganda battle, an acrimonious exchange, or a constructive effort with a promise of more to come. We want the constructive effort and so do our friends, allies, and the American people."

What I said was on Ronald Reagan's wavelength but not on his staff's, I could see. Three days later, I was back at the president again. "Early this week," I said, "I gave you my views on the attitude we should take toward your meeting with Gorbachev." I then handed him a memorandum giving him substantive details, focusing on arms control and the way to handle the central and sensitive issue of SDI. I argued that the choices being set up in the current debate, "full speed ahead" or "bargain it away," were false choices. Our orientation should be how best to ensure that we get the full benefit of SDI's enormous potential and that we make it a permanent fixture of our strategic posture. We should seek massive reductions in offensive nuclear weapons. "We want SDI positioned in the agreement as the key to implementation of the offensive nuclear reductions, all of which would be consistent with the continuation of a vigorous research program within the terms of the ABM Treaty. We would want to clarify," I said, "the development and testing of SDI permitted by the treaty."

I put together talking points to show the president how he might express these matters to Gorbachev. I had long since learned that the president's mind was engaged not so much through briefing books as through an active process that involved him in give-and-take and a feel for his operational role. My talking points included the idea that we "cannot excise from men's minds the knowledge of how to make nuclear weapons, particularly nuclear missile systems. Unless you and we have nonnuclear defenses capable of countering such delivery systems, there would exist an enormous temptation for men to build them clandestinely in the hope this would enable them to exercise immense power in the world." The talking points helped to engage President Reagan actively, to set him thinking about his personal role. But the occasion itself was a long way off. I wanted to see him get involved, but I didn't want him to leave his fight in the dressing room.

Three years remained in the Reagan presidency. Not even Cap Weinberger claimed that SDI would be remotely deployable by the end of Reagan's second term. I wanted to make SDI a part of, and reason for, an agreement with the Soviets for massive arms reductions. That way, SDI would become an institutionalized and accepted reality, a legacy that Ronald Reagan's successor would want to honor. A big problem loomed on the horizon, however: the ABM Treaty and its interpretation. Our SDI program could proceed very well for at least three or four more years while remaining within the present interpretation of the ABM Treaty. But the drumbeat was increasing to find a way to abrogate the treaty now, a move, I felt, that would be extremely unwise.

I telephoned the president to congratulate him on a September 17 press conference. Nancy came on the phone. She had initiated correspondence with Raisa Gorbachev and had received a reply that pleased her. I agreed to arrange for the two women to meet at the Geneva summit.

The Run-up to Geneva

The president invited Shevardnadze to the White House during the opening sessions of the annual meeting of the UN General Assembly, as he had invited Gromyko a year earlier. On Friday, September 27, at a meeting in the Oval Office, Shevardnadze presented the president a new Soviet arms control proposal: a 50 percent reduction of offensive strategic weapons to a level of 6,000 "charges," defined as an explosive weapon that could hit the territory of the other side. This proposal was clever and was weighted heavily against us. The 6,000 charges would include the intermediate-range missiles we had deployed in Europe but not Soviet missiles of similar range, since these would hit our allies, not the United States. It would cover all such weapons on carriers at sea, but the Soviets had no carriers. Our bomber weapons would be covered, but the Soviets had relatively few of these weapons. It would ban our Midgetman but permit the Soviet SS-24s and SS-25s. The 6,000 limit would not touch 70 percent of the Soviet intercontinental ballistic missiles. And under the proposal in Gorbachev's letter, SDI would get the ax.

In Gorbachev we were clearly dealing with a new kind of man, one ready to make radical changes but not ready to bring the Soviet Union into real parity—in terms of missiles and warheads—with us. Nevertheless, I regarded the proposal as a breakthrough of principle, even though the specifics were not remotely acceptable; it was a victory for the president's policy of seeking significant reductions in offensive nuclear arms. The Soviet preoccupation with our SDI program was obviously a prime motivation for their desire to reach an agreement with us. Radical cuts in arms would be possible, but they would require tough negotiating. And on a personal level, the president found himself, happily, in an unexpected encounter. Eduard Shevardnadze came across as a real human being. Ronald Reagan started telling jokes to Eduard Shevardnadze—jokes about Communists—and Shevardnadze laughed. What a change!

I welcomed the Soviet position and said that we should stress that this was a "counterproposal": Ronald Reagan had been the first to call for reductions; now, at last, the Soviets in their counterproposal had *also* put forward reductions. That in itself was a triumph for the president. Yet the Soviet proposal was unacceptable except for the 50-percent-reductions and 6,000-charges ideas. We wanted reductions that would enhance security *and* reduce the risk of war. What Winston Churchill had called the "balance of terror" was getting out of balance. Weaponry with first-strike potential was building up, and we wanted any arms control agreement to reduce the incentive for a first strike. Equality in the resulting offensive forces and verifiability of the result were also essential characteristics of any agreement. And how could we handle SDI in a way that would highlight its importance and thereby enhance its staying power even after Ronald Reagan had left the White House? I went back to the idea I had earlier discussed with the president: strategically significant reductions by the Soviet Union would have an effect on how the United States would go forward with eventual deployment of strategic defenses.

Cap Weinberger, Richard Perle, and others at the Pentagon were totally opposed to this approach. They wanted to press forward with SDI at full speed no matter what. To them, the ABM Treaty was an obstacle to be sidestepped. I was clear in my mind that we had to abide by the ABM Treaty, but I was becoming increasingly aware of the controversy over what the treaty meant and the controversy over what testing and development were permitted under it.

The ABM Treaty: The Debate Heats Up

As preparations for the summit moved forward, our work was punctuated by the growing internal controversy over the 1972 ABM Treaty. In one of our daily sessions, Paul Nitze said: "We don't want to amend the treaty; we want to agree on its meaning." The 1972 treaty contained a crucial provision as Article V (1): "Each Party undertakes not to develop, test, or deploy A.B.M. systems or components which are sea-based, air-based, space-based, or mobile land-based." For thirteen years through three administrations, this short text was interpreted as prohibiting the development and testing of space-based ABM systems.

But "Agreed Statement D" in the treaty permitted testing and development of ABM systems based on "other physical principles" than those known when the negotiations were under way in 1972. SDI was based on new ideas. Would not the broader scope indicated in Agreed Statement D apply to the research undertaken in the SDI program?[5]

The argument intensified within the administration and came to a head, Nitze reported to me, in a contentious meeting of the Senior Arms Control Group on October 4. Nitze, who was personally involved in the ABM Treaty negotiations, was convinced by this time that Agreed Statement D did indeed allow for broader scope for SDI research.

On Sunday, October 6, as tension over this issue was rising within the administration, on Capitol Hill, and among our allies, Bud McFarlane on "Meet the Press" stated that the ABM Treaty did indeed permit research, testing, and development of the new systems.

"I think that the President is guided by the ABM Treaty, and the terms of that treaty," Bud said, "are very explicit in Articles II, III, IV and V, plus Agreed Statement D. They make clear that on research involving new physical concepts, that that activity, as well as testing, as well as development, indeed, are approved and authorized by the treaty. Only deployment is foreclosed, except in accordance with Articles XIII and XIV. So our program is compatible with the treaty, and will remain so." The detailed nature of Bud's answer indicated that he had planned deliberately to set his position out in public on this occasion. Bud had stopped just short of the extreme Pentagon position that amounted to abrogating the ABM Treaty. He had, in effect, *declared publicly that the U.S. was unilaterally changing its long-held position on the treaty*. No such decision had been

---

5. Agreed Statement D reads: "In order to insure fulfillment of the obligation not to deploy ABM systems and their components except as provided in Article III of the Treaty, the Parties agree that in the event ABM systems based on other physical principles and including components capable of substituting for ABM interceptor missiles, ABM launchers, or ABM radars are created in the future, specific limitations on such systems and their components would be subject to discussion in accordance with Article XIII and agreement in accordance with Article XIV of the Treaty."

made! And there would now be hell to pay. I was appalled and angry at this arrogation of power.

First thing Monday morning, Paul Nitze stated his own view to me and a few others. "It is unwise to go to such an extreme position now. It is more than a public relations point." He was personally persuaded that a broader interpretation of the treaty was justified but did not think this was the time to assert that idea. State's legal adviser, Abe Sofaer, who had studied the treaty intensively, said that the Americans who had been responsible for negotiating the treaty in 1972 had "tried but failed" to persuade the Soviets to accept restrictive language on ABM development. The Soviets had insisted on the flexibility of Agreed Statement D. Our negotiators, however, had explained it to Congress as though they had won the argument. The treaty as drafted was broad in its flexibility, but our negotiators had portrayed it as narrow and restrictive—and therefore as consistent with reliance on offense, or Mutual Assured Destruction—as the method of deterrence. The Soviets had insisted on the broad approach during the negotiations, Sofaer said, and we were justified in taking that position now.

I was beginning to realize what a formidable fellow my new legal adviser was. Abe, as he insisted on being called—not Judge, as people kept saying—was a merry, noisy perpetual-motion machine. He roamed the upper floors of the department, trying hard to penetrate the walls erected to keep out snoopy lawyers. I encouraged that trait. But when he had got his teeth into a problem and had reached his considered conclusion, Abe's exuberant personality transformed itself into that of chief justice of the Supreme Court. His authoritative voice and manner mirrored a brilliant mind and a resolve that would not retreat. "The president is not limited with regard to research, development, or testing of SDI," proclaimed Sofaer.

A few hours later, former Secretary of Defense Harold Brown came to my office. He set out his view of the ABM Treaty: its language was unclear, but its *spirit* was undeniable. Brown put it this way: "The treaty meant to limit work on new systems to research and development and some testing— testing of 'other physical principles.' But when you got to a component that would be part of a system, then you can't test or develop it," Brown asserted.

"How do you test a principle?" I asked.

"The test just can't be of a component of a system that would substitute for an ABM part," he answered.

I shook my head. With this conversation, I had entered the higher realms of arms control theology.

Bud had jumped the gun. No administration position on the question of the ABM Treaty had yet been agreed upon. And what Bud stated publicly was *not* the traditional position of the United States, or the position of our allies; nor was it in accord with what Congress had been told about the meaning of the ABM Treaty's language; nor was it the position previously taken by the administration. And it certainly was at odds with current Soviet views. The Soviets were saying—ridiculously—that the ABM Treaty did not even permit us to do research on SDI.

"The Russians," Nitze said, "will use McFarlane's statement to show we are playing ducks and drakes with the treaty."

But we didn't need to gut the treaty to do what we needed and wanted to do on SDI. We would be in the research stage for years. And, during that time, we could use the strength of SDI to press the Soviets into deep offensive weapons cuts. It made no sense for Bud McFarlane to fuel this controversy now!

Worse than that, it was a seizure of presidential authority by a member of the president's staff. Such a precipitous change, furthermore, could stir up Congress, the press, and our allies to so constrain SDI that it would atrophy. That is what the Soviets wanted, and that result—unilaterally cutting back SDI while getting nothing in return from the Soviets—would deprive us of our critical leverage to get true arms reductions out of Gorbachev.

CBS's "Evening News" that night led with the story: "In a major policy shift, the Reagan administration says there are no treaty limits on SDI testing." In the *New York Times* on October 8, Bernard Gwertzman raised the question whether the main policy-making role had shifted to the NSC adviser. However we got into this mess, Bud was outrageously out of line. No matter how strongly Bud and others felt about the necessity to change our stance on SDI testing, his statement on "Meet the Press" was irresponsible. This was a matter of such great importance that only the president should decide, not the senior arms control advisers or members of the cabinet, including me.

I had breakfast with Cap Weinberger and Bud on Wednesday, October 9, and told them my view with the bark off. I said to both that they were trying to change our treaty interpretation in a sweeping way. "This is a decision for nobody but the president," I told them. I rode down in the elevator with Bud and said that he must get a coordinated memorandum prepared giving the president the options and putting the decision to him. "Any decision so sweeping as to say that the treaty places no limits on what we can do is a presidential decision," I said. He was furious. I was furious, too. The point was, this decision was for the president, and the considerations went beyond the negotiating record with the Soviets.

Abe Sofaer privately gave me his considered view on the SDI testing issue. Abe said he had read the entire negotiating record. The American negotiators back then knew what they were doing. The Soviets back then were unwilling to deal with future systems, unwilling to restrict them. They were much more interested in defense than we were and far less willing than we to settle for deterrence through Mutual Assured Destruction. Our negotiators battled successfully to get the Soviets to agree to limit "deployment" but could never get them to agree to bar "development" or "testing" in connection with systems based on "other physical principles." "The more I look at the record, the clearer it becomes," Abe told me. On the other hand, our negotiators did not explain it that way to Congress, so, in effect, Congress had consented to ratify the narrow and traditional interpretation of the treaty.

The allies were now in an uproar over the issue of the interpretation of the ABM Treaty. The British wanted to consult before we came to a decision. Chancellor Kohl said that our stance put him into an untenable position and, our embassy reported, had made a "passionate attack" on the McFarlane statement. Senator Sam Nunn, ranking Democrat on the Senate Armed Services Committee, and House Foreign Affairs Committee Chairman Dante Fascell had come out in opposition to the McFarlane statement. Paul Nitze had just returned from a European swing and reported universally strong negative reactions to McFarlane's reinterpretation. Kohl, he said, was furious and felt that we had made a big political blunder by making such a change at this time. I agreed.

By that time, I was persuaded that Abe was right and that the treaty, as negotiated with the Soviets, did permit us to go ahead with certain testing and development of SDI. But there was the presentation to Congress during the ratification process, the pattern and practice long adhered to, and the impact on our allies and our bargaining posture. My deepest problem with Bud McFarlane was the outrageous way this matter had been handled procedurally, which amounted to the usurpation of presidential power, with the result that all the factors in the decision had not been properly weighed and put carefully to the president. I expressed all this to the president. He shared my concern about the process and was ready to review the whole issue. He was, in a sense, on both sides of the issue.

Our position, I felt, should be that we were studying the ABM Treaty carefully as a result of all the questions raised about it—and by Soviet actions that Moscow claimed were in conformity with the treaty but were in fact clear violations of any interpretation. I was especially concerned with the Soviet construction of the Krasnoyarsk radar. We had perceived an important area of ambiguity about the testing and development of systems based on "other physical principles." Nonetheless, our SDI was a research program. We could do research and address the questions we needed to answer *within* the confines of the ABM Treaty as construed earlier in the year in congressional testimony by Pentagon officials responsible for the program.

So we would continue with the SDI program as currently conceived. That combination would give us the best of both worlds, I felt. We would be able to research the key questions of strategic defense. We would also have something to fall back on and to bargain with by "clarifying" the treaty. So all this flurry of concern could be made to be useful to us. If we went too far—as Bud had, and Cap still wanted to—we could badly erode allied and congressional support for what we were doing. Trying to shift the rules at this point would be self-defeating. I went over this line of thinking carefully with the president on October 9. By this time, Bud seemed to be coming around to my point of view.

In a speech to the North Atlantic Assembly on October 14 in San Francisco, I included a critical passage. I had made the passage known to other key people in the administration, and I had gone over it carefully with the president. The president agreed. I said that the ABM Treaty "can be variously interpreted as to what kinds of development and testing are permitted, particularly with respect to future systems and components based on new physical principles." Our view is "based on a careful analysis of the Treaty text and the negotiating record, that a broader interpretation of our authority is fully justified." Then I came to the key sentence. "This is, however, a moot point; our SDI research program has been structured and, as the President has reaffirmed last Friday, will continue to be conducted in accordance with a restrictive interpretation of the Treaty's obligations." The audience applauded. "Furthermore, any SDI deployment would be the subject of consultations with our Allies and to discussion and negotiation, as appropriate, with the Soviets in accordance with the terms of the ABM Treaty."

I had set out not only to create an opening for a revised reading of the ABM Treaty but also to convey an assurance that the United States was not about to abrogate the ABM Treaty, a pillar of the policy of deterrence that had helped keep the world from nuclear war for so long. My speech received wide media attention and seemed to have a calming effect. I flew directly from San Francisco to Brussels, where on Tuesday, October 15, I further explained our position to the allies and then flew home to Washington that afternoon. Bernie Kalb gave the press a statement saying that the State Department "does not recognize jet lag."

Back on Track

Toward the end of October, the United Nations celebrated its fortieth anniversary. Before dawn we saw the lights of the UN Secretariat Building go on with windows lit to give the message: "UN: 40." On October 24, President Reagan addressed a full house of the General Assembly. "When Mr. Gorbachev and I meet in Geneva next month, I look to a fresh start in the relationship of our two nations," he said. "We must review the reasons for the current level of mistrust." He quoted Andrei Sakharov: " 'International trust, mutual understanding, disarmament and international security are inconceivable without an open society with freedom of information, freedom of conscience, the right to publish and the right to travel and choose the country in which one wishes to live.' " Nothing can justify the continuing and permanent division of the European Continent, the president declared. As for arms control, Reagan said that "within their [the Soviets'] proposal there are seeds which we should nurture."

Before going off to breakfast with Shevardnadze at our mission in New York on October 25, I looked at a cable Max Kampelman sent from Geneva: there was a division evident within the Soviet delegation. The Soviets were starting to criticize each other in private statements to Kampelman. Even more intriguing was Max's report that one delegate claimed that Shevardnadze would be willing to discuss a U.S.-Soviet agreement not to withdraw from the ABM Treaty for ten years, during which time reductions in offensive weapons would take place. That was very interesting. In my view, continued observance by the United States of the ABM Treaty while offensive reductions took place would work to our advantage: the *prospect* of SDI would keep the reductions coming, and SDI would still be moving along. The Soviets, perhaps, were realizing that they would experience benefits because their reductions in offensive weaponry would be in the context of not having to confront a major SDI deployment. The prospects of our being able to deploy a credible strategic defense by the mid-1990s were dim. So, in agreeing to a period of nonwithdrawal, I said, "we will be giving them the sleeves from our vest."

I had made sure that we had a hearty breakfast for Shevardnadze and his group when they came to our room at the U.S. mission at the United Nations. "We ate before we came," they said. "We're ready to work." So we started in, intensively, with simultaneous translations. I got no indication of the idea mentioned in Max Kampelman's cable and did not probe for it, but I felt that they were clearly eager to make this first summit of the decade a success. They invited me to Moscow in seven days to further the preparations. "The Soviets," I told President Reagan, "are clearly reaching for it."

A Soviet Jumps Ship

Nothing in foreign policy proceeds in a straight line. Events intrude that can threaten to derail progress on issues of the most fundamental importance. On Thursday, October 24, a Soviet seaman named Miroslav Medved had jumped overboard from his ship, the *Marshal Konev*, lying off New Orleans, waiting to take on a cargo of grain. Medved swam to shore, asked for help, and was taken to the local office of the Immigration and Naturalization Service (INS), an agency of the Justice Department. There, in a Kafkaesque interview, his request for asylum fell victim to poor interpretation and poor judgment, and the INS officers returned him to his vessel against his will, thinking he was a stowaway. Subsequently, the New Orleans office filed a report, and on Friday the INS in Washington and the Justice Department called Mark Palmer, deputy assistant secretary in our European bureau, to bring the matter to State's attention. Palmer quickly called the Soviet embassy to demand the return of Medved to shore. The Soviets refused. He demanded consular access to Medved on board the ship. Again the Soviets refused.

Over that first weekend, the diplomatic to-and-fro continued. We sent Tom Simons, formerly our Soviet desk officer, to New Orleans to put some seniority on the ground, along with Louis Sell, a talented, midgrade, Russian-speaking foreign service officer. We called Aleksandr Bessmert-nykh in New York and told him that Shevardnadze had to intervene so that we could gain access to Medved. If necessary, we said, we would board the vessel and forcibly take Medved off. A hurricane was building in the Gulf, and the notion of our officers trying to force their way on board the vessel in such weather was nightmarish, but we were prepared to do it. The idea of "force" did not mean using weapons, but going aboard uninvited could be dangerous, so the INS and port authorities would carry arms.

We stared the Soviets down and, with Shevardnadze, were able to appeal to reason. We got permission to board the ship. The seas were rough, and even without the confrontational aspects we feared, boarding was risky. Sell and the federal officers boarded the vessel, got Medved off, took him to the officers' quarters of the local naval air station, gave him a private room with television, and tried to make him feel safe and at ease. He spoke of being drugged after his forcible return to the vessel. He was in a state of high tension, but at the end of his stay on shore, he said again and again that he wished to return to his ship. We had no doubt that he had been threatened and intimidated and told that his family would be endangered if he did not return. But he insisted he wanted to go back, so we returned him to his ship. Then we had to fight a rearguard action with Senator Jesse Helms, who had taken an interest in the case, and William von Raab, head of the U.S. Customs Service in the Treasury Department, who wanted to prevent the vessel from leaving New Orleans.

Eventually the ship loaded up and left with Medved on board. Commander Paul Yost of the Coast Guard was ordered to provide the same protection to the vessel that it would any other vessel. And so the last picture of the Medved case, much to the distress of the Coast Guard, was of the *Marshal Konev* proceeding through the waters, surrounded by small boats of political protesters attempting to stop it, but with the Coast Guard vessels providing protection in the name of "marine safety." Subsequently, through our embassy in Moscow, we periodically got assurance that Medved was alive, and later we learned that he had become a university student.

Meanwhile, the interagency process on arms control was on track and working well for a change. We would have a further arms control proposal to present to the Soviets well in advance of the Geneva summit. We produced a counter to their 50-percent-reduction and 6,000-charges ideas. Our proposal was to apply such reductions to "comparable" strategic weapons and to subdivide the 6,000 charges into 4,500 ballistic missile warheads and 1,500 air-launched cruise missiles on 350 long-range bombers. We also wanted to clarify what testing was permitted by the ABM Treaty.

Another positive development was the Soviet decision that they did *not* want a "private channel" to conduct U.S.-Soviet business: the official channel would be the "real" channel. Ever since I came into office, a hodge-podge of voices in the White House, in Congress, and in the State Department had argued that only a "two-track" process—one public and nominal, one secret and real—could make progress. Bud McFarlane was unhappy. He had a note hand-delivered to me in New York, where I was attending UN meetings. He complained about the collapse of the secret channel idea and implicitly blamed me. Bud wanted to be the secret negotiator and felt that I was thwarting him.

I picked up the phone and called him. "I'm very distressed with your note," I said. "I rack my brains about what I've done to cause it. I want to put it right before we meet with the president on Friday." Having said that, I launched into a long rundown of what we had to do to get ready for Geneva. Bud responded as though no note had ever been written.

Just then, on October 31, another asylum case popped up. A Soviet soldier, Aleksandr Sukhanov, darted into our embassy in Kabul, Afghanistan, saying, reportedly, that he did not like the war and wanted to go home. He did not want to defect, he said. Soviet troops soon were surrounding our embassy; they wanted him back. If we made him return, the young soldier said, he would be sentenced to ten years' hard labor. I feared that was an understatement. I protested the Soviet action. I spoke to the president, and he agreed to a two-step approach: assure the soldier he could stay if he chose to do so, then allow a Soviet embassy official to come into the neutral ground of our embassy to ask the soldier, in a nonthreatening way, what he wanted to do. In the past, we had returned such soldiers when the Soviets gave us guarantees about no retribution. This was different from the case of the seaman in New Orleans, where the ship and therefore the man were entirely under our control. In Kabul, under the glare of floodlights, Soviet troops ringed our embassy. They cut off the electricity. We protested vehemently. They eased off. The Soviet soldier remained in our Kabul embassy and refused to be seen by any Soviet official. On November 3 he asked to meet with Soviet envoy Fikryat Tabeyev. For over an hour he met with Tabeyev and our chargé at the U.S. embassy in Kabul, who took notes. The Soviet soldier said that he wanted to go home. We allowed him to do so.

The summit meeting, I knew, was only a few weeks away, but I sometimes felt we would never get there. Rocks on the road were plenty, some put there by chance, some by calculation, some by the struggle over substance of our national security posture. Would we stumble?

CHAPTER 30

Classroom in the Kremlin;
Summit in Geneva

Time was short. Ronald Reagan and Mikhail Gorbachev would meet in Geneva in a few weeks. On November 2, 1985, I was on my way to Moscow. Word from the intelligence community and other Soviet specialists around the government was that the Soviet Union would never, indeed *could* never, change no matter how bad their internal economic and social problems were. I didn't see it that way. The generational shift in the Soviet leadership, I thought, was very significant. The old guard Communists had either ignored internal problems, as did Gromyko, or covered them up, as did Brezhnev. Gorbachev and Shevardnadze were from a distinctly different mold. It was more than a difference in personality. Because this new generation of leaders from the provinces had dealt with real problems in the Soviet system, they might accept the fact that change was imperative.

If they looked hard, they would see not only social and economic failure but moral failure as well. Anatoly Shcharansky stood for countless Soviet Jews who were oppressed. Other Soviet minorities had also been held down and kept back by the Communist party's rejection of individual rights and of religious freedom. Human rights had to be on top of our agenda with the Soviets: only when the Soviets changed human rights practices and recognized the importance of these rights to their own society could Soviet-American relations change at the deepest level.

I had given great thought to my meeting with Gorbachev and decided to bring up subjects of importance to both the Soviet Union and the United States but not related to the problems between us. I was determined to engage him on the subject of the "information age," its pervasive impact, and its implications. The computer and the technology of instant communication were already transforming the worlds of finance, manufacturing, politics, scientific research, diplomacy, indeed, everything. The Soviet Union would fall hopelessly and permanently behind the rest of the world in this new era unless it changed its economic and political system. "Just

586

look around," I would tell Gorbachev. "The successful societies are the open societies."

At the center of the problem for the Soviets was their attitude toward the rights of individual human beings. A society that is closed and compartmented simply cannot take advantage of the new technology. Furthermore, technology breaks through borders, so the state has more and more difficulty insulating its citizens from information about what is going on elsewhere. This line of thought was the way, I felt, to lead the Soviets to realize that improved human rights practices were in their own interest.

My idea was controversial within my delegation. "It's a classroom in the Kremlin; it's condescending," one of State's Sovietologists told me. "The Soviets will resent your presentation deeply; it will set us way back in our efforts to get somewhere on the issue of human rights."

I disagreed. "The question of political and economic freedom is central to everything the two superpowers do or can do. It has to be addressed." I would put forward the ideas of economic and political freedom in a way that engaged Gorbachev's clear interest in new ways of thinking.

I arrived in Moscow on November 4 and set right to work, meeting first with Shevardnadze. At a mansion in Moscow dating from czarist days and subsequently taken over by the Foreign Ministry, we started with a private session. I raised the issue of human rights first. Shevardnadze listened carefully, cautiously, without commitment, but without resentment. We then moved into a larger room for the plenary session. Shevardnadze had equipped the room for simultaneous translation and said with a smile, "I hope you'll like this bit of technology transfer."

It was a tough day. "As tough as testifying," Paul Nitze said. The Soviets were cordial but gave the impression of being ragged in their internal organization, of not having their act together. On arms control issues, they simply went through the motions, asking questions the answers to which they already knew. Yuli Kvitsinsky said to Nitze, summarizing their views, "The U.S. will not get chocolate until it gives sugar": no reductions in offensive weapons unless we abandoned SDI. Whatever important substance they might have to put forward, I assumed, would emerge in my meeting with Gorbachev, to occur the next day.

I arrived back at Spaso House, our ambassador's grand old Moscow residence, in time for a late dinner. The night before my arrival, the Soviets, after years of fruitless American requests, had repaved the street in front of the residence. Looking out the window at the little square below, Paul Nitze said, "It looks like they even painted the mud in the park." High up in the dome above the cavernous ballroom that forms the center of Spaso House, the family parrot could be heard whistling the "Marseillaise." I went down to dinner with the Hartmans. "The roses on the table," Donna

Hartman said, "come from the bishop of Antioch, who has a church here under a special agreement. Antioch was destroyed by an earthquake in 983, or something like that. So his seat moved to Damascus. His church here is under fewer regulations than others and so has developed the busiest practice in town baptizing and marrying people." The Soviets were facing something of a dilemma: the thousandth anniversary of the introduction of Christianity to Russia. This historical event was too important for the Kremlin simply to ignore; on the other hand, the Communist party rejected religion. So the regime had decided to recognize the occasion by stressing the architectural splendor of the churches and restoring some of them. It would be a way of paying tribute while avoiding spiritual content.

I assumed that our conversations would all be pleasant and light, for we knew the Soviets had bugged Spaso House—and virtually everywhere else, as far as I could tell. Art Hartman surprised me, however, by saying, "Ninety percent of what I want to say, I can say right here. We want our message to get across to the Soviets, and this is one of the few ways we can get them to listen to us. So I hold all of my briefings for congressional delegations in Spaso House."

As we were talking, the news came in that Vitaly Yurchenko, who had been a high official in the KGB before he defected in Rome in July and then proceeded to the United States, had disappeared. He had been debriefed extensively by the CIA. On November 2, he had slipped away from his CIA handler and later surfaced at the Soviet embassy in Washington, claiming that the CIA had drugged him, kidnapped him from Rome, and then forced him to make statements about defecting. The Soviet embassy had delivered a protest to us demanding that Yurchenko be given safe passage out of the United States to return to Moscow.

Art Hartman told me that Mark Palmer, deputy assistant secretary for European and Canadian Affairs, had come to him with a protest of his own. He wanted to register his objections to my proposed presentation to Gorbachev on human rights. "I care deeply about human rights, and I think George Shultz is all wrong. He is the secretary of state and can do what he wants, but when he has real experts, he should at the least ask for our advice," he told Hartman. He didn't like my "information age" classroom in the Kremlin or my approach to the matter of human rights.

The problem, I felt, was that the "experts" were too often mired in their own pet positions. They were hooked on the idea of trading Soviet actions on human rights for U.S. actions on trade. Shevardnadze kept telling me that the Soviets would do what made sense from the standpoint of their society. I was groping for a way to get the Soviets to see that their own society would benefit from better treatment of individuals.

Palmer and my other advisers didn't know that I planned to go even further. They thought that in Washington they had talked me out of my idea to ask the Soviets to allow me to take Soviet dissidents Anatoly Shcharansky and Ida Nudel with me on my aircraft as I left Moscow. But I still would make this request to the Soviets, even knowing that they would refuse. It was one more way of underlining to them the importance of the issue.

Pull and Haul with Gorbachev

Gorbachev sent us word that he hoped for a small meeting. He would have with him only Shevardnadze, Dobrynin, and his interpreter. I decided to keep my delegation to the same size, with only Bud McFarlane, Art Hartman, and our interpreter joining me. I was sorry not to include Paul Nitze, given his acute powers of observation. No one had a longer or more astute baseline of observation from which to compare Soviet leaders than Nitze. We met in Gorbachev's Central Committee office. Translation was consecutive.

Gorbachev, I could see, was in a feisty mood. He went immediately on the offensive, declaring that "disinformation" in the United States about the Soviet Union made it impossible to build a healthy relationship. He knew all about us, he said, how Weinberger and I had worked in the same company. Gorbachev picked up a book from the table next to him. It was *The United States in the 1980s*, a collection of policy essays by scholars of the Hoover Institution at Stanford. "I know all about your ideas," he said. In this he was right on target; Ronald Reagan had looked to the Hoover Institution for help in his administration.[1]

"Look," I said, "the person to focus on is Ronald Reagan. He is popular. He speaks with authority. If he makes an agreement, he can get support for that agreement. That's important in any negotiation, to know that the person you are dealing with can deliver."

I must have touched a raw nerve. He lectured me about agreements made but not ratified, referring to SALT II.

I pushed back, "Deeds are more important than words. SALT II was withdrawn by Carter after you invaded Afghanistan."

"Leave arguments like that for the press," he interrupted, animated. "We are not uninstructed on these issues. You shouldn't be using arguments like that with people like us, who know the real story. SALT II was dead and buried even before Afghanistan. Don't use arguments like Afghanistan. It shows you don't respect us. The U.S. got out of SALT II because you didn't want to be constrained by it." Speaking of linkage between arms control and regional issues, he said, "You ought to put that one in mothballs. It's old hat."

---

1. I had been a member of the advisory committee for the Hoover project that produced the book.

Gorbachev then took off on the military-industrial complex. "If you need help in employing 18 million people, let us know; maybe we can buy something to keep them busy," he said sarcastically. I thought Dobrynin was egging him on and was surprised that Dobrynin, who should have known better, had apparently been feeding him so much nonsense.

I told Gorbachev that he was dead wrong about the importance of military spending to the U.S. economy. "Military procurement accounts for no more than 3 percent of our GNP," I countered, "and our economy can easily get along without that. The reason for our military buildup is the threat from the Soviet Union." I used this opportunity to get back into the discussion. I told Gorbachev that most of what he had said I didn't agree with. "I don't want to go back over all the points. I want to raise the essential question: where do we go from here? That is the essential question."

Having changed the subject, I delivered two letters from President Reagan and turned to the Geneva meeting. "I have not the slightest doubt the president has a great desire to see a more constructive relationship between our two countries which will enable us to deal with each other in a realistic and pragmatic way: realistic in that each side should know that we operate under two very different systems. You think yours is better; we think ours is better. But there is a responsibility on us as the two great powers which is tremendous and which leads to the conclusion that both must work for a more constructive relationship." I went further. "We know the present state of our relationship is unsatisfactory. The reason for the coming meeting is to do better. That is the way the president wishes to approach in a very serious manner the upcoming meeting in Geneva."

Gorbachev seemed to settle down a bit. He interrupted the translation to say, "If that is so, maybe we can succeed."

I went on to point out that the reason the Geneva meeting was important was not just a negative one. Certainly the negative one—the avoidance of war, especially nuclear war—was critically important. But there were positive reasons as well. "For example, what sort of world do we want to build for the future? This sort of reason weighs very heavily with the president. The world is changing very rapidly. You want to see progress, and so do we. This progress is going to be a reflection of what happens in the world and how we handle the opportunities open to us."

I recalled comments Gorbachev had made at our meeting after the Chernenko funeral about the number of new countries in the world and his view about the changes this would bring about as they all struggled to succeed. "You were right," I said, but change will come not only from "the creation of new national entities but also from the great variety that will exist and the stimulus this will bring to innovation and creativity. But there will obviously be differences in developments in different parts of the world. The United States and the Soviet Union will be interacting all over the world as it changes, sometimes in volatile situations which may not even be created by the two great powers but will affect them. We need to see how we can interact constructively in these situations."

I then talked about epochal changes being brought about by the information age. "Science and technology are moving quickly, and this affects everything, including military weaponry, but it also affects how we produce things and how we live. We have left the era of the industrial age and have moved into what we might think of as the information age, in which we will have to think about new ways of working, new ways of making decisions. Society is beginning to reorganize itself in profound ways. Closed and compartmented societies cannot take advantage of the information age. People must be free to express themselves, move around, emigrate and travel if they want to, challenge accepted ways without fear. Otherwise, they can't take advantage of the opportunities available. The Soviet economy will have to be radically changed to adapt to the new era."

Far from being offended, Gorbachev lighted up, "You should take over the planning office here in Moscow, become the new head of Gosplan [the Soviet ministry charged with economic planning], because you have more ideas than they have." He went on to say, with a twinkle in his eyes, "The next time you come to Moscow you should forget about your government duties and come as a businessman and economist."

Turning to the Geneva negotiations, I referred to Shevardnadze's speech at the United Nations in which he spoke about the central importance of deterrence and stability and the threats to achieving a stable deterrent. "When you look at SALT I and the ABM Treaty," I told Gorbachev, "there are certain assumptions both on the offensive side and on the defensive side, but those assumptions haven't held up. And so now we have a situation that's quite different from the one we expected when those two treaties were signed. One assumption was that as we constrain defense under the ABM Treaty, offensive forces would be significantly reduced. But obviously that hasn't happened. We both today have more missiles and more warheads. This accounts for our interest and perhaps even the Soviet interest in radical reductions."

"The second assumption," I said, "was that while defenses were being held in check, critical-path items would be constrained in order to stop the creation of a national antiballistic missile defense. We abandoned our strategic defense plans, even though you kept yours around Moscow, as was permitted under the ABM Treaty." Then, referring to the phased-array radar under construction at Krasnoyarsk, I said, "I want you to know that we believe certain things you have done are contrary to the treaty." I went on, "And you have all of these developments in science and technology and the development of ballistic missiles with extraordinary accuracies and the MIRVed and mobile systems."

Gorbachev interrupted. "Are you saying that the ABM Treaty is obsolete because of the quality of weapons? Just what are you suggesting?"

"No," I responded. "The ABM Treaty is of tremendous importance, and the president has ordered that all of our activity should remain within the bounds of the treaty in its narrow definition. But we need to ask a question even before the research results are available on SDI; we've got to ask the question, how do you manage deployment or a transition to an increased dependence on defense? None of this is new to you. How do we have a cooperative transition?"

Gorbachev interrupted vociferously, saying to McFarlane, "I'm amazed that you would base your judgment on the advice of a lawyer who had previously only had experience prosecuting drug and pornography cases."[2] What struck me about this comment from Gorbachev was the disclosure of how closely he followed small details of the debate in the United States over the meaning of the ABM Treaty. Gorbachev continued, "The Strategic Defense Initiative is an attempt to justify an ABM system by unworthy means, and we're smart people. We know what's going on. We know why you're doing this. You're inspired by illusions. You think you're ahead of us in information. You think you're ahead of us in technology and that you can use these things to gain superiority over the Soviet Union. But this is an illusion. Other people have recognized this."

I interjected, "There aren't any illusions on the part of the secretary of state or the president about the capabilities and strengths of the Soviet Union. That's why we're sitting here today."

Gorbachev responded, "Well, we don't have illusions, either, but I can tell you that I know that you do." Gorbachev then said rather solemnly, "You can rest assured that we will not help the United States get out of its ABM Treaty obligations. We will not assist you with the politics of it or in a technical way so that you can take the arms race into space."

"Look, we'll figure out for ourselves what our policy is on defense," I responded. "In fact, yours is the same. All you have to do is watch your programs and you, the Soviets, are doing the same thing. We don't see anything wrong with defending ourselves."

"The Soviet Union will not retreat in ABM," Gorbachev said. "You are full of illusions. First, you believe that the Soviet Union is less economically powerful and therefore it would be weakened by an arms race. Second, that you have the higher technology and therefore SDI would give you superiority over the Soviet Union in weapons. Third, that the Soviet Union is more interested in negotiations in Geneva than you are. Fourth, that the Soviet Union only thinks of damaging U.S. interests in regions around the world. And fifth, that it would be wrong to trade with the Soviet Union

2. Gorbachev was referring to an opinion made public by a lawyer from the Defense Department, Philip Kunsberg, not Abe Sofaer, the legal adviser to the secretary of state.

because this would just raise its capability. These are all illusions, and you apparently are failing to draw lessons from history. The Soviets know how to meet their challenges.

"The big question is," Gorbachev asked, "is the United States interested in improving relations? You've got this big budget; a large part of it is due to military expenditure. Eighty percent is financed by borrowing money, and you've got high interest rates. Perhaps the Soviet Union could place orders in the U.S. and relieve the U.S. economy of having to be dependent on making arms. Maybe the U.S. administration has lost its way in trying to find a policy toward the Soviet Union."

I responded with some heat, and he said, "Well, Dobrynin tells me that people in the United States are still listening to those who think in terms of illusions. Are you afraid that you'd lose your jobs if you admitted this?"

In an attempt to lighten the air, I laughed, "I've got news for you. I've got a tenured position at Stanford University, so I don't worry about those things."

After more pull and haul, Gorbachev said, "I'm not attempting to have an argument, but we've been talking very frankly, perhaps like you do in your office."

I felt he was trying to diffuse the heat. I responded positively, "We think there's an opportunity to make progress, and we should work at that."

I invited McFarlane into the conversation. After he made extended remarks on the reasons why the stability of deterrence was deteriorating, he started in on defense and SDI: "You have been portraying me as having an aggressive intent toward the ABM Treaty. That's wrong."

Gorbachev interrupted. "You only invented this interpretation of the ABM Treaty last spring. You got a new idea on what Article V meant because you wanted to get out of the ABM restrictions and you needed the broad interpretation. We're very suspicious of what's going on. SDI is not compatible with the ABM Treaty. The Soviet Union isn't trying for unilateral advantage, and you shouldn't try, either."

Gorbachev asserted, "The Soviet Union will only compromise on the condition that there is no militarization of space. I hope this is not your last word. If so, nothing will result from the negotiation. There will be no 50 percent reductions. You are operating from a different logic. If you want superiority through your SDI, we will not help you. We will let you bankrupt yourselves. But also we will not reduce our offensive missiles. We will engage in a buildup that will break your shield. We don't want war, but neither are we going to allow unilateral advantage. Therefore, we will increase nuclear arms. But we are patient, and we still have hope."

Gorbachev then turned to Geneva. "The Geneva meeting is an important starting point, but using it as a get-acquainted meeting is too restricted. And so is just setting an agenda for the future. We realize that the difficulties which have piled up over the years will not be solved in one meeting. So we take the view that if there is only the fact of the meeting, that it would be a disappointment to our people and the world. So what we should be thinking about is the interests of the world and how they can be served by moves that would lead to a major political impetus to get a drastic improvement of our relations. We need policies that meet the preoccupation with world problems. The great question is of war or peace. That's what preoccupies people everywhere. We should have as our intent the development of a dialogue to reduce confrontation and to encourage détente and peaceful coexistence. That is what the world wants."

He shifted subjects. "The countries of Latin America are being robbed by transnational corporations, and they need to raise their productivity. This is not the hand of Moscow. And Africa and Asia are both in that same sad situation. The Soviet Union will continue to support national liberation movements, but you should give up your illusions—you, the United States, should give up your illusions, and then we can move to go on together, even on such questions as human rights." I was immediately struck by his reference to human rights. Maybe we were getting through to this new personality. He was a far cry from Gromyko.

Gorbachev concluded by agreeing to discuss in Geneva regional and bilateral issues as well as arms control, and by this time he knew we would bring up human rights. He had virtually accepted that in his last comment. Our four-part agenda was on the table.

Postscript

I was pleased with my day. I had a toe-to-toe encounter with Gorbachev. I liked it. He probably got some matters off his chest with me that would not come up again with the president. I hoped he learned something from my comments. He didn't take offense when I interrupted; I think he even enjoyed it. He talked a lot, but he also listened. SDI obviously hit a raw nerve. That was good: SDI had brought them to the table. And I was glad to see that we had succeeded in getting human rights on Gorbachev's mind.

"What's the headline? What's the headline?" Bernie Kalb asked me as we were getting ready to leave.

"Stalemate on Eve of Summit," I said with a laugh. Gorbachev had been acting, posturing, I felt, trying to show how tough he was. His refrain was that everything was tied to SDI: nothing positive was possible in our relationship until the United States gave up SDI; SDI was leading to a new arms race. Rather than offensive cuts, the Soviets would now have to speed their nuclear buildup, he claimed.

Through it all, I sensed a deep commitment on Gorbachev's part to communism as an ideology. He was a new presence, no doubt, but his

A light moment with the president in the Oval Office, November 16, 1984.
Ronald Reagan Presidential Library

Soviet Foreign Minister Andrei
Gromyko comes to the White
House on September 28, 1984,
his first visit since the Soviets
invaded Afghanistan in 1979.
Ronald Reagan Presidential Library

West German Chancellor
Helmut Kohl's departure
ceremony at the White House,
November 15, 1984.
Ronald Reagan Presidential Library

Cap Weinberger, Vice President Bush, Arthur Burns, Rick Burt, Bud McFarlane, and I with President Reagan in the Oval Office, November 15, 1984. Ronald Reagan Presidential Library

Paul Nitze, President Reagan, and I in the Oval Office, December 1984. Paul signs on as my special adviser on arms control.

Ready to pilot the F-15 Eagle. Nellis Air Force Base, Nevada, 1985.

After my counterterrorism speech, 1984. Hy Rosen

Andrei Gromyko and I at the Soviet mission in Geneva, January 7, 1985. "Time flies when you're having fun." L. Bianco, Geneva

The Shultz-Weinberger debate on the use of force, 1984. Hy Rosen

Happy days. President Reagan, Vice President Bush, and I at the White House, January 10, 1985. Photograph by James M. Thresher, *The Washington Post*, reprinted with permission

Facing a crucial vote on appropriations for the MX missile, Cap Weinberger and I testify in an unusual three-hour session before the Senate Armed Services Committee, February 26, 1985.

Feeling svelte, with sumo wrestlers from Japan and Ambassador Nabuo Matsunaga in the Benjamin Franklin Room of the State Department's Diplomatic Reception Rooms, 1985.

Bud McFarlane, President Reagan, and I discuss the controversial visit to Bitburg on *Air Force One* en route to West Germany, May 6, 1985.

Jim Baker, President Reagan, and I at the final session of the Summit Seven meeting in Bonn, May 1985. Allen Wallis is on the right. Ronald Reagan Presidential Library

Opposite: I deliver a speech at Yad Vashem, the Holocaust Memorial, on May 10, 1985.

After Bitburg, Shimon Peres and Yitzhak Shamir flank me at Yad Vashem, the Holocaust Memorial, Jerusalem, May 10, 1985.

I show Prime Minister and Mrs. Rajiv Gandhi Thomas Jefferson's standing desk, at which he is said to have penned parts of the Declaration of Independence, June 12, 1985.

Dancing with the first lady at the White House, July 1985.

Ronald Reagan
Presidential Library

The Reagans come to dinner at my house: President Reagan inscribed this photo: "Welcome to our house, George and O'Bie," as he had arrived before I did, July 30, 1985. Ronald Reagan Presidential Library

My address to the General Assembly at the fortieth anniversary of the United Nations, September 23, 1985.

Greeting new Soviet Foreign Minister Eduard Shevardnadze at the White House, September 27, 1985. Ronald Reagan Presidential Library

Sinking a putt—en route to Geneva on *Air Force One*, November 1985. My gallery includes Bud McFarlane, Don Regan, and Mike Deaver. Ronald Reagan Presidential Library

I throw a pass to Redskins receiver Art Monk, winner of the NFL Player of the Year Award, 1985. Aron C. Chrapp

With Norman Mailer in the New York Public Library before addressing the International PEN (Poets, Playwrights, Editors, Essayists, and Novelists), January 12, 1986.

President Reagan (seated), Don Regan, Cap Weinberger, Vice President Bush, John Poindexter, and I in the Oval Office, February 25, 1986. Ronald Reagan Presidential Library

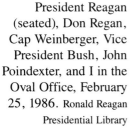

Prime Minister Brian Mulroney of Canada and I during his state visit, Washington, D.C., March 1986.

Corazon Aquino, triumphant as president of the Philippines, March 1986.

Taking off my shoes before entering the Blue Mosque, Istanbul, March 23, 1986.

Above, left: "Bad call?" at the White House
Tennis Tournament, April 7, 1986.
Ronald Reagan Presidential Library

Above, right: On "Meet the Press," June 1,
1986. Reni Newsphotos

At left: "I'm glad you asked that question. . . ." Foreign Policy Association
speech, June 4, 1986.

I greet El Salvador's President José Napoleón Duarte in Bogotá, Colombia, August 7, 1986.

Wearing a "Cory" doll during Corazon
Aquino's state visit to Washington,
September 1986.

approach was to *repair* his system, not *replace* it. He was granting nothing in the ideological contest between communism and freedom. Gorbachev had been combative; he had sought to intimidate me. What he got was an argument, an exposition of my point of view, and a challenge for a break-through on the treatment of Soviet Jews and other dissidents and refuseniks persecuted in the Soviet Union.

Back at the embassy in the secure bubble where I briefed my delegations on the day's events, a further report came in about Yurchenko. He had escaped from his CIA handler as the two were having dinner at a George-town restaurant by excusing himself to go to the men's room and then climbing through a window to the alley outside. The belief around the administration was that Yurchenko had gotten fed up with the way he was being treated, especially with the way information that he gave to the CIA leaked subsequently to the newspapers. The CIA said he had defected in the expectation that the wife of a Soviet diplomat in Canada would leave her husband and join him: she didn't, and Yurchenko didn't want to stay any longer in America. In an interview on neutral ground, we verified that he wanted to leave, so he was entitled to do so. But to botch such a catch, in my view, was a real black mark on the professionalism of the CIA. The case seemed symbolic to me: a high Soviet official had rejected his society for ours, but our own intelligence service had blown it.

My trip ended with a final session with Shevardnadze, who focused on the positive. I, too, thought my meeting with Gorbachev had been positive: a candid, direct, even if combative, exchange. The verbal sparring was fine with me. But I was disturbed that Gorbachev and Shevardnadze were so ignorant of—or misinformed about—U.S. positions and statements that we had made to Ambassador Dobrynin in Washington and that our ne-gotiators had made to the Soviets at the talks in Geneva. There was a disconnect somewhere in the Soviet chain of command. This made it es-pecially important that I had talked straight and talked tough to Gorbachev, to counter notions about the United States that were far off the mark.

As I left Moscow for the airport, my motorcade suddenly slowed to a crawl. Another motorcade roared by, kicking up the pebbles on the shoul-der of the road; it was Shevardnadze, hastening to arrive before me to bid me farewell in proper protocol style.

After we were airborne, I went forward to the cockpit of the plane and saw before me fingers of colored light rising above the curving night ho-rizon: the aurora borealis. The sun was hidden, but its light spiked through the earth's magnetic field, an awe-inspiring sight.

By midafternoon, Thursday, November 7, I was back in Washington. Ambassador Dobrynin came in to talk with me alone. His message was amazing: it was something of an apology. And the Soviets *never* apologize. Dobrynin said that the Soviets wanted the summit to go well: Gorbachev would not be as tough on President Reagan as he had been on me. Apparently, they had scared themselves. I hadn't been alarmed by the vigorous exchange. I thought it was good.

From Acrimony to Accomplishment

The substance of the relationship was a puzzle. We had produced a further proposal—a counter-counterproposal—and made an effort to see that our ideas were raised and discussed first by our negotiators in Geneva rather than by me in Washington or Moscow. We wanted to maintain the focus on the designated negotiating table when business was to be done. But here was Max Kampelman, home from Geneva and in my office, telling me that his Soviet counterparts had simply called our ideas unacceptable and had raised again old demands that they knew were out of the question.

Yet at the same time, Max said, there was an almost plaintive effort by the Soviets to appear to make progress. "In the last few weeks the Soviets have tried hard to see whether we could come up with words for a joint summit communiqué. At times they seem rather desperate: 'Can't we find some words?' " The mere thought of a joint communiqué with the Soviets alarmed Cap Weinberger and others in the Defense Department. They were driving Bud McFarlane wild with charges that he had to "stop Shultz" from doing any such thing.

Max was turning out to be excellent as head of our team at the Geneva negotiations. In a gentle, reasonable voice he would surround his arguments with every nuance of style and care—and respect for his interlocutor. But his words were woven with steel cables. Kampelman described his Soviet counterpart, Yuli Kvitsinsky, with whom Nitze had jousted in "the walk in the woods": "Kvitsinsky is imaginative, a doer; he tries," Kampelman reported. "He protects himself by putting his thoughts in our mouths and then reports these thoughts to Moscow. Kvitsinsky says that he needs a statement that neither side will withdraw from the ABM Treaty for ten years and something on antisatellite efforts—that's what he means by constraining SDI. My impression is that Kvitsinsky thinks this at some point will be doable. But he cannot be relied upon to tell the truth or to report accurately to Moscow," said Max.

"Yes," I noted, "in Moscow, Kvitsinsky reassured Paul Nitze by saying, '*This time* I'm telling the truth!' "

As the pace quickened in preparation for the Geneva summit, it became clear that the Soviets very much wanted a joint communiqué. On our side, the Defense Department and the CIA now wanted to look at and weigh in on everything, and their own personnel were split between those who insisted we must not sign anything "jointly" with the Soviet Union and those who were willing to do so but insisted on stuffing the communiqué draft with impossible language that neither the Soviets nor any other government would accept. It was a technique to doom a communiqué by setting impossible goals.

The president did not like the acrimony and decided that we should put "on hold" efforts with the Soviets to develop what they described as a possible joint communiqué. But he did agree with me on the importance of developing language for what we called an "agreed statement" privately so that I would have some ideas and language "in my pocket" should we have an opportunity for something constructive in Geneva. We would just skip over this interagency squabbling.

I had decided by this time that "communiqué" smacked too much of the détente days and that we should call whatever emerged an "agreed statement." I wanted to use words that meant the same thing to both sides. That would mean expressing what we agreed upon in language that avoided phrases of the past like "peaceful coexistence" and "nonuse of force."

On November 13, I went over to the Defense Department for breakfast with Cap. I reviewed for him the twenty-six items that we planned to take up with the Soviets. I was on top of my brief and felt confident. The breakfast went well, to my surprise.

Later, I went to see the president in a positive frame of mind. Although the president had stopped the effort to produce a joint communiqué in order to end the bickering within the administration, I wanted to turn this decision into something that could still allow progress and would take advantage of the president's own positive instincts. "Let's do it differently," I said. "No precooking of a full communiqué with the Soviets, so you and Gorbachev won't spend your time ratifying somebody else's work. Let's make it a *real* summit and see what comes out in the atmosphere you and Gorbachev produce. We'll turn out an agreed statement in Geneva if we have something worth saying as a result of the meeting." This was right down the president's alley. He readily agreed.

I was feeling good. We were on to something. At 6:40, Dobrynin came to my office, and I talked to him alone. A new relationship was possible, I told him. U.S. and Soviet positions were coming closer together. At this summit the leaders themselves should do "real" work: the two could agree upon and announce significant steps forward. Dobrynin kept returning to the Soviet hope for a precooked joint communiqué. "No," I said, "whatever emerges will be a real product of the meeting. The president wants a meeting of the bosses: Reagan and Gorbachev. Two leaders." Dobrynin seemed intrigued.

First Impressions in Geneva

We were wheels up from Andrews at 8:35 Saturday morning, November 16, bound for the Geneva summit. As we flew in over the snow-blanketed

Alps, a harsh wind swept the white flakes into the air, creating a fine haze over Cointrin Airport as we landed. President Reagan went to his residence, La Maison de Saussure. The villa, owned by a Swiss businessman, was being rented by Prince Karim Aga Khan. His son had left instructions for President Reagan to please be sure to feed the fish while he was there. Upon arrival, the president began immediately to follow instructions.

I went to the Intercontinental Hotel, which overlooked the Soviet compound and was my usual port of call in Geneva. Don Regan and Bud McFarlane stayed with the president in a building near his villa. Eight miles down the shore of Lake Geneva was the site selected for the sessions of the summit when we were host, Fleur d' Eau, a stately home on grounds of about seven acres. A gravel path wound down from the veranda to a swimming pool, now covered with ice and snow, next to which stood a small, cozy pool house. The advance team of security agents had a blazing fire going in the stone-lined fireplace.

Just before our departure for the summit, both the *New York Times* and the *Washington Post* obtained and published a letter from Cap Weinberger to President Reagan urging the president *not* to give Gorbachev a commitment that the United States would continue to abide by SALT II and, in the same vein, not to agree to any narrow interpretation of the ABM Treaty, so that SDI could proceed unhampered.

Reactions around Washington and in Moscow were similar: Weinberger's letter must have been written and leaked deliberately to hamstring the president and sabotage the summit. Soviet propagandist Georgi Arbatov remarked that the letter appeared to be "a direct attempt to torpedo the whole arms control process." The press for some time had been speculating that Cap's absence from the Geneva delegation was a snub and sign of his declining influence. This was not true, but it fueled the feeling that the letter was Cap's revenge. The *Washington Post* reported on November 19, "The individual who last Friday provided the Post with Weinberger's letter and the executive summary [of a report he had submitted on Soviet treaty compliance] refused yesterday to discuss for publication the reasons for that action. The Post source continued to ask that neither his or her name nor place of work be mentioned." The president was angry about the leak.

Bud McFarlane, when asked whether the leak "was intended to sabotage the summit," responded, "Sure it was." The fact that Weinberger's letter was not classified suggested that the Pentagon was asking for a leak. Once the summit began, however, this storm simply blew away.

Along with the leaked Weinberger letter came an attempt from Bill Casey to head off any effort to improve relations with the Soviets. In his view, an improvement in relations would amount to a return to a Nixon/ Kissinger–era détente and would serve Soviet interests, enabling them to strengthen themselves at home while giving up none of their objectives internationally. This was Bill Casey's eleventh-hour effort to block movement at the Geneva summit.

In the study of my suite at the Geneva Intercontinental I found a copy of Gorbachev's new book, *A Time for Peace*, and a tangerine on my desk, obviously placed there by someone on my staff. In the other half of the room, sitting on a Victorian-style carpet, was an eight-foot-high box with a glass door: in effect, a small, secure telephone booth. This was my "security bubble." I took my team in one by one to discuss their roles at the summit; there was barely room for two. Richard Perle wanted to be part of the team to negotiate whatever joint statement might emerge. He had done a great job at the January meeting in Geneva with Gromyko. I told him he was more than welcome but that Roz Ridgway would be in charge. No problem; he worked well with her. I also told him that I felt the Defense Department had misled President Reagan about what could be achieved in the SDI program within the restraints of the ABM Treaty. The Defense Department made it seem as if there could be no SDI without lifting treaty restraints. Perle and I argued a bit, but we had learned to spar easily and amicably and had developed a mutual respect.

The president and Nancy, with the big event about to take place, were looking everything over with care. We went together through Fleur d'Eau, approved the physical arrangements, and went through a game plan of the upcoming events. The president wanted to start with a private talk, just the two leaders, in a relaxed setting. He and Nancy looked over the pool house, a short walk from the main house and down by the lake. The president thought he might use it toward the end of the day. Keep the fire going there, too, was the message. Nancy encouraged the idea of private meetings, and I agreed with her. Ronald Reagan was at his best in personal exchanges. He had a knack for making friends, creating a sense of warm, genuine human interaction and intimacy and, in the process, sizing up the other guy.

The president convened our delegation for a run-through of the program. He wanted to hear whatever points anyone on the team wanted to raise. I argued strongly—and, in the end, successfully—that we propose to Gorbachev a press blackout while the sessions were under way. No one in either delegation, if the blackout was adopted, could brief the press on the discussions except through authorized statements by each side's respective spokesmen. That had worked very effectively in Geneva the previous January, I argued. A blackout would allow us to negotiate directly with each other and not indirectly through the press.

The Summit Begins

On Tuesday, November 19, the summit began. Ronald Reagan greeted Mikhail Gorbachev at 10:00 A.M. with an engaging smile. Flashbulbs lit the landscape. The image was dramatic: the hatless, coatless seventy-four-year-old who had bounded out energetically in the bitter cold to greet the leader twenty years his junior. In the photos, Gorbachev—in topcoat and brown fedora—looked older than the president. President Reagan steered his guest into a side room for what was planned to be a meeting of about twenty minutes. Thirty went by, then forty. Jim Kuhn, the president's personal assistant and keeper of the schedule, approached me asking whether he should go in and give the president an opening to break up the meeting. What did I think?

"If you're dumb enough to do that, you shouldn't be in your job," I said, perhaps a bit harshly, as Don Regan, I discovered later, had sent him to me with the question. The rest of us, Americans and Soviets, sat around the large table that had been set up in the villa's dining room, engaged in casual conversation, and stared through the high windows at the frozen scene outside. While the president and Gorbachev met, I spent the time in conversation with Shevardnadze. We agreed to go through our own agenda when our bosses were meeting as a way to prepare ground for them. We started on regional issues, beginning with a mutual assessment of developments in Southern Africa.

After about an hour and a quarter, the leaders emerged, smiling. The president later told me that he and Gorbachev hit it off well. The president described how he brought up the importance of human rights and said that the balance of their talk had been a short version of what had followed at the big table.

Gorbachev opened by giving President Reagan a firm line: the United States should not have illusions about being able to "bankrupt" the Soviet Union; neither could we gain military superiority over the Soviets. "Make no mistake," Gorbachev said, "we can match you, whatever you do." It was the same line he had given me in Moscow, but with his punches pulled now for the president. Gorbachev was pleasant. Reagan was more stern and direct, talking of the Soviet post–World War II buildup and their responsibility for the cold war.

Gorbachev replied that the war had left the USSR far behind and that they had caught up with the West. The president, to emphasize the difficult problem of trust in our relationship, recounted how the Soviets in World War II had refused to let U.S. bombers land and refuel in the USSR after our runs over Nazi targets.

During a break, Georgi Kornienko, deputy foreign minister and a man I had come to know, exploded at me. "Your president was totally *wrong*, I know," he said, "because I was stationed at a Soviet base where your bombers came in to refuel. What can we think of a president who is so misinformed?" I later checked the story out and found that Kornienko was right. But the negotiations to authorize such refueling had been painful, slow, and acrimonious. Many times I would try to correct the president on particular facts of a favorite story. It rarely worked. Once a certain arrangement of facts was in his head, I could hardly ever get them out. Usually, as in this case, there was an underlying kernel of truth, even if aspects were off the mark.

After adjourning for lunch, Gorbachev brought up Afghanistan. He talked about withdrawal of Soviet troops "as part of a general political settlement between us." He even indicated that the United States could "help" the Soviets get out. I thought I saw the beginning of an opening there, but no one else picked up on this. Gorbachev described the "process" that our two nations should use to advance the relationship. He envisioned contacts at various levels, starting with foreign ministers and ranging through a wide variety of topics. As I listened, I thought to myself, Gorbachev could be reading right out of the president's own briefing book.

Gorbachev then moved on to arms control. He had a set of questions about SDI, which he claimed was taking us into a new arms race, as it would require the Soviets to increase their offensive weaponry while developing their own SDI. Theirs would be cheaper and better than ours, Gorbachev assured us.

President Reagan did not pick up at all on Gorbachev's lightly veiled hint about pulling out of Afghanistan. Instead, the president cited Afghanistan, Cambodia, and Nicaragua as examples where Soviet intervention and troublemaking were undermining peace. He then talked about the substantial reductions of battlefield nuclear weapons—and withdrawals of such weapons—undertaken unilaterally by the United States since 1969.

In midafternoon, coffee was brought in. The president said to Gorbachev, "We get along pretty well talking alone" and suggested they walk down to the pool house by the lake. Comfortable chairs and a blazing fire awaited them. Outside it was unbearably cold. "There's nothing like a little shared hardship to form a bond," I remarked. While they were talking by the fire, Shevardnadze and I and all the others chatted among ourselves. The two leaders returned an hour later, having discussed inconclusively our approach to arms control. Both were obviously in a good mood. The president made an important announcement to us. They had agreed on reciprocal visits: first Gorbachev to a Washington summit, then Reagan to a Moscow summit. I was surprised and encouraged, as much by the obvious rapport between the two men as by their quick agreement without hesitation on reciprocal visits for two follow-on summit meetings. Such agreement was one of our main objectives in Geneva. The president's brand of personal diplomacy seemed to be working.

At the end of the afternoon in our postmortem with the president, the general conclusion was that the tone had been good and that Gorbachev had come toward our positions on quite a few topics. Gorbachev was long-winded, but his talk had content. He was not filibustering. He made far fewer misstatements of fact about the United States with the president than he had in the preparatory meeting with me in Moscow. Beyond agreement on home-and-home summits, the big story of the day, everyone felt, was the extended time that the two men had spent together. Personally, I thought the big story was that they had hit it off as human beings.

The Soviets had let me know that they wanted to get work going on a joint communiqué. I thought we should listen to whatever they might say and, at the same time, let them see what an agreed statement, as we would call it, might look like. I was still not authorized by the president to proceed with a real negotiation. I authorized Roz to meet and learn what she could about the Soviet ideas.

I then left for the dinner the Gorbachevs were hosting at the Soviet mission. The evening was pleasant and cordial, and the Gorbachevs were warm hosts. The first course at dinner was caviar. Shot glasses were filled with vodka. Shevardnadze raised his glass, as though to make a toast, and said with a smile, "Mr. President, I have to come all the way to Geneva to get vodka." Gorbachev joined the laughter. The incident showed me the easy relationship that existed between Shevardnadze and Gorbachev. Suddenly everyone was talking about visiting California, visiting Moscow. It was wonderful in a way, but there was little real movement yet on key issues of substance. It would be hard for President Reagan to be disagreeable to Gorbachev after this. "You know," Reagan had told Gorbachev, "people have come to think of us as enemies. We don't have to be."

Wednesday morning, Roz Ridgway came in to report on her night's work. "There is not a single formulation of ours they can accept," she told me in obvious frustration. So Gorbachev's mood had not been translated into a new approach by his staff. "Their tone is quite measured, but we have a real problem," Roz explained. "They have a game to go through—letting us know they wanted to develop a communiqué weeks ago and making us pay now for holding back then. We face the same old sourness. We have a lot of work ahead."

Day Two

The second summit day, Wednesday, November 20, was tough from start to finish. The Soviets were hosts. Gorbachev began by inviting President Reagan into a side room in their embassy for a private session. We had predicted this would happen, and the president had decided to use the opportunity to take up human rights issues again. When the two leaders emerged, they were not smiling. The atmosphere had been highly charged. The president told me that after he made his points, Gorbachev attacked human rights practices in the United States, citing discrimination against blacks and women and unemployment figures, which he contrasted with full employment in the Soviet Union. The president had argued back. The exchange had been intense. Again, that sounded good to me. The Soviets were talking with us about the subject. They weren't stonewalling. Maybe we could move forward through this process of mutual criticism.

In the plenary session, we turned to strategic arms. Regan, McFarlane, Nitze, Ridgway, and Hartman joined the president and me on our side, facing our Soviet counterparts. Gorbachev again harangued us about SDI. President Reagan exploded. The two leaders went back and forth, interrupting each other and expressing their views with vehemence. Ronald Reagan got the floor. He spoke passionately about how much better the world would be if we were able to defend ourselves against nuclear missiles. He was intense as he expressed his abhorrence at having to rely on the ability to "wipe each other out" as the means of keeping the peace. "We must do better, and we can." The depth of the president's belief in SDI was vividly apparent. Ronald Reagan was talking from the inside out. Translation was simultaneous. Gorbachev could connect what the president said with his facial expression and body language.

When the president finished, there was total silence. After what seemed an interminable time, Gorbachev said, "Mr. President, I don't agree with you, but I can see that you really mean what you say." Ronald Reagan had made an immense impression on Mikhail Gorbachev, who must have realized that he could not talk, con, bully, or in any other way manipulate Ronald Reagan into dropping his SDI research program. Ronald Reagan had nailed into place an essential plank in our negotiating platform.

Showdown on an Agreed Statement

Meanwhile, I got a green light from the president to work on an agreed statement with the Soviets. "You told us before you wanted no communiqué, but here you work with us on it," one Soviet said to me. At the end of the day, Gorbachev and Reagan were sitting together just chatting casually while I organized teams to keep working the text. I stood for a while with Gorbachev, along with Shevardnadze, Kornienko, and Dobrynin, after the president's motorcade left. In the presence of his delegation, and deliberately, I was able to get Gorbachev to express his agreement on some of the essential ideas for the joint statement: 50 percent reductions in strategic arms, the possibility of an interim INF agreement, the process of follow-up meetings, and the importance of an exchange of people and a cultural agreement. On the basis of Gorbachev's public concurrence with his delegation surrounding him, I thought Roz would have a relatively easy time finishing her work. As I was taking my leave, Sam Donaldson yelled at Gorbachev, "Do you think that women understand throw weight?" a reference to Don Regan's statement that women were interested in people, not issues like throw weight.

Back at my hotel, I called together our working group. "You should be prepared," I told them, "to spend the night exploring how the areas where views are similar might fit together; now is the moment to shoot for an agreed statement." Suddenly the entire delegation was eager. Those who had most vehemently attacked the idea of a joint statement in sessions back in Washington now wanted to be part of the all-night drafting team. Everyone was pumped up. "Okay," I said. "Roz is chairman." Drafters would be Richard Perle, Mark Palmer, and Bob Linhard, an air force colonel and arms control expert on the NSC staff. Others could be present as needed. "You'll have a rough night," I said. "The Soviets can call it anything they want; to us it is an agreed statement."

Nancy Reagan had orchestrated a wonderful dinner that night at Maison de Saussure. Both Reagan and Gorbachev were relaxed. They spoke with warmth in their toasts at the dinner table, and the toasts had real content. We then moved into the library for coffee. Arrangements for the next day were not at all settled. There would be a final ceremonial meeting at the International Press Center. The agreed statement, I thought, would shape up satisfactorily. But what would the leaders do? I said to the president and Gorbachev, "You can't just sit there while a statement is being presented. You are the leaders. You each must say something." I sensed reluctance. Each was hesitant, I surmised, to risk being seen on worldwide television while the other might level criticism. "Agree to speak for three minutes each, along the lines of the toasts you gave at dinner," I urged. They both knew they should speak, and each was looking for a little reassurance from the other.

Just then I received a message that Roz Ridgway urgently wanted to speak to me on the phone. I stepped out. Roz told me that the Soviets were "stonewalling." At their lower levels, they had concluded from a Reagan speech, delivered before coming to Geneva, that a broadened exchange of people and a cultural agreement were of central importance to the president. So, in classic Soviet style, the Soviet negotiators now told Roz that we had to agree to their terms on a civil aviation agreement being negotiated in Moscow or there would be no cultural agreement. Gorbachev had agreed on the exchanges, and having been told earlier about this point of contention, I had confirmed with Gorbachev himself—in front of his negotiators—the Soviet agreement on these points in my conversation at the end of the afternoon. I had told all this to Roz.

Instinctively, I saw Georgi Kornienko's hand and knew exactly what he was doing. He was not acting in accordance with what Gorbachev had said. Kornienko was responsible for the fact that negotiations on an agreed text had stopped. The Soviets' new demand had led Roz—based on the discussions she and I had had on "old style" Soviet negotiating and linkage—to snap her briefing book shut, saying, "So be it. We aren't going to negotiate that way." With that, she left and made her call.

After hearing this from Roz, I returned to the dinner party and took Kornienko on in a vehement way. I was genuinely upset. All other conversation ceased. I accused Kornienko of trying to prevent the general secretary's approach to the agreed statement from being carried out. I turned directly to Gorbachev. I reminded him of our own conversation at the end of the afternoon. The president was startled by my suddenly explosive demeanor, and Gorbachev was struck by this as well. Our interpreter heard Gorbachev say to Kornienko, "We don't go back on our agreements."

After dinner I called Roz. "Do not change *anything* in our position," I told her. "Wait for the Soviets to get back in touch with you. I am sure they will."

They did. And negotiations started again at midnight. New instructions had been given.

At 1:00 A.M., now Thursday, November 21, I was awakened by a trumpet playing outside the hotel. I thought that it might be a Swiss army version of taps. At the same time, a messenger came in with a text sent over by Roz from the U.S. mission and the news that she was on her way. Roz arrived in my suite shortly thereafter. "We're finally getting somewhere," she said. I looked at the text.

"I can see you are. You're going to make it," I said smiling.

"I'm enjoying this," Roz replied. All the while, the trumpet playing continued, but the army-style music had now given way to other melodies. Finally, I heard "Amazing Grace," after which the odd musical interlude ceased. Roz went back to work and by 6:00 A.M. had achieved excellent results.

At 7:30 A.M., I gathered our delegation in my suite to go over the agreed statement produced the night before. After the summit, the entire delegation would fan out around the globe to brief our allies and friends on what had been achieved at Geneva, the first summit of the decade.

The statement covered our four-part agenda. The 50 percent reduction idea, "appropriately applied,"[3] was endorsed, as was a call for "early progress" toward an "interim INF agreement." I took this as the first sign that we might succeed in breaking INF out for special treatment. Nuclear and chemical nonproliferation, the conventional arms reductions talks, and efforts in Stockholm to agree on confidence-building measures were all treated in positive terms. A statement right out of an earlier Reagan speech was included, "The sides . . . agreed that a nuclear war cannot be won and must never be fought." This statement about nuclear weapons would be cited by Reagan and Gorbachev again and again in subsequent meetings.

The statement also announced agreement on an arrangement to ensure air safety in the northern Pacific, negotiations for resumption of air services,

3. The key issue now was how to reduce strategic weapons so that the result would leave us equal, even though the exact weapon structure would differ, since the two sides had historically developed different force structures.

the opening of consulates in Kiev and New York, an important and ambitious people-to-people exchange program, and cooperation on fusion research. The statement called for a process of dialogue, regular meetings of foreign ministers, periodic discussions of regional issues, and the encouragement of "greater travel and people-to-people contact." A start was made in the area of human rights with the sentence "They [Reagan and Gorbachev] agreed on the importance of resolving humanitarian cases in the spirit of cooperation."

Roz and her team had done a masterful job. All in all, I thought, the statement reflected well the positive and serious spirit created by the two leaders.

A Momentous Day

Thursday, November 21, was a big day for Ronald Reagan. We all went with him to the International Press Center, where the final ceremony would take place, beginning at 10:00 in the morning. The agreed statement was available. We all milled around in the holding room offstage. I said to Kornienko that it had turned out well and was the product of a lot of give-and-take.

"Yes, and we did all the giving," he said sardonically.

Reagan and Gorbachev each spoke in direct and positive terms. The personal chemistry was apparent. The easy and relaxed attitude toward each other, the smiles, the sense of purpose, all showed through.

The first Reagan-Gorbachev summit had come to an end. The fresh start that the president wanted had become a reality in Geneva, not least because the two leaders had come to like and respect each other. They had agreed; they had disagreed. We had heated moments; we had light moments. We had come in order to get to know each other as people by working hard on the issues, and we did, as did the two leaders, who spent almost five of the fifteen hours of official meetings talking together privately.

Precedents were being established that could be useful in big meetings with the Soviets down the line. The two-day news blackout had worked well, as it had in my previous meeting with Gromyko in Geneva. The press grumbled, but not too much. The key was that there were no leaks and no scoops. The great benefit of a blackout was that the leaders and their delegations could concentrate on the business at hand rather than dissipating energy on efforts to get out to the press your side of the story or knock down this or that account.

Then there was the matter of our—and their—large delegation of high-ranking people. When I had first proposed taking representatives of all key players to my January negotiation with Gromyko, I ran into opposition from those in the State Department who wanted to keep the delegation small and from others who resisted attending a meeting in which they would play, at most, a supporting role. Ken Adelman protested that he didn't want to be "part of a traveling road show." I disarmed him with the simple question "Has it occurred to you that experts might actually be needed?" They were, and the wide involvement brought a new sense of cohesion in the administration and support for what we were doing.

The combination of private or very small meetings of key people followed by larger meetings with specialists working on particular issues worked effectively. Ronald Reagan's one-on-one meetings with Mikhail Gorbachev were clearly productive, and I was finding Eduard Shevardnadze to be a person I could talk with in an easy and straightforward way. The Soviets, I could see, also valued these personal interchanges.

Most of all, the precedent of serious and direct talk had been established. We could find issues where agreement was possible and, without the hesitations of the past, go ahead and agree. We could disagree, sometimes passionately, as on SDI, without getting set back or discouraged. And we could see the real possibilities of a better relationship built not on seeking such a relationship for its own sake but on constructive efforts to deal with problems of real concern. So, all in all, I felt that the summit—and a summit it was—was a great success.

With the ceremony in Geneva over, we boarded *Air Force One* and headed to Brussels, where the president briefed thirteen heads of NATO governments and two foreign ministers. They expressed their firm support and heard him respond actively and articulately to their questions. Then we were off to Washington.

At 9:20 P.M., Washington time (by then the time was 3:20 A.M. in Geneva), Ronald Reagan stood before a joint session of Congress and, on television, before the American people. "I called for a fresh start, and we made that start," the president said. "We understand each other better, and that's a key to peace. . . . We remain far apart on a number of issues, as had to be expected." He went on, "We're ready and eager for step-by-step progress." He concluded, "As our forefathers who voyaged to America, we traveled to Geneva with peace as our goal and freedom as our guide. For there can be no greater good than the quest for peace and no finer purpose than the preservation of freedom. It is 350 years since the first Thanksgiving, when Pilgrims and Indians huddled together on the edge of an unknown continent. And now here we are gathered together on the edge of an unknown future, but, like our forefathers, really not so much afraid, but full of hope and trusting in God, as ever."

When the president finished with "God bless you all," he also finished a momentous day: he had zeroed in on the character of the human being in the other chair. He was genuinely impressed by what he saw and felt in his first encounter with Mikhail Gorbachev. That impression, apparently reciprocated by Gorbachev, would define Ronald Reagan's outlook and his new sense of the possible with the Soviets.

CHAPTER 31

People Power
in the Philippines

On September 15, 1982, I greeted President Ferdinand Marcos and his wife, Imelda, on their arrival in Washington, something I always did when a head of state arrived for a State visit. Such occasions are opportunities for important exchanges and are also full of pomp and circumstance. The White House dinner was set in the Rose Garden that night. Tiny white lights on the trees and shrubs gave the appearance of a fairyland. In the course of the visit, a personal relationship developed between the two presidents and the two first ladies. Cap Weinberger, at a Pentagon ceremony that was part of the visit, presented three medals to Marcos in recognition of his valor in World War II.

But I was uncomfortable. I had been concerned about the Philippines since I had come into office as secretary of state and worried about what seemed to me a rapidly deteriorating economic and political situation over the previous two years.

I first met President and Mrs. Marcos in the Philippines in 1974, when I was treasury secretary, and knew them as intelligent, energetic, and cunning people. Ferdinand Marcos reputedly had received the highest score ever recorded on the Philippines bar examination and was said to be the most decorated Filipino in the Second World War. He had a flat face and high, round cheekbones. His black hair swelled in a wave over the top of his head. He raised his brow when he wished to be gracious. Marcos was almost always dressed in black trousers and a cool white barong shirt. He was a shrewd politician who ruled like a monarch in the trappings of democracy. Marcos lived and worked in Malacañang Palace, the sixteenth-century residence built for the Spanish governor-general, where the walls are of woven wood and look like rattan mats. Marcos had been president of the Philippines since 1965 and had ruled through martial law for over eight of those years.[1] He ended martial law in 1981 but retained most of the powers that it had provided him. He had established himself as staunchly pro-American and anti-Communist.

There are over 7,000 islands in the Philippines, only about 1,000 of which are inhabited. Many of the deserted islands are tucked with lagoons and white coral beaches. Old, rusted tramp steamers slip in and out of these small green dots of land. This island nation, with its tremendous diversity and poverty, is hard to govern. In many ways, the Roman Catholic church more than the government is the unifying force.

President and Mrs. Marcos entertained O'Bie and me at a grand luncheon during a brief stop in Manila in June 1983, on my way to an ASEAN (Association of Southeast Asian Nations) meeting in Bangkok. The meal was served in the ballroom of the palace under enormous carved chandeliers that looked like inverted tarantulas. Ferdinand and Imelda sat with my wife and me on a raised dais overlooking the large luncheon crowd. I was uncomfortable with this arrangement. Halfway through the luncheon the entertainment began. At either end of the hall were two orchestras that had not surrendered their amateur standing. They pressed out medleys of Broadway hits. The local star of *Annie*, Lea Salonga, sang "Tomorrow." There were also richly costumed performances including the "tinikling," in which dancers depicting a wedding couple stepped rapidly in and out of rhythmically slapping poles of bamboo. If one of them missed, I thought, surely a leg would be broken. The performance was flawless. The events were separated by a fashion show, of all things, during which I found myself thinking, What am I doing here? At the end of the show, Imelda Marcos was prevailed upon to give us a song in Tagalog, and President Marcos then gave a toast equating the private-sector economy with the Tree of Life. I almost laughed, as I well knew that state-sanctioned monopolies were in fact the dominant businesses. When the meal was over, we left the ballroom through an arcaded reception chamber along a gauntlet of young women dressed in white and clapping their hands while singing, "I'll take Manhattan, the Bronx and Staten Island, too." The Philippines presented an incredible and odd juxtaposition of imagery and reality.

Earlier in the day, I had called on President Marcos in his office. His ladder-back chair stood on a small platform raised above the floor where I and others in his audience gathered. It struck me as odd. Another chair and a hint of dynasty recently added to the platform was reserved for Imelda, a former beauty queen and muse of Manila, now a minister and

1. Marcos imposed martial law in 1972 to enable him to remain as president longer than the two terms allowed by the Philippine Constitution.

mayor of Metro-Manila and called by many "Super Ma'am." She clearly intended to succeed Marcos.

While Marcos, his family, and his political intimates prospered, his economic policies and political dominance had a debilitating effect on the people of the Philippines. He seemed to have lost the distinction between public and private: between what belonged to the government and what belonged to him. Growth in GNP had slowed to less than 2 percent in 1982 and continued to slide. Several important businesses had been adversely affected by a financial crisis stemming from scandalous behavior of a prominent member of the Philippine business community. The "crony companies" that monopolized key sectors of the economy were characterized by "behest loans" (requested of banks by the palace), excessive profits, and kickbacks to presidential favorites. From my standpoint, I was concerned about Clark Air Force Base and the Subic Bay Naval Station, two of the most important elements in the U.S. presence and strategic posture in the Pacific. The environment surrounding these historic facilities was turning sour. Marcos's support for us and the erosion of support for him among the people of the Philippines were creating political opposition to our bases.

The performance of Ferdinand and Imelda Marcos had a disturbing quality to it. The gap between reality and the perception of reality they sought to create was too wide. Where would Marcos take the Philippines? As matters stood, we and our bases were linked to him and to a large degree dependent on him. I felt uneasy.

A Cowardly and Despicable Act

Only two months after my visit to the Philippines, on August 21, 1983, Benigno S. Aquino, Jr., was shot in the head as he set foot on the tarmac at Manila Airport after more than three years of exile in the United States. Aquino was a popular opposition leader, heroic and charismatic, and an implacable and outspoken critic of President Ferdinand Marcos. Opposition to Marcos had been fueled by years of corruption, the accumulation of great wealth by a small sector amidst vast poverty and corruption, and the repressiveness of martial law. For reasons of security, even Aquino's family and close friends did not know what flight he was on. He traveled under an assumed name. Nevertheless, thousands of supporters were in the airport area. He was expected on one of the incoming flights. Military guards were on hand. The alleged assassin, who was wearing an airline maintenance uniform, was immediately killed in a burst of gunfire from the soldiers.

The State Department issued, that same day, a powerful statement: "The murder of Senator Benigno S. Aquino in Manila on August 21 is a cowardly and despicable act which the U.S. Government condemns in the strongest possible terms. The U.S. Government trusts that the Government of the Philippines will swiftly and vigorously track down the perpetrators of this political assassination and bring them to justice and punish them to the fullest extent of the law. . . ."

Aquino's assassination triggered widespread resentment, distrust, and anger. Marcos appointed a five-person commission of inquiry a few weeks after the assassination; on October 10 the commission dissolved itself in response to popular doubts about the impartiality of its members. In the meantime, a huge rally to mourn the death of Aquino had ended in violence. Marcos said that the opposition had misread the ability and the will of the government.

A congressional resolution on October 26 called for a "thorough, independent, and impartial investigation" and expressed support for "genuine, free, and fair elections" scheduled for the Philippine National Assembly in May of 1984. A few days before the passage of the resolution, Marcos, under pressure at home and from the United States, had reluctantly appointed a panel of distinguished private citizens to conduct an investigation.

Protest and opposition continued to mount. In May 1984, opponents of Marcos made large gains in voting for seats in the National Assembly. Marcos said in a May 15 interview on CBS News, "I would presume our instructions to our people to allow the opposition to win some seats might have been taken too literally." It was an incredible statement for Marcos to have made, but there it was. The private investigative panel report on October 23, 1984, rejected the government assertion that Aquino's assassination was the work of a lone Communist gunman, pointing instead to a military conspiracy. The panel members differed on how high up in the military command structure the conspiracy went, but four of the five members named General Fabian C. Ver—commander in chief of the Philippine armed forces and a close associate of Marcos—as part of the conspiracy.

During a presidential campaign debate with Walter Mondale on October 21, 1984, President Reagan had been asked, "What should you do and what can you do to prevent the Philippines from becoming another Nicaragua?" in light of his earlier criticism of President Carter for "helping to undermine two friendly dictators who got into trouble with their own people, the Shah of Iran and President Somoza of Nicaragua."

"I know there are things there in the Philippines that do not look good to us from the standpoint right now of democratic rights," President Reagan responded. "But what is the alternative? It is a large Communist movement to take over the Philippines. I think that we're better off trying to retain our friendship and help them right the wrongs we see rather than throwing them to the wolves and then facing a Communist power in the Pacific."

The Philippine opposition reacted sharply, saying, in the words of Ramon Mitra, an opposition leader in the National Assembly, "Our alternative to

Marcos is certainly not Communist. The alternative to Marcos is a democratic government. But if there is one thing that may lead to Communism
here, it is Marcos staying in power."

A State Department spokesman clarified to the Associated Press that
the president did not mean to suggest the only alternative to communism
was Marcos: "I don't think that the President was narrowing the situation
that far. I think there is certainly recognition on everybody's part that there
are other forces working for democratic change in the Philippines."[2]

The Philippine economy continued to decline. Real GNP fell by 7.1
percent in 1984 and 4.2 percent in 1985. Investors lost confidence, capital
flight grew to an estimated $1 billion, and foreign banks refused to renew
short-term credit after the revelation that foreign exchange reserves had
been overstated by $600 million and foreign debt understated by $2 billion.
All this aggravated the problems of a country saddled with huge foreign
debts. The value of the peso fell by 60 percent between October 1983 and
October 1984. Unemployment climbed to 25 percent.

A U.S. Approach Takes Shape

By early February 1985, I made the problems of the Philippines and their
impact on our bases at Clark and Subic Bay the main topic for a Family
Group meeting with Cap Weinberger, Bill Casey, and Bud McFarlane, held
over lunch in the Old Family Dining Room in the White House. Bill Crowe,
still commander in chief in the Pacific but soon to become chairman of the
Joint Chiefs of Staff, joined us, bringing to the discussion his professional
knowledge about the Philippine armed forces.

We focused on the problems facing the Philippines. Critical decisions
would have to emerge from a Philippine process. But the United States
could help. I proposed that we promote the revitalization of institutions
by working with diverse Filipino leaders: businessmen and professionals
who could push for an open election process and a free market economy;
those in the Catholic hierarchy who were concerned about elements in the
church that sided with the Communist insurgency; military professionals
who wanted to stop Marcos's politicization of their institutions; and responsible members of the opposition who wanted to work constructively
for democratic reforms.

There were three main issues. First, the Communist insurgency was
growing. I felt, and Bill Crowe agreed, that the problem would be almost
impossible to contain without truly professional Philippine armed forces.
Loyalty to Marcos had become a prime test within the officer corps, and
despite the presence of many able and well-trained men, the result was a

2. Reported in the *New York Times* on October 23, 1984, p. A3.

catastrophe. As Bill Crowe put it, "They can't shoot, they can't move, and they can't communicate."

Second, Marcos, through various authorized monopolies operated by his friends, was running the country as if it were his personal property, strangling any chance of a competitive private sector. Structural change in the interests of a healthy economy was essential.

Third was the problem of succession. Marcos's health was poor: how poor, we did not know. He was becoming more and more isolated, more dependent on his wife, Imelda, for his knowledge of Philippine developments, and more preoccupied with his own survival. Maneuvering among potential successors was intense, with Mrs. Marcos clearly trying to position herself as the heir to power. If she succeeded, we felt sure, the result would be massive disorder and violence. I knew that the astute prime minister of Singapore, Lee Kuan Yew, concurred in this judgment, as did many within Marcos's own inner circle, although they were afraid to say so publicly.

A rough consensus emerged among Casey, Weinberger, McFarlane, and myself through our discussions. We saw Marcos as a survivor, not a reformer, but also as someone who would respond to pressure. We all agreed our objective should be to do everything we could to strengthen institutions—political, military, business, financial—and to enlist Marcos, a man of undoubted ability and intelligence, in the effort if we could. We would try to swing him into action to bring about reform. We were especially concerned about General Fabian Ver, who was on leave as chief of staff. A military court had been constituted to try Ver and others for conspiracy in Aquino's assassination. It was expected in the Philippines that such a court would acquit him. If General Ver was reappointed chief of staff, that act would be inflammatory within and outside the military. Our ambassador, Steve Bosworth, would have to press Marcos on this as well as the other issues we had identified. That would make Bosworth unpopular with Marcos. We would need to supplement his efforts with a special presidential envoy at some appropriate point.

I went through all of these matters with the president. He agreed with our judgments and our course of action, while hoping, as we all did, that somehow Marcos would shift gears and work with us on reform. I could see that Ronald Reagan wanted to support this man who had been a friend of the United States over many years, a staunch anti-Communist, and head of a country that was host to important U.S. military bases.

As the year proceeded, however, I became increasingly convinced that Marcos was the problem, not the solution. He was highly unlikely to change and probably was so locked into corrupt arrangements that he could not change, even if he wanted to.

I felt the National Security Council system was working well on the

Philippine problem. We had able and knowledgeable people on hand in Washington and in the Philippines. We achieved general agreement on a coordinated course of action. We had a basis for discussion with key members of Congress, who, like us, were increasingly concerned about developments in the Philippines.

Mike Armacost, who had been ambassador to the Philippines before becoming under secretary of state, stopped briefly in Manila during an Asian swing in early June. He found important elements of the military ready for reform and encountered a political process characterized by lively debate. But his overall impression was disturbing: security conditions were deteriorating, and Marcos was simultaneously losing credibility and gearing up to perpetuate his tenure in office. Armacost appraised the opposition as unimpressive, with little in the way of a program beyond getting rid of Marcos.

In late September 1985, I went to New York for the annual opening of the UN General Assembly. Only a few delegates saw the Philippine foreign secretary, General Carlos P. Romulo, a world-class statesman who had been a delegate at the founding of the United Nations. A Philippine patriot who had come ashore with General Douglas MacArthur at Lingayen Gulf to free his country from Japan, General Romulo did not come to the UN General Assembly or make any calls on fellow foreign ministers. I knew and admired him and made an appointment to see him in his suite at the Waldorf-Astoria. In ill health, he told me that this would be his last visit to the United Nations but that he could not bring himself to greet colleagues in the great hall of the General Assembly. He said he was too ashamed of what was going on in the Philippines and of the conduct of the Marcos regime. I felt saddened to see the distress of this great man in the twilight of his life.

Back in Washington, I related this encounter to President Reagan. The story seemed to affect him more than all the previous briefing papers and discussions we had had on the Philippines put together. He knew and admired General Romulo and spoke at length about a moving address he had heard Romulo deliver some years earlier.

By early September 1985, Marcos was saying pointedly that Bosworth did not represent the views of President Reagan. A presidential envoy was needed. Senator Paul Laxalt was the man for the job: he was a savvy politician and was well known to be a close friend of Ronald Reagan. That would give Laxalt clout. I knew his mission would be dicey. Marcos was already making quiet threats about our tenure at our military bases and had hinted to the Soviets that they might gain access to Philippine naval facilities. Still, we had to push ahead. I told the president, "The reforms we are urging are in the interests of the Philippines as well as in our interests. The reforms enjoy widespread support. They can provide an agenda for other political candidates if Marcos turns his back on you."

At a National Security Planning Group meeting on October 4, the president approved the idea of sending Senator Laxalt as an envoy carrying a presidential letter to Marcos. The plan was for the president's letter to introduce Laxalt as "one of my closest friends," to underline "deep concerns about the trends and problems" in the Philippines previously discussed by Ambassador Bosworth, and to express particular concern about the Communist insurgency and "the interlocking political, economic, military, and insurgency problems." By putting President Reagan's authority behind the points Bosworth had been making, we sought to underline to Marcos that Bosworth was speaking for Ronald Reagan, as was Laxalt.

On October 16, 1985, Senator Laxalt and President Marcos met in Malacañang Palace. The visit was bracketed by protests against American support for Marcos, protests that were suppressed with excessive violence by the regime. Laxalt delivered President Reagan's letter, said his piece, listened, and, in the process, seemed to establish himself as a direct and reliable link to Ronald Reagan. He reviewed the deteriorating military, political, and economic picture with Marcos and urged him to take action.

Marcos questioned the accuracy of Laxalt's information and gave him a private letter for President Reagan. Laxalt said nothing to the press, but Marcos's spokesman offered decidedly defensive statements: President Reagan "has not been getting the whole picture of what is going on"; "we were not overrun by two previous insurgencies, and we will not be overrun by this one."

The most disturbing note was Marcos's assertion to Laxalt of his intention to reinstall General Ver as chief of staff of the armed forces "when"—not "if"—he was acquitted by the court now deliberating on the Aquino assassination case. Marcos also had pointed to "coup plotting" by reformists in the military and threatened to arrest Lieutenant General Fidel V. (Eddie) Ramos, acting chief of staff, unless the plotting stopped. Marcos knew that Ramos, a West Point graduate, was well regarded by the U.S. military. Nevertheless, the Laxalt visit undoubtedly made Marcos uneasy and may have spurred him at least to think about reform, if only to demonstrate his responsiveness and his command of the situation. He needed to burnish his image and to improve the appearance, if not the reality, of the situation.

"The letter Marcos gave Laxalt for you," I told President Reagan, "is a disappointing response to your serious effort, as a friend and ally, to persuade him to face up to the reforms he must make if he is to turn back the Communist insurgent challenge that directly affects the future of the Philippines and our bases in that country." The president was clearly quite uncomfortable with my harsh assessment. In his head, he knew as I did that Marcos was blundering badly, yet he felt an instinctive loyalty to Marcos and flashed to me a giant warning of caution.

A Snap Election

On November 3, 1985, in a dramatic remote interview on ABC's "This Week with David Brinkley," Marcos announced that he was moving up by a year the date of the presidential election scheduled for 1987. The election would now take place on January 17, 1986, he said, and this would be the way to settle the "silly claim," as he described it, that his government was inept. Members of the U.S. Congress, as well as others, he said, would be invited to observe the voting. He dismissed charges that earlier elections had been marred by fraud as "sour grapes" and "a publicity stunt." He asserted, "If all these childish claims to popularity on both sides have to be settled, I think we'd better settle it by calling an election right now, or say give everybody 60 days to campaign and to bring the issues to the people, I'm ready. I'm ready."

The fat was in the fire. Marcos, perhaps reacting to Laxalt's visit, had decided on a snap election, apparently hoping to get himself reelected before the opposition would have time to organize itself and mount a serious challenge. Some opposition leaders called the election a ploy by Marcos's "U.S. masters" to improve his image, but others got busy. The eight opposition parties struggled to unify themselves and in the end decided on one candidate: Corazon Aquino, widow of the assassinated opposition leader. She was totally inexperienced in politics and said so, but seemed to have good political instincts. She said immediately that she would not announce her decision until after Marcos signed into law a National Assembly bill calling for the balloting. He did so and then adjusted the election date to February 7, 1986.

On December 2, a three-judge court acquitted General Ver and twenty-five others in the slaying of Benigno Aquino. The ninety-page decision defiantly supported the contention put forth by the military that Aquino was killed by a lone gunman, not by a military conspiracy. Marcos immediately accepted a request for reinstatement by General Ver as chief of staff. The verdict was greeted with great skepticism in the United States and conflicted with the findings of the private panel of a year earlier. At the State Department, deputy spokesman Chuck Redman said, "Recall that in October 1984 the Agrava Commission, a board of respected, independent-minded citizens, unanimously refuted the government contention that a lone Communist gunman killed Senator Aquino. The board found the murder to be the work of Philippine military personnel who were charged with the crime and the cover-up. It's very difficult to reconcile the exemplary, thorough work of the Agrava Board, and the conclusions it reached after a year of hard work, with the outcome of this trial."

Members of Congress also spoke up, particularly Stephen Solarz, the Democratic chairman of the Asian subcommittee of the House Foreign Affairs Committee. He called the trial "a mockery of justice" and started beating the drums for the administration to shut off military aid to the Philippines as long as General Ver held his post.

On December 5, the opposition leadership announced their slate: Corazon Aquino would be their candidate for president, and Salvador H. Laurel, a former senator, would be the candidate for vice president. In an interview with *New York Times* executive editor A. M. Rosenthal and foreign editor Warren Hoge on December 15, *Times* correspondent Seth Mydans reported, "The opposition candidate for president, Corazon C. Aquino, said today that if she is elected next Feb. 7 she will probably put President Ferdinand E. Marcos on trial for the murder of her husband. 'I will file charges against him,' she said, later modifying this to say: 'Maybe I will be one of many. Maybe it doesn't even have to be me.' " She seemed uncertain, Mydans reported, of the implications of her threat to put Marcos on trial if she won the election. Mrs. Aquino was modest and self-effacing. "The only thing I can really offer the Filipino people is my sincerity," she said, continuing that she was not a politician, that she became a candidate only reluctantly. "I'll have to admit to you, I'm getting so many crash courses at this point in my life." She was apparently thrown off balance and even intimidated by the close and persistent questioning. "He [Marcos] will be given justice which was denied my husband. Can't we leave it at that? You really want Marcos to shoot me, don't you?" Referring to Marcos, she went on, "He has never met anybody like me. I mean he knew my husband because my husband was a politician. I am not a politician, so he never knows, or at least I think he doesn't know everything I'm going to do. Marcos is probably thinking, 'Oh gosh, what is this crazy woman talking about?' "[3]

When Abe Rosenthal came to Washington in mid-January, he reported firsthand. "That empty-headed housewife has no positions," he told me. "She is a dazed, vacant woman." He was distressed at the idea she might replace Marcos. He passed the same assessment along to President Reagan and Nancy, and Don Regan, at a White House dinner. His words made a deep and lasting impact on them.

Mike Armacost said after Rosenthal left, "Makati businessmen [the business establishment] are advising her [Mrs. Aquino], and they are sound." He thought Abe's view was off the mark.

On January 13, Ambassador Steve Bosworth said in an interview in Manila that the United States could work with any democratically elected government there. This was taken as a pro-Aquino, anti-Marcos statement, and the Filipino Parliament produced a resolution calling for Bosworth to be declared persona non grata. I wanted us to be neutral: we should simply call for a fair election on February 7. But the prospect of a healthy Marcos

3. Reported in the *New York Times* by Seth Mydans on December 16, 1985 , p. A1.

taking hold and instituting needed reforms seemed increasingly remote.

The Marcos forces were not allowing Aquino access to national television and were playing on fears in the United States that the alternative to Marcos was chaos and new opportunities for the Communist insurgency in the Philippines. Although Marcos had said that U.S. and other observers would be welcome during the election period, there was debate and uncertainty over just how a delegation of American observers should conduct themselves. Would they seem to be interfering in Philippine affairs? Would they wind up being co-opted into lending legitimacy to a process likely to be deeply flawed? Still, the presence of a U.S. delegation would be a deterrent to fraud.

Bernie Kalb, a veteran of Vietnam reporting, said, "Observers can be fooled so easily. In Saigon I asked Senator Hickenlooper where he was going to observe. He said, 'In the better neighborhoods.' " I urged that a congressional delegation be formed. Senator Dick Lugar had thought the problem through carefully, and he was ready to take on the task. So was Dante Fascell. I discussed the idea carefully with both of them. We knew that 86,000 voting precincts couldn't be observed directly, but observers would see a significant sample of the election process and represent the idea that a fair election was vital to the future of American-Philippine relations.

Tension was rising. Word from the Marcos camp made him sound increasingly desperate. We were told that the Marcos people were considering abducting Mrs. Aquino. I said to get word back that we had heard that rumor and would not countenance any such action.

On January 22, 1986, after seeing the president in one of my regular private meetings, I stayed to talk to NSC adviser John Poindexter.[4] He picked up a newspaper reporting the Bosworth interview and showed me the headline,"State Dept. Assails Marcos." "The president doesn't want that," he said.

"If we say we are for free elections, we are accused of assailing Marcos. Those charges can't be allowed to stop us," I replied.

"The president defended Bosworth because of Laxalt's praise of Bosworth," Poindexter said. "But you have to watch it."

I was quite aware that President Reagan wanted Marcos to change, not leave. However bad the Philippine situation might be, Ronald Reagan felt that Marcos had been a friend and ally of the United States, and Reagan stood up for people when the going was tough. That trait was criticized but also admired. Reagan had been outraged by the way the United States turned its back on the shah of Iran; he did not want to treat Marcos that way, to have it said that the United States abandoned its friends. I under-

---

4. Poindexter had succeeded Bud McFarlane in December 1985.

stood the president, but I worried about other dangers as well. If Marcos won in a clearly fraudulent election, that would disillusion people in the Philippines and encourage extremes in the opposition. Congress would cut off American assistance to the Philippines, a step that would only serve the Communist insurgency and endanger our bases.

Whatever was said in the United States by authoritative people, owing to our historic and continuing relationship, always received close attention in the Philippines. Congressman Solarz held hearings. They were well publicized and full of information damaging to Marcos. The *New York Times* questioned the accuracy of Marcos's record as a World War II hero. The State Department was accused of trying to oust him. I worried about our activism.

Mort Abramowitz, State's director of intelligence, had just returned from a trip to analyze the situation in the Philippines and had become passionately anti-Marcos in the process. I felt he had rendered himself incapable of making an objective intelligence assessment, and I said as much in my morning staff meeting with the principal officers of the department. "We have to choose our words and actions carefully," I said. "We will not serve our interests by the appearance that the United States is trying to oust Marcos." A battle instantly broke out in the meeting. Ed Rowny recalled the Vietnam War and said that correspondent David Halberstam had undermined President Diem, who had later been assassinated. Bernie Kalb leaped to the defense of journalism: "*Facts* undermined Diem!" he cried out.

"The high biases that people around here have should be kept under control," I said. "Otherwise, we ourselves may influence an election that we want to be fair and to be an expression of Philippine sentiments."

I asked Mort Abramowitz to come to my office. "The intelligence community, including you," I told him, "must be very careful about getting involved in policy views, especially in hotly contested issues." I had a real problem with the CIA in that regard. Abramowitz said he knew that I was concerned about intelligence biased by a point of view. He insisted that the written product of his bureau was objective; he would not allow himself or his people to grind their axes in written analyses. But he did hold views, he said, and felt that he could separate himself from his bureau and provide me with those views as an adviser rather than an analyst. "The problem," I said, "is that when someone is pushing a particular view, that view colors his appraisal of the facts. It undermines the integrity of the intelligence product and creates a feeling—fair or not—that the books are being cooked. So stop being an advocate or get out of the intelligence loop."

On January 31, Corazon Aquino, through one of her advisers, asked Ambassador Bosworth for U.S. protection. The threats from the Marcos camp were ominous, he reported. Bosworth was inclined to ask her to stay at his official residence and to tell Marcos that he had done so right away. I turned back this idea. I told Bosworth to tell Mrs. Aquino, "We are prepared to work with you and others to find a safe Philippine environment." I did not want to damage her by the symbolism that would be generated by U.S. protection, or to turn her into the U.S. candidate. At the same time, I wanted to do what was possible to prevent harm to her during this volatile time.

I was struck that Mrs. Aquino thought no non-American place in the Philippines was safe for her. Some Philippine specialists around the department had earlier told me that the Aquino family had a long record of anti-Americanism; her request for help was therefore a turning point of sorts. "Even Cardinal Sin's residence, she feels, is not secure enough," Gaston Sigur, the NSC staff specialist for Asia, told me. Should something happen to her, I knew, we could never forgive ourselves for not ensuring her safety. I decided that we should encourage her to find "a Philippine solution." We would stay in close touch, I ordered, and we would be ready to provide a safe haven for her as a last resort—but we wouldn't tell her that.

An estimated 1 million Aquino supporters turned out in central Manila on February 4, just days before the election. It was one of the biggest rallies in the history of the country. The next day Mrs. Aquino had a final campaign message: "As the old dictator lurks in his palace with his dwindling band of cronies and his false medals for comfort, I warn him: Do not cheat the people on Friday."

Jaime Cardinal Sin, the powerful Roman Catholic archbishop of Manila, issued a statement on February 5 that could be interpreted only as a strong endorsement of Corazon Aquino. Mrs. Aquino, he said, was an honest and sincere woman who "will also make a good president. I am tempted to ask: Is this a presidential election or is this a contest between good and the forces of evil, a fight between the children of light and the children of darkness?" Although Marcos issued an invitation to Cardinal Sin that they pray together for clean elections, the cardinal turned it aside: "I think they can pray without me. It's better that they pray and ask the Lord for mercy and compassion."[5]

Haiti 1986

Suddenly, in the middle of January 1986, the subject of Haiti emerged with some prominence. A situation was unfolding there that caught attention as far away as the Philippines. On January 13, 1986, the topic of Haiti

5. As reported by Seth Mydans in the *New York Times*, February 6, 1986, p. A8.

arose at the morning staff meeting. I doubt that Haiti had even been mentioned in such a meeting more than three or four times before in my term of office. Our embassy reported that the regime was in danger; widespread violence was threatened. In the fall of 1985, I had used the certification process to put American aid to Haiti temporarily on hold, an action intended and taken as a signal of our dissatisfaction with the repressive Duvalier regime. Many people in Haiti took my action as support for efforts to bring down Baby Doc. A general strike was in the works.

Haiti was not part of the cold war context. Soviet and Cuban ambitions, so aggressive and confident in seeking to advance the Communist cause elsewhere in the hemisphere, seemed to lose heart in contemplation of the morass of problems in Haiti. The island country had been ruled with an iron hand by François ("Papa Doc") Duvalier and now was ruled by his son, Jean-Claude ("Baby Doc"). They lived high in a country of abject poverty. American businesses had little if any desire to invest in Haiti. The policy of the United States was one of trying to gain improvements in human rights through the tenuous leverage of threats to cut off U.S. assistance. Haiti had natural beauty despoiled by the destruction of its forests. Anyone flying over the island of Hispaniola could instantly see where the border divided Haiti from the Dominican Republic: the Dominican side was lush green; the Haitian side was dry and barren. The capital of Port-au-Prince pumped its sewage into the bay, and the wind blew the pervasive smell back. Private citizens seeking political appointments as ambassadors did not press for Port-au-Prince; we sent a series of good professional foreign service officers to head our embassy there. Most became captivated by the Haitian people and their culture but could do little to promote change. They hoped for something better, but the Duvaliers—Papa Doc and now Baby Doc—seemed to have established a firm hereditary dictatorship.

On January 27, with the Haiti certification question again before me, Elliott Abrams took a strong stand on Haiti in a small-group session with me. "We *cannot* certify human rights [progress] on Haiti," he said. "It would destroy our credibility on [progress in] Central America. People think *we* are keeping him in power. It's not so." The reaction from the others in the Latin America bureau was, "Don't sell Duvalier short." Both views might be right, but I was clear that we should not link ourselves, by our aid, to practices totally at odds with our own values.

On Friday, January 31, Port-au-Prince National Radio reported that Baby Doc Duvalier had fled Haiti. But Duvalier was, in fact, still in his palace. Confusion reigned and with it uncertainty. As violence in the capital increased, Duvalier declared a "state of siege" and denied he would leave. Larry Speakes told the press that the Duvalier government had fallen when, in fact, it had not.

*   *   *

I was interviewed on Monday morning, February 3, on ABC-TV's "Good Morning America." I said that the United States wanted to see a government in Haiti "that is put there by the democratic process." We "stand by our views and our principles and, of course, all of our instincts to help people who desperately need it in a humanitarian way, and we do that." My words, combined with my appearance and the firmness of my demeanor, made a strong impact in Haiti. Under instructions, our ambassador in Haiti, Clay McManaway, was undertaking almost nonstop meetings in Port-au-Prince, using every means at his disposal to get the message to Duvalier that he should leave peacefully.

By Wednesday, February 5, events were moving fast. The Haitian ambassador to Switzerland had asked the Swiss for asylum for Duvalier. The Swiss said no. Prime Minister Edward Seaga of Jamaica had been in touch with Duvalier and told us that Duvalier would leave Haiti not later than Saturday. Ambassador McManaway, worried about a general breakdown of order in the capital, asked us to position U.S. Navy ships near Haiti in case we needed to evacuate American citizens (about 6,100 in the country, to our knowledge) and asked me to consider "low overflights" of Port-au-Prince as a symbol—if needed—of U.S. involvement in support of a successor government once Duvalier was gone.

Late in the afternoon of February 6, McManaway reported that he and the French ambassador had been called in to see Duvalier. He wanted to leave at midnight. The United States was asked to provide transportation and security. I checked directly with President Reagan. He agreed. McManaway, on instructions, had suggested to Duvalier that he pass on his authority to the military, who would then be pressed by us to name a civilian prime minister and cabinet to serve as a provisional government until elections could be held.

I told Elliott Abrams to call the French ambassador and say that the United States felt "it would be constructive" if France would agree to take Duvalier. In a conference call with Weinberger and Poindexter, I brought them up to speed on McManaway's conversation about how the next Haitian government would be formed. Cap, uneasy about the air force involvement despite earlier agreement to provide a plane, raised the idea of using a CIA aircraft. "No," I said. "People will say that Duvalier has been on the CIA payroll. The U.S. Air Force should fly him and should do so openly. Get an air force plane going. We'll be in very close touch with the French. They like the idea of doing this in association with us."

On Friday, February 7, also the day of the Philippine elections, Duvalier and about twenty of his followers left Haiti on a USAF plane for Grenoble, France. The French had agreed to give him "temporary" asylum. Haitians swarmed into the streets seeking the *tontons macoutes,* the bands of thugs who, in the pay of the Duvaliers, had terrorized Haitians for decades.

Lieutenant General Henri Namphy, commander of the armed forces, announced that he would head a governing council as a transition until elections could be held.

In the days following, I found my statement on "Good Morning America" the previous Monday, February 3, cited in many press accounts. "Shultz's Words Heeded; Duvalier Saw Omen in Televised Remark," read a *Washington Post* headline on February 10. I felt I hadn't said all that much, but *Washington Post* correspondent Edward Cody reported, "Secretary of State George P. Shultz's declaration on a U.S. news show Monday morning proved decisive as events unfolded toward Duvalier's downfall after 15 years as ruler of Haiti. . . . In the heated atmosphere of Haiti at that moment, his [Shultz's] comment was explosive."

The president and I, and the administration, were given credit for critical pressure on a dictator. More significantly, the media analysis raised the question of whether our approach to Duvalier at this time might indicate the end of an era, as they put it, of unquestioning American support for right-wing dictators who are pro-U.S. and anti-Communist but otherwise odious. Duvalier's departure and the press speculation about that departure were fully noted in the Philippines. I began to feel that we might well have given Marcos a potent signal.

An Election in the Philippines

The U.S. delegation to monitor the Philippine elections was headed by Senator Dick Lugar and Congressman Jack Murtha, two strong and level-headed men. They had arrived two days before the polling day and were already awash in allegations of fraud and widespread intimidation. Observer groups were also present from nineteen other countries, and they gave the same reports. By the evening of February 8, the day after the vote, both Marcos and Aquino were claiming victory. Election commission reports indicated that Mrs. Aquino was ahead. Marcos disagreed. Obviously, in a nation as far-flung and unlinked by modern communication as the many islands of the Philippines, a real count could not be completed for days. The tension would be enormous over this period. There was coup talk in Manila.

I heard from our Manila embassy that the Marcos forces were holding back on reporting votes from the provinces, waiting to see what would be needed after the big city votes were tallied. I recalled my Chicago days and the allegations that Mayor Daley held back the Chicago returns, "You gotta wait for downstate."

The Washington intelligence community, Mort Abramowitz told me, was predicting a 55 to 45 percent Marcos victory. The American media were reporting a different view. Yet another novel development of the "information age" came to the fore: Cable Network News, CNN. Via CNN millions followed the Philippine drama as it was occurring. The American television networks and press were all over Manila, reporting constantly, first on the voting and the atmosphere at the polling places and then on the counting. The Filipino media, in turn, were simultaneously rebroadcasting the American coverage back to the Philippines. So the Filipino people were watching themselves and hearing themselves analyzed primarily through American eyes. From the U.S. media, the Filipino public was getting the strong impression that Corazon Aquino had won and that Marcos was not going to accept her victory.

A Critical Meeting

Sunday morning, February 9, was cold and damp. I lit a fire in the fireplace in my living room and looked out the window as I heard people coming up the steep walk to my front door.[6] Patches of snow covered the ground. I called this meeting to appraise the election results, to consider what actions we would take, and, by letting everybody see that all views were being considered, to maintain the consensus on Philippine affairs that I had so laboriously formed over the past year. Paul Wolfowitz had the latest cable from Bosworth: the international observer group was sharply critical of the election but would give no final judgment yet; Senator Lugar felt there was nothing we could do now. The media were calling for action, but the analysts at our embassy in Manila and in Washington and the officials I had gathered were saying, "The time is not ripe, let the dust settle."

"Obviously there has been a great deal of fraud," I said. "If we wait weeks to say anything, basic attitudes will be shaped. So we should be part of the shaping process, even though action on our part is premature. We know the result: fraud, denial of the meaning of votes, and an outpouring of people who want democracy. It's too easy to sit back and say we don't know enough yet. The Marcos era is over," I said.

"We need to send an emissary out there," I said, suggesting Vice President Bush. "Big stakes for the U.S. are riding on a decent outcome, and we should send the first team."

"Let's rule him out," Bill Crowe said. He didn't explain why, but we all knew the vice president had praised Marcos for his democracy during a stop in the Philippines in 1981. In Manila on June 30, 1981, Vice President Bush had said to Marcos, "We love your adherence to democratic principle and to the democratic processes."

6. Those who came to the meeting were Admiral Bill Crowe, Mike Armacost, Paul Wolfowitz, Charlie Hill, Nick Platt, Gaston Sigur, John Whitehead, Mort Abramowitz, Peter Rodman, and Rich Armitage.

Nevertheless, I thought, George Bush had been a truly effective diplomat at critical times, and he carried the prestige of high office. "It's a matter of weeks," I said. "The situation will unravel. Now do we go—and say to Marcos, 'You are through. We are keeping our bases.' We should insist on that. Move in hard. Move decisively," I said. "The Bosworth cable says we should stand back and wait. No. That means high-level meetings, leaks, and endless speculation. That doesn't appeal to me a damn bit."

Bill Crowe and Mike Armacost pointed to other troubles coming. General Ver was likely to move on the reformers in the Philippine military, who were scared. Marcos had contacted the CIA in Manila to "get approval" to put down the independent poll-watching group Namfrel (National Movement for Free Elections). He was told no, we wouldn't stand for such an action.

Mike Armacost suggested we send Phil Habib. Gaston Sigur said Paul Laxalt was the one to tell Marcos, "The president has changed his mind." A consensus was emerging that the United States should "accelerate the succession." The clarity of the election fraud made the case for intervention easier. There had to be reform in Philippine politics and within the military if the country was to deal effectively with the New People's Army (NPA), the Communist guerrillas, numbering some 12,000 to 15,000. Throughout the 1980s, every time the United States tried to deal with a regional conflict anywhere, the cries of "another Vietnam" were immediately heard; this time, such a fear might be warranted. The potential for chaos was evident. Our bases could be caught up in such chaos. We could be drawn in, and quite possibly on the wrong side, I thought.

Bill Crowe and I discussed how we were beefing up security at Clark Air Force Base and at Subic Bay. Clark was the problem, with its sixteen-mile perimeter fence; the area around it was an active New People's Army region. I felt that we should hold reinforcements "over the horizon" in case Marcos or the NPA moved against the bases; to reinforce visibly now would make us look worried and might give people ideas.

"Sounds good to me," Crowe said.

The president had scheduled a press conference on Tuesday, February 11. I would see him Monday, describe the emerging situation carefully, and give him my view: our objective should be to have Marcos move out in a gradual and orderly way. But I knew the president's own view was heavily conditioned by the record of the United States having turned its back on friends before.

"The president's attitude will be quite different from that of this meeting," John Whitehead noted. "He will be inclined to call Marcos and congratulate him on his victory."

George Bush had dinner at my home that Sunday evening, February 9, and I asked him whether he would undertake a mission to Manila. He was ready but questioned whether he was the right person in view of the perception that he had been a supporter of Marcos in past years. Dick Lugar would be returning from Manila on Monday. I would consult with him, talk to President Reagan, and then we would decide whether to send an envoy and, if so, who that should be.

By Monday, February 10, evidence of massive voting fraud was accumulating, and the delegation of forty-four observers from nineteen countries who had come to monitor the election said jointly, "The electoral anomalies which we have witnessed are serious and could well have an impact upon the final result. Occurrences of vote-buying, intimidation and lack of respect for electoral procedures were present." "They had seen no instances of fraud committed by Mrs. Aquino's supporters," the *New York Times* reported on February 10, continuing, "The 30 computer workers who quit the official vote count in protest gathered at a Manila church, where they accused the Marcos government of rigging the tally. In a separate statement, a group of 20 American observers said it had 'witnessed and heard disturbing reports of efforts to undermine the integrity' of the electoral process."

Senator Lugar headed back for Washington, where he would meet with the president and me on February 11. In the meantime, White House spokesman Larry Speakes said that Marcos had won the election and pointedly did not criticize him. He urged the two sides to work together in an act of reconciliation. At the State Department, I reacted angrily to this statement, and the White House later said, "The President feels that there has been violence and fraud, which is regrettable, but the outcome is not yet clear. The President will be meeting with [Senator] Lugar to determine what the situation is on the ground, but without illusions that the American observers can have a definitive judgement. That decision can be made only by the Filipino people."

Perceptions were what counted now. The perception from all private and public reporting was that Mrs. Aquino had won and should be the next president, that President Marcos would reject the outcome of a clear though flawed democratic process, and that the United States faced a monumental decision.

The Filipino people had taken the democratic process seriously and put their faith in the fairness of that process. They cared about their country, and they wanted to express their views through voting, but the image before them was of a dishonest election. So the United States faced a big moment: we represented democracy to those people. I could not see Marcos giving up, yet Aquino clearly appeared to be the democratically elected candidate. Could a process of internal reconciliation take place in which Marcos, to govern effectively, would feel forced to reach out to the reformist movement? No. Marcos had poisoned the well of reconciliation. Most likely, I feared, we were headed for the worst outcome imaginable: an election perceived to be phony; a leader perceived to be a dictator; a reform movement supported by the people perceived to be defrauded; a Communist guerrilla force able to take advantage of these setbacks; a Congress demanding a cutoff of U.S. assistance to Marcos; and an American media that had tasted blood.

John Whitehead came in to talk at the end of the day. He was worried that any action by the United States now would just bring trouble. "We should wait for chaos to develop and then respond to it. If we talk sternly to Marcos before there is popular unrest, we will be held responsible by him for creating it."

Perhaps so, I argued, but "if the U.S. does not take a stand, then the extremist opposition to Marcos will take over from Aquino and eventually bring Marcos down. The U.S. will then face a radicalized Philippines. And that could well lead to another Vietnam."

I had asked Phil Habib to spend some time at the State Department and with me. I could see critical developments in several parts of the world and had asked Phil to be on hand. He, like Whitehead, was cautious about major action in the Philippines. "We should move slowly and subtly," he said. "Wait for Marcos to see that he can't govern." Then we could push for change. Habib was opposed to a big vice presidential visit: "too high a profile."

Our embassy in Manila reported in. Imelda Marcos told our embassy that Marcos had won; the election was over. The opposition campaign was "sordid," she said, and stressed that she and her husband were not "fair-weather friends" of the United States.

A Stand for Democracy

In my view the election fraud was inescapable and unacceptable; the election had shown the strength of democratic yearning among the people. The political dynamics at work in the Philippines, not the United States, would undermine Marcos. The United States, I felt, must take a stand in favor of democracy, and that meant taking a stand that respected the results of the election.

Ambassador Bosworth cabled that there had been a major, systematic effort at fraud directed right out of Malacañang Palace:

> The bottom line conclusion is inescapable: Mrs. Aquino would have won if there had been an even minimally fair count. The opposition, therefore, will not accept the National Assembly proclamation [of Marcos's victory]. Our urging that they join together in national reconciliation on reform would not change their position. Such a U.S. position would however subject the

U.S. to charges of "whitewash" after our principled emphasis throughout the campaign on free and fair elections. This election has effectively cost Ferdinand Marcos most of his remaining political legitimacy and credibility, both in the Philippines and in the U.S.

Bosworth's message concluded, "Our overriding policy objective is to manage our way into the post-Marcos era."

Since Dick Lugar and Jack Murtha were returning to Washington on Tuesday morning, I pushed my meeting with the president off until then, so that we could hear their report directly. The press was full of stories on the Philippines, and the White House staff felt that President Reagan would have to make a public statement that day. I had asked that Cap Weinberger be present with the president and me so that he, too, would hear what they had to say.

Lugar was sober, measured, detailed, and devastating in his description of massive election fraud. He was extremely impressive. Murtha supported Lugar's assessment and said that everyone in the bipartisan observer group shared the same conclusions. "The fraudulent election has fatally impaired Marcos's legitimacy," I told the president. "The moderate elements in the Philippines regard the election as stolen." Neither Aquino nor her followers would accept the declaration of a Marcos victory. "Marcos is incapable of undertaking reforms," I continued, "and reforms are crucial: a more professional military, an open and competitive economy, less political intimidation. The stage is set for violence, and that plays into the hands of the Communists. The protection of our strategic interest lies in fostering a transition to a more democratic government."

I recommended sending Phil Habib to the Philippines to assess the possibilities of our assisting in such a transition. We agreed that the president would make a statement, saying that fraud had occurred and that he was sending Phil Habib to talk with leaders in the Philippines. I went back to State and reviewed the situation with Habib. "Ronald Reagan will never pull the rug out from under a friend, but he's beginning to see that Marcos has pulled the rug out from under himself," I told Habib. "We are in the post-Marcos era. The erosion of his moral authority cannot be stopped. But however Marcos leaves office, we will not be the ones to push him out."

"He's doomed by his own faults," Habib agreed, "but he won't go easily. There are no flies on Marcos: he's a smart guy."

When the president spoke about the Philippines at his February 11 press conference, he followed his own script. He announced that he was sending Phil Habib to the Philippines as a special envoy. The United States would be neutral, he said; there had been "the possibility of fraud, although it could have been that all of that was occurring on both sides." The media analysts immediately took this as an endorsement of Marcos. When Senator Lugar was asked about the president's statement, he said that his observer group had seen no evidence of fraud on the Aquino side and that he didn't know where the president had gotten that idea. Larry Speakes told Bernie Kalb, "Shultz is trying to push the president further than he wants to go." Speakes said his comments on Monday had been soundly based on the president's feelings.

I telephoned President Reagan after his press conference and told him there was no evidence of fraud by the Aquino side. My words did not seem to change his view. We had hard evidence that Marcos had committed fraud, but the president was just not ready to accept that. His position of "neutrality" was read as putting us behind Marcos. People were distressed by the president's stand. I had never seen Mike Armacost so upset. I erupted at Mike, in a friendly way. "The president is the president," I said. "He has strong views; that is how he got to be president. So don't fight the problem, just keep working away within the realm of what's possible and what's proper." Look, I said, "I know how you feel. I'm working on it and I'm not getting anywhere. The president does not want to push Marcos over the brink. We have to wait for events to happen; we cannot move the president under present circumstances. The Filipino people will have to throw Marcos out. Ronald Reagan will *not* push out a friend."

Phil Habib left on February 13 and was set to see Marcos as soon as he arrived in Manila. Meanwhile, Senator Lugar said that he and other observers estimated that if the election had been honest, Corazon Aquino would have 60 to 70 percent of the vote. And two key senators, Republican Majority Leader Bob Dole, and Sam Nunn, ranking Democrat on the Armed Services Committee, spoke up independently. In a letter to President Reagan, Senator Nunn said that Marcos and his allies were "in the process of making an all-out effort to steal the election by massive fraud, intimidation and murder." Senator Dole warned that the United States should be ready to consider moving our bases because of "unrest" that could be expected in the Philippines.

Our embassy learned that Marcos had ordered those in charge of the electoral system to declare him the winner before Habib was to meet with him. On February 15, the National Assembly declared Marcos and his vice presidential running mate, Arturo Tolentino, the winners with 53.8 percent of the vote. But the Roman Catholic bishops of the Philippines, with their enormous following, described the election as "unparalleled" in its fraud and endorsed nonviolent resistance to the Marcos-engineered outcome.

Steve Bosworth encountered Imelda Marcos at a social occasion. She complained about the unfairness of it all. "We were born poor," she said, "while Aquino was born rich. And to think we could have lost all this," adding, "All's fair in love and war and elections." At about the same time, our embassy picked up rumors that Mrs. Marcos had hinted she might have a couple of Americans killed so that martial law could be declared. We sent an officer to confront her people to make sure that it wouldn't happen.

I continued to emphasize the facts to the president, facts that were now so public and clear that they could not be denied. On February 15 a White House statement read: "It has already become evident, sadly, that the elections were marred by widespread fraud and violence perpetrated largely by the ruling party. It was so extreme that the election's credibility has been called into question both within the Philippines and in the United States." The statement represented a major shift in the president's view of Philippine developments. What caused this shift? The accumulation of evidence. But Ronald Reagan still, I knew, had no intention of abandoning Marcos, nor could he conceive of Marcos's departure from office.

People Power

On February 16, in a speech before hundreds of thousands of supporters, Corazon Aquino claimed victory and announced her own seven-point program of nationwide nonviolent protest to bring down the Marcos regime. This was the launching of "people power," an immense and unprecedented outpouring of what seemed like an entire nation taking to the streets to demand a change, not by violence or threat but simply by an overwhelming human presence, a living, breathing river of humanity moving through the capital. Mrs. Aquino called for people to protest. Church spokesmen supported her call, but the eruption was also a spontaneous expression of a national will for change. The crowds called for "Cory." The call was carried live on CNN to millions of viewers worldwide.

Marcos reacted by declaring on February 16, "I am the President. They are not going to drive me out, because the people are behind me." But he also accepted the resignation of General Ver and replaced him with General Ramos. Meanwhile, anti-Marcos sentiment was swelling in the U.S. Congress. On February 17, Senator Lugar, who had become a voice listened to most carefully, said that Marcos "ought to step aside." Economic troubles continued to deepen as the value of the peso fell sharply.

On Wednesday, February 19, Phil Habib put through a secure call. "The dominant view here is that Marcos is finished, but it will have to be the U.S. that gives him the boot. Marcos doesn't have the strength, will, or ability to do what's needed to govern effectively. The situation is very bad. At the moment, I'd say don't do anything more. Keep quiet and let the elements out here sort it out." Habib didn't want any American action. "When Congress mouths off about how Marcos must go and how we will cut off aid, then the elements out here say, 'Hell, the Americans will take care of it,' " he said. "I was given a list of pro-Marcos people by an aide to Marcos. I went to see them, and all four told me, 'Marcos has got to go, and you Americans have got to get rid of him. You're the Godfather. *You* do it.' It was dumbfounding. Cardinal Sin said to me, 'Tell the president to pick up the phone and tell Marcos to go,' " Habib said.

Habib did not favor such an approach, and President Reagan would never agree to it. Habib urged us to consider an evolutionary change: the two camps would somehow merge; Marcos would eventually step aside with dignity and honor; there would be new elections and a new constitution. The trouble with Aquino, he said, is that "she doesn't have a party; she has a movement. There's no organization there."

I valued Habib's report but did not agree with his conclusion that a reconciliation of forces was possible. Ronald Reagan wasn't going to dump Marcos, and Marcos was never going to go gently. I asked Habib to take a plane back to Washington. He said he could arrive at Andrews by mid-afternoon, Sunday, February 23. "Get going," I said. I wanted him on hand in the morning. I called the principal players to set up a meeting at my house to hear Phil's report.

I had tried to keep my public profile down and use the information I had at hand and public statements made by others as a basis for talking privately to President Reagan, trying to make sure the unvarnished facts and their implications were clear to him. On February 19, however, when I testified before the Senate Budget Committee, most of the discussion was about the Philippines. I assailed the "fraud and violence on a systematic and widespread scale" that had been carried out by the supporters of Marcos. The election did not produce a "legitimized and credible government," I said. I argued that we should keep our aid in place for the time being and asserted, "We have a big stake there. We have a stake in freedom. We have a stake in democracy. Let's put that first, over and above the bases. The bases are important. They are important to the Philippines and to other countries out there, in addition to ourselves." I was making the point that we should not be willing to accept a fraudulent election simply to keep the bases; in fact, the way for the United States to lose the bases would be to accept a fraudulent election under these circumstances!

On February 19, the Senate voted 85 to 9 to declare the Philippine elections "marked by such widespread fraud that they cannot be considered a fair reflection of the will of the people of the Philippines." Steve Solarz led a similar charge in the House.

By February 20, only one country had extended congratulations to Marcos on his reelection: Mikhail Gorbachev's Soviet Union. On Saturday, February 22, it was clear that the next twenty-four hours would be crucial. Just then we learned that General Ramos and Defense Minister Juan Ponce (Johnny) Enrile had resigned—a stunning development. They were holed up, along with supporters, at Camp Aguinaldo, a principal military establishment on the outskirts of Manila. Marcos told them to "stop this stupidity and surrender." Ramos and Enrile told military units to "disobey all illegal orders," especially orders to fire on civilians. Cardinal Sin called for "peaceful change." These were powerful voices. The regime of Ferdinand Marcos was crumbling, and that was happening at the hands of Filipinos, not Americans.

Philippine army opponents of Marcos inside Camp Aguinaldo were telephoning our ambassador, Steve Bosworth, to discuss the tight spot they were in, fearing that Marcos would soon send in troops to vanquish them. Mrs. Aquino was on the island of Cebu, urged to go there by the army rebels as a precaution for her safety. We began to get reports that Marcos was mustering troops to assault Camp Aguinaldo and crush the popular movement. Marcos, I feared, was not going to blink. Ambassador Bosworth reported that nothing we said would have any effect on Marcos.

We made a statement through Larry Speakes in support of Enrile and Ramos, saying that their words and actions "strongly reinforce our concerns that the recent Presidential elections were marred by fraud, perpetuated overwhelmingly by the ruling party, so extreme as to undermine the credibility and legitimacy of the election and impair the capacity of the Government of the Philippines to cope with a growing insurgency and a troubled economy. Many authoritative voices in the Philippines have been raised in support of nonviolence. We support these voices and expect them to be respected. We also support resolution of the issues involved by all the people of the Philippines as quickly as possible."

Early Sunday morning reports were that 25,000 or more Filipinos were in the streets. A cable from Ambassador Bosworth was brought to me at home: Marcos would not give up his office unless President Reagan put the issue to him directly and urged him to accept a dignified transition from power.

The president was at Camp David that Sunday, February 23, when I had asked all the chief officials involved to come to my house to hear from Phil Habib. It was bright and chilly, and I lit a fire in the living-room fireplace as people began to gather for what we all knew would be a critical discussion.[7]

---

7. The first to arrive were the foreign service officers on my staff—Charlie Hill and Nick Platt. They were followed by Secretary of Defense Cap Weinberger, National Security adviser John Poindexter, Marine Commandant General P. X. Kelley (representing the Joint Chiefs of Staff), Admiral Bill Crowe, commander in chief, Pacific Forces (soon to become chairman of the Joint Chiefs of Staff), Presidential envoy Phil Habib, Deputy Director of Central Intelligence Robert Gates (sitting in for Bill Casey), Deputy Secretary of State John Whitehead, Assistant Secretary for East Asia Paul Wolfowitz, State Department spokesman Bernie Kalb, Assistant Secretary of Defense Rich Armitage, Under Secretary of State Mike Armacost. Gaston Sigur, Asian specialist on the NSC staff, would have been included but was in Japan; through his special personal relationship with Prime Minister Nakasone, we would keep the Japanese government posted on Philippine developments as we saw them.

I was determined to manage this discussion carefully. *"No one,"* I told my State Department colleagues, "is to speak about what we should do"— Phil Habib was full of ideas on that score—"until everyone in the room has been brought around to the recognition that Marcos is no longer able to govern." I was determined to avoid having proposed actions stated at the outset, as that would only start fruitless argument. I had learned from experience that you cannot involve people in the difficulties of solving a problem until they have agreed on what the problem is. I wanted the meeting built on a foundation of accumulated fact that would lead inescapably to a conclusion we all would acknowledge as correct. And when we went to President Reagan, I wanted us to go with a unanimous view.

Armacost began by reporting on the situation at the moment. It was then nighttime in Manila. Marcos had tried to use his troops to assault the rebels in Camp Aguinaldo, but crowds of citizens had turned them back. Bob Gates, deputy CIA director, added that nonetheless the balance of military power in Manila heavily favored Marcos.

Habib, just back from the Philippines, reported that Marcos was isolated, looked "horrible," and refused "to realize that he faces a widespread movement to dump him." If Marcos crushes the army rebels, Habib said, "he will move against Aquino next."

The talk continued, as the fire crackled, until all the bits of information about the relative political and military strengths of those involved, as well as the details of the situation on the ground at that hour, were on the table. I asked Habib what he thought about the claim of *New York Times* editor Abe Rosenthal that Mrs. Aquino was "vacant" and incapable of leadership.

"He's wrong," Habib said. "She has her own following and the church's power with her. She is simple but not stupid. She draws crowds. She has a spiritual calm. She prays. The cardinal called her a Joan of Arc. I reminded him of what the church did to Joan of Arc." Habib laughed.

I felt that now, after this extensive review of realities in the Philippines, the time had come to draw some conclusions. "I'll put forward some propositions," I said. "First, although it's possible for Marcos to keep control through military power, it is not possible for him to govern effectively anymore." Everyone present agreed. "Second, if Marcos succeeds in liquidating the army rebels and if he prevails, that development would play into Communist hands. Now the church and Aquino reject the left and are the alternative to the left. A semipolice state imposed by Marcos would destroy the ability of Aquino and the church to provide a democratic alternative to the Communists. So we don't want that to happen." All agreed. "Third," I said, "the United States has, historically, been badly damaged by the way we have been involved in tidal shifts like this—most recently the fall of the shah. We have paid a heavy price for our past handling of these matters. We have gotten the worst of both worlds: we have gotten on the wrong side, and we have appeared disloyal to our friends. So we have a big stake in decent treatment of Marcos the person."

Cap Weinberger broke in. "I have a different conclusion regarding the shah. We never considered the alternative correctly. Our liberal establishment turned away from the shah but did not consider the alternative. So the question is not whether we get Marcos to live with Solarz, but what happens in the Philippines."

"That's my fourth point," I said. "But we all think that if Marcos tries to stay, that's bad. Now the next question is, what happens in the Philippines if he goes?"

"There is now a national movement that has emerged from the democratic process and which is backed by the church," Habib said. "The probability is that Aquino won the election. She unified the opposition. From our standpoint, the mass of Philippine opinion, unlike in Iran, hopes *we* will solve the problem. So, the question comes down to whether we can have some control of the situation," Habib concluded. "Everything points to an early move to bring a transition into being."

NSC adviser John Poindexter noted his talk with Senator Sam Nunn the previous night. Nunn favored a Reagan message to Marcos offering asylum. Paul Wolfowitz remarked, "Marcos wants honor; he wants to retire in the Philippines."

Habib followed on, "And he doesn't want to hand over to Aquino— that would be an admission of fraud in the election. So we need something in between. We need a way for him to retire and go somewhere for medical treatment. I was horrified at Marcos's appearance. His mind is sharp, but otherwise he's broken down."

Mike Armacost thought that a message from President Reagan would not be enough to get Marcos to step down; it would eventually take urging from within the Marcos family and clan as well. Habib said that Prime Minister Lee Kuan Yew of Singapore had concluded that Marcos would have to go but that he would have to be pushed.

"So," I concluded, "this group comes out unanimously the same way?" They all nodded and murmured their agreement. That was a solemn and important moment: there was unanimous agreement, among people who often disagreed, that Marcos could no longer govern and the more quickly he left office the better. Corazon Aquino was visibly and vividly the winner and the alternative.

"Remember," Phil Habib said, "Marcos plans in forty-eight hours to take the oath of office on television, with public meetings of support for him organized around the country."

Poindexter went to the kitchen telephone, out of earshot, and called the White House. He returned to the living room to say that the National Security Planning Group, which included many of the same people then sitting around my fireplace, would meet in the Situation Room. The president, back from Camp David, would be there at three o'clock that afternoon, in time to make a decision before dawn on Monday, Manila time, as there were strong indications that Marcos would attack the army forces at Camp Aguinaldo.

The group broke up, and I went to my office in the State Department to prepare carefully for the afternoon meeting. I drafted talking points for myself: the United States should make a public statement against the use of force in the Philippines, making clear that we would stop our military aid if Marcos moved against the opposition. Senator Laxalt should carry a message from President Reagan to Marcos telling him of our judgment, if the president concurred, that he could no longer govern effectively and that he would be welcome to come to the United States. Habib's job would be to return to Manila and help with the transition. Phil Habib went with me to the private elevator. We rode down to the basement, got in my car, and headed for the White House.

When we arrived at the Situation Room, troubling reports began flowing in: the U.S. defense attaché in Manila reported that Marcos's troops had cleared a road into the camp. Civilians had been moved out of the way. An armored column had left Camp Bonifacio and was headed toward the area. Marcos might order the use of gunships and artillery. Attack was expected at "first light." The army rebels had telephoned the U.S. embassy to ask whether they had U.S. support. Civilians were being teargassed. The rebel army officers were on the radio calling for more civilians to come into the streets to support the opposition to Marcos. Mrs. Aquino was on the radio calling for the people to come into the streets. Our embassy reported that Marcos's troops were moving forward. The crowds were fighting them with sticks. Two helicopters landed inside the rebel camp, and those on board defected to the rebels.

President Reagan was troubled; he was ready to listen. Phil Habib gave his firsthand report. Habib concluded with the blunt statement "The Marcos era has ended." This was followed by total silence. It was a dramatic moment.

I then went forward with the evidence: "Marcos can no longer govern effectively. An effort by him to remain in power by military force will destroy the democratic alternative to the Communists. The United States must find a way to support the democratic forces for change and to treat Marcos with respect and courtesy. We should be ready to bring him to the United States."

Chief of Staff Don Regan, who had been unable to attend my morning meeting, objected. He felt that it was too soon to press for the departure of Marcos. He cast up the image of the Ayatollah Khomeini replacing the shah and argued that there was no certain successor to Marcos.

I reminded President Reagan of the consensus among his advisers. "Mr.

President, there's not a person here, other than Don, who believes Marcos can stay in power. He's had it."

The President Turns a Corner

President Reagan listened carefully. Then he turned the corner: he authorized a message to Marcos in response to threats of the use of force, urging Marcos "to avoid an attack against other elements of the Philippine Armed Forces," and continued, saying that the United States "cannot continue our existing military assistance if the government uses that aid against other elements of the Philippine military which enjoy substantial popular backing."

At 6:45 on Sunday night, President Reagan approved a second message to Marcos: it was time for Marcos to make the transition from power.

On Monday, February 24, the private messages were supplemented by a public statement issued by the White House calling on forces loyal to General Ver not to use force: "We urge those contemplating such action to stop. Marcos has pledged to refrain from initiating violence, and we appeal to him and those loyal to him and all other Filipino people to continue to do so. Attempts to prolong the life of the present regime by violence are futile. A solution to this crisis can only be achieved through a peaceful transition to a new government."

The president of the United States had made the decision to support a transition and had informed Marcos of that decision. He recognized that Marcos had lost any claim to support in the Philippines. But he was still deeply disturbed at the thought of the fall of a longtime friend and anti-Communist ally. Ronald Reagan had turned the corner intellectually but not emotionally.

Don Regan, always close at hand, was not in a mood to accept Mrs. Aquino as Marcos's successor. Abe Rosenthal's comments about her had poisoned the well in the White House, and Don Regan was fighting me and the problem all the way.

That same day, Ambassador Bosworth reported that he had gotten to Marcos in the palace and had given him our message. "He rejected it. He is staying put. Marcos said it is a ridiculous conclusion we have drawn: he is in full control. He has no intention of doing what we suggested. He rejects our conclusions."

Mike Chinoy of CNN reported from Manila: "As dusk fell, government troops again clashed with the opposition, opening fire on demonstrators near the presidential palace. And after dark, crowds of people set up barricades to block Marcos forces from moving on the rebel-occupied TV station. Inside, they broadcast urgent appeals for more people to come to the scene, amid increasing signs of an imminent government attack. Similar scenes were being repeated on a larger scale at rebel headquarters, where Mrs. Aquino appeared before hundreds of thousands of people to urge them to stand firm and continue to put their bodies on the line to keep the rebellion alive. So, three days after the rebellion began, there is no sign of a peaceful settlement. And both sides are bracing themselves for the worst."

An editorial in the *Washington Post* that day, Monday, February 24, recounted: "President Reagan has not been 'licensing rebellion.' He has been affirming the democratic process in [an] effort to assure that the Philippine people will be masters of their own destiny. This is the right policy." On Manila television Marcos announced he would not resign and called for his supporters to come from the countryside and bring their weapons.

Throughout the day we worked intensively, consulting with Congress and following through on the president's Sunday decision. I was on Capitol Hill giving a large group of senators a private briefing on the situation when Marcos telephoned Senator Laxalt with word that he was "willing to bargain." He wanted to stay in the Philippines and have a significant advisory role in any new government. Laxalt and I rushed to the White House to inform the president and review the unfolding situation.

Mike Armacost telephoned me in my car, "We've been in indirect touch with the family. They have talked conditions about getting out." He concluded, "Steve Bosworth's view is that the only thing remaining is *how* we get him out."

Senator Laxalt called Marcos and delivered the message agreed on in our meeting with the president: President Reagan and the first lady were very concerned about his safety. "Power brokering won't work," Laxalt told Marcos. We would negotiate about his security if he was willing to leave. Marcos replied that this was very disappointing news. "There were long silences," Laxalt reported. "He was very emotional. Marcos said he would go through with his inaugural ceremony in a low key and then telephone me on Tuesday. I was very direct on 'no power sharing' and that he should go out with dignity. There was a long pause. I thought he'd passed away on me. I assured him we would do nothing to expose him until we heard from him Tuesday." Laxalt told Marcos that he should "cut and cut clean."

I told Laxalt that we had been talking to the Marcos family independently. "If we can get Marcos out through some approach that is already under way, we will."

On Tuesday, February 25, Marcos and Aquino both staged inaugurals in Manila. At dawn that day in Washington the final preparations were completed for Marcos to leave the Philippines on a U.S. Air Force plane. At 8:00 A.M. in Washington, Marcos was on his way to the airport to depart from the Philippines for the United States.

Recognition and Legitimacy

Up to this point we had focused almost entirely on the problem of how to get Marcos out. Now came the matter of recognizing his successor. Through an early morning phone call from the State Department, I learned that the Aquino camp had made known through the media that "the Aquino government" needed the legitimacy that U.S. recognition would give. I headed for my office.

The moment had come, I concluded, for the United States to declare its recognition of a new Philippine government. Nick Platt, executive officer of the department, was furious because no one was in from our East Asia bureau to draft a recognition statement. I worked over a text and wrote, "We pay special tribute to Mrs. Aquino for her role in revitalizing the democratic process in the Philippines. Her commitment to non-violence has earned her the admiration of all Americans."

I telephoned Poindexter and said that I had faxed a recognition statement to him and that I thought I should come to the White House, go over the statement with the president, and then read it to the press and take questions. From his tone I gathered that Poindexter was reluctant to have me do that.

I arrived at the White House at 9:00 A.M. and immediately ran into trouble. Don Regan and I met outside the Oval Office. We stepped inside. The president was not there. Don Regan was scathing and vehemently against what was happening. "Wait a minute! Wait a minute!" he told me. "How did we get to her? How did she become president? I'm serious, George, I'm serious. How can we say she is president of the Philippines? She hasn't won an election or been ratified by the Assembly!" I looked through the tall windows of the Oval Office and saw the president outside.

Snow had fallen overnight. Ronald Reagan was out in the Rose Garden throwing snowballs for some cameramen. His pitcher's arm sent them scurrying and laughing. He turned and came into the Oval Office, stomping snow off his feet, and looked at the statement I proposed to make. The president objected: the words about Corazon Aquino and the democratic process were too strong; those words would make us look as if we wanted to dump Marcos. We argued.

"If we equivocate about Aquino's position at this moment," I said, "it can turn a triumph of democracy into a catastrophe. Forces on all sides, left and right, are waiting to see if we hesitate. The Filipino people are sending a message. It's loud. It's dramatic. It's clear." The president nodded his agreement.

I walked over to the White House pressroom, with Bernie Kalb alongside, at about 10:00 A.M. Bernie said, "Mr. Secretary, you're accelerating history." I stepped up to the podium and read the statement on behalf of the United States recognizing Mrs. Corazon Aquino as the leader of the government of the Philippines:

> The President is pleased with the peaceful transition to a new Government of the Philippines. The United States extends recognition to this new Government headed by President Aquino. We pay special tribute to her for her commitment to non-violence, which has earned her the respect of all Americans. . . . The United States stands ready as always to cooperate and assist the Philippines as the government of President Aquino engages the problems of economic development and national security. We praise the decision of President Marcos. Reason and compassion have prevailed in ways that best serve the Filipino nation and people. In his long term as President, Ferdinand Marcos showed himself to be a staunch friend of the United States. We are gratified that his departure from office has come peacefully, characterized by the dignity and strength that have marked his many years of leadership.

I responded to a question: "As we assess the overall picture and we assess his role in the Philippines over a long period of time, he has been a constructive force. And as he continues on his life, we wish him to have a life of dignity and honor." We had offered Marcos a safe haven, and that safe haven should be respected, I said.

Strains with the President

I knew that my relations with the president and the White House had been badly strained by the turn of events in the Philippines and my role in them. No one could argue that the result was wrong. I had worked on the problems of the Philippines for over a year in close collaboration with the president and my colleagues. The president had signed off personally on every step we took. Nevertheless, in his gut, Ronald Reagan felt aggrieved that his former friend and ally had gone down the drain. Somehow, I am sure, he felt I should have found a way to save Marcos. And Don Regan was wildly upset at the recognition of Corazon Aquino. The United States had to move promptly and decisively. And we did. The United States was well served by that decisive support for democracy.

Nevertheless, I knew I was not on the president's wavelength. The White House staff, particularly Don Regan, was closer to the president's feelings than I was. I had engaged in intense arguments with the president,

McFarlane, Poindexter, and others in December 1985 and January 1986 over proposed sales of arms to Iran, sales that were essentially a trade of arms for hostages. Cap Weinberger had been my only real ally opposing such a swap. The president had heard me out, but he didn't like what I said or agree with my assessment of what had been proposed. I could feel a certain distance developing then, even though I still had my regular private meetings with the president and he still listened, joked, discussed, and was relaxed with me.

The general reaction in the Philippines, the United States, and in democracies around the world was wildly enthusiastic at the turn of events in the Philippines. The president and Don Regan, however, were not the only people upset by this dramatic chain of events. Henry Kissinger wrote in the *Washington Post* on March 14, 1986: "Whatever else may be said about the Marcos regime, it contributed substantially to American security and had been extolled by American presidents, including President Reagan, for nearly two decades." We were guilty of applying a "double standard," Kissinger maintained, being harder on Marcos than on far worse dictators elsewhere. Kissinger had "grave concerns about the implications of these actions for the future." Our bases at Clark and Subic were in jeopardy, he said. Were we going to practice "interventionism" everywhere? "What will be the impact on world security—or human rights—if Asian countries decide that they must distance themselves from their intrusive and changeable friend?" The "preconditions for democracy" were lacking in the Philippines as in many developing countries. "Knowing what in fact constitutes democratic reform is something the West has clearly not thought through." He did acknowledge, "My misgivings about the prevailing self-righteousness include no doubt about the impeccable democratic credentials of Aquino."

I did not agree with Henry's analysis, though his comments pointed up the need for some careful damage control in a few countries, particularly South Korea and Indonesia. What transpired was fundamentally a peaceful revolution generated by the people of the Philippines and sparked by an unusual coalition: an appealing new leader with a name made famous in opposition and assassination, Marcos defectors, and the Catholic church. If the U.S. government had held on to a failing Marcos, propping him up despite his loss of legitimacy among his own people and fraud in the election, we would have lost the confidence of the Filipino people. Our support for people willing to fight for freedom would not ring as true. Furthermore, the Reagan Doctrine could not hold up if the freedom fighters we would support were only those fighting Communist regimes. Nevertheless, "people power" in the Philippines disturbed leaders in many other countries, perhaps even leaders in countries of the Warsaw Pact. I knew we would need to work carefully with President Chun Doo Hwan of South Korea in our effort to bring about an orderly transition to democracy in that country.

Postscript

The president and Nancy left Washington on April 26, 1986, for a thirteen-day trip to Asia. I accompanied them on what would become the longest trip they would take in his presidency. Had there been no upheaval in the Philippines, he surely would have visited Ferdinand Marcos in Manila, but Manila was not on the itinerary. We made our way slowly westward: first stop, Honolulu.

I was host to a small dinner in a restaurant on the thirty-fifth floor of a modern skyscraper. Through the wall of windows I saw the forest of other gleaming towers that cluster around Waikiki; the beach and surf were too far below to be visible, but from a tiny corner of space between the buildings I could see Diamond Head far off, lit by the fading sunset. John Poindexter recounted that his family name came from a Norman ancestor who had accompanied William the Conqueror when he took England in 1066. Did his comment, prompted by nothing in particular, provide an insight into how Admiral Poindexter viewed himself? I wondered.

Don Regan came to the dinner but was called away almost instantly to the telephone. When he returned after what seemed like a half hour, he said that the call had been from "my friend" (President Reagan), who had just been "set up." As Ferdinand and Imelda Marcos were now in exile in Hawaii, the Reagans wanted to telephone them as they passed through. I and others had to argue hard to keep the president from making a personal visit to Marcos. The telephone call had turned into a videotaped and media-saturated publicity event. Mrs. Marcos wept at length, while the Reagans, trapped, could only hear her out. I thought this experience might change the president's attitude toward Marcos a bit, but it didn't affect his attitude toward Mrs. Aquino. Later he told me, as we discussed a proposed visit of Mrs. Aquino to the United States, "I have a wait-and-see attitude toward Aquino."

"The Filipinos are waiting to hear you say you support her government," I replied.

"I'll support a legitimate government—when she gets elected," the president responded.

"She thinks she *did* get elected," I said. After the president's Asia trip, I went on to Manila, where I persuaded Mrs. Aquino to accept the invitation for an official visit to the United States. She was worried about her reception. Knowing President Reagan's instinctive personal charm and friendliness, I assured her that she would be treated with respect in the White House and with wild enthusiasm in the Congress.

A comment by Prime Minister Lee Kuan Yew was reported to me: "We have moved from a situation of certainty to one of uncertainty." With Marcos, disaster was certain; with Mrs. Aquino, the future was uncharted, but there was at least a chance for progress.

Corazon Aquino's triumphal visit to Washington in September 1986 marked a high point of support for her in the United States. As she left the podium after her dramatic address to a cheering joint session of Congress, one of the escorting senators, Bob Dole, said, "Cory, you just hit a home run!"

Beaming, she shot back without skipping a beat, "I hope the bases were loaded."

Soon, however, came a series of serious coup attempts by military insurgents, and support from many Philippine leaders expected to be in her corner turned lukewarm. She had campaigned for them when they had stood for election, and then many of them refused to support her on critical issues, from economic reform to the continuation of the U.S. bases. She was plagued by periods of ineffective administration in her own presidential office and proved unable to come to grips with the widespread corruption that so plagued the country. Added to these problems of leadership and governance came natural disasters as well: earthquake, typhoon, and volcano damage ravaged the islands. Acute problems remained unresolved, which resulted in increasing criticism.

Still, Cory Aquino had made important accomplishments: from a standing start, she quickly formed a cabinet with many strong members; produced a new constitution and saw it ratified by an overwhelming margin; revitalized the democratic process through national and local elections; began a process of economic reform that turned decline into real growth in excess of 5 percent through the end of the decade; made progress in professionalizing the military despite many problems; kept the Communist insurgency at bay and turned it back in some areas; stood up to the debt problems she inherited; and saw the ratio of debt to GNP improve dramatically. Taken together, these were big steps forward and marked a sharp improvement from the situation she found when she took office. She aspired to turn over a functioning democracy to an elected successor. This great goal she achieved. And the winner of the next presidential election, Fidel (Eddie) Ramos, was the candidate she supported energetically.

The rise to power of Corazon Aquino and the fall of Ferdinand Marcos marked an important shift in American official thinking: support for authoritarian governments that opposed communism could not be taken for granted. The United States supported people who were themselves standing up for freedom and democracy, whether against communism or against another form of repressive government.

CHAPTER 32

Confronting Terrorism:
Evolution of a Policy

On July 19, 1982, just three days after I was sworn in as secretary of state, David Dodge, acting president of the American University of Beirut, was kidnapped as he left his office. On August 8, 1988, as my motorcade sped along a narrow road leading down from the airport to La Paz, Bolivia's capital, a dynamite bomb exploded just seconds after my car passed by. Twelve days later, I attended the funeral of President Zia of Pakistan and then brought home the body of the U.S. ambassador to Pakistan, Arnold Raphel. They were killed when their plane was blown up in midair.

Terrorism marked my time in office from beginning to end. I was confronted by it personally: on six different occasions somebody tried to knock me off. I worked hard to develop strong policies and sound laws to counter terrorist efforts. And I learned a lot, sometimes through bitter experience, about how to view and how to handle this danger.

Terrorism is hardly a new problem. The bomb-throwing anarchists of the Industrial Revolution come quickly to mind. In more recent times, ethnic and separatist groups have used the tactic: Basques in Spain, Armenian nationalists, the Irish Republican Army. By the 1970s, small groups of leftist fanatics (the Red Brigade in Italy, the Baader-Meinhof gang and the Red Army Faction in Germany, to name but a few) had acquired advanced technological means and the support of Communist movements in Eastern Europe and of Middle East dictatorships. State-sponsored terrorism had by 1980 become a weapon of unconventional war against the democracies of the West, taking advantage of their openness and building on political hostility toward them. It was an ugly fact of international life that some states provided terrorists with important resources—weapons, financing, passports, safe houses, training areas. In return, the terrorists committed acts of violence that served a government's interests while enabling the government to deny responsibility. In 1980, there were some 278 terrorist incidents and more casualties than in any year since the U.S.

government began to collect such statistics twelve years earlier. Americans, especially U.S. diplomats, had become primary targets.

The U.S. government had policies for dealing with terrorists, but I did not think they were sufficient or effective. As I looked back in the spring of 1984, the recent record of terrorism was disturbing: in 1979, American embassy personnel were taken hostage and held in Tehran for 444 days; Pope John Paul II was shot in St. Peter's Square in May 1981; Anwar Sadat was assassinated in October 1981; Israel's ambassador to Great Britain was shot and severely wounded outside a hotel in London in June 1982; and bombs were placed on Pan Am flights to Honolulu and Rio de Janeiro in August 1982. The list continued: a car bombing of the American embassy in Beirut in April 1983 and then the truck bombing of our marine barracks on October 23, 1983, with 241 men killed. A second bomb exploded that same day at French headquarters, killing 59. On November 17, the French retaliated by targeting a terrorist training camp, the Sheik Abdullah barracks in Lebanon's Bekaa Valley, which had been linked to the suicide bombings of our marine barracks and the French headquarters. The barracks were under the control of Hezbollah, the Party of God, a Shiite Muslim group supported by Iran.

Terrorist acts continued: bombings at Harrod's in London and at Orly Airport in Paris, the murder of four members of the South Korean cabinet in Rangoon by North Korean agents, destruction of a Gulf Air flight in the United Arab Emirates.

On December 12, 1983, in a coordinated ninety-minute series of bombings, six targets in Kuwait were hit, including the American and French embassies. Five people were killed; some eighty-six were injured. The Kuwaitis reacted quickly, and seventeen men involved were apprehended, tried, and found guilty. I strongly supported the Kuwaitis' tough application of the rule of law to these terrorists. They were imprisoned, but not executed. Fourteen of them were members of "al-Dawa," an Iranian-backed Shiite Muslim group, and the other three were from Beirut, where they were followers of Hezbollah and had close family ties to leading terrorists. They became known as the Dawa prisoners.

In the first three months of 1984, Malcolm Kerr, the president of the American University of Beirut, was murdered, and three other Americans, including CIA Station Chief William Buckley, were taken hostage in Beirut. The hurried withdrawal of the marines from Beirut in February 1984 left a clear message: terrorism works. And when terrorism works, one consequence is assured: far more lies ahead.

Development of a Program

On March 24, 1984, I gathered specialists on counterterrorism for an all-day Saturday seminar. Brian Jenkins of the RAND Corporation chaired the session. I wanted to look at this issue with a fresh eye—we probed how to think about terrorism and what could be done to combat it. Since the problem was international in character, an effective counterterrorism policy would need to command vigorous support abroad as well as in the United States. At this time, National Security Decision Directive 138 was in preparation. Signed on April 3, the directive was notable primarily for the arguments it stimulated. A passage authorizing operations to "neutralize" terrorists encountered fierce opposition: those opposed argued that it sounded as if it authorized assassination. The word "proactive" was substituted to describe preemptive operations against terrorists: a good word, but the argument disclosed great reluctance even to consider offensive action against terrorists. The Long Commission report on the bombing of the marine barracks had stated, "It makes little sense to learn that a State or its surrogate is conducting a terrorist campaign or planning a terrorist attack and not confront that government with political or military consequences if it continues forward." I agreed with the commission that terrorism constituted a form of warfare for which we were ill prepared.

To start with, our thinking about terrorism was confused. How many times had I heard it said, "If you want to get at terrorism, you have to get at its 'root causes.' " Someone would commit a terrorist act, and then that person or that group would say, "That's because I'm a Palestinian," "That's because I hate Indira Gandhi," "That's because I'm a North Korean and I hate the South Koreans," "That's because I'm hungry," that's because of any untold number of grievances of one kind or another that people might express. As Senator Claiborne Pell so often—and so fallaciously—put it, "One man's terrorist is another man's freedom fighter." If we got ourselves in the frame of mind that these terrorist acts could be justified and legitimized—and that somehow *we* were to blame—then we would have lost the battle.

What does a terrorist do? A terrorist attacks a society by spreading unease, terror, and death among the civilian population. Society constantly faces a similar problem with common criminals—who always have some reason for committing a murder, rape, or theft. If we are ready to allow that line of argument, then we don't recognize murder as murder, crime as crime, or terrorism as terrorism. And we've lost. The first objective must be to try to get into people's heads what the nature of the terrorist threat was and what it wasn't and to get their thinking straight.

Do poverty and injustice cause terrorism? We should work for social betterment but not legitimize terrorism in the meantime. Does political oppression cause terrorism? We should work for human rights and diplomatic solutions to conflicts. But terrorists often launch their assaults just when progress is being made. Terrorists fear negotiations and seem spurred to terror in an effort to derail progress. They reject the fundamental character of democracy and negotiated peace or social progress. Whenever even a glimmer of peace emerged in the Middle East, radical Palestinians and rejectionist states would step up their assaults on innocent people. In my firm view, people who engage in terror do not want peace or justice, and people who want peace and justice do not engage in terror.

I started to speak out on the subject. Public debate, I felt, could be a way to sharpen our thinking and strengthen our policy. On April 3, 1984, at a meeting of the Trilateral Commission, I said we had to take on the challenge of terrorism boldly and to be willing to use force under the right circumstances. "Certainly we must take security precautions to protect our people and our facilities; certainly we must strengthen our intelligence capabilities to alert ourselves to the threats. But it is increasingly doubtful that a purely passive strategy can even begin to cope with the problem. This raises a host of questions for a free society: in what circumstances—and how— should we respond? When—and how—should we take preventive or preemptive action against known terrorist groups? What evidence do we insist upon before taking such steps?"

As the threat mounted—and as the involvement of such countries as Iran, Syria, Libya, and North Korea had become more and more evident— it had become increasingly important that the nations of the West face up to the need for active defense against terrorism. Once it becomes established that terrorism works—that it achieves its political objectives—its practitioners will be bolder, and the threat to us will be all the greater.

The lesson of Vietnam was continually being cited to reject any use of military force unless in exceptional circumstances and with near total public support in advance. Does this, I asked, "mean there are no situations where a discrete assertion of power is needed or appropriate for limited purposes? . . . The need to avoid no-win situations cannot mean that we turn automatically away from hard-to-win situations that call for prudent involvement." Few cases would be as clear or as quick as our operation in Grenada. On the contrary, most other cases would be a lot tougher. "But we cannot opt out of every contest," I said. "If we do, the world's future will be determined by others—most likely by those who are the most brutal, the most unscrupulous, and the most hostile to our deeply held principles."

On June 9, at the London economic summit, I worked hard, with the president's support, to get a strong statement on terrorism signed by the leaders of the seven largest industrial democracies. Margaret Thatcher's voice was powerful and determined. We achieved agreement for "closer cooperation and coordination between police and security organizations and other relevant authorities, especially in the exchange of information, intelligence and technical knowledge." More importantly, we agreed on "consultation and as far as possible cooperation over the expulsion or exclusion from their countries of known terrorists, including persons of diplomatic status involved in terrorism." It was a significant step. Some nations allowed terrorist cells to lodge within their borders with impunity in return for a pledge not to conduct terrorism against targets in the host state. Such a pact with the devil at the expense of innocent civilians in other neighbor states had become a growing, deeply pernicious practice. I placed great value on authoritative statements using the words "expulsion" and "exclusion," even though they might not have an immediate impact. A tone and an attitude were being established, a priority recognized, a signal being sent to governments: terrorism must be confronted.

I tried to translate these ideas into action at home. The executive branch was itself so fragmented that it was impossible to orchestrate all counter-terrorist efforts effectively or even to get agreement that there should be a specific counterterrorist effort. With the cooperation of Congress, we began to add more resources to our collection of intelligence, to enhance embassy security, and to initiate training foreign law enforcement officers in counterterrorism. This last measure was important: the U.S. government had been blocked from doing such training since the Vietnam War era because of sentiment in Congress that we would enhance the ability of dictators to suppress popular movements against their regimes.

Still, I felt we needed to do more. But I remained frustrated. Can a country abide by the rule of law and effectively counter terrorists? This serious question deserved an answer: my answer was yes. When Benjamin Netanyahu, the Israeli embassy's deputy chief of mission,[1] asked me to speak to the Jonathan Institute, a foundation dedicated to public education on the nature of terrorism, I agreed. In my speech on June 24, 1984, I raised the difficult issue once again, stating: "It is time to think long, hard, and seriously about more active means of defense—about defense through appropriate preventive or preemptive actions against terrorists before they strike." To walk on this slippery slope, I knew, we would need spikes in our shoes, but I also knew that terrorists had to see costs to themselves and active opposition.

The terrorist toll continued to mount. A Venezuelan airliner was hijacked on July 29, 1984. In July and August, mines were found in the Red Sea, and clear evidence later established that the mines were planted by Libya. A suicide van bomb severely damaged our new embassy in Beirut on September 20; two U.S. military officers were killed. Within a day, we had

---

1. The brother of Lieutenant Colonel Jonathan Netanyahu, who led, and was killed in, the Israeli mission to rescue passengers from an aircraft hijacked by terrorists to Entebbe, Uganda.

clear evidence of where the incident had been planned and rehearsed and who was responsible. Reconnaissance photographs of the Sheik Abdullah barracks in Baalbek showed a replica of our embassy's *chicane*—the concrete barriers designed to slow down approaching vehicles. We could deduce that the suicide driver had practiced how to drive quickly through the maze. If we moved swiftly, we would likely catch terrorists there and destroy their facilities—and would show that the United States *could* take decisive action. But Cap Weinberger and the Joint Chiefs raised question after question. They would not move. And the president would not move without them.

On October 12, 1984, Britain almost lost its prime minister, Margaret Thatcher. A bomb placed by the Irish Republican Army blew up a large part of the hotel in Brighton where she was staying.

I spoke out again, this time at the Park Avenue Synagogue in Manhattan on October 25. In the hours before I delivered the speech, the draft had been circulated around the government in Washington. Calls began to come in complaining that I was going too far. Minutes before I was to speak, just as I was finishing dinner in Rabbi Judah Nadich's residence with his family, a telephone call came in from the vice president's office. George Bush, I was told, was "unhappy" with my text, feeling that it conveyed a belligerent approach that we would not be able to carry through. There was also irritation that, through my speech, I was setting U.S. policy on my own, without going through the usual bureaucratic processes—and that it was not a policy anyone else wanted. I felt confident that I was expressing views completely consistent with the president's, and I went ahead with the speech. "We cannot allow ourselves to become the Hamlet of nations, worrying endlessly over whether and how to respond. A great nation with global responsibilities cannot afford to be hamstrung by confusion and indecisiveness. Fighting terrorism will not be a clean or pleasant contest, but we have no choice. . . . We must reach a consensus in this country that our responses should go beyond passive defense to consider means of active prevention, preemption, and retaliation. Our goal must be to prevent and deter future terrorist acts. . . . The public must understand *before the fact* that occasions will come when their government must act before each and every fact is known—and the decisions cannot be tied to the opinion polls."

The next morning, Vice President Bush was campaigning in Ohio and was asked whether he agreed with my position and the risk it might pose to civilians. The vice president said, "I think you have got to pinpoint the source of the attack. We are not going to go out and bomb innocent civilians or something of that nature. I don't think we ever get to the point where you kill 100 innocent women and children just to kill one terrorist." I agreed, of course, that any action would have to be pinpointed, but the critical proposition was to let terrorists know that action was possible.

President Reagan, when asked about the apparent conflict between Bush and me, said of my speech, "I don't think it was a statement of policy." This created the impression that the president was disavowing the position I had taken. But my speech was read again, and White House spokesman Larry Speakes was instructed to say that Shultz's speech "was administration policy from top to bottom." In fact, the idea of action, preemptive or retaliatory, had many opponents.

A few days later, Vice President Bush telephoned me to say he was sorry about the confusion and that he was "not sniping away" at me. It was a great speech, he said, but "the press is dying to show divisions in the administration." He had been misled, he said, about precisely what I had said. I was glad to have his support for the idea that we must push forward in the fight against terrorists.

The Debate Escalates: The Proper Use of Force

My Park Avenue Synagogue speech did not end the debate over the proper use of force to combat terrorism or the larger debate over the proper relationship of power and diplomacy, nor did it change American policy. I regarded strength and the credible possibility of its use as an essential element of policy. Cap Weinberger went public with an elaboration of his views in a speech at the National Press Club on November 28. He escalated and codified the debate when he promulgated the six-point "Weinberger doctrine." In his own words:

> First, the United States should not commit forces to combat overseas unless the particular engagement or occasion is deemed vital to our national interest or that of our allies.
>
> Second, if we decide it is necessary to put combat troops into a given situation, we should do so wholeheartedly and with the clear intention of winning.
>
> Third, if we do decide to commit forces to combat overseas, we should have clearly defined political and military objectives. And we should know precisely how our forces can accomplish those clearly defined objectives. And we should have and send the forces needed to do just that.
>
> Fourth, the relationship between our objectives and the forces we have committed—their size, composition and disposition—must be continually reassessed and adjusted if necessary.
>
> Fifth, before the U.S. commits combat forces abroad, there must be some reasonable assurance we will have the support of the American people and their elected representatives in Congress. We cannot fight a battle with the Congress at home while asking our troops to win a war overseas or, as in the case of Vietnam, in effect asking our troops not to win but just to be there.
>
> Finally, the commitment of U.S. forces to combat should be a last resort.

One journalist called this "the Capgun Doctrine." Cap's doctrine bore relevance to a major, conventional war between adversarial armed forces. In the face of terrorism, or any other of the wide variety of complex, unclear, gray-area dangers facing us in the contemporary world, however, his was a counsel of inaction bordering on paralysis. (And his doctrine would have stopped us dead in our tracks on Grenada.)

There had to be some way to deal with violent threats that lay between doing nothing or launching an all-out conventional war. Diplomacy could work these problems most effectively when force—or the threat of force— was a credible part of the equation. What was left unstated was the Defense Department's deep philosophical opposition to using our military for counterterrorist operations. There was the Joint Special Operations Command (JSOC), a group of commandos trained to rescue Americans held by terrorists. But Cap set down conditions that must exist before the JSOC could be employed that were so restrictive as to mean that they would virtually *never* see action.

The argument turned into a battle royal between Cap Weinberger and me over the use of force. To Weinberger, as I heard him, our forces were to be constantly built up but not used: everything in our defense structure seemed geared exclusively to deter World War III against the Soviets; diplomacy was to solve all the other problems we faced around the world; if the time ever came when force seemed to be required, how would prior "reasonable assurance" of support from the American people be obtained? By a congressional vote for action against a terrorist group or for a rescue operation for Americans in danger? Only if and when the population, by some open measure, agreed in advance would American armed forces be employed, and even then, only if we were assured of winning swiftly and at minimal cost. This was the Vietnam syndrome in spades, carried to an absurd level, and a complete abdication of the duties of leadership.

My view is that democratically elected and accountable individuals have been placed in positions where they can and must make decisions to defend our national security. The risk and burden of leadership is that those decisions will receive, or not receive, the support of the people on their merits. The democratic process will deal with leaders who fail to measure up to the standards imposed by the American people and the established principles of a country guided by the rule of law. The idea that force should be used "only as a last resort" means that, by the time of use, force is the *only* resort and likely a much more costly one than if used earlier.

The *Wall Street Journal* wrote: "Mr. Shultz's sensible anti-terrorist policy of 'active prevention, pre-emption and retaliation' has Washington quaking in its boots. White House and Pentagon officials have been falling over themselves to say he didn't really mean to say any terrorist could actually ever get hurt by use of American force, let alone that we would ever launch

an attack that carried any risk of accidentally harming an innocent by-
stander. Mr. Shultz's speech seems to have provoked an outburst of the
impotence it deplored."[2]

As Bill Safire put it, tellingly, in his *New York Times* column on December 3: "Secretary Weinberger's purpose in enunciating the doctrine of
only-fun-wars is to undermine Secretary of State George Shultz's position
in the battle for President Reagan's strategic soul. Mr. Shultz has been
putting forward the more traditional, less simplistic theory that power and
diplomacy must be used in tandem if we are to stop the erosion of our
national interests." Bill Safire mailed me a copy of his column, on which
Henry Kissinger had written: "Bill—one of your best. We must never be
in the position where our only options are waging total war or accepting
total defeat."

George Ball, under secretary of state in the Kennedy and Johnson administrations, said in the *New York Times* on December 16 that my "obsession
with terrorism" was distorting my "normally judicious view of the world."
He hit a responsive chord. Caution and worry and inhibition were para-
lyzing an effective response to terrorism: on Capitol Hill and in the Pentagon, among Democrats and Republicans, on the left and on the right,
all too many people of influence and authority seemed to have an endless
litany of reasons to refrain from the use of power as an instrument of
American foreign policy. I had a different perception of American attitudes. When the next major terrorist threat or action came, if we had clear
evidence of responsibility and could isolate the target and moved quickly
and decisively, such an act of leadership would be supported by the American people.

A Scale of Responses

But as the debate over the use of force raged in Washington, terrorism
raged in the world at large. On October 31, 1984, Prime Minister Indira
Gandhi had been assassinated in New Delhi. Another American, Peter
Kilburn, a librarian at the American University of Beirut, had been taken
hostage on December 3. The following day, a Kuwaiti airliner with 161
people on board had been hijacked by Shiite terrorists and flown to Tehran.
Two Americans were murdered. A rescue attempt was out of the question,
as Iran was a wholly hostile environment in which a commando team could
not operate without risking its own safety. The hijacking concluded without
any direct U.S. action. The *New York Times* said on December 16, "The
'Shultz Doctrine' Is Rendered Moot in Iran."

We, of course, did not want to strike back in a way that would worsen

2. October 30, 1984.

the situation. But the moment might come when we could use force to good effect. Beyond force and the willingness to use it we had to have a strategy.

Our first response was to gain a better understanding of terrorism and how to counter it. The so-called Stockholm syndrome noted by psychologists had to be understood so that hostages—and nations—could resist the tendency of victims to sympathize with the cause of their captors or attackers. This, in effect, underlay the notion that "one man's terrorist is another man's freedom fighter," a slogan that served terrorists who would inflict horror on innocents.

The second need was reliable intelligence—not an easy job when nation-states were supporting terrorists. More resources had to be dedicated, especially to the delicate task of collecting information from human sources. Cooperation with other nations on intelligence sharing would be crucial but difficult for the United States, with our profusion of government leaks. The slightest hint of identification of an intelligence agent could cost a source his or her life.

And third, we needed to improve security measures at U.S. embassies. Every day when I entered the State Department, I saw two plaques on the wall commemorating members of the Foreign Service who had died in the line of duty. The first plaque spanned a period of 187 years. Most of the people listed there died from accident or disease. The more recent plaque, however, was filled in twenty years. And most of the dead were murdered by terrorists. Diplomacy had become a dangerous profession. Five American ambassadors had been killed by terrorists since 1980.

Fourth, we needed to strengthen international efforts to improve airline safety. In 1970, the Popular Front for the Liberation of Palestine hijacked three airliners in a single day. Since then, we and the international community had developed near-universal screening of airline passengers for weapons and explosives. At the time, some people criticized the cost and effectiveness of defensive measures. When the effort began in late 1970, I was director of the Office of Management and Budget. My role was to play devil's advocate—to try to poke holes in anything that was going to cost a bundle of money. But I didn't find holes, and I supported the increased security effort. Early on I remember people complaining: "Why do I have to stand in line at the airport to go through this thing?" We had to create a new mentality. And we did. Before long if a person went to an airport and didn't have to go through security measures, that individual would have been uneasy, and for good reason.

Strategy, intelligence, and defense were only part of the policy we had to build. Terrorists were waging war. Every nation has the right under international law to take defensive action. Part of that defense is to be prepared to take the offense when the proper occasion arises. Terrorists must realize that there are tangible costs to them, that they stand to pay a price for their crimes. The use of force as part of the rule of law had to be brought to bear on terrorists.

The first goal of an action program was to pressure states that sponsored terrorism to stop. The link between terrorists and their state sponsors had to be exposed and then broken. A key part of our program to take the offense was to streamline international legal procedures and promote closer cooperation among law enforcement agencies. Extradition treaties with Britain, the Federal Republic of Germany, Belgium, Canada, and Spain needed to be changed. Terrorists should not be able to escape justice by availing themselves of legal protection intended for refugees seeking political asylum. With good police work and good international cooperation, we would apprehend terrorists, put them on trial, and bring them to justice.

Meanwhile, more hostages were taken. The kidnapping of Peter Kilburn in December 1984 was followed in January 1985 by the abduction of the Reverend Lawrence Martin Jenco. In February, CNN Beirut bureau chief Jeremy Levin, who had been taken eleven months earlier, escaped from the hostage holders, apparently with some assistance from Syria. On March 8, 1985, a massive car bomb in Beirut killed 80 and wounded 200 in an apparent attempt to assassinate Sheik Mohammed Hussein Fadlallah, the spiritual leader of Hezbollah, the Iranian-supported Shiite group thought to be hostage takers themselves and implicated in our marine barracks bombing, our embassy bombing, as well as others. On March 16, Terry Anderson, the Associated Press bureau chief, was taken hostage. In May, David Jacobsen of the American University of Beirut was taken captive. On June 9, Thomas Sutherland, also of the American University of Beirut, was added to the hostage ranks. On June 11, 1985, Shiite extremists hijacked a Jordanian airliner in Beirut, forced it to Cyprus, then to Sicily, and on to Beirut, where they blew up the aircraft after releasing the passengers. A Palestinian terrorist then took over a Lebanese airliner and flew it to Cyprus, where he surrendered but was allowed to fly to Amman, Jordan. The momentum was disturbing.

The Hijacking of TWA Flight 847

Bureaucratic battles in Washington were suddenly overwhelmed by the eruption of a terrorist event of great magnitude. TWA's Flight 847 bound for Rome, the daily flight familiar to Americans in the Middle East who picked it up in Athens on their way to other European cities or en route to America, was hijacked on Friday, June 14, 1985. One hundred and fifty-three passengers and crew were on board, mostly Americans. The terrorists demanded the release of 766 Arab prisoners held by Israel and the 17 Dawa prisoners held in Kuwait. The hijackers wanted to go to Algiers but lacked enough fuel, so they ordered the plane to fly to Beirut International Airport, where they released nineteen women and children, took on fuel, and ordered the plane to Algiers, where more passengers, mostly women and children, were released. The terrorists then ordered the pilot, the experienced Captain John Testrake, to fly them back to Beirut. There, to show they meant business, the terrorists beat U.S. Navy diver Robert Stethem, shot him in the head, and tossed his body off the aircraft onto the tarmac. In the ensuing confusion, more terrorists from Beirut scrambled aboard the plane, which took off again for Algiers.

The Algerians told us they could handle the crisis on their own; they wanted no help from the United States in the form of advice or trained rescue teams. When American TV had reported that a U.S. Delta Force team was in the Mediterranean area, the Algerians had become alarmed.

Terrorists had found in Beirut a permissive environment. There they could be among their fellow terrorists to rest and refresh themselves while continuing with their hijacking. I wanted to keep them on the ground in Algiers so that they could not get back to Beirut.

Israeli Defense Minister Yitzhak Rabin told our embassy that Israel had planned—even before this hijacking—to release over time all or nearly all of the 766 prisoners (mostly Shiites who had been captured in attacks against Israelis in south Lebanon) demanded by the hijackers. Israel was opposed to releasing them under direct terrorist threat, but, Rabin said, if the United States asked Israel to release the Shiite prisoners in exchange for the Americans held by the hijackers in Algiers, "it would be hard for Israel to refuse." He was putting the monkey on our back, but he did give us an avenue to follow. We told the International Committee for the Red Cross—which was now in touch with the Algerians—that Israel had conveyed to us that it had planned *before* the hijacking to release all or nearly all the Shiite prisoners they held and that they could convey this to the Algerians. This would give the Algerians something to work with as they tried to talk to the hijackers and pressure them to give up.

The terrorists were now talking about particular prisoners held in Greece and Cyprus and Israel whom they wanted released. The Greeks and Cypriots complied instantly, probably seeing this as an opportunity to get rid of prisoners whose captivity would lead to future terrorism directed at their own countries. In exchange, the terrorists released a Greek citizen. The deal was a clear-cut violation of international treaties in which over 120 nations, including Greece, agreed to refuse such deals with hijackers.

The Algerians continued to hold the plane on the ground. I did not, however, have confidence that they would make the tough decisions (such as shooting out the tires) necessary to keep TWA 847 grounded there. We were told that forty-eight American men were on board and that eight to ten other Americans may have been taken off the plane in Beirut to be held there as hostages. Our best option was to keep the plane in Algiers where the Algerians could try to bring the crisis to an end by somehow persuading the terrorists to release hostages or conceivably by agreeing at some point to let our "shooters," as the JSOC commandos were known, take over the plane. Everyone agreed that our approach should be "anything but Beirut." If the hijackers returned there, they would be resupplied with arms and ammunition and supported by local terrorists for round-the-clock shifts. Such support would preclude any rescue attempt. It appeared that after they had accomplished their objective of trading hostages for prisoners, they wished ultimately to get to Tehran and to the protection of the Iranians.

On Sunday, June 16, TWA 847 left Algiers for Beirut. The Algerians did not try to stop the departure. Clearly, Beirut International Airport had become home base and haven for terrorism. Our ambassador, Mike Newlin, reported that Algerian President Chadli Bendjedid felt continuing press speculation that an American commando rescue team was in the Mediterranean region had led the hijackers to decide suddenly to order the TWA pilot to take off. Bendjedid also did not want such an American presence on the ground or the embarrassment of declining to allow U.S. commandos on his territory.

American television carried live the arrival and touch down of the TWA jetliner at Beirut International Airport. I suddenly realized that the American media were there—in Beirut—in among the terrorist establishment, and that they were not only going to cover the crisis, they were going to be *part* of it. Television was reporting that food and newspapers were being taken out to the plane, now parked on the tarmac. The hostages, the television reported, sent out a message from the plane addressed to President Reagan: "We implore you not to take any direct military action on our behalf. Please negotiate quickly our immediate release by convincing the Israelis to release the 800 Lebanese prisoners as requested. Now."

Admiral Stansfield Turner, who headed the CIA in the Carter administration, appeared on television and said that the United States should make the exchange the hijackers demanded. And the world was treated to a stunning sight: a terrorist leering at the TV camera as he yanked the pilot's head out the cockpit window and put a gun barrel to his temple. This media circus was playing into the terrorists' hands and making U.S. efforts to deal effectively with this life-and-death crisis far more difficult. That day we ordered the aircraft carrier *Nimitz* and the missile destroyer *Kidd* to positions off the coast of Lebanon.

The Israelis were now virtually inviting us to ask them to release all or nearly all of the many Lebanese Shiite prisoners they held in exchange for the release of TWA 847 and its remaining passengers. They were putting the responsibility on us. If people were killed, we couldn't say it was because of Israel's refusal to swap prisoners for hostages. These Lebanese Shiite prisoners had been taken in April from the El Ansar camp in Lebanon to Atlit in Israel in violation of the Fourth Geneva Convention dealing with treatment of civilians in wartime. The United States had opposed this violation publicly when it occurred. Nonetheless, if we asked the Israelis to make a trade of prisoners for hostages, we would be repudiating our own policy against making concessions to terrorists, and we would be inviting terrorists to take further hostages as bargaining chips in order to gain one thing or another: the possibilities were endless—and dangerous. Americans would be put at risk all over the world by such capitulation.

In a meeting in the Situation Room that same Sunday, June 16, President Reagan suggested that we tell the terrorists to release the hostages, and we would then see that Israel released its prisoners. That, I felt, would amount to a direct swap of hostages for prisoners. I was strongly opposed. I argued strenuously that our policy of not making deals with terrorists also meant we should not encourage others to do so. I said, "You can't square that circle, Mr. President." He agreed.

After the meeting, President Reagan publicly warned the hijackers, "for their own safety," to release the hostages and, in response to a reporter's question about the prisoners in Israel, said, "The decision isn't so simple as just trading prisoners. The decision is, at what point can you pay off the terrorists without endangering people from here on out once they find out that their tactics succeed." The president was strong and clear about the underlying reason for his stand.

We now knew that the Amal militia, a Shiite group of Lebanese led by Nabih Berri, a part-time resident of Dearborn, Michigan, was deeply involved with the hijackers on the ground. Whether Amal had been part of the terrorist plans from the start or was now engaged in order to serve its own interests was unclear, but Nabih Berri was trying to make himself a middleman and in so doing was becoming part of the terrorist effort. Through a phone call from Bud McFarlane, who had gotten to know Berri when McFarlane was our Mideast special envoy, we disabused Berri of the idea that he could persuade us to pressure Israel as part of a deal.

President Reagan sent a letter to President Assad of Syria: Assad had leverage on Berri, and we asked him to work on Berri to try to end the crisis. Berri told our ambassador to Lebanon, Reg Bartholomew, that the hijackers now had three demands: first, free the Dawa prisoners held by Kuwaiti authorities; second, free the hundreds of Israeli-held Shiite prisoners that had been transferred from the Ansar camp in Lebanon to Atlit in Israel; and third, free two prisoners held in Spain on terrorist charges.

The statements coming out of Israel were creating a real problem for us. They continued to indicate to the media that if the United States did not ask the Israelis to trade, then the TWA 847 crisis could not be blamed on Israel. The public perception was that Israel and the United States were at odds on antiterrorist policy. The practical effect of the line of argument they were putting out would set a terrible precedent from Israel's own perspective: grab some Americans and you can pressure the United States to pressure Israel, and successfully. I had to explain the U.S. position emphatically to the Israelis.

Although I was tempted to contact Prime Minister Peres about this problem directly, I decided that any phone call or exchange of cables could easily be misinterpreted. I decided to have my executive assistant, Charlie Hill, contact Benjamin Netanyahu, Israel's ambassador to the United Nations. They could talk directly, and Netanyahu could then communicate with Peres. Hill told Netanyahu that the United States was holding the line against terrorism, while Israel, usually the champion and leader in antiterrorism, was undercutting us. Netanyahu fully agreed and passed our views right back to Jerusalem. He said he couldn't understand why Israeli officials had been taking such a self-defeating and dangerous line. Netanyahu had been interviewed on Israeli radio the day before, had praised the United States for standing firm, and had seen this statement of support cut out by the Israeli censor; it didn't make sense to him. I, too, was surprised by the censorship, one of the costs, even in a society as open as Israel, of being in a perpetual state of war with most of its neighbors.

The public Israeli position was shortly brought back into line by our own statement of principle: we do not make concessions to terrorists, and we do not encourage others to do so. The Israeli government then stated publicly that it would not release the prisoners as part of an arrangement to gain the freedom of the TWA 847 hostages—even if the United States made such a request.

By this time, the media coverage was revolting me. The terrorists controlled not only the aircraft on the ground but the entire airport and the surrounding area. Reporters were everywhere, in essence serving the ends of the hijackers: television footage of the staged terrorist displays of their hostages played as straight news events. Reporters asked the terrorists, "Do you have a message for President Reagan?" On one day, viewers would see interviews of the aircraft crew; on the next day, the fare would include a hostage press conference; the following day, a "spontaneous" mass anti-American demonstration. The terrorists were providing, on a daily basis, compelling TV footage, and television was providing them worldwide advertising time for their views. The ability of the terrorists to manipulate the media to serve their ends was deeply disturbing. Instant global communication put people around the world in immediate touch with events that were out of control: the violent, the unscrupulous, and the gullible were linked in a bizarre partnership.

The press was after a big and compelling story, full of human drama. The terrorists reveled in the publicity and used it for their purposes. The process encouraged other terrorists to use the dramatic hostage-taking technique. And the barrage of reporting made our operational tasks that much more difficult, since we had a hard time taking steps that would not be reported, in effect, to the terrorists. Certainly the proven technique of isolating the terrorists simply could not be used in this case.

The intense publicity enhanced the value of the hostages to those holding them and made our own effort much more problematic as we sought to raise the costs of hostage holding to the terrorists while trying to lower the value of the hostages to their holders. I did not know how to solve this dilemma except to bolster the security of our own deliberations and plans.

On June 18, a reply to President Reagan's letter came in from Assad in the form of a question: "Can we understand that the U.S. will exert efforts for the release of the Lebanese prisoners, especially since the U.S. considered the holding of them in Lebanon and their transfer outside Lebanon as a violation of the Geneva Convention and made the U.S. government's position public?" Before I could weigh in on the answer, White House spokesman Larry Speakes, at his 10:00 A.M. briefing, stunned reporters by saying that the United States "would like Israel" to "go ahead and make the release" of the Ansar prisoners now held in Israel. Out that went on CNN.

Furious, I went to the president and pointed our how badly Speakes had hurt our policy. He agreed. The White House staff was told that from then on, *all* questions about this crisis were to be referred to the State Department: State had the action on this. I insisted that the White House put a tight lid on its people.

President Reagan then responded to Assad: no deals by us, and we would not ask others to make deals with terrorists, either. If anyone was blocking the release of the prisoners held by Israel, it was the hostage holders at Beirut International. As our reply went back to him, Assad was in Moscow, his patron and military supplier.

In his press conference on June 18, President Reagan put us back on track: "America will never make concessions to terrorists—to do so would only invite more terrorism—nor will we ask nor pressure any other government to do so." He added, "Those in Lebanon who commit these acts damage their country and their cause, and we hold them accountable." The next day, both the president and I repeated this forceful message: as he put it, "We must not yield to the terrorist demands that invite more terrorism."

Intelligence reports were telling us that the terrorists responsible for the hijacking were Lebanese Shiites of the Party of God—Hezbollah—and that the hijackers were led by a relative of one of the Dawa prisoners whose release from Kuwaiti hands the hijackers were demanding. The reports were confirming what we had thought. Our chief fear was that the TWA

Flight 847 hostages would be taken into Beirut itself or into the Bekaa Valley to join the other hostages seized previously by Hezbollah and other Iranian-supported terrorist bands. That would be a terrible development. We had indications now that most of the hostages had been removed from the plane. We had to move swiftly to end this crisis—but without violating our own counterterrorist policy. It was an odd paradox: we would not make a deal, and the deal the terrorists wanted—the release of the Shiites held by Israel—was being blocked by their very demand for a deal. The sole impediment blocking Israel's implementation of their announced policy concerning the release of the Shiite detainees was the refusal of the terrorists to free the passengers of TWA 847.

As we continued to work at this delicate problem, news came in that a terrorist bomb had exploded at the airport in Frankfurt, Germany: three were dead, forty-two were wounded.

Ambassador Mike Newlin in Algiers reported that the Algerians had been in contact with Nabih Berri, who told them that he could bring about the release of all the TWA 847 hostages but that he must have "a date certain" on which Israel would release the Ansar prisoners. At a National Security Planning Group meeting on June 20, I proposed that we seek Israel's intentions in a "precise" way. The president agreed and authorized me to proceed.

Precision was my guideline. I wanted to know from Jerusalem what would happen to the prisoners held in Israel if there were no TWA hostages. I did not want to cross the line of connecting the prisoners' release in Israel to the hostages' release in Beirut. Accordingly, Netanyahu was asked to put a carefully phrased question to Prime Minister Peres: "What can we expect Israel to do about all the Ansar prisoners on the assumption that there are no TWA 847 hostages being held?" It was, we stressed to the Israelis, not a request, not a suggestion, and not a change in our policy. We were seeking clarification of their intentions. Netanyahu asked only one question in reply: "Are you using any other channels?"

"No" was my answer.

I was wrong. Without telling me, the question had been put through the CIA to Mossad, its Israeli intelligence counterpart. I conjectured that Bud McFarlane had initiated the request. Bill Casey telephoned me with the Israeli answer: "We have intended to release gradually the Shiite detainees in accordance with security developments. However, we do not intend to release them under blackmail from the hijackers." The Israeli respondents went on to elaborate: because they were now under pressure to release the detainees, they would not release them, and they "would rather *not* have" a U.S. request to accelerate their original timetable for release.

I respected the Israeli answer, but it was not exactly on the point and gave me nothing to work with. Beyond this, I worried that the nearly incessant free-lance style of Bud McFarlane and Bill Casey and—beyond that and even more disturbing—the NSC's obsessive desire for an operational role would result in a disaster sooner or later.

I went to the president and told him that I had been blindsided by McFarlane's unreported use of the CIA to communicate with the Israelis. I called it a blunder. Bud McFarlane, who was present, said he was shocked. He had not authorized any such contact, he told me.

We had misinformed Netanyahu; another contact in another channel had been made. We called Netanyahu to tell him again that his channel was the sole authoritative approach. Our question was precisely formulated and was being asked by the secretary of state on behalf of the president, and we wished to receive a reply from their prime minister. So we put the same question again: "What can we expect Israel to do about all the Ansar prisoners [now held at Atlit in Israel] on the assumption that there are no TWA 847 hostages being held?"

Television coverage continued to broadcast the terrorists' announcements. At 2:00 P.M. Thursday, June 20, a "press conference" in the Beirut airport cafeteria was broadcast. Hostage Allyn Conwell expressed fear about what would happen should negotiations fail and expressed hope that the United States would do nothing to jeopardize the hostages' lives. The network then cut live to Arlington National Cemetery, where Robert Stethem, the navy diver who had been murdered by the hijackers, was being buried.

The media were now reporting that the United States had made a "request" to Israel to release the detainees; it was now up to Israel, they intimated. This was a terrible development: the Israelis were understandably confused and irritated.

The tension was immense, and the television coverage saturated the public. On Friday, June 21, hordes of Hezbollah supporters stormed onto the runway at Beirut International Airport screaming, "Death to America! Death to Israel!" Television captured it all live as it was happening. The *New York Times* that same day carried a story by Bernard Gwertzman: "The Reagan Administration has told several friendly governments that if the 40 American hostages are freed unconditionally by the hijackers in Beirut, Israel will follow with the release of the 766 detainees, Administration officials said today." That was not correct. The hijackers themselves, by their demand, had held up Israel's stated plan to release the detainees. It was important to keep that clear. The Israelis would believe we had deliberately leaked this news to the *New York Times* to send a signal to, or pressure, them.

We called Netanyahu once again to clear up any misunderstanding that might have been caused by the erroneous news reports. We still wanted an answer to our carefully phrased question; we were not trying to influence what that answer would be. Press coverage of the hostage holding continued at a saturation level. And this undifferentiated entity, the press, on the one hand urged us to "make a deal" and then criticized us on the assumption that we were making one. Undoubtedly, the press, while doing its job, was complicating our task of getting the captives released, as we worked to knock down false stories. Our best hope was to continue to work through our channel, to which the press had no access.

Late in the morning on June 21, Prime Minister Peres's reply came in; it carried the approval of Foreign Minister Shamir and Defense Minister Rabin:[3]

1. If the hijacking had not taken place, we would have continued with a gradual release of the detainees, depending upon developments in southern Lebanon.

2. We have not set a timetable for their release.

3. In view of the hijacking, we are not inclined to do this in a way that would appear to give in to the terrorists.

4. Israeli law says that detainees may appeal to a board headed by a district judge.

5. As the result of such an appeal board decision, we have to release some thirty-one detainees next week.

It should be noted that one-third of the detainees are not Shiites, but Palestinian members of terrorist organizations apprehended in Lebanon.

It was a complex and indefinite response: some prisoners would be released on general principles, some by legal procedure, and some might not be released at all. The Israelis were going to proceed on this matter as their law provided, just as they would have if there had been no hijacking; but just *how* they were not prepared to say.

At noon on June 21, Shimon Peres called me from Israel to say he supported the tough position we had taken. He expressed his concern for the hostages and their families, saying, "We feel about them as we would our own people." I told Peres what the president had said: that we must not yield to terrorist demands. As we were talking, I heard the crash of doors slamming in the outer hall, the sound of people running, and the muffled clamor of excited voices. A crazed man with a rifle had gained entrance into the building and was on my floor, right down the hall, within twenty-five yards of my office, inside the security guard post and the limited-access doors. A few minutes later came word that the intruder, the son of a State Department secretary, had shot and killed his mother and then shot and killed himself. This human tragedy also demonstrated that our own security

3. Although the media later called this the first high-level U.S.-Israel contact since the hijacking, that was in fact far off the mark.

system at State was in need of urgent attention. The man had used a temporary pass, given family members of State Department employees, allowing him to enter without going through security and the metal detectors. I changed the policy immediately.

Ambassador Reg Bartholomew in Beirut had been in touch with Nabih Berri and reported over the tacsat. Berri professed to be trying, with some optimism, to get the main group of hijackers to give up, but a hood-wearing inner group of terrorists, he claimed, was not under anyone's control—not Iran's and not Hezbollah's; it seemed that they were related by family to the Dawa prisoners held by Kuwait. The Dawas were the ones whose release the inner group wanted—not the detainees held by Israel. This chain of terror all began, we were told, when Saddam Hussein, the ruler of the secular Baath party–run nation of Iraq, had moved to suppress the Dawa group, a Shiite Islamic movement in Iraq. The Dawas had taken up opposition to Sunni governmental rule and to Western influence and had conducted terrorist acts against a variety of mostly Western targets in Kuwait, where they had been captured and imprisoned. They were, in fact, convicted murderers carrying a Dawa banner. So Shiite activists in Iran, Iraq, Kuwait, and Lebanon all formed something of a network forged partly by family ties. It was this dimension that now surfaced in the TWA 847 crisis. Kuwait would not release the Dawa prisoners, who had been tried, convicted, and sentenced in Kuwaiti courts, and the United States supported Kuwait entirely in this position.

Phil Habib, who was roaming the corridors of State, eager, I thought, to be dispatched to Beirut to negotiate this crisis, was outspoken in his desire for a deal. "Get Israel's commitment to release the 766, then go make a deal for the TWA release," he said. Abe Sofaer supported this approach. He saw a difference between Israel's agreeing to do what it had intended to do all along and a deal in which real concessions were granted. The United States had, he pointed out, publicly condemned Israel for moving the Lebanese prisoners to Atlit as a violation of international law.

"No. No deal," I said. At the same time, I wasn't going to kid myself: anything that would produce the release of the TWA 847 hostages was going to be regarded in the media as some sort of a deal. So be it; I was proceeding on a straight track, and I would stick to it.

Ambassador Newlin reported in from Algiers: the Algerians had questions. They wanted to know the number and date of release of the detainees that Israel would set free in accordance with its judicial process. We replied that the Israelis had announced publicly that they would release thirty-one prisoners early the following week. The Algerians asked whether Israel intended to go ahead with additional releases even if the TWA 847 hostages were not freed. We replied that we did not expect Israel to make any more releases except as a result of further successful judicial appeals. And, finally, the Algerians wanted confirmation of the report that one-third of the detainees in Atlit were Palestinians, not Lebanese Shiites. (The Algerians said they could not imagine that the Shiites would knowingly seek to secure the release of Palestinians.) We replied that the Israeli Ministry of Defense had stated publicly that only 570 of the 766 were Shiites. I relayed the Algerian questions and our answers back to Israel through our channel.

I now got word from President Assad that he was working to end the crisis; he had "sent an envoy" to Beirut. That had the feel of a positive development.

On Monday, June 24, Israel released thirty-one of the Ansar prisoners from Atlit, announcing that this step had nothing to do with the hostages at Beirut International Airport. Nabih Berri announced to the press that 31 releases meant nothing; Israel would have to release all 766 detainees.

That afternoon I went to the White House Situation Room for a National Security Planning Group meeting, primarily to consider ideas that Bill Casey had proposed: shut down Beirut International Airport by jamming its communications; blockade the port of Beirut; close the Beirut-Damascus roads, etc. I welcomed the emergence of these ideas, even if most of them were virtually impossible to implement. The one workable suggestion, which I advocated, was to declare that any country that serviced an aircraft coming from or going to Beirut International Airport would lose its landing rights in the United States. The meeting was long. Nothing was decided.

I wanted to avoid a public perception that we were as stymied as in fact we were. The president canceled his planned trip to California. I had argued against such a cancellation; I did not want him to repeat Jimmy Carter's mistake of virtually making himself a prisoner in the White House. But the Reagan staff prevailed, saying the president's absence at this time would project a bad image. On June 25 we learned that Nabih Berri had gone to Damascus; perhaps the Syrians were in fact at work. The Soviets now made it known that they had weighed in with Syria to resolve the crisis.

The president was increasingly wound up about getting this hostage crisis resolved; he wanted action. He had been impressed by an article I had given him about the Iran hostage crisis that stressed that negotiations for a solution mattered less than the environment in which they were conducted: if you surround a situation with force, that can work wonders for negotiations. The president told me that the article had made the biggest impression on him of anything he had read in a long time. In response, the NSC staff produced a "time line" of steps for the United States to take, starting with the shutting down of Beirut International Airport and leading eventually to "declaring war on terrorism," specifically on any nation that used its state apparatus to support terrorism. The time line of escalation was designed to change the environment so that governments and people in the region would see and worry about the consequences to them of the hostage crisis. The list of steps would meet resolute opposition from the Department of Defense, but I welcomed the talk about possible action. That might help engender an atmosphere of impending danger for the hostage holders and their supporters, which might help break this situation open. In international crises, "logic doesn't travel," Bernie Kalb said.

"Threats do," I said, "if the threats have some credibility." While I was counseling a hard line, others were counseling a soft line. Cap Weinberger in private and George Bush in public, in Bonn, said we should simply ask Israel to release the Ansar prisoners now held in Atlit.

On June 26, the president received a message from Assad, who said he was making progress. What if the hijackers were informed that Syria would guarantee the release of the Lebanese prisoners after the TWA passengers were freed? I flashed back our answer to Assad via our embassy in Damascus:

> It has been the position of the U.S. throughout this event that the hijacking and hostage-taking is preventing the planned release by Israel of Atlit prisoners. Therefore you may inform the Syrians that the President believes that Syria may be confident in expecting the release of the Lebanese prisoners after the freeing of the passengers of TWA 847, without any linkage between the two subjects. This is the President's view only if this refers to all passengers and crew and if "Lebanese prisoners" refers to the Lebanese Shiites now held in Atlit.
>
> You should in addition urge that Syria do all it can to bring about the release of all hostages in Lebanon in addition to the hostages from TWA 847.
>
> The U.S. reaffirms its publicly stated position regarding the illegality of the transfer of prisoners from Ansar to Atlit. The U.S. will be active on this issue.

Our ambassador to Syria, Bill Eagleton, had been on his way back to the United States when the TWA hijacking took place. We had asked him to hold his travel in Madrid, but he had not returned to Syria. As a result, the American diplomat in Damascus who was now working on this issue with Assad and the Syrian government was our chargé d'affaires, April Glaspie. It was a tough assignment: she was solid and quick.

A Shift of Gears

In every crisis there comes a moment when a shift seems imminent and the mental attitudes seem to change everywhere at once. People we had not earlier heard from began to call in—from Paris, Bern, Rome, the

United Nations, Beirut, and elsewhere. Diplomatic volunteers emerged from all over the landscape, offering to get involved in "the release." It was ludicrous. Jesse Jackson was in touch with Nabih Berri, who was now proposing to various parties that all the TWA passengers would be released by the terrorists into the custody of a Western embassy in Beirut, or a third country, or to the United Nations, or some such trustee that would hold them until Israel released all the prisoners from Atlit.

Of all those who now sought to be intermediaries, the Swiss approach alone had special merit, because the Swiss themselves would have no part in becoming hostage holders. If the Swiss received the hostages, they said they would set them free at once and would guarantee that Israel would thereafter make releases from Atlit. From the U.S. point of view, that statement was too sweeping, not differentiating between the groups being detained in Atlit. I passed my thoughts back to the Swiss, adding that they should seek the release of all forty-seven Americans, including the seven who had earlier been taken hostage by terrorists in Beirut: we wanted a total of forty-seven Americans out. I said we would not give up on those seven.

Shimon Peres telephoned me from Israel. I told him of the Swiss scenario. "We shall be as forthcoming as necessary from your point of view," Peres said. "Maybe one or two gentlemen" would not be released, he said, but Israel intended to release the Shiites and maybe some beyond the category of the Shiites. Peres hoped that we would try to use this occasion to get Jews held captive in Lebanon released also. I said I would push for that. We reported all this to April Glaspie.

A flash cable came back from her: she had gone over our message with advisers to Assad. The Syrians agreed that our position was "good" and that "the end should be in sight." Unfortunately, the Syrians did not "envision" the release of the seven non–TWA 847 Americans held hostage in Beirut. A critical point in getting what appeared to be a breakthrough was the one-line cable we had sent her authorizing her to tell the Syrians that "the U.S. has no plan of action against Syria." The Syrians had evidently been highly concerned about the presence of our warships off the Lebanese coast and the growing talk in Washington of using force. The possibility of American retaliation against Syria and discussion of the time line of escalation had had an effect. The Swiss option was shelved. In this unfolding drama, Syria and Iran now came to center stage.

Within a very short time we learned that the Syrians had informed Nabih Berri that they had received the guarantees they had requested; the American hostages could be sent to Damascus; Israel would set the prisoners free from Atlit. Syria was ready to take responsibility for these undertakings and thereby resolve the crisis. Intelligence reports also revealed that the Iranian government had sent word to Hezbollah in Beirut to facilitate an end to this crisis. There were indications that Hezbollah leaders in Beirut wanted an end to the pressure they were feeling now; perhaps they, too, feared U.S. military action. We had given no guarantees at all and made no deal, but the states supporting terrorism in the region appeared to have concluded that the U.S. reaction to this event meant that the hijacking and holding of the remaining TWA hostages was no longer in their interest.

My remaining concern was that the seven American hostages being held in Beirut be included in the release of the TWA 847 captives. I instructed our people to "keep pushing" for them, but my hopes were fading. Hezbollah, Syria, and Iran may have concluded that hijacked hostages were becoming a burden, not a benefit, but the hostages previously taken seemed to be in a different category. Probably, I thought, they were being held by what had been described earlier as the "inner group" of terrorists whose attention was focused on the Dawa prisoners.

Late at night on June 27 came word that Israeli television had reported that the United States and Israel had reached an understanding that Israel would release all 735 Lebanese prisoners only after all the U.S. hostages had been released. The Israeli government quickly denied the statement, but all the parties were now setting the stage for how they would perform the final act.

For our part, we reiterated our demand for the seven other hostages and began an effort to get international agreement that the use of Beirut International Airport as a home for terrorism would not be tolerated. I knew that an international effort would not coalesce, but I was determined to push forward an understanding within the U.S. government that the next time terrorists headed toward Beirut International Airport, we would move militarily to make the airport unusable.

On Saturday morning, June 29, we got word that the hostages from TWA Flight 847 had been brought together in preparation for being moved overland in Red Cross trucks from Beirut to Damascus, where they would be handed over to our people at the American embassy. Suddenly word came that four of the TWA hostages had been kept behind, still held by Hezbollah who were said to be seeking a "nonbelligerency" guarantee from the United States.

Assad was now out on a limb; he had publicly stated that all would be freed. April Glaspie came up on the tacsat to say that this development appeared to have stung Assad: he was "frustrated, humiliated, and pulling out all the stops to get the hostage holders to release everyone." There were signs that Iran and Hezbollah had held back four hostages to stick a finger in Assad's eye; Iran and the Shiites were making a statement to us and to Assad about their role in Lebanon. Assad had ordered Syrian troops to make an all-out sweep of the Bekaa Valley in search of the seven non-TWA American hostages, who were reportedly held by Iranian-supported Hezbollah.

We'll just keep pushing, I thought. By late Saturday night the Syrians were seeking further public statements from us about American behavior toward Lebanon in the future; they also wanted the Atlit prisoners transferred to Syria rather than returned to Lebanon. In Middle East negotiations, the last moment, I knew, is almost always used to try to squeeze out the last drop. I told spokesman Bernie Kalb simply to release a restatement of our long-held policy toward Lebanon: "The United States reaffirms its longstanding support for the preservation of Lebanon, its Government, its stability, and its security, and for the mitigation of the suffering of its people."

As for the Syrian request about the Atlit detainees, we told them that was a separate matter and such proposals could be taken up "after the present situation is clarified." On Sunday morning, June 30, the Syrians told us that the problem was "solved": a Hezbollah representative had been sent from Damascus to Beirut; all the TWA hostages would be "marshaled" in a Beirut schoolyard and then travel by convoy to Damascus and taken to the airport there for evacuation.

Mindful of the massive media presence throughout this crisis, the Syrians first took the convoy to the Damascus hotel known because of its clientele as the "Sheraton-Terrorist" for a press conference. From there the hostages were driven to the airport, where they would board aircraft able to provide them with medical care. The crisis had been a massive television event. One newspaper's television critic even suggested that the terrorists had decided to close the show because they realized that "the viewing public was getting sick of it."

On Sunday night, President Reagan and Nancy came to my home for a long-planned dinner. Actually, they got there before I did, since I had been delayed by a wind-up press conference on the ending of the TWA crisis. With a mischievous smile, the president greeted me at my door with a handshake and "Welcome home." We all felt a sense of relief that the TWA 847 hostage crisis had been resolved successfully. Nancy, departing from her usual practice, had a hard drink "just to celebrate with you boys." Our elation and relief were, however, diminished by our regret that the seven other previously seized Americans still remained captive and that Robert Stethem had been murdered. We were getting the impression, however, that Iran, not Syria, was in the position, if any country was, to call the shots when it came to the remaining American hostages.

Monday around noon I took a telephone call from Shimon Peres. He told me some 300 detainees would be released from Atlit in the next 48 hours; most would be Lebanese Shiites. The process of further release proceeded for weeks and weeks, and entirely on Israel's terms. Not until September 10 were all the prisoners in Atlit released.

President Reagan sent a letter to President Assad recognizing Syria's role in ending the crisis; he also called Assad on the telephone. The conversation had been stiff and cold. President Reagan made it clear that while we appreciated Syria's help, we wanted Syria to end its support of terrorism. Assad rejected the Reagan message. No doubt Assad felt that the president did not appreciate his pivotal role in resolving the crisis. He also no doubt underestimated the strength of Ronald Reagan's concern about terrorism and the taking of Americans as hostages. Publicly, nothing was said about the sour exchanges. While the Syrian press exulted in the international praise flowing in, the leader of Syria seethed.

Looking back at the episode, I thought that the most effective tactic we used was our relative silence. The president had agreed—after unfortunate statements by Larry Speakes and others—to put the lid on comments by U.S. officials except as specifically authorized. The relative silence created a threatening aura that astounded the world's observers and the terrorists; even some of our allies were alarmed. This threatening aura served our purposes more effectively than simply moving U.S. warships to the eastern Mediterranean. Silence can instill fear.

I also reflected on the widespread readiness to take the easy way out, to make the trade the terrorists sought, and to make whatever rationalization was handy for doing so. I was attacked for my insistence on what seemed to many like a fine distinction, a distinction without a difference. But there was a big difference between what we did and an outright deal. I felt, too, that Ronald Reagan had internalized the point that a trade for American hostages puts Americans at risk all over the world. To provide terrorists a reward for release of hostages, as the president had stated publicly, endangers "people from here on out once [terrorists] find out that these tactics succeed."[4]

4. From a presidential news conference on June 18, 1985.

CHAPTER 33

Terrorism:
Attack and Counterattack

On Monday, October 7, 1985, Palestinian terrorists seized an Italian cruise ship, the *Achille Lauro*, as it lay off Alexandria, Egypt. The ship, when I got the news, was at sea "somewhere" in the eastern Mediterranean. This crisis was in stark contrast to the TWA 847 hijacking of three months earlier. The dramatic difference? There was no media coverage on the spot. In fact, no one knew where the spot was. I was called at my home in the early morning hours and consequently got to my office at 6:30 A.M. on Tuesday, October 8, 1985. A message came in from our embassy in Damascus. The Syrians said the ship's hijackers had asked to come to the Syrian port of Tartus so that the Italian and American ambassadors to Syria could negotiate with the terrorists. The Syrians would permit the ship to come to Tartus if we wanted them to do so. That, I knew, would initiate another circus of media coverage as negotiations were conducted.

At 7:10 A.M. I got Cap Weinberger on the phone to ask whether ships from the Seventh Fleet had been ordered to search for the *Achille Lauro*. No, he said, they haven't been ordered to move because we don't know the location of the cruise ship. I let that one pass and urged that he have the U.S. Navy search and pursue. "The cruise ship is faster than our ships," Cap said. "It can outrun us." I hung up. This was absurd: a cruise ship can't outrun a U.S. Navy destroyer! Besides, we have airplanes, radar, many ships—we shouldn't have to outrun the cruise ship to locate it!

I had the same feeling I had when the TWA 847 hijacking crisis began: no one was taking charge of our response. So I appointed myself. I felt strongly that we had to find the ship and keep it away from Syrian waters. I did not want another media circus to complicate our problems as it had in Beirut. The *Achille Lauro* had over 400 passengers aboard, about 19 of them Americans. As usual, the hijackers demanded the release of terrorists, this time fifty convicted Palestinian terrorists, members of the Palestinian Liberation Front, held in prison in Israel. I telephoned Cap again to tell him that I wanted to keep the ship "in Egypt's orbit"; I did not want the ship to be in the hands of Hafez Assad. We were close to the Egyptians; they would be easier to work with. Cap said that the ship was twenty-five to thirty nautical miles off Port Said at the head of the Suez Canal. Egyptian helicopters were observing it. A U.S. Navy destroyer in port in Haifa could be sent to interdict the *Achille Lauro*, Cap said. I briefed Bud McFarlane on all this, and he agreed with the way I proposed to handle the situation.

From this point on, the crisis proceeded on an almost split-second time-table. Our check with the Italians indicated that they had no plan but, on a contingency basis, they had sent a commando team to Akrotiri, a British Royal Air Force base on Cyprus.

I telephoned Ambassador Nick Veliotes in Cairo to tell him that we wanted to make the handling of this problem a cooperative American-Egyptian effort and to ask the Egyptians to try to keep the *Achille Lauro* in Egyptian waters. Nick was totally in the dark, and he said the Egyptians were, too. Cap's intelligence was apparently far behind the reality: the ship had not been seen for twelve hours, Nick reported, and the Egyptians were not monitoring it. At 8:30 A.M., word came from the Egyptian defense minister that the ship was "confirmed" to be about fifteen miles off Tartus, Syria.

Dick Murphy, assistant secretary of state for Near Eastern Affairs, argued that we should want the ship to enter a Syrian port. Legally, the receiving nation—Syria—would be responsible for the event. The Syrians would be quick and decisive, Murphy thought: they would storm the ship, and the crisis would soon be at an end. If the ship put in at the port of Beirut, it would be another TWA 847 scene, but not if it went to Tartus, Dick believed. I agreed on the importance of keeping the ship out of Beirut, but I didn't agree with relying on Syria. I told Murphy to contact the Syrians immediately, tell them what we knew, and ask them not to allow the ship into a Syrian harbor.

I was at the White House at 9:30 A.M. on Tuesday, October 8, for the official arrival of Singapore's Prime Minister Lee Kuan Yew and his meeting with President Reagan. In the prebrief for the meeting I pushed for a quick presidential decision to order U.S. forces to take action to intercept the ship. The terrorists had already killed someone, we believed, and had to be stopped. The president was not ready to make such a decision. Bud McFarlane scheduled a National Security Planning Group meeting for 1:00 P.M., after the president's meeting with Lee was over, at which options could be put before the president. I was upset: we should not waste three hours before deciding. Once again the Defense Department seemed to resist any notion that our armed forces take action. Meanwhile, the "intelligence community" was spreading confusion with a barrage of inconsistent assertions about the ship's location. By noon, all our sources agreed that the *Achille Lauro* was offshore of Tartus and that Syria had refused to let the ship come into port. After that, the Syrians said, the ship had broken radio contact and was heading west. I talked to Admiral Bill Crowe, chairman of the Joint Chiefs, who said he would present an operational plan for the president's consideration at the 1:00 P.M. NSPG. I told him that the navy should keep the ship away from the port of Beirut and prepare a SEAL team to board it at sea. We had word from the Jordanians that Abu Abbas, a member of the PLO executive council and part of a pro-Arafat faction, was the leader of the terrorists aboard the ship, although he himself had remained onshore in Egypt.

Because of Prime Minister Lee's visit, I was not able to attend the National Security Planning Group meeting, so I sent Under Secretary of State Mike Armacost in my place. At midafternoon, Armacost reported that the group had agreed to "a disposition track," which seemed to mean surveillance of the ship from "over the horizon," and coordination by the Joint Chiefs with British and Italian commando forces at the Royal Air Force base at Akrotiri. The president would make his decision on any use of force on Wednesday morning, Mike said.

The early morning television news on Wednesday did not make the *Achille Lauro* a big story: there was no "footage." Without a media presence on the scene, there was far less confusion and less amplification of the terrorist "demands" than in the TWA hijacking. State's Near East bureau reported at 7:30 A.M. that the ship was now "in the Egyptian orbit," at anchor twenty miles off Port Said. The information came from the Israelis.

Incredibly, the Defense Department had never located the ship during its odyssey to the eastern Mediterranean and back. At 8:00 A.M., the BBC international service reported that the ship's captain had said on his ship-to-shore radio that everyone was in good shape on the ship and that the hijackers wanted a boat so they could come ashore. Our embassy in Cairo, now in the thick of it, within minutes reported the hijackers were proposing a deal to Egypt. They would surrender if they would not be extradited or prosecuted, and if they would be released into the custody of the PLO. The Egyptians, Italians, and British all agreed, and Nick Veliotes recommended that we also agree. "No. Terrorists should not go free," I replied. But I knew that the Egyptians would probably go ahead anyway.

The president decided that morning, "It is Egypt's call"; the government of Egypt had jurisdiction over this matter. If any American citizen was harmed, President Reagan said, we would expect Egypt to arrest and prosecute the terrorists responsible. And the United States would pursue, through international legal processes, all the hijackers—whether Americans had been harmed or not. We should tell the Egyptians, however, the president said, that the United States does not understand the logic of allowing the perpetrators of violence and terrorism to get away. I did not like this stance. We seemed to be on both sides of the issue. I wanted the Egyptians to take the hijackers into custody. Mike Armacost telephoned Clair George at the CIA and said, "Follow those guys." ABC TV's Peter Jennings wanted a two-minute live interview from my office for his evening newscast. The terrorists had committed a crime, I said, and they should be made to answer for it. They should not be allowed safe conduct to another country. The BBC minutes later reported Egyptian Foreign Minister Esmat Abdel Meguid's statement that the terrorists *had* been promised safe conduct out of Egypt. The deal had been cut. The ship came in to port.

Benjamin Netanyahu telephoned us at State to say that the Israelis believed this to be a PLO ploy: Abu Abbas had masterminded the hijacking, and now the PLO in Tunis sought credit for negotiating an end to it. The media were now part of the action, and their reports suggested the Israelis had a point. Ted Koppel interviewed Yasser Arafat, who, basking in the media limelight, assured Koppel that if Italy, where government officials were friendly with the PLO, requested extradition, Arafat would cooperate.

By this time, Nick Veliotes had gone aboard the *Achille Lauro* in Port Said harbor. Nick reported that Leon Klinghoffer, an American tourist who was handicapped, had been shot by the terrorists and thrown, in his wheelchair, into the sea off Tartus. The Palestinians had threatened to kill other passengers, but the ship's captain had dissuaded them.

The Israeli intelligence analysis expanded on Netanyahu's thesis. The *Achille Lauro* had been intended originally only as transportation for the terrorists. Their target was the ship's next port of call, Ashdod, Israel, where they would slip off the ship and try to terrorize Israeli citizens. Apparently fearing exposure after a ship steward found them in their cabin cleaning weapons, they commandeered the ship. The PLO instructed them to return to Port Said from off Tartus. Then the PLO contrived to appear as "negotiating" an end to the crisis. Arafat wanted a medal for helping to put out a fire he had set.

With the news of the murder of Leon Klinghoffer, I sent a flash cable instructing our embassy in Cairo to press Egypt to arrest and prosecute the terrorists, and since the president was in Chicago on October 10 on a speaking engagement, I tried to reach President Mubarak on the phone. I got Foreign Minister Meguid at 1:20 P.M., told him about Klinghoffer's murder, and urged Egypt to go after the terrorists. The Egyptians felt that they had made their deal and their internal political situation left them no choice but to turn the hijackers over to the PLO. I had a strong sense from the tone of our conversation, however, that Meguid wanted us to take some action. Attorney General Ed Meese agreed to press for an indictment so that we could demand extradition of the terrorists from Egypt.

Before we were able to get this process under way, we discovered that the Egyptians were driving the terrorists to the airport while claiming that the terrorists had left Egypt before they had news of the murder. The Egyptians were letting the murderers go while holding the *Achille Lauro* passengers for interrogation! I was furious.

We urged the Tunisians not to let the aircraft carrying Abu Abbas and the *Achille Lauro* hijackers land. Mike Armacost and Mort Abramowitz, the head of State's intelligence bureau, were working in close coordination with the NSC staff, the CIA, and the Pentagon to keep the plane out of Tunis. At one point, Mort said, "Well, an aircraft can be intercepted." We had thought the same thing when TWA Flight 847 was moving back and forth across the Mediterranean but could not get an effort coordinated before the plane was on the ground at Beirut International Airport. This time we had a chance to carry through.

President Reagan was alerted, and he authorized a quick effort to see what might be feasible. On the NSC staff, Lieutenant Colonel Oliver North coordinated actions among the White House, the Pentagon, and the CIA.

At 5:30 P.M., word came that an Egypt Air 737 charter (what amounted to a getaway plane) was in the air carrying the hijackers to Tunis. From *Air Force One*, on which President Reagan was traveling back to Washington, he authorized action. F-14 Tomcats off our U.S. Navy carrier *Saratoga* were ordered to divert the Egyptian charter plane to Sigonella, a NATO base in Sicily. The Egyptian pilot's requests for permission to land at Athens and Tunis airports were denied. Our F-14s were instructed *not* to fire at the Egyptian aircraft or to try to shoot it down. They were to use whatever other means of persuasion they could, however, and the Egyptian pilot did not know he was not in danger. By 5:45 we had "acquired" the Egyptian plane. Our pilots encountered no resistance at all. The F-14s simply instructed the Egyptian pilot to follow them to Sigonella, and he did so. I instructed Nick Veliotes to say to Egyptian Defense Minister Abu Ghazala, "Let us take this problem off your hands."

Nick did and reported back that Abu Ghazala was "thunderstruck" to learn we had diverted the plane: it was a great idea, Abu Ghazala thought, but he wanted Egypt to get credit for taking Abu Abbas to Sigonella.

At 6:30 P.M., I called McFarlane's deputy, Admiral John Poindexter, who was on duty at the NSC staff in Washington while Bud was traveling with the president. With the Egyptian airplane only minutes out of Sigonella, we had to get a U.S. plane revved up and ready to take the terrorists on board and then on their way to the United States. They were guilty of a felony under U.S. law, and we could apprehend them legally, because the aircraft was properly viewed as noncivilian in its use as a getaway vehicle. "Quickly" was my urging.

"Cap is against it," Poindexter replied. "He's afraid of trouble with the

Italians." Cap was in Canada and could make his views known only on the telephone. At this point, State, Justice, the NSC staff, and the president were all on the same wavelength.

The Italians refused to let the plane land at Sigonella and began scrambling F-104s of the Italian air force to maneuver our F-14 Tomcats off. At 6:40 P.M., President Reagan, Cap, and I were on a conference call. I argued as forcefully as I could for "just doing it": landing at Sigonella and moving Abu Abbas and the other terrorists to a U.S. aircraft for immediate takeoff.

Exuberant, Ronald Reagan exclaimed, "Good enough!" and ordered us to go ahead. Cap was still opposed, but the president told him to telephone the Italian defense minister and have Chairman of the Joint Chiefs Bill Crowe telephone his Italian counterpart to ask each of them to let the plane land at Sigonella. Cap found Defense Minister Giovanni Spadolini furious over our alleged violation of international law and our violation of Italian sovereignty: Spadolini was going to take it up immediately with President Bettino Craxi. Bill Crowe reported that his counterpart at the head of the Italian military was quite calm: no problem with him. President Reagan weighed in with President Craxi, who gave permission to land.

By 7:15 P.M., the Egyptian 737 was on the ground at Sigonella, and a U.S. military airplane was available there to take the terrorists on board. Six Palestinians were on the Egyptian plane: four were the hijackers of the *Achille Lauro*, and two were the Palestinians to whom the Egyptians had turned over the hijackers; one of the latter was Abu Abbas. At 8:45, I telephoned Italian Foreign Minister Giulio Andreotti.

As I was calling, Mike Armacost rushed in. "There's a stalemate on the ground at Sigonella," he said. U.S. forces had surrounded the Egyptian aircraft, but far larger numbers of Italian forces surrounded us! NATO allies were confronting each other in an armed face-off. I told Andreotti that the United States was in the process of transferring the Palestinians from one aircraft to another to bring them to the United States to stand trial.

"I absolutely cannot give authorization to that," Andreotti told me. "They should stand trial in Italy." As I was talking to Andreotti, Abe Sofaer, State's legal adviser, was on the other phone in my office talking to Admiral Poindexter. Sofaer was offering Poindexter legal advice as Poindexter relayed reports from our military at Sigonella. We had no legal right, Sofaer said, to use the base for other than NATO activities. We had to persuade the Italians or give in to their plan.

"An American has been murdered, and trial here is appropriate," I said to Andreotti. He absolutely would not budge. That was it. I said thank you, and we hung up.

It was over. I called President Reagan. We had done a great piece of work, I said, and almost carried it off. President Reagan called President

Craxi, but the Italian decision was firm. At least the terrorists were in Italian hands, and the Italians were on the spot to deal with them through their legal system.

Fallout

At that moment, however, I also worried: would the fallout from this event damage our relations with Egypt? Would our use of the base at Sigonella be jeopardized? And with due respect for the Italian judiciary system, which had handed out some stiff sentences to terrorists, I felt that Abu Abbas would eventually go free to strike terror again.

Netanyahu called in from New York. "The U.S. just did something magnificent," he said. "So now, guess what? There's a resolution up to-morrow in the General Assembly to invite Arafat to the UN."

"A hero's welcome? What a farce!" I said when told of this latest news.

On October 11, the Italian government charged the four terrorists who had been on the *Achille Lauro* with murder and let the other two, including the ringmaster and known terrorist, Abu Abbas, go free. Our lawyers had stayed up all night to file a request for his provisional arrest under our extradition treaty with Italy, but the request was denied. Abbas was later tried "in absentia" in Italy and found guilty of hijacking. They had already set him free, and he would soon be visibly involved again in PLO affairs. I could only conclude that the Italians were trying to buy immunity from the PLO. On October 12, Egyptian President Mubarak accused the United States of "an act of piracy" for forcing the Egyptian aircraft to Sigonella. On October 16, a body found on the Syrian coast was identified as that of Leon Klinghoffer. The same day, the Italian coalition government collapsed over the Sigonella affair, but it "revived" itself by the end of the month. Our relations with Italy and Egypt settled down. Importantly, we had acted, the depth of our concern about terrorism had been vividly emphasized, and four terrorists were in jail.

I was not surprised that Italy had released Abu Abbas and his cohort or that Yugoslavia, where he had gone originally, had turned down our request to detain him. But I was disappointed and angry. Both countries had signed treaties requiring them to extradite or prosecute terrorists, and Italy had an extradition treaty with the United States. Particularly astonishing to me was an argument put forth that those who had seized the *Achille Lauro* and had killed Leon Klinghoffer were not "pirates" because they had acted for "political" rather than "economic" motives. Such an argument was a license for terrorism.

"How can this happen? What's wrong with the law?" I later asked Abe Sofaer. "What do all those treaties mean if they are to be systematically disregarded?" Abe did not try to defend what had happened. He pointed out that this time, most of those responsible for the hijacking and murder had been caught. And in 1986, they were tried and sentenced to substantial terms. "That's better than the usual result," he said. And Italy and Egypt had agreed to work on a Maritime Terrorism Convention to plug the loopholes that some believed existed in the definition of piracy. But Abe fully agreed with me that plenty was wrong with the law and that new conventions were not enough to remedy the situation.

Sofaer later wrote a piece for *Foreign Affairs* (Summer 1986): "Terrorism and the Law," which summed up what was wrong with international law and how recent changes in legal doctrine had been advanced to support and justify terrorism. I wanted Abe to pursue this issue forcefully. And he did. By the time we were through, we had had a significant impact on the legal issues that confronted us as we confronted terrorism.

On December 17, 1985, on a swing through Eastern Europe following the annual NATO foreign ministers' meeting, I had held a joint press conference in Belgrade, Yugoslavia, with Foreign Minister Raif Dizdarevic. In reply to a question, Dizdarevic said that although Yugoslavia condemned terrorism, "one must also view the causes that lead to it, because we believe that by the elimination of causes of terrorism, the phenomenon itself can be controlled and eliminated." I landed on him strongly.

Nothing was more odious or dangerous, in my view, than the line of argument that "root causes" justify and legitimize terrorist acts. *New York Times* diplomatic correspondent Bernard Gwertzman reported on December 18: "The Secretary, his voice rising in intensity and his face turning red, said: 'Hijacking the Italian ship, murdering an American, torturing and holding a whole bunch of other Americans is not justified by any cause that I know of.' Pounding the table with his fist, he added: 'It is wrong! And the international community must step up to this problem, and deal with it, unequivocally, firmly, definitively.' After his outburst, Mr. Shultz turned to Mr. Dizdarevic and said quietly, 'You probably feel the same way.' "

Actually, I was even more angry about Iraq, with whom we had reestablished diplomatic relations earlier in 1985 on assurances of an end to its connections with terrorist groups. Abu Abbas had flown from Italy to Yugoslavia and then, according to our unconfirmed information, on to Iraq. "With respect to Yugoslavia, he [Abbas] passed through," I said in a press conference on my plane. "With respect to Iraq, he seems to have been welcomed there. That is different and it constitutes more of a problem."

The fight against terrorism was frustrating. Many people fell for the "root causes" argument; many governments allowed a terrorist presence on their soil on the understanding that their nationals would not be attacked; many states used terrorists actively. But at least the United States had taken action against the *Achille Lauro* terrorists and helped put four of them in jail, even though the mastermind got away. Terrorists and their sponsor states were now on notice that the United States would and could take action and that the rule of law could apply to them.

Qaddafi and Terrorism

Back in February 1983, I had appeared on "This Week with David Brinkley" after a publicized incident involving the deployment of U.S. air warning (AWACs) planes to Egypt and the subsequent cancellation by Libyan strongman Colonel Muammar Qaddafi of a Libyan action planned against Sudan. "Qaddafi is back in his box where he belongs," I said. He didn't stay there. Fifteen Libyan-sponsored terrorist efforts were identified by State's counterterrorism unit in 1984. Some failed, such as an attempt to assassinate Egypt's president, Hosni Mubarak. Some caused trouble, such as the laying of mines in the Red Sea. Some ended violently, such as the Libyan hijacking of an Egyptian airplane in November 1985 in which sixty people died.

Then, in December 1985, twenty people, including five Americans, were killed by simultaneous terrorist attacks at El Al ticket counters in the Rome and Vienna airports. All were civilians, and the Americans included a young girl, whose blood-splattered body was shown on TV around the world. Qaddafi hailed these killings in airports as "heroic." The Palestinians who carried out the attacks were carrying Tunisian passports that records showed had been confiscated by Libya. In response to these attacks, on January 7, 1986, the United States severed all economic ties with Libya. I had pressed for retaliatory action against Libyan military targets, but Cap Weinberger and the Joint Chiefs were opposed.

An important principle was at stake. We had to make clear that Libya could not avoid responsibility for attacking American civilians and others by using Palestinian terrorists to do the job. Abe Sofaer noted, however, that as sound as this principle seemed, international lawyers would argue these murders were not "attacks" on the territory of the United States that enabled us to engage in self-defense under the UN Charter. I was skeptical of the need to announce so obvious a policy, and we had warned Libya on prior occasions against such use of terrorists. The president decided to wait, however, and he issued a clear warning on January 7, 1986: if Libya used terrorists to attack our citizens abroad, we would treat that as equivalent to an attack by regular Libyan forces warranting necessary and proportionate acts of self-defense.

On January 15, 1986, I addressed the National Defense University on the subject of low-intensity warfare. I wanted to make clear my belief that the law allowed, as common sense required, necessary and proportional responses to state-sponsored terrorist acts outside a nation's territory. If nothing else worked, the use of force was necessary, or the UN Charter was nothing more than a suicide pact. "There should be no confusion about the status of nations that sponsor terrorism against Americans and American property. There is substantial legal authority for the view that a state which supports terrorist or subversive attacks against another state, or which supports or encourages terrorist planning and other activities within its own territory, is responsible for such attacks. Such conduct can amount to an ongoing armed aggression against the other state under international law." Later, Margaret Thatcher issued a blast at what I had said.

Free-Lance Diplomacy

Our deliberations at the State Department were conducted against a cacophony of banging, sawing, and general thumping. The reconstruction of the seventh floor that I had authorized months ago was now creating a "treaty room" in the corridor just outside my new office. The noise whenever we met approached the deafening. One morning, Charlie Wick paused in his presentation and asked, "What time does this conference room land at La Guardia?"

At this time the behavior of William Wilson, our ambassador to the Vatican and a close personal friend of the president's, came to the fore. Qaddafi, in a media interview on January 5, 1986, said he had met "in the past few days" with an American diplomat. Mike Armacost reported to me that back in November 1985, Wilson "evaded his security people, went to the airport, and flew south under deception." Wilson's move had been reported by the regional security officer in Rome, but his report had been destroyed. I told Armacost to investigate how the report on Wilson had been destroyed. I told Poindexter what I had heard about Wilson. I knew that only the president could make the decision, but, I said, Wilson had to go, for the president's sake as well as to protect the integrity of our policy. Poindexter responded that Wilson had admitted visiting Qaddafi. Wilson claimed that he had done so on the authority of Bill Clark, who, when NSC adviser, had authorized Wilson to maintain continued contacts with Qaddafi. Poindexter and I agreed that from this point on Wilson was *not* authorized to contact the Libyans in any fashion and that we would have to keep a close check on his behavior.

The extent of William Wilson's maneuvering with Libya continued to emerge. I learned that someone in the White House in late 1985 had sent a back-channel message to Italian Foreign Minister Andreotti asking Andreotti to tell Qaddafi not to attach too much importance to President Reagan's public statements accusing Libya of being a center of global terrorism. A second "White House" message had asked Andreotti to convey to Qaddafi that the United States would not be opposed to "détente" with Libya. Andreotti had been reluctant to approach Qaddafi with these messages. A third request then followed, reportedly from President Reagan himself, asking Andreotti to request that Qaddafi receive an American emissary. This apparently was what led up to Wilson's visit to Qaddafi, which neither Max Rabb, our ambassador in Rome, nor I was aware of. Such a trip was unauthorized and went against administration policy. Wilson, I was told, "was received by [Libyan Foreign Secretary] Turayki, then at length by Colonel Qaddafi."

Wilson was pulling strings inside the White House, but whose strings I did not know. Was it even possible, I wondered, that Wilson had misled the president into asking the Italians to set up a meeting for him in Tripoli? I was certain that Ronald Reagan was not going soft on terrorism or on Colonel Qaddafi.

Reports about Wilson kept coming. Just as we were sending messages and people—such as Under Secretary of State Ed Derwinski—to the allies to seek cooperation in the effort to stop Qaddafi's terrorist actions, we were learning that some of our allies, through their intelligence services, were aware that Wilson had secretly met with Qaddafi.

On Thursday, February 6, I asked Wilson to come to my office and confronted him with the evidence I had on his trip to Libya and meeting with Qaddafi. Wilson said that he had been authorized by Bill Clark, when Clark was NSC adviser, to be in contact with the Libyan leader and he assumed that that permission was still in effect. He said that he had talked to Bud McFarlane about it. I said that whatever he had been up to with Libya, it was now "at an end." His trip was going to leak, and I would say that what Wilson had done was without authorization.[1]

Pressure on Qaddafi

On March 6, 1986, Vice President Bush issued the report of a task force on terrorism, which he chaired. "We should reiterate the willingness of our Administration to retaliate and retaliate swiftly when we feel we can punish those who were directly responsible," Bush said in a press conference that day.

---

1. The story of Wilson's visit to Libya did surface in mid-March, and was reported by Leslie Gelb in the *New York Times* on March 23, 1986. Both Clark and McFarlane denied authorizing Wilson to be in contact with Qaddafi. In mid-June, Qaddafi described his conversation with "a good man who supports the Arab cause." According to Qaddafi, as reported in the *New York Times* on June 14, 1986, Wilson had said to him, "In fact the problem between you and us is not concerned with the Gulf of Sidra or the Palestine issue. We know that the Gulf of Sidra is a Libyan gulf." I never saw a report from Wilson on the content of his talk with Qaddafi.

On March 24, during a U.S. naval exercise held in the Gulf of Sidra, north of the coast of Libya, U.S. aircraft were fired on by Libyan SA-5 missiles. The United States had a long-running dispute with Qaddafi over the Gulf of Sidra, the deep bay that shapes in a concave form Libya's Mediterranean coastline. Qaddafi drew a line across the bay, east to west, from headland to headland, and called it "Libyan waters." This was a flagrant violation of international law and of freedom of navigation on the high seas. Qaddafi was a frightening figure to many governments in the region; so it was left to the U.S. Navy to deal with his unilateral claim to this part of the Mediterranean Sea. This our navy did by periodically notifying all concerned that our ships would, at a specified time, transit through the waters wrongfully claimed by Qaddafi. As Qaddafi's ambitions mounted and his state-supported terrorism spread, he grew bolder in ordering his forces to respond to our naval transits.

We set such a naval exercise for late March 1986, and we fully expected Qaddafi's air force and navy to respond aggressively. Some press accounts accused the administration of deliberately provoking Qaddafi by our movement into the Gulf of Sidra, but that was not the case. The freedom of the seas is crucial to America and to all other maritime nations, and such challenges are necessary on an almost regular basis; without them, government after government around the world would slowly encroach outward until ships at sea would be intolerably restricted whenever near a coastline. (In early March, our navy would make a similar challenge into the Black Sea waters wrongfully claimed by the Soviets: another instance of our normal challenge program.)

As we planned for the contingency that Libya would attack our ships and planes, I favored a U.S. response that would hit Libyan military installations on shore. The Defense Department opposed this. If Qaddafi's forces threatened ours during the Gulf of Sidra exercise, Cap wanted to reply "tit for tat" and hold it to that. If a plane was fired at, it could fire back. Cap won the debate.

Under the prevailing rules of engagement, when Libya on March 24 launched two Soviet-made SA-5 missiles against our carrier-based aircraft, our pilots were allowed to fire back: hostile targets had displayed an "intent" to attack us. I regarded these rules of engagement as disappointing, but Cap had prevailed. As this exercise was taking place, I was in Ankara, Turkey, on a long-delayed visit to our two quarreling NATO allies, Greece and Turkey. I discovered our pilots actually had *not* been authorized to fire back as I had assumed they would be. Instead, I learned that a National Security Planning Group "task force" had been convened back in Washington to discuss possible U.S. responses. This was preposterous. "We need action, not another damn meeting," I said. Our planning had been that we *would* retaliate when fired upon. If an NSPG was being convened now, that could mean only that, with me out of town, Weinberger was seeking a way *not* to retaliate.

As further reports came in, I learned that Libyan MIG-25s had been ordered to fire at our aircraft if they could "lock on" to us as their target. They had tried and failed. Another missile launch at us was detected at 0600 Greenwich mean time on March 24. The National Security Planning Group meeting was canceled. Now we did strike back. About time, I thought. Aircraft from the carrier *Yorktown* hit a Libyan patrol boat operating outside of Qaddafi's Gulf of Sidra line. A U.S. Navy A-7 fired air-to-surface missiles at an SA-5 base at Sirte, Libya, and knocked out the radars there. I was told that Soviet advisers were stationed at Sirte. When the radars came back into operation, we hit them again.

By Tuesday, March 25, I learned that a second and third Libyan patrol boat had been sunk and we had conducted a second strike at a Libyan surface-to-air missile launching site. Representative Dante Fascell was saying that the administration was not in compliance with the War Powers Act. Don't fire back unless Congress says you can—another formula for paralysis. And King Fahd was expressing worries about Vice President Bush's upcoming visit to Saudi Arabia; demonstrations might occur. "This is not to say the vice president is not welcome," the Saudis assured us, but they were worried that this confrontation was giving Qaddafi more importance than he deserved. I did not agree.

I knew that the reports of military action could not be considered accurate: the first intelligence or military reports almost never are. Nonetheless, at last we had acted. The American public's response seemed to be positive. Larry Speakes announced to the press the names of those who had been with the president in the Oval Office when he made the decision on March 24. No one from the State Department was mentioned. Pettiness about "principals only" overcame the common sense of having State's point of view represented. While I was abroad, John Whitehead and Mike Armacost had urged that Congress be kept informed, but their counsel had been ignored and neither was invited to the decision meeting. Complaints were now flowing in from Congress, and the State Department was told to take on the job of damage control.

Still on March 25, Libya further escalated the threat level. The Italian ambassador in Tripoli was summoned by the Libyans and told that bases on Italian territory would be subject to Libyan military retaliation in the event that "American aggression against Libya escalated." Italy informed NATO of this threat. We learned later that Qaddafi, on the same day, sent a message to Libyan people's bureaus, his term for their embassies, in East Berlin, Paris, Rome, Madrid, and other European capitals, to plan terrorist attacks against American targets. In the Gulf of Sidra, our naval exercises proceeded with no further Libyan military challenge.

On March 27, Libya summoned all foreign ambassadors in Tripoli to inform them that a "state of war" now existed with the United States and that Libya considered all American installations under the jurisdiction of NATO to be targets. In Libya, there was joyous celebrating as it was reported, falsely, that three American aircraft had been shot down.

The Saudis informed us that King Fahd had contacted Qaddafi to urge him to refrain from further military actions. King Fahd found Qaddafi "furious, disoriented, incomprehensible." The Soviets called for a session of the UN Security Council and produced a fiercely anti-American draft resolution. And the Soviets, in response to the U.S. air strike against Libya, "postponed," as inappropriate under the circumstances, Foreign Minister Shevardnadze's scheduled trip to Washington that had been planned as a follow-up to the discussions at the Geneva summit meeting. But underneath the public statements of concern, complaint, or outright condemnation of what we had done, we heard governments of the region telling us, in effect, sotto voce: we hope that, having paid the political price, you will go on to finish the job against Qaddafi. Even the Soviets, I felt from subsequent discussions, were embarrassed by the behavior of Qaddafi, whose arms and military training they supplied.

Prime Minister Craxi of Italy told close associates that he hoped the United States would continue on, take out Libya's military infrastructure, and bring about Qaddafi's downfall. Of course, Craxi indicated, public opinion in Italy meant that he could not openly support such an effort; indeed, he would have to oppose it. Some Italian officials did not support our effort at all, as I discovered when I went on to Rome. In my meeting with President Francesco Cossiga, he quoted approvingly Mikhail Gorbachev's statement that "Qaddafi is a fact." Live with it was his message.

I lit into him. The United States, I said, was not going to acquiesce in what appeared to be a new principle of international relations: that evil wrongdoers should not be confronted. Foreign Minister Andreotti had nothing good to say about Qaddafi, but he was unhelpful in a different way: he called for the International Court of Justice to take up the question of whether the Gulf of Sidra was international or Libyan waters.

Egyptian Foreign Minister Meguid was also in Rome. On the evening of March 28 we met in the study at the Villa Taverna, the American ambassador's residence. To the Egyptians, Qaddafi was a curse. "I hope your blow to Qaddafi will temper his behavior," Meguid told me.

Our naval exercise in the Gulf of Sidra had been scheduled to continue until April 2, but suddenly it was over. At dinner in Rome I talked with the chief of naval operations, Admiral James Watkins, who had come out to the Mediterranean area. Once our forces had engaged Libya's and put them down, Cap Weinberger had called off the balance of the exercise. Watkins was unhappy; if we had gone on to "clobber" Qaddafi, he said, everyone would have cheered.

On Sunday, March 30, I was over the Atlantic on my way back to Washington. A wire-service report was handed to me. Qaddafi had held a mass rally in Tripoli. At the end of his oration, an ox with the image of Ronald Reagan on its side was slaughtered.

On April 2, a bomb placed by a terrorist under a seat on TWA Flight 840 en route from Rome to Athens exploded, blowing four Americans, including a nine-month-old baby, out through the fuselage. It was not, we quickly determined, a Qaddafi-directed operation. But CIA director Bill Casey called me on the secure phone to say that our intelligence system was picking up indications of Libyans targeting U.S. diplomatic missions and other facilities used by Americans in Europe and elsewhere. On Saturday, April 5, as I awoke, reports were coming in that a bomb had gone off in a discotheque called La Belle in West Berlin. Two people were killed and 155 were wounded, including 50 to 60 Americans. Intelligence reports made the connection to Libya unmistakable. We were "reading their mail": we had intercepted a Libyan communication from East Berlin saying that their operation had been carried out successfully "without leaving clues."

We had two carrier battle groups in the Mediterranean: the *America*, at Livorno, and the *Coral Sea*, at Málaga. I called NSC adviser John Poindexter. "The president will want to do something—Tuesday or Wednesday night," he said.

"The sooner the better. I'm all for it," I replied. I said it was important not to go into a big, visible meeting this time. We had a "smoking gun." I wanted to inform European heads of government so that they, too, would know about the clear link to Qaddafi. The intelligence we had on the terrorists was of the sort that usually would not be released, for the very fact that we possessed such knowledge would indicate how we got it and thereby "compromise" and make ineffective the use of that method in the future. But Bill Casey said he thought releasing the intelligence "should be possible given the circumstances."

On Monday, April 7, I met with the president, Casey, Poindexter, Deputy Secretary of Defense Will Taft (representing Cap Weinberger), and General John Wickham (representinging the Joint Chiefs) at the White House. We discussed potential targets: air and naval bases; one terrorist training camp, Sidi Bilal; three infrastructure targets; Qaddafi's desert camp, an intelligence center that we knew was a command post, and Qaddafi's residence. I argued against hitting Qaddafi's residence. We wouldn't get him, and, I thought, it would be seen as an attempt by us to kill him that failed. We decided to approach Britain and France to permit F-111 flights from a British base with overflights across France. We also would consult Italy, Egypt, Algeria, and Tunisia.

I noted that the Joint Chiefs and Will Taft, Weinberger's deputy, had now dropped the Pentagon's usual insistence that no American military action could be taken until we had confirmed that public opinion fully supported it before the fact. Cap was on an extended trip in Asia, but I heard that he was on board this time. Mike Armacost remarked that he, too, would be traveling when our proposed attack was to occur. "I'll be in Pakistan this weekend for the riots," he said with a sardonic smile.

Ambassador Dobrynin was back from Moscow and had had breakfast with me that morning. I told Dobrynin about Qaddafi's direct involvement with the La Belle disco bombing (without disclosing why we were so sure) and about Qaddafi's other terrorist operations against us and others. Dobrynin made no comment. As we came down from breakfast in the elevator, the deputy of our Near East bureau, Arnie Raphel, said, "So we can check off the box marked 'consult with the Soviets.' " I wasn't just getting my ticket punched. It was important to have informed the Soviets, an uneasy supporter of Libya, of our strong objections to Libya's actions.

That afternoon, President Reagan went to Baltimore to the opening game of the baseball season. The president sat in the Orioles' dugout. The catcher, Rick Dempsey, came over and sat down next to him and started telling him how to take care of Qaddafi. The press was speculating that something was up: they had picked up on the fact that State and Defense were no longer split on retaliation. On Wednesday morning, April 9, I met with the president; he listened to advice from me and others, particularly the military leaders who would carry out the operation. He had chosen the potential targets: (1) Tripoli air base, Tarabulus naval base, Benghazi naval base, Benina air base; (2) a terrorist training camp at Sidi Bilal; (3) Qaddafi's intelligence headquarters, his desert encampment, and his bunker, residence, and guard barracks.[2] We had considered much more devastating attacks, for instance, on Libya's oil installations, but rejected those options as disproportionate.

Bill Crowe said that to prepare these strikes, he would need until Monday or Tuesday. The president sent a "direct" message to Margaret Thatcher requesting permission to stage USAF F-111s out of Britain. He also, on the advice of the intelligence people, decided not to provide our allies with details of how and what we knew about the Libyan terrorists. He decided to move the carrier *Enterprise* from the Indian Ocean to the Mediterranean. This meant asking Egypt to allow a nuclear-powered warship to transit the Suez Canal, something they had never agreed to before. From American diplomatic posts in every part of the world came reports of ominous surveillance of our people by Libyan agents. We also learned that the French had narrowly prevented a massacre by Libyan operatives of civilians outside our embassy in Paris.

Thursday morning's television news reported that "intense preparation"

2. The president also approved additional, subsidiary targets.

was under way for retaliation and noted that the president did not deny to the press that he had already ordered military action. "If and when we could specifically identify someone responsible for one of these acts, we would respond," President Reagan said.

Prime Minister Thatcher said yes to our request for use of U.S. F-111s from U.S. bases in Britain, but she made it clear that we needed to make public our evidence against Qaddafi, that we should limit the targets to those with clear terrorist connections, and that our retaliation should be "proportionate." She now agreed with us that such attacks justified resort to self-defense. I felt that despite intelligence community concerns, we would have to make public what we knew about the Libyan involvement in the La Belle bombing. I went over our target plans with British Ambassador Oliver Wright.

President Mitterrand of France was equivocating about granting overflight rights; he wanted us to send our multilingual roving ambassador, Dick Walters, to Paris to talk about the operation. Mitterrand liked him. Walters left for Paris. We were now briefing Congress in general terms. I worried. We had briefed allied heads of government in detail but not Congress; we were afraid of leaks. Many members of Congress seemed constantly to oppose any use of any attribute of American power—and a leak about this operation would have forced us to postpone or cancel it. And there were War Powers Act problems. Dante Fascell, who was toughminded and action oriented, still seemed to feel that the president should get a resolution of authority from Congress before doing anything.

On Monday morning, April 14, the media had picked up all the indicators that we were about to strike. NBC-TV reported that European leaders felt the president was just bluffing in order to pressure them to adopt stronger economic sanctions against Qaddafi. The president "should put his gun back in his holster" was the sentiment being registered. German Foreign Minister Hans-Dietrich Genscher was on his way to Washington reportedly to tell us that there was insufficient evidence to justify an attack against Libya.

I was in Kansas that day, giving the Alf Landon Lecture in honor of the former Republican candidate for president at the invitation of Senator Nancy Landon Kassebaum, Landon's daughter. I knew that the strike against Libya was set for 7:00 P.M., Washington, D.C., time. Word came from the Pentagon that Cap Weinberger wanted the president to delay action until Tuesday morning. I left immediately after the lecture for Washington and arrived at Andrews Air Force Base at 4:25 P.M. A meeting with congressional leaders had already begun. I went straight to the White House. Strangely enough, the meeting was being held in the Old Executive Office Building, in room 208, a large conference room that had recently been fitted with the communications and display equipment needed to conduct worldwide operations outside the White House Situation Room.

I walked in and was handed a note from Will Ball, assistant to the president for congressional relations, saying that the meeting had been disjointed so far and suggesting that I get people to understand "our broad purpose and how we have *carefully* weighed our options." I was hearing the sound of footsteps in retreat. I reminded everyone of Qaddafi's many acts of terror, the incontrovertible evidence in the La Belle case, and our ability to hit military and terrorist-related targets. The group seemed to take on new resolve.

The attack proceeded. Seldom in military history, I thought, had a punch been so clearly telegraphed. At 6:30 P.M., Peter Jennings announced, "An attack is imminent." At 7:00 P.M., Tom Brokaw said: "American ships and planes are moving." The U.S. Air Force confirmed that more than forty F-111s had left England on night operations. Qaddafi was no doubt hearing it all, too, in the middle of the night in Libya. Then on television, over a telephone line from Libya, came "Tripoli is under attack!"

President Reagan spoke on national television from the Oval Office at 9:00 P.M. on April 14, 1986. He announced that at seven o'clock that evening, "Air and naval forces of the United States launched a series of strikes against the headquarters, terrorist facilities and military assets that support Muammar Qadhafi's subversive activities." He went on,

> Colonel Qadhafi is not only an enemy of the United States. His record of subversion and aggression against the neighboring States in Africa is well documented and well known. He has ordered the murder of fellow Libyans in countless countries. He has sanctioned acts of terror in Africa, Europe, and the Middle East, as well as the Western Hemisphere. Today we have done what we had to do. If necessary, we shall do it again.

He concluded his address:

> We Americans are slow to anger. We always seek peaceful avenues before resorting to the use of force—and we did. We tried quiet diplomacy, public condemnation, economic sanctions, and demonstrations of military force. None succeeded. Despite our repeated warnings, Qadhafi continued his reckless policy of intimidation, his relentless pursuit of terror. He counted on America to be passive. He counted wrong. I warned that there should be no place on Earth where terrorists can rest and train and practice their deadly skills. I meant it. I said that we would act with others, if possible, and alone if necessary to ensure that terrorists have no sanctuary anywhere. Tonight, we have.

The next morning, I went over to see the president. I congratulated him on his tough decision. He felt, and I agreed, that we had emphatically put down a marker that the United States was ready and able to take military action against states that perpetrated terrorism. We had come a long way since the initial reaction to my speech at the Park Avenue Synagogue.

Margaret Thatcher had come through in staunch support of our effort by allowing American planes to take off from British bases. The French, by contrast, refused us even overflight rights. The result was a longer and more difficult mission for our F-111s. And the Egyptians said there was not enough time to change their policy on nuclear-powered warship transits. The head of the European Community, Hans van den Broek of the Netherlands, telephoned me to say that our military action "would do serious damage to the transatlantic relationship." I went up to Capitol Hill to a Republican Senate Inner Circle dinner. The senators, members of the president's own party, had questions all over the landscape. Not one said "We're with you." They all seemed to be waiting to see whether the operation was a success and to hear the public reaction.

The public response in the United States and Europe supported the president's actions. His standing in public opinion polls soared. That made an impact on congressional critics. More important, Qaddafi, after twitching feverishly with a flurry of vengeful responses, quieted down and retreated into the desert. The Europeans, more alert now to the dangers posed to them by Libya, alarmed at the use of force by the United States, and anxious to show cooperation with a popular U.S. action, took action of their own. We had finally gotten their attention. They forced drastic personnel reductions in the Libyan people's bureaus, and the activities of those remaining were restricted and watched. This action alone significantly curbed Qaddafi's terrorist capacities.[3]

Triumph in Tokyo

Terrorism was by now very prominently on the international agenda. Polls in the United States showed the public more concerned about terrorism than any other issue. Ronald Reagan's willingness to act, the widespread public support for his action in and outside the United States, the lack of support for Qaddafi, even among Arabs, all gave strength and drive to our continuing fight against terrorism. The annual meeting of the leaders of the seven leading industrial democracies would take place in Tokyo from May 4 to May 6, 1986. I was determined that a strong statement must emerge from this meeting. The president was in full agreement. Not at all to my surprise, Margaret Thatcher was equally determined and was forceful and articulate on the need to confront the threat posed by terrorism. I circulated what I regarded as a powerful statement on the subject. We

3. On May 20, 1986, a few weeks after the air strikes against Libya, Ambassador Wilson resigned his post at the Vatican.

developed a well-coordinated U.S. strategy. The president hit the subject hard during meetings of the heads of state, I startled my fellow foreign ministers with my vehemence—I wanted to get them energized—and Jim Baker enlisted the ministers of finance.

The result was a strong joint declaration by the Summit Seven.[4] Libya was on everyone's mind. We "strongly reaffirm our condemnation of international terrorism in all its forms, of its accomplices and of those, including governments, who sponsor or support it. We abhor the increase in the level of such terrorism since our last meeting, and in particular its blatant and cynical use as an instrument of government policy." And it declared: "Terrorism has no justification." So much for the "root cause" argument. The communiqué then stated forcefully, "It [terrorism] spreads only by the use of contemptible means, ignoring the values of human life, freedom and dignity. It must be fought relentlessly and without compromise."

That ringing statement was followed by the commitment to take actions individually and collectively that would place restrictions on the activities of states that sponsored terrorism, apply the rule of law through improved extradition procedures and immigration and visa requirements, and strengthen cooperation among the police, security, and intelligence services of our countries.

The declaration was issued on May 5. I met with the large U.S. press contingent to explain it. In response to a question, what message does this send Qaddafi? I replied, "You've had it, pal." That phrase was played on television and caught the headlines. It rang true. He was isolated.

By midyear of 1986 I felt that our war against terrorism and the policy that informed it were taking shape in an effective way: those who argued that terrorism was justified because of economic or political grievances now knew they would be taken on whenever they put this argument out. Our legal position had been carefully developed and articulated. Most importantly, we had shown that we possessed the will to take military action against a state found to be directly supporting terrorism. We had achieved an unprecedented sense of unity among the major democracies on cooperative approaches to stopping terrorism. The point had been driven home by Ronald Reagan's own public statements, including his flat assertion: "America will never make concessions to terrorists—to do so would only invite more terrorism."[5]

4. The United States, Great Britain, France, West Germany, Italy, Japan, and Canada.
5. From a presidential press conference on June 18, 1985.

CHAPTER 34

The Year
of Maximum Leverage

The success of the Geneva summit in November was still in my mind as I looked toward 1986. Roz Ridgway had come to real prominence at Geneva. She was the first woman to head a regional bureau of the State Department, and her Bureau of European and Canadian Affairs was at the center of important action. With noble features and steel-gray hair, her presence was commanding. The Soviets respected her stern diplomacy.

I called Roz to thank her for the great job she had done at the summit. "It beats keeping house," she responded. And Assistant Secretary of Defense Richard Perle, whom the press had earlier dubbed the "Prince of Darkness," who would sell his soul to prevent an arms control agreement with the Soviets, was proving to be a helpful force. "He is floating in a cloud over the success of the Geneva summit," John Whitehead told me. "He is glowing about his part. You brought him in. At dinner the other night he said he had always felt like an outsider before. Now he feels he is on the team." I had not co-opted Perle. He had played a big role in developing the president's original arms control proposals and by now could see that these proposals were at the center of the negotiating stage.

At Geneva, Gorbachev was preoccupied with the idea that we were developing what the Soviets called "space strike weapons." Just before the summit, Dean Rusk sent me a letter expressing the same concern. If that was Gorbachev's fear, I felt we should tell him that we were willing to negotiate assurances against the stationing of offensive arms in space. That should be possible without impairing the eventual development of a defense against ballistic missiles. Paul Nitze told me that Richard Perle thought this Soviet fear was worth our attention and that Perle would try to work on it with Lieutenant General James Abrahamson, head of the SDI program. "One plan is to put rods up there that could penetrate missile silos on the ground," Nitze said, "so the Soviets' concern is not entirely misplaced. We need to get at it."

Momentum to Maintain

As we rounded into the new year, I felt that 1986 would be our year of maximum leverage. Support for the U.S. defense budget had peaked. Support for the president's Strategic Defense Initiative would not increase but decrease from now on, especially when people started to face up to the enormous costs of the program. And, by 1987, the question of who would succeed Ronald Reagan would command increasing attention. The momentum we had worked so carefully to create must not be allowed to drain away: we had twelve months or so in which to crack the Soviet shell, to achieve significant arms reductions and some agreed-upon arrangement on the Strategic Defense Initiative that preserved the research and made SDI the propellant that would lead the Soviets to agree to deep reductions.

Bud McFarlane finally had resigned on December 4, 1985. The question was, why just now? Everyone seemed eager to analyze him. Speculation abounded: it was a midlife crisis; he was near a nervous breakdown; he was hypersensitive and couldn't bear criticism; he wanted the kind of mysteriously secret yet widely publicized and powerful role that Henry Kissinger had created as NSC adviser, but was thwarted. I felt he left in part out of frustration over the inability to get the administration's national security people to work together effectively as a team. The effort to make progress on any front was complicated by the continuous struggle over what the direction was that represented progress. No decision could ever be regarded as final or implemented with confidence as policy.

I knew that I would never be free of the need to "battle it out" on U.S. policy toward the Soviet Union with the phalanx of staff people who were always kibitzing whenever a White House meeting was under way. The cabinet table and all the chairs against the wall had been filled on December 3, 1985, for a meeting on a bill authorizing the president to restrict credits to the European Community as a means of disrupting their nonstrategic trade with the Soviet Union. The president was not present. The discussion turned into another debate on Soviet policy. Flamboyant right-wing hard-liner Pat Buchanan, now in the White House as the president's director of communications, led the attack: the Soviets get foreign exchange from trade, so we and the Europeans should not trade with them.

"That's *not* the president's policy, and I'm carrying out the president's policy," I told Buchanan. My mind flashed to the agonizing process I had undertaken to defuse the acrimony caused by U.S. trade sanctions imposed in the Siberian pipeline dispute back in 1982. It had taken me months to craft an agreement worked out with the Europeans to end the pipeline dispute and institute strong controls on trade in strategic goods while permitting trade in other areas.

Now here I was, four years later, listening to advocates of "lightswitch diplomacy" again propose trade as a weapon to influence change in Soviet behavior. Ed Meese said the president's powers to curtail trade with the Soviets should be greater.

"That would be worse," I said. "Government power hanging over the market is a threatening and disruptive force." I had to go through that kind of debate, rearguing fundamental principles again and again. At the end of the meeting, I remarked, "There are more people in this room than the total membership of the NSC staff and the Economic Policy Committee. Someone is going to go right out to the press and talk about tough Pat Buchanan and soft George Shultz. So let's put the story out this way: 'the President does not think this bill would be helpful now.' "

"In every debate . . . the participants must reargue basic premises," Suzanne Garment wrote on December 6 in the *Wall Street Journal*. She was right. I talked to Vice President Bush and Don Regan about this constant effort to go back to square one on every issue. "Bud's not leaving for family reasons," Bush said. "The president should be told of Bud's concerns about the lack of cohesion in the national security community." Don Regan seemed to agree with Bud's concerns, though the two had bitter, strained relations. Someone, I said, needed to be preeminent in managing the president's foreign policy—as John Foster Dulles had been under Eisenhower and Kissinger had been under Nixon and Ford. One central person has to orchestrate things on behalf of the president.

I was determined to do this job. There were two inherent problems, however, that I knew I could never resolve. The president was terribly reluctant to discipline or fire anyone: when people know that, they are ultimately impossible to control. I was also increasingly uneasy about CIA director Bill Casey. He had very strong policy positions, which were reflected in his intelligence briefings. He claimed he was objective. But his views were so strong and so ideological that they inevitably colored his selection and assessment of materials. I could not rely on what he said, nor could I accept without question the objectivity of the "intelligence" that he put out, especially in policy-sensitive areas. Casey felt I was too willing to negotiate and too indifferent to leaks—an assessment that I regarded as far off the mark. His view and mine were starkly different: they could not be reconciled.

A Push on Afghanistan

The Soviet invasion of Afghanistan late in 1979 and their continued military effort to conquer the Afghan people represented a deep and running sore in East-West relations. In early December, I reviewed the situation there. Our State Department analysts put stock in the pessimistic assessment of the Pakistanis: the Soviets were in Afghanistan for the long haul. Their Spetsnaz troops had hurt the mujaheddin freedom fighters, and there had been no major victories for the Afghan resistance for months. The Afghan people were war weary, and Soviet policy was "buying them off." The Soviets seemed to be winning.

Out of State's review I came to certain conclusions, not unlike those in arms control. There would be a narrow window in the next year or two in which pressure on the Soviets might be effective. So we should do all we could to strengthen the Afghan resistance in the next twelve months. A key was the Soviet helicopters: the resistance did not have the weapons to deal with them, and the helicopters were wreaking havoc. Some captured Soviet-made SA-7s, British Blowpipes, and Swiss Oerlikon antiair weapons had been supplied and had been used to knock down some Soviet choppers, but the situation was not improving much. Mort Abramowitz, director of State's Intelligence and Research Bureau, said, "I believe we are not putting significant pressure on the Soviets. We should put in an American weapon: the Stinger." This hand-held missile could be employed very effectively against helicopters and low-flying aircraft.

Again, as with every important issue, interagency conflicts arose. The CIA was running the war, but the Defense Department controlled the Stinger missile and did not want Stingers used for fear they would fall into Soviet hands and thus compromise our technology, or be sold to Third World terrorists for use against American targets. These were justifiable concerns, and controls to deal with them would need to be worked out. In the State Department some people worried that any American weapons system that could turn the tide would so antagonize the Soviets that it would sour our overall effort to improve relations. I strongly disagreed. We should help the freedom fighters in Afghanistan to be as effective as possible. So despite the obstacles to employing the Stingers, I felt that we should use them. Unless we hurt the Soviets in Afghanistan, they would have no interest in dealing with us to end the war there. I pushed Mort's idea, in the end successfully. Bill Casey was a strong ally in this effort. The president decided to go ahead. The Stingers, even when parceled out with care, made a huge, perhaps even decisive, difference. The Soviets could no longer dominate areas by helicopter or by accurate bombing from low-flying aircraft. High-level bombers were ineffective against the dispersed and mobile forces of the Afghan freedom fighters.

Foray into Eastern Europe

In mid-December 1985, I was in Brussels for the North Atlantic Council meeting of the allies. From there I traveled to Bonn and then Berlin, where I went to the Berlin Wall. On a miserable night in a chilly, driving rain, I looked eastward, searchlights glaring in my eyes as I encountered that depressing mass of concrete: a fitting way to experience a monument to totalitarianism, I thought, and a fitting place from which to proceed to a few countries of Eastern Europe and, in doing so, to let them know that we did not concede to the Soviets the role of permanent dominant power there. I flew to Bucharest, a gloomy city that seemed to have lain unimproved since the 1920s except for unfinished and ugly high-rise buildings that were sprinkled about, the twisted rods of their structural beams sticking out, making them seem more like bombed-out buildings than ones still under construction.

Budapest, my next stop, was quite different, not just because of its natural beauty. But beautiful—stunning—it was, with the historic Danube flowing through high bluffs and with ancient buildings of an earlier Parliament restored to something approaching their magnificent past. Real progress was being made in Hungary as the stranglehold of socialism over economic life was slowly and methodically being pried loose. The Hungarians just hoped that their Soviet overlords would not take too much notice of how much better life was there.

"Don't come here with your big trombone," Janos Kadar, the prime minister, told me. He also made clear to me that he did not like our policy of judging his country by the degree to which Hungarian policies differed from the Soviet line. Kadar had come far, but he was irremediably tainted by the brutal and bloody stamping out of the Hungarian uprising of 1956 in which the term "freedom fighter" had become common parlance.

Hungary needed a new generation of leadership. Kadar pressed for an invitation to visit America. I sidestepped, but made clear that we welcomed lower-level visits as a way to help Hungarians see and understand life in the United States.

On the way to the airport, I stopped at a large market where both state farm-grown produce and privately raised fruits and vegetables were sold. The differences in the quality of the produce and in the attractiveness of their display presented stark contrasts. The public stalls dominated the middle of the hall and were the most accessible. Vegetables were heaped in piles, to be picked over. At the private stalls, which ringed the perimeter, goods were arranged attractively, and an attendant was ready to sell you what you wanted. The prices were higher, as was the quality. A smiling old woman, tending her private stall, gave me a bag of garlic. "It's a blessing," someone said. "It keeps away the werewolves," another added.

After a brief stay in Belgrade, Yugoslavia, where I met with Foreign Minister Dizdarevic, we left for home. As my plane took off from our refueling stop at Shannon, Ireland, en route to Washington on Wednesday, December 18 (our ancient Boeing 707 was surely the last airplane in the air force inventory unable to fly nonstop from Western Europe to the East Coast of the United States), I discussed our policy toward Eastern Europe with my traveling colleagues. I had suffered through a sporadic series of administration meetings on the topic, each of which invariably had collapsed in deep animosity between those advocating that the United States exert "relentless pressure" against leaders and countries they saw as "incapable of change" and those who, like me, saw glimpses of a desire for change and who wanted to respond to encourage such change. Our policy was stuck now on the former course.

I decided, having assessed the situation during my Eastern European trip, to push harder for a change in course. The current United States policy was known as "differentiation." The idea was that in response to domestic or foreign policy moves by a country away from Soviet-style policy, the United States would reciprocate with positive moves of our own. The problem always was determining what constituted a change worth recognizing and how to respond without raising the stature of leaders committed to or trapped in the Soviet system. "We've got to get away from the idea that if they don't change radically, we won't help out," Roz Ridgway said. "We need to help them play their game, not our game."

The game of the more venturesome and bold East Europeans was to probe constantly for the line that the Soviets had drawn and then to come as close to it as possible, hoping in the process to push that line out farther and farther. Most people in the Reagan administration wanted to have no contact with the East Europeans unless they took a giant leap way over that line in order to win American benefits on trade or relief on debt. When pressed too far, they often had to back away. "If we ask them to do too much, we get nothing. A policy of erosion is more likely to bring results," I said.

Small steps that accumulated could wind up being a big step, even if little seemed to be taking place at any one moment. Work with small steps would be a promising and reasonable shift on our part. But Roz had been wounded often in the fierce interagency battles. So I decided to give Deputy Secretary of State John Whitehead the lead on this job. That would give Roz the political-level cover she needed and identify our efforts with the number-two man at State, who also had strong credentials in the Republican party. John took on this assignment with enthusiasm and flair. "I know I'm still learning this business, but could you tell me why we can talk to Gorbachev but can't talk to Jaruzelski?" he asked in a State Department meeting. This was met with stark silence—no answer. Such a distinction made no sense. A shift in policy was needed.

I felt that as the Soviets moved to try to improve their relations with us, we should say to them, without being provocative or antagonistic, "Don't get in the way of the countries that are allowing their societies to evolve differently from yours." The East Europeans clearly did not want the United States to appear to embrace them too warmly or to make noise about their departures from the Soviet line. Soviet propaganda attacks on me during my short swing to Romania and Hungary alerted me that I was walking on highly sensitive terrain—as sensitive then as at any time in the cold war.

"We are entering a time of major potential change in international affairs," I said to Roz. "Yet with our budget deficit, we are going to be strapped financially as never before in the cold war. We are going to have to run our foreign policy largely on *ingenuity*. We want to make it as hard as possible for the Soviets to extract economic benefits from Eastern Europe. We want the Soviets to see it as costly to be there." I wanted *no talk about policy changes*: that would simply activate the administration's most rabid elements. Instead, we would probe the possibilities and move to meet them from a new angle.

My Literary Lionization

The ferment produced by the superpower contest was not limited to debates within the Reagan administration. The power of Communist ideology, I was convinced, was on the wane, even though Soviet military capability was formidable. My own role in an oddly striking conference reminded me of other aspects of the superpower confrontation and of the importance, in our society at large, of the commitment to the tenets of a free society and to freedom of speech.

Early on the dark, cold evening of January 12, 1986, I was escorted up the grand staircase between the famous inquiring lions of the New York Public Library by Vartan Gregorian, the ebullient scholar-librarian. In the south wing reading room, for this event designated a holding room, I was greeted by Norman Mailer and his wife, Norris Church. Mailer, then the president of American PEN (Poets, Playwrights, Editors, Essayists, and Novelists), and I chatted amiably for more than half an hour while the crowd settled in—actually it remained a most unsettled gathering—into the north wing. The event was delayed in starting, and the crowd milled about. The dark rooms, with their high ceilings, made the din of voices echo deeply. Bernie Kalb loved it: it was New York; it was intellectual; it was intense. He spent fifteen minutes talking with a woman he thought was author Susan Sontag, only to learn later that she was a media colleague, Susan Stanberg.

The occasion was the first meeting of the International PEN in the United States in twenty years. Founded by John Galsworthy, H. G. Wells, and others shortly after the First World War, "PEN's chief business," said novelist Richard Stern, "is rescuing the world's writers from the political and social consequences of their work. The word is older than the state. Words form and reform states. Those who run states know the power of words and attempt to control them. PEN, as much as any group, not only stands for the liberty of the word but does something about it. It gets international petitions to parliaments and heads of state. Frequently it helps unlock prison doors."

I was surprised and pleased, if somewhat apprehensive, to have been invited to speak to this gathering. I was surely asked, although it was never openly admitted, to be the representative of "the state"; Norman Mailer was the representative of the world of writers. "The Writer's Imagination and the Imagination of the State" was the topic of the conference.

Outside, in the hall between the north and south reading rooms, a letter of protest about my presence was handed out. Also distributed were copies of an article in *The Nation* by the novelist E. L. Doctorow—not exactly warm notes of welcome.

> It is difficult for me to understand why he was invited. What has Shultz written?[1] What is his connection to the world of letters? Has he ever been on the boards of libraries or publishing houses? Has he ever as Secretary of State championed the cause of universal free expression that so concerns the international community of writers?
>
> At the last international congress held in the United States, in 1966, no member of the Johnson Administration was invited to address the writers. The late Ignazio Silone was heard then to remark what a pleasure it was to go to one of these congresses and not hear from the presiding politicians of the host country. Indeed, America is one of the few nations in the world in which writers don't have to ask for the endorsement of the government. I imagine the looks on the faces of the hundreds of foreign guests convened in the public library when they realize that American PEN has put itself in the position of a bunch of obedient hacks in the writers union of an Eastern European country gathering to be patted on the head by the Minister of Culture.

Well, whatever I was—or was not—there for, it was preposterous to put me into a category with Communist-bloc cultural commissars. The evening's events began with an "election." Someone asked for nominations. A man stood up in the back of the room and spoke. Hardly anyone could hear him. He turned out to be from East Germany. The chairman did not ask for a voice vote, a vote by acclamation, or anything. He simply declared Norman Mailer president of International PEN. Then I was to present the "keynote" address. As I rose to speak, protesters all over the densely packed room ostentatiously walked out. "I recognize that I'm not standing here today simply because of my achievements as an essayist," I said. "It wasn't until I read the *New York Times* on Friday that I realized that I've become the latest PEN controversy. In Norman's world, that's a high form of flattery—and that's how I take it. And I salute you for taking this decision in favor of free speech."

1. Actually, I had authored or coauthored nine books.

As if inflamed by hearing the words "free speech," Grace Paley stood up in the crowd and shouted her demand that the petition against my presence be read aloud from the podium. I persevered:

> I regard the creative literary writer as an individual of primary importance for the entire range of thought, culture, and human existence. . . . America is proud to have you here. Diversity, debate, contrast, argumentativeness are what we as a people thrive on. So, as individuals, each of you is truly welcome here. And PEN as your collective spirit and organization is welcome as well, for the larger and noisier PEN has become, the more it has been able to do for freedom around the world.
>
> Freedom—that is what we are all talking about and why we are here. And the writer is at the heart of freedom. There is no more striking image of freedom than the solitary writer, the individual of imagination, creativity, and courage, imposing through language the perceptions and prescriptions that can illuminate and, perhaps, change the world. The writer needs freedom, but the writer also is the creator of freedom. No government or ideological system has ever yet succeeded in stopping the writer, although some are trying very hard. . . . There are countries in which writers know that if their art appears to threaten the political fortunes of their rulers, they may be silenced, imprisoned, even killed. Equally tragic, there are countries in which writers choose to aid the apparatus of repression.
>
> By contrast, there are other countries—and I'm proud to say that the United States is one of them—where writers can speak, write, and publish without political hindrance. . . .
>
> In the computer age, reading and writing will not become obsolete, as many have so facilely asserted. . . . There is no escaping the reality that our culture is built upon, and relies upon, the written word. . . . Indeed, the awesome power of the writer resides in the fact that it takes only paper and pencil to do it. No apparatus, consensus, or license is required. . . .
>
> And this gathering is only one of many recent testaments to our commitment to maintain the free marketplace of ideas. . . .
>
> Let us remember today those writers who exist in states where the typewriter or mimeograph are regarded as dangerous weapons, where writers have no independent right to publish, and where a free press has no free access. Let us work to support the solitary writer in a suppressive society. Let us take heart that many governments and their censors have found that it is not so easy to stop all the writers, every last solitary individual with a pen and paper or typewriter and friends who will smuggle out what he or she writes. . . .
>
> I am optimistic about the future. As the world gets smaller, the importance of freedom only increases. The yearning for freedom is the most powerful political force all across the planet. You are among its champions. You can be proud of what you have done for that cause.

And don't be so surprised by the fact that Ronald Reagan and I are on
your side.

That last line did it. The hall went into an uproar: they were infuriated
with my presumption of identifying with their cause. As Norman Mailer
rose to speak following me, the hoots and catcalls mounted. "Read the
protest!"

"Up yours," Mailer shouted.

A disturbing feature of my experience with PEN as a gathering of influential intellectuals was the extent to which some among their ranks
rebuked the open society's state while expressing both fear of and a thrilling
attraction to the totalitarian state—even on artistic grounds. Cultural critic
George Steiner put the point this way:

> The haunting paradox is this: Historical evidence goes a long way to suggest
> that great literature flourishes under political-social repression. . . . The ge-
> nius of Russian poetry and fiction runs unbroken from Pushkin to Joseph
> Brodsky, from Turgenev to Solzhenitsyn, victims all of suppression or
> exile. . . . The liberalities of the privileged West are no guarantor of true
> creativity. Where everything can be said, the writer is not, as Tolstoy pro-
> claimed him to be, "the alternative state," the compelling counterimperative
> of clairvoyance and of conscience. The "censorship" of the free and mass-
> market economies is wonderfully light compared to that of the East German
> or South African truncheon. But it corrodes, it trivializes. . . .

Why do so many intellectuals seek to define themselves in bitter opposition to democratic government, to a free and open society, emphasizing
and exaggerating our shortcomings? Nevertheless, I hoped my words had
let the reluctant PEN audience see that Ronald Reagan and I stood for
freedom, whether or not they approved of him, or me, or my appearance
before them.

A New Soviet Agility

The secret, multinational effort to get Anatoly Shcharansky out of the
Soviet Union appeared on the verge of the possible in early January. An
East German deal maker had put together a package involving prisoners
held in the United States, West Germany, and East Germany, which seemed
defensible as a straight "spy swap," with Shcharansky's freedom thrown
in as a sweetener.

UN Ambassador Dick Walters stopped by. "The Soviets have stopped
drinking vodka. I'm worried about Gorbachev," he said. "When Prime

Minister Mendès-France urged milk on the French instead of wine, he soon vanished from the scene."

The trouble was that the Soviets hadn't stopped drinking. Gorbachev was trying to get more discipline and performance out of the Soviet system. But as Margaret Thatcher had said, the system, not the management of the system, was the problem. Until Gorbachev could bring himself to face that fact and throw the system out, I felt his economic programs would not succeed.

On Wednesday morning, January 15, I talked with Ambassador Dobrynin, who was sending me an urgent message from Gorbachev. I looked it over quickly and phoned NSC adviser John Poindexter. "I have just received an extremely important letter to the president from Gorbachev," I said. "Dobrynin says that Gorbachev will go public with the content in Moscow in a few hours. This is very different from anything we have seen before and is a matter of high priority. I will have a restricted group take a look at it. A messenger will hand-deliver it to you for the president in five minutes."

I called in Paul Nitze, Roz Ridgway, and Jim Timbie. The essence of Gorbachev's message was: let's go to zero in nuclear weapons and ballistic missiles, by the year 2000. The particulars were booby traps, but he made that goal look operational and more serious by proposing a three-stage process to get there. And he announced the extension of the unilateral Soviet moratorium on nuclear testing. I passed around the letter for the others to read.

Nitze was fascinated. "I wonder whose work of art on the Soviet side this is."

While accepting the president's general concept of massive reductions in nuclear weapons, even to zero, the Gorbachev letter was also packed with all the old obstacles: defining our intermediate-range missiles as strategic, but not theirs; including the British and French nuclear systems in their proposal, although they altered the form of inclusion in a way that moved toward our position; conditioning all reductions on our agreement to give up SDI.

The proposal was a blockbuster that Gorbachev clearly intended, by going public within hours of providing it to us, to use for propaganda purposes. I telephoned Cap Weinberger. "I'd like Paul Nitze to talk to Richard Perle about the letter right away." We had to produce our public position quickly to counter Gorbachev's attempt to gain a propaganda advantage.

I felt that we should welcome the fact that Gorbachev proposed large-scale reductions; we should *not* put out the word that this was just another warmed-over Soviet propaganda ploy. I telephoned Bill Casey. "Bill, something of considerable significance has come in from Gorbachev. We need to make a decision about a fast public response. I'd like Doug George [CIA arms control expert] to come over here right away. Have him come to Paul Nitze's office. Richard Perle is coming. I want a representative from every interested agency."

At 2:00 P.M., I went over to see President Reagan, having in hand a careful summary and preliminary analysis of Gorbachev's proposal. The Soviets had moved conceptually in the president's direction by advocating big reductions. But we faced a real dilemma. At the Geneva summit, President Reagan had made a comment to Gorbachev, which I had later called to his and McFarlane's attention. Although I had not been present, I had read the interpreter's notes of the president's one-on-one conversation with Gorbachev in front of the fire in the pool house at Fleur d'Eau: if there was agreement that there would be no need for nuclear missiles, then one might agree that there would also be no need for defenses against them. The president said at first that he had never made the statement. But here was Gorbachev, in this letter, calling for the elimination of nuclear missiles and a related end to SDI. Gorbachev knew that we could not agree to his formulations, but in setting them out, he had accepted the fundamental concept of massive reductions in nuclear arms that was central to the president's agenda.

I said to President Reagan, "This is our first indication that the Soviets are interested in a staged program toward zero. We should not simply reject their proposal, since it contains certain steps which we earlier set forth."

The president agreed. "Why wait until the end of the century for a world without nuclear weapons?" he asked. He recalled that he *had*, in fact, made that statement to Gorbachev in the pool house at Fleur d'Eau. I wanted to get the president's initial reaction out to the public immediately. Otherwise, we would leave the stage entirely to Gorbachev. Again, he agreed. He put out word that he welcomed the Soviet proposal and would study it carefully. And the next day he said in response to questions, "We're grateful for the offer. . . . It's just about the first time that anyone has ever proposed actually eliminating nuclear weapons." He smiled when I later reminded him of the many times he had publicly and privately said that his dream was to see a world free of nuclear weapons.

I had argued in the past with Ronald Reagan that we could not "uninvent" nuclear weapons and that nuclear deterrence had kept the peace. Still, he was firm in his belief that the United States and the rest of the world would be better off without them. I came to feel that utopian though his dream might be, the shared view of Reagan and Gorbachev on the desirability of eliminating nuclear weapons could move us toward the massive reductions in medium-range and strategic ballistic missiles that Reagan had proposed back in 1981 and 1982. I supported those goals wholeheartedly.

*   *   *

How should we proceed diplomatically? The naysayers were hard at work, even in my own building. Peter Rodman said that the elimination of nuclear weapons meant a neutralist Europe, the end of our NATO strategy, a disaster for the West. No one could accept the thought of a world moving toward the elimination of nuclear weapons. Richard Perle declared to the Senior Arms Control Group in mid-January that the president's dream of a world without nuclear weapons—which Gorbachev had picked up—was a disaster, a total delusion. Perle said the NSC should not meet on the idea, because then the president would direct his arms controllers to come up with a program to achieve that result. The Joint Chiefs' representatives agreed with Perle. They feared the institutionalization and acceptance of the idea as our policy.

I did not see it that way, "I know that many of you and others around here oppose the objective of eliminating nuclear weapons," I told my arms control group on January 17. "You have tried your ideas out in front of the president from the outset, and I have pointed out the dangers, too. The president of the United States doesn't agree with you, and he has said so on several very public occasions both before and since the last election. He thinks it's a hell of a good idea. And it's a political hot button. We need to work on what a world without nuclear weapons would mean to us and what additional steps would have to accompany such a dramatic change. The president has wanted all along to get rid of nuclear weapons. The British, French, Dutch, Belgians, and all of you in the Washington arms control community are trying to talk him out if it. The idea can potentially be a plus for us: the Soviet Union is a superpower only because it is a nuclear and ballistic missile superpower."

"I'm worried about us losing our grip," Rodman responded. "If we broaden the negotiations out this way, we could fritter away our leverage. The Soviets are setting up SDI as the one obstacle to a nuclear-free world."

The next day, I talked with Paul Nitze and Richard Perle. Perle insisted that Gorbachev's letter was not serious, just propaganda. "We must not discuss it as though it was serious," he said. The worst thing in the world would be to eliminate nuclear weapons.

"You've got a problem," I said with a laugh. "The president thinks it is a *good* idea. Don't worry, we can say 'fine' to the three-stage approach and then front-end load our program in the first stage. Gorbachev's language makes the INF zero option operational; all else is a transition to it." We could, I felt, design a first stage that would convert Gorbachev's language into our own proposal to eliminate INF missiles and achieve deep reductions in strategic arms.

At this point, I began to realize that the "zero option" for the INF talks about medium-range missiles should be the centerpiece of our next arms control effort. We should work to eliminate that entire class of missiles, as the president had first proposed in 1981 and as our allies had endorsed. Gorbachev had included a conditioned elimination of INF missiles in Europe in his first stage, even though that proposal was hedged and limited so that Soviet intermediate-range missiles in Asia were not affected. We should, I said, put forward again the idea of a "global ceiling." We would say that deployments in Europe could be anywhere between X and zero, with zero being the best outcome, and we would seek to get deployments in Asia as close to zero as possible. Gorbachev's letter was silent on what Soviet deployments would be in Asia; we could not allow the Soviets simply to shift their weapons from one side of Eurasia to the other. "If the general context of his letter has the goal of zero"—and that's what Gorbachev in response to Reagan initiatives has put forth—"then his overall goal legitimizes zero for a given category," that is, for intermediate-range missiles.

"There is no doubt," I said, "the creation of SDI has produced this proposal to reduce nuclear weapons to zero." We had to make clear to Congress that the Strategic Defense Initiative had brought this new proposal—and its acceptance of deep reductions in our nuclear stockpiles—into being. "If the Congress threatens the SDI program, they threaten arms control," I said.

While the Soviets were clearly coming around to our agenda, to the idea of deep reductions in our nuclear arsenals, they also suddenly presented us with a broad, active, and more flexible Soviet diplomacy. Foreign Minister Shevardnadze had just completed a successful trip to Japan. The contrast between him and Gromyko was breathtaking. He understood there was more to the world than the United States, the Soviet Union, and Europe. He could smile, engage, converse. He had an ability to persuade and to be persuaded. We were in a real diplomatic competition now—we couldn't just sit around and say that the Soviet positions were "nothing new" or a "catastrophe for the free world." The Soviets were awake. We had to engage them. They were presenting a face that looked more reasonable, but the underlying bone structure was tough. Soviet supplies to Angola and Nicaragua were being stepped up. Gorbachev was proving to be a skillful and adroit tactician in the politics of the Politburo and was now solidly entrenched. He had quickly put his own people in key spots. He had great capability and agility and toughness.

What would cause him to alter course, I felt, would be a combination of U.S. determination and strength combined with persuasive arguments that the Soviet Union would benefit from a different approach to its own people and to its foreign relations.

I went to the president on January 24 and told him I wanted to set up a special group to work on our broad approach to arms control and our ability to initiate and react to the Soviets in this new stage. My idea was not to create a new decision-making body but rather to get all the key people together outside the petrified, stultified "interagency process." I wanted to create the general understandings within which detailed new proposals would be developed, thereby speeding up the process and rising above the usual carping. I advised the president that we had to respond to Gorbachev seriously. "Your response is going to be controversial," I said, "because your arms control community disagrees with your desire to get rid of nuclear weapons."

"If any nation is likely to conduct a first strike, it is the Soviet Union. So why isn't this a problem we want to get rid of?" President Reagan responded. I had been discussing the problem of nuclear weapons with the president practically since my first day on the job. I was interested in his use to the press of the word "grateful" in response to Gorbachev's letter. Was he expressing a perception that Gorbachev understood him better than his own advisers?

By late January, the spy swap that we hoped would free Anatoly Shcharansky looked good. The swap would take place in Berlin. I wanted Shcharansky separated from the spies right away. "Take him to Tempelhof, fly him to Frankfurt, and link him up with El Al," I said. I wanted his wife, Avital, to be there under our escort, but I didn't want her told until the last minute, to avoid disappointment if the swap fell through.

President Reagan himself was a worry: he deeply wanted Shcharansky out, but he did not want to compel anyone, even convicted spies, to go back behind the Iron Curtain against their will. "We aren't going to *force* anyone back to Czechoslovakia, are we?" he asked. I assured him we were not.

Senator Ted Kennedy, we knew, had been negotiating with the Soviets about a trip he might make to Moscow on three conditions: Shcharansky or Sakharov was released; Kennedy could meet dissidents; Kennedy could appear on television. The Soviets had indicated this was no problem. I mentioned this to the president and suggested that we foster bipartisanship on human rights and make common cause with Kennedy. He agreed.

Charlie Wick, director of the U.S. Information Agency, had gone to Moscow to discuss cultural exchanges. Everywhere he went, he found Soviet officials who had been told to "make it work." Wick was encouraged about prospects for cultural exchanges, which had been agreed to at Geneva. Gorbachev had created a remarkably positive atmosphere, Wick said.

But back in Washington, and especially from the CIA and its lead Soviet expert, Bob Gates, I heard that the Soviets wouldn't change and couldn't change, that Gorbachev was simply putting a new face on the same old Soviet approach to the world and to their own people. "The Soviet Union is a despotism that works," Gates said.

Gorbachev might not succeed, but he was trying something boldly different. The Soviets were managing their foreign policy in an entirely new way.

Soviet experts across the board in the U.S. government were forever counseling President Reagan that the Soviets had an inferiority complex and that he should guard against statements that might unnecessarily antagonize them. Before the Geneva summit and after my two meetings with Gorbachev, I had told Ronald Reagan, "Mr. President, the man you are about to meet does *not* have an inferiority complex."

Roz Ridgway remarked to me later, "We used to be able to count on their stodgy bureaucracy; now I think *we* have the stodgy bureaucracy."

Before the year of the missile, 1983, the Soviets had tried to best us through propaganda and threats. The West stood up to the threats and deployed controversial INF missiles. Now the Soviets had learned that propaganda had to have substance behind it. They were adding substance. And the substance of their proposals was actually pointing to the possibility of real change.

Gorbachev was proving to be an energetic advocate of appealing positions. On Saturday, January 25, I was to hold the first session of the new steering group on Soviet issues. On Friday, reviewing the situation with my State Department team, I said, "We are now facing a bold and agile Soviet leader who is even tougher and more of a challenge to us than his predecessors. He is pouring military equipment into hot spots. When we ran our Gulf of Sidra naval challenge to Qaddafi, he put a Soviet command ship offshore. In a crisis, this is a leader who is capable of action. We're now in a fast-stepping game." We would have to think boldly, something that many in Washington weren't used to—and tried to avoid at all costs.

The issue of where the superpowers, let alone other countries, were heading with nuclear weapons was of immense consequence. Ronald Reagan had long and openly advocated a world without nuclear weapons. Gorbachev had now said, in essence, "Okay, let's sit down and figure out how to get there." Paul Nitze was troubled. "What are the preconditions for a nonnuclear world?" he asked me rhetorically. "They are extreme and unacceptable," he replied to his own question. I knew what bothered him: the nuclear balance had kept the peace for over forty years. Without the balance provided by nuclear weapons, the Soviets would have by far the world's preponderant conventional military force. Nitze had been through this problem before. "In 1961," he said, "the Soviets' public line beat ours by calling for total disarmament. It was all propaganda."

Roz Ridgway broke in. "At dinner last night, Dianne Feinstein [Mayor of San Francisco] said, 'Of course people can imagine a nonnuclear world—everybody does.' She was astonished that we had questions about its desirability." But Roz was troubled, too. "The loss of nuclear weapons would mean the loss of a special American preeminence; it would change the way we walk down the street. And it can't be done without a gigantic conventional military buildup."

Art Hartman bolstered her point. "In Europe, our allies are up against huge Soviet conventional power. The threatened use of nuclear weapons in order to deter the Soviets is essential to them."

"The trick is," I said, "to whack away at the first phase within the overall goal while keeping the incentive—our military modernization and SDI—as an insurance policy and a stimulus to continued reductions by the Soviets. If we back off from the president's vision of a world without nuclear weapons, we will lose all the steam behind his effort to bring about genuine arms reduction.

"We want to respond to Gorbachev with the powerful vision the president has projected," I told them. "We want a staged approach. The first stage must be fail-safe; that is, we must keep SDI as the motivator. And the second stage must be built on the fulfillment of key preconditions; that is, we have to address the immense asymmetries in Soviet and American conventional power, such as in armor. The interagency process is not going to put the issues to the president in the proper way. That process will just be used, as in the past, as a way for those who don't support the president's approach to gather material to leak to the press in order to derail the process."

"Yes," Nitze said. "At the last meeting of the Senior Arms Control Group I suggested that the session be interrupted periodically for filing breaks."

"We should just draft the letter that we feel the president should send. And we should say that, as we go forward, we will abide by the ABM Treaty," I told them.

The group dispersed, but Nitze stayed behind. "That was a bitter debate yesterday in the SACG [Senior Arms Control Group]," he said. "The idea of a nonnuclear world had to be ventilated, but I don't know whether we can keep Richard Perle in line. It's good to talk to him; it's important to have him on our side, but just as important to stand up to him at times. The interagency process is always difficult," Nitze went on. "Acheson had little trouble, though. Truman backed him, and Acheson and Marshall got along. I was the director of policy planning for the secretary. The Joint Chiefs knew I reflected Acheson's views and that the president would back Acheson. There was no point in a reclama. We got all kinds of things done. As for defense, Lovett was a great wit and handler of the Hill, but he was not good as a strategic analyst or as a decision maker. As secretary of defense, you need three requirements: an ability to work with Congress; an ability at big-time management; and an ability at war strategy. Only Forrestal had all three." Nitze's depiction of the good old days bore little resemblance to current working arrangements involving State and Defense.

When I had my next discussion of these matters with President Reagan, I could see that anyone trying to talk him out of his vision of a world free of nuclear weapons was wasting his breath. I told him I would send him a draft for his letter of reply to Gorbachev.

Roz Ridgway and her team in the European bureau wrote a first draft, and Paul Nitze and I worked it over. The main point of our approach was to ensure that SDI continue to be researched and developed as a guarantee and a lever for deep reductions in nuclear weapons. But I did not want to say that directly to Gorbachev in this letter. I wanted to retain the president's vision of a world without nuclear weapons, stress the first phase of arms reductions, and build the notion that the path to such a world would require that a host of difficult but related issues be dealt with: verification, conventional forces, chemical weapons, and regional conflicts and flash points.

Shcharansky Is Released

Reports on our negotiations for the swap for Shcharansky were coming in fairly frequently now. Shcharansky was to be released across the Glienicke Bridge into West Berlin on February 11. On Monday, February 3, a leak about the coming release appeared on the front page of the *New York Times*. When I said, "No comment," that was taken by the TV analysts as confirmation. As usual, a mob of people had been present in the Oval Office the previous week when the Shcharansky release was mentioned, so the leak may have come from there. But there were other possibilities. The Soviets had also leaked the story to the German press, probably deliberately, to get press credit. That was a good sign; a leak from their side usually meant that the release had approval at the top.

Our people in the European bureau were now in contact with the intermediary who was arranging the release. A disturbing message came in asking us to get Avital Shcharansky to write a letter to Anatoly urging him to "cooperate" with the arrangements. I feared that this might be used to induce Shcharansky to sign something unwise or otherwise to give in to Soviet authorities. I said no to the request. "You don't need to worry," said Avital. "If Anatoly is asked to compromise, he just won't do it." Given all the leaks and the increasing certainty that the release would take place, I had decided that Avital should know the scenario for the release so she could plan to be in Europe at the time. She should consult with Prime Minister Peres right away, we advised. Avital said she would walk over to his house (it being Shabbat) that evening, Friday, February 7.

During this period the president's senior advisers met frequently on Soviet issues, and the sessions began to fall into a predictable pattern. I would describe how the Soviets were moving in our direction and point to steps we should take to keep that positive movement going. Cap Weinberger would then say that we were falling for Soviet propaganda. CIA director Bill Casey or his deputy, Bob Gates, would say that CIA intelligence analysis revealed that Gorbachev had done nothing new, only talked a different line. And most of those present would try to stimulate the president's fear that any U.S. diplomatic engagement with Moscow would jeopardize the future of SDI.

I telephoned Poindexter that same day to suggest that the president reply to Gorbachev's letter of January 15 with a handwritten note to show his personal commitment to this whole process. I had developed ideas on content, working with Roz Ridgway and Paul Nitze. Mark Palmer at State and Jack Matlock at the NSC started working on a draft.

On Tuesday, February 11, 1986, Anatoly Shcharansky crossed the Glienicke Bridge to West Berlin. The spies being held on each side were not released until he was met by our new ambassador, Rick Burt, who was so moved that he took off the special cuff links, bearing the emblem of the Great Seal of the Republic, that I presented to each American ambassador. He pressed them into Shcharansky's hands. Rick cabled me later in the day to request a new set. (Shcharansky told me later when I met him in Washington, that he was not wearing the cuff links, that he had never worn cuff links—or a necktie—in his life, and though pleased with the gift, he hoped I wouldn't be offended if he didn't wear them in the future.) Within a few hours after his release, Anatoly and his wife were in Shimon Peres's office and chatting with me on the phone. "It's a great moment in the history of our people," Peres told me.

The Debate About Gorbachev

That day, February 11, I reviewed the Soviet position in Afghanistan. There were signs of serious movement, not just another "peace offensive." The key for the Soviets, if they wanted to get out of the morass they were in, would be to change the Kabul government sufficiently to convince the rebels to cease their attacks on the regime. The Soviets kept telling us that our arms supply to the rebels was the core of the problem. That was nonsense. We and the Afghan resistance were responding to the Soviet invasion of, and armed presence in, Afghanistan. As for solutions, the Soviets would first have to show they were serious about withdrawing from Afghanistan. If we even talked to the Soviets about cutting back on our supplies to the mujaheddin, that would undermine their morale. "Our problem is harder than just dealing with the Soviets," I told State's analysts. "We are committed to the freedom fighters in Afghanistan. We should hang back and not say anything that might cause our side to unravel." I could not agree that we should partially reduce the flow of arms in return for a "partial" Soviet withdrawal.

Dobrynin was called to Moscow for a Central Committee meeting. I met with him alone in my office on February 11 and told him we were disappointed that Gorbachev's letters to the president had not addressed our proposals in the START and in the defense and space talks. We wanted to see progress in these areas. He could convey to Gorbachev, as a personal message from President Reagan, that we were prepared to work energetically on an INF agreement independent of the negotiations on START and defense and space. Gorbachev appeared to be attempting to link the setting of a date for a second summit to changes in our positions in the arms control negotiations.

"This is not a constructive linkage," I told Dobrynin. "If you feel uncomfortable with another summit meeting this year, we should put it over into 1987. The president thinks there is ample time."

That seemed to take Dobrynin aback, and he assured me that the Soviets had no such linkage in mind.

I wanted to disabuse him of the notion that the setting of a summit date was a bargaining chip. I also wanted the Soviets to know that the INF negotiation was in our view the most "pregnant."

At this point, highly disturbing news arrived. A "high-level American official" had urged French and Japanese officials to put pressure on their respective governments to oppose the INF agreement that the president was seeking. Probably as a result of this, we had already started to hear such opposition from the lower levels of the Japanese government—a puzzling development at first. That someone on the president's own arms control team would try to enlist foreign governments to help thwart American policy was a shocking indication that the debate within the administration had become pathological.

The text proposed by the NSC staff for the letter from President Reagan to Gorbachev was equally subversive: the draft did not even mention INF in setting forth the president's proposed agenda for U.S.-Soviet work as we headed toward the next summit. The State Department text, by contrast, had called for intensive work on arms control issues, *particularly* INF.

Our evidence was that the "high American official" who had asked the French and Japanese for help in blocking INF was in the Defense Department. I showed our evidence to Poindexter, who said that such an action constituted "grounds for dismissal." He said he would "let the president see how he is being set up." On February 21, the president handed Poindexter a note on which he had written that the secret approach to the French and Japanese (and probably to other allies) was "a despicable act." The president left it up to Cap Weinberger to deal with this breach of discipline and of loyalty to the president.

"These people," I said, "are out of control." To my knowledge, Weinberger did nothing.

The president's handwritten letter, sent to Gorbachev on February 23, welcomed Gorbachev's January 15 proposal to eliminate all INF missiles from Europe but insisted that any INF settlement be global in scope, covering missiles deployed by the Soviets in Asia as well.

On April 7, 1986, I had breakfast with Dobrynin, who was back in Washington only briefly. He had suddenly been appointed a top adviser on world affairs to Gorbachev in Moscow. Many people speculated that he would dominate Shevardnadze, the newcomer to foreign affairs. I didn't agree. I knew them both; it would not be Dobrynin who would prevail in such a contest. Shevardnadze was a close friend of Gorbachev and he also knew his country well. "Gorbachev is a politician," Dobrynin told me. "He has to get results for his constituencies." So what could he get out of a summit meeting in Washington?

"INF and START are the big issues to work on," I said. "We have put out sensible proposals for each."

"What about SDI? Is there anything new?" Dobrynin asked.

"The president will not curtail his research program," I responded.

Dobrynin made an important declaration: "Gorbachev thinks INF is possible." Then he commented, "There have been some questions in the press about whether Gorbachev is in control. Let me tell you, *he is in control!*"

Yes, I thought, but he is in control of a declining power. At the end of our meeting, I took Dobrynin up to the eighth floor and to my private dining room for lunch. Out on the balcony, on this bright spring day, we could see all Washington stretched out before us, from Capitol Hill far up to the left, to the Lincoln Memorial straight ahead, to Arlington Cemetery and the Custis-Lee Mansion on the right. Dobrynin said he had seen this sight many times in his decades of service in Washington and asked whether I could give him a panoramic photograph of it all. "Of course," I said. Dobrynin seemed wistful and subdued, as though he hated to leave America, the country in which he had been ambassador for almost a quarter of a century. I soon found out that no such photograph existed. It took six months to get a good panoramic photograph shot and framed. Then some security people raised concerns about such a picture hanging in the Kremlin, apparently fearing it would help the Soviet air force with plans to bomb the Washington Mall. I mailed it to Dobrynin, anyway.

After Dobrynin left, Nitze, Kampelman, and I reviewed the scene. The crucial first breakthrough had to be the elimination of INF missiles. We had to break the Soviets' political position: we had to make them understand that we would keep our missiles in Europe until they agreed to eliminate the whole category, worldwide. The deeply intrusive verification terms we would demand could never be granted by the Soviet Union we had known; if we could get them to accept our requirements, verification could become the crowbar with which we could pry open the entire USSR.

Writing a START treaty would be an excruciating undertaking, but agreement on the basic elements could be achieved in a reasonably short period of time. Insofar as SDI was concerned, we should find a way to give the Soviets some reassurance in the near term without compromising the research program. We wanted to structure whatever was agreed upon regarding SDI in a way that made clear that SDI was the motive force behind movement on the other two issues.

On April 9, I met with Dobrynin once again, this time at a farewell party for him in his role as "dean of the diplomatic corps" in Washington. The room was jammed with his fellow ambassadors from countries throughout the world, including his successor, the ambassador from Sweden, Count Wilhelm (Willy) Wachtmeister. I wanted a light touch that would end on an appropriately upbeat note.

> The other day, I told President Reagan that Ambassador Dobrynin was going to become Secretary of the Central Committee of the Communist Party of the Soviet Union. The President looked at me and said, "You mean to tell me that all along this guy's been a Communist?"
>
> I said, "Don't worry. It's okay. Even Richard Perle talks to him."
>
> In order to make Anatoly feel right at home here this evening, I have prepared an eight-hour-long speech.
>
> Anatoly has asked that a news blackout be imposed on this ceremony so that Moscow won't know what's going on here this evening. That's because this transfer of power is a violation of the Brezhnev Doctrine. It's the first time ever that a Communist handed power over to a Count. . . .
>
> Anatoly has been in Washington a long time. So long, in fact, that he still thinks of Senators as a baseball team. . . . To make it easier on Anatoly, I once gave him a chair with the State Department seal on it. And he has just brought me a handsome clock from Moscow.
>
> So I'd like to offer a toast tonight to Anatoly Dobrynin and to the possibility that at some point before too long—before our respective security agents reassemble his chair and my clock—we will see progress toward a more stable and sustainable Soviet-American relationship.

Dobrynin enjoyed the toast so much that he pulled the notes I had away from me when I sat down.

In late May 1986, I convened one of my Saturday seminars, this one to think and talk about the Soviets, particularly Gorbachev after one year in office. He was a new force, moving away from the dogmas of Brezhnev. But Gorbachev still did not grasp the realities of the information age: he still wanted to reform communism, not get rid of it. Robert Gates, most prominent among the CIA analysts, said that nothing had happened or could happen, that Gorbachev was just another in the succession of hidebound Soviet leaders. I was fascinated to hear some variations from that view from younger CIA analysts included in the meeting at the suggestion of Mort Abramowitz. I saw that there was at least healthy ferment in the agency. I was learning more by listening to the divergent arguments set forth here than to the tidy, distilled conclusions formally presented to me by the CIA.

Paul Nitze, who had been in Europe in March, had read Gorbachev's latest six-hour speech on his plane ride home. Paul's analysis was sobering and revealing. "The first fifty pages," Paul said, "are the grossest kind of ideological argument. Then he goes into the sins of the Brezhnev era and then the mechanics of how to get things going again. The foreign affairs section is pedestrian and has nothing new in it. But when the speech gets to the purification of the Communist party, it has real conviction and reads like Gorbachev wrote it himself. An activist is Gorbachev," Paul said, "but his *summum bonum* is the party."

As long as that was the case, I felt, and as long as he continued to make six-hour speeches in the traditional Communist party boss way, he would not take the crucial steps required to save his country from failure. Gorbachev saw that the condition of the Soviet system was terrible, but then he stopped short of what was needed. "His goals could be met," I told the group, "if he would change the Soviet system. So we need to keep trying to influence Gorbachev in that direction." I could see the Gorbachev boldness reflected in the arms control negotiations: we got glimmers that the Soviets now could envisage a mutually beneficial agreement with us in INF and START. They now could contemplate real arms reductions but had a hard time with on-site verification, for that would require the unveiling of their closed society. They were an elite under stress, intellectually and politically. And they were a society under stress economically and morally as a result of the long night of repression.

The line of analysis the CIA was circulating dovetailed with the Defense Department's emphasis on the magnitude of the Soviet military buildup. Both painted a picture of a mighty nation confronting us everywhere—confident, unchanging, and determined. Their message was to fight back wherever confronted and forget about negotiating agreements with the Soviets. Build strength and never negotiate. Indeed, we should throw off any past arms control agreements that constrained us in this massive confrontation.

I did not agree. The picture they conjured up of the Soviet Union did not match the reality I saw. The Soviet leadership, and Soviet society, seemed increasingly in disarray, and the USSR's strength—outside the field of nuclear missiles—was highly questionable. Their society was demoralized and their economy unresponsive. Looking around the world, we could see that the Soviets' onward thrust in Central America had been blunted and contained in Nicaragua; their efforts in Yemen and the Horn of Africa had faltered; they had nothing to offer in the Middle East but support for rejecting the peace process; and our efforts in Southern Africa, Southeast

Asia, and Afghanistan were gaining strength. The Soviets' Eastern European empire was held together by military force and a rigged economic dependence on Soviet markets and oil. Most important of all, the Soviet Union had nothing to offer the Third World on economic development. Their ideology was a known failure in practice. One need only contrast West Germany and East Germany, South Korea and North Korea: economic success contrasted vividly with economic failure. Social scientists could not have designed a more revealing laboratory experiment.

"My conclusion is radically different from that of Casey and Weinberger," I told my colleagues. "The Soviets have lost the ideological battle. Their idea is receding; ours is moving forward."

Tension and Stalemate

As the winter months had passed into spring, a certain sense of stalemate and sourness had set in. The year 1985 had been a tough one in the espionage community, so much so that many called it "the year of the spy." Marine Private Robert Cordrey's conviction on charges of trying to sell nuclear, chemical, and biological warfare information to the Soviet Union was announced on January 8, 1985. On May 20, 1985, retired navy warrant officer John Walker, Jr., had been arrested and charged with espionage, and it soon appeared that he had headed a family of spies that for as long as twenty years had provided information of great importance to the Soviets.

In mid-June, I had ordered steps to tighten security at our embassies and reduced the number of Soviet employees in Moscow. A CIA employee, Sharon Scranage, had been arrested by the FBI on July 11, charged with passing intelligence information to Ghanaian authorities. In September, Edward Lee Howard, a CIA employee who had been stationed in Moscow but who was now under suspicion and on leave, slipped out of sight and turned up in Moscow the following August, no doubt compromising whatever human sources we had developed there.

On November 21, Jonathan Pollard, an analyst for the Naval Investigative Service, had been arrested and admitted that he had delivered classified material to Israel. On November 23, Larry Wu-Tai Chin, a retired employee of the CIA, had been charged with spying for China for over thirty years, undetected despite passing lie detector tests. On November 25, Ronald Pelton, a former communications specialist in the supersecret National Security Agency, had admitted selling intelligence to the Soviets for over five years. Lie detector tests had missed him, too. I was not surprised. I was convinced that many people could train themselves to beat the tests and that even with untrained populations, the tests were wrong in a disturbing number of cases. I had my own fight with the intelligence community when I objected to the generalized use of lie detector tests. Concern about Soviet espionage in the United States and directed at the United States in third countries was at a high pitch.

A long-term source of aggravation for the FBI, whose job it was to keep track of Soviet activities and ferret out spies, was the Soviet mission to the United Nations. The numbers assigned had long been far larger than those from any other country, and the count was 275 in the spring of 1986. We knew which people were attached to the KGB, and all were watched—a big job. The president decided, with support from all his key national security advisers, including me, that the time had come to reduce this Soviet presence. The undertaking would be delicate, we knew, since we are obligated by the treaty under which the United Nations operates in New York not to interfere with UN activities, including the staffing of the missions of member countries. We maintained, however, that we had the right to look after our security interests.

On March 7, 1986, the United States, having earlier informed the Soviets and the secretary-general of the United Nations, announced that the size of the Soviet mission must be reduced to 170 by April 1988 in increments of 25 every six months. The Soviets and the UN secretariat, where an additional 310 Soviets were employed, protested. The U.S. government insisted.

The Soviets, through *Tass* on March 8, called our move "unprecedented" and "hostile" and on March 11 went further: "The U.S. Administration has to realize that such actions reinforce distrust toward its policies and by no means create a favorable background for a summit meeting. . . . Of course, the Soviet side cannot pass over such illegal actions by the United States and will be forced to draw the appropriate conclusions for itself."

On March 13, on a mission cleared by the State Department in advance, two of our naval ships, equipped with extensive and sophisticated electronic capability, moved within six miles of the Soviet Black Sea coastline. This was part of the worldwide navy program to assert our rights of "innocent passage" and was not the first time in the Reagan administration when we had made such an assertion close to Soviet shores. It was, however, the first time since the Geneva summit. The Soviets reacted sharply and warned against any repetition.

On April 14, the United States launched a limited air strike against Libya in response to Libyan terrorism against Americans. Foreign Minister Shevardnadze subsequently canceled his scheduled visit to Washington. We had, of course, informed the Soviets that we had solid evidence of terrorist acts against Americans by Qaddafi and set forth why we felt our actions were necessary. In the aftermath of the Libya raid, I watched for a Soviet response: there was none. In 1982, after Israel had demolished the Syrian air force's Soviet-supplied planes, the Soviets had rushed Syria large quantities of advanced weaponry, manned with Soviet personnel. This they did not do for Qaddafi. They moved a Soviet command ship offshore, but that was all. We hit Qaddafi, and he stayed hit. No one came to his defense or to his side politically.

Chernobyl and Its Diplomatic Fallout

The president and the first lady left Washington on April 25, 1986, for a thirteen-day trip to Indonesia and Japan. We made our way slowly westward. As we were leaving Honolulu for Bali, Indonesia, on April 28, distressing news reached *Air Force One*. Abnormally high levels of radioactivity had been reported by Sweden, Finland, and Denmark, all downwind from the Soviet Union. Experts in these Scandinavian countries first checked their own reactors and found no problems. Sweden demanded information from the Soviets. On April 28, a clipped statement from the *Tass* news agency was read on Soviet television: "An accident has occurred at the Chernobyl nuclear power plant as one of the reactors was damaged. Measures are being taken to eliminate the consequences of the accident. Aid is being given to those affected. A Government commission has been set up."

I was initially surprised at this announcement, because the Soviets *never* reported disasters, hoping to give the impression, to their people and to the rest of the world, of a society miraculously free of the troubles that beset others. But as this disaster was observed by satellites in space and was recorded by sensitive technology in other countries, word of the extent and consequences of Chernobyl was beamed back to the USSR. Gorbachev could not cover up the incident or control reports of it. Months earlier, in Moscow and Geneva, I had tried to describe to Gorbachev the power of the information age: the Soviet Union no longer had a monopoly on information reaching its people or the people of the Warsaw Pact countries. The East Europeans were downwind of the large-scale radiactive fallout from what amounted to an uncontained and sustained nuclear explosion. They, too, heard about this catastrophe, an event of immense human importance, from the West rather than from their ally, the Soviet Union. I had told Gorbachev during our meeting in the Kremlin in November 1985 that the information age was going to cause the system of the Soviet Union to change. The Soviets, I had argued, would need to be part of the information age if they were to be part of the modern world. For this to happen, they would need to be far more open, with far more scope for individual initiative. In any case, important developments anywhere would quickly be known everywhere. As we flew on from Honolulu, I wondered whether Gorbachev would recall our talk as he tried to cope with this disaster.

On *Air Force One*, I drafted a proposed presidential message:

Dear Mr. General Secretary:

I have been informed of the bulletin issued by the Council of Ministers concerning the nuclear accident at Chernobyl. I want you to know that we have experts trained to deal with the medical and toxic consequences of such events, as well as specialists skilled in the techniques required to bring damaged reactors under control. I am prepared to order a team of such experts to get under way at once to assist the Soviet Union in dealing with this situation, should you wish me to do so. I do not intend to make this message public.

Ronald Reagan

Don Regan wanted to send the message; John Poindexter didn't. I could see another classic White House spat in the works. Poindexter said that he wanted to put the question of what, if anything, to offer the Soviets into the hands of an NSC-chaired "lower-level group" that would consider suggestions made by the Department of Energy. The group would report to the vice president and then send the president its recommendations. I threw up my hands. "We need a quick response!" I argued. A small group was convened in Washington, and technical capabilities were identified. The president approved a message, and the State Department announced on April 29 that the United States had offered humanitarian and technical assistance.

After the Soviets issued the initial bulletin on Chernobyl, the Soviet leaders attempted a news blackout, but ham radio operators outside the Soviet Union transmitted reports, which were received within the Soviet Union, about the extensive and continuing nuclear accident. Despite all efforts at denial and control, the information age had inundated the Soviet system. Perhaps, I thought, the combination of my arguments and this traumatic event would really register with Gorbachev.

As the world watched the two superpowers, assessing which was stronger and more confident as they faced off on the big issues of the global scene, another accounting went on simultaneously, at a lower, less visible level. Like boxers who know when they have scored a point, or been scored upon, while the ringside fans are still counting up the dramatic punches, the United States and the Soviet Union both knew in the early summer of 1986 that the United States was pulling far ahead. Reagan had starred at the Geneva summit; we had challenged the Soviets' use of their UN personnel for espionage and were insisting on a reduction in their numbers; our navy had run a successful Black Sea challenge; we had struck at Libya while the Soviets watched; the balance was shifting our way in Afghanistan, Angola, Cambodia, and Central America; and Chernobyl revealed fresh flaws in the Soviet fabric. Although the world at large did not see it yet, the Soviets were ready for a fall.

When Shcharansky came to see me on May 13, he, too, detected the change. "From childhood, I was taught one rule: in any competition, socialism will win, a law of nature," he told me. "Suddenly I read a Gorbachev speech saying that if the Soviet Union does not do something radical, socialism could lose. That is a stunning statement to someone raised in the system."

The Soviets on the Ropes

I talked to the president at some length the next day. "The Soviets," I said, "contrary to the Defense Department and the CIA line, are not an omnipotent, omnipresent power gaining ground and threatening to wipe us out. On the contrary, we are winning. In fact, we are miles ahead. Their ideology is a loser.

"They have one thing going for them: military power," I said. "But even there they have only one area of genuine comparative advantage—the capacity to develop, produce, and deploy accurate, powerful, mobile land-based ballistic missiles." I elaborated on this point, which I had made to President Reagan many times: "There's only one thing the Soviet Union does better than we do: that is to produce and deploy ballistic missiles. And that's not because they are better at engineering. They're not. Our political system resists basing ballistic missiles on our own territory. But their ballistic missiles threaten our security directly. Not since we beat the British at the time of our revolution has anything threatened our country like the ballistic missile does.

"So we must focus on reductions in ballistic missiles," I said. "Reductions are the name of the game. The only way to achieve reductions is through negotiations. The negotiation of large reductions in strategic missiles is the most important objective for the security of the United States. We have a tremendous amount to gain by bringing the number of strategic missiles down. We must start in 1986.

"Your successor," I told President Reagan, "should be able to decide whether to deploy a defensive system. Keeping an SDI research program alive is important but difficult. To keep it alive," I said, "we have to be willing to give up something in SDI. An agreement for massive reductions in strategic missiles can use SDI research and potential deployment of a strategic defense as a means to win Soviet compliance on continuing reductions. So we should give them the sleeves from our vest on SDI and make them think they got our overcoat.

"We want a summit in 1986," I said. "Gorbachev was weak at Geneva in November 1985 and still is. He will not want to agree to a summit when he would be doing so from a position of weakness. So we have to look for something that will entice him into a summit meeting with you. This is the moment when our bargaining position is at its strongest."

President Reagan said he liked my approach, as did Don Regan and John Poindexter, who were also present. The president was firm on massive reductions. He had made INF and START proposals years earlier, in 1981 and 1982. He wanted to be sure the sleeves we gave were from our vest. He would not compromise our research program for strategic defense.

I sent the president a draft of a letter for him to send to Gorbachev, just as a way of making these ideas operational. Let's get started on our mutual objective of eliminating nuclear weapons by working first on major reductions in strategic systems, the draft said. While pressing in this way for START, I remembered that Dobrynin had told me that Gorbachev felt INF was possible. I thought so, too. A verifiable treaty on significant reductions of such weapons would be a far-reaching step. And the political impact of removing all of those missiles—the zero-zero outcome—would be historic. Within the administration, Cap Weinberger still fought against the entire approach. On the NBC-TV "Today" show, Weinberger remarked, critically, "A lot of people think that arms control is more important than anything else." What was important, Weinberger kept asserting, was gaining strength to deter war.

The Debate Resumes: Abandon SALT II?

In 1985, the president had debated whether he should continue to abide by the limits set out in the unratified SALT II Treaty. The outcome of the debate then was to maintain the policy of staying within the SALT II limits. Practically speaking, we had no operational need to exceed them. Cap Weinberger and others kept the question very much alive. I favored that we maintain the current policy on the grounds that the Soviets were in a better position than we were to add to the arsenal of strategic ballistic missiles. The Joint Chiefs of Staff agreed with me. But I also recognized that the arguments against that policy were powerful.[2]

On May 27, President Reagan announced that the United States would no longer abide by the SALT II limits. I expected the uproar from our NATO allies (including Margaret Thatcher) and Congress, not to mention the Soviets. But I am not sure the president and Weinberger were prepared for the magnitude of what hit them. I defended the decision, I felt, more effectively than its advocates. The president decided to dismantle two older submarines rather than put them in dry dock, as advocated by Weinberger.

2. The SALT II Treaty had not been ratified; Ronald Reagan had long argued that it was "fatally flawed," since, among other problems, the fundamental unit of account was launchers rather than warheads. Furthermore, the Soviets had themselves clearly violated the related ABM Treaty by construction that was well under way on the phased-array radar at Krasnoyarsk, and arguably they had violated the SALT II Treaty by testing a new type of strategic ballistic missile.

He thereby stayed within the treaty limits for the moment while saying he had no obligation to do so. Nevertheless, in Congress and among our allies, the feeling of confrontation created unease.

"Star Wars": The Soviet Focus

On May 29, the Soviets privately presented a new proposal at Geneva. They had obviously prepared their proposal before our SALT II decision, but nonetheless went ahead with their presentation, while warning that Soviet forces would be increased if the United States exceeded the SALT II limits. They had moved away from their position that research, testing, and development of "space strike weapons" be prohibited in exchange for a 50 percent reduction in what they defined as strategic weapons. Now they offered an entirely different kind of trade-off: research, testing, and development of SDI components could go forward in what they called "the laboratory"; we would both agree not to exercise our rights of withdrawal from the ABM Treaty for fifteen to twenty years, followed by an indefinite period of negotiations over subsequent steps; and strategic arms, defined more agreeably to us, would be reduced by 30 percent. (On June 11, the Soviets further adjusted their definition of "strategic" by agreeing with us that forward-based aircraft systems would not be included.)

Soviet restrictions on our work on SDI were unacceptable to us, the period of nonwithdrawal was too long, and their proposed reductions were too modest. Still, this was promising: it was the first real opening we had received in space and defense negotiations in Geneva. We were approaching the moment of truth, I was convinced. The key was to shorten the period during which we could not deploy so that no practical restriction was actually placed on us.

When I met with President Reagan on June 3, however, he had reversed his position. He was afraid that *any* discussion with the Soviets about strategic defense would be used as a way to scuttle SDI. I tried to convince him that we could give up those deployment rights that we could not exercise anyway—we lacked the technical capability—and hold the line there. That would be giving the Soviets the sleeves from our vest! But he remained apprehensive, and we reached no agreement.

That evening I called in Paul Nitze. "I keep trying to explain to the president that this approach, which you and I have advocated, is the best insurance policy for the continuation of SDI and the best way to make SDI valuable to his successor," I told Paul. "The question is, are we willing to discuss what the ABM Treaty means? The Soviets have come toward our position. They have moved from saying the ABM Treaty bans any work on SDI, a ridiculous position, to asking us how we might agree that the treaty limits SDI, particularly on deployment rights, in return for an agreement on offensive reductions."

Cap Weinberger was denigrating the Soviet proposals on television, and pressure was building against a positive American response. A cable came in from Max Kampelman in Geneva: "It is imperative that we not shut the door."

On June 11, I asked President Reagan to authorize me to advise the Soviets that he took their arms control message seriously; that if Gorbachev wanted to suggest a mid-November summit date, he would accept it; and that we noted and valued the recent positive steps in human rights cases in the Soviet Union. The president agreed. I called in the new Soviet ambassador, Yuri Dubinin, and gave him all three points. So we had locked in a positive reply. But that was just the beginning. Paul Nitze said simply, "The battle [with Weinberger and Perle] is Sisyphean."

Weinberger was working ceaselessly to convince the president that any negotiation that even mentioned SDI would kill the program. The reality was that the right outcome in negotiations could *preserve* it. I felt this point was gradually settling into the president's thinking. I found it impossible to argue with Weinberger. But Perle was engaging and constructive. Behind Perle's opposition I could sense a willingness to look for ways to reach an agreement with the Soviets that was in our interest. Until that agreement came along, however, Perle would fight tooth and nail against giving the Soviets the slightest benefit of the doubt. That was all right with me. If State Department officials leaked details of the Soviet START proposal in order to present it in a good light, Perle said, the office of the secretary of defense would feel compelled to respond with a negative leak to protect SDI. He proposed that State and Defense adopt a "no first leak" policy.

Perle, Nitze told me, was angry at me because he thought I had tried to get him fired. I talked to Perle, told him of my information about statements in opposition to INF made to French and Japanese officials. He assured me that he had not been responsible. I accepted his word. By this time, I knew from my own sources that he was not the culprit. The air was cleared, and our relations proceeded amicably. Increasingly, I found Perle one of the most creative and reliable thinkers on arms control matters.

An Astonishing Proposal from Cap

The president convened an intimate and restricted group in the Situation Room on June 12 to consider the Soviet proposals. Cap Weinberger surprised the president and me with a dramatic and radical proposal. When Gorbachev had proposed at the beginning of the year a phased program to eliminate nuclear weapons, the president was enthusiastic, but no one else in his administration was. I had tried to convert the idea into an asset on which we could build a solid first phase of reductions. Now came Weinberger with a proposal to eliminate all ballistic missiles. Everyone was astonished.

The president looked at me. I smiled. "I compliment Cap on having the imagination to present such a bold idea," I said. I recalled to the president my sentiments about the Soviet comparative advantage in ballistic missiles. The president was intrigued. We left the meeting on the note that Cap's idea should be studied carefully but quietly to see how we might make it a part of our reply to the latest Soviet offer.

Actually, I had previously heard from Max Kampelman some rumblings of what Cap presented in the Situation Room. Fred Ikle, under secretary of defense, had raised the idea with Max Kampelman, as he apparently had also with the Joint Chiefs of Staff and with Poindexter's deputy, Don Fortier. Ikle pointed up the special danger from fast-flying ballistic missiles, which cannot be recalled once launched. Ikle had taken the argument to its logical conclusion. I thought this idea was unlikely to go anywhere but that, with Weinberger making the suggestion, the result would be to break a logjam in thinking about strategic issues within the administration.

During these months, the president from time to time heard the views of writer Suzanne Massie. Massie was the author of *Land of the Firebird: The Beauty of Old Russia*, a book about traditional Russian culture under the czars; her husband Robert Massie had written a best-seller on czarist Russia, *Nicholas and Alexandra*. When Suzanne Massie had finished talking to the president, he would send her over to me. She was buoyant with enthusiasm for what she saw as signs of a renascence of Russian spirituality. Although I was not swept up by her rhetoric, I felt that her frequent travels to the Soviet Union had revealed to her undercurrents of great power; I had felt them myself. Suzanne Massie gave a glimpse of a different Soviet reality from the one I read about in my secret briefing papers. There might well be a vast historic transformation developing, I felt, but the dimensions went beyond religion and reached into the realm of economics, politics, and the changes wrought by the information revolution as well.

A Grand Compromise?

I told the president on Wednesday, June 18, that the Soviets had moved with proposals across a wide front and in a sophisticated manner. At Geneva, I said, the Soviets had made clear, substantive changes in their position, and they were talking about our agenda, just as we had wanted. "The Soviets are ready to bargain," I said. "The U.S. should respond." President Reagan agreed that we must reply positively to the Soviets. "The surest way to preserve SDI is to turn it into the leverage by which offensive cuts would proceed," I argued. Still, President Reagan talked only about going ahead full steam on SDI and then sharing it with the Soviets. "Yes," I said, "but that would be far down the line; we need some way to get us there." Ronald Reagan agreed with me in general, but he never swerved from his single-minded focus on SDI.

On Thursday, June 19, at a high school commencement in Glassboro, New Jersey, the site of the 1967 Johnson-Kosygin summit, President Reagan announced, "There have been fresh developments. The Soviets have made suggestions on a range of issues, from nuclear power-plant safety to conventional force reductions in Europe. Perhaps most important, the Soviet negotiators at Geneva have placed on the table new proposals to reduce nuclear weapons. Now, we cannot accept these particular proposals without some change, but it appears that the Soviets have begun to make a serious effort. . . . This could represent a turning point. . . . An atmosphere does exist that will allow for serious discussion."

On the same day, Weinberger sent a memo to Poindexter: "I am deeply disturbed that the State Department, without our concurrence, sent out a cable Tuesday night, which described the new Soviet START proposal for use by our embassies in discussions with allied governments." The Defense Department had tried to block the cable, which simply informed our close allies of the most recent Soviet proposals. The cable had been properly cleared through the NSC process. Cap said it should have contained an "appropriate U.S. assessment." As a consequence, he said, "the cable is a messenger for the Soviet position without conveying the President's views." He urged that a Defense Department–drafted cable with a negative and critical assessment be sent out as soon as possible. Cap had stated the problem. Agreement with Weinberger on an assessment would take forever; in the meantime, our allies would know about a Soviet initiative without hearing from us about it. That was a formula for creating distrust within the alliance.

I decided to give the matter a rest. The president was going to his ranch in Santa Barbara, while I had to go to the ASEAN foreign ministers' meeting to be held in the Philippines starting on June 26. I would arrive early to see how Cory Aquino was doing and visit Hong Kong, Singapore, Brunei, and Palau as part of the trip. My visit to Brunei[3] would mean I had paid my respects at each of the ASEAN countries, and a stop in Palau would emphasize our continuing interest in the island countries of the Pacific. I had landed on Palau as a marine in World War II, and I felt we tended to forget the strategic importance of the Pacific islands and our historic ties to them.

3. I did not raise the question of support by Brunei for the Contras, but I did conclude from my conversations with the sultan that he supported ASEAN and our efforts to counter Vietnam's occupation of Cambodia and was concerned about aggressive communism around the world.

On my way to Asia, I sent President Reagan a message headed "Arms Reduction: Getting to the Payoff Stage." This was the time to press for an arms control agreement. I argued that we build on the positive points in the Soviet proposal tabled in Geneva on May 29, and I again advocated that we propose a trade-off of 50 percent reductions in nuclear arms for a willingness to forgo deployment of a strategic defense for the period during which reductions would take place.

I sent another message to Poindexter from Hong Kong after thinking further about Cap's objection to State's cable to our allies describing the latest Soviet proposal:

> . . . First, just for the record, State sent the June 17 cable describing the Soviet proposal only after receiving clearance from the NSC secretariat. Even so, the delay caused by the Department of Defense's unwillingness to release even the most basic information to our embassies and allies already had cost us at NATO and elsewhere. Our allies are pretty smart people; it only hurts us when we appear to be treating them like children.
>
> Second, we have an urgent need to develop a balanced USG [U.S. Government] analysis of the Soviet proposal. But Cap, in his message to you, uses this inaccurate bureaucratic complaint to advance an unbalanced, negative assessment of the Soviet proposal. As the Glassboro statement makes clear, Cap's view is not the President's view.
>
> The real problem with OSD's [Office of the Secretary of Defense] position is that it would block any effort to reach a negotiated solution; OSD seems to be saying that the only acceptable outcome is a wholesale Soviet capitulation to our most far-out positions. Were we to go in this direction, we would see a rapid erosion of public and Congressional support for SDI, and the Soviets would have little choice but to initiate a massive offensive buildup.
>
> The reality is that the new Soviet proposals represent substantive steps forward compared to their previous positions on forward-based systems, cruise missiles, and linkage to defense and space. The Soviets no longer count missiles as warheads in the START limits, no longer propose to ban SLCMs [sea-launched cruise missiles], and no longer link reductions to a ban on all "space strike arms." And they subsequently have picked up on some of our ideas and applied them to the problem of the verification of mobile ICBMs. While their new proposals are far from acceptable as they stand, the Soviets have made real moves in our direction on some of the central START issues.

While I was in Singapore, a flash cable from Washington arrived with the news that Ambassador Dubinin had brought a letter from Gorbachev. Many Sovietologists in the U.S. government had worried that Gorbachev might not want to expose his arms control ideas to *his* "interagency process," and so, with urging, especially from the NSC staff, a private channel or set of special emissaries to carry on the work between us had been proposed. No, Gorbachev indicated that he wanted the work done through "existing channels," our respective embassies, with the foreign ministers, Shevardnadze and me, taking the lead. This was helpful to me, in the face of the NSC staff's constant efforts to become the U.S. special channel or emissary.

Yet I recognized that I could easily get bogged down in *our* interagency process. I had long since concluded that any serious issue would have to be lifted above that quicksand and decided by President Reagan himself. Gorbachev suggested that Shevardnadze and I meet in New York in September, on the eve of the reconvening of the General Assembly, and review whether a summit meeting in the late fall looked promising or not. The topics: nuclear testing and the subjects under negotiation in Geneva: space, START, and INF. The Soviets were picking up on our ideas and playing them back to us as though they had just invented them. That was fine with me. The more Gorbachev wanted to play the role of "creative world statesman for peace" by *coming toward our agenda*, the more we should stand back and applaud him in that performance.

Poindexter sent me a draft presidential letter to Gorbachev that he had worked out with Weinberger. They made use of the ideas of nonwithdrawal from the ABM Treaty and elimination of ballistic missiles, but in what I regarded as a peculiar way. I sent their draft privately to Nitze for comment. He pointed up problems, particularly with our allies. When I returned to Washington, I focused my work on a response to Gorbachev's May 31 proposals.

The debate within the administration over our response to Gorbachev soon leaked. On July 10, the front page of the *Washington Post* carried a Walter Pincus–Lou Cannon article, headlined "Star Wars' Compromise Discussed: If Soviets Slash Weapons, Reagan Might Delay Deployment." Sourced to "administration officials," the story said that Weinberger and Shultz "disagree so sharply over whether the United States should consider such a swap that the schism ultimately will have to be resolved by President Reagan," adding, "Reagan has reached no decision." That was wrong.

The president had been working over ideas and a draft response with a small ad hoc group of key advisers, which included Weinberger, Casey, Poindexter, and me. A letter finally emerged that covered much familiar ground, including reductions by 50 percent in strategic weapons. But, at the end, the letter contained a new proposal. For seven and a half years, both sides would consent not to withdraw from the ABM Treaty. For five years, each side would confine itself to research, development, and testing consistent with the ABM Treaty. If either side then decided to deploy strategic defenses, then that side would be obligated to offer and negotiate a plan for sharing "the benefits of strategic defense" and for *eliminating offensive ballistic missiles*. If no agreement was reached on this plan by the end of the seven and a half years, either side would be free to deploy after six months' notice.

This was a different version of the approach Nitze and I had advocated: a restriction on SDI that did not really restrict us and the reductions we sought in strategic weapons. And it now included Cap's idea of eliminating ballistic missiles. The letter was made known to our allies and then was sent to Gorbachev on July 25, 1986. The compromise on the ABM Treaty was promptly leaked. But the proposal to eliminate ballistic missiles was not revealed publicly until an August 25 article in the *Wall Street Journal*. There was little comment on what I had regarded as a radical idea, perhaps because no one took the idea seriously.

Suzanne Massie came in, fresh from the Soviet Union. What she said confirmed my own thinking and instincts: the Soviet Union was on the road to collapse. There were shortages of everything, and the people now realized that they had to turn to free enterprise. Chernobyl was of great symbolic importance, she felt: it showed that Soviet science and technology were flawed, that the leadership was lying and out of touch, that the party could not conceal its failures any longer. "Chernobyl," she said to the president and me, "means 'Wormwood,' a reference to bitterness and sorrow from the Book of Revelation. There are many biblical allusions in Russia now," she said. I thought that Chernobyl was a turning point in having made a dramatic impact on Gorbachev. I learned that he had calculated, as I had, the relation of Chernobyl's release of explosive power to that of a single nuclear warhead. Gorbachev also saw the information age at work. News came relentlessly to his country and to the downwind countries of the Warsaw Pact—but from the West. The information age means that lies are almost impossible to sustain.

Former President Richard Nixon had gone to Moscow in July. When he returned, he gave President Reagan a twenty-six-page report on his meeting with Gorbachev. Nothing he had said to Gorbachev made a bigger impression, Nixon said, than when he told Gorbachev that Reagan, even after he left office, would have an enormous influence on American opinion when it came to the Soviet Union. If Gorbachev failed to reach an agreement with the United States while Reagan was president, Gorbachev might still find that ex-President Reagan would be a powerful critic of the kind of deal he would try to strike with Reagan's successor. Nixon concluded that Gorbachev wanted the first major U.S.-Soviet agreement to be achieved with Ronald Reagan.

I was sure that it could be done. My goal was an INF agreement by mid-1987 and a structure for START that would permit an agreement on that by mid-1988. As the August 1986 vacation period began, it seemed to me that our foreign policy was poised to "cash in" on all the efforts the Reagan administration had put forward over the past few years to build up our strength and leverage.

Obstacles to Success

Notwithstanding the promising prospects, unease in the White House over my efforts in the Philippines lingered. I was uneasy, too, with *them.* I was at odds with the intelligence community over lie detector tests. I had opposed arms sales to Iran, an ill-conceived and misguided effort.[4] I was subjected to a kind of low-level guerrilla warfare from the White House staff. I had been involved in a bruising battle with Bill Casey and Pat Buchanan in mid-July over a speech about sanctions on South Africa. I did not favor sweeping new sanctions imposed by legislation but did favor additional strong steps to be taken by executive order.

A presidential speech was decided on, with my reluctant agreement, presumably to dramatize the president's anti-apartheid views. A Buchanan-NSC draft speech competed with one we originated in the State Department. Casey, who worked with South African intelligence, weighed in. The approved draft, changed at the last moment without telling me, left out steps we had agreed on and did not hit unequivocally at the central problem of apartheid. Pat Buchanan had gotten his way with the draft. The speech inflamed Congress at the worst possible time and subsequently caused an unnecessary override of a presidential veto in the Republican-controlled Senate by 78 to 21, the first override on a foreign policy issue since President Nixon was defeated on the War Powers Resolution in 1973. I felt this loss doubly: on the substance, a meritorious position was defeated and an erosion of control of foreign policy had taken place; I could also see my further separation from the White House, Casey, and the president.

On August 5, 1986, I gave the president my letter of resignation. He did not accept it. I didn't want to abandon him, but I felt that he must correct the indecisiveness and backbiting involved in the current NSC and White House processes. I also knew that when it came to anti-Communist dictators, he and I were just not on the same wavelength. And I was sick and tired of fighting the same battles on Soviet matters over and over again. "You might well be better off without me," I told him.

On August 8, I was at home on vacation at Stanford when Don Regan called me on the tacsat that had been set up in my study. The president had been very distressed by my letter and conversation with him and wanted me to stay, Regan told me. Was I tired or did I have a physical problem, or a family worry? "You are on his mind," Don said. "The president does not want you to go because of the way the White House operates." That was exactly why I did feel I should go. "The president feels that together the two of you can accomplish a hell of a lot in the next two years."

I went all over the problems again for Don. "The environment is a very

---

4. See Chapters 37–39 and 42 for a full discussion of what became known as the Iran-Contra affair.

frustrating one to work in. I find it difficult to pull together a team in the national security field. The situation is debilitating. I am constantly under attack. I get no sense of support. I feel I'm out there operating on my own. Maybe somebody else can do it better."

Don recognized the problem. "We take to the field in the next four or five weeks in one of the most important games ever for the U.S.," he told me. "If we can't work coherently, the president himself may have to bang heads and make sure the group is united: no deviating, no undercutting, no sniping!" The president would never do that, I knew. That was not in his nature.

"I suggest a two-stage approach," I told Don. "I'll be back next week, and we'll talk. Then I'll give my thoughts to the president."

When I got back to Washington, I saw Don Regan and outlined for him "the problem with the way the White House operates." I went over the obstacles to forming a team to deal with the Soviets; the leaks and statements out of the White House and the Defense Department aimed at freezing U.S. policy; the inability to get good people in important jobs because of the small-minded White House personnel approach; the multiple channels—State and CIA—going out to foreign governments, such as South Africa, that allowed them to play different parts of the administration off against each other; the withholding and politically motivated distortion of intelligence: I documented it all. Even hardheaded Don Regan was stunned by some of the things I told him. Taken together, the actions portrayed White House and NSC staffs that were operating on the fringes of loyalty to the president and of common sense.

Paul Nitze headed a team of experts that went to Moscow in mid-August and returned to say that the atmosphere was good. There were seven on the U.S. team: Paul Nitze, Ed Rowny, Max Kampelman, Mike Glitman, Ron Lehman, Bob Linhard, and Richard Perle. Ken Adelman asked to be included, and I agreed. Adelman said that I regarded him as "the eighth dwarf."

"Do I look like Snow White?" I asked.

"I felt the Soviets were instructed to be serious about narrowing differences," Paul said, "but the people they selected for their team find it hard to deal with such instructions." The Soviet delegation was composed of the same people who had been negative all through the negotiations in Geneva. Bessmertnykh had remarked privately about his own delegation, saying, "We perhaps made a mistake in the composition." The Soviets were fascinated by SDI but showed no signs of interest in our July 25 approach. The least progress of all was on START. With INF, Nitze felt we were getting somewhere. He asked me a crucial question, "Do we put the brakes on an emerging INF agreement until we see Soviet movement toward radical reductions in strategic arms?" "No," I said without a moment's hesitation.

"Wherever we see the possibility of progress, we should be ready to go forward."

I went to my farm in the Berkshire Hills of Massachusetts for a few days of rest at the end of August. The president was on vacation in California. I was mulling over how best to persuade him to change his White House and NSC decision-making process. I was ready to leave if that would help, though I was also ready to stay and work flat out in a clarified and improved environment.

Just then, a fresh Soviet-American crisis flashed onto my screen, followed by a surge of events over the next three months that taxed to the limits my capacity for steadiness under tension and work under fire.

CHAPTER 35

Victim Made Hostage:
The Nicholas Daniloff Case

The summer holiday was coming to an end. Meetings between U.S. and Soviet arms control teams in Moscow and now in Washington were proving productive in substance and positive in tone. I was to meet Foreign Minister Eduard Shevardnadze on September 19 and 20, 1986. These would be our first meetings since the summit in Geneva ten months earlier. But I was uneasy about my relationships in Washington. I was planning to talk to the president again about the disarray in the national security process and my readiness to step aside. I would have that talk, I thought, after he returned from Santa Barbara and I from my stay at my farm in New England. But other traumatic events intervened.

Nicholas S. Daniloff, the *U.S. News & World Report* correspondent in Moscow, had been arrested by the Soviets on August 30 and was in Soviet custody on a charge of spying. He had been set up, or so it looked to me. After being handed a package allegedly containing some material stamped "top secret," Daniloff had been arrested. The Soviets obviously had taken an American to trade for Gennadi F. Zakharov, a Soviet scientific attaché assigned to the UN Secretariat in New York, who had been arrested by the FBI on August 23 after he exchanged money for classified documents provided by the FBI to a student Zakharov had approached. While the Soviets persistently used the personnel of their enormous mission to the United Nations for espionage activities, they rarely employed for espionage Soviets who worked at the UN Secretariat and did not have diplomatic immunity. Zakharov's spying was a departure from practice and therefore was doubly disturbing.

We had arrested a real spy in a sting operation, and the Soviets had taken a reporter to use in bargaining for a swap. The wire services soon were carrying a story, datelined Santa Barbara, indicating the United States would consider a "swap" of Daniloff for Zakharov, a breathtakingly stupid

728

thing to say. Someone in the California White House had blundered badly.[1]

On Friday, September 5, 1986, I drove from my farm in western Massachusetts to Cambridge to address a convocation marking the 350th anniversary of the founding of Harvard University. The Cambridge audience was responsive right at the outset to my statement: "I know that I have come to the right place to voice a message of outrage at the detention of Nick Daniloff, Harvard Class of 1956. The cynical arrest of an innocent American journalist reminds us of what we already know: Our traditions of free inquiry and openness are spurned by the Soviets, showing the dark side of a society prepared to resort to hostage-taking as an instrument of policy. Let there be no talk of a 'trade' for Daniloff. We, and Nick himself, have ruled that out." The audience applauded the principle of no trade, and I hoped that this public statement put the earlier comment from the summer White House to rest. "The Soviet leadership must find the wisdom to settle this case quickly in accordance with the dictates of simple human decency and of civilized national behavior," I said.

I had hoped to go back to the farm for the weekend but returned to Washington to deal more effectively with the Daniloff case and with the hijacking of a Pan Am jet in Karachi by Arab terrorists. By the time I was back in my State Department office Friday afternoon, we had reports that the Pan Am plane had been stormed by Pakistani commandos. Later, passengers said they escaped after the terrorists panicked when a generator failed. The terrorists opened fire and survivors escaped in the chaos through emergency exits. This incident was over. But the Daniloff arrest was building into a major confrontation with the Soviets.

That evening, I was assured that Daniloff was not working for the CIA. The Soviets were talking tough, however, saying that they had a strong case on him. "If they do, the Soviets won't blink" on this one, State's Soviet specialists told me.

The Daniloff arrest soon catapulted into the crisis category. Predictably, administration hard-liners took it as a way to advance their own agenda. If we traded Daniloff for Zakharov, we would be capitulating to Soviet strong-arm tactics and equating a spy with an innocent citizen. Reciprocity was absolutely unacceptable. I agreed. If we did not trade, then we would have to find other points of pressure on Moscow. I agreed. The counterintelligence community in Washington wanted us to order most of the Soviets at their UN mission out of the country. Deputy CIA director Bob Gates, speaking for Bill Casey, and Cap Weinberger were ready to suspend

---

1. Throughout the Reagan administration, statements put out by the White House spokesman's office when the president was at his ranch caused me trouble. Apparently worried that Reagan's vacation time would fail to produce enough "news" and convey a sense of drift, the staff at Santa Barbara would often react to world events in an ill-considered way and without checking with Washington or even, I suspected, with the president at Rancho Cielo.

all preparations for a Reagan-Gorbachev summit. Others saw a chance to halt the entire effort to better the U.S.-Soviet relationship. I did not agree. Such wild pendulum swings were not only counterproductive but also dangerous. We had to be tough, I felt, but we should not cancel important meetings: I did not want to revert to the days when the doctrine of "linkage" put everything on hold whenever an unexpected problem or confrontation arose.

President Reagan, in an initial effort to work out the problem, had sent a message to Gorbachev on September 5 personally assuring him that Daniloff was not a U.S. spy and calling for his immediate release. Then Mike Armacost, who had been tracking events since we first received the news of Daniloff's arrest, came in with information that knocked me back hard: five years earlier, Daniloff had delivered a package to our Moscow embassy that wound up coming to the CIA, and the agency had followed up the lead to try to establish a "relationship" with the source. The Soviets observed this CIA effort and linked it to "the source's" contacts with Daniloff. But the U.S. government never paid or used Daniloff. He simply delivered the package. "But," Mike added, "the CIA doesn't always come clean. They are prohibited from dealing with journalists, so if there is something there, they have an interest in covering up. They *say* they are clean."

The next day, late Saturday afternoon, September 6, Soviet Ambassador Yuri Dubinin asked to see me. While I was waiting for Dubinin to arrive, I called NSC adviser John Poindexter, who was with the president in California. He was drafting a memo recommending that the president approve retaliation against the Soviet mission to the United Nations, ordering it to reduce personnel there in an accelerated series of steps down to zero until and unless Daniloff was released. Poindexter would scarcely listen to me when I said, "We should wait for Gorbachev's reply to the president's message. We should be strong: do things in addition to saying things, but we must not cut off our meetings with the Soviets. I'm going to tell Dubinin that we want Daniloff released this weekend."

That evening, Dubinin brought with him Gorbachev's reply, asserting that Daniloff had long engaged in impermissible activities and that a Soviet investigation was under way. The issue should not, Gorbachev said, act to the detriment of our relations. I had now read Poindexter's proposed memo to the president, and I called him to say I was opposed to the idea of changing the size of the Soviet UN mission on the basis of the Daniloff case. We were already working to reduce its overblown size to 170 people. That action had to be taken on its own merits and not be linked to Daniloff.

Linkage would just create a legal trap for the Soviets to spring on us, stemming from our agreement with the United Nations by which that organization was located in New York. Poindexter agreed and said he would quash the memo. A great sense of careless haste and tension was evident, as though he, and others, were relieved, even delighted, to have this excuse for a confrontation that could derail the momentum for a better U.S.-Soviet relationship. Gorbachev's reply had been ambiguous and suggested that he felt Daniloff's activities should be investigated even if he was arrested on a trumped-up charge.

More information about Daniloff came to me that Saturday from David Gergen, former White House communications director and now editor of *U.S. News & World Report.* Gergen brought to our Soviet desk documents and photos stamped "Secret" in Russian. Daniloff had acquired them in the USSR and had sent them to his magazine. I called Poindexter on the secure phone and asked him to pass this information on to the president. "The Soviets will know of this," I said. "Daniloff has violated Soviet law—and it has nothing to do with his being employed by the U.S. Government. I'm speculating, but the Soviets may have been accumulating information on him until they got a basis for taking action." They undoubtedly did pick up Daniloff in retaliation for the FBI's arrest of Zakharov, I told Poindexter. "But is there a real case under their law? Maybe yes. Some American reporters go around the world systematically violating laws about classified information, just as they do in Washington, where no reporter gets punished for taking government documents. So when you say the Soviets have nothing on Daniloff, I doubt that on the basis of what Gergen showed us."

Poindexter said he had not heard of the Gergen information. Poindexter at this time was said to be under severe pressure from right-wingers for trying to curtail the activities, unspecified, of Lieutenant Colonel Oliver North, and North in retaliation was, according to rumor, drumming up a campaign against Poindexter. Poindexter's performance as national security adviser had been criticized in the press. What truth there was to all this, I did not know, but I did see that Poindexter seemed determined to take as hard a line toward the Soviets as possible.

Debating Alternatives

On Sunday afternoon, September 7, the president telephoned me from his ranch near Santa Barbara. Armand Hammer, chief executive officer of Occidental Petroleum and a longtime friend of the Soviet Union, had been in Moscow at the time of Daniloff's arrest and had intervened on his behalf: he was now seeking a meeting with President Reagan. Such volunteer diplomacy was a hazard and a waste of everybody's time. "Hammer is anxious to be part of a negotiated trade," I told the president. "If we want a trade, we can contact the Soviets to discuss it without his help." I had the sense that Ronald Reagan, agonizing about Daniloff as an innocent victim made hostage, was much more uneasy about Daniloff's situation than was Poindexter and that the president was more disposed to considering alternative ways to secure Daniloff's release.

My Sunday afternoon telephone call from the president evolved into a conference call among the president, Don Regan, Poindexter, and me. I had just received word that the Soviets had charged Daniloff with espionage; a conviction could bring the death penalty. We talked back and forth about sending a message over the "hot line" to Gorbachev. I told the president that he should not make up his mind until he got back to Washington and we all had an organized discussion: policy-making by telephone could become a problem; too much could be misunderstood and the options often were not formed fully or intelligently.

Poindexter broke in. "No trades!" he snapped, and then argued for a tough hot-line message. Poindexter was approaching this problem with almost messianic zeal. Ronald Reagan kept musing about a trade. If the Soviets would release Daniloff now on some face-saving ground, such as health, he said, then we could guarantee that after trying Zakharov, we would release him. "If you want a deal," I said, "we can get a better deal than that." But I knew that a "straight trade" could turn any foreign reporter in Moscow into a potential hostage. Poindexter was beside himself at this point. Finally, I persuaded the president to let me come to him with some genuine alternative. "We have to be aware," I said, "that the Soviets can produce material that will lend credence to their charge." Poindexter scoffed, but the president agreed to wait for my suggestions.

That Sunday night, a hot-line message went out from President Reagan to Gorbachev anyway: Daniloff must be released or "serious and far-reaching consequences" would result. "If he continues to be held, we can only consider his detention an attempt by Soviet authorities to create a hostage, and react accordingly." The message bothered me. We had not thought through the "consequences," and we did not have all the facts.

The Soviets came right back over the hot line, rejecting the president's message. That was not good, and we had opened the hot line to an unintended use rather than restricting it to time-urgent matters of war and peace.

After the initial slipup of the Santa Barbara "trade" story, the situation had been turned around. President Reagan publicly called Daniloff's detention "an outrage," called on the Soviet Union to act "responsibly and quickly," and said, "Otherwise there will be no way to prevent this incident from becoming a major obstacle in our relations." We had a firm position. We had Gorbachev's reply: the Soviets were urging us not to let this event affect the U.S.-Soviet relationship; they were also signaling us that Daniloff had done something that justified their investigation.

What Happened to Daniloff?

Monday morning, September 8, I called in Tom Simons and Mark Parris, the senior foreign service officers specializing in Soviet affairs, and told them to find out precisely how much we knew about Daniloff's activities in the Soviet Union. I had just been told that Daniloff had been assigned there for *ten years*. That was a shock in itself. "I want it straight. What happened?" I was concerned over the ignorance of people who were advocating the toughest countermeasures. "There's a tendency to say any trial in the Soviet Union is a farce," I said. "My guess is that the Soviets have been setting up Daniloff for years." The White House and NSC staffs did not want to research the facts about Daniloff and put them before the president: they wanted action now.

Shortly after 9:30 Monday morning, Bill Casey called me. Almost as though he had heard my request to Simons and Parris for the facts, Casey said that he wanted me to be "up-to-date on all the things Daniloff was on the periphery of." I asked him to have the material brought to me immediately. Maybe, I thought, the CIA was going to tell me the truth.

Two hours later, a courier arrived from Langley with Casey's material on Daniloff. It made the following points:

- A "source" in 1981 produced the single most significant document the CIA had obtained on Soviet strategic missiles. The agency was not able to follow up to get more from this source.
- In January 1985, Daniloff received an envelope—after getting a telephone call from a Soviet citizen, Father Roman Potemkin, saying that he was sending some materials to Daniloff.
- Daniloff gave the envelope to the public affairs officer at the American embassy in Moscow. The envelope was addressed to our ambassador. The CIA saw that the handwriting was the same as that of the 1981 source.
- The CIA tried to reach Potemkin but got no response.
- In April 1986, Daniloff told the public affairs officer that Potemkin objected to the CIA attempt to reach him. Daniloff said that he (Daniloff) did not want to be involved further. The CIA told him they were trying to keep him out of the agency's follow-up effort.
- A "Soviet penetration" in April 1986 told the CIA that they had tried to approach the wrong person and that the KGB was convinced that Daniloff was working for the CIA.

I showed this material to Abe Sofaer. "The CIA has really reamed Daniloff," Abe said. He then investigated the matter further, talking to both David Gergen and former Secretary of State Cyrus Vance, who was acting as counsel for *U.S. News & World Report*. He soon came back. "Based on my reading of his activities," Abe concluded, "Daniloff can credibly be prosecuted under Soviet law, and a Soviet journalist who became similarly involved with the KGB in the U.S. could be credibly prosecuted under our law." I was shocked and deeply disturbed.

This put a whole new light on the case. And the case was moving fast. At 2:10 that afternoon, Tom Simons and Mark Parris came to my office. "We have an offer," Simons said, "from the KGB at the Soviet embassy via John Wallach.[2] They want both Daniloff and Zakharov remanded to the custody of their respective ambassadors in Moscow and Washington—without a commitment to anything further. They want a positive signal from you before making this proposal officially."

President Reagan was on *Air Force One* en route to Denver. I called Poindexter and asked him to get word to the president. To accept the Soviet idea would be giving the two cases a certain equivalence, but Daniloff had now been charged, and remanding him to the custody of our ambassador would get him out of jail and spread the problem out a bit. I also knew that Soviet jails were extremely unpleasant and unnerving places. Poindexter resisted: this was tantamount to a trade, he said.

I told Poindexter about the material in Casey's report. "The CIA compromised Daniloff. There is a real equivalency building here. We should move fast," I said. Poindexter didn't want to accept the Soviet offer. The argument was pointless. I hung up. I knew that as soon as the president heard the Soviet proposal, he would take it faster than I could snap my fingers.

More damaging information was coming in. A CIA officer in Moscow had named Daniloff in a letter to "Potemkin" when he sought to make contact with the "source" of the information brought to the embassy by Daniloff. What idiocy: that was not only clumsy and unprofessional, but also was a wanton endangering of Daniloff without his knowledge. Now the problem was much more than Daniloff's activities—the CIA had exposed Daniloff to the KGB!

Poindexter telephoned to argue once again for his option: we would order the Soviets to get fifty people out of the Soviet mission at the United Nations by October 1 and threaten to do more. Then we would accept the Soviet idea to remand the two prisoners to their ambassadors. I didn't follow the logic; it seemed like a formula for making the crisis semipermanent. I asked to see the president, and we set 9:00 A.M. Tuesday, September 9, to review the situation. When we met, I found President Reagan poorly informed about the case, and I felt that Poindexter clearly did not want him well informed.

2. An American reporter for Hearst Newspapers and director of the Chautauqua Conference on U.S.-Soviet Relations.

I gave the president my recommendations: under the law, we had to try Zakharov, but we would ask the court to remand him to the Soviet embassy pending that trial; Daniloff would go to the American embassy residence; the Soviets would then expel Daniloff from the USSR; Zakharov would be tried quickly; if he was convicted, we would seek to trade him for Soviet refuseniks; if acquitted, we would expel him. The president seemed relieved to hear my proposal and was happy to authorize me to try to make it work.

Earlier that morning, I had talked to Casey about the CIA blunder. As a result, Casey said he would send over to the Soviet embassy a statement from him saying that Daniloff had received an unsolicited package addressed to the U.S. embassy and that he had delivered it, and that the CIA followed up on this, entirely independently of Daniloff. This was a start, in my view, but not remotely enough, as Casey's statement did not admit the CIA blunder in naming Daniloff and did not spell out clearly that Daniloff did *not* work for the CIA.

If Daniloff had not been a reporter but rather a businessman, at least some in the American press by this time would have been tearing the administration to shreds, accepting the Soviet charges as true, denouncing the CIA and Daniloff, and citing Reagan's tough statements as proof the United States was not serious about better relations with the USSR. But Daniloff was a journalist. The press was being careful. This was helpful.

An Unpopular Agreement

On Wednesday, September 10, Ambassador Dubinin came in to confirm officially what we had been told by John Wallach: remand the two to their embassies. I replied that I preferred to try to reach agreement on a complete solution rather than take interim steps. At this point, I feared that the Soviets would insist on a one-for-one trade and that President Reagan would agree. For an American to be held captive and mistreated overseas was a matter of personal agony for Ronald Reagan. If a straight trade was agreed to, then as soon as Daniloff was out, the State Department would issue a warning to U.S. citizens in the Soviet Union that they risked being taken hostage. I also would make a point with the Soviets that their behavior would lead to their isolation. We would, of course, proceed with our previously announced plan to cut back on the number of Soviets at their UN mission.

To underline Casey's message to the Soviet embassy in Washington, I had Deputy Chief of Mission Richard Combs give an "oral message" to the Soviet Foreign Ministry in Moscow on September 11: "Nicholas Daniloff has never had any connection of employment with the U.S. government, nor has he undertaken tasks on the instructions of any U.S.

government agency. He has never participated in arranging any espionage connections. He was not aware of any intelligence operations nor did he knowingly participate in any."

When Combs told the Soviets that Daniloff was not aware of any subsequent message that others in the U.S. government had sent, including those to people Daniloff knew, the Soviet deputy foreign minister, Aleksandr Bessmertnykh, replied that there were more facts on Daniloff than had yet emerged. The case against him was airtight, he implied.

I called Ed Meese to ask whether the Justice Department properly could approach the judge in the Zakharov case to inform him that we would be filing a motion to remand the prisoner into the custody of the Soviet ambassador. As calls went back and forth within the administration, it became increasingly clear that President Reagan would be satisfied with a one-for-one trade: just get Daniloff's agony over with. By early afternoon, preliminary steps were falling into place. Roz Ridgway was our action officer, and Oleg Sokolov of the Soviet embassy was theirs. We agreed to the Soviet proposal to remand them both because remanding was step one of our own proposal. The judge was set to hear the Zakharov case in chambers. As soon as Daniloff's release was confirmed, we would turn Zakharov over to the Soviets.

At this point, controversy arose over an imminent event. The Chautauqua Institution, devoted to improving U.S.-Soviet relations in citizen-to-citizen dialogue through meetings alternately in the United States and the Soviet Union, had scheduled a "town meeting" in a Soviet city, Riga, Latvia, for mid-September. Administration hard-liners wanted the meeting canceled. I didn't. I felt that our point of view should be expressed vigorously to as many Soviet citizens as possible. This was an opportunity: part of the meeting would be televised, at least locally. My only hesitation involved personal risk taken by the participating individuals themselves. The president sided with me. I invited all those who planned to go to meet with me on September 11 in the State Department. I said that the Chautauqua Institution had a long and distinguished record of "free and open debate." I told them, "It is ironic that an effort so motivated is put in jeopardy by the very kind of act that demonstrates so clearly the differences between our two societies. The seizure as a hostage of Nick Daniloff is an unacceptable act to which we will not become reconciled. He is a hostage. He is not an agent." They would be traveling in the Soviet Union without diplomatic immunity, I reminded them, and would talk to Soviet citizens and ask them questions. "Is that spying? You have to ask yourself: are you going to be a potential hostage because you talked to a Soviet citizen? Are you going to be a potential hostage if somebody deposits something in your mailbox?"

That evening, September 11, the Soviets told us they were ready to proceed with the first step: remanding to the embassies. Zakharov and

Daniloff would be released simultaneously: at 10:00 A.M. in New York City and at 6:00 P.M. in Moscow on September 12. The arrangement was unpopular around Washington. Was this letting the Soviets bully us into treating a spy and an innocent hostage alike?

The public had no way of knowing that the U.S. government was in no position to stand on principle after the way the CIA had implicated Daniloff in an espionage effort.

The first thing the next morning, I telephoned Poindexter to bring him up to speed. "This step will be unpopular, so you may want to blame it on those wimps in the State Department," I told him. "The president can have it both ways: talk tough, yet get Daniloff out."

Daniloff was released from Lefortovo prison on Friday, September 12. The president was happy, and Daniloff was jubilant. I felt very unsatisfied about the arrangement, but I saw no real or better choice. Bob Gates had put together a chronology of CIA contacts with Daniloff. He said Daniloff was "part of a small subset" of aggressive reporters willing to be in contact with the U.S. government. This was not espionage, but what the Soviets had on Daniloff—though he was innocent and had been "set up"—was sufficient to build a case against him. I felt strongly that we had a special obligation to Daniloff because of what the CIA had done to him. None of this was known to the public. So the administration was taking a lot of criticism in the press for having "caved in" to Moscow.

Bill Safire on Monday, September 15, in the *New York Times* called the remanding a step on the road to "this generation's Yalta." He envisioned any possible summit meeting as involving a spineless Ronald Reagan. But Safire did not know the Soviets had enough on Daniloff to keep him in jail forever—even though he *was not*, and never had been, a spy.

Also that day, a message arrived from the Soviets: "Dual remanding has brought a positive outcome. Further on, mutually acceptable solutions can be found. Your proposal is not acceptable [that Zakharov go on trial in a U.S. court]. If you do not want to seek mutually acceptable outcomes, you will be responsible for the outcome." The Soviets were now stiffening their position. Our ambassador, Art Hartman, believed that the Soviets regarded the FBI arrest of Zakharov as a deliberate test and provocation of them at a crucial moment just prior to major meetings with us.

On Tuesday, September 16, Daniloff, now at the American embassy in Moscow, sent word to us that when he was interrogated by the KGB, they showed him a transcript of a telephone conversation between the CIA in Moscow and "Potemkin" in which a CIA officer had mentioned Daniloff by name over the phone. I was stunned to hear such an outrage. Over the phone? I was incredulous at such stupidity, in Moscow especially, where everyone knows that telephone lines are bugged and conversations recorded. This was even worse than the earlier CIA mishandling. Mentioning

Daniloff in this way was virtually to broadcast to the Soviets that he was working for the CIA.

I had to conclude that CIA incompetence had put Daniloff in a Soviet prison and was now to blame for his being trapped in the Moscow embassy. In his own account, *Two Lives, One Russia*,[3] Daniloff later wrote:

> Almost as soon as we entered the embassy, Combs said he wanted to talk to us in the bubble. Ruth [Daniloff] and I followed him and sat down around the oblong table. He asked me to describe the interrogation, particularly the sequence concerning Father Roman [Potemkin]. I was about to recount Sergadeyev's outlandish claims—his assertion that Stombaugh [CIA station chief] telephoned Roman, the phony letter from Stombaugh—when Ruth interrupted, her voice shaking with anger. "Don't tell him anything, Nick!" she shouted. "You know where he is going to send it and why he wants it. Believe me, those people have done you enough harm already. You don't have to tell them anything!" I did not understand what she was talking about or why she was so upset. Then Ruth dropped the shocker: the Stombaugh letter was real. Real. Not a forgery at all! Stombaugh had really telephoned Roman, had said he was a friend of mine, even though we had never met. The CIA station had shamelessly used me without my knowledge. The embassy had acknowledged this to the Soviet Foreign Ministry and admitted everything to Ruth. But she had never breathed a word of it to me in prison for fear of undermining my morale. My head reeled. I could hardly believe what I was hearing.

I went to President Reagan on the afternoon of September 16 to be sure that he was aware of the full story behind Daniloff. I brought Abe Sofaer with me. Abe told the president that as a former judge and prosecutor, he could get a conviction of espionage in a U.S. court of a Soviet on whom we had the evidence they had on Daniloff. Abe added that he had gone over the evidence carefully with Stephen Trott, assistant attorney general in charge of the Justice Department's criminal division, and that Trott concurred with Sofaer's opinion. I told the president that we had a special obligation to Daniloff since the CIA had compromised him. President Reagan said that Daniloff was innocent and should not be equated with a Soviet caught in the act of spying. We got up to leave. Then Sofaer turned to the president. "The legal standard is not truth in the abstract. Guilt is determined on the basis of evidence. Daniloff is in truth a hostage and not a spy, but he could be found guilty in a U.S. court."

The president had visibly reacted to Sofaer's parting remark. Still, to Ronald Reagan, Daniloff was an innocent American in trouble, and he wanted to get him out of the Soviet Union. The president agreed that I

---

3. *Two Lives, One Russia*, by Nicholas Daniloff (Boston: Houghton Mifflin, 1988), pp. 280–81.

should go back to the Soviets that night to say again: we are aware that you have certain information about Daniloff, but he is not a spy, and you should not let your information lead you to believe otherwise.

Roz Ridgway passed a message to Sokolov at the Soviet embassy on Tuesday, September 16:

> The U.S. Government is aware that Soviet authorities have in their possession certain information about Nicholas Daniloff. . . . We want to be sure that you understand that we know—despite whatever appearance you may construct to the contrary—that Daniloff is not a spy and has never worked for the U.S. Government or any U.S. agency. The U.S. could not participate in resolving this situation in a manner that could be interpreted as indicating that he had such a relationship.

Twists and Turns in Washington

I received a message late that night that Foreign Minister Shevardnadze— who was due in Washington for meetings on September 19 and 20—had put Ambassador Dubinin in a car and sent him racing down the turnpike from New York to Washington to see "appropriate officials" urgently. The atmosphere in Washington was hostile. Cap Weinberger had privately and publicly urged that my meetings with Shevardnadze be canceled. The president had agreed with me that I should go ahead. I wondered whether Shevardnadze would be the one to cancel. When Dubinin got to the State Department, he wanted merely to go over arrangements for Shevardnadze's meetings with me. I was pleased at this sign that the Soviets were ready to try to work out our problem and also to focus on the many other issues and opportunities before us.

On September 17, the president, with the support of his advisers, ordered twenty-five Soviet KGB officials to leave the Soviet mission at the United Nations by October 1, 1986, or face expulsion. This order stood by itself and was not linked to Daniloff. We had informed the Soviets the previous March that they must reduce the overblown size of their mission from the current 275 to 170 in steps of 25. By October 1, they were to be down to no more than 218. Now we were also telling them *who* must leave. The original issue was the number of people and their intelligence-gathering practices. But the order would be taken, without any doubt, as linked to Daniloff's detention in Moscow. UN ambassador Dick Walters reported that the secretary-general's office saw our move as a violation of the Headquarters Agreement that obligates the United States to allow foreign missions to operate at the United Nations without political interference from the United States. Secretary-General Javier Pérez de Cuéllar maintained that we should have ordered the Soviets to reduce their Washington embassy: by aiming at the Soviet mission at the United Nations, he said, we were creating trouble for ourselves. The Soviets could take us to arbitration before a UN tribunal and they would win, the UN's legal adviser told Walters.

In Washington, the State Department and I were taking our lumps from the right wing for being "soft on the Soviets." President Reagan jokingly told me not to read the conservative publication *Human Events*, "because you're all over it pleading to hold a summit." The usual group of NSC staffers was telling the press that State and I were bent on reaching agreement with the Soviets no matter what. They argued we should force the Soviets to back down on Daniloff. If the Soviets didn't, well, there would be no summit and Daniloff could rot in Moscow forever, but our principles would be intact.

The Soviets had bluntly rejected our earlier proposal. Despite their rejection, I had the president's support in trying to get Daniloff out in a way that would *not equate him* with Zakharov and to try to trade Zakharov for one or more Soviet dissidents. As for the Soviet mission at the United Nations, I thought we were right to do what we did, regardless of the Daniloff case. I was as determined as others in the administration to reduce the Soviet mission to a proper level.

A message came in from the Soviets that afternoon. It was not a "blink" but a "half blink." The Soviet message came through Sokolov, their deputy chief of mission, to Deputy Assistant Secretary Tom Simons:

> We regard the action in New York as unjustified, unfounded, unlawful and untimely. It looks like a step toward escalation of tensions in our relations, although the moment in our relations is very important and responsible. This is a moment when we face the task of overcoming existing differences in our relations; rather than doing that, your action adds new differences. We proceed from the necessity that at this time both sides should display caution and restraint rather than encourage emotions which hardly benefit the relationship. We hope the U.S. side will be guided by the same approach. We are not in a hurry to make or pass final conclusions or judgments or to counterreact to these steps. Minister Shevardnadze would like to wait for his discussions with Secretary Shultz to discuss the matter further.

When I read this message, I was bolstered in my determination to see this incident through the right way. I felt that the Soviets wanted a summit with us and that they would reduce their UN mission and release Daniloff on terms we could accept. The Soviets clearly were worried. I picked up the secure phone, got the president, and told him of the message and my interpretation of it. At a meeting earlier in the day to discuss Shevardnadze's arrival, Weinberger had argued again that we should cancel all contact with the Soviets until they unconditionally released Daniloff and gave us full satisfaction for the death of Major Nicholson. At that meeting, President Reagan had decided that I would deal with Shevardnadze on Daniloff as well as on the long-term issues but that he, the president, would not talk to Shevardnadze about anything but Daniloff and Nicholson. I knew that Shevardnadze did not want to get into a public standoff with the president and, perhaps, hoped even to avoid meeting him at all.

Throughout this affair, the facts of the CIA's incompetent misuse of Daniloff's name had not come out at all in public. Public knowledge would not work to our advantage, since expectations would then shift toward an even-up trade. I didn't want an even-up trade: I felt sure we could do better than that.

David Gergen of *U.S. News,* after talking with Daniloff, asked us for a copy of Daniloff's statement at the embassy in Moscow recounting his KGB interrogation. I talked to Ed Meese, who correctly pointed out that if information on all of Daniloff's doings in Moscow were to be made public, it would almost guarantee that the Soviets would put him on trial. We checked with Daniloff to make sure he understood the ramifications of releasing the full story right now. *U.S. News & World Report* then decided not to publish the whole story, and Bill Casey weighed in with them, saying the CIA's operations in Moscow would be damaged by such publication. The confrontation continued with the public totally unaware, and with only a very few people in the government aware, of what really had happened.

John Whitehead greeted Shevardnadze when he arrived in Washington in the early afternoon of September 18. The Soviets bristled at reporters' questions about Daniloff, but on the ride in from Andrews Air Force Base, Shevardnadze stressed that this issue "should not deflect" the United States and the Soviet Union from our main tasks.

I frankly had anticipated that Shevardnadze might refuse to come to Washington at all. The Soviets were the target of ceaseless press criticism, justifiably so, for arresting Daniloff, and Weinberger and other "sources" in the administration were piling on. But Shevardnadze came. He and his team were obviously under instructions to hold our relationship on course. I felt empathy for him because of the spot he was in. Events and ill-disposed people seemed to be conspiring to create an atmosphere that ensured that U.S.-Soviet relations would be perpetually hostile. There were plenty of reasons beyond Daniloff for strain and animosity, but I was determined to get through to Shevardnadze so we could work as constructively as possible. As Shevardnadze was arriving, President Corazon Aquino was making her triumphal visit to Washington, and I was squiring her to a joint session of Congress and to state occasions. No crisis can ever get undivided attention.

I was alternately delighted and distressed, relaxed then tense, during these hours. Cory Aquino's visit was a joyous occasion. I was glad to see Ronald Reagan enjoy a friendly conversation with her.

Meanwhile, a special CIA-KGB liaison had been set up in Vienna as one more channel of communication. Bill Casey called me at 7:30 A.M. on September 19 and reported that the four-hour meeting there did not go well. Instead of easing the tension, each side was exacerbating it, trading tough cold-war charges in efforts to face each other down. The Soviets were particularly agitated by the feeling that we were "treating them as less than a superpower." Casey asked me to call him right away if anything positive on Daniloff emerged from my meeting with Shevardnadze and said that he would relay the information to Vienna. On the public front, the Friday morning news carried Gorbachev's assertion, for the first time in public, that Daniloff was "a spy who was caught in the act." The media pointed out that Gorbachev's statement amounted to calling the president a liar.

I had long since learned in negotiations that personal confidence and a personal touch can be helpful. I decided to break with precedent. I went to the Treaty Room, near my office, to meet Shevardnadze as he arrived. I watched him get off the elevator and walk through the series of stately rooms on his way to the central area used for signing ceremonies and other special events. The last time we met, he had been pink cheeked and confident; now he seemed peaked, thin, and nervous. I peeled him off from his entourage and took him to my private office. "We have a lot of sensitive matters to talk about," I said, "and we will just have to try to work our way through them as human beings. I want you to know that I value our personal relationship and that while you are here, you will be treated with courtesy and respect, whatever the strains of U.S.-Soviet relations."

We got down to work: each of us stated our respective positions. Our meeting went on for two and one-half hours. I went over and over with Shevardnadze a scenario of: (1) Daniloff is released; (2) Zakharov, after trial, is released; (3) Soviet refuseniks are released. Each of the three steps can stand alone, I said. I wanted Daniloff released first in a manner as disconnected in appearance and reality from other releases as possible. Shevardnadze didn't say yes, but he didn't say no. He said the Soviets wanted an immediate trade of Daniloff for Zakharov and no trial for Zakharov.

"No, we cannot do that," I said flatly.

Shevardnadze told me he had a letter from Gorbachev to the president. I had arranged with the president that I would call him to bring Shevardnadze over at the moment I thought was appropriate. I picked up the phone in Shevardnadze's presence and asked the president whether we could come to the White House. I told the driver to take us in through the southeast gate to avoid the reporters and staff that hang around the West Wing. I walked Shevardnadze up behind the Rose Garden and into the Cabinet Room. The president was ready, but Shevardnadze now became agitated. He had not expected to see the president this morning, and he suddenly realized that he did not have with him the letter from Gorbachev. He dispatched an aide to fetch it.

Shevardnadze met with President Reagan for an hour and could not conceivably have emerged without knowing that the president was truly angry. Ronald Reagan usually cannot help smiling, but he was not smiling that day. Near the end of the session, Gorbachev's letter was brought in to Shevardnadze, who belatedly handed it to the president. The president did nothing to relieve the tension. He made it obvious to Shevardnadze that no progress could come in the U.S.-Soviet relationship without Daniloff's release. I knew Ronald Reagan was an accomplished actor, but this was no act.

Gorbachev's letter to President Reagan contained a proposal that clearly intrigued the president, as it did me: Gorbachev and Reagan should meet for two days sometime very soon as a prelude to a summit meeting in Washington. He proposed London or Reykjavik. I was amazed: two NATO capitals. We would not even consider such a meeting while the Daniloff case was unresolved, the president made clear. If such a meeting was to be held, I told the president privately, we should prefer Reykjavik, an isolated city where the host government would not interfere in what would surely be tense marathon negotiations and where ceremony would be at a minimum.

When we returned to the State Department, Shevardnadze and I continued our meetings, first in a plenary session and then just the two of us. The Conference on Security and Cooperation in Europe (CSCE) meeting in Stockholm on confidence-building measures was approaching a successful end, except for a few important sticking points. Shevardnadze and I discussed them privately and agreed on a message we would each send our negotiators. Our suggestions broke the remaining deadlock. As a result, agreement was announced on September 21 on measures that included, for the first time, on-site inspection of military maneuvers.

Paul Nitze and his team of arms controllers who had met in Moscow and Washington with their Soviet counterparts reported to Shevardnadze and me: no breakthrough, but forward motion and a constructive atmosphere.

I gave Shevardnadze in our private meeting two lists with names of people who wanted to emigrate from the Soviet Union and who, we felt, should be allowed to do so: one was a list of Soviet Jews given me by Morris Abram, chairman of the National Conference on Soviet Jewry; the other was a list of Soviet dissidents. As we talked, reports were brought in to me from the Vienna CIA-KGB liaison meeting. The Soviets were getting tough: they were going to fight us tooth and nail on the UN ouster. Zakharov was merely a poor, innocent student, they said; they could try, convict, and keep Daniloff in the Soviet Union forever. In our private talks, I stressed Daniloff; Shevardnadze stressed a summit.

Every aspect of superpower relations seemed to have become like an exposed nerve. A Soviet dancer had defected in Boston from the Moiseyev Dance Company, then touring the United States. Rumors of assassination attempts against Gorbachev were reported in the media. While Shevardnadze and I were meeting, the Soviets protested the printing of these rumors and demanded that the State Department censor the American press.

Not until that Saturday, September 20, did it begin to penetrate to the White House—Regan and Poindexter and the president himself—that the Daniloff case was highly complex and that the United States's case was weak. That was the day when I finally felt sure that we would resolve the problem on our terms and that we were headed for a summit.

I called over to the White House to reaffirm my view that Reykjavik was the place for the summit. I wrote out in advance the positions I would take with Shevardnadze and sent them over to President Reagan so that he would know exactly what I would be saying.

I told Shevardnadze that we reacted favorably to Gorbachev's proposal for a meeting soon in Reykjavik, but that in the present atmosphere, "we cannot put such a positive response into effect. The Daniloff problem must be resolved as soon as possible. No summit meeting can be held until Daniloff is out of the Soviet Union." On the Soviet mission to the UN issue, I also told him that we wanted the Soviet mission to be reduced to no more than 218 people by October 1, 1986. If the twenty-five people we had declared persona non grata brought their overall number below 218, they could fill those slots, but not with intelligence agents. By a year later, we wanted the number down to 170 people.

Shevardnadze heard me out. He then suggested that we meet in New York to "get all these cases out of the way." For purposes of reciprocity, he focused on the idea of the Soviets expelling twenty-five Americans from the Moscow embassy and then allowing us to replace them, even with intelligence agents. I knew the great effort involved in training foreign service officers for duty in Moscow and that the careers of those expelled would be short-circuited. I said we couldn't accept that.

Despite all the tension and cliff-hanging about the future of superpower contacts, I was well aware and appreciative of how much easier it was to deal with Shevardnadze than with Gromyko. The difference was absolutely dramatic. We could have a real conversation, argue, and actually make headway in resolving contentious issues. Shevardnadze was comfortable and candid with the press when he wanted to be, whereas Gromyko just repeated the ideological line and compulsively denounced every aspect of American policies and actions. There was also a remarkable difference between the positions I had heard from Shevardnadze at our first meeting in Helsinki and what I was hearing now: real give-and-take and real progress were perceptible. When I finished my session with Shevardnadze, at about 6:00 P.M., I called the president, Don Regan, and John Poindexter to report that prospects looked better.

Pressure and Patience: Breakthrough in New York

I arrived in New York on Monday, September 22, for the opening of the UN General Assembly. I would attend for two weeks and would meet with some heads of government and most of the world's foreign ministers. Oil magnate Armand Hammer was still meddling with his volunteer diplomacy. He had been in touch with Shevardnadze and was passing us details of various bad deals that would end the episode to the Soviets' advantage. I knew it was hopeless to try to stop Hammer, who was incorrigible. All I could do was make clear to the Soviets that Hammer in no way spoke for the United States and that we had no interest in his proposals. Hammer was telling them, I knew, that he was authorized by the president to negotiate for Daniloff's release.

I saw Shevardnadze on Tuesday. The Soviets wanted either no trial for Zakharov or Daniloff or trials for both. As a sweetener, after both were out, Shevardnadze said, "We might give you a present" of a dissident release. Gorbachev had approved the release of the renowned Soviet physicist Yuri Orlov, who had been prominent on the list I had given Shevardnadze in Washington. On the matter of the Soviet mission staff, Shevardnadze took a tough line. His proposal was constructive, I told him, but unacceptable. Back and forth we went haggling over the terms—at our UN mission and at the Soviet UN mission. Each day a new formula was proposed and knocked down.

The battleship *New Jersey* was to conduct an exercise off the Soviet coast in the Sea of Okhotsk. This maneuver was one of those the U.S. Navy periodically ran to challenge the sealing off of any international waters from general use. In this case, the challenge was to Soviet efforts to restrict use of waters that were legally international but politically sensitive: places where the Soviets did not want us to go. I supported the navy's efforts but questioned whether this was the time to have an American battleship making news near the port of Vladivostok. I was told that the Soviets knew the navy was coming to their coast. If we canceled the exercise now, we would "look weak." This was a classic case: whenever U.S. diplomacy

reached a crucial moment, some irritant like this always seemed to
pop up.

Suzanne Massie had gone to see President Reagan, who then sent her
on to see me. Her message was that Gorbachev almost certainly had not
ordered Daniloff picked up—it was the "theys" of the regime. Gorbachev,
she said, now was referring to "they," as in "they" got Khrushchev. He
was under pressure from hard-liners, and his room for maneuvering was
narrow. She had urged the president not to push Gorbachev too far on the
Daniloff matter, for she felt such pressure would serve those in the USSR
"who want to stop this process of improvement."

The *New Jersey* maneuvers and Massie's analysis were interesting in
juxtaposition. The president wanted to approve the *New Jersey*'s movements in the Sea of Okhotsk and cited Richard Nixon: the Soviets want a
summit and so would find a way *not* to let the *New Jersey* derail that. Massie
wanted us to go easy; Nixon wanted the navy to go forward. Both based
their opinions on speculation about Soviet attitudes. I was skeptical of
efforts that tried to convert one's own version of what was "in the minds
of Soviets" into policy for America. We should pursue our interests, issue
by issue. I agreed with the president: let the navy proceed with the
maneuver.

At our third big meeting of the week, in New York on Thursday night,
September 25, Shevardnadze and I made no progress. We agreed to meet
again on Sunday. Of special significance, I thought, Shevardnadze told me
that Gorbachev wanted him to get the Daniloff case settled so we could
meet in Reykjavik from October 10 to October 12. At Reykjavik, Gorbachev hoped to make a breakthrough on the INF negotiations so that he
could sign an INF treaty when he visited Washington. The Soviets were
now absolutely rushing toward our positions. This would have been embarrassing for them but for the air of activism and dynamism that Gorbachev and Shevardnadze projected. They seemed creative, but they were
being creative with *our* ideas!

I returned to Washington the next day and met with President Reagan at
the White House in the early afternoon. Regan and Poindexter were present, too. We discussed in excruciating detail the phasings of what we would
accept from the Soviets: how many hours would pass between the release
of Daniloff and that of Zakharov, when and how various steps would be
publicly announced, and so on. I took care to get everything down in
writing and read my notes back to the president. I wanted to be absolutely
sure I was operating with clear presidential authority.

I arrived at the Soviet mission in New York at 8:30 P.M. on Sunday and
did not leave until well after 11:00. After some very hard dealing, Shevardnadze and I agreed:

- Day 1: the Soviets permit Daniloff to leave the USSR.
- Day 2: twenty-four hours after Daniloff's departure, Zakharov pleads *nolo contendere* (no contest), a legal equivalent of guilty, and the United States expels him.
- Day 3: as soon as Zakharov departs, the U.S. announces that Yuri Orlov and his wife will be allowed to leave the Soviet Union by October 7.
- The Soviets acquiesce in our reduction of the number of personnel at the Soviet mission to the United Nations.
- On Tuesday, September 30, we announce that Reagan and Gorbachev will meet in Reykjavik on October 10–12, 1986.

Shevardnadze also gave me his commitment to work on getting other dissidents and refuseniks released. I trusted him to do this.

Shevardnadze and I had met on the Daniloff problem three times in Washington and four times in New York. These meetings had been intense and personal. Most of the time only our interpreters and one other person on each side were present. Roz Ridgway was with me and her Soviet counterpart, Aleksandr Bessmertnykh, joined Shevardnadze. No papers were exchanged for signature. At the moment of agreement, we went over the points carefully with each other. I was within my instructions, which President Reagan had signed off on personally. At the end, Shevardnadze and I sealed our agreement with a handshake. We had been through a tense and extended effort together. The experience built personal confidence in each other, and trust.

Aftershock

Back in my office on the thirty-seventh floor of the UN Plaza Hotel, I phoned NSC adviser Poindexter to give him the details. "That's a good night's work," he said. This was the first pleasant sentence I had heard from him since Daniloff was seized.

As soon as agreement is reached by the negotiators, it usually starts to collapse in the hands of those who implement it, no matter how carefully cleared at the top the agreement has been. A thousand problems of coordination, communication, transport, bureaucracy, and law suddenly loom up and threaten whatever has been resolved. In this case, a sudden effort to draw back after Daniloff was released on Sunday, September 28, threatened my credibility and, more importantly, threatened the credibility of Ronald Reagan.

By noon on Monday, September 29, the Soviets were wildly upset. According to CNN at 12:20, Daniloff was already out of the USSR. But

Zakharov's lawyer was getting nothing but blank stares from the U.S. attorney in New York. Then a flash cable came in from embassy Moscow: Daniloff's Lufthansa jetliner was still on the ground at the Moscow airport because it had been overfueled; it would be delayed while the surplus was off-loaded. Fears arose that this would allow the Soviets to take control of Daniloff until we broke through whatever was holding up the legal processing of Zakharov. We got a lucky break. Daniloff's aircraft was serviced without incident and was wheels up for Frankfurt, Germany, by 1:05 P.M.

By midafternoon, Abe Sofaer reported that the Department of Justice was fighting against the decision to release Zakharov. They said they had a full confession from Zakharov and were talking about seeking a life sentence. Earlier, John Poindexter, after a discussion with Ed Meese, had solemnly assured me that there would be a swift hearing by a judge in chambers of a nolo contendere plea by Zakharov; now I was told that no court date had been set at all. Hysteria was mounting.

We worked on the problem frantically through the night, to no result. Before I left for Washington early Tuesday morning, September 30, I telephoned Ed Meese at 7 A.M.: "We have to talk," I said. "Here's the problem," I said. "I told the Soviets on instructions from the president that Zakharov could plead nolo, described as a technicality to get him released without trial. Now a bitter scenario has developed between the judge and the prosecutor. Effectively, Zakharov is about to be tried and convicted of espionage in a public court and with the media present. That is miles away from what I told Shevardnadze. The Soviets feel they've been deceived. Abe Sofaer says there is lots of flexibility. The judge can hear a plea in chambers. The Soviets may think we've broken the deal. If so, we may not get Orlov out. Then the president faces a loser's choice: go to Reykjavik without Orlov or cancel Reykjavik. The president and his policy could be derailed. And Shevardnadze is on the line too. He recommended to Moscow that Daniloff just be released, period. The judge is to meet the attorneys in an hour in New York. If it goes according to what I've just described, the president could be out of business fifteen minutes later. So I'm calling you with an urgent plea. A lot is riding on this."

Ed Meese said he'd go right to work on the problem. I knew he would. Meese had been a part of these arrangements, and he would not want to see President Reagan undercut in this way.

At the White House, on a dedicated phone line to the courthouse in Brooklyn, we tracked events minute by minute. I worried that the deal could blow up in our faces. At 9:55 A.M. there was a brief public hearing. At 10:04, Zakharov was convicted on the basis of his nolo plea, given five years' probation, and allowed to return to the USSR. A minute later, I announced Zakharov's release and the freedom of Yuri Orlov. At 10:15, President Reagan announced that he would meet Gorbachev in Iceland.

At 4:40 P.M., Daniloff and his wife arrived at Dulles Airport. Yuri Orlov and his wife, Irina Valitova, also a dissident, arrived in New York on October 5. On October 9, the Soviets announced that Jewish refuseniks Viktor and Inessa Flerov would be allowed to emigrate to Israel.[4]

Casey on the Offense

The Daniloff affair ended with an argument between me and Bill Casey. I was not surprised. Casey had been angered by my comments to the president about the inept performance of the CIA after I had discovered what they had done with the information that Daniloff provided them. On October 7, Casey sent a memo to the president, Don Regan, Poindexter, and me emphasizing the importance of information that could be received from the human sources involved in the Daniloff case and expressing his resentment of me. "When officials of this government imply or state that this effort to renew highly valuable information . . . was 'unprofessional' or 'bungled,' . . . it makes our officers wonder whether they are expected to reject information from Americans who volunteer it in Moscow or ask follow-up questions about it. When anyone suggests such a limitation on the few officers we have in Moscow, . . . we are sending a very bad signal to our officers, our general public, and the Soviets."

I had never, nor had anyone on my staff, told the press about the CIA's treatment of Daniloff, with the result that I took much more criticism than was warranted for what, under the circumstances, was as good an outcome as we could achieve. Brent Scowcroft, for example, who, given his experience as President Ford's national security adviser, might have been expected to wonder whether there was more here than met the eye, was quoted in the *New York Times* on October 1, 1986: "I really don't think the Administration did very well."

When I got Casey's letter, I replied:

> I appreciate your detailed explanation of the handling of the Daniloff case by CIA [officers] in Moscow. . . .The question is not whether the CIA should have sought to find a way for followup; the question has to do with the way [the agency] conducted [its] followup activities.
>
> In a place like Moscow, I do not think that the importance of the information sanctions putting at risk private US citizens who do not have diplomatic immunity. I understand that when Daniloff was called back twice to

4. In December, Irina Ratushinskaia and Igor Gerashchenko were allowed to go to London, and the Soviets allowed the dissident physicist and Nobel laureate Andrei Sakharov to leave his exile in the closed city of Gorky and pardoned his wife, Elena Bonner. In October of 1987, Ida Nudel was allowed to emigrate to Israel, as were Josif Begun and his family. Shevardnadze made no comment to me about these releases, but when I noted to him later that they had all been part of our discussion, he smiled. I thanked him for following through.

the embassy, [a CIA officer], along with the Deputy Chief of Mission, was present and questioned Daniloff. . . . Daniloff reports that at the time he asked not to be involved further in any matter relating to the letter. It seems to me that the [CIA] officer should have taken every precaution to protect Daniloff. Surely it was not necessary to refer to "Nicholas" or "the journalist" to establish his *bona fides*. . . .

Daniloff is the source of allegations that the CIA had "bungled." I imagine in his forthcoming book he will elaborate on this thesis.

Daniloff himself recounts how [Potemkin] had pursued him with calls. The implication is that the . . . papers were all along a setup. In any event, I believe good tradecraft always assumed this is a strong possibility in the Soviet Union, and special precautions should be taken to protect private individuals who have volunteered information but who do not have diplomatic immunity.

The affair was managed in a way that achieved Daniloff's release without equating him with the Soviet spy, that obtained the release of several heroic Soviet dissidents, and that nailed down our effort to reduce the size of the Soviet mission to the United Nations. We also managed to keep our discussions on other matters going forward constructively throughout this heated, tension-filled period. As a result, a breakthrough at the CSCE in Stockholm had been achieved during this time. We used the Soviet desire for the Reykjavik meeting—though President Reagan also wanted that event to take place—as an additional pressure to bring the Daniloff case to a satisfactory conclusion. Now we turned to what would become the most dramatic and controversial—the most productive and the most misunderstood—of all U.S.-Soviet summit meetings: Reykjavik.

CHAPTER 36

What Really Happened
at Reykjavik

If observers sometimes regard the everyday practice of diplomacy as cold and bloodless, no one could possibly miss the drama of a summit. There the decision makers face each other. No safety screen stands between the issues and the highest authorities. But what produces drama can also lead to problems and risks.

Unpredictability was not a comforting prospect for meetings between the leaders of the two nuclear superpowers in an era of cold war antagonism. So the practice arose of choreographing every move and reaching agreement in advance on virtually every substantive detail of U.S.-Soviet summits. The events themselves were significant, but they were so highly programmed that the space reserved for innovation by the leaders was carefully circumscribed. Replete with ceremonial pomp and the focus of a vast media spotlight, summits had become something of a theatrical performance on a grand scale.

Ronald Reagan did not like the format of a summit fully stage-managed from the bottom up. He had objected to his experiences in 1981 and 1982 at the economic summits held in Ottawa and Versailles with the heads of the seven leading industrial countries of the world. He found himself in the midst of a foregone conclusion, consumed by communiqués negotiated before the event, and barred from personal interchange with other leaders on whatever he, rather than his staff, wanted to discuss. Ronald Reagan wanted to talk, to get to know his counterparts, to understand them and have them understand him. I had helped him break out of the programmed pattern at the economic summit he chaired in Williamsburg in 1983: there was no prenegotiated communiqué; much more time than in the past was given for the leaders to meet alone and engage in real conversation. With this new pattern, the leaders reached real agreement on policy at the end of the meeting. Reagan and Gorbachev followed the same top-down pattern

751

in Geneva in November 1985, and despite tense moments at the end, the result was excellent.

Even for Ronald Reagan, however, Reykjavik broke the mold. The site was selected so that protocol and ceremony could be avoided; the media were put on hold by a strict news blackout; both leaders knew that they would be engaging on the hard questions face-to-face without the script available beforehand. We had little more than a week between the announcement of this meeting at the end of the Daniloff affair and our departure for Iceland. The event was not even supposed to be called a summit; this was to be a "meeting." But in the eyes of the world, Reykjavik would become the epitome of the very word "summit."

Preparations for Reykjavik

Despite the short interval between announcement and event, preparations for a summit had been going on for a long time: every issue that might arise had been placed on the table, and most had been debated extensively over a period of years, in the case of strategic arms, for decades. Meetings with the Soviets on arms control during the summer in Moscow and in early September in Washington and on other issues during Shevardnadze's mid-September visit in Washington had served to recapitulate where matters stood across the board and moved some positions forward. We had consulted carefully with our allies throughout the negotiation process and arranged for authoritative meetings with them just before the event in Reykjavik. We had on hand a big black book of fully cleared U.S. positions on every conceivable proposal. We were ready for anything, certainly ready to put forward our own positions with confidence and to respond to whatever the Soviets might put on the table. This summit would not be prenegotiated. But we were prepared.

On the American side, I had established a new pattern for these high-level meetings with the Soviets, going back to my negotiations with Gromyko in Geneva in January 1985 and solidified at the November Reagan-Gorbachev summit meeting in Geneva. Representatives from all concerned agencies were included in the U.S. delegation, and everyone was briefed immediately after each meeting of the Soviet and American leaders. I felt experts should be on hand to help evaluate whatever might arise. I also wanted to encourage the sense of inclusion that comes from being present at, and part of, such key events. The president's talking points were available to each person on the delegation, and each was invited to make comments and suggestions. It was, frankly, the only way to keep the internecine fighters and leakers of the bureaucracy under some semblance of control.

The prospect of a summit hastened the pace of ongoing negotiations so that completed documents or agreed frameworks would be on hand to lend content and purpose to these events. The danger, I was very well aware, was that the drive to meet a deadline would lead to unwise compromise or ambiguous language.

There was a unique sense of uncertainty in the air. The meeting had come about so suddenly. Nothing seemed predictable. The midterm elections were only three weeks away, and the president had been on the road campaigning. Republican prospects in some key Senate contests did not look good. At the same time, the president was having trouble with Congress: his veto of a bill applying heavier sanctions on South Africa had been overridden in the Republican-controlled Senate, and the Democrat-controlled House of Representatives was trying to force a sharp curtailment of nuclear testing and was challenging President Reagan's decision to abandon SALT II. The atmosphere was one of hectic pace, divided opinion on important issues of foreign policy, and challenge to the political preeminence of the president.

I studied every aspect of our four-part agenda as I prepared myself to be of maximum assistance to the president at Reykjavik. Arms control would be central. I looked over this landscape with particular care. Initial proposals and a long history of counterproposals from each side, most recently in General Secretary Gorbachev's letter of January 15, 1986, in President Reagan's letter of July 25, 1986, to Gorbachev, and Gorbachev's letter of September 15, 1986, to Reagan. The exchange had placed an immense amount of detailed content on the table. That was especially true in the START and INF areas.

The area of space and defense was the most difficult and contentious and also the least worked over in prior negotiations. Both sides engaged heavily in research on how to defend against ballistic missiles, and the Soviets had deployed and modernized a ground-based ABM system around Moscow. Such a deployment was allowed under the ABM Treaty. But a dispute raged within the United States and with the Soviets about the nature of permitted research under the ABM Treaty. The Soviets wanted to restrict our Strategic Defense Initiative effort. The president wanted to conduct the research, development, and testing needed to establish whether a survivable and effective system of defense against ballistic missiles was possible. That could be accomplished consistent with the traditional interpretation of the ABM Treaty but no doubt could be done more cheaply and with greater confidence if that treaty was interpreted broadly. Debate about the appropriateness of the "broad interpretation" was intense in the United States.

There was also a doctrinal and operational problem with the difficult transition from offense-based to defense-based deterrence. The prospect of defense would lead—or so the Soviets threatened and many arms control experts argued—to increases in offensive weapons so that defenses could be overwhelmed, exactly the opposite of our objectives in the Strategic Arms Reductions Talks (START). Furthermore, the argument went, the deployment of an effective strategic defense would leave the side that first deployed it in a position to launch a first strike on the other without fear of effective retaliation. Deterrence would be undermined since Mutual Assured Destruction would no longer be mutual, much less assured. Under these circumstances, the emergence of a credible and deployed strategic defense would, unless managed in a mutually agreeable way, create a transition period of uncertainty and potential danger. The side without potential defenses might be tempted to use its weapons before they became obsolete.

Two additional ideas had come forward to deal with these doctrinal dilemmas. The Soviets proposed that each side agree not to exercise the right of withdrawal from the ABM Treaty for an extended period, thereby forgoing for that period the ability to deploy. The Soviets first proposed fifteen to twenty years, with an indefinite period for negotiation about what could happen after this nondeployment period. The president accepted this idea but proposed seven and a half years.[1] The other idea dealt with offensive forces. Gorbachev in his letter of January 15, 1986, had proposed the elimination of nuclear weapons by the end of the century, including the missiles that would deliver those weapons. The president, in a little noted but deeply felt proposal, had put forward in his correspondence to Gorbachev on July 25, 1986, the idea that the side that wished to deploy defenses be obligated to present a plan for "sharing the benefits of strategic defense" *and* for eliminating offensive ballistic missiles.[2] If ballistic missiles were eliminated before deployment of defenses against them, then no capability for a first strike would exist. The doctrinal dilemma would disappear, and the original objective of the president's Strategic Defense Initiative, freeing the United States from the threat of attack by ballistic missiles, would be attained. The deployment of defenses would be justified, anyway, the president argued, as an insurance policy against cheating or against some other power that might acquire offensive strategic missiles. I had pointed out many times to the president that ballistic missiles were the only area of Soviet advantage and represented the first real external threat to our homeland since the time of the American Revolution.

I told the president that we were in a strong position, that the handling of the Daniloff case had shown the Soviets that we could be tough and creative. We were entering the crucial phase, I said, in his effort to achieve deep reductions in nuclear forces.

We heard rumors that Gorbachev would come to Reykjavik with a blitz

---

1. The president proposed this in his July 25, 1986, letter to Gorbachev.
2. The president's plan recognized that if such a program was agreed to with the Soviets, then other nuclear powers would need to be drawn into agreement as well.

of proposals, but there were no official exchanges about the agenda except on the timing and composition of the meetings. After a preliminary one-on-one between Reagan and Gorbachev, Shevardnadze and I would join the two (along with note takers and interpreters) for three sessions: morning and afternoon the first day and morning on the second. No social events were scheduled. This would be a working occasion.

Arrival in Iceland

The town of Reykjavik had the compact build and serious, energetic manner of the northern fishing village it was and essentially still is. The president took over our ambassador's residence. I stayed at the Holt Hotel, which fronts on a narrow street not far from the water. The rooms were small and taut, as if to give the cold, dark, outer world as little space to penetrate as possible. I had been to Iceland before; I found it a comforting yet exhilarating place. The air was cold and fresh and stimulating. Yet, at this time of year, it was also foreboding, with its endless hours of darkness.

The past is a living presence for Icelanders: the sagas of the medieval settlers of the island comprise almost a bible, constitution, literary masterpiece, and cultural icon woven together. When I visited the Iceland Museum and viewed the ancient bundles of brown sealskin pages curled in a thick roll under glass, I felt a certain awe at the hardiness of both mind and body of those who settled this rugged land.

Late in the evening, Thursday, October 9, I met with Paul Nitze and Roz Ridgway, who had just come from Brussels, where they had briefed the NATO allies in detail about our approach to Gorbachev. They found "deep desperation" there among the allies, who considered our stance on virtually every issue to be too difficult for Gorbachev to accept. They hoped, and let Roz and Paul know they expected, that we would show more flexibility in the direct meetings to come.

Friday morning, before meeting with the president, I convened our entire delegation in our embassy's cramped conference room. With representatives from all the Washington agencies involved in arms control and others dealing with human rights, regional issues, and bilateral problems, the room was jammed. I went over procedural plans and listened to suggestions. The size of our diplomatic delegations was a joke to some. The "core thirty-four," someone dubbed the Reykjavik team. The key working members of the delegation actually numbered about twelve. It was a far cry from the small, intimate, secret talks between envoys in the era of classic diplomacy, but this approach of mine was working effectively to ease the contentious atmosphere within our "team."

I argued that everyone should be on the inside, to feel a sense of participation and responsibility and to be part of an effort to produce something significant for ourselves and our allies. I also successfully argued for a rule of silence: no one was to talk to the press. We would report to the public when we had something to say and then only through our official delegation spokesman. Anyone who violated this rule would be expelled from the delegation. In this way I hoped to avoid leaks to the press designed to stimulate outside pressures on the negotiations as they were under way.

The press accepted this approach so long as the blackout was observed impartially and the news was made available at the conclusion of the meeting. But reporters did not like the blackout. They had no one to quote for colorful inside detail on the talks; they could not play one assessment of a delegation member against that of another, thereby highlighting dissension in the team. They were "out of the action."

The response of someone in the press corps was to produce a little tin can like those used by Icelandic fisheries. The label read, "Iceland Waters Blackout." The instructions: in the event of a total news blackout, open the can; the ingredients: the substance of the Reagan-Gorbachev talks. The can was empty. If the press wasn't getting anything, there must not be anything there.

In sharp contrast, the Soviets were conducting a full-scale media blitz in the days before the summit. When we arrived at Reykjavik, we found that the composition of their delegation differed markedly from that of previous times. Usually, as Paul Nitze had pointed out, about half the Soviets' delegation could be linked to the KGB, but this time they numbered only a handful. Instead, the Soviet team was packed with officials associated with the media and propaganda. But as the substantive talks began, the Soviets agreed to our news embargo: neither side would tell the press what was transpiring in the negotiations until the sessions were concluded.

Friday evening, October 10, marked the culmination of tense negotiations with congressional leaders. The House of Representatives, with strong support from the Democratic leadership, was about to hand the Soviets two big gifts on the eve of the Reykjavik summit. One would mandate U.S. observance of the unratified SALT II Treaty, thereby handing the Soviets a victory over the president. The other would impose on us a moratorium on nuclear tests, once again a victory for the Soviets. The president's position, after extensive pulling and hauling within the administration, was that (1) as long as we had nuclear weapons, we needed to test them so as to improve them and ensure their safety and reliability; (2) verification measures needed to be strengthened in the signed but unratified Threshold Test Ban Treaty (TTBT) and Peaceful Nuclear Explosions Treaty (PNET), after which the president would submit the treaties to the Senate for consent to ratify; and (3) we were prepared to negotiate a step-by-step approach to limiting nuclear tests as the number of nuclear weapons declined. (The Soviets advocated a comprehensive test ban, reflecting in part their lead in the testing process, and had instituted unilateral moratoria on testing.)

Finally, in a telephone call from Reykjavik, President Reagan persuaded Speaker of the House Tip O'Neill to agree to withdraw the two proposals for House votes. "I'm delighted that now we can go forward united," the president told Tip. It was a great relief to get that problem behind us, at least for a time.

The Summit Begins

Saturday, October 11, was day one. My morning began with an intelligence report called "The President's Daily Brief." Collected and put together on a regular overnight basis, this document was brought to the president, the vice president, the secretary of state, the secretary of defense, and the national security adviser each morning by an experienced CIA briefer. This day, the briefer called attention to a veiled message the CIA was sending to the president and me. The Soviet army, we were told, was opposed to Gorbachev because he was open to making agreements with the United States. Soviet commanders were even contemplating assassinating him. The only way Gorbachev would survive, according to the message, was for him to be perceived as successful at the summit.

I left the Holt Hotel in a driving rain. As we approached the embassy, I could see the American flag snapping in the wind. I joined the president there for a final review and at 10:20 we left for Hofdi House, arriving before Gorbachev, as the president was host for the first meeting. Hofdi House, a grim structure set on a bare plain at the edge of the North Atlantic, looked like the haunted house Icelanders proclaimed it to be. The British had sold it in 1952 after pictures had unaccountably fallen off walls and an alarmed ambassador decided to move. The Iceland government had proposed a local hotel for the meeting site, but security people on both the U.S. and Soviet sides preferred this isolated structure, which could be guarded more easily. I was happy to get inside, where everyone was shedding dripping raincoats and blowing on their hands to warm them.

Gorbachev and his party arrived at 10:30 A.M. After a brief session for photographers, the two leaders met alone, and the rest of both delegations moved to the second floor. Each delegation had two small rooms and a bathroom with a shared large meeting room in between. Our rooms were on the left as you ascended the stairs, and theirs were on the right. After about thirty minutes, Eduard Shevardnadze and I joined Ronald Reagan and Mikhail Gorbachev in a small room off to the right of the entry hall. The meeting table was set near a window, giving a vista of the gray and turbulent sea beyond. President Reagan sat at one end of the small table, and General Secretary Gorbachev at the other, with Shevardnadze and me diagonally across from each other, close enough to our leaders to whisper or pass notes back and forth. There were two interpreters and two note takers.

In their private session, the president, as host, invited Gorbachev to speak first. I learned from the president and our note taker at lunchtime that Gorbachev had told the president that he wanted to present new Soviet proposals as soon as Shevardnadze and I joined them. President Reagan had pointed up at the outset of his remarks the critical importance of human rights and regional issues. He also said, with respect to arms reductions, "There is a Russian saying: *doveryai no proveryai*, trust but verify. How will we know that you'll get rid of your missiles as you say you will?" Gorbachev had replied that he accepted strict verification, including on-site inspection.

President Reagan had pushed for large cuts in the warheads on strategic arms, to 4,500 for ballistic missiles as compared with the Soviet proposed limit of 6,400–6,800, adding that even 4,500 should be seen as an interim goal on the way to the complete elimination of ballistic missiles. He and Gorbachev had confirmed to each other their mutual objective of eliminating all nuclear weapons, with parity and equality at each of the steps of reduction along the way.

With Shevardnadze and me now present, Gorbachev launched into a lengthy presentation of sweeping proposals on strategic and intermediate-range arms, space and defense, and nuclear testing. When he finished, he handed President Reagan a paper entitled, "Directives for the Foreign Ministers of the USSR and the USA Concerning the Drafting of Agreements on Nuclear Disarmament." Gorbachev was brisk, impatient, and confident, with the air of a man who is setting the agenda and taking charge of the meeting. Ronald Reagan was relaxed, disarming in a pensive way, and with an easy manner. He could well afford to be, since Gorbachev's proposals all moved toward U.S. positions in significant ways.

Gorbachev proposed that strategic weapons be cut in half: land-based and sea-based missiles, including the heavy ICBMs that gave us the greatest concern, and bombers as well.[3] On INF, he would accept our definition of strategic weapons, thereby equating missile systems by their range rather

3. Both leaders had said they wanted to eliminate nuclear weapons, and both had called, in the START negotiations, for a reduction by 50 percent in offensive strategic arms. The position of the two sides differed substantially on what was meant by 50 percent, partly as a matter of bargaining tactics but more importantly because the makeup of strategic weapons possessed by each side varied greatly. The differences between these weapons systems made for difficulty in how to equate them, how to count a strategic bomber, for example, as compared with a ballistic missile with strategic range, and therefore in how to calculate 50 percent. In addition, particularly in view of the Soviet lead in the number of ballistic missiles deployed, we naturally insisted that the end result must be equality.

than by their presumed target.[4] He proposed the total elimination of all Soviet and American missiles in Europe. He dropped what had once been a firm demand to include British and French weapons as part of the American count or in some other implicit way to be included in an INF agreement between us. He emphasized that this was a major concession on his part, since British and French systems were sizable, growing in number, and improving in quality. He argued that with massive reductions in nuclear weapons under way, agreement on a comprehensive test ban should be possible. He proposed a freeze on deployment of short-range INF systems, knowing that we had none deployed. The freeze would be followed by negotiations to reach some permanent understanding about these weapons. I thought to myself, if we have none and they have 120 and the deployments are frozen, we would be frozen into a permanent disadvantage. "What it really amounts to," Gorbachev said to Reagan, "is your own zero option proposal of 1981." He was in part right, but also critically wrong. He did not want to include intermediate-range nuclear systems in Asia, only in Europe.

Ronald Reagan listened quietly to Gorbachev's dynamic presentation of "Soviet proposals," which amounted to, in reality, his significant movement toward *our* proposals. Gorbachev went on to address the critical subject of SDI and the ABM Treaty: "We propose a compromise in which we adopt the U.S. approach of a nonwithdrawal commitment and a period of negotiations following it." While the commitment and negotiation period were in effect, "both sides would observe the ABM Treaty strictly and in full. What is important here is to get a mutual understanding that permits research and testing in laboratories, but not outside of them, covering space weapons that can strike objects in space and on earth." His "compromise" was a nonwithdrawal period of "not less than ten years" followed by "a period of negotiations of three to five years concerning how to proceed subsequently." Gorbachev concluded, "The Soviet Union is interested in

4. The Soviets had defined strategic to mean any weapon belonging to one side that could hit the other, thereby including our INF missiles deployed in Europe but excluding theirs deployed in the Soviet Union and aimed at targets in Europe and Asia. Before Reykjavik, in the intermediate-range nuclear forces (INF) negotiations, the president's original proposal that this class of weapons be totally eliminated remained our stated goal, but we had proposed many interim steps on the way to such an agreement. Always, however, we held to the principles that the outcome must be equal and the limits global in scope. We also insisted that intermediate-range weapons systems of shorter range than the principal ones at issue (the longer-range INF weapons) be covered by any prospective INF agreement and that the same principles of equal outcome and global scope must apply. We had no short-range INF missiles deployed, whereas the Soviets had about 120 deployed. The Soviets had not wanted to discuss their missile deployments in Asia and wanted to count the small but growing numbers of warheads on British and French systems. We insisted, as did the British and the French, that the negotiation concerned only U.S. and Soviet weapons.

effective verification by any means necessary, including on-site inspection."

When President Reagan got his turn, he commented briefly on various shortcomings of Gorbachev's proposals. He reacted particularly to the ABM proposals. "The point is," he said, "that success with SDI would make the elimination of nuclear weapons possible." He went on: "Representatives of each side should be able to be present at tests, and if testing shows that a defensive system is practical, there would be an obligation to share and to agree on the elimination of ballistic missiles."

"The pursuit of SDI will necessitate a buildup of strategic arms," Gorbachev interjected.

"We are accused of wanting a first-strike capability," Reagan responded, "but we are proposing a treaty that would require the elimination of ballistic missiles before a defense can be deployed; so a first strike would be impossible."

Gorbachev seemed to me somewhat taken aback at President Reagan's pleasant but argumentative reaction to his sweeping proposals. Gorbachev acknowledged that he had put many new ideas on the table and suggested that since the time for the end of this morning session had come, we should take a break. He hoped, he said, that the president would study the Soviet proposals carefully. The president agreed to do so.

I was relieved. Gorbachev had introduced new and highly significant material. Our response, I knew, must be prepared with care, capturing the extensive Soviet concessions and pointing up deficiencies and difficulties from our standpoint. I was glad we had on hand a knowledgeable team with all the expertise we needed. They could rework the president's talking points during the break. Excitement was in the air. I felt it, too. Perhaps we were at a moment of breakthrough after a period, following the Geneva summit, of stalemate in our negotiations.

Gorbachev's Strategy: Concede and Press

I assembled our team in the claustrophobic quarters of our embassy's "security bubble," a small, vaultlike enclosure mounted on blocks between the floor and ceiling of the room in which it was installed. There weren't enough chairs to go around. I reviewed the morning's session and the Soviet proposals. Everyone was surprised. Gorbachev's proposals were heading dramatically in our direction. He was laying gifts at our feet—or, more accurately, on the table—concession after concession. The president joined us, joking. "Why did Gorbachev have more papers than I did?" Looking at the transparent walls, floor, and ceiling of the "bubble," he laughed. "If there was water in here, could we keep goldfish?"

"This is the best Soviet proposal we have received in twenty-five years," Paul Nitze said. Richard Perle pointed out that by accepting the zero option in Europe, the Soviets had conceded a great deal to us. But they could simply shift those missiles to Asia for a time and then move them back to Europe whenever they wished. I dispatched a team to work on the president's talking points to help frame his responses in the afternoon session. Included in his responses, the president agreed, would be his suggestion that a working group meet that evening to review carefully what had been accomplished during the day and, possibly, to prepare some agreed documents setting out the progress made. Nitze, Kampelman, Linhard, and Matlock did not go to Hofdi House that afternoon; they used the time to prepare for the evening session.

That afternoon, beginning at 3:30 and running until 5:45, President Reagan spoke from the heart, explaining why the United States would go forward with research on a strategic defense system in space. He vividly described his horror of a nuclear ballistic missile attack against which there was now no defense. The American people, he said, should not be left defenseless. SDI would eventually make possible the elimination of all nuclear ballistic missiles, he felt. Any testing of SDI would take place in the presence of observers from the other side. If tests showed that the system worked, the United States would be obligated to share it with the Soviet Union. Then an agreement could be negotiated on the elimination of all ballistic missiles and on sharing SDI. Ronald Reagan presented a visionary, revolutionary, far-reaching concept, and his presentation made clear how devoted he was to that vision.

Gorbachev was highly irritated by the president's presentation. "You will take the arms race into space," he said, "and could be tempted to launch a first strike from space."

"That's why I propose to eliminate ballistic missiles and share SDI with you," replied President Reagan.

Gorbachev said regretfully that he did not believe that the United States would share SDI with the USSR. "If you will not share oil-drilling equipment or even milk-processing factories, I do not believe that you will share SDI," he scoffed.

"We are willing to eliminate all ballistic missiles before SDI is deployed, so a first strike would be impossible," the president declared again. Gorbachev, Reagan continued, was refusing to see that if SDI research was successful, it would become possible to eliminate all nuclear weapons. The president said he was willing to sign a treaty that would bind future American administrations, one that could supersede the ABM Treaty.

Tempers flared. Gorbachev hotly supported the ABM Treaty as the one agreement that had kept the world from nuclear war, and Reagan firmly pointed out that the treaty held vast populations hostage to a balance of terror.

Gorbachev asked for answers to his proposals. START? The president welcomed the Soviet proposals, responded to them, and suggested that a joint working party deal with the subject that evening. Zero option for INF? The president said Soviet missiles in Asia must be included. The two men agreed that this issue should also be referred to the joint working party. The ABM Treaty? The president spoke eloquently again about the need to free humanity from fear. "I'm older than you are," President Reagan said. "When I was a boy, women and children could not be killed indiscriminately from the air. Wouldn't it be great if we could make the world as safe today as it was then?" Gorbachev reiterated his proposal. Again, they decided to refer the question of defense and the ABM Treaty to the working group.

The discussion turned to regional issues and human rights, with the president emphasizing, as he had at Geneva, the importance of these issues. "We arm because we don't trust each other," the president argued, "so we must get at the human rights problems and regional disputes that are the sources of distrust." Gorbachev pointed up human rights problems in the United States: crime, unemployment, discrimination. Yet he also seemed more ready than Soviets had been in the past to discuss these issues, on a reciprocal basis.

President Reagan again suggested that we each put a group of our senior people to work that night on arms control issues. Agreement was quick on a meeting at Hofdi House at 8:00 P.M. I made an urgent suggestion to the president that a second working group be convened on human rights, regional issues, and bilateral problems. The president agreed and proposed that to Gorbachev, who also agreed without hesitation. And so the first day ended.

We had not made any concessions but had received more movement from the Soviets than anyone had thought possible. President Reagan stood his ground effectively. He had advocated radical ideas: the elimination of nuclear weapons and ballistic missiles. These were ideas that he had put forward on other occasions, public and private. There was a tendency within our own government and among our allies not to take these ideas seriously. But Ronald Reagan was serious. So was Mikhail Gorbachev. Two serious men agreed that, as President Reagan said, "significant progress is possible."

A Marathon Begins

The whole nature of the meeting we had planned at Reykjavik had changed. The working groups meant that a U.S.-Soviet negotiation had been launched. The president had informed Gorbachev of the composition of our working groups. Paul Nitze would chair our side of the arms control negotiations and Roz Ridgway the negotiations on other issues. Roz would bear down particularly on human rights, seeking to elevate that subject so that it would become a recognized part of our joint agenda. We knew that her counterpart would be Aleksandr Bessmertnykh. Over dinner, we speculated about who would chair the Soviet side on arms control.

A new face had appeared in the Soviet delegation, Marshal Sergei Akhromeyev, the top military man in the Soviet Union, comparable in rank to the chairman of our Joint Chiefs of Staff. Nitze had chatted with him in the Hofdi House room shared by the two delegations. Paul was impressed with the acuity of his mind and his command of the issues.

"I'm the last of the Mohicans," Akhromeyev said to me in an informal moment.

"What do you mean by that?" I asked him, puzzled, as my mind flashed instantly to James Fenimore Cooper's book. He explained that he was the last active commander who had fought the Nazis in World War II. "But that phrase, 'the last of the Mohicans,' where did you get that?" I asked.

"In boyhood," he replied, "I was raised on the adventure tales of James Fenimore Cooper." Literature can bridge cultures, I saw. This Soviet military man seemed far more at ease with himself, more open, more ready for real conversation, than had the professional negotiators of times past with whom we customarily dealt. We took Akhromeyev to be a man with a sense of history and an awareness of the American way. Our Soviet experts thought he would not be in their working group. He wound up as its chairman and did practically all the talking.

At 2:00 A.M., sound asleep at my hotel, I was awakened by Paul Nitze. He, along with Kampelman, Perle, Linhard, Hill, and Timbie, crammed themselves into my small sitting room. The Icelandic chill pervaded the room. I put a sweater on over my pajamas and over that a bathrobe. Nitze was agitated. He saw a chance to make real progress, but Rowny in particular in our delegation objected to any show of flexibility on our part: the Soviets would have to meet our positions entirely. Nitze went on, "On START, they would reduce by 50 percent in every category, but we could not agree to the unequal outcome that such a process would yield." Nitze had insisted on equal numerical end-levels on warheads and delivery vehicles. We proposed a limit of 6,000 warheads and 1,600 delivery vehicles. "On INF, Asia is still a problem." Paul paused. "Akhromeyev is a first-class negotiator. Communism is a flawed system and it will fail, but Marshal Sergei Akhromeyev is a man of great courage and character. If anyone can help the USSR toward its best aspirations, he can. But he is a good man in a bad system."

"Akhromeyev was agreeable," Richard Perle said. "Then they caucused, and Karpov, we judged, argued with Akhromeyev for departing from Gorbachev's proposal: 50 percent reductions, category by category, resulting in unequal outcomes."

"So the military man is reasonable, and the Foreign Ministry man blocked him," I said with a laugh. That was just the opposite of the message provided in the CIA's "intelligence" report of twenty-four hours ago.

"We're supposed to reconvene at 3:00 A.M.," Richard Perle noted. "The problem is that 50 percent cuts across the board will leave the Soviets with more than we would have in every category where they now have more on their side."

"We must stand our ground on equal outcomes," I told them. Everyone agreed. "They have put something new on the table. We shouldn't be bound by the detail of our old position," I said. "Sunday's discussion will be less precise, but potentially bolder, because Reagan and Gorbachev will be bargaining with each other, not with their hard-line advisers. What the president will need from us in the morning is boundaries of positions and words he should stick to."

On INF, I told the group, "try to get to the point where we agree in a precise way on everything but Asia." On START, "your job is to make use of—not just reject—their offer of a 50 percent cut in heavy ballistic missiles. Apply the 50 percent cut, then say that equality is their long-standing position. But we can't seek strict equality, as there are asymmetries in the two force structures. You guys have got to get loose from just restating our old position. Get SDI deployment worked into the equation so that continuing reductions in offensive weapons are clearly the result of a continuing SDI program."

To Nitze I said, "This is your working group, and you're the boss. It's not a meeting in which everybody has a veto. There's no rule or requirement for unanimity on our side." So, shortly before 3:00 A.M., Nitze led the group back to Hofdi House.

"I'm really sorry to have disturbed your sleep, Mr. Secretary," Nitze said.

"Who do you think Akhromeyev woke up?" I laughed. Nitze went back to work. I went back to bed. But I tossed and turned, mulling over how to handle the coming day's inevitable pressure—and potential.

At 7:10 A.M., Nitze reported in. The working parties had agreed on START: big reductions in heavy ballistic missiles and equal outcomes of 6,000 warheads and 1,600 delivery vehicles on each side. And Nitze had achieved a critical breakthrough with Akhromeyev on bomber counting rules: a strategic bomber would count as one, no matter how many gravity bombs or short-range attack missiles were on board.[5]

"Damn good! It's what we came for!" I said, and pumped Nitze's hand.

5. This was a genuine breakthrough, since the "bomber counting" rule was a real stumbling block in deciding the meaning of an equal outcome when the force structures were sharply different. We had more bombers than the Soviets, but one gravity bomb on a bomber could not remotely be equated to a warhead on a ballistic missile.

"The last sentence on sea-launched cruise missiles took an hour and a half," Paul said. And they had come close to agreement on INF except for the Asian question.

"A terrific night's work, Paul," I told him.

"I haven't had so much fun in years." He beamed. "Akhromeyev is very sound," Nitze said. "Great guy. We had a good exchange. Karpov was fuming. Arbatov was terrible. On our side, Rowny was negative."

The long night's work was coming our way. We had won a 50 percent cut in strategic weapons to equal numerical outcomes, and, on INF, the Soviets had held to their new position that British and French systems need not be included. "The president's call for the total elimination of all ballistic missiles is the crucial point of our position," I told Nitze, "because the more they cut, the less need there is for a full SDI; and if they cut entirely, there is no need for argument about SDI. Gorbachev is making these proposals and will expect credit for them. Fine, let him keep making them. His proposals are the result of five years of pressure from us."

Day Two

For the Sunday morning session we took our whole delegation to Hofdi House. People wandered about the upstairs sitting rooms, where huge oil paintings of subjects such as American astronauts in surreal landscapes hung on the walls. The president, in our premeeting discussion, agreed that our working group had made great progress in fleshing out and strengthening material developed during the first day. But the president also saw, as we all did, that much work remained.

When the president and the general secretary reviewed the night's work, their faces fell. The president said the group had done well on START and on human rights and bilateral issues, but nothing had been pushed forward in other areas. President Reagan said he was disappointed. What about INF? Gorbachev said he was very disappointed. The agreement on START was good, but what about the ABM Treaty and SDI?

I thought, here are *stunning breakthroughs* in Soviet-U.S. arms control negotiations—they both know that—and they are both disappointed! I was far more impressed with the accomplishments so far than they were. But I also agreed with the president that now was the time to press Gorbachev in order to get as much out of this meeting as possible before the negotiators returned to the traditional framework in Geneva.

The weather was alternating every half hour or so between dark, driving rain and brilliant sunshine, and the course of our work mirrored the weather. Round and round we went. On INF, the president finally won from Gorbachev agreement to limit Soviet missiles in Asia to 100 warheads, matched by our right to deploy 100 in the United States, presumably in

Alaska, aimed at targets in the Asian part of the Soviet Union. The Soviets also recognized that short-range INF missiles would need to be dealt with as part of any final agreement. The president agreed to this outcome as an interim step but put Gorbachev on notice that he would continue to press for the elimination of *all* long-range INF weapons.

At one point I needed copies of a text I had drafted for us and for the Soviets. I asked for copies to be made, only to discover there was no copier in Hofdi House. Observing Charlie Hill frantically and fruitlessly searching the basement of the building, a helpful Soviet security agent offered us the use of Soviet carbon paper. "Ah," Akhromeyev commented upon receipt of his carbon copy, "another triumph of Soviet technology!"

By the end of the session, which went from 10:00 A.M. until 1:30 P.M., well beyond the scheduled two-hour time, important developments were in hand: a refinement of language from the night before setting out accomplishments in START; resolution of the Asian aspects of INF so that we now had a package with the earmarks of the kind of agreement we had been seeking; the makings of an approach to the prickly issue of nuclear testing that had caused the president so much trouble in Congress; and forward movement on the issues of space and defense, though without approaching anything that could be called an agreement. Gorbachev, I could see, was totally dissatisfied with where matters stood on the space and defense issues.

The exchange between Reagan and Gorbachev on INF had been particularly interesting, with argument and movement from both sides. The atmosphere was one of constructive problem solving. Gorbachev talked about his huge concession in agreeing not to count British and French systems in what he viewed as the U.S. total. The president insisted that he must address the issue of missiles in Asia. When Gorbachev finally agreed to a limit in Asia of 100 on each side, the president looked over at me with a questioning look. I whispered to him, "We should keep after complete elimination, but this is a good deal, better than we were willing to accept before we came here." The president then agreed to Gorbachev's proposal.

An immense amount of difficult work remained before an INF agreement, in all its thorny detail, could be completed, but Ronald Reagan and Mikhail Gorbachev achieved the essence of what became the INF Treaty there at Reykjavik. I wondered why Gorbachev held on to the 100 missiles in Asia. I came to feel that this was a test of sorts. Would President Reagan settle for something that was less than precisely what he wanted? An answer of yes would mean to Gorbachev, I speculated, that Ronald Reagan was truly willing to reach an agreement with the country he had once called an "evil empire."

The language Roz Ridgway and Aleksandr Bessmertnykh had worked out the night before held up and provided an outstanding breakthrough:

the Soviets had acquiesced by agreeing to recognize human rights issues as a regular, open, and legitimate part of our agenda. That was a magnificent triumph.

With so much in the works and so close to fruition—but with the SDI-ABM issues totally up in the air—Gorbachev said at one point, "We've accomplished nothing. Let's go home."

Finally, the two leaders agreed, after a rather testy exchange, to add one more meeting. It would begin at 3:00 P.M. They designated Shevardnadze and me, with teams of advisers, to meet at two o'clock to try to work out agreed language that captured the progress made so far and develop a better way to handle the contentious space and defense issues. As the president was the host for the morning session, the Soviets left Hofdi House first. We had much work to do, I knew, so I stayed at Hofdi House with a key group while the president and Don Regan returned to the embassy for lunch. With me were Paul Nitze, Max Kampelman, Richard Perle, Bob Linhard, Ken Adelman, General John Moellering, and John Poindexter.

The president earlier had proposed to Gorbachev an approach to space and defense issues that posed three questions for our Geneva negotiators to address. The questions had not sparked interest from Gorbachev, but he had not brushed them off entirely. Maybe, I thought, we could instruct our negotiators to address those questions in a way that would allow us to move our positions forward and closer together. The questions were: How can activities with respect to the investigation of strategic defenses be synchronized with our shared goal of eliminating ballistic missiles? What should the conditions and time frame be for increased reliance on strategic defenses? Until these conditions are met, what common understanding can be reached on activities under the ABM Treaty on advanced strategic defenses?

Just then I got word that the Soviet side had broken the press embargo and had released a statement that the two sides were close to agreement on deep cuts in strategic weapons and a zero-zero outcome on INF.

President Reagan was back in his quarters in our ambassador's residence, and Gorbachev had returned to his delegation's headquarters in a Soviet cruise ship that lay offshore. We had agreed, I told members of my working group, to zero INF nuclear weapons in Europe. That would come as a shock to many people. We had to get word out to our European allies and to Japan and Korea: the Europeans had worried that we were not serious enough about arms control. Now they would need reassurance of a continuing U.S. commitment to Europe and the courtesy of hearing this information from us before any public announcement.

Chancellor Helmut Kohl had fought the battle of his political life to get Pershing II missiles deployed in West Germany. His had been an especially difficult fight. And the idea of ballistic nuclear missiles on German soil capable of hitting targets well inside the Soviet Union, maybe even Moscow, was a particularly sensitive point, a raw nerve, to the Soviets. Kohl had felt their pressure and stood up to it. His success had played a major part in obtaining Soviet agreement to our proposal in INF. I told Roz Ridgway to get on the phone to Horst Teltschik, Kohl's equivalent to our national security adviser, to counterparts in the other basing countries, and to Japan (which had sent a special representative to Reykjavik).

At this point the global INF limit we had agreed on was 100 INF missiles on each side, with the Soviets' in Asia and ours in the continental United States. We would go to work on eliminating the last 100 and achieving agreement on a zero-zero outcome globally. West Germany, Britain, Belgium, the Netherlands, Italy, and Japan—all would have to be told right away what was happening here. I directed delegation members to get the word out: we had broken through the problem of INF in a manner totally consistent with our guiding principles and original objectives.

That afternoon, we were back at the negotiating table. Shevardnadze and I sat on opposite sides of a long table, each of us flanked by our delegations, protagonists in the long cold war struggle over nuclear arms and ballistic missiles. I opened our discussion with what I regarded as a solvable drafting problem: the issues in nuclear testing. I found Shevardnadze cold, almost taunting. The Soviets had made all the concessions, he said. Now it was our turn: there was no point in trying to perfect language on other issues. Everything depended on agreement on how to handle SDI: a ten-year period of nonwithdrawal and strict adherence to the terms of the ABM Treaty during that period. That was their bottom line.

Bob Linhard, an air force colonel and arms control expert assigned to the NSC staff, with Perle looking over his shoulder, was scribbling away on a draft, which he then passed to the other American delegates, who one by one nodded in assent. Then Poindexter passed it to me. I read the draft carefully. Linhard had combined in an interesting way ideas we had put forward earlier. Richard Perle had tried out something close to this on me before we came to Reykjavik. Poindexter had suggested to the president during our private dinner the night before, reflecting our feeling that something bold from us might be called for, that we should consider using in a dramatic way Weinberger's idea of eliminating ballistic missiles. The president had not objected.

I said to Shevardnadze, "I would like to explore with you an idea that I have not discussed with the president, but please hear me out. This is an effort by some of us here to break the impasse. I don't know how the president will react to it. If, after we break, you hear some pounding in our area, you'll know that is the president knocking my head against the wall." I then read:

Both sides would agree to confine itself to research, development and testing which is permitted by the ABM Treaty, for a period of 5 years, through 1991, during which time a 50% reduction of strategic nuclear arsenals would be achieved. This being done, both sides will continue the pace of reductions with respect to the remaining ballistic missiles, with the goal of the total elimination of all offensive ballistic missiles by the end of a second 5-year period. As long as these reductions continue at the appropriate pace, the same restrictions will continue to apply. At the end of the 10-year period, with all offensive ballistic missiles eliminated, either side would be free to deploy defenses.

Shevardnadze immediately questioned why we would want the right to deploy defenses at the end of ten years. By that time, it was almost 3:00 P.M., and the leaders had returned to Hofdi House. Each side caucused. President Reagan was entirely comfortable with the Linhard idea. He regarded it as his own idea dressed up in the lingo of arms control. His most ardently held goal as president was his desire to work to rid the American people of the threat of annihilation from ballistic missiles carrying nuclear warheads. The caucus on each side proceeded feverishly, delaying the start of our afternoon meeting until 3:25.

Gorbachev led off by reading out what amounted to a Soviet counterproposal:

The USSR and the United States undertake for ten years not to exercise their existing right of withdrawal from the ABM Treaty, which is of unlimited duration, and during that period strictly to observe all its provisions. The testing in space of all space components of anti-ballistic missile defense is prohibited, except research and testing conducted in laboratories. Within the first five years of the ten-year period (and thus by the end of 1991), the strategic offensive arms of the two sides shall be reduced by 50 percent. During the following five years of that period, the remaining 50 percent of the two sides' strategic offensive arms shall be reduced. Thus by the end of 1996, the strategic offensive arms of the USSR and the United States will have been totally eliminated.

President Reagan responded that "this seems only slightly different from the U.S. position."

"There are important differences," I interjected. The president then proceeded to read out the same position I had given Shevardnadze, thereby putting presidential authority behind the Linhard idea.

Back and forth went Ronald Reagan and Mikhail Gorbachev.

Reagan argued: "I've given you the ten-year period you wanted, and, with no ballistic missiles, you cannot fear a first strike or any harm from SDI. We should be free to develop and test during the ten years and to deploy at the end. Who knows when the world will see another Hitler. We need to be able to defend ourselves."

Gorbachev knocked back: "Leave open for negotiation what will happen at the end of ten years, prohibit testing in space and confine research and testing to the laboratory." He was candid enough to say what his proposal was aimed at: "For ten years the ABM Treaty will not be gone around, and there will be no deployments in space *while* [emphasis added] offensive weapons are being eliminated."

Gorbachev obviously knew, but did not say directly, that the restrictions he wanted would make the successful development of a strategic defense extremely remote. No doubt he worried that if SDI research proved successful in the near term, the United States would simply not wait for the ten years to expire before deploying. I sensed, too, that SDI was, in a powerful way, propelling the Soviet concessions, in part because they feared that we were further along technically than we actually were. (I also remembered thinking of this likelihood when the president delivered his SDI speech in March 1983.)

President Reagan saw that a restriction of SDI research to the "laboratory" meant that the research would be badly hampered and far less productive than he wanted it to be. He would not agree to such a restriction. He asked Gorbachev, "If you feel so strongly about the ABM Treaty, why don't you dismantle the radar you are building at Krasnoyarsk in violation of the treaty?"

I had asked for a copy of the Soviet proposal. We had one typed. The president called on me to address the differences between the two texts. I identified what happened during the ten-year period, what happened at the end, and the difference in the second five-year period between "strategic offensive arms" in their proposal and "offensive ballistic missiles" in ours. We went back and forth on these points without resolution but agreed at 4:30 to take a break to assess within each delegation where matters stood.

During the break, after discussion among all advisers, the president agreed that we should not change our proposals, but we worked out a new text, putting our proposals into the Soviet format. When the leaders reconvened, the president read out our revision:

> The USSR and the United States undertake for ten years not to exercise their existing right of withdrawal from the ABM Treaty, which is of unlimited duration, and during that period strictly to observe all its provisions while continuing research, development and testing, which are permitted by the ABM Treaty. Within the first five years of the ten-year period (and thus through 1991), the strategic offensive arms of the two sides shall be reduced by 50 percent. During the following five years of that period, all remaining offensive ballistic missiles of the two sides shall be reduced. Thus by the end

of 1996, all offensive ballistic missiles of the USSR and the United States will have been totally eliminated. At the end of the ten-year period, either side could deploy defenses if it so chose unless the parties agreed otherwise.

"What has happened to the laboratory?" Gorbachev asked. "Why shift to just ballistic missiles in the second five-year period?"

The two leaders argued back and forth about their differences. Shevardnadze pondered and stared out the window. I kept drafting, trying to find the language of acceptance. As I wrote, their words rose to an increasingly intense crescendo.

"We are so close!" Reagan said.

"Mr. President, may I draw your attention to the fact that our proposal allows us to take account of all positions as they may emerge after ten years," Gorbachev responded. "To sum up: there would be a ten-year period in which the two sides would not withdraw from the ABM Treaty but would adhere strictly to it. You can conduct *laboratory* [emphasis added] research. After the ten years, and during the ten years, we can completely eliminate all strategic weapons."

"If we both eliminate nuclear weapons, why would there be a concern if one side wants to build defensive systems just in case?" Reagan asked pointedly. "Are you considering starting up again with weapons after ten years? I have a different picture. I have a picture that after ten years you and I come to Iceland and bring the last two missiles in the world and we have the biggest damn party in celebration of it!"

"Mr. President, we are close to a mutually acceptable formula. Don't think we have evil designs. We don't," Gorbachev answered.

"A meeting in Iceland in ten years: I'll be so old you won't recognize me. I'll say, 'Mikhail?' You'll say, 'Ron?' And we'll destroy the last two," Reagan said.

"I may not be living after these next ten," Gorbachev remarked.

"I'll count on it," Reagan responded.

"Now you can go smoothly to age 100. You have already passed through the danger period. I'm just entering it. Beyond that, I'll have the burden of having gone through all these meetings with a president who doesn't like concessions. He wants to be a winner. We must both be winners," Gorbachev said forcefully.

"I can't live to 100 worrying that you'll shoot one of those missiles at me. Fifty percent. We both got it. You told your people ten years and you got it," Reagan said. "I told my people I wouldn't give up SDI; so I have to go home saying I haven't. Our people would cheer if we got rid of the missiles."

"Well, what we say about research and testing in the laboratory constitutes the basis and the opportunity for you to go on within the framework of SDI," Gorbachev said. "So you would not have renounced SDI on your side. I am a convinced opponent of a situation where there is a winner and a loser in our meeting. If that is the case, then after agreement and ratification, the loser would take steps to undermine the agreement. So that cannot be the basis. There has to be equal footing. Otherwise you can say that the agreement is in keeping with the U.S. position, and I can't say it is in the interests of the USSR. So the documents should be deserving of ratification in the interests of both sides."

"What's wrong with saying 'research, development, and testing as permitted by the ABM Treaty'?" asked Reagan. "Then, when we meet in Washington in the summer, we could discuss whether testing is allowed under ABM provisions."

Periodically throughout the discussion the president drove the level of tension up with pronouncements about the aggressive intentions of Marx and Lenin and about the horrors of continued reliance on Mutual Assured Destruction to keep the peace—a fate, he said, that the ABM Treaty inflicted on humanity. At one point, after the president had started to quote Lenin, Gorbachev laughed, "Well, at least we've gotten past Marx and on to Lenin." But Gorbachev would not be drawn into an argument or debate about ideology. Then, in the pull and haul over "strategic" versus "ballistic," Reagan said, "It would be fine with me if we eliminated all nuclear weapons."

Gorbachev shot back, "We can do that. Let's eliminate them. We can eliminate them."[6] But Gorbachev, referring to the many concessions he had made, said that he wanted only one concession in return, SDI. I felt that Gorbachev had instructions or had agreed—perhaps with the Politburo—that he had to get the scalp of SDI.

President Reagan did not give up. "Listen once again to what I have proposed: during that ten-year period strictly to observe all provisions of the ABM Treaty, while continuing research, testing, and development which is permitted by that treaty. It is," he said, "a question of one word."

Gorbachev responded that the president should agree to that word: "If we are to agree to deep reductions and elimination of nuclear weapons, we must have a firm footing, a front and a rear that we can rely on. I cannot go back to Moscow and say we are going to start reductions and the U.S. will continue to do research, testing, and development that will allow it to create weapons and a large-scale space-defense system in ten years. If I go back and say that research and testing and development can go on outside the laboratory and the system can go ahead in ten years, I will be

6. I was criticized in the aftermath of Reykjavik for not "stopping" Ronald Reagan from offering to eliminate nuclear weapons. I responded that President Reagan had taken that position publicly and privately many times: before and after national elections. I knew that no one could stop him from taking this position in which he believed deeply and on which he had campaigned.

called a dummy and not a leader. You are asking me to allow you to develop a system that will permit the U.S. to destroy the Soviet Union's offensive nuclear potential." This was "not an acceptable request," he said.

President Reagan countered, "There will be no offensive weapons left to destroy, and space defenses could not be deployed for ten years or so."

The stalemate proceeded. Gorbachev reiterated that the president should agree that "the testing in space of all space components of missile defense is prohibited, except research and testing conducted in laboratories." Gorbachev then said with resignation that he had tried to move everywhere he could. "I tried to do so. My conscience is clear before the president and his people. What depended on me I have done." Finally, Gorbachev said, "It's 'laboratory' or good-bye."

President Reagan wrote a note and pushed it over to me. "Am I wrong?" I looked at him and whispered back, "No, you are right."

The Soviets, I thought, had agreed to our long-standing proposals. They had done so, I believed, because of SDI. They wanted SDI to wither and die. If President Reagan had agreed—by this compromise—to let SDI die, we would have had no leverage to propel the Soviets to continue moving our way. I admired the president for hanging in there. If he had given in on SDI, all the other progress we had achieved with the Soviets would have been problematic. Gorbachev came to Reykjavik prepared to make concessions because of the pressure of SDI, but he also came to kill SDI, and he went to the well once too often. Confining SDI to the "laboratory" meant that Gorbachev was trying to impose an interpretation on the ABM Treaty that was more restrictive than that held by the most ardent supporters of a strict interpretation among congressional Democrats and the mainstream of the arms control community.

Appearance versus Reality

Ronald Reagan, disappointed but resigned to the inability to resolve this impasse, stood up, as did Gorbachev. They gathered their papers. "Please pass on my regards to Nancy," Gorbachev said. It was dark when the doors of Hofdi House opened and we all emerged, almost blinded by the klieg lights. The looks on our faces spoke volumes. As one reporter said, "We read their body language as they came out, and it said, 'Close, but no cigar.' " As I later watched the TV news footage of President Reagan and me leaving Hofdi House, I saw that more than body language conveyed a message: our faces looked stricken and drained.

"I still feel we can find a deal," Reagan said to Gorbachev as they parted below the steps of Hofdi House.

"I don't think you want a deal," Gorbachev replied. "I don't know what more I could have done."

"You could have said yes," Reagan said.

"We won't be seeing each other again," said Gorbachev. That last remark was overheard by many people, and a rumor flashed out that U.S.-Soviet relations had collapsed, that Gorbachev refused to meet Reagan again. From the context, I knew that this was *not* what he meant: Gorbachev was saying simply that the departure schedules of the two meant that they would not meet again in Reykjavik. But the rumor added to the mounting perception that a terrible failure had just occurred.

The president, Don Regan, and I rode back to the American ambassador's residence in the president's limousine. I would hold a press conference in a short while. I told him I thought I should just report what happened. The president agreed.

Back in the residence, we three and Poindexter slumped in chairs in the solarium. "Bad news. One lousy word!" the president said.

"The haggling was not over one word," I said. "It was over what the word stood for. And we were nowhere near agreement on 'strategic arms' versus 'ballistic missiles.' " The sweep of what had been achieved at Reykjavik was nevertheless breathtaking. The president reaffirmed that I should go before the press and report what had happened, holding nothing back. And I did.

Certainly no major diplomatic meeting ever concluded with such a complete recounting of what had gone on behind closed doors. There were no leaks from Reykjavik. Everything was set out on the record. I described the deliberations at a press conference immediately after leaving the embassy residence, and the top members of our team were dispatched to brief governments around the world.

At my press conference, I looked worn and exhausted, and I was. And that is what the cameras and the analysts registered—my appearance. The words I used, including words of near success of breathtaking magnitude, registered far less to the viewing audience than did my demeanor, which reflected deep disappointment that—at least temporarily—a dazzling array of Soviet concessions had been scuttled. The reality of the actual achievements at Reykjavik ironically never overcame the perception conveyed by the scene of Reagan and Gorbachev parting at Hofdi House and my own depressed appearance at my press conference.

"One of the Most Amazing Events . . ."

Paul Nitze told me, "As I was bidding farewell to Marshal Akhromeyev upstairs at Hofdi House, he said to me, 'I hope you will forgive me. I tried. I was not the one who let you down.' And as he turned away, Akhromeyev said, according to his translator, 'Someone must bear the responsibility.' Aleksandr Bessmertnykh said, 'That's not accurate,' and he corrected the translator, 'Someone must bear this cross.' "

As I flew on to Brussels to brief our allies, I thought about Akhromeyev's words. Far-reaching concessions to the American positions had been put forward, orchestrated by Gorbachev, over the two days: it was an elaborate chesslike performance. At the end, Gorbachev pulled the rug out. Was his plan to entice Reagan to abandon SDI or else all his concessions would come off the table, at least in a formal sense? That would explain Akhromeyev's parting remark to Nitze.

Gorbachev's approach had been brilliant, but he neglected two points: President Reagan's deeply felt commitment to a new, defense-based concept of deterrence; and the fragility of the Soviet arms control concessions. Without SDI as an ongoing propellant, these concessions could wither away over the next ten years. I knew that the genie was out of the bottle: the concessions Gorbachev made at Reykjavik could never, in reality, be taken back. We had seen the Soviets' bottom line. The concessions could, I felt confident, be brought back to the negotiating table. At Reykjavik, we had reached virtual agreement on INF and had set out the parameters of START. And we had gotten human rights formally on the negotiating table.

At NATO, when I briefed the foreign ministers of the allies on what had happened, their reaction was positive: the negotiations had been a striking success in bringing out Soviet positions that had not emerged earlier.

When the summit finally ended on Sunday, the press had registered on our appearances, our visible discouragement, and called the summit a "failure," a time of "bitter disappointment." Congressman Ed Markey criticized that Reagan "had a chance to cash in 'star wars' for the best deal the Russians have offered us since they sold us Alaska." But the reality was that Reykjavik was a stupendous success. At NATO, the foreign ministers felt Reykjavik was an astounding achievement.

Back in Washington on Tuesday morning, October 14, I shared my thoughts with the president. I thought of Christopher Columbus, who at the time was said to have failed because he only landed on a couple of islands and didn't bring back any gold to Spain. But after a while people realized that he had come upon a New World. "In a way, you found a new world this weekend," I told the president. "Some of the critics used to say that your positions were too tough. Others used to say that they were unrealistic—like zero-zero. But at Reykjavik you smoked the Soviets out and they are stuck with their concessions.

"So we have to move fast to lock them in. We should instruct our Geneva team to move the positions up to reflect what Gorbachev has given; consolidate our achievement in INF, testing, human rights, and other areas,"

I said. "Substantively, where do we go from here? I feel we should just stop referring to a future summit. But I will see Shevardnadze in Vienna in early November, and possibly in Finland in early December. We should move at this 'working level' on these occasions and others." As Rod McLeish had expressed it on National Public Radio, Reykjavik was "one of the most amazing events in diplomatic history."

The achievements at the Reykjavik summit were greater than those in any U.S.-Soviet meeting before, but the popular perception of the outcome in Iceland at the time was one of near disaster or near farce. Over the years, that perception hardened into accepted truth.

At Reykjavik, Reagan and Gorbachev agreed that human rights would become a regular and recognized part of our agenda. They reached the basis for a first step of 50 percent reductions in Soviet and American strategic nuclear forces over a five-year period—something others considered impossibly ambitious. They reached agreement on even more drastic reductions in intermediate-range nuclear weapons, down from a Soviet total of more than 1,400 warheads to only 100 Soviet INF missiles worldwide. That reduction would cut by more than 90 percent the Soviet SS-20 warheads then targeted on our allies and friends in Europe and Asia. This breakthrough would eventually lead to a zero-zero outcome: the total elimination of an entire category of nuclear weapons for the first time in history.

Reagan and Gorbachev created a format for negotiation about space and defense, involving a nonwithdrawal period, consideration of what could be done at the end of the period, and argument over the research, development, and testing activity allowed under the ABM Treaty. Gorbachev must have calculated that with only SDI standing in the way of major reductions in START and INF, pressures would mount in the United States, let alone Europe and Japan, in opposition to SDI. Public reaction seemed to work in exactly the opposite direction: if Gorbachev is so concerned about SDI, then there must be something to it, so let's support SDI.

Beyond this, President Reagan and General Secretary Gorbachev went on to discuss further steps to enhance global stability. President Reagan proposed to eliminate all ballistic missiles over the subsequent five years. Gorbachev proposed to eliminate all strategic offensive forces. They talked about the eventual elimination of all nuclear weapons. The very scope of the talk was historic, even if disturbing to those who could not accept such a radical shift in the nuclear balance. Reykjavik was the most remarkable superpower meeting ever held.

Yet there were many second thoughts and criticisms that the president had gone too far. Admiral Bill Crowe, on behalf of the military chiefs, told the president that the chiefs were alarmed at the idea of giving up ballistic missiles. Apparently, they had not taken Cap Weinberger seriously when he made that proposal, nor had they objected when the idea found its way into a letter from President Reagan to Gorbachev. I wondered to myself, later, whether I would have been wiser not to use the Linhard idea in my meeting with Shevardnadze. But I think that had I not introduced the idea, President Reagan would have proposed it himself. In truth, the world was not ready for Ronald Reagan's boldness.

The outcome at Reykjavik portended such a departure from the past that it split my colleagues in the State Department. Paul Nitze saw the outcome in the perspective of the long years of the cold war. "The Kremlin sees a nonnuclear world as removing the one really fatal threat to them. So it is attractive to them," he said. "After all, no one is going to attack them conventionally."

Rick Burt and Roz Ridgway, however, thought our policy would create a major danger to the alliance—a view that Henry Kissinger would soon take up. "The Western Europeans, unable to rely on an instant U.S. nuclear response on their behalf, will make their political accommodation with the Soviet Union," he said. Others agreed that the path we were pursuing would strain the Western alliance, even distance us from our closest friends, which, they felt, was what the Soviets wanted all along. In this view, we had walked into a trap at Reykjavik. That was an argument I didn't buy.

"A love affair with the status quo has started," Roz said. "A lot of people are starting to love the bomb."

Not me. I recalled the fear and tension in 1983 when INF missiles were deployed, and I knew that we were doing the right thing in trying to achieve drastic reductions in these vast nuclear arsenals.

What happened at Reykjavik seemed almost too much for people to absorb, precisely because it was outside the bounds of the conventional wisdom. Ronald Reagan was attacking that accepted wisdom across the board. Reagan's presidency was turning out to be the most radical since FDR's. That simply was not commonly perceived or appreciated. Reagan had stood up to totalitarianism, and its weaknesses were now exposed; he had stood up for freedom fighters, and their cause was gaining strength; and he was turning back the tide of the arms race. We were on the verge of eliminating intermediate-range nuclear weapons in Europe—perhaps everywhere— and we were even contemplating the notion of a world without nuclear weapons.

Post-Reykjavik: Explain and Defend

Meanwhile, a storm was brewing over at the White House and the Pentagon: "What did the president agree to at Reykjavik?" Many at the staff level were trying to walk the cat back. Eliminating offensive ballistic missiles would be okay, but not all nuclear weapons. I was probed on the subject at the National Press Club. Poindexter tried to talk President Reagan out of the idea of eliminating nuclear weapons. "It would be a catastrophe to eliminate nuclear weapons," Poindexter said.

"Face it," I responded to Poindexter, "the president's aim is to eliminate nuclear weapons. We shouldn't apologize or be defensive about it." We certainly were not going to change Ronald Reagan's mind. "I have watched Ronald Reagan for two decades," I told Poindexter. "When he gets an idea in his head, it stays there. Cuts in marginal rates of taxation. SDI. Elimination of all nuclear weapons. He won't go away from those ideas. Don't write him off." But to Weinberger, Poindexter, and many in the State Department, Reykjavik was regarded as a blunder of the greatest magnitude.

Telling me he could no longer sit in National Security Planning Group sessions with Weinberger being so "arrogant and negative," Paul Nitze tendered his resignation. Looking back on his work over almost forty years of the cold war, Nitze said he felt that the United States had great assets and that it must use them to outwit the Russians. But the administration would not permit us to do anything new, he felt. I told Nitze I could not accept his resignation. He stayed.

I set myself two tasks immediately. One was to try to explain our achievements at Reykjavik to the public. To this end I agreed to give a major speech at the University of Chicago[7] in November. Nitze and I realized that we must develop something other than the total elimination of nuclear weapons—that goal was too idealistic. We wanted an "insurance policy" that would include defenses (SDI) and a small offensive nuclear force. I would develop that theme in my speech.

Second, I wanted to offer the president, privately, my thoughts on how his major objectives might be realized in a comprehensive way. I drafted a memo, at the top of which I wrote "One Eye Only," in an effort to draw attention to the pervasive "Eyes Only" cult of secretiveness. I carried the memo over to him and delivered it personally. I later showed a copy to Don Regan, but no one else ever saw it. I told him that the move away from nuclear to conventional weapons would be expensive. Nuclear weapons gave "more bang for the buck" and were a way in which we offset larger Soviet conventional forces. We must try to eliminate this conventional asymmetry but even so, I said, "As long as I have talked to you about budget matters, and this goes back well before the 1980 Campaign, you have had some very clear priorities: (1) provide for strong defense and

7. The nuclear age began when Enrico Fermi conducted the first controlled release of nuclear fission in a squash court underneath the university's abandoned football stadium in December 1942.

national security; (2) reduce the marginal rates of taxation; (3) reduce the general level of government spending; (4) balance the budget."

I went on, "Your fourth priority (curing the budget deficit) is having the effect of undermining your first priority (security). And while the marginal rates of taxation are now down, they won't stay down unless something different is done about the budget deficit."

I then argued that the real threat from the huge budget deficit came from "its devastating impact on the net U.S. savings available for investment. We now rely on funds (savings) from abroad to finance much of our investment, thereby bringing about rapidly increasing ownership of America by foreign investors and governments. Beyond that, the large net inflow of funds leads to a large trade deficit, in turn a force behind moves to protect U.S. markets with most undesirable consequences."

The only way to cure the deficit, I argued, was to combine "control over the entitlement programs" with "improvement in the revenue base." I proposed "a substantial tax on the price of gasoline at the pump to avoid losing the conservation gains made in recent years and to avoid falling back into the oil trap" and "a way of addressing the problem of rapidly growing 'entitlements.' That is the place where the spending is most out of control, but where there is tremendous support for the programs. As for run-away agriculture, I could comment, but my secretary wouldn't type it." The president thanked me for my observations but made no comments on the substance of my proposals.

I also tried my best to consolidate all the ground we had gained at Reykjavik. To those who worried about Soviet superiority in conventional arms, I argued in a speech to the National Press Club on October 17, "As we reduce nuclear arsenals, we'll have to address the conventional balance and deal with chemical weapons. We're working with our allies on how to address these important issues, and we have put the Soviets on notice that they must be addressed. And, I might say, they've done likewise with us— they see those same points."

I remarked, "Many people have asked why I seemed and looked so tired and disappointed immediately after the meeting ended in Reykjavik. The answer is simple. I was tired and disappointed." That got a laugh.

There were more general lessons from Reykjavik. For one, there was a significant value in thinking big. In this leader-driven atmosphere, many contentious issues that had long been blocked—INF reductions in Asia, counting rules for bombers, the problem of British and French systems, the importance of an equal numerical outcome in START—were broken out of bureaucratic stalemate and resolution was reached. Even though the Soviets withdrew these concessions at the end, I knew that we could reel them in again subsequently. I also saw the importance of prior engagement on issues. We had worked over START and INF extensively in Geneva, but because of fierce objections from extreme proponents of SDI, we had not really been able to engage the Soviets extensively on how to approach this complicated issue. There was a lesson here: we should not be afraid to engage out of fear of being outnegotiated.

I also saw, once again, how poor the quality of our intelligence was about the Soviet Union. We had no accurate help from the intelligence community about what to expect; in fact, the message we received from the CIA about what to expect in Reykjavik was exactly contrary to what transpired. The Soviet military was well represented and in the person of Marshal Akhromeyev presented the most reasonable Soviet face.

I took the criticism of Reykjavik seriously. Yet contrary to public perception, the accomplishments were immense. The Soviet agreement that human rights belonged on the regular agenda of U.S.-Soviet relations was astonishing. I thought we had in fact arrived at an enormous turning point. I recognized full well that the nuclear age could not be abolished or undone: it was a permanent reality. But we could at least glimpse a world with far diminished danger from possible nuclear devastation. A better world was possible. As I often said to the critics of Reykjavik and proponents of the status quo, "What's so good about a world where you can be wiped out in thirty minutes?" I had never learned to love the bomb—or the ballistic missile that carried it.

Part VI

SETBACK

CHAPTER 37

Revelation:
Arms Sales to Iran

The autumn of 1986 was a season full of promise for the foreign policy agenda of the United States. We were six years into the Reagan presidency. They had been years of sweeping change in the nation and the world. The political ideas of democracy and freedom and the economic ideas of free and open markets were taking hold over much of the globe. The relationship between the United States and the Soviet Union had changed dramatically from stark confrontation to the emergence of mutual problem solving, with a real possibility that such cooperation might continue on an expanding scale. The Reykjavik summit, with all the controversy over the revolutionary arms control measures put forth there and the disappointment at the lack of closure on any of them, nevertheless showed clearly that major breakthroughs were in prospect. And Communist societies had embarked on a process of internal economic and political reform—halting, but reform. All of this and more was under way and beginning to take hold by the end of 1986. At that auspicious moment, the Iran-Contra affair hit the country, hit the world, and most of all, hit Ronald Reagan.

I had been secretary of the treasury under Richard Nixon when the effort within the White House to cover up the Watergate break-in unfolded. The cover-up led to the deterioration of an administration just returned to office by an overwhelming margin. The Nixon presidency was destroyed by the futile attempt to cover up, and the potential achievements for the balance of Nixon's term were largely aborted. Now here we were in the Reagan administration with so much potential before us, yet with the same danger of having unfolding events destroy not only these prospects but the Reagan presidency itself.

On Sunday, November 2, 1986, just two days before our midterm elections, I learned that David Jacobsen, an American held hostage in Lebanon for over seventeen months, had been released. I was instantly full of foreboding about what lay behind it. I sensed that the situation could be explosive. A courier had earlier brought me the text of a White House statement to be released to the press. The word "hostages" had the "s" crossed out by hand wherever it appeared. Apparently the White House had expected the release of several or all of the hostages but then had to settle for one.

I knew little about the dealings with Iran for hostages held in Lebanon and nothing about what had led to Jacobsen's release. But I did know about some earlier hostage-release attempts and had fought fervently against what I viewed as an arms-for-hostages exchange. About eighteen months earlier, in the late spring of 1985, I got the first smell, by accident, that NSC adviser Bud McFarlane and some of the NSC staff wanted, with Israel's involvement, to send arms to Iran in an effort to attain the release of Americans held hostage. In four major battles between mid-1985 and fall 1986 I had fought to stop such a deal, and each time I felt—or had been assured—that my view had prevailed. But this snake never died, no matter how many times I hacked at it.

The day after Jacobsen was freed, the revelation came, in *Al Shiraa*, a Beirut Arabic language magazine, of a trip to Tehran by Bud McFarlane, by that time a private citizen but dispatched by the White House. This, I feared, was just the beginning.

In the early afternoon, more details came in to State. Hashemi Rafsanjani, speaker of Iran's Parliament, was reported to have said that McFarlane had come to Tehran secretly in September 1986 with four other Americans on a plane carrying military equipment for Iran purchased from international arms dealers. They had been held in a hotel room for five days, and then were released. Rafsanjani said, "The envoys carried Irish passports," and they brought "a Bible, signed by President Reagan, and a cake." The cake, in the shape of a key—supposedly the key to Iranian-American friendship—had been eaten by hungry revolutionary guards at the airport. The story was so bizarre it was almost beyond belief.

A meeting of the foreign ministers of the countries sponsoring the Conference on Security and Cooperation in Europe (CSCE) started in Vienna during the first week of November. I had declined to be present at the opening, feeling that the secretary of state should be in the United States on election day. But by late that afternoon, November 4, I would be on my way to Vienna. The president and his staff were in California. Out of touch with them, I was preoccupied with the events that were rapidly unfolding and was mulling them over and over, trying to remember what I had known and acted upon since that first whiff of trouble in the spring of 1985.

Before I left for Vienna, I talked to some of my key people: John Whitehead, Mike Armacost, Jerry Bremer, Charlie Hill, Nick Platt, and Chuck

Redman. "We are right where some of us a long time ago said we didn't want to be—but feared we would be," I said. I then reviewed with the group what I could recall on the subject: in the summer of 1985, a message came from Bud McFarlane describing an approach for arms sales to a "possibly changing Iran" and the potential for release of hostages. David Kimche, director general of the Israeli Foreign Ministry and a former official in Israel's intelligence service, had brought the proposal to Bud. Shady characters were involved as intermediaries. I turned Bud off. Kimche came back. In two meetings with the president and other key advisers, I had opposed *any* arms sales to Iran whether or not connected with release of hostages. Cap Weinberger agreed with me completely. Telling foreign officials one thing while we did another,[1] would, I had argued, violate our own policies, blow our integrity, and earn us the total contempt of everyone, including the Iranians. Questionable characters were involved who were clearly playing us for suckers.

State Department spokesman Chuck Redman wanted to know what to say to the press. "Chapter and verse have to come from the White House. We don't have it," I said. I told him to direct all questions to the White House. I told Charlie Hill, my executive assistant, and Nick Platt, State's executive secretary, to pull everything together so that I could see what I had known and when and what I had done about it. Over at the White House, I said, they had a tendency to indulge in wishful thinking, to say that they were looking toward a better relationship with Iran after Khomeini and that the arms were to help Iran protect its Soviet border. That wouldn't wash, and Redman should not join in peddling it.

"It's amateur hour over there," Jerry Bremer said with disgust. "A bunch of kids working with Ollie.[2] Television is onto him. They are tracking him." Bremer was hopping mad, and wounded. As ambassador-at-large for counterterrorism, he had been on the road almost incessantly, trying, with considerable success, to talk our friends and allies out of supplying arms to Iran or Iraq or rewarding those who sponsored terrorism. He was totally undercut and discredited in their eyes by this deal. So was Redman, State's press spokesman. So was I, the secretary of state. But, most importantly, so was the credibility of the president of the United States and the credibility of U.S. policies of not trading for hostages and not selling arms to countries sponsoring terrorism—and that included Iran.

"We, as a litany, have said repeatedly that we do not provide arms to Iran," Redman noted, "so I can say it's all in the context of—"

Hill interrupted, "The policy hasn't changed. It has been violated."

---

1. The United States, as a part of its Operation Staunch, had an embargo on sales of arms to Iraq and Iran in the attempt to dry up the weaponry fueling the Iran-Iraq War.

2. Lieutenant Colonel Oliver North, whose name always seemed to come up when hostage-release ideas arose in the White House.

"And as to any violations, we refer you to the White House," volunteered John Whitehead.

"Take our position and stay there," I told Redman. "Don't start throwing smoke."

"Carrington[3] was not responsible for the British being surprised by the war over the Falklands, but he resigned," I said. "This could be the kind of thing where somebody has to resign and take the rap. The hostages keep growing in number. This deal encourages that."

Chuck Redman reported that the White House press office had told him they would handle all questions and we should religiously direct inquiries to them. Redman had done so at the noon press briefing at the State Department and had run into heavy pressure from the press corps: why was State referring everything to the White House? Whatever the real story was, it looked as though White House spokesman Larry Speakes was not informed, either. NSC adviser John Poindexter had released a statement: "As long as Iran advocates the use of terrorism, the U.S. arms embargo will continue." What was that statement supposed to mean? Iran was clearly still sponsoring terrorism. Was this the start of a cover-up? I was determined *not* to let that happen.

On November 4, as I boarded the Air Force 707 at Andrews Air Force Base, ABC-TV correspondent John McWethy, scheduled to fly to Vienna with me, was suddenly pulled off the trip to cover the emerging Iran story. The buzzing of the reporters on the plane was: the White House made a deal with terrorists; Secretary Shultz was cut out of it; and Shultz is distancing himself from it.

From my plane I fired off a cable to Poindexter, reflecting on these developments and making my first effort to get the facts out into the public domain as rapidly as possible and to avoid a cover-up. My usual in-flight press conference, I wrote Poindexter, was dominated by questions about whether the United States had violated its own antiterrorism policy by making an arms deal with Iran in order to get hostages released. I noted that Jacobsen's release came just two days before our election, and that fact in itself would stimulate speculation that the deal was triggered at a moment designed to affect the election. "The only way to contain the damage," I said, "is to give the essential facts to the public" as quickly as possible: get everything out in the open, and fast.

Poindexter's cabled response the next day only sharpened my apprehensions. "Not only will such [a decision to put out the facts] complicate our efforts to secure the release of other hostages, but may also undermine opportunities for eventually establishing a correct relationship with Iran and possibilities for an active U.S. role in ending the Iran-Iraq War. . . . At

---

3. Lord Peter Carrington, former British foreign minister, later secretary general of NATO.

some point we will have to lay out all of that but I do not believe that now is the time to give the facts to the public. . . . I have talked with the Vice President, Cap, and Bill Casey. They agree with my approach." He went on imperiously, "Today I am establishing compartments. One is operational and I am willing to brief Jerry Bremer into it providing he reports only to you. The second is on policy and long-term strategy toward Iran. I would like to include only Armacost and [Deputy Assistant Secretary Arnold] Raphel in this one. . . . When you get back I will give you my views on what is happening. . . . It is very significant that Rafsanjani's statement that Bud went to Tehran in September[4] and other facts are wrong . . . since he knows the facts, I believe he is trying to send us a message." The general tone of Poindexter's response was frigid and unyielding.

My plane touched down in Vienna before dawn on November 5. That evening I was at a reception of freed Soviet dissidents and refuseniks and Europeans active in pressing human rights concerns on the Soviet Union. It was a teeming crush of people, each of whom had a hurried and moving tale of oppression to tell me, along with an impassioned plea for America to do something about the absence of freedom in the USSR. Later, I learned that over at the side of the large room, Michael Ledeen, whom I had never met but who had been mentioned to me when an arms-for-Iran scheme arose in the past, had shouted to Charlie Hill over the din, "Now you know that you can't *not* know about this operation!" A couple of months earlier Ledeen had pressed to "brief" me at, he said, Bill Casey's request—topic: Iran. I had not agreed, feeling that if Casey wanted to tell me something, he did not need and would not use an unofficial intermediary. But now, Ledeen's comment suggested that something irregular and mysterious had been going on.

I was amazed that despite the revelations and the immediate uproar in the country, in Congress, and in the press, Poindexter and the White House–National Security Council staffs were apparently intent on plowing ahead with what sounded to me like *more* "arms-for-hostages" swaps. In his cable, Poindexter was oblivious to and unconcerned about the uproar in the press and seemed convinced that an operation of enormous significance was under way. He seemed to feel that the administration could simply "stonewall" the press, Congress, and the public about the arms-for-hostages swap despite revelations indicating that we had violated two of the president's most important policies.

"I don't mean to compare it directly, but it is somewhat like Watergate," I said to my staff. "They get in and can't get out, so they stonewall and get in deeper." At this moment, in Vienna, I didn't know precisely what to do, but I did know that I was not going to go along with this, as Poindexter suggested. And I was certainly not going to instruct Bremer to go trailing

4. The trip had actually occurred in May 1986.

around after the NSC staff; I did not want him to get lashed up with Oliver North.

The scene in Washington was difficult to follow from Vienna, but reports from State were that the media were dominated by one story: the United States had dealt "arms for hostages." Walter Pincus, in the *Washington Post* on November 6, linked the release of three hostages over a period of nearly a year and a half to administration-approved arms transfers to Iran. If true, nothing could be worse: it would be a message to the terrorists that American citizens were the currency we would accept if they wished to purchase weapons. Press stories were that the United States had allowed three shipments of arms, each related to the release of one hostage. And during this period three more hostages had been taken. It was, in the words of columnist Charles Krauthammer, "commerce without end."

A political tidal wave, I felt sure, was bearing down on President Reagan and would, in my opinion, destroy his presidency unless the arms-for-hostages dealings were stopped immediately.

The danger of the situation was borne in on me while I was still in Vienna. At 6:30 A.M. on November 7, my last morning there, Irish Foreign Minister Peter Barry came to see me in my hotel suite, hopping mad because of press reports that Bud McFarlane and four others had traveled to Tehran using Irish passports—either forged or stolen. I received instructions from Washington telling me how to respond to him. I did not follow them. "I'm not going to start lying to friends and allies," I told Roz Ridgway. I had to tell him I knew almost nothing of the operation in general and absolutely nothing of the details. All I could do was refer him to Washington. I did not know the answers to good and proper questions. The meeting was as humiliating as any I ever held as secretary of state. I could only sit in anguish as my colleague told me how this had infringed on Ireland's sovereignty and severely damaged America's reputation. Suddenly, Ireland had been dragged into an affair it knew nothing about by the use of Irish passports apparently forged by officials of my own government without my knowledge.

Because of my lack of information and the White House statement that questions would be handled there, I continued to refer to the White House all the questions I was getting from the press. Their chatter was that I was in limbo, poised between silence and resignation. I could also feel, even halfway around the world, growing White House unhappiness with what they saw as my "distancing myself" publicly from the whole Iran affair. They were right: I had in the past opposed any arms-for-hostages deal whenever I got wind of it; I continued to oppose it now that the truth was bursting out; I would oppose it fiercely in the future.

I was deeply troubled. Poindexter still was not telling me what had happened. In the air on my way home and about an hour and a half out of Andrews, a report was telephoned to me that White House spokesman Larry Speakes was answering press questions about my role. Has Shultz resigned? No. Did Shultz know all about this Iran deal? Yes. Was he involved from the start? Yes. The operation was handled through normal procedures throughout, Speakes allegedly claimed. This was totally untrue, but at the moment, with my plane bumping down through the clouds, there was nothing for me to do but finish the gin rummy game I was playing with O'Bie. When our game was over, she looked at me and asked, "Are you going to resign?" I didn't answer.

This explosive affair would have a crushing impact, I felt, on my own effectiveness and credibility with other governments and on my ability to carry out the president's foreign policy agenda. I had preached to and pressured them steadily in the effort to create an internationally agreed upon policy against capitulating to terrorists and against selling arms to Iran. I had to get the truth from Poindexter and try to bring the situation under control. From my standpoint, the week had been terrible. The Republicans had lost control of the Senate in the Tuesday elections; the meeting in Vienna with the Soviets had been a bust; and the credibility of the United States had been badly damaged by our government's violation of its own policies.

When I arrived back at my house Friday night, I found a message from Poindexter. It was a warning from him against any "leaks." Again, I sensed that far from admitting that arms-for-hostages trades had been tried in the past, Poindexter was seeking secretly to carry this disastrous operation forward despite all the devastating revelations.

Back in my office on Saturday, November 8, I heard that the White House team was fully engaged in going ahead with further arms-for-hostages deals and was implying, without revealing details, that far bigger stakes were involved than the hostages. Oliver North, I was told, was even this weekend headed off somewhere on a secret mission. I hardly knew North, but I did know that Poindexter and others at the White House regarded him as a key "operator" on the NSC staff. I was being kept entirely out of the loop, and I was also being given an unmistakable signal: I should get on the team and cease my opposition. That I would not do.

Clearly this massive, secret White House operation was totally contrary to the long-standing policy that Ronald Reagan and I had constructed to deal with terrorists. The policy could be summed up succinctly by the precept "Make sure that terrorism does not pay." If hostage takers find that they can "sell" their hostages, their crimes will never cease.

I telephoned the national security adviser's office that Saturday morning and invited John Poindexter to have lunch with me. Word came back that he was too busy. He would be tied up all day and could not see me. No calls came from the White House at all that day.

The *New York Times* front-page headlines on Saturday, November 8, 1986, reported: "Reagan Approved Iranian Contacts, Officials Report; No Mention of Weapons; Secret Approaches Sought to Improve Relations and to Help Free Hostages" and "Shultz Reaffirms His Opposition to Negotiations With Terrorists."

So that Saturday afternoon I mulled over the crisis. "This has all the feel of Watergate," I said. "People close to the president get hooked into something and then start lying because they think they'll never be called to account." I thought the situation over and over and, as I talked, Charlie Hill carefully wrote down my assessment of where we stood and what we must do:

- The exposure of this deal has revealed that major aspects of the president's foreign policy constructed over six years have been gravely damaged. If we do not act *now*, some of his major achievements will not endure. And the morale and structure of his administration could start to collapse.
- After years of work, the keystone of our counterterrorism policy was set: No deals with terrorists. Now we have fallen into the trap. We have voluntarily made ourselves the victims of the terrorist extortion racket. We have spawned a hostage-taking industry. Every principle that the president praised in Netanyahu's book on terrorism[5] has been dealt a terrible blow by what has been done.
- We have assaulted our own Middle East policy. The Arabs counted on us to play a strong and responsible role to contain and eventually bring the Gulf War to an end. Now we are seen to be aiding the most radical forces in the region. We have acted directly counter to our own major effort to dry up the war by denying the weapons needed to continue it. The Jordanians—and other moderate Arabs— are appalled at what we have done. And our hopes of getting united allied action against Syria have foundered as the allies see us doing precisely what we have relentlessly pressured them not to do.
- We appear to have violated our own laws. Certainly we have corrupted ourselves in the eyes of the law. At this moment there are Israelis and others on trial in U.S. criminal courts for doing what the U.S. government has now revealed itself to be doing.
- Our credibility is shot. We have taken refuge in tricky technicalities of language to avoid confronting the reality that we have lied to the American people and misused our friends abroad. We are revealed to have been dealing with some of the sleaziest international char-

5. Benjamin Netanyahu, ed., *Terrorism: How the West Can Win* (New York: Farrar, Straus & Giroux, 1986). The president had read this book on the trip to the Tokyo summit meeting and had come back to the senior staff area several times from his cabin on *Air Force One* to read passages to us that he particularly liked.

acters around. They have played us for suckers. There is a Watergate-like atmosphere around here as the White House staff has become secretive, self-deluding, and vindictive.

So it must be stopped. How?

1. A statement by the president is needed reaffirming his policies on terrorism and the Middle East.
2. I am prepared to back the president all the way, with the public, with Congress, with other nations, as having undertaken an effort for humanitarian reasons that we will now close out.
3. The operation must be totally closed out and Ollie North returned to the Marine Corps. Counterterrorism policy will have to be explicitly returned to the management of the State Department.

If this operation is the wrong way to achieve our goals, how *do* we achieve them?

Iran: There are signs of a new post-Khomeini situation. We have a channel through Yaqub Khan [the Pakistani foreign minister] that can most reliably assess the facts there and the real possibilities for progress. There is an unavoidable geostrategic fact: *any* Iranian government that wants to stay free of Soviet influence *has* to turn to the U.S. But in this operation *we* have put *ourselves* in the role of petitioners.

Terrorism: We have been hurt badly, but if we move quickly, we can recover. The fact that Syria has been caught red-handed by the British[6] offers us an immediate objective that can restore allied unity, calm the moderate Arabs, and pressure those holding the hostages who cannot function over time without Syrian acquiescence and help.

But almost every aspect of our foreign policy agenda will suffer unless the president makes the decision now to halt this operation and let me clean up the mess.

My Battle Begins

From this framework I set to work. My attention shifted from what had happened to what was still going on and to what had to be stopped and reversed. I had to persuade the president to call off the Iran arms-for-hostages operation, to get the NSC staffers out of the action altogether, and to return direction of our Iran policy and the hostage crisis to me. No battle of my official life would be more brutal and intense.

6. The British had apprehended a Syrian terrorist who planted a bomb in the luggage of his fiancée about to board an El Al flight at Heathrow Airport.

My objective now was to get President Reagan to see how badly he was being served by the arms sales to Iran, *especially* as tied to freeing hostages, and to see how badly he was being served by members of his staff, who were not being honest with him. I had to stop completely any further arms-for-hostages deals. I knew my job was on the line, but proud as I was to be secretary of state and conscious as I was of possible achievements of great significance, I knew I could not want the job too much.

I had to level with the president and fight his staff. If I got tossed out, so be it, but if I prevailed, the turnaround would save the presidency. If his staff prevailed, Ronald Reagan's presidency would go down in a welter of misguided policies, misinformation, and a cover-up of reality. My credibility with the president could only be enhanced by his knowledge that I was the easiest guy in Washington for him to get rid of.

On Sunday morning I stood in my living room and looked out the window at the street below. A television camera crew had been stationed there for hours in anticipation that I might emerge and announce my resignation. Some friends and associates, Nick Brady, Chuck Redman, Charlie Hill, and Nick Platt, came over and together we sat in the den and watched "This Week with David Brinkley." The show was full of talk about whether I would—or should, or would be forced to—resign.

I mulled over the question, but by Monday morning I was clear in my mind that I owed it to Ronald Reagan to do all I could to get him and his presidency through this crisis—and then I would offer to leave if he wished. "If I leave," I said, "I don't want to go out with virtue on my sleeve. I want to go in a manner that gives support to the things about the president's policies that I have worked for and agree with and that gets the president in a position where the next secretary of state can be effective on terrorism and other issues. So the name of the game is to help the president and not worry about me because I will one way or another get along." A telephone call came in from Charles Krauthammer: my resignation would be a disaster, Krauthammer said. "The wrong man always resigns in cases like this."

I Review the Record

I asked Abe Sofaer to have his staff, in collaboration with Charlie Hill, glean from the record the details of my role, awareness, and actions since the arms-for-hostages idea was first raised. From a preliminary review of the material immediately available, my recollections were refreshed, and events I had forgotten took on more meaning to me now than they had at the time they occurred.

Going back over this material was an eye-opener. What I read about and what I remembered amounted to a series of isolated, fleeting moments, punctuated by assurances that the effort had ended. These moments did not add up to anything in my mind until I put them together. Even then I could see that the information I had was fragmentary at best and perhaps was not even representative of what had in fact happened.

My first indication that something odd was taking place had come on May 30, 1985. Ambassador Sam Lewis in Tel Aviv reported that someone named Michael Ledeen—described to me as a free-lance academic with a conspiratorial bent—was in Israel talking to Israeli officials about intelligence on Iran. Ledeen was said to be traveling "on a secret mission from the White House," under orders from the National Security Council staff. Sam Lewis said that he did not know what was going on. Lewis had been told at the Israeli Ministry of Defense that Ledeen's mission was "too hot to talk about" but that Defense Minister Yitzhak Rabin would tell me about it when he met with me in Washington on June 3. When Rabin came to see me, he did not mention Ledeen or any White House mission. I did not inquire, as I obviously was not going to ask the Israelis to inform me about a White House matter.

The next day, when I was in Lisbon on June 4 for a meeting with NATO foreign ministers, Bud McFarlane telephoned to tell me of his own scheduled meeting in Washington with Rabin. Bud made no mention of Ledeen or Iran. So I sent a message to McFarlane objecting to Ledeen's secretive mission and warning against the potential bias implicit in any Israeli intelligence involving Iran. Israeli intelligence "could seriously skew our own perception and analysis of the Iranian scene," I told Bud. The United States was trying to shut down the Iran-Iraq War by denying arms to both sides and by trying to persuade other nations to do the same. The Israelis, by contrast, were glad to see their enemies demolishing each other and, beyond that, wanted to maintain at least a subterranean relationship with Iran and thereby with Iranian Jews. Bud replied by cable that Ledeen had been in Israel "on his own hook" on an Israeli initiative; McFarlane continued that he was "turning it off entirely." I was skeptical. The story didn't add up. That would turn out to be only the first of several times when I was assured that an Iran-oriented initiative of some kind had been closed down. I was troubled by McFarlane's tendency to dissemble when it served his purpose.

Within two weeks of his assurances to me, on June 17, 1985, McFarlane circulated a draft National Security Defense Directive (NSDD) proposing a change in our policy toward Iran to involve the "provision of selected military equipment as determined on a case-by-case basis."

I opposed this forcefully, stating in writing that "to reverse our present policy and permit or encourage a flow of Western arms to Iran is contrary to our interests, both in containing Khomeinism and in ending the excesses of his regime. It would seem particularly perverse to alter this aspect of our policy when groups with ties to Iran are holding U.S. hostages in Lebanon. I therefore disagree with the suggestion that our efforts to reduce arms flows should be ended. I cannot agree that the NSDD as drafted should be signed by the President."

Cap Weinberger was more blunt. He called the proposal "absurd" and said that this would be like "asking Qaddafi over for a cozy lunch."

Instead, I proposed another course of action, a two-track policy that would (1) continue to try to restrain arms flows to both Iran and Iraq and to support a mediated end to their war and (2) encourage the Europeans and the Japanese to broaden their commercial contacts with Iran as a means to end Iran's isolation and offer Iran an alternative to the Soviets. I heard no more about this proposed NSDD, nor to my knowledge did anyone else at the State Department. I concluded that the matter had been dropped.

June and July of 1985 were dominated by the hijacking of TWA Flight 847, with its high-profile coverage, the murder of passenger Robert Stethem, and the highlighting of hostage issues. I and others worked hard to achieve the release of the TWA passengers held hostage in Beirut, but the seven American hostages who had previously been taken captive were not released. Pressure mounted on the White House and from the White House to "do something." Ronald Reagan felt a deep sense of personal responsibility for the fate of those seven unfortunate Americans.

On July 14, 1985, while in flight between Perth and Canberra, Australia, I received a message from Bud McFarlane. He said that David Kimche had met secretly with him the week before and had asked Bud to confirm that the United States was, in fact, *not* interested in pursuing the approach to Iran earlier discussed with Michael Ledeen. McFarlane cabled that he had so confirmed. He then told me that "today" an unnamed emissary had reopened the issue on behalf of Israeli Prime Minister Shimon Peres. The emissary said that in a recent meeting between the Israelis and some Iranians, including Manucher Ghorbanifar, the Iranians had allegedly expressed "their hope and that of what they portrayed as a significant cadre of the hierarchy . . . to develop a dialogue with the West" and emphatically with the United States.

The Israelis, allegedly pressing "for some tangible show" of the Iranians' ability to deliver, were told that the Iranians could in the short term achieve the release of the seven Americans held in Lebanon. But, McFarlane repeated, in exchange the Iranians said they would need to show "some gain" and sought specifically the delivery from Israel of 100 TOW missiles. "They stated," McFarlane continued, "that the larger purpose would be the opening of the private dialogue with a high-level American official and a sustained discussion of U.S.-Iranian relations." That sounded to me like an unacceptable exchange of arms for hostages, cloaked in a strategic guise.

In his cable McFarlane reviewed the imponderable questions, as he put it, raised by this proposal, including "our terrorism policy against negotiating with terrorists . . . notwithstanding the thin veil provided by Israel as the cutout on this specific matter." McFarlane noted our long-term interest in the possibility of new ties with Iran and the importance of doing something soon about the seven hostages. He said, "We can make a tentative show of interest without commitment and see what happens, or we could walk away. On balance I tend to favor going ahead." He said the emissary—Kimche, I assumed—who was leaving soon, asked for a prompt signal. MacFarlane said that he would abide fully by my decision.

This position, indicating a willingness to talk but without commitment, was consistent with the administration policy of maintaining contact with people who might eventually provide information or help in freeing hostages. I replied to McFarlane that same day: "I agree with you that we should make a tentative show of interest without commitment. I do not think we could justify turning our backs on the prospect of gaining the release of the other seven hostages and perhaps developing an ability to renew ties with Iran under a more sensible regime, especially when presented to us through the Prime Minister of Israel." I pointed out, however, "the fraud that seems to accompany so many deals involving arms and Iran and the complications arising from our blessing an Israeli-Iran relationship where Israel's interests and ours are not necessarily the same."

I suggested that Bud McFarlane give the emissary "a positive but passive reply, that is, tell him that the United States is receptive to the idea of a private dialogue involving a sustained discussion of U.S.-Iranian relations. In other words, we are willing to listen and seriously consider any statement on this topic that they might wish to initiate." I told McFarlane I thought that he should manage this probe personally but the two of us should discuss its sensitivity and the likelihood of disclosure after my return. I was uneasy about my response, but I well knew the pressures from the president to follow up on any possibility of gaining the release of our hostages. I felt that Bud would in fact go ahead no matter what I said and that I was better off to stay in close touch with him and thereby retain some influence over what happened.

On July 16, 1985, I saw a report stating that Ghorbanifar—one of Israel's Iranian contacts mentioned by McFarlane—was well known as "a talented fabricator." My yellow light turned to red. This matter would need careful handling. McFarlane could be deceived into unwise actions, I feared.

On July 19, just back from the Far East, I visited the president in his room at Bethesda Naval Hospital. He was recuperating from successful surgery to remove a malignant polyp from his colon. Bud McFarlane was there when I arrived. I gave the president a tour of world issues: impressions of the Far East, developments on the Middle East peace process and on

Soviet matters. Bud was enthusiastic about the idea of a joint U.S.-Egypt military operation against Qaddafi. He did not mention the Israeli discussions with the alleged representatives of Iran.

In early August 1985, the scheme to deal arms to Iran for our hostages in Lebanon suddenly reappeared. On August 6, 1985, during one of my regular meetings with the president, Bud McFarlane again brought up the idea of talks with Iran. McFarlane said he had met again with David Kimche, who reported that the Israelis and people purporting to represent Iran had held three meetings during which the Iranian representatives said Iran was in a shambles and a new government was inevitable. The military and the Iranian people, the Iranian intermediaries reportedly said, were "still pro-American" and "want a dialogue with America." They also wanted arms from the United States and 100 TOW missiles from Israel. All this would be totally deniable, Bud said. The Iranians said they could produce four more hostages and wanted a meeting somewhere.

McFarlane said that Prime Minister Shimon Peres wanted to know explicitly whether I was informed. At this point what I knew was what Bud had told me and nothing more. I also argued strongly to the president and McFarlane that arms sales to Iran would be a grave mistake and that discussion of the possibility should be stopped. I thought that the president agreed, though reluctantly.

McFarlane startled me on September 3, 1985. He telephoned me that he had been told by his interlocutor, whom he did not identify, that the Iranians wanted more arms than originally indicated and that such transfer should take place before any hostages were released. I said, "No. No arms." I wanted all seven hostages out before any other step in relations could be considered. I felt Bud agreed.

The next day, September 4, Reg Bartholomew, our ambassador to Lebanon, called on the tacsat to say that the NSC staff had alerted him to cooperate with Lieutenant Colonel Oliver North, who was handling an operation that would lead to the release of all seven hostages. On the same day, our records indicated that North wanted the State Department to issue him a passport in another name. North would go to the eastern Mediterranean to provide military liaison if the seven were released. Bartholomew was told that all seven would be brought to a beach north of Tripoli, Lebanon, where our people would meet and get them safely offshore. The department issued such a passport to North—which I later learned was under the name of "Willie B. Goode," apparently an expression of the staff-level skepticism about North as a continuing problem.

Through the first half of September, McFarlane periodically reported that the release of all seven was "working" and would soon be accomplished. On September 14, 1985, Benjamin Weir was released, but the CIA kept this news from the State Department and from becoming public knowledge until September 16, apparently worried because Weir had a note from his captors intended to dramatize an additional demand: the release of Shiite terrorists, known as the Dawa prisoners, held in prison in Kuwait after being tried and sentenced there. The next day, Ambassador Bartholomew told Hill that McFarlane had informed him directly that the other hostages would be released in three batches without publicity. Weir had no information about the other hostages and said he had been released only to bring pressure for the release of the Dawa prisoners. Bartholomew's speculation was that Weir's situation was separate from whatever might transpire on the beach north of Tripoli.

Bartholomew was pessimistic. He said he knew precious little about the origins of this effort or who was involved. He thought the chances of gaining the release of any more hostages now were slim to nonexistent. On September 17, NBC carried a story about an Iranian aircraft carrying Iranian Jews to Israel and suggested that Israel would send spare parts to Iran in return. The Israelis denied it, and I was told shortly thereafter that the report had been false.[7] The McFarlane-North operation to free all hostages had failed. On Saturday, September 21, McFarlane telephoned to discuss further the indications that Iran might be ready, unconditionally, to start improving relations with the United States. At that moment it appeared that Weir had been freed by terrorists who wanted to publicize their demand for their Dawa cohorts to be released from Kuwait. Any hope for the release of the other American hostages had been dashed for the time being. I was left very uncomfortable and unsettled, fearing that I had not heard the last of arms-for-hostages schemes.

Early in the evening of November 19, 1985, the first day of the Geneva summit meeting, after a grueling session with the Soviets, I rushed back to my suite in the Intercontinental Hotel to change clothes before going to the dinner that General Secretary Mikhail Gorbachev was giving for President Reagan. I had been told that my suite was one that Arab potentates always used, so our security people assumed it was totally bugged. They seemed particularly suspicious about an enormous tray of Swiss chocolates, which seemed to require their daily inspection and consumption. Another consequence of their concern was the cramped, soundproof security bubble that they installed in the study of the suite. The phone inside was ringing as I was getting dressed for dinner. Bud McFarlane was on the line: four hostages would be released on November 21. The Israelis would send a plane with 100 Hawk missiles to Portugal, where they would transfer them to another aircraft. If the hostages were released, the airplane

7. If there was any quid pro quo as far as I could see, it was that the Israelis were ready to release some Shiite prisoners from detention at the Atlit camp, as they had informed me they would at the time the TWA hostages were released. That might induce the hostage holders to let the remaining American hostages go free.

would fly to Iran. If not, it would fly to Israel. Israel would buy replacements for the Hawks from the United States and they would be paid by Iran.[8]

This was arms for hostages, plain and simple. With stony anger, I told McFarlane that I had been informed so late in the operation that I had no conceivable way to stop it. I hoped that the hostages would be released, but I dreaded what I feared would be an unfolding nightmare.

November 21, 1985, the supposed release date, arrived and passed. No prisoners were released. On November 22, the release apparently slipped again, allegedly to get airspace clearance from Turkey. Also on that day, Bob Oakley, who was then in charge of State's antiterrorist efforts, reported that he had heard from "corridor talk" that the hostages would be released that afternoon in exchange for 120 Hawks at $250,000 each, worth $30 million in all. This was a $30 million weapons payoff. It was appalling to me. I recalled that Bud, at some point in Geneva, had told me he had cleared the plan with the president.

On December 4, 1985, Bud McFarlane resigned as national security adviser. I had seen his resignation coming for a long time. Bud had a capacity for strategic thinking, but in his position as NSC adviser to the president, he yearned to make things happen through his own secret diplomacy. Somebody—especially me—always seemed to be saying no to Bud. His relations with Don Regan were tense and strained. Over time he became more and more morose. Even when his manner was calm and measured, underneath I sensed he was churning. I had worked with him closely and successfully on Soviet affairs, where he made a genuine contribution. But I felt that he never found real satisfaction in the NSC adviser's role as coordinator: he wanted to be the action man.

On December 5, 1985, Vice Admiral John Poindexter, who was appointed to succeed McFarlane as NSC adviser, told me that he had set up a meeting about Iran, arms sales, and hostages for Saturday, December 7. I told him that the operation should be stopped, that Iran was playing a big role in Lebanon, through the Shiites, whom even Syria could not influence. "We are signaling to Iran that they can kidnap people for profit," I said. I raised the problem of notifying Congress. I told him I had been opposed to the operation from the start, that I favored improving relations with Iran if there was a logical prospect of doing so, but *not* through breaching important U.S. principles and policies by allowing terrorists to "sell their hostages." I warned Poindexter that if this operation leaked—and I felt it

8. Don Regan, in his memoir published in May 1988, placed me at a meeting on November 19, 1985, that I did not attend. Regan described in detail how McFarlane briefed President Reagan and him on the intricate structure of the proposed arms sales to Iran and release of hostages. Because I was *not* at this meeting, McFarlane had called me that evening to brief me by telephone, as I describe above. Donald T. Regan, *For the Record* (New York: St. Martin's Press, 1988).

inevitably would leak—the fact that we had violated our principles would be clear, and our effort to block arms transfers from other countries to Iran would be seen to be perfidious. I found no reassurance, I told him, in the fact that Israel was handling the sales. "This thing has got to be stopped," I told him.

I told Poindexter that I was uninformed, that State had been cut out of the cable traffic. He promised cooperation, told me that the emphasis of the project was on relations with post-Khomeini Iran more than on the hostages. He told me that 3,300 TOWs and 60 Hawks were being discussed.

I learned from Poindexter why the transfer of Hawks to Iran that Bud described to me while I was in Geneva had "misfired." Iran had rejected the shipment as "too old," I was told, because they bore 1979 markings. So that ill-considered episode was over, I thought. I also learned that the meeting scheduled for December 7 would take up the possible sale by Israel of Hawks and perhaps some Phoenix missiles out of Israeli stock to be compensated by TOWs from the United States. I was ready to express once again to the president my opposition both to the project and to dealings with the operators who were allegedly representing Iran.

On December 7, 1985, the president convened the meeting in the White House family quarters on this issue. I had prepared my views carefully and in detail. Also present were Cap Weinberger, John Poindexter, deputy CIA director John McMahon standing in for Bill Casey, Don Regan, and Bud McFarlane. Poindexter suggested that McFarlane, who was still active in this operation even after his resignation, contact the Iranians in London to ask them to release the hostages without receiving any military equipment. If they would do so, we would be prepared to reach a better understanding with Iran. I thought the prospects for success were minimal, but I did not object to that approach.

Poindexter then suggested that if the Iranians rejected this first proposal, McFarlane should be authorized to ask other countries to sell arms to Israel to replace those Israel would transfer to Iran: that idea I opposed *vigorously*. Such an effort was still trading U.S. arms for hostages, I said, and it would be a more complicated deal that would make us even more vulnerable: arms for hostages and arms to Iran were both terrible ideas! I argued that this was a betrayal of our policies and would only encourage more hostage taking. Cap Weinberger expressed the same point of view with genuine and unmistakable conviction. He got the president's attention by opening with a question. "Mr. President, do you really want to hear my opinion?" He stopped and looked at the president. He was very effective.

No decision was made at the meeting. But my sense was that the point of view that Cap and I argued had won the day. Later that day, Poindexter told me privately that when the project had fallen apart during Thanksgiving week, he had recommended to the president that we disengage. The president did not want to disengage, he said.

On December 10, 1985, I was in London on my way to a NATO foreign ministers' meeting when I was told that Bud McFarlane had come to London with the proposal I had supported—the one that did *not* include any arms sales—and that proposal had been flatly rejected by the Iranians. A meeting had been held in the White House that day, and I was informed through my staff that the operation was *completely turned off*. Once again, I felt that there had been a lot of debate, that no arms had actually been exchanged, and that the effort was over. I was relieved, but still wary.

Leaks and Lie Detectors

On November 8, 1986, the day I had returned from Vienna into the maelstrom of arms sales to Iran for hostages, the only message I had received from the White House was the pointed one from Poindexter about the danger of "leaks." The problem was an old one in Washington and had become an obsession with many in the Reagan administration. I was distressed by leaks and, somewhat to the disappointment of many journalists, held all my interviews "on the record." Once when I discovered the identity of someone who leaked in the State Department, I fired him. My approach to management has always been clear-cut: start by trusting people. Trust creates trust and loyalty in return. If you find someone who can't be trusted, get rid of that person, the sooner, the better.

A year earlier, in the fall of 1985, a sudden furor had bubbled up around Washington over lie detector tests for government employees. The arrest of Jonathan Pollard as an Israeli spy, coming on top of other espionage cases and a stream of leaks to the press by officials in the know, had alarmed the NSC staff. With strong support from the CIA, the FBI, and the Defense Department, an NSDD (National Security Decision Directive 196) was hurriedly engineered that would have instituted a massive program of random lie detector testing affecting employees throughout the government who had access to sensitive information. I had strongly and repeatedly opposed the use of lie detector tests as a managerial tool, and my view was well known. News of the NSDD appeared in the press on December 11, when I was in Europe for a NATO foreign ministers' meeting. I took the position in response to questions that this was a domestic problem and I would not address it while abroad.

The day of my return, December 19, 1985, I met with reporters to introduce the members of an Advisory Commission on South Africa that I had just established. The questions turned to NSDD 196 and lie detector tests. "Personally, I have grave reservations about so-called lie detector tests," I said, "because the experience with them that I have read about—

I don't claim to be an expert . . . but from what I've seen, it's hardly a scientific instrument. It tends to identify quite a few people who are innocent as guilty, and it misses at least some fraction of people who are guilty of lying. And it is, I think, pretty well demonstrated that a professional—that is, say, a professional spy or a professional leaker—can probably train himself or herself not to be caught by the test." Actually, I knew of cases where the CIA had been fooled and badly misled when a trained agent of another country repeatedly and successfully passed their polygraph tests.

Don Oberdorfer of the *Washington Post* then asked me whether I would take such a test if asked to do so.

"Once," I answered.

"Once?" he followed up.

"Once," I repeated. "The minute in this government I am told that I'm not trusted is the day that I leave." I then walked out of the room.

All hell broke loose. The CIA put out a rebuttal almost immediately, concluding, "The director of Central Intelligence and his predecessors voluntarily have been polygraphed, believing in the importance of setting an example that all those with access must do what they can to protect our secrets and to cooperate in identifying those who do not."

After the press conference, I told a few members of my staff: "You cannot work effectively in an organization where you are not trusted, and under this NSDD everybody takes the lie detector test sooner or later. It is not acceptable to apply lie detector tests across the board as a condition of employment. The scale required for these tests is so great that there is bound to be sloppy administration. It is a very dangerous instrument to put into the hands of our government—there have been so many ugly periods in our government. The NSDD is wrong. I have spent a fair amount of time with the president giving my view on this. There was a meeting in the Situation Room at which I took this position. Poindexter has misconstrued the lie detector totally, saying it is like fingerprints or a blood test. I said, 'No, it's not.' "

The fact was that the president had signed the NSDD, and I was saying I would not stand for it. As Bernard Gwertzman wrote in the *New York Times* on December 20, "This was the first time that Mr. Shultz had publicly dissociated himself from a Presidential decision. It raised questions about whether he intended to remain in the Administration if there was no change in the directive. Since becoming Secretary of State in July 1982, Mr. Shultz has prided himself on publicly defending an Administration policy once it has been put into effect, even if he opposed it originally."

The State Department press corps saw the CIA statement as an unmistakable reference and challenge to me. Casey saw me in the White House corridors that afternoon and said, "Sorry about that, George, but I had to do it." I went to the Oval Office at 1:00 P.M. on Friday, December 20, 1985, and I made my arguments to the president. He agreed not to go forward with the NSDD. At 2:45, Poindexter telephoned to read me a statement that he had drafted to put out in the president's name. He had not yet cleared the statement with the intelligence agencies.

> Some questions have arisen about the President's views on the use of polygraphing. He opposes new mandatory requirements of polygraphing a broad spectrum of U.S. Government employees. He feels that polygraphing should be limited to use in investigating espionage cases.
>
> Secretary Shultz fully shares the President's view of the seriousness of espionage cases and agrees with the need to use all legal means which can contribute to the counter-espionage effort and help safeguard our national security interests.

This statement sounded to me too much like the president eating crow. I offered to put out a statement:

> I had a chance to talk fully with the President today on his view on the use of polygraphing. He told me that he opposed the broad use of polygraphing throughout the government as a routine matter. He feels that it has potential usefulness in particular investigations of cases in which espionage may be involved. I fully support the President's view of the seriousness of these cases and the need to use all legal means to conduct the counter-intelligence effort and protect our national security interests.

I could have given them a statement that would have been hard for Casey, with his compulsory lie detector tests, to live with, but I didn't. At 4:10, Poindexter telephoned me again with yet another draft statement prepared after discussions with the National Security Agency (NSA) and CIA. He read it to me, and we worked over the wording, taking out language that might be interpreted as allowing regular testing of government employees for security-clearance purposes. When we had finished, the statement, which the president agreed to, read as follows:

> Some questions have been raised about the President's views on the use of polygraphs. The President believes the polygraph can be a limited though sometimes useful tool when used in conjunction with other investigative and security procedures in espionage cases. Under this policy polygraphs may be used as an investigative tool in espionage cases. Departments and agencies may, as some do now, use the polygraph as a condition for access to certain types of sensitive information.
>
> Secretary Shultz fully shares the President's view of the seriousness of espionage cases and agrees with the need to use all legal means in the investigation of such cases.

I was satisfied with this. My aim was to stop the White House from imposing a vast government-wide process of regular polygraphing of all government employees who had access to sensitive information, even when no grounds whatsoever existed for suspecting them of any impropriety or wrongdoing. I was not trying to stop the CIA or the Defense Department from managing themselves as they wished, but I was determined that they would not manage the State Department through the ruse of establishing an intimidating government-wide regulation. I resisted, spoke out, and the NSC staff and intelligence agencies backed away or were forced to do so by President Reagan.

The difference on this issue between Bill Casey and John Poindexter and me meant that the CIA would not work with or provide information in many instances to State Department officials because they were not subject to regular lie detector testing. In truth, Casey was already screening me and the State Department out anyway. I realized when Don Rumsfeld had come into the State Department that he, as a former secretary of defense, had access to a wide range of intelligence information that I did not get. Apparently I was not to be trusted. But the problem was becoming more fundamental: even when intelligence was provided to me, I increasingly recognized that the intelligence on many sensitive issues reflected the strong ideological policy views of Bill Casey. The stamp was there. Clearly, at the top level in the CIA, policy and analysis were intermixed.

Arms Sales Emerge Again

After the developments following the December 7, 1985, meeting, I heard nothing more about the issue of contacts with Iran for almost a month. Then, on January 7, 1986, I was suddenly called to a meeting with the president in the Oval Office on further developments regarding Iran. The new developments were much the same as they had been before. The snake had not died. All the key players were present: Vice President George Bush, Don Regan, Cap Weinberger, Bill Casey, Ed Meese, and John Poindexter. I again argued fiercely and with passion against *any* arms sales to Iran, especially arms sales connected to the release of hostages. "Strangely enough, I agree with George," said Cap. No one else did. Cap and I were isolated.

I had an uneasy, uncanny feeling that the meeting was not a *real* meeting, that it had all been "precooked." I had the sense that a decision had already been made, though none was explicitly stated. I was bewildered and distressed by this turn of events.

I learned a year later that the actual decision *had* been taken the day before, on January 6, when John Poindexter presented President Reagan with a draft "finding" authorizing arms sales to Iran. The president signed it. I heard no discussion of a finding during the January 7, 1986, meeting or at any time until *after* the public revelation of arms sales in November 1986, after Jacobsen's release.[9] In order for any arms sale to Iran to be legal, the president would have to make a finding authorizing the secret sale as being in the national security interests of the United States. Such findings were usually notified to the Senate and House committees dealing with intelligence. But I learned after I finally heard about the finding that the president had decided not to give such a notice in this case. Beyond the question of a finding, however, the dominant consideration in my mind was the gross violation of our policies of no arms sales to Iran and of no swaps of arms for hostages.

At lunch with the Family Group[10] on January 17, 1986, I talked bluntly with Bill Casey about how disturbed I was with the CIA and its performance. "The CIA has a strong policy view; I always have to stop and ask myself: what is it that I am reading? What message does the agency want me to get?"

Casey mumbled that he was "aware of the problem." What Casey really wanted to talk about was lie detector tests. The pressure against me for my opposing position had never slackened. I remembered that Anne Armstrong, formerly ambassador to Great Britain and now head of the President's Foreign Intelligence Advisory Board, had once hit me hard. "I took a polygraph test," she said, "and I didn't get on *my* high horse." FBI director William Webster had also once told me that administering lie detector tests was "an art form." It made people nervous, and you could get people to confess all kinds of things just with the threat of a polygraph, he explained. You could keep people in line by intimidating them was the impression I got from Bill Casey and other disciples of lie detector tests. Discipline has its place in running an organization, but management by intimidation never appealed to me.

At this same lunch, after my argument with Casey, Poindexter said that he was proceeding with efforts to construct a better relationship with Iran and that he feared leaks about prospective meetings would throw him off track. I knew very well that he had me and the State Department in mind. I told him, in a remark I would learn to regret, that in view of his concern about leaks, I didn't need to know in advance about every operational move. I wanted to know about anything affecting our foreign policy and expected periodic briefings on his activities. (My remark to Poindexter would later be cited to me again and again, and I was to agonize about it

9. The operative finding, I learned on November 10, 1986, was dated January 17, 1986.
10. Casey, Weinberger, Poindexter, and I held periodic luncheons in the Old Family Dining Room of the White House.

myself. But when the facts came out in congressional hearings in 1987, I could see a pattern of deliberate deception, lies, and misrepresentations to me that made clear that my remark to Poindexter had been virtually irrelevant—it was certainly not central to why I was kept in the dark.)

Hostages: More Dealings with Iran

On January 31, 1986, a rumor had come in about Oliver North, who was said to be working with the pope as well as a plethora of shady international characters. Millions in payoffs were said to be involved. The Anglican emissary Terry Waite was said to be linked to the effort. The whole thing seemed so implausible, even nutty—that it was viewed at State as comic relief.

But at the Family Group lunch on Tuesday, February 11, I was surprised, and trapped, again. All the hostages would be out Saturday or Sunday, February 22 or 23, Casey and Poindexter said, as part of an operation already under way. I feared from what they recounted that arms might already be on their way to Iran. I felt frozen: I could not, at the last second, try to stop this effort, but I dreaded its consequences. Again, however, nothing happened.

Days later, on February 28, Poindexter outlined another approach: the Iranians wanted a high-level dialogue on issues other than the hostages. He said the White House had chosen Bud McFarlane for the mission and that Bud would go to Frankfurt to meet with Ghorbanifar. No arms were mentioned. I said that McFarlane should be given precise instructions to govern his negotiations and that I wanted to clear those talking points. I was shown what I was told were Bud's instructions: no arms were involved. Poindexter said that the hostages would be released when McFarlane met the Iranians in Frankfurt.

On March 11, 1986, Poindexter told me that the arrangement had fallen through, allegedly because McFarlane objected to some aspect of it. I had thought the entire arrangement was naive and extremely unlikely to succeed, and I was not surprised when it did not materialize. On March 18, Ambassador Reg Bartholomew informed me that we had information that some of the American hostages were being held in a Hezbollah prison in southern Lebanon and that our embassy was seeking to confirm that and to work with the U.S. military on a possible assault on the place. Nothing was imminent, Bartholomew said, and indeed, the operations probably would never come off. We did not want to mount "another Son Tay," he said.[11] Nothing came of that effort.

11. The U.S. raid on a North Vietnamese prison said to hold American POWs but which proved to be empty.

*   *   *

On May 4, 1986, in Tokyo—where I was attending the economic summit—
I received a cable stating that Ambassador Charles Price in London had
reported to Under Secretary Mike Armacost that an embassy officer in
London had learned from Roland (Tiny) Rowland, a British entrepreneur
with interests in Africa, of a deal involving arms and grain for Iran from
various countries. The embassy officer reported that Adnan Khashoggi, a
Saudi operator, had suggested that Rowland meet with Amiram Nir, Prime
Minister Peres's special adviser on counterterrorism, and Ghorbanifar.
Rowland did meet with them and reportedly learned from Nir of various
arrangements to get arms to Iran with the use of Swiss banks. Armacost
cabled that Price reported that Rowland said that he was told: "The scheme
is okay with the Americans. It has been cleared with the White House.
Poindexter allegedly is the point man. Only four people in the U.S. Government are knowledgeable about the plan. The State Department has
been cut out."

As soon as I got this message, I sought out the president. He, Don
Regan, and John Poindexter were in one part of the Okura Hotel, and I
was in another. The president was not available. I couldn't locate Poindexter, but I did find Don Regan. I expressed strong opposition across the
board: on policy, legal, and moral grounds, as well as my concern for
exposing the president to a seamy and explosive situation. "Stop!" I said.
"This is crazy." I told Regan to go to the president: "Get him to end this
matter once and for all." The deal was all wrong. "If this activity continues," I said, "the president will be gravely damaged." Regan seemed
to share my concern: he seemed alarmed and said he would talk to the
president.

When I later expressed my concerns to Poindexter, he did not share my
view at all. He claimed that we were not dealing with "those people"—
that we were not involved in "that deal."

"The president is very exposed," I told him. I later learned that Poindexter told Ambassador Price that there was no more than "a smidgen"
of reality to this story.

After the Tokyo summit, I went to South Korea and the Philippines.
The president and his party went home. Back in Washington on May 22,
Poindexter sprung the trap on me again: all the hostages would be out
immediately, and the price was a shipment of TOWs.[12] Again, I held my

12. I did not refer to this incident or the similar brief and aborted effort which I was
informed of on February 11, 1986 (at the Family Group lunch mentioned earlier) in my
congressional testimony. I had not remembered them, and my executive assistant, Charlie
Hill, had not found references to them in his review of notes he had taken. They were located
when the Independent Counsel's office, under the direction of Lawrence Walsh, subsequently
went thorugh all of Hill's voluminous notes, spending far more time doing so than Hill was
able to take from his ongoing operational duties. The Independent Counsel also found a note
in the files of Defense Secretary Cap Weinberger referring to a conversation he had with me

breath—and again, it didn't happen. On May 28, while at the United Nations, I was informed that the whole effort was dead. In Washington, on May 30, Armacost confirmed that "it has petered out." In mid-June, both Bill Casey and John Poindexter told me directly that at the end of May, the operation had been brought to an end and that the people involved had been told to "stand down."

Rumors and rumblings popped up intermittently from the lower levels, and my concern never abated through the early summer of 1986. On July 15, 1986, Prime Minister Junejo of Pakistan came to Washington on an official visit, bringing with him his foreign minister, Yaqub Khan, who I regarded highly as experienced, astute, and trustworthy. Khan knew the Iranian scene well. With the president's agreement, I worked out careful talking points with Poindexter for possible use by Khan with the Iranian foreign minister in a secret probe on our behalf. We put the idea to him. He agreed to play the role as an intermediary. That was the fourth time I had moved to control or block a twisted arms-for-hostages scheme. There must be only one channel to Iran on the question of hostages and future U.S.-Iran relations, I told Poindexter repeatedly. From now on, our dealings with Iran must go through Khan's professional hands to officials of the Iranian government, I insisted. At the end of July, Father Lawrence Jenco was released, for reasons of health, I was told. Two more hostages, Frank Reed and Joseph Cicippio, were seized by terrorists in early September 1986. Then came the release of hostage David Jacobsen on November 2, followed by the explosive revelation on November 4, 1986, of arms sales to Iran.

When I lined up this whole scenario before me, a story with fragmented coherence emerged. The president was in trouble and key administration policies had been grossly violated. I felt I should have asked more, demanded more, done more, but I did not see *how*. I had argued vigorously and passionately on a number of occasions with the president against arm sales to Iran, especially as linked to hostage-release efforts, and even with Cap Weinberger strongly on my side, I had not moved him.

I felt that the president was clearly being deceived and misled by his staff in the White House. I knew that now I must fight *for* the president by fighting *against* members of his own staff.

---

on May 13, 1986, in which he told me about a possible arms sale to Iran. I did not recall this conversation, and so its contents were not reflected in my testimony either. These incidents do not change the picture presented of my consistent opposition to the arms-for-hostages efforts and the fragmentary nature of my knowledge of what those on the NSC staff and CIA were doing.

CHAPTER 38

A Battle Royal

The presidency of Ronald Reagan was in deep trouble, whether the president and his White House staff realized it or not. I had to drive that point home to them. I somehow had to bring an end to arms sales to Iran in exchange for hostages, however dressed up the deals were in the strategic guise of a change in relations with Iran. I had to break through the disposition to stonewall the public and Congress: that was a sure road to a disastrous cover-up. And I had to get policy on Iran and on antiterrorism back on track, into my hands and away from the NSC staff. A tall order, but I was convinced that my success in this fight was essential to save the Reagan presidency.

My dilemma was that while the White House clearly had taken us down the wrong path, the president was still surrounded by people who were asserting—here in November 1986, *after* the revelation of efforts to trade arms for hostages—that a further hostage release was imminent. I did not want to abort the possibility of a release, but I was battling to shut this operation down. What bothered me immediately was a comment made on television by Vice President Bush. His close friend and adviser, Nick Brady, had telephoned me Saturday night, November 8, 1986, to ask whether I planned to resign. I didn't answer but told Brady, "What concerns me is Bush on TV saying it is inconceivable even to consider selling arms to Iran for hostages. The vice president was in one key meeting that I know of, on January 7, 1986, and he made no objection to the proposal for arms sales to Iran, with the clear objective of getting hostages released in the process. Cap and I were the only voices of dissent. The reality of whatever happened is just emerging. Who knows what will be revealed? The vice president could get drawn into a web of lies. If he blows his integrity, he's finished. He should be very careful how he plays the 'loyal lieutenant' role now."

The next morning, Sunday, November 9, Nick Brady came to my house to talk about what I had said on the telephone. Shortly before he arrived, the vice president's assistant for national security matters, Don Gregg, telephoned Nick Platt to say that Bush was worried. "What is Shultz's disposition?" Bush wanted to know. He had apparently heard from Brady of my warning that his television statement did not square with the proposal put forward during the critical January 7 meeting we had both attended.

After Nick Brady and I watched "This Week with David Brinkley," I turned off the television and said to Nick, "The vice president should not rush out with statements until he knows all the facts or he'll get himself in the glue." Bush, I said, had been perfectly aware that arms sales to Iran— along lines that Cap and I had argued was an "arms-for-hostages deal"— had been proposed in the administration and that he had, on at least one occasion to my knowledge—in the January 7, 1986, meeting—not objected to the proposal. So it would not square for him to say to the media that such a step was "inconceivable."

Not long after Nick left, Vice President Bush telephoned to invite O'Bie and me to dinner that night. We couldn't accept because of an earlier obligation, but we went over for a drink with him and Barbara in the late afternoon. I put my views to him: I didn't know much about what had actually transpired, but I knew that an exchange of arms for hostages had been tried on at least one occasion. And I knew such an action would never stand up in public. Bush admonished me, asking emphatically whether I realized that there are major strategic objectives being pursued with Iran. He said that he was very careful about what he said.

"You can't be *technically right*; you have to be right," I responded. I reminded him that he had been present at a meeting where arms for Iran and hostage releases had been proposed and that he had made no objection, despite the opposition of both Cap and me. "That's where you are," I said. There was considerable tension between us when we parted.

(I was astonished to read in the August 6, 1987, *Washington Post* the account of an interview by David Broder during which Vice President Bush said, "If I had sat there and heard George Shultz and Cap express it [opposition to Iran arms sales] strongly, maybe I would have had a stronger view. But when you don't know something, it's hard to react. . . . We were not in the loop." Cap called me. He was astonished, too: "That's terrible. He was on the other side. It's on the record. Why did he say that?")

Facts and Rumors

That evening, Bud McFarlane telephoned me. He told me that he had made no trip to Tehran that I didn't know about. I didn't know what prompted his call and did not want to discuss the matter with him.

Every few hours the mood of the crisis seemed to shift and to worsen. The issue on Monday, November 10, changed to the constitutional implications. The *Washington Post* ran the headline: "Hill Probes of NSC Planned; Arms Deal With Iran Seen as Attempt to Circumvent Congress." The view was emerging that what had happened was a back-room operation run by staffers who, given their positions in the bureaucracy, would not be subject to congressional or public scrutiny.

Early that same day, Poindexter finally telephoned me. There would be a meeting at 11:30 A.M. with the president at which Poindexter would brief Vice President Bush, me, Cap Weinberger, Bill Casey, and Ed Meese on what "really" was going on.

"Good idea," I said, "but my opinion hasn't changed. We should shut the operation down. I thought that it had been shut down last May or June." Poindexter and Casey had both explicitly told me that.

Poindexter said that in August 1986, "Rafsanjani's nephew" got in touch with the White House and had been "a valuable channel" ever since then. "Rafsanjani wants to end the [Iran-Iraq] war," Poindexter told me. He went on to elaborate on his theory that in Rafsanjani's public revelation of the McFarlane trip to Tehran, in which he incorrectly stated facts of which he had personal knowledge, Rafsanjani was sending a signal to the United States that he was still "with us."

After he hung up, I recalled an old Bernie Kalb line, "Is that what they told you, Missy?" an old Asia hand's way of noting hopeless gullibility.

With everyone alert to the slightest nuance, reports and rumors were flying in. The State Department's Near East bureau picked up a report that the release of Father Jenco in July 1986 had been arranged by Oliver North in return for arms valued at $24 million. The corridors of the State Department buzzed with rumors of several such schemes. It was insane if true. All along, the only sensible approach had focused on getting *all* the hostages out at once *without any trade of arms* in exchange. To let the terrorists sell hostages to us one by one was to create a hostage-taking industry. I could scarcely believe that Casey, Poindexter, and North could be so foolhardy and gullible, but now I did believe it.

Most incredible of all were the rumors reaching us on this morning of November 10 that an arms-for-hostages operation was still under way at this very moment. An Iranian aircraft reportedly had been expected in Vienna to pick up an arms shipment, but it had not come on time, and "the Iranians are no longer answering Ollie's telexes." I decided to collect all the facts I could find in order to put them in front of Ronald Reagan to open his eyes and get him to order a halt to the continuation of this madness.

The latest swap was supposed to produce the hostages Terry Anderson and Thomas Sutherland and the remains of Beirut CIA Station Chief William Buckley. Iran also, as part of the rumored deal, was supposed to deliver a Soviet-made T-72 tank to our base on Diego Garcia Island in the Indian Ocean. If the arrangement worked, so we heard, President Reagan would authorize a military operation to rescue three other hostages, presumably those held in the Hezbollah prison that Ambassador Bartholomew had reported on in March.

North was saying that Iran, as part of this effort, had agreed eighteen months ago to cease terrorist acts against the United States and that they had kept that deal. That is why, I was told, Poindexter had put out the statement that the American arms embargo was in effect "as long as Iran advocates the use of terrorism." It was a rhetorical trick. It was also preposterous. Frank Reed had been kidnapped in Beirut on September 9, 1986, Joseph Cicippio on September 12, 1986, and Edward Tracy on October 21, 1986, and the other hostages were still being held.

Incredulous as I was about everything Poindexter and others reported, I saw that he and North were continuing their efforts—undaunted by the disasters of their own making. They had entangled themselves with a gang of operators far more cunning and clever than they. As a result, the U.S. government had violated its own policies on antiterrorism and against arms sales to Iran, was buying our own citizens' freedom in a manner that could only *encourage* the taking of others, was working through disreputable international go-betweens, was circumventing our constitutional system of governance, and was misleading the American people—all in the guise of furthering some purported regional political transformation, or to obtain in actuality a hostage release. And somehow, by dressing up this arms-for-hostages scheme and disguising its worst aspects, first McFarlane, then Poindexter, apparently with the strong collaboration of Bill Casey, had sold it to a president all too ready to accept it, given his humanitarian urge to free American hostages.

"Ultimately," I said, "the guy behind it, who got it going, and the only guy who can stop it, was and is Ronald Reagan." Perhaps the most important achievement of the administration was President Reagan's restoration of the faith and confidence of the American people in the integrity and strength of the presidency. Even Arthur M. Schlesinger, Jr., had said so on television a few weeks previously—now this.

I consulted Abe Sofaer, State's legal adviser, about the legal aspects of such arms transfers. The president could provide an exception to any executive order, Abe said, but he would have to do so in a recognized, regular manner. The president could not, however, override statutes, and specifically, one prohibiting arms exports to any nation that the secretary of state had designated as a supporter of international terrorism. Iran was on the terrorist list. Abe said he had checked with the White House counsel, Peter Wallison. "They say they haven't the foggiest notion what is going on," Abe told me.

Calls were flooding in. Nearly everyone I knew had a view on whether I should resign or not. A terse message came in from Shimon Peres in Israel: "Hello. Don't go."

At 11:30 on November 10, the president's national security group gathered in the Situation Room. The president opened. He had watched the Sunday talk shows, he said, and we were being taken apart without justification—because what we were doing was right, and legal, and justifiable. We were trying to turn around a strategic situation in the Persian Gulf area, to move Iran toward a constructive role, to help the Iranians with their problem with the Soviets. And, of course, he added, we wanted the hostages back.

Poindexter then made a long presentation. There had been a "finding" on January 17, 1986. CIA director Bill Casey had been told, presumably by the president, not to brief Congress on it. The finding emphasized, Poindexter said, our strategic objectives toward Iran. Potential moderates in Iran would be given credibility with the military there by getting an arms relationship with us. That, Poindexter suggested, was why we had to give arms to Iran before expecting to get hostages freed in return.

"This is the first I ever heard of such a finding," I exploded. Cap was equally astounded.

This all started, Poindexter maintained, when Lieutenant Colonel Oliver North tried to find out about Israeli arms shipments to Iran: he stumbled onto an Israeli warehouse in Portugal and challenged the Israelis to explain it. Their reply was that they had to develop a relationship with the Iranians because Israel was concerned about Jews in Iran. This led, said Poindexter, to a "Ghorbanifar-Kangerlou [the Iranian intelligence chief] channel" and an operation that culminated in Bud's trip to Tehran in May 1986. None of this achieved anything, Poindexter said, so that channel was closed.

Subsequently, Poindexter went on, another channel more directly related to the Iranian government was opened through the nephew of Rafsanjani. As a result of discussions in this channel, the Iranians had pursued the release of the hostages in many ways, Poindexter told us, including through Anglican emissary Terry Waite and Lebanese contacts. A number of meetings had been held in Europe and the United States. The Israelis sold 500 TOWs to Iran. Poindexter had learned about this sale after the fact. Then, Poindexter said, we agreed to replenish the Israeli TOW stockpile. Two hundred and forty Hawk missile battery parts also were shipped, followed by a second shipment of 500 TOWs just the previous week, for a total of 1,000 TOWs. These were small amounts, defensive in nature, Poindexter said, and designed to establish good faith. They could not affect the outcome of the Iran-Iraq War, he said. I was astonished to learn of all these arms sales.

"So what are the results?" Poindexter asked. No more American hostages had been taken for over a year; Iran had stopped terrorist attacks, he said. "Well, there were three hostages taken recently," Poindexter corrected himself, "but there is a special explanation for that." The special explanation, I reflected, must be that the additional hostages can be traded for more arms! His tale was ludicrous.

We have achieved, Poindexter went on, solid contact with Rafsanjani. We have convinced Iran that it can't win the war, that the hostages have to be returned, and that the Soviets are a threat to them. Poindexter then sketched for us his view of the political scene in Iran: there were conservatives and clerics opposed to Khomeini; among them was Foreign Minister Velayati; in the middle of the road was Rafsanjani: the revolutionary guards were with him. In other words, Poindexter said, some of the radicals were changing—becoming more moderate. The most radical elements, Poindexter said, were for war, terrorism, revolution. Those radicals were the ones who sent armed pilgrims into Saudi Arabia during the Haj; and they were the ones who were linked to Hezbollah in Lebanon and who were responsible for the last three hostage takings. Khomeini's heir apparent, Ayatollah Montazeri, was an "independent player." In other words, the Iranian political situation was fluid and susceptible to influence in a way that would be positive for us, said Poindexter.

As for American policy, Poindexter said, there was no problem. The moderate Arabs knew that our policy was unchanged. We assured Iraq of our neutrality. And the Saudis, he said, had their own contacts with Iran. Egypt supported our contacts with Iran. Only Jordan had not yet been reassured. As for our European allies, Poindexter said, they all traded with Iran anyway, so they couldn't complain about what we were doing.

A Flash of Candor

I started asking tough questions about Poindexter's preposterous assertions. I could see immediately that Poindexter, and the president, regarded me as a problem. I asked about the 500 TOWs that Poindexter said had been shipped the previous week. He replied that the shipment had been arranged by Oliver North and CIA operative George Cave at a meeting in Europe with the Israelis. North had reported to Poindexter that another two Americans would be released by the end of this week. "So if the 500 TOWs plus other items have been supplied to Iran in the context of hostage releases," I asked Poindexter, incredulously, "How can you say this is not an arms-for-hostages deal?"

The president jumped in, asserting, "It's not linked!"

Poindexter undercut him. "How else will we get the hostages out?" he asked me in an accusing tone. In that flash of candor, Poindexter had unwittingly ripped away whatever veil was left to the rationale of a "changed Iran" as the reason for our arms sales.

I responded that as we crossed the line of conspiring with the Israelis on arms sales to Iran, we gave Israel a clear field, and they would then supply Iran with equipment that really mattered.

CIA director Bill Casey then produced a draft statement to be released to the press. The purpose was to say that all the president's advisers were fully aware of this operation and supported it. "Everyone must support this policy," the president said. That I was *not* prepared to do. President Reagan was being ill served by advisers who were putting forth schemes for arms-for-hostages swaps—which this was—despite the refusal to call it that. I continued to ask questions about the structure of arrangements, which always came down to a trade of arms for hostages. Poindexter was furious at me.

"Our policy is what we *do*, not what we *say*," I argued forcefully. The session ended with a dangerous electricity in the air. At the meeting, Cap had said that he agreed with my position, but he was not as vehement now as I had seen him earlier. As I returned to the State Department, I felt that I had become the most unpopular man in town. I was in a quandary, however, because of Poindexter's assertion that hostages would be released in a few days. I feared doing anything that might block an imminent release. I was thoroughly frustrated.

What Poindexter had described was absolutely outrageous. The arms transfer could not be justified. I could not support this program in public, and I could not acquiesce with its continuation. President Reagan, in his desire to free the hostages, had allowed himself to be sold a bill of goods. Poindexter had fabricated a high-toned rationale for a sordid swap, and the president had accepted it. "Iran is playing us for suckers," I said, "and we are paying extortion money to them."

A Misleading Press Release

My overriding responsibility would have to be to get the president to understand the true nature of this terrible operation and to order it stopped. That would not be easy, for President Reagan simply did not seem to grasp what was actually going on. I would have to marshal my arguments carefully and powerfully so that he could not brush them aside. I went to Andrews Air Force Base and boarded my plane for the Organization of American States General Assembly in Guatemala City, scheduled for the next day, November 11. Not long after we reached cruising altitude, a telephone call came to the aircraft from the Oval Office. A press release had been prepared; the White House wanted to read the proposed release over the phone and have me agree to it. The president, Vice President Bush, Casey, Meese, and Weinberger all had already cleared it, I was told. The message was written down by a member of my staff:

The President today met with his senior national security advisers regarding the status of the American hostages in Lebanon. The meeting was prompted by the President's concern for the safety of the remaining hostages and his fear that the spate of speculative stories which have arisen since the release of David Jacobsen may put them or others at risk. During the meeting the President reviewed ongoing efforts to achieve the release of all the hostages as well as our other broad policy concerns in the Middle East and Persian Gulf. As has been the case at a number of meetings with the President and his senior advisers on this matter, there was unanimous support for the President's decisions. While specific (garble) [decisions] at the meeting cannot be divulged, the President did ask it be reemphasized that our policy of not making concessions to terrorists remains intact.

At the conclusion of the meeting the President made it clear to all that he appreciated their support and efforts to gain the safe release of all hostages. Stressing the fact that hostage lives are at stake, the President asked his advisers to ensure that their departments refrain from (garble) [making] comments or speculating about these matters.

"That's a lie," I said in disgust. "It's Watergate all over again." I asked the USAF communications specialist to get Poindexter on the phone for me. It took a while, and the patched-in voice at the other end was faint, but we could understand each other. "I have your message, and it is not accurate," I said with stony anger.

I told him that I could not accept the release as drafted. I did *not* support this operation and I would *not* join in lying about it. "It says there was unanimous support for the president's decisons. That is not accurate. I can't accept that sentence. Drop the last word [decisions]." There was sharp disagreement. Poindexter said he would change the sentence to read "there was unanimous support for the president." I said that helped. "Eliminate 'in a number of' before 'meetings,' " I added. Even so, I said, it's misleading. I won't object to the statement, but I am very uncomfortable with it.

"*That*," Poindexter replied, "is most unfortunate" and hung up.

"They are distorting the record," I said afterward, "and there's no end to it. They are lying to me and others in the cabinet right now." I knew that Oliver North had not stumbled on an Israeli warehouse in Portugal; this effort had begun much earlier; Bud McFarlane was working at it in May 1985. Bud always gave me the impression that as national security adviser, he wanted to be like Henry Kissinger, to do big and dramatic things *secretly*. As Henry brought off "the opening to China," so Bud had the idea of an "opening to Iran." McFarlane hoped to bring off this coup, run secretly out of the NSC staff, and hand to the president the triumph of "winning Iran back to the West." But Kissinger had dealt with *officials* of the Chinese government and did not violate any U.S. laws in doing so; this operation with Iran, on the contrary, was conducted with disreputable international arms merchants and shady operators. And somewhere along the line Oliver North and Bill Casey had become involved, and hostages had come to dominate the whole scheme. The Iranians must have learned, no doubt with help of media hype, that the president would do just about anything to get hostages released.

A Lonely Battle

As my plane droned on, I said that unless this operation was stopped now, it would ruin a great presidency and make a shambles of American policy. "I will have to keep fighting the operation and refuse to be part of it." Back on August 5, 1986, reflecting my sense of difference with the president on the Philippines, my disagreement with him the previous January on arms sales to Iran, the unease I felt in the national security community over my refusal to go along with lie detector tests applied as a routine tool of management, and the constant sniping I felt from low-level White House operatives, I had handed the president a letter starting, "I hereby submit my resignation as Secretary of State."

President Reagan had said that he would not accept my resignation, that he would work with me to straighten out our problems and that we *were* on the same wavelength. I asked him to put the letter in his desk drawer for future discussion, and he did. So the president had my letter of resignation and could pick it up at any time. As we began our final approach into the Guatemala City airport, I knew that I would have to make a hard and unwelcome statement to the president.

The situation was beginning to remind me of Richard Nixon's attempt to get me to use the Internal Revenue Service to go after his "enemies list." I wouldn't go along with that then, and I wouldn't go along with an arms-for-hostages deal now. On occasions like this, you look for allies to help prevail on the president. But I felt alone. What had been going on here was a staff con job on the president, playing on his very human desire to get the hostages released. They told the president what they wanted him to know and what they saw he wanted to hear, and they dressed it up in "geostrategic" costume. And they kept me as well as others who had constitutional responsibilities to advise the president in the dark. A responsible staff should have kept the president fully informed and should have continuously warned him of the legal and constitutional problems created by the actions taken or not taken. They should have called his attention repeatedly to the violations of his own policies and warned him that the intelligence about Iran was fragile at best and obtained from parties with strong interests and biases of their own.

I recalled a brief incident a few days earlier that had puzzled me at the time, but now seemed to have meaning: I had been over in the West Wing of the White House and by chance had an extra minute on my hands. I dropped in on Poindexter to leave a paper on the Middle East with him. I stuck my head in his outer office and asked his secretary whether the admiral was in. "Yes," she said, "and he's alone. Go right in." I knocked, opened the door, and surprised Poindexter, who was huddled in a meeting with Oliver North, NSC staffers Howard Teicher and Alton Keel, and a bearded man I did not recognize. I excused myself and left. I could not understand how they could have been in there without the secretary, whose desk was only a few feet away from Poindexter's office door, knowing of it.

I asked my secretary, Lora Simkus, who once had worked at that same NSC office desk, if there was another entrance to Poindexter's office. "No," she said, "only one, and the women who sit in that outer office, Wilma[1] and Flo, are perceptive people with long experience over there; they would certainly know who was in that office with Poindexter." Was I being given a message that something was wrong?

On the Guatemala trip I drafted and redrafted and redrafted yet again the case I would make to the president to try to convince him to halt this operation—permanently. I wanted to awaken him to the reality of what was taking place. I would have to persuade him that something was deeply wrong and that he had a big problem on his hands. I had to warn him that his staff was "rearranging the facts."

When I returned to Washington on Wednesday, November 12, I talked to Charlie Wick, the U.S. Information Agency director. Wick was a pal of the president and Nancy from way back. I went over my views, and Wick agreed with me entirely. He said he would try to get to Nancy Reagan first, and then to the president, to persuade them to pay attention to what I would be saying.

At two o'clock that afternoon, the president met with key members of Congress. Vice President George Bush, John Poindexter, Cap Weinberger, Don Regan, Ed Meese, Bill Casey, and I were there. We met in the Situation Room, which was highly unusual for a meeting with the congressional leadership.

Poindexter opened with a long discussion about our strategy toward Iran. He was vague to the point of prevarication when it came to mentioning hostages. He did not give any sense that arms transfers to Iran might have been linked to the hostages, but admitted that arms had been sent. He read out the January 17 "finding" on policy toward Iran but said nothing about its origin. Poindexter said the operation had been conducted throughout by "a representative" of his and a representative of Bill Casey's.

---

1. Wilma Hall, the mother of Fawn Hall, Oliver North's secretary, who was a witness in the Iran-Contra joint hearings in July 1987.

Senator Robert Byrd turned to me. "The press says you didn't agree with this policy." I replied that I made a practice of not revealing the advice that I gave the president. The president wrote something on a pad and pushed it over to me. "Thank you," it said.

Senator Byrd saw through Poindexter's presentation. "Iran is a terrorist country. You are selling arms. You want others *not* to sell arms. It's selling arms for hostages," he said, "and it's a bad mistake." The meeting then trailed off into a pointless wrangle between Jim Wright and Cap Weinberger over arms control talks with the Soviets.

Afterward, I got Don Regan alone and went through the problem with him. Don was from the world of finance, and I figured he should know how to make a tough decision when one had to be made. I told him that the president was in deep trouble. He had to help me get Ronald Reagan out of the line of fire and turn this mess over to me to clean it up. We discussed how a presidential speech or press statement might terminate the whole operation and put Iran policy and terrorist policy back in my hands.

Leaks from the Situation Room session with the leadership flowed out immediately. NBC-TV reported that at the session the president had admitted for the first time that arms had been transferred to Iran, and arms-for-hostages became an even hotter media story. The lid had now come off.

Poindexter's threatening insistence that any public revelation would jeopardize further hostage releases was now irrelevant. Bud McFarlane, in an op-ed piece published November 13, 1986, in the *Washington Post*, sought to explain his role by saying that his model indeed had been Kissinger's approach to China in the early 1970s. George Will's column in the *Post* that day dealt with me: "Given the passion Shultz has invested in the principle of not dealing with terrorists, he may now feel like resigning not because he was responsible for what was done, but because he was not. In any case, someone should sober up Uncle Sam before he staggers into another of the world's sharp edges."

There was truth in that. My past position—being cut out—was, if humiliating, explicable in terms of my not knowing what took place; my present position—being cut out of what the president was treating as a major American foreign policy effort—was not sustainable. I would have to get the president to see that grave mistakes were being made, get control over the mess, or go.

The President Explains

On November 13, in a nationally televised address, President Reagan stated that he had authorized a small shipment of arms to Iran, but not as part of a trade for hostages: "That no concessions policy remains in force, in spite of the wildly speculative and false stories about arms for hostages and alleged ransom payments. We did not—repeat—did not trade weapons or anything else for hostages, nor will we."

The president's speech convinced me that Ronald Reagan still truly did not believe that what had happened had, in fact, happened. To him the reality was different. I had seen him like this before on other issues. He would go over the "script" of an event, past or present, in his mind, and once that script was mastered, that was the truth—no fact, no argument, no plea for reconsideration, could change his mind. So what Reagan said to the American people was true to him, although it was not the reality. He had stated publicly that our policy was no arms for hostages. If no more arms were sent, then I could work with that renewed statement of policy.

I telephoned Don Regan: stop the NSC staff effort; transfer the president's policy as stated in his speech to me, and I will try to put our policy and our behavior back together, I said.

Regan seemed to agree. He seemed eager to get the operation out of the hands of the NSC staff, away from the president and out of the White House. He asked me once more to go on one of the Sunday talk shows. I agreed and accepted one of the flood of requests for me to be interviewed on television.

I knew that I was engaged in all-out diplomacy with my own president and his administration, aimed at gaining the authority to do the job I had been hired to do. Everything now depended on getting the arms-for-hostages operation stopped and getting the policy as a whole under control and back to the State Department.

The president's November 13 speech did not have many takers; the story he recounted was not believed. The *Wall Street Journal* on November 14 quoted Senator Pat Moynihan, who said that the secret Iran negotiations were "the worst handling of an intelligence problem in our history." Barry Goldwater, in the same paper, said: "I think that's a dreadful mistake, probably one of the major mistakes the United States has ever made in foreign policy." And others heard in the president's speech an underground message that he was still willing to trade. There was chaos in the White House. Don Regan, interviewed on TV, said no more arms for hostages; Poindexter, on television, suggested that there would be further arms transfers.

In my regular sessions with the president, when I tried to get him to focus on demanding issues elsewhere in the world—Soviet relations, arms control, the Middle East—he could not concentrate. Poindexter, who in earlier days had been eager to join me whenever I saw President Reagan, was now arrogant and aloof. Poindexter almost had to be dragged into the Oval Office when I was there, and when I spoke, he feigned boredom, doodled, and looked out the window. I was getting a strong message.

I recalled how I had resigned as Nixon's secretary of the treasury. Nixon had put on a wage-price freeze in 1971. I opposed it. He did it again in 1973. Herb Stein, chairman of the Council of Economic Advisers, had said to him, "Mr. President, you can't walk on water twice." In a rare flash of humor, Nixon replied, "I can if it's frozen!" I opposed the freeze the second time but again defended it in public. Then I handed in my resignation. Nixon refused it. So I just dropped out for a while—no public appearances. Finally, I went to White House Chief of Staff Alexander Haig and said, "I'm not showing up for work tomorrow, so you better get a new secretary of the treasury." And he did—Bill Simon.

But this time I wasn't going to drop out. I would fight to get the Reagan presidency back on track, and if I couldn't, I'd go. No successor could function in this job, I felt, unless this terrible situation was put right.

I went to see President Reagan at 1:30 P.M., Friday, November 14. Poindexter was there. I told the president that it was time for me to go but that for the next few weeks I would try to get him through this crisis and then be on my way. The president again said he didn't want me to resign. "I want you to stay. I want to talk later about it." He still believed that what had been done was right and was not a trade with terrorists for hostages. That evening, in my office at the State Department, I watched "World News Tonight." ABC's "Person of the Week" was Oliver North. A poll indicated that 57 percent of the American public felt that Reagan had gone back on his vow of no deals with terrorists; one by one, fact after fact set out by the president in his speech was taken apart and discredited by the television report. It was a sad day for the Reagan administration. For the first time, the president had gone before the American people to make his case and try to clear things up, and they had not believed him. That was devastating to him, I knew.

I also wanted to talk to the president about human rights in Chile and the idea that we would vote against a proposed World Bank loan to that government. Our action would be a signal to Chilean President Augusto Pinochet and to the people of Chile. The president did not agree to this slap at the anti-Communist dictator. He and I argued. I knew a lot about the Chilean economic program because economists trained at the University of Chicago, known in Chile as the "Chicago boys," had been the architects of their successful use of free market ideas. But I opposed Pinochet's regime of political repression. The president raised the idea, possibly to provoke me, of a State visit by the Chilean dictator. It was a measure of how far apart we were. There had been a time when the president would simply have trusted my judgment on such an issue, but not since the fall of Ferdinand Marcos. Poindexter was snide, challenging every point I made, conveying the impression that I already was off the administration rolls.

I Face the Nation

The program I agreed to appear on was CBS's "Face the Nation" on Sunday, November 16. On Saturday, I was to go to Camp David with Margaret Thatcher to see the president. I wanted to have some time there to go over with the president what I would say on television, with the aim of getting control of the policy shifted away from Poindexter and back to State. I drafted a paper for the president to approve. I proposed to state on "Face the Nation":

- The president's counterterrorism policy is a good policy. I support it.
- But the way it has been conducted in the past is under intense scrutiny. All the record will come out for everyone to judge.

For the future:

- Policy toward Iran will be directed and conducted by the State Department;
- Our policy to end the Gulf War continues. There will be no arms transfers to Iran or Iraq as long as they remain intransigent;
- We are working night and day to get the hostages released. But we will not pay for them. A consensus exists in the administration that this is the right policy: concessions to terrorists only produce more hostages;
- We do not want a relationship of permanent hostility with Iran. The president's policy provides a way to go forward toward a constructive situation. That will be done quietly and in recognized, structured State Department channels. The president wants it this way, and we have indications that Iran does, too.

At Camp David I was not able to get even a moment alone with the president for a serious discussion. So I handed the paper to Don Regan, saying that I proposed to express administration policy "this way" on television tomorrow. He read my notes.

"I understand," Don said, "but we are not in a position to do what you're asking for."

Sunday, November 16, was a gloomy, gray day. A camera crew was a now-familiar presence stationed outside my house, waiting for me to emerge—perhaps to announce my resignation. State Department colleagues Hill, Bremer, Platt, and Redman came over early. This was my first television appearance since the "revelation." Jerry Bremer, director of State's anti-terrorist efforts, referring to Margaret Thatcher's presence at Camp David, pointed up the absurdity of what the White House had done. "Maybe you should tell Mrs. Thatcher that as the Irish Republican Army does not conduct terrorism against Americans, we have decided to open a quiet dialogue with them, and as a signal of our serious intent, we are making some token arms shipments to them."

"Don't tell me things like that," I said, laughing, "I might use them."

Our discussion continued. My main fight was with an NSC staff that had developed an operational capability and a fervent will to use it—often unwisely. With authority, ambition, and power, the NSC staff could operate without anyone's full knowledge, even the president's, and was not subject to congressional oversight. Laws that limited the behavior of regular government agencies could be read as not applying to the NSC staff. And there was the bizarre situation of the NSC adviser having his own spokesman and appearing in the media: Poindexter would be interviewed on NBC's "Meet the Press" at about the same time as my appearance on "Face the Nation." Here we had, as a primary foreign policy figure of the administration, the NSC adviser—who is not even subject to confirmation by the Senate and is not obliged to testify before Congress. The NSC staff had turned into a "wildcat operation." There used to be a "passion for anonymity"—no longer. Arthur Burns always took the position "Either you are a private adviser and have nothing to say publicly, or else you are a public figure. You cannot have it both ways." If Poindexter was to be on "Meet the Press," then he had no reason not to testify before congressional committees. When Poindexter explained something, he was frequently pedantic, pedagogical, and patronizing: once Poindexter had lectured me, "You see, George, the Arabs don't like the Israelis." I could imagine that when he had briefed the president on this operation, he would have been pretty dogmatic.

Lesley Stahl, the moderator of "Face the Nation," was a solid, tough questioner. She was relentless that morning. "I don't want to badger you," she said once, pursuing her point.

"No, you can badger me," I came back. I wanted to set straight where I stood. "It is clearly wrong to trade arms for hostages. So that is our policy . . . it isn't the right thing for governments to trade arms or anything else for hostages, just because it encourages taking more."

She persisted: "Will there be any more arms shipments to Iran, either directly by our government or through any third parties?"

"It's certainly against our policy," I answered swiftly.

"That's not an answer," she asserted. "Why don't you answer the question directly? I'll ask it again. Will there be any more arms shipments to Iran, either directly by the United States or through any third parties?"

"Under the circumstances of Iran's war with Iraq, its pursuit of terrorism, its association with those holding our hostages, I would certainly say, as far as I'm concerned, no," I responded.

"Do you have the authority to speak for the entire Administration?" she followed up.

"No," I said, looking her straight in the eye.

On that stark note, the program ended.

Afterward, Lesley gripped Nick Platt's arm. "I need a drink."

"I never should have come on," I told her.

"We were all amazed you did," she replied. I felt I had done as good a job as possible for the president. But I had thrown down the gauntlet in my final exchange. I felt I had to do it. Now it was up to the White House to respond.

When I returned home, I was in a rather gloomy mood. I almost expected a telephone call from the White House—"you're out." I felt I was alone and without support from others at the top level of the government to stop further arms deals. Bob Strauss called about my appearance on "Face the Nation": "You were somewhere between A+ and fabulous," he said. I felt a little better.

On Monday morning, press and television accounts were laden with reports on arms to Iran. Andrea Mitchell, on NBC's "Today," reported that Poindexter indicated more arms sales were to come, while Shultz opposed more arms "but can't say it won't be done against his advice." The *Washington Post* headlined on November 17: "Shultz Sees No Benefit for U.S. In Further Iran Arms Shipments; Disapproval of Deal Is Undisguised." The *New York Times* headlined: "Shultz Declares He Opposes Giving More Arms To Iran; Officials Appear Divided; Secretary Says That He Can't Speak for Administration on Issue of Shipments."

That afternoon, I was to deliver a major speech at the University of Chicago, setting out the achievements at the Reykjavik summit and pointing toward future steps in negotiations with the Soviets. I flew off to Chicago half-expecting to be ousted from office before returning to Washington that evening.

The White House Blinks

When I got back to the capital, I was met by Nick Platt. "The White House blinked," Platt said. My public declaration on "Face the Nation" finally flushed out of the White House the statement earlier that day from spokesman Larry Speakes that I *did* speak for the administration and that "The President has no desire, the President has no plans, to send further arms to Iran." The president and the secretary "are in complete accord on this," Speakes said. Poindexter had argued, I learned, for a response of "No comment." Later when the president was asked directly whether he was going to make any more arms shipments to Iran, he replied, "We have absolutely no plans to do any such thing." In this peculiar way the whole issue had come to a head in public and shifted the weight of the argument in my direction. The White House simply could not stand up to saying publicly that we would continue to sell arms to Iran.

Reviewing the intelligence analyses from the CIA that evening, I read through a piece on the "power struggle" in Iran that was wholly at odds with the briefing that Poindexter had given in the Situation Room a few days before: Khomeini was firmly in power, and Rafsanjani was carrying out the ayatollah's resolute policy of opposition to the United States; recent events in Iran suggested that no Iranian leader other than Khomeini has the power to initiate a rapprochement with the United States or even to offer such a suggestion for debate. So much for the wooing of the Iranian moderates. Doubting the reliability of CIA material on Iran, I could not, however, credit this as a serious piece of analysis, even though it matched my own views on the situation in Tehran. The thought crossed my mind that perhaps someone in the CIA had "blinked," too.

Bernard Gwertzman of the *New York Times*, who had an uncanny ability to get inside a story, wrote on November 18, in a front-page article headlined "All Eyes on Shultz," that "Secretary of State George P. Shultz appears to have swayed White House policy on Iran in his direction, at least for the moment."

I wasn't so sure. The damage to the Reagan presidency continued to mount. Former Presidents Ford and Carter spoke harshly of the Iran operation. A poll taken by the *Los Angeles Times* showed that only 14 percent of the American people believed the president was telling the truth in his speech. A cabinet crisis was building, the media seemed to agree, and the president would have to fire some people or be seen as no longer in charge.

In one sense I felt that, bit by bit, I was edging the White House staff back into line, but the NSC staff was fighting back. Bob Pearson, a foreign service officer assigned to the White House, passed the word that my "Face the Nation" appearance "had not hit the applause meter" over there. The NSC staff, he said, "thinks State has kicked over the traces, is off the train, and should not be allowed to criticize the president." Poindexter was said to be furious over foreign service reporting that other nations, especially those in Europe and the Middle East, were appalled at what the United States had done. Resentment ran deep.

The media played my "Face the Nation" appearance as an act of defiance, suggesting that I had shaken some sense into the president and his White House staff, but noting that the NSC staff—as though they were some autonomous entity—was proceeding with the operation, and was determined to knock me off.

Inaccuracies Abound

Bill Casey was going to testify before the congressional intelligence committees at the end of week. Mike Armacost, who had been in touch with the CIA, reported that Casey was preparing written testimony; Casey did not want the State Department "to be briefed on what had happened." At this point I felt I could have no confidence in any CIA "briefing." What we needed was access to the full record of what had taken place. Armacost asked the CIA for the full record. "We'll get back to you," they replied. Right now, Armacost said, Casey's people at CIA were scrambling to try to back up Poindexter's assertion that Iran had abstained from terrorist activity over the past eighteen months.

I shook my head. "The facts are to the contrary. They can't rewrite reality." Three more hostages had been taken in September and October 1986 by Iranian-backed groups.

Early in the afternoon on Tuesday, November 18, Abe Sofaer came into my office. He and White House legal counsel Peter Wallison had met with the legal counsel of the NSC staff, Paul Thompson (incredible but true, the NSC staff had its own legal counsel), with the CIA General Counsel David Doherty, and with Assistant Attorney General Charles Cooper.

Wallison had convened the meeting to try to find out what had taken place regarding Iran arms shipments so that he could help the president prepare for his coming press conference. He asked Thompson, who knew more than anyone else present, what had gone on. Thompson, Sofaer said, had refused to comment, saying Poindexter had ordered him not to provide information to anyone who had "no need to know." Sofaer got the impression that only he, from State, and Wallison, from the White House, were in the "no need to know" category. Sofaer and Wallison then asked at least to be given what the CIA and NSC staff planned to provide to the congressional intelligence staffs. Again they were refused. In that case, Sofaer said, neither the State Department nor the White House counsel could be asked for legal opinions on the policy. "I'm not able to make a legal analysis because I can't get the facts," Sofaer had said.

"They were going to tell congressional staffers what they wouldn't tell the White House or State Department—it was shocking," Sofaer told me. He conjectured that the manner and timing of some of the arms transfers to Iran might be such that no decision or "finding" by President Reagan could render them legal. If so, they could now be involved in a Watergate-style cover-up of an illegal act ordered by the president or his aides. Thompson, Sofaer said, had reported to the group that Poindexter felt Congress was "calming down," having realized that the operation was justified on intelligence grounds. "He's kidding himself," Sofaer added.

*   *   *

Did I have myself to blame for any of the aggrandizement of the NSC staff? I agonized. Ever since my first days as secretary of state, I had sought to make the national security adviser my channel to the White House and, on day-to-day matters, to the president. I tended to rely on Clark and McFarlane and Poindexter to be my daily representatives in the Oval Office. I could not be there all the time. I *had* to rely on the NSC adviser to get my views to the president accurately and quickly and to keep me posted on whatever happened when I was not there. I could count on my twice-a-week private meetings with the president, I felt, to keep in close touch with him, to seek his views, and to let him know what I was doing and thinking. I felt it was critical to try to make the NSC process work so that material given to the president would reflect the views of all relevant departments or agencies. That process built up the stature of the NSC adviser and his staff. I operated on the assumption that those who do the nation's work, especially at the top of the government, do it in reasonably good faith, and that I should not allow myself to end-run the process because of bureaucratic difficulties as long as I was working in harmony with the president.

But our paths had started to diverge with the fall of Marcos, to which President Reagan was never really reconciled. The Reagan Doctrine meant support for freedom: support for freedom fighters against Communist regimes *and* support for efforts to move authoritarian regimes in a democratic direction. The president had a hard time opposing a leader claiming to be pro-American and anti-Communist. The divergence in our viewpoints was picked up by the NSC staff, which, after the fall of Marcos, increasingly displayed a pattern of arrogance toward the State Department, at the very same time that the NSC's own standing diminished. Throughout the summer and fall of 1986 the stock of the NSC staff around town dropped. The media, in a low-level fashion, began to characterize the NSC staff as ineffectual and Poindexter as not up to the job. Still, I wanted to move forward by consensus, but the result was even more arrogant and independent behavior by the NSC staff. Low-level White House officials began to try to deny me use of aircraft for official travel; this was sniping of a petty kind, but it was another irritant. The White House staff had gotten to Al Haig that way, and they were trying now to get to me. This was only one of many reasons I had submitted my letter of resignation in August 1986. I had stayed on only after the president and Don Regan assured me that my problems were recognized and would be dealt with to my satisfaction.

I knew that President Reagan was fundamentally oriented to the merits of issues, and I knew that, by and large, he and I saw the major issues the same way. Since the departure of Jim Baker, Mike Deaver, and Ed Meese from the White House, the situation there had gone downhill. There was increasing insularity and less political savvy in the White House. I looked back with renewed respect to those Baker-Deaver-Meese days. All three had been immersed in national politics and had developed the antennae of sensitivity and subtlety so keenly needed around any president. Don Regan and John Poindexter had never really been involved in politics.

At 10:30 P.M. that night, November 18, the Israeli ambassador to the United Nations, Benjamin Netanyahu, telephoned in agony over the Iran arms shipment revelations. He had become a compelling voice for a tough counterterrorist policy for the West. Now Israel had "done a deal" with the masters of terrorist acts. Netanyahu said he had been "hiding out, refusing all interviews and public appearances." His message for me was: "Don't resign; your antiterrorism policy is in jeopardy." Yitzhak Shamir asked Netanyahu to get word to me that "Shamir admires the role the secretary has taken and that it would be a tremendous loss if he goes." Netanyahu also let me know that the Israeli government was in a panic that Israel would be used by the White House as "cover"; that is, Congress would be asked to excuse the president because the scheme was Israel's. He had seen the front page of the coming morning's *Washington Post*: "Israeli Reportedly Set Up First U.S.-Iran Arms Deal." Netanyahu wanted me to suggest to Peres and Shamir that Netanyahu be asked to talk to Nancy Reagan about this crisis.

A Disastrous Press Conference

The news early Wednesday morning, November 19, contained more speculation about my departure. On the radio I heard that "White House aides" were saying I would resign and that Senator Paul Laxalt would be named secretary of state. NBC-TV news reported rumors that I would demand a change in the policy or resign. "White House aides" were said to be "furious" with me but feared that my resignation would make the situation worse. ABC's Peter Jennings, on "World News Tonight," said, "President Reagan's televised news conference tonight . . . will be the most important of his presidency." That was true. I would try to use my meeting with him in the afternoon to affect his handling of that press conference.

I found a clipping on my desk from the November 13 *Wall Street Journal*. Karen Elliott House had written: "If some malicious Merlin were trying to concoct a scheme that, with one stroke of a wizard's wand, would undermine American principles, policies, people, interests and allies, it would be hard to conjure up anything more harmful and humiliating than secretly shipping supplies of American weaponry to the world's primary terrorist state in exchange for a handful of hostages. . . . In the process, Mr. Reagan seems to have cuckolded his own secretaries of state and defense." She was right on the mark in her appraisal.

I saw the president at 1:30 on November 19 and put my argument to him again as gravely and persuasively as I could: terrible mistakes had been made. The time was long past to tell the full story, to put a stop to any further arms sales to Iran, and to return to adherence to our own stated policy—the policy we had followed before this fiasco—and to conduct that policy properly through the accountable departments of the government. I read to the president a statement that I wanted him to make on television, declaring that there would be no more arms sales and that our Iran policy would be managed by the secretary of state.

The president responded by saying, again, that the operation was a good one and that Iran—the CIA had assured him—had tempered its support for terrorism.

I flatly and strongly disagreed and countered that "even if the Iranians agreed to cease targeting Americans in return for arms—which, in reality, they *have not*—that's a terrible deal to make! Terrorism is an international problem, and we must treat it that way." I presented to the president detailed factual material Jerry Bremer had assembled that revealed Iran had clearly *not* ceased support for terrorism: three new American hostages had been taken as recently as September and October 1986 by Lebanese groups associated with Iran. There was much more.

"This is news to me," Reagan said.

"Mr. President," I said, "you are not fully informed. You must not continue to say we made no deals for hostages. You have been deceived and lied to. I plead with you," I said, "*don't* say that Iran has let up on terrorism."

"You're telling me things I don't know!" the president said.

"Mr. President, if I'm telling you something you don't know—I don't know much—then something is terribly wrong here!"

But I could see I had not convinced him. As I left, I told him, "What I said the other day stands." He knew I meant my offer to resign. Despite our differences, he seemed to want me around, perhaps out of an instinct that, unwelcome as my statements were, I was leveling with him.

Poindexter's office was bustling with activity, gearing up to put the president's views across after his televised appearance that evening. When I walked in, Poindexter was barely civil. He agreed with nothing I said. The White House would go forward, he indicated, with this operation. After the president had convinced the public of its correctness that night, a "media blitz" would follow in which I would be "expected" to participate. Everyone, including me, was fully informed and on the team, he told me. My temper was building with each absurd development. There would be more arms sales to Iran. Poindexter gave me a clipping from the *Economist* saying that it was a mistake to pay ransom unless it was for "another, wider goal": "greater interests are sometimes at stake." This was for a higher goal, Poindexter said. I would have laughed had I not been so incensed by the folly of this self-delusion and where it might lead. Bill Safire, on November 13 in the *New York Times*, had the answer to Poindexter's notion. "One difference between French appeasement and American appeasement is that France pays ransom in cash and gets its hostages back while the U.S. pays ransom in arms and gets additional hostages taken." True, I thought, but both were driven by expediency, not strategy or principle. It was almost unbelievable to me that the White House still would not see that for a government to trade arms for hostages or anything else for hostages wasn't either right or sane: it only encouraged the taking of more!

I looked around for Don Regan but couldn't find him. Back at the State Department I concluded that I had struck out completely. The president's staff was continuing to deceive him, but he was allowing himself to be deceived. He eagerly bought the sophistry of Poindexter and improved it in the telling. He felt sure that if he explained it all to the American people, they would agree that everything had been done the right way. Outside the Oval Office everyone seemed tense, pale, and nervous.

Later in the afternoon, I received from the White House the text of the statement the president planned to deliver in opening his televised press conference in a few hours. The statement made the case for a high-minded and strategically significant effort that, if continued, would be run by Poindexter. I heard that the statement had been drafted by Poindexter and North. The NSC staff was proceeding as if they should manage such policies in the normal course of events. But by straining to justify what had been done, by defining it as a "mainstream, wholly rational aspect of foreign policy," they had created a situation under which its continued secret control by a handful of unaccountable staff officials could not conceivably be sustained.

Calls now flooded in from the press asking whether I had resigned "twenty minutes ago." I told Chuck Redman to answer, "The secretary of state went to the White House today for his regularly scheduled meeting with the president. He was secretary of state when he went in, and he's secretary of state now."

The only one in the White House who I felt might in any way understand my view of this matter was Don Regan. I telephoned him on the secure line that Wednesday afternoon, November 19. I went over for Don the same points I had made to the president: the fact that deals had been structured in such a way as to be clearly arms for hostages; the evidence that Iran was still involved in terrorism; why it was disastrous for intelligence and operations to be intermingled, as they had been in this case, because the operators start "cooking the intelligence" to win support for what they want to do; the idiocy of running operations out of the White House, depriving the president of any insulation. "I've struck out everywhere— you're my last hope," I said with emotion.

Don then read to me what the president would say in a few hours.

"That's terrible!" I said, "I pray he doesn't say anything like that!" Don

Regan himself, I felt, was increasingly awake to the fact that he, too, had been misled.

The Wednesday evening television news again featured speculation on my resignation. One line had me demanding a change in direction by the president; the other, sourced to the White House, said that the president and I had "composed our differences."

The president strode into the East Room of the White House at 8:00 P.M. He started the press conference with a statement:

> I understand this decision is deeply controversial and that some profoundly disagree with what was done. Even some who support our secret initiative believe it was a mistake to send any weapons to Iran. I understand and I respect those views, but I deeply believe in the correctness of my decision. I was convinced then and I am convinced now that while the risks were great, so, too, was the potential reward . . . .

> To eliminate the widespread but mistaken perception that we have been exchanging arms for hostages, *I have directed that no further sales of arms of any kind be sent to Iran.* [emphasis added.] I have further directed that all information relating to our initiative be provided to the appropriate Members of Congress. There may be some questions which for reasons of national security or to protect the safety of our hostages I will be unable to answer publicly. But again, all information will be provided to the appropriate Members of Congress. . . .

> We, as I say, have had nothing to do with other countries or their shipment of arms or doing what they're doing. And, no, as a matter of fact, the first ideas about the need to restore relations between Iran and the United States, or the Western world for that matter, actually began before our administration was here. . . .

> I don't think a mistake was made. It was a high-risk gamble, and it was a gamble that, as I've said, I believe the circumstances warranted. And I don't see that it has been a fiasco or a great failure of any kind. We still have those contacts. We still have made some ground. We got our hostages back—three of them. And so, I think that what we did was right, and we're going to continue on this path.

The president's statement that there would be no further arms shipments to Iran was a crucial victory. But the fact that he still maintained "what we did was right, and we're going to continue on this path" was incredible to me. Many of the president's statements were factually wrong. He was defensive and lacking in his usual confidence. "The president was extraordinarily badly prepared for this press conference," I told Jerry Bremer, who had watched it with me. "He is surrounded by people who are interested in protecting themselves, not in serving him. He therefore has not received the full flow of facts. Congress is going to tear this place apart unless changes are made." I told Bremer to work on the transcript so that I could show the president the erroneous points he had made and try once more to convince him that he was not getting the straight story from the his staff or from Bill Casey and the CIA.

A Tough Encounter

I telephoned the president at the conclusion of his press conference. I told him that he had made "a great many factual errors." I said I wanted to come over to the White House in the morning. I would show him, chapter and verse, what the errors were. He was shaken by what I said and agreed to listen to me.

"Iran furor strengthens Shultz's hand" read the headline in the *Christian Science Monitor* the next morning, Thursday, November 20. Other commentators also seemed to sense that I now had a shot at turning this fiasco around. The next step, I felt, was for Poindexter not only to give up control of the operation but also to leave the White House altogether and return to the navy. I would be willing, given the emergency, to turn State over to my deputy, John Whitehead, and become acting NSC adviser for a month. I would clean house and then turn the job over to whoever would be permanently appointed. I went over to the White House, put this idea to Don Regan, and went through all the incorrect statements the president had made on television the previous night. Don said that the president had told Vice President Bush and Poindexter of my charge that he had been factually misled. The president wanted to "think it over at the ranch" and then convene a meeting of us all "to go over what everybody knows and get it all together."

"That's a formula for catastrophe!" I said to Don. "We have to make decisions. Here they are. Make them! The longer you wait, the worse it gets. It's not a matter of getting our lines straight! Think of the future!"

Don was uncharacteristically subdued. We broke off our meeting. I said I would call and push him on this again in the afternoon.

Back in my office I met with Abe Sofaer and Mike Armacost to go over the information we had gathered at the State Department about the arms-for-hostages attempts so they would be prepared to assess the testimony that Casey was scheduled to give on Friday up on the Hill. Casey and his deputy, Robert Gates, were "now at the White House for some big meeting," Armacost said. Armacost had noticed that the contractor named in the Iran affair—Southern Air Transport—had also been involved in support for the Contras. This set off a warning bell in the back of my mind. It sounded as if the list of revelations had not yet been exhausted.

Abe Sofaer asked me to authorize him to tell White House counsel

Wallison and Attorney General Ed Meese of the evidence that we had that
administration officials knew of arms shipments that had been made before
the January 17, 1986, finding. I told Abe to do so, and he passed on to
the deputy attorney general, in Meese's absence, the information that Bud
McFarlane had told me in Geneva about the November 1985 shipment of
Hawk missiles to Iran. Meese sent back a message saying he knew all about
the problem—but also of factors that made the shipment legal. I didn't
know what that meant.

Don Regan telephoned me. He said he now tended to agree with me
and the president should hear me out. I told him that I was scheduled to
go to Ottawa on Friday. "Time's a wasting," I said. "We both should ask
to see the president now—this afternoon—in the family quarters." I insisted that Don be there: "If I'm by myself, the president transforms the
message in his mind."

The president, Don said, "just doesn't realize it's a problem. He says,
'Gee, we didn't do anything wrong.' So you have to convince him." For
the first time, Don told me, he was ready to join me in the effort to persuade
the president that he had massive problems and had to make changes in
policy and personnel.

Charlie Wick telephoned to say he had talked to the first lady. Nancy
felt that I was not being helpful. Wick had tried to convince her that I was
trying to protect the president and that the only way out of this fiasco was
to put me in charge of our dealings with Iran. Wick thought she understood
and would be helpful.

At 5:15, November 20, I showed up at the family quarters. The president
and I, along with Don Regan, sat at the end of the long foyer in an area
Nancy Reagan had arranged in a way that created a relaxed sitting room.
The content of our discussion was tough. I had detailed material on statements the president had made that were wrong. He had accepted as accurate information provided him by the CIA and the NSC staff that was
in fact laden with error—all coordinated, insofar as I could see, by Poindexter. For nearly an hour I went at it with the president. We argued back
and forth, hot and heavy. I never thought I would talk to a president of
the United States in such a direct and challenging way.

President Reagan didn't seem to resent my efforts, but I didn't shake
him one bit. To him, the problem was with the press. I told him about Bud
McFarlane's telephone call to me in Geneva in November 1985 describing
an arms-for-hostages deal. "Oh, I knew about that," the president said,
"but that wasn't arms for hostages." I replied that no one looking at the
record would believe that. The president said his information was different
from mine: "George, I know what happened, and we were doing the right
thing." He refused to recognize that there was a problem. So I never even
reached the point of discussing steps that should be taken. You can't solve

a problem until you recognize there is one. Unfortunately, Nancy was not present. I had hoped for her help.

The president gave me plenty of time, and I gave it my best shot, but I didn't move him an inch. He still wanted to have a meeting on Monday at which everyone could exchange information. I would go down my list again on Monday and say we were "facing a catastrophe."

My meeting with the president then degenerated into a discussion about Pat Buchanan. He had asked the president to be named ambassador to NATO. The president said he liked the idea. (Don Regan had told me Nancy wanted to get Buchanan out of the White House.) Pat Buchanan at NATO? Pat's stock in trade was confrontation and division. What we needed at NATO was cohesion. I was amazed that such a preposterous idea was even being considered.

On Friday morning, November 21, a copy of Bill Casey's testimony—to be given to Congress later that day—was on my desk when I arrived. I read it carefully. The testimony was filled with material I had not known about. Then I was off to Ottawa for a long-scheduled day of talks with Foreign Minister Joe Clark. The news was full of small-scale sniping. Bud McFarlane had said that he had told me "repeatedly and often of every item that went on in this enterprise." That was not true. Don Regan blamed everything on McFarlane: "Let's not forget," Don was quoted as saying, "whose idea this was. It was Bud's idea. When you give lousy advice, you get lousy results." Now Bud said dealing with Iran was a mistake; White House aides were "flabbergasted" that McFarlane would say a mistake had been made. And so on.

While I was in Ottawa, a disturbing piece of news was passed to me from the State Department. Bill Casey's testimony, I was told, had been "altered" from the draft I had read just a few hours before. The CIA and NSC staff were apparently changing their story to indicate that they did *not* manage the November 1985 arms shipment and didn't know what the shipment contained. I passed word back that Abe Sofaer must get into this to try to prevent Congress from being misled.

Abe was already on the job. He had been shown the latest copy of Casey's prepared text. It said that no U.S. government official knew of the November 1985 arms shipment to Iran. I had told Sofaer to inform himself about all of our information on arms dealing with Iran. He had read the notes about what had happened in Geneva when McFarlane's secure telephone call stunned me with news that a complex arms deal to gain the release of American hostages was then under way. And Sofaer knew that Casey's deputy at the time, John McMahon, had known about the arrangement, declaring then that no more such shipments would be made without a finding. So Sofaer knew that Casey's testimony was untrue and untenable.

Sofaer had a duty to inform the attorney general that the draft testimony was wrong, and he did so. Casey's testimony was then changed again. Meese's assistant told Sofaer that when Meese asked the president about the shipment, the president replied, "I didn't know about it. I never approved it." Meese said he would "confront" McFarlane on Sunday, November 23, with the evidence—a note taken by Charlie Hill, my executive assistant, of my conversation during Bud's phone call to me in Geneva on November 19, 1985—that McFarlane obviously knew about the shipment at that time. An attempt was under way, I worried, to pin everything on McFarlane, who was now out of the government, while trying to exonerate those who were still in the administration.

Meese Investigates

Early in the afternoon, a secure call came through to Ottawa to tell me that Abe Sofaer had been called by Assistant Attorney General Charles Cooper: Ed Meese, he said, was deeply concerned and had asked the president for authority to investigate all aspects of this matter, with full access to all individuals and materials. Proof of the November 1985 arms shipment was taking its toll. The president had agreed and had given Meese a mandate to seek to uncover facts inconsistent with what the president had been told of this operation. Maybe, I thought, my tirade in the family quarters yesterday had gotten to the president after all. I knew that such an investigation would not be accepted by Congress or the press as sufficient, but I welcomed Meese's effort as a "start," as a possible help to me in my thus far futile attempts to change the president's mind. I said I would make myself and all our records available. According to Cooper, Meese wanted to start his investigation by interviewing me in my office first thing Saturday morning, November 22. He was specifically looking for information, Cooper said, to indicate whether the president had been misled about the November 1985 arms shipment.

At 8:05 Saturday morning, Ed Meese and Charles Cooper, both wearing the slacks and sports jackets that government officials like to put on to come to work on Saturdays, walked into my office to interview me. Charlie Hill was present; he and Cooper both took extensive notes. I asked that copies of the notes be exchanged after the interview so each of us would have complete records.

Ed Meese was, at this time, perhaps the most derided high official of the Reagan administration. He was a favorite target of the *Washington Post*'s editorial page cartoonist Herblock, and the press in general portrayed him as sometimes a marauding bulldog, sometimes a sinister clown. In fact, I saw him as a kind of unfathomable St. Patrick, talking the snakes out of their holes; what he would do with those snakes afterward, I was never sure.

"The president," Ed Meese said, "asked me to pull together facts that seem to be eluding us—to get some picture of what you and I didn't know about. Not views but facts." Abe Sofaer's intervention to point out the misrepresentation in Casey's testimony, Meese said, was "fortuitous." The key question revolved around the arms shipment of November 1985.

Then, for an hour and a quarter, Meese questioned me in detail about my knowledge and involvement with the arms-to-Iran-for-hostages proposal. "Our president's stock-in-trade is being straight," I said to Meese, "but he is now in a position where he is saying things that demonstrably are not true—although he is not consciously doing so. I told the president this and he didn't like it at all."

"We have to get the facts so he knows the facts. And no cover-up," Meese responded.

I went through, chapter and verse, what I knew. I told Meese, "You should know that I went to the president Thursday night and saw him in the family quarters along with Don Regan. I had called the president after the press conference to tell him, 'a lot of your statements won't stand up to scrutiny.' And I described Bud's phone call to me on November 19, 1985, in Geneva regarding the arms shipment to Iran that month. The president said he knew all about that, but that wasn't arms for hostages. I had told him that no one looking at the record would believe that." Meese told me that the president had no notes and had trouble remembering meetings. As to my November talk with Bud, was there any contact that I knew of between Bud and the president on this topic then? "Not to my knowledge, though I don't know," I said.[2]

We went over the many inconsistencies, even in the varying statements Poindexter had made in the past few days. On Monday he talked about 1,000 TOWs, and during the week the number shifted to 2,000. "The number was 2,008," Meese said.

The president, I said, told me the number was small and for defensive purposes. "He's been sold a bill of goods and is way out on a limb he shouldn't be on," I responded.

Toward the end of our session, Meese said, "Certain things could be a violation of a law. The president didn't know about the Hawk shipment in November 1985. If it happened and the president didn't report it to Congress, it's a violation. [The president] said to me 'if it happened, I want to tell Congress and not have them tell me.' " So the aim of his investigation, Meese told me, "is not to write the history of it, but to give the president the right general picture and point to any possible laws broken." We dis-

2. At this stage, having been devoting my efforts to stopping this ongoing operation, I had yet to review my own record in detail, and I had not recalled on the spot that Bud had told me in Geneva that he had cleared the November 1985 arms shipment with the president. This information was included in the notes taken by Charlie Hill and was provided to all the investigative authorities and in my subsequent congressional testimony.

cussed the ins and outs of the legal requirements. Cooper and Meese were
definitive in their view that the president had not known of the shipment
that might be illegal, and that the shipments he did know of were not
illegal. I had already told them that the president had said to me that he
"knew all about" the November arms shipment.

"I hear what you are saying," I said to Meese, "but I would not want
to be the president arguing it in public. Another angle worries me. This
could get mixed in with help for the freedom fighters in Nicaragua. One
thing may be overlapping with another. There may be a connection."

Meese did not reply to this suggestion. I was recalling Mike Armacost's comment to me two days earlier that a contractor in the Iran arms deliveries,
Southern Air Transport, had also been used in support of the Contras.

After Meese and Cooper left, Armacost and Sofaer came in to tell me
about the testimony they had witnessed a day earlier on the Hill. There
were lies: Poindexter's statement that he had heard of the November 1985
shipment only yesterday and Casey's assertion that he thought it was a
shipment of oil-drilling bits. There were also omissions: in the early draft
of Casey's testimony Southern Air Transport had been mentioned, but
then it was edited out, and Casey did not mention it at the hearing. "They
may have shifted funds between the two trades—Iran and Central
America," Armacost speculated. Sofaer had spotted these omissions and
had told Meese of them that day. "The president is in the hands of people
who are lying," Sofaer concluded.[3]

Nick Brady had asked O'Bie and me down to his place on Chesapeake
Bay for the weekend. We drove down to the Eastern Shore, where we
relaxed with Nick, Jim Baker, and their wives. "You saved the vice president's political life by telling him to wait for the facts before speaking out
about arms shipments," Nick said to me.

In the *Washington Post* on Sunday morning, November 23, a lead story
declared "White House Shake-Up Plotted." The president's California
friends and Nancy Reagan, the story said, wanted Weinberger to replace
me, Drew Lewis to replace Don Regan, and Jeane Kirkpatrick to replace
Poindexter. That same morning, Cooper telephoned Charlie Hill to confirm
the text of Hill's November 19, 1985, note which revealed that McFarlane
had known of the shipment at that time. Meese would confront McFarlane
with this on Sunday afternoon, Cooper said.

Netanyahu called to give me a message from Yitzhak Shamir, who had
telephoned in the middle of the night, Israel time: Shamir was "terribly

3. Sofaer had told Charlie Hill after my meeting with Attorney General Meese on November
22, 1986, that he had gotten ahold of the Defense Department price list for TOWs and
compared it with what the Iranians were charged. There was a substantial discrepancy. Sofaer
telephoned Cooper at the Justice Department and said that a profit had been made and
suggested that the money might have been used for another project.

worried" that I was about to resign. The next morning came a letter from Shimon Peres to the same effect.

"Get Rid of Shultz"

Monday morning, November 24, 1986, was a day to read the Washington press the way a Kremlinologist reads *Pravda*: everything in it was likely to be a message dropped into the hands of reporters in the hope of influencing decisions and events. The news about me had a sour tone. CBS-TV reported the rumor that Ed Meese and Bill Clark wanted me fired for disloyalty and Don Regan dismissed for failing to protect the president. The revolving door was set to spin any day now. The story continued: influential friends of the president were urging him to get rid of Shultz. Senator Bob Dole said, "I think right now they ought to circle the wagons, either that or let a couple of the wagons go over the cliff." And "White House Aides and Senators Criticize Shultz on the Iran Affair; Reagan Friends Said to Discuss Staff Changes to Bolster President" read the headline in the *New York Times* that day.

I found out later that on November 23, Bill Casey had written the president, "The public pouting of George Shultz and the failure of the State Department to support what we did inflated the uproar on this matter. If we all stand together and speak out I believe we can put this behind us quickly." Casey continued, "You need a new pitcher! A leader instead of a bureaucrat. I urge you to bring in someone like Jeane Kirkpatrick or Paul Laxalt, who you may recall I recommended for State in 1980. You need this to give your foreign policy a new style and thrust and get the Carterite bureaucracy in State under your control. Otherwise, you will not be doing justice to yourself or to your Presidency. Time is short."

A secretary who had recently joined my office staff asked me, "Why do they want to fire you?"

"It's like I'm the baseball manager and the team is losing," I said. "So they want to get rid of the manager."

Dante Fascell, chairman of the House Foreign Affairs Committee, called hearings that Monday and wanted Mike Armacost to testify. It would not be appropriate, I felt, in a politically charged battle, to ask a professional foreign service officer to answer for political decisions. I asked John Whitehead to take over. He had only three hours to prepare. He did a tough job in a magnificent way. Shock waves reverberated around town as Whitehead openly defended me, denounced arms for hostages, said Iran supported terrorism, and pointed out the impossibility of coping with operations run clandestinely by the NSC staff. CNN's Ralph Begleiter reported: "John Whitehead today declared open warfare on the White House basement . . . not since Watergate have we heard such tearing of flesh." The congressional committees were not asking me to testify because, I was told, they recognized that the day I testified would be my last day in office.

In the afternoon, a National Security Planning Group session was called so that, I presumed, Meese could present the results of his quick probe into this affair. The meeting was as perplexing as it was peculiar. Meese said almost nothing while Poindexter took charge, reviewing the Iran operation just as he had before, as if no objections had ever been raised. Bill Casey followed with an account of how well placed we were regarding intelligence on Iran. George Cave, an alleged expert, then gave the CIA's intelligence assessment about Iran. Poindexter stressed that our effort toward Iran was correct and that it would continue on course. I interrupted with a starkly different view. I made no impact whatsoever. Cap spoke at length, but he placed his emphasis on the importance of a tilt toward Iraq in the Iran-Iraq War. He was opposed, but he did not take my side of the argument with the vigor he had in such sessions long ago. Poindexter ignored what I said.

The point of the meeting, Poindexter said, was to inform us all—present were President Reagan, Vice President Bush, Weinberger, Casey, Regan, Poindexter, Cave, Meese, and me—that we would be sending an emissary around to other countries to explain our goals and that we would proceed without changing the project or the policy.

The president remained unmoved by my words. We were right in what we were doing, he said, and it was only the press that was to blame for calling it into question. The president was in a steamy, angry mood clearly directed at me—which sent an unmistakable message: understand me, and get off my back. He was determined that he was totally right. He was angry in a way I had never seen before.

Don Regan said that the NSC had a chronology on the November 1985 shipment. Poindexter interjected that McFarlane ran the operation all by himself until December 4, 1985, and no one knew what he did. I didn't believe that. I said that I knew something of what he did. Once again, it looked like they were rearranging the record.

Ronald Reagan pounded the table. "We are right!" he said, "We had to take the opportunity! And we were successful! History will never forgive us if we don't do this! And no one is to talk about it!"

"But there will have to be testimony," Meese interjected. The president was frustrated, angry, self-righteous, and seemed completely swayed by Poindexter. I assumed that Meese's silence meant that he was still collecting evidence in his investigation. I had to leave while the meeting was still going on for a previously scheduled appointment with South African Zulu Chief Buthelezi.

About six o'clock that evening, Whitehead, Armacost, Hill, Platt, and I were sitting around the fireplace in my office, trying to puzzle all this out when a call for Whitehead came from Poindexter. The climate at the White House had abruptly changed. Poindexter's attitude was entirely different now: understanding, cooperative, mild. He wanted to assure Whitehead that the uproar over his testimony was no problem; Poindexter would tell the president it was okay. He said he hoped State would "get involved" with Iran policy. "State can take the lead if it wants to," Poindexter said. In fact, he went on, "I want to get out of it. I haven't been able to do anything else for weeks."

I was stunned. I told Whitehead to call Poindexter back immediately to firm up the details of how State would take charge of Iran policy and this operation. Whitehead called, and Poindexter, ready to hand it over, said he was "delighted" that we'd agreed to take over.

A Dramatic Shift

"We just crossed the Great Divide," I said. Something dramatic must have happened. What, I did not know. I could not believe that Poindexter had simply had a change of heart or was putting this issue aside in order to attend to other matters. I was mystified but elated at this dramatic shift from the White House.

A National Security Planning Group meeting was called on Tuesday, November 25, at 10:15 A.M. The president called on Ed Meese, who gave us explosive news: some funds from the sale of arms to Iran had been diverted to support the Contras. Poindexter and North were both out. Al Keel, Poindexter's deputy, would become acting NSC adviser. CNN reported that the president would make an announcement at 11:30. At 12:05 President Reagan came on television to announce the reassignment of Oliver North and John Poindexter. Then came Attorney General Meese, who stated that from $10 to $30 million in payments made by Iran for U.S. arms in 1986 had been diverted to rebels fighting the Sandinistas in Nicaragua. The president had not been informed. A complete investigation would be conducted by the Department of Justice. A special review board would look into the operations of the NSC staff, an effort that turned into the Tower Commission, named for its chairman, former Senator John Tower.

Meese had now publicly declared not only that the president had no knowledge of the diversion of funds, but also that he did not know of the November 1985 arms shipment and was not informed of the operational details. I was disturbed because the president had told me he knew about the November 1985 shipment. I was disturbed as well when I looked over the copy of Cooper's notes of my Saturday interview with Meese. In sharp distinction to Charlie Hill's notes, which made clear who was speaking throughout the session, Cooper's notes at key points ran Meese's statements and mine together; from these notes a reader might conclude that *I* had stated that the president was unaware of the November arms shipment and had not approved it, when in fact Meese had made that remark.

The attention of the press, the Congress, and the public now shifted dramatically from "Iran" to "Contra." "The State Department announced yesterday," said the *Washington Post* on November 26 "that it has been given control over U.S. policy toward Iran, effective 'immediately.' " State's statement, I would come to learn, was not exactly right. Chuck Redman had asked whether he could go that far, and I had said yes. The test was yet to come whether I would succeed. The editorial page of the *New York Times* on November 26, 1986, said:

> Suddenly, the clouds part on what the State Department has been doing. The President asserted that the secret efforts with Iran had caused the Ayatollah Khomeini to ease off on terror. Monday, John Whitehead, the Deputy Secretary of State, dissented frontally. State Departments do not lightly war on the White House.
>
> Some part of Government had to preserve credibility: That may explain why Secretary of State George Shultz, a consummate loyalist, three weeks ago started distancing the Department from the White House. These were all signals that the secret had to be worse than Iran. It is.

I did distance myself, but not because I knew that the secret was "worse than Iran." The arms-for-Iran decision was bad enough for me. I did not want Ronald Reagan to be yet another American president destroyed in office, and I did not believe that America deserved that either. The way to avoid that outcome was for me to slay the arms-for-hostages snake once and for all and to get the Iran arms sales for hostages and Contra aid stories out fast and in all their details.

We had important work to do in the next two years and significant prospects for real success in our foreign policy. I felt relieved and ready to start putting our foreign policy back together. The president, I reflected, may have been hit harder than I had realized by my assertions the previous Thursday evening that he was being misled and was not being given the facts by his NSC staff. He had been immediately receptive to Ed Meese's suggestion of an investigation. Meese had uncovered shocking behavior by the NSC staff. The president had acted quickly, getting rid of the key offenders and making instant public disclosure. President Reagan instructed me and everyone involved to make available all the information we had to the various investigating groups. The president had my full support. But any thought that I now had a clear track to move ahead on Iran and other foreign policy issues would be quickly put aside. This snake was far from dead.

CHAPTER 39

The Snake
Would Not Die

I went to see President Reagan on November 26, 1986, and asked Chief of Staff Don Regan and acting NSC adviser Al Keel to join me. "I'm ready to sign on for the duration," I told the president.

"That's what I want. I'm relying on your advice, and I'm looking to you as my point man on foreign policy," the president responded.

We had a long talk about the State Department. The president, I could sense, continued to feel that State was against him. "The president is the only constituency the State Department has. It's in State's interest to have a strong president. Only a strong president can make foreign policy succeed," I told him. I knew he had been uneasy with my opposition to the Iran arms-for-hostages schemes. I hoped now he would realize how hard I had been trying to protect him from being misled by his staff about developments in Iran and from the distortions that come from mixing together operations and intelligence. I told President Reagan that I would no longer deal with him exclusively through the NSC adviser: I would come to him directly, and I would invite the White House chief of staff to be present when I did.

"Anytime you want to see me, you can," the president said.

"And privately whenever you want," Don Regan added.

I went through how I intended to bring the Iran mess, and our Iran policy, under control. The president seemed to like my proposals. Given Iran's long border with the Soviet Union and the history of tension between those countries, Iran needed the United States, I told the president. We didn't need to chase after the Iranians.

"That's right," the president replied.

"We don't need to pay them for a relationship," I said. But we would make clear to them the circumstances under which a relationship with us would be possible.

The president was subdued. He normally reminded me of a star shortstop eagerly waiting for the batter to hit a hard-to-handle grounder at him—because he knew he could handle it. But at his last press conference, Reagan had fumbled the ball. His message had not generated public confidence. He wasn't used to this. Now his own confidence was shaken, not from a feeling that he had done something wrong but because he saw that his support among the American people had slipped. Part of my task, I knew, was to help him rebuild his self-confidence and restore the confidence in him of the American people.

The mood I had found all over the White House was tense; nerves were raw. No sense of remorse was detectable anywhere. The attitude was very stiff. After I left the Oval Office, Don Regan's mood changed. He launched into me, saying that I had "distanced" myself from the White House and that now he was the one who had to cope with the mess.

"I'm signed on," I told Don, "but don't take me for granted. The president sets policy, and we'll carry it out, but we don't need the NSC staff to tell us how to write cables." I told him he should consult Cap and Casey and me about the new NSC adviser.

Don asked me who I thought should succeed Poindexter. We both respected Frank Carlucci but did not think he would be willing to come back into government. Some months earlier I had sounded him out for a top position in the State Department, and he had declined. Shortly after my conversation with Regan, Bill Casey telephoned me. He liked Carlucci but preferred Zbigniew Brzezinski for the NSC job. I respected Brzezinski, but I thought that bringing back the NSC adviser from the Carter administration was a crazy idea. Casey was acting as though nothing remotely unusual had been happening.

While I was with the president, Mike Armacost, under secretary of state for political affairs, was attending a meeting at which Iran policy was supposed to be handed over to State's control, where it could be reshaped into an entirely different kind of effort. I had designated Armacost to be point man for the State Department on everything to do with Iran. Rodney McDaniel, filling in for Al Keel, was sitting in the NSC adviser's chair. "Shall we keep the Ollie channel open?" he asked.

"It was surreal," Armacost reported. How could they *still* talk of keeping the North channel open?

That afternoon, I went to Quantico, Virginia, to give a graduation speech to the marines who would be posted to U.S. embassies. My boot camp training had been at Quantico, and as a young marine I got kicked around there to beat hell. The marines were glad to see me, and I was refreshed to see them, living, as they were, in a land of little ambiguity.

On Friday morning, November 28, I invited Cap Weinberger to meet with me in my office. We agreed on the importance of getting a first-class national security adviser. The right and proper role was that of a coordinator, not an advocate. We talked over people we both had confidence in and could trust. Both of us thought Frank Carlucci would fit the bill: Cap and I had recruited Carlucci to work with us when I was director and Cap deputy director at the Office of Management and Budget in 1971. Frank also had been Cap's deputy when Cap was secretary of health, education, and welfare, as well as in the early years when Cap was secretary of defense. The meeting was refreshing and constructive. We placed a joint call to Don Regan and discussed our views with him in detail. Don took Frank's name to the president, who knew Frank well. He agreed. Carlucci was offered the job amid the building Iran-Contra controversy.

The front-page headlines on Monday morning were not heartening. " 'I'm Not Going to Back Off'; Reagan, Facing a Deepening Crisis, Expresses Defiance, Hits News Media"; "Dole Urges Recalling Congress for Inquiry; Special Session Asked on Iran-Contras Affair"; "GOP Leaders Warn Reagan," headlined the *Washington Post* on December 1, 1986.

Carlucci called me that day. I assured him of my wholehearted support and recounted how we all agreed that his name should be put forward to the president. "You're everybody's choice," I said. He asked me about reporting relationships. I urged him to insist that he report directly to the president but that he keep Don Regan completely informed. He asked whether I was going to stay on, and I assured him that I would. He worried about the president's continued support for the Iran initiative.

"He's having a hard time. He's been wounded and sold a bill of goods. But he stands in there. He has flexibility for the future." The president hadn't dropped out. "He isn't frozen," I told Frank. Early on Tuesday, December 2, Carlucci telephoned to say he had been to see the president and had signed on. When Carlucci quickly recruited General Colin Powell, Cap Weinberger's former executive assistant, some of my State Department colleagues questioned my judgment, saying I had, in effect, turned the NSC staff over to Cap. "Don't worry," I said, "Carlucci and Powell are able and straight people. We'll get along just fine." I reminded them that Carlucci had started out as a foreign service officer.

The Same Old Game?

That afternoon, Bill Casey called me. He told me that Amiram Nir, the Israeli who had been involved in our arms dealings with Iran, had called to inform Casey that he was going to meet Kangerlou, director of intelligence for Iran's revolutionary guards, in Geneva to discuss hostages; Ghorbanifar would be there. Prime Minister Shamir wanted the meeting to happen but also wanted to be sure we had no objections.

Though I was relieved that Casey was informing me, I thought that this continuing effort was idiotic. How could the same gang of operators still be working the same scheme? Because the meeting involved representatives of two other governments, I did not see what we could do to stop it, but I told Casey to make clear that the United States was in no way involved. I told Mike Armacost to double-track through his own channels with the CIA and make sure that *this* U.S.-Israeli link was severed. As far as I was concerned, the same people would probably talk about the same old swindle. So there must be *no* "green light" from the United States: Israel should be perfectly clear about that. From now on, the Israelis were on their own.

Casey was not to be trusted. He had now changed his story in testimony to Congress on December 2 and admitted that he *had* known about the arms-for-hostages trade described by Bud McFarlane in his phone call to me in Geneva in November 1985. I heard that Casey had tried to get his deputy, John McMahon, to cook up a way to place that shipment ex post facto under a presidential finding. McMahon, I was told, had resisted.

Later in the day on December 2, the president asked that an independent counsel be appointed to look into the whole affair. Clearly, the Meese investigation would not be enough, and the Tower Commission[1] had been directed by the president to "conduct a comprehensive study of the future role and procedures of the National Security Council staff in the development, coordination, oversight, and conduct of foreign and national security policy," which, though a crucial task, would not be sufficiently broad.

That evening, I reported to President Reagan on King Hussein's response to an earlier presidential letter trying to explain the Iran events to the king. "The king fails to see how our arms shipments constituted neutrality. He is convinced that the weapons have prolonged the war, strengthened the pro-war faction in the Iranian government, and encouraged more hostage taking, and he is worried that our actions offer the Soviets an opening to expand their regional influence. Arguing that TOW missiles and Hawk spares greatly increase Iran's fighting power against the very armor and aircraft upon which Iraqi survival depends, Hussein fears that we have opened the way for other countries to ship arms to Iran without concern for our [arms] embargo." I agreed with the king's assessment and told the president so. He was uncomfortable, but he recognized that he was getting straight, even if unwelcome, reports from me.

The media were producing new revelations by the minute. John Poindexter repeatedly invoked the Fifth Amendment in testifying before the Senate Intelligence Committee on December 3 (the first time in history that an admiral on active duty in the U.S. Navy had done so, Representative Lee Hamilton later noted). The White House grapevine was alive with

---

1. Named by the president on November 26 and composed of former National Security adviser Brent Scowcroft, former Secretary of State Edmund Muskie, and former Senator John Tower, chairman.

rumors that the first lady had "turned against" Don Regan, portraying him as "not having the class to quit." That night, I found a note from Bud McFarlane under my door at home. "I wanted to reach you to clarify that my public statement about keeping you informed—that of course could only apply to my term of service through December 4, 1985," the date, twelve months ago, when he had resigned as NSC adviser.

The president still seemed intransigent, unrepentant, but he had set in motion the right processes of digging out the truth. When I told the president about the Nir-Kangerlou-Ghorbanifar meeting in Geneva and that I had ordered that the United States get out of that loop, he was taken aback. He said nothing, but I could sense that my action had riled him.

Because of the president's mood—and Bill Casey's—and because of the continuing Israeli activity in this matter, I feared that despite the press, congressional, and public uproar, some version of the operation was still alive. Those who were responsible for the operation now seemed desperate to succeed and thus to vindicate their judgment in the face of overwhelming criticism.

The CIA's George Cave, who had accompanied Oliver North on past operations, was pressing for authorization to contact the Iranians again. I said Cave could see his contacts but only to advise them that from now on anything they wished to convey should come through the State Department. I was coming to realize more and more how heavily Casey and the CIA were involved in these contacts with Iran. Cave had to be phased out of the picture: we could not allow the continuing involvement of someone who had gone to Tehran with McFarlane. The Iranians would conclude that no change in our policy had taken place. I had heard Cave, at Casey and Poindexter's behest, brief the National Security Planning Group about what he called the big policy turnaround that Iran had made because of this project. Not only was the briefing flagrantly in error, but having Cave—who was an *operator* in this affair—serve as the *intelligence analyst* assessing Iran violated the cardinal rule of any professional intelligence service: do not mix operations and intelligence analysis!

The Chain of Command

On Saturday morning, December 6, I found a cable on my desk from Ambassador John Kelly in Lebanon. Now that revelations were flying thick and fast, Kelly wanted me to know that over the past two months he had had numerous contacts with the NSC staff regarding arms for hostages about which he had not informed me. His cable read:

> I met in Washington in July or August 1986 with Robert McFarlane, who
> briefed me on the hostage negotiations involving arms to Iran as an induce-

ment. Between the dates of October 30 and November 4, 1986, I had numerous conversations with Lieutenant Colonel Oliver North and Richard V. Secord relating to the hostage negotiations with Iran. During that period I received and sent numerous "back channel" messages to and from the White House—Admiral John Poindexter—concerning the hostage negotiations.

I was livid. I immediately thought of Reg Bartholomew, Kelly's predecessor, who had been on the tacsat to us whenever anything of note came into his sight. I asked that the letter that the president signs and provides to each new ambassador be pulled out of the files, in order to show that Kelly had been specifically instructed—as all American ambassadors are—to report through the secretary of state as the channel to the president and the rest of the U.S. government. For Kelly to deal with the NSC staff on a serious issue without informing me was a clear violation of that instruction.

When Nick Platt found the letter sent to Kelly, I was astonished to see that the key sentence—"I expect you to report to me through the Assistant Secretary for Near East and South Asia Affairs and on some subjects to me directly"—had been omitted. This language had been the center of a bureaucratic struggle over the proper channels to and from our embassies that went back to the time of President John F. Kennedy and before. Could that key sentence have been omitted by chance or clerical error? Before Kelly had gone to the Beirut embassy as ambassador only a few months ago, he had made the rounds in town, including at the NSC staff. Had the text of this letter been tampered with in the White House to take Kelly's direct and secret dealing with Poindexter out from under the regular responsibilities imposed upon American ambassadors? I had no way of knowing. But from Kelly's cable, I could now see why Poindexter would not accept my advice to him on November 4 to get the whole story out: for even as I was giving that advice, Poindexter and others were working on another arms-for-hostages swap.

On Monday, December 8, 1986, I testified before Dante Fascell's House Foreign Affairs Committee: this was my first comprehensive statement about my knowledge of and behavior on all these Iran-related events. I was on the razor's edge. Some critical information was classified, some not. I did not want to give a partial picture to the committee and to the public, but that result was inevitable in view of the classification problem and my lack of comprehensive knowledge. I based everything I said on the hard written evidence in my possession or my firm recollection. My record was far more specific and detailed than that of others in the administration, even though my role was marginal, mostly an effort to stop the initiative from going forward. Those who were extensively involved were unable, or unwilling, to comment in depth on what they had done. Having gone through the record that had been assembled for me, I spoke about what I knew from that record.

The committee was friendly and seemed relieved to hear from me. Peter Jennings reported on ABC, "Ninety plus percent of the Committee were very sympathetic to Shultz's position." But Sam Donaldson noted that he could not believe the White House would be very pleased, as "Shultz said the skimming action was 'illegal'—the first time that's been said." John McWethy reported, "We saw a glimpse of the depth of Secretary's Shultz's feeling; it was embarrassing for a man of his stature." The next day, the *Washington Post* described it on the front page as testimony "that riveted and sometimes astounded the committee." What astounded them was the extent to which a secretary of state could be cut out of a major operation. In the effort to inform the committee of the information I had in my possession and to let them see just how far out of control the process had gone, I told them about Kelly's cable, which became a news item in itself: I was, said NBC News, "so frozen out that the U.S. Ambassador in Beirut, John Kelly, was talking secretly with the White House and National Security Council staff members without Shultz's knowledge. Shultz did not know until last weekend."

Bill Safire called: "You're too popular. Take some heat on behalf of the president. Let the press denounce you."

I had left Washington in the afternoon on December 8 for the annual NATO foreign ministers' meeting in Brussels. I appreciated Geoffrey Howe's invitation to meet him first at Chevening, the country home allocated to the British foreign minister, to talk with him along with the foreign ministers of Germany and France. They were all looking for reassurance that U.S. negotiations for arms reductions and efforts to improve U.S.-Soviet relations would continue, despite the disarray in Washington. "The going will be rough." I told them, "but the president and his policies will stay in place." They hoped I was right. I hoped I was right, too.

In the meantime, I had summoned Kelly back to Washington. Mike Armacost and Nick Platt had talked to him and reported to me that Kelly on August 8, 1986, had met with McFarlane (then a private citizen but still working on this operation) at the Center for Strategic and International Studies on K Street, where McFarlane had told Kelly of the president's decision to transfer arms to Iran. Kelly had then talked to NSC staff member Dennis Ross, who said nothing to Kelly on this subject, and to Robert Earle, who was in on the Oliver North operation and who told Kelly to keep the project on "close hold." Kelly left Washington for Beirut, having said nothing about his conversations with McFarlane and Earle to anyone at the State Department.

Kelly told Armacost and Platt that on about October 30, 1986, he had been instructed to telephone a number in Germany and ask for a Mr.

Goode (North traveled on a passport in the name of Willie B. Goode). North told him that the project was "cooking" and that Kelly should get ready to facilitate the movement of released hostages. Shortly thereafter, Poindexter had instructed Kelly to communicate with the NSC staff only through "back channels" and not to inform the Department of State. Kelly said that he had asked Robert Earle to inform State and the Joint Chiefs and had been told by Earle, "We'll take care of that." Kelly had been in contact, he said, between October 30 and November 4, 1986, with Oliver North, Robert Earle, Craig Coy, Richard Secord, and a Colonel Dutton. He also saw Terry Waite, the archbishop of Canterbury's envoy (who seemed to Kelly to be cooperating with Oliver North). Kelly said he had received the last "back channel" message on November 4. I was furious about Kelly's failure to discuss with the department what he had learned in August as well as his conduct during this more recent episode. The congressional committees wanted Kelly to testify; I said not until he had talked to me.

I told Nick Platt to start working on a message to every American ambassador, reasserting that the chain of command ran to and from the ambassador through the secretary of state and that only the personal intervention of the president himself—not others in his name—could override that chain of command; otherwise, no exceptions.

In Brussels, at NATO, I found myself arguing hard to persuade our European allies that the Reagan presidency was still in business and that it would work effectively through its second term. They were aghast at the spectacle of yet another American government in disarray and in danger of unraveling further, particularly when the prospects for major changes in East-West relations were looking far more promising than in a long while. Here we were in sight of the first nuclear arms reduction agreement in history.

While I was in Europe, Mike Armacost, whom I had designated to take charge of Iran policy, left town on a long-scheduled trip to Southern Africa. As soon as he left, Bill Casey and his followers moved their own Iran operation back on the rails again. On Saturday afternoon, December 13, just as I was getting started on a huge pile of work on my desk after coming in from my arrival at Andrews Air Force Base, John Whitehead brought me up-to-date. Armacost and Casey had agreed at a meeting on Friday, December 12, that a State Department official and George Cave would meet with Iranians to inform them that future contacts with Iran would *not* deal with arms for hostages, would *not* mix policy and intelligence, and would be maintained through the Department of State.

Casey agreed; everything was satisfactory, he said. Casey then went straight to the White House to get the president to overrule State on the need to cut the link between operations and intelligence analysis. Casey wanted to stay in the loop and in command. At 5:00 P.M. on Friday, Casey telephoned John Whitehead. "The president is not happy with the way this thing was left," Casey said. He was about to leave for Long Island to rest over the weekend; Whitehead should call acting NSC adviser Al Keel to get the president's instructions.

"I thought State and CIA just agreed on this," Whitehead said.

"Call Keel," said Casey, and hung up.

Keel told Whitehead, yes, the president had called him in. Casey had called Don Regan, and Regan had gone to see the president to say that Casey wanted to keep going with Iran but Shultz was trying to shut it off. The president said he wanted to keep the contacts going so that the "dialogue" that had been established could be built upon. So the agreement between Casey and Armacost had been overturned: the Cave channel would stay open and would, Keel said, "continue to be used for both policy and intelligence discussions," again mixing operations and intelligence analysis, again a fundamental violation of professional intelligence work.

Deputy CIA director Bob Gates told John Whitehead that Vice President Bush had talked to the CIA's Thomas Twetten, head of their Near East division, to confirm that "policy and intelligence" were still to be conducted through the CIA channel.

The CIA and the NSC staff, with apparent support of President Reagan and Vice President Bush, were proceeding just as though nothing had happened. Congress was being misled right now—a month and a half after the revelation first appeared. What was worse, Whitehead said, "we have just learned that the CIA has told the Iranians that the State Department is just a 'temporary impediment' and that after it calms down, Cave and Secord will be back in action. The president is being ripped to pieces, and the CIA is reassuring the Iranians!"

Foreign service officer and Farsi speaker Charles Dunbar was to meet the Iranian representative, Mehdi-Najat, in Frankfurt on December 13 with CIA official George Cave at his side. I insisted that they go together so there would be no impression of a divided U.S. administration. Dunbar was to tell the Iranians: we do not want to be in a perpetual state of animosity with Iran; we are willing to continue with private—but official— contacts; we want all Americans held by terrorists released; the arms-for-hostages effort is *over,* completely.

I met with Ambassador John Kelly on December 13 and heard his story. I would review what he told me and get back to him, I said. I explained the key points that troubled me the most: he was the only ambassador (of three) who had been contacted by the NSC staff on this operation who had *not* informed the State Department. His conduct on the scene was in sharp contrast to that of his predecessor, Reg Bartholomew. Kelly had been told of the operation before leaving to take up his post at a time when he was in consultations with Washington; he failed to check out the operation with State. He failed to inform me of his role even after I had made public statements opposing trading arms for hostages. He was a smart, experienced professional who knew all the ins-and-outs of the business; his silence could not be regarded as an oversight. He claimed to have sent the CIA a message on November 10 asking that they inform me of preparations for a possible military attempt to rescue hostages. The CIA told State it had no record of his message; the officer there who would have seen all such traffic did not know of such a request.

An Explosive Report

That same day, December 13, State's Charles Dunbar reported in by secure telephone. He and CIA's George Cave had met the Iranian, Mehdi-Najat, in Frankfurt, West Germany. The Iranian had urged that the project continue as before, saying, "Much has been accomplished by North, Secord, and Cave." Mehdi-Najat wanted the United States to produce more military equipment for Iran, and he referred, Dunbar said, to a "nine-point agenda" on which the United States and Iran had agreed to work. Cave talked openly to the Iranian about future U.S. help with their military requirements. Mehdi-Najat stated that Iran had been pressuring Kuwaiti authorities—at Poindexter's request—to release the Dawa terrorists from prison, as their release might make it easier to gain the release of Americans held hostage in Lebanon. Dunbar followed his instructions and read his talking points to the Iranian. Openly scornful, Mehdi-Najat was supported in his attitude by Cave. Dunbar "should go back to Washington and get briefed on where this situation stands. A lot of commitments have been made, and we are far down the road," the Iranian said.

This was horrendous. I could hardly believe what I knew to be an accurate report. President Reagan, Vice President Bush,[2] Bill Casey, and Don Regan had *all* either supported or known about a change in the instructions that would keep the previous dealings with Iran alive. The president himself was withdrawn and, to a degree, out of action. I asked my secretary to call the White House Saturday and say I wanted to see President Reagan. The White House staff referred my request to NSC staffer Rodney McDaniel, who telephoned my staff to ask, "What does Shultz want to see the president for?" So I called over myself and wound up with the president's

2. Vice President Bush sometimes would not state his position in meetings on the ground that he owed it to the president to provide his thoughts and recommendations privately. Therefore, while it was possible to know with certainty what the vice president heard at a meeting, it was not always possible to know with confidence what the vice president's position was on a particular issue at a particular time.

scheduler, David Chew. "We really want to give the president a day off on Sunday," Chew said. I persisted.

On Sunday morning, December 14, Al Keel telephoned me to say that a meeting probably could be arranged between me and the president "if you *really* want it." I told Keel that I did. I was upset. The president needed to take strong steps, not partial steps that looked weak and made people think there was no change and no leadership. The situation was still unraveling. The president was roped in and refused to see the real picture. Bill Casey had the bit in his teeth and apparently was able to enlist the support of Don Regan and the president. Whatever the president told me, I didn't have confidence that key people around him would deal squarely with me. When that happens, you're out of business.

At eleven o'clock Sunday morning, I went to see President Reagan. I told him that this was a very crucial moment in his presidency. It was a moment, if ever there was one, for him to be decisive on both procedure and substance. "We must have a clear chain of command," I said. "John Kelly should be fired." I went over my dispute with Casey over his persistent and continuing drive to control the operation, with the result that policy was melded with intelligence analysis. I explained why this was a problem and reminded the president that this mixture had led to erroneous reports in the past—reports that had seriously misled him.

Then I went through the material that emerged from the meeting the previous day of George Cave and Dunbar with the Iranian, Mehdi-Najat, in Frankfurt: there was a nine-point agenda that the Iranian seemed to regard as a set of U.S. commitments. There was a dedicated telephone line for Iran to use at any time with the CIA. There was Cave's continuing talk of further arms transfers. There was the indication that the United States had put itself on the side of Iran in the Iran-Iraq War. And there was the revelation, I told him with anger, that Iran, at Poindexter's request, had been pressuring Kuwait to let the Dawa terrorists out of jail.

President Reagan was dumbfounded by this news. His reaction was visceral. He could not believe that we had agreed, in effect, to press Kuwait to release the convicted Dawa terrorists in exchange for the release of U.S. hostages in Lebanon. It was as though someone had kicked him hard in the belly. I felt that for the first time Ronald Reagan was convinced that he really had been misled and that terrible violations of our policy had taken place. "I'm glad to be in the position personally of seeing how shocked you are. The CIA and Cave have to get out of this," I said, "or Iran will never get the message that we now are serious and that they can no longer play games with us."

The next day, Monday, December 15, the news was even worse. After Dunbar left to return to Washington, a second meeting was arranged between Cave and Mehdi-Najat in Frankfurt. "Who *is* this Mehdi-Najat?" I kept asking. All anyone seemed to know was that he was a "revolutionary guard who does not portray himself as anything." After cutting Dunbar out, Cave was back in business on his own. As a result, the Iranians wanted to push ahead with the "nine-point agenda" that was said to cover the release of Shiite prisoners held by Israel, the release of Dawa terrorists held by Kuwait, the overthrow of Saddam Hussein—and thereby Iran's victory in its war with Iraq—and extensive arms shipments to Iran: more Hawk missile parts, the repair of American Phoenix missiles in Iranian hands, more TOWs, and cameras for Iranian F-4 aircraft. The Iranians wanted arms merchant Albert Hakim and General Richard Secord to continue to play a role.

At 9:30 A.M. that Monday, I went back to the White House to see the president. George Bush, Don Regan, and Al Keel were also present. I went over chapter and verse again—how the Armacost-Casey agreement of last Friday, when I was in Europe, had been overturned by Casey as soon as Armacost left town. I described the Saturday Frankfurt meeting that Cave and Dunbar had with Mehdi-Najat and the revelations that had emerged from that meeting: the CIA was *still* trying to trade arms for hostages; the CIA was pressing another nation, Kuwait, for the release of jailed terrorists; and the CIA was pursuing an agenda with Iran that clearly put us on Iran's side in the Gulf War. When I told them of the dedicated Iran-CIA telephone line, everyone in the room seemed astonished. When I informed them of the effort to get Kuwait to release the Dawa prisoners, they were appalled, as the president had been on Sunday. "We have an obligation," I said, "to pass this information on to Congress. It is explosive. There needs to be a clear separation between policy and intelligence, but the CIA has been doing both. The State Department *must* conduct U.S. policy with regard to Iran." I let everyone know that *I had asked to testify* before the Senate Intelligence Committee the next day, December 16, to set out in a closed session what I knew of this whole story.

Then I stressed the need for discipline within the administration. I recounted John Kelly's actions. I told them of the sentence inexplicably missing from Kelly's letter, a significant departure from the standard letter that the president sends to every ambassador. The discomfort of the others in the Oval Office was palpable; they did not want to make any changes, not least because of resistance to seeing me take a more leading role. "Mr. President, you must be decisive!" I said sharply. As for Kelly, the others were all on his side: Vice President Bush had earlier sent me a message through his assistant, Don Gregg, saying how highly the vice president regarded Kelly and that he "hopes it can be worked out."

They thought I was overreacting to what Kelly had done and not done.

I asked Don Regan, "How long would a branch officer at Merrill Lynch keep his job after something like this?" Don, who had been the head of Merrill Lynch before entering the Reagan administration, smiled ruefully.

"I don't think he [Kelly] should be relieved, but you can admonish him," the president said to me.

"Okay," I said, "but Mr. President, you have agreed to send to all ambassadors a cable reaffirming that the chain of command runs through the secretary of state, and I will needle everyone unmercifully until this cable is sent out."

"Does this mean a State takeover?" Don Regan snapped. He was red-faced and bristling.

"Of course not," I snapped back. "It means a presidential takeover and the conduct of the president's foreign policy in the normal way."

As the meeting was breaking up, I reminded the president that I would now inform Congress of all this new information. "Bill Casey is bad news," I said to Vice President Bush as we left. Casey had grossly distorted the proper conduct of government, and I was going to make it my crusade to stop him from continuing these renegade operations.

The meeting ended at 10:15 A.M. At 11:00, back at the State Department, a call came in from Fox Butterfield of the *New York Times*: "Bill Casey has been taken to the hospital; the CIA says that it is a reaction to medication." The pressure on Casey must be great, I thought.

The basic message from those at the White House, I felt, was that they were terribly uneasy about me. They certainly did not want to turn things over to me. They wanted to keep a string on everything. But if Ronald Reagan did not reestablish his authority soon and his chain of command through proper channels, he would start to drift again and his presidency could go down the drain.

On December 16, I saw Kelly again. "I have discussed your situation with the president directly, with the vice president present. We conclude that you should be admonished and asked to return to your post. You should understand the nature of your responsibility to report through the chain of command. You got a letter from the president with a sentence missing." Kelly interrupted to say that he was not relying on that letter to defend himself, that he knew the rules. "We'll put out a new message on the chain of command to all ambassadors," I continued. "I'm personally disappointed that somehow you didn't find a way to report in. I do have the sense that your activity in helping [hostage David] Jacobsen get out was an outstanding job. You are pretty well known to Vice President Bush, and the president is well aware of your role in the Jacobsen release."

"So the president knew what was going on then?" Kelly asked.

"He knew what it took mechanically at least to get him [Jacobsen] released," I responded. "You are available to the Congress and to the FBI to give them the facts. Basically, you should return to your post."

"What am I being admonished for?" Kelly asked. "For not finding a way to inform the department?"

"The material you were told by McFarlane, by the CIA, by the NSC staff. And the work to get Jacobsen out. You should have checked in in some fashion. If I'm not available, Murphy, Hill, Platt would be."

"May I see the press statement that will go out on this?" Kelly asked.

"It hasn't been written yet," I said. "You should see the statement when it is drafted."

"Thank you, sir," Kelly said, and left.

Kelly went from my office directly to the office of Charlie Hill. "I accept being admonished," Kelly said, "but Shultz is opening the way to more difficulty. Congressional staffers are going to ask why I was admonished, and I'll say that I thought Shultz knew. I'll say that [Ambassador for Counterterrorism] Oakley knew about arms going to Iran and that he told Shultz." That was absurd—and worse. Kelly was making a threat. It didn't work.

Hill called Kelly on his threat. "Just tell the Congress the truth as best you can. Be open," he said.

On the afternoon of December 16, I went up to Congress, on my initiative, to testify in a closed hearing before the Senate Select Committee on Intelligence. I had told the president, the vice president, Don Regan, and Al Keel the day before that I would seek this opportunity to inform Congress about what had happened, including the most recent developments. I told the senators everything I knew, based on the documents available to me and on my firm recollection—the same story I had dredged out of my records and memory in early November, and the same story I would set forth again and again as the investigation deepened. When I told them about the two Frankfurt meetings between Cave and Mehdi-Najat, the senators were dumbfounded. The general reaction from the committee was that I should have pressed harder during the course of this episode, but they also recognized that I had had reasonable grounds to believe—having been so told on at least four occasions—that arms sales were no longer an element in our contacts with Iran. Senator Bill Cohen, having heard me testify that day, said to me six months later, "You are the only witness whose story in this sorry episode has never altered from the time the revelations first came out."

Privately, that evening, Don Regan informed me that Bill Casey had a brain tumor and that he might be out of action "forever." Robert Gates, as Casey's deputy, became acting CIA director. I later wondered whether Casey's brain tumor had affected his judgment and behavior—and, if so, to what degree and for how long.

The Nine-Point Agenda

I telephoned Bob Gates on the secure line at 9:30 A.M. on December 17. "I've seen Dunbar's report of the Saturday [December 13] meeting and learned of Cave's subsequent meeting with Mehdi-Najat, on his own, *without* Dunbar, which was not in accord with our understanding," I told Gates. "Out of these meetings and the Iranian's reactions we've learned of stuff we never dreamed of before. I need to know the facts and take action."

George Cave had told Dunbar that Poindexter had pressed Kuwait to release the Dawa prisoners and that NSC staff people pressed the French to pressure Kuwait also. He had mentioned a nine-point program, which included points on the Dawas and on weapons.

"So I would like to know," I told Gates forcefully, "what is the nine-point agenda? I want to see it. And I want to know about the weapons parts of the arrangement and about the role of Secord and Hakim. If we pressed Kuwait, that's shocking. I reported to the president about the Saturday meeting, and I will tell him of [Cave's] subsequent meeting. We must go to the Kuwaitis and say that the president has no intent to press them to release the Dawas." My fury was no doubt apparent to Gates, even over the telephone.

Gates asked how I had learned all this. "Cave told Dunbar," I said. "Cave hung around with North and Secord. So Cave is knowledgeable— distressingly. And the Iranians do *not* believe that the arms sales are over. We have to tell them firmly, and we have to take Cave totally out of this business," I stressed. "Cave should not have had a second meeting by himself." Gates said that he would cooperate fully and get me the information I wanted. "And I will act on it," I said.

Gates telephoned back in an hour. He said that the second Cave meeting was no big deal, that the State Department was trying to stir things up. Cave had stayed on in Frankfurt to see his son, Gates said, and the Iranian had initiated a contact because he wanted to talk to Dunbar. But Dunbar had left for Washington, so Cave met Mehdi-Najat alone. And we really had not pressed Kuwait to let terrorists out of jail, Gates told me. I was very skeptical. I had been lied to many times before about this operation.

Gates continued: Poindexter and North had gone to the Kuwaiti foreign minister only to urge Kuwait "to open a dialogue with Iran." Then Poindexter and North had told the Iranians that the United States had no leverage with Kuwait regarding the Dawa prisoners, so Iran, they said, should open contact with Kuwait. And as for the French, Gates said, Ollie North had simply talked to them about seizing the Dawa prisoners on French criminal charges after they were released by Kuwait. Once again, I thought of Bernie Kalb's line, "Is that what they told you, Missy?"

Gates said he couldn't provide the nine-point agenda to me because it was "an NSC document" and "has been constantly changed." This last phrase is Washington bureaucratic code for "I have the document, but I can delay any response to your request because the document is not final." Gates said he thought the nine-point agenda would be among the NSC staff documents seized and sealed by the Department of Justice. I asked Gates to provide me with whatever documents Cave had been using.

At the end of the conversation I felt that Gates, unlike Casey, was in a certain sense trying to be straight with me. But I was still distressed by the way Gates tried to make the nine-point agenda sound innocent and trivial when clearly it was scheming, idiotic, and disgraceful.

So North and Poindexter had dealt with the foreign minister of Kuwait. I sent a cable to him saying that some indication may have been given to Kuwait about the Dawa prisoners that was at odds with stated U.S. policy. I was sending this message to assure him that President Reagan's policy of no deals with terrorists was in effect and that Kuwait would receive no pressure from us concerning those prisoners. I told the Near Eastern Affairs Bureau to work with the CIA to bring about the following: State would handle contacts with Iran; policy and intelligence would be kept distinct; Cave would not work on Iran issues; the January 17, 1986, "finding" would be rewritten to eliminate the concept of selling arms to Iran.

On December 18, the CIA sent over a draft of the "nine-point agenda" dated October 8, 1986. It apparently was a document that Cave had worked out with the Iranians:

1. Iran will pay Hakim the price of 500 TOW—and if so desired—Hawk parts that remain from the previous agreement.
2. Nine working days later—should Iran agree—500 TOW as well as Hawks together with donated medicines will be delivered to Iran.
3. Prior to fulfilling the provisions of para. 4, Albert [Hakim] will submit the plan for the release of the Kuwaitis (seventeen persons) [the Dawa prisoners].
4. One and one-half American hostages (one with certainty and possibly two through persistent effort) to be released from the Lebanese through Iran's effort (three to four days after the delivery of the cargo mentioned in para. 2).
5. Through a method for opening of credit to be studied by Albert and Ali by tomorrow night: 500 TOW with a maximum of 100 launchers to be delivered to Iran within four days after fulfilling the provisions of para. 4. Iran will pay for 1,500 TOW (500 received and 1,000 future ones) and the 1,000 TOW will be delivered within nine days.
6. The U.S. shall start and implement the technical support (both in goods and expertise) for Hawks as well as the rejuvenation of military information (intelligence) and maps and special commo [communications]. And

it (the U.S.) will submit to Iran the price schedule and timetable for the delivery of Ali's items.

7. Prior to return of (Ayub?) to Tehran, the question of Muslim [Shiite] prisoners in Lebanon and the process for their release by the parties involved shall be discussed with Secord.

8. Iran shall pursue its efforts for the creation of the (proper) background for the release of other hostages.

9. Steps to be taken for the submission of items in para. 6, second sentence.

What a shocking document: dangerously amateurish and totally at odds with the rigorously stated policies of the United States of America. It was dated October 8! Now, in mid-December, Poindexter was gone; North was gone.

Casey, the streetfighter, had clearly been driving this catastrophic effort.

How to Handle Hostages

As 1986 came to an end, I felt that I was slowly getting things under control. The key to this resolution was the departure of Bill Casey.[3] The zeal seemed to go out of the operation when he left the CIA. It was as though a festering boil had been lanced.

President Reagan could still not bring himself to believe that the concept underlying this Iran initiative, let alone the execution, was fatally flawed. Ronald Reagan respected me, I knew, and recognized that I had been fighting for his interests and that I had been right in my claim that he was being deceived. Poindexter's effort to get the Kuwaitis to release the Dawa prisoners drove that point home to him more than anything else had before. But I was sure that the president felt that somehow I should have been able to make his Iranian hostage-release effort work.

I wished we had been able to bring about the hostages' release, but certainly not through any arms deal, which created a hostage-taking industry.

The key was quiet, patient work to "lower the value and raise the costs of taking and holding hostages," I said. That strategy is tough to follow in a free and open society. Politicians must learn how to handle the inevitable pressure to "do something," and the population at large and the media must also appreciate the importance of raising costs to terrorists and to denying them gain and massive publicity from their actions. The searing publicity about Ronald Reagan's well-intentioned but ill-fated effort ironically contributed to this educational process.

3. I had known Casey for years. We had been friends in the Nixon administration. Our relationship had degenerated in recent years, but I was saddened by his tragic end.

The way this effort had been handled made clear to Iran and its friends in Beirut that we placed a high value on the hostages. Of course, we did, but the right strategy is to let the hostage holders know that they will not get any kind of ransom in exchange. Moreover, as the value of the hostages in the eyes of the holders is reduced, the costs of holding hostages need to be escalated in whatever ways possible.

We should always be willing to talk to any credible person about our hostages. The hostages should know that we would never cease our efforts to gain their release. But we owe the millions of Americans at risk throughout the world the assurance that they will not be turned into targets by the known willingness of our government to pay money, sell arms, pressure another government to pay money, or, in any other way, make it profitable to take Americans hostage.

A Different Approach

On the last day of January in 1987, *Wall Street Journal* correspondent Gerald Seib, who had gone to Tehran at the invitation of the Iranian government, was taken captive by the Iranians as "a spy of the Zionist regime." Seib was the latest in the list of Americans held hostage, but this time the state sponsors of terrorism had acted directly rather than through their agents in Lebanon, as had been the more recent practice.

On Monday, February 2, a group from the *Wall Street Journal*—Warren Phillips, Karen Elliott House, Norman Pearlstine, and Albert Hunt—came in to talk to me about Seib. The *Journal*'s editorials had skewered me in the Daniloff affair, charging me with making a deal with the Soviets to swap a guilty Soviet spy, Zakharov, for an innocent American reporter, Daniloff. They, of course, did not know that the Soviets had constructed a powerful case against Daniloff on the basis of careless and unprofessional work by CIA officers in Moscow. I was interested to hear what their attitude would be now that one of their own people had been captured.

I described for them how the State Department was proceeding. We were raising hell with the Iranians, but privately. As the United States had no embassy in Tehran, we were using the Swiss, Turks, and Japanese as intermediaries. My message was this: Iran had made a big mistake in taking Seib. They would get nothing out of us for Seib's release. And we would see to it that Iranian interests suffered as a result of this act of terrorism.

What would I advise the *Journal* to do, they asked. "What I recommend is something that may go against your grain—you may not instinctively want to do what I advise," I told them. "If you don't express public outrage, you may feel odd, but making a gigantic public issue out of this just raises the value of the hostage in the eyes of the terrorists. It is absolutely the *wrong* action to take. Terrorists take hostages so they can, in effect, 'sell them'—sell them back for the highest price they can get: for changes in U.S. policy, for changes in American behavior, for arms, for money, for the release of terrorists sentenced to prison in the West. If we make such deals, or if we convey an attitude that 'there's nothing in this world we won't do to see that he is freed,' we will only prolong his captivity by raising his value."

"We could put out the word that respectable reporters won't go to Iran as long as he is held," Karen Elliott House said.

"But they will go, and the Iranians know it, so that's not a credible line," I replied. Other suggestions were raised, none of which made sense to me: show Iran evidence that Seib was not working for Israel (but how do you prove that?); inform them that he was not Jewish but Roman Catholic (that was intolerable—what if a hostage *was* Jewish?).

"The right strategy," I said, "is, first, to avoid giving the impression that Seib is a valuable property and, second, to make clear that this action is going to cost Iran more than it can possibly hope to gain."

"Should Seib's parents make a personal appeal?" someone asked.

"These people are not responsive to human compassion, and such family involvement only raises the value of their asset," I said. The ill-considered efforts led by McFarlane, Poindexter, Casey, and North—with the president's blessing—had only made matters worse by demonstrating that we would pay heavily for hostages.

They accepted my arguments. I continued with the strategy I had set out to them. Two days after this meeting, on February 4, Seib was released. He was turned over to the Swiss embassy, and on February 6 he was flown to Zurich. Just what had caused the Iranians to shift gears, I did not know. But I did feel that this was one hostage crisis that was handled correctly. The people at the *Wall Street Journal* deserved credit for their good sense.

I had now signed on for the duration and had left all my considerations of resignation behind me. I reflected on the letter that Bill Casey had sent to the president in mid-November urging him to "get a new pitcher": that is, get rid of me. Now Casey was gone; I was not. There was a message, I thought, in the fact that the president had not taken Casey's advice.

The operation had now been stopped, but the crisis of the Reagan presidency was not over by any means. For the first six months of 1987, the sense of uncertainty and tension over its future mounted as the time for testimony before the now-established Joint Congressional Committee on the Iran-Contra Affair—set for late spring and summer of 1987—approached. The investigative process had just begun.

Part VII

ON THE MOVE AGAIN

CHAPTER 40

The Struggle to Get
Back on Track

Washington officials scattered in December for the end-of-year holidays, though in 1986, I found it hard to celebrate. The White House staff and the president seemed in a daze, grappling to understand what had happened and why, and even why—stemming from the Iran-Contra events—they faced a problem. Lee Annenberg telephoned twice to make sure that O'Bie and I were coming to her annual New Year's Eve party for the Reagans in Palm Springs. I heard that the president's friend, Bill Wilson, was campaigning to get me fired and that within the California kitchen cabinet of advisers, the view was that if only I had gone along, everything would now be fine. Were the Annenbergs sending me the message that they were on my side and that I must be present to defend myself on New Year's Eve? Columnist Charles Krauthammer summed up the mood in Washington as the year came to an end: "This presidency is over: 1987 will be a Watergate year—and the following an election year."

At the Palm Springs party, I found everyone very friendly to me and some even complimentary. Nancy Reagan said she was "disgusted" with Poindexter and North. "They should be court-martialed," I heard her say to Cap Weinberger. Walter Annenberg was heated and eloquent about the imperious behavior of the NSC staff back in the Nixon days when he was ambassador in London. But I could not get anyone energized about the need to pick up the pieces and put them together again.

All the talk and the advice seemed to roll off Ronald Reagan's back. He looked healthy—but hurt. He was tentative and deferential, humbled. I had never seen him like that before. On our New Year's Eve golf outing, I rode on the cart with him. We bantered; he told a joke or two. But we had no real discussion of substance. Whether at a party, on the golf course, or in a policy discussion, the president just didn't seem ready to engage.

The Troubled Washington Scene

Back in Washington on Saturday, January 3, 1987, President Reagan telephoned my home and, finding that I was out playing tennis, told O'Bie he wanted to send something over to me. When I got home, a package had arrived with a note from him: "Here are some pretty sound thoughts from a friend who wants to be anonymous." Enclosed were papers on the Middle East, Nicaragua, arms control, and other issues. I read them: I could see that the author was knowledgeable, a little off the reservation but in interesting ways, and with some views similar to my own. (I later learned that the author was Bud McFarlane.) This was a presidential initiative to me about ideas that had merit and showed movement on key issues. I took this as a sign that Ronald Reagan was reengaging again after a period of demoralization as the Iran-Contra issues unfolded and his own popularity with the American people sagged—that he wanted me to know he was relying on me, reestablishing his relationship with me on substantive issues. I hoped that the relaxed time with old friends in the California desert had been a tonic for the president. I was encouraged.

Frank Carlucci was now national security adviser, having replaced John Poindexter. We knew each other well. I invited Carlucci to my home on Sunday morning, January 4, where we had a lengthy and frank talk about the substance and procedures in foreign policy. I told him that I had no confidence in the intelligence community, that I had been misled, lied to, cut out. I felt that CIA analysis was distorted by strong views about policy. I continued to read "The President's Daily Brief," in part to know what was being put before him. The CIA, I told Carlucci, had been unable to perceive that change was coming in the Soviet Union. When Gorbachev first appeared at the helm, the CIA said he was "just talk," just another Soviet attempt to deceive us. As that line became increasingly untenable, the CIA changed its tune: Gorbachev was serious about change, but the Soviet Union had a powerfully entrenched and largely successful system that was incapable of being changed; so Gorbachev would fail in his attempt to change it. When it became evident that the Soviet Union was, in fact, changing, the CIA line was that the changes wouldn't really make a difference.

Carlucci heard me out, but I could see that as a former deputy director of the CIA, he was offended by my attack on the agency. I was discouraged by our first long one-on-one session. If he was uneasy with my views of the CIA, I was uneasy with the desire he expressed to rebuild the NSC staff into analysts, policymakers, arbiters, and operators all rolled into one. While I was relieved to have a man of Frank's competence and integrity on the job, we did not get off to a good start.

*   *   *

My other colleague in a new capacity was Robert Gates, now acting director of the CIA. On January 5 he telephoned me in the early afternoon. Frank Carlucci had told him, he said, of my complaints about the agency. So I repeated them for Gates directly. "I don't have any confidence in the intelligence community," I told Gates. "I feel you all have very strong policy views. I wouldn't trust anything you guys said about Iran no matter what. I feel you try to manipulate me. So you have a very dissatisfied customer. If this were a business, I'd find myself another supplier. I feel bad about my state of mind, as I have historically been a supporter of the agency. Now I feel that the CIA is an alternative State Department with its own strong policy views. I want to have my confidence rebuilt. The DCI [director of central intelligence] should not be part of the policy process; heavy involvement just can't help but influence you. In the policy business you develop a bias. The CIA should be objective, and if it is not, that means what you say must be discounted."

We agreed to talk further, and in the late afternoon on January 20, 1987, Gates came to my office. "I want to express my attitudes and get your reaction," I told him. "Here is this 'intelligence community,' which I've known something about over the years, since I was budget director and reorganized the intelligence budget process. Later, as treasury secretary, I worked hard to help the CIA develop its capacity in economics and used the agency's excellent work on crop estimates in the USSR and on estimates of the changing patterns of supply and demand and of explosive price changes for oil in the early 1970s. I was a member of the President's Foreign Intelligence Advisory Board. So I've known and respected the CIA and tried to help. But since becoming secretary of state, I've gradually come to be very disappointed in the intelligence community. You have fantastic technical capability. But there must be an attitude toward me and the State Department that is very wary—you deal out intelligence as you deem appropriate. I feel an effort is made to manipulate me by the selection of material you send my way."

The CIA has very strong foreign policy views on Central America, Southern Africa, Iran, Afghanistan, and the Soviet Union, I told Gates. "I agree with some of those views, but not with others. The CIA gets involved operationally. With Iran, your involvement clearly colors your analysis. The intelligence follows the point of view. When the CIA runs covert operations, you must build a wall around those operations." I reviewed at length my struggle against the CIA over Iran policy. "On Iran, I'm struggling to help the president. I see what is being fed to him. Cave[1] is in the meeting, and the president is told Iran has stopped supporting

1. George Cave was the CIA member of the Oliver North team in dealing with Iran. See Chapter 39 for an account of his involvement in analysis and operations and his briefing of the president and others, including me, at a National Security Planning Group meeting on Monday, November 24, 1986.

terrorism. This is what happens when policy and analysis get mixed up. The president gets bum dope. The director of central intelligence was *involved*. He had a conflict of interest with the president, and he was the president's trusted adviser. Then I find out we provided intelligence to Iran about Iraq. I felt ashamed when I read it. It's awful. Your nine-point agenda: it's revolting! I'm not blaming the nine-point agenda on you. Then Armacost works out talking points for the Frankfurt meeting,[2] and Casey calls the president and changes the talking points to include policy. Then Cave sticks around and has a second meeting. So I'm very dissatisfied. We need good intelligence. On our Moscow embassy, the intelligence community assaults us. State has made mistakes, but your assaults are almost joyful," I told Gates.

"So you have a big, powerful machine not under good control," I said. "I distrust what comes out of it. I put Mort Abramowitz in charge of State's intelligence bureau because he understands policy. But I told him, 'Now you are *out* of the policy business!' I almost threw him out of his job when he got involved with our Philippine policy. The CIA should have nothing to do with policy. You have to keep objectivity in analysis. But the intelligence community is not a constructive part of my life; it is a problem. It is telling the president things that I'm not aware of and that I don't trust. This is a severe statement, but it is my belief. I have to stop and say to myself, 'What point are they trying to make?' I am in a bad frame of mind and hope you can straighten me out. You have a high standing," I said.

Gates responded: "I am deeply disturbed by your attitude. The intelligence community is not a monolith. There are great differences. The analytical part of the CIA is separate from the director of operations, very separate. 'The President's Daily Brief' is not seen by the managers of covert operations—not seen before distribution by me or Casey. It is the genuine view of analysts who are not in operations. So all you see from us is done in isolation from the director of central intelligence, his deputy, and covert operations. Analysts don't know the details of covert operations except for one or two in order to review them and put realism into such operations. They are basically isolated. The dissemination of reports is done automatically, not by me or Casey. You get them all. The clandestine service thinks the State Department is more secure than the Department of Defense. So point one is, separation is real."

I knew that was *supposed to be* the policy, but I also knew that the policy was *not* always the reality. I had seen the result of a lack of separation between analysis and operations in the case of Iran. I felt that Gates was

2. See Chapter 39 for a description of this important meeting, held on December 13, 1986, as a result of which I learned shocking details of Oliver North's dealings with Iran. Among the issues of a nine-point agenda under negotiation was U.S. involvement in seeking release of the Dawa prisoners, in jail in Kuwait for terrorist acts.

giving me an idealized picture of what was an altogether different reality.

"The national intelligence officers [NIOs] represent the director of central intelligence at SIGs [Senior Interagency Groups], IGs [Interagency Groups], and other meetings," Gates continued. "They are inclined to offer their own opinion and venture beyond a legitimate intelligence role. NIEs [National Intelligence Estimates] don't do that. But national intelligence officers have strong views. So I need to rein in NIOs so they represent the intelligence community's views, not their personal opinions. This is an area that affects what you see. I'm trying to correct it. Then there is Casey's role. At the NSC table, he gives his own views."

"If he is replaced," I told Gates, "I think his successor should *not* be a member of the cabinet; that stands for the policy process. Casey is the only director of central intelligence ever to be in the cabinet."

"You are important to us," Gates said, deflecting my remark. "We have trouble with the Department of Defense. We have terrible fights within the CIA. This lends credence to our objectivity, I feel. I have given the analysts a very hard time on Gorbachev analysis. He is changing all the rules. There is turmoil, and we haven't conveyed that. Iran is a special case. Our people are outraged at the idea of 'moderates' there."

"Send them my compliments," I said.

"I spoke to our employees," Gates said. "I told them the CIA is too passive. We let the NSC staff establish the ground rules and the compartmentalization. Iran left the CIA as unhappy as anyone. My message is: I can understand your feelings, but on most problems it is less because the CIA has a point of view than that it doesn't agree with the [State] Department's view. We won't let them cross from description to prescription. So I urge you to call us on your questions. The odds are extraordinarily high you are reading our analyst's view and not my or Bill's agenda. Your heartburn, I believe, comes out of meetings, not out of reports. Meetings are where the personal views come out."

I didn't agree with his assessment, but I would do my best to make a fresh start with Gates. I also knew that he was, as a top official of the agency, a part of the very developments that caused me such deep concern. I was wary. He sat at the top of an extraordinarily well financed and powerful outfit.

Almost as though the fates decided it was time for some comic relief, the allegation arose that I had a tattoo of a tiger on my rear end. Speculation abounded. Did I or didn't I? If I did, under what circumstances could this have happened to the staid secretary of state? On January 23, in the midst of a blizzard that was disrupting Washington, I was to testify on the Hill. Despite four-wheel drive and tire chains, I was late arriving at the hearing room. As I entered, stomping the snow from my boots, the committee chairman introduced me by saying, "The secretary of state is here, and I'm sure has something on his hind." The next day, at the noon press briefing, State Department spokeswoman Phyllis Oakley was barraged with questions about, as one reporter put it, "the tale about the tail." "I'm not in a position to comment," Mrs. Oakley replied. I myself adopted a "neither confirm nor deny" policy.

Swimming Against the Tide

A big problem was that President Reagan kept saying—and he truly believed it—that we had not traded arms for hostages. I had to keep trying to make him realize that indeed we had. The president had completely buffaloed himself about this matter. Conducting the business of the U.S. government in early 1987 was like swimming against a powerful tide. The entire surrounding environment of Iran-Contra threatened to catch the administration in an undertow, as Watergate had in the Nixon years. Clearly, the American people felt that Ronald Reagan had been hurt— and had disappointed them. But Iran-Contra was different from Watergate in innumerable ways. A most important difference was that the people wanted Ronald Reagan to recover and to see his presidency restored.

Washington continued to be disrupted by heavy snowfall. The temperature was not far above zero on the night of January 27, 1987, when President Reagan emerged from the White House for Capitol Hill to deliver his State of the Union message. He sought to take responsibility for the Iran-Contra mess, saying "mistakes were made," but he made clear that his greatest regret was that the hostages had not been released. Indeed, only a few days earlier, Terry Waite, the archbishop of Canterbury's aide, disappeared after leaving his Beirut hotel to meet with Hezbollah representatives. And then, on January 24, four professors (three of whom were Americans) from Beirut University College—Alann Steen, Jesse Turner, Robert Polhill, and Mithel Eshwan Singh—were taken hostage.

In attempting to reconstruct our counterterrorism policy, I had to be more vigilant than ever. The situation, I feared, might now actually become even worse. The president's speech did not convey a strong message that there would be no more arms-for-hostages deals. At about this time an opportunity developed that enabled me to pursue an alternative approach aimed at getting the hostages released,[3] thereby giving me an additional

3. Jean Sutherland, wife of hostage Tom Sutherland, called on me and presented what she regarded as an opportunity: the possibility of an indirect dialogue with Sheik Hussein Fadlallah, the spiritual leader of Hezbollah. During eighteen months of exchanges through a third party, Fadlallah's view seemed to shift from advocate to opponent of hostage taking. Nevertheless, in the end, so far as we could tell, he could do nothing to bring about the hostages' release. The hostage holders continued to demand the release of the Dawa prisoners held in Kuwait in exchange for the hostages' freedom. Such a swap was totally unacceptable to us. When the Dawa prisoners became "free" after the Iraqi invasion of Kuwait in August 1990, I felt that our hostages would finally somehow be released as well. In fact, all were out before the end of 1991, the last being Terry Anderson.

argument in my effort to keep the president from going back to yet another version of an arms-for-hostages fiasco.

The president told me that he and Ed Meese visited Bill Casey in the hospital and found Casey alert but hardly able to speak. Casey gave the president his resignation; the president asked him to serve as "counselor to the president." Casey was moved deeply and had tears in his eyes, the president told me. The president then named Robert Gates, without consulting Carlucci or me, to succeed Casey as CIA director. This nomination was subsequently withdrawn amid uncertainty about Gates's own role in the Iran-Contra affair. Bill Webster, director of the FBI, was then installed as director of the CIA in order to give that agency fresh and experienced leadership.

Channels of Confusion

Meanwhile, the world seemed to have been turned upside down since the Reykjavik summit in October 1986. I wondered what the Soviets would do now as they saw the president weakened. I knew that a wounded presidency would have a big impact on my own effectiveness. The president agreed that I should propose to the Soviets that we send Paul Nitze and Richard Perle to Moscow to probe how best to move forward. Word came back from Moscow: Nitze and Perle were "not what we have in mind." The presence of Perle, the Soviets said, would make talks "pointless." They were misjudging Perle, who was tough-minded but creative. Our initiative went nowhere.

The Soviets by early 1987 seemed to be communicating with us via Larry Horowitz, an aide to Senator Ted Kennedy. I trusted Kennedy but was apprehensive: I was leery of back-channel communications. Frank Carlucci pointed out that Horowitz was sending telex messages about the Soviets that could easily be intercepted by European governments. Carlucci thought that the Soviets might be using this kind of channel to alarm our European allies and increase tensions within NATO. I told Carlucci how futile I thought it was to try to puzzle out the Soviets' purpose behind their words and pattern of conduct, but I agreed with Frank that we should move the dialogue back into regular channels, where we knew that it was Gorbachev speaking to us.

We heard through Senator Kennedy's aide that the Soviet delegation in Geneva would be headed by Yuli Vorontsov, who would also be designated their representative for any private-channel communications. That sounded to me as though someone in the Kremlin also wanted to get back to the proper channels. With the president's approval, I instructed Max Kampelman, our overall coordinator of U.S.-Soviet arms control negotiations in Geneva and therefore Vorontsov's opposite number, to inform Vorontsov that he would be our representative in any private-channel communications.

Frank Carlucci, I then discovered, wanted to work with former Ambassador Dobrynin in a separate U.S.-Soviet channel and wanted to travel to Moscow to conduct negotiations. It was like Bud McFarlane all over again. I put my foot down hard: no. I would not accept the insertion of the national security adviser into an operational role, particularly as Carlucci's first item of business. Don Regan and Carlucci were trying to convince the president to place central operational duties in NSC staff hands again. Carlucci claimed to me that the president and Don Regan thought the arms control effort needed someone closer to the president than Kampelman.

"This is idiotic!" I told Mike Armacost. "Frank Carlucci should know better than to try to go running around the world being the negotiator. The Ted Kennedy channel is bad enough. This is worse. What a disappointment—the White House is going to screw everything up again! They are running scared when it comes to the Soviets. They're demoralized and amateurish." I then argued to President Reagan that the Kampelman-Vorontsov channel in Geneva should be the only private channel. He agreed.

The uproar about what channel to use with the Soviets masked the real problem: the massive, continuing refusal of many key players in the administration to exercise any creativity in our policy, whatever the channel. Cap Weinberger had opened a presentation at a Situation Room meeting by saying, "Max [Kampelman] and the Communists want to . . ." I hit the roof, and so did Max.

Despite the back-channel, multiple-channel processes that had been going on with the Soviets and constant rumors that they wanted to move ahead rapidly on arms control, no substance emerged on that topic either via Kampelman in Geneva or Art Hartman in Moscow. Instead—and I welcomed this—the Soviets, Art Hartman informed me, wanted to talk about Afghanistan. They were ready to discuss a timetable for Soviet troop withdrawal and a government of national unity that would include the Afghan freedom fighters and even leaders of armed Afghan groups outside Afghanistan. We would be premature to engage on the agenda as they stated it, I thought. We would not accept a government broadened out of the present regime. Nevertheless, it was an important blink, and I was encouraged.

There was intense debate in Washington about the Strategic Defense Initiative. SDI provided our strongest leverage, but SDI's most ardent advocates were endangering its continuation far more than its opponents were. "I'm so resentful of the way Weinberger proceeds," Nitze told me on January 15. "The president is intolerant of anyone not fully behind SDI, and Weinberger uses this. He [Weinberger] goes and testifies and says we must deploy right away. What he proposes violates the ABM Treaty. It's not just a research system under his new concept. Now he proposes a space-based system based on kinetic energy. That will take a lot of engineering work—mainly to get the weight down. Deployment in space is in violation of the ABM Treaty." Paul pointed out that we were far away from the point where a deployment decision could be responsibly considered. Weinberger simply wanted to break the ABM Treaty. Weinberger's advocacy would create a backlash in Congress that could kill SDI *and* strip us of our negotiating leverage with the Soviets.

Although the Soviets continued to say nothing of real substantive importance to us about arms control, they proposed at the end of January that I go to Moscow. Max's counterpart, Vorontsov, hinted that both START and INF were doable. Max was now reporting that his sessions with Vorontsov were busy, constructive, and fruitful. If we made some progress in the next week or so, I was ready for Moscow. But as always, tough negotiations would be taking place within our own side. The ultimate shoot-out with Cap Weinberger was not far off, as he continued to urge the president to take steps beyond what was remotely feasible on SDI.

On the other hand, in diplomacy even bad ideas have their uses. All Cap's talk about the United States actually "deploying" a defensive system in the near future was likely to make our offer at Reykjavik of a ten-year period of no deployment all the more attractive to the Soviets. Cap's purpose, however, was to get all that was agreed to at Reykjavik tossed on the scrap heap. At a National Security Planning Group (NSPG) meeting on February 3, Weinberger pressed the president to go forward with a phased SDI deployment and to state publicly that our broad interpretation of the ABM Treaty would make such a step permissible.

I urged a different approach. On behalf of the president, I asked Abe Sofaer to undertake a careful study of the ABM Treaty, building on his examination of the negotiating record and looking at the interpretation of the treaty presented to the Senate by the Nixon administration, the Senate ratification debates, and the record of subsequent conduct.

However Abe's study might come out, I knew that if we adopted the "broad" interpretation at a time when Weinberger was talking up deployment, that would mean a confrontation with Congress and a setback in our ability to get the funds from Congress that the SDI program required. Bill Crowe, chairman of the Joint Chiefs, agreed with me and said so to the president. Crowe also stated flatly that abandonment of the ABM Treaty at this time would prove more advantageous to the Soviets than to us. When proponents of SDI leaked purported statements by the president in this NSPG meeting indicating his readiness to deploy and his impatience with the ABM Treaty, a torrent of criticism was unleashed in Congress and among our allies. Congress was right for the wrong reasons. In reality, we were nowhere near being able to deploy a strategic defensive system that even remotely approached the aspirations of SDI.

*   *   *

I sent a note to the president. "Obviously, instantaneous deployment is not even conceptually possible," I said. Each phase of SDI deployment, I argued, must make a contribution to stability. And the first phase should be undertaken only when the overall structure of deployment could be envisaged with clarity and confidence. At this stage, that was not possible.

"A related but separate question," I said, "involves permitted activity under the ABM Treaty. We have stated that a broad interpretation is warranted by an examination of the negotiating record—but we have designed the SDI program within the framework of the narrow interpretation. The project engineers now want to make some additional tests at some point down the road, and planning for the tests should begin now. Such tests cannot be performed within the framework of the narrow definition of the ABM Treaty. I believe that shifting our interpretation from narrow to broad is warranted, but many people dispute the validity of the broad interpretation. So, if such a decision is to be effective and consistent with support for funding SDI, we must engage in a convincing process of examining the evidence collaboratively with the Senate."

I then outlined the steps Abe Sofaer planned to take and urged that the president agree to this cooperative process. I also again warned the president, "As we move toward a less threatening world from a nuclear standpoint, either through defense against ballistic missiles or fewer of them, or both, we must recognize the enhanced importance of defense against cruise missiles and bombers, and of conventional forces."

I had clashed with Cap Weinberger on all of these points. On Wednesday, February 4, I saw the president for my regular private meeting. As I reviewed my arguments personally with him, I found him far more subdued and realistic than Cap; he seemed to realize that Weinberger's zeal for SDI, which far surpassed our present ability to deploy, had needlessly stirred up a potentially devastating resistance to the entire SDI program.

Suzanne Massie had come to the State Department on February 3 carrying a handwritten message that she said was from Gorbachev for Reagan: "U.S. assistance in national reconciliation in Afghanistan would be very positively regarded in Moscow. The Soviet side in that case might be of help in untangling some other regional conflicts. That would also facilitate reaching compromise on the problems of arms reductions."

President Reagan had sent the message over to me with his own comment on top: "I know that you are seeing Suzanne Massie this evening. She delivered this handwritten note from Gorbachev. He asked her to deliver this to me personally. They don't want to go public with this proposal if we are going to say no. I don't think we can say yes—if they plan to withdraw troops but leave a Communist government." The president was right. But I was skeptical that this message actually came from Gorbachev. It had been given to Suzanne Massie by Radomir Bogdanov, deputy director of the Soviets' Institute of the USA and Canada and a KGB officer. I welcomed any indication that the Soviets felt they needed to get out of Afghanistan, but I could see that they were trying to extract a high price from us for doing so, particularly in pairing Afghanistan implicitly with Nicaragua. The Soviets also seemed to condition progress on arms control upon our letting the Soviets depart from Kabul on their terms. This was yet another instance of the confusion that multiple, unofficial channels create.

Cracks in the Soviet Bloc

Changes in the Soviet Union were affecting not only the Soviet position in Afghanistan, but also, more importantly, they were having a deep impact on the Eastern European satellite nations of the Soviet bloc. When I had visited Vienna in November 1986 for the CSCE meeting that included all of the Warsaw Pact countries, I had Roz Ridgway and Tom Simons meet with the Poles to encourage them to initiate internal changes that moved away from the Soviets. The Poles were interested. I talked this over with John Whitehead, whom I had earlier asked to give special attention to the idea of encouraging change in these countries. John suggested that he make an extended trip to Eastern Europe. I agreed. I could have spent only a day in each capital; Whitehead could stay longer and dig in.

My effort to encourage change in Eastern Europe was actively opposed by many on the NSC staff, in the CIA, and in the Defense Department—people who believed that we should shun all "evil empire" leaders and avoid visits to them that would "enhance their credibility." For a time Chief of Staff Don Regan even tried to deny John Whitehead the use of an air force plane to keep him from traveling to this emerging area of positive opportunity. Don eventually relented. Whitehead's trip was finally designated a "presidential mission."

On February 9, Whitehead returned from a swing around Eastern Europe. "Things are changing," he declared. What he had seen had charged him up: the changes in the Soviet Union were releasing the Eastern Europeans to undertake change themselves, in some cases, faster and deeper than was appreciated in the West. The Soviets, preoccupied increasingly with their own internal problems, were becoming less instantaneous and less ominous in their negative response to deviations from Communist orthodoxy elsewhere in the bloc. As a result, some leaders in Eastern Europe were taking a longer and longer lead off first base every time they had a chance. I began to think that one of them might steal second and break the bloc open before long. All the leaders that Whitehead met, even the most hard-line of the Communists, were so eager for good relations with the United States that they backed off every confrontation.

In Poland, for example, Whitehead was informed upon arrival that Solidarity leader Lech Walesa would not be able to come to Warsaw to meet with him. "Why not?" Whitehead asked.

"He works in the shipyard in Gdańsk, and he has used up all of his vacation days," Whitehead was told. Solidarity had been declared illegal, and Walesa was restricted to Gdańsk and not permitted to travel.

"If Walesa is not permitted to come to Warsaw," Whitehead responded, "I will fly to Gdańsk instead of meeting here in Warsaw with General Jaruzelski, as I am currently scheduled to do." Whitehead stood up, shook hands, left the room, and drove to his hotel. It was a bold, savvy move. Whitehead realized how embarrassing it would be to the Communists if, in this first high-level American visit in many years, a representative of President Reagan came to Poland, visited Walesa, and had not even seen Jaruzelski.

The Communist authorities folded. "Everything is okay," they sent word later to Whitehead. "You misunderstood about Walesa. He's on his way here now from Gdańsk." The tales of Whitehead's travels were a delight to me.

Whitehead met with Lech Walesa at the U.S. ambassador's residence, occupied by John Davis, then deputy chief of mission. The meeting was private, but we ensured that press and photographers were present for Walesa's arrival and greeting at the door by Whitehead and Davis. The pictures, which appeared around the world the next day, demonstrated strong U.S. support for Solidarity without a word being uttered. The pictures did not make the Polish press.

Whitehead's session with General Jaruzelski took place as scheduled. For almost three hours, the atmosphere was tense and confrontational. Jaruzelski was a forbidding figure, Whitehead recounted. He carried himself erectly and stiffly and never smiled. His eyes were obscured by heavily tinted lenses, from which Jaruzelski could see out while Whitehead looked into his silver-mirrored lenses. Jaruzelski did not say a word of greeting; he just shook hands. He showed no reaction to John's comments on Polish relations with the United States, but when John turned to human rights, Jaruzelski exploded. "Mr. Whitehead, I cannot allow you to continue. You are interfering in our internal affairs. I cannot allow you to do that. We are a sovereign nation. You have your system. We have ours. I do not interfere with yours, and you must not interfere with ours."

"You are right, Mr. President," Whitehead told Jaruzelski. "We have no right to interfere in your internal affairs, but we do certainly have a right to choose our friends. And in choosing our friends, we prefer to be friendly with countries that treat their people decently. What I am here to propose," Whitehead said in keeping with our planned approach, "is a simple, step-by-step process in which you will agree to make some small concessions to our concerns in the human rights area, and we will respond by making equivalent concessions to your concerns in the trade and investment area. By this process we would expect that our relations would steadily improve, just as fast as you are willing to go."

Jaruzelski said with considerable anger: "I know that I am hated in your country. Two years ago I went to New York, but I was not allowed to go to Washington, and the president would not see me. Your secretary of defense said that I was 'a Russian general in a Polish uniform.' For me, there could be no worse insult. I am a Pole for many generations. We would not survive if we tried to be independent of the Soviets. Who do you think is responsible for keeping us still a separate country and not just another Soviet republic? Someday you in America will realize who is the real Polish patriot who has kept his country alive all these years."

"These last personal remarks were bitter," Whitehead said, "but revealing." Jaruzelski cared about approval from the outside world, I could see. That made me hopeful that he would move ahead on our step-by-step process, and eventually he did.

Our work for change in Eastern Europe was promising: I congratulated John on his deft performance.

Road Blocks to Moscow

The president was again focused on moving forward with the Soviets, but I had a tough time juggling the great array of issues involved in the midst of the ever-expanding daily revelations about the Iran-Contra affair. On February 9, 1987, I learned that Bud McFarlane was in Bethesda Naval Hospital after an apparent suicide attempt. I was especially distressed: I had not been in touch with Bud even though he had reached out to contact me. Abe Sofaer had advised me not to talk to him or any other former members of the NSC staff involved in the Iran-Contra affair.

I was also still being accused of "not supporting the president." On February 20, Congressman Jack Kemp called for my resignation on that count. I was about to leave for China when the news broke on February 26 that the report of the Tower Commission was out. Cap Weinberger and I—despite our vehement and continuing opposition to the arms-for-hostages effort—were criticized for having "distanced" ourselves from the president and I was admonished for requesting "to be informed only as necessary to perform his job." In a grudging concession, the report said that "Shultz may have been actively misled by VADM Poindexter."

Word came to me in Hong Kong on February 28 that Don Regan had resigned, after having learned on television that he had been replaced. I was not surprised. By this time, Don had lost the confidence of the president and, for that matter, had lost his own confidence in the president. He had tried to run a tight ship, as in his days at Merrill Lynch, but the ship had sailed away from him. Judging from his support for Frank Carlucci's efforts to give the NSC staff a continuing operational role, I felt he had not learned the basic lesson of the Iran-Contra affair. Political Washington was ready to see him go. The *New York Times* "quotation of the day" was:

> Dear Mr. President:
> I hereby resign as chief of staff to the President of the United States.
>   Respectfully yours,
>   Donald T. Regan

The new chief of staff was Howard Baker. This was great news: Howard was an extraordinarily able man and an experienced politician, having retired a year earlier as Senate majority leader. The White House staff operation would be in good hands. I could work easily with Howard, who had been a friend since my days in the Nixon administration.

Almost as though out of the blue, on February 28, Mikhail Gorbachev not only publicized his Reykjavik offer to eliminate all intermediate-range missiles in Europe and limit those in Asia to 100 warheads, but he expressed a willingness to separate negotiations on this INF issue from our continuing differences on SDI. It was a significant move. Ronald Reagan's bold zero-zero proposal, made back in 1981 and derided then by many in the arms control community and in the media, was on its way to being vindicated.

My prospective trip to Moscow suddenly became more promising. After back-and-forth cables between me in Asia and Max Kampelman in Geneva, I agreed to meet Shevardnadze and Gorbachev in Moscow in mid-April. The meeting, announced on March 6 by Frank Carlucci at the White House, would enable me to force my way through the interagency bureaucracy. Perhaps all of the talk in Washington about the "broad" definition of the ABM Treaty and "deploying SDI" had played a part in inducing Gorbachev to take this step, to shift the focus of the debate, and perhaps to try to slow us down on SDI.

Back in Washington, the Tower Commission report had inflamed Cap Weinberger, and he asked the White House to make a correction. On March 9, Colin Powell, Cap's former executive assistant who was now deputy to Frank Carlucci at the NSC, sent over to me a statement that the president planned to make in his upcoming Saturday radio talk. Referring to Cap and me, he would say, "It turned out they were right and I was wrong." I didn't like the tone of this: the president should not be put in the position of publicly apologizing to members of his cabinet. I told the president he need not say anything on my account. He responded that the White House lawyers told him not to say that he was wrong and had crossed out the sentence, but he had written it back in: he wanted to recognize that Cap and I had given him good advice.

The real problem with the Tower report, Arthur Liman said when I first met him on March 12, was that it missed the ball completely in not perceiving CIA director Bill Casey's central role. "Oliver North's rabbi was Casey; his father was McFarlane," said Liman, chief counsel of the Senate side of the Iran-Contra investigation. What really bothered me about the Tower report was its whitewash of the flaws in the national security system. Already Frank Carlucci had initiated a pattern of meeting with the Soviet ambassador and other ambassadors as well without the State Department's knowledge, which gave an inestimable advantage to those governments to play one side of the U.S. administration against another.

"In the case of the Iran initiative, the NSC process did not fail, it simply was largely ignored," the Tower report asserted. The report's recommendations were that the national security adviser should be "primarily responsible for managing this [NSC] process on a daily basis." The report based the notion of the NSC adviser's primacy on the theory that cabinet secretaries would inevitably represent departmental interests and that the adviser "is perhaps the one most able to see things from the President's perspective," since "he is unburdened by departmental responsibilities."

The report recommended that the NSC adviser (and, by extension, other NSC staff members) "chair the senior-level committees of the NSC system." Despite all this, the report astonishingly declared that "we urge the Congress not to require Senate confirmation of the National Security Adviser." So the report would put the NSC adviser, who is not accountable to the Congress, in a senior position over cabinet officers who *are* accountable. I was incredulous. Was *this* the lesson learned by the Tower Commission from its review of NSC staff performance in the Iran-Contra affair? Brent Scowcroft, a former NSC adviser under President Ford, I felt, must have dominated the thinking of the commission. I vehemently disagreed with these recommendations.

The President Turns a Corner

I was worried about how the president would do in his first televised press conference of the year, to be held on March 19. I need not have been. He turned a corner: he admitted that his policy had deteriorated into a trade of arms for hostages, accepted "full responsibility," renounced his Iran initiative, and barred a recurrence. "But it could be that the policy was flawed in that it did deteriorate into what I myself, when I went on the air recently, said was arms for hostages," the president said. "No, I would not go down that same road again. . . . We had quite a debate, and it was true that two of our Cabinet members were very much on the other side. And it turned out they were right, because, as I say, it did deteriorate."

Then the president fielded a question: "If I could follow up, Mr. President, you're still arguing that somehow this event deteriorated; it went awry as it went along. I want to know whether you think it was wrong or right in the beginning."

The president responded: "Well, if I hadn't thought it was right in the beginning, we never would have started. . . . But we're not going to try the same thing again, because we see how it worked."

I was enormously relieved to hear these words from the president himself. Tom Shales in the *Washington Post* reported, "If it was a fight, Ronald Reagon won it. He seemed clear-eyed, assertive, emphatic and confident from the very outset of last night's televised press conference. The press, by contrast, occasionally came across as rude and self-important." Other reporters remarked that the president was in command and seemed almost eager to provide the public with an explanation of the initiative. Still, I knew we had a long struggle ahead to regain our confidence and sense of direction. But by this time, I felt confident we were back on track.

CHAPTER 41

Breaking Through
to the Soviets

I was set to arrive in Moscow on April 13, 1987. I thought of this as a real opportunity, extending beyond the traditional issues on our agenda. I wanted to engage in deeper discussions with Gorbachev and Shevardnadze about the shape of the future: the shape of the world five to ten years ahead. Arguments about specific problems tended to consume all the time and therefore set the tone of the relationship. I wanted to look at a different range of problems and opportunities that did not set us against each other but would affect us both in powerful ways. Gorbachev seemed highly alert to a new set of realities. The information age was changing the basis for material and intellectual advance: that is what I wanted to get across to the new Soviet leaders.

I wanted to push for a Soviet decision to leave Afghanistan. Mike Armacost, who had just returned from Moscow, brought back news that the Soviets were putting out the line that their withdrawal would be a defeat for the United States. "Some defeat," I said, laughing. "We could stand defeats like this in Angola, Nicaragua, Cambodia, and Eastern Europe."

Spy Trouble

The situation at the American embassy in Moscow was terrible. The place looked shabby and dispirited, Armacost reported. Our personnel, short-handed and forced to do all the work previously done by 260 Soviet nationals as well as their own jobs, were exhausted. The embassy building was a drab and dusty rabbit warren, and the housekeeping was terrible. Stacks of old newspapers clogged corridors, wastebaskets were unemptied, light fixtures shone a dirty yellow, and extension cords snaked around the floor. The new embassy building, a half-constructed shell, sat down the hill from the old building. This was itself a cause for astonished complaint:

why was our new embassy in a low area, while the new Soviet embassy building in Washington was high on Mount Alto, with a commanding view and clear surveillance lines over the whole city?

The decisions made back in the Nixon administration permitting the Soviets to build on Mount Alto had been a big mistake. At the time, however, the reasoning, including that of the intelligence agencies, was different: the location of the Soviets on Mount Alto gave us a clear line of sight on them, and our location in Moscow denied that to them. The debate, I found, was endless and aggravating. Now I felt we had no choice but to make the old embassy structure more secure and better maintain it, tear the new structure down as insecure, and start construction all over again. I was determined that the Soviets would not move into their new Mount Alto quarters until we received satisfaction and security for our own embassy in Moscow. This was U.S. policy.

Back in January, the marines had announced that Sergeant Clayton Lonetree, a marine security guard at our Moscow embassy, had confessed to passing classified information to a Russian woman with whom he had been involved intimately. I was told on March 24 that a second marine, Corporal Arnold Bracy, was said to have confessed, too: the two embassy marines, while they were on watch together, were alleged to have allowed Soviets to roam through the embassy, go through the "burn bags" for secret papers, and generally have the run of the place at night. The marines were the keepers of all the safe combinations; if the marines had been subverted, the Soviets might have had access to *everything*.

Our embassy in Moscow had been a constant topic of Washington political controversy. Soviet espionage efforts to watch and subvert our people were relentless. The debate was heated as to whether Soviet citizens should continue to be employed by the embassy or whether all jobs should be filled by American citizens. After much soul searching, I became convinced that we should incur the expense involved and replace all Soviets employed in our Moscow embassy. By April 19, 1985, Ambassador Art Hartman had submitted a long-term plan to accomplish this in two phases. First, we would replace Soviets in sensitive jobs, such as drivers and switchboard operators. The replacement process was well under way when the Soviets, in the October 1986 round of espionage expulsions, removed any further debate by prohibiting Soviet citizens from working at our embassy. All Soviet nationals had been withdrawn, leaving the U.S. professional staff with an enormous assortment of chores to perform, from cleaning toilets to standing in line at stores to buy staples for use at the embassy. Electronic eavesdropping and KGB penetration of our embassy, in the context of alleged marine treason, had created an atmosphere so tense and apprehensive that our people were writing everything out by hand: they would not dictate into a tape recorder or even use a typewriter for fear that the

Soviet listening devices would pick up the text. In the information age, the alleged prowess of the KGB had forced our embassy back almost into the preindustrial age.

My trip to Moscow would be drastically affected by this situation. All American embassy communications out of Moscow had to be shut down. Would I have the ability to communicate with the president and the State Department from Moscow? A specially shielded van with an "autonomous communications package" could be flown in; for it to work, I was told, our experts needed to ensure that we had fifteen square feet of "clean" space somewhere on the embassy premises in which to spot the equipment. At the moment, we didn't have it. No room, no telephone, no typewriter, no airwave, not even any outdoor space, could be considered "secure."

The more I heard about the marines in Moscow, the worse the situation sounded and the more difficult to escape the reach of the KGB. Art Hartman described the problem: young men with a fighting spirit were given a passive mission in an isolated, socially impoverished area. Along came Russian women telling the men they were Finnish; therefore they were not suspected of being linked to espionage. A Russian woman working as an embassy cook was fired; then she was hired privately by an American and continued her work for the KGB. A Russian woman working as an embassy barber was fired, so the marines went to a Moscow hotel barbershop where another female, who turned out to be a KGB agent, cut their hair. Every step to improve the situation seemed to make it worse. Nonetheless, I felt that strong, alert supervisors and well-trained marines could do the job right. We could turn the situation around—and must.

At an NSPG meeting on March 27 to address the problem, the damage assessment was huge. Vice President Bush raked Art Hartman over the coals, recalling a cable that Art had sent some months earlier disparaging the criticism of embassy management. The vice president was not alone in his criticism.

The mood of the town was boiling mad—at the Soviets and, among some, at the very existence of our diplomatic relationship with them. Lieutenant General Bill Odom, head of the National Security Agency, said there was "no way" that the United States could get a secure communication facility in place in Moscow in the short time before my scheduled arrival there. Scores of marines had been interviewed and interrogated, I was told, and it was now alleged that on at least thirty occasions, our embassy's supposedly secure interior areas had been penetrated by Soviet agents admitted by marines, sometimes for hours at a time. At the NSPG a photograph was passed around of one of the marines at the annual Marine Ball with his girlfriend—said to be a KGB agent. The U.S. counterintelligence experts were telling me that this was the worst intelligence defeat for the United States since World War II. (Eight of our assets allegedly had been "rolled up" and four killed—more likely, I thought, as a result of information provided by CIA defector Edward Lee Howard, who had just arrived in Moscow.) Fingerpointing and blame placing were widespread—by those outside the administration at the administration and by those inside at each other. There was a sense of fury everywhere.

The foreign service culture reflected American culture: friendly and open, with a desire to get to know people and understand them, to reach out to dissidents in Communist countries and discuss with anyone who would listen the way of thinking in the United States. So we built facilities— embassies—in places that were easily accessible. By contrast, the Soviets kept their people in and walled the world out; they did not encourage interaction. We did not want to live in fortresses. But Soviet espionage had caused us to draw inward. We were not good at being insular, and the effort to "wall ourselves in" strained and demoralized people who served in our embassies in the Communist world. We had focused on defending against Soviet technological techniques of espionage, but the marine scandal appeared to exemplify the oldest trick around.

I asked Ambassador Bill Brown, a marine, a Russian-speaking foreign service officer who was then our envoy to Thailand, to go to Moscow as my man on the spot: to investigate and make recommendations to bring the security situation under control. Responsibility for managing the embassy belonged to the State Department; that meant me. So we had to investigate the problems and manage the security issues. I recognized also that to take responsibility was a way to assert authority.

At the end of March, the media were linking my trip to Moscow with the security disaster there, and the idea was spreading in Congress that I should not go—as a deliberate rebuke to the Soviets for their alleged success in demolishing our embassy security system. Others inside the administration had their own alternatives. Cap Weinberger wanted me to demand that the Soviets meet me in Geneva. Lieutenant General Odom wanted the meeting held in Helsinki and urged us to close our Moscow embassy altogether until we (meaning the NSA, his agency) could vouch for its security. Cap and others argued that we should take everything off the table that had been achieved at Reykjavik. My only ally on the White House staff for going forward and pursuing our agenda with the Soviets— without being derailed by "linkage" to the security debacle—was the amiable and steady Howard Baker. His backing was a big boost. My main support came from the president, who was furious at the Soviets but determined that I should go to Moscow and try to build on the momentum for Soviet change.

I met with our technical security experts. Lieutenant General Odom favored a secure communications van: it could be flown to Sheremetyevo Airport outside Moscow on an air force plane and kept on board. When I wanted to talk to the president, I could take the long ride to the airport,

In the Iran-Contra hearings, I testify about the battle royal over setting policy toward Iran and my fight to stop, for good, ongoing efforts to sell arms for hostages. July 23, 1987. Paul Hosefros/*New York Times* Pictures

Addressing the XVI General Assembly of the Organization of American States, Guatemala, November 11, 1986.

Roz Ridgway and I at the North Atlantic Council, Brussels, December 10, 1986.

John Whitehead greets Lech Walesa in early February 1987 at the American ambassador's residence in Warsaw, Poland. The picture, which appeared in European newspapers, carried a powerful message.

I confer with Hans-Dietrich Genscher and Peter Carrington at NATO, June 11, 1987.

"WELL, BACK TO THE REAL WORLD"

Iran-Contra: after the Shultz testimony, August 1987. From *Herblock at Large* (New York: Pantheon Books, 1987)

In Prime Minister Shamir's office, Jerusalem, October 16, 1987. Matty Stern, USIA, Tel Aviv

"George, I'm home," says Ida Nudel in Jerusalem. O'Bie is at the right. October 1987.
Matty Stern, USIA, Tel Aviv

Eduard Shevardnadze, Mikhail Gorbachev, Frank Carlucci, and I in Moscow,
October 23, 1987.

After the success of the Washington summit, Nancy Reagan, Ken Duberstein, Howard Baker, Charlie Wick, President Reagan, and I share a laugh at the White House, December 1987. Ronald Reagan Presidential Library

Garner, *Washington Times.*

Mikhail Gorbachev and I in Moscow—all smiles before what turned out to be a traumatic meeting, October 23, 1987. (Paul Nitze is in the background.) Ronald Reagan Presidential Library

"It's time to go," I say at a White House departure ceremony. With me are Colin Powell, Howard Baker, Nelson Ledsky, Frank Carlucci, and Roz Ridgway, February 1988.
Ronald Reagan Presidential Library

Charlie Hill at Spaso House, Moscow, February 1988.

Margaret Thatcher, President Reagan, and I at a NATO meeting in Brussels, March 2, 1988.

With crowds in the streets of Kiev, April 1988.

Colin Powell, President Reagan, and I in the Oval Office, April 1988.

I confer with Mikhail Gorbachev as President Reagan talks with Eduard Shevardnadze and Andrei Gromyko during the Moscow summit, May 30, 1988. Ronald Reagan Presidential Library

President Reagan toasts Margaret Thatcher in the White House on her last visit during the Reagan presidency, June 2, 1988. Ronald Reagan Presidential Library

In the office of Egypt's President Hosni Mubarak, Ittihadiyya Palace, Cairo, June 7, 1988.

With Deng Xiaoping in the Great Hall of the People, Beijing, July 15, 1988.

I am awarded a Princeton tiger by the traveling press on my final Asia tour as secretary of state, July 1988.

A tête-à-tête: Nancy Reagan and I in the Oval Office, August 1988. Ronald Reagan Presidential Library

Arriving at La Paz, Bolivia, August 8, 1988. Descending the stairs are: Luigi Einaudi, Elliott Abrams, Chuck Redman, David Greenlee, O'Bie, and I.

A terrorist bombs my motorcade, missing my car by a few seconds. La Paz, Bolivia, August 8, 1988.

Nancy Reagan, pleased with her reception after her speech on the use of illegal drugs, UN General Assembly, October 25, 1988. Ronald Reagan Presidential Library

I demonstrate my farewell gift—a suitcase containing a miniature train, each car of which represented a NATO country—from the NATO foreign ministers. President Reagan is ready to take the controls as Ken Duberstein looks on, December 14, 1988.
Ronald Reagan Presidential Library

The "Shultz Plan" for Arab-Israeli peace, 1988. "WELL, AT LEAST THEY AGREE ON SOMETHING." Paul Conrad, copyright 1988, *Los Angeles Times* Syndicate, reprinted with permission

I receive the Medal of Freedom from President Reagan, January 19, 1989.
Ronald Reagan Presidential Library

My eyes well up as I bid farewell to the State Department. "California, here I come!"
January 19, 1989.

get in the van, drive it off the plane, and race around the airport while sending my message to Washington. I regarded the plan as ridiculous. It deepened my doubts about our intelligence services. Such schemes, I sometimes suspected, were advanced in the hope of thwarting *any* contact with the Soviets. "Come on," I said to Odom, "we can fly in a White House Communications Agency [WHCA, pronounced walk-a] van, drive it into the embassy compound, and keep it under guard at all times. I can go to it when needed and communicate with the president without Soviet eavesdropping."

Pressure was mounting. The State Department was under assault. The idea of lie detector tests for all State employees in sensitive spots surfaced again. The CIA never seemed to miss a chance to apply its own management techniques to everyone else. Henry Kissinger was telling people that I should not go to Moscow under these circumstances. Opinion on Capitol Hill toward the State Department and the idea of improving relations with the Soviet Union was intense and negative. State's congressional liaison people reported that Congress was seething: proposals were surfacing to break relations with Moscow, shut down our embassy, and impose the death penalty on Americans involved in treasonable security violations.

I received a cable on April 9 from Jack Matlock, who had just taken over as our new ambassador in Moscow. (The message had to be hand-carried to Frankfurt, Germany, and telegraphed from there.) Matlock had talked to Dobrynin. The Soviets were moving our way again. They wanted, Dobrynin said, to sign the INF Treaty before the end of 1987 and, if possible, reach agreement on the basic elements of a START Treaty in time for a summit in late 1987.

Abe Sofaer was deep into his study of all the records of the ABM Treaty, as Senator Sam Nunn blasted away at him. Abe was feeling for the first time the heat of a Washingtonian attack on his character. He had come to town as "the judge," with an air of distinguised invincibility, and now found himself in a street fight. His wife, he said, was distraught at the personal attacks on him—assertions that he was compromising his own legal integrity to serve the political desires of Ronald Reagan. I was thoroughly convinced that Abe was doing his study properly. The trouble was that the ABM record was ambiguous and the issue was intensely political.

Abe said he was finding that our negotiators back in 1972 had tried to nail down every point and that had they succeeded, the treaty certainly would have confined our work on SDI within what was known as the "narrow" definition of the treaty. But the Soviets had insisted on language (Agreed Statement D) that kept the treaty from covering forms of equipment based on new discoveries in science that might come about in the future ("other physical principles"). When our negotiators came before the Senate to urge ratification of the treaty, they tended to argue that the treaty was watertight and restrictive. In practice we followed this "narrow" definition of the treaty. So Abe was saying that the treaty language and the negotiating record were, in fact, "broad" and therefore seemed to permit more extensive testing in support of SDI research. Sam Nunn was saying that what was presented to the Senate for ratification was "narrow" treaty language and that if we were to change, Senate action would be required. The president, in Nunn's view, could not unilaterally change the meaning of a treaty as presented to the Senate, regardless of what the treaty itself said. The Senate's constitutional role and prerogatives were involved. If intellectually stimulating, the debate was politically devastating.

The immediate question was, what about me and my trip to Moscow? Rumors were circulating that marine guards had been subverted at our Leningrad consulate and Vienna and Budapest embassies. The security agencies were still backtracking on whether any facility I might use in Moscow could be certified as secure. And Congress was on the warpath. Representatives Dan Mica and Olympia Snowe, chairman and ranking minority member of the House Foreign Affairs Subcommittee on International Operations, went to Moscow and declared that our embassy had been "fully compromised."

A National Security Decision Directive (NSDD) had been issued and was cast in stern language: I was given tight instructions, almost as if to assure that I not come back from Moscow with any progress toward an agreement. While the president supported me in going forward with this trip, he had sided with Cap Weinberger in giving me almost no room to maneuver, even drawing back here and there from positions we had taken at Reykjavik. The tightness of my instructions had been promptly leaked, attempting to put as much of a chill on my mission as possible.

On April 10, the day before I was to leave for the Soviet Union, Senator Edward Kennedy came to see me bringing with him his aide, Larry Horowitz, who had served as a channel from the Soviets earlier in the year. They came into my back office, where I was sitting on a sofa, reading, with my leg propped up, following doctor's orders, having pulled a muscle playing tennis. There was banter about my "lying down on the job" and "getting a leg up on Cap."

Horowitz said that he had been in Moscow: Soviet officials had asked him to "clarify" some points for me before my trip. First, Horowitz repeated what Senator Kennedy had stressed: "They [the Soviets] said your trip would be the most important contact since Ronald Reagan came to office." The Soviets, he said, were changing their definition of "laboratory." By saying that SDI research should be confined to the laboratory, they meant only to say that the ABM Treaty prohibited testing and deployment, "but the definition of what is testing would be flexible. So the Soviets want you to know that research outside the laboratory would not be considered testing," Horowitz said. I told Kennedy that I appreciated his serious interest—and I did—but that back-channel and special-channel dealing was not the right way to proceed in negotiations with the Soviets.

President Reagan gave me a note to carry to Gorbachev attributing the arms race to the "fundamental distrust" between the two governments and referring indirectly to the situation at our embassy in Moscow as having deepened distrust and increased tensions. The general view in the administration by this time, including that of the president, was that little chance remained for my trip to produce any progress.

Despite all this, I departed for Helsinki and Moscow on Saturday, April 11, after seventy senators had voted "yes" on a resolution *opposing* my Moscow trip. The *Congressional Record* showed that all 100 senators voted. Only ten Republicans voted against the resolution calling on me not to go. The three days were likely to be tough, I knew.

As the airplane took off from Andrews, I wondered whether the Soviets might understand that sending me home in failure would not serve their interests. In terms of negotiating psychology, this might present an opportunity to get something out of them on this round.

The tension was pervasive even as I arrived in Helsinki, where I always stopped before going on to negotiations in Moscow. Jack Matlock, our new ambassador to the Soviet Union, came to Helsinki, where we could discuss, without being bugged, our approach to the meetings that would start the next day in Moscow. When I went to our Helsinki embassy, someone asked me to pose for a photo with the marine security detachment there. I had never seen such jumpy marines. I looked at transcripts of the Sunday television talk shows from Washington: the commentary was highly critical of the Moscow embassy "security collapse" and of my role and that of the State Department.

The investigation of what had happened at our Moscow embassy was revealing a culture of suspicion, of intelligence gathering and counterintelligence surveillance, that was disturbing to me. A siege mentality had set in, and our Moscow presence had become almost a mirror image to that of the Soviets. Our embassy had been transformed from an office in which diplomats work on U.S.-Soviet problems to something more like an "intelligence collection platform." Intelligence agency activities—theirs and ours—dominated the operation of the structure and the behavior and tasks of the embassy's personnel. Our people there were unwittingly becoming less a symbol of American commitment to freedom and openness and more a closed society of self-suspicion.

Bill Brown did such a sensitive and impressive job in conducting his security investigation that it actually seemed to lift morale. But he let me know that he had come to conclude that lie detector tests should be required for State's employees. I remained adamantly opposed. People deserve to be presumed innocent and to feel trusted unless there is evidence to demonstrate otherwise. "The results of lie detector tests are not sufficiently reliable to be accepted as evidence in a court of law, and they are not reliable enough to detect trained professional spies," I said. If the security experts felt that the only way to deal with the security challenge was to transform the American system into one resembling the Soviet system, then they'd lose me for good.

A Different Moscow

When I arrived in Moscow on Monday, April 13, a light snow covered the runways and the fields surrounding the airport. I was determined not to be distracted by the atmosphere generated by our embassy problems and by the reactions to those problems in Washington.

I plunged in on Monday morning with Foreign Minister Shevardnadze. We met briefly alone, then with our full delegations to designate working groups on our four-part agenda: human rights, bilateral issues, regional problems, and arms control. Shevardnadze and I laid the groundwork for my upcoming meeting with Gorbachev on Tuesday afternoon.

With all of the tension, yet also with a sense of openness and change in the air and the possibility of forward movement on breakthroughs that had been achieved—and then withdrawn—six months before at Reykjavik, I decided to try something different at the large, semisocial luncheon after my first session. I knew the Shevardnadzes were fond and proud of their native Georgia. I had got hold of the music and a tape of a torch singer singing "Georgia on My Mind." When the time came for my toast, I gave the music and the lyrics, translated into Russian, to the Shevardnadzes; then I sang the song with feeling, played the tape, and introduced a quartet of our embassy Russian speakers, who then sang "Georgia on My Mind" in Russian. The room burst into laughter and applause. Eduard and Nanuli Shevardnadze were surprised and delighted. When the noise died down, Eduard looked at me. "Thank you, George, that shows respect," he said. He had a capacity for fun, and his humanity showed through. To me, he displayed a confidence in himself that Gromyko, with all his imperious dignity, never convincingly imparted. Shevardnadze and I were developing a personal relationship based on mutual respect. We could deal with difficult issues despite the atmosphere of tension.

The Seder at Spaso House

After my second session with Shevardnadze in the afternoon, I finally went to Spaso House, our ambassador's residence, where I unpacked and prepared for the evening's gathering: a seder, the annual Passover celebration of Jews throughout the world of their ancient passage to freedom from enslavement in Egypt. In the ballroom of this czarist-era mansion, where aristocratic belles once waltzed with epauletted officers and courtiers, candlelight transformed the heavily draped room into a warm and welcoming place of sanctuary.

There, waiting for me, were the Jewish refuseniks, each with a different experience of repression and each denied elementary human rights: to worship as they choose, to emigrate, to teach Hebrew and Jewish culture to their children. I put on a yarmulke and walked slowly around the room, talking to each in turn. I knew all the names, all were individuals who had had the personal courage to stand up to authority against great odds and maintain their beliefs. I brought pictures to the Slepaks of grandchildren they had never seen, a book or memento for others. I expressed the emotions that I felt: "You are on our minds; you are in our hearts. We never give up, we never stop trying, and in the end some good things do happen. But never give up, never give up. And please note that there are people all over the world, not just in the United States, who think about you and wish you well and are on your side."

All of us there knew that every guest present was undertaking a risk by coming together for this central celebration of Judaism—and in a room in the American embassy. The American press and TV covered the Moscow seder, and news of it was broadcast to Jewish communities all around the world, providing a sense of hope and identification. The event moved me deeply, as it did all my colleagues who were present. I came away inspired by the courage and the strength of spirit of these men and women.[1]

Human Rights in the Information Age

When Shevardnadze and I resumed later that evening, I naturally had human rights on my mind. I had thought long and hard about how to present this subject most effectively. I had argued the merits of human rights issues, had insisted that the Helsinki Accords meant that each signatory nation had undertaken solemn obligations, and had reluctantly used the inducement of greater trade in exchange for more emigration, as embedded in U.S. law by the Jackson-Vanik Amendment, passed during the Nixon era of détente. Now, following the arrival on the scene of Gorbachev and especially, I felt, Shevardnadze, we were seeing progress in terms of the numbers of people the Soviets were allowing to emigrate. At Reykjavik, we had achieved the breakthrough of establishing human rights as a legitimate topic for our agenda. Shevardnadze always emphasized that the Soviets would make changes that were sensible from their standpoint,

---

1. All of the prominent refuseniks at the seder had been allowed to emigrate by the time of Passover the following year, 1988.

not in response to our pressure or "to please you." I racked my brains for a better way to respond to his point, which I felt was honestly stated. So I developed a different approach. I asked Shevardnadze for a half hour of private time with him and former Ambassador Dobrynin, who allegedly was relied upon by Gorbachev.

I told Shevardnadze I had listened carefully to his comments and wanted to develop for him why a changed approach to human rights "was in the Soviet interest." I then went through carefully a line of argument in which I believed firmly and had introduced briefly, from a different perspective, to Gorbachev in the Kremlin in November 1985. I argued that the economic progress the Soviets sought from what they called "radical reforms" could not be achieved "unless the Soviet system is changed sharply, in ways that stimulate the creativity and drive of individuals. In the information age, success will come to societies that are open and decentralized and provide lots of room for individual initiative. Countries throughout the world are seeing this truth.

"The gap," I argued, "will widen between nations that adapt to the information age and those that do not. Your interests and ours will not be served if the future is marked by growing economic asymmetry between East and West. But that will happen if the Soviet Union does not become a full participant in the information revolution. Such a Soviet failure will heighten tension, suspicion, and insecurity. Neither of us want that.

"The degree of constraint that you now exercise over information flows, economic opportunities, and consumer choices," I went on, "will not permit sufficient development of the human potential needed to keep pace with the more open societies. There is no way to get there from here without lifting many of the restraints you place on your people. You believe that human rights consist of jobs, housing, health care, and economic benefits. The only way your society is going to be able to fulfill those rights is to permit your people a greater degree of what *we* regard as human rights: freedom of speech, movement, expression, and personal choice.

"Conversely," I said, "a society like yours is going to find, I believe, that the economic well-being of its people is likely to diminish to the extent that human rights are restricted. And practically speaking, when human rights are allowed to flourish, and economic 'rights' consequently flourish also, then the problem you face with regard to pressure for emigration will diminish. In this way a range of problems that has severely aggravated our relationship could over time be substantially eased.

"We do not view Soviet change on human rights issues as a concession to the United States," I said. "But change would build support among the American people for further improvement in our relations. The reality is that when a nation's leaders engage in the suppression of criticism of government, in the limitation of the free flow of information, in a lack of due process for individuals, the international community can never be sure that such a nation will be bound by its commitments. Therefore, I say to you with deep conviction that a change in the relationship between the state and individuals, giving individuals more freedom and more rights under a rule of law, including the right to emigrate, is very much in the interest of the Soviet Union."[2]

Shevardnadze paid close attention. He did not interrupt. When I finished, he thanked me and said that his note takers had recorded what I had said. He did not respond further.

A System Falling Apart

Tuesday, April 14, 1987, I went to the Kremlin, this time to meet the chairman of the Council of Ministers, Nikolai Ryzhkov, whom I had first met in Stockholm at the funeral of Olof Palme in March 1986. The subject was economics—for three hours. Here I received my first extensive exposure to Soviet recognition at a high level that their command-and-control system was not working. "I couldn't believe what I found here. They were trying to plan every detail of our huge economy," Ryzhkov told me. He knew the old system was falling apart. But I recognized that they clearly did not know what to do.

We talked about foreign trade. I told Ryzhkov that they could not expect to see exports and imports flourish until they were able to break loose from barter arrangements. "You need an internal market and a convertible currency in order to take part in multilateral, currency-based exchange," I said. He agreed but maintained that they could change only gradually.

"Gradualism will run you into trouble," I told Ryzhkov. "You have to have one system or the other. Trying to have both at the same time will mean that they run into each other." I left impressed that he saw how immense his problems were but dismayed that he had no clear vision of what to do next. He struck me as very much the manager, as had been his prior experience. I hoped he would realize that he had to change the system, not better manage it.

Breaking Through to Gorbachev

At 3:00 P.M. the door to St. Catherine's Hall opened, and I walked into a grand and imposing chamber. Gorbachev entered from the other end at

2. In September 1989, after I had left office but while he was still the Soviet foreign minister, Shevardnadze and his wife invited O'Bie and me to dinner in New York, where we had the opportunity for a relaxed conversation. I asked him whether he remembered that particular presentation. "Oh yes," he replied, "I went over the notes carefully with Gorbachev and others in the leadership. What you said had a profound impact."

precisely the same moment. We met halfway, exchanged greetings, bantered briefly with a small press contingent, and then proceeded to an intense four and a half-hour session. I had with me Paul Nitze, Roz Ridgway, and Jack Matlock. Across the table sat Gorbachev, Shevardnadze, Dobrynin, and Dubinin.

I opened with my objections to the Soviets' excessive intelligence effort, so overdone, I said, that they were threatening to turn our relationship over to the KGB and the CIA. Gorbachev disingenuously took the line that it was good to know more about each other. Not in such an "overbearing" way, I responded. I told him that seventy senators had voted that I should not take this trip to Moscow.

"Well," Gorbachev declared "you acted correctly in coming here." Then he said flatly that there had *not* been a physical intelligence penetration of our embassy.

"Can I tell the president," I asked, "that it is against your policy and rules to allow your intelligence agencies to physically penetrate our embassy building?"

"Yes, this is precisely so," he responded. I had raised this subject in my first meeting with Shevardnadze, and he had told me that I was being deceived. The top Soviet leadership had made unequivocal statements to me that were totally at odds with the story that had official Washington in flames.

"Where do we go from here?" Gorbachev asked me. "The U.S. administration does not see what is going on in the Soviet Union. You think we are weak. You pocket our concessions. So what have you brought?" I reviewed our positions on INF and START: sharp reductions to global and equal levels, that was our approach. "At Reykjavik," Gorbachev said, referring to INF, "you agreed to 100 on each side globally and none in Europe—do you still agree?"

"Yes," I said, "we agree. That is not what we want; we want zero globally, but we agree to that as a step in the right direction." I argued for a global zero on the grounds that, from the Soviet standpoint, they were only sticking their fingers in the eyes of the Japanese, the Koreans, and the Chinese. And from both our points of view, I said, verification of zero was easier and more certain than of any finite number. "The United States has allies, so I am not just speaking for the United States," I added.

"I have knowledge about your instructions," Gorbachev responded. "You are here to probe. You have come on an intelligence mission. You will not come to a conclusion, and you will blame it on your need to go and consult your allies." I told him again that we would agree to 100 warheads on each side, with none in Europe.

I felt that I had just made a major impact on Gorbachev: he had not believed—to this point—that Ronald Reagan would ever make an agreement with the "evil empire" or that Reagan would ever agree to anything less than *exactly* what he wanted. Now, suddenly, I felt that Gorbachev saw Reagan in a new light. He was hearing from me that as a step forward we still agreed to something less than precisely what we wanted.

I then raised the issue of short-range INF missiles. "Well, whatever you do, we're going to get rid of the systems in East Germany and Czechoslovakia," Gorbachev told me. "The remainder [what would be left in other Warsaw Pact countries] is a new number, and there should be a freeze," he said.

"I'm glad to hear that you are getting rid of some systems. But there cannot be a freeze. We must have equality and the right to match your deployments," I responded. We went back and forth.

Gorbachev then proposed to treat short-range INF missiles in the same way as the long-range INF category: zero in Europe and 100 in Soviet Asia and in the United States. I rejected that approach.

"These weapons are easily moved. The only sensible outcome is equality on a global basis," I told him. By the end of the discussion, Gorbachev himself proposed a global zero. I insisted on the right to match any Soviet deployment. He proposed elimination of all short-range INF weapons on a global basis and in a short period of time.

I could not accept his offer right there: this was a matter for the alliance to discuss. But I thought we *would* wind up accepting this offer and that, in the end, the idea of global zero would be extended to long-range INF missiles as well. The logic and the motivation would push in that direction. So I responded, "We have a Soviet offer on the table. Equal limits on a global basis. You have put forward the limit of zero. Some of our allies may prefer a finite number. I will take this offer back to them. I owe you an answer."

Gorbachev responded sarcastically: "You are just on an intelligence mission. What kind of leader are you? Why can't you make a decision?"

Shevardnadze interjected, "I am amazed that the U.S. is objecting to unilateral Soviet elimination of operational short-range missiles."

"Our alliance works," I responded, "because we consult one another. You will get a prompt response."

Gorbachev still did not seem to grasp the nature of the NATO alliance. But he said, "There is a possibility of success. I have fewer doubts that the administration wants an agreement, but I still have doubts."

An Interlude: The Information Revolution

At this point, about two hours into our meeting, Gorbachev suggested we take a short break. I took this as an opportunity to engage him in a line of discussion I had talked over carefully with President Reagan before leaving for Moscow. I walked to the end of the table and set up two brightly colored pie charts showing the distribution of world GNP at various times, including a projection to the year 2000. "Here is what is happening," I said. "The U.S. and the Soviet Union are now the two great powers. Others are not in a position to think about global developments the way we are. Typically, over the years, high-level Soviet-American exchanges have dealt with controversy: arms, human rights, communism versus capitalism, regional hot spots. There are big changes going on in the world economy. It's not just bipolar to multipolar; the world is in the midst of a highly complicated evolution—or revolution. The implications are not entirely clear, but we can see an outline of the future taking shape. The central feature is the great growth of the global economy: a general rise in GNP, gigantic expansion in goods and services, a huge increase in trade flows. As the world's output expands overall, the distribution of that output is more and more dispersed."

Gorbachev looked at the charts. I could see he was intrigued. "As a result, more and more nations are achieving economies of a size that permits them to divert major resources into one or more major undertakings at a world-class level. The list of nations able to take on an influential world role in a particular field—computers, weapons, finance, and so on— is going to be truly astonishing. China, Singapore, Korea, Israel are examples of very different countries clearly heading into this top category in one or more areas. What drives this growth?" I asked rhetorically.

"Science and technology," Gorbachev responded.

"Yes, but," I said, "hitched to an incentive-based, market-oriented economic system. Examples: in agriculture, nations are becoming free from a burden as old as civilization—the struggle to feed themselves. Malthus, who believed there are inherent limits to food production, is turned on his head. Biotechnology, plant strains, fertilizers, genetics, waste- and spoilage-reduction technology, have brought about a revolution. More important has been the rediscovery that if a farmer can get a price for his product that covers the cost of production plus a little more, the incentive for production is enormous. The net result of all this will be that the world can feed itself and at a relatively small cost," I told Gorbachev.

"In industry, almost every natural resource—take copper, for example— now has its substitute. Scientific and chemical processes now replace minerals in the ground. This is good news for some nations and bad for others. But for all it is a spur to move beyond the industrial age to the information age," I emphasized. "Manufacturing is often global in scope. Here is a shipping label for an integrated circuit used in manufacturing by an American company. The label reads, 'Made in one or more the following countries: Korea, Hong Kong, Malaysia, Singapore, Taiwan, Mauritius, Thailand, Indonesia, Mexico, Philippines. The exact country of origin is unknown.' " I had a picture of this label. Gorbachev looked at it with some skepticism.

"The military scene is being transformed by the increasing ease with which formerly militarily insignificant nations can now obtain or even produce weapons only somewhat less sophisticated than the best we have today, such as the Chinese Silkworm missiles now possessed by the Iranians. With the rise of ethnic (such as Tamil terrorism in Sri Lanka), regional (such as the Vietnamese occupation of Cambodia), and religious (Islamic fundamentalism) tensions, this means that small conflicts can become unprecedentedly explosive," I said.

"And the financial world was transformed years ago. The London market, the New York market, and the Tokyo market are big, but today, the only way to conceive of the financial market is globally. The information age has put the world on an information standard. Markets react almost instantly to a major event anywhere.

"What are the philosophical implications of all this?" I asked. "Here are my thoughts. This is a scientific revolution. There was a time when a government could control its scientific establishment and be basically successful. No longer. To keep up today and in the future means that scientists will have to be in constant touch with the 'thinking community' around the world. And this is an information revolution. The inability of one nation to be predominant in the international financial world is going to be repeated in field after field. The key is going to be knowledge-based productivity, even in defense: an aircraft carrier is really one big information system," I said.

"So the old categories no longer hold true. In our GNP accounts, we have classifications that distinguish between capital and labor. That distinction is central to Marxist thought as well. But that dichotomy is becoming obsolete because we have entered a world in which the truly important capital is human capital, what people know, how freely they exchange information and knowledge, and the intellectually creative product that emerges."

As I talked, Gorbachev interjected occasionally, but basically he listened carefully. He was engaged and interested. "We should have more of this kind of talk," he told me. I agreed.

Moving In on Old Issues

After about twenty-five minutes, Marshal Akhromeyev walked in with a jaunty step and upbeat, confident manner. We turned to START and SDI. Gorbachev said that the idea of a 50 percent cut in strategic forces, first agreed on at the Geneva summit, could now be described in numerical terms: 1,600 launchers and 6,000 warheads—the Reykjavik formula we had worked so hard to pin down. We had an extensive argument about the importance of sublimits on various types of weapons. We insisted; the

Soviets resisted. Nitze and Akhromeyev had a long argument about their negotiation in Reykjavik. In the end, our prized "bomber-counting rule," which Nitze had fought so diligently to achieve there, was still intact. We had, by this point, consolidated the INF and START concessions first tabled at the Reykjavik summit. I was quietly elated.

"Defense and space" was our next debate. Gorbachev complained about our "lawyers," threatened a Soviet reaction to any violation of the ABM Treaty, and said, "Your administration has painted itself into a corner." He offered to help us "untie the knot" by considering laboratory work to cover ground-based research in various scientific institutions and research centers "conducted without launching an object into outer space." The ABM Treaty, he went on, "should not be changed but observed."

"That is what we are doing, and there is nothing about a laboratory in the ABM Treaty," I said.

Then why, Gorbachev asked, "are you avoiding discussion of what is permitted and not permitted under the treaty? I have heard about Kampelman's response, and I urge you, George Shultz, to develop new instructions." I repeated that our program was consistent with the ABM Treaty. In exasperation, Gorbachev said, "U.S. policy is one of extorting more and more concessions. Two great powers should not treat each other that way."

"I'm weeping for you," I responded with a smile.

Gorbachev, saying he had now covered his agenda, invited me to raise any subject of interest to me. I turned to human rights, first expressing appreciation for recent developments and hoping that important further moves would be made.

"The Soviet side is prepared to consider any proposal that emerges in the humanitarian area," Gorbachev told me. He then launched into a bitter attack on me and my attendance at the seder at our embassy the previous evening. "You deal only with a certain group of Jews, people who do not like it here and have complaints, and show no interest in the millions of other Soviet Jews, who are out of your field of vision." He suggested that my activities were "stimulating" discontent.

"I welcome your comments as indicating that if Jews want to practice their religion, to learn Hebrew, to teach it to their children, that is all right with you," I replied. And I asked that emigration be truly open. "Then you will know who wants to leave. Perhaps, as in Hungary, open opportunity to emigrate would not find many takers. Try it." I added. "I've got a deal for you. I've got a great big airplane. If you don't want them [the refuseniks], there isn't a person in my party, including the reporters, that wouldn't give up his seat for those people. And you can just put them all on and get rid of them if you don't want them. We'll take them."

He did not respond but instead launched into an attack on the treatment of minorities in the United States as contrasted with the Soviet Union, where, he said, "we have quite a record on relations between nationalities, self-determination, and autonomous areas for even the smallest group." He suggested that our ambassador, Jack Matlock, "get in touch with the Central Committee to develop recommendations to the U.S."

I regarded all this pull and haul as real progress. Gorbachev did not understand the United States, but he was willing to discuss human rights in the Soviet Union as long as the transcript showed that he had hit back.

I brought up regional issues, and we quickly turned to Afghanistan. The Soviet Union wanted to leave, Gorbachev said, but the United States kept putting "sticks in the spokes." The United States would not agree to a modified version of the present government. Gorbachev argued that "what exists is each country's national interest; it is not just the United States that has a national interest. The art of foreign policy is to seek a balance of such interests."

"Our attitude is not pro-U.S. but pro-Afghanistan," I replied. I continued to feel we were gaining on the Afghan problem and that we should keep the pressure on in Afghanistan and the dialogue going on regional issues. "Solutions" Gorbachev went on, "are not for one or the other to make alone, but only in common." At the right time, I thought, but not quite yet. The Soviets must leave.

We then turned to the issue of nuclear testing, a subject on which Gorbachev had concentrated considerable effort and prestige and on which the Reagan administration had a real difference of opinion with many Democrats in the House of Representatives, including Speaker Jim Wright and Majority Leader Tom Foley. Once again, Gorbachev and I returned to formulations that had emerged at Reykjavik. A key issue on the way to any substantive agreement was the capacity to verify the fact and the size of a nuclear test. We differed with the Soviets on methodology. I proposed that we each observe tests in the other's country in a massive joint verification experiment. Gorbachev and I achieved agreement in principle to negotiate such an approach to verification.

And so we ended at 7:30 P.M. I was exhausted. But I was also exhilarated. The meeting had been tremendously productive.

I went back directly to the embassy, where O'Bie and I scooped out sundaes at an ice cream social for the whole American contingent serving in Moscow. We relaxed a bit and had a good time. At 9:30 P.M., I went back to work with Shevardnadze until midnight.

Afterward, I met again with my own team. It was 12:35 in the morning when I went down to the Winnebago, packed with communications gear and counterbugging devices, that was parked in the basement of the American embassy housing complex. Within seconds, I was speaking by secure telephone to President Reagan at his ranch in California. I told him that

I had "consolidated all of the concessions we had achieved at Reykjavik on INF and START and had made great progress on short-range INF missiles." The president asked about likely reactions among our allies. "Some Europeans want zero," I said, "some want a number. I think they'll have a hard time arguing for something other than zero."

Gorbachev and I had worked out a statement on negotiations on nuclear testing that was "totally within the framework of your instructions," I told him. "We are being followed here by Jim Wright, and the Soviets asked if we agreed with his position on the limit of one kiloton. So this could keep Jim Wright out of mischief." I added that these negotiations about verification could also lead to ratification of the Threshold Test Ban Treaty (TTBT) and the Peaceful Nuclear Explosions Treaty (PNET), on which he had agreed with Tip O'Neill to go forward on the eve of meeting with Gorbachev in Reykjavik.

"It's not peaches and cream," I told President Reagan. "It's been a rough day. Gorbachev talked about a summit with content: an INF agreement, a Threshold Test Ban Treaty, and some overall points on START and space if these come out of negotiations. He talked about fall to the end of the year. I didn't bite except to say that everything should be carefully prepared and it should be preceded by a visit from Shevardnadze. But I was low-key and didn't focus on it. If we look too interested, they will raise the price."

The president authorized me to talk in positive tones about a summit and said he had heard I had discussed human rights. I told him about the seder and said I was scheduled for an unprecedented thirty-minute interview on Soviet television on Wednesday. "The Soviet Union *is* changing, and the strong policies you've kept in place—and the pressure—have made a real difference."

A little after 2:00 A.M., Wednesday, April 15, I was back in the Spaso House sitting room, looking at the familiar floodlit American flag rippling on its pole outside as Jack Matlock poured himself, Paul Nitze, and me a vodka. "Let's send the clock to Shevardnadze," I said. I had brought Shevardnadze a wonderful Geochron clock, the kind that illuminates the path of the sun as it moves across the face of the earth, showing where it is day and night. The clock had been adapted for Soviet current. I had hesitated earlier whether to present a gift, given the embassy security situation. Matlock reminded me that the Soviet security people would regard the clock as a possible espionage device. "They'll tear it apart and probably never be able to reassemble it," he said.

The Feel of Change

Five hours later, on Wednesday morning, I was up and out of bed. Soon I was off to Peredelkino, where, at his dacha, Boris Pasternak had written

Dr. Zhivago. Peredelkino was like a scene out of the movie. Rough, woodsy country houses enclosed by sagging picket fences were scattered among birches and tall firs. Snow whirled about us as O'Bie and I entered a high, dark, narrow Russian Orthodox church, where a service was under way. Old Russian women were bowing their heads to the floor and crossing themselves rhythmically over their bent shoulders. Afterward, we walked through hardening slush and a tiny cast-iron fence to Pasternak's grave, set among crowded crosses festooned with dead flowers. In the midst of mud, logs, and sawdust—with snow falling densely and Russians gathered around, some with tears in their eyes—someone said to me, "Here you can feel the true soul of our land." I placed fresh flowers on Pasternak's grave.

This rural scene, evocative of the depth and passion of the Russia so vividly depicted by Pasternak, provided a striking and revealing contrast to the bland, faceless character of Communist Moscow.

I went from Pasternak's grave to a nearby dacha for a plain but ample feast with a few Soviet intellectuals. We talked about developments inside the Soviet Union, particularly *glasnost*, the new openness. A book written by one of them, a Russian novelist, twenty years earlier had just been published. I heard about more probing theater, more open reporting and commentary. "We are past the point of no return," one said. They all seemed to agree. I hoped they were right, and I was impressed with their enthusiasm. We were making new contacts, breaking new ground.

On Wednesday afternoon, Speaker of the House Jim Wright, Majority Leader Tom Foley, and Republican Congressman Dick Cheney, who had just arrived in Moscow on a fact-finding mission, met with me in the tiny space left inside the new security van, crammed with electronic gear. The three would be seeing Gorbachev in a few hours. I reported fully to them on the substance of my sessions and gave them my appraisal of the dramatic changes taking place. I wished them luck and asked that they not undercut me with Gorbachev. I later heard that they were supportive, especially of the effort to make progress on verification of nuclear tests.

Afterward, I proceeded to Osobnyak to sign a space agreement with Shevardnadze and then on to the Novosti building for a press conference and TV interview with a well-known Soviet commentator, Valentin Zorin. I had agreed to appear for as long as they wanted, on one condition: the full interview must be shown. "No cuts," I said. They agreed. They kept their promise and broadcast everything I said, even, remarkably, my comments about Afghanistan: "The Afghan people want you to leave their country; they do not want your armed forces to be in their country. How many soldiers do you keep there, 120,000?" But my final two sentences were televised *without* translation: "It is a very devastating war, and they do not want you there. They want peace with you, but they do not want you occupying their country."

Reactions

Red Square is one of the great sights in the world. I stopped there briefly, then went on to the airport. As my aircraft was in flight to Brussels, where I would consult with our allies, I was handed a wire-service report: "UPI: The Soviet Union attacked the U.S. position on arms control within hours of Secretary of State George P. Shultz's departure Wednesday, saying it was inadequate for any agreement."

While I caught up on some sleep, members of my delegation worked through the night to perfect the arguments I would present to our allies at NATO headquarters outside Brussels in the hope of assuaging their fears and winning their assent to the course we were on. Roz Ridgway and Richard Perle once again worked well together. In the morning, when I looked at what my team had done, I saw the most tightly reasoned, compelling set of talking points I had ever used. The agreement that we had in the works was breathtaking in its asymmetry: the Soviets would take out vastly more weapons than would we.

In my room in the hotel in Brussels, I saw the *International Herald Tribune*: "Shultz Reports 'Progress' Toward Euromissile Pact: NATO Fears Erosion of U.S. Shield," ran the headline. Such fear of a denuclearized Europe was genuine. As Barry James of the *Herald Tribune* reported, "Mikhail S. Gorbachev's proposal to eliminate all short- and medium-range missiles from Europe is likely to create difficulties for America's European allies, according to NATO officials and defense experts. British official sources said Wednesday that Mr. Gobachev's proposals would be welcome provided they did not entail the denuclearization of Europe. Prime Minister Margaret Thatcher has stated repeatedly that she considers nuclear weapons essential to keep the peace. Earlier this week, a West German spokesman said his government was ready to back Mr. Gorbachev's call for immediate talks on eliminating short-range weapons, but could not accept the Soviet demand for a freeze on their deployment pending the outcome of such talks."

I heard that Gorbachev thought he had "put me in a corner." If so, it was a corner that I liked: he was offering to eliminate weapons that he had and that we did not have.

I had to assure the allies that we would retain the many U.S. nuclear weapons that were deployed in Europe and were not affected by the INF negotiations. Insofar as short-range INF weapons were concerned, I put a clear choice to our allies, saying we would support whatever alliance decision emerged: we would accept global zero, or we would accept a finite number. But, I added forcefully, if a finite number is chosen, then we *must* deploy. A theoretical but unexercised right to deploy would not be acceptable. (As it turned out, the allies, especially the Germans, agonized for a couple of months before agreeing on what I regarded as the inevitable outcome: they accepted that short-range INF weapons be eliminated on a global scale.) My fellow foreign ministers were elated by the results of my three days in Moscow. As I left NATO, Geoffrey Howe, the British foreign minister, summed up the general feeling, "This is good news for all of us— in the East and in the West."

On this encouraging note, I left for the United States. After refueling, I flew on to Southern California, where I switched to *Marine One*, the president's helicopter, for the trip into the Santa Barbara mountains and to the president's Rancho Cielo. The president and Nancy greeted me warmly and took me into their striking yet unpretentious ranch house. The president was full of questions about Gorbachev, changes in Moscow, the seder, my TV interview, and the content of my meetings with Gorbachev. He had read my reporting cables completely. He was excited by the possibility of making progress toward the achievement of goals he had long sought. He congratulated me. My three days in Moscow had been extraordinary in content, in promise, and in tone. So much for seventy senatorial skeptics.

Cap's Further Twist

I returned to Washington and soon encountered yet another effort by Cap Weinberger to shift our position in a way that would set back the progress achieved in Moscow. President Reagan and I, no less than Cap, preferred the total elimination of long-range INF missiles, but the president had agreed at Reykjavik to a major asymmetrical reduction that would leave 100 warheads on each side, with none stationed in Western Europe or within range of Western Europe. I was convinced that if we wound up accepting the proposal that Gorbachev made to me of eliminating all short-range INF missiles, he would eventually agree to the elimination of the longer-range INF missiles as well. The arguments for him were as compelling as for us. Verification would be vastly simplified. From his standpoint, his strains with the Chinese and the Japanese would be eased. I was convinced that he regarded Ronald Reagan's agreement to 100 warheads on each side as a test of the president's willingness to conclude an agreement with the Soviets that was a compromise from his preferred position. I therefore opposed Cap's urgings that we now shift to an insistence on a zero outcome. That could kill the whole deal and, ironically, could jeopardize our best chance to achieve the zero outcome we all wanted. President Reagan agreed with me.

On May 15, in what I could interpret only as an act of defiance and sabotage of a president weakened by the Iran-Contra affair, Cap engineered a statement in the communiqué of a meeting of NATO defense ministers calling for the elimination of *all* long-range INF missiles. Cap sought to reopen in a public and embarrassing way an issue he had lost in debate with President Reagan. "Nothing was agreed at Reykjavik," Cap said. He went on in press remarks virtually to endorse a suggestion of former President Nixon and former Secretary of State Henry Kissinger to link an INF agreement to one that would also reduce conventional arms. A White House statement had already rejected this linkage of two subjects being negotiated in totally different negotiating groups and on different timetables. Since Nixon and Kissinger opposed the INF Treaty in any case, I could only interpret this linkage as a backdoor attempt to block the treaty, rallying the Republican right to try to force President Reagan to accept conditions that could not be fulfilled in any remotely immediate time frame.

President Reagan did not change his position. Cap's standing with Howard Baker and Frank Carlucci, let alone me, sank further with this effort.

A Scandal Evaporates

Seven months after my extraordinary April visit to Moscow, the great marine spy scandal evaporated. Sergeant Lonetree, whose original confession had unleashed this furor, told a different story when interviewed carefully as part of an investigation to assess damage. The Naval Investigative Service had become convinced that even though Sergeant Lonetree had provided some information to the Soviets, he had never let the Soviets into the embassy building nor had he conspired with Corporal Bracy to do so. Indeed, Bracy had repudiated his original "confession" almost immediately, and ultimately all charges against him were dropped. Logbooks showed that Lonetree and Bracy had never stood watch together in the manner described in Bracy's repudiated statement. The embassy communication center's electronic monitoring devices also showed no record of entries that were not authorized or reported.

So the KGB had *not* penetrated our embassy, after all. I remembered the flat statements of denial of Gorbachev and Shevardnadze. What must they have thought was going on in Washington? The marine spy scandal had been whipped up and fueled by investigative zealots interacting with a media and Congress all too ready to believe, even relish, wrongdoing.

Once again I was confirmed in my opposition to "linkage," which would have prevented me from taking advantage of a tremendous opportunity over an issue that turned out to be a massive false alarm. More importantly, I was convinced that we now had broken through to new ground with the Soviets.

CHAPTER 42

Testimony on Iran-Contra

On January 28, 1987, my day was full, from breakfast with Cap Weinberger to testimony before the House Budget Committee, my regular Wednesday session with the president, a controversial meeting with Oliver Tambo, president of the African National Congress, and a long session with Bernardo Sepulveda, foreign minister of Mexico. At 6:35 P.M., Senators Daniel Inouye and Warren Rudman, joined by Abe Sofaer, State's legal adviser, came to my office. We sat around the fire and talked for over an hour.

The two senators were the chairman and ranking minority member of the Senate side of the joint committee investigating the Iran-Contra affair. They had asked for this appointment. They told me that the Senate would approach its task in a nonpartisan manner. They would have one counsel and staff that would serve both the Democrats and the Republicans. Arthur Liman had been signed up as chief counsel. Abe Sofaer, reacting to this information, said that Liman was a distinguished and fair attorney. The senators told me that they did not know where this investigation would lead but that they were determined to dig out the truth, whatever that might be.

They assured me—and this was the purpose of their unusual visit—that they were well aware of the promising but tense situation with the Soviets. They were not on a witchhunt, and they were not out to destroy the president or undermine our ability to deal with the Soviets and others. Their investigation would let the chips fall where they may, the senators said, but as a duty of responsible government, they would let me know if any devastating information turned up. I told them I appreciated their nonpartisan approach. In the meantime, President Reagan and I would get on with the nation's business.

On May 5, the House-Senate committee investigating the Iran-Contra affair opened joint hearings, a massive undertaking. Watching the opening session briefly on the television in my office, I heard commentator Peter Jennings describe the experience, there in the hearing room, of listening to "the cadence of the American voice" in the unmistakably charged tones of democratic inquiry. The Iran-Contra hearings dominated the town: more than Topic A, they occupied much of the whole alphabet. Explosively, the first witness, retired Major General Richard Secord, said, "I was told by Admiral Poindexter in January of 1986 that not only was he pleased with the work that I was doing, but the President was as well.On a few occasions I heard Oliver North offhand and I think in a humorous vein remark that in some conversations with the President he had mentioned that it was very ironic that some of the Ayatollah's money was being used to support the Contras. Whether he actually said this to the President or whether he was joking with me, I am not sure. It was not said to me in a way that I took it as a joke." In light of the president's clear statements that he did not know of this diversion of funds to the Contras, I did not believe this secondhand story.

The hearings were a spectacle, but they also demanded a vast effort, drawing off some of the most talented people on the Hill and enormous numbers of support people in both the legislative and executive branches. It would be difficult, I feared, to accomplish much in American foreign policy. But there were important subjects that needed to be addressed energetically: INF and other negotiations with the Soviets, freedom of navigation in the Persian Gulf, and the Iran-Iraq War. I found myself also caught up in yet another frustrating battle over the way the NSC staff should operate.

The Empire of the Staff

By mid-May, I was engaged in a steady—though initially unexpected—struggle with Frank Carlucci over the proper role of the NSC staff in policy formulation and execution. The Tower Commission had chided me a few months earlier for not doing enough and for distancing myself. I felt it were off-base in not perceiving how vehemently I had opposed the effort and that, in view of my known opposition, I had been cut out. What bothered me even more about the Tower report, given its mandate to look at the NSC system, was the set of recommendations the commission had come up with: recommendations that, if anything, offered the NSC staff an opportunity to *increase* its authority—exactly the opposite of the remedy needed.

The Iran-Contra disaster had come about in part because the NSC staff had improperly used the power of the White House while escaping the accountability of the rest of the executive branch. So I could not accept the Tower Commission's recommendation that the NSC staff should chair interagency groups, including cabinet-level meetings, thereby controlling their agenda and pace.

NSC adviser Frank Carlucci in late March 1987 had proposed a National Security Decision Directive (NSDD) that would vastly increase the power of the national security adviser over the interagency process along the lines recommended by the Tower Commission. NSDD 276 put the national security adviser in the chair and established him as a member of a senior review group that was declared to be "the Cabinet level interagency group for the consideration of national security issues." It also established a policy review group, chaired by the NSC adviser's deputy and made up of deputy secretaries or under secretaries of cabinet departments. I refused to go along with this proposal, so a struggle ensued as the NSC staff battled to expand the powers of the very entity whose uncontrolled powers had brought us the Iran-Contra fiasco in the first place.

On May 12, 1987, I confronted Carlucci directly about NSDD 276. I told him that I had no problem with informal meetings of the National Security Council being coordinated by the national security adviser. In fact, I had created the Family Group forum with the idea that the meetings would be managed by the NSC adviser. But it would be a grave mistake, I said, for the NSC adviser, a nonstatutory member of the National Security Council, someone *not* in the cabinet and *not* subject to confirmation by the Senate or to the accountability of appearances before congressional committees, to be designated in an NSDD as the chairman of NSC meetings. "Frank Carlucci is not a member of the NSC," I said. "You are the staff of the NSC. You serve the principals of the NSC, especially but not exclusively the president." Frank replied that in working up this draft NSDD, he had just been trying to do what the Tower Commission had recommended.

"The Tower Board's recommendations have already been forgotten," I said. "Stop chewing on that nail."

Every week or so I would learn of some NSC staff private channel that had been kept from me. On May 13, Max Kampelman told me that he had learned from Larry Horowitz, Senator Kennedy's assistant, that the channel to the Soviets that Kennedy first discussed with me earlier in 1987 in fact went back a long way and was managed by the NSC staff. The channel had started, Horowitz told Kampelman, with Senator Kennedy in contact with Brezhnev's successor, Yuri Andropov. The action officers then became Horowitz, Dobrynin, and Poindexter. When Horowitz had asked, as the exchanges continued, whether the State Department should be brought into it, Poindexter had said no. Only when the scandal over NSC staff behavior was revealed in late 1986 did the senator bring the existence and content of this channel to me at the State Department. Now I was getting signals that the Soviets still wanted to pass messages in this manner. I didn't like such back-channel activity, but I would listen to whatever the

Soviets chose to pass on to me. I also was determined not to be a "reverse sinner," so I kept the president and Carlucci fully aware of everything I was hearing.

To make clear, for the record, my view of where the NSC staff should be placed in the chain of command, I sent a memorandum to Carlucci detailing how and why I disagreed with his proposed NSDD 276; he did not like my view and did not yield. "Forgive my annoyance," Carlucci told me, "but I did not return to government in order to be an executive secretary."

Impact on Soviet Relations

Paul Nitze and Max Kampelman, who, as the hearings started in May 1987, were in closest touch with the Soviets, feared that the spectacle of the presidency in disarray was leading the Soviets to think they could exploit our weakness. The Soviets had just backed away from an idea they had proposed through the Horowitz channel. "I think they really now don't want a deal, except an INF agreement on their terms," said Nitze in a meeting in my office. "I think the chance that we can get an agreement—START or INF—is now close to zero."

"Do you think we should back off this INF agreement?" I asked Paul.

"I'm just turning it over in my mind," he told me. "I'm the only one who leans this way. We could be tougher—insist on the INF deal we want. Zero-zero is better than 100-100. So I'd be tougher: zero-zero on a global basis." Paul was having second thoughts about the whole negotiation.

"The question is," I said, "is the INF agreement itself desirable? I think it is, and we should move ahead. This would be the first-ever reduction in—let alone elimination of—an entire nuclear weapons system."

"I've seen Soviets try before what they did with Horowitz," Nitze responded. "They say, 'You are too weak to be worth negotiating with. We no longer have respect for you.' It's a pressure tactic, but there is something to it. 'How can the president get this potential INF agreement through the Senate ratification process?' they can ask."

My own view was clear: continue to hold steady in negotiations and continue to work for an INF agreement.

Frank Carlucci called. The president and Nancy, he told me, were talking about having Gorbachev come to the United States and visit their ranch at Thanksgiving. "Oh, stop," I said. "Let the summit idea alone; quit pressing."

By the late spring of 1987, the whole world seemed to be watching the Iran-Contra hearings. Our ambassador in Nicaragua, Harry Bergold, reported that the Ortega regime had ground to a halt: "They just all watch the hearings on CNN," he said. I was not watching the hearings much. There was too much work to do, and I also wanted to be as little influenced as possible by the statements of others. I wanted to tell my own story without reference to what others had said. I would stick to my own record.

I saw brief segments of testimony from early witnesses—some of whom I had never even heard of—acting as though they were properly conducting the nation's business when they were, in fact, acting in violation of the law and against ordinary precepts of common sense. I thought of my friend Arthur Burns, a truly great public servant, lying near death at Johns Hopkins University hospital. In his professional life he represented the epitome of honesty and intellectual integrity. He insisted that statements be meticulously accurate. Someone who is careless with facts is usually careless in thought and therefore unsound in judgment, he said. Arthur was a man with immense ability and wisdom. That was why he was so powerful and so respected. What a contrast to these characters.

On May 20, 1987, I met with the president to discuss the Soviet proposal for eliminating short-range INF missiles. I felt sure that if we accepted the Soviets' proposal of zero short-range INF missiles, Gorbachev in the end would agree to zero long-range INF missiles as well. In recent days, we had been checking with the allies. Deep concern existed that elimination of all INF weapons would somehow disassociate, or decouple, America from the Western European democracies and leave them to face Soviet pressure alone. Reassurances about the large U.S. nuclear arsenal remaining in Europe would be essential, I knew. Chancellor Kohl's view would be central, and Bob Linhard had been in touch with Horst Teltschik about it. On May 28, the message from Bonn was: the short-range INF's (Pershing Ia's) must go "at the end of the process." At the economic summit in Venice in early June, Chancellor Kohl told the president and me that Germany had now resolved its problems with the proposal for zero short-range INF missiles that Gorbachev had made to me during my April meeting with him in Moscow. With this decision, we were now positioned for a final drive for the INF Treaty. All the key elements were in place.

The media's assessment of the Venice summit was painful to read. The president was portrayed as out of the action. Reporter David Hoffman in the *Washington Post* wrote on June 11 that the president "has rather suddenly begun to show his age and lame duck status." I felt the *Post* assessment was off the mark. The president had been an active participant, and much was accomplished in rallying support for our efforts to protect the international waters of the Persian Gulf from disruption by Iran.

I departed from Venice with my staff for the next meeting by boatcade: three U.S. Navy launches, *Whidbey Island, Nashville,* and *Spartanburg County,* escorted us to the airport. I then flew to Reykjavik, where the NATO foreign ministers were meeting. Upon arrival, I checked in by telephone with Washington. The press was quoting me as having called Oliver North "a loose cannon." Those were not my words. I hardly knew North, but the characterization seemed to fit.

The Struggle for Accountable Authority

After the Venice economic summit with the president and the NATO meeting of foreign ministers in Reykjavik, I had to go directly to the annual meeting with ASEAN foreign ministers and to other stops in the Asia Pacific. It was not a good time to be away from Washington. My talks with Frank Carlucci about how the administration's work in foreign policy should be coordinated went nowhere. Frank could see that his position as national security adviser had its counterparts, as governments elsewhere emulated the American national security system. Teltschik in Bonn was one. Frank regarded Dobrynin, now in Moscow, as another and wanted to establish direct communication with him on current U.S.-Soviet arms control issues. So Carlucci, like McFarlane and Poindexter before him, wanted to deal and negotiate with them directly.

This was nonsense—and dangerous, I said to Carlucci. Multiple tracks in negotiations lead to confusion and give our adversaries the chance to play one track off against the other. Furthermore, I said, "The secretary of state has been formally nominated by the president, examined and confirmed by the Senate, and is required to testify before the Congress on any and all aspects of American foreign policy. So the secretary is accountable to the Congress and responsible to the president."

President Nixon had made recommendations to improve the organization and operation of the federal government, but they were never approved by Congress. The idea was to disperse power away from the president. Everybody wants to report to him, with the result that so many people formally do so that presidential oversight is impossible. Nixon felt that accountable people other than the president must take some responsibility. If everything goes to the president for decision, White House staffers end up deciding most issues, and they are not accountable. A cabinet secretary tends to reflect departmental views and can lose sight of the presidential perspective. Then the White House staff starts to monitor and override the cabinet, presumably to make sure that the president's views are taken into account. All too often, that simply means the staff's views.

Nixon's answer was to group cabinet officers according to areas of interest—national security, economics, human resources, natural resources—and to provide key cabinet officials offices in the White House, where they would absorb the White House view. When I was secretary of the treasury, I had a White House office as well as one in the Treasury. I was the president's manager of economic policy and made decisions on his behalf where presidential guidance was clear. I didn't stop any cabinet officer from seeing the president. But I had a White House orientation as well as that of the Treasury Department. I started my day in the White House office with a meeting of all administration top officials on economic matters. When I had been director of the budget, I also had an office in the White House. And I felt that the secretary of state should have a White House presence, as Henry Kissinger did when he held that post. Nixon had a good idea then, and the idea was still good now.

While traveling to Iceland I learned that NSDD 276, embodying the Tower Commission's exaltation of the NSC staff, had been "wheeled" (a facsimile of the president's signature made by an automatic pen) on the instruction of Carlucci, no doubt with the president's authorization. I had specifically asked to discuss it directly with President Reagan, but that had not occurred. The document, which formalized NSC staff chairmanship of interagency groups of accountable presidential appointees, including cabinet officers, set up a process that was not proper. It amounted almost to a palace coup. I had lost the bureaucratic battle, but I was not going to lose the real battle over substance. I would work with the president and ignore the NSDD.

The Icelandic sun set at quarter past midnight and rose again about 1:00 A.M. It did not make for a good night's sleep. By June 15, I was in Manila; by June 17, in Singapore. There in my hotel suite I could look out upon a vast atrium. Observation elevators zipped up and down at astonishing speeds. Plants of jungle richness draped over each balconied floor, level on level, creating a hanging garden. From the orchestra far below in the lobby, a woman plaintively sang the theme from *Dr. Zhivago* against a background of splashing fountains. I went back to my desk and wrote a message that I intended to hand to the president at our next meeting. I had been away too long.

After my return to Washington on June 23, I gave my memorandum, a fierce attack on NSDD 276, to the president. In it I described the NSDD as a blow to cabinet government. Coming at a time when the evidence was undeniable that the NSC staff operated beyond the scrutiny of, and kept information from, the properly established officers of government, I wrote, "NSDD 276 perpetuates and institutionalizes the very flawed processes that your administration now confronts in these [Iran-Contra] investigations." If this process is the wave of the future, I went on, the change should not be made by an NSDD but by a statute. But I could see that President Reagan was not interested in what he regarded as a bureaucratic struggle.

I received a letter from the president dated July 13 replying to my concerns about NSDD 276: "None of the arrangements put in place by NSDD 276 will be at the cost of your authority or that of any other members of my Cabinet. It is important to note that the committees chaired by the National Security Adviser and his deputy are not freestanding groups, but instead feeder systems for the NSC and NSPG which I chair." I wasn't sure what the president's message to me meant. I decided that he was encouraging my instinct simply to ignore the directive.

Run-up to My Testimony

The White House seemed to have lost all spirit. Frank Carlucci was unhappy with his job, and my opposition to his NSDD 276 played a big part in that feeling. Howard Baker was demoralized, too; he worried that the nomination of Robert Bork to the Supreme Court was going to be a disaster. I regarded Bork as an outstanding legal scholar, and I wrote the members of the Senate to express my support.

The testimony of Oliver North on July 7, 8, and 10 at the joint hearings of the House and Senate on the Iran-Contra affair was producing "Olliemania." Polls showed widespread support for North and a sense that Congress was making him the scapegoat. This development deeply dismayed Congress and encouraged many in the White House to believe that the problems generated by the Iran-Contra events had been put to rest and that, anyway, nothing so terribly wrong had occurred. "White House Exuberant Over North Success; Reagan Moves to Capitalize On Apparent Turn in Public Opinion," announced headlines in the *Christian Science Monitor* on July 14, 1987. I was astonished by a call from a friend, the former president of a major bank, who remarked that he was captivated by North.

The objective of these hearings was presumably to find the truth and clear the air so that the country could get going again. But Oliver North's performance was clothing with an aura of heroism and propriety what was, in fact, a rogue operation and an immense constitutional threat: the creation by the director of central intelligence and the NSC staff of a combined policy-and-operations unit operating beyond the reach of the law and beyond the checks and balances of the American system of separation of powers. A "staffocracy" had been created: government by a unit of government that was totally unchecked but which functioned with the implied authority of the presidency. This was a growth on the American body politic that was not subject to its system of safeguards and defenses. The process was a disaster waiting to happen; and happen it did in the Iran-Contra affair.

Admiral John Poindexter testified for five days, from July 15 to 21, just before me. He said flatly that he had *not* informed the president of the diversion of funds to the Contras, thereby corroborating the president's repeated statement that he had not known of the diversion. At the cabinet breakfast in the White House on July 16, the general feeling was upbeat: "Congress is on the run," Howard Baker said.

"Wait a minute," I said, "Congress has been lied to. Documents have been shredded. The ultimate staff man took over decisions from the people elected by the country." The mood in the room was not friendly.

On the evening of July 16, Margaret Thatcher had arrived for a brief visit. She focused on our negotiations with the Soviets, but the occasion provided her as well an opportunity to assess the president's mood and standing and at the same time to provide the support implicit in a visit from such an important head of government. We also discussed the Iran-Iraq War, the U.S. effort, with British support, to protect the safety of international waters in the Gulf, and, most especially, our effort in the United Nations to bring about a strong resolution designed to stop the bloody Gulf War.

By Monday, July 20, our efforts to rally support in the United Nations were coming to a head. I traveled to New York, had lunch with the secretary-general and representatives of other permanent members of the Security Council, and then moved on to a three-hour session in the Security Council chamber. The occasion was genuinely momentous, with the United States and the Soviet Union on the same side of a delicate and difficult issue of international security.[1]

On the two Saturdays before my testimony, I spent most of the morning and early afternoon with Abe Sofaer, Libby Keefer, Mike Kozak, and Charlie Hill. Sofaer, as State's legal adviser, had organized the work: assembling my records, following the hearings, and analyzing the material. Libby Keefer from Abe's staff was in charge of that effort and Mike Kozak from the legal adviser's office helped as well. We met with members of the staffs of the joint committee and, for several hours, with Mark Belnick, executive assistant to Chief Counsel Arthur Liman. Belnick, who would undertake the initial interrogation of me, had assembled an extensive set of documents for use in his questioning and a chronology of Iran-Contra events of which I had knowledge. My main preoccupation was to try to convey to Congress my sense of why this policy had gone out of control and how such a disaster could be avoided in the future. To me, both matters required attention to the flaws in the national security decision process and its oversight.

I devoted much of Tuesday, July 21, to preparations. By July 22, the day before my appearance, I was engaged primarily in other activities, including my regular private meeting with President Reagan. His only comment on my impending testimony was to reassert his instruction to provide a full account to the committee. My impression was that he and Howard Baker,

---

1. See Chapter 43 for a full discussion of this dramatic event.

as an attorney as well as chief of staff, were being especially careful not to say anything even remotely suggestive to the prospective witness.

I left for home at the relatively early hour of 6:45 P.M. and got a good night's sleep. The next morning, I was ready for what I knew would undoubtedly be my most important appearance before a congressional committee.

On July 23, just before I left my office to start my Iran-Contra testimony, I received word of a Gorbachev interview with an Indonesian newspaper, *Merdeka*, in which he agreed, as I had hoped and expected he eventually would, to eliminate all long-range INF missiles. In the same interview, he made another statement that caught my eye, "In principle, Soviet troop withdrawal from Afghanistan has been decided upon." Both pieces of news were stunning vindications of the president's powerful agenda, seeking drastic reductions in nuclear arms and an end to the Brezhnev Doctrine. I went off to the hearings buoyed by these developments: this was important progress.

On Trial

Senators Daniel Inouye and Warren Rudman and Congressmen Lee Hamilton and Dick Cheney, the chairman and ranking minority member on both the Senate and House sides, invited me to their small caucus room just before the hearing. They then accompanied me into the hearing room and into what would be two days of highly charged and fully televised interrogation. The room was jammed. I was the first witness with cabinet rank. The chips were down, and I knew it. I had a strong story to tell, and I was ready to tell it.

Lee Hamilton, chairman on the House side, called the hearing to order at 9:00 A.M. I felt that the senators and representatives were almost holding their breath. He asked whether I had an opening statement. I said, "No, but I would like to make a few remarks."

"Please proceed," he said.

"I have testified on the general subject of these hearings on four different occasions," I opened. "You have that testimony. . . . So I don't choose to read it out again." After explaining that the president had told me to respond to questions about my conversations with him, I added,

I have on numerous occasions—including, I think, before your committee right here, Chairman Fascell—been asked about what advice I gave the President on this, that, or the other subject. And I have always taken the position in 10½ years as a member of the Cabinet that those conversations are privileged, and I would not discuss them. This is an exception, and I have made this material available at the President's instruction, but I mention it because if I am testifying before you on some other subject sometime and you try to use this as a precedent, I won't buy it. I am just putting you on notice right now.

The chairman then turned to Mark Belnick. In questions and answers with building drama, Belnick took me through in great detail and with great precision what I knew and what I did not know of the Iran-Contra affair. He asked me whether I was a statutory member of the National Security Council. I replied that I was. Then I named the other members and said, "I find in these discussions often people refer to the NSC when they really mean the NSC staff. There is a difference." On my knowledge of the various presidential findings, Belnick asked, "When were you first informed, Mr. Secretary, that the President also had signed a third Finding on December 5, 1985?"

"When it emerged in the course of these hearings," I replied, with a sense of chagrin and outrage.

He asked about the meeting in Frankfurt on December 13, 1986, between Iranian representative Mehdi-Najat and George Cave of the CIA and Charles Dunbar, the Farsi-speaking foreign service officer whom I had sent to read out a statement and to represent State. Dunbar had stumbled onto the nine-point agenda, which included pressure to release the Dawa prisoners.[2] Dunbar had phoned in this information, and I immediately had sought a meeting with the president. I recounted to the committee: "And the President was astonished, and I have never seen him so mad. He is a very genial, pleasant man and doesn't—very easygoing. But his jaws set and his eyes flashed, and both of us, I think, felt the same way about it, and I think in that meeting I finally felt that the President deeply understands that something is radically wrong here."

Belnick went into the question of my alleged desire not to be informed: "Admiral Poindexter testified that he did not withhold anything from you that you did not want withheld from you. With this in mind, Mr. Secretary, . . . let me ask you, first, whether you ever told Admiral Poindexter or any other member of the administration that you did not want to be kept informed of the Iran initiative?"

SECRETARY SHULTZ. I never made such a statement. What I did say to Admiral Poindexter was that I wanted to be kept informed of the things I needed to know to do my job as Secretary of State. But he didn't need to keep me posted on the details, the operational details of what he was doing. That is what I told him. . . . The reason for that was that there had been a great amount of discussion of leaks in the administration, justifiably so.

2. See Chapter 39 for an account of this meeting.

I think it is a terrible thing that goes on in Washington, leaks from everywhere, constantly, and we are all very concerned about it. And there had been, in connection with what to do about it, discussion of the idea of giving very large numbers of people who were—who had access to classified information, lie detector tests on a regular, random basis, which I opposed.

While I was on a trip abroad in the latter part of 1985, a directive encompassing that idea was signed. So I didn't comment on it when I was abroad, but when I got back here I did comment on it, registered my opposition, talked to the President about it, and it got changed.

Now that, I recognized, put me at odds with the intelligence and national security community, to put it mildly. . . . So I felt it would probably leak, and then it wouldn't be my leak.

So that was the background of this. It had to do with the problem of leaks.

But that doesn't mean that I just bowed out insofar as major things having to do with our foreign policy are concerned.

And then your previous question, the things that were being talked about, to consider that that statement would mean that I shouldn't be informed of things like that is ridiculous.

MR. BELNICK. The main events you wanted to be kept informed of?

SECRETARY SHULTZ. Yes.

MR. BELNICK. And that was true not only with respect to Iran, but with respect to all areas of foreign relations activity, including activities engaged in by the NSC staff in Central America?

SECRETARY SHULTZ. Not only did I want to be informed, but when I found out things, sometimes by chance, I did my best to act on those things.

MR. BELNICK. With these claims in mind, and Admiral Poindexter's testimony, let me review—

SECRETARY SHULTZ. They are not claims. They are just descriptions of what I said and my view of what I said.

MR. BELNICK. Yes, sir.

Let me review certain events with you.

We went through the many instances in which I had been misled or lied to by McFarlane and Poindexter. Then Belnick asked me about my attitude in 1984 toward solicitation of funds for the Contras from third countries:

MR. BELNICK. You had also said and expressed your position that in no event would you agree to the U.S. Government serving as an intermediary or a conduit for aid to the Contras from any third-country source; is that correct?

SECRETARY SHULTZ. That's correct, and I questioned—without being a lawyer, I questioned the legality of any such arrangement. . . .[3]

MR. BELNICK. Did you have a view then as to the wisdom of the policy of approaching third countries for assistance at that time, June, 1984?

SECRETARY SHULTZ. I am a very strong supporter of the idea of helping those people in Nicaragua who are ready to fight for the freedom and independence of their country to do so. . . .

But our major concern should be to conduct ourselves so that we maximize the chance of persuading the Congress to come back on board and give support. And I felt that if we, if we actively solicited third countries, we would be cutting against those objectives in our arguments with the Congress, and beyond that it seemed to me that since this is a matter of vital interest to the United States, we couldn't, we didn't want to get ourselves in the position where we have to rely on what we can persuade other people to do to serve our vital interests. We have to step up to those ourselves. That was my thinking.

MR. BELNICK. On the legal side, did you conclude and express the view at the NSPG meeting that you ought to get an opinion from the Attorney General as to whether the United States could help the Contras with assistance from third countries?

SECRETARY SHULTZ. Yes. There was a back-and-forth argument about the subject of legality, and I am always a little hesitant to express myself on those subjects surrounded by lawyers, as I am here and everywhere.

MR. BELNICK. Sir, there is [sic] never enough.

SECRETARY SHULTZ. But I have noticed in . . . my experience in the Government that when you go to an official, professional lawyer . . . who is holding office and you say, "I want an opinion, I want you to write it down and sign your name to it," that that gets their attention. It is better than a casual, you know, "I guess it is OK" kind of thing. . . .

MR. BELNICK. . . . Did you ever receive the legal opinion from the Attorney General that was discussed at the June 1984 meeting?

SECRETARY SHULTZ. No. The subject seemed to die down. . . .

He then explored my shift of view about solicitation of funds from third countries.

MR. BELNICK. . . . And my question . . . is why your views had so changed in the 2 years between June 1984 and now, May 1986?

3. When funds from any source come into the hands of the U.S. government, those funds are then subject to whatever restrictions apply to appropriated funds. On the other hand, no U.S. law can prohibit a third government from contributing funds directly—so that the money does not come into U.S. possession—to a group, such as the Contras, in another country.

SECRETARY SHULTZ. The whole atmosphere had changed. Congressional attitudes had changed and the law had changed. And so I thought under those circumstances, it was perfectly proper to do it, in fact, perhaps even desirable if we could do it in the right way.

MR. BELNICK. And the change in the law to which you refer was the change which expressly provided that the State Department could solicit humanitarian aid for the Nicaraguan opposition, subject only to the strictures of the Pell amendment; am I correct?

SECRETARY SHULTZ. That is correct. . . . I think it is important to recognize that the Pell amendment, which has the structure of a restriction, is, in effect, an authorization so long as you pay attention to the restriction. . . .

Belnick moved on to the matter of the accuracy of the information provided to the president by his advisers.

MR. BELNICK. And did you begin developing the view, particularly as of November 10—we'll talk about the additional press guidance that you got on that day—that the President's advisers were misleading him and not giving him the facts concerning what had actually transpired in the Iran initiative?

SECRETARY SHULTZ. I developed a very clear opinion that the President was not being given accurate information, and I was very alarmed about it, and it became the preoccupying thing that I was working on through this period, and I felt that it was tremendously important for the President to get accurate information so he could see and make a judgment.

His judgment is excellent when he is given the right information, and he was not being given the right information, and I felt as this went on that the people who were giving him the information were, in a sense—had—I think I even used the word with some of my advisers, they had a conflict of interest with the President and they were trying to use his undoubted skills as a communicator to have him give a speech and give a press conference and say these things and, in doing so, he would bail them out. . . .

So I was in a battle to try to get what I saw as the facts to the President and get—and see that he understood them.

Now, this was a very traumatic period for me because everybody was saying I'm disloyal to the President, I'm not speaking up for the policy, and I'm battling away here, and I could see people were calling for me to resign if I can't be loyal to the President, even including some of my friends and people who had held high office and should know that maybe there's more involved than they're seeing.

And I frankly felt that I was the one who was loyal to the President, because I was the one who was trying to get him the facts so he could make a decision, and I must say as he absorbed this he did, he made the decision that we must get all these facts out.

But it was—it was a battle royal.

MR. BELNICK. Mr. Secretary, in that battle royal to get out the facts which you waged and which the record reflects that you waged, who was the other side?

SECRETARY SHULTZ. Well, I can't say for sure. I feel that Admiral Poindexter was certainly on the other side of it, I felt that Director Casey was on the other side of it, and I don't know who all else. But they were the principals.

Belnick then went into the change in the instructions engineered by Bill Casey for the December 13 meeting. Senator Nunn interjected with a question: "Mr. Chairman, I don't know, perhaps everyone got the point, but I didn't quite get the point about what changed. I don't know whether the Secretary could go back over that? We just talked about a change that took place, and I'm not sure the substance of that change is clear."

MR. BELNICK. Mr. Secretary, the change the Senator is referring to is the one you discussed, were the ground rules which said this channel would be used for intelligence only, was now put back to be a channel for both policy and intelligence, and the question, as I understand Senator Nunn, is what was the significance of that change? What did it really mean to say that a channel that you had insisted and thought would be used now only for intelligence was going to be a channel that would be used for both intelligence and policy?

SECRETARY SHULTZ. I meant that the battle to get intelligence separated from policy and control over the policy was very much in play and the Director of Central Intelligence wanted to keep himself very heavily involved in this policy which he had been involved in apparently all along. That's what it meant. To me that's what it meant.

MR. BELNICK. Mr. Secretary, did it indicate to you that State had not— that your belief that State had now been given control over the policy towards Iran might not, in fact, be the case, and that, in fact, nothing had changed?

SECRETARY SHULTZ. Well, a lot had changed by this time. It wasn't that nothing had changed, but as you well know, or maybe you don't—you are not a Washingtonian—nothing ever gets settled in this town. You have to keep fighting, every inch of the way. . . .

MR. BELNICK. As you testified earlier, . . . you reported your discovery [of the nine-point agenda and the discussion of the Dawa prisoners] to the President on December 14, and based on his reaction, you felt that now at last you had gotten through?

SECRETARY SHULTZ. The President was stunned, and he was furious, as I have said before, and this just had a big impact on him. He had no idea of this at all, I am sure.

MR. BELNICK. At that point, Mr. Secretary, the argument which had begun in 1985 was finally over?

SECRETARY SHULTZ. I hope so.

MR. BELNICK. So do I.

At 12:25 P.M., the joint committee recessed. Although I had been testifying for almost three and one-half hours, it seemed like an instant to me. Someone called to me as I left the hearing room, "Mr. Secretary, are you glad to get this off your chest?" I didn't answer, but I *was* relieved. I had answered all the questions head-on, directly and easily. But I also knew that Belnick's job was to get out the record, and to the extent I had been able to reconstruct it, I had that record well in mind. I had a quick lunch back at the State Department. I decided to forgo further conversation with my staff in favor of peace and quiet. I stretched out on the couch in my office. Even though I was not able to drift off to sleep, the fifteen minutes of rest was helpful before the long afternoon in the witness chair that awaited me.

Lessons to Be Learned

Chairman for the day, Congressman Lee Hamilton, called the afternoon session to order at 2:30. I was confident but careful. The morning session had gone well. Now would come questions from the members of Congress: interpretations, meaning, motives, attitudes would be scrutinized. Senator Daniel Inouye was the first interrogator. He reviewed my long record of public service and said he had found the Iran-Contra story "sad and depressing and distressing" as well as "shocking and at times frightening." He ended with a question that was an invitation to me to comment on the process of governance: "And more importantly, Mr. Secretary, if you could also touch upon and advise us as to how we can prevent this from happening again and thus avoid the suffering of national self-doubt and international humiliation that follows such an ordeal?"

I responded at length:

SECRETARY SHULTZ. . . . The first point I think we need to keep before us is that a tremendous amount has gone right for America in the last few years. In fact, in many respects we're on a roll. And our efforts to help people move toward democracy and freedom, our efforts to show that a form of economic organization and economic policy that emphasizes markets and incentives, enterprise, things that have worked for us and we believe in, those things have gone forward.

The Coin of the Realm

I stressed the importance of honesty and trust for effective work in government. I was concerned that the spectacle of government being presented in the hearings would cause young people, especially, to avoid careers of public service:

> And I would say with respect to the revelations that were brought out this morning and that I've been learning about of the deception and so on, and people coming and telling you that they lied to you and so on, as they did to others, that's not the way life is in government as I have experienced it. It is—government in the Congress and in the Executive Branch is basically full of people who are here because they want to help and they're honest, they work at it. We argue. But I would say, for example, right now in the State Department, the people I work with, I have never worked with more able and more dedicated people who just work their tails off when they see the substance in what we are doing and what we are trying to achieve.
>
> So . . . I want to send a message out around our country that public service is a very rewarding and honorable thing, and nobody has to think they need to lie and cheat in order to be a public servant or to work in foreign policy. Quite to the contrary: If you are really going to be effective over any period of time, you have to be straightforward and you have to conduct yourself in a basically honest way so people will have confidence and trust in you.

I then told a story that had made a strong impact on me. "I had the great benefit, when I first came here in the Cabinet almost 20 years ago, to have a great American take me under his wing, and many of you know him, Bryce Harlow, a wonderful man, very experienced in the ways of Washington, and, boy, nobody was sharper at figuring the angles and getting things his way. He was sensational. But everybody listened to him, there was never any mark on Bryce. Why? He drummed it into me when I first came here. He said, 'Remember, George, one thing: Trust is the coin of the realm; trust is the coin of the realm. Be careful when you make a promise to somebody because you want to be sure you are ready to carry it out. And no matter how tempting it may be if you are trying to persuade somebody to vote for this or that or the other to say yes to something that they want, don't say yes unless you are prepared to work your heart out to get it or think you can deliver it.' So trust is the coin of the realm."

Intelligence Separated from Policy

I had long since concluded that the mixing of policy and intelligence had served us badly:

> I believe that one of the reasons the President was given what I regard as wrong information, for example, about Iran and terrorism was that the agency or the people in the CIA were too involved in this. So that is one point. And I feel very clear in my mind about this point. And I know that long before this all emerged, I had come to have great doubts about the objectivity and reliability of some of the intelligence I was getting, because I had a sense of this.

Let Accountable People Run Things

Then I discussed the critical issue of accountability and the problem of relations between staff people and those in the direct line of authority.

> A second point has to do with accountability. . . . The Executive Branch ought to be so organized that to the maximum extent possible the people who are running things are accountable people. Accountable people are, number one, the President and the Vice President, they are accountable to the American people, they run for election, just like in the Congress the accountable people, in my opinion, are the Members of Congress, the Senate and House, you run for election, you are accountable to your constituents.
>
> In the Executive Branch there are also a lot of other people who are accountable in a different way. They are people who get nominated by the President for a post and they are examined and so on and they get nominated, and then they appear before you. I appeared and spent 2 days—before the Senate Foreign Relations Committee—of examination. And then the full Senate votes.
>
> So they examine you and then that's not the end of it, by any means. From then on you are accountable in the sense that you can be called to testify.
>
> And it's not only the Cabinet officers, but all the Presidential appointees. . . . And there's hardly a day goes by when the Congress is in session when—if there's not somebody from the State Department who is an accountable officer, an assistant secretary, under secretary, or deputy secretary, whatever, that isn't appearing before . . . some committee of this Congress answering questions, presenting testimony, and in that sense being accountable. . . .
>
> I heard the question put to Admiral Poindexter, did he tell the

President about this fund diversion, and he said no, he decided that he wouldn't do that, and of course the President has said that he had no information about the fund diversion. . . . But in a sense . . . the deeper question is how could it be that a staff person was the sole possessor of such a piece of information and had operational control over it and his colleagues didn't know about it and he had that decision in his hands.

That decision shouldn't be in his hands in the first place.

So I believe that the Tower Commission was absolutely right in saying that the staff of the National Security Council should not be involved in operations at all.

I believe that the Tower Commission, in its recommendation that the staff of the National Security Council chair the meetings of Cabinet officers, the adviser, and the deputy, the sub-Cabinet and so on down the line, thereby putting the National Security Council staff at the center of the process—I think the Tower Commission recommendation on that is totally wrong.

I think the chairmanship and all that stands for should be in the hands of the accountable departments, whatever the subject may be, and the National Security Council staff should not be anywhere near the size that it is now. It should be much smaller and it should perform a very, very important job, which is a tough job, and that is the job of coordinating, the job of being up on their toes and running whenever there is a problem and you have a real time thing that you have to cope with . . . like, for example, when the decision was made to try to bring down, get forced to land a plane that we knew about that was carrying terrorists and the President made the decision to get that plane down.

That was a good operation in the sense that it worked well together, it was coordinated well by Admiral Poindexter, the President was very decisive and very quick, and the job was done and we got the terrorists down, and one of them was subsequently let go but the others weren't, and we were able to deliver the message: There's no place to hide, Mr. Terrorist. . . .

And, finally, I commented on the interaction between the executive branch and the legislative branch:

So I think—looking at it from the Executive Branch standpoint, we have to respect the fundamental duties of our colleagues on the Hill, but we have to expect them to respect ours and what that means is, as many have pointed out, that while we have a system of separation of powers in the way it is constituted, it inevitably means we also have a system of sharing powers, and there isn't any real way to say here is the answer by some kind of a formula.

You have to have a sense of tolerance and respect and a capacity to work together and a desire to do it, for us to share information, for you to put forward your ideas, not to keep telling us all the time how to run things, but keep tabs. . . .

I am a great respecter of staff and you cannot operate without it and there is a lot to be done by staff work and interacting of staff work, but that is really not the way for us to do our business together primarily.

The way for us to do things is basically to deal with each other and you can only do that from your standpoint if you feel when you are meeting with the accountable people that they really are the ones who are running things. . . .

So these are some of my reflections. Intelligence separated from policy. Let the accountable people run things. And be sure that the accountable people are tied in with the President.

In a sense, the President should feel that the Cabinet is his staff.

A Grilling

Then came questions from each of the twenty-six members of the joint committee. Senator Rudman returned to the matter of the Dawa prisoners, questioning whether I accurately judged the president's reactions. I responded, "I am sure of it. I have known Ronald Reagan for almost 20 years, and I have worked closely with him before he was President and during his Presidency. And we have our mostly agreements, sometimes disagreements, we have had plenty of discussions, and I think I know him as a human being pretty well. And I know that I have not misjudged his reaction."

Rudman went on about the president's decisiveness, and I responded, "He is comfortable with himself. He is decisive, he steps up to things, and when he decides, he stays with it. And sometimes you wish he wouldn't, but anyway, he does. He is very decisive, and he's very strong."

In response to a question from Senator Sarbanes about administration of policy by staff people, I said ruefully, "Let me just say that a minor aspect of all this that galls me, as you look at almost any part—this is minor, but it nevertheless, it galls me. Our guys, to the extent that the staff people who were doing this, they got taken to the cleaners. You look at the structure of this deal. It's pathetic that anybody would agree to anything like that. It's so lopsided. It's crazy. People say you can't trust the State Department to negotiate a tough deal. Well, I'll tell you."

MR. SARBANES. Let me ask you to respond to this final question.

Admiral Poindexter, in talking about the use of the proceeds of the Iranian arms sales for the Contras, also addressed using it for a series of other covert projects, and he was asked was that the first time you ever heard about that, and he said, "It is the first time that I've heard it discussed in that depth; I don't at all doubt that Colonel North and Director Casey may have discussed that; frankly, it is an idea that has some attractive features in my mind."

Is it an idea that has any attractive features in your mind?

SECRETARY SHULTZ. None.

MR. SARBANES. Would you explain why?

SECRETARY SHULTZ. Because it is totally outside of the system of government that we live by and must live by. . . .

The questions continued until 6:05 P.M., when the chairman adjourned the hearing for the day. A buzz filled the room. I returned to my office for a brief postmortem.

Reactions to my testimony dominated the news. An ABC-TV commentator said that "there had never been such laundering of views by a public official." CBS-TV reported that there were leaks coming from the White House staff that "Shultz is a crybaby." Peter Jennings said on ABC's "World News Tonight" that evening, "It really was one of those rare occasions, an education in government both good and bad. . . . The Secretary of State was eager to tell his story." ABC's Brit Hume, on Capitol Hill, reported, "Shultz had been accused of failing to support the President on Iran and of failing to oppose him enough. Either way many said he should have quit. Shultz had waited a long time for this and he was ready."

John Whitehead came in to tell me that Lou Harris, the poll taker, had telephoned to say that never in his long experience had he seen one performance change the course of events as mine had today. I had provided a narrative, an account of history, he said, that relieved the Senate and House members' concerns somewhat and yet also provided an explanation on which the White House could stand: what happened had happened because of a renegade NSC staff.

Senator Sam Nunn on the "Today" show the next morning said: "This witness [Shultz] believes in our form of government, the Constitution, the rule of law. He says it was arms for hostages. So he's credible." To which, on the same program, Senator Paul Trible added, "And he never said 'I can't recall.' He testified with precision. An eloquent soliloquy on trust in government." Nice words, but I knew a tough day lay ahead.

Day Two

At 9:00 A.M., July 24, Chairman Hamilton gaveled the hearing to order once more and, one by one, recognized the members for their turn at questions or, in some cases, extended statements expressing their views of the Iran-Contra events.

Congressman Henry Hyde was among those who criticized me for not stopping the Iran initiative:

> MR. HYDE. . . . You could have stopped it dead in its track and if you couldn't, you and Secretary Weinberger sure could.
>
> Now, it is easy to be critical of you talking to the President and not saying, "Mr. President, if you do this, because I love you and respect you, you got to do it without me and you got to do it without Cap."
>
> I cannot believe if you had been that forceful and that committed to opposing this flawed initiative as much as Poindexter and North were committed to advancing it, you couldn't have stopped it dead in its tracks and I ask you if that is not so.

"I doubt it very much," I responded. No one had even a remote idea of the extent of my struggle to try to get this ill-conceived and disastrous effort shut down—especially in the long, ongoing battle royal *after* the revelation of the arms-for-hostages deals with Iran. After an extended description of all the efforts I made over an eighteen-month period to block the Iranian arms initiative as it went through its various stages, I summarized:

> Now, I said right here in this room the first time I testified on this subject in public session, I said, "I don't give myself A-plus in all this," and I looked and I asked myself, did I do enough, could I have done more?
>
> But I have to tell you, Congressman, that as this hearing has gone on and I've seen in the form of these PROF[4] notes and so on the systematic way in which the National Security Council staff deliberately deceived me, I might say long before I made the comment to Admiral Poindexter about not needing to know about the details, this was not something that started after that. . . . my sense of "did I do enough" has to a certain extent given way to a little edge of anger about it. . . .
>
> MR. HYDE. Mr. Secretary, my time is up. I just want to say I guess the bottom line with me is I'm glad you didn't resign, but I wish you had gone up to the brink. Thank you.

---

4. PROF notes were computer messages through which NSC staff members communicated with each other. They apparently did not realize that material deleted from the computer was still held in the computer's backup files and could be retrieved. As a result, the notes became available to the committee.

As the day wore on, the questions, mostly from Republicans, became more critical of me for not fighting harder against the president's decision to proceed with the original Iran initiative.

Chairman Hamilton concluded the hearing: "Mr. Secretary, you have spent 2 full days with us. And I know that is a large hunk of time for a Secretary of State. And we deeply appreciate it. And I will not try to sum up. I simply want to say that I think the importance of your testimony for us is that you have really changed the focus of the committee's work. Up until your appearance, we really have been focusing on the question of what went wrong, and in a sense, that is the easy part of our work, though it hasn't been easy. And I think from now on, as you have said several times in the course of your testimony, we have to begin to focus on what needs to be done, what kinds of constructive suggestions we can come up with to make this system of ours work better."

At 5:25 P.M., he rapped his gavel: "And we stand in recess."

I felt suddenly drained of adrenaline, yet I was tremendously relieved that my testimony was over, and I was satisfied that I had done my best to answer the questions candidly and to express my own thoughts on the larger lessons of governance to be drawn from the Iran-Contra affair.

Reaction to my testimony was highly but not exclusively favorable. The Republican right was upset because I had taken issue with the glorification of North's testimony and had placed the emphasis on underlying problems of governance and what should be done to rectify processes that had clearly gone awry. The Democratic left was upset because I had successfully defended Ronald Reagan and the continuation and productivity of his presidency.

Elizabeth Drew, commenting on PBS, noted, "Secretary Shultz has become a political issue within the party. . . . There is some GOP and White House feeling that Shultz is making himself look good at the expense of the president." Cokie Roberts, also on PBS, said, "Republican loyalists are attacking one side of Secretary Shultz. Democrats are attacking the other. So he's getting it from both sides. But there's a very, very friendly attitude here [in the hearing room] toward him." When the hearings ended, Elizabeth Drew said, "Shultz saved them [the Senate and House committees holding the joint hearings]; he provided the model of rectitude they were seeking."

There was plenty of criticism, however, mostly to the effect that I should have threatened to resign, or resigned. "Washington is a resigning town," I remarked. Nothing else holds the special excitement of a rumored resignation. The problem was that a line of thought had grown up in Washington that if you don't like what's going on, then you should pull out. If you don't like apartheid, pull out of South Africa; don't stay and fight for change. If they are shooting at your troops in Beirut, pull out. If there is a risk to your navy in the Persian Gulf (the reflagged tanker *Bridgeton*, escorted by the U.S. Navy, had just hit a mine on the way to Kuwait on July 24), pull out. Maybe leaving would make you feel better—and safer— but I decided that it was not my way, not as events had played themselves out in the Iran-Contra affair. For in order to get the ongoing arms-for-hostages efforts shut down for good, it had been essential for me to stay in there and slug it out.

A warm and supportive telephone call came in from President Reagan and Nancy. But my relations with Frank Carlucci did not get easier. "You have been stirring up a State Department war with the NSC," he told me when my testimony was over. Feeling in the NSC staff was running high. He had ordered the staff not to comment on my testimony, he told me. "The president signed NSDD 276," Carlucci said. "You can talk to him all you want—he won't take it back." Over the weekend the NSC staff had staged its annual picnic, Carlucci told me. Three former NSC advisers had attended—Kissinger was not among them. One of them had picked up a knife and plunged it into a cake, saying "*That* for the State Department." Frank was grim. I thought back to Bud McFarlane's cake in the shape of a key. "What is it about NSC advisers and cakes?" I asked with a laugh.

Still, Frank was basically a good person, and he had assembled a far more professional staff than I had dealt with before. Colin Powell, his deputy, was wonderful: savvy, smart, straightforward, and energetic. A crush of critical work lay before us. We had plenty of problems, but, more importantly, immense opportunities. As we all became immersed in the substance of critical developments, I felt, our procedural differences would fade into the background. I could see real possibilities with the Soviets, important activity in the Persian Gulf and in the Middle East, and a new turn of events stirring in Central America. I would put Iran-Contra behind me and work flat out on the president's and the nation's foreign policy.

CHAPTER 43

Signs of a Sea Change:
Reflagging in the Persian Gulf

I headed to my farm in the Berkshires to relax for the weekend after a tense two days of testimony in the Iran-Contra hearings. I played a round of golf with old friends. I felt better. I had worked hard in the first half of the year to get our foreign policy back on track. In my testimony, I did my best to be candid and open and to elevate the debate to the underlying principles of government that were involved.

We had a year and a half remaining in the Reagan presidency. Was the foundation laid in the first term still usable? How much life was left in our policies? As I had struggled through the Iran-Contra summer of 1987, I began to realize that forces of change were moving our way. The president had come through a period of immense uncertainty, and his administration was still alive.

Signs of a sea change with the Soviets were clearly evident during my April 1987 visit to Moscow, as well as in the unanimous vote of the Security Council on the resolution mandating a cease-fire in the Iran-Iraq War and in Gorbachev's agreement to eliminate all long-range INF missiles. Evidence of a sea change was also to be seen in the Persian Gulf, the Middle East, Central America, Chile, and South Korea. It was as if our foreign policy, more successful than I realized in the difficult first half of 1987, seemed to be fundamentally transformed as we approached the dog days of August.

A Decision to "Reflag"

In 1987, the Iran-Iraq War dragged into its eighth year in a series of battles involving human slaughter on a massive scale and raising fears that Iran was about to overrun southern Iraq and then go on to threaten Saudi Arabia and the Gulf Arab states. Over a million people had been killed or wounded since Iraq had invaded Iran in September 1980. In January 1987, Iran had launched a major offensive, driving into Iraq just north of Baghdad and south of Basra, near the Persian Gulf. Iran was mining the Gulf, menacing commercial shipping, and threatening to close the Gulf and strangle the states of the Arabian Peninsula, let alone Iraq. Iran sought to position itself to dominate the entire region. In November 1986, Kuwait approached members of the Gulf Cooperation Council about the idea of superpower protection for shipping in the Persian Gulf. By early December, the Kuwaitis had reached a tentative agreement with the Soviets on a chartering plan and raised the question of reflagging their ships with the United States. The idea of the Soviets playing a key maritime role in the Gulf had no appeal to us, as the Kuwaitis well knew. We were at first reluctant to raise the level of our direct involvement in the Gulf by making Kuwaiti ships our direct responsibility, registering them as American vessels. But we did step up our presence in the Gulf.

On March 23, 1987, we offered to extend military protection from attack by either Iran or Iraq to Kuwaiti vessels proceeding through Gulf waters. On April 6, Kuwait formally proposed transferring the registration of some of its oil tankers to American flag registry. The U.S. Navy would then have more of an obligation to escort such commercial shipping up and down the Gulf, and the Iranians would have no doubt of U.S. intentions to keep the sea lanes open.

The Kuwaitis had made the same proposal to the Soviets. Despite strong feelings throughout the administration that we should not be part of an effort by the Kuwaitis to draw the Soviets into the Gulf, I felt we should not object to some Soviet presence: to object would only heighten Kuwait's bargaining power with us. For once, on an issue involving the use of our military force, Cap Weinberger and I were on the same side—for reflagging, despite the evident risks to our men and vessels that would accompany an expanded U.S. presence in the Gulf.

My main concern was that if the United States made this effort, we should be prepared to see it through. The ability of our forces to defend themselves, let alone others, had not been impressive in recent crises. Iran would be very likely to test us. With Beirut in mind, they might well expect that, as soon as our sailors came under fire and casualties occurred, Congress would call the navy home. I did not want to let the United States get drawn into the Iran-Iraq War. But it was critical that Iran not come to dominate the Gulf and therefore the Arabian Peninsula. I wanted the United States to keep trying, against all odds (the Chinese, Koreans, French, and Soviets were all selling arms and making money on the Gulf War), to restrict the flow of weapons to both Iran and Iraq and to maintain the freedom of international waterways, a cause that the United States had always led.

*   *   *

On May 17, two Exocet missiles from a French-made Iraqi F-1 fighter aircraft struck the U.S.S. *Stark*, a navy frigate then seventy miles north of Bahrein. Thirty-seven crewmen were killed. The United States immediately protested and demanded an explanation. Because of the hostage crisis going back to Iran's seizure of our embassy in Tehran in 1979, official Washington and public attitudes had been conditioned to view Iran as the primary threat and Iraq as a fragile counterforce holding back the tide of Khomeini's human waves. The attitude of many in the administration was to dismiss the attack: call it "inadvertent," an accident. I insisted that such commentary be "shut off."

We should let the Iraqis know that we would shoot down any plane that moved in a potentially threatening way toward any of our ships. The next day, a message flashed in from our ambassador to Iraq, David Newton, in Baghdad reporting that Iraq had expressed its deepest regrets and condolences. The Iraqis proposed a joint investigation. If Iraq was involved, Baghdad said, that could only have been an accident. Iraq promised an apology if the investigation showed Iraq to be at fault. I passed this message to the president with the comment that we must not let up. Recordings of the pilot's voice indicated he had erred.[1] Saddam Hussein admitted that Iraq was responsible and apologized. (Iraq, after a long and difficult negotiation not concluded until the Reagan administration left office, paid record-breaking compensation for the attack on the *Stark*: $27 million, an average of $730,000 for each of the 37 seamen killed.)

On May 19, 1987, President Reagan approved the announcement that, in response to Kuwait's request, the United States would reflag eleven Kuwaiti tankers so that the U.S. Navy could escort them. Amid general trepidation on the Hill, the Senate voted 91 to 5 to require the administration to report on the security situation in the Gulf before reflagging began.

At the end of the month, most press commentary was hostile to the president's decision, emphasizing that the United States took little oil directly from the Persian Gulf and missing the point that oil is a fungible commodity in world trade: whatever happened in the Persian Gulf would affect the United States as the world's largest user and importer of oil. Our allies were not rallying to our side, and Saudi Arabia would not allow our planes to use their airfields as a base for providing air cover for any of the escorted convoys. Once again, the signal was being sent to the world that if the United States took on this responsibility, Congress, the press, and the public would probably seek to compel us to pull back at the first sign of danger to our forces. Under those circumstances, other countries did not want to be associated with our effort.

1. "I got a [tanker]!"

Reflagging Set in Motion

By early summer, reflagging had begun. The Kuwaiti corporation that owned the tankers chartered itself in Wilmington, Delaware. From a road map of the region, new names were chosen for the ships from small towns across the Delaware River in South Jersey: Bridgeton, Surf City, and so on. President Reagan convened a National Security Planning Group on the Gulf situation. The navy laid out a detailed plan for escorting tankers with sound rules of engagement. The president approved. When the meeting was over, I made calls to congressmen to inform them of our plan and to point out that the more worries they expressed publicly, the more likely the Iranians would feel they could gain from attacking us.

The eight congressional leaders I talked to stressed the risks and the need for formal consultations under the War Powers Act. The attack on the *Stark* showed that American forces would be in danger, they argued. Prince Bandar, the Saudi ambassador, said the Saudis and the Gulf States feared another American pullout. If Saudi Arabia joined us in protecting Gulf shipping and Iran confronted us, Bandar suggested, the Saudis feared the United States might withdraw, as we had in Lebanon. The Gulf Arabs then would be dangerously exposed to Iran's advance. Our precipitous withdrawal from Beirut in 1984 was foremost in Arab minds. The assumption, not unfounded, was that Iran could take enormous losses inflicted by us, but *any* appreciable casualties on our side would lead Congress to compel us to bring our forces home.

Our allies hung back. They feared an escalating involvement as U.S. and Iranian forces interacted. They did not want to be drawn in. Silkworm missiles, which Iran was acquiring from China, were perceived as a threat to all forces in the region. The United States would probably have to hit at Iran itself, some allies feared, if we saw Iran deploying these missiles into batteries along the eastern shore of the Gulf. The prospect that reflagging would force us to choose between quitting or escalating was too much for many people. Even worse, White House rhetoric cast the United States as the major adversary of Iran, possibly in an effort to make President Reagan seem to be "standing tall" at a time when the Iran-Contra hearings threatened the future of his administration.

The Soviet role was hotly debated. The cold war view was, keep the Soviets out of the Gulf. Bill Safire in the *New York Times* on June 8, 1987, said we were "stumbling toward a New Yalta" if we cooperated with the Soviets in protecting the Gulf and in arranging an international conference for the Arab-Israeli peace process.

I did not want to see a major Soviet role in the Gulf, but I did sense that a beginning of a new era of U.S.-Soviet cooperation—on several sensitive fronts—might be possible for the first time since the cold war began.

A few in the media caught that scent. While I was in Venice at the economic summit, on my bedroom television set I heard Morton Kondracke on "This Week with David Brinkley" say: "I smell here something historic going on. The United States traditionally has tried to keep the Soviet Union out of the Persian Gulf. Now we seem to be saying that the Soviet Union is the co-guarantor of security in the Persian Gulf. This is . . . a major step . . . are we going to do this for the Middle East as well?"

Three Soviet minesweepers were then on the way to join two Soviet frigates on patrol in the Gulf. We should, I felt, handle this development in a way that made it a useful adjunct to our own far larger and riskier step. Chief of Staff Howard Baker agreed with me.

The Venice summit on June 9 pronounced on the Gulf: "We reaffirm that the principle of freedom of navigation in the gulf is of paramount importance for us and for others and must be upheld. The free flow of oil and other traffic through the Strait of Hormuz must continue unimpeded. We pledge to continue to consult on ways to pursue these important goals effectively."

I pointed out in a press conference that same day, "We are not alone in this by a long shot. For example, the British so far this year have escorted 104 vessels in the gulf—British vessels as they come in and out." In response to questions, I said that "effective measures" meant that "we call for a cease-fire, and if either country declines, then we will . . . call for mandatory sanctions on the sale of arms. Now whether the Soviets will join in that or whether the Chinese will join in that, we don't know yet. But that's what we're going to take into our discussions in the Security Council."

At the same time, I well knew that France was reluctant to be associated with us in the Gulf. Germany and Japan pointed to restrictions in their constitutions that prohibited military participation, and Giulio Andreotti, the foreign minister of Italy, after meeting with a high Iranian official, said that his country was not interested in taking part either. Altogether, international support for the present and prospective U.S. effort was uneasy and, with the Soviet Union, presented us with a strange bedfellow.

I was moving around the world for most of June. Before President Reagan and I left for the economic summit, I talked with the president, NSC adviser Frank Carlucci, and Howard Baker about possible developments in the Gulf. I said I supported a strong response to challenges that might come from Iran. During my travels, I kept in close touch with the situation in the Gulf. The CIA's analysis of the situation alarmed people. At an NSPG meeting on June 16, I was told, Judge William Webster, who had succeeded Bill Casey as CIA director, warned that the Kuwaiti reflagging effort would almost certainly lead Iran to attempt to force a reversal of that decision, including possible attacks on U.S.-flagged vessels protected by the U.S. Navy.

Once again, I found that being away from Washington led to misunderstanding. When I arrived home from my ASEAN trip, I read the press clips. Elaine Sciolino reported in the *New York Times* on June 24, 1987: "Contributing to the Administration's difficulties is Secretary of State George P. Shultz's noticeable absence from the debate, raising speculation, despite State Department denials, that he opposes the policy, or is reluctant to get involved in an open-ended commitment in the Middle East." The speculation was wrong. I wanted to use our forces to ensure free and safe navigation in the Gulf. I saw this as a way to thwart Iran's ambitions and possibly lead to an end to the long, bloody war.

On June 25, I found opposition growing in Congress. Senator Claiborne Pell proposed a bill that would have prohibited U.S. reflagging to protect Kuwaiti shipping. I felt we had to press Congress to a vote. Admiral Bill Crowe told me that the navy would be ready to go with its escort mission on July 3 and assured me that our warships could take care of themselves and the ships they escorted.

Something New: The United Nations

That same day, June 25, I received a memo from Frank Carlucci asking me to take "personal charge" of an effort at the Security Council to halt the Iran-Iraq War. "The Administration needs to demonstrate clearly that we have a diplomatic—and not just a military—strategy for dealing with the danger in the Gulf," he said. That was exactly the kind of argument I made to the White House on Central America and Soviet policy, usually encountering resistance. I agreed that there had to be a diplomatic track, but I felt that first the United States had to show a willingness to act in defense of reflagged Kuwaiti vessels and, for that matter, of the Gulf Arab states. If we precipitated a foreign ministers' meeting in New York prematurely, the likely result would be all rhetoric and no results and might require us to put the reflagging-escort idea on hold. Initially, I groused about the idea. I quickly realized, however, that Frank was preaching my own sermon to me, and I got going on the diplomatic track.

"There is no support in Congress for our Gulf policy," Carlucci told me on June 26. "So we need to draw attention away from the reflagging idea." Maybe, he said, we should declare we would "protect" shipping there but not go so far as to escort tankers. Now I feared the White House, as well as Congress, was drawing back from the idea of protecting the reflagged ships. If we flinched, the Soviets would gain unilaterally in the area. If, instead, we went forward, we might stop Iran, give heart to Kuwait, start a new cooperative chapter with the Soviets, and help end this protracted war. Something of a sea change was possible. Howard Baker had met with Senator Bob Dole and Congressman Bob Michel; Sam Nunn had weighed in. Their question was "Where is Shultz?" I was totally in support of the president's policy, Baker told them. They were reassured.

When I saw the president later that day, he agreed that I should go to work in New York. Action in the United Nations, if the Soviets and Chinese would agree, could be the diplomatic track we needed. The president also agreed that UN action was most likely if the administration and Congress were lined up behind a strong and undelayed reflagging and escort operation. I wrote to my fellow foreign ministers saying I would go to New York to address the UN Security Council.

Iran Acts: Unwisely

On June 27, the Iranians attacked two tankers in the Gulf, one Norwegian, one Liberian. Iran, the BBC reported that day, "has 20,000 trained revolutionary guards to attack U.S. ships in fast, Swedish-made coastal craft." Joint Chiefs Chairman Bill Crowe knew all about suicide patrol boats, he told me, and he had no doubts about our ability to handle them. He was completely confident about the escort role of the U.S. Navy in the Gulf. He had been there, knew those waters, and knew our ships and our capability. Other rumors increased the tension: the American hostages had supposedly been transferred from Beirut to Iran to be put on "trial"; Iran had laid mines outside Kuwait's harbor in anticipation of an assault on one of Kuwait's main islands; and Silkworms had been moved to launch sites in coastal Iran.

On Sunday, June 28, I appeared on "Meet the Press" and made the point that only the United States could defeat Iran's effort to close down navigation in the Persian Gulf and choke off the flow of oil through that critical waterway. If Iran was successful, I argued, nations friendly to us would be intimidated and the whole region could be radicalized. The United States wanted an end to the Iran-Iraq War through diplomacy: we remained officially and formally neutral and were open to communication from both Iran and Iraq. The immediate crisis lay in making Iran understand that it could not close the Gulf to commercial shipping.

I joined the congressional leadership for a meeting with President Reagan on June 30. The president was confident and decisive. I also argued the case, putting my full support behind him. Key Democrats—Senators Nunn, Wright, Boren, and Byrd—all indicated a willingness to support the president in this effort, but they remained disturbed that it was really Kuwaiti ships we were defending.

On June 30, the Senate Foreign Relations Committee passed two resolutions: one urging the president to delay reflagging for twelve months and the other threatening to invoke the War Powers Act to stop the escorting operation. Howard Baker, on "This Week with David Brinkley" on

July 5, was asked by Sam Donaldson about the Soviets' suggestion "that all vessels that are foreign to the Gulf be removed." Baker said that "if the Soviets remove theirs, perhaps we'll take a fresh look," sounding an uncertain note that did not express our policy and that I feared could invite an Iranian strike.

A Crucial Vote

Our diplomatic efforts proceeded with increasing prospects. The fact that the U.S. Navy was seriously engaged was increasingly evident to the other countries in the Security Council, let alone to Iran and Iraq. By Monday, July 20, our efforts to rally support in the United Nations were coming to a head. I traveled to New York for informal discussion with the secretary-general and representatives of other permanent members of the Security Council and then for a three-hour session in the Security Council chamber. The foreign ministers of France, West Germany, and the United Kingdom came to New York for this genuinely momentous occasion. Our relations with the Soviets had progressed to the point where we could collaborate on an important and difficult issue, the Iran-Iraq War.

The United Nations' most severe action was under consideration. In accordance with the rotation procedure in the Security Council, France held the chair. A representative of each country on the Security Council spoke. Foreign Minister Jean-Bernard Raimond of France presided: he was fair, judicious, and steady. At the end, he called for a vote. I raised my hand in support of the resolution. Aleksandr Belonogov, permanent representative from the Soviet Union, raised his hand as well, as did Huang Jiahua, the representative of the People's Republic of China. Representatives of every other nation at the table followed suit.

Nothing like this unanimous vote on an issue of real importance and difficulty had ever happened before in the history of the United Nations. A thaw in the cold war was clearly under way. Constructive action through the United Nation was now possible. I was proud to be the representative of the United States on this dramatic occasion.

The unanimous vote in the Security Council for UN Resolution 598 called for withdrawal of all forces to internationally recognized borders and for a total cease-fire in the Iran-Iraq War, an important and neutral step, because a cease-fire restricted to the Gulf would have served only Iraq. Iran nevertheless denounced the resolution as a "vicious American diplomatic maneuver." The resolution was adopted under Articles 39 and 40 of Chapter VII, the UN Charter's most forceful provision. Compliance was mandatory under international law. Even though measures of enforcement were not dealt with, the adoption of this obligatory resolution was a historic step. I recalled for the delegates: "September marks the eighth year of the war. The bloody fighting has now lasted longer than either the first or second world wars. . . . More than a million people—civilians as well as military personnel—have been killed or wounded. Cities have been razed by artillery and aerial attack. Chemical weapons have been used, and they honor no distinctions between combatants and non-combatants."

"The Security Council," I said, "was designed to quell precisely this kind of conflict." This binding resolution, scrupulously evenhanded, sought "to create the framework for an equitable and lasting peace, with neither victor nor vanquished, without loss of territory by either of the combatants." And I emphasized, "Importantly, the resolution records the Council's decision to meet again to consider further steps to ensure compliance."

Face-off with Iran

Two days later, on July 22, three U.S. Navy ships escorted two reflagged tankers up the Gulf toward Kuwait. At 2:00 A.M. on Friday, July 24, the president was awakened to hear that the *Bridgeton* had hit a mine. The convoy continued. Cap Weinberger ordered minesweeping helicopters to the Gulf. I requested Germany, Britain, France, the Netherlands, and Italy to contribute to the minesweeping effort. The *Bridgeton* made it to port by July 27 with a hole as big as a tractor-trailer in her hull.

The U.S. Navy was patrolling parallel to the convoy and had not swept the mines ahead of the tanker. People were snickering, saying that the *Bridgeton*, first in the convoy line, had been escorting the navy instead of vice versa. Questions were raised at the Pentagon about escort operations. Insurers and shipping companies were saying that when we escorted vessels in the Gulf, the risk of attack went up, not down. In a public statement on July 31, the British turned down our request for minesweepers; I remembered their opposition to our action in Grenada. Ours was a "deadend policy," the British said, and they wanted no part of it.

That same day, July 31, in an ominous outburst of violence in Mecca, thousands of Iranians on pilgrimage there fought with Saudi police. Four hundred people were killed. The Saudi and Kuwaiti embassies in Tehran were smashed. These simultaneous actions appeared to be a deliberate attempt by Iran to strike at the heart of the Saudi nation—and its guardianship of the Islamic holy places. The next day, Iranian officials called for the "uprooting" of the Saudi royal government.

Even as we were trying to end the Iran-Iraq War, a regionwide conflagration threatened. Suddenly the Iranian threat to Saudi Arabia was all too real. Iran began to conduct naval maneuvers in Saudi territorial waters, reportedly training for suicide missions by speedboats against the U.S. Navy. Iran's vituperative anti-American rhetoric reached its highest level in years.

But President Reagan did not waver, and our navy continued with its mission. Our demonstration of strength served our diplomacy. Our ships and aircraft showed readiness to shoot. The British and French finally did send minesweepers in mid-August, and Italy, the Netherlands, and Belgium followed soon after. With U.S. ships and Soviet ships already patrolling the Gulf, we had assembled the largest international flotilla since the Korean War. By Labor Day, I was beginning to see signs of a shift in Iran's diplomatic posture, which was becoming more conciliatory toward us and the UN effort. Deputy Foreign Minister Larijani of Iran passed a message to us through Foreign Minister Hans-Dietrich Genscher of Germany that Iran wanted to avoid escalation of the war and conflict with the United States in the Gulf. Tehran is "open to suggestions," Larijani said.

UN Secretary-General Pérez de Cuéllar was invited to come to Tehran on September 10 to talk about UN Security Council Resolution 598. The diplomatic process for ending the war had begun. An international effort through a coalition of key countries, using the United Nations as its founders originally intended, had been created. The United States and the Soviet Union were on the same side of a security issue for the first time since the beginning of the cold war.

The U.S. Navy drove the final spike into this affair in late September. The navy had been tracking *Al Fajr*, an Iranian amphibious landing craft fitted for minelaying. On September 21, the *Al Fajr* was observed and photographed dropping cylindrical objects. A navy helicopter hit the craft, and the next morning, forty miles off Bahrein, U.S. naval forces met no resistance when they boarded the *Al Fajr* and found mines on board.

On September 23, the Iranians informed the secretary-general that they would be "working within the framework of UN Security Council Resolution 598, to address implementation." We heard later that day that Iranian President Khomeini (who was then at the United Nations and who had said flatly that the *Al Fajr* was not laying mines) and his circle had been shocked by our attack; they had not believed the U.S. Navy would ever act against them directly.

Against this background, the view from many quarters was that we should use this advantageous moment to try to cram UN Resolution 598 down Iran's throat. I did not agree. I talked to President Reagan. He shared my view that we should give Iran a stake in this war-ending crisis. Iran wanted a commission of inquiry to report on how the war started, and they were justified in demanding that, for Saddam Hussein had launched the war. So I got an agreement to stretch out and sequence the steps envisioned in Resolution 598 without violating the integrity of the resolution. Soviet

Foreign Minister Shevardnadze agreed with me and, when I saw him in New York on September 24, he called U.S.-Soviet cooperation in trying to bring this war to an end "precious." I regarded his attitude as one more sign of a genuine and positive change in the Soviet worldview and in their attitude toward the United States.

In mid-October I went to the Middle East to advance the peace process. President Hosni Mubarak of Egypt praised us for our earlier retaliation against Iran: "For years no one has stood up to them." With the end of the Gulf War in sight, Mubarak was focused on Iraq. He had, he said, been working on Saddam Hussein to "shift gears" to a more moderate stance toward Israel. Iraq, he said, had a powerful military machine, and unless Iraq shifted its policy, no comprehensive peace between Arabs and Israelis would be possible.

The Iranians tested us again several times, and we struck back. On October 8, 1987, our helicopters sank three Iranian gunboats. On October 16, an Iranian (Chinese-made) Silkworm missile hit the reflagged tanker *Sea Isle City* at its Kuwaiti anchorage. Three days later, the U.S. Navy destroyed an Iranian oil rig used as a gunboat base, and the president banned all imports from Iran. Our resolve eventually made an impression. On August 8, 1988, both Iran and Iraq accepted a cease-fire under UN Resolution 598.

Throughout this reflagging and escort operation, I admired Ronald Reagan's resolve—not only for making a correct but tough decision, but for sticking with that decision in the face of widespread criticism and adverse and threatening developments.

Taken as a whole, the reflagging episode gave a new shape to international relations in response to a dangerous conflict. We had gained the cooperation, even though reluctant, of a diverse group of nations unused to cooperating with one another. We had worked hard to bring the Soviets to take a responsible position rather than play their usual spoiler role. Our creative use of the United Nations proved effective and established a precedent for collective action in the future. President Reagan's persistence enhanced the standing of the United States and contributed, in a decisive way, to the termination of the long, bloody war between Iran and Iraq. After the setback wrought by the Iran-Contra affair, Ronald Reagan was back in business.

CHAPTER 44

Signs of a Sea Change:
A New Mix in the
Middle East Peace Process

By early 1987, I had become more convinced than ever that the most promising way to approach the Palestinian-Israeli conflict lay in some form of shared, overlapping, or interwoven sovereignties across Israel, the West Bank, and Jordan. That way, I felt, Israel could find security and full recognition as a state, Palestinians could govern themselves and gain the attributes of citizenship in the international community, and Jordan could find stability, security, and prosperity through a degree of integration with its neighbor to the west. So, with this endgame in mind, I felt the idea was to figure out what interim steps would best get the parties there.

The parties to the conflict would have to be induced somehow to enter into direct, face-to-face negotiations through a doorway over which the text of UN Resolution 242 was inscribed. But the words associated with that resolution, "territory for peace," would have to be treated with flexibility. Just as peace is an ambiguous concept, so too is territory, especially with regard to who is sovereign over that territory. The many functions of government would have to be controlled in different ways, with total or mixed control following a variable pattern and distributed in different ways among Israel, Jordan, and the Palestinians. I discussed my thoughts with a few of State's Middle East team. Our ambassador to Israel, Tom Pickering, immediately saw the concept of "mixed sovereignty" in a creative and positive light. I had a muted sense that the Near Eastern Affairs Bureau people, led by Dick Murphy, regarded my views with some skepticism: to them, Resolution 242 was the bedrock concept of all Arab-Israeli diplomacy, and territory was a clear-cut and unambiguous geographic reference; any attempt to tinker with 242 or avoid it would lead to trouble. Nonetheless, in my own mind, I knew where I thought the process should come out, and that helped me as I sought a way to get there.

The process would start with an international conference, as King Hussein insisted. That was a way to give the king the legitimacy taken from him by the Arab decision at Rabat that gave the PLO the role of representating the Palestinians. It was also a way to overcome the Arab reluctance to engage in direct negotiations with Israel. Second, the conference would have to lead immediately to direct Arab-Israeli negotiations, which, third, would be accelerated faster than the pace prescribed at Camp David in 1978: a transitional or interim stage would still be necessary during which Palestinians and Israelis might gain in mutual confidence, but the final status talks ought to get under way promptly. Shortly after King Hussein reinvented the international conference idea in 1985, we had sketched out to him a conference model that would address all of his requirements but would dispatch them quickly so that face-to-face talks could begin. Dick Murphy had moved around the Middle East for months, especially between Israel and Jordan, promoting this idea, but to no real avail.

On April 7, 1987, Jordanian Prime Minister Zaid Rifai brought us a message from Syrian President Assad: if Jordan and the United States agreed on an international conference on King Hussein's terms, Syria would agree to attend. But a conference on the king's terms—a real, continuing, empowered international assembly—could result in a ganging up against Israel and would be especially dangerous as long as the Soviets remained the weapons supplier and superpower patron of Iraq and Syria, nations dedicated to Israel's elimination. On the other hand, I thought, it was possible in 1987 that the Soviets, now adjusting foreign policy across the board, might join the United States as cosponsors of a brief conference, a ceremonial event to launch direct talks.

A Breakthrough?

Israeli Foreign Minister Shimon Peres had secretly arranged to meet King Hussein in London on the weekend of April 10, 1987. I sent Ambassador Wat Cluverius, our roving envoy on the peace process, to London in case we could be of help.

In Helsinki, I stopped on my way to Moscow at the Finnish government's Kalastaajatorpa guest house, with its lake still frozen hard enough to walk on although it was mid-April. An emissary from Shimon Peres, Yossi Beilin, arrived to brief me on what had happened when King Hussein and Peres had met in London on April 11. He portrayed the meeting as a breakthrough: King Hussein and Foreign Minister Peres had reached an agreement on the holding of an international conference. Peres felt, Beilin relayed, that it would prove to be "the most historically significant step for

Israel" since the Biltmore Conference in May 1942 produced the ideas that aroused world Jewry's support for an Israeli state in what was then Palestine. "It is an agreement," Beilin said, "the first ever. They [Peres and Hussein] didn't sign. Each wrote the paper and then shook hands. This handshake had the feeling of an historic event." The two had agreed, Beilin said, that the secretary-general of the United Nations would invite the permanent members of the Security Council (the United States, the Soviet Union, Great Britain, France, and China) and the parties to the Arab-Israeli conflict to negotiate a peaceful settlement based on UN Security Council Resolutions 242 and 338, to bring comprehensive peace to the area, to provide security to its states, and to respond to the legitimate demands of the Palestinian people.

All participants in the conference would agree that the purpose of the negotiation was the peaceful solution of the Arab-Israeli conflict based on Resolutions 242 and 338 and the peaceful solution of the Palestinian problem in all its dimensions. The conference would invite the participants to form geographical, bilateral committees to negotiate the issues between them. In other words, Beilin explained, the international conference would meet simply to say to the parties, go to work.

Jordan and Israel would agree that the international conference could not impose any solution or veto any agreement arrived at between the parties; negotiations would be conducted in the bilateral committees directly; Palestinian issues would be dealt with in the committee of a joint Jordanian-Palestinian delegation and an Israeli delegation; participation in the conference would be based on the parties' acceptance of 242 and 338 and the renunciation of violence and terrorism; other issues would be decided by mutual agreement between Jordan and Israel; all agreements would be subject to the approval of the governments of Jordan and Israel. All these provisions had been incorporated into an agreed-upon document, Beilin said.

King Hussein had taken a tough line on the PLO. He had said to Peres that the Palestinian problem was Jordan's problem and he would deal with it. He said the PLO would fall into line when it saw the process going forward without it.

Beilin said his report should be regarded by the United States as a formal request of both parties, King Hussein and Foreign Minister Peres, that the international conference proposal, as described, be "taken over as the initiative of the United States." To launch this effort, a visit by me to Israel was needed, Peres felt. "Don't let it evaporate," Beilin said. "It's in your hands now."

The idea of a carefully controlled international conference that would meet to propel the parties into direct, bilateral negotiations was one I had sketched out earlier in an in-house memorandum on July 7, 1985,[1] and subsequently. I had explored the idea with Shimon Peres when he was prime minister. Yet this urgent request was extraordinary: the foreign minister of Israel's government of national unity was asking me to sell to Israel's prime minister, the head of a rival party, the substance of an agreement made with a foreign head of state—an agreement revealed to *me* before it had been revealed to the Israeli government itself! Peres was informing me, and wanting me to collaborate with him, before going to his prime minister. The situation was explosive, especially because Shamir and his Likud party were vociferously denouncing the idea of an international conference of any kind. Shamir, in his Passover message to President Reagan on April 1, had stated that it was "inconceivable that there may be in the U.S. support of the idea of an international conference, which will inevitably reintroduce the Soviets into our region in a major role."

If I portrayed the Peres-Hussein agreement as an American initiative, I would be deceiving—a deadly practice in diplomacy and one that would inevitably be discovered. If I took it to Shamir as the Hussein-Peres agreement that it was, Shamir would certainly veto it on the spot. At the same time, I wanted to do all I could to capitalize on this development. During my Moscow meetings with Shevardnadze in April, I raised regional issues. Our talks were difficult. When we came to the Middle East, I went over the issues laboriously with him and discussed at length the international conference idea. "Do you agree that the negotiating is to be done by the parties directly and bilaterally and that all the international conference can do is promote that?" I asked him.

"Yes," Shevardnadze said, "I agree."

I was not worried by the Soviet role in such a ceremonial event; the real problem would be to persuade the Arabs and the two parts of the Israeli government to agree.

When my highly productive meetings with Shevardnadze and Gorbachev in Moscow ended, I flew to NATO headquarters in Brussels to brief allied foreign ministers and then to California. At Rancho Cielo on April 16, I went over with President Reagan both the substance emerging from my discussions with Gorbachev and Shevardnadze and the atmosphere of genuine change in Moscow. I also reviewed the situation in the Middle East. We agreed that the next step would be to find out King Hussein's views directly. And Peres would have to take this agreement to Shamir himself; the United States could not do that for him. Chief of Staff Howard Baker, who was at the ranch, was uneasy. He believed that if we proceeded, we

---

1. I envisioned a conference in Washington, attended by representatives of the five UN Security Council permanent members. It would be a one-day affair and meet simply to provide international legitimization for direct Israeli-Jordanian/Palestinian negotiations that would start in the United States.

were likely to take a fall for intervening in Israeli politics, perhaps even causing the collapse of the government, and we would be inviting the Soviets, with their long record of troublemaking, back into the Middle East.

Seizing the Moment

Back in Washington on April 20, I received word from Dick Murphy that Peres had informed Shamir about what he and King Hussein had agreed to in London. The Jordanians told us that they fully confirmed the description of the event that Peres had given me through his emissary in Helsinki. On April 22, I telephoned Prime Minister Shamir to tell him that I had been informed of the London agreement by his foreign minister and by the king of Jordan. I was ready, I told him, to come to the Middle East to work with him, seizing upon this very positive moment to go forward in the peace process.

Shamir replied that he wanted to think the idea over for a day or two, but I could sense that he was dead set against it. Two hours later, Eli Rubinstein, Shamir's quick-witted aide, telephoned from Jerusalem to give us Shamir's answer. Prime Minister Shamir did not want to say this to me directly, but the London document had no appeal for him; he would not welcome a visit by me. An international conference would amass pressure on behalf of the Arabs against Israel. If the United Nations was involved, there was no way the PLO would not be involved. "So Shamir is very upset," Rubinstein said. "This international conference has become a passion. He is utterly against it. It goes to the core of Israel's national interest. Nothing personal toward the secretary, but an international conference? 'A healthy head into a sick bed,' that's the prime minister's view."

I detected that Shamir was convinced he could establish a personal relationship with King Hussein and deal with him directly, without the wider involvement of others. The king had sent a warm nonsubstantive message to Shamir. I told Paul Boeker, our ambassador to Jordan, to suggest to King Hussein that he follow up with another message telling Shamir why Jordan needed the conference and trying to address Israel's concerns. Boeker passed the message on. I'll see what I can do, the king responded.

The next day, April 23, word came from Peres: he was pleased with the way I had handled the issue with Shamir; he recognized that he would have to risk breaking the government over this; he would "not be a party" to Israel's missing this opportunity. "In London, Israel and Jordan had been in direct negotiations and had achieved agreement. Would the Israeli prime minister now turn away from this opportunity?" Peres asked.

*   *   *

On April 24, Israeli Defense Minister Moshe Arens appeared in my office, sent by Shamir. Arens said this London agreement had come as a total surprise to him. I told him everything I knew about it, including the idea that the United States take it over as our own initiative. "I regard Shamir as rejecting this whole approach," I told him.

"You read us right," Arens replied.

"I don't agree with the prime minister's arguments. This represents a possibility that never existed before. My instinct is to work on it," I said. "But since Shamir is opposed, I'm filling up my calendar. But it's too bad." The apparent calm on the West Bank is deceptive, I told Arens. "Now is the time for neighbors to try to come to terms with each other before real trouble breaks out."

Arens stressed the impropriety of what Peres had done. "I was astounded to learn that Peres negotiated an agreement, even *ad referendum*. This has never happened in Israeli history before," he said.

Arens and I debated the value of an international conference. The heart of Arens's objection was that almost all of the parties present at such a conference would take a position diametrically opposed to Israel's—or even to Israel itself. Such a gathering was too risky; real, direct negotiations might not take place; the conference could get out of control; it was too slippery a slope.

I argued back long and hard: King Hussein had no choice but to ask for some sort of an international conference to give legitimacy to his role as negotiator for the Palestinians. The idea that he would deal alone with Israel was a nonstarter: he could never deliver on an agreement reached in that way. I described for Arens in excruciating detail exactly how a conference could work and be kept under control, but he would not budge.

The fundamental problem, Arens countered, was that the Soviet Union, as the United States's cold war adversary, would always adopt radical Arab views, and King Hussein would then be unable to take a more moderate stance. Nothing could go forward, Arens concluded, until Shamir and the king met face-to-face. Our conversation ended on this sour note but with what amounted to a request for help in arranging such an encounter.

I sent a message to King Hussein saying that Shamir's bedrock objection to the conference was in large part based on his resistance to Soviet participation. I emphasized the importance of a meeting soon between the king and Shamir and said, "Assurances on Soviet participation that Your Majesty could give would be very important in that context."

By early May, Jordan had disclaimed the London agreement, leaving Peres out on a limb, testy, and tending to blame me. Soon the issue of "how to engage" in the peace process became the hottest topic in Israeli politics. And it became apparent that Shimon Peres did not have the votes to win in the Knesset. Fiery charges flew back and forth between Peres and Shamir.

On May 17, 1987, in a speech to the American Israel Public Affairs Committee (AIPAC), I set out my view that an international conference convened strictly to initiate direct negotiations could provide an opportunity for Israel, despite the divisions in Israel over the issue.

Peres was at the AIPAC meeting, and I talked privately with him. Shocked by the criticism and lack of support in Israel for his London agreement, Peres went out of his way to say that he did not blame me. His aides, however, were deeply bitter. Before long, they were telling the press that I was responsible for the collapse of this unprecedented agreement.[2]

Having defeated Peres over this issue, Shamir and his inner circle began to consider seriously the arguments I had put forth to Moshe Arens for a strictly limited conference. On June 14, in Manila, I received a message indicating that Shamir might agree to a conference of the superpowers or the five UN Security Council permanent members if they would meet to "endorse direct negotiations" and then adjourn. I decided to try to make some version of that happen.

At the end of July, with my Iran-Contra testimony over, I talked to President Reagan about further efforts in the Middle East, and we agreed to push once again on Shamir and Peres to see whether there was some way to move things along. I decided to send Charlie Hill, my executive assistant, to Israel on an informal and exploratory mission. He was well known to the Israeli leaders and had the advantage of a low profile. The problem was how to reduce the risks of an international conference. Shamir told the press on August 6 that the visit was "mission impossible," an international conference was out of the question.

Shamir's Game Plan

Shamir had his own game plan in mind. Shamir secretly sent his aide Dan Meridor to see me. "Greetings from the prime minister!" he said when we met in the late afternoon of August 6. His visit concerned a highly confidential matter, he said. The Israeli embassy did not know he was in Washington. He had come to report that Shamir and King Hussein had met on July 18. The king had been the host, in his house outside London. He had provided a kosher meal for Shamir: "First time for Yitzhak Shamir." Meridor chuckled. The meeting had gone on for five hours, beginning formally, ending warmly. Shamir had put forward a long list of cooperative steps that could be taken jointly by Israel and Jordan and went

2. The front page of the *Christian Science Monitor*, on July 17, 1987, headlined: "SHULTZ UNDER FIRE: Peres aides say US has let Soviets seize Mideast initiative."

over the interim arrangements for Palestinian self-rule that had been launched by the Camp David process. This was the way to proceed, Shamir said, not by way of an international conference.

"But," I told Meridor, "if we deliver to you the kind of international conference that would get to direct negotiations, one that would be cosmetic and that would not be continuing, would Prime Minister Shamir say yes to it?"

"We are against an international conference," Meridor said. "Of course, if King Hussein said, 'I want direct negotiations, but I want the five permanent representatives [in the UN Security Council] to urge me to do it'— fine, no problem."

Still, it was obvious that Shamir wanted to focus on his own private contacts with the king. The two had agreed, Meridor said, that Shamir would send an emissary to Amman soon. Was there a chance here, I thought, that Shamir had caught a mild case of peace fever? He might want to compete with Peres as a peacemaker but do it in his own way—secretly with King Hussein and without the backdrop of an international conference.

King Hussein also sent word to me about his meeting with Shamir in London, but his description of the meeting diverged dramatically from Meridor's. In effect, the king was saying, Shamir is hopeless, that he couldn't work with him, whereas Shamir, in effect, was saying that he could work directly with the king and didn't need any help from outside. Each insisted that I not reveal his assessment of the London encounter to the other. I specifically asked King Hussein for permission to reveal to Shamir that I had received the king's read-out of the session. The answer was no. Both parties seemed to disparage and discount the importance of the United States in all this.

The damage the presidency was suffering because of the Iran-Contra affair was palpable. My own worry stemmed from the feeling that while the Middle East scene seemed quiet on the surface, a dangerous explosiveness was rumbling underneath. Shamir continued to stress his new private link with King Hussein, indicating that he would actively pursue it in the period just ahead. He would inform us as soon as his special emissary returned from the next session with the king.

Hill spent time with people on both sides of the Israeli political scene, and from his talks with Shimon Peres came the idea that the next Reagan-Gorbachev summit might become the international conference. I liked that idea and mulled over how to create an international doorway through which the parties could enter into direct negotiations.

I heard periodically about Prime Minister Shamir's attempts to arrange the visit of an Israeli emissary to Jordan and of his hopes to meet the king again, in Europe in the fall, but nothing ever took place. King Hussein's version of the July 18 London meeting had turned out to be the decisive one.

A Startling Idea

On September 11, I put my thoughts to President Reagan: he and Gorbachev, as an adjunct to their Washington summit planned for the end of the year, would invite King Hussein and Prime Minister Shamir, as well as representatives of Syria, Egypt, and Lebanon, to meet in the United States under U.S.-Soviet auspices and with the secretary-general of the United Nations in attendance.[3] This gathering would call on the parties to launch direct negotiations: the Jordanian delegation would include Palestinians with whom Israel was willing to meet. The accepted purpose would be to achieve a peace treaty between the Arab states and Israel. I would manage the process in Washington and pursue it by traveling to the Middle East shortly thereafter. Shamir could avoid the dreaded words "international conference" by calling the meeting a summit; in the meeting the king could find the international cover he needed to negotiate directly with Israel.

"This may sound like a startling idea," I said to President Reagan: "Why should we invite the Soviets into the Middle East? But something profound is happening. A new global reality is taking shape." Ronald Reagan's policy toward the Soviet Union was succeeding, and with that success was coming a new set of challenges and opportunities. What Nixon did in his opening to China, I told the president, was rightly seen as a historic turning point. Nixon created a connection between the leader of the democratic world and the leader of the most populous nation of the Communist world. "What you are doing," I said, "is of even greater significance—working to turn the Communist world's superpower onto a totally different course, more open, with a more acceptable foreign policy and a different perspective toward the world economy. So the question is whether we should work to co-opt the Soviets in some areas." We were on the same side of the Kuwaiti reflagging operation, I noted. "The Soviets' yearning for equal status remains so strong—even as their relative power declines—that we may be able to design an approach on the Middle East that gives them status but restricts their substantive influence."

"I'll think about it," the president responded. He seemed—understandably—to be growing weary of the Middle East and the incessant maneuverings of its leaders. But I knew his interest in the Middle East ran deep and that he would think my idea over carefully.

3. As joint chairmen of the Geneva Conference of 1973 on the Arab-Israeli conflict, the United States and the Soviet Union in this role would provide a semblance of renewal of a still-convened, if in name only, international conference.

*   *   *

The next day, Saturday, September 12, Simcha Dinitz, a diplomatic pro who had earlier been Israel's ambassador to the United States, came to my office on instructions from Peres. Dinitz brought to me, on Peres's behalf, an idea similar to what I had just put forward to the president. Too much planning and preparation could kill the idea, he said, tying it down to so many detailed agreements that the negotiations that followed would be doomed to deadlock. "My experience in diplomacy," Dinitz said, "is that big ideas at times help us escape stumbling blocks of details. Israel could never have planned or prepared for Sadat's visit. That is what we now need, something so swift and dramatic that people must ignore details."

I told Dinitz that he was trying to take me into something I had already been trying to develop. Then I went over for him, as I had earlier with Prime Minister Shamir, my views on what should be the eventual substantive outcome of the whole process: not territory for peace in the literal sense, but sovereign control over various functions dispersed among Israel, Jordan, and the Palestinians, with varying patterns of control, depending on the subject—security, health, water, education, to name a few. Such an approach, I argued, could meet the differing needs of Palestinians and Israelis.

On September 23, while I was attending the opening of the UN General Assembly, I got word from President Reagan that I could go ahead with the "international conference" idea. "But the first guy who vetoes it kills it," he said.

I telephoned Prime Minister Shamir on September 27 to say I would like to meet with him before going to Moscow to prepare for the upcoming summit. He said he would welcome me. My presence in Israel just before arriving in Moscow would be a signal of special interest in the plight of Soviet Jewry. I had an invitation to the Weizmann Institute that would constitute the "reason" for my visit.

On October 7, Abba Eban came by to see me, as he periodically did when in America. Eban, as Israel's first ambassador to the United Nations, had been famous to Americans in the 1950s. Tall, stout, dignified, articulate, and intellectually domineering, Eban had become one of those figures more admired abroad than at home. In a meeting with Eban, there was almost no point in even trying to speak, so after a while I just sat back and listened. One remark he made echoed my own worries about the situation there: "All looks fine. But there is rumbling underneath. The urgency of it all doesn't scream at you, unfortunately."

On the Columbus Day holiday, I sent Dick Murphy to Canada, where he met with Prime Minister Margaret Thatcher for over an hour, during a refueling stop at Uplands Canadian Forces Base. There he briefed her and

Foreign Minister Geoffrey Howe on what I intended to do in the Middle East. King Hussein would be in England when I would talk with him, and perhaps, I thought, she could help out there. Murphy reported in colorful style what must have been a lively meeting. Prime Minister Thatcher, he said, was intrigued by the idea. "This is a way to kick it into life at last," she said. "It's putting a stiletto to Yitzhak Shamir's throat. I like that!" But, she cautioned, in classically grave Thatcher style, "beware you don't get a Russian knife between your shoulder blades." Warming to her objections, she proceeded to raise alarms. "Beware of our chum who is still in Afghanistan. This is so fast! This is an astonishing U-turn in America's approach to the Soviet Union!"

"Margaret," Murphy reported Geoffrey Howe as saying with a deep sigh, "you've badgered George for five years about doing something just like this; now don't send a message of apprehension."

"No, no, no!" Thatcher threw up her hands in protest. "I'm all in favor." But she was also skeptical of Shamir and reserved about giving a prominent role to the Soviets.

On the eve of my departure for Israel, Eli Rubinstein called in one of the regular Israeli attempts to smoke out what I had in mind and rid me of any foolish expectations. "Apart from an international conference, Shamir is ready to consider any approach." Rubinstein sighed genially.

In the early morning of October 16, over the eastern Mediterranean, Israeli Air Force F-16s suddenly appeared alongside my plane to escort us into Ben-Gurion Airport, an impressive sight. People on our aircraft crowded to the windows to look.

Shamir: Attracted and Appalled

Friday afternoon I met with Prime Minister Shamir. After I had gone over every detail of our proposal, I was surprised to hear him say, "This is a very new idea, and I can't help but respond positively. But," he said, and my heart sank, "there are very many problems, and we must think them through." The magnitude of the idea had dawned on Shamir and his people; he seemed at once attracted and appalled by it. I made precisely the same proposal in a separate meeting with Peres, who told me privately that he fully agreed but would say nothing in the interest of maximizing the chances of a favorable reaction from Shamir. I admired his restraint.

I had wanted to meet with a group of Palestinians from the West Bank and Gaza, but they canceled, I was told, because of threats from the PLO. Maybe. But I had made a mistake in letting our embassy set the meeting in my hotel, the Jerusalem Hilton, which was ringed by armed Israeli security guards. When I saw the guards, I realized the Palestinians would not regard that environment as neutral ground and that pictures taken of them coming and going would be used against them, possibly in a deadly way.

After sundown Saturday, I took Murphy with me to Prime Minister Shamir's residence. Moshe Arens was present. If Shamir agreed, I said, I would go to London to put the idea to King Hussein, and then to Moscow to present it to Gorbachev. "Everybody will describe the idea in a different way," I said. "It is a summit. It is an international event. It is a renewal of the Geneva Conference." Shamir asked dozens of questions, all implying that, on reflection, he could not say yes. He spun out the chess moves, all of them depicting a situation growing out of control. "Okay," I said, "I don't want to waste your time. Just say no."

He didn't want to say no, he told me, but there were "insurmountable obstacles." Shamir suggested that after Sunday's cabinet meeting, Eli Rubinstein and Yossi Ben-Aharon, another of his close associates, go over all the problems with Dick Murphy and Charlie Hill; then Shamir and I would meet again on Sunday evening.

Sunday was a rainy, chilly gray day. I was at the Weizmann Institute, accompanied by Dick Murphy, hearing about activities there, making a speech, and receiving an honorary degree. Hill and the two Shamir aides sat in a hotel room and went through every detail of every possible concern and all of the myriad "understandings" or "assurances" that Israel would require before entering such a risky process as this. When the long debate ended, Eli Rubinstein, as always full of Yiddish stories, told about the Jewish mother in Central Europe who made her little boy wear so many clothes to keep warm that he couldn't step over a branch across the path or fly to Israel. "We don't want to strap this up in so many belts and suspenders that no one can move," Eli said. When I heard that story, I realized that Shamir's answer just possibly might be yes, although most of the betting was still on no.

As I was leaving for the prime minister's residence, Murphy said, "If Shamir's answer is no, this will be a brief, pleasant evening. If his answer is yes, we'll be up all night negotiating an MOU [memorandum of understanding] with them."

But that was not the way it turned out. I had a private dinner with Shamir. We talked about problems in the region, my negotiations with the Soviets, the problems of Soviet Jewry, the Israeli economy. After dinner, two or three people on each side joined us, and we turned to the issue at hand. Our session was brief and direct. "Well, Mr. Secretary," Shamir concluded softly, "you know our dreams, and you know our nightmares. We trust you. Go ahead."

That was it. No more had to be said. He had rolled the dice with us. More important, a sense of trust was evident and essential. I was moved. I would use that trust carefully.

The next evening, at King Hussein's Palace Green residence in London,

I put the proposal to him as one from the president of the United States to the king of Jordan. I went over it in great detail and made clear that he need not respond at that moment. I knew he would need to think it over and consult. We had plenty of time before the Washington summit would take place. He and his advisers, Tahir al-Masri and Marwan Kassem, were taken aback by the idea and were astounded at Shamir's agreement. They grew more and more serious and seemed intrigued as I continued to explain the idea. We agreed that King Hussein and I would meet again the following day.

When I returned to my hotel in London, O'Bie told me that the Dow Jones industrial average had fallen 508 points, the largest one-day decline in the history of the New York Stock Exchange. I could hardly believe it, but my mind remained focused on the Middle East.

A Surprising Blow

The next day, Tuesday, October 20, I met again with King Hussein. He had made up his mind: his answer was no.

The king gave me two reasons. His nerves went raw at the very mention of Shamir. "I can't be alone with that man," he said in an aside to Murphy. He did not believe that Shamir would ever permit negotiations to go beyond the issue of "transitional" arrangements for those living in the West Bank and Gaza. And he also did not believe Shamir would ever give up an inch of territory or work on a "final status" agreement for the territories. So, no, that was that, said the king.

A third reason was implicit but unstated. The king knew that President Assad of Syria would reject this approach and felt that the Soviet Union—whatever its publicly cooperative stance with us might be—would in the end support Syria's rejectionist and violent opposition to any serious step toward peace. Again, I thought the king was mistaken about the Soviets: with this remarkable opportunity, and with the United States and the Soviet Union acting together, I was convinced that Syria could be contained and a new chapter opened for Palestinians and Israelis.

I made all these arguments forcefully to the king. But at that moment, in London, no amount of arguing with the king could change his response. I left the king and went to Heathrow Airport to head for Moscow. In a small holding room I briefed my delegation on the king's decision. They were downcast.

"Stop talking about it," I told them. "It's over. No more memos. No need for a postmortem." I told Murphy to go over to the Foreign Office to tell Geoffrey Howe what had happened. Margaret Thatcher would be surprised, and disappointed. She had assumed without question that King Hussein would agree.

The Intifada *Erupts*

On November 9, 1987, Ambassador Tom Pickering came in from Israel. "I have kept this out of the cables," he said, "but your visit to the Middle East has resulted in a sea change in Israel." Peres was moving away from the idea of a full-blown international conference that King Hussein wanted. "Shamir and his crowd are very interested in keeping the Shultz proposal alive." As a result, Pickering thought, we have a foundation laid for Israeli agreement to a controlled conference in the future.

One month later, on December 9, 1987, the "rumbling" below that I had sensed exploded to the surface: the Palestinian *intifada* burst out in the West Bank and Gaza. Young people throwing rocks defied Israeli soldiers. Increasingly, the soldiers fired back, as Israel sought to repress the uprising. The scene was ugly. Rebellion—not intimidated by increased use of force by the Israeli army—became the order of the day. The Israel Defense Forces were drawn into acts of violence, highly publicized around the world, that fractured Israel's image, distressed Israel's friends, and encouraged Israel's enemies. The *intifada*, too, was a sea change: an expression of the Palestinians' dissatisfaction with the conditions of their lives in the occupied territories. The uprising was not "led" but seemed rather to "explode" in a kind of spontaneous combustion. It caught the attention not only of the Israelis but also of Arab rulers throughout the Middle East. Somehow the status quo—uncomfortable but apparently stable and enduring—was far less secure.

CHAPTER 45

Signs of a Sea Change:
Toward Democracy
in Central America,
Chile, and South Korea

Whenever I went to El Salvador, a U.S. Army helicopter would fly me from the airport, over the cloud-covered mountains, to land on a soccer field in the capital, San Salvador. After one of these flights, the pilot described his helicopter as "ten thousand pieces of metal, each one trying to tear the others apart." The imagery seemed an apt description of the way the U.S. government, with fiercely held and wildly disparate views both in Congress and within the administration, went about policy-making toward Central America in the mid-1980s.

A New Turn in Central America

In Washington, staff members in the White House and in the departments, including State, were skeptical of, and in some cases were actively trying to sabotage, my efforts to establish a diplomatic track in Central America. Meanwhile, the lack of such a track gave congressmen a rationale for depriving the Contras of their ability to contribute to the pressure needed for our diplomacy to work. And many individuals, in the Senate and House, in the CIA, the NSC staff, the Pentagon, and White House, and even at State, felt free to conduct their own foreign policies toward Nicaragua and Central America.

Daniel Ortega ceaselessly tried to define the struggle as a bilateral one between Nicaragua and the United States, while we insisted that the problems were regional, affecting Central America as a whole. Work on these problems required close coordination between Washington and Nicaragua's non-Communist neighbors. Those countries, however, were relying privately on the United States to protect them from Sandinista ambitions

950

while scoring points in their domestic political arenas by denouncing, or keeping their distance from, Washington's efforts in the region. My own struggle was to find some way to get U.S. policy, the "Contadora process,"[1] and the "Core Four" countries on the same general path—and all this in a wildly politicized and divisive atmosphere.

Phil Habib returned to Washington, having completed his mission to the Philippines in March 1986. He had contributed masterfully to U.S. efforts during the transition from Ferdinand Marcos to Corazon Aquino. The president and I then sent him to Central America to work on the thorny diplomatic problems there. "Habib can do anything" was the aura around him. He had the confidence of the president and me and of the Congress. There was no real diplomatic process under way for Central America then, and I told Habib to assess the prospects for a negotiated outcome of the conflicts there, particularly those involving Nicaragua.

Phil had returned from Central America with new insights. The Contadora process, he said, was dominated by Mexico, whose foreign minister, Bernardo Sepulveda, was biased in favor of the Ortega regime and would never be helpful to us.[2] That I knew. The Central American nations, weary of being lectured by their Mexican and South American brethren, were ready to think for themselves. This was welcome news. Oscar Arias had just been elected, on February 3, 1986, president of Costa Rica. Arias would be a genuine spokesman for democracy in the region. "Arias has no use for the Sandinistas," Habib said, "and is a man of such integrity and independence that no one could ever accuse him of parroting the Washington line." So the best way forward was to work with the Central American Core Four countries and move them to the forefront of the diplomatic effort.

I gave Habib a four-point charter for his mission. The United States sought: a definitive, verifiable end to Sandinista support for subversion; removal of Soviet, Cuban, and other radical security and military advisers from Nicaragua; limitation and reduction of Sandinista military capabilities to levels that would restore regional military equilibrium; and fulfillment of the Sandinistas' 1979 commitment to the Organization of American States (OAS) to govern through democratic practices.

"Try to achieve a comprehensive and verifiable agreement on these points," I told Habib, "and a plan to implement them that would get the

1. The Contadora process, a regional effort to bring peace to Central America, involved the sponsoring countries of Mexico, Venezuela, Colombia, and Panama and the Central American Core Four—El Salvador, Guatemala, Honduras, and Costa Rica—plus Nicaragua.
2. I had many meetings with Sepulveda, but after a reasonably positive outcome of our first meeting in April 1983, we were increasingly on opposite sides of most issues, not just those involving Central America.

Sandinistas beyond the point of no return simultaneously with steps the United States would take in support of regional stability and economic development." We should, I said, focus our efforts on encouraging the Core Four countries to pursue more actively their own efforts to consolidate democracy in Central America. As Habib correctly pointed out, none of these points had anything to do with winning a war or overthrowing the Ortega regime by military force.

Habib was perfect for this job. In him, the Central Americans would see a top professional diplomat working to achieve a negotiated outcome to the agonizing problems in Central America. But the hard right in Washington deeply distrusted such negotiations, resented Habib's appointment, and sabotaged his efforts. NSC adviser John Poindexter and hard-liners on the NSC staff argued that Vice President Bush should not even attend the inauguration of Oscar Arias as president of Costa Rica on May 8, 1986, as a rebuff to Arias for his opposition to the Contras. Habib and I personally urged George Bush to go, and he did, to very good effect. When Bush and Habib appeared in San José, the Costa Rican crowd gave them a spectacular welcome.

Over a period of time and with Habib's help, the Central Americans increasingly took the lead, despite attempts by Mexico, on the pro-Ortega side, and NSC staffers, on the overthrow-Ortega side, to derail their effort. Gradually, Oscar Arias convinced the other Central Americans that the right negotiating path pursued four points, which were actually similar to those I had discussed with Habib. Arias strongly emphasized the importance of democracy, and he became the spokesman for democratic change inside Nicaragua. His blind spot—an unwillingness to recognize the importance of pressure from the Contras to spur the Nicaraguans to the negotiating table—always baffled me. But I never doubted his sincerity of purpose.

Renewed Pressure: Contras and Elections

On May 24 and 25, 1986, the presidents of Costa Rica, Honduras, Guatemala, El Salvador—and Nicaragua's Ortega—held a summit meeting at Esquipulas in Guatemala. They issued a declaration, later to be known as Esquipulas I, which stated each nation's right to choose its own economic, political, and social system, without external interference, so long as the choice was "the product of the people's free will." This last point expressed the essence of the declaration. If ever one free election could be held in Nicaragua, I was convinced, that would be enough to spell the end of Daniel Ortega and the Sandinistas' Marxist regime. As the diplomatic effort proceeded, Habib was almost constantly at the side of the heads of government and foreign ministers of the Core Four, urging them to concentrate on a sustainable approach to a negotiated settlement. Meanwhile, he worked to neutralize the Mexicans and get the other Contadora nations (Venezuela, Colombia, and Panama) to let the Central Americans take the lead. The Nicaraguans sought to make progress contingent on the ending of U.S. aid to the Contras. While the Central American presidents found it difficult publicly to support Contra aid, privately (with the exception of Arias) they realized how important it was.

On June 25, 1986, in the House, and on August 13, in the Senate,[3] President Ronald Reagan and all of us working with him on the problems of Central America achieved a spectacular and crucial success: the president's request for $100 million in aid to the Contras and $300 million in additional economic support for Costa Rica, Honduras, Guatemala, and El Salvador was approved. The administration, led by the president and with intense effort by me, worked hard on this vote. The outcome was a moment of triumph for us, especially for Ronald Reagan.

The Nicaraguan *comandantes* and their leaders helped our efforts with Congress by demonstrating, with remarkable ineptness at key moments, that their Soviet- and Cuban-backed regime did pose a serious military threat to its Central American neighbors. In late March 1986, some 1,500 Sandinista troops crossed into Honduras. On March 25, the United States provided $20 million in emergency aid to Honduras and the next day airlifted Honduran soldiers to the front. The Sandinistas retreated from Honduran territory.

As the year-end approached, the Sandinistas crossed the border again. It was nearly midnight, Saturday, December 6, 1986, when Chairman of the Joint Chiefs Bill Crowe and I telephoned the president to awaken him. I told the president: "We have a problem in Honduras and [there is] an action we recommend. . . . All your advisers support this. An attack [by Nicaraguan armed forces] on Thursday against Honduras has become a big issue there. The Hondurans sent aircraft against Sandinista troops inside Honduras today. To test our will, Honduras has asked us for fifty helicopter sorties to take their troops to landing zones [near the border] inside Honduras. President Azcona made the request tonight to Ambassador Briggs. . . . We recommend you authorize assistance tonight."

The president was well aware of the possibility of this hostile move by Nicaragua into Honduran territory. What was new was the urgent request from Azcona. "I agree completely," the president responded, "Go ahead."

U.S. support for the territorial integrity of Honduras was crucial, in part to meet a threat to Honduras but also to send a message to Communists

---

3. The Senate had earlier voted its approval, but the August vote was on the language as agreed with the House.

and anti-Communists alike that the United States would not allow Nicaragua to use its massive (in Central American terms) military machine against others in the region.

The presence of Contras inside Honduras put President Azcona in a tough spot, however, as he was playing host to a force conducting military operations in neighboring Nicaragua. The announcement on December 8, 1986, by Honduran and Contra officials that the Contras would move to positions inside Nicaragua by spring helped Azcona. This important move was made possible by the renewed flow of assistance to the Contras from congressionally appropriated funds.

Contact with the Comandantes

Throughout 1986, the State Department had been engaged in an unusual kind of contact with some of the *comandantes* of the Nicaraguan government, and I felt that we had come to know quite a bit about them. When I persuaded the president to select Harry Bergold, a foreign service officer with long experience in dealing with Communist regimes, to be our ambassador in Managua, I asked Harry to get to know the country, including the Sandinista leaders, and to send me regular letters on a completely personal basis. I wanted insight and feel to supplement the factual but flat official reports that came my way. Throughout the year, Harry's reports came in, brief gems conveying a sense of the plight of the country and the blind sides of its leaders.

During a time of wild and divisive tension over Nicaragua in Washington, Bergold went among the Contras in their remote camps and was out in the countryside with members of the inner circle of the Sandinista Front as well, including Tomás Borge, the only surviving founder of the Frente Sandinista de Liberación Nacional (FSLN).

At the Sandinistas' seventh anniversary ceremony on July 19, 1986, Bergold noticed that Bayardo Arce was the only *comandante* who sang every word of the Sandinista hymn. "He stood there belting it out while Daniel Ortega on one side of him and Carlos Nuñez on the other seemed to be only moving their lips to the music." Bergold asked Arce to explain. "He said it all came from fighting on the barricades in Esteli in early 1979. The Sandinista fighters would shout lines from the Sandinista hymn across to their comrades on other road blocks as a prearranged identification. 'If you didn't have the words right, you got blown away,' explained Bayardo Arce."

Bergold described the scene on November 7, the anniversary of the Bolshevik Revolution, which was celebrated by the FSLN:

All the things present in Moscow—or almost all—were to be found in Managua on the day of its parade. . . . But the important part of all this is that the parade went very well, without flaws; nothing like it has ever been seen in Nicaragua. Nicaraguans see this force as being purely their own, representing a level of military capability previously unknown in this country. They have no sense of what a puny sword they are rattling by the standards of the great powers. . . . The crowd was young, befitting a country where 75 percent of the population is under 24 years of age. . . . "How can the Contras possibly think they can defeat this army?" was the subliminal message flashed to all who watched the performance.

Whatever the message of the parade, the fact was that the Soviets and Cubans were systematically working to nail Nicaragua into the Socialist camp and, in effect, to create the potential for Soviet military bases on the American mainland. I remembered Scoop Jackson's concern that the real target of the Soviet challenge in Central America was Mexico.

A New Peace Plan

On January 7, 1987, Foreign Minister Rodrigo Madrigal of Costa Rica met with Phil Habib and Elliott Abrams in Miami to go over the outlines of the evolving peace plan being developed by President Oscar Arias, following Esquipulas I. The elements were new elections in Nicaragua, a cease-fire and amnesty, and a regional peace treaty. This meeting was followed by a period of intense diplomatic activity led by Arias and the Core Four Central American countries and actively supported by Habib. Phil worked hard to tighten up the Arias proposals and to close loopholes that we knew the Ortega regime would exploit. But he had competition that complicated his job.

As Habib tried to shape a better set of proposals, members of Congress, Senator Christopher Dodd of Connecticut[4] in particular, were in close contact with Central American governments. Dodd conducted his own negotiations, making suggestions that undercut Habib and were far too soft. The sponsoring Contadora nations, with Mexico in the lead, were virtually representing Nicaragua and tried to pressure the Core Four into accepting an agreement that compromised both unwisely and unnecessarily on key provisions. Beyond this, church and political action groups in the United States were fueling public and congressional opposition to our tough policy toward Nicaragua. And the hard-liners from all corners around town were busy sniping at Phil Habib. Despite all of these potshots, by the first

4. Senator Dodd was chairman of the Senate Foreign Relations Committee's Subcommittee on Western Hemisphere and Peace Corps Affairs.

months of 1987 we had reestablished a diplomatic track. I considered this to be real progress, particularly since the Central American countries themselves were increasingly taking direct responsibility for their fate.

The focus of attention then turned to the next meeting in Esquipulas, which would be held in midsummer 1987. The recklessly undisciplined scene in American foreign policy was vividly on display: a delegation from Congress was planning to attend. Habib was beside himself. "Did you ever hear of U.S. congressmen sitting in on a negotiation between foreign countries?" he shouted at me. "This town is in trouble! You are the strong man—do something!" I had tried, but unsuccessfully. Once again, it was an example of "everybody wants to get into the act," augmented by congressional love of travel abroad, especially when associated with a highly publicized event.

Oscar Arias had given a superb speech, statesmanlike yet realistic, in September 1986 at the United Nations. He was the only leader in Latin America with the courage to speak his convictions openly:

> The heroic fight for the freedom of the Nicaraguan people . . . has taken a political course that does not respond to that people's yearning for freedom. . . . This unwanted and unforeseen political course has transformed Central America into another stage for the East-West conflict. There is no letup for anyone along the path chosen by the commanders, who betrayed a revolution aimed at returning democracy to several generations that only knew oppression. . . . There is no letup for neighboring nations, which already sense the threat of a new, totalitarian dogmatism, and are already suffering the consequences of a frontier of sorrow and disillusionment.

But often the eloquent statesman would slide off toward the saintly, and his eyes would grow sad and visionary. Arias seemed to believe that the world could be set right simply by righteous declarations and the renunciation of the use of force. Costa Rica was a relatively prosperous and peaceful country and proud of its commitment to exist without a national army. Once when I encountered Arias in such an idealistic and melancholy mood, I recalled the time the president of Switzerland had told me that the Swiss realized "the good life" in that neutral nation was made possible because of "America's willingness to defend democracy." Arias, I perceived, did not share that recognition. I knew he did not appreciate how important the growing Contra pressure was to the success of his negotiating efforts in Contadora.

"How firm should I be with Arias?" Habib asked. "He doesn't want to change a thing in his plan. The Democrats in Congress tell him it's perfect. It isn't. Some of it is crazy. Parts of it don't make sense, like how you get a cease-fire. Cease-fires are complicated."

"Go over with him what needs to be changed," I told Habib, "and describe it as 'amplification.'"

Esquipulas II was set for August 7, 1987. On July 30, I had lunch with Speaker of the House Jim Wright. NSC adviser Frank Carlucci had been talking with Wright about the possibility of a common legislative-executive branch position. I was not fully posted on what had transpired, but suddenly I found myself the point man in this effort, as Carlucci had gone off on a foreign trip.

Getting close to Jim Wright was not a pleasant experience. He would flash a Machiavellian smile two or three times during a single sentence, at points when his words made a smile inappropriate. It struck me that he thought his smile would soothe and reassure his listener when in fact it was disconcerting and created suspicion. He could smile at you while he cut your throat. But Wright was working with us to achieve a bipartisan executive-legislative branch approach that could move us forward. And importantly, the wording of our prospective agreement made clear that if the Ortega regime refused to move toward democracy, we would provide further military aid to the Contras. Wright faced strong opposition from liberals in his own party, who opposed Contra aid under any circumstances. Wright and I worked over language in an effort to develop a set of points that the president and he could both accept. My goal was to achieve a bipartisan agreement that could lift us out of the quagmire of partisan divisiveness.

On August 3, joined by Chief of Staff Howard Baker, I met again with Jim Wright on the Hill. Wright had produced a peace plan for Central America that incorporated most of the points we had discussed previously and which were essential from the administration point of view. "I'm taking a big risk with this," Wright confided. "If the Nicaraguans spurn this, I'm on the hook to support Contra aid."

"That's right," I responded.

We agreed that it would be cast as a congressional plan endorsed by the Reagan administration. I felt that the plan had the potential to take us to a new level on Central America, where bipartisan support could allow a realistic appraisal of the situation and create a readiness to be forthcoming, backed by a readiness to be tough if Nicaragua did not respond constructively. This plan would be a great surprise. I was, in fact, amazed to find no reporters waiting when I emerged from our meeting. No one had leaked what was taking place. I gathered together Phil Habib, Elliott Abrams, and others from our Latin America bureau, and we studied the text word by word. After taking note of their suggestions, I went to see President Reagan. With the help of Howard Baker, and despite opposition from José Sorzano, Frank Carlucci's Latin America hand on the NSC staff, I persuaded the president that with a few changes I knew Wright could accept, this was a good document. The text that emerged incorporated the improvements I wanted in the peace plan developed by Oscar Arias.

On August 5, President Reagan unveiled the text of the Wright-Reagan plan to the press and announced that we were sending it to the Esquipulas II meeting in Guatemala. I complimented Speaker Wright for his support of the initiative. Suddenly, his support weakened, and at the last minute, he backed away and said he could make no commitment to support renewed Contra aid if this proposal failed to evoke a serious response from the Ortega regime. Wright flashed his smile. I couldn't locate his backbone.

The plan sent to Guatemala specified three "legitimate" concerns of the United States:

1. That there be no Soviet, Cuban, or communist bloc bases established in Nicaragua that pose a threat to the United States and the other democratic governments in the hemisphere;
2. That Nicaragua pose no military threat to its neighbor countries nor provide a staging ground for subversion or destabilization of duly elected governments in the hemisphere; and
3. That the Nicaraguan Government respect the basic human rights of its people, including political rights guaranteed in the Nicaraguan Constitution and pledges made to the Organization of American States (OAS)—free speech, free press, religious liberty, and a regularly established system of free, orderly elections.

On the basis of these concerns, the plan called for:

1. An immediate cease-fire in place subject to OAS verification. The United States then would halt military aid to the Contras; the Sandinistas would stop receiving military aid from Cuba, the USSR, and communist bloc countries; and a plan would then be put in place to demobilize "both Sandinista and resistance forces." Then, "an independent multiparty electoral commission will be established to assure regular elections open to free participation by all."
2. Withdrawal of foreign military personnel and advisers from Nicaragua and its immediate neighbors that are in excess of the normal and legitimate needs of the region.
3. After the cease-fire is in place, negotiations to begin among the five Central American nations and the United States on reductions in standing armies in the region, withdrawal of foreign military personnel, and on the restoration of a regional military balance.
4. Acceptance by Nicaragua of a "plan of national reconciliation" that would give the Contras amnesty and "equal rights to participation in the political process. There shall be a plan for demo-

bilization of both Sandinista and resistance forces. In accordance with the implementation of this plan, the United States simultaneously shall cease all supply of resistance forces."

5. An end to the U.S. embargo on trade with Nicaragua and resumption of normal trade and aid after these changes had been made.

6. Immediate commencement of the negotiating process, which should conclude by September 30, 1987.

If the Ortega regime did not engage on these terms, the United States and the Contras would be "free to pursue such action as they deem necessary to protect their national interest."

The policy expressed in this document, consistent with the president's address to a joint session of Congress in April 1983, went beyond the idea of containing Nicaragua's aggressive capabilities and intentions. The plan emphasized the critical importance of achieving a democratic form of government in Nicaragua. This call for democracy was a conceptual breakthrough with the Democratic leadership of the House. Without doubt, because of this—and because of the implicit threat of renewed aid to the Contras—Jim Wright continued to meet strong opposition from liberals within his own party.

Arias commented publicly that the Wright-Reagan plan could be helpful. Daniel Ortega denounced our effort, saying he would deal with the United States bilaterally and would never meet with the Contras. The next day, August 7, in Guatemala City, a peace plan emerged from the meeting of the Central American nations, including Nicaragua. Ortega signed the document, called Esquipulas II. Its thrust was similar in general terms to the Wright-Reagan plan, but the language was looser and with less attention given to enforcement mechanisms. The Central American presidents called for a cutoff of aid to the Contras but also for an end to Soviet aid to the Sandinistas and for free elections in Nicaragua. The Wright-Reagan proposal had created an important and helpful pressure.

A constructive process was under way, and I felt that we could work with Esquipulas II. The Sandinistas had made concessions they would not otherwise have made, I thought, in part because they saw a militarily tough U.S. proposal that had bipartisan support. Esquipulas II and the Wright-Reagan plan shared and emphasized a conceptual common ground of great importance: the essence of a peaceful solution in Central America hinged upon the emergence of democracy in Nicaragua.

Once a free election occurred in Nicaragua, I felt sure that the Ortega regime's exit would be assured. NBC-TV news that evening reported that leading Democrats leaped to embrace the Esquipulas II plan and gave Ronald Reagan some credit.

Esquipulas II: Opportunity or Hornet's Nest?

I asked Habib to come to my office that evening. I toasted him and "a great agreement." We were relaxed and elated. Habib reminisced about how, in the awful days of the Vietnam War, Dean Rusk would invite foreign service officers up to his office for a drink at the end of the day. Habib was a deputy assistant secretary in the Near East bureau then. "Dean was a fine man," Habib said. "Life in Washington was easier in earlier days; after the Vietnam War started, life changed." The tensions and emotions stirred up by Vietnam were still with us as we addressed the problems of Central America. Phil and I also toasted the Contras, for the pressure they created on the Sandinistas ultimately played a critical role in getting Ortega to the negotiating table and his signature on this document.

I called President Reagan and went over the Esquipulas II plan for him in detail. "It's got a good thrust to it; it starts a process that will, with hard work, lead to democracy in Nicaragua," I said. "And to our relief and astonishment, its measures have simultaneity[5]—so it's a victory." When I put the phone down, Elliott Abrams, always preoccupied with the Contras, expressed a different view. "I am very worried about this agreement. Communists win these kinds of negotiations. This could be the end of our policy."

Habib was livid at Abrams's response. "You made the decision that we would work with this agreement," he exploded to me furiously. "If you hadn't been on the phone tonight to the president, the White House would have rejected it!"

I tried to calm the waters and told Phil and Elliott to get a good night's sleep. Habib had plenty of enemies because of his aggressive effort in trying to achieve a diplomatic solution. Carlucci, I knew, wanted Habib out, and Elliott was constantly sniping at Habib.

On August 8, President Reagan issued a statement that I regarded as a moderate victory for my point of view: "I welcome this commitment to peace and democracy by the five Central American Presidents . . . there is much work to be done by the parties involved. . . . The agreement emphasizes reconciliation, democracy, and full respect for political and civil rights. We are encouraged by that emphasis." And, keeping his foot on third base, the president added, "The promise of this agreement can only be realized in its implementation."

I went to the White House on August 10 to talk about prospective work with Oscar Arias and the Esquipulas II agreement. I recommended that

---

5. We were concerned that the structure of events called for in any plan require critical actions by Nicaragua simultaneously with actions by the United States so that we would not give up our leverage prematurely. Esquipulas II recognized this in principle.

Habib go to Central America immediately, but I met a storm of opposition as the hard-liners caught their breath and tried to reverse course. NSC adviser Frank Carlucci, his staff man José Sorzano, and my own assistant secretary, Elliott Abrams, were all putting roadblocks in the path that Phil Habib and I wanted to follow. The president told me he was afraid that he and Habib and I were going to be "skinned" by the right-wingers in Congress. For one thing, they hated Jim Wright and resented the fact that the president had made an agreement with the Speaker. They also mistrusted me, Habib, or anyone else to negotiate effectively with Communists. We would, they thought, either be duped into an unsatisfactory agreement that benefited the Communists more than us, or if a good agreement was reached, the Communists would never abide by its terms. Their real bottom line, however, was a fixation on the Contras, whom they increasingly viewed as an end unto themselves. The right-wing ideologues did not want a negotiated settlement that would end Contra aid. I supported the Contras, but as a source of pressure to further our true objectives: democracy in Nicaragua and peace in Central America. The Contras could then safely and effectively be able to take part in the political process.

A substantial momentum with real tailwind had now been created with Esquipulas II for a peaceful settlement. We had chips on the table and a strong hand. The Core Four countries also supported our effort. Now we were being shut down in our own country by the hard right. Key players in high places in the Reagan administration simply did not want a negotiating effort to succeed.

When Habib heard my report of the August 10 White House meeting, he concluded ruefully that his usefulness had ended, and he gave the president his resignation. This was a real blow. Tom Enders, Tony Motley, Dick Stone, and Phil Habib had all been forced out for trying to seek a two-track policy in Central America involving diplomacy as well as military strength. I could see once again an obsessive preoccupation with the Contras, a belief held by Elliott Abrams and by members of the NSC staff that the Wright-Reagan plan, let alone Esquipulas II, would undercut our base of support for Contra funding. I disagreed strongly. I felt, and said, that support for the Contras, a close call in Congress under the best of circumstances and a probable loser after the Iran-Contra revelations, would disappear if we opposed the kind of outcome and process envisioned in the Wright-Reagan plan and in Esquipulas II. What we needed was to achieve a reasonably fair election in Nicaragua.

On August 15, true to form, the Nicaraguan government security forces forcibly suppressed planned peaceful marches, using dogs, nightsticks, and electronic shock batons. Nevertheless, after further progress in a meeting of the Central American foreign ministers on August 19 and 20, the Contras on August 21 formally accepted Esquipulas II—subject to assurances that they would be able to negotiate directly with the Nicaraguan regime. There was much hand wringing over this by hard-liners, who felt I had somehow forced the Contras to surrender. The reality was that we had achieved, however painfully and precariously, a basis for cooperative movement toward peace, stability, and democracy in Central America—a basis that incorporated a shared understanding between key leaders of the executive and legislative branches and between the United States and the Central Americans.

On August 27, I met President Reagan in Los Angeles and enlisted his support for a plan of action. Elliott Abrams, with misgivings, agreed to the plan, as did the NSC staffers who worked this issue. Their agreement, however, was basically to the support for the Contras included in the proposal. Ronald Reagan seemed genuinely in favor of a negotiating effort, although he was concerned, as we all were, that the Contras be treated fairly and with honor. Our new emissary, replacing Habib, would be Morris Busby, a talented foreign service officer with wide experience in Latin America. The president, I could assure Busby, was ready to work once again at a negotiated outcome while still supporting the Contras as a way to provide continuing pressure and as an insurance policy in the event of a breakdown in negotiations.

A Chance for Freedom and Peace

Three developments had come together over the past summer to shape an important opportunity for peace. In the United States, the Wright-Reagan Plan had transcended party divisions and made clear that the leadership in this country agreed on basic U.S. security objectives in Central America: that pursuit of U.S. interests called for a democratic Nicaragua that was neither a military threat to its neighbors nor a platform for Soviet and Cuban activities hostile down the line to the security of our own country.

The second development had been the increasing success of the Contras in pressuring the Sandinistas. Their improved military performance since January 1987, following the infusion of renewed support from the United States, and their sustained effort to broaden their political base, transformed them into a serious challenge and potential political alternative to Nicaragua's Communist regime.

The third development had been the signing of the Esquipulas II plan on August 7. Central America's Core Four presidents had affirmed their belief that with the continued support of the United States, peace and democracy were attainable in the entire region, including Nicaragua. Nicaragua had responded to these pressures and had committed itself, in writing, to a process of democratization, including freedom of the press, political pluralism, and the lifting of the state of emergency.

On September 10, 1987, I set out the administration position before the Senate Foreign Relations Committee. My testimony included a notification to Congress that "at the appropriate moment," depending on developments in the region, we would request further assistance to the Contras. That statement made the testimony controversial, but it was a necessary ingredient to ensure implementation of Esquipulas II. In reality, this plan gave us an important new foundation on which to build. "In 1980–81, a lot of people thought it was too late to end the spreading turmoil and violence in El Salvador and Nicaragua or to stop the spread of communism in Central America," I said. "They thought the United States would ultimately either have to use U.S. troops or else simply have to become accustomed to having the Soviet Union as the dominant power from Panama to Mexico." Now, I concluded, we should "make this present chance for freedom and for peace a success."

In October came the announcement that Oscar Arias had won the Nobel Peace Prize. The report I watched on "NBC Nightly News" October 13 said, "What particularly galls the Reagan administration is that President Arias won the Nobel Prize for a plan that calls for an end to American support for the Contras." In fact, Esquipulas II, on which Arias had been the moving force, called for much more than an end to Contra aid. If it could be brought to fruition, it would bring democracy to Nicaragua and peace in Central America—results for which the president and I had labored throughout the Reagan administration.

Jim Wright's Rogue Diplomacy

My job was to maintain as strong a negotiating effort as possible, holding Nicaragua to a regional forum and calling on the Sandinistas to meet with the Contras and to start the process of reconciliation called for in Esquipulas II. Daniel Ortega resisted a meeting with the Contras, as that would constitute his recognition of their legitimacy, and he sought direct and bilateral negotiations with the United States.

On November 9, President Reagan, in a speech to the Organization of American States, took an important step. He announced that I would be ready to talk with the Ortega regime in a regional setting, including representatives of the Core Four, on one condition: that the Sandinistas agree to talk with the Contras through Cardinal Miguel Obando y Bravo, who had an acknowledged role in Nicaragua as mediator in the reconciliation process. I followed up by saying that the talks could start as early as that week.

Frank Carlucci told me that the right wing was furious that the president had said that I would meet with Ortega. "Our policy for three years has been to be ready to meet in a regional setting," I reminded Carlucci. "The right thinks they have enormous influence in the White House, but the president just goes on making them furious." Ronald Reagan was a hard-liner, but with a major difference from most of his hard-line supporters: he was willing to negotiate with his adversaries and was confident in his ability to do so effectively. The trouble was that Congress frustrated his brand of a hard line by its off-again, on-again attitude toward the Contras. And the president did not impose the discipline within his administration needed to allow the negotiating track to proceed in an unambiguous way.

Meanwhile, Daniel Ortega himself on November 12 was up on Capitol Hill, working the Congress and getting much encouragement for his effort to engage in bilateral talks with the United States, excluding the other Central America governments altogether. The president's policy, which I was trying to implement, remained: support the Nicaraguan opposition, keep the Ortega regime in a regional negotiation, and work closely with the Core Four governments in the negotiating process. Gradually, this effort had begun to have an effect. But I was subject to undertow from many directions. Senator Dodd and others would telephone me from time to time with suggestions they had received from "the embassy." I had learned long ago that they meant the Nicaraguan embassy in Washington. I was barely able to stifle my outrage at these efforts that undermined the U.S. policy of dealing with Nicaragua on a regional basis and that portrayed the United States to our adversaries as a country inviting them to go around the presumptive authority of the president on foreign affairs.

A foot of snow fell on Washington in a storm that left the city crippled. "Something funny is going on," Elliott Abrams told me. Speaker Wright's office had told the press that on Friday, November 13, Wright and Ortega would hold a press conference at the Papal Nunciature (the embassy of the Vatican in Washington) at which the cardinal would be present. Ortega was going to produce a peace plan, and Wright would accept it, I was told. If that was true, Speaker Wright was springing a big surprise. And how could the Catholic church be the mediator if it accepted one side's—Ortega's—position? Jim Wright was trying to blindside President Reagan and me, subvert our policies, and become the de facto secretary of state in the process. This was outrageous! The press was being told that I knew all about this plan and approved of it. When I had seen Wright that very day, he had said nothing whatsoever about what he proposed to do.

At 10:30 on the night of November 12, Wright telephoned me with a convoluted story designed to make me appear to be trying to thwart both Congress and the Catholic church in their efforts to make peace in Central America. I told him that Ortega and the Contras should negotiate a cease-fire and that I hoped the cardinal would facilitate that effort. I also reviewed for him the importance of keeping our own position moving in line with that of Oscar Arias and the Core Four countries of Central America. So,

I told him, I would not be part of any Ortega-Wright-Obando meeting, if that was what he was setting up for tomorrow. The Speaker said he was going ahead; my comments made no difference to him, nor did our policy and advice.

The Speaker of the House was succumbing to a Sandinista scam. Only Congress could appropriate money, but now Wright was using that authority to conduct foreign policy. The Speaker was bent on eliminating the middle men: President Reagan and me and the rest of the executive branch of the government, constitutionally designated to conduct the nation's foreign policy.

Near midnight, Elliott Abrams received a telephone call from the papal nuncio, Archbishop Pio Laghi, who put Cardinal Obando on the line. Elliott talked the cardinal out of taking part in a public show in the morning. The cardinal said he would meet with Wright and Ortega, but he would not be part of any press conference or "photo op." That was good. I regarded the cardinal as a stand-up guy.

The next morning, Daniel Ortega, Jim Wright, and Cardinal Obando y Bravo met at the Nunciature. Ortega reportedly presented an eleven-point plan, but Wright did not reveal the plan when he emerged after his two-hour meeting. Even members of Congress were appalled: what the Speaker had done, said Senator John McCain, was "unseemly at best, unconstitutional at worst."

That night Friday, November 13, Jim Wright was interviewed by NBC-TV's Tom Brokaw, who asked Wright whether his role in this instance was appropriate. "In a meeting that you had with the Secretary yesterday, Mr. Shultz advised you against any Americans getting involved in these negotiations." Wright leaned forward and said, "In the first place, Tom, I don't take orders from the Secretary of State, and I don't take orders from anybody else except the people who have elected me." That was Jim Wright. But he had seized almost enough rope to hang himself. "What Is Jim Wright Doing? . . . he overreaches recklessly," said the lead editorial in the *Washington Post* on November 16, 1987.

Cardinal Obando y Bravo had informed me that Wright, in the meeting at the Nunciature, had proposed that negotiations be conducted by a non-Reagan administration U.S. group composed of Paul Warnke, a former arms control negotiator in the Carter administration, and two staff aides to Wright. Ortega had endorsed Wright's proposal. The cardinal confessed that he was vastly confused by this. "What is going on?" he wanted to know.

Jim Wright had spun out of control. He was looking increasingly foolish and was so portrayed in the press. "He's down; kick him," Abrams encouraged me.

"No. That would make things worse," I said. "We should try to get him back to the Wright-Reagan peace concept and the implied support for the Contras."

Wright asked to see the president, and we met at 10:00 on Monday morning, November 16, at the White House. The president was present briefly but had to leave, so I talked to the Speaker at length, with Howard Baker and Colin Powell joining in. We talked with the bark off. I told Jim Wright that he had set back the peace process in Central America. He had undercut promising efforts to keep the Nicaraguans in a regional setting and force them to deal with the Contras, and he had damaged a promising effort to force the Sandinistas to conduct a real election. We pressed him on the need for continued aid to the Contras. Clearly shaken by the episode, Wright nevertheless said he would not help with the Contras. Baker, Powell, and I hit him hard, and he appeared crestfallen and anxious to justify what he had done. When I asked him about using Paul Warnke as the negotiator, Wright said that was not his idea; "they" had pushed it. "Who is 'they'?" I asked.

Ortega and his people, he replied. So Wright had been pushing Daniel Ortega's strategy on the cardinal, who was justifiably mystified. But Wright was beaten now. That afternoon, when Senator Dodd telephoned me, he, too, was subdued and seemingly cooperative. He was astonished, he said, that Wright failed to realize he was helping Ortega wriggle out of the regional negotiating approach produced in Esquipulas II and agreed to by the United States as well as President Arias.

That night, Wright was on television news again, trying to defend himself and slamming "a small cadre of people in the State Department." The *New York Times* on November 17, in a pro–Jim Wright editorial headed "Speaker of State," asserted that "diplomacy abhors a vacuum." Throughout this brouhaha I tried to remain reasonably calm and composed, letting Wright be the one who was openly aggressive and threatening. "He has taken a lot of rope," I observed, "and he is hanging himself." That was part of the Iran-Contra fallout in Washington, as Congress's power expanded. The trouble was that Wright was also hanging our policy.

I tried to get control of the deteriorating situation. Bob Strauss and I discussed the stakes and the problems involved on November 17 over lunch. I wrote down a series of points that Strauss and I turned into a draft statement, a kind of Shultz-Wright treaty that could serve as the basis for executive-legislative peace on the proper way to conduct American foreign policy with regard to Central America. I called Howard Baker, who checked with the president and others in the White House.

The word back from Baker was that if I could get Wright's agreement to the statement, that would be constructive: go ahead. I informed Elliott Abrams and had him look at the language. I telephoned Wright on the Hill at 1:45 P.M. Bob Strauss got on the phone, too. We went over the idea and general content of the statement. Wright asked if I would meet him in his office in the Capitol.

"Just don't pray with him. Jim Wright can outpray anybody," Bob Strauss counseled me as I left for the Hill. I took Strauss with me; his instincts about the Washington political scene were sharper than those of anybody else I knew. "There are a lot of guys in the House who disagree with what Jim Wright did but who support him, anyway," Strauss said, "just because they're sick of the Senate doing it all."

This time Speaker Wright didn't argue or bluster; he agreed with my draft text without modification, and the two of us went before the cameras and joined in presenting a common approach on Central America:

1. We want the Guatemala City agreement [Esquipulas II] to succeed in bringing peace and freedom and democracy to Central America.
2. We believe that efforts toward that objective should be concentrated in Central America and continue to be guided primarily by Central Americans.[6]
3. We strongly encourage Cardinal Obando y Bravo to undertake his mission of mediation and peace.
4. The United States has vital interests in this outcome, as was stated in the Reagan-Wright Plan.
5. As the Cardinal's efforts lead to serious negotiations, the United States will be ready to meet directly in a regional setting[7] with representatives of the countries of the region.
6. Neither of us wants to create unnecessary problems. We want to work together to bring about solutions.

I hoped that this statement would put us back on track, but I quickly discovered how wrong I was.

The House Republicans were deeply angered by my agreement with Jim Wright. Dick Cheney told me that I had made a bad mistake: Jim Wright had serious ethical problems (this was the first I had heard of such a charge); the Republicans and the swing Democrats had been planning a revolt against the Speaker, but I had given him a new lease on his political life. I felt that I had persuaded Wright to capitulate on every point of difference between him and the president's policy. But that seemed to make no difference now. House Minority Leader Bob Michel was steaming mad, ready to criticize me openly, I learned. By this time I could see I had made a mistake. The deal was good on the merits, but it was bad politics. I started making calls to the Hill in an effort to calm the waters. No matter how

---

6. This amounted to Wright's confession that he had been wrong in letting himself become an agent of Ortega's Washington lobbying campaign.

7. Again, this amounted to an admission by Wright of his being duped by Ortega.

often I enumerated what I had persuaded Wright to sign onto and what we were trying to accomplish in Central America, I made no headway. "White House aides, still seething at Wright, also are irritated at Shultz for making peace with the speaker," reported the *Wall Street Journal* on November 20, 1987. "Officials complain that the secretary of state made the decision to make up largely on his own, and didn't let the White House in on his plans soon enough."

Howard Baker did not come to my rescue, even though he had given me a green light. Nevertheless, my position within the administration was strong as we approached climactic events with the Soviets and elsewhere. On November 17, I had gone to a farewell ceremony at the Pentagon for Cap Weinberger, who had resigned. I had long known and worked with Cap and regarded him as a Renaissance man and a man of integrity. But I often disagreed with his judgment and his rigidity. He and I had battled over all too many issues, most of which were going my way by now. Jim Wright had tried to play secretary of state but now was neutralized. I would continue the frustrating effort to work the Central America problems on a regional basis and work the Congress to renew military support for the Contras and thereby give our diplomacy the strength needed to be successful.

An Endgame Without an End

The peace process in Central America dragged along. On March 23, 1988, in Sapoa, Nicaragua, Sandinista and Contra leaders reached agreement on a cease-fire that stuck, despite some isolated violations. Their accord, also an act of formal and mutual recognition, included a general amnesty and a guarantee that the Contras could "incorporate themselves" into the political and civil life of Nicaragua. This agreement represented clear progress. Virulent adversaries were talking and even agreeing. Nevertheless, individual Contra leaders were skeptical, and they tended to drift back into Honduras. The Sandinistas had again pledged "unrestricted freedom of expression," but in mid-July, the government arrested demonstrators, suspended the opposition newspaper, *La Prensa*, and closed a radio station operated by the Roman Catholic church. Skepticism was confirmed.

I was not able to wrestle the Nicaraguan problem to the ground before leaving office, but I felt that resolution was in sight. The Soviets, who had used their support for Cuba and Nicaragua as one of the few needles they could keep in our side, were less and less able to sustain their assistance levels. Other regional problems were gradually being resolved in a manner consistent with U.S. objectives, in Afghanistan and Namibia most visibly.

By this time, with American support, the tide had turned in Central

America. Costa Rica, long the region's leading democracy, continued to stand for freedom and the rule of law. El Salvador, Honduras, and Guatemala had elected governments that were offering their people the chance of a better future, despite widespread poverty and internal strife, particularly in El Salvador. Nicaragua remained the odd man out in this otherwise encouraging picture, an obstacle to Central American unity, a threat to its neighbors, and a country by 1988 in total disrepair: income per capita was half the pre-Sandinista level, inflation was running out of control, and resistance to the draft was open and widespread.

I was confident now that the opposition to Ortega was both broad and deeply rooted and that it would continue to increase the pressure on his regime. Nicaragua was isolated in Central America, and the Sandinistas were increasingly seen as the agents of catastrophe within Nicaragua. The end of the Sandinistas' rule was in sight, I was convinced.[8]

Chile Feels the Heat

Nicaragua was not the first place where the Communist bloc had sought to implant a new Cuba on the mainland of the New World. In a 1970 election in Chile, a pro-Cuban Marxist coalition under Salvador Allende received 36 percent of the vote, a plurality, and was elected. The United States, with CIA involvement, had sought his defeat. "Chile voted calmly to have a Marxist-Leninist state," reported U.S. ambassador Nathaniel Davis, "the first nation in the world to make this choice freely and knowingly." The Allende government never attained majority support in the Chilean Congress and quickly proved inept and unable to retain the Chilean people's support. In September 1973, during a military coup launched against him, Allende was killed; claims of murder were widespread.

General Augusto Pinochet came to power, bringing dictatorship and repression to the political scene. But he did restore prosperity to the economy. Chileans trained in free market economics at the University of Chicago applied the ideas of classical economics, opening the Chilean economy to international competition, eliminating subsidies, relying on market signals to direct investment, seeking fiscal balance and a stable monetary policy. These policies worked. Moreover, openness in economic life created increasing strain on the closed, repressive political system. Nevertheless, for years Pinochet pursued a dual policy and kept himself entrenched in office. The United States was almost universally blamed for bringing him to power and helping him stay there.

8. On February 25, 1990, despite major advantages for Ortega, Violeta Chamorro was elected president of Nicaragua.

The Reagan administration came into office with a critical view of the way President Carter had approached human rights issues. I, too, was critical of what I called "lightswitch diplomacy," an effort to turn trade and investment on and off in order to try to influence a country's human rights practices. A guideline text for the Reagan administration had been an article by Jeane Kirkpatrick in the November 1979 issue of *Commentary* distinguishing between totalitarian regimes, which were Communist and invasive of individual rights, and authoritarian regimes, which were anti-Communist and less intrusive in nonpolitical aspects of individual life. In the first years of the Reagan presidency, an effort was made to "understand" Pinochet's problems, in the hope of moderating the repressive practices of his authoritarian regime. Certainly important was the fact that Pinochet's economic policies were working well at the start of the 1980s. So, as the United States tried to work with the Chilean government, various U.S.-Chile relationships that had been suspended during the Carter years were revived.

By the start of the second Reagan term, however, I was convinced that the U.S. approach was not working. We understood Pinochet: he was not changing. But he did not understand us: we wanted a more open government, the rule of law, and a government headed by elected officials.

I wanted to see Pinochet's authoritarian rule give way to real democracy to accompany Chile's prosperity. But in my attitude toward Pinochet, as in my view of Ferdinand Marcos, I was not really on the wavelength of the president and many of his advisers: to them, Pinochet was a friend of the United States and a bulwark against communism. Pinochet made everyone uneasy, but he was on our side.

In 1980, Pinochet had decided that Chile needed a constitution, and one was produced that provided for a plebiscite to determine the future shape of the government. According to one story, Pinochet wanted the constitution, which he had worked on for a number of years, to provide for a sixteen-year term for him beginning in 1981. Chilean friends, however, had apparently persuaded him that such a lengthy term would not fit the Chilean people's concept of legality and that he ought to split the sixteen-year term into two eight-year terms. In order not to run too much of a risk in an election, a plebiscite referendum would be held between the terms, with only one name on the ballot.

Pinochet accepted that advice reluctantly, but he did accept it, and those provisions were included in the 1980 Constitution. In addition, he had to permit voter registration because, having asserted that the Allende registration system was fraudulent, Pinochet's followers had destroyed all the voting records. The Pinochet government also decided that to make the plebiscite credible, there had to be political parties. Political parties were legalized and registered. Then there had to be a law on media, particularly on the use of television in political campaigns, so in due course a law was passed regarding the access of political parties to television.

Once Pinochet decided he wanted a constitution, a next step was implied, and a next. Traditions have an impact in a society like that of Chile. Chile's history of democracy dated back to the early twentieth century and had been reasonably rigorous since the 1920s. Pinochet clearly thought that he could control the political process and gain legitimacy without giving up any of his authoritarian power and control. In reality, Pinochet's constitutional ploy gave democratic forces within Chile something to work with and gave the United States something to support.

I persuaded the president to ask Harry G. Barnes, our ambassador to India and a career foreign service officer, to go to Chile as our ambassador. Santiago was a less prestigious post in the foreign service pantheon than New Delhi. Barnes was not wildly enthusiastic about the shift, but I thought he might be just the man for this job. The oddly pro-Soviet Indian government had complained to me about Barnes, who spoke Hindi fluently, traveled the countryside constantly, and was in close touch with people in all walks of Indian life. That did not please the government, and I was aware of their unease. To me, their discomfort was a sterling recommendation for Barnes, a wizard at languages, to go to Chile. He would similarly immerse himself in Chilean life and culture in his new post.

Before Harry Barnes went to Santiago in the fall of 1985, I worked out with him a threefold policy: continue support for Chile's economic programs, make clear our view that basic human rights must be respected, and push Chile to move promptly, through discussions among the political parties and the government, toward a return to democracy. I knew that Chile did not need much in the way of lessons in democracy. The ideas and traditions were already built into Chilean society.

Barnes quickly made his presence felt. Beyond official calls, he saw people in the opposition political parties, calling on them as he did government officials instead of asking them to come and see him, an unexpected gesture to the Chileans. Barnes also became acquainted with human rights organizations in Chile. He attended a candlelight service in the cathedral commemorating a declaration by a number of church groups on the importance of human rights. Television cameras covered the service. One newspaper the next day carried a cartoon showing Barnes with a candle in his hand and next to him a terrorist wearing a ski mask with a bomb in his hand. The government of Chile wanted to equate advocacy of human rights with terrorism.

In the spring of 1986, I worked with Dick Schifter, assistant secretary of state for human rights affairs, Elliott Abrams, and others in an unpublicized but tough fight within the administration to develop a dramatically different position toward Chile. At the March meeting of the UN Human

Rights Commission in Geneva, the Reagan administration for the first time sponsored a resolution critical of the repressive practices of the Chilean government. Our resolution, which called on the Pinochet government to stop the use of torture and the abuse of human rights by security and police forces and to put in place democratic institutions, received the consensus backing of the forty-three-member commission. Our sponsorship, let alone support, was a shock and surprise to many people. The government of Chile attributed the resolution to its "enemies," but this event made an impact.

"The United States," Barnes reported, "is genuinely real to many Chileans, partly because of the democratic example and link to Chile's past practices, partly because of the number of influential Chileans educated in the U.S., and partly because of our common economic philosophy. Whatever the reasons, we are seen as a model with inherent power: what we think, what we say, and what we do count a great deal in hemispheric and world affairs."

In that context our influence in Chile cut two ways. The government, political parties on the right, and many in the private sector welcomed our approval of their economic policies. But the political right was disappointed when we did not take their free market economics as sufficient to justify the political repression that also existed. They felt that if their economic policies were right, the United States should be satisfied. I disagreed. So, with the date for the autumn 1988 plebiscite on the horizon, we became more insistent about the importance of democratic reform as well as economic performance.

The Chilean government became more and more upset, and they appealed to their friends in the White House. The Pinochet government was isolated within Latin America, isolated from Europe, and isolated from most of the rest of the world. U.S. criticism of Chile reinforced that sense of isolation. And this pressure from the United States indirectly bolstered the efforts of Chileans working to restore democracy.

Some members of the democratic opposition in Chile thought the United States went too far in praising the government's economic policies. On the whole, though, most realized that our support of the economic policies of the Pinochet government was understandable. But more significantly, the Reagan administration was now clearly supporting both a prompt return to democracy and greater respect for basic human rights. Chileans took comfort in U.S. solidarity with their democratic cause. So, while the Pinochet government and its supporters felt our pronouncements and actions—concrete or symbolic—constituted "interference" in their internal affairs, the democratic elements viewed them as gestures of support and respect for what mattered. Interference, such as that implied when a country joins the United Nations and thereby accepts the Universal Declaration of Human Rights, was just right.

*   *   *

On July 2, 1986, in a general strike called by the opponents of Pinochet, five people were killed, two hundred were detained, and tear gas was fired into crowds of anti-Pinochet protesters. The strike seemed to stiffen the regime's resistance to change, but it also dramatized problems of leadership within the resistance. Those who supported democracy, we counseled strongly, must separate themselves from the Chilean Communists. Evidence came to us that supplies of arms from Cuba were flowing to the Chilean Communists. That would only play into Pinochet's hand.

Also in July, Harry Barnes and his wife, Betsey, attended the funeral of a young student, Rodrigo Rojas de Negri, originally from the United States, who had been burned to death after being doused with gasoline in one of the demonstrations. The Pinochet regime was blamed for this atrocity. The presence of the American ambassador at the funeral was seen as a challenge to Pinochet's regime. Visiting Chile shortly thereafter, Senator Jesse Helms attacked Barnes for attending.

On September 7, an attempt was made to assassinate Pinochet. Five members of his police and military escort were killed. "We are in a war between democracy and Marxism, between chaos and democracy," Pinochet said on television. He imposed a state of siege. The violent left was a menace for proponents of a return to democratic government. The United States condemned the attack, but we expressed our concern, through the State Department spokesman, with "the re-imposition of a state of siege which provides the government sweeping powers of censorship, repression and forced resettlement, without any recourse to judicial review."

As part of the Chilean government's tactics of intimidation, the Vicariate of Solidarity, the Catholic church organization that worked on human rights problems, came under considerable pressure from the government to turn over its records of human rights violations. I authorized Ambassador Barnes to call on the Vicariate's director in a highly visible way to show the United States's support for the human rights work of the Vicariate. The meeting was reported on the evening television news and in the press the next morning. Ambassador Barnes and the director of the Vicariate were shown in earnest conversation. That message of solidarity from the United States was as important as some of the more tangible help we later provided in areas such as voter registration and help to the democratic opposition in checking the Pinochet government's voter tallies.

In a police state, such actions by our ambassador and by Chileans seeking democracy were not trivial. The Ortega regime in Nicaragua played to liberals in Congress hoping to undercut the administration's policy, while the Pinochet regime in Chile played to the right wing in Congress for the same purpose. Senator Jesse Helms and members of his staff were viscerally opposed to what Barnes and I were doing in Chile and made their displeasure known. And like-minded staff people at the White House were equally opposed to our policy.

In November 1986, I received a blow from the White House. Chile had applied for a loan of $250 million from the World Bank. I had authorized Elliott Abrams to say in July that the United States would vote against the loan. As the date for the vote arrived in November, at the height of my struggle to stop arms sales to Iran, I was set back. My relations with Poindexter and others in the White House were enormously strained at the time. The president was uneasy about a rebuff to Pinochet. From somewhere on his staff the suggestion emerged that Pinochet be invited to the White House for an official visit! In the end, I received authority only for the United States to abstain on the loan vote. The loan went through, projecting a message that was ambiguous at best.

Still, I continued with our efforts to bring about democratic change in Chile, and I felt we were having a real impact when I received a message in July 1987 from Ricardo García, newly appointed as foreign minister. He reminded me that he had previously been minister of the interior, "in which function I made progress in institutionalizing and promulgating laws designed to bring Chile to full democracy," and he pledged the "total identification of myself and the external actions of Chile with the democratic principles that govern the free nations of the western world." Pinochet, I knew, had the power to remove his foreign minister at any time; in this cynical world one has to be suspicious. Nevertheless, García's words were important and undoubtedly reflected a growing desire in Chile to be regarded with respect in the United States and elsewhere in the world.

During the summer of 1988, a development occurred with the potential for personal misfortune and policy setback. Barnes became the subject of a right-wing attack. I gave Barnes my backing and, of far greater significance, so did the president. An effort to sabotage Barnes, the U.S. spokesman for democracy in Chile, was transformed into a demonstration of support from the man whose support mattered the most, Ronald Reagan.

As the plebiscite approached, the U.S. Congress voted to give $1 million to the National Endowment for Democracy for use in Chile to support the openness and honesty of the electoral process, and the Agency for International Development (AID) provided money for voter registration efforts. Through Barnes and our embassy we sought to maintain a dialogue with all parts of the political spectrum except for the Communist party on the left and the extremist, undemocratic parties on the right.

The plebiscite was set for October 5, 1988. Pinochet was the only candidate. As polls showed that the vote would be close, rumors abounded that the election would be postponed. We were concerned that any violence from the right or the left might provide the excuse for such an action. Election day finally came. The election itself came off in good order and was closely watched by outside observers as well as by Chileans themselves. When the votes were counted, Pinochet lost. He received only 43 percent of the vote. The no vote was 54 percent. Pinochet was astounded. The plebiscite triggered a competitive election held in December 1989 in which Pinochet was not a candidate. On March 11, 1990, as a result of a contested election, Patricio Aylwin, candidate of the Coalition for Democracy, was sworn in as the civilian elected president of Chile.

The democratic revolution of the decade of the 1980s culminated in a victory for the Chilean people. The economic policies of free and open markets developed by the "Chicago boys" had brought to Chile the healthiest economy in Latin America. This experience with freedom in the marketplace fanned the desire for freedom in the political arena. Chile's democratic culture asserted itself. Like Ferdinand Marcos before him, Pinochet was one more dictator fooled by the power of the electoral process, a difficult process to rig in the knowledge and information age. The democratic sweep in the Americas moved yet another step forward.

A Political Miracle in South Korea

Democracy is not culture bound, but unlike Chile, South Korea had no tradition of democracy to guide it as it approached the time to choose its president through an electoral process. There had been many points of tension during the cold war, but one of the coldest and most intense was the Demilitarized Zone (DMZ) in Korea. No sooner had the Koreans freed themselves from Japanese domination after World War II than they saw their country divided as Communist North Korean troops swept south, crossing the thirty-eighth parallel on June 25, 1950. So began the Korean War, in which over 33,000 Americans were killed and twice that many from the Republic of Korea. Thereafter, U.S. forces became a permanent fixture on South Korean soil. Hostility and justifiable concern for security were an ever-present part of life in the Republic of Korea throughout the cold war decades.

To Ronald Reagan, South Korea was a stalwart ally and a valiant symbol of resistance to communism. The first foreign head of state to visit the White House in the Reagan era was President Chun Doo Hwan of South Korea. That sent a signal to the world, urgently needed, that the United States was committed to South Korea's security. But more than anticommunism was involved; in 1981 when he came into office, Chun had pledged a peaceful transfer of power to his elected successor when his term would end in February 1988. That would be an unprecedented event in Korea. History had made Koreans fixated on security, and from the days of Syngman Rhee in the 1950s, the South Korean government had kept a tight lock on the political life of the nation, even as its economy opened and flourished. The Republic of Korea's citizens enjoyed many freedoms, but in 1981, Korea was not a democracy. The opposition, particularly among students, was restive and increasingly given to violent protest. I knew South Korea from the days when I was a businessman and admired that country's economic performance. When I became secretary of state, I wanted to do all I could to help President Reagan see that President Chun fulfilled his pledge.

I realized that South Korean politics were volatile and that reform would be met with increased discontent and dissent. From the time that President Chun in 1983 lifted the ban barring some 250 people from political activity, protests in the streets became a regular fixture of Korean life.[9]

September 1983 had brought the downing of Korean Airlines Flight 007 by the Soviets, which had both heightened superpower tension and left the South Koreans outraged and frustrated. A month later, in early October, in Rangoon, Burma, a terrorist bomb killed sixteen South Koreans, including Foreign Minister Lee Bum Suk and three other cabinet ministers who were members of a visiting South Korean delegation. President Chun was spared only because his motorcade had been delayed. Communist North Korea was immediately suspect for this terrorist act. Chun said upon his return to Seoul, "I cannot control the raging anger and bitter grief of this atrocity." I could share something of his feeling at the news of this atrocity; it had a personal dimension for me, since Lee Bum Suk and I had developed an easy and productive working relationship. The Republic of Korea's government exercised great forbearance and resisted the temptation to retaliate. But this tragedy drove home the deep animosity projected by the North Korean government toward South Korea and the necessity for South Korea to be vigilant on security concerns.

President Reagan was scheduled to visit Korea the very next month, from November 12 through 14, 1983, after a four-day visit to Japan. The South Koreans immediately asked whether the president intended to go through with his planned visit. He assured them that he was more determined than ever to stand at their side: his support registered.

The intense concern with security was evident as President Reagan's motorcade drove from Kimpo Airport into the heart of Seoul along its wide boulevards. In Paris the grand boulevards were designed to be too wide for demonstrators to build barricades; in Seoul they were designed to be wide enough for aircraft to land in the event of war. The twelve-mile route was lined with thousands of Koreans, many of them children. They jostled on the edges of the sidewalks, cheering and giggling and waving

9. Chun had left the eight-year-old ban in force for 305 others (including Kim Young Sam and Kim Dae Jung, prominent opposition leaders).

small flags. They carried posters and banners saying "Welcome Ron" or "We Love Nancy" or "Great Regard for Ronald W. Reagan."

At noon President Reagan addressed the Korean National Assembly, whose leaders received him first with ginseng tea. The president took a silver pen from his coat pocket and squirted two doses of Sweet and Low into his cup. His hosts were astonished.

The president's speech was remarkable. Somehow, even to people who speak a different language, the president's spirit and vision came through. He spoke, as he had in Japan and elsewhere, of his dream of a world free of nuclear weapons.

After a full day of meetings, we dined in a grand and gilded room at the Blue House as guests of President Chun. After dinner we withdrew to red velvet chairs in a nearby hall to watch an ancient shamanistic dance expressing resentment and defiance. These were emotions common to a people squeezed onto a small peninsula that is an appendage of the great Chinese landmass, a country that had felt the anguish of occupation over many decades of domineering Japanese rule, after Japan annexed Korea in 1910 and tried to stamp out its culture and language.

Seoul struck me like a river pouring out of the mountains. The city swept around the rocky outcroppings that jutted from the middle of the city and seemed to throw sprays of blue- and red-tiled houses on the hillsides. On Sunday, November 13, we moved to the Demilitarized Zone in eight helicopters, flying low over the patchwork of frozen rice paddies. At the DMZ, dressed in U.S. Army parkas and brown helmet caps to protect against the prickly cold, we were shown antitank walls and dragons' teeth, depots and artillery emplacements. Jeeps pulled us to the top of Hill 229, where, under a camouflaged awning, we peered across the desolate DMZ at the North Korean lines two miles away. Here the cold war was hot with tension.

We walked along a path formed by barbed concertina wire to a rocky clearing near a row of sandbagged mortar bunkers. The area was covered by a canopy of camouflage netting, and the president took his seat for a church service in the front row of folding auditorium chairs that had been arranged before a small white altar. Soldiers sang hymns. "We are seated, literally and figuratively, at the edge of freedom," the chaplain said. He was right. Beyond the altar lay a minefield. A group of Korean orphans in white stood in front of an armored personnel carrier next to the altar. They sang "God Bless America." President Reagan walked down the makeshift aisle, nodding to the soldiers on each side. Their applause was muffled by their thick black gloves.

Security was the number one topic on the minds of the Koreans. We made our mutual pledges of determination and support. Then President Reagan delivered our central message: the importance of President Chun's commitment to step aside as president at the end of his term in 1988 and to turn power over to an elected successor, a commitment that we well knew would be difficult to fulfill.

The South Koreans had never experienced a peaceful and democratic change in leadership. So the president and I kept on putting down our markers. And President Reagan did so here in a way that was pleasant but unmistakably clear. Chun Doo Hwan had made a commitment, and we wanted him to realize that the United States expected him to keep it. The talks were forceful, and I appreciated that this was a nation under fire and a leadership under abnormal stress.

The Pressure of Democratic Politics

On April 26, 1985, President Reagan once again received President Chun in the White House, a meeting that had been eagerly sought by Chun. South Korea was emerging onto the world stage, having been selected as the site for the September 1985 joint meetings of the World Bank and International Monetary Fund and for the 1988 Summer Olympics. Chun sought continuing reassurance from the United States on the security front. The president and I again emphasized the critical importance of Chun's commitment to a democratic succession. He had opened the political process somewhat to greater expression of political opinion, and he exercised moderation and patience with the emerging opposition political parties.

One year later, in the spring of 1986, the situation in South Korea had become as tense and delicate as any I had encountered. The overthrow of Ferdinand Marcos in the Philippines in February 1986, the U.S. role in the transformation of the Filipino political scene, and our support for Corazon Aquino had suddenly turned the world's gaze on the Republic of Korea. Would Korean "people power" bring the ouster of Chun Doo Hwan? Would Seoul become the next Manila?

On March 23, 1986, the largest antigovernment rally since Chun came to power erupted in the large South Korean city of Pusan. Kim Young Sam, a well-known dissident, led the opposition, as pressure mounted for direct elections and constitutional reform. Chun played the crisis deftly and fairly, I thought, but efforts to restore order fueled further protests. On May 3, four days before I was to arrive in South Korea following the economic summit in Tokyo, antigovernment demonstrations turned violent; many people were injured, and hundreds were arrested.

When I arrived in Seoul on May 7, the atmosphere was brittle with tension. Our ambassador, Jim Lilley, advised me to avoid political topics in my public remarks: the slightest mention of democracy or of positive steps that the government had made in trying to inch the system toward greater political openness would, it was feared, cause trouble for the United

States and the South Korean government. I disagreed with that advice.

"What we would like to see is the continuation of that movement [toward democracy] in a stable and orderly way," I responded to a question at a press conference just before my arrival. "Part of the process of becoming a genuinely democratic nation, it seems to me, is taking in the fact that the way to have change take place is a nonviolent way and that violence is not tolerated as a part of the democratic way of changing things." I was criticized, but also respected, for speaking about both sides of the democratic coin.

In my meetings, I stressed that the Republic of Korea was not like the Philippines under Marcos—it was moving in the right direction under tense and volatile conditions. If there was a lesson to be learned from Manila, it was that both the people and the authorities had sought to avoid violent confrontations. The most difficult trick I had to accomplish during my stay was to demonstrate firm American support for President Chun while encouraging the process of political liberalization.

I decided to meet with Lee Min Woo, the head of the main opposition party, the New Korea Democratic party, while our top Asia hand, Assistant Secretary Gaston Sigur was to meet with other opposition leaders, including Kim Young Sam and Kim Dae Jung, who had been released from prison in late December 1982 after serving over two years of a twenty-year sentence for his political activities. He had written me that his release was the result of "humanitarian and political efforts" that I had undertaken.[10] My meetings took place, but Sigur's were canceled by the opposition leaders at the last minute, apparently because of the considerable political tension at the time and my own statements supporting orderly change. When my schedule took me on to other stops in Asia, I sent Gaston Sigur back to Seoul, where he continued to try to help the South Koreans make their way through the minefield that had to be crossed to reach a working, democratic system of governance.

A Further Turn of the Wheel

Protest and turmoil in the first part of 1987 led me to fear for the worst. I was concerned about possible violent confrontation providing the basis for the government to call off or postpone the upcoming election. On February 6, Sigur, in a speech delivered in New York—and widely noted in South Korea—warned against any military interference as the process of political transition moved along. On March 6, 1987, I met with President

10. He wrote this to me in a letter on January 3, 1983. The Reagan administration at various levels, with our ambassador, Richard Walker, as the point man, had been arguing with President Chun for the release of political dissidents, including Kim Dae Jung. As part of a Christmas amnesty, 1,200 dissidents were released a day after Kim's release.

Chun again in Seoul, and again he assured me he would go through with his pledge to carry out a peaceful and democratic transition in 1988, although debate over constitutional issues concerning the structure of the electoral process continued hot and heavy. I was asked publicly if I agreed with Sigur's speech and said that I most assuredly did.

After meeting with President Chun, I made this firm declaration: "The United States, as a friend and ally, supports the aspirations of all Koreans for continuing political development, respect for basic human rights, and free and fair elections. President Chun's commitment to leave office in 1988 will set a historic precedent for the peaceful transition of power. We will support all those who are urging moderation and nonviolent political change."

The months that followed continued with protests, forced resignations, detentions, and the declaration of a state of emergency. The opposition distrusted the procedure of having the president elected by the National Assembly and instead advocated direct election of the president by popular vote. Chun seemed unyielding. On June 24, President Chun met with opposition leader Kim Young Sam and agreed to end the house arrest of Kim Dae Jung; riots followed and Kim Dae Jung was jailed again.

In a Single Stroke

On June 29, Roh Tae Woo, the candidate of the ruling Democratic Justice party, stepped into the limelight. Dramatically, he accepted political reforms, most particularly direct election of the president. In a single stroke, he revolutionized the situation and established himself as a strong and independent political figure. Even the opposition was impressed. "What Roh Tae Woo showed today was great determination" said Kim Young Sam. "On second thought, drop the word 'great,' " he amended.

Two days later, President Chun approved the changes advocated by Roh and once again released Kim Dae Jung. Chun said, "Let us work another miracle by developing Korea into a model of political development deserving to be so recorded in world history; we must not be content with having newly become a model of economic development." Within days, large additional numbers of political dissidents were released.

In the Reagan administration, we were deeply pleased but deliberately quiet. We did not want to be a visible part of the Korean electoral process, now well under way. Roh Tae Woo came to Washington in September 1987 and met with President Reagan and with me. I was struck by his readiness to engage in the give-and-take of conversation, a welcome contrast to the formal and stiff manner of Chun. Again, President Reagan and I had to walk a fine line, supporting change without intervening improperly.

On December 16, 1987, Roh Tae Woo won the presidency of the Republic of Korea with a plurality of 37 percent of the vote. The opposition, including Kim Young Sam and Kim Dae Jung, had not been able to settle on a single candidate, so their split vote enabled Roh to win a genuinely contested election. And in February 1988, Chun Doo Hwan made history: he presided over the first peaceful transfer of power through an electoral process in the history of South Korea. Roh Tae Woo was inaugurated on February 25, 1988.

Hurdle and Opportunity: the Olympics

There was one more massive hurdle and opportunity ahead: South Korea was to host the 1988 Summer Olympics. I had looked over the preparations and arrangements as they were put together. The South Koreans were doing a masterful job. The great worry was whether there would be terrorism. Would North Korea take the Olympics as a target for attack? Toward the end of 1987, on November 29, Korean Air Lines Flight 858 had exploded between Abu Dhabi and Bangkok, on its way to Seoul. Almost all of the 115 people killed were South Koreans. On January 15, a woman who identified herself as a North Korean agent confessed to planting a bomb on the plane, after which she and her partner in crime did not reboard the plane in Abu Dhabi. Her partner committed suicide after being apprehended in Bahrein. She had failed in her attempt to follow suit. Their objective, she said, on orders of the North Korean government, was to destroy the plane in order to disrupt the 1988 Olympic Games and create fear and unrest in South Korea.

I worked hard to help South Korea attract countries to the games, providing assurances of the extensive steps taken to safeguard the security of the athletes. The Soviets decided to attend, having boycotted the Los Angeles Olympics. The Chinese also decided to take part. The problem of terrorism from North Korea had been underlined by the bombing of Flight 858. When Foreign Minister Shevardnadze was in Washington on March 23, 1988, I discussed the subject with him and took him over to the White House for lunch with the president. "What about the possibility of terrorism from the North during the games?" President Reagan asked Shevardnadze directly.

"Do not worry," Shevardnadze replied. "We [the Soviet Union] will be at Seoul to compete. There will not be any terrorism." And there wasn't.

The 1988 Olympics marked the acceptance of the Republic of Korea as a legitimate and responsible member of the international community. President Roh on October 18, 1988, became the first Korean leader to address the UN General Assembly, an appearance made at the invitation of the majority of the members. Roh called for a new era of relations with North Korea. He could do so on a stunning record of South Korean success. For over forty years, the South Koreans had in place a strong security regime for defense against any renewed aggression from the North. Economic growth had been phenomenal. And now their progress toward democracy had further demonstrated to the world which of the two Koreas had the best system. A new prospect for progress on the Korean peninsula was in place. The South Koreans had added to their economic miracle a political miracle as well.

The March Toward Democracy in the 1980s

Ronald Reagan from his first day in office and I from the day I became secretary of state a year and a half later were consistent advocates of political and economic freedom. We supported with enthusiasm the inauguration of civilian elected presidents in Argentina in December 1983 and in Brazil in March 1985, and we heralded the march toward democracy that occurred during the Reagan presidency, in our hemisphere and beyond.

When President Reagan came into office in 1981, about half of the people of the Americas lived in countries with democratically elected leaders, the great bulk of whom lived in North America. By 1988 the proportion of people in the Americas living in countries with democratically elected leaders had risen dramatically—to 96 percent. Cuba, Nicaragua, and Chile were the odd men out. And by the end of 1988, democratic change had come to Chile. We had earlier seen in the Philippines how a dictator, Ferdinand Marcos, had been displaced by an election that he himself had called in the false expectation that it could be rigged in his favor.

I was firmly convinced that this broad sweep toward freedom and democracy, so evident in the Western Hemisphere, would rise in importance throughout the world. Given a real choice, I was confident, people would turn in a democratic direction.

During the Reagan years three strongmen—Marcos, Chun, Pinochet—had run up against the electoral process in this new and insistent information age. These were developments from which I and countless others derived great satisfaction. But the real point was the opportunity for progress open to the people involved. We should be willing to help them make the most of it.

CHAPTER 46

The Long Road
to a Washington Summit

Ronald Reagan wanted a summit in Washington. He was proud of the United States; he wanted to show our country off. I agreed. But, despite the important achievements at Geneva and Reykjavik, the fact that they took place neither in the United States nor in the Soviet Union registered a point: our relationship was still uneasy. A home-and-home pattern, as Reagan and Gorbachev had agreed to in Geneva, would express important movement toward more stability. But now, in September 1987, almost two years had passed since the Geneva summit, and uncertainty shrouded the possibility of both leaders meeting in Washington.

I wanted to use the prospect of a summit, which I felt Gorbachev wanted as much as Reagan did, to move the Soviets in our direction on human rights, arms reduction, and the resolution of regional conflicts that had a major East-West overlay. I had my mind especially on Afghanistan and Southern Africa. Such an effort would require us to maintain a certain diffidence about summitry. But attitudes around the White House were anything but diffident. Referring to Nancy with a good-natured laugh, Colin Powell said, "She's already bought the groceries for Thanksgiving. Gorbachev's going to the ranch whether he wants to or not." To impress the Soviet leader, Powell said, the White House arrangers were planning a flight path for the Gorbachevs that would take them over all sorts of Southern California real estate, endless private houses, many with swimming pools.

Actually, I thought Gorbachev would benefit from seeing California, with its natural beauty and economic dynamism. The Reagan ranch held its own meaning: a simple, though quietly elegant adobe house in an extraordinary setting, where the Reagans had put much effort, with Ronald Reagan cutting brush and fixing fences. He was part of this land.

The hours just before Eduard Shevardnadze was to arrive in Washington in mid-September were unusually tense. We would have to make progress toward a summit during the Shevardnadze meetings if the event was to happen before the end of the year. At the White House and at the State Department voices were strained. Doors and drawers were slammed. An accident on the Roosevelt Bridge, a stuck elevator, holes not punched in a briefing book paper—all seemed to rattle people excessively. I put it down to Iran-Contra and to the uncertainty of what the Soviet approach to us might be. Would they regard us as a mortally wounded administration, or despite this latest in the series of Washington upheavals that had engulfed recent presidents, would they be ready to do business?

I felt confident that my meetings with Shevardnadze would be productive. All the basic elements needed for an INF Treaty were in hand and simply needed to be put together to form the whole.[1] My April mission to Moscow had convinced me, to the consternation and disagreement of authoritative voices in the CIA, on the NSC staff, and at the Pentagon, that change was moving rapidly in the Soviet Union.

The clear movement toward an INF agreement was not universally welcomed. This prospect alarmed the Republican right in Congress and some important former officials, notably former President Nixon, former Secretary of State Kissinger, and former NSC adviser Brent Scowcroft. They seemed to see in the INF Treaty the beginning of the end of the Western alliance: the beginning of a process of denuclearization of Europe (following removal of INF weapons) that would leave Western Europe vulnerable to Soviet conventional forces and bring about a "decoupling" of the United

1. My April 1987 visit to Moscow had produced the Soviet proposal of equality at zero in short-range INF missiles. On June 1, Chancellor Helmut Kohl had informed us of his agreement to this proposal, and the step was formalized at a meeting of NATO foreign ministers in Reykjavik on June 12. The meeting had also produced important language, creating a "firebreak," as Margaret Thatcher put it, between the elimination of short-range INF weapons and even shorter-range U.S. nuclear weapons stationed in Europe. Denuclearization of Europe was a concern of Thatcher's, Mitterrand's, and some officials of the German government. The Germans, however, were deeply troubled because they focused on the remaining short-range nuclear weapons and the implication of these weapons as they saw it: Germany might become a nuclear battleground. Their view seemed not to recognize the large numbers of warheads on air-launched missiles based in other countries. We, too, were concerned that there be no "third zero." Then, on July 22, Gorbachev had announced his agreement to eliminate long-range INF missiles: this meant we were now agreed on what became known as the "double zero."

By midsummer, a new problem had arisen: how to handle the Soviet demand for elimination of the Pershing Ia missiles (comparable to short-range INF missiles) owned by the West German government, but with nuclear warheads that belonged to and were controlled by the United States. These were German weapons that, like the nuclear weapons owned by the British and French governments, were not included in this negotiation between the United States and the Soviets. President Reagan had won the point of exclusion of British and French systems in his session with Gorbachev in Reykjavik, but the question of the German missiles was not addressed. We regarded the missiles as German; the Soviets saw the weapons as American. We agonized, along with Kohl, and on August 26, Kohl announced that the Pershing Ia missiles would be dismantled after the INF Treaty was signed and implemented. The United States, we said, would then treat the warheads in the same fashion as others covered by the INF Treaty.

States from Europe. I disagreed, as did our NATO allies. Our remaining nuclear capability in Europe would still be formidable and would enable us to exercise the full scale of possibilities called for by the doctrine of flexible response. In fact, if the United States reversed its stand now on our willingness to eliminate INF missiles, after maintaining this position throughout the volatile predeployment period, such a reversal would be political dynamite in Europe!

The vocal opposition of Nixon, Kissinger, and Scowcroft had clearly slowed down serious work on our sweeping effort for strategic arms reductions (START). I argued vigorously to the president that START was of even greater significance than INF and that the United States would benefit more from a strategic arms agreement than would the Soviets. In an unconstrained environment for building and deploying heavy intercontinental ballistic missiles, I argued, the Soviets could move forward far more easily than could we. Serious work on START meant that we would have to reexamine positions we had taken earlier. The president said he understood and agreed: we should go forward on START.

Shevardnadze and Gunfire

At eight o'clock sharp on Tuesday morning, September 15, 1987, Eduard Shevardnadze arrived at the State Department. We went immediately to my private office, where we had a year earlier started our work together on the release of Nicholas Daniloff. Shevardnadze, now the master of his brief, was ready to work. As we sat down in the small study behind my larger, more formal office, one of my security agents entered abruptly and quickly drew the curtains. I looked at him quizzically. "There's a guy at the Vietnam Memorial with an M-16," he said, "and threatening to fire." Such events seemed to be occurring with greater frequency. A few weeks earlier, as I was walking into the Pentagon's river entrance, I heard gunfire nearby, and suddenly was crushed inside a circular wall of security guards. This incident, annoying but inconsequential, was well reported in the Washington press. What was Shevardnadze to think, I wondered, of this underside of Washington, D.C., fast becoming known as the murder capital of the world.

Shevardnadze and I turned to the task at hand. We agreed quickly on the establishment of working groups on human rights, regional issues, bilateral problems, and arms control in all its dimensions—the four-part agenda I had set forth in my Senate testimony in June 1983. We fell easily into what was becoming a familiar pattern: our respective delegations met with each other and then with us. Our work together had become increasingly confident and productive.

Shevardnadze gave me a letter from General Secretary Gorbachev for

President Reagan confirming all the basic elements needed for an INF agreement:

> With success we would be able to provide a firm basis for a stable and forward-moving development not just of the Soviet-U.S. relationship but of international relations as a whole for many years ahead. We would leave behind what was, frankly, a complicated stretch in world politics, and you and I would crown in a befitting manner the process of interaction on the central issues of security which began in Geneva. . . . We believe that the time has come to remove the cloak of dangerous secrecy from the military doctrines of the two alliances, of the U.S.S.R. and the U.S.A. [the Warsaw Pact and NATO]. In this process of giving greater transparency to our military guidelines, meetings of military officers at the highest level could also play a role.

I felt we could not have asked for a better tone, spirit, and substance than were evident in this letter.

Gorbachev's letter contained a clear indication that the Reagan Doctrine had brought results: "I have in mind, in particular, the growing desire for national reconciliation." Gorbachev was letting us know that he was ready to work to defuse tensions in hot spots around the world. We were supporting the opposition to Marxist regimes in many lands: Afghanistan, Angola, Nicaragua, Cambodia. The free and Communist worlds faced each other on the Korean Peninsula. Were the Soviets ready to see at least some of these conflicts resolved?

Most gratifying was Shevardnadze's statement to me that the Soviets would now move to expand human rights, that their overall policy had changed. "Give me your lists [of people who wish to be allowed to emigrate]," he said; "we'll be glad to look at them."

We adjourned at 10:40 so that I could brief President Reagan on our progress before Shevardnadze's arrival at the White House, where in a Rose Garden ceremony we would sign an agreement to establish Nuclear Risk Reduction Centers in each country. This was an idea developed by Senators Sam Nunn and John Warner, the chairman and ranking minority member of the Senate Armed Services Committee. Richard Perle and Bob Linhard had done an outstanding job in leading the negotiation for the United States. The agreement, in effect an extension of the hot line, would create an open and instant communications link between the two countries, in order to further reduce any risk of a nuclear exchange due to error or miscalculation. The line would be the means, for example, of notification of missile test firings and exchanges of information useful in verifying arms control agreements. The president hosted lunch at the White House. My sessions with Shevardnadze continued in the afternoon, over a dinner on the barge of the chief of naval operations, and then throughout the next day and the day following. Shevardnadze had come to work. He said nothing about the debilitating Iran-Contra affair.

The next afternoon, Wednesday, September 16, Shevardnadze and I were to convene with our working group on regional issues. He drew me aside. "I would like to talk with you privately before we go into the larger meeting." We walked into my back office while others waited in my larger adjoining office. "We will leave Afghanistan," he opened with a quiet directness. "It may be in five months or a year, but it is not a question of it happening in the remote future. I say with all responsibility that a political decision to leave has been made." This was a development of immense importance—and a dramatic moment.

Shevardnadze asked me for our help, particularly in dealing with the threat of the spread of Islamic fundamentalism: "A neutral, nonaligned Afghanistan is one thing, a reactionary fundamentalist Islamic regime is something else." He was clearly worried about the Islamic republics in the Soviet Union. This was confirmation of a huge breakthrough in the making.

I pointed up the importance of a short timetable for withdrawal of Soviet troops and for disproportionate numbers to be withdrawn at the beginning, known as "front-end loading." His concerns were not easy to address, I said, but our interest was in a neutral, nonaligned Afghanistan being governed by Afghans. We did not try to agree on anything.

The meeting was a private sharing of critical information. Gorbachev and Shevardnadze had both said publicly on earlier occasions that the Soviets would withdraw from Afghanistan, but we saw no evidence on the ground to lend credence to their statements. This private assurance was different. I had enough confidence by this time in my relationship with Shevardnadze that I knew he would not deliberately mislead me.

We then joined our waiting working group and listened, on Afghanistan, to the same old arguments. I said nothing, but I looked over at Shevardnadze and he at me as we shared a knowing glance.

Beyond arms control and Afghanistan, we talked about the Iran-Iraq War and the importance of following through on UN Security Council Resolution 598, mandating a cease-fire on all fronts in the war. Although the Soviets were reluctant to favor mandatory sanctions against Iran, they were willing to consider them. No doubt the large Islamic population in the Soviet Union lay behind this hesitation. At the same time, the Soviets were agitated about the large U.S. presence in the Persian Gulf. I assured Shevardnadze that as the need for an American naval presence in the Gulf receded, so would the number of our ships.

I invited NSC adviser Frank Carlucci to join me on Thursday morning to make him part of our effort. The subject was arms control, and Frank had considerable expertise to provide. A sticky detail involving the Pershing Ia issue arose. By contributing an important suggestion for solving the problem, Frank registered with Shevardnadze as a person of standing and ideas.

At three o'clock, we moved to the James Madison Room on the floor above my office. I had invited, with Shevardnadze's agreement, all the members of all the working groups. Extra chairs were brought in, but there was still not enough space, so many people stood along the walls. The U.S. and Soviet chairmen of each working group reported to the assembled multitude, over fifty people. The reports were factual, candid, and devoid of the usual polemics. Compartments between people and subjects had been broken down. A sense of the whole, of common purpose and possibilities, was clearly emerging. People were talking openly now about subjects they would hardly breathe to each other before. I felt that we had turned an important corner.

A far more normal atmosphere had emerged, where the emphasis had shifted toward solving rather than creating problems. Perhaps most noteworthy was the discussion of human rights matters under the leadership on our side of Assistant Secretary of State Dick Schifter. Dick was dedicated to this cause, and in a sensitive, patient, insistent manner, he produced results. Mark Parris, our Soviet desk officer and an experienced, skeptical, and astute observer of the Soviet scene, said to me afterward, "Today produced the most forward-looking attitude I've felt since I've been in this business."

Shevardnadze and I went to the White House in the late afternoon to give President Reagan a full account of our three days of hard work. He was enthusiastic about the progress we had made and the prospects it foreshadowed for the future. We were able to announce in a formal joint statement that we had "agreement in principle to conclude a treaty" reducing to zero all INF missiles and that we expected that treaty to be ready for signing when President Reagan and General Secretary Gorbachev met in Washington in the late fall. The exact dates for the meeting would be set, we announced at the suggestion of the Soviets, when I visited Moscow in October.

The *Washington Post* on Friday, September 18, 1987, carried the banner headline "U.S., Soviets Agree on Missile Treaty Outline." The NBC-TV morning news analysis noted, "The president virtually froze out the Pentagon and other administration hard-liners, giving the lead to Secretary Shultz." I telephoned former secretaries of state to brief them on what we had achieved. Al Haig was reserved in his reaction. He did not like the reduction in NATO nuclear capability. All the others gave their full support except Henry Kissinger. This, he said, "undoes forty years of NATO." He would have to express his reservations in public, Kissinger said. On the other hand, he conceded, if we were going to sign a treaty, it would be terrible to have it defeated by the Senate.[2] Soon Jeane Kirkpatrick joined the ranks of our critics.

2. Henry Kissinger expressed his criticism of INF and of the Reagan administration's approach to arms control and Soviet relations in an article in *Newsweek*, October 12, 1987.

Congress greeted our success by voting to curb SDI research, thereby diminishing our leverage, and the Senate Foreign Relations Committee released a report on September 20 declaring that the Reagan administration's reinterpretation of the 1972 ABM Treaty to allow development of exotic missile defenses was "the most flagrant abuse of the Constitution's treaty power in 200 years of American history." The committee statement reflected the growing intensity of the dispute over the meaning of the ABM Treaty. Abe Sofaer's examination of the negotiating record disclosed a different picture from the meaning presented by the Nixon administration at the time of ratification. The Senate, with Sam Nunn at the forefront, was up in arms and demanding that the complete INF negotiating record be available to the Senate during the ratification debate. The *New York Times* headlined on September 21: "SENATE COMMITTEE THREATENS DELAY OF NEW ARMS PACT."

We were being assaulted both from the right and from the left as we tried to solve problems with the Soviets and to achieve the first treaty ever that actually *reduced* existing levels of nuclear arms. These extremes—left and right—were, deliberately or otherwise, undercutting the president's effort to move forward from INF to START. But the carpers and the doubters and the undercutters did not dampen my spirits, or, more importantly, the spirits of Ronald Reagan. I felt completely comfortable about our course of action, and I was buoyed by the fact that the president never wavered.

I got a boost from an unexpected corner when I turned on Monday night football on September 21. An NFL players' strike was about to start, and the players' representative and former Oakland Raiders star, Gene Upshaw, was quoted as saying, "Someone—he knows who he is—can step in and prevent the strike." Frank Gifford commented, "If they're talking about Secretary of State George Shultz, he's been busy."

In New York, something was wrong. Shevardnadze, in his speech at the annual meeting of the UN General Assembly, made some hostile comments about President Reagan for having lectured him that the Soviets needed to change their system. I now knew that Shevardnadze was in the forefront of those in the Soviet Union who wanted reform, and I also knew that President Reagan had *not* lectured Shevardnadze in their meeting in Washington. There were, I was well aware, people in the Kremlin, just as there were in Washington, who did not like the change of course in the U.S.-Soviet relationship. With strength returning now to President Reagan, we would prevail in the United States against the naysayers, I felt confident. I wondered whether the critics in Moscow were more dangerous.

I continued to work on the human rights issue as I prepared to go to Moscow at the end of October. I had given Shevardnadze a chart brought to me by Morris Abram, on behalf of the American Jewish community, which made a dramatic point about the number of Soviet Jews waiting to emigrate. I heard that Shevardnadze showed it to Shimon Peres when they met in New York. What registered with me was that Shevardnadze had clearly looked at the chart, understood its message, and cared enough about the message to discuss it with the Israeli foreign minister.

On October 15, 1987, I was asked, if at all possible, to be available in the afternoon for a phone call from Jerusalem. At 3:18 P.M., the call came through in my office in the State Department. On the other end of the line came "This is Ida Nudel. I'm in Jerusalem." She paused, then said, "I'm home." I could hardly speak for the rush of emotion I felt. This was the one of the most moving moments of my years as secretary of state. Her story was heroic even among the many tales of intrepid Jewish refuseniks. This courageous woman's name was on the list I had given Shevardnadze at the time of the Daniloff negotiation, and she had been present at the well-publicized seder I had attended in Moscow early in April. I had met twice with her sister in Jerusalem and heard her moving plea. I had always said we would never give up our effort on Ida's behalf but had never said anything to Ida or her sister that could mislead them. Ida gave Ronald Reagan and me much of the credit for forcing such promising change in human rights in the Soviet Union. I was not sure what was causing it, but the signs of change were unmistakable.

Shevardnadze had said to me, "The Soviet Union is taking actions because we judge them to be in our own interest." I harked back to my having made that very argument to him the previous April in Moscow. The Soviets could not keep pace in the information and knowledge age unless they opened up their society and allowed individuals more freedom. Was my line of argument having some impact?

A Changing of the Guard

In October 1987, Cap Weinberger let it be known that because of the ill health of his wife, Jane, he would be resigning as secretary of defense. His world was collapsing around him. His approach to the defense budget was "never compromise." By now, his technique was well understood in Congress, with the result that no one even tried to reach accommodations with him. Cap had become a marginal figure in the debate. President Reagan had rejected Cap's effort to go back on the Reykjavik decision to agree to a global limit of 100 long-range INF missiles on each side. Now the policy that I had urged on the president and to which the president had agreed and adhered had paid off. Gorbachev had agreed to the total elimination of INF weapons. We were going forward with the Soviets, and the relationship was showing sure signs of dramatic improvement.

The question was, who would become Cap's successor? Cap seemed to favor Will Taft, his own deputy. Frank Carlucci came to me and asked for my support. I felt that Frank would make an excellent secretary of defense.

I had been getting along with Frank increasingly well in recent weeks. My problems with Frank as director of the NSC staff stemmed from his desire to be in operational charge of important diplomatic and cabinet-level interagency groups. He was able and experienced and straightforward. I took my views quietly to the president and found him like-minded. No announcement was made immediately. I urged the president to move Colin Powell up to be the national security adviser. As deputy, Powell had proved to be extraordinarily knowledgeable and gifted intellectually. He had a great touch with Congress. I had known of him going back to the 1970s, when he had been a White House Fellow in the Office of Management and Budget at the time I was director. If we went into the final year of the administration with Carlucci, Powell, and me in the key foreign and security policy posts, that would be by far the best team, and in fact, the first genuine team, assembled in the entire Reagan presidency. And with Chief of Staff Howard Baker and his deputy Ken Duberstein running the White House staff for the president, we once again had on hand the needed political savvy and experience.

Having in mind Carlucci's prospective move to the Defense Department and my experience that greater cohesion in our policy resulted when the NSC adviser was included in important meetings with the Soviets, I invited Frank to accompany me on my trip to Moscow. He accepted with a sense of keen anticipation. Despite his long years of service in the U.S. government as deputy in the OMB, HEW, CIA, and Defense, he had never been to Moscow.

Our job would be to get firm agreement on INF and, with that in hand, to set a date for a Reagan-Gorbachev summit in Washington. The president expected me to produce both. At the same time, hard-liners in Washington were increasing the pressure to block both. I told the president that the way things were going, the conservatives in his party could end up opposing him on the INF Treaty, while the Democrats in the Senate could be his leading supporters. That brought him up out of his chair but did not change his mind in the slightest. He felt that the conservatives in the end would always support him.

Off to Moscow

On Wednesday, October 20, 1987, after stops in Israel, Saudi Arabia, Egypt, and Britain, I arrived in Helsinki for a day's layover before going on to Moscow. The members of my delegation coming directly from Washington would use the time to get adjusted to the time zone before undertaking important negotiations, and we would all have time to devote exclusively to discussion among our delegation, including our arms control negotiators coming in from Geneva, and Jack Matlock, our ambassador, coming in from Moscow. We would then fly into Moscow early on Thursday morning in time to start our meetings by 10:30 A.M.

Early Wednesday morning, I was told that the entire Moscow area, including Sheremetyevo Airport, was totally fogged in, and those conditions were expected to continue at least through Thursday. The Soviets suggested that we come by night train and volunteered to produce the necessary cars. After discussing the situation with Pat Kennedy, the tireless and ingenious manager of these trips, I decided that we should accept their invitation so that we could start on time. After all, a great deal was riding on this effort. The Soviet special train would be made up in Leningrad and sent into Helsinki. A Finnish engine would pull it to the border, where a Soviet engine would be hooked up and take us on to Moscow. This would be, we speculated, a "Potemkin" train, like the Potemkin village set up on the Volga by Catherine the Great's minister to impart a vision of progress when there was none. But the whole idea seemed like fun, and everybody— Americans, Finns, and Soviets—took this departure from routine in the spirit of a holiday outing.

At 3:00 in the afternoon, we learned that the Soviets had failed to come up with a train. But by some miracle and on four hours' notice, the Finnish government did. At 7:15 P.M. on Wednesday evening, we boarded a special train carrying our complete delegation, including all the security people and thirty-five members of the American press. The mayor of Helsinki saw me off at a floodlit, crowd-packed ceremony in the city's grand railway station. "Good-bye! Happy journey! Finland brings the superpowers together!" the mayor cried out as the train pulled out of the station.

The cars were clean and comfortable. My compartment included a bathroom with a shower! The trip took on a festive air. I wandered through the cars to say hello to everybody, including all the press corps. Our communications group set up a secure satellite hookup in a baggage car and proudly showed it off. They were determined that the secretary of state should not be out of touch at any time. I appreciated their efforts, and to prove it, I placed a call to Washington.

At 10:00 P.M., we halted at the Finnish border town of Vainikkala. A Soviet locomotive with a big red star on the boiler came out of the darkness and hooked us up. The scene might have come right out of *Dr. Zhivago*. Then, across the Soviet border—at Vyborg, a name that revealed that this was territory taken from Finland by Stalin—we halted again. There was a small nineteenth-century-looking train station painted in a bland yellow that seemed intended to brighten the gloom of official structures. About thirty brown-suited, green-capped Soviet guards swarmed on board. The odor of their unwashed uniforms was penetrating. They all spoke German— apparently the language of choice between Finn and Russian border officials. Most of them roamed up and down the corridor, looking desultorily into each cabin while the women among them inspected the *"briefkasten"* filled with our passports. *"Alles ist in Ordnung* [All is in order]," one said and then commented, *"Nebel. Schrecklich* [Fog. Terrible]." Then they all scrambled off, and we rolled on. The roadbed inside the Soviet Union, unlike that on the Finnish side, was rough and jolting.

Ed Rowny, usually grumpy and lugubrious, pulled out his harmonica and played "Siberian Sleighride" and then explained to the amazed reporters that he had started out playing with Larry Adler's Harmonica Rascals in vaudeville. Then he played "Wabash Cannonball," which became "Moscow Cannonball." Soon everyone was asleep as the train rolled on. When I woke up, we were edging into Moscow station.

Peter Jennings, on ABC's "World News Tonight" on October 21 said, according to a transcript given to me at the Moscow station, "Secretary of State George Shultz . . . tonight got on a train in Helsinki, Finland, to go to Moscow because the airport is fogged in. We asked ourselves why he was in such a hurry to get to Moscow. We thought it might have something to do with the fact that President Reagan is going to give a news conference tomorrow and might want to say something about a summit." Summit fever was raging.

The festive air of the improvised train ride was matched by the reception we received at the Moscow train station. The Soviets were pleased with themselves. The train ride had been their idea, and they had been able to produce a Soviet locomotive that had hauled us from the Finnish border on into Moscow. I went directly to the by now familiar Osobnyak, the Soviet Foreign Ministry meeting house on Alexei Tolstoy Street, where Shevardnadze and I and our delegations typically met. We greeted each other warmly and started in.

Shevardnadze: Full Steam Ahead

Shevardnadze was all business. He set out a suggested extensive schedule, complete with a layout of working groups parallel to those we had set up so successfully in Washington. All this was preparatory to a Friday session with Gorbachev beginning at 11:00 A.M. and expected to last until 1:00 in the afternoon. We invited the entire Soviet delegation and ours for lunch at Spaso House at 1:30 P.M., on the advice that Gorbachev would adhere to the schedule he announced. I agreed with Shevardnadze's procedural suggestions, but knowing something that he did not know, I raised an additional question on what I called "the personnel side." Would it be possible, I asked, for him to arrange that Minister of Defense Dimitri Yazov might be present on some occasion so that Frank Carlucci and I could meet him? I had long sought to bring together the defense ministers and the top military officers. Cap Weinberger had always resisted this, and I thought it would be a pleasant surprise to the Soviets when they would read shortly that Carlucci had been appointed secretary of defense. Shevardnadze replied that, as it turned out, Yazov would be present at the luncheon he was giving me immediately following our initial session.

After meeting briefly with all the members of the working groups, Shevardnadze and I and our immediate associates (Carlucci and Roz Ridgway on our side, Dobrynin and Bessmertnykh on theirs) returned to the adjoining room and continued our pattern of private talks. We started with human rights. By this time, while I emphasized individual cases that we were especially concerned about, we were also working on broader issues: changes in their laws, the misuse of psychiatric institutions, freedom of religious practice, the right to travel and to emigrate, especially problems of Jewish emigration. I noted the particularly rapid progress recently in the permission of ethnic Germans to emigrate, and I asked whether this might reflect a Soviet perception that Soviet Germans had an ethnic homeland in Germany.

I told Shevardnadze, through a story designed to make the argument that there was also a Jewish homeland, how deeply moved I had been by my recent conversation with Ida Nudel and by her first words, "I'm in Jerusalem. I'm home." So, Israel, I said, is a homeland for Jews, just as much as Germany is for Germans. Shevardnadze had been quoted as saying, when he had recently met with Jewish leaders in Uruguay, that any Jews who wished to leave the Soviet Union would be allowed to do so. "If that represents Soviet policy," I said, "an important change has occurred. And the increased liberality we see in the granting of visas for travel to the United States, this increased ability for Soviet citizens to come and go, is an encouraging part of a pattern that seems to be developing and that we welcome."

Shevardnadze was responsive, while insisting that this discussion had to be a "two-way street," with comments by him on human rights problems in the United States. He spoke about the Soviet proposal of a human rights conference to take place in Moscow as an agreed follow-up to the CSCE conference then taking place in Vienna. "The Soviet Union will not perish if this meeting does not occur," he said in such a way that I knew the proposal was a matter of great importance to him. He acknowledged to me that there were no substantive barriers now to Jews who wished to leave, except for those who had been exposed to "state secrets." I knew that there would be plenty of problems, but I also knew that significant change was taking place.

We moved on to other subjects. The problem of short-range INF missiles, examined in further excruciating detail, seemed finally resolved to the satisfaction of the Soviets. The existence of nuclear-tipped ballistic missiles of any range on German soil was an obvious neuralgic point with the Soviets.

That afternoon at our embassy I met with refuseniks and individuals separated from their spouses because of being denied exit visas. I went back to the Osobnyak for still another three-hour session that evening. By the end of this session, we had covered the complete range of subjects on our four-part agenda. My talks with Shevardnadze were going very well.

But at breakfast at Spaso House on Friday morning, October 23, the working group attempting to settle the remaining technical issues of the INF Treaty reported to me that no progress had been made in their meetings throughout the night. The Soviet team was "pathetic," out of touch, uninstructed, and ignorant—or feigning ignorance—of issues Shevardnadze and I had already resolved. "The bad guy was Obukhov. He's under permanent suspicion by the KGB," Nitze said, "because he's got a degree from the University of Chicago, where he studied with Hans Morgenthau, so he has to live it down." I didn't know quite what to make of this development other than to recall that on earlier occasions in Moscow, the pace had been slow until the key meeting with Gorbachev. We would discover at 11:00 this morning what Gorbachev had in store for us.

A Gorbachev Surprise

At 10:45, the KGB notified Marty Dougherty, the head of my security detail, that they were ready to lead us into the Kremlin. We were whisked through the main gate, leaving the sense of city behind, and entered a different world of grassy expanses and birch trees separating the stately buildings. The Soviet chief of protocol met us, led us up a stairway, through a long corridor to a splendid holding room that could only make one wonder at the elegance of life in czarist times.

At precisely 11:00 A.M., I walked from my end of St. Catherine's Hall and Gorbachev from his. We met, as was traditional, in the middle of the room. Our delegations followed. A small pool of reporters was present. Gorbachev engaged in a little banter. One of the reporters shouted something about a trip by Gorbachev to the United States. "I think it's going to happen," he said. Summit fever was everywhere, and the press took this comment as confirmation that an agreement about dates for the Washington summit was coming. The reporters were herded out, and we started in.

On my side of the table sat Frank Carlucci, along with Paul Nitze, Roz Ridgway, and Ambassador Jack Matlock, plus our note taker, Mark Parris, and our interpreter. We looked across not only at Gorbachev but at Shevardnadze, Dobrynin, Marshal Akhromeyev, Deputy Foreign Minister Bessmertnykh, Ambassador Dubinin, Gorbachev adviser Chernyaev, and the Soviet interpreter.

Gorbachev was smiling and positive in his manner. He noted that my presence in Moscow so soon after Shevardnadze's lengthy meetings in Washington spoke for itself and suggested that the U.S.-Soviet relationship had entered a more dynamic phase. The Soviets welcomed this, said Gorbachev. But, he continued, "The most important thing is substance. I feel that there, too, something is emerging."

I agreed and noted what I had said in my toast the day before: "Ten years from now, people will record the Reykjavik summit meeting as having accomplished more than any previous summit."

Reykjavik had been "a kind of intellectual breakthrough," Gorbachev responded. Its shock effect, he said, had been similar to that caused by the reaction to the recent plummet of 500-points [on October 19, 1987, just four days earlier] of the U.S. stock market, a sense that something big had happened. "When people settle down," he said, "they realize that a new stage in the U.S.-Soviet political dialogue has started, especially in security issues."

In introducing Frank Carlucci, I told Gorbachev that Carlucci and I had worked together since the 1970s and that few people in government had such varied and extensive experience as he. Gorbachev quipped, "Carlucci must have learned from all this experience that no agreement is possible without taking into account the interests of both parties," but, he went on, "I know that when Nitze and Akhromeyev get together, they invariably seek to achieve some advantage over the other."

"This is the first time I've heard that about Akhromeyev," I interjected with a smile, "although I know it is true of Nitze."

Gorbachev then asked for and got a report from me and Shevardnadze about our discussions. Gorbachev wanted to talk about the Persian Gulf. I could see that he was concerned about the large U.S. presence in the Gulf and worried that we were setting ourselves up to stay there. I assured him that our presence would diminish as the need for it diminished, and once again pushed for agreement on sanctions under UN Security Council Resolution 598. "We want to see U.S.-Soviet cooperation in UN diplomacy continue to work well, as it has, because that might end a poisonous war," I said. "Nothing could strengthen the standing of an organization like the UN like success in dealing with a difficult problem." In the negotiations with the secretary-general, I said, Iran was playing games, not taking Resolution 598 seriously, and we needed to follow through. Otherwise, "Iran will make a fool of the UN Security Council. The Council's credibility is on the line."

Gorbachev asserted that an INF agreement could be completed soon. The main issues should be resolved in Moscow, leaving only technical questions, drafting and editorial work, for the negotiators. He then challenged me. "Why is deployment of INF missiles continuing? Perhaps we should consider a joint moratorium effective November 1, even before signing the treaty." Such a move, he said, would correspond to the political decision that had been made to conclude an agreement.

I did not buy that argument. We should not give up what they were seeking in the negotiations until the negotiations were satisfactorily concluded. He said the "root problem" was "strategic arms" and "offensive arms in space." He then suggested a modified version of the Reykjavik proposal, or as he described it, the "essence" of the Reykjavik formula: a 50 percent reduction to equal levels in strategic arms and a ten-year period of nonwithdrawal from the ABM Treaty. In turn, these undertakings would involve strict observance of the ABM Treaty and a discussion of "what could be in space and what could not be in space." He then proposed a set of sublimits involving each leg of the strategic triad, all within the 6,000-warhead limit agreed to at Reykjavik.[3]

I raised questions. About the ABM Treaty, "Did I understand that Moscow called for a ten-year nonwithdrawal period? And for compliance with the ABM Treaty as negotiated?"

He interrupted. "In the form we observed it before 1983, there was no difference in interpretation until then."

I pointed to the legitimate questions of interpretation of the ABM Treaty and said that the Soviet side had sought to establish what I called a "narrower than narrow" interpretation of the treaty.

"No, what I now mean is the actual practice of both sides before 1983," Gorbachev replied. The key, he said, would be that there should be "no weapons in space. The important word is weapons," he said.

On START (Strategic Arms Reductions Talks), I summarized what we had already agreed to: a 6,000-warhead aggregate ceiling, a 1,600 bomber-launcher limit, a sublimit of 1,540 heavy missile warheads, a bomber-counting rule, and the reduction of throw weight by 50 percent. I said that we thought the next step was to limit the number of ballistic missile warheads, and our proposed ceiling was 4,800. I raised the problem of verification of any agreement on mobile missiles and invited Gorbachev to demonstrate how they would propose to solve that problem before he came to the United States.

"The basis exists for work on a key provisions agreement" that could be ready in time for a Washington summit, Gorbachev responded. "We should now look to the negotiators in Geneva to come up with an agreed principles statement," he said.

I argued that the leaders must make the major decisions. Gorbachev's response was quick, "Reykjavik is now history, but a second Reykjavik is not possible. We cannot once again have an extemporaneous discussion."

Gorbachev suddenly turned sour and aggressive. He produced a State Department document entitled "Soviet Intelligence Activities: A Report

---

3. His proposals were 3,000–3,300 ICBM warheads, 1,800–2,000 submarine-launched ballistic missile warheads, and 800–900 air-launched cruise missile warheads.

on Active Measures and Propaganda, 1986–87."[4] This document, he said, contained "shocking revelations," in particular the pamphlet's treatment of a "Mississippi peace cruise." He had commended this event to President Reagan during the Geneva summit as an example of good people-to-people activity. Now, he said, "you are alleging that this same cruise was being used by the Soviets to deceive Americans." I had no knowledge of this pamphlet and asked to see it. He held on to it, waving it at me: "We have no interest in Moscow in nourishing hatred for the United States. Can the United States not live without portraying the Soviet Union as an enemy? Is it a must to do so? What kind of a society would lead to such an approach?"

We have a genuine desire to improve relations, I said, but "there is much skepticism in the United States about the Soviet Union" because of your past actions. "Jimmy Carter, a man of good will, certainly learned a lesson when the Soviet Union invaded Afghanistan. The shooting down of the Korean air liner is another episode."

"You ought to begin with Gary Powers and the U-2 incident," Gorbachev interjected.

"Gromyko in Madrid said to me and all the other foreign ministers, 'Yes, we did it, and we'll do it again.' He sent a chill through the room," I replied, returning to my point about the shooting down of KAL Flight 007.

"How much did the United States pay for the pension of the pilot who flew KAL 007?" Gorbachev asked.

"I will not dignify that comment with a response," I snapped. Gorbachev said that he would ignore my remarks. "You should read Gromyko's speech. It appalled everyone," I told him. I went on to object to more recent Soviet efforts to spread rumors that the United States had invented AIDS and was trying to spread it. I was determined that Gorbachev would get a real argument whenever he went on the offensive like this. I suspected that Dobrynin put him up to it, so a tough argument might also put the former ambassador on the spot.

After some additional comments, Gorbachev mellowed, suggesting we "conclude this sharp exchange on the note on which I began, a desire to improve relations. How would you like to conclude the meeting?" he asked, more or less inviting me to make some comments about the summit.

"From the standpoint of content there is much work to do, but I have nothing to add to what has already been said," I said. "The agenda we have agreed on is broad, and we need to address all the issues, from human rights and Afghanistan to various security issues, and we constantly need

4. The document had been published by the State Department early in October in compliance with a statute passed in 1985 requiring each year a report on anti-U.S. propaganda. The content was supplied largely by the CIA and other intelligence agencies.

to be looking for areas where we can take constructive action." I noted real possibilities in Southern Africa. President Reagan, I said, hoped that Gorbachev would come to the United States and was prepared to receive him with respect and dignity and friendship. The most convenient time for the president would be late November. "You referred to a reciprocal visit to Moscow, as had been agreed in Geneva, and I am sure the president would like to see the Soviet Union, and not just Moscow," I told Gorbachev.

He pushed for more on the prospective agenda. "The program," I said, "would reflect the broad nature of the relationship itself. Certainly, there would be an INF Treaty to sign; there should be sessions between you and the president supported by advisers and possibly working groups on a wide range of substantive issues. Some discussions could be held in a special setting, such as Camp David or Williamsburg. The official program," I continued, "will demonstrate respect for the general secretary of the Soviet Union. Opportunities will also be presented for exposure to members of Congress and to Americans from various walks of life. It would be very desirable for you to travel beyond Washington. I have had the privilege of seeing a fair amount of Mikhail Gorbachev," I said, "and I am convinced that you would be liked and respected in America. Your direct, engaging, and curious manner will strike a responsive chord among Americans," I told him.

Gorbachev interjected, "Well, what about the questions of strategic arms and space?"

I didn't know what could emerge, I said.

"The agenda does not seem to measure up to what would be necessary at a summit and raises the question, would we two leaders gain or lose in our own countries and the world," Gorbachev countered. "It was right to have the first summit in Geneva and there have been many meetings between you and Shevardnadze, so what would be better, a summit meeting or something else? People will not understand if the two leaders keep meeting and have nothing to show for it, especially since both agreed and said publicly that strategic arms were the key."

In every meeting that I had had with Gorbachev, he always precipitated at least one episode of tension and acrimony. But I also felt something unusual was transpiring now. I couldn't quite place my finger on what it was, but I was determined not to fall into the trap of trying to adjust substance in order to persuade him to come to Washington. So I responded that if Gorbachev could not come to Washington, then perhaps "we should consider other ways to conclude an INF accord. The accord is virtually complete and should be signed, ratified, and put into effect," I said.

We should both do some thinking to "clarify what should be done," Gorbachev responded. "I will report to the Soviet leadership, and I assume you will report to the president."

"Of course," I replied. "Meetings of the leaders of the two superpowers should be possible without the world shaking. There is much to discuss," I said, "and it isn't necessary that every central issue be resolved." In any case, I would report to the president and "give some thought to alternative ways to have the INF Treaty signed." I could tell that he did not appreciate that suggestion.

Gorbachev kept saying that if we worked hard between now (late October) and a prospective summit toward the end of the year, we could accomplish a great deal in strategic arms and space. I said I doubted it, although we would work on the problem. I felt once again that Gorbachev was trying to exact a price in exchange for his agreement to come to Washington. I was determined not to bite on that apple. Gorbachev then said, "The dialogue is not over. I have the advantage that I can write directly to the president."

"We will look forward to your letter," I responded.

"Okay, these have been good talks." Gorbachev concluded our session briskly. He then moved around the table to shake hands with all the members of our delegation.

By this time, it was 3:00 in the afternoon, and our luncheon at Spaso House had long since been canceled. I went from my meeting with Gorbachev to the security bubble in our embassy, where I called President Reagan and described what had happened. I told the president that if he wished to take a different approach, I knew I still had time to turn the situation around. Perhaps a date could be set for the summit, but, I said, "I think we should just pass. We shouldn't push for this." The president, disappointed though I knew he must be, agreed with me.

I had one more meeting scheduled with Shevardnadze, basically to hear reports from our working groups. Some of the groups had substantial accomplishments to report, particularly on nuclear testing and nonproliferation of chemical weapons, human rights, and a few of our bilateral issues. Toward the end, Shevardnadze noted, "Although the working groups have not discussed strategic offensive weapons and the ABM Treaty, we talked about them for three hours with the general secretary."

"Four and a half hours," I corrected.

"Almost five, " said Shevardnadze,"but only three of them on this topic." Shevardnadze commented that the format of our meetings was good and that we should use it in the future. He said that he would characterize our talks to the press as "both constructive and businesslike: the atmosphere has been good and all the exchanges have been productive."

I went on to my press conference. The expectation was that I would announce the dates for the summit, regarded as the key objective of the whole meeting. Toward the end of my opening statement, I said that we had not agreed on any date for the summit, and so I was searching around for alternative ways to have the INF Treaty signed, since it was practically completed. I did not in any way raise objections to Gorbachev's refusal to set a summit date, though he had encouraged every expectation in advance that he would do this. I did not want to dig him into a hole any deeper than he had already dug for himself.

"This Boxer Has Been Hit"

In fact, I felt that I had seen something distinctly different in Gorbachev during our meeting. I said to our delegation when we reached our security bubble, "Something has changed." I was reminded of a line from Carl Sandburg's poem "Chicago." I had always viewed Gorbachev as supersure of himself, "Laughing even as an ignorant fighter laughs who has never lost a battle." Today, I said, "he no longer looks to me like a boxer who has never been hit. This boxer has been hit."

The news that, contrary to widespread expectations, no date had been set for the summit led some in the U.S. media, apparently forgetting Iran-Contra, to call this the worst single week in the Reagan administration: the stock market had plummeted on "Black Monday"; Robert Bork's nomination to the Supreme Court had been defeated in the Senate; and Soviet-U.S. relations had stalled out.

Nevertheless, when I briefed the NATO foreign mimisters in Brussels on Saturday, October 24, I reassured them and said I thought they shouldn't be too concerned. I reported on the positive developments from the Moscow meetings, including the narrowing of differences on the number of ballistic missiles to be allowed in START.[5]

I had just arrived in Washington that same evening when a cable came in from our embassy in Moscow. Deputy Foreign Minister Bessmertnykh had told Ambassador Matlock that Gorbachev had "blundered": my meeting with Gorbachev "did not go as planned." The Soviets would try to patch things up with us, he indicated. I could imagine that this was so, from the point of view of the Soviet Foreign Ministry. But Gorbachev knew something, I felt, something connected with Kremlin politics, that the bureaucrats in the ministries did not know.

Whatever the problem was, the Soviets quickly moved to repair the damage. "There is no reason to discuss the visit of Shultz to Moscow in terms of failure," Bessmertnykh told Matlock. On October 27, Matlock telephoned me on the secure phone from Moscow. Gorbachev had reversed himself; he wanted a summit. Shevardnadze wanted to visit Washington on October 30 to set the date for it. A letter was coming to President Reagan.

---

5. Our proposal was 4,800. Gorbachev had proposed sublimits of 3,000 to 3,300 ICBM warheads and 1,800 to 2,000 submarine-launched ballistic missile warheads. We did not at all agree on this distribution, but, adding these ranges together put them at 4,800 to 5,300. In other words, the Soviets could consider a number as low as 4,800.

I called the president immediately. "Gorbachev just blinked," I said.

Shevardnadze arrived in Washington early on the morning of October 30. The letter he carried from Gorbachev proposed that the summit begin on December 7, that the two leaders sign the INF Treaty, and that they try to go as far as they could in achieving a breakthrough on the START Treaty so that they could sign it by the time the president visited Moscow sometime in the first half of 1988. Gorbachev reiterated his proposal for a ten-year period of nonwithdrawal from the ABM Treaty, but he did not insist that the treaty be "strengthened," rather that it must be "strictly observed." He no longer demanded an agreement on "key provisions" as a condition of the summit.

Also on October 30, the news broke that Gorbachev had been fiercely criticized in the Central Committee session that had taken place on October 21, just before I arrived in Moscow. Boris Yeltsin had confronted Gorbachev, charging that his program of reform, *perestroika,* was losing its drive and that Gorbachev was losing the confidence of the people. We already knew that Gorbachev was being attacked from the right by Ygor Ligachev, so now, with Yeltsin hitting him from the other direction, Gorbachev's leadership was being challenged doubly within the Communist party. Ligachev, on his right, was telling him to slow down, and Yeltsin, on his left, was telling him to speed up or he would lose the momentum of his program. I must have sensed, sitting across the table from him, Gorbachev's awareness of this new vulnerability.[6]

Intelligence Assessment

I never heard anything from our "intelligence community" about the reasons for Gorbachev's conduct during my Moscow meetings, so I decided to seek out their views in a different way. I asked Bill Webster and Bob Gates to bring their Soviet analysts over to the State Department for a discussion about what was happening in the Soviet Union. We gathered in my office on Friday, November 6. The lower-ranking analysts were bursting with information and interesting angles on developments in the Soviet Union. They pointed to two factors that may have affected Gorbachev during my Moscow trip: he was under pressure from both sides, those who wanted to slow down reforms (Ligachev) and those who denounced the "foot draggers" (Yeltsin). And the U.S. attack on an Iranian oil platform,

6. In response to questions in an interview with Tom Brokaw (as reprinted in the *New York Times* on December 1, 1987), Gorbachev said, "No, there was no mistake. No. You know, we will follow the path of perestroika firmly and consistently, we will follow the path of democracy and reforms firmly and consistently, but we will not jump over phases. We will not allow any adventurism. . . . And what happened with Yeltsin—well, look, in fact it's a normal process for any democracy."

in retaliation for an Iranian attack on a reflagged Kuwaiti ship, just before my arrival had thrown a controversial topic into the center of the Kremlin's internal political struggle.

Bob Gates described Gorbachev as a Leninist: "He's tried to jump back over Stalin to a time when Leninism was not encased in Stalinism. So this goes back to the NEP [Lenin's New Economic Policy]. It's a way to recapture the dynamism of the past." Gates said there was consensus in the Politburo on the need for "a breathing space with the West." The Kremlin was seeking "a period of dampened tensions with the West" while they revived themselves internally and gathered strength for another era of conflict with us. "Gorbachev hasn't cut military research and development and has poured in more weapons to regional conflicts," Gates said.

I disagreed with Gates's assessment, I told them. The Soviets were admitting that the Brezhnev Doctrine was dead; the Reagan Doctrine was driving spikes into that coffin. The Soviets wanted to get out of Afghanistan, and I felt they were fading in other regional hot spots. I was hearing more and more about the possibility of change in at least some of the Warsaw Pact countries. I felt that a profound, historic shift was under way: the Soviet Union was, willingly or unwillingly, consciously or not, turning a corner; they were *not* just resting for round two of the cold war. I called attention to a recent Gorbachev speech to foreign delegations in Moscow that had even talked about reexamining the Soviet actions that destroyed the "Prague Spring" in Czechoslovakia in 1968.

The fact was, here in mid-November, the Soviets were practically begging us to help them get out of Afghanistan. John Whitehead had just returned from Eastern Europe, which he reported was "moving fast toward us" and away from the Soviet Union. Moscow was transfixed as Boris Yeltsin, a new rival of Gorbachev's, tried to pull him faster toward a freer system. We should, I thought, work with Gorbachev in order to pull him in the right direction—and as fast as possible.

"We are," I told the president on November 18, "the psychologically superior party, and we need to stay that way: we can continue to afford to let [Gorbachev be] the innovator as long as he keeps innovating in our direction," as he had, dramatically, on INF and in Afghanistan. I reminded President Reagan of the little plaque he had given me, which I kept in my private office. He had one like it on his desk, too: "There is no limit to what a man can do or where he can go if he doesn't mind who gets the credit."

Fascinating as it was to speculate on the sources of Soviet conduct, we should not, I told the president later, base our policies on our speculation about what was going on over there. Our knowledge was thin; we could be wrong. We should continue to maintain our strength while seeking agreements that served our interests. I also told the president on December 1: "The mandate for change he [Gorbachev] brought to the job has worn thin as the gap between the grandiose objectives he has declared and the sobering realities they confront has become more apparent. The Yeltsin affair has revealed fault lines in the Soviet leadership we do not fully understand but which probably limit Gorbachev's freedom of action. He is thus probably prepared to go even further than he has so far to achieve a predictability in U.S.-Soviet relations which will enable him to focus on getting his own house in order. If sustained, the steps we are asking for as the price for that predictability could bring about real change in Moscow's approach to the world and its own citizens."

The Devil Is in the Details

There were still ninety-five bracketed items of disagreement in the INF draft, despite the fact that all main points had been resolved. Some were at the level of whether our inspector at a Soviet missile factory could carry a flashlight! Shevardnadze and I agreed to meet again, this time in Geneva, with our arms control negotiators all at hand. But beyond INF, we received, on November 19, further movement in the START negotiations. A special channel, code-named CALYPSO, had been set up earlier between Dobrynin and me to convey important messages on arms control. The channel had been virtually dormant until now. Suddenly the channel was used: the Soviets were ready to accept the number of 4,800 ballistic missiles if we would agree on the freedom to mix between land-based intercontinental ballistic missiles (in which they were relatively strong) and ballistic missiles based on submarines (in which we were relatively strong). Complete freedom to mix would mean that within a total of 4,800 strategic ballistic missile warheads, either party could have whatever proportion of whatever type of missile it wished. This was an important piece of information. President Reagan had called for a 5,000 limit in 1982: 4,800 was even better and was our current position. But sublimits, particularly on their heavy ballistic missiles, were essential, and they had earlier agreed to a sublimit of 154 such missiles, each of which carried ten warheads. So the Soviets had moved toward us on the overall limit, but had moved away on essential sublimits.

The Soviets very much wanted Gorbachev to be invited to address a joint session of Congress. Congress had balked at the suggestion, and the Soviets were hurt. Congress was reacting in part against extending such an honor to the world's top Communist but also to sloppy work by Soviet Ambassador Dubinin. I had offered to try to set up the invitation, but Dubinin had insisted on working the Hill himself, and he simply did not understand what he was up against.

On November 22, I was on my way to Geneva to see Shevardnadze for a final push on arrangements for the summit and on an INF agreement. This time, I had our new NSC adviser, Colin Powell, with me. His upbeat personality was refreshing, and his confident optimism was much like that of Ronald Reagan himself. Colin was amused by the experience of flying in our ancient 970, a Boeing 707 that looked impressive rolling up to the red carpet at a foreign airport but that groaned and creaked and wiggled in flight—and not infrequently broke down. He had flown on this aircraft once before, he told me. "I was flying somewhere with Cap, and a rotor blade in the engine cracked. We called back to Andrews for advice on getting a new part. They said, 'Yeah, we know all about that. What you do is get a file and file it down real smooth and then it's good for another forty hours.' "

I told Colin about the time the plane broke down in Alaska and the part involved was so obsolete that they had to bring a mechanic out of retirement in Tennessee and fly him up to Alaska to fix it. We had such a good time swapping stories that we soon imagined ourselves passengers on a flying death trap. (Actually, the U.S. Air Force did an amazing job of keeping those old 707 aircraft flying, waiting patiently for the political process to produce more up-to-date equipment.)

Once again, I had as much or more trouble with my own delegation than I had with the Soviets. "These negotiations," Jim Timbie said, "are like a slumber party; the one thing that isn't done is the name of the event." We spent more time negotiating with ourselves than with the Soviets. I got a strange message from the White House saying that I must arrange for the president and Gorbachev to sign the INF Treaty at precisely 1:45 P.M. on Tuesday, the first day of the summit. No one knew why. Actually, the time worked well in our schedule. The Soviets kept asking, "All right, but why?" I didn't try to answer.[7]

At 10:00 A.M. on November 23, I arrived at the Soviet mission in Geneva. I remembered the Reagan-Gorbachev meetings that had taken place here. I had heard that Marshal Akhromeyev would be in Shevardnadze's delegation, so I felt confident the Soviets were prepared to make final decisions. The military sign-off would be present. Akhromeyev appreciated seeing another general in the room: Colin Powell. We agreed quickly on a schedule, including two social occasions, dinner at our ambassador's residence and a lunch on Tuesday at the Soviet mission. The atmosphere was entirely positive. We moved through issues, resolving key points that would unlock others for our negotiating teams.

"The INF negotiations are a kind of academy, preparing the two sides for more difficult verification problems in START," Shevardnadze said.

I agreed and suggested, therefore, that "where difficulties arise, we should err on the side of *more* rather than *less* verification." Shevardnadze

7. I learned when Don Regan's memoir, *For the Record,* was published in May 1988 that the timing originated with an astrologist consulted by Nancy Reagan.

agreed. Other issues were gradually falling into place. We went through the prospective summit schedule in great detail. Gorbachev's time was limited: he could not travel around the United States. I sensed that he did not want pictures beamed back to his country of the bountiful United States of America. By late afternoon on Tuesday, November 24, we were finally able to resolve the last issue on INF. Akhromeyev joked that he might have to seek asylum in neutral Switzerland. My work with Shevardnadze and him had been warm and congenial. Eduard and I went out to meet the press together at about 5:00 P.M. "Minister Shevardnadze and I are shaking hands," I said. "The reason is that we have now completed agreement on all of the outstanding INF issues." Shevardnadze responded, "We have completed some very important work. I think that what we have done is in the interest of all the nations of this planet."

I felt relieved, even triumphant, about the INF agreement. And I felt confident about our emerging ability to resolve outstanding issues in many areas of tension. The INF agreement was important in the many precedents set by its terms, which were almost exactly what Ronald Reagan, to the scoffing of arms control experts, had proposed back in 1981: reduction to the point of elimination of an entire class of nuclear weapons! The numbers eliminated were asymmetrical, reflecting the far larger number deployed by the Soviets. They would eliminate about 1,500 deployed INF warheads and we would eliminate about 350. The verification procedures were far more extensive and intrusive than ever before, involving complete inventories of all weapons, on-site inspections, short-notice inspections, and continuing monitoring of the sites where the weapons to be eliminated had been produced. All those were "Reagan proposals" that had been dismissed by the people "who knew everything" as impossible to attain! There had been nothing even remotely like this ever before. Ronald Reagan had an agenda, and that agenda was not just a dream.

INF was about to become a reality.

Canisters and Critics

Long before preparations for the Washington summit of December 1987 were completed, we were discussing the summit to come, to be held in Moscow. The Soviets had agreed. We were establishing a pattern of regular head-of-state contact. There was still plenty of argument and anguish in the INF talks, despite the fact that Shevardnadze and I had settled all the real issues. "The devil is in the details," everyone pointed out. Our teams worked night and day to complete the actual texts in both English and Russian.

Suddenly, our Geneva team was confronted with what Roz Ridgway and I regarded as an old Soviet trick: an effort to use the pressure of time to gain some marginal or unrelated advantage. The Soviets, in working out the details of the inspection regime in East Germany, took the position that our inspectors must enter the country through "its capital, Berlin." We had always refused to accept Berlin as the capital of the German Democratic Republic. Should our negotiators find a way to accommodate this issue? Roz reported this problem to me, and I told her: "Hang tough: do not change our position." Roz called Bessmertnykh, who seemed incredulous that we would take such an inflexible position. As the time passed, the Soviets shifted gears: we learned in Geneva that the Soviets "would accept Leipzig" as the entry point for INF inspections in East Germany.

President Reagan was enthusiastic about the INF Treaty, feeling justifiably that he had achieved exactly what he had sought for over six years, only to be derided by the "experts" as "not being serious" about arms control. He was enthusiastic, too, about the Gorbachev visit to Washington. This was a chance to develop further a relationship that promised major change in world affairs. I shared the president's enthusiasm.

But there were many vocal critics of the INF Treaty and of the very idea of the flag of the Hammer and Sickle flying alongside the Stars and Stripes all over Washington.

On December 3, Ronald Reagan blasted back at his INF critics in an interview, calling them uninformed and accusing them of accepting the inevitability of war. On NBC-TV news on December 7, Senator Bob Dole, Republican leader in the Senate and an active candidate for the Republican presidential nomination in 1988, said, "I don't trust Gorbachev," and accused the president—taking his cue from Nixon and Kissinger—of "stuffing this [INF] treaty down the throats of the allies." A group of conservative senators—Malcolm Wallop, Jesse Helms, Steve Symms, Larry Pressler, and Dan Quayle—announced on December 4 their opposition to the treaty. Senator Quayle said in the Senate that President Reagan's comments were "totally irresponsible" and that he was "appalled" by them. Quayle, taking his cue from Nixon, Kissinger, and Scowcroft, now joined by Weinberger, would try to work out an amendment to the INF Treaty that would link withdrawal of U.S. INF missiles in Europe to reductions in the imbalance between U.S. and Soviet conventional forces, a clear effort to sabotage INF. Such a link would, he well knew, kill the implementation of the INF Treaty.

Howard Phillips, chairman of the Conservative Caucus, a right-wing public policy organization, laid on the wood in an op-ed piece in the *New York Times* on December 11, 1987:

President Reagan is little more than the speech reader-in-chief for the pro-appeasement triumvirate of Howard H. Baker Jr., George P. Shultz and Frank C. Carlucci. . . . The center of the Administration's policy is the President's unfounded assertion that Mikhail S. Gorbachev is "a new kind of Soviet leader" who no longer seeks world conquests. The summit meetings and so-called arms control treaties are a cover for the treasonous greed of those who manipulate the Administration. . . . Mr. Reagan is no longer in any way accountable to the millions who recognize that we are in a deadly, strategic end-game with the Soviet Union, militarily the most powerful regime in world history.

What rubbish, but amazingly and distressingly, it had a following. Ronald Reagan's opponents comprised a strange and uneasy set of bedfellows.

Despite the cold war fear and antagonism that we encountered for trying to forge a better relationship with the Soviets, I was refreshed to see how much people outside the field of the battle perceived that a turning point had come. In December each year I gave a dinner in the State Department at which the Kennedy Center Honors for performing artists were awarded. As I stepped up to the podium, the guests fell quiet, and then, just as I was about to speak, they burst into spontaneous applause. I took the applause to be an expression of relief, which many of them expressed to me in the receiving line: a great anxiety about the world seemed to be lifting. At one point before I stood up to speak, I heard my dinner partner, Leontyne Price, humming quietly as she picked up some background music. I asked her whether she would open the ceremony with a song. So my opening remarks were: "In this room loaded with talent, and in the spirit of the spontaneity of the evening, I've cooked up a little deal with my dinner partner." Leontyne Price sang "America the Beautiful," softly at first, and then making the rafters ring.

I had, in the run-up to the summit, much on my mind. I remembered that Gorbachev had been intrigued at my remarks about technology and the information age during our meeting in the Kremlin the previous April. I sought a way to present to him again a vision of where the world was heading and of the revolutionary implications of a world in which access to ideas becomes the key to scientific and economic progress. On December 4, anticipating Gorbachev's imminent arrival, I had arranged to speak at the World Affairs Council in Washington and set out these same thoughts once again.

The speech was scarcely reported—no hard news. But I had my address translated into Russian and distributed to Gorbachev, Shevardnadze, Akhromeyev, and others in the Soviet party. Questions and comments subsequently came my way and to my staff. I felt sure that the ideas in my speech were having an impact on the thinking of these Soviet leaders.

On December 7, O'Bie and I greeted the Gorbachevs at Andrews Air Force Base at 5:30 P.M. I rode into Washington with him. He was upbeat, positive, animated, and eager. He talked about the changes taking place in his country and his desire to close out the cold war with the United States. "What about critics in the U.S.?" he asked.

"The vast majority of Americans support what President Reagan is doing," I responded. "The move forward in our relations is not like coming into a dark room and throwing on the light." It would be more gradual than flicking a switch.

He liked my image: "It applies to *perestroika* at home."

"The concept for our relations should be building a relationship by solving problems," I said.

"I work very hard," he told me; "I drive people and wear them out. I go at it all the way. If I tire, someone else will take over." At that moment, he looked as if he would never tire. Compared to Moscow in October, I thought, Gorbachev has come up for air.

When I returned to the State Department, I found that a crisis had erupted over a small point. The Soviets refused to give us the required photograph of the SS-20 missile—the key Soviet missile that was to be wholly eliminated by this treaty. They provided a photograph of a canister, arguing that the SS-20 was assembled inside the canister and there were no pictures of the missile itself. Some on our team said we should "let the point go by," that it was not important. I did not agree. Nor did Max Kampelman: "I think that getting the photograph should be a condition for signing the INF Treaty." Max said, "Otherwise, the Soviets would be in noncompliance with the treaty before it is even signed. It's required by the text: a photograph of the missile, not the missile hidden inside its canister." In a meeting with Shevardnadze shortly after his arrival in Washington, I was insistent on this point. At 7:30 the next morning, Obukhov, their INF negotiator, handed Kampelman a photocopy of the supposedly nonexistent picture of the SS-20. He said that the original photograph was on its way. Everything required was now in hand.

The Washington Summit

At the Washington summit, ceremony, substance, and spectacle were woven together, shaken up by the unexpected, and projected to the world in the information age. The main event was the signing of the INF Treaty. An expectant and excited crowd waited in the East Room of the White House. "Ladies and gentlemen," the announcer said, "the president of the United States and the general secretary of the Communist party of the Soviet Union." Ronald Reagan and Mikhail Gorbachev strode together down a broad red carpet and onto a stage.

Ronald Reagan took the microphone: "It was over 6 years ago, November 18, 1981, that I first proposed what would come to be called the zero option. It was a simple proposal one might say, disarmingly simple. Unlike treaties in the past, it didn't simply codify the status quo or a new arms buildup; it didn't simply talk of controlling an arms race. For the first time in history, the language of 'arms control' was replaced by 'arms reduction'— in this case, the complete elimination of an entire class of U.S. and Soviet nuclear missiles."

Reagan continued, quoting again the old Russian maxim "*Doveryai, no proveryai*—trust, but verify."

"You repeat that at every meeting," Gorbachev interjected with a chuckle.

Reagan nodded, smiled, and answered, "I like it." The room erupted. The easy and friendly relationship between the two leaders came through in their words and their body language. The message was received with relief by people in both countries and around the world.

Gorbachev then took his turn: "For everyone, and above all, for our two great powers, the treaty whose text is on this table offers a big chance at last to get onto the road leading away from the threat of catastrophe. It is our duty to take full advantage of that chance and move together toward a nuclear-free world, which holds out for our children and grandchildren and for their children and grandchildren the promise of a fulfilling and happy life, without fear and without a senseless waste of resources on weapons of destruction. . . . May December 8, 1987, become a date that will be inscribed in the history books, a date that will mark the watershed separating the era of a mounting risk of nuclear war from the era of a demilitarization of human life."

Then the two leaders signed the treaty, one copy in a red leather binder for the Soviet Union and one in blue for the United States. They walked back down the hall to the State Dining Room, where each, with the benefit of simultaneous translation, addressed his own country and the world.

The atmosphere was electric with a sense of historic importance. I was as elated as everyone else. But I also had the job of keeping content on track. The day had been exhilarating for the president: a ceremonial arrival on the South Lawn of the White House, a first small meeting with Gorbachev, and now this dramatic event in the early afternoon. The president, I could see, was on an understandable high. We had ahead of us a one-hour meeting scheduled for 2:30 in the Cabinet Room, deliberately chosen so that as many members as possible in both delegations could be part of at least one meeting. The room was crowded, with people seated all along the walls as well as at the cabinet table. After a photo opportunity with the press, the meeting started. I was concerned. I could see that as far as the president was concerned, this meeting was a total anticlimax. He was not up for it, nor was he concentrating now.

The president gave Gorbachev, as the guest, the privilege of speaking first. Gorbachev initiated a discussion of problems in the Soviet Union and his efforts, through *perestroika*, to reform the Soviet system. Wonderful, I thought: this opening would allow a promising opportunity to learn more about Gorbachev's ideas for reform and even to have some effect, in our discussion, on shaping his ideas.

Soon the president interrupted Gorbachev with a story about the differences between our two countries: "An American scholar, on his way to the airport before a flight to the Soviet Union, got into a conversation with his cabdriver, a young man who said that he was still finishing his education. The scholar asked, 'When you finish your schooling, what do you want to do?' The young man answered, 'I haven't decided yet.' After arriving at the airport in Moscow, the scholar hailed a cab. His cabdriver, again, was a young man, who happened to mention he was still getting his education. The scholar, who spoke Russian, asked, 'When you finish your schooling, what do you want to be? What do you want to do?' The young man answered, 'They haven't told me yet.' That's the difference between our systems," said the president.

Gorbachev colored. However telling the president's story might be, this was not the moment for it. I was disturbed and disappointed. Discussion of Soviet internal problems and Gorbachev's ideas for dealing with them would have been revealing to us and possibly helpful to him.

Gorbachev then switched topics, suggesting that we move on to discuss conventional arms: the subject of multinational negotiations then going on in Vienna as part of the CSCE process. He said that he had noticed interest in the subject on the part of some opponents of the INF Treaty. The president readily agreed. I was upset. I knew the president was not well informed about the subject, and I had no written material at hand to give him for guidance. As the discussion proceeded, the president looked to me to respond. I did so, but reluctantly. The principal in such a major meeting should always be the main interlocutor, with occasional comment from others.

After the president and I escorted Gorbachev and his party to their cars on the ellipse outside the West Wing of the White House, the president, Howard Baker, Colin Powell, and I met in the Oval Office. I criticized the president's Cabinet Room performance. Howard Baker agreed. The president said he realized what had happened and asked what we should do about it. "No more big meetings in the Cabinet Room," I suggested. "You do much better in smaller groups and in the intimacy of the Oval Office." The president should also have had brief talking points on specific issues so that he could lay down the main arguments before inviting others to supply details, if needed. This was the only low point in the summit; fortunately, it did not last long or do any real damage.

That night at the White House state dinner, Ronald Reagan was back on the front burner. The event was marvelous in every way. I was seated at the same table as Akhromeyev. "I am the Marshal of the Soviet Union and have had many honors in my career, but I have never been as proud of anything as when I was a sergeant fighting for my country at Leningrad— until now," he told me. "My country is in trouble, and I am fighting alongside Mikhail Sergeyevich to save it. That is why we made such a lopsided deal on INF, and that is why we want to get along with you. We want to restructure ourselves and to be part of the modern world. We cannot continue to be isolated." I was stunned by this volunteered story and the analogy to the battle of Leningrad, a hallowed memory, I knew, for Akhromeyev and for the Russian people.

Wednesday, December 9, was my day to engage in ceremony, but it turned out to more than ceremony. After the morning meeting in the Oval Office, I was host to the Gorbachevs at a grand luncheon in the elegant diplomatic reception rooms of the State Department. Everyone wanted to come, and the crowd was the largest ever for such an event.

The guest list was high-powered: key members of Congress, all former ambassadors to the Soviet Union, outstanding Americans from business, finance, agriculture, labor, the arts, members of the cabinet. I had a moment before the receiving line started to show the Gorbachevs my favorite piece of furniture: the desk designed by Thomas Jefferson, where he stood as he wrote portions of the Declaration of Independence. The Gorbachevs had done their homework: they had a personal word with each guest. The receiving line took about three-quarters of an hour. No one seemed to mind the wait.

I had thought carefully about my toast and decided to make it short and, I hoped, instructive. "What should we both be keeping in mind?" I asked. I talked about the unique nature of the relationship, the need to recognize the differences in values, the need for realism, "avoiding extremes, either of hostility or euphoria, through the ups and downs of our relations." In the spirit of "clarity and candor," I said, quoting a December 5 statement issued by the heads of government of the European Community, "Respect for human rights and freedom is a prerequisite for confidence, understanding and cooperation." I turned to a point I sought to emphasize to Gorbachev and the Soviets on every possible occasion:

> In five to ten years, our world will be vastly different from the one we know today, and from the postwar world of the past 40 years, which has conditioned so much of our thinking. . . . The material substances of daily life are being transformed. The speed of human transactions is accelerating. Scientific, economic and political matters are now global in dimension. And through all these changes, runs the thread of knowledge: its discovery, its rapid transmission as information, and the education needed to use it. . . . The recognition that openness to ideas, information and contacts is the key to future success.

Gorbachev responded at some length:

> Urging us on is the will of hundreds of millions of people, who are beginning
> to understand that as the twentieth century draws to a close, civilization has
> approached a dividing line, not so much between different systems and ideo-
> logies, but between common sense and mankind's feelings of self-preserva-
> tion, on the one hand, and irresponsibility, national selfishness, prejudice—
> to put it briefly, old thinking—on the other. . . . What matters now is that
> we cannot let those opportunities pass, and must use them as fully as possible
> to build a safer and more democratic world, free from the trappings and the
> psychology of militarism. . . . While moving closer to each other, we have
> come to appreciate even more the role and importance of Soviet-American
> relations in the current development of international affairs, together with
> our enormous responsibility, not only to our own people, but also to the
> world community.

Then he referred to the many individuals who had helped bring about
these events and said he wanted to "pay tribute to the many who dedicated
to it their intellect, energy, patience, perseverance, knowledge and a sense
of duty to their nation, and to the international community. And first of
all, I would like to mention Comrade Eduard Shevardnadze and Mr.
George Shultz." Shevardnadze and I each rose and walked from our respective tables for a handshake as the room echoed with applause.

Later, as we walked to the elevator, Shevardnadze said to me, "George,
that was not a luncheon; it was a political event. Thank you."

How far we had come from the days of tension with Brezhnev, Andropov,
and Gromyko. A transformation had occurred.

Very early on the last morning of the summit, I met with Paul Nitze and
others from our arms control working group. Carlucci, Powell, and I were
in constant communication. They still had not found a way to pin down a
top limit on ballistic missiles, and the problem of how to handle the ABM-
related issues in the final joint statement was unresolved as well. I discussed
the options with Nitze, cleared ideas quickly with Carlucci and Powell, and
set off for a meeting with Shevardnadze at the Soviet embassy. I took Nitze
with me. Our greatest problems were with the ABM Treaty issues. We
wanted to be sure that any agreed language would not curtail the pursuit
of the president's Strategic Defense Initiative. We also wanted to advance
toward our objectives (acceptance of as broad an array of permitted research activities as possible, recognition of the desirability of explicit discussion of a more defense-oriented form of deterrence, specification of a
nonwithdrawal period short enough so that possible deployment would not
be inhibited, and the automatic right to deploy at the end of the period if
either party chose to do so).

I recalled for Shevardnadze Gorbachev's words in a prior day's discussion, "If you want to deploy at the end of the nonwithdrawal period, that is up to you." I made some suggestions on bracketed language and handed Shevardnadze a proposed revised text. He seemed agreeable but reserved the right to check with Gorbachev, as I did with Reagan. We agreed to postpone the start of the final meeting between the leaders so that we would have time to go over the material with them. Then off we both went to Vice President Bush's breakfast with Gorbachev.

On his way from the breakfast to the White House, Gorbachev suddenly stopped his motorcade, got out, and to the crowd's delight, mingled and pressed the flesh. The almost adulatory scene, I thought, must have played as well in Moscow as it did in the United States. Gorbachev, with his open manner, easy repartee, and spontaneity, proved to be a captivating figure in the United States and around the world.

The final meeting was short because of Gorbachev's late arrival and was followed by a televised walk around the White House lawn by the two leaders alone. We assembled for lunch, but there were still open items on the joint statement that would be issued at the end of the day. So Carlucci, Powell, and I and our Soviet opposite numbers left so we could resolve these remaining issues. We gathered in the Cabinet Room. Carlucci whispered to me, "Why don't you suggest 4,900 as the limit of ballistic missiles?"

"You do it as secretary of defense and look right at Marshal Akhromeyev when you speak," I suggested. Frank did.

Akhromeyev agreed: *"Da."* We had jumped the last hurdle!

Real progress had been made during the summit in many areas, including START, and this was reflected in an outstanding joint statement. On ABM issues, Max Kampelman put it well, "We kicked the can down the road." We made slight progress and avoided the potential of this issue to blow up everything else.

The leaders took their leave of each other by 2:30 P.M., their words and mood not dampened by cold and drizzly weather. Reagan called the summit "a clear success," and Gorbachev spoke of his impression that "there is a growing desire in American society for improved Soviet-American relations." After they said their farewells, I went immediately to provide a lengthy briefing on the summit, first to the Senate and then to the House. The reaction was genuinely positive: not a sour note.

Gorbachev held a press conference in the late afternoon. I watched on television, prepared to leave for the Soviet embassy as soon as it was over in order to be part of the American contingent escorting the Soviets to the airport. I was in a hurry. Right after Gorbachev's departure, my plane would leave for Brussels, where I would brief the NATO foreign ministers. Gorbachev's opening statement went on and on for almost an hour, and his answers to questions were long. Finally, at 7:45 P.M., his press conference concluded, and I left for the Soviet embassy. I was placed in a holding room. Before long, in bounced Gorbachev. "George, I understand you watched my press conference," he said, and invited my comment.

"You went on much too long," I said with friendly candor.

He clapped me on the back. "Well," I said, "at least there's one guy around here who tells you what he thinks." He laughed, in high spirits.

At this point, the protocol officers took over and guided us to our respective cars—Vice President Bush with Gorbachev, me with Shevardnadze—for the short ride to Andrews Air Force Base. Floodlights illuminated the tarmac as we jostled around in the wind and rain. Gorbachev and Shevardnadze, I could see, were tired but excited. I waved good-bye as they boarded their Soviet aircraft, then moved on to my own. My plane took off right behind theirs.

In Brussels the next day, I took part in still another ceremony, this one underlining the degree to which the INF Treaty was an achievement, not just of the United States but of our whole NATO alliance. I signed, along with the foreign ministers of the five countries where our INF missiles were based (West Germany, Great Britain, Belgium, the Netherlands, and Italy), an agreement giving the Soviets the right to conduct on-site inspections of the missile bases of our allies.

In the statement on our NATO meeting in the morning, we called INF a "treaty without precedent in the history of arms control" and "all the more meaningful because it opens the way to progress in other arms control areas." Geoffrey Howe congratulated me on "not only a momentous week, but a week of hope for all mankind." The treaty, said Hans-Dietrich Genscher, "doesn't reduce but increases the security of Western Europe." Jean-Bernard Raimond expressed his reserve by refusing language calling INF "historic." "We will not know for twenty-five years whether anything is historic," he argued. How French. But he joined the general sense of remarkable progress in our joint effort to improve our security and lessen tensions in East-West relations.

And so the summit ended for me. The results were a tribute to the persistent effort of Ronald Reagan to stick by his basic objectives, to maintain our strength and the cohesion of our alliances, and to be willing to recognize an opportunity for a good deal and a changed situation when he saw one. President Reagan had the courage of his conviction that Gorbachev represented a powerful drive for a different Soviet Union in its foreign policy and in its conduct of affairs at home. Mikhail Gorbachev had come into power in 1985 with a difficult set of problems. He was perceptive enough to see them and bold enough to be decisive in dealing with the critical foreign policy issues we faced. I admired and respected both leaders, and I had told them so. I went to sleep in Brussels feeling exhausted but quietly triumphant.

CHAPTER 47

Interlock:
The Shultz Initiative

The problem of the Arab-Israeli conflict is so compelling, and the conduct of the participants often so repugnant, that secretaries of state, over the years have been repeatedly tempted to give "the speech." This was a favorite idea of the State Department's Near East bureau: have the secretary "go public," heaping blame on all the parties. That would show 'em. Let them stew in their own juice.

In the winter of 1987–88, the flames of the intifada were raging, fueled by the frustration of Palestinians living on the West Bank and Gaza. Israel's methods of suppression were alienating even its most ardent supporters. Leaders in the Arab world were bitterly critical of Israel but also worried about the intifada, the powerful manifestation of frustrated people erupting on their own: young Palestinians throwing rocks in acts of sheer defiance of Israeli authority. Palestinians were not fully accepted anywhere, and Arab populations, stirred by Islamic fundamentalism, were restive. This was the time for the speech, said my team. No speech unless I could put together new ideas for a solution, I told them. In this way, I kicked off a brainstorming process that produced not a speech but what became known as the Shultz initiative.

The Intifada Rages

The intifada created a wholly new situation, one that in its own way altered the fundamental concept of the peace process. The "territory for peace" formula of UN Security Council Resolution 242 in 1967 assumed that any solution would be negotiated between Arab states and the state of Israel. This traditional conception of the peace process arched over the heads of those Palestinians who lived on the land in question. They were not seen as a group speaking and voting on their own behalf. The Palestinians' only representation in the political struggle was through those on the outside, the Palestine Liberation Organization, whose leaders were neither elected nor effective. The Palestinian inhabitants of the territories were assumed to be quiescent, enduring, silent observers of the military and political conflicts that raged over them. Now that had changed, and the situation would never be quite the same again.

Yasser Arafat appeared worried by this new challenge to his leadership, and talk of a Palestinian government in exile began—Arafat's way to try to consolidate his control. But the PLO was not in the lead in this uprising, and chances were, I thought, that it would never fully regain its earlier monopoly over Palestinian politics. There was a fresh opportunity now, I felt, to try to push these changes in the right direction and far more rapidly than the usual pace of the peace process. The intifada bore promise of a new generation of Palestinians, with new leaders trying to take hold of their own affairs. Israel had always wanted to deal with the Arab inhabitants of the West Bank and Gaza: now that might be possible. Instead of deporting indigenous leaders when they challenged Israeli authority, Israel could start to talk to leaders who were legitimizing themselves. Maybe we could help identify leaders who could get a new dialogue going.

The scene in Israel and the occupied territories was ghastly: "Israeli Police Storm Temple Mount: Witnesses Say Tear Gas Fired Inside Two Islamic Holy Places," headlined the *Washington Post* on January 16, 1988. "Israeli police for the first time fired tear gas into two of Islam's most sacred mosques as Palestinians demonstrated against Israeli occupation after Friday prayers at Temple Mount," reported the *Post*'s Jonathan Randal. The reaction of Arab governments to this event seemed oddly muted. Was the situation, I speculated, so volatile that they feared they might lose control of their own Islamic populations?

Four days after the Temple Mount clash, Israeli Defense Minister Yitzhak Rabin declared that the intifada would be dealt with by "force, power and blows," portraying this as a way to reduce the use of live ammunition and the killing of demonstrators. But he also said—repeatedly—that "there is no military solution to this problem." Images of Israeli brutality appeared almost nightly on American television and elsewhere throughout the world. Concern was intense in the American Jewish community. Violinist Isaac Stern came to see me, spoke of his shock, and said that on his upcoming trip to Israel, he would refuse to meet with any Israeli leaders.

Meanwhile, some interesting signs emerged from the Palestinians living in the West Bank and Gaza. I received a list of fourteen "demands" dated January 14. While much on the list was familiar and unpromising, the last six points emphasized pragmatic issues—elections, taxation, land, and water—all reminiscent of the autonomy negotiations at the opening of the 1980s: pragmatic issues long since derailed after the Israeli invasion of Lebanon.

On January 19, I asked whether Eli Rubinstein, Shamir's aide, could come to Washington to talk about what might be done. Shamir readily agreed. Foreign Minister Peres had already sent Yossi Beilin to urge us to appoint a special envoy to work intensively between Israel and Jordan on the future of the West Bank.

A long letter—six and a half single-spaced pages—dated January 20 arrived for me from Prime Minister Shamir, who said he intended to set up a special team to draft an Israeli peace proposal. He spelled out his thinking in some detail, really a restatement and elaboration of the Camp David framework. But I knew that such an approach would get nowhere with the Arabs, especially now, given the political heat generated by the intifada. I felt that we needed a new blend of Camp David features. Speculation was rising that we were about to come up with something. "U.S. IS CONSIDERING A NEW INITIATIVE FOR MIDEAST PEACE: ISRAEL WANTS ENVOY SENT" was the headline on the front page of the *New York Times* on January 22, 1988.

A New Peace Process

On Sunday morning, January 24, I got together three foreign service officers who were experienced and creative on peace process issues. "We need to put basic ideas together in a new form," I said, "with enough substance to encourage direct negotiation and enough process to enhance the prospect that further substance can be developed through direct negotiations." We would make use of key ideas drawn from the Camp David Accords, without referring directly to Camp David: too many Arabs had committed themselves to oppose it. We would restart the talks on self-rule for the Palestinians of the West Bank and Gaza, converting them to talks about "transition arrangements." Israel wanted such talks, and the Palestinians would benefit from more control over their own lives. The Palestinians would be reluctant to agree, however, if negotiations on the "final status" of the occupied territories were not clearly in the picture. So we would try to speed the process up by getting to final status negotiations quickly, whether or not transition arrangements had been agreed upon or had been put into effect. We would repackage and streamline the Camp David framework—to try to force its pace and speed its implementation. I went over my ideas carefully with President Reagan and NSC adviser Colin Powell. They agreed on the general structure and on the need to reactivate the peace process—if the parties were willing to be responsive.

When Eli Rubinstein came in on Tuesday, January 26, we went so far as to talk over a possible timetable with him: the following month, in February, I would go to the Middle East to present the concept; then events would move forward at a rapid pace.

- March 1988: the U.S. would seek a tacit Arab-Israeli understanding that would halt the violence of the intifada and halt the expansion of settlements in the occupied territories during negotiations.
- April 1988: negotiations on autonomy would begin, and the United States would table a draft agreement.
- October 1988: negotiations for transition—autonomy—arrangements should conclude, and the autonomy agreement should be signed. A three-month campaign period for elections in the territories would begin.
- November 1988: Israeli elections probably would be held in any case.
- December 1988: negotiations on final status for the territories would begin on an established date even if the autonomy talks were incomplete. This was the new and important element: an"interlock" would be established—an overlapping, locked-in connection between transition (autonomy) talks and talks on final status.
- January 1989: elections for the Palestinian self-governing authority would be held.
- February 1989: Palestinian self-government would be inaugurated.
- Somewhere at an early point in this effort, an international conference or some other kind of international event would kick off the process.

This diplomatic calendar produced an obvious question: why should the Arab side negotiate seriously for autonomy if final status talks were going to start in any event? I was ready to give the Arabs my answers. Because the Arabs would see a guaranteed start to final-status talks coming quickly, they could accept Camp David–style autonomy talks, knowing full well that self-rule was not a substitute for an outcome on the final status of the occupied territories. The transition arrangements would provide a distinct improvement in the quality of their lives, and final status talks would inevitably take a considerable period to come to a conclusion. My feeling was that the Israelis should perceive that the same "interlock" connecting the two issues would induce the Palestinians to negotiate seriously and to forswear violence and that the more serious and responsible the Palestinians were about autonomy, the more serious and responsible the Israelis were likely to be in the final status talks.

My plan was detailed, fast moving, and complex. The Palestinians in the occupied territories had come center stage with a vengeance, and Israel's brutal crackdown was doing great damage to its own interests and its international reputation. The peace process could be accelerated, I felt, if the pressure in the situation caused both parties to want progress. Diplomatically speaking, my effort was comparable to a "two-minute drill" at the end of the fourth quarter of a football game; that was about how much time was left in the Reagan administration. Still, I was going to give this initiative everything I had, to engage the parties themselves in a bold effort to break through the impasses. I felt I had a real chance to move thinking forward and, by creating an active and visible peace process, to lessen the dangers of escalating violence.

Eli Rubinstein reported back the next day, January 27, that he had gone over the concept with Prime Minister Shamir. "He trusts you. So he would like to be positive," Rubinstein said; "he is ready to go with negotiations based on the principles of Camp David. His answer can't go beyond this general point—he'd have to see the details, of course." Shamir had seen our timetable and would understand its implications. His response was positive, at least in that he was ready to engage in a diplomatic process.

Also that day, I met with Egyptian President Mubarak, who was visiting Washington. I put the idea in general terms first to his foreign minister, Esmat Abdel Meguid, and then to him. They complained that this was "Camp David," which had been denounced by Palestinians and other Arabs. Meguid suggested that the plan include an agreed date for the start of talks about final status in order to gain Arab confidence that such talks would really begin. Fine, I said. When I then explained my plan in greater detail to Mubarak, he heartily supported the ideas and became a strong proponent of my effort through this initiative, to activate the peace process.

Later that same day, I met with two Palestinians from the occupied territories, Hanna Siniora and Abu Rachme. After receiving a request from me, Shamir had lifted the travel ban on Mr. Siniora so that I could meet the two men in Washington. At the same time, Shamir's aide Yossi Ben-Aharon told our ambassador that my decision to meet the two amounted to "a decision to negotiate with the PLO." I did not want to put the two on the spot, so I stayed away from discussing the substance of my initiative; our meeting was itself a message. The two talked of the PLO's leading and essential role.

"The PLO has a reality problem," I told them. "Until the PLO accepts Israel's right to exist and Resolution 242, and until the PLO renounces the use of terrorism, it can have no place in our diplomacy."

I needed some additional readings from the region before deciding whether and when to make a trip to the Middle East. I called in Phil Habib and Dick Murphy. Dick would go to Saudi Arabia, Syria, and then Israel. King Hussein would be a key player. President Reagan telephoned the king to emphasize the importance of the initiative and arranged for Phil to be received in Amman. Habib reported in from Amman on January 31 that King Hussein "agreed to the concept in principle." In fact, Habib said,

"While I expected to receive a tepid or equivocal response, the king welcomed the approach." Increased U.S. activism was essential for peace, the king said. But "the king also left little doubt that an international conference remains central in his thinking." That, I knew, would spell trouble with Shamir.

In Israel, Ambassador Tom Pickering followed up with Shimon Peres's aide, Nimrod Novik, and Shamir's aide, Rubinstein. Pickering reported that Novik said yes, Rubinstein, no. Rubinstein did not reject the "interlock," but he could not accept that final status talks could begin before the end of 1988. On February 4, Pickering reported that Shamir "appears to be really pleased and gratified by the Secretary's initiative, the renewed U.S. involvement, and the fact that he [Shamir] is finally part of an ongoing and possibly fruitful peace process." Shamir had told Pickering the previous day that the initiative had "brought us to an important phase; it is a very positive and significant step."

Word then came from Jordanian Foreign Minister Tahir al-Masri that he recognized the significance of the "interlock" and that, therefore, Jordan would drop its former insistence that the transitional period not be implemented until agreement had been reached on the final status of the territories. This response was the kind of movement I needed to break the logjam.

"Interlock"

Earlier, Phil Habib and Bob Strauss, on behalf of the Council on Foreign Relations, had asked me to be the speaker at a small, off-the-record session on the Middle East. I had agreed, feeling that an informal conversation with a few knowledgeable council members could be a helpful variation on my periodic Saturday seminars. As February 9, the date for this session, approached, the character of the meeting, predictably, had changed. A large crowd, including ambassadors from key countries, had signed up to come. Instead of a small, intimate group, I would speak and answer questions in the Loy Henderson Room, a large auditorium in the State Department, which holds several hundred people.

I intended to deliver a carefully crafted speech, since what I said would be reported back to capitals, even though the council's traditional rule was that sessions were "off the record." Draft after draft was prepared; I didn't like any of them. So, with my own thoughts carefully engraved in my mind, I proceeded to the auditorium and went to the podium to speak without any notes to the assembled crowd. Everyone could see that they were hearing my thoughts unvarnished, without the filter of a cast of people who might have prepared a script, a text, or even a set of talking points.

I first reminded the gathering that progress had been made over the years: "There is a peace treaty between Egypt and Israel that has lasted. It has been possible recently to work out the method for dealing with the Taba dispute.[1] Egypt has stuck with the peace treaty despite a lot of pressure and, being, in effect, boycotted by its fellow Arab neighbors. The Arab countries have now come back to Egypt, even as Egypt has held its position. . . . An Arab bank has been established on the West Bank. . . . It is impossible for such a thing to get started unless there are some pretty detailed and careful discussions between the banking authorities in Israel and banking authorities in some other countries."

"What these achievements show," I pointed out, "is that under the right circumstances negotiations can work." I called our approach a new blend of substance and procedure. We would work for genuine and sharp improvement in the conditions of life on the West Bank and Gaza, including the handling of land, water, and police, implemented by a transition authority that would be identified through some kind of electoral process. I set out the idea that negotiations over the final status of the occupied territories should start a date certain, not far beyond the six-month timetable I had in mind for completion of negotiations over transition arrangements, so that "the actual final status negotiations would get started rapidly.

"So here you have, basically, three substantive things: one dealing with things that can be done quickly; another dealing with the issues of final status; and a third dealing with the interrelationship between them, a kind of interlocking between these two areas of substance," I said. And I added that we would go forward on the basis of Resolution 242 and "the formula of territory for peace." I said that a strictly procedural international conference, given all these understandings in advance, ought to be workable.

Then came questions and answers. In response to a question I agreed that there must be the possibility of "an Israeli-Syrian negotiation, an Israeli-Lebanese negotiation, as well as an Israeli-Jordanian-Palestinian negotiation." And I added that Syria might accept, "although it seems doubtful."

The subject of "territory for peace" was especially sensitive, and I attempted to start people thinking in fresh ways about these concepts: "As I've been trying to scratch my head and speculate about where our world is going . . . the meaning of sovereignty, the meaning of territory, is changing, and what any national government can control, or what any unit that thinks it has sovereignty or jurisdiction over a certain area can control is shifting gears." I concluded, "The complication will wind up being help-

---

1. Israel had retained a small piece of territory claimed by Egypt as part of the Sinai. Taba was located on the Gulf of Aqaba, and the Israelis had developed the site into a resort. After much pulling and hauling and tremendous effort by Abe Sofaer and Dick Murphy, Egypt and Israel had agreed to arbitrate the dispute. In the end, the Egyptian view prevailed.

ful." In fact, I had already talked informally and privately with Shamir and Peres and with King Hussein about the necessity to realize that sovereignty was taking on new meaning. Control over various functions in a territory could be shared. Who controls what, I argued, would necessarily vary over such diverse functions as external security, maintenance of law and order, access to limited supplies of water, management of education, health, and other civic functions, and so forth. In the emerging world, people had a right to define themselves but would not be able to wall themselves off, I said. Constructs based on a rigid view of sovereignty and unambiguous borders would not be adequate to provide the vision needed for the future.

Bombarded

Before I could schedule a shuttle to the Middle East, the tide swiftly turned: the Israelis started to bombard me from all sides. I had said that a purely ceremonial, noncontinuing, nonsubstantive international "event" would need to be part of the initiative. This caused great distress in Shamir's office. An emissary from Shamir, Knesset member Ehud Olmert, came to Washington on February 14 with a message for me. "We are unhappy with the details of your program: the timetables, the vagueness of the international event or happening," he said. "If the secretary expects us to accept the principle of territory for peace, I don't think anything will start."

A warning from Benjamin Netanyahu soon followed. "We are coming to a confrontation . . . in this environment any negotiation will be tough."

Two monkey wrenches had been tossed into the works: first, Shamir had consulted with Menachem Begin and emerged opposed to any alteration of Camp David. My "interlock" idea indisputably was a new departure. Second, the Near East bureau of State and our embassy were out of sync with me regarding the nature and importance of an international conference. I did not regard it as key to this initiative; it was needed merely as a ceremonial kickoff event. They, thinking of King Hussein, placed more emphasis on the international conference than did I. Their concept of the international conference idea set the alarm bells ringing in Jerusalem.

Murphy and Habib, back from the Middle East, reported that my basic "interlock" concept was known and grasped—accepted or not—by all the parties. Although I had not intentionally tried to keep the content of my initiative secret, the American press did not have the details and was treating my upcoming trip as something of a mystery, thereby heightening the drama. I decided to try to keep it this way: the less public debate over the initiative, the more leeway the leaders in the region would have to consider my proposals on their merits. I would not go public with the idea until I had gone through one or two rounds of discussions with the leaders in the region themselves.

During a mid-February visit to Moscow, I raised my ideas about the Middle East with Gorbachev and Shevardnadze but quickly concluded that they were out of touch with the subtleties and realities of the region. Furthermore, the Soviets' current idea of an international conference was just what I and the Israelis did not want: a conference with authority to weigh in on outcome. With the cold war winding down and with Soviet preoccupation with their own internal problems growing, the day was not far off, I thought, when Moscow might be a constructive force in the Middle East. But that day had not yet arrived.

Under Pressure in Jerusalem

While I was in Moscow, a cable came in from Jerusalem. My Middle East team had explained the initiative to Palestinian leaders from the West Bank and Gaza. They had been attentive, nonpolemical, and responsive, more so than ever before. They wanted to meet with me when I arrived from Moscow.

By the time I arrived in Jerusalem on February 25, however, the media were reporting Arafat's decision that "no Palestinian national personalities will meet with Shultz by decision of the PLO." They had issued, I was told, "Underground Order #8: stay inside today and tomorrow, demonstrate after Friday prayers. Get into the streets on Saturday." Arriving at the hotel, I received a message from the Palestinians: "Meeting with you is impossible." I was told that the PLO decision had put their lives on the line.

Overnight it had snowed, and Jerusalem was patched with white as I left for my meeting at the prime ministry with Yitzhak Shamir. He told me he had spoken at length with former Prime Minister Menachem Begin, who was adamant about the need for a full five years of experience with autonomy, as called for by Camp David, before the Palestinians and Israelis could address final status. My idea of a faster process and an "interlock" was a mistake, Begin had told Shamir. Shamir and I now debated the issue vigorously but inconclusively. I had consulted carefully in advance with Shamir and had received initial encouragement from him. Now he was singing a different song. I was concerned.

I had invited Palestinian representatives to meet me that evening at the American Colony Hotel, a famous spot in the predominantly Arab part of Jerusalem. When I went there, I would be the first secretary of state to have gone to East Jerusalem since the Israeli army captured that part of the city in 1967. I knew that the Palestinians would not appear: the PLO directive to boycott my meeting made that certain. Both Shamir and Peres advised me not to go under such circumstances, saying that showing up alone would be a humiliation for the United States. I disagreed.

I decided to go anyway in order to make a statement to the Palestinian people through the press. When I arrived, I encountered a scene of high drama. Klieg lights lit the golden stones of the courtyard of the old hotel and picked up the color of fruit trees in the background, their bright oranges topped with the snow that still spotted the city. I looked into the cameras. Had the Palestinian leaders come to meet me, they would have heard me say: "Peace has its enemies. Even small steps toward peace can be significant in moving beyond mistrust and hatred. In a small way, I want to do that this evening." I went on, "Palestinians must achieve control over political and economic decisions that affect their lives" and "be active participants in negotiations to determine their future. . . . Negotiations work. Negotiations [can] produce agreements which meet the fundamental concerns of all parties. Experience shows you that you can have an agreement with Israel, and it will be kept by Israel. . . . Now is the time to get to work. We have a workable plan, and we are ready to commit our efforts to it." The Arab translator's "voice-over" of my words competed with the call to prayers of a muezzin in a nearby mosque. The juxtaposition of the two disparate voices made me think of the depth and longevity of the conflict and of the many constituencies whose views would have a bearing on any possible outcome.

Back in my hotel room, I watched the Arabic channel of Israeli television and saw footage of myself, interspersed with elaborate commentary, being repeated over and over. Later, in Jordan and in Egypt, people told me how important it was that I had gone to deliver my message to Palestinians on the West Bank and Gaza despite the PLO boycott. Apparently, my message had made an impact. Nevertheless, emotions ran high and brought out the negatives, threatening to foreclose a fundamentally workable and novel plan. "Shultz's peace initiative may already be dead," Shamir was quoted. On the PLO side, the line was "Anyone who would meet with Shultz would be a traitor to the Palestinian people."

The next morning, I was in Amman, Jordan, to touch base with officials there. King Hussein was in London, where I would see him later. The Jordanians said they liked my ideas, but that this was basically a PLO matter. I disagreed. Jordan had to play a leading role, I argued. In Damascus, I had a long talk with Hafez Assad. He asked questions and insisted that there could be no partial solutions and that Syria would talk to Israel only *after* Israel returned the Golan Heights to Syria. Until that happened, there was nothing to negotiate, Assad said. He asked me to keep him informed of what I was doing and said he was interested. My presence, I knew and worried, tended to lend him stature. Assad did not hesitate to use violence or terrorism to further his ends. Nevertheless, I also knew that it was important to the other Arabs that I consult with him.

On my return to Jerusalem on Sunday, February 28, I heard that Shamir and his advisers regarded my initiative simply as an attempt to arrange an international conference. "Shamir never could accept an international conference and has always said so; it has always been a red line for him," said Eli Rubinstein. Again and again, we had stated that the international conference I had in mind was merely a ceremonial, procedural way station to direct negotiations. I felt that the Israelis were simply using this issue as an excuse to deflect the real concept and opportunity. I was throwing them a life jacket, but they were refusing to put it on.

I was feeling great frustration: I was engaging with people who both did not listen and would not comprehend. I got a boost when the Sunday evening news carried word that Egypt "endorsed" my plan. President Mubarak had said he would help, and he was doing so. Later that evening, I saw Yitzhak Shamir again. It was an evening of tough remarks. The sum of it was that the international conference was unacceptable and the "interlock" moved too far too fast. But "I'm not saying no; let's keep working," Shamir told me. This refrain was becoming a cliché, and I was getting tired of it.

After another round in Amman and then back in Jerusalem with no real progress, I felt that the peace issue would continue to split Israeli politics. Shimon Peres supported what I was doing and said so publicly. Sooner or later, I thought, an Israeli party or leader would accept, or develop, a peace effort compelling enough to occupy the center of the Israeli political stage, which was now nearly vacant. With a coalition built around the peace issue, a political movement could move effectively toward peace and capture the Israeli electorate.

"Near Jerusalem, Israeli plainclothes security officers checked out a time bomb this morning, but it proved to be a dud. That is just how many Israelis view George Shultz's peace mission," John Cochran reported on NBC-TV on February 29, 1988. I was not amused, either by the bomb or the characterization. Prime Minister's Shamir's aide and adviser Yossi Ben-Aharon remarked as we departed on March 1, "I marvel at you Americans—how you keep coming up with these ingenious peace efforts and pursue them with such optimism."

Optimism was not what I was feeling at that moment, but I did feel that progress was possible, even if improbable. The parties themselves were their own worst enemies. I hoped that Yitzhak Shamir would somehow seize the moment to come to the fore and exert the leadership so sorely needed to make peace for Israel with its Arab neighbors. As I left to see King Hussein, Shamir's final words to me, spoken with deep emotion, were: "The people are there. Somehow we will find a way to live together peacefully. Tell King Hussein that when I say I'm ready to negotiate final status, I am. And what does final status mean? It means sovereignty." The last word came out with almost a strangled gulp.

The remark called to mind a careful talk I had with Shamir earlier about the changing meaning of sovereignty. "Territory is a divisible concept," I had told him. "Different attributes of sovereignty over territory can be treated in different ways."

I met King Hussein at his mansion at 7 Palace Green in London on March 1 and went over my initiative in detail. He raised problems: the PLO must play a central role in negotiations; any direct negotiations must take place within the setting of an international conference that could weigh in on issues of substance. Once again I heard the refrain: he would not say yes, he would not say no, but "keep working." I could not take any encouragement at all from his comments. I went over to our London embassy to work with my team on a draft letter summing up the initiative and its value and answering the chief objections I had encountered. I knew the letter would become public and wanted that to happen, but only *after* I had delivered it in person to each of the parties.

Later that day, I went on to a NATO heads-of-government meeting in Brussels, where I worked with President Reagan on his remarks about U.S.-Soviet affairs. As it turned out, he spoke extemporaneously and with great impact. But my own mind was still absorbed with the Middle East. In comparison with the international politics of the Middle East, NATO was tame and refined. I laughed as I saw my scruffy, baggy-pants Middle East team, pistachio nutshells dropping from their pants cuffs, shuffling down the corridor among the elegant Eurocrats.

Trying to Lock in Interlock

I finished work on the letter I would take back to each of the parties—basically the same text for each—in an attempt to get them to engage further and keep the process alive through the months ahead. Then I retraced my steps: first to 7 Palace Green, London, with King Hussein on March 3; then to Jerusalem with Prime Minister Shamir and Foreign Minister Peres early on March 4; to Damascus with President Assad in the early afternoon; and on to Cairo and President Mubarak by evening. "Here is my letter," I said to each. "I'll return to get your answer."

Seeing me coming at them again, they struck me as boxers who had gone fifteen rounds and suddenly had been asked to go five rounds more. The steam had gone out of their punches. The press corps traveling with me was totally baffled: they did not know why I was returning to the area. I had told them on March 4 that I would not brief along the way. I was anxious to move rapidly and to talk to each leader before my letter leaked to the public.

But by the time I returned from my meeting with President Mubarak to my plane at the Cairo airport, my last stop, the press corps all had copies of the letters I had been delivering. I was met with a round of applause as I entered the cabin. "What an ingenious plan," remarked someone, who seemed to express the general sentiment. When Shimon Peres had finished reading the letter, he looked up at me and said, "I have to tell you, from a professional standpoint, this letter is a masterpiece." This was my letter:

March 4, 1988

Dear ——:

I set forth below the statement of understandings which I am convinced is necessary to achieve the prompt opening of negotiations on a comprehensive peace. This statement of understandings emerges from discussions held with you and other regional leaders. I look forward to the letter of reply of the Government of —— in confirmation of this statement.

The agreed objective is a comprehensive peace providing for the security of all the states in the region and for the legitimate rights of the Palestinian people.

Negotiations will start at an early date certain between Israel and each of its neighbors which is willing to do so. These negotiations could begin by May 1, 1988. Each of these negotiations will be based on the United Nations Security Council Resolutions 242 and 338, in all their parts. The parties to each bilateral negotiation will determine the procedure and agenda at their negotiation. All participants in the negotiations must state their willingness to negotiate with one another.

As concerns negotiations between the Israeli delegation and the Jordanian-Palestinian delegation, negotiations will begin on arrangements for a transitional period, with the objective of completing them within six months. Seven months after transitional negotiations begin, final status negotiations will begin, with the objective of completing them within one year. These negotiations will be based on all the provisions and principles of United Nations Security Council Resolution 242. Final status talks will start before the transitional period begins. The transitional period will begin three months after the conclusion of the transitional agreement and will last for three years. The United States will participate in both negotiations and will promote their rapid conclusion. In particular, the United States will submit a draft agreement for the parties' consideration at the outset of the negotiations on transitional arrangements.

Two weeks before the opening of negotiations, an international conference will be held. The Secretary General of the United Nations will be asked to issue invitations to the parties involved in the Arab-Israeli conflict and the five permanent members of the United Nations Security Council. All participants in the conference must accept United Nations Security Council Resolutions 242 and 338, and renounce violence and terrorism. The parties to each bilateral negotiation may refer reports on the status of their negotiations to the conference, in a manner to be agreed. The conference will not be able to impose solutions or veto agreements reached.

Palestinian representation will be within the Jordanian-Palestinian delegation. The Palestinian issue will be addressed in the negotiations between the Jordanian-Palestinian and Israeli delegations. Negotiations between the Israeli delegation and the Jordanian-Palestinian delegation will proceed independently of any other negotiations.[2]

This statement of understanding is an integral whole. The United States understands that your acceptance is dependent on the implementation of each element in good faith.

Sincerely yours,
George P. Shultz

In the days after I left the Middle East, I was bombarded by scathing attacks from the Israeli media as well as from official circles: the American initiative was a surrender to terrorism, violence, and pressure. Was Israel now expected to wipe away the Camp David Accords, for which it had paid so high a price? The U.S. proposal was "an act of capitulation conceived in sin," the Israelis said. "Shamir is obligated to resist with all his power, and his power to resist is very great," I was told.

In private sessions during his visit to Washington on March 16 and 17, Shamir and I went over and over my initiative. "I want to remove any hard feelings," he said. "Some of my interviews may have hurt you, that was not my intention," he said. "In October 1987, my answer came first, so let King Hussein answer you first now.[3] The most difficult obstacle is this international conference." Again came the refrain "I won't say I reject that [my idea of a procedural international conference], but I oppose it." He concluded, "I can say that I welcome the efforts of the United States to work for peace. I have strong reservations about an international conference. A few months ago, I accepted a proposal to give international legitimacy to the parties who need it. I am ready to consider a similar proposal."

On March 26, I met with two American professors who were members of the Palestine National Council, Edward Said of Columbia University and Abu Lughod of Northwestern University. Since this organization was, in a way, the parent organization of the PLO, I knew some quarters would attack me, saying I was breaching Kissinger's 1975 pledge that the United States would not negotiate with the PLO until it accepted UN Resolution 242 and Israel's right to exist. Later, a third requirement was added: the PLO must give up terrorism. But these were American citizens; no one could justifiably complain about a U.S. government official meeting with U.S. citizens.

2. President Assad's letter was different in that it spoke of a negotiation between Israel and Syria rather than between Israel and a Jordanian-Palestinian delegation.
3. He was referring to my proposal in October 1987 that the Reagan-Gorbachev summit meeting in Washington be used as the international event that would kick off direct negotiations.

As I was on my way to the Middle East on my April shuttle, twenty-four senators urged me to refrain from any "other" meetings with the PLO, claiming that my session with the two Americans of Palestinian descent "sets a dangerous precedent." I was disappointed at what I regarded as their narrow and myopic view. I had long since concluded that diplomacy means—and needs—contact. The very purpose of diplomacy is to talk with people with whom you disagree, so I had concluded that the Kissinger conditions, while they made a point of tremendous importance, also created a certain problem for the United States. Still, I agreed that the PLO had no place in a Middle East peace process until it accepted the U.S. conditions—really the fundamental premises for responsible diplomacy. I was not going to reach out to the PLO or water down the long-standing U.S. position, especially because I saw some signs now that the PLO might be ripe to change its stance on meeting the three conditions.

I arrived in Israel on April 3. "I delivered a letter when I was last here," I said to Shamir and then Peres; "I've come back now to see whether anyone answers the mail." Horror stories of violence and suppression on the West Bank and Gaza still permeated the Western media. Although Israeli censors kept many of the worst scenes from the Israeli public, people knew very well that the situation there was deplorable. When I was leaving Ben Gurion Airport, one of the Israeli drivers for our embassy was moved almost to tears. "Please don't stop; keep trying," he implored. The *New York Times* "Quote of the Day" on April 4 came from my arrival statement: "This is the time and the season to move decisively toward peace."

But peace was not the mood I encountered. Outside my Jerusalem hotel window I was greeted by a giant color cartoon of Yasser Arafat—some forty feet high and fashioned from plywood, his huge face leering, his belt hung with skulls. "Welcome, George," said the poster. The message: my effort played into PLO terrorist hands. "Peace in our time," read signs of the protesters, a reference to Neville Chamberlain "selling out" to Hitler at Munich.

In my meeting with Yitzhak Shamir, I tried to get him inside the four corners of the letter I had left with him. Shamir proceeded to tear it apart, selecting and rejecting from it.

"It's a skeleton we want to put flesh on," I countered, "not a skeleton whose bones we want to dismember." I saw no disposition in Shamir to give me anything at all to work with. I offered to take a message from Shamir to King Hussein. Shamir then gave me a paragraph that urged direct Israeli-Jordanian negotiations. I made the same offer to Peres: he drafted a message urging King Hussein to accept my initiative. I was frustrated by Shamir's inflexibility and by the fact that divided government, as had existed in Israel since late 1984, meant that no one could be held responsible and accountable.

When I arrived in Jordan, I found King Hussein candid and gloomy: he again gave me nothing but wanted me to "persevere." I saw President Assad in Damascus the same day. Every meeting with him was an exercise in agony. This time we sat for over three hours in an airless room. I was near suffocation before Assad twirled his finger and the air-conditioning began to hum. Again the same message: I can give you nothing, but "continue."

Losing Altitude

I recognized the reality of the message, the same at each stop: my presence and perseverance, by giving people a reason to talk and a basis for hope, helped the parties keep the lid on this boiling cauldron of Middle East politics from completely blowing off. But no one truly wanted substantive change.

My mission was useful, but I was dissipating my own credibility at the same time. Still, I kept at it, because I felt an active peace process was needed in such a volatile situation. At the least, I was forcing people to consider new ideas. At a later date, these ideas—including my interlock concept and my notion of mixed sovereignty in the occupied territories— might have a better chance.

I had given a television interview in Jordan, answering questions about the initiative as fully and frankly as I could. The Jordanians censored the interview as "inflammatory" and tried to convince me they had done me a favor. Prime Minister Rifai said that showing the interview on television "would seriously have damaged Shultz's credibility in the Arab world." That was disconcerting, but I did hear some good news and more encouraging public words in Israel: "Focusing today on the nature of the interim and final agreements, Shultz again displayed infinite patience, giving everybody the feeling that they are partners to the program and to the efforts to make it a living thing. . . . The U.S. today proved again that it is making a supreme effort to bring an end to the deteriorating conflict in the Middle East," said commentator Yigael Goren on Israeli television on April 5. The message in *Ma'ariv*, the same day, was "Secretary Shultz's message was as simple as it was reasonable. Unfortunately, the prime minister is not going to buy it."

To the audience in the United States, John Cochran on NBC's "Today" reported, "Secretary of State George Shultz continues to be a remarkable example of the power of positive thinking . . . [he] compared his mission to trench warfare." I laughed. "Trench warfare would have been easier."

I had been on an Israeli TV interview show at my request explaining and advocating my ideas. The *Jerusalem Post* reported on April 6 the results of a poll showing that "60 percent [of the Israeli public] thought that Israel should accept his plan for an international conference," and this was the least appealing part of my proposal to the Israelis.

When I left the region, I made it clear that I was not giving up and that I would be back. "He [Shultz] is wearing us down. How can we get him to go home and stay home," the press reported an Israeli official as saying. The problem was, I was *not* wearing them down. Back in Washington, AIPAC's Tom Dine passed his view to me, "The pro-Israel community [in the U.S.] has lost its enthusiasm for the initiative. Inactivity is the word." Earlier they had supported my initiative enthusiastically, and seventy leaders in the American Jewish community had journeyed to Israel to make that view clear to Israeli leaders. By this time, I concluded, Israeli leaders, especially Shamir, had weighed in with the Americans and turned them sour.

I returned to the Middle East in June, basing myself, for the first time in American diplomatic practice, not in Jerusalem but in Cairo, and making my shuttles to and from Egypt as the hub. President Mubarak had all along supported my effort fully, and I wanted to convey the message that he was an essential part of this effort. In my arrival statement on June 3, I asked: "What is the Arab-Israeli conflict? It is the competition between two national movements for sovereignty on one land. . . . The fate of Zionism and Palestinian nationalism are interdependent." I intended to stir things up with this equation of Israel and Palestinians in the same utterance with the words "national" and "sovereignty." In Jerusalem, Amman, and Damascus, the leaders urged me to keep going, but there was still no movement from anyone.

My peace initiative did seem to give Arab moderates something to point to as evidence that their approach could be more effective than that of the radicals, and, I was told, it helped stave off a radical outcome to the Arab summit in Algiers in early June. The PLO signaled at the summit that it sought a role in peace process diplomacy. The "moderate" PLO statement was described on June 8, 1988, in the *Wall Street Journal* as "an explicit declaration of the PLO's willingness to recognize Israel and accept a two-state solution." I was skeptical, but still some change in PLO thinking might be under way, I thought.

A Legacy

With only four months to go before a new American president would be elected, time was running out. Although King Hussein had urged the Arab summit in early June not to reject my initiative, I knew there was little more I could do. In the region, the status of my initiative was captured by an Israeli political cartoon: an Israeli and a Jordanian, each with a club, and a Palestinian with a stone were holding me down and beating me mercilessly. The caption read: "Well, at Least They Agree on Something!" The press reflected this assessment as well. The *Economist* thought that I was preparing the stage for an American showdown with Israel after Reagan and I left office. And the *Washington Post* in an editorial on June 9 observed, "Israel wasted a very large opportunity during the Reagan years. . . . This leaves Israel more dependent on its one foreign patron and more estranged from the Palestinians, necessarily its one partner in any reach for peace." The *Post* spoke the truth.

In June the PLO had circulated an essay written in English by a close adviser to Arafat, Bassam Abu Sharif, and intended for a wide non-Arab audience. The essay indicated a readiness to accept—and to negotiate directly with—Israel. A week or so later, moderate Palestinians living in the West Bank and Gaza gave their support to the document. Were the Palestinians genuinely trying to change their approach to Israel? Israel had always been able to say that it was ready to talk but had "no Arab partner." Now Palestinians wanted to say that "no Israeli party" could be found on the other side of the table.

Disappointed and angry that Arafat had denied the Jordanians a negotiating role—even as the PLO enjoyed a presence in Amman to monitor and coordinate the intifada—King Hussein, on July 31, 1988, announced that Jordan was cutting legal and administrative ties to the West Bank, including the salaries Jordan had paid since 1967 to about 30 percent of the local Palestinian public bureaucracy. This action harmed both the Jordanian and Palestinian economies far more than King Hussein intended: a run on Jordanian banks ensued, and the Jordanian dinar, still common currency in the West Bank, suffered a rapid devaluation. King Hussein's decision to cease representing the Palestinians altogether did, however, turn the spotlight on the PLO. If the PLO failed to change its policies, the newly emergent voices produced in the territories by the intifada might start speaking themselves without much reference to the PLO. In my view, that would be a potentially positive development.

Only a few weeks after King Hussein announced his decision, he asked us to pass a message to Shimon Peres: the king's decision to remove Jordan from the peace process was taken in the hope that it would cause the PLO to "see the light and come to terms with reality." In a press conference on August 7, 1988, the king said that Jordan never again would assume the role of speaking on behalf of the Palestinians. By seeming to close out the idea of a Jordanian-Palestinian delegation and of a West Bank in some manner affiliated with Jordan, the king's decision appeared to mark the end of my initiative. I did not agree with that assessment: the ideas would remain of continuing importance, even though I could not pursue them further in the limited time remaining to me in office.

I had crafted my initiative to provide an incentive for each party to sign on: for Jordan, an international conference as cover for its participation in direct negotiations; for Israel, protection against pressure resulting from such a conference. The initiative would be propelled by the Israeli desire to achieve a change on the West Bank and Gaza through the granting of autonomy and by the Arabs' desire for a rapid, guaranteed advance to negotiations on the final status of the territories. When these talks started, the United States would be ready to put forth proposals to bridge differences based on President Reagan's September 1, 1982, "Fresh Start" Middle East peace initiative: Palestinian confederation with Jordan—and perhaps with Israel as well—with the elements of sovereignty dispersed or blurred where the realities and needs of land and water use and security in such a small area would be best served.

My initiative had not achieved the direct negotiations I had sought, but through it I had brought some new elements to the negotiating table. The initiative included some novel ideas for future peacemaking efforts. On September 16, 1988, I gave a major address at the Wye Plantation near Washington, again setting out the key elements of the initiative, which I considered to be my legacy to the next American administration.

"The status quo between Arabs and Israelis does not work," I said in my address, and I noted, "Jordan's disengagement from the West Bank hasn't ended Jordan's involvement in the peace process. Jordan has its own interests to pursue." I pointed out the ominous fact that "ballistic missiles and chemical weapons continue to proliferate. The use of chemical weapons by both sides in the Gulf War and Iraq's use of these weapons against the Kurds are grim reminders of the dangers these weapons pose to the conduct of international relations."

I highlighted the idea of the "interlock" between transitional arrangements regarding self-rule and negotiations about the final status of the occupied territories. I said that the parties must recognize "the strategic reality of Jordanian-Palestinian interdependence." I called for the right kind of an international conference to launch and support direct negotiations "without interfering in them" and emphasized that "direct negotiations are at the heart of this negotiating process." And I stated flatly, knowing full well the difficulties of finding people simultaneously acceptable to the Israelis and legitimate in the eyes of the Palestinians, "the right of Palestinians to participate actively in every stage of negotiations."

High-Stakes Poker with the PLO

Beginning in mid-August, feelers from the PLO came into my office. Bill Quandt, NSC staff specialist on the Middle East in the Carter years and now at the Brookings Institution, was asked by Muhammad Rabia, a Palestinian-American close to Arafat, whether the United States or Israel would respond to a PLO move at this point to meet the U.S. "conditions." I passed back our long-held position: "If the PLO meets the three U.S. conditions, we will start talks with them." On September 3, Quandt came to see Dick Murphy with a document reportedly approved by the entire executive committee of the PLO. They asked for a U.S. reaction to the text, which clearly did not add up to acceptance of our conditions. I did not want to be drawn into a series of indirect exchanges with the PLO in this fashion. Nonetheless, something seemed to be cooking in the PLO camp. Murphy told me on September 7 that the PLO had shared this draft with the Soviets and the Egyptians. Perhaps King Hussein's decision, although it had derailed my initiative, was stimulating the PLO to take some initiative of its own.

On September 8, Murphy told me that Quandt had shown him a PLO statement that met the U.S. conditions: acceptance of UN Resolution 242, an end to violence, and recognition of Israel's right to exist. It would require only "minor changes" to be acceptable, he thought. From us, the PLO wanted a commitment to start a dialogue and to accept the Palestinians' right to self-determination. While I felt that cutting this Gordian knot would be a useful legacy for the next American administration, I would not consider acceptance of "self-determination," since, in this case, that had become a code signifying acceptance of an "independent Palestinian state." The PLO by then had promoted its idea to quite a few interested parties and observers, and I was feeling pressure from both directions. A prominent Jewish congressman urged me to make the call for Palestinian self-determination; if I did, "I'll only criticize you mildly," he said. I would not in any way endorse an independent Palestinian state, but I told Murphy to point out to anybody who asked that our conditions were clear and unequivocal—and that the United States would respond once those conditions were met.

On September 12, I was informed that the hard-line PLO leadership had accepted a document that met the conditions. So what would the United States do? "Open a dialogue," we answered. That same day, I reviewed these developments with the president and showed him the language we were told the PLO would put out, and what we would say in response. President Reagan thought our approach was just right, but Ken Duberstein, who had replaced Howard Baker as chief of staff, was deeply concerned that U.S.-PLO talks might upset George Bush's presidential campaign.

"We really have no choice," I said. "If the PLO meets our conditions, we have to honor our commitment to start a dialogue." Echoes of all this discussion reached Israel. On September 12, I received a letter from Prime Minister Shamir emphasizing what we well knew: he had no trust at all in the PLO. "American beckonings only strengthen them and hamper efforts to deal with non-PLO Palestinians," he said.

          *   *   *

Hearing no more from the PLO, we did nothing. Quandt urged us on September 20 to do something, because our silence could be read as lack of interest. He suggested that we pass a message through him that we would be "unable to handle" a positive PLO decision until after our presidential election. I felt that no such comment was needed and that we would in fact build pressure on the PLO by silently holding to our long-held position.

The speech I had given at the Wye Plantation a few days earlier was, I thought, rock solid on Palestinian issues, but they apparently were yearning for a sign from us and thought they saw two of them: my mention of Palestinian "political rights," a phrase I had also used before the Knesset Foreign Affairs and Defense Committee, and my assertion that any party to negotiations could bring any position (for example, self-determination) to the table. That was the U.S. position going back to President Reagan's September 1, 1982, Middle East peace initiative, but some people now saw it afresh.

In October the PLO sent a message through the CIA in the form of a question: was it really true that I was standing pat and not negotiating with Quandt? I was informed of this question and felt we must continue to hold to our position, make no response, in this poker game. On October 19, Quandt telephoned Dan Kurtzer in our Near Eastern Affairs Bureau: his Palestinian sources said the Palestine National Council would meet on November 8 or 9 to consider a declaration of independence and a peace process program. This would be stage one. Stage two would depend on what they could expect from the United States "in reply to a more forthcoming statement" toward meeting the American conditions. In other words, what came out of the PNC meeting would not be the final word from the PLO. I suspected that the PLO believed our lack of engagement with them stemmed from a U.S. desire to avoid a dialogue with the PLO, or even a debate about the possibility of one, during the presidential election campaign. The timing of this PNC session suggested they had held off consideration of a significant move until both the American and Israeli elections were over.

On November 9, 1988, the day after George Bush's landslide victory, I was handed a report that the PLO representative at the United Nations, Zehdi Terzi, had informed the president of the Security Council that the PLO would request a visa for Yasser Arafat to come to the United Nations that month. The United States, as host nation, had signed a headquarters agreement with the United Nations under which we agreed not to block representatives from attending the sessions unless the security interests of the United States were threatened. The PLO had "observer delegation" status at the United Nations and Arafat was PLO chairman. But U.S. law also barred the admission of PLO members to the United States on the grounds that the PLO supported terrorism and therefore the presence in our country of PLO members threatened our national security interests. If a PLO member applied for a visa, our law provided, it could be granted only if the secretary of state personally recommended it to the attorney general, who then would decide, in an independent step, whether or not to grant the visa. Over the years, certain PLO officials had received exceptions to our law in order to exercise the PLO's observer status at the United Nations.

There was no exact precedent for me to follow when it came to a visa for Arafat. He presented a special case. He was the head of the PLO, an organization whose members had recently been involved in acts of terrorism. At the latest PNC meeting, Abu Abbas, mastermind of the *Achille Lauro* hijacking in which terrorists had killed Leon Klinghoffer, had been present and in friendly association with Arafat and had reportedly laughed about his crime. The standard procedure, our consular people told me, would be for a foreign government or organization to deliver a diplomatic note to me. On the basis of this note, I, and subsequently the attorney general, would decide yes or no. I decided to wait until Arafat formally applied for a visa and then make the decision. I would not regard Arafat's request to the United Nations to be equivalent to an application submitted to the United States.

At the PNC meeting in Algiers, Arafat on November 15 proclaimed an independent state of Palestine "on our Palestinian territory, with holy Jerusalem as its capital" and hinted at recognition of Israel. I put the U.S. position out quickly: "The way to deal with the issues of peace and the occupied territories is through direct negotiations; unilateral declarations have no weight." Some analysts at State saw Arafat's statement as a successful step in wresting concessions from hard-liners at the PNC conference. A close look, however, revealed an attempt to trade the meeting of our conditions for a U.S. commitment to a Palestinian state. And Resolution 242 was described as no more than a basis for an international conference. The language was blurry and ambiguous.

Meanwhile, pressure on me was mounting to grant Arafat the visa. The CIA and the FBI informed me that the United States could not consider Arafat's presence in itself to be a threat to national security. Former President Jimmy Carter telephoned me on November 22 to urge a visa for Arafat. He and former President Gerald Ford had met with George Bush the preceding day, Carter said, and all had agreed that the PNC meeting in Algiers had showed forward movement and moderation. It "would be a great mistake" to turn Arafat's request down. "I urge you in the strongest terms to approve the visa," Carter said. Prince Bandar of Saudi Arabia wrote to me. This is an historic moment, he said; "a positive gesture is needed to break the psychological barrier." I thought that, on the contrary, my continued demonstration of firmness would be far more likely to cause the PLO to meet our conditions.

On November 24, Arafat and members of his entourage formally applied for visas at the American embassy in Tunis. I knew I must decide quickly. I read over all the legal opinions and memoranda provided me by the various agencies and offices concerned. I listened to an endless string of advisers who came to my office on November 25, mostly to advise that I must grant the visa. I thanked them, but we all knew that under U.S. law, this decision was one to be made by the secretary of state: I would bear the weight of responsibility alone.

In Stockholm, the Swedes had hosted a meeting between the PLO and a group of prominent American Jews. On November 25, a representative of Swedish Foreign Minister Sten Andersson came to see me with a document the two groups had drafted. I regarded their statement as an improvement on what had come out of the PNC conference, I told the Swedes, but it was not yet even close to meeting the U.S. conditions for a dialogue with the PLO.

Struggling with the decision I must make on Arafat, I focused on the issue of terrorism, as required by U.S. law. The law, the arguments, and the precedents on this issue ran the gamut. The United States had granted Arafat a visa for the United Nations in 1974. Earlier in 1988 Congress had made a move to close the UN office of the PLO because of its involvement in terrorism. I had argued that the granting of observer status to the PLO was a UN decision. If the United States denied Arafat a visa, why not deny a visa to Terzi, the PLO's regular UN representative? Simple: he was a functionary, not a leader. But the PLO had clearly committed numerous acts of terrorism since the 1985 hijacking of and murder on the *Achille Lauro*. No evidence connected Arafat himself to any specific act of terrorism, but he was the head man. He had, through his continued association with Abu Abbas—whom he did not repudiate—condoned the murder of Leon Klinghoffer.

The next day, November 26, 1988, I made my decision: I did not recommend to the attorney general that Arafat be granted a visa. That amounted to a decision to deny. I issued a carefully worded statement: "The Congress of the United States conditioned the entry of the U.S. into the U.N. headquarters agreement on the retention by the U.S. Government of the authority to bar the entry of aliens associated with or invited by the United Nations 'in order to safeguard its own security.' In this regard, U.S. law excludes members of the P.L.O. from entry into the United States by virtue of their affiliation in an organization which engages in terrorism."

We had, I said, "convincing evidence" of PLO terrorism against Americans and others. I gave some of that evidence and asserted, "As chairman of the P.L.O. Mr. Arafat is responsible for actions of these organizations which are units of Fatah, an element of the P.L.O. of which he also is chairman and which is under his control." I cited Arafat's associations with Abu Abbas, "a member of the Executive Committee of the P.L.O. who has been convicted by the Italian judicial system" of the hijacking of the *Achille Lauro,* resulting in "the murder of an American citizen, Mr. Leon Klinghoffer." Arafat "knows of, condones and lends support to such acts; he therefore is an accessory to such terrorism."

The reaction was swift. Secretary-General Pérez de Cuéllar denounced my decision. The pope, referring to the PNC, suggested that its positive gestures needed a response. German government officials were quoted as saying, "Washington" had lost touch with reality. The British press said I had "sandbagged" Margaret Thatcher, who had been impressed enough with the PNC statement in Algiers to tell the president and me, "When people do things that we like, we should welcome it." The Egyptians, our ambassador reported, were "going crazy" and wanted to send an envoy to President Reagan to get the decision overturned. Vice President Bush privately told Colin Powell that he did not agree with what I had done, but when he heard that President Reagan had endorsed my decision, he said he would continue his "no comment posture."

On December 1, I received a boost in the form of a letter of support signed by sixty-one senators. But William F. Buckley, Jr., wrote that my denial of the Arafat visa was indefensible: bad politics and bad morally. In editorials the *New York Times* said I "erred badly." It was the wrong decision, the *Washington Post* echoed. Jim Baker was "surprised by the decision" and "did not understand Shultz's logic in deciding to bar Arafat," reported John Goshko on November 29 in the *Post.* I telephoned Jim Baker about the matter on December 2. He said he was not opposed, just not familiar with the issue. And the ranking American in the UN system, Joseph Verner Reed, criticized my decision in a letter to President Reagan, which Reed himself released to the public. He called my decision "baffling and contradictory" and said it did "incalculable damage to U.S. credibility." I was infuriated.

"The U.S. and Israel stand alone tonight in the matter of Arafat and the UN," said CBS-TV on December 1, 1988. "Though the President supports Shultz's very personal decision, there are those in the White House who suggest things might very well be different in the next administration."

On December 2, the UN General Assembly voted 154 to 2 to move their debate on "Palestine" to Geneva so that Arafat could attend and speak. Our UN ambassador, Vernon (Dick) Walters, who had evaporated from the scene when the heat was on me to grant Arafat a visa, materialized again, saying he wanted to go to Geneva to represent the United States at Arafat's address.

That same day, the Swedish ambassador, Count Wilhelm (Willy) Wachtmeister, delivered a message to me from Foreign Minister Andersson stating that Arafat himself would go to Stockholm to meet the American Jewish group. Would I please inform the Swedes of the U.S. position?

Yes, I said. The next day, Saturday, at 3:30 in the afternoon, Wachtmeister came to my house, where I gave him a letter for Andersson that stated our long-standing position on the PLO and the precise conditions for a dialogue with the United States. I made clear that this letter was for the use of the Swedish foreign minister in response to his request and not for Arafat and the Americans in Stockholm.

I told Wachtmeister I would not negotiate any change in our position— not with the PLO or the Swedes or anybody else. I thought that my resolve to hang tough on Arafat's visa request should be convincing evidence that the U.S. position would not change. To open a dialogue with us, the PLO, not the United States, would have to do the changing. To make sure that the Swedes knew the U.S. position was unalterable, I gave them a copy of my speech at Wye Plantation in September and said that if any questions arose, that speech expressed the authorized U.S. position.

On December 6, Wachtmeister came back with a statement produced in a meeting between Andersson and Arafat in Stockholm. Arafat would make this statement at his Stockholm press conference on December 7, he told me. "Does this statement meet the U.S. conditions?" he asked.

Without a doubt, it did. I took the text over to President Reagan; he agreed.

"We win," I told the president. Once again in the Reagan presidency, a firm policy had caused others to meet conditions set out by the United States.

Then I walked over to Vice President Bush's office. "It's terrific progress. I will support a dialogue. I'm all for it," Bush said.

I went back to State and called in Wachtmeister. "Tell Andersson that if Arafat makes this proposed public statement, we will reply that U.S. conditions have been met." As the proposed Arafat statement also made reference to the PLO position on an independent Palestinian state and an international conference, I told the Swedes that we would say that we continued to disagree with those positions. Later in the day I briefed Jim Baker, who was delighted.

Yasser Arafat, however, did *not* make the promised statement on December 7. "They have cold feet," Wachtmeister told me. Instead of a public announcement, Arafat had signed the statement and given it to Andersson; Arafat was going to Tunis to try to obtain the PLO Executive Committee's approval for what he had done. Wachtmeister then handed me a copy of the actual document signed by Arafat.

On December 12, Andersson told me that the PLO Executive Committee had approved Arafat's statement. "Arafat will read it exactly as written in

PALESTINE LIBERATION ORGANIZATION

STOCKHOLM

منَظَّمَة التَّحـريرالفِـلِسْطينيّة

ســـتوكهولم

Mr. Sten Andersson
Minister for Foreign Affairs

SWEDEN

REF.   STOCKHOLM   December 7, 1988

Dear Mr Sten Andersson,

In continuation to our discussions that took place in Stockholm
on the 6th and 7th of December 1988 about the text presented by
Mr. Shultz, the Secretary of State for Foreign Affairs of the
United States of America concerning the beginning of dialogue
between the PLO and the American Administration I hereby enclose
the text that we present and that has my approval and which I
have signed. We will work to have it issued officially after
being presented to the Executive Committee later on.

Please accept the expression of my highest consideration,

Yasser Arafat
Chairman of the Executive Committee
of the Palestine Liberation Organization

Postadress   Telefon   Postgirokonto   Telex
Tulegatan 49   08/34 41 14 FAX   430 01 46-0   15868 QODSONA S
S-113 53 Stockholm 08/16 05 60 Off.
Sweden

As its contribution to the search for a just and lasting peace
in the Middle East, the Executive Committee of the Palestine
Liberation Organization, assuming the role of the Provisional
Government of the State of Palestine wishes to issue the following
official statement:

1. That it is prepared to negotiate with Israel within the framework
of the International Conference a comprehensive peace settlement
of the Arab-Israeli conflict on the basis of U.N. resolutions
242 and 338.

2. That it undertakes to live in peace with Israel and other
neighbours and to respect their right to exist in peace within
secure and internationally recognized borders, as will the
democratic Palestinian State which it seeks to establish in the
Palestinian occupied territories since 1967.

3. That it condemns individual, group and State terrorism in all
its forms, and will not resort to it.

the course of a speech he will give in Geneva on December 13," Andersson said. He asked again that we restate the American position as I had set it forth in my Wye Plantation speech.

"If Arafat makes the statement as written, with no conditions or contradictions, we will respond that it meets our conditions and proceed promptly to discussions with the PLO," I told Andersson.

By this time, a wave of near-hysteria was sweeping through Middle East watchers on three continents. Everyone knew that something was brewing. Rumors abounded. People tried either to take credit for or to kill the prospective development. Messages—usually false messages—flew back and forth. I shut my ears to all the noise except for what the Swedes and I communicated to one another.

I informed the Israelis on December 12 of the Swedish assertion that Arafat would publicly meet our conditions on December 13. Israel's ambassador to the United States, Moshe Arad, was taken aback: "This is the most significant message I have received from you. A very delicate plateau has been reached. I'm still trying to grasp the new reality and what it means for our relationship. I didn't expect to see it before the end of this administration." Arad reported this development to Jerusalem.

Instantly a request came back from Shamir: please do not react to Arafat's statement until you have heard from Israel. Then Shamir warned me, with a shot across my bow, "There will be great difficulty in our relationship if the U.S. moves to open a dialogue with the PLO." I responded that if the PLO met the U.S. conditions, we would move promptly to be in touch with them. That was our long-standing position, and we would honor it.

On December 13, Arafat gave a speech, but he did not read his signed statement as promised. I told President Reagan, "In one place Arafat was saying, 'Unc, unc, unc' and in another he was saying, 'cle, cle, cle,' but nowhere will he yet bring himself to say, 'Uncle.' "

Suddenly I was inundated with alternative channels and alternative language, all attributed to the PLO and claiming to be authoritative. The Swedes were apparently scrambling for ways to let Arafat off the hook: they proposed that Arafat simply "endorse" a speech by Andersson on the conditions. "Close, but no cigar," I said to Andersson. Senator Rudy Boschwitz came in, and I brought him up to speed. "The one constant is our policy," I said; "we are in the catbird seat."

In Geneva, at a press conference on December 14, 1988, Arafat finally said "Uncle." I heard a tape recording made in Geneva. Arafat was explaining his Geneva speech the day before, describing the PLO position in terms that, while crafty, undeniably met the conditions for a dialogue with the United States.

I called Colin Powell at 3:40 in the afternoon and said I was sending the text over for the president. At 4:30, I asked Jim Baker to come to my office so I could show Arafat's statement to him as well. "Arafat's statement meets our conditions," I told him.

"It's just great to have this done. Congratulations," Jim Baker responded.

At 5:14, Colin Powell called back: the president agreed and authorized me to make a public statement that the PLO had met our conditions for a dialogue. At 6:30 that evening, I went down to the pressroom and announced: "The Palestine Liberation Organization (PLO) today issued a statement in which it accepted U.N. Security Council Resolutions 242 and 338, recognized Israel's right to exist in peace and security, and renounced terrorism. As a result, the United States is prepared for a substantive dialogue with PLO representatives."

I wanted to control this dialogue carefully, so I designated Robert Pelletreau, our ambassador to Tunisia and a top-notch professional, as the only authorized channel. I stated flatly, "The United States does not recognize the declaration of an independent Palestinian state." And, I emphasized, "The United States' commitment to the security of Israel remains unflinching."

In a reference to the Arab "three noes" of 1967 (no recognition, no negotiation, no peace with Israel), Bill Safire on December 15, 1988, in the *New York Times*, called this the "three yesses": yes to Israel, yes to forswearing terrorism, yes to 242. Safire amplified perceptively:

> In the end, our unrelenting pressure paid off. "We totally and absolutely renounce all forms of terrorism," read Yasir Arafat, "including individual, group and state terrorism. . . . we want peace." . . . For weeks the P.L.O. leader has been trying to entice the departing Reagan Administration into talks with half-concessions and phony "yesses."
>
> Secretary of State George Shultz was not having any of that. Others, from Margaret Thatcher to a group of dovish Jewish citizens of the U.S., read the murky Arafat tea leaves and saw what they wanted to see, but the Reagan Administration, to its credit and credibility, demanded straight answers.
>
> I think the key in forcing the P.L.O. leader to act was the denial of his visa to the U.S. That was an action that brought almost universal denunciation upon Secretary Shultz's head, but one that carried more weight than any form of cajoling or persuasion.

I had stood firm, and the denial of a visa to Arafat had been tough evidence that I would continue to do so. The waters had swirled, roared, and tumbled around me. When they receded, the PLO had made a new decision, while the United States had held fast to a constant position.

Reactions varied widely, mostly following preconceived hopes. Some people were excited by the prospect that the PLO, long thought indispensable to progress in the peace process, would now be involved. Others were furious that an odious organization and its chieftain had been legitimized. The Israelis launched into their familiar tactic, when something went against their perceived interests, of "damage magnification," blowing out of all proportion the negative side of this development and ignoring the positive possibilities. Some Arabs were ecstatic. Others responded warily, with the familiar tendency to view any development with a conspiratorial bent. Our ambassador to Tunis reported that "Arab diplomats fear the U.S. dialogue with the PLO is motivated by an American desire to take pressure off Israel"—to defuse the intifada and thereby get Israel out of that jam. More generally, though, the reaction to the PLO decision was rather like the way the stock market anticipates news: when the news actually breaks, the market doesn't react; it has already absorbed the idea.

I was skeptical of the PLO's ability to maintain a consistent and constructive position, but I was glad that a self-imposed prohibition to American diplomacy was now a matter of history. I was also glad to have forced some important words out of Arafat's mouth. Words are important. Once issued, they can never be taken back.

Representation:
A Lesson from My Days with Nixon

I had no high expectations for the PLO before or after they met our conditions. Their capacity for change and accommodation was, by their past performance, a question mark at best. Nevertheless, in my discussions with the Israelis, I repeatedly emphasized the importance of having as opposite numbers in negotiations Palestinians who were not involved in terrorism but who were legitimate, who truly represented their constituencies. At some point, sooner or later, Israel would have to face up to that truth. Over an informal and private dinner at his official residence, I discussed my views with Prime Minister Shamir on April 15, 1988. "You need strong representation on the other side of any bargaining table," I said. To deliver on any deal, the deal makers must have the full confidence of their constituencies. To underscore my point, I told Shamir a long story about my involvement in the desegregation of the schools in the American South, an account meant to dramatize for him the importance of credible and legitimate representation if the outcome of a negotiation is to get support. He listened patiently as I recounted my own personal story from a page of U.S. history.

As late as 1970, I told him, the schools in seven of our Southern states were still segregated by law. The *Brown* v. *Topeka Board of Education* decision by the Supreme Court in 1954 had declared such segregation unconstitutional. Time passed. Tension mounted. The whole subject was intensely controversial, with great arguments over the problems of busing in areas where the schools were segregated.

In March 1970, President Nixon had declared the *Brown* v. *Board of Education* decision to be "right in both constitutional and human terms" and expressed his intention to enforce the law. He decided to form a cabinet committee to work on this process in a direct, managerial way. Vice President Spiro Agnew was made chairman, and I was the vice chairman. Our problem was how to manage the transition to desegregated schools in the seven affected states: Alabama, Arkansas, Georgia, Louisiana, Mississippi, North Carolina, and South Carolina.

Agnew wanted no part of this problem and basically declined to participate in the committee's deliberations. So I wound up as de facto chairman. I had strong help from Presidential Counselor Pat Moynihan, Special Counsel Len Garment, and Ed Morgan, a savvy former advance man for the president. I first formed biracial committees in each of the seven states. We determined, with the president's agreement, that politics should have nothing to do with the selection of the people for these committees. We wanted people in equal numbers of black and white who were truly representative of their constituencies. And so, with great care, we picked strong, respected leaders from each of these states.

This was a key point. I told Shamir, "We didn't pick people who agreed with us or with each other. We picked people who were respected by those they would represent."

The first group invited to Washington came from Mississippi in the late spring of 1970. I took them into the Roosevelt Room of the White House, right opposite the president's Oval Office, and started in. The discussion was civil, but the deep divisions were evident. The blacks argued that desegregation of the schools would be good for education and that it was absolutely essential. The whites were resistant. Both sides were tough but truly representative. I let them argue and get it out of their systems. There came a point in the meeting, after about two hours—and this happened with regularity as groups from the other states came in—when I felt that it was time to shift gears. By prearrangement, I had John Mitchell standing by. He was known throughout the South as the tough guy, and on the whole was regarded by the whites as "their man." I asked Mitchell, as attorney general, what he planned to do insofar as the schools were concerned. "I am attorney general, and I will enforce the law," he growled in his gruff, pipe-smoking way. He offered no value judgments and did not take part in the debate about whether this was good, bad, or indifferent. "I will enforce the law." Then he left. No nonsense. Both the blacks and the whites were impressed.

This message from the attorney general, I explained to Shamir, allowed me to move our discussion forward from "whether" to "how," to managerial and administrative topics. The fact was, desegregation *was going to happen*. The only question for these outstanding community leaders was, *how would it work*? Would there be violence? How would the educational system in their community be affected? What would be the effect on their local economies? They had a great stake in seeing that this effort was managed in a reasonable way, whether they liked it or not, I told them.

The same was true on the West Bank and Gaza, I told Shamir. "The status quo is not stable. Change will come. The questions are, how and to what."

When lunchtime arrived, back then in the spring of 1970, I took the whole group over to the diplomatic reception rooms in the State Department, where we were surrounded by the artifacts of colonial America. I pointed out the desk designed by Jefferson on which he wrote portions of the Declaration of Independence: "dedicated to the proposition that all men are created equal." I sat with the two strong men I wanted to cochair the Mississippi advisory committee.[4] I argued that if they would accept, the committee would immediately have great credibility with whites and blacks; their acceptance would thereby enhance the ability of the committee to attain its goal: a desegregated school system with the least possible disruption and the greatest chance to enhance the quality of education for their children.

I saw that I was making headway, so I left them alone for a bit, much to the consternation of an observer from the Justice Department. "I learned long ago that when parties get that close to agreement, it is best to let them complete their agreement by themselves," I told the perplexed observer. "That way, the agreement belongs to them—it's theirs—and they will try hard to make it work." As lunch ended, these two tough, respected leaders shook hands on their own deal. We were in business in what many regarded as the most problematic state.

Gradually, after we returned to the White House, the whole group came around, and individuals started to make suggestions about how to handle this or that potential problem. A small kitty out of HEW flexible funds had been set aside, so I was able to say to the committee members that if they judged that funds were needed for minor expenditures, I could provide them on a fast-track basis. That seemed to help.

When I felt the time was right, again by prearrangement, I let President Nixon know that we were ready for him. We then walked across the hall and into the Oval Office, where he met each of them and sat them down. President Nixon spoke to them with a great sense of conviction and with considerable emotion. Looking around the room, he said, in essence,

4. Warren Hood, the president of the Mississippi Manufacturers' Association, and Dr. Gilbert Mason, president of the Biloxi chapter of the NAACP.

"Here we are in the Oval Office of the White House. Think of the decisions that have been made here and that have affected the health and the security of our country. But remember, too, that we live in a great democracy where authority and responsibility are shared. Just as decisions are made here in this office, decisions are made throughout the states and communities of our country. You are leaders in those communities, and this is a time when we all have to step up to our responsibilities. I will make my decisions, and I count on you to make yours. We must make this work."

By the time he got through and people were ready to leave, they were charged up to get their backs into making the school openings and subsequent operations of the schools go forward as smoothly and constructively as possible.

The group went home to Mississippi, and they were able to provide real leadership. They were strong people, and they were accepted as legitimate and valid representatives within their communities of the true feelings that people had. We went through the same process with representatives of five other states before the school year was to start. The last state to go was Louisiana. I suggested to the president that we hold this meeting in New Orleans. We would go to the South, where the action would take place. I would do my part in the morning. He could fly down from Washington and do his part with the Louisianans at the end of the morning meeting. Then, in the afternoon, we would invite the cochairmen from each of the seven states to join the president and me for an overall discussion of the school openings.

I remembered well a meeting in the Oval Office to discuss this possible set of events, I recounted to Shamir. Vice President Agnew strongly warned the president not to go. He said, there you will be in that room, Mr. President, half the people there will be black, half will be white. The schools will be opening, beginning the following week. There will be blood running throughout the streets of the South, and if you go, this will be blood on your hands. This is not your issue. This is the issue of the liberals who have pushed for desegregation. Let them have it. Stay away.

President Nixon looked at me, the nonpolitician in the crowd. I thought he had already decided to go and didn't need arguments from me. But I told him what I thought: "Well, Mr. President, I can't predict what will happen. The vice president may very well be right about violence in the streets, but this is your country. You are the president of all the people, and it seems to me that we have seen some very reasonable and strong people come up here. You've met with them and have had a big impact on them. We should do everything we can to see that the schools open and operate peacefully and well."

The president decided to go ahead with our plan. Down we all went to New Orleans, except for Vice President Agnew, who stayed home.

I left the night before the president and started in the morning with the biracial Louisiana group. The going was tough, much more so than with any other state. As I struggled, I thought, maybe my problem was the closeness of the school opening, maybe the more restricted amount of time, maybe we just missed the ambience of the White House. President Nixon was due to arrive about noon to put on his final touch. As noon arrived, I had not achieved the degree of agreement that I usually had by the time the president met with the group. We took a recess. I went out to meet with the president. "Mr. President," I told him, "I'm sorry to tell you that I haven't got this group to the point you usually find when you meet with them. They're still arguing. I'm afraid this time you're going to have to do the job yourself."

Nixon came in. He listened. He talked. He raised the sights of everyone. He stepped up to the problem, did a wonderful job, and brought them all on board.

That afternoon we had our meeting with the cochairmen from the seven states. The meeting was highly publicized throughout the South. President Nixon talked eloquently about the importance of what was going to happen and the stake that everyone had in seeing it go smoothly. There were strong pledges of cooperation from whites and blacks alike. A sense of determination in a joint, compelling enterprise filled the room.

Riding home on *Air Force One*, we gathered around to discuss the day's activities—Pat Moynihan, Len Garment, Bryce Harlow, the president, and I. We felt very good about the day's activities. Bryce Harlow, who was from Oklahoma and the only real Southerner in the crowd, said that he thought things would go pretty well in the South. But, he said, wait until this process of desegregation comes to the North. The lawyers from Boston have been coming South preaching all these years. But wait until they have to face desegregation in their own communities.

The president said, "How do you figure that, Bryce?"

He said, "Well, Mr. President, people in the South have been living with the Negro for all these years, side by side. In the South, we love the Negro as a human being, but we hate the Negro as a race. In the North, it's just the opposite. There is no experience of living together as human beings, so Northerners love the Negro as a race, but they hate the Negro as an individual. Therefore, and since this all comes down in the end to individual human relationships, it will go better in the South than in the North."

As the schools opened, we worried about how this would be covered on television. Len Garment went around to the leading networks and told them that they should report the facts as they were. He said to them, "Suppose a hundred schools open, and there is violence at one of them. What is the story? I think the story is that the schools opened 99 percent peacefully." The schools opened, and all went well. The openings were peaceful, much to the amazement of almost everyone. The leaders in their communities had done a fine job. They stood up to their responsibilities.

After having told this long, involved story, I looked at Shamir. "There are two big lessons in this story as I see it," I told him. "The first is that if you are to give legitimacy to an effort, involve people who truly represent their own constituencies, not people who think the way you do and are easy for you to talk to. The other big lesson has to do with the human relationships involved. Jews and Palestinians have been living side by side throughout the region for centuries. I have traveled around in the Middle East a fair amount, and I have heard many expressions of admiration, respect, and affection for human beings across ethnic lines. Just as in our South, there are personal relationships of long standing. Although deep and abiding hatreds exist—and the intifada and Israel's harsh reaction are intensifying those hatreds—there is also personal rapport and respect to be nurtured.

I hoped also that Shamir would gain inspiration from the example of President Nixon, who had courageously stepped up to this historic and difficult problem and had given the leadership needed at a critical moment. "The moment must come," I said, "when strong Arabs and Israelis step up to their possibilities as well as their problems, when 'whether' turns to 'how,' and when the job of creating better and more stable conditions of life begins."

That was my exit from the peace process: I left with ideas on the table that I hoped could be taken up anew by new players. I remembered my first visit to Jerusalem in 1969 and the words of Mayor Teddy Kollek, "Jerusalem is like a beautiful mosaic. The colors don't run into each other, but if you put them together in the right way, they can make a beautiful picture." I also remembered Shamir's statement to me that "somehow we will find a way to live together peacefully."

Somehow, but how?

Tough decisions on all sides were needed, made with a foresight that eluded the Middle Eastern scene. Otherwise, the drift would continue toward spiraling violence and positions that become more and more irreconcilable. The United States had, and has, a unique ability to bring together all the parties and to help them overcome hatreds and forge solutions to their deep-seated problems. But those who reside in the Middle East, and those who lead them or aspire to, must in the end bear the burden of responsibility for conditions where they live.

CHAPTER 48

The Struggle
to Oust Noriega

On Saturday, May 21, 1988, at 10:35 A.M., all the key people in the national security agencies of the executive branch gathered in the White House.[1] The subject: how to get military dictator General Manuel Antonio Noriega out of Panama and whether, in negotiating with him, we were wise to use the possibility of quashing an indictment—which had been brought against him in February on drug charges—as a lever to get him out of power and out of Panama. President Reagan had decided almost two weeks earlier in a meeting with Attorney General Ed Meese to do so.

On May 10, in a meeting in the Oval Office attended by Vice President Bush, the details of a potential deal with Noriega had been spelled out. I could see then that the vice president was uneasy. He wanted the dropping of the indictment to be described as "in the nature of a plea bargain" and counseled that we must orchestrate Latin support for the deal and be sure that House Speaker Jim Wright was on board. Mike Kozak, a lawyer in State's Latin America bureau who had played a role in achieving the Panama Canal Treaty in the 1970s, was our negotiator. Toward the end of the meeting, I said, "So we can take this as a decision for Kozak to go ahead?" All agreed: President Reagan, Vice President Bush, everybody.

But here we were, eleven days later, with the deal almost in hand, arguing the fundamentals all over again. Nothing ever gets settled in this town, I thought once again. At one point the president turned to me, "George, you and I seem to be pretty lonely here." Vice President Bush, Treasury Secretary Jim Baker, Chief of Staff Howard Baker, and his deputy, Ken

---

1. In addition to President Ronald Reagan, Vice President George Bush, and myself, also present were Secretary of the Treasury Jim Baker, Attorney General Ed Meese, Secretary of Defense Frank Carlucci, Chief of Staff Howard Baker, NSC adviser Colin Powell, CIA director William Webster, Deputy Chief of Staff Ken Duberstein, deputy to the NSC adviser John Negroponte, Under Secretary Mike Armacost, Assistant Secretary Elliott Abrams, and Mike Kozak.

Duberstein, and Attorney General Ed Meese all were arguing with the president that we should back off from negotiating with Noriega.

President Reagan, in exasperation, said, "I'm not giving in. This deal is better than going in and counting our dead. I just think you are wrong as hell on this."

A Long and Sorry History

Panamanian strongman Manuel Antonio Noriega was known to be a canny and ruthless operator with his eye focused on his own interests. "You can't buy him; you can only rent him," I said. But attitudes in the U.S. government toward Noriega were mixed. The Defense Department had a large base and the headquarters of the Southern Command (SouthCom) in Panama, with responsibility for the security of the Panama Canal. The CIA, beyond its own installations, had had Noriega on its payroll for a number of years. The Drug Enforcement Agency (DEA) of the Justice Department had worked with Noriega on drug interdiction and had given him a special commendation for his work in helping them in some major drug busts. The State Department in general and Elliott Abrams in particular regarded Noriega as a menace, powerful and not remotely trustworthy.

I had attended the inauguration on October 11, 1984, of conservative economist Nicolás Barletta as Panama's president, trying as best I could to foster a transfer of power from the armed forces to an elected civilian government. But that was not to be. Barletta resigned under pressure from Noriega on September 27, 1985, and the elected vice president, Eric Arturo Delvalle, with Noriega's blessing, stepped into the unenviable job of trying to govern a nation under the thumb of the military dictator. I had never had even indirect contact with Noriega until November 1986, when, in the midst of the uproar over the emerging Iran-Contra scandal, Elliott Abrams informed me that Noriega had passed word to Lieutenant Colonel Oliver North that he was willing to send Panamanian guerrilla teams inside Nicaragua to destroy power lines in an effort to shut down the country's electrification network. I told Elliott, "Noriega should be told to expect no dealings of any kind with or for us until he cleans up his own act."

Panama Responds to an Indictment

On February 4, 1988, without adequate consultation with the State Department or, as far as I could learn, with the White House, the Department of Justice had indicted Noriega under drug trafficking and racketeering laws. In mid-February the Senate Foreign Relations Committee held hearings, widely publicized in Panama, in which José Blandón, a former adviser to Noriega, accused him of a wide range of crimes.

Anti-Noriega sentiment rose in Panama. A general strike took place, and people filled the streets. Panamanians assumed the United States meant business; they could now dare to express themselves. On February 25, Delvalle fired Noriega as head of the Panama Defense Forces (PDF).

In turn, at 1:00 A.M. the following morning, Noriega convened the National Assembly and, in a twelve-minute session of dubious constitutionality, had Delvalle replaced by Manuel Solís Palma, minister of education, as president of Panama. The United States continued to recognize Delvalle and, at his instruction, impounded in the United States all the funds that would otherwise have flowed to the government of Panama from the operation of the Panama Canal. Delvalle went into hiding. Opposition civic and political groups announced their intention to join with Delvalle in forming a government of national reconciliation.

The mounting crisis in Panama was deepened by the shortage of cash. Noriega ordered all Panamanian banks closed to prevent remaining funds from being withdrawn. The government of Panama was unable to meet its payrolls. This was the moment for the United States to move decisively. Abrams proposed and I supported vigorous actions designed to exploit Panamanian developments.

State's proposals were denounced by Bill Crowe, chairman of the Joint Chiefs, as "harebrained." We could not do anything involving our bases, he declared. That set the tone. Others in the White House, who were down on Abrams, agreed with Crowe. The proposals went nowhere.

My strategy at this point, approved by President Reagan, was to generate as much pressure as possible on Noriega and couple that with a proposal that he seek asylum in a third country. Spain volunteered. We would agree not to extradite Noriega as long as he stayed in Spain. With the indictment still operative, the result would be to hold him in exile there and out of Panama.

An attempted coup failed on March 16, and Noriega's government imposed a "state of urgency" on March 18, in effect suspending constitutional and political guarantees. I sent Mike Kozak and Bill Walker of State's Latin America bureau to meet with Noriega. They obtained a vague commitment from him to step down sometime before the next Panamanian elections, scheduled for May 1989, but Noriega rejected the idea of political asylum in Spain with a guarantee against extradition.

Through internal argument and inaction, our moment had passed: we had missed our chance to convert into decisive pressure on Noriega the dissatisfaction in Panama over the cash squeeze and the isolation caused by Noriega's indictment in the United States on drug-related charges.

Ten days later, in an act of open defiance of American and world opinion,

Noriega sent his armed guards to storm a meeting of the opposition in a Panama City hotel. Scores of people were beaten and arrested. As April began, the Defense Department announced that our forces in the Canal Zone would be augmented to beef up security around our bases. Noriega, however, was not going to give in under such symbolic pressures. If we were to have any hope of removing him from office by negotiation, we had to have something beyond an appeal to the best interests of Panama. Noriega was focused on his own interests.

On April 8, President Reagan raised the ante by invoking the International Emergency Economic Powers Act of 1977 (IEEPA), freezing all assets of the government of Panama in the United States and prohibiting any payments by a U.S. individual or organization to the government of Panama. The cash squeeze tightened.

Pressure and Diplomacy

NSC adviser Colin Powell joined me at the Helsinki airport early Thursday morning, April 21, 1988, and we flew to Moscow together to prepare the way for the Reagan-Gorbachev Moscow summit to begin in late May. In the air we received a message from SouthCom and our embassy in Panama setting out their joint suggestions for a strategy of additional pressure against Noriega. We would draw in—and draw down—the number of nonessential American personnel: this was to create a sense of impending danger in Noriega's mind. We would exploit potential dissension against Noriega within the Panama Defense Forces. We would engage in selected shows of force to heighten further the tension within the Noriega camp. We would also support political action by Delvalle aimed at turning public opinion against Noriega.

On the same short flight, Powell received a message reporting that a three-man U.S. Marine sentry post south of Howard Air Force Base in Panama had come under fire from what was thought to be a force of about thirty intruders: a Panamanian hospital was reporting one Cuban killed and three wounded as a result of the firefight.

Then came a message from Mike Kozak in Panama, where he had met with Noriega. Kozak said that Noriega was preoccupied with the narcotics indictment and that the economic sanctions were working better than we had expected. Noriega said he was looking at legislation that would set a five-year term for the head of the Panama Defense Forces. Under this legislation, he could step down "with dignity" on August 12, 1988. Kozak concluded, "The indictment is our real leverage. It's a great personal affront to him and he's afraid of it."

Colin Powell and I talked this over in the security bubble of our Moscow embassy. "I can't see how we could lift the indictment," I said. "The indictment stands for our commitment to fight drug trafficking. It is also our strongest leverage to see that he keeps any deal that we might strike with him. And we cannot bind future administrations," I argued. Colin agreed entirely. I sent back instructions: stick with the indictment; play with the idea of not seeking extradition; try for something to move Noriega out much earlier than August 12.

The next morning, April 22, in Moscow, I heard a report of four armed attempts to penetrate the perimeter of U.S. positions in Panama. Some participants in the intrusions reportedly were evacuated by a Cuban boat lying offshore Panama City. It sounded as if Noriega and some pals were trying to put the squeeze on us. Mike Armacost, under secretary for political affairs, cabled us with his recommendation that we send Mike Kozak and his deputy, Gerry Clark, a U.S. Army lieutenant colonel, back to see Noriega right away with the following proposal:

- The United States would suspend economic sanctions in order to permit a dialogue among the Panamanians without outside pressure.
- The U.S. arrest warrants for Noriega and others would be withdrawn.
- The Panamanian Assembly would establish a five-year maximum term for PDF commanders.
- Noriega would restore freedom of the press, assembly, and political activity and then take a "long vacation" from his job.
- A government of national reconciliation would be agreed upon by Panamanians.
- Delvalle would remain as president unless he voluntarily chose not to do so.
- The United States would recognize the government and let Panamanian funds flow out of escrow.
- Noriega would leave Panama not later than August 12, 1988, and he would not return to Panama, if ever, before the 1989 elections were held.
- The United States would not try to extradite or "snatch" Noriega while he was out of Panama and would not oppose a motion by Noriega's lawyers for judicial review of the indictment if such a motion were to be made after the 1989 elections.
- The United States would provide reconstruction assistance to the new government of Panama.

Armacost added that Mike Kozak thought this proposal would not be enough for Noriega, who would insist that the indictment be quashed.

The USAF radio operator had a swatch of messages on Panama for me as I flew from Moscow to Kiev on Saturday, April 23. Radio transmitters provided by the United States had arrived in Panama on Thursday, two days earlier, and the Civic Crusade, a collection of groups opposed to Noriega, would be able to start broadcasts against Noriega in about a week. The U.S. Southern Command was preparing a "show of force" for the following Tuesday, a jet fighter flyover of Noriega's headquarters, the *Comandancia.*

But a depressed papal nuncio, the representative of the Vatican in Panama, told our embassy people that Noriega was noticeably more confident than a month ago; many diplomatic missions, he noted, had quietly gone back to business as usual in dealing with the Noriega regime, which, the nuncio said, "is rotten, but still hanging on the vine."

On April 26, 1988. a *Washington Post* editorial gave its assessment: "It seems that everywhere but inside the Reagan administration a consensus has developed that Gen. Noriega has turned to his own political benefit the pressures the United States has applied to Panama. . . . The quick American fix has failed. A slow Latin fix has a better chance."

Nevertheless, after eight weeks of debate within the U.S. government, we finally had induced Noriega to discuss his departure, and we had a plan for moderate pressure. But as Tuesday, April 26, ended, Elliott Abrams came in to report: "After six hours of talks between Kozak and Noriega, Kozak says there is no way Noriega will leave his job with that indictment hanging over his head."

"No dice," I replied.

"Jim Baker is prepared to fold," Abrams said. "He is totally out of sympathy with our approach." The National Security Planning Group also was softening, he said. "They are willing to fold on any deal. They, including Treasury, aren't sticky on the indictment point; we at State are."

The top story the evening of April 26 on ABC's "World News Tonight" with Peter Jennings was that "hostile forces" probed near Howard Air Force Base in Panama; twenty-five unidentified personnel were detected by infrared sensors from the air; Cuban advisers and shipments were said to be involved. On the same day, Noriega's thugs had sacked the headquarters of the Civic Crusade, blocking their planned protests for that day.

At 6:40 P.M., Kozak called in on the tacsat. After six more hours with Noriega, he felt Noriega was serious. "He wants out. The indictment is the key," Kozak said. "He won't leave until it is quashed."

It was a strange conjunction. Noriega was behaving more aggressively with commando probes of U.S. installations. At the same time, he was conducting a canny diplomacy, convincingly serious, but tough on his key concerns. On the U.S. side, we had the interagency group in agreement on an action plan for the first time, but the plan wasn't being carried out. (There was no Tuesday flyover of Noriega's headquarters as had been agreed.) Our problems were not helped by the Panamanian opposition's comments either: Delvalle had just stated that while Noriega must step down, he need not leave Panama.

On April 25—in a backgrounder known to have been given by Treasury Secretary Jim Baker and publicized the next day in the United States and especially Panama—Baker, in effect, informed Noriega that the Treasury Department was weighing a long list of exceptions to the economic sanctions and that "any time you use" economic sanctions, "you end up hurting American business, whether it's Iran or Libya or Nicaragua or Panama." He went on to identify—and rule out—force as our remaining option: "There are other things that you can do, but they all involve putting our military assets into play, and we're not going to do that. The question is what kind of Panama you pick up when it's over. If you put military assets into play, you're likely to pick up a less pro-U.S. Panama."[2]

Noriega Negotiates

Mike Kozak, back in Washington on Friday, April 29, and steaming over public statements from key players that were undermining his efforts, recommended that we quash the indictment and lift the sanctions. Then Noriega would have a law passed limiting his term to five years, commit himself to leave Panama on August 12, and stay away "on a long vacation" until after the 1989 elections.

"No quashing," I said.

"It's like a plea bargain," Kozak responded. "It's the only way to get him out." The Panamanians were keen to find a face-saving formula, Kozak said. "Noriega wants the sanctions lifted; then he will take action. The indictment and economic pressures are our leverage. The indictment really gets to him. He says the guys who testified against him are people he rolled up for us! He says it's political pressure against him, and he wants it off first. He coughed up the August 12 date as the institutional end of the five-year PDF term. He would pass such a law. Would he leave Panama? He said it can't be a condition, but he gave me a plan under which he would be out of Panama."

Kozak went on, "I asked about the 1989 elections. Noriega said no to any imposed conditions. I said, 'What are your plans, then?' He said, 'We Panamanians are not good at planning.' He said he would spend a month getting his affairs in order and then go abroad. 'I guarantee I will stay out of the political process,' he said." Noriega had raised the idea of his becoming Panamanian ambassador to China. Kozak thought he might be serious, remarking, "He is said to be part Chinese." But the fundamental

2. *New York Times*, April 26, 1988, p. A9.

point, Kozak stressed, was the indictment: "Noriega says, 'Unless the indictment is off the books, I don't leave office.' I can see no deal unless we get rid of the indictment," Kozak concluded.

On Wednesday, May 4, Mike Armacost and the interagency team he was working with produced recommendations for a set of additional pressures: further drawdowns of nonessential personnel to create a sense of alarm; a presidential proclamation restricting visas to the United States for Noriega's supporters; U.S. military approaches to the PDF in an effort to wean military units away from Noriega; and nonattributable U.S. support for opposition activities, which would include communications equipment and pamphlets, if legal problems could be overcome. I checked off on all these "stronger" steps, but they were far short of what was needed.

"What about a military show of force?" I asked Armacost.

"Given Jim Baker's backgrounder and the Defense Department's penchant for immediately reassuring our Congress and public—and thereby Noriega—that such exercises would not lead to the actual use of force, they would have no beneficial effect and would be seen only as a provocation," Armacost replied.

On Friday, May 6, I spoke with Howard Baker about Elliott Abrams and our Panama policy. "Elliott Abrams is tolerated by Congress," Howard said, "only because of their respect for you. Abrams doesn't get along with the NSC."

"He used to," I replied. "This Panama policy is not my policy, Howard. I wanted a much more vigorous policy."

"Yes, you did," Howard said, "and I'm sorry that I didn't support you then."

On May 8, the PDF harassed the ambassador's security team at Paitilla Airport, forcing his plane to land at Howard Air Force Base. Government harassment of Canal Company employees suspected of ties to the Civic Crusade raised employee concerns for their personal safety. Such harassment could complicate Canal operations, our embassy reported.

The Indictment in Play

On May 9, President Reagan, who had been kept fully informed of Kozak's discussions, met with Ed Meese and, I was told, decided that he would use the indictment as leverage in bargaining with Noriega. Given President Reagan's earlier reluctance to make such a move, I was surprised. But by this time I had come to share the president's view. This was the decision Kozak had been waiting for.

At 8:30 A.M. on Tuesday, May 10, Kozak came on the tacsat to Abrams: "We have a deal!" Noriega's aides, Kozak said, were drafting documents that would be deposited with the papal nuncio for safekeeping. Noriega wanted a $67 million deposit from Japan to help inject some liquidity into the Panamanian financial system. He claimed that Japan had been on the verge of lending this sum to Panama before the action was stopped in conjunction with the U.S. effort to dry up financial liquidity in Panama. Japan's deposit was needed, Noriega maintained, to help restore that liquidity.

Noriega would make a speech, Kozak said, and then at a press conference say that he would go on vacation. Kozak would see all the documents beforehand, including those relating to restoration of political rights in Panama. Noriega would leave and stay out of Panama from August 12 through the 1989 elections except for two short family visits. The papal nuncio would hold the chronology.

"So," Abrams said, "the question right now is whether we will go to the Japanese." As for the indictment, Abrams continued, an exchange of letters would commit the United States to file documents with the court, as in a plea bargain, and that after August 12, if Noriega retired, we would seek dismissal of the indictment. According to Kozak, "If Noriega is faking, he's fooling his own representatives."

A phone message alerted me that the arrangement for Noriega's departure had leaked and was likely to be in the press tomorrow. I feared that Noriega would use the leak to close out the whole arrangement.

As I was waking up Thursday morning, May 12, CNN was reporting a deal to drop drug charges against Noriega if he left the country. Senator Alfonse D'Amato was quoted as vigorously opposed to dropping charges before Noriega left Panama. The word was that most other senators agreed with him. The Panamanian media were reporting that the United States would lift sanctions if Noriega would step down—no need for him to leave Panama; he could even run for president in 1989, so the story went. Noriega was manipulating the media adroitly.

Kozak reported by tacsat: conditions had been deteriorating since the news of the agreement had been leaked. Nonetheless, he said, Noriega's staff was energetic, and the lawyers were working on the resignation documents. State Department spokesman Chuck Redman thought that Justice Department officials had leaked the deal to try to kill it and were telling reporters that the president gave the go-ahead over Ed Meese's objection.

Kozak had met Noriega on the evening of May 11 and again the following day. They discussed the whole agenda and reached agreement on detailed questions of timing. "All this is very ticklish, but we are still going forward," Kozak said. Noriega and Kozak tentatively agreed that the announcement would be made on Saturday. Lawyers for both sides were working on the last details.

Noriega stepped up actions against the opposition: vigilante squads were active, unexplained detentions mounted, rumors of torture of opposition figures appeared, all of which kept the opposition preoccupied with their own safety and off the streets. Congressional opposition to the leaked agreement mounted, and I heard rumors that a Justice Department prosecutor was going to resign.

Assessing the Deal

I spent Friday morning, May 13, in Brussels briefing our NATO allies about summit preparations. While I was in the air on my way back to Washington, I received a report from Mike Armacost about the current state of the Kozak-Noriega negotiation: Kozak was to see Noriega in a few hours for a final handshake. On "day one" we would lift sanctions and Japan would deposit $67 million in the Panama National Bank—after Noriega announced his resignation and stated that he would withdraw as PDF commander August 12; Noriega would call on the Assembly to limit the PDF commander's term to five years; he would call for a government of national reconciliation; he would call for passage of a law, within three to five days, to grant civil freedoms; the exiles would be allowed to return; amnesties and pardons would facilitate the government of national reconciliation effort; the PDF would participate in the national reconciliation dialogue; the government of national reconciliation would supervise the restoration of the economy and the election; and the PDF would become a professional military organization under civilian control. The United States would welcome these announcements and reaffirm our respect for the Panama Canal Treaty.

Noriega's lawyers, Armacost said, would file a motion to dismiss the indictment for want of prosecution. The United States would join in that motion as of August 12. Noriega would, at a press conference, say he intended to travel. He would leave Panama from September until after the 1989 election. Kozak would sign a document saying the United States would not try to extradite or seize Noriega between "day one" and August 12. All of the above, Armacost reported, would be registered with the papal nuncio as depositor. The Japanese ambassador was to meet Kozak today about the $67 million loan. The agreement would be announced on Saturday at 11:00 A.M. in Washington, at noon in Panama. Attorney General Meese was to go over all these provisions once more with President Reagan at 9:30 A.M. on Friday, Armacost said.

"The deal has eroded," I said. "Noriega won't be out of the country by August 12 under this approach. He will be able to screw up the process of establishing a government of national reconciliation. We should continue to recognize Delvalle as president and back up his decisions. We can't have a period when no one is president. We can't be part of the national reconciliation process. We should be clear that we will take firm action if Noriega betrays the letter or spirit of this arrangement." I sent a flash cable to President Reagan:

> I have just been briefed, here on the aircraft from NATO Brussels to Andrews, on the shape of the arrangement negotiated by Mike Kozak and Noriega and his aides. I greatly admire what Mike Kozak has achieved, under very difficult conditions. He has gotten the most from the relatively weak hand we have had to play. . . .
>
> I believe that certain additional points should be made clear to Noriega in order to firm up both the letter and spirit of this arrangement:
>
> 1. We will not tolerate meddling by Noriega in the GNR [government of national reconciliation] process; he cannot expect to dictate or become a beneficiary of the next government.
> 2. We cannot accept a situation in which Panama has no President (i.e., if Delvalle and Solís both resigned before the GNR process was completed, thus leaving Noriega as the only de facto authority in Panama). So we should continue to recognize Delvalle as the legitimate Head of State until the GNR is ready to operate.
> 3. We should insist that, while the PDF needs to participate in the GNR dialogue, the GNR process and its results must be unmistakably in civilian hands.
> 4. And both we and Noriega should have it clearly in our minds that we will take strong and decisive measures if he goes back on the deal or starts playing games with it.
>
> I want to stress again that I fully support this arrangement which Mike Kozak has brought about. The above points will add muscle to our position while remaining compatible with this negotiated outcome. . . .

The answer came back within an hour: the president wants one more meeting on Panama. The meeting would take place before my arrival, as my plane had been delayed by strong headwinds. The president wanted to know if there were any other points I wanted to make. "Stress to the president that we must be clear and determined that if Noriega does not carry through on, or deviates from, the arrangement, we will take stern action. Noriega should make no mistake about this," I told Armacost.

I arrived at Andrews Air Force Base at 2:30 P.M. and went straight to my office at State. Armacost had returned from seeing the president and was waiting for me. "The meeting was stimulated by Meese," Mike said. "The president was ready to go ahead, but Meese was getting cold feet because of political pressure from D'Amato and law enforcement people in the DEA [Drug Enforcement Administration] and the U.S. Attorney's office. The vice president is nervous about it. The president in the meeting today was strong; he said: 'What's the alternative? Force?' "

"This is when you need a decisive president," I said to Armacost, "and Reagan is."

"Jim Baker is nervous," Armacost continued; "Howard Baker chimed in to say that the deal is salable if it gets Noriega out of the country in return for the indictment. The consensus of the meeting was to have Kozak go back to Noriega to work on the link between the indictment and Noriega's departure from Panama. Elliott conveyed this to Kozak in Panama, and both Kozak and Cooper [the lawyer assigned to the negotiation by Justice] said that it would be impossible, that Noriega wanted a pardon. Cooper feels he can't go back again to Noriega; he may call Meese." Armacost continued: "The Japanese are not yet prepared to deposit the $67 million. They fear it will instantly disappear. It's unresolved." Kozak had reported that he had conveyed a threat of stronger action—as I called for in my cable—to Noriega.

"I screw around with the gringo," Noriega had said to Kozak, "but I'm not stupid."

Pressure on the President

Pressures for the president to stop this negotiation were mounting. Ed Meese and Jim Baker had told the president that going through with the Noriega arrangement would be "as big a problem for him as 'Irangate,' " Colin Powell informed me,

"If the fearful kill this deal because it's not tough enough," I told Powell, "then we have to support tougher measures—like go in and get him. They are too timid to allow tough measures and too timid to allow this moderate deal. We can't stay where we are. If we don't do this, we'll need to agree on stronger measures." I told Colin he should set up a meeting to put the decision to the president again.

We had about an hour and a half to come to a decision if we were to have any hope of keeping to the Saturday, May 14, announcement schedule. "Noriega starts drinking and getting pretty bombed about this time Friday afternoon," Armacost said.

Late in the day word came from the White House: the arrangement was off at least until Monday because of the opposition of Vice President Bush, Jim Baker, and Ed Meese. The president would hold another meeting at which we would focus on what would have to be done if the vice president prevailed and the present arrangement was rejected. I summoned Kozak back to Washington immediately.

Armacost was frustrated. "The alternatives are a military option or turn out the lights down there. Defense would never do the first; the second is just to limp off. Jim Baker now says the deal is okay if we can get Noriega out of Panama on August 12 and then drop the indictment. Kozak says we can't get that. The vice president is strongly against any deal because it's giving in to a drug lord. Bush and Baker want us to build up pressure on Noriega."

"For God's sake," I said, "we have been asking for that for months, and all those guys have denied it to us!"

"We should announce publicly that Kozak and Cooper had been called home," I said. "Kozak should tell Noriega and his representatives that they have pushed this too far and may have lost the deal. Then we should do some things, so that Noriega, who is feeling his oats, gets the message that he has gone too far. We need to set him back a bit," I told Armacost and Abrams. "What has happened is what we predicted: we missed the market. Meese precipitated this with the indictment. We had to talk the Justice Department out of indicting the entire Panama Defense Forces. You can't indict a head of government and not follow through on it. Back then, in February, in the Situation Room, Jim Baker had looked at the president and said, 'Did you sign off on this indictment?' The president said, 'No.' " I thought it was outrageous for a de facto head of another government to be indicted without consultation with the president!

The Plot Thickens

At 7:00 A.M. on Monday, May 16, the telephone rang. I was at home waiting for Shimon Peres to arrive for a breakfast meeting. Mike Armacost was on the line. Noriega's lawyers had urged him to say he would depart on August 12 in return for a U.S. commitment not to seek extradition until after the 1989 elections. Noriega rejected the deal out of hand.

At 9:10 A.M., my breakfast with Peres was interrupted by a call from Vice President Bush. He was dead set against going ahead with an arrangement with Noriega in any of its variations: such a deal sent the wrong message about our opposition to drugs. There was no support for the deal among any group, he said. We should not pursue any such arrangement, he said: we should sit back and analyze the situation for a couple of weeks, then maybe consider a little more military muscle. Delvalle had no support: we backed the wrong horse. And, he felt, the schedule for Noriega's departure—not leaving until September—was wild from a campaign standpoint. The vice president said he wanted it on the record that he called me and took a position against this deal.

I told the vice president I would make sure his view and his call were both registered fully for the record. I agreed that there was a huge momentum now against any such arrangement. "But if not this, then what? If we back away, we leave this guy in charge of a whole country and with all his drug affiliations and Cuban support." I saw only two alternatives:

to use our resources more fully, as I had advocated six to eight weeks ago; or to throw up our hands and leave the Noriega problem to the Latin Americans.

Late that morning, May 16, the president convened a meeting in the Oval Office—a showdown of sorts. Jim Baker argued on behalf of the vice president against any of the possible arrangements to get Noriega out. Ed Meese was against the deal on the table. I gave the reasons for going ahead. Colin Powell agreed with me. President Reagan, too, agreed that we should go ahead: try to negotiate Noriega out even if it means dropping the indictment.

Kozak was to go back, see Noriega, and put the proposal to him again, saying that if Noriega rejected it, or welched on it, the United States would have left only a military option. The president knew a negotiated outcome would be unpopular even if it succeeded, but he was firm.

At 8:10 A.M., Tuesday morning, May 17, Elliott Abrams, having just talked via tacsat with Kozak in Panama, rushed to my office. "The money is the last piece," he said.

"I have never understood why so much money, or any money, is important," I told Elliott. I was against any U.S. effort to try to come up with money as part of this negotiated package. Private financial flows would quickly resume, I knew, once the political conditions stabilized. I stewed about the money question. Any such negotiated deposit, even if it would all benefit the Panamanian people after Noriega was gone, would appear to be a payoff. I called Abrams back to my office. "Any funds we might arrange to deposit or have deposited by someone else in the Panama National Bank would be a bribe, pure and simple, a bribe." If Noriega departed, we did hope to see liquidity return to the Panamanian economy. But just to deposit it would risk turning the money over to Noriega. "Don't let Noriega get his hands on it," I said; "let money flow back in a normal manner."

"They want it for payrolls," Elliott said. "Justines [second in command in the PDF] has stressed this. They would write checks against it. We can prevent Noriega from stealing it."

"Let those who own the money structure their arrangements so they get their money back. Elliott, you are only months away from finding yourself in the private sector. Soon you'll realize that $20 million is a lot of money," I said.

At 11:30 A.M. on Wednesday, May 18, Kozak reported in from Panama. He was very unhappy. "This deal will work," he said. "If we cut it off now, the pressure will be lifted from Noriega," Kozak felt. He said Ambassador Art Davis also felt the effort should continue. At that moment, word came from Colin Powell: the president was still comfortable with the deal and wanted to keep working on the negotiations, but drop the financial part. Vice President Bush had telephoned the president again, Powell said, to argue against the deal. Powell felt that no other plan was available to us because neither Defense nor the CIA would cooperate with stronger action in the future—they never agreed to go after Noriega in the first place.

"So it's back to the deal," I told Powell. "The president wants it that way. But no to any money other than what would flow in normally when sanctions are lifted." (Both Texaco and Citicorp had indicated they would put funds into the Panamanian financial system once this happened.)

I called Colin Powell back at 12:20 P.M. "We are instructing Kozak to say to Noriega that now is the time to decide; that he, Kozak, has been instructed to return to Washington and that he, Kozak, needs an answer. If no answer comes, we will take it as a 'negative.' We want to make sure Noriega knows we are not leaving it open."

"Okay," Colin replied.

At 3:20 in the afternoon, Abrams came in. Kozak had met with Noriega's representatives. They said they wouldn't even go back to Noriega with a deal without money. Kozak was arguing against his instructions: we should figure out how to get the money, or we should delay, he felt.

"It's not liquidity he is after; it's a bundle," I said. "Kozak is to say he wants to see Noriega in person. He should put the proposition to him and, in doing so, say there is no money. The governments we approached refused because they don't believe they would get the money back and don't trust that it would be properly employed. And, frankly, we share their suspicions. Kozak should say, 'There it is; there's the deal; we must have an answer today; I'm being called home. So that's it.' "

At 6:40 P.M., Kozak called in on the tacsat, "They are looking for Noriega so I can meet with him. He's 'touring.' Last night Noriega said *he* would comply with it all if *we* would comply with it all. But he and his people see some nefariousness on our part. I'll try to convince him that economic alternatives exist. He has it loud and clear that political support for this arrangement is zero in the U.S. It's hard to find Noriega. The system doesn't always know where he is. It's not necessarily stalling or bad faith. They go off sometimes down here."

I returned to the department from Capitol Hill and went to the tacsat booth in State's operations center. Mike Armacost, just back from the White House, showed up there, too. In sharp contrast to the situation at the time of the fall of Ferdinand Marcos—when everybody was on board but the president—now nobody but me was on board except the president. We arranged for an aircraft to arrive in Panama at 7:30 A.M. Thursday, May 19, and to leave at 9:30 A.M. with Kozak on it, bound for the United States.

Noriega Agrees

The next morning, Thursday, May 19, just as my car was running into the thickening morning traffic coming down Massachusetts Avenue at 7:00 A.M., I turned to the pile of bulging folders on the seat beside me. The *Washington Post* was on top. The headline read: "Bush Splits With Reagan On Handling of Noriega." The vice president would not, the article said, "bargain with drug dealers." Then I looked at the *New York Times* headline: "Joint Chiefs' Head Skeptical on Noriega Policy." Elaine Sciolino reported, "Admiral Crowe has urged that military force not be used to remove General Noriega, something Mr. Shultz has advocated as a viable option."

When I arrived in my office, Kozak was on the tacsat again: "Noriega says he has kept his word. He accepts what we have negotiated and will comply with it. He needs to talk to the PDF commanders. He can be ready in twenty-four hours. He says that I can come with him to see that he's not stalling. If I want to see him to hear all this directly, okay, he says. The bottom line is that Noriega will commit immediately to the agreement as originally negotiated. So he will announce it tomorrow. Money: Noriega says he understands that we tried. But he says we created the economic problem, and he can't go forward and not have the banks open. He understands our accountability problem. They are urgently seeking a formula that does not involve us in an unaccountable transfer. When civil rights are restored, the banks must open. But the point is that Noriega will commit immediately to the plan as originally negotiated, understanding that the transfer as planned then can't be done. But he has to have some way to have the banks open. He wants to go," Kozak concluded.

Colin Powell called me back within minutes of receiving this report. "The president is on board, the vice president is in a state, and the two of them are debating furiously."

"We have authorized our negotiator," I told Powell. "He put the proposition down. We cleaned it up on the financial front. Noriega has swallowed it. Now, if we take it off the table, that's not the way to negotiate."

Colin replied that the vice president was fighting vehemently against the whole effort.

"The vice president is conducting an election campaign; let the president conduct the presidency," I said. "The guy has blinked. He has accepted the deal. The vice president can't have it both ways. We solve the problem, and he can carry on like D'Amato. Will it help if I march over there?" I asked. "I'm on my way."

The White House meeting was wild. The president and vice president were toe-to-toe, with Attorney General Meese pitching in. Faces were tense. Vice President Bush said law enforcement people would be totally disillusioned with the president's stand on crime and drugs, that the whole

Miami field office would resign, that people in other countries taking strong stands would be undercut, that Americans were on fire about this, that August 12 was a key date in the campaign, that we couldn't argue against negotiating with terrorists if we negotiate with drug dealers. "It's just plain wrong," Bush said. "The president should withdraw from any deal; there is no deal with Noriega that makes sense."

"George, I'll say in public that you opposed it," the president said to Vice President Bush. "If it goes wrong, I'll say I was wrong. The only alternative is to send in troops."

"We could study it, ask the CIA to come up with something," the vice president countered.

"I have urged the whole U.S. government repeatedly to come up with something," I said. "All the resources are with the CIA and Defense, and they won't do anything."

At the end of the meeting, Meese said he had changed his mind: he had been 51 percent for going ahead; now he was against it: "Don't do it," Meese told the president. Howard Baker wanted us to renegotiate the whole deal.

President Reagan held firm. "Go with it," he said, "and all those who oppose can go on the record as opposing it."

Money Trouble

We got Kozak on the tacsat: "The president says go—start the process."

Kozak replied that the dean of the Panama banking community had approached a Colombian-owned bank that would deposit into the Banco Nacional de Panama increments of $10 to $15 million, bank to bank. The Colombian bankers would watch to see that it was used properly. It would be a line of credit. They wanted a telephone call from Elliott Abrams to the bank president saying we didn't object. It would be a form of guarantee that when we recognized the post-Noriega government and we released the frozen funds, we would say you couldn't take the funds for just anything; you had to pay off the Colombian bank loans. We would give this position to the papal nuncio. "Noriega will speak in public twenty-four hours after the documents are deposited with the nuncio," Kozak reported.

I did not like this at all. I sent a tacsat message back to Kozak: we could make a statement that we did not object to any normal financial arrangement they made, but the frozen funds did not belong to the United States. We could not make any undertaking or any statement as to their disposition under a government of national reconciliation.

Kozak was worried. "That could scotch the deal," he said. "The president of the Colombian bank says okay; he wants the secretary to call the Colombian foreign minister. The bankers want some guarantees. All we would have to do is say that we recognize the government of national reconciliation, knowing that funds are earmarked for repaying the loans."

"Noriega gave his intermediaries full authority," Kozak stressed. "He is ready to shake hands as soon as they tell him the agreement is set up in principle. The intermediaries are talking to the Panamanian foreign minister now. It would be helpful if the secretary could add that the U.S. will conduct itself in a way to assure that the Colombian bank remains whole at the end of the day—just a statement of attitude." When all this was reported to me, I replied that I would not say anything about supporting a financial arrangement; it was damned important that we had stopped the first financial arrangement.

At 5:30 P.M., Kozak called in that the Panamanian foreign minister had called Julio Londoño, the Colombian foreign minister, about the bank-to-bank arrangement. Londoño's only concern was whether this would cause hostility toward Colombia from the United States. Would Shultz please call Londoño?

My staff received a call from the *New York Times* asking for comment on the rumor racing around town that "the floors of the White House are awash in blood and that the vice president is furiously trying to get Kozak pulled back and the deal killed." No comment.

I swallowed and telephoned Foreign Minister Londoño at 6:30 P.M.: "I understand the National Bank of Panama is arranging with a Colombian bank for this purpose on an urgent basis and on the basis of it being for use only for government of Panama functions, official functions. It's up to the Colombian bank whether to make this arrangement. If it does, we will not oppose it," I told him.

Londoño replied that the bank was not a state bank of Colombia, so its board of directors would make the decision. "It will be important to the directors to know if there would be any backing or guarantee by the U.S. of a formal or confidential nature to the bank," Londoño said.

"The U.S. is not able to make such a guarantee," I replied. "So you can't offer that to them. They will have to look to the capability of the National Bank of Panama over the long term."

At 7:15 P.M., Vice President Bush telephoned me to ask about the state of play. I told him: "Here is what has taken place. The Panamanians want to have liquidity. They asked us to make arrangements for a deposit. We tried Japan and Taiwan, and they said no. We told the Panamanians that. The Panamanians then went to a Colombian bank headed by 'the dean of the banking circle in Panama' and asked if his bank would make deposits. He said yes—under controlled conditions. He asked if I would call the Colombian foreign minister to say we did not oppose it. I said it's up to the Colombian bank, but the U.S. would not oppose it. They are interested in knowing the status of the money frozen here. It belongs to the duly constituted government of Panama, of which Delvalle is the president. The new government of national reconciliation would come into control of the funds. We have not intervened. We had nothing to do with arranging it. We simply have said we wouldn't oppose it. We are not telling them to do it, and we didn't say we favored it. I was asked if we guaranteed it. I said no."

Vice President Bush said that if there was a Colombian bank involved, that meant drugs—and the CIA knew which banks were drug banks. He was very upset. I assured him that his view was clear and that I was aware of his position from top to bottom.

I got word to Kozak of this call and stressed that there was no U.S. commitment to guarantee any funds the Colombian bank might deposit and there would be no guarantee. Just after midnight, the senior watch officer conveyed a message from Kozak: "I will meet the nuncio at 8:00 A.M. The money issue remains a most important one."

Midmorning on Friday, May 20, I learned from Colin Powell that CIA director Bill Webster had told the president that the Colombian bank in question "is one of the dirtiest," and the vice president was citing this to kill the arrangement. The president had said, "Where is Kozak? Stop him in his tracks and get him back here." Powell said that every political figure around was urging the president to kill the deal.

Within the hour, Kozak reported in by tacsat: "We just met with the nuncio. He is happy to be the custodian and very pleased with the plan. He will help get the opposition to support the plan. He says the U.S. has done a masterful job with what is possible. He has influence, and he is very supportive." He went on: "Londoño telephoned the bank president late last night. The Colombian government fully supports the deposit. The Panamanians are now trying to get the bank directors to see the urgency of the situation. Money is the key point." He stressed, "The arrangement for it has to be in place. If that happens today, we will deposit the legal documents with the nuncio. Noriega will then consult with the PDF within a day or less and the process will flow from there. It's all in place on their side."

Kozak was told that the deal was now on hold in Washington because the Colombian bank was involved in money laundering. He was appalled. "There's no alternative to this. Where will we be when Noriega is still here parading around like a banty rooster? The only other way is military. The word of the U.S. is destroyed this way. We told the Panamanians ten days ago that the president accepts this plan. Noriega says he does, too. We haven't kept our word to the people around Noriega who are trying to move him out. The U.S. has shown an inability to follow a constant line. It's a humiliation," Kozak concluded.

I telephoned Colin Powell at 11:30 A.M. "Kozak met and had a very satisfactory session with the nuncio. All is in place. The nuncio is pleased to play that role and very complimentary of what the U.S. has done. No papers were left. If the green light is given, Kozak will go back and deposit the papers. The Colombian bank has not yet made a decision. The Panamanians won't go ahead without a way to get liquidity, but that's their thing; we are not involved. The Colombian foreign minister called the bank and said the Colombian government supported the deposit and they are now awaiting word. Kozak has been told to stand still until further notice."

Shoot-out in Washington

I arrived at the White House at 1:30 P.M. on May 20. The battle I walked into there raged through most of the afternoon. Vice President Bush raised hell about the bank. Bill Webster repeated that it was the dirtiest bank in Colombia. Howard Baker and Ken Duberstein said we had created a political catastrophe.

"We have to get a decision," I said. "Mr. President, you supported this approach, but I think you now feel it is time to break it off and go on to something else."

"No! George," the president said, "you read me wrong. This is the only way we have." He said he wanted to talk to Kozak directly, to ask him whether he believed Noriega would keep to his bargain.

"Okay, we'll bring him back," I said.

On Saturday, May 21, the *New York Times* headlined: "DEAL FOR NORIEGA TO LEAVE PANAMA REPORTED GAINING; BUSH OPPOSES THE TALKS; VICE PRESIDENT'S SPLIT WITH REAGAN WIDENS."

At 9:00 A.M. on Saturday, May 21, Mike Kozak, Gerry Clark, Elliott Abrams, and Mike Armacost walked into my office. "We meet with the president at 10:30," I told Kozak. "He wants to hear from you. Of all the elected officials in America, the president is the only one who favors what you have been negotiating. You will be attacked by the vice president in this meeting. He will do everything he can to derail you, Mike," I said. "So just relax."

"Noriega," Kozak responded, "doesn't make commitments lightly or answer questions lightly. When he does, I feel he sticks with it. He gave us a date. He had to cough it out. But he has stuck with it. The people around him have clearly worked hard and want this to go forward."

"The Senate voted 83 to 10 that the indictment should not be dropped in order to get Noriega out," Abrams told me. "I asked Chris Dodd why Dole had come out against it so hard. He said, 'Isn't it obvious? Sheer hatred for Bush.' So Bush will have to be more against it than anybody."

As the American presidential election season heated up, Michael Dukakis and Jesse Jackson lashed out at the reported agreement with Noriega. The *New York Times* carried the story that morning. "You tell me how I and people like me can go to those children and their parents today and tell them to say 'no' to drugs when we've got an Administration in Washington that can't say no to Noriega," Michael Dukakis declared at a rally in Sacramento, California, on May 20.

Kozak and I were greeted by a tense and mostly antagonistic group of people as we walked into the Oval Office that Saturday, May 21. The cast of characters included all the key players in this prolonged drama.[3] The meeting was even wilder than the previous showdowns: Kozak was astonished to see this debate raging before him. The president seemed to be waiting for the vice president and his other advisers to say, "Mr. President, we feel your decision is wrong, but we will stand behind you and carry it out." But they didn't say that.

Kozak, at the president's request, reviewed what had happened: acting on presidential instructions, he had reached agreement with Noriega; the Noriega team tried to add to the deal, but we stiff-armed them, and the deal held; now it remained to implement the arrangements. Kozak did a masterful job of describing the negotiations and answering questions about the arrangements. But no one switched sides or came on board to support the president. CIA director Bill Webster, who the previous night had telephoned Armacost to tell him, in a contrite mood, that he had gone too far in denouncing the Colombian bank, now read off to the president a massive array of charges against it. I saw instantly that if even a portion of what he said was true, I would have to extricate myself and the administration from even the noncommittal phone call I had made to Londoño.

The dialogue was intense:

CHIEF OF STAFF [HOWARD] BAKER: This is the worst political situation I can think of. I don't know if the madness of our friends will spill over. I don't know the effect on the trade bill and INF. Sometimes a good idea just won't fly. This is a good idea, I've defended it, but I don't think it will fly. It will flounder and cause us grief.

PRESIDENT REAGAN: But that's based on the fact that no one has told the people of this country the indictment [as long as Noriega is in Panama] isn't worth the paper it's printed on. What of the political fallout when Noriega stays there after all these months of trying to get rid of him, and now we say we can't do anything about it.

CHIEF OF STAFF BAKER: I hope we can do better than that. But now it's best to stop the fire from spreading to other things.

---

3. Present were President Ronald Reagan, Vice President George Bush, and I, as well as Treasury Secretary Jim Baker, Attorney General Ed Meese, Defense Secretary Frank Carlucci, Chief of Staff Howard Baker, NSC adviser Colin Powell, CIA director Bill Webster, Deputy Chief of Staff Ken Duberstein, Deputy to the NSC adviser John Negroponte, Under Secretary Mike Armacost, Assistant Secretary Elliott Abrams, and Mike Kozak.

PRESIDENT REAGAN: Howard, none of you seem to agree with me for a minute. You're just leaving the son-of-a-bitch there to do what he's doing.

ATTORNEY GENERAL MEESE: We can do all the things George [Shultz] suggested before and add all the Station can do and a lot more.

SECRETARY SHULTZ: Our chances now are worse than they were two or three months ago when I suggested those options. Those things you mention, a lot of people in this room think are harebrained, because that was the way they were described. Those levers are not in our hands now: the opposition unity and the street demonstrations and the faith in the U.S. are gone. Under this agreement, Noriega pays a heavy price because he's out of power. It can help us lift our position up in Central America. Once we've indicted him, we have to do something about it.

The argument turned to congressional reactions and the counsel to delay:

MR. DUBERSTEIN: I have not been able to recruit one ally on the Hill in our contacts there. It's really due to the hysteria in the country now on drugs, even if there is no alternative way of dealing with Noriega.

PRESIDENT REAGAN: I still say I think—all you say is true—but who created the hysteria? Those same people on the Hill and in the press. I'm as mad at that U.S. attorney down there right now as I am at Noriega. That indictment doesn't mean a thing [as long as Noriega is not in the jurisdiction of the U.S.]. There is no alternative to this deal except troops. Now what danger is there if you go down and say that we want to put it all on hold due to the summit?

MR. KOZAK: The danger is that we've been trying to keep down the leftist forces and keep Noriega under control. The leftists keep creating provocations, and then he and his guys back them off. I don't know how long they can go on doing this.

CHIEF OF STAFF BAKER: Isn't it better to wait but not tell Noriega why? Making a direct link to INF is bad. But it is a good idea to wait and consult more.

PRESIDENT REAGAN: In eight years as Governor and almost eight years as President now, I've always said I would never make a decision just based on the political ramifications. That's what I'm being asked to do today. If the people know the facts, as Thomas Jefferson always said; but this disgraceful media telling people we are giving in to a drug merchant! It's not giving in to use the indictment to get rid of him.

Meese chimed in:

ATTORNEY GENERAL MEESE: And there are more indictments possible; they are now being worked on.

PRESIDENT REAGAN: And what will we do with them? When we started all of this, we all said our policy is the removal of Noriega, getting him out of Panama—from the very beginning.

ATTORNEY GENERAL MEESE: That's still our goal.

PRESIDENT REAGAN: It doesn't sound like it. We've got a fixed departure here in this agreement.

ATTORNEY GENERAL MEESE: But we would be giving him the same deal that Colombia is not giving the cartel despite the incredible risks they face. We can't be perceived as giving in.

PRESIDENT REAGAN: But this drug dealer is a military leader with total control of the country.

ATTORNEY GENERAL MEESE: There are things we can do. For example, we can go to 100 percent searches of Panamanians coming in, we can tighten up.

PRESIDENT REAGAN: That would just annoy a lot of innocent people.

SECRETARY [JIM] BAKER: And what would Nancy be able to say when she addresses children about drugs?

SECRETARY SHULTZ: She can say we extracted a heavy price from this man: he had to resign from the PDF and leave Panama.

ATTORNEY GENERAL MEESE: But we have left him with all his assets, and he gets no punishment and keeps the money. There is no drug dealer we have ever indicted who wouldn't agree to that deal.

PRESIDENT REAGAN: How can you say that this is no punishment? He is an absolute dictator with life and death power, and he uses it. And now instead he has to get out and become a tourist.

SECRETARY BAKER: I agree with Ed that any indicted drug dealer would accept this deal.

PRESIDENT REAGAN: But we can't do anything about that indictment. It is useless [as long as he's in Panama].

Then came a law enforcement appeal:

ATTORNEY GENERAL MEESE: I can't stress too strongly the law enforcement view. All the law enforcement people I know strongly oppose this. Mr. President, for the first time in twenty years, you'll be doing something which the law enforcement community is strongly opposed to. The impact on our policies will be so severe.

PRESIDENT REAGAN: You've just lowered my respect for people in the law enforcement field. How is it better to leave him in charge?

ATTORNEY GENERAL MEESE: Let me use this simile: we don't give in to the demands of a criminal even if he is holding hostages. So we can't give in to the demands of a dictator even if he holds a country hostage. Even you would not be able to explain this to the American people.

PRESIDENT REAGAN: None of you has shaken me a bit as to the rightness and wrongness of this. But should we go back and put it on hold? Tell him we're not ready with all that's going on here. That puts you [Kozak] in a tough spot. Tell him we're a bunch of jerks who can't make up our minds.

Alternatives were explored:

SECRETARY BAKER: You continue to maintain that he's got to go, and if he acts, we've got a different situation and can react.

PRESIDENT REAGAN: What you guys are settling for is that we have to go in there with considerable loss of life, and how does that look to the rest of Latin America? . . .

SECRETARY SHULTZ: I cannot see us supporting a major invasion force to get a person out of Panama. To send an armada, to risk our kids' lives and theirs. There has got to be something in between war and nothing.

SECRETARY BAKER: You've made some suggestions. We, including I, rained all over them. What's wrong with those ideas?

SECRETARY SHULTZ: They were good ideas then. The Panamanian people were out in the streets then, and the opposition was united. The idea was that we'd get behind them. Now the Panamanian people are disillusioned. They have been put back in the box by Noriega. Now to regenerate all of that is difficult or impossible. Perhaps we do need some covert action. Anyway, we don't assassinate people. So, this deal here is the best thing we can get, I think.

PRESIDENT REAGAN: I do too.

The president restated his firm convictions:

PRESIDENT REAGAN: What if you had this opportunity with Hitler, to get him out before he did all that he did? I hate the way I feel here, being so damn stubborn. But I'll work my ass off to explain this to the public. We thought from the beginning [of this negotiation] that the indictment was trading material. I just can't walk away from this.

CIA DIRECTOR WEBSTER: We've dropped spy indictments in prisoner exchanges.

PRESIDENT REAGAN: He'll be scot free down there, waving his machete around.

At the end, President Reagan would not be budged. He was deeply convinced that what he had negotiated was the only way to try to solve the problem. As the meeting was breaking up, Ed Meese said, "Mr. President, as recently as a month ago, we worked with Noriega to confiscate drugs going through the Canal."

"Ed Meese! You worked with Noriega? I'm shocked," I said.

Back to the Money

When I returned to the State Department, I instructed Ambassador Tony Gillespie in Bogotá to get to Londoño right away with a message from me: "The U.S. has considerable evidence about the involvement of the Colombian bank with drug money. Under these circumstances, I must withdraw my statement that 'it is up to the Colombian bank whether to make this arrangement, but it if does so, we would not oppose it.' "

On late Sunday morning, May 22, when I returned to my house after appearing on "This Week with David Brinkley," I found Kozak waiting for me.

"We've got a big problem," he said. "Your message to the Colombians withdrawing your statement of 'no objection' came exactly at the time when Colombia and Panama were about to agree on providing for post-Noriega liquidity. Your message came across as the U.S. not wanting Colombia involved because they are all drug dealers. [President of Colombia] Barco went ballistic. Your withdrawal drove him crazy."

"Look," I said, "the fact is that if this agreement for Noriega's departure is reached and a new political process starts and we lift economic sanctions, the liquidity problem will resolve itself. Funds will start to flow. The financial aspect is not the key."

The President Decides Once Again

On Sunday, May 22, I telephoned the White House to say I wanted to meet with the president. The same group as before convened at 8:00 P.M. in the living quarters of the White House. The mood was even worse at this Sunday night session than it had been on Saturday. Vice President Bush and Treasury Secretary Jim Baker were adamant and cutting in their opposition to the president. Once again, Ronald Reagan was troubled but unshaken by their arguments. I reported that I had retracted my statement to Londoño.

Colin Powell quietly supported going ahead. Ken Duberstein said we had not one supporter in Congress. All the others reiterated the political stupidity of the negotiations. Every argument was reviewed over and over. Finally, Howard Baker said, "Mr. President, you've decided this five times." In the end and all the way through the evening, the president was firm: Kozak was to get back to Panama right away. On the money question, I could say we were not opposed to an arrangement Panama might make; we could urge U.S. companies to be helpful, but we must not solicit funds for liquidity. Kozak left on a U.S. Air Force plane for Panama at midnight.

Kozak met with Noriega's representatives at midday and reported the outcome in a tacsat call: "The hangup is money. They say the Colombian government had committed itself to provide $70 million and then backed away, offended by the Shultz message which they took as a slander against the government of Colombia." Kozak said he had made all the arguments about how money would just flow in normally once Noriega was gone and the sanctions had been lifted, but the Panamanians weren't buying it.

On Tuesday morning, May 24, Kozak called on the tacsat: "Noriega's representatives are willing to go forward tomorrow if the U.S. will give general assurance to the effect that if normal market forces do not restore the liquidity of the Banco Nacional, the U.S. will take steps X, Y, and Z. I said no," Kozak reported. "I'll ask to see Noriega at midday and say, when the president and the secretary fly off to the summit tomorrow, it's over."

At midafternoon, Kozak had turned optimistic. "It seems positive. Noriega has gone around briefing staff and the relevant leaders. I think they'll play it out to the eleventh hour," Kozak said. "They are postured to go with a speech tonight or tomorrow without the money or to say it's all fallen apart because we welched on the deal to provide money. I can't tell which way it will go. I've asked to hear it from Noriega directly."

At 5:15, Kozak reported again: "It's in its final throes. We are getting somewhere. Noriega and Solís are fine-tuning how it will go. They got a commitment from Texaco. Noriega wants a statement made in the White House that will cover four points. Here's the text he wants:

> In order to further restoration of civilian democratic rule in Panama and to stimulate the economic recovery and financial liquidity which is essential to that process, the President has directed the following:
>
> 1. That the economic measures pursuant to IEEPA[4] be suspended immediately;
> 2. That the U.S. will interpose no objection to financial flows to Panama from third countries, and that U.S. firms be encouraged to restore normal business operations in Panama;
> 3. That the additional U.S. military forces deployed to Panama in light of the crisis be withdrawn as soon as possible;
> 4. That certain arrangements be implemented which will result in the dismissal of the indictments against General Noriega.

"If it's a go," Kozak said, "I'll go over for a handshake and we'll deposit the documents."

I reacted negatively to the last three points and to the idea of a White House statement putting these ideas together and making a commitment

4. International Emergency Economic Powers Act (IEEPA) invoked by President Reagan on April 8, 1988.

about the disposition of our military forces. Kozak was dismayed. He felt Noriega's request was reasonable and that the United States had planned to say these things all along. My rejection of these points, Kozak felt, meant that his credibility was shot; he no longer could negotiate in Panama.

The four points covered matters we would be willing to consider as time went on, or, on the last point, deposit our agreement as agreed with the nuncio. But Noriega had overplayed his hand. I wanted him to realize that. "Let's pack for Moscow," I said.

Noriega Accepts Again

Shortly after 8:00 P.M., Tuesday, May 24, I got a message from Kozak: "We have a deal." When confronted with the fact that Kozak was being pulled back and everything would be taken off the table, the Panamanians "caved." I informed my staff that I would not be traveling on *Air Force One* with the president; I would stay back for one day. I could catch up with the president in Helsinki.

I got a conference call set up so I could outline the situation to President Reagan, Vice President Bush, Howard Baker, and Colin Powell. Vice President Bush asked whether Delvalle would support the deal. I said I couldn't guarantee that he would. The president said, "Go ahead."

At 2:00 A.M. Wednesday morning, there had been no handshake and no trip to the nuncio. The Panamanians were requiring a statement again— something that mentioned withdrawal of U.S. forces. We said no. Nonetheless, the process seemed to be going forward. Armacost was in charge of pulling it all together: talking to opposition figures, nailing down arrangements for restoration of civil liberties, the return of exiles, the release of political prisoners.

At 7:05 A.M., Kozak was on the tacsat: "Noriega will speak at 8:00 A.M. It's all in line. But Noriega went to bed leaving orders not to be awakened until 6:00 A.M., which is now. So I'm waiting for a call to have the handshake. It still seems to be a go."

At 8:30 A.M., I called Colin Powell to tell him, "Noriega is going over the details; Kozak is standing by." We discussed what the president would say. The White House idea was for the president to be videotaped in his cabin aboard *Air Force One* en route to Helsinki making his statement about Panama; the plane would then land somewhere and drop the tape off.

"The president," Colin said, "is convinced he is right on this one and wants to go for it."

At 9:35 A.M., Kozak called on the tacsat. The Panamanians he had been dealing with had disappeared, he reported. The Panamanian press was reporting that some Panama Defense Forces officers—"bad apples"—were insisting that Noriega remain in power, apparently fearing for their own skins should their boss depart. "Noriega's followers see themselves as dead meat once he's out. So they are fighting hard against it now," Kozak said.

At 10:30 A.M., Kozak called: "Justines is at the *Comandancia* [Noriega's headquarters]. There's a confab with the majors who are trying to stop Noriega."

Chuck Redman came in. "The press is aware that you stayed behind. The networks are getting ready to go live with the story."

At 1:00 P.M., Kozak called again: "There is a storm going on in the military here!" And at 3:50 P.M., Kozak came up on the tacsat again. He had been at Noriega's residence for two and a half hours. "Noriega said that junior officers threatened a coup when presented with this. So he couldn't do it now. So I [Kozak] said, 'That's it. The whole deal is off the table.' Noriega said the junior officers accused him of selling out the PDF to the opposition. Noriega said he had not had time to work on his people; he had been dodging them. He'd had no time to prepare them for this. 'The junior officers just don't understand it. I can prepare them,' he said. 'It will take two weeks.' "

That was it. It was over. We had been at this effort for four months.

I called the president aboard *Air Force One*: "Mr. President, Kozak had a lengthy meeting with Noriega. It's apparent that Noriega saw clearly that our proposal and our negotiation would get him out of power and out of Panama, and they [Noriega and his fellow PDF officers] could not bring themselves to agree to it. I will make a tough statement and answer questions and then join you in Helsinki."

Kozak was back on the tacsat offering his resignation as I went to the pressroom to say that negotiations were over and all offers were off the table, that at the final moment, Noriega would not carry through with the arrangements his representatives had negotiated.

The inconclusive outcome of these negotiations was welcomed on Capitol Hill. Republican Senator D'Amato called the proposed agreement "nothing more than surrender on our part." Democratic House Majority Leader Tom Foley said, "All in all, ironically, he saved the administration from some very bitter criticism." And Senator Bob Dole, Republican leader in the Senate, commented, "Noriega must go if we are to achieve our goals in Panama. But sending him to retirement with a legal golden parachute would have been the wrong step at the wrong time."

My plane was wheels up from Andrews at 6:30 P.M. I was concerned about Kozak, who had, as a career man, been way out in front on this negotiation. He was carrying out instructions from his president, but those instructions had been vigorously opposed by the probable next president. Two letters were cabled to him.

Dear Mike:

As you emerge from this arduous, sensitive and significant negotiation, I want to tell you what a superb job you have done for the President and for our country. The outcome today should convince the critics of the integrity of our approach and the essentiality of achieving our goal. You come home with pride in your work and with the gratitude of all your friends and colleagues.

Sincerely,
George P. Shultz

Dear Mike:

Last Saturday in the Oval Office when you reported on your negotiations in Panama, I was more convinced than ever that we were doing the right thing. What has come through even more since then has been the personal courage you have shown. With no security and no communications, you went without hesitation right into the lion's den. As George Shultz said, you were "playing in a rough league." You did a fine job. Welcome home. We're proud of you.

Sincerely,
Ronald Reagan

As my plane headed across the Atlantic on the way to join the president in Helsinki and Moscow, I thought about this inconclusive negotiation and about Ronald Reagan's performance. I thought the outcome could well have been different if President Reagan had been supported in his decisions and if the execution of his decisions had been firm and accelerated. No one can know for sure.[5]

Ronald Reagan had gone through a tense fight with his closest advisers and political associates. He was virtually isolated. He was also impressively sensible, clear in his mind, and decisive. He stood his ground when almost everyone opposed him, even threatened him by suggesting a parallel to the Iran-Contra affair. He saw the immediate political difficulties, but he refused to make a decision based on the politics involved. He was ready to fight flat out to convince the American people to support him in what he regarded as the right course for the United States. He was, I thought, genuinely presidential. I admired and respected his strength under fire.

5. But one conclusion is for sure: a negotiated outcome, with all its downsides, would have saved many lives, American and Panamanian, and much suffering and economic disruption in Panama.

CHAPTER 49

The Last of the Superpower Summits: Making the Most of It

Ronald Reagan, as we started in on 1988, was looking less and less like a lame duck. In fact, he was flying high. The Moscow summit to be held in late May would be an important moment in superpower relations: the challenge was to use that moment to achieve important results, before, during, and after the main event. The possibility of fundamental change was real. My task was to help turn possibility into reality.

I had in my mind a set of domestic and diplomatic objectives as I settled in for a final year of work on the Soviet relationship with President Reagan and our new team: persuade the Senate to give its advice and consent to the ratification of the INF Treaty; make progress on START, with the object of having a treaty ready for signature by the time of the summit (I knew that decisive action by the Soviets on the Krasnoyarsk radar station would be an important ingredient for success); get the process of Soviet withdrawal from Afghanistan under way; build on this achievement to move forward on independence for Namibia in the tangled situation in Southern Africa; and continue efforts on human rights so that positive changes in Soviet behavior would warrant our agreement to a human rights conference in Moscow as part of the conclusion of the ongoing CSCE meeting in Vienna, opening the way to promising negotiations on reductions in conventional arms in Europe.

I felt we had a genuine chance to attain all these objectives. One of the reasons for my optimism was the new team. Frank Carlucci, Colin Powell, and I had really clicked at the Washington summit. We had confidence and trust in each other. We tossed the ball around and used our comparative advantages effectively. President Reagan could see this for himself and gave us his full support. He was pleased. We all worked easily with Chief of Staff Howard Baker and his deputy, Ken Duberstein. I made a suggestion to Frank Carlucci and Colin Powell that we meet every morning we were all in town at 7:00 A.M. in Powell's White House office: no agenda, no staff, no substitutes, no output other than the most important—better understanding among the three of us of our respective problems and agreement about who would handle what and how. Our staffs were uneasy at first, but gradually they got the message: the bosses were working together closely, so maybe they should, too.

I had been reading Gorbachev's book *Perestroika*, published in 1987. The writing sounded like him. The vision was that of a pragmatist, still imprisoned by an ideology but looking for changes that would work. Success, I thought, would depend on his willingness to abandon, not just modify, a failing system.

The Battle over Ratification

Our problem with INF ratification would not be with Gorbachev and the Soviets. Shevardnadze, in a casual but puzzled way, had asked me during his October 30, 1987, visit to Washington, "Do you think the INF Treaty will be ratified by the Senate?"

"We have the votes," I replied, "but there is articulate opposition from several quarters, so we will have a contentious process but a clear outcome."

Shevardnadze persisted, "The two nuclear testing and SALT II treaties have never even come to a vote; there must be resistance to any treaty with us." The Soviets, he said, had made major concessions, questioned by many in their own military, to get an INF agreement. "We paid the political price of those concessions. We hope those concessions are not wasted."

I could see what was on his mind. "This treaty is far more solid than SALT II," I said, "and Ronald Reagan is far stronger than Jimmy Carter. He'll get INF through the Senate." I sounded confident and I was, but I also realized that the INF's road through the Senate would be rough.

Opposition came from many sources. One was fear that the INF Treaty would lead to a denuclearized Europe, leaving the West vulnerable to superior Soviet conventional forces. Richard Nixon, Henry Kissinger, and Brent Scowcroft made this fear, which I regarded as unjustified, respectable. On this conceptual base, the treaty was attacked by the tactic of adding to it "killer amendments"—requirements that had to be met *before* the treaty could go into effect, such as the Soviet withdrawal from Afghanistan or the equalization of conventional strength between NATO and the Warsaw Pact countries. Those objectives were desirable and even attainable, but they were moving on totally separate tracks. Confusion and complication would result from such linkage, which would in all likelihood be rejected by the Soviets. For some opponents, that was the aim: to kill the treaty and to use the divisive process as a way to combat the closer ties clearly developing between the United States and the Soviet Union.

An added complication that proved difficult to handle arose from the debate over the administration's effort to broaden the interpretation of the ABM Treaty. What put the fat decisively in the fire was the threatened assertion from the White House that the president could simply declare a change from the interpretation presented to the Senate in the ratification hearings. Senator Sam Nunn, chairman of the Senate Armed Services Committee, led the charge, declaring such an action would be an infringement of the Senate's constitutional prerogative. What was the Senate ratifying? he asked: if the Senate could not rely on the presentation of the administration, it must examine the negotiating record for itself. So we had a solid treaty, very much in the U.S. interest, popular in the United States, Western Europe, Japan, and around the world. But we also had our problems.

We organized to take on these problems, fielding a first team dedicated to the ratification task. Mike Glitman, the chief INF negotiator, was given an office on the Hill and spent all his time there, ready on a moment's notice to answer questions from any senator or senate staffer. Key people—Max Kampelman, Paul Nitze, and Ed Rowny—testified and met regularly with senators. I led off with a detailed presentation, complete enough to become a kind of bible on the subject.

I responded to the objections of Nixon and Kissinger in *Time* and subsequently in the *New York Times*.[1] To the central charge that we would not have sufficient nuclear capability left to implement the NATO doctrine of flexible response, I countered in *Time*:

> Even after an INF agreement, NATO would retain a robust deterrent. More than 4,000 U.S. nuclear weapons would still be in Europe, on aircraft that could retaliate deep into the Soviet Union and on remaining missiles and nuclear artillery. NATO is planning or undertaking modernization of several of these systems. Also, several hundred submarine-launched ballistic-missile warheads would remain available to the Supreme NATO Commander. Thus, even after eliminating LRINF [long-range INF] missiles, we could continue to discourage a Soviet attack without relying exclusively on strategic systems.

Again and again, I articulated our arguments in support of the treaty. My opening statement to the Senate Foreign Relations Committee on January 25, 1988, gave a history of the negotiation and a demonstration that we had achieved by 1987 what President Reagan had set out as our objectives in 1981 and which Congress had endorsed in 1981. "And both the Senate and House voted for that [the elimination of INF missiles]," I said. "The Senate voted unanimously. And I might say that every member of this committee who was in office in November 1981 voted for that resolution. So, the outcome you voted for and endorsed in November 1981 is

1. *Time*, May 18, 1987, and the *New York Times*, December 13,1987.

the outcome that is in this treaty." And I commented on the relationship of strength to the ability to succeed in negotiations with the Soviets: "As we and our allies move forward, we must draw the right lessons from INF. We succeeded in getting a good treaty because we persisted in our approach. If we and our allies had not gone forward with deployments or if we had not had the courage of our convictions at the bargaining table, none of this could have been achieved."

Arguments were one thing, but the politics of Senate constitutional prerogatives in passing on treaties was something else. We made available to the Senate the complete and voluminous INF negotiating record. I said in a letter to Senator Byrd, "This is the most complete body of material ever presented to the Senate for the purpose of assisting it in the vital role of providing its advice and consent." Max Kampelman and I worked out a formula with Senators Byrd and Nunn to meet their concerns about senatorial prerogatives, but suspicious supporters of a broad interpretation of the ABM Treaty blocked that formula, fearing that our language could be turned against them in the ABM battle.

The hearings before the Senate Foreign Relations Committee had started with my testimony on January 25, 1988, but that same day, Senator Nunn said that the Senate Armed Services Committee would refuse to take testimony until I confirmed that administration testimony was "authoritative" and that the president could not reinterpret the INF Treaty without consent of the Senate.

The dispute was finally defused with an authorized statement by me: "All INF testimony of Executive Branch witnesses, within their authorized scope, is authoritative. We will inform the relevant Committee of any instance in which a witness's testimony is not authoritative in any respect," and "I can assure you that the Reagan Administration will not depart from the INF Treaty as we are presenting it to the Senate." Those seemingly innocuous sentences relieved an immense amount of tension over the constitutional issues involved in treaty interpretation.

Meanwhile, a group of key senators went on a European tour, in effect, to take testimony from European leaders, who, according to Henry Kissinger, did not support the treaty. What the senators found was enthusiastic support for the treaty and a conviction that failure to ratify would be considered a devastating blow in Europe.

Returning for a second round of testimony before the Senate Foreign Relations Committee on March 14, I got into a heated exchange with Senator Jesse Helms, who led off by accusing the administration of "confusion, misstatements and . . . even misrepresentation" in our testimony.

"Are you accusing me of sitting here deliberately misrepresenting facts?" I snapped.

"No, sir, no sir," Helms responded.

"That is what I thought you said." I told him.

"I did not say deliberate," Helms said.

"I do not know what I am doing here if the committee thinks I am misrepresenting things," I said with bristling indignation.

"You'll have to decide why you're here," Helms replied.

The Democrats weighed in on my side. "He is here because we invited him," said Senator Pell, the chairman. Other Democrats (Alan Cranston and Brock Adams) praised administration testimony and called it candid and thorough. Which is the president's party? I thought to myself.

Finally, on March 30, the Foreign Relations Committee voted 17 to 2 to report the INF Treaty favorably to the full Senate. The Armed Services Committee had further questions. A dispute arose over the application of the INF Treaty to "futuristic" weapons, such as lasers, particle beams, and microwaves, which might operate over the ranges covered by the treaty. We said those weapons were covered. The Soviets confirmed their agreement with our statement. In the end we were, in effect, required by the Senate to gain Soviet written agreement with our statement, especially after Cap Weinberger and Ken Adelman, both of whom were by then out of the administration, wrote letters to Senator Dan Quayle saying they felt the subject of futuristic weapons was not addressed.

Senator Quayle came at me repeatedly with complaints about this issue. Finally, I said to him, "Dan, you have to shut down! We can't have the president's achievement wrecked by Republicans!" And the real opposition was all from the GOP side. I told the president that on April 15. He agreed and could only shake his head in dismay.

By May 10, three weeks before Ronald Reagan was due in Moscow for the summit, with ratification of the INF Treaty expected to be the centerpiece, another dispute erupted. This time the problem arose in technical talks being led by Defense Department officials over the implementation of verification measures. A senior White House official, unnamed, was quoted in the *New York Times* on May 11—"It's been bungled bad"— and put the blame on me for being preoccupied with other concerns in the Middle East and Panama.

I met with Shevardnadze in Geneva on May 11 and 12 with a complete range of arms-control advisers. The U.S. opponents had looked for details they could use to derail and delay a vote on the treaty, hoping by this process to stop this step of critical importance in U.S. and allied relations with the Soviets. The Soviets were bewildered, and to a degree, so was I. But with hard work and long hours, we got the job done. All the technical issues, really issues normally faced in the implementation of an agreement, were wrestled to the ground—finally. Shevardnadze and I witnessed the formal signing of an agreement on futuristic weapons. I felt that surely, by this time, the Senate had had its pound of flesh.

On the evening of May 23, I went with several colleagues to see a new play, *A Walk in the Woods*. I had been in office long enough, I mused, to be witnessing a cultural production depicting an event from the early days of my own tenure. The drama portrayed the Soviet negotiator, Yuli Kvitsinsky, as flexible and the American, Paul Nitze, as hidebound and troublesome: a portrait totally at odds with the reality.

That afternoon, I had gone to Capitol Hill twice to meet with groups of senators to urge them to vote on INF in time for the Moscow summit. We were due to leave on May 25, with a stopover in Helsinki before going on to Moscow. Opponents of the treaty, Republicans, argued that this was an artificial deadline and seemed unconcerned at the prospect of sending the president to Moscow in a posture of weakness in his own country.

On May 25, Senator Robert Byrd, Democratic majority leader, said, "I think the president's hand would be strengthened and that it would be in the interests of the country to have the instruments of ratification in his hands." But Senator Helms, ranking Republican on the Foreign Relations Committee, fought back, saying the president had been "misled and misguided" in signing the treaty.

Finally, the dam broke. On Friday, May 27, the Senate voted to give its "advice and consent" to ratification of the INF Treaty. The margin was 93 to 5. The nays were from four Republicans and one Democrat.

But the naysayers' real pint of blood was taken from the efforts to conclude a START Treaty. Strategic arms were much more complex, had a much greater bearing on our strategic defense posture, and presented far more difficult issues of verification than did INF. I drove hard in early 1988, with full support from President Reagan, to convert our agreements on the main elements of START into a completed treaty. We made headway on outstanding problems and developed a joint text with bracketed items to show areas of disagreement. The demonstration of the immense difficulty we had encountered over INF ratification gradually took the edge off the push on START. The Soviets could not help but wonder whether their concessions to gain our agreement to a treaty would be negated by the subsequent ratification process. And our team realized the immense burden of proof they would necessarily carry into a START ratification process that was certain to be brutal.

By the end of February, President Reagan had said in an interview, probably "the time is too limited" to complete a START Treaty in time for the Moscow summit, although it could be completed perhaps before he left office.

On March 1, I had drafted a message for President Reagan to send to Gorbachev: "I want you to understand fully that I hope we will be able to complete a treaty that serves both our interests by the time we meet in Moscow. . . . I have told our negotiators to press forward with great energy, not to get a fast treaty but to get a good one. Assuming we can resolve the very real and tough problems involved, including those of verification, we intend to 'go for it.' "

The air did not completely go out of the START balloon; I just couldn't keep pumping the necessary air into it. I was deeply convinced then that a treaty reducing strategic arms and putting in place an extensive verification infrastructure in the Soviet Union would have been enormously in our interests.

In light of the subsequent dissolution of the Soviet Union and the attendant concerns about the location and control of strategic and other nuclear weapons, I am even more convinced of the wisdom of Ronald Reagan's objectives. How much safer we would all have been if those arsenals had been declining in magnitude in a manner where we could have seen firsthand just what was taking place. The verification infrastructure that would have been put in place by a START Treaty also could have made far more surefooted any further moves by reciprocal unilateral steps. Ronald Reagan's critics—primarily on the conservative and Republican side of politics but also including large segments of the arms control community—did not serve us well.

Afghanistan:
The End of the Brezhnev Doctrine

Ever since Shevardnadze had told me privately in September 1987 that the Soviets would leave Afghanistan soon, I had been convinced that this would occur. Such a departure would be the first-ever retreat by Soviet forces from a territory or country they dominated. That would mark a clear break with the Brezhnev Doctrine, initially demonstrated at the time of the Soviet invasion of Czechoslovakia in 1968. Its meaning was simple and chilling: once a country was in the so-called socialist camp, it was not allowed to leave. The Soviets said to the rest of the world: "What's mine is mine; what's yours is up for grabs."[2]

The Reagan Doctrine presented a direct challenge to this Soviet posture. We supported resistance groups, freedom fighters, in several countries dominated directly or indirectly by the Soviets: Afghanistan, Angola, Cambodia, and Nicaragua. And we supported the pursuit of freedom across the globe, with increasing impact in the Warsaw Pact countries and even in the Soviet Union itself. If the Soviets left Afghanistan, the Brezhnev Doctrine would be breached, and the principle of "never letting go" would be violated. The stakes were high.

2. This was the characterization of the Brezhnev Doctrine I had used in a speech to the Commonwealth Club in San Francisco on February 22, 1985.

There was no doubt why the Soviets wanted to leave: the war was bloody, and the resistance by the Afghan mujaheddin was fierce. In March 1985, with Bill Casey pushing hard and with me in full agreement, the president had stepped up sharply our level of assistance to the mujaheddin. And President Reagan's decision in April 1986 to provide the Afghan resistance U.S. ground-to-air Stinger missiles sharply reduced the Soviets' ability to fly helicopters and low-level aircraft against guerrilla targets. The tide of the conflict shifted.

Before and during the Washington summit, I had worked hard at nailing down the terms of a Soviet withdrawal. The United Nations had provided a forum for a diplomatic track on this issue for years. Pakistan had felt a domestic political need for such a process, and we were content to take part, along with the Soviets, as a potential "guarantor" of any agreement that might be reached. In December 1985, our negotiators in Geneva had taken the position that upon Soviet withdrawal from Afghanistan, our support for the mujaheddin, having served its purpose, would cease.

As the possibility of Soviet withdrawal became increasingly real, and as the Soviets made clear their intention to continue supplying arms and other support to their allies in Kabul, this position seemed to me incomplete and unwise, to say the least. We had to have the same rights as the Soviets. If they could supply their puppet regime, we must be able to supply the Afghan freedom fighters. The Soviets, of course, tried to lock us in to an unbalanced outcome. On Wednesday, January 6, 1988, Shevardnadze told the Afghan press agency that the United States agreed to cut off aid to the rebels as part of a withdrawal agreement. That was incorrect and spelled trouble and misunderstanding on an important ingredient in the unfolding Afghan drama. President Reagan had made exactly the opposite assertion just before the Washington summit. I hit the ball back in a press conference in Washington on January 7, setting out the U.S. position.

I insisted on reciprocity: we would stop the flow of arms if the Soviets did the same; if the Soviets continued military supplies to the Najibullah regime, we would do likewise for the mujaheddin. We would not abandon our friends to superior firepower. The Soviets regarded this, not surprisingly, as a shift in our position. Shevardnadze said to me at our meeting in mid-March, "Your delegation in Geneva took a position when you weren't paying much attention. Now you see an agreement might be reached, and you are now involved. You've changed the U.S. position." We had sharpened our position, but only in the light of Soviet insistence on continuing their own supply operations.

Mike Armacost, who managed our dialogue with the Soviets on regional issues, had, like me, become convinced that the Soviets would leave. The CIA thought otherwise: the Soviet talk was political deception; we were foolish to take them seriously. Armacost told me he bet Bob Gates twenty-five dollars and Fritz Ermarth, the agency's national intelligence officer on the Soviet Union, fifty dollars. I started checking out views of what would happen when the Soviets left. On January 15, I telephoned Gates. Two years earlier the CIA had put out an estimate that any Soviet troop withdrawal that was not stretched out over at least a year and a half would result in the collapse of the Najibullah regime. "Is that still your view?" I asked.

Yes, even more so, was Gates's reply: the Kabul regime would unravel and fall if the Soviets withdrew. The CIA was our principal intelligence source, since they, through our supply operation, were in close and constant contact with the mujaheddin. The view from the CIA was clear and unequivocal: the Najibullah regime would disintegrate, perhaps even with the announcement of Soviet departure. I hoped they were right, and their view seemed to make sense intuitively: the regime was identified with a foreign force and had conspired in an effort to repress the people of Afghanistan. Uncounted multitudes were dead or wounded, and millions were in refugee camps in Pakistan and Iran.

Foreign service officer Jon Glassman, posted in Kabul, had a different view. He was in charge of the embassy that I had insisted be kept open as an observation post despite widespread pressure to close it down for security or symbolic reasons. "Once the Soviets have withdrawn," Glassman reported, "and so long as Islam is not threatened, many Afghans in the countryside will be anxious to put away their guns and simply ignore the Kabul regime—as they traditionally have done." He continued: "Similarly, the Kabul population, notably business interests, many of whom fear a fundamentalist Islamic regime's ascension and who have for the most part lived comfortably and profitably for years, would probably be willing to accept a continuation of the regime." I doubted Glassman was right about the willingness of the mujaheddin to put down their guns, but he might well be on the mark in assessing the willingness of many war-weary Afghans to accept Najibullah's continued rule. Glassman's analysis strengthened my own conviction. We must have an insurance policy in case the CIA assessment proved wrong. I did not want to achieve the departure of Soviet troops at the cost of cutting off the very people who had fought the invaders and who still would seek freedom from the Soviets' puppet regime. Maintaining the right to continue to supply the Afghan freedom fighters grew more important in my eyes. They had to have the ability to keep pressure on the Kabul regime.

On February 8, 1988, Gorbachev had announced to the Soviet people that Soviet forces would start withdrawing from Afghanistan by May 15 and would complete their withdrawal in ten months. We heard from President Zia of Pakistan on February 11. A visit from Soviet Deputy Foreign Minister Yuli Vorontsov, President Zia wrote, "has left us with no doubt that the

Soviet Union is sincere about their withdrawal." In this letter, President Zia reversed a position with which we had agreed and had persuaded the Soviets to accept. Earlier the Soviets had asked for our help in establishing an interim transition regime comprising some sort of coalition that would include Najibullah and the resistance forces. In agreement with Zia that such a regime would inevitably lend an element of legitimacy to Najibullah, we declined and persuaded the Soviets that their approach was not workable. Now Zia wanted us to take up this "rejected possibility" with the Soviets. It was needed, he argued, to ensure stability for the return of refugees "with dignity and honor" and to keep him from having to sign an agreement in Geneva with the hated Najibullah regime. After consulting with President Reagan, I sent word to Zia that our top priority must be to get the Soviets out of Afghanistan as soon as possible, but that if he did not want to sign an agreement with Najibullah, then we would "respect and support that judgment."

When I met with Gorbachev in Moscow on February 22, he told me that we had asked him to declare an intent to withdraw and "to set a date. That has been done." He asked that we work urgently to complete the Geneva accords. He criticized "some who are impudent enough to say the Soviet Union is announcing withdrawal for propaganda purposes."

"Not the American side," I responded. "We take what you say at face value. In my case, Shevardnadze told me this privately, earlier."

At this juncture, I reluctantly took up Pakistan's desire to see a transition Afghan government established. Gorbachev blasted the idea: "You said earlier that a coalition government could not be created with bayonets; we agreed." He went on, "The Soviet Union cannot dance the polka with these parties." I dropped the subject.

The key sticking point was our insistence on reciprocal arrangements: whatever the Soviets could do, the United States must also be able to do. Shevardnadze and I went over this point time and again. We did not agree. He told me that the Soviet Union had "state to state" agreements with Afghanistan going back to 1921 and would insist on maintaining them. I stuck to our position.

Dobrynin got word to Ambassador Matlock on March 12 that "Gorbachev feels betrayed by the U.S. demand for simultaneous cessation of arms to Afghanistan and by Zia's insistence on a change of government in Kabul before signing in Geneva." Gorbachev thought that he had agreed with the president in Washington that if they would leave unconditionally, the United States would stop sending arms to the resistance. This had led Gorbachev, the Soviet message said, with great difficulty and not without opposition, to put together his policy announcement on February 8, 1988, that Soviet troops would start to leave on May 15 if a settlement was reached in Geneva by March 15. Now he was, Dobrynin complained, "faced with two new demands and cannot accommodate them." The Soviets had cut their deal with Najibullah, we were told, and could not go back on it without damage to their prestige elsewhere. The Soviets were aware, Dobrynin said, that the United States believed Najibullah could not survive a Soviet departure. "Our assessment is that you may well be right, and we are willing to let nature take its course: *Que sera, sera*," he said, "but nature must take its course after we leave and not be pushed by us beforehand."

Jack Matlock predicted that the Soviets would not budge on the symmetry point. "They can't be seen to back down under pressure." But, of course, that was exactly what they were doing by withdrawing from Afghanistan.

On March 20, Shevardnadze arrived in Washington with a full delegation, set to push forward in preparation for the Moscow summit. I made Mike Armacost my action officer for the Afghan endgame. His Soviet counterpart, Anatoly Adamishin, proposed an "internal understanding" that since there was no mention of military supplies in the Geneva Declaration on International Guarantees, the United States would be legally free under this formula to render military assistance to the Afghan resistance, and the Soviet Union would be legally free to render military assistance to the Kabul regime.

This posed a problem for us, although the Soviets were trying to accommodate our concerns about symmetry. We could not keep the supply pipeline open without Pakistani help. The Pakistanis were extremely nervous about any arrangements that allowed continued weapons supply to both sides unless the Soviets stated explicitly that Moscow would not accuse Pakistan of violating the accord. This the Soviets refused to do.

On Shevardnadze's last afternoon in Washington, we had a three-hour meeting on Afghanistan, with Armacost and Colin Powell joining me on our side. Shevardnadze, in strong and emotional terms, argued his case. The Soviets had done everything we asked: announced their intent to withdraw, set a date, and established a short, front-end-loaded withdrawal schedule. All we needed to put an international imprimatur on an historic agreement, he argued, was "this one last piece."

We knew the mujaheddin had a large stockpile of arms, and we assumed the Kabul regime did as well. We continued to be ready for any reciprocal arrangement. We tried out a variety of ways to say the same thing. Shevardnadze finally asked for a "yes" or "no" to his request for an end to U.S. supplies of arms to the mujaheddin. I suggested we pause for a few moments. I took Armacost and Powell to my back office. We talked the matter over and over. We knew Shevardnadze was in charge of the Politburo effort on Afghanistan. He was on the spot. But we could not see any reason to change our position. We went back into my larger office to rejoin Shevardnadze. I restated our position. He paled, threw up his hands. The meeting had been one of our most difficult.

The outcome of my Shevardnadze meeting was reported to the Pakistanis. They were worried. The Pakistanis had by this time accepted the agreement after some six years of work under UN auspices. What would the impact on them be of a refusal to sign now? And, if Pakistan signed, it agreed to "prevent within its territory the training, equipping, financing and recruiting of mercenaries from whatever origin for the purpose of hostile activities against the other High Contracting Party [Afghanistan]." But that was precisely what it had been doing and what we insisted on continuing as long as the Soviets continued to supply Najibullah.

After some discussion through our embassies, two phone calls were arranged. First, Pakistani Prime Minister Junejo called me to urge us to sign the accords and to pledge that regardless of the language the Pakistanis would agree to, they would continue to provide a home to the mujaheddin and be a place through which U.S. arms and other supplies would flow to them. Several hours later, President Zia, the truly authoritative figure in Pakistan, called President Reagan with the same message. I heard the president ask Zia how he would handle the fact that they would be violating their agreement. Zia replied that they would "just lie about it. We've been denying our activities there for eight years." Then, the president recounted, Zia told him that "Muslims have the right to lie in a good cause."

By this time, some senators were sharply critical of what I was doing about Afghanistan, asserting that I was about to agree on a "secret deal" to let the Soviets keep supplying their surrogate while we would cut off the freedom fighters. They were wrong. I had told Junejo that we would make our position clear to the public, and the Soviets certainly would then level heavy criticism at Pakistan. "Not a problem," Junejo said; "they have done so before. We can take it." This was a brave assertion; Pakistan had never publicly acknowledged their role in supporting the mujaheddin; now they were willing to take the heat when we asserted publicly that our supplies would continue.

On March 30, Ronald Reagan and I sat out on the White House patio. The trees on the Mall were just starting to carry that light green glow of a Washington spring. I went over all arrangements with the president. Zia had called once again and reaffirmed all the points I had nailed down with Junejo. We were in business.

There would be no secret understandings. We would make our position public. President Reagan authorized me to let Shevardnadze know that we would sign, but that at the signing we would express our intent to continue to support our friends.

In April, a new problem arose. The Soviets, speaking for Najibullah, wanted the language calling on the parties to respect "existing international borders" dropped, claiming that it might lend weight to the Pakistani position on the disputed Afghan-Pakistani boundary.[3] "This is the key," I was told. I rejected the appeal; the language stayed in. Shevardnadze sent me a message on April 4 again urging we drop border language; if I would do so, "then we are in business." I declined, but Pakistan came up with alternative language: "so as not to violate the boundaries of each other." Najibullah flew to the Soviet city of Tashkent to meet Gorbachev, and *Tass* reported on April 7 that they agreed there was no longer any obstacle to signing the Geneva agreement.

We were clearly at the final decision point on a matter of immense significance. A good indicator was the heat I was taking from some on the hard-line right who, I suspected, did not really want the Soviets to leave Afghanistan; they preferred to "bleed" them to death through the indefinite continuation of the war. I also encountered some reluctance in my own team, who worried that my signing in Geneva would somehow convey U.S. and Soviet equivalence when it came to Afghanistan. I ignored the nay-sayers. I wanted to get the Soviet troops out, and if I signed, they would start rolling north on May 15.

I sent a message to Shevardnadze on April 8, pushing him to acknowledge that the United States would be free to continue to supply our side in Afghanistan, through Pakistan. An answer came back the next day saying that all was agreed but failing to be specific on this point. I cabled Shevardnadze right back, stating that we would accept no restrictions on our right to supply and that we would assert this publicly at the Geneva signing ceremony. I was focused on ensuring that this point not be lost or eroded.

A Turning Point

I went to see the president on Monday, April 11, to go over what we had accomplished and what we would say about it in Geneva. All the White House advisers were with him. They were nervous. He was confident. The Soviet withdrawal from Afghanistan was a tremendous triumph, one of the biggest events of Ronald Reagan's two terms and a turn of seminal significance in Soviet internal as well as external policies.

Just before taking off for Geneva and the signing, I went up to Congress on April 13 to go over what was to take place. "This is an historic moment," I asserted. "Soviet withdrawal is due to begin May 15. Preparations are already under way. . . . Without a Geneva agreement, Soviet withdrawal could be protracted and incomplete. This would prolong the agony of the Afghan people, and probably expose Pakistan to continued cross-border reprisals. For all these reasons, it's in our interest to sign onto the Geneva

---

3. The issue was whether the de facto "Durand" line would become de jure by the use of the words "internationally recognized" in this text.

agreements." I went on, "The President made clear to General Secretary Gorbachev last winter in Washington, and I have repeatedly told Shevardnadze, that the obligations of guarantors must be symmetrical. The Soviets rejected our preferred means of establishing symmetry, a moratorium on arms supplies to parties in Afghanistan, which I proposed to Shevardnadze on March 23. . . . We have told the Soviets that we assume our position on military supplies does not pose an obstacle to a Soviet signature at Geneva."

On the airplane to Geneva on April 13, I was handed a proposed draft statement that the United States would make there. It stated that "if the USSR undertakes, as consistent with its obligations as guarantor, to provide military assistance to parties in Afghanistan, the U.S. retains the right, as consistent with its obligations as guarantor, likewise effectively to provide such assistance." That was upside down and poorly drafted; it should say that we retain the right, *period*. I redrafted it: "The United States has advised the Soviet Union that the U.S. retains the right, consistent with its obligations as guarantor, to provide military assistance to parties in Afghanistan. Should the Soviet Union exercise restraint in providing military assistance to parties in Afghanistan, the U.S. similarly will exercise restraint."

I was told that we had already provided the Soviets with the first version. "It's not right," I said; "it says 'if the Soviets supply, we retain the right.' We have the right and can supply, period." This was one of those moments in diplomacy, I feared, when hasty and poor draftsmanship could result in long, vituperative disputes for years.

In my Geneva hotel room I heard that the Soviets were having real trouble with Najibullah; he was balking. His Afghan regime's representative here was refusing to sign. The Soviets had Vorontsov working him over to gain his "compliance." I sat down at the dining-room table and started signing the various parts of the accords. An aide came in and said I should put on a tie and be photographed. I declined. I saved one of the documents so I could sign it ceremonially with Shevardnadze.

The ceremony that took place in the Palais des Nations in Geneva was strange. There were no handshakes. There were four signators: the Afghan regime (whose legitimacy we did not recognize) and the Pakistanis were the principals; we and the Soviets were the guarantors. We all entered the grand room and went to our places. We simply signed and left. Afterward, I made a public declaration asserting "our right to provide military aid to the resistance. We are ready to exercise that right, but we are prepared to meet the restraint with restraint."

And so the process of Soviet withdrawal was given an international basis. The troops had started to move out even before the end of May, when the Moscow summit was under way. Reporting the CIA's confident analysis,

I had told President Reagan on April 11, "The resistance struggle against Moscow's client regime will continue. The intelligence community expects that the regime will not long survive the withdrawal of Soviet troops; it may fall even before they get out. We have taken steps to ensure that resistance forces inside Afghanistan have ample stocks of equipment and weaponry. We have preserved our right to supply the resistance and have made clear we intend to exercise that right if the Soviets continue to supply Kabul. Although the Najibullah government will sign the Geneva accords, we shall continue to deny it our formal recognition."

This CIA prediction turned out to be completely wrong. Najibullah maintained a position of control in a situation of disarray in Afghanistan. That was disappointing. We owed the Afghans a continuing effort. But the fact of overwhelming importance was that the Soviets had been forced to withdraw. The Reagan Doctrine of support for people who fight for freedom had won out over the Brezhnev Doctrine of perpetual control by the Soviets of territory they had seized. This was a new day and a major signal to restive Soviet satellites throughout the world.

At Geneva, Shevardnadze had said: "The importance of these instruments and of this moment can hardly be exaggerated . . . we fully agree with those who regard the Geneva Agreement as the first example of a peaceful resolution of regional conflicts on the basis of the principles of new political thinking."

I agreed heartily with Shevardnadze's statement. The Soviets had been rolled back. The Brezhnev Doctrine had been breached. What impact this would have elsewhere in the Soviet empire remained to be seen, but the event was monumental. Now I wanted to move quickly to carry the momentum on to other regional issues, most particularly to a solution in Namibia and Angola. I would make use of the Moscow summit to further that objective.

Human Rights and the Moscow Summit

Ronald Reagan and I both gave pride of place to human rights. He took the subject up at each of his meetings with Gorbachev and with most visitors from the Soviet Union to the Oval Office. I pounded on the subject at every opportunity, increasingly emphasizing to the Soviets the advantages to them, in the emerging knowledge and information age, of changing the way they dealt with their own people. I remembered Ronald Reagan's first "deal" with the Soviet leadership, when, in 1983, the Soviets allowed the Pentecostals, who had sought refuge in our Moscow embassy, to emigrate. President Reagan had agreed not to crow about it or claim credit. And he didn't.

President Reagan's approach to human rights with Soviet leaders, especially Mikhail Gorbachev, was essentially this: "Human rights represent a matter of principle for me. I'm not playing games. I'm not trying to push you in a corner publicly. I understand politicians even in your circumstances have to worry about how they look and don't want to be pushed around in public. I'm not grandstanding. I simply want people to be allowed to get out, and if you let them go, I won't crow about it. I'm worried about the people, not making points."

The Soviet approach to human rights was changing: our dialogue was deep and extensive; emigration and travel were increasing; political prisoners were being released; dissidents, including all those who attended the April 1987 seder in our Moscow embassy, were being allowed to leave; more leeway was emerging for religious practice inside the Soviet Union; and *glasnost* was bringing far greater freedom of expression. Ambassador Jack Matlock, then serving his third tour in Moscow, commented on the amount of time he now spent reading the Soviet papers. "They are full of interesting material," he said, "unlike the old days, when they contained so little of interest that they were hardly worth reading."

Back on December 16, 1986, Gorbachev had telephoned Andrei Sakharov, a giant of a man in every respect and honored throughout the world for his advocacy of human rights. Sakharov's six years of internal exile in Gorky, a closed city, thus came to an end. He and his wife, Elena Bonner, were allowed to return to their apartment in Moscow. This event, affecting a man of towering intellect and moral authority, made an impact even on some of Gorbachev's most severe skeptics.

I had gone to Moscow on February 21, 1988, to continue our across-the-board negotiations, to prepare for the Moscow summit, and as a matter of my private agenda, to see Andrei Sakharov. At 6:50 in the evening, sandwiched between meetings with Shevardnadze and a session with human rights activists, I walked up the stairs to Sakharov's modest apartment. He and his wife were warm and cordial. We plunged into a far-ranging conversation about arms control issues, then *glasnost*, then human rights. I asked him what he thought about the idea of a human rights conference to be held in Moscow as one outcome of the CSCE negotiations in Vienna. Such a conference was generally regarded as a concession to the Soviets. "You must insist on Soviet departure from Afghanistan and on the release of political prisoners—prisoners of conscience," he told me. His estimate of the number of true political prisoners was significantly lower than ours. "But," he said, "then you should welcome a human rights conference in Moscow. Such a meeting, lasting several weeks, would call real attention to this subject in Moscow, where the attention could make a difference." I later recounted Sakharov's view to President Reagan and to human rights activists in Congress. Sakharov's assessment deserved heavy weight, I thought, in any decision on this vital matter.

When I met with Shevardnadze later that evening, he went on the offensive about human rights. "The United States," he asserted, "systematically denies women and blacks the opportunity to advance, to undertake important tasks." Seated across from him were Roz Ridgway and Colin Powell. Their presence was a partial response to the charge. I told him that we had made real progress but had lots more work to do.

On April 21, I arrived in Moscow for what I knew would probably be my last visit there heading a delegation as secretary of state. We would move as close as possible to final arrangements for the Moscow summit meeting only five weeks away. The high point would be my meeting with Gorbachev on April 22, but I looked forward also to getting some feel of how the new policies I heard about in Moscow were being received away from that central city. I would go to Kiev and Tbilisi to see for myself. That would be my first opportunity to see areas of the Soviet Union outside Moscow since I had visited Sochi and Leningrad as secretary of the treasury in 1973.

Another Encounter with Gorbachev

I felt a certain sense of nostalgia as my car rolled through the Kremlin gates and as I walked to the grand holding room and then into St. Catherine's Hall. Gorbachev had been under attack for his reforms, I knew. A chemistry teacher in Leningrad, Nina Andreyeva, had written a strong declaration against reform entitled "I Cannot Betray My Principles," published on March 13 in *Sovetskaya Rossiya*, an official Russian newspaper. The article was widely regarded as a planted challenge. Gorbachev's response, reportedly following an intense battle in the Politburo, appeared in *Pravda* on April 5. This struggle was continuing as I arrived. On April 21, Gorbachev had ordered the Kremlin gates closed all day as he met there in marathon sessions with provincial party bosses. He emerged the victor in what was called the most important political confrontation in the Communist party leadership since he had assumed power. At the celebration of Lenin's birthday on April 22, a speech by a Gorbachev protégé, Georgy Razumovsky, firmly restated Gorbachev's proreform policies. Ligachev was "called back from vacation" to stand and listen.

When I saw Gorbachev on April 22 in the midst of this drama, his attitude reflected his strengthened position. He was self-confident, behaving as though he had no rivals at all. He soon flew into a tantrum. He had scrawled notes to himself with a felt pen on all four sides of a file folder—which probably had held staff-prepared talking points that he had thrown out. He was angry over a speech President Reagan had given in Springfield, Massachusetts, the previous day, April 21. I had not seen the speech, nor had Colin Powell, who was with me. I listened to Gorbachev's opening blast, trying to figure out what in the president's speech had triggered his outburst. "The U.S. Administration," said Gorbachev, "is not abandoning stereotypes, not abandoning reliance on force, not taking account of political realities and the interests of others. I have to conclude that there is backward movement and an attempt to preach to us, to teach us." He went on and on. "So how am I to explain this? Is this summit going to be a catfight?" Gorbachev demanded. He seemed to be at a fever pitch, though much of his performance was theatrical. The message was clear: tell the president not to make a speech like that in Moscow.[4]

When Gorbachev finished denouncing the president's Springfield speech, he turned to Nixon's criticisms of the INF Treaty. "Nixon has taken a break from the labor of writing his memoirs to take part in political debates. I can understand why because the stereotypes Nixon took so long in building are being abandoned. But the dead should not be allowed to take the living by the coattails and drag them back to the past. We should not let old politicians prevent us from building up relations," Gorbachev protested. "Why should we fritter away the capital that has been built up over many months?" he asked. "If we cannot protect the atmosphere we had at the beginning of the year, I don't see how we can have a successful visit." We needed to resist, he went on, people "who want to put sticks in the spokes of Soviet-American normalization."

Having unburdened himself of his concerns and frustrations, he now moderated his approach, as I had come to realize he often did after such an outburst. Gorbachev said they were ready "to prepare a visit so that it will be a major political event . . . not only the government but the people of the Soviet Union will give the President a very friendly reception, showing respect not only to the American people, but also to the President himself."

My turn finally came. Not knowing the president's Springfield speech, I just ignored that subject. "More stable and constructive relations" are widely appreciated in the United States, I told him, and I pointed to a recent vote in our House of Representatives supporting the INF Treaty, 393 to 7. "I didn't think there was anything that could get that big a majority in the House." I reviewed "the flow of the relationship" since Geneva and identified important achievements in each part of our four-part agenda. We exchanged ideas about future possibilities.

*   *   *

4. I later learned that the Springfield speech, given to a World Affairs Council audience, contained language on human rights, Afghanistan, and the importance of strength in dealing with the Soviets that was considered standard Reagan rhetoric in the United States but always offended the Soviets. U.S. newspapers, in the scant attention paid to the speech, focused on other parts of the speech: "Soviet-American relations have taken a dramatic turn into a period of realistic engagement"; "negotiations are under way between our two governments on an unparalleled number of issues"; and "this single, startling fact: the Soviets have pledged that next month they will begin withdrawing from Afghanistan."

Gorbachev then launched into what I regarded as truly remarkable statements for the Communist boss of the Soviet Union. "The Soviet Union does not pretend to have the final truth. We do not impose our way of life on other peoples." That is totally at odds, I thought to myself, with Communist ideology and past practice. "We've told you we want to cooperate, we want dialogue, we want to find answers together with the United States." He commented on "the pragmatism typical of American policy" and said he thought there was "inertia inherent in pragmatism." Then he recalled "a time in this very room, this St. Catherine's Hall, when you and I looked at charts you brought on what the world would look like in a few years in terms of economic power and changes in forces and roles. I welcomed that talk. I have thought about it a lot and not just by myself. I have consulted experts." If the trends continue as you outlined, he continued, "our two countries have a lot of reason to cooperate."

I was impressed and delighted to see that the ideas I had put to him on earlier occasions had registered. State's Sovietologists had initially accused me of running a "classroom in the Kremlin," but Gorbachev had evidently seen more in my "Global Trends" presentation than they had perceived themselves. I said I would welcome more opportunities for such talks but that current issues seemed to take up all the time. Gorbachev replied that we would have time after we both left office and then confided, "I hope you don't divulge this to the press," that the coming party congress would, "if I prevail," put "a limit on the time Party and Government officials could spend in their positions." Term limits in the Soviet Union: that was extraordinary!

I thanked him for the confidential information. The problem was "to get people who are in charge, in office, to sense the trends and to build them into their thinking." In that way, I said, leaders could "shape what is done" to "change the balance of problems and opportunities in the direction of opportunities."

"The present leadership in both countries is at a watershed. A new generation of political leaders is coming to better reflect the trends of the world than leaders did in the past," Gorbachev responded.

He then went directly to the subject of human rights. I could see his ambivalence. He was ready to move but did not want to be our "pupil." "The United States does not understand that we have different values. The United States values private initiative, private property. Its media, its philosophy, its politicians all protect that. That's the choice of the United States," Gorbachev said. "Whereas in the Soviet Union, we're just beginning to develop new forms of cooperation and individual work. And people are asking if that means a return to private property, to capitalism, to the exploitation of the working class. We are just beginning to develop these forms, and the charges [against private initiatives] have nothing to do with reality. Matlock can read about it every day."

"I have been to one of your cooperative [private] restaurants," I told him. I could see that he still struggled with the idea of a private "profit-making" enterprise: profit to him was exploitation.

"You've got more money in your pocket than the average Soviet citizen," he replied. "But the authorities have to work hard to prove that these new forms are consistent with socialism. Values are different. The Soviets don't impose their values, and when the U.S. tries to impose its values, this only results in aggravation and a bad atmosphere. Maybe that's what the American side wants. The Soviet side is criticizing itself a lot, and it's pretty hard for the United States to add to that."

"We accept that there's diversity in government arrangements in the world," I responded. "Countries have to balance the needs for efficiency and the needs for equity, for social justice in society. Everyone has to make that choice. But if you go too far either way, it does not work. Discussion on how to organize we regard as healthy. There is nothing wrong with it. We have learned from criticism."

Gorbachev challenged me, "I would be interested in what you have to say about U.S. society, whether you engage in self-criticism on human rights."

"There is great freedom to criticize in the United States," I replied. "We're worried about our problems. Drugs are a problem; crime is a problem. They'll be big issues in the upcoming election campaign. Our standard of living is on the whole high, the market system is working well, but there are problems. Ours is a country of great diversity. At the lower end of the income scale, especially in the inner cities, there are undesirable conditions. We have worked hard on it. Sometimes we are successful; sometimes we are not. There has been a tremendous struggle on the general subject of civil rights. We have a way to go, but we've made headway. In the sixties and seventies, that struggle was intense. I was engaged in it. So we take the point seriously. There is no lack of criticism. And I think that on the whole we benefit from it.

"I have been impressed with your willingness to criticize," I continued. "No one has criticized all aspects of Soviet society and the economy as severely as you. But there are some things that are registered internationally in the Helsinki Final Act and in the Universal Declaration of Human Rights that cut across the board. You have signed them; we have signed them. We do not think it is interference to hold up that standard and ask questions. I think there has been tremendous progress, even in my time. I would like to see that preserved and built on. When I started, the two sides wouldn't even discuss the issues. Now we have an organized and systematic review under way. Shevardnadze has asked me many questions. He has raised issues about life in the United States; he has raised cases. I don't mind. I try to respond. I think things have moved in a healthy way."

Gorbachev then shifted gears. "Both the Soviets and the United States have said that Islamic fundamentalism is a dangerous phenomenon," he said. "Both have stated that there are dangers if Iranian fundamentalism is allowed free rein. Then the United States supported Islamic fundamentalism in Afghanistan, probably seeing some advantage in that. And now the Afghan fundamentalists want to move their center to Iran, where they feel an affinity." Gorbachev then concluded, posing a question: "So, in short, when is George Shultz right, as in correct?"

"I am almost always right," I said with a smile.

Gorbachev laughed and congratulated me. Our meeting ended on a cordial note, with Gorbachev saying, "I am pleased to meet again with old friends, and I hope no one will be able to wipe out what we have done together over the past three years to improve relations. Life demands that."

Gorbachev's reaction to the president's Springfield speech had gotten us off to a testy start, but our session had gone far in drawing out the profound change taking place in Gorbachev's thinking, in Soviet actions, and in the U.S.-Soviet relationship. I felt that this discussion would help set the tone at the Moscow summit. A new day was dawning. Reagan and Gorbachev could dramatize that fact to the whole world.

A Dramatic Visit to Kiev and Tbilisi

I was ready to go on to Kiev and Tbilisi. The Soviets had at first refused to let me fly on *Air Force 970*: I would have to go in a Soviet plane, they said, for security reasons. I protested, and Shevardnadze heard about the matter. "Let him go on his own plane," he said. "We'll save money." That was a real example, I thought, of "new thinking."

In Kiev, I heard from local authorities about the accident at Chernobyl that had occurred two years earlier. It was still on their minds, still an ongoing problem. A shift in prevailing winds at the time of the accident had been fortunate for residents of Kiev, but they were still concerned about the effects on food supplies and possible contamination in their city. Later, I visited Babi Yar, where Soviet citizens, starting with Jews, had been slaughtered by the Nazis during World War II. The memory of German cruelty was dramatized to the citizens of Kiev by an arresting sculpture of bodies falling into the low ground before us.

In Tbilisi, the capital of Georgia, the tension between the Georgians and Soviet authority was palpable. I wanted to visit the centuries-old church, a popular focal point in this republic, which was converted to Christianity long before Russia was. My visit caused a great stir. Some people in the streets shouted, I was told, "Shultz is a believer. He is a man of peace." The scene in the small, dark Greek Orthodox church was gripping. The KGB made itself felt, trying to keep people from approaching me, shoving them back. The singing in the crowded church resonated with emotion. Dubinin, Bessmertnykh, and Sukhodrev, who accompanied us everywhere, seemed terribly uncomfortable. "This is a Christian nation," Sukhodrev said as he looked around uneasily.

The Georgian priests handed out lighted candles. The Soviet officials took the candles but held them warily, as if they were about to explode.

The patriarch asked me to say some words to his congregation. I spoke of the importance of religion in our lives and the staying power of religious belief through the centuries, despite repressive efforts of government. When I returned to my seat, I saw that my hosts from Moscow were ready to leave for the next stop on our heavy schedule. I looked over at O'Bie. "I'm enjoying this," she said. So we stayed on for a while longer, despite the discomfort of those who brought us.

My visits to Kiev and Tbilisi were a dramatic contrast to the drab and tense atmosphere of Moscow. The Soviet Union, I became more convinced with every encounter, was in the process of genuine and far-reaching change. Who knew where it would ultimately lead or end? Whether or not Gorbachev would move toward a system of markets, enterprise, and private property remained to be seen. But I could feel the new openness of glasnost everywhere.

Ronald Reagan Goes to Moscow

Finally, all arrangements in place, Ronald and Nancy Reagan set out for their first trip to Moscow on May 25, 1988, with a stop in Helsinki to adjust to the time change. On arms control, I knew the chances of progress toward a strategic arms reductions treaty were minimal, but the Vienna negotiations to create a mandate for a new round of talks on conventional forces in Europe were moving toward a conclusion and needed a boost. On regional issues I took with me Assistant Secretary of State Chester Crocker, in an effort to highlight the negotiations for Namibian independence and to enlist Soviet support for our efforts. Cuba and Angola were key countries involved, and both were clients supported by the Soviets.

Ronald Reagan expressed the overriding and powerful theme for the Moscow summit. On May 27, in his address in Helsinki's Finlandia Hall on the eve of his departure for Moscow, he said in stirring words, "There is no true international security without respect for human rights. . . . The greatest creative and moral force in this new world, the greatest hope for survival and success, for peace and happiness, is human freedom."

He went on to ask bluntly "why Soviet citizens who wish to exercise their right to emigrate should be subject to artificial quotas and arbitrary rulings. And what are we to think of the continued suppression of those who wish to practice their religious beliefs?" I supported these sentiments by attending a seder in Helsinki, well publicized in order to let the Soviets know the strength of our views on emigration and religious freedom. The president let the Finns know that he understood the heroism of their own continuing struggle for independence from their aggressive neighbor and for maintenance of a free and open political and economic system. From that moment, a new chapter was opened in U.S.-Finnish relations.

The Reagans also made known that they would, by a personal visit, demonstrate their concern for Yuri and Tatayana Zieman, Jewish refuseniks who had first applied to emigrate in 1977. The Soviets painted the apartment where the Ziemans lived and repaired their street. But they also sent Bessmertnykh to Helsinki with a message delivered to Roz Ridgway. They were "confident" that the Ziemans would be allowed to emigrate if "the issue is not forced," but if the Reagans went ahead with their plan for a visit, the Ziemans might never be permitted to leave. President Reagan decided that he had accomplished his purpose. He considered the Soviet statement, delivered by a special high-level official, to be a commitment. Two months later, after a little further follow-up, the couple was allowed to emigrate to the United States.

On the first full day at the summit, May 30, in the late afternoon, the Reagans met the Ziemans, along with ninety-eight refuseniks and human rights activists, at a truly inspiring reception at Spaso House. Tables were elegantly set, complete with gold-embossed White House place cards. The occasion delivered a message of our respect: we are on your side. Three guests spoke of their own hardships, and yet focused on their continued hope for the future. Some had spent years in prison and had just been released; others were seeking to emigrate; all had felt the heavy hand of Soviet repression. Each was courageous to come. We, having invited them to this public event, recognized fully the responsibility to follow their treatment closely. Their very attendance was risky for them, and we did not want any reprisals to be taken against them. Ronald Reagan was eloquent. He praised the positive steps already taken by Gorbachev, but insisted that much more remained to be done, quoting Pushkin, "It's time my friend, it's time. The heart begs for peace, the days fly past, it's time, my friend, it's time."

I included Chet Crocker in a side meeting with Shevardnadze the next day; we discussed the promising possibilities of gaining independence for Namibia. The behavior of the two Soviet clients, Angola and Cuba, would be critical to success. I wanted to achieve a sense of drive to further these complex negotiations being so deftly orchestrated by Crocker. Shevardnadze, with some reluctance, agreed to help and to use the tenth anniversary of the passage of UN Resolution 435 on Namibian independence,

September 1988, as a goal. We would consult with the Soviets all the way. If they helped, so much the better, but our discussion at least gave some assurance that the Soviets would not take up the role of spoiler.

I had a small personal triumph at the summit. I regard Red Square as one of the great sights of the world. I was determined that Ronald Reagan should have the chance to see Red Square for himself. The White House image makers were opposed: too much risk of pictures with the backdrop of Lenin's tomb. While we were in Helsinki, I told President Reagan how striking the square is. "Red is our translation for a Russian word for 'beautiful.' Red Square acquired its name even before the Communists came to power." I suggested privately to the president that he say to Gorbachev, "Mr. General Secretary, I understand that Red Square is quite a sight to see, and sometime during the course of this visit, I'd like to see it." I even had this typed on a small card as a reminder. I told the president, "I'll bet that Gorbachev will say 'great idea,' and he'll wind up being your tour guide."

That's just about what happened, providing the most memorable photographs and TV scenes of the visit—and a powerful visual symbol of the immense change well under way. There the two men were, easy in their relationship, greeting Soviet citizens. Gorbachev held a baby. Reagan's winning smile came through. Body language and imagery told the story: a dangerous cold war era was ending. In fact, Reagan enjoyed the scene so much that he took another piece of advice from me: go see Red Square at night. After our private dinner at a dacha with the Gorbachevs and the Shevardnadzes, the president asked his driver to return again to Red Square, where he and Nancy saw the dramatic lighted images, featuring the famous St. Basil's Cathedral.

The *New York Times* picked up another sidelight to our trip as well:

> Toward the end of the Moscow summit meeting, Tony Dolan, the proudly conservative White House speechwriter, slipped out to Red Square for a final peek at the gilded onion towers of St. Basil's Cathedral.
>
> Alas for the archimandrite of Reaganism, Mr. Dolan [author of the Springfield speech] was sighted by Secretary of State George P. Shultz, who was also making an unscheduled stop on the square.
>
> Next day, Mr. Shultz gleefully told colleagues that he had seen Mr. Dolan "worshiping at Lenin's Tomb." "I was not visiting Lenin's Tomb," Mr. Dolan indignantly sniffed to an inquirer this week, "I was in Red Square selling subscriptions to the *National Review*."[5]

On May 31, Ronald Reagan addressed the students at Moscow State University, standing at a podium against a backdrop of a gigantic bust of

5. *New York Times*, June 8, 1988, p. A26.

Lenin. I was seated along the side of the room and could watch the students as they listened, connecting the words and the body language through simultaneous translation. Skeptical at first, they were drawn quickly into the president's message.

He talked about the future:

> I want to talk about a very different revolution that is taking place right now, quietly sweeping the globe without bloodshed or conflict. . . . It's been called the technological or information revolution, and as its emblem, one might take the tiny silicon chip, no bigger than a fingerprint. . . .
>
> Linked by a network of satellites and fiber-optic cables, one individual with a desktop computer and a telephone commands resources unavailable to the largest governments just a few years ago.

He talked about freedom and creativity and entrepreneurship: "In the new economy, human invention increasingly makes physical resources obsolete. . . . The explorers of the modern era are the entrepreneurs, men with vision, with the courage to take risks and faith enough to brave the unknown."

He took a popular and humorous shot at the bureaucracy. The room erupted in laughter. He quoted from Boris Pasternak's *Dr. Zhivago*, banned in the Soviet Union until recently, and he spoke against a symbol he particularly loathed—the Berlin Wall. "In my conversation with General Secretary Gorbachev, I have spoken of how important it is to institutionalize change—to put guarantees on reform. And we've been talking together about one sad reminder of a divided world: the Berlin Wall. It's time to remove the barriers that keep people apart."

He concluded on an inspiring note: "A people free to choose will always choose peace. . . . Your generation is living in one of the most exciting, hopeful times in Soviet history. It is a time when the first breath of freedom stirs the air and the heart beats to the accelerated rhythm of hope, when the accumulated spiritual energies of a long silence yearn to break free."

This was precisely the message to deliver. And Ronald Reagan delivered it magnificently. I wondered whether Gorbachev connected it with my own earlier discussions with him about the new information age, an age that would force the pace of change.

A moment of tension came suddenly during the last plenary session in St. Catherine's Hall on June 1. Gorbachev had given Reagan a brief statement during their first one-on-one session in the Kremlin, just after our arrival in Moscow. "Proceeding from their understanding of the realities that have taken shape in the world today, the two leaders believe that no problem in dispute can be resolved, nor should it be resolved, by military means. They regard peaceful coexistence as a universal principle of international relations. Equality of all states, noninterference in internal affairs, and freedom of sociopolitical choice must be recognized as the inalienable and mandatory standards of international relations." Gorbachev proposed that we include this in the final communiqué. President Reagan looked it over, saw nothing difficult in it, and said he would talk it over with his delegation.

I argued strongly that this represented a return to détente-era declarations that could be variously interpreted, had not stopped the Soviets from invading Afghanistan, and implied, by the phrase "peaceful coexistence," a willingness to leave unchallenged areas of Soviet conquest and control. In the negotiations over the joint statement conducted by Roz Ridgway and Aleksander Bessmertnykh, Roz, who strongly concurred in my view, had successfully argued our objections. Now, at the last minute, Gorbachev threw it back on the table in a blazing and pugnacious manner. He handed the original Soviet text across the table, saying to President Reagan, "You had no objection to this last Sunday."

I had seen these sudden Gorbachev mood changes before, in almost every one of my meetings with him in the Kremlin. I objected, as did Roz and Frank Carlucci. We called for a recess in the meeting. Our delegations and the press were waiting in nearby St. Vladimir's Hall to witness the signing of the ratification papers of the INF Treaty. We persuaded the president that he should not accommodate Gorbachev.

President Reagan went back to Gorbachev and stood toe-to-toe. "I'm very reluctant to put this in. I don't want to do it," he said flatly. Then he was silent.

We could see that the issue was important to Gorbachev. I speculated that the statement might have been drafted by Gromyko, who, now occupying the largely ceremonial post of president, may have been reaching back to an earlier era favored by Kremlin conservatives. Gorbachev insisted. But he had also learned by now that Ronald Reagan, once settled on a position, was very unlikely to change. He sighed, put his arm around Reagan, and they walked together to the final ceremony.

On the way out, Bessmertnykh said quietly to Roz, "He almost buried our masterpiece."

Through all the pomp and circumstance, state dinners, visits with intellectuals and dissidents, an unscheduled tour at the Arbat,[6] Ronald Reagan personified an optimistic and forward-looking America. As he had in China four years earlier, he spoke of the values that made America the greatest land of freedom and opportunity in the world. And he inspired the young

6. A street near Spaso House where Soviets are free to sell paintings and artifacts and where the arrival of the Reagans caused the KGB to display its capacity for brutality in controlling a friendly crowd.

people with his message that a vibrant future beckoned them in the name of freedom.

Gorbachev Comes to the United Nations

On November 12, the Saturday after George Bush was elected president of the United States, Ambassador Dubinin called me urgently asking to see me the next day upon his return to Washington. Fine, I told him.

When he arrived at my office, he told me that Gorbachev had decided to come to the United Nations in early December to make an important address. Could he meet with President Reagan and President-elect Bush? I said I was sure the president would certainly want to see Gorbachev. I told Dubinin I would get back to him quickly.

I called in Roz Ridgway and then Colin Powell. I could see that we must react positively. Gorbachev had yet to make an appearance at the United Nations despite having held office for over three years. He was coming. We recommended to President Reagan that he be gracious about the visit.

Ronald Reagan, it turned out, was more than ready for one more round of discussions with Gorbachev. Arrangements were made for a luncheon meeting on Governor's Island, an easily secured Coast Guard base in New York harbor, on December 7. George Bush agreed to be present as vice president, though he did not seem to welcome this event. James Baker, his secretary of state designate, did not attend. Gorbachev would join us after his address at the United Nations, and before the event was over, the three leaders would be photographed together against the dramatic backdrop of the Statue of Liberty.

I sat in the U.S. chair in the grand assembly hall of the United Nations. Gorbachev entered the room with the cheers of the world body ringing in his ears. Applause, let alone enthusiastic applause, was most unusual in this chamber where Khrushchev had pounded on his desk decades earlier. Gorbachev's speech had two parts, the first philosophical, the second operational: announcing troop reductions of 500,000 men, including military units in various Warsaw Pact countries. This hard news caught all the headlines. I thought the first part of the speech, which went virtually unnoticed, was far more important.

Gorbachev displayed a perception of a very different future: "The world in which we live today is radically different from how it was early in, or even in the middle of, the present century. . . . The idea of the democratization of the entire world order has turned into a mighty sociopolitical force."

He had taken on board the vast implications of the information age:

> At the same time the scientific-and-technical revolution has turned many
> problems—economic, food, energy, ecological, informational, and demo-

graphic—which not so long ago we dealt with as national or regional ones—
into global problems. Thanks to the latest means of communications, mass
information, and transportation, the world has, as it were, become more
visible and perceptible for everyone. International contact has been simplified
in an unprecedented way. Today it is hardly possible to preserve some sort
of "closed" societies.

The world economy is becoming a single organism, outside of which not
a single state can develop normally, whatever social system it belongs to or
whatever economic level it has reached.

He put the 1917 Russian Revolution in the past; his speech never mentioned Marx, and he referred to Lenin in passing only once: "There
emerges before us today a different world, for which it is necessary to seek
different roads toward the future, to seek—relying, of course, on accumulated experience—but also seeing the radical differences between that
which was yesterday and that which is taking place today."

His comments on the use of force and the importance of tolerance of
differences led me and many others to think immediately of the countries
of Eastern Europe:

Everyone, and the strongest in the first instance, is required to restrict himself
and to exclude totally the use of external force. . . . The compelling necessity
of the principle of freedom of choice is also clear to us. . . . This objective
fact presupposes respect for other people's views and stands, tolerance, a
preparedness to see phenomena that are different as not necessarily bad or
hostile and an ability to learn to live side by side while remaining different
and not agreeing with one another on every issue.

He spoke about the relationship of the Soviet Union with the United
States:

Look how our relations with the United States have changed: Little by little
mutual understanding has started to be built up, elements of trust have arisen,
without which it is very difficult to move forward in politics.

On human rights Gorbachev seemed almost to be adopting a Western
point of view.

I would like to add my country's voice to the high assessments of the significance of the General Declaration of Human Rights adopted 40 years ago
on 10 December 1948. . . . The most suitable way for a state to mark the
declaration's anniversary is to improve its own conditions at home for the
observance and defense of citizens' rights. . . . We have gone substantially
and deeply into the business of constructing a socialist state based on the
rule of law. . . . There are now no people in places of imprisonment in the
country who have been sentenced for their political or religious convictions.

Hearing these words, I thought of Sakharov's conditions for a human rights conference in Moscow. And once again I thought of my exchanges with Gorbachev in the Kremlin, starting in 1985, about how the Soviet Union would have to open its society and value the rights of the individual if it was to succeed in the information age.

And he added a grace note that was welcome, though unexpected:

> We acknowledge and value the contribution of President Ronald Reagan and the members of his administration, above all Mr. George Shultz. All this is capital that has been invested in a joint undertaking of historic importance.

The lunch conversation itself was free flowing. There were two highlights for me. In an exchange between Bush and Gorbachev involving investment, Bush said, "We're a nation of investors, and an investor wants to know what conditions are like today. But an investor is even more interested in the prospective situation. So, Mr. General Secretary, what is it going to be like in the Soviet Union three or four or five years from now?"

Gorbachev replied without missing a beat, "Mr. Vice President, even Jesus Christ couldn't answer that question!" He laughed.

And, in an exchange involving me, after the president had noted some continuing differences, "Krasnoyarsk, for instance," Gorbachev said he had put an end to the problem "to make things easier for the new president." He added, "Shultz has spent so much time on Krasnoyarsk that I have transferred it from the military to the scientists."

I interjected, "I listened carefully to your address and, concerning Krasnoyarsk, the word you used, in my translation, was 'dismantle.' "

Gorbachev replied with a smile, "I bet you wrote that down. I can confirm the translation. Another victory for the secretary."

At the end of the luncheon, President Reagan said to Gorbachev, "This is my last meeting with you, and I raise a glass to what you have accomplished, what we have accomplished together, and to what you and George Bush will accomplish together after January 20."

"I can join in that toast, and will the vice president do so as well?" asked Gorbachev.

"Yes, I do," George Bush said.

"Good, then that is our first agreement," Gorbachev said jovially.

Gorbachev was ready to engage, and I hoped the Bush, Baker, Scowcroft team would also be ready to move ahead. The opportunity was there for the taking. Gorbachev, with the important exception of Soviet strategic ballistic missiles, had a weak hand. Ours was the winning hand, and I felt we should play that hand with energy and with a vision in mind of the different and promising world of the future.

CHAPTER 50

The End of Colonialism
in Africa

Slavery—its reality, its abolition, and its legacy—has marked the conscience and consciousness of Americans throughout our time as a nation. It has imposed an intense sensitivity and responsibility upon us, not only for our domestic racial situation but also for the problems of black Africa. So I was especially gratified that through a sustained effort in the final year of the Reagan administration, we were able to bring to fruition one of the administration's longest-sought goals, a dramatic change in Southern Africa: the independence of Namibia, Africa's last colony, the withdrawal of foreign forces from Angola, and reason for hope that change for the better in South Africa might be on the horizon.

The United States pursued its strategy in this long endeavor through intricate, though largely unnoticed, diplomatic maneuvers, followed with patience and persistence over the six and one-half years of my stewardship as secretary of state. The central figure in this complex effort was Assistant Secretary of State Chester (Chet) Crocker, a historian and specialist on Africa recruited from Georgetown University into the Reagan administration. Chet was canny and knowledgeable, softly insistent and determined.

Elegantly tailored, sporting a dapper mustache, and with a twinkle often present in his eye, Crocker could have stepped out of the Foreign Office in Whitehall in the era between the world wars. But Crocker was thoroughly American and utterly committed to his mission. His most notable characteristic was his absence—from Washington, that is. He was no striped-pants, home-office policymaker. He was, rather, incessantly on the road, crisscrossing Africa. Speaking softly, without benefit of a big stick, he worked together with me and his immediate team to put together, piece by piece, an irresistible diplomatic plan.

I was drawn to this effort in considerable part out of my own involvement in civil rights activities in the 1960s and 1970s. I had worked on the private retraining of workers, mostly black, as change caused displacement in the

1109

meat-packing industry. I had, as secretary of labor, broken, with a sledge-hammer called the Philadelphia Plan, the quota system (zero) against blacks in the skilled construction trades. One of the high points of my public career had been my part in the desegregation of the Southern school system.[1]

No sight that I saw as secretary of state so struck me as the Slave House and "door of no return" on Goree Island, off the coast of Senegal. The Slave House, I was told, was the spot where in 1619 the first shipload of African slaves embarked on their voyage to the Virginia colony. Untold thousands followed from the small stone rooms of confinement through the stone archway into confinement once again on ships for a voyage that a great many did not complete. When I saw Goree in 1987, it was becoming a site of pilgrimage where people could come, as I did, and see this reminder of man's inhumanity to man.

I walked from the Slave House to the nearby eighteenth-century, two-story building that once housed the American consulate—the first U.S. diplomatic mission to be established in West Africa. When I returned to Washington, I gave my support to the dramatization of a contrast: establish this former consulate building as a museum and center for the study of the African diaspora, with particular focus on the achievements of African-Americans. Let people walk from the Slave House to the contributions and the achievements of the descendants of those who came to America from Africa.

Disarray in Southern Africa

The tormented lands around the southern edges of Africa displayed nearly every aspect of the problems facing the entire continent: poverty, disease, political turmoil, racial tension. Angola, a colony of Portugal since the age of exploration, had become, after decolonization, a battleground between rival nationalist groups and a base for Soviet-backed guerrilla forays beyond its borders.

The Popular Movement for the Liberation of Angola (MPLA), under the leadership of Jose Eduardo Dos Santos, and with large-scale Soviet support and the use of Cuban troops, became the generally recognized government in the capital city of Luanda, along the coast, and in much of the northern interior. Dr. Jonas Savimbi, a dynamic and charismatic personality, led an opposition force, the National Union for the Total Independence of Angola (UNITA), with headquarters in Jamba, in the southeastern corner of the country. In a reaction against American in-

1. See Chapter 47, pages 1045–50.

volvement in Vietnam, the Clark Amendment in 1976 had prohibited U.S. aid to Savimbi. He received the help of a South Africa glad to see this opposition to an ideologically hostile Communist state on its border.

Soviet-backed revolutionaries, the South West Africa People's Organization (SWAPO), operated into Namibia from Angola. Still a colony of South Africa, mineral-rich Namibia was an anachronistic remnant of a bygone era. The United Nations in UN Resolution 435 had called in 1978 for Namibian independence, but South Africa, Namibia's master, would not let go. Soviet influence and Cuban troops in next-door Angola were prominent among the many reasons for South African resistance to the all-too-real possibility of "the red flag in Windhoek," Namibia's principal city.

South Africa was reviled everywhere for its policy of apartheid, and the country's leader, Pieter W. Botha, was ironically a personal embodiment of the policy. He was moderate in comparison with his predecessors, and he introduced a number of piecemeal reforms. But when black unrest exploded in response to the limited scope of his modest changes, he introduced in 1985 a state of emergency, a draconian measure responsible for thousands of deaths, some 30,000 detainees, and a curtailment of basic freedoms.

The economies of all the countries of Southern Africa were inextricably tied into the dominant economy of South Africa. Interdependence was the handmaiden of deep antagonism and distrust. Black allegiances in South Africa were diverse, but the African National Congress (ANC) commanded a wide following, with its designated leader, Oliver Tambo, and its hero, Nelson Mandela, long jailed in South Africa but widely respected throughout the world as a figure of integrity and dignity. The ANC was strongly influenced by Communist ideology and had been involved in terrorist activity in South Africa. After being driven underground in the early 1980s, the ANC had become a political and military ally of Moscow.

In Mozambique a Soviet-supported government under the presidency of Samora Machel held uneasy sway. A guerrilla movement, RENAMO (Resistençia Naçional Mozambiçana), was a creature of South Africa and a remnant of the discontented leftovers from the Portuguese past and from the days of white rule in Zimbabwe, then Rhodesia. RENAMO, from all the evidence I saw, did not at all possess the natural base of support of Savimbi and, a careful report confirmed, engaged in terror and cruelty on a large scale.[2]

The entire region was pitted by small but ugly battles. In Angola, crack Cuban troops, dispatched in the service of international communism,

2. The Gersony report was released on April 20, 1988, and the acts of brutality it disclosed shocked even the supporters of RENAMO.

fought to put down Savimbi's guerrilla fighters, who sought to force the Luanda regime to accept national reconciliation. The South African Defense Force regularly probed beyond their borders to keep their adversaries off balance. They ran commando raids into Mozambique, which undermined the slight stirrings there of movement away from Soviet influence. The South African Defense Force also sent commandos into Zambia, Botswana, Angola, Lesotho, and Swaziland. Everywhere I looked, with the exception of Botswana, the scene in Southern Africa was grim: communism, colonialism, racism, violence, and despair. No real democracy, no sound prosperity, no true independence anywhere.

A Complex and Difficult Strategy

Our approach to these problems was straightforward, if little understood. The U.S. policy was constructive engagement. In South Africa, the United States would maintain its presence and involvement and would use that presence and involvement to speak and work against apartheid. We would promote democracy and oppose racism without reservation. Our effort to achieve Namibian independence, important in its own right, was also an important part of a strategy to abolish apartheid. With independence attained, apartheid in that South African–dominated state would come to an end. So we sought the independence of Namibia, but we knew that South Africa would not accede as long as Cuban troops and heavy Soviet influence were present in Angola. Beyond that, the United States, too, sought the removal of Cuban forces, an enforcer of the Brezhnev Doctrine. Moreover, since the removal of Cuban troops would leave Dos Santos on his own, that would also make national reconciliation in Angola, a goal we shared with Savimbi, more attainable on terms acceptable to Savimbi. Looking at the region as a whole, we sought reduced cross-border violence, a reduction of Soviet-Cuban meddling, an end to South African attacks on its vulnerable neighbors, and an end to internal conflicts fueled by racism and Marxist dictatorships. That was the ambitious sweep of constructive engagement.

Therefore, in the structure of our diplomacy, we tied Namibian independence to Cuban withdrawal from Angola. Many states in Africa and elsewhere objected on the grounds that UN Resolution 435 called for Namibian independence without any conditions. Our insistence that we would not ignore the Cubans gradually won at least tacit acceptance.

The United States had inherent prestige to back our diplomatic effort but until 1986 no military or economic muscle. We were able, however, to use the pressure provided by UNITA, with its South African support, as a basis for the argument to Dos Santos that he could not win a military victory. If he wanted peace in his country and the buffer against South Africa that the independence of Namibia would bring, he would have to face up to the conditions the United States presented. Savimbi, too, could see that he could not overpower the Dos Santos regime. While many of his supporters on the right in the U.S. wanted a military victory, Savimbi himself knew better.

On the other side of South Africa was Mozambique, where Soviet weight was less than in Angola and where Cuban troops were neither present nor desired. The U.S. strategy, supported strongly by Margaret Thatcher among others, was to befriend Samora Machel and draw him away from the Soviet camp. South African forbearance in its support of RENAMO would be needed. I took care to know who and what the United States was supporting and funding. Despite heated demands from the right-wing fringes of the administration and Congress, I steadfastly insisted we refuse to give backing to the atrocity-prone RENAMO.

The implications of the administration's, mainly State's, strategy ran far beyond the aspirations of the people of Namibia to control their own lives and territory. Independence would mean an end to South African–imposed apartheid in Namibia. What might the end of apartheid there mean for South Africa itself? A precedent, an experiment, a recognition that the white regime finally must face the inevitability of change? Who could know how the experience of being part of something that succeeded—the achievement of Namibian independence and freedom of Angola from foreign forces—might affect all of Southern Africa.

This improbable cast of nations and characters made for a unique challenge. The United States had a long-standing adversarial relationship with Castro's Cuba. We had no diplomatic relations with Marxist Angola. Our policies of support for Savimbi's UNITA guerrillas and opposition to RENAMO's guerrilla effort were under constant domestic political attack alternately from the right and the left wings in Congress. Bill Casey's pursuit of different foreign policy goals, using the CIA as his platform and his source of influence, was also a continuing problem for Crocker and me as we pursued what had been approved as administration policy. And our relations with South Africa were severely strained because of racial policies that were anathema to us.

Confronting us at every turn were the Soviet Union and cold war tensions that rose higher and higher through the early and middle years of the 1980s. Beyond this, domestic politics created intense and apparently irreconcilable pressures. To moralists, apartheid in South Africa was the only real issue; they wanted all our effort focused to end it. To strategists and all-out cold warriors, the Soviet client state of Angola and the Cuban troops active there were the most urgent challenge. To legalists, gaining compliance to UN Resolution 435's call for Namibian independence was foremost. To some, Savimbi "the freedom fighter" should be perpetually spurred into battle. To others, Savimbi "the warlord" was an instrument of American imperialism. Zealous advocates of any given cause saw little reason to address a comprehensive solution to the issues of the region and seemed unwilling to understand the subtle interrelationships involved.

The tensions created by varying objectives were always difficult to manage but became far more so when they erupted in the full-scale pressures of Washington politics during 1985 and 1986. The media glare and the political circus of posturing politicians made implementation of our strategy difficult. At times, I thought, this is Central America all over again, with wildly divergent and polemical views threatening to destroy people and block solid, constructive efforts. Tactically, Chet and I sought to work quietly—to cruise along invisibly—drawing people into an evolution of their positions and a willingness to accept workable compromises.

Near-Stealth Diplomacy?

I told Chet Crocker early on that we would triumph only by steady diplomacy. But even more, he and I would need near-stealth diplomacy, allowing us to make progress when the spotlight was trained on other scenes.

So Crocker and his deputy until early 1986, Frank Wisner, a foreign service officer who could convey friendliness and ferocity all at once, worked dynamically yet quietly and subtly through the first Reagan term. South Africa's military assaults into Angola in 1983 and the UN Security Council's Resolution 546 of January 6, 1984, calling for member states to aid Angola, took center stage briefly. The United States abstained on this vote, to the temporary consternation of the Angolans. They soon, however, resumed diplomatic activity with us. By mid-February, we had brokered a disengagement agreement at Lusaka, Zambia, under which the South Africans were to pull back from Angola, the Cubans would hold well north of combat areas, and the Angolans would curtail SWAPO guerrilla action into Namibia. The MPLA regime had accepted the concept of withdrawal of foreign forces from Angola, both South Africans and Cubans. And Chet Crocker had begun to go among the parties, negotiating on a calendar detailing the terms of withdrawal. This was news that the Angolans, interestingly I thought, did not want fully shared with the Soviets. Chet and I felt this Angolan acceptance of our concept was clearly a preliminary breakthrough.

A second breakthrough came with the Nkomati Accord, a nonaggression pact signed on March 16, 1984, by South Africa and Mozambique. Samora Machel called the accord "the only rational alternative for our future to be free of the specter of violence and destruction." Although the accord was periodically violated by the South African Defense Force, who continued to give support to RENAMO and to make sporadic forays into Mozambique, it was nevertheless a sign of some movement by both countries. And the accord gave Machel and the South Africans an uneasy but real point of contact with each other. Mozambique would be watched closely by Angola to see whether a regime could move to give up Marxism-Leninism and still survive—and whether a regime could survive an agreement with South Africa. South Africa would be watched to see whether it had made up its mind to conduct a regional policy aimed at stable, even if strained, relations with its neighbors.

The landslide victory of Ronald Reagan on November 6, 1984, had a sobering effect on all the parties: they now knew that this determined man would be on hand for another four years, so they would have to deal with him and his representatives if they were to make any progress.

So the pace picked up, but at year-end 1984 and in the first half of 1985, South Africa's internal strife drew world media attention. Anglican bishop Desmond Tutu, winner of the Nobel Peace Prize, met with President Reagan on December 7, 1984, and denounced U.S. policy toward South Africa as "immoral, evil, and un-Christian" and by implication called for our total disengagement; militant black Africans demonstrated against Senator Edward Kennedy when he visited South Africa on January 13, 1985; the South African government on January 31 offered freedom to Nelson Mandela in return for a pledge of nonviolence, but Mandela refused to accept any conditions. The U.S. Congress began to search desperately for opportunities to cast a new vote against apartheid. As the glare of this publicity threw Crocker's movements into blinding light, we began to lose control of our policy: the scene became cluttered with volunteer diplomats who wanted to take center stage.

In the hope of winning broader public support for our policy, I gave a major speech on Africa on April 16, 1985. Largely ignored by the media and disregarded by Congress, it was cited by right-wingers within the administration as proof that I was "selling out," because of my strong criticism of South Africa and my support for negotiations with the likes of Cuba and Angola.

Ronald Reagan, a true proponent of democracy and individual liberty, was, at the same time, disposed to give the benefit of the doubt to an anti-Communist leader, even if authoritarian and dictatorial. So the president was likely to nod in assent when some adviser—or even an out-of-office Bill Clark, who suddenly emerged from right field as an informal lobbyist for and confidant of the South Africans—would suggest we invite P. W. Botha to the White House. A wild idea, I thought. Similarly, President Reagan could be led to agree with the proposition that all freedom fighters—UNITA and RENAMO alike—deserved unquestioned support. The South African government's Washington lobbyists, John Sears and Stuart Spencer, found easy access to White House corridors.

Within the administration, Bill Casey viscerally and unswervingly opposed all that Crocker and I were doing; his CIA officers ran channels to the South Africans from CIA headquarters at Langley and used CIA representatives in the field to undermine Crocker with Savimbi and other black African leaders. As early as September 1983, I had to take steps to reconvince Savimbi that Crocker was not leading him into a Cuban trap, charges emanating from what supposedly was our own side. My problems with Bill Casey and those he used in the CIA were not confined to Southern Africa but were represented in our cross-purposes there. He worked with South African intelligence, gave the benefit of the doubt to South Africa, and distrusted any negotiation or potential agreement with a Communist government. I spoke publicly and clearly for radical change in South Africa and worked for an agreement with Angola and Cuba for the removal of Cuban troops from Angola, for national reconciliation there, and for Namibian independence.

With the media's upsurge in coverage of South Africa stimulating the Congress to get into the act, tension grew in the summer of 1985—both between the executive and legislative branches and between contending forces within the Reagan administration. The internal struggle came to a head in August 1985, when Ronald Reagan realized that Samora Machel of Mozambique had accepted an invitation, cleared in advance by the White House, to make an official visit to Washington. The news came at a time when South Africa, with Bill Casey's encouragement, was particularly vigorous in supporting South Africa's surrogate force, RENAMO, against Machel's government. In late August 1985, Casey's CIA briefers were showing their audiences in the administration and Congress a map of Mozambique colored to indicate—falsely—that RENAMO controlled virtually the entire country.

The president looked at me during one of our private meetings and spoke sharply: "When did I agree to meet this guy?" I told him when and tried to go over, once more, the importance of Machel's evolving defection from Marxism and Moscow toward our own strategy for withdrawal of foreign troops from Angola and for Namibian independence. Margaret Thatcher, I reminded him, was very much in favor of this approach to Machel. President Reagan was nevertheless uneasy, and worried that he was being led into a trap. South Africa's lobbyists ran a full-page ad in the newspapers that displayed the worst anti-American, pro-Soviet statements Machel had ever uttered. I felt disaster looming, and I dreaded even the thought of the coming visit.

On September 19, 1985, I escorted Samora Machel into the Oval Office.

Photographers arrived in waves to record the two presidents seated side by side, smiling. When the discussion became relaxed, as President Reagan always sought to achieve in such meetings, Machel began to take Reagan by storm: the president was charmed and impressed. Machel regaled us with anti-Soviet jokes and derogatory anecdotes about communism gleaned from his trips to Moscow. The president loved nothing better. And the tale-telling carried over into a medley of stories, which Machel told with great flair and an irresistible smile, about white South Africans: a Boer goes into a bar to get a scotch and water. He asks for Chivas Regal. The bartender says, "I don't have any." The Boer asks for Johnnie Walker; "I don't have any." So the Boer asks in consternation, "Well, what do you have?" "Black and White," says the barkeep. "Okay," says the Boer gruffly, "but pour it into separate shot glasses."

By the end of their talk, the two were calling each other "Ron" and "Samora." When their session was over, President Reagan stopped me outside the Oval Office: "I don't want to sound naive, but I think that guy is sincere."

"If we can take him away from the Soviets, that would be a ten-strike," I replied.[3]

Stormy Weather

We weathered the storm of 1985, but not without coming close to shipwreck. The South African government responded to its internal challenge and to rising foreign pressures by engaging in new forms of outrageous conduct. A repressive state of emergency was declared in mid-July. Earlier South Africa had conducted a military raid into Gaborone, the capital of neighboring Botswana, and had sent commandos far into northern Angola to strike at U.S.-owned oil installations. The outside world had to register its disapproval with action. The president and I recalled our ambassador for consultations. To Congress, the answer was further economic sanctions involving the forced withdrawal of American businesses, but by this time, no sanctions from America could inflict as much damage on South Africa as it was inflicting on itself. On August 27, 1985, the South African government suspended stock and currency trading as the rand fell to its lowest point in history; on September 1, principal repayments on foreign loans were stopped.

On September 9, hoping to preempt a great sanctions battle with Congress, the president signed an executive order that imposed limited sanctions on dealings with the South African government and banned

---

3. Machel was killed in a plane crash on October 19, 1986. I regretted that he did not live to lead his country further along.

krugerrands from the United States. Neither the president nor I had changed our views on the importance of maintaining an American business presence in South Africa, but I saw this action as a necessary response to South African behavior and compatible with a continued American presence.

With Savimbi's UNITA and Angola, we also faced a shifting scene. The Soviet Union, which had provided Angola an estimated $2 billion over the previous five years and had sent hundreds of advisers, sparked and supplied an Angolan-Cuban assault that threatened Savimbi's Jamba headquarters. South African troops came in to provide critical support. Congress also reacted by agreeing, in a foreign-aid authorization bill signed by President Reagan on August 8, 1985, to repeal the Clark Amendment that had barred us from aiding anti-Marxist elements in Angola since 1976. The Clark Amendment had contributed to Angola's present Marxist misery, and I was glad to see it go. I thought a show of strength on our side would lead to a stronger diplomatic posture. By early October, we were still trying to use our new leverage to prompt the Dos Santos regime into action at the negotiating table. The Angolan leader met Mike Armacost in October, but his remarks were inconclusive.

With the Clark Amendment out of the way, a debate began to rage: should the United States now provide aid to Savimbi's UNITA? Savimbi's supporters in both parties avidly desired to register American support in a public way. By mid-October of 1985, several bills had been introduced in Congress to do just that. I wrote to House Minority Leader Bob Michel, discouraging support for a bill that would provide, through an open vote, nonlethal aid in the amount of $27 million: "This bill is ill-timed, and will not contribute to the settlement we seek. I feel strongly about Savimbi's courageous stand against Soviet aggression, but there are better ways to help." The last phrase was a way of reminding Michel of the far greater importance of covert and lethal assistance. The point was that the aid had to be delivered, and to obtain the cooperation of an acceptable neighboring state, delivery had to be deniable. Explicitly open assistance would not work. Angola's neighbors, Zaire and Zambia, could not openly support an insurgent group in another African state! And we had no intention of sending our aid through the South Africans in Namibia; our goal was to reduce Savimbi's dependence on Pretoria.

Conservatives in Congress, always suspicious of me and the State Department, went on a virtual rampage. Congressman Jack Kemp called for my resignation because I opposed open assistance to Savimbi. He did not want to listen to the realities; the conservatives wanted an open vote as a matter of thumping their collective chests.

On November 8, 1985, I had a stinging set-to with Jack Kemp in the Cabinet Room. The president turned pale at our harsh exchange, as Kemp harangued for an open vote for an open program and I tore into him, stating all the reasons why an open program would be a disaster. "Why don't you try thinking, Jack," I snapped. "How are you are going to get aid delivered? Zaire and Zambia cannot openly support insurgents in another African state. And the aid has to go through there! If the aid isn't delivered, it's worthless to Savimbi."

Four days later, at a National Security Planning Group meeting on Angola held in the Situation Room, the president decided to ask Congress to authorize a program of covert and lethal assistance to UNITA. I had taken considerable heat, however, and was somehow further tagged by congressional conservatives as soft on freedom fighters. In reality, the reverse was the case. I wanted to give more muscle to our diplomacy, and I insisted that our attention focus on national reconciliation in Angola, Savimbi's objective, as well as independence for Namibia, and withdrawal of all foreign forces from both countries—the Cubans out of Angola and the South Africans out of Namibia.

Washington's focus in early 1986 shifted to apartheid and to P. W. Botha, South Africa's president. I learned indirectly that contacts were under way between Bill Casey and South African military intelligence—and that NSC adviser John Poindexter was involved. I was immediately uneasy. The subject under discussion was a possible visit by Botha to the United States and a meeting with President Reagan. Suddenly, Poindexter and Casey were all over me on this issue. Bill Clark, one of Poindexter's predecessors as national security adviser, claimed he had learned from the South African government that Botha was ready to take steps toward dismantling apartheid but "needs to show something for it in return." The quid pro quo sought was an official visit to the White House, Clark said: the visit would be a "home run" for the president. The problem was Crocker, Poindexter complained, who was refusing to agree to a Botha visit. I, too, strongly opposed such a visit.

Suddenly, our South Africa and Southern Africa policy, which had been run by Chet Crocker and me with an intentionally low profile, had become the obsession of the White House. Poindexter and Casey and various lobbyists for the South Africans, private and congressional, were working hard on Ronald Reagan to persuade him to issue an invitation to Botha. To me, such an invitation would be idiotic, both politically as well as diplomatically. Welcoming Botha at the White House would grant the South Africans legitimacy at the worst possible moment. Our shunning of Botha was itself a sanction, one that had an effect; now was not the time to let up.

On January 21, 1986, Bill Clark phoned me. After a brief rundown on his lobbying and advising activities overseas (he was about to go to Baghdad at the request of Saddam Hussein), he came to the point. Would I implore the president to bring Botha to Washington? Botha "desperately wants to get rid of apartheid, and he needs this invitation to do it. But Crocker is standing in the way," Clark said. I hung up quickly and with an uneasy feeling.

Botha's emissary, General Pieter van der Westhuizen, came to town. Botha was ready to fly to the United States instantly, Crocker was told on January 22. He "could be here on Saturday." With this news I went to see President Reagan to argue the issue out. From my session with the president I had the clear impression that Clark had talked to Reagan and brought him around to the view that the South African government was not all that bad, that Botha wanted to do the right thing, and that a White House invitation was the key. After our session, however, Reagan's conclusion was that he was willing to meet Botha *if and only if* the South Africans made some real change to get rid of apartheid. We agreed that Chet Crocker should send van der Westhuizen back to Pretoria with the message that an invitation "would require a clear and significant quid pro quo up front."

"Van der Westhuizen recounted," Crocker said, "that this whole thing had been created by Bill Clark." But Crocker didn't buy it; Chet's evidence was that the effort had been created by Bill Casey and van der Westhuizen and then was followed up and encouraged by Clark.

On January 28, 1986, Dr. Jonas Savimbi came to Washington at our invitation; he made a powerful impression that sent a message to the People's Republic of Angola. And it showed that visits can carry substance as well as style. The CIA had been putting out the analysis that Savimbi's UNITA was on the ropes—in the hope of increasing congressional willingness to fund a covert program. I had no doubt that he needed assistance. Savimbi's demeanor and statements, however, convinced me and many others that he felt secure. His circle of friends in the world was quietly widening. The moment was ripe for us to mount further efforts to promote direct MPLA contacts with Savimbi, so Crocker went to work to bring that about.

Proponents of a Botha visit focused on the speech he was to give on January 31, 1986, at the opening of the South African Parliament. Botha did suggest some changes: termination of the detested pass laws[4]; a readiness to set up a "national statutory council," including blacks, to serve in an advisory capacity; and an important commitment to equality before the law. But the speech did not come remotely close to what was necessary to justify an invitation to Washington. Beyond this appraisal, I had argued to President Reagan against the idea of a U.S. reward to Botha and his government for making concessions to us. Such an approach was fundamentally off course. The South African whites, I argued, must deal directly with

4. Every South African was required to carry a card identifying him or her as black, white, Asian, or colored, Depending on that identification, rules varied as to where you could go, when you could go, what curfew must be observed, and so on. You were forced to carry, in the form of this card, a constant reminder of apartheid and its impact on your freedom, rights, and acceptability.

South African blacks, who themselves needed to feel political progress as rising from their *own* efforts and achievements—not from U.S. efforts. U.S. engagement, with both blacks and whites, should be directed to that end.

In mid-February, Crocker saw South African Foreign Minister Roelof (Pik) Botha, no relation to President P. W. Botha, in Geneva. The South African government could not meet anything close to our price for a visit, Crocker was told. The very idea of a Botha visit had been impossible from the start, the South African said, "but the idea came from your side." Efforts for a Botha visit did not stop. In mid-March, Chet Crocker told me that Bill Casey, during a visit to South Africa, had raised the issue once again. The effort did not go anywhere but did give President Botha a continuing signal that there was more than one avenue through which to deal with the president—and more than one policy.

Contrary to what the foreign minister had told Crocker in Geneva, South African behavior turned rough again in the spring of 1986. Their troops launched attacks against alleged ANC sites in and around the capitals of Zambia, Botswana, and Zimbabwe. The United States strongly condemned the raids and expelled the South African embassy's military attaché. The news revived congressional interest, and new economic sanctions were proposed as violence inside South Africa worsened. Republicans in Congress urged President Reagan to speak out in unequivocal terms that would dramatize our opposition to apartheid and to South African behavior.

Setback in Congress

I was uneasy. I well knew how difficult it was to control the content and tone of a presidential speech once it got into the White House speechwriting mill. I also knew that Ronald Reagan's true feelings were not unequivocal. He was at least as concerned for the whites in South Africa as for the blacks, and would say so. I shared his concern that one terrible system not be changed to another and saw no problem in having him say so, as long as he also let blacks know that he understood *their* aspirations for equal political and economic opportunity, a sharing of power, and an end to racism.

For over a month Chet Crocker and I struggled back and forth with the White House speechwriters. I wanted to include some fresh actions to go with the words: termination of South African Air landing rights in the United States; establishment of visa procedures that would keep out of the country white extremists and people suspected of potential violation of U.S. laws; the expulsion of South African military attachés from the United States and the withdrawal of ours from Pretoria; the prohibition of new investment in South Africa unless the company doing the investing adhered

to the Sullivan Principles;[5] expanded U.S. support for regional development of transport links among South Africa's neighbors (Zimbabwe, Zambia, Mozambique, and Malawi) as a means of reducing South Africa's
stranglehold over their economies; and expanding consultation with allies
on stockpiling of strategic minerals in which South Africa had a commanding position. I wanted also to place the United States firmly behind
negotiation, including talks with the ANC. We would have to talk with the
ANC ourselves if our advice was to have credibility.

Pat Buchanan, with help from Casey and Poindexter, cut back the thrust
of Chet's and my proposed language covering the actions that had been
agreed upon. Crocker and I struggled and fought against the NSC-
Buchanan draft. We lost the battle.

On July 22, 1986, the president delivered a major address on South Africa.
Buchanan had produced a polarizing message, with language chosen carefully to signal to the South African government that the president understood its problems. The president's delivery demonstrated that he was fully
in tune. Key parts of Crocker's and my original ideas were missing. The
president did not say much about the desperation and fear of blacks but
spoke eloquently about the security of the whites "in this country they love
and have sacrificed so much to build." And the president again urged
Congress "to resist this emotional clamor for punitive sanctions." There
were many positive ideas in the speech, but they were lost. A confrontational president was projected into the atmosphere of deep and building
resentment against South Africa.

Congressional and media commentary on this address was immediately
negative. A bipartisan storm slammed into the White House. I tried to
restore calm in testimony on July 23, saying what should have been said
in the president's speech. In the White House, they now could see that
great damage had been done. Too late.

With moderate Republican Senator Dick Lugar in the lead, legislation
carrying further economic sanctions against trade, investment, and financial
dealings with South Africa passed on August 15 by 84 to 14, a vote in
which the president was deserted by 75 percent of his own party. When
this bill, after agreement with the House, later arrived at the White House,
the president exercised his veto. On October 2, his veto was overridden
by 78 to 21, despite strenuous efforts by Crocker and me while I was in
the midst of the intense negotiations to gain the release of Nicholas Daniloff, held hostage in Moscow. This was the first time since President Nixon

5. The Reverend Leon Sullivan established a set of principles for employment and community policies that were subscribed to by most U.S. firms active in South Africa. Use of
these principles meant that U.S. firms were in the lead in the training and promotion of blacks
and in support for community services that advanced the health and educational opportunities
of blacks.

had been overridden on his veto of the War Powers Resolution in 1973 that a president had experienced such a loss on a foreign policy issue: it represented a true erosion of presidential control over foreign policy issues. I took some heart when pollster Lou Harris telephoned me to say that, 60 percent to 30 percent, the American people opposed sanctions that would cause American companies to get out of South Africa. Harris told me that the results surprised him: "People seem to support what you are doing—but you're not presenting it right." I had to agree.

A few weeks later, General Motors announced the sale of its South African operations to local investors, and other U.S. companies, including IBM, decided to pull out as well. In many instances, sanctions were turning black employees over to employers less inclined to train, promote, and help black employees than had been the Americans.

The president made a statement of his own when, with my recommendation, he appointed as our new ambassador to South Africa Edward Perkins, an experienced foreign service officer and America's first black ambassador to the apartheid state. Quiet, low-key, and dignified, Perkins went about the business of systematically opening doors to our message, pressing South Africans to listen to each other and serving as a personal embodiment of our own principles of equal opportunity.

With political attention focused inside South Africa, Crocker found running room on Angola and Namibia and regained his negotiating stride. Savimbi had agreed to negotiate with the Dos Santos regime, and in an unprecedented meeting, Crocker conferred with the African National Congress's Oliver Tambo in London on September 20, 1986. That was followed by my own meeting with Tambo on January 28, 1987, shortly after my return from a trip to Africa, during which I enlisted support from key African leaders for national reconciliation in Angola. I decided to meet Tambo despite an official State Department report that same month stating that the ANC was "deeply beholden" to the South African Communist party and despite political pressure on me to extend a PLO-type ban on American contacts with the ANC.

Tambo and I debated the sanctions issue, and I urged him to cut loose from Soviet influence. "It is a sure loser," I told him. The ANC and its jailed leader, Nelson Mandela, had important constituencies in South Africa. Sooner or later, I felt, South Africa would be forced to deal with them, and I should be willing to do so myself, setting an example and avoiding the establishment of a ban on dealing with the ANC.

The war in Angola escalated, as once again the Soviet-supported forces of Angola and Cuba sought a military solution. They did not prevail. UNITA defeated an Angolan force in late October 1987 in the largest battle of the twelve-year conflict. South African help was of critical importance to Savimbi. U.S.-supplied antitank and antiaircraft missiles played an important role, and I was glad that covert U.S. lethal aid had gone forward. When the moment had come, a few months earlier, to increase such support from $18 million to $40 million, the president's conservative base gave him full support. As the fighting continued, Crocker kept working ceaselessly on three continents to move the positions of the several parties closer and closer.

The Last Lap

As 1988 opened, there was a breakthrough. In late January, the Cubans, in exchange for the seat at the negotiating table for which they had been pressing, agreed to withdraw their troops from Angola. Then Crocker, in Luanda, talking directly to the Cubans and Angolans, produced, for the first time, a formal agreement in principle for Cuban troops to be withdrawn totally from Angola in the context of an overall agreement that would also get South Africa out of Namibia. This agreement was an immense achievement, but implementation would not be easy. A specific timetable was not in hand.

In Angola, unlike Afghanistan, there were no imperatives pushing the Soviets. Crocker felt that the Soviets would not pressure the Cubans to get out quickly (before the end of the Reagan administration) or the Angolans to accept reconciliation with UNITA, unless I made it clear to Gorbachev that this issue was important to them and to us. On April 14, I took part in the UN-sponsored ceremony in Geneva marking the Soviet decision to leave Afghanistan. I wondered whether this was an implicit precondition to their change of view toward the problems of Angola and Namibia. In the course of my conversations in the Kremlin with Gorbachev and Shevardnadze on April 21 and 22, 1988, I pointed up the issues. I found them discouraged about Angola and interested in steps that would enhance the credibility of the United Nations. I decided to work on this interest at the coming summit meeting in Moscow.

On May 3 and 4, Crocker brought the South Africans together with the Cubans and Angolans in London to work on a formula for withdrawal from Angola and Namibia. The South Africans and Angolans followed up with their own meeting in Brazzaville, Congo, on May 13. Margaret Thatcher used heavy verbal artillery on Pretoria: her strong words had a critical impact on getting Botha to reengage. Geoffrey Howe, Helmut Kohl, and Hans-Dietrich Genscher were also constructive. I knew we were getting somewhere when other Western Europeans began to climb on the bandwagon and the Cubans started giving the press their own spin on the talks. Crocker was everywhere.

I was encouraged by Crocker's report to me on his meeting with Soviet Deputy Foreign Minister Anatoly Adamishin in Lisbon. (The Portuguese, as former colonizers of Angola, played a facilitating role.) Adamishin reported that the Dos Santos regime recognized the reality of their internal problems, their inability to enforce a military solution, and the necessity for a political solution. Crocker used this report to move the Soviets further toward letting their dependent, the Angolan regime, share power with Savimbi. This move, as with Soviet withdrawal from Afghanistan, was another step toward dismantling the Brezhnev Doctrine.

At the Moscow summit in late May and early June 1988, I worked hard on Shevardnadze, using the theme of making the UN process work and exposing him directly to Crocker's persuasive personality. I suggested that an Angola-Namibia agreement could be signed by early autumn. We agreed on an objective of September 29, the tenth anniversary of the passage of UN Resolution 435, calling for the independence of Namibia and setting out an elaborate electoral procedure for the establishment of a new constitution and government.

Chet conducted further talks among the parties in Cairo in June and in New York City in July, and what became known as "the Governor's Island Principles" were initialed—fourteen points for a peaceful resolution of this vast complex of issues.[6] These meetings coincided with the final climactic confrontation of South African forces with forces from Cuba and Angola in southwestern Angola. By early August, we were able to devise the means to obtain a cease-fire and a disengagement of forces.

In a meeting with Chet Crocker in late July, I had told him that many issues were being resolved our way around the world and that his project was one of the trickiest and most intriguing. The pace was quickening: a meeting with the Soviets in Geneva, followed by another tripartite round. Chet's new deputy, Chas Freeman, had just come in from the Ivory Coast and talks with Savimbi. The Cubans were hinting openly that their withdrawal could be speeded up if UNITA and the Angolan ruling party, MPLA, and Dos Santos moved faster to compose their differences. That was the track we were on, national reconciliation, but the Cubans were in a delicate spot and could not be seen forcing the hand of their nervous allies. They hoped we would reassure Luanda by cutting aid to UNITA— something we had no intention of doing.

6. The key points were:
  • implementation of Resolution 435;
  • independence for Namibia via elections;
  • total Cuban troop withdrawal, with on-site verification;
  • respect for the sovereignty and inviolability of borders;
  • noninterference in internal affairs;
  • abstention from threat or use of force;
  • right of Southwest Africa to self-determination, equality of rights;
  • provisions for verification and monitoring;
  • five permanent UN Security Council members as guarantors;
  • international cooperation for development for Southwest Africa;
  • recognition of the mediating role of the U.S. government.

Savimbi told Freeman that he, Savimbi, was the only man who could make Dos Santos "the real president of Angola." He was right. Savimbi held one-third of the country and had the allegiance of all the tribal groups in that territory. The key piece of economic infrastructure, the Benguela railroad, could not operate without Savimbi's assent. Savimbi said he was willing to take the second, third, or fourth government position under Dos Santos. But anyone who had met Savimbi could feel his dynamism and charisma, and I could see why Savimbi would feel confident of himself— maybe too confident—in any reasonably fair political process.

In Geneva in August, Angola, Cuba, and South Africa provisionally agreed on the text of a treaty containing the core principles of a settlement but leaving the big issue of a Cuban withdrawal schedule for discussion at the next round. The parties also signed a key protocol that effectively ended the cross-border war and outlined the remaining negotiating agenda. The Cubans, Chet reported, were conducting themselves in a statesmanlike way, which made a positive difference.

Almost relentlessly, this process moved step by step toward its conclusion. United Nations Security Council Resolution 435, an initiative from the Carter era, was now being achieved by a sustained, intensive U.S. effort. This was a twelve-year American diplomatic effort spanning two administrations. The Geneva protocol called for an immediate cease-fire, the removal of South Africa's remaining troops from Angola by September 1, and the presentation then of Cuba's timetable for total withdrawal of its troops from Angola. On November 1, 1988, according to the protocol, the United Nations would begin supervising the process of independence for Namibia.

But as often happened when success was near, efforts to subvert success emerged. Crocker, calling in on September 9 from Brazzaville, Congo, said he felt confused and beleaguered. Something was working negatively on Savimbi. Communications in and out of Savimbi's headquarters in Jamba, in southern Angola, were sporadic and unclear. Chet feared that South Africans were feeding phony intelligence to Savimbi to make him fear a massive Cuban surprise attack, because the Cubans, this so-called intelligence maintained, would back away from the agreement. And, as had been the case throughout this diplomatic marathon, right-wing staffers from Congress, fueled by information from the CIA, were meddling—visiting Savimbi, trying to convince him that Crocker and I would sell him out by depriving him of South African support while leaving loopholes in the agreement regarding Cuban troop withdrawal.

Congress itself was about to launch into another debate aimed at imposing further sanctions on South Africa, ironically including Namibia, at the very time when the United Nations, under the proposed agreement, would be starting to oversee Namibia's transition to independence. This

moral posturing by Congress, oblivious to the flow of international negotiations, was likely to damage the negotiations at a critical moment.

I telephoned Senator Claiborne Pell, chairman of the Foreign Relations
Committee, on September 7 to tell him that Chet Crocker was in Brazzaville
and we were getting very close to success. "The South Africa bill couldn't
come at a worse time: It is an intrusion into the negotiations," I told Pell.
I asked him to put the vote off for a week and offered to send Freeman
up to the Hill to brief the Senate on the course of the negotiations. Pell
replied that they would vote the bill no matter what.

"Would you be interested in the facts of what's going on in the negotiations?" I asked Pell.

"No," he responded. When Pell called me back an hour later to talk at
great length about what he was really interested in—foreign service ambassadorial assignments—I threw up my hands. As it turned out, Pell
outflanked himself: Senator Jesse Helms attacked Pell for refusing to let
me brief on the status of Crocker's diplomacy, and the South Africa bill
got pushed back. I was on the same side as Jesse Helms. "Yes, it could
ruin both your reputations," someone said to me.

As the autumn days passed, Crocker and his delegation raced between
Brazzaville and Washington in an effort to push the Cubans, Angolans,
and South Africans to keep to their negotiating deadlines. Once the troop
pullouts started, they would create a momentum that would be irreversible,
but we had to get them started. A delay would mean that troops would
still be present in the region when the dry season started, and renewed
fighting then—when we were no longer in office—could cause a decade's
work to collapse. But the Cuban withdrawal schedule proved to be a stubborn obstacle, consuming the months of September, October, and November. I sent a message to Shevardnadze pressing him to get Angola and
Cuba on board the compromise schedules Crocker had tabled: the dry-
season danger of fighting was real. I interpreted Shevardnadze's reply on
November 4 as indicating that the MPLA and Cubans might be ready to
make the concessions necessary for an agreement. Crocker and I proceeded
on that basis.

The election of George Bush on November 8, 1988, and his immediate action on naming my successor led me to worry momentarily that
the Angolans or Cubans, or their Soviet backers, might try to stall, waiting
to see if they could get a better deal once Crocker and I were gone. But
now the Soviets appeared to be helping. At Geneva, on November 11–15,
Crocker's persuasive efforts produced agreement between negotiators
for Angola, Cuba, and South Africa on the schedule for Cuban troop
withdrawal from Angola linked to the UN plan for Namibian independence.

On December 6, Crocker telephoned me to say that the South Africans, at a meeting in Brazzaville, had formally agreed to accept the accords. "You have brought off a huge triumph," I told Chet. When he returned from Africa and walked into my morning staff meeting, he received a spontaneous, standing burst of applause. "Once in a while," I said, "after long effort, something works. Chet, you have conducted a brilliant piece of diplomacy."[7]

A Crown on Success

The treaty had something in it for everyone, woven together as it was with strands of common interest that the parties themselves had not recognized existed. Savimbi got the departure of the Cubans, a development that would sooner or later require the Angolan regime to accept a role for UNITA in the government. The Angolan regime could see a buffer state between itself and South Africa in the form of an independent Namibia devoid of South African troops. South Africa could claim to have ousted Cuba from the continent, a result that would transform the regional balance of military power and could justify at home its agreement to free Namibia. Cuba could boast that it forced the South Africans to yield and to implement the UN resolution. The Soviet Union was able to off-load a deadbeat client, Angola, while getting credit for constructive work with the United States. And Namibia was able to throw off the shackles of apartheid and colonialism.

Savimbi well knew that the United States would stand up for freedom and for those, like himself, willing to fight for it. As the Reagan administration and my own term in office neared its conclusion, I received a gift from him in thanks for America's support of his UNITA freedom fighters and their long struggle in the bush of southern Angola against the Communist regime in Luanda. I opened a big, orange-covered cardboard case to find within a Soviet-made Kalashnikov automatic rifle. The gift symbolized one of the striking turnabouts in the history of the cold war: the Reagan Doctrine replacing the now-retreating Brezhnev Doctrine. The image of Soviet-backed Communist guerrillas fighting from the bush to seize power had now been replaced by American-backed revolutionaries operating from jungle camps to oppose the Communist domination of their countries—and supplying themselves by capturing Soviet- and Chinese-made and supplied weapons!

As I prepared for the signing ceremony at UN headquarters in New York City, I realized that this would be the third time within the past year and a half that the United Nations had played a useful role in resolving a difficult

7. Chet Crocker tells his own story of these developments in *High Noon in Southern Africa* (New York: W. W. Norton, 1992).

issue. It was a measure of the end of the cold war and a statement that better U.S.-Soviet relations would bring positive results in many areas, including the usefulness of the United Nations. The unprecedented unanimous vote in the Security Council in July 1987 had prepared the way for an effective cease-fire in the bloody, protracted Iran-Iraq War; the signing ceremony in Geneva in April 1988 had sealed the commitment of the Soviet Union to withdraw its troops from Afghanistan; and now the United Nations would provide the setting for the dramatic withdrawal of Cuban troops from Angola and of South African troops from Namibia, and for the independence of a Namibia free from apartheid.

None of these developments could have occurred without the dramatic change in the relationship between the United States and the Soviet Union that took place during the Reagan presidency. The Soviet attitude toward its relationship to world events had altered profoundly. The Brezhnev Doctrine was dead, with the execution due in some considerable part to its opposite number, the Reagan Doctrine. The cold war was ending, and the resolution of contentious issues provided the hard evidence of that tremendously important development. In this new setting, I thought, the evidence also suggested a new usefulness to the United Nations.

On December 22, 1988, I represented the United States at the signing ceremony at the United Nations of the Angola-Namibia Accords, which created Namibia as an independent state.[8] It was an incongruous assemblage, where attitudes ran from unholy to ungracious to vicious. But the point was that everybody came. The three ministers made speeches, their words appropriately toned down from their true attitudes. As Chas Freeman described it in the summer 1989 *Foreign Affairs*. "The Angolan managed a polite dig at South Africa and the United States. The Cuban was polemically sarcastic about both, and took a barely disguised swipe at the Soviets as well. The South African wound up with remarks that declared his country's solidarity with Third World resentment of Western domination of the global economy." What an incredible task it had been to get all their names on a single document!

I wanted Chet Crocker to sign for the United States, but that act was required of me as secretary of state. When the moment came for the ceremony's official photograph, I made sure Chet Crocker was prominently placed at the center of the group. Every one of the assembled foreign ministers joined in paying tribute to Chet; they recognized that his personal commitment and creative diplomacy had been indispensable to this success.

Although deep problems remained, the colonial era in Africa had ended.

---

8. The trilateral Angolan-Cuban-South African Treaty contained the linkage formula and a set of reciprocal obligations. It incorporated by reference the specific Cuban withdrawal schedule contained in a separate Angolan-Cuban Treaty.

CHAPTER 51

Turning Point

Here we stood at the end of the Reagan presidency, ready to turn over power to our successors, ready to hand over a legacy of promise at a rare fluid moment in history when the world could be changed profoundly and for the better.

In the late summer I convened periodic sessions with State Department principals and managers to go over what should be done to help the new team. We set up office space for the new people to use between the day after the election and January 20, telephones, secretarial staff, computers, foreign service officers to be special assistants, and, most important, briefing materials that laid out in detail where every issue of our foreign policy stood.

What a contrast, I thought to myself, with the world in turmoil when I entered office in 1982, or the sense of showdown at the end of 1983, when the controversial deployment of INF missiles in Europe was met with a defiant Soviet walkout from arms control negotiations and by expressions of intense hostility. America's foreign policy back then was regarded by many intellectuals as unraveling: democratic governments were the rare exception outside of the Western alliance, and the "capitalist" model for economic development was judged harshly.[1] Now, in 1988, explosive regional issues were on the road to settlement and the human rights environment in the Soviet Union, though still unsatisfactory, was nevertheless transformed and moving in the right direction. The INF Treaty, finally ratified, was a watershed agreement, not only because of its terms but also because it showed that large-scale reductions in nuclear weapons were

---

1. In a widely used textbook, *America, Russia, and the Cold War, 1945-1984*, 5th ed. (New York: Alfred A. Knopf, 1985), Cornell Professor Walter LaFeber pointed to "a larger crisis within the capitalist world" (p. 312), to Reagan's "foreign policy failures," and "ideological inflexibility that prevented his (and his advisors') understanding the new power relationships" (p. 314). "As [Reagan] neared the end of nearly four years in the White House one consequence was, as a close military advisor of the president worried, that the American-Soviet relationship had turned 'as bad as it's been in my memory' " (p. 314).

possible: the United States and the Soviets *could* work out a complex problem of great importance. The treaty was also a tribute to the strength and cohesion of the NATO alliance in deploying Pershing II and cruise missiles in the face of politically explosive protest in the basing countries.

On September 25, 1988, I moved to New York for the first two weeks of the General Assembly of the United Nations. The next day, Ronald Reagan addressed the world body for the sixth time, his final appearance there. He was able to talk of the "hope of peace" in many troubled lands, to say credibly that the differences between East and West were easing, and to point to "talk in the East of reform and greater freedom of the press, of assembly, and of religion."

As I went from meeting to meeting over my two-week stay, seeing foreign ministers and heads of government from every part of the world, I could hear echoes of the president's refrain. It was as if the whole world had breathed a deep sigh of relief. An immense tension had gone out of the system. The world had changed. Margaret Thatcher had it right. In an interview with the *Washington Post* and *Newsweek* on November 17, during her last official visit to Washington during the Reagan administration, she said flatly, "We're not in a Cold War now." Despite this new reality, many in the United States seemed unable or unwilling to grasp this seminal fact. But to me, it was all over but the shouting.

The years of the Reagan presidency were, in the sweep of history, a turning point, building on the ideas and the institutions put in place in the critical period right after World War II. For the bigger part of the century, the world had witnessed a titanic struggle between two visions of the future. Both were revolutionary: one based on freedom and flexibility, the other based on central power and control. When our country's military strength was built up to a point where our Soviet rivals recognized they could not match us, when they perceived that we might actually use our strength to repel aggression, and as their own system indisputably failed the Soviet people even as it abused them—then came the turning point.

In the spring of 1985 I had written in *Foreign Affairs*: "The United States is restoring its military strength and economic vigor and has regained its self-assurance; we have a President with a fresh mandate from the people for an active role of leadership. The Soviets, in contrast, face profound structural economic difficulties and restless allies; their diplomacy and their clients are on the defensive in many parts of the world."[2]

This was made evident by Gorbachev's concessions at Reykjavik in October 1986. The backdrop to this drama was our incessant push for human rights. The Soviets' early and adamant refusal even to listen to us began

2. "New Realities and New Ways of Thinking," *Foreign Affairs*, Spring 1985, p. 707.

to crumble, all the more rapidly when Gorbachev started to realize that not only were human rights the core value of the West that any nation would have to accept if it wanted a sound relationship with us, but also that human rights were essential as a practical matter for any society hoping to succeed in an era propelled by knowledge and information.

Now, in 1988, the United States had turned the tide against the Soviets in strategic terms, but the end of the cold war and the transformation of East-West relations was by no means the only arena in which a new world was emerging. Hardly noticed or appreciated was the growing strength of our relations with Canada—by far our largest trading partner—capped by the momentous U.S.-Canada Free Trade Agreement. And the change in the Asia-Pacific region was of fundamental importance. The American security umbrella, plus our willingness to keep our own large and expanding market open—from which we have benefited enormously—and our encouragement of open economic and political systems have enabled the highly diverse people of the Asia Pacific to develop and prosper to an unprecedented degree. Just as the end of the cold war presented new opportunities and problems in Europe, the emergence of many strong economies, particularly but hardly limited to Japan, did the same in the Asia Pacific. I worked hard though quietly in this area, and I considered the strength of these relationships at the time President Reagan and I left office to be of critical importance.

At the dawn of the nuclear age, Albert Einstein had commented, "Everything has changed but our way of thinking." Ways of thinking are hard to change, but the most important development of all during the Reagan years was the dramatic shift in the conventional wisdom: ideas about open and democratic forms of governance and the rule of law, and private enterprise, and market-based forms of economic policy were moving to the center of the stage. An era was over. A new era in a new world was beginning.

It was as though a gigantic experiment had been conducted and the world was the laboratory. One group of countries had organized themselves through totalitarian and repressive government, with apparent order and discipline and an ability to develop formidable military power. To this was added an economy planned and managed from the center, with little room for individual incentive and none of the motivation that comes from the ownership of private property. The other group of countries organized political life more or less openly, with the rule of law and elected leaders and with economic systems based on markets, incentives, and private property. Both groups had access to vast raw materials and extraordinary human talent. The essence of the contrast lay in issues of liberty, security, and economic and social well-being: the issues that frame, test, and define societies. Ideas have consequences. And it was Ronald Reagan who shaped those issues with big ideas and who put those ideas across.

Understanding Ronald Reagan

President Reagan was leaving the country far better off than he found it. The situation in foreign affairs had been transformed in one of the truly revolutionary periods in the international politics of the century. A sea change of immense importance had occurred.

I thought about Ronald Reagan the man and the rhythm of his time in office. He had frustrated me with his unwillingness to come to grips with the debilitating acrimony among his national security advisers, with over-reliance on his immediate staff, with a sometimes wishful approach to an issue or program. He could rearrange facts to make a good story better, and he could allow himself at times to be deceived, sometimes almost knowingly. He and his administration paid the price, most dearly in the Iran-Contra affair.

Sometimes President Reagan simply did not seem to care that much about facts and details. That bothered the press and it bothered me. On occasion I would try to correct the inaccurate chronology of a favorite story about something he had done earlier in his presidency. When he told me how the release of the Russian Pentecostals was linked to his subsequent lifting of the grain embargo against the Soviets imposed by Jimmy Carter, I pointed out that he had lifted that embargo shortly after taking office, over two years before the Soviets allowed the Pentecostals to emigrate. He nodded in agreement and kept right on telling the same story. More importantly, no matter how often I pointed out to him that he had indeed traded arms for hostages in the Iran-Contra affair, he found that almost impossible to accept.

Over time, I began to see another side to his love of storytelling: he used a story to impart a larger message—and sometimes that message was simply more important to him than the facts. He was a gifted storyteller, who could use a story effectively to make his point take on a deeper and more vivid meaning or to defuse a tense situation. People, he felt, believe in and act on the stories they hear and tell about the past. Stories create meaning. Facts are the unassembled parts of an apparatus that do not operate until put together in an individual's own unique way. Stories bring facts to life. To Ronald Reagan, today's events always seemed rooted in some piece of wisdom, some story he had incorporated long ago. When he quoted the Russian proverb "Trust, but verify" to General Secretary Gorbachev at the signing of the INF Treaty, it was simply another way of conveying his favorite saying of "Mr. Dooley"—Finley Peter Dunne—Midwestern America's Irish-American humorist: "Thrust ivveribody, but cut the ca-cards."

I understood what a central role Nancy Reagan played in his life, and an experience I had with her as the administration came to a close was in its own way vintage Ronald Reagan. On October 25, 1988, I had accompanied her to the United Nations, where she would speak on behalf of the administration about the problem of illegal drugs. She had fought a battle over the text of her speech, particularly her emphasis on the obligation of the United States itself to do a better job of curbing the use of drugs. Those opposed argued that such a statement would only make more difficult our efforts to persuade other countries to fight against the suppliers of drugs. I disagreed with them and agreed with Nancy. President Virgilio Barco of Colombia had told me, "The profits to be made from selling drugs in the United States are staggering, and those profits are fueling what amounts to another government in my country."

Nancy insisted that we come early to the UN session at which she would speak. "If I want people to listen to me, I should come in time to listen to them," she said. She sat in the delegate's seat and I right behind her in the seat assigned to the U.S. alternate. When we arrived, well before her announced time to speak, the large room was virtually empty. She looked around and then turned apprehensively to me, "George," she said, "doesn't anyone want to hear what I have to say?"

"People know when you are scheduled to speak and the room will be full by then," I reassured her. By the time she spoke, the room was jammed and the atmosphere expectant.

She surprised the delegates with her candor: "If we cannot stem the American demand for drugs, then there will be little hope of preventing foreign drug producers from fulfilling that demand. We will not get anywhere if we place a heavier burden of action on foreign governments than on America's own mayors, judges and legislators. You see the cocaine cartel does not begin in Medellin [Colombia]. It begins in the streets of New York, Miami, Los Angeles and every American city where crack is bought and sold."

Afterward, delegates from all parts of the world came over to her with their congratulations. The critics of her speech had been dead wrong: delegates told her that her candor would make them even more resolute in their efforts to combat the production and trafficking in illegal drugs. Nancy had spoken the simple truth, a trademark of her husband.

Before he became president, Ronald Reagan had been a successful governor of California, and had left office there after eight years as a popular figure: the state was much better off when he left than when he arrived. Now he had achieved on a national level, and most especially on an international level, a changed landscape—and for the better. He had faults, at which critics hammered away. But what about his great achievements, his success? That question must be addressed by critics and historians. What did he bring to the party? I remembered Bud McFarlane, in the months before his resignation, shaking his head and saying in bewilderment, "He knows so little and accomplishes so much."

In truth, Ronald Reagan knew far more about the big picture and the matters of salient importance than most people—perhaps especially some of his immediate staff—gave him credit for or appreciated. He had blind spots and a tendency to avoid tedious detail. But the job of those around him was to protect him from those weaknesses and to build on his strengths. Some of them did just the opposite. He had a strong and constructive agenda, much of it labeled impossible and unattainable in the early years of his presidency. He challenged the conventional wisdom: on arms control, on the possibility of movement toward freedom in the Communist-dominated world, on the need to stand up to Iran in the Persian Gulf, on the superiority of market- and enterprise-based economies. The world learned when Ronald Reagan faced down the air-traffic controllers in 1981 that he could dig in and fight to win. The world learned in Grenada that he would use military force if needed. He did not accept that extensive political opposition doomed an attractive idea. He would fight resolutely for an idea, believing that, if it was valid, he could persuade the American people to support it. He changed the national and international agenda on issue after issue. He was an optimist; he spoke the vocabulary of opportunity. He had a vision of what he stood for and what we aspire to as a nation.

Critics said Ronald Reagan read too many letters and not enough briefing books. I often wished he would spend more time on the briefing books, mastering details more fully and following up more aggressively on the management of foreign policy. But the letters buoyed him up and also gave him a continuing sense of contact with the people, selective though the letters might be. The shoot-from-the-hip, saber-rattling, jackbooted image was not in the nature of the man. He had and could express a clear and simple view of a complex world. Every Sunday he brought acorns down from Camp David to feed the squirrels outside the Oval Office. The squirrels at the White House hadn't had it so good since Ike cleared the area to put in a putting green. His most endearing aspect was his fundamental decency. He appealed to people's best hopes, not their fears, to their confidence rather than their doubts.

Ronald Reagan had clear objectives, and at the end of the day he truly did look for the right thing to do. I remembered vividly his argument with Vice President Bush—and with almost everyone else—over his approach to getting strongman Manuel Noriega out of power and out of Panama. To those who told him that he had "no support in Congress" for his proposed course of action, he countered simply and fervently that he would take his case to the American people and argue it flat out: he would do what he felt was right for the country, whether it was popular or not.

Ronald Reagan was not at the end of his presidency what he was when he started out: he was not a man who would stay labeled or stay put. He was ever changing, on the move, ever evolving in new and surprising ways. He was a doer, a pragmatist, a man who enjoyed hard physical tasks, as in the ranch work he loved to do. But that brush clearing and fence fixing was a symbol, too; he wanted to be doing it himself because from the land came not only strength and clarity, but a vision—the vision of the West and the endless horizon. The American people liked Ronald Reagan and reelected him in one of the biggest landslides in history because he trusted them and he conveyed to them that they need not be bound, tied down by class, or race, or childhood misfortune, or poverty, or bureaucracy—they, the people—could make something of themselves; indeed, they could remake themselves, endlessly.

But beneath this pragmatic attitude lay a bedrock of principle and purpose with which I was proud to be associated. He believed in being strong enough to defend one's interests, but he viewed that strength as a means, not an end in itself. He was ready to negotiate with his adversaries. In that readiness, he was sharply different from most of his conservative supporters, who advocated strength for America but who did not want to use that strength as a basis for the inevitable give-and-take of the negotiating process. All too often, they lacked confidence in the ability of democratic leaders, including Reagan, to negotiate effectively with our adversaries. Ronald Reagan had confidence in himself and in his ideas and was ready to negotiate from the strength so evident by the mid-1980s.

He was a fervent anti-Communist who could comprehend and believe that people everywhere would choose to throw off the Communist system if they ever had the chance. And he worked hard to give them that chance. He favored open trade because he had confidence in the ability of Americans to compete, and he had confidence that an integrated world economy would benefit America. He stuck to his agenda.

The points he made, however consummate the delivery, were unmistakably real in his mind and heart, an American creed: defend your country, value your family, make something of yourself, tell the government to get off your back, tell the tyrants to watch their step. Ronald Reagan conveyed simple truths that were especially welcome because "nowadays everything seems so complicated." What he said ran deep and wide among the people.

Reagan as president was a Republican, a conservative, a man of the right. But these labels will mislead historians who do not see beyond them, for Americans could see some of Ronald Reagan in themselves. You couldn't figure him out like a fact, because to Reagan the main fact was a vision. He came from the heartland of the country, where people could be down-to-earth yet feel that the sky is the limit—not ashamed of, or cynical about, the American dream. Not far from Ronald Reagan's small town of Dixon, Illinois, is Jane Addams's small town of Cedarville; not far from Cedarville is Ulysses Grant's small town of Galena. And not far from Galena is Carl Sandburg's Galesburg. Reagan had something of them all: his heart going out to the people; his will ready to fight for the country;

his voice able to move the nation. And, as Carl Sandburg wrote it,

> The republic is a dream.
> Nothing happens unless first a dream.

Transition and Farewell

On November 7, the day before the election, I reviewed the scores of transition papers and then one big comprehensive book produced for my successor. I found the content and the insights impressive and on the mark, much better than anything I had seen in my brief moment of transition.

At 8:00 A.M. on November 9, the day after George Bush's landslide victory, I received a phone call from the president-elect: "George, I just wanted to let you know that I'd like to announce Jim Baker for secretary of state this morning unless that would disrupt something you have under way."

"Go ahead. I think highly of Jim. I welcome his appointment," I said.

Bush then asked me who the top foreign service officers were and I gave him some names. "I'm thinking of taking a senior foreign service officer and making him UN ambassador, noncabinet," he said. I urged him to do so. He had thought about this since the days when he himself had been UN ambassador.

"When you announce Jim Baker," I suggested, "say something good about the Foreign Service. It will send warm waves through the building." I drew up a statement of strong support for Jim Baker and got ready to go down to the pressroom to read it as soon as the president-elect had made his announcement. I did not expect or want to stay on in this demanding job, but I thought this move was a little abrupt. I was still going strong on a number of fronts, and I hoped the announcement would not make it more difficult to tie up some important loose ends, to the benefit of the incoming administration.

My last trip as secretary of state was to Vienna on January 17, 1989, to sign the CSCE Treaty setting up a new and promising approach to rectifying the huge imbalances in conventional armaments in Europe and, on the basis of tough and insistent negotiations, agreeing to a conference on human rights in Moscow in 1991. We had insisted throughout the two years of this effort that we would not settle simply for words on human rights in the concluding document. Plenty of good words had already been agreed to, we argued. We insisted on deeds by the Soviets and their satellite states. Through our strong efforts, and helped by the determined posture of Margaret Thatcher, by the end of our administration we had brought the Soviets to end the jamming of radio and television broadcasts, to release political prisoners, to allow refuseniks to emigrate along with an increasing flood of other Soviet citizens emboldened by the new atmosphere, to restore the permissibility of religious teaching, to end the abuse of using psychiatric institutions as places of political detention, and in countless other ways to push the Soviets to transform *glasnost* from a word into deeds.

I recalled Gorbachev's address at the UN a few weeks before and his statements on human rights and the rule of law, including his declaration that there were no longer any prisoners of conscience in the Soviet Union. As I worked in early January to persuade President Reagan that we should agree to a prospective CSCE human rights conference in Moscow, I argued Andrei Sakharov's point of view that such a gathering of human rights activists could spur on human rights progress in the Soviet Union.

But I worried. George Bush and Jim Baker seemed concerned and wary that Ronald Reagan and I had become too impressed with Soviet person-alities—Gorbachev, Shevardnadze—too ready to believe that genuine change was occurring in the Soviet Union. Brent Scowcroft had been named early on as NSC adviser, and I knew he would be influential. He had opposed the INF Treaty, had raised severe doubts about the prospective START Treaty, and was highly skeptical about the reality of change in the Soviet Union and Eastern Europe. I was apprehensive that the "new team" did not understand or accept that the cold war was over. I heard that a "top-to-bottom policy review" would be undertaken. Fair enough. But President Reagan and I were handing over real momentum. I hoped it would not be squandered.

In the last days before January 20, 1989, good will and good humor came to the fore. The Senate paid me a bipartisan tribute. Colin Powell told a group at a dinner in my honor that the NSC adviser and the secretary of state had not gotten on so well since the days when Henry Kissinger held both jobs simultaneously. Everyone roared, including Henry.

Ronald Reagan presented me with the Medal of Freedom at his last official event, a farewell luncheon at the White House. I was proud to receive that honor from him, as we had fought together for the idea of freedom throughout his presidency. We knew that the price of freedom is eternal vigilance and a willingness to act in its defense. We knew that on this matter of principle we could not compromise.

When I returned to my office, I was surprised to find gathered there some forty members of my State Department team. They had created a special Thomas Jefferson Award for me, noting that the day marked the 200th anniversary of his confirmation as our first secretary of state.

As O'Bie and I went down the back elevator for the last time, it stopped to our surprise at the balcony level overlooking the diplomatic lobby with all the flags of the nations recognized by the United States hanging there. The lobby was packed with our State friends and colleagues. My eyes welled with emotion. We walked down the stairs and out the front door as a contingent from the Marine Band played "California, Here I Come!"

Index